BRADSHAW'S
CONTINENTAL RAILWAY GUIDE

Published by Collins
An imprint of HarperCollins Publishers
Westerhill Road
Bishopbriggs
Glasgow G64 2QT
www.harpercollins.co.uk

1st edition 2016

Originally published in 1853 as Bradshaw's Continental Railway Guide and General Handbook Illustrated with Local and other Maps 'special edition' from 1853 and also Bradshaw's General Shareholders Manual and Directory 1853

A catalogue record for this book is available from the British Library

ISBN 978-0-00-820127-2
ISBN 978-0-00-820476-1

10 9 8 7 6 5 4 3 2 1

Printed in China

This facsimile edition is sourced from the National Library of Scotland's original copies of Bradshaw's Continental Railway Guide and General Handbook Illustrated with Local and other Maps 'special edition' from 1853 and also Bradshaw's General Shareholders Manual and Directory 1853
Continental Railway Guide – Hall.149.d
General Shareholder's Manual – N.73.b
www.nls.uk

PUBLISHER'S NOTE

This Bradshaw's Continental Guide has been recreated from the Bradshaw's Continental Railway Guide and General Handbook Illustrated with Local and other Maps 'special edition' from 1853 and also Bradshaw's General Shareholders Manual and Directory 1853.

Maps which appear as pull outs throughout the original text have been moved to a section after the main book.

In order to make the original documents easier to interpret this edition has been published at a slightly enlarged scale.

SECTION 1

BRADSHAW'S CONTINENTAL RAILWAY GUIDE

PRIZE MEDAL!!

WATHERSTON AND BROGDEN'S GOLD CHAINS,

By Troy Weight at realisable value and Workmanship, at Wholesale Manufacturers' Prices.

THE GREAT EXHIBITION having established the advantage of purchasing from the Wholesale Manufacturer, wherever it can be accomplished, and thereby dispensing with an intermediate profit, WATHERSTON & BROGDEN beg to announce that, in obedience to the numerous calls made upon them, they have thrown open their Manufactory to the Public at the same prices they have been in the habit (for the last half century) of charging to the Trade in London, India, and the Colonies.

WATHERSTON & BROGDEN beg to caution the public against the **Electro-Gold Chain and Polished Zinc Gold,** so extensively put forth in the present day under the titles of **"Pure Gold"** and **"Fine Gold,"** and to call attention to the genuine Gold Chains made from their own ingots, and sold by Troy Weight at its bullion or realisable value.

The system of weighing Chains against Sovereigns being one of the greatest frauds ever practised on the Public, WATHERSTON & BROGDEN guarantee the Gold in their Chains, and will re-purchase it at the price charged; the workmanship according to the intricacy or simplicity of the pattern.

EXAMPLE.

Intrinsic value of a Chain of 15-Carat Gold, weighing 1½ oz. ...	L.3 19 7
Supposing the workmanship to be	2 0 0
TOTAL	L.5 19 7

By this arrangement, the purchaser will see at a glance the proportion charged for *labour* compared with the *Bullion* in a Gold Chain; and being always able to realize the one, will have only to decide on the value of the other.

N.B.—Australian and Californian Gold made into articles of Jewellery at a moderate charge for the workmanship.

An Extensive Assortment of Jewellery, all of the first quality, made at their Manufactory,

16, HENRIETTA STREET, COVENT GARDEN, LONDON.

[L.O.—3

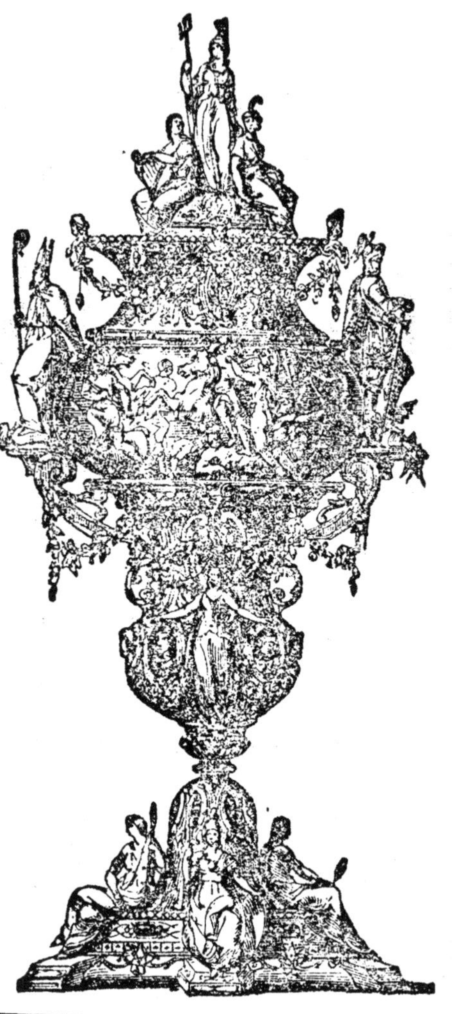

ELEGANT PERSONAL REQUISITES.

ROWLANDS' MACASSAR OIL.

THE successful results of the last half century have proved, beyond question, that this unique discovery possesses singularly nourishing powers in the growth and restoration of the Human Hair, and when every other specific has failed. It prevents hair from falling off or turning grey, strengthens weak hair, cleanses it from scurf or dandriff, and makes it beautifully soft, curly, and glossy. In the growth of Whiskers, Eyebrows, and Mustachios, it is unfailing in its stimulative operation. For children it is especially recommended, as forming the basis of a beautiful head of hair. Price 3s. 6d., 7s.; or Family Bottles (equal to four small), 10s. 6d.; and double that size, 21s.

ROWLANDS' KALYDOR.

An Oriental Botanical Preparation, of unfailing efficacy, in thoroughly purifying the skin from all pimples, spots, redness, freckles, tan, and discolorations; in producing a healthy freshness and transparency of complexion, and a softness and delicacy of the hands and arms. During the heat and dust of summer, and in cases of sunburn, stings of insects, or incidental inflammation, its virtues have long and extensively been acknowledged. Price 4s. 6d. and 8s. 6d. per Bottle.

ROWLANDS' ODONTO, OR PEARL DENTIFRICE,

A White Powder. Prepared from Oriental Herbs with unusual care, transmitted to this country at great expense, this unique compound will be found of inestimable value in preserving and beautifying the Teeth, strengthening the Gums, and in giving sweetness and perfume to the breath. Price 2s. 9d. per Box.—**Beware of Spurious Imitations.**—The only GENUINE of each bears the name of **"ROWLANDS'"** preceding that of the article on the Wrapper or Label.—Sold by A. ROWLAND and SONS, 20, Hatton Garden, London, and by Chemists and Perfumers.

[L.O.—4

No. 73, 6th Mo. (June,) 1853.

BRADSHAW'S CONTINENTAL RAILWAY, STEAM NAVIGATION, & CONVEYANCE

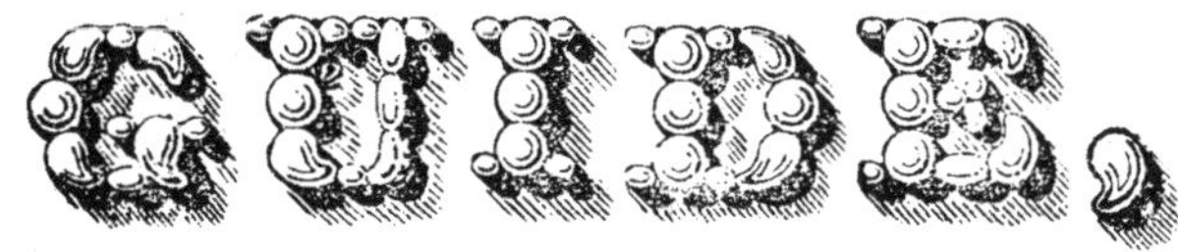

A TRAVELLER'S MANUAL

FOR THE

WHOLE CONTINENT OF EUROPE:

CONTAINING EVERY INFORMATION CONNECTED WITH RAILWAYS, STEAM NAVIGATION, AND CONVEYANCES;

AND PRACTICAL INSTRUCTIONS FOR TRAVELLERS.

THE SAILING OF THE ROYAL MAIL PACKETS,

&c., &c., PUBLISHED OFFICIALLY IN THIS WORK,

BY AUTHORITY OF THE LORDS OF THE ADMIRALTY.

PRICE ONE SHILLING AND SIXPENCE,

Sent Post Free for 2s.

ACCOMPANIED WITH A WELL EXECUTED MAP OF THE RAILWAYS OF EUROPE.

A SPECIAL EDITION, PRICE 3s. 6d.,

Sent Post Free for 4s.,

CONTAINS AN ADDITIONAL AMOUNT OF USEFUL INFORMATION, TOGETHER WITH SPLENDID MAPS OF FRANCE, SWITZERLAND, AND PLANS OF THE CITIES OF PARIS, BRUSSELS, ANTWERP, GHENT, MAYENCE, THE HAGUE, OSTEND, FRANKFORT-ON-THE-MAINE, BERLIN, MUNICH, AND ALSO OF THE RHINE.

LONDON:

PUBLISHED BY W. J. ADAMS (BRADSHAW'S RAILWAY PUBLICATION OFFICE), 59, FLEET-STREET.

MANCHESTER :—BRADSHAW AND BLACKLOCK, 47, BROWN-STREET.

LIVERPOOL :—T. FAIRBROTHER, 2, OLD HALL-STREET.

PARIS:

PUBLISHED BY GALIGNANI & Co., 18, RUE VIVIENNE; J. DAWES, 3, PLACE VENDOME;

BOULOGNE-SUR-MER :—MRS. MERRIDEW, 60, RUE DE L'ECU, near the Port.

FRANKFORT-ON-THE-MAINE—C. JUGEL.

BRUSSELS.

Sole Continental Agent and Manager—W. MIDDLETON, 94, Montagne de la Cour, Brussels, to whom ALL Continental Advertisements for insertion in the Guide MUST be sent before the 20th of every month.

Gerant—Mr. W. MIDDLETON, 94, Montagne de la Cour, Brussels.

NOTICE TO TRAVELLERS.

Tourists who make use of this GUIDE, and may find any inaccuracies therein, are earnestly requested to communicate personally or by letter with the Editor, on their return to England; or, should they be permanently resident abroad, to do so through friends in this country, in the course of their regular correspondence, requesting such friends to communicate with the Editor. Travellers would also oblige by forwarding in like manner any suggestions as to economy in travelling, interesting and cheap tours, detours, &c., that they may think useful. Much good would also accrue were the Hotel Keepers to communicate with our Continental Agent—Mr. MIDDLETON, 94, Montagne de la Cour, Brussels—respecting their Hotels, new roads opened, new conveyances started, or new facilities offered by themselves to Travellers wishing to penetrate beyond the beaten tracks.

We avail ourselves of the present opportunity of expressing our cordial thanks to those kind friends who, either personally or by letter, have furnished us with valuable hints respecting those continental cities which they have recently visited; and we would again solicit from future travellers similar favours, as the most certain means of rendering our GUIDE more increasingly useful to the large number of individuals who, either on business or pleasure, are constantly visiting the Continent of Europe. We have introduced, at the end of the Special Edition, a few leaves of writing-paper, which we think will be useful to travellers for putting down such stray remarks and notes; and if tourists would put them under cover, and direct to our office, we shall feel obliged.

We have to request that all Correspondence and Information relating to the CONTINENTAL GUIDE be addressed direct to our London office, 59, Fleet-street.

The recommendation of Hotels is confided exclusively to our Representative, the Continental Manager, whose address is given on the Title Page, and who is engaged in selecting the best and most respectable throughout the Continent, in order to render the GUIDE a valuable reference in respect to those and other Establishments in the principal cities of Europe.

Our only object being to assist the tourist, and protect him from imposition, we wish it to be understood, that if a traveller has JUST GROUNDS of complaint against any of the houses recommended, and will communicate (post paid) with the Manager on the subject, an inquiry will be made into the case, and, if necessary, the particular recommendation will be immediately revised or suppressed.

A SPECIAL EDITION of the CONTINENTAL GUIDE is now issued, containing an additional amount of information, together with *thirteen Maps*, price 3s. 6d.

To those Continental Companies who have transmitted their Time Bills direct to our London Office we feel much obliged; and if all Companies would do so, our obligations would be much increased, and the correctness of our information indubitably guaranteed.—We shall feel obliged to those gentlemen who favour us with information on printed forms to post them with merely a strip of paper across for direction, in the same manner that newspapers are dispatched.

AUX VOYAGEURS ET NOS CORRESPONDANTS.

Nous sommes bien obligés à toutes les Compagnies du Continent qui ont transmis directement leurs Feuilles d'Arrivées et de Départs à notre Bureau de Londres et nous serions très reconnaissants à toutes les autres compagnies qui feraient le même. L'exactitude de nos informations serait alors parfaitement garantie.

AN UNSERE GEEHRTEN CORRESPONDENTEN UND REISENDEN DES AUSLANDES.

Denjenigen Eisenbahn, Dampfschiffahrts, &c. Gesellschaften und unseren Auslandischen, Freunden welche uns ihre Fahrpläne und sonstigen Beiträge an unser Londoner Bureau (No. 59, Fleet Street), direct zugesandt haben, sprechen wir hiermit unseren verbindlichsten Dank, aus und bitten wir zugleich sämmtliche verehrlichen Geselschaften und das Reisende Publikum uns ihre Fahrpläne, &c. fur unseren "Continental Railway, &c. Guide," frühzeitig mitzutheilen damit derselbe ein vollständiges und zuverlässiges Hülfsmittel der Reisenden werde; Drucksachen bitten wir uns nur unter Kreuzbänd zugehen zu lassen.

TO ADVERTISERS.

In consequence of the increasing sale of the CONTINENTAL GUIDE, Messrs. B. & B. beg to acquaint their advertising friends, that from and after this date, the following SCALE OF CHARGES will be adopted:—

	£	s.	d.
Whole Page	£3	3	0
Two-Thirds of Page	2	5	0
Half	1	14	0
One Third	1	4	0
One Fourth	£0	18	6
Sixth of Page	0	12	0
One Eighth and Under	0	9	0

ANSWERS TO CORRESPONDENTS.

We have great pleasure in calling the attention of British and American Travellers to the following communication from Charles S. Goodrich, Esq., United States Consul at Lyons; (that gentleman will please accept our best thanks.) He will perceive, on reference to page 20, that his suggestions have been attended to; and we shall still further extend the information in the next edition, by giving in their proper place, the names and residences of the United States Consuls on the Continent, as well as those accredited by Great Britain.

CONSULATE OF THE U. S., AMERICA.

SIRS,—Like other American residents and travellers, I feel under obligations to you for the information, instruction, &c., in your "Guide." Excuse me for making a suggestion or two. Probably more than half of your readers—and those who greatly rely on your information as contained in your various publications—are *American* citizens. These last would probably feel as much obliged, and as grateful for *special* information, as the English subjects. It has occurred to me, that you would do a favour, in your next edition, to many American residents and travellers, if you would make the same reference to American Consuls, &c., in the various cities of the Continent, that you do in regard to the English. I am well aware, that our government officers abroad are not as fixed and stable as yours; still, this is no serious objection to your noticing them for the benefit of their voyaging fellow-countrymen.

Again, in this city of Lyons, with a population in the city and suburbs of some 275,000, and by far the largest silk manufacturing town on the Continent, the British Government have no Consul or Agent of any kind. I have been surprised at this; and it is a subject of remark by English residents and English travellers. Scarcely a day passes, that some one or more English subjects do not apply to me for aid, instruction, or information, or to be extricated from some difficulty. They say they have no Consul here; and they feel as though they had claim on the only Consul here who speaks their language. They often do not speak the language of the country, and this is the source of some trouble. Then again, there are others that require papers to be legalized—these, of course, I *cannot assist*. But wherever and whenever I can, I do and act for them, and take the same trouble for them, that I do for my own fellow-citizens. If the British Government do not choose to station a Consul here, they ought at least, I should think, to refer their subjects to some proper individual. Until that is done, and so long as I hold this post, I shall take pleasure in aiding and assisting, in any way that I can, any and all who speak my language, and who solicit my interference in their behalf. Excuse, yours, &c.,

CHAS. S. GOODRICH,
Consul, U. S., America, Lyons, Fr.

The Editors of Bradshaw's Continental Guide.

ST. B.—The manager received your letter with much pleasure; and was gratified with the satisfactory testimony you bear to the utility and value of the "Continental Guide." He immediately inquired into the case you considered an exception to the general correctness of our notices of hotels; and he is persuaded your suspicions are unfounded. He submits the following remarks to your consideration:—

The list of wines in the saloon of the hotel gives the prices of each description, viz., Medoc, or Vin ordinaire, 3 fr. 50 c.; St. Julian, the wine you had, and which is much superior to the ordinaire, is 6 fr.; and if you asked for St Julian, you cannot reasonably object to paying the usual price.

The price of the apartment you occupied is 10 frs. per day, therefore 14 frs. for two nights and a-day is not exorbitant.

The charge for wax lights is invariably made throughout the Continent; and it is alleged, that as St. B. used them during two evenings, the lights were burning considerably more than *two minutes*.

With respect to the "*ver cassé*," this was not a fictitious casualty, as the entry is made in the books of the hotel in the handwriting of the landlady, to whom the circumstance had been reported. There may have been a mistake. The said hotel is considered deserving our designation. The prices are probably somewhat higher than at an inferior house; but in this, as in other things, one must pay for quality, situation and rank.

The majority of the proprietors of hotels recommended in this Guide, are aware of its influence and they are mostly particularly anxious to justify our recommendatory notices. Exceptions there may be; but in such cases we have only to give the authenticated facts complained of in these columns, and to caution our countrymen against the house, to bring the person to his senses. We intend, however, to use this power in an honourable manner; and we only ask our readers to assist our efforts in the same spirit, as *gentlemen and men of the world*, and they will then perceive the "Continental Guide" is exercising a salutary effect in their behalf throughout the Continent.

Will the gentleman who sent us the numerous suggestions and alteration for our Guides in the month of February last, and who answered our notice in the March Guide, again take the trouble to send us his name and address, (which most unfortunately has been mislaid), when we will communicate with him.

We have not space to reply at length to any other correspondents. The following will please accept our best thanks for their communications:—MADAME C. N., LONDON; MR. R. B. T., UTRECHT; Messrs. G. & K., LEIPSIC; and Mr. W. M., ST. ANDREWS.

GENERAL INSTRUCTIONS TO CONTINENTAL TRAVELLERS.

Soap.—Travellers should be particularly careful to provide themselves with this useful article before proceeding to the Continent; if they fail so to do, they will find this form a serious item in their hotel bills, soap being a rare article in Continental Hotels, and if supplied to travellers, is always charged.

Shoes.—These should be double-soled, with three rows of hob-nails, and without iron heels, which are dangerous, and liable to slip in walking over rocks. They should also be so large as not to pinch the feet in any part, and should be worn some time before, in order to conform them to the shape of the foot. Good Shoes may always be obtained in Switzerland fit for mountain excursions, and they should be kept in constant repair. The waiters at the Swiss Inns will attend to all commissions of this sort.

Stockings.—Woollen are preferable to cotton; the latter cut the feet in a long walk. Worsted socks, or cotton stockings with worsted feet, are decidedly the best.

Gaiters are useful in wet weather to keep the socks clean; they also prevent small stones from falling into the shoes.

Trowsers.—Cloth are preferable to linen, which afford no protection against rain, or changes of temperature in mountain regions. Tweed stuff is very suitable.

Coats.—A frock coat is better than a shooting jacket, which will do well enough in remote places, but looks strange, and will attract attention in the streets of a foreign town. A very serviceable article is a *blouse*, (kitter, in German) somewhat resembling a ploughman's smock-frock in England, and which is very extensively worn by all classes on the Continent. It may be worn either over the usual dress, or substituted for the coat in hot weather. Brown is the best colour, blue being worn by labourers only. This garment may be purchased in any German town. The light great-coat, now so generally worn in England, is perhaps preferable to the blouse. A waterproof Mackintosh life preserver may be useful in some situations. Felt hats are very comfortable.

Knapsacks may be purchased much cheaper abroad, and much better than in England.

Portmanteaus are better purchased in England than any where else. The dimensions allowed in the French mails are 27 inches in length, 15 in breadth, and 13 in height.

Polyglot Washing Books, will also be found useful.

Black Glass Spectacles, to screen the eyes from the glow of the sun in southern climates, and the dust and cinders whilst riding in the railway carriage.

Purses.—A stout leathern purse or canvas bag, to hold silver crown pieces and dollars, cards, or pieces of parchment for writing directions for luggage, (it being necessary many times to address every package,) and one or two leather straps, to keep together small parcels, will be found very useful.

Writing-case.—Portable writing and dressing cases are better procured in England, and will be found useful.

Umbrella.—A strong substantial one, that will also serve as a walking-stick, is the best.

Remedy for Sea Sickness.—*The Creozote*, which is advertised as a remedy for toothache, is believed to be equally efficacious in the distressing malady commonly known as sea-sickness. It may be had of any respectable druggist, and is to be thus taken:—About half an hour before the passenger embarks, he is to take three drops in a small quantity of water. When on board, if he feels a little nausea, let him pour two or three drops on a bit of sugar, which he will swallow; and this he may repeat every hour if he have nausea, or if sickness come on after the stomach has been relieved.

Passports.—The rigid regulations of the Continental Police, and the Passport custom, are the two greatest annoyances experienced by English travellers on the Continent. But they should recollect that it is a matter of necessity, from which there is no exemption; and, by care and attention, what is a nuisance may be greatly modified, and vexation and inconvenience avoided. More than half the embarrassments our countrymen get into are caused by their own neglect. Perhaps impressing on their minds, that without "papers" they are, in the eye of the law on the Continent, thieves, vagabonds, and suspected persons, may induce them to pay more attention to these instruments. They too often only get a glimpse of the truth when they come into collision with the police. Mere unpoliteness to an *employé* is punishable with fine and imprisonment, as "insulting a deputed officer of the crown in the execution of his duties." For particulars in reference to the regulations under which Passports are issued for the various countries, &c., see pages 19 and 20.

We insert the following notice here, as it is important:—

AMERICAN TRAVELLERS.—American Travellers intending to visit Austria, by way of Dresden and Prague, must have their Passports *visé* by an Austrian and American Ambassador or Consul, at London, Berlin, or Frankfort, or in some other town where an American representative resides.

Landing on the Continent.—No sooner does the steam boat reach port, than the traveller finds himself pestered by discordant cries dinned into his ears by the porters and employées of the different Hotels. Showers of cards will be poured on him, and the prices charged bawled out lustily. To avoid all this as much as may be, let him determine on his Hotel *beforehand*, and name it at once, when the agent for it will immediately step forward, and take the new arrival under his protection, and escort him to the Hotel.

Custom-house Regulations.—Passengers, on landing, are not permitted to take their baggage with them on shore. The Custom-House Porters, who are responsible for its safety, convey it direct from the vessel to the Custom-House, where the owner, to save personal attendance, had better send the Commissionaire afterwards with the keys. The Commissionare will also obtain the necessary official signature of the police to the traveller's passport. The landlord of the inn is responsible for his honesty. The search into the luggage is frequently more severe in the presence of the traveller than otherwise; and he that would keep himself in good temper, and not begrudge a fee of two francs to the Commissionaire, will do well to employ him.

Hotels.—It is not necessary, in travelling on the continent, for a gentleman and his wife (supposing they wish to live with economy) to take a sitting-room as well as a bed-room, as is the custom in British Hotels. On arrival at an Hotel abroad, state what sort of a bed-room you wish to have, and go and choose it at once: as a general rule, the *higher* you ascend, the *less* you pay. You may drink tea there, if you like, and you always dine in the public rooms, when there will be plenty of ladies to support you. The neat little German beds have silk coverlets thrown on them during the day, and the washing apparatus is made for concealment; and you may receive visiters in your sleeping apartment as well as in a drawing room. If you require no more than two wax candles, tell them to take the others away, otherwise they will be charged in the bill.

Porterage of Luggage.—Travellers will save themselves much trouble and overcharges by always asking the proprietor of the hotel to which they go, to settle with the porter for luggage.

PRACTICAL INFORMATION FOR TRAVELLERS IN FRANCE.

Travellers landing at Calais, and intending to proceed immediately to Paris, may avoid an inspection of their baggage till they reach Paris, by making a declaration to that effect at the Custom-house. Travellers proceeding THROUGH FRANCE to Belgium direct, will avoid examination by the French Custom-house authorities by making a similar declaration as to their destination.

The Traveller upon his arrival at Boulogne, Calais, or other French port, is not allowed to take any luggage on shore with him save a small parcel; but if he arrives at night, he is allowed his carpet bag.—His baggage is removed to the Custom-house for the purpose of being examined, after which he may clear it himself if he thinks fit, but it is usual to employ a commissioner, who is entitled to receive for his trouble only that which he had previously agreed for.—No traveller can be charged any thing for his luggage beyond the following sums, which include the expenses of landing, warehousing, and conveying to any part of the town.

Packages under 10lb. weight.	0	Francs	7 sous.
do. from 10lb. to ½ cwt.	0	,,	14 ,,
do. from ½ cwt. to 2 cwt.	1	,,	0 ,,
do. from above 2 cwt ..	1	,,	10 ,,

Nothing is due for objects of little weight, such as walking-sticks, umbrellas, hat boxes, cases, or small baskets, when they form a portion of other luggage belonging to the same person or the same family.

Every object and package taken from the warehouse without being carried home, pays 35 c. (7 sous.

A traveller employing a commissioner owes him nothing beyond these charges, but what he may have agreed to pay him. All complaints and claims are to be addressed to the Agent General, whose office is on the spot, or by writing to the President of the Chamber of Commerce.

NOTICE —All articles not being WORN, such as wearing apparel, must be declared at the Custom-house. Travellers not conforming to this regulation, would incur not only the confiscation of the articles not declared, but also the payment of a fine.

IN TAKING FURNISHED APARTMENTS, the stranger should have a written agreement, with an inventory, signed by both parties, containing a precise account of the furniture, even to a plate. He must also have a stipulation therein that the landlord pays the furniture tax, otherwise the party will have to pay, notwithstanding the furniture is the property of the landlord.

A TENANT must answer for the effect of fire in his rooms, unless he can show that the fire was occasioned by accident.

SERVANTS in France are engaged by the month: masters possess the right of discharging their servants when they think proper, according to a regulation established by the JUGE-DE-PAIX, and servants can leave their places when they like; but in this case they are only paid by the day.

Summer Visiters are not subject to the payment of taxes; personal and furniture taxes are levied only on foreigners who are residents at the time the annual lists are revised in November.

Carriages are hired at the rate of two francs per hour, and, if the journey is ever so short, the charge of two francs is expected unless an agreement to the contrary is made beforehand.

English Postage Stamps count for nothing in the French Post-Office.

Permits.—At Boulogne and Calais, Permits can be had one hour before the departure of each steamer, or from 1 to 3 p.m., preceding the night of departure of the packet, when it starts between ten at night and five in the morning. If the passenger with his permit goes on board from ten to eleven o'clock, or one hour before the vessel leaves, he will not be allowed to come on shore again without permission of the police.

Passengers proceeding to England will be allowed to take with them any quantity of spirits less than a pint, and half a pint of Eau de Cologne, free of duty. Travellers, however, should bear in mind, that if articles liable to duty are contained among their luggage, they must make declaration of such at the French or English Custom-house; which will avoid forfeiture or other subsequent unpleasantness. Letters for posting found among passengers' baggage at the French or English Custom-houses, subject the sender and bearer to penal consequences at the instance of the authorities of both countries.

Switzerland and Mountainous Districts.—Those travellers, whether equestrian or pedestrian, who intend ascending mountains, should be provided with a frock of oiled silk, as the best protection against the weather in places where the labour and heat attendant upon the ascent would render an additional outer garment a severe incumbrance. A mountain-pole, which can always be procured in the neighbourhood, is also of considerable service, and a belt round the waist. The best restorative is tea, and it can be procured good in Holland, and in most of the large towns of Germany. Provisions should also be conveyed in a knapsack or haversack, of which the Guide will take charge, and the contents of which he will expect to share. The traveller should never lose sight of his Guide, as he may frequently be in considerable danger without being aware of it, especially in the neighbourhood of glaciers. Persons subject to giddiness, should be cautious of venturing into certain situations.

Luggage, &c.—Passengers landing at Calais for Belgium may have their baggage declared for transit, when it will not be examined till they arrive at the Belgian frontier. Travellers from Cologne declaring thence for England, may have it passed through France and Belgium in like manner, thus saving great annoyance, and sometimes great expense. As on most Continental Railroads no baggage is free of carriage to the traveller, but every pound has to be paid for, this mode of conveyance becomes both troublesome and expensive.

It may be premised as a general rule, that travellers would do well, and spare themselves considerable annoyance and inconvenience, by taking with them as little luggage as possible, particularly if intending to travel on the Belgian or German Railways.

Ladies who are anxious and wishful for comfort in their mountain excursions, should provide themselves with a saddle, recently constructed by Whipping, of North Audley-street; it can be easily packed, as the crutch is separable, and the girths, crupper, &c., are made to fit a horse or donkey. This saddle can be put into an oil cloth bag, and attached to the carriage.

Language.—Every traveller should, if possible, make himself acquainted with the language of the country, before he goes to travel in it. To know the language is to have a double purse. The French language will suffice for Belgium, the Rhine and its vicinity, Switzerland, Piedmont, and the chief towns of Northern Italy. It is not generally known in the German States, nor in the provincial towns of Italy, nor in the Tyrol. In Holland, and many parts of Germany, you are more likely to be understood, when you ask your way in English than in French. When parties do not understand, or speak the language, they ought to employ an interpreter, and should be particular in their arrangement with the person engaged. They should be satisfied as to his character and intelligence, and have a very explicit understanding as to the amount of remuneration to be paid him for his services.

German Railways.—The Second Class carriages on the German Railways are much superior to our own, and few persons travel first class.

Expenses—Money.—It is altogether impossible to fairly calculate the exact expense of travelling on the Continent. That depends more or less on the habits and means of the traveller and his mode of journeying, and likewise on the rate of charges made in the various countries. It may, however, be remarked that, unless the expenditure be very lavish, 20s. per day for each individual ought to cover all expenses—even when travelling by post. Pedestrian excursions in remote situations can hardly exceed from 5s. to 10s. per day. The chief expense arises from locomotion, the cost of Hotel living being almost insignificant. The cost of locomotion will be considerably increased when the traveller proceeds quickly. The above amount will be very probably near the mark when the tourist journeys 70 or 80 miles a day, if only 40 or 50 miles, the expenses, then, are not likely to be more than 15s. per day.

Travellers when setting out on their tour, should take especial care to inform themselves as to the currency of each respective country through which they purpose passing, with a view of making themselves practically acquainted with its representative value. And in no case should they transact an exchange unless through their Banker, or through the agency of a respectable Broker.

Circular notes will be found the most economical and safest mode of carrying money on the Continent to meet expenses. They have this great advantage, over letters of credit, that the bearer may receive his money at different places instead of at *one* fixed place. The traveller having calculated his expenses as near as he can, pays over the sum to the Banker, and receives in return notes to the same amount, without any charge. Each of these notes are equivalent to the sum of £10 or more, and in addition he receives a general LETTER OF ORDER, addressed to the Foreign Agents of the House in the different parts of Europe: for further particulars see page 23. There being over 200 of these agents dispersed throughout Europe, the tourist will always find himself not far removed from his supplies. The notes are drawn to order, and the holder should *not endorse* them until he receives the money. The cheques are so concerted with the agents as to render a successful forgery of the name almost impossible. The value of the notes is subject to the current usance course of Exchange on London, at the time and place of payment, and subject to *no commission.*

English Bank Notes are convenient in Belgium and in all parts of Germany, but the exchange is lower than that of the Circular Notes. A small supply of English gold should be taken to defray steam boat expenses, as also to provide against shortcomings where Circular Notes cannot be exchanged. Throughout Germany, English sovereigns bear a high premium, and ought to be taken at all the hotels at their full value, but the best course to adopt is to apply to some *authorized* money-changer when the traveller requires to change them, and not at Inns or Hotels. The value of Napoleons, sovereigns, and 10-guilder pieces, are liable to be depreciated by steam-boat clerks and waiters, who presume upon the traveller's ignorance.

Persons changing Circular Notes will take the money of the country, if he intends to remain there, but if not, the best coin to take is Napoleons, as they bear a high premium. For the best Continental gold coin to take from England, see page 23.

Travellers should be provided with the legal coin of the country he travels in, and not take more than is necessary to defray his expenses whilst in it, as almost every state has a distinct coinage. This course prevents all danger of loss. In all their transactions with Hotel Proprietors, Coach Officials, &c., they should have a *distinct* arrangement, in presence of witnesses, *before* availing themselves of any accommodation or services. At hotels and inns through the journey, the Bill of Fare should be called for, and *seen*, and the prices *accurately* ascertained. This course, if followed, will prevent much after unpleasantness, and preserve the traveller against imposition—a very plentiful commodity on the Continent.

FOREIGN RAILWAYS BEING CONSTRUCTED.

AUSTRIA.—Laibach (Illyria) to Trieste—Troppau (Gallicia) to Bochnia.
BELGIUM.—Charleroi to Marienbourg—Liege to Mastricht.
EGYPT.—Alexandria to Cairo.
FRANCE.—Epernay to Rheims—Poitiers to Angouleme—Chalons to Lyons, Valence, and Avignon, with a branch to Grenoble—Le Mans to Alençon—Chartres to Mans, Laval, and Rennes—Chartres to Seez, Argentan, Caen—Caento Lisieux, Bernay and Rouen, and Bernay and Paris—St. Quentin to Herculine.
GERMANY.—Emden to Lingen, Osnabruch, and Minden—Lingen to Rheim—Carlsruhe and Stuttgart—Frankfort to Aschaffenburg, Würzburg, and Bamberg—Kaufbeuern to Lindau.
HOLLAND.—Rotterdam to Utrecht—Arnheim to Emmerich.
HUNGARY.—Pesth to Debreczin—Odenburg to Raab.
ITALY.—Brescia to Verona—Busalla to Genoa.
NORWAY.—Christiania to Lake Morsen (50 mes.)
PRUSSIA.—Konigsberg to Warsaw, by the Vistula.
RUSSIA.—St. Petersburg to Warsaw.

RAILWAYS PROJECTED.

ITALY.—Rome to Bologna and Ancona—Civita Vecchia to Rome—Sienna to Rome.
SPAIN.—Santander to Valladolid and Madrid—Aranjuez to Almanza and Alicante, besides several others.

CONTENTS.

THE SPECIAL EDITION.

It also contains maps of the following places:

Europe, France, Paris, Brussels, Antwerp, Ghent, The Hague, Ostend, Frankfort on the Maine, Munich, Berlin, the Rhine, and a Map of the Namur and Liege Railway.

INDEX.

Note—For convenience of reference, the Guide is now divided into two parts, viz., Tabular and Descriptive. In the following Index the Traveller will find no difficulty in ascertaining which portion is referred to, by recollecting that the Tables end at page 124, and the Descriptive matter begins at page 140; consequently, all below 124 refer to the Time Tables, all above 140 to the Descriptions.

List of Abbreviations used in this Guide.

Money.—fr., franc; c. or ct., cent.; th. and thl., thaler; rth. and rthl., rix thaler; sgr., silver groschen; ngr., new groschen; pf., pfenning; guild., guilder; fl., florin (gulden); g. or guld., gulden (florin); kr., kreuzer; rbl. roubel; kop., kopeck; marc., mark current; shil. and sh., Hamburgh shilling; btz., batz; rp. rappen; zwanz., zwanziger (Austrian lire); Aust. lire or L., Austrian lire (zwanziger.)

Distance and Time.—Dis., Distance; h., hours; m., miles; G. M., German miles; E. M. English miles.

Conveyances.—D. diligence; S. steamer; C. private carriage; M. mule.

PASSPORTS.

We strongly recommend British subjects travelling on the Continent to procure a Foreign-Office Passport, taking care to have it properly visé by the authorities of the various countries intended to be visited, before leaving London. It is essential, in accordance with the latest regulations, that the bearer should attach his or her signature before presenting it for a Foreign *visa*. This is absolutely indispensible—more especially as regards Austria—as the legation of that government in London will refuse to visé any Passport unless this is complied with. Application for a Foreign-Office Passport must be accompanied by a letter from a Banker or Banking Establishment in any part of the united kingdom, recommending the applicant as a British subject, and giving in full the name and address. If a Bank recommendation cannot conveniently be obtained, the letter of a member of either house of Parliament will answer the purpose. Officers in Her Majesty's service, travelling on the Continent, *en route* to join their regiments or stations, are entitled to a Foreign-Office Passport without fee. A Foreign-Office Passport may include several persons travelling in company; and is not limited in duration, if only viséd for every journey.

The following are the Regulations respecting Passports, issued from the Foreign Office for the present year:—

"1st.—Applications for Foreign-Office Passports must be made in writing, and addressed to Her Majesty's Secretary of State for Foreign Affairs, with the word 'Passport' written upon the cover.

"2nd.—The Fee on the issue of a Passport is 7s. 6d.

"3rd.—Foreign-Office Passports are granted only to British subjects, including in that description Foreigners who have been naturalized by Act of Partiament, or by Certificates of Naturalization granted before the 24th day of August, 1850: in this latter case, the party is described in the Passport as a 'Naturalized British subject.'

"4th.—Passports are granted between the hours of twelve and four, on the day following that on which the application for the Passport has been received at the Foreign Office.

"5th.—Passports are granted to persons who are either known to the Secretary of State, or recommended to him by some person who is known to him; or upon the written application of any *Banking Firm* established in London or in any other part of the United Kingdom.

"6th.—Passports cannot be sent by the Foreign Office to persons already abroad. Such Persons should apply to the nearest British Mission or Consulate.

"7th.—Foreign-Office Passports must be countersigned at the Mission, or at some Consulate in England, of the Government of the country which the bearer of the Passport intends to visit.*

"8th.—A Foreign-Office Passport granted for one journey may be used for any subsequent journey, *if countersigned afresh* by the Ministers or Consuls of the countries which the bearer intends to visit.

"*Foreign Office*, 1853."

* The countersignature, or *visa*, of the Prussian or Sardinian authorities in London, is not required.

The other parties authorized to grant Passports, are Ambassadors and Consuls of Continental States, and English Consuls residing at Foreign outports. Ambassadors Passports are gratuitous. Consuls' Passports can be obtained without difficulty, requiring only a fee, varying from 5s. to 10s. English Consuls abroad can give Passports to British subjects, and so can the French Consuls resident at our own ports; but it is always prudent to provide for emergencies by securing one in London before leaving. An Ambassador's Passport is obtained by addressing a written or verbal communication to his secretary, and stating therein both Christian and surname, age, height, profession and address. This is required to be left one day in advance, at the office; and if the applicant call himself on the following day, the Passport is delivered. Those residing in the provinces may obtain a Passport from the Foreign Ministers in London. (See page 21 for Prussia, the Rhine, Nassau, &c.)

When different members of a family travel together, they can all have their names included in one Passport; but friends, servants, &c., must each have one distinct.

As every police official abroad is authorised to inspect it, the Passport must, under all circumstances, be carried about the person. To protect it from the effects of constant friction, it is desirable to have it bound in a pocket-book, which should contain some blank leaves to receive the *visas*, as the official signatures are termed, or to have it sewed on a sheet of parchment, with blank leaves in the centre, and fold and endorse it with the traveller's name, so that he may easily distinguish it from others.

It will be always essential for the traveller to remember that he cannot pass from one country to another without the Passport is *visé*, or countersigned, by the Ministers of those countries through which he intends to pass. Thus, as the Austrian Ambassador in London neither gives nor countersigns any Englishman's Passport except that issued by the Secretary of State, it is indispensable to the traveller bound to Italy, or any part of the Austrian territories, to obtain it at Paris, Frankfort-on-the-Maine, or some one of the great continental capitals.

When desirous of leaving a seaport abroad, in some cases the traveller must obtain a permit from the authorities; should the Passport be in proper form, however, this is instantly given on application.

SCOTLAND.—Passports for all places on the Continent are issued by the Lord Provost, from his Office, City Chambers, Edinburgh.—Fee for each passport, 5s.

PLACES IN LONDON WHERE PASSPORTS, PASSES, OR VISES, are to be obtained; and other necessary information.

At the Foreign Office, Downing Street, West, or on the recommendation of a banker. Fee, 7s. 6d. Passports to all parts, (excepting Italy, see page 21.). Office hours from 12 to 4. All applications for Foreign Office Passports must be accompanied by a Letter of recommendation from a Banking establishment, or a Member of either House of Parliament. *It is imperative that this* *recommendation should give the address of the Parties, in addition to their names, in full, and must notify that they are* British Subjects.

AMERICA.—Hon. Mr. Ingersoll, 45, Portland Place. Passports and Vises granted to American citizens from 11 to 3. For the information of Americans travelling on the Continent, we subjoin a list of those places where a Consul of the United States is resident:—In Austria—at Vienna, Trieste, and Venice; Baden—at Mannheim; Bavaria—at Augsburg and Nurnberg—Belgium—at Antwerp; Denmark—at Copenhagen and Elsineur; France—at Paris, Havre, Bordeaux, Marseilles, Sedan, Lyons, Nantes, LaRochelle, Bayonne, Napoleon, and Vendee; Greece—at Athens; Hanseatic Cities—at Hamburg, Bremen, and Frankfort; Hanover, Hesse Cassel, and Hesse Darmstadt—at Darmstadt; Modena—at Carrara; The Netherlands—at Amsterdam Rotterdam; Portugal—at Lisbon; Prussia (Westphalia)—at Aix-la-Chapelle, and Stettin; Pontifical States—at Rome, Ancona, and Ravenna; Russia—at St. Petersburg, Riga, Archangel, Odessa, and Helsingford; Sardinia—Genoa and Nice; Saxe-Mein—at Sonneberg; Saxony, Leipsic, and Dresden; Spain—at Bilboa, Cadiz, Denia, Malaga, Barcelona, Vigo, and Port Mahon; Sweden and Norway—at Stockholm, Gothenburg, and Bergen; Switzerland—at Basle and Zurich; Turkey—at Constantinople, Smyrna, and Candia; Tuscany—at Leghorn and Florence: Two Sicilies—at Naples, Palermo, and Messina; Wurtemburg—at Stuttgardt.—The above will be found useful in many respects to British as well as American travellers; as in many towns will be found an agent accredited from the United States, where a British Consul is non-resident—in which case English and Americans will meet with equal courtesy and attention.

AUSTRIA.—British subjects must be provided with a Foreign Office Passport, countersigned by the Austrian Ambassador, and by the Ambassadors or Consuls of each of the countries through which they may pass. The *visa* for Passports of the Foreign Office is granted at the Austrian Legation, Chandos House, Chandos Street, Cavendish Square, without any charge whatever; *and it is expressly desired that no fees may be given to the servants.* Office hours from 12 to 2. The Consul is Baron Rothschild, but he neither grants nor *visas* Passports. The words, "British Subject," must be written in the body of the Passport, otherwise, the *visa* will be refused. AMERICAN TRAVELLERS who intend visiting Austria, should take care to have their Passport *visé* by an Austrian and American Ambassador or Consul, at Berlin or Frankfort, or in some other town where an American representative dwells.

BADEN—At the Consul's Office, 1, Riches-court, Lime-street, City. Fee 2s. 6d.

BAVARIA.—At the Minister's, 3 Hill-street, Berkeley-square, when personally known to him; otherwise, at the Consul's Office, 33½, Great St. Helen's, Bishopsgate-street. Fee 5s.

BELGIUM.—Consul's Office, Adelaide Chambers, 52 Gracechurch Street. Hours, from 11 to 4. Passports for Belgium only, are granted to British subjects on payment of 6s. 6d. Visas, 3s. 9d.—Ambassador's residence, 50 Portland Place. British subjects on entering Belgium are required to be provided with either a Belgian Passport, or a British or other Passport countersigned by a Belgian authority. When only traversing Belgium, going to Prussia, British subjects will require British Passports. Should this form be omitted, they may procure a British Passport at the British Consulate in Ostend or Antwerp. On landing in Belgium without a Passport in due form, travellers are exposed to be conducted, by the Police, either to the Consul or to the Bourgmestre, before they are enabled to obtain a Passport and continue their journey in Belgium. Travellers proceeding through Belgium to the Rhine, must enter their luggage for Cologne, where it is examined.

BRAZIL.—Legation, 5, Mansfield Street, between 11 and 2.—Gratis.

SICILY.—A Special Passport is required for Sicily. It can easily be obtained, on application to the Ambassador at Naples.

DENMARK.—At the Consul's Office, 6, Warnford-court, Throgmorton Street, Bank, between 10 and 4.—Fee 10s 6d.—Ambassador's residence, 44, Mortimer Street.

FRANCE.—Passengers can land at any French port without Passports. But before proceeding to Paris, or the interior of France, the possession of a Passport is indispensable. British travellers can obtain Passports for travelling in France and upon the Continent from the British Consuls resident at Boulogne, Calais, and other French outports. The British Consular Passport, which costs 4s. 6d., and which is in force one year (twelve months), merely requires to be *visé* by the Police authorities, for which no charge is made. This Passport can be made to include all the members of a family and its domestics. Should the traveller intend stopping only a short time in Paris, the Passport ought to be countersigned as speedily as possible, and the next place he intends to visit specified. In all excursions about Paris, the Passport should be carried about the person, as admission to many places may be gained through its exhibition alone. Travellers with Foreign Passports are subject to a *visa* on entering Calais, the expense of which is two francs. Before returning to England it is necessary to send it to the British Ambassador, Rue du Faubourg St. Honoré, where it can be countersigned, between the hours of 11 and 2. It must afterwards be taken to the Prefecture of Police, open on week-days from 10 to 4, and on Sundays from 10 to 1, where it is again countersigned. Before a traveller can leave a French port, *a permis d' émbarquement* must be obtained; it is given gratis at all hours on exhibiting the *passe* or passport in regular form, and is received by an officer of police as the traveller goes on board the packet. Travellers who intend visiting the Continent may obtain Passports and *visas* at the General Consulate Office, **No. 47,** King William-street, London Bridge (corner of Arthur-street East). Passes and Passports are issued at this office for France only. Parties visiting the Continent with a French *passe* or passport should observe the following distinction:—if intending to proceed further, they can do so by having their passport, when in France, visé by the Minister or Consul of the country they intend visiting—but a Passe extends to France only, and cannot be visé for any other country. Foreign Office Passports, after being duly visé, are endorsed to France only; in order to proceed further they must again be visé in France by the Minister or Consul of the country to which the traveller is desirous of proceeding.—These remarks apply to British and other subjects, and not to French citizens.—Passports are delivered to French parties for all parts of Europe, &c.—The fees are as follows:—for Passport, 5s.; Passe, 5s.; Visa to a Foreign Passport, 4s. 3d. To natives of France, the fees for Passport or Passe, 4s. 3d.; Visa, 2s.

GREECE.—At the Consul's, 25, Finsbury Circus; between 11 and 4.—Fee 2s. 6d.

HAMBURGH and HANSEATIC REPUBLICS of LUBECK and BREMEN.—Consul's Office, 12, Copthall Court, Throgmorton Street.—Fee 5s.

HANOVER.—Secretary to Embassy, 4, Hobart-place, Eaton-square, between 10 and 3. Also at the Ambassador's (Count Kilmansegg's), 44, Grosvenor-place, between 10 and 3. Gratis. The porter, 1s.

HANSEATIC REPUBLICS (LUBECK, BREMEN, HAMBURG).—Chargé des Affaires, 3, Stratford Place; Passports granted to none but Hanseats; Passport Chancery, 12, Copthall Court, Throgmorton Street; Consulate General, 12, Copthall Court, Throgmorton-street, City, from 11½ till 3

HOLLAND.—Passports and *visas* granted at the Consul's Office, 123, Fenchurch Street. Fee, 5s. Ambassador's residence, 20, Lowndes Square. The strictness respecting Passports is now as great in Holland as in other states—no one should travel through the Dutch states without one. A Prussian, Belgian, or French Passport will answer the purpose. An examination of Passports and Luggage takes place at Emmerich, on board the Steam-boat, on ascending and descending the Rhine.

ITALY.—Travellers should pay very particular attention to the manner in which Italian Passports are managed. Every foreigner, before being permitted to enter the Papal States, is required to have his passport *visé* by the Papal Consul, or Nuncio resident in the capital last visited by him; and, if taking the French route, much convenience will be the consequence if he procure the *visa* of the Nuncio at Paris, on setting out. If this be impossible, the Papal Consular *visa* at some important town, will suffice. The Austrian *visa* is also available for *all* parts of Italy. At each town the passport is examined and countersigned, for which a fee of two pauls has to be paid; and, in garrison towns, the same formality is observed on leaving. In sea port towns, the *visa* of the British Consul is necessary. The traveller, before quitting Rome on his return, should obtain to his passport the *visas* of the representatives of the various dominions through which he purposes to travel. If travelling from Milan through Geneva, into France, the signatures to his passport of the British, Sardinian, and French Consul Generals at Milan, will be necessary.

LASCIA PASSARE.—Persons journeying in their own private conveyances, should provide the above to be forwarded to the frontier, and also to be left at the Porta del Popolo, as it will cause to be avoided the formalities of the Custom House. This they can do by writing to their bankers or correspondents. Travellers by public or post-carriages, cannot be permitted this privilege.

MEXICO.—Legation, 6, Arundel-street, Coventry-street, Haymarket, between 12 and 4: delivered the day following on personal application

NAPLES and SICILY.—Passport Office, 15, Princes-street, Cavendish-square, Mondays and Thursdays, between 10 and 12; delivered, gratis, following day, between 2 and 3. For persons *going by sea*, Consul's Office, 15, Cambridge-street, Hyde-park-square, between 10 and 12.—Fee 10s. Ambassador's residence, 16, Park Lane. Visas to Passports from 12 to 2, not later. The Sicilian Minister will grant passports only to Sicilian subjects. Englishmen visiting that portion of the Continent must obtain their passports at the Foreign Office, Downing Street, and the Italian minister will visa them gratis.

NICARAGUA.—Consul's Office, 1, London-street, Fenchurch-street.

OLDENBURG.—Chargé d'Affaires residence, 3, Stratford Place. Passports granted to none but Oldenburgs. Passport Chancery, 12, Copthall Court, Throgmorton Street; Office hours, from 11 to 3½.—Consul's Office, 12, Copthall Court, Throgmorton Street. Fee, 5s.

PERU.—Ambassador's residence, 15, Portland-place.—Consul's office, 6, Copthall-court

PORTUGAL.—Embassy, 12, Gloucester Place, between 11 and 4; delivered, following day. Also at the Consul's Office, 5, Jeffery's-square, St. Mary Axe.—Fee 5s.

PRUSSIA, the Rhine, Duchy of Nassau, Brunswick, and Grand Duchy of Hesse—British subjects are now allowed to enter the Prussian dominions with a Passport from the British Secretary of State for Foreign affairs, without the counter-signature of the Prussian Ambassador or Consul, but the *visa* of the Ambassadors or Consuls of each of the countries through which they may pass must be obtained. Consul's General, Mr. Hebeler, 106, Fenchurch-street. On entering Prussia, from Belgium, the Passport is taken from the traveller at Herbesthal, but must be applied for at the Bureau de Passports at Aix-la-Chapelle, at the railway station. Travellers arriving at Berlin or Minden will be required to exhibit their Passports before leaving the station. The Prussian Government has issued instructions to their authorities throughout the Prussian dominions, stating that Passports granted by Foreign Consuls, in Foreign States, are contrary to the police regulations, and are not to be relied upon; and directing them to cause the necessary steps to be taken for insuring the strict observance of these regulations for the future. We therefore repeat our recommendation to travel on the Continent with a Foreign-Office Passport, properly *visé* by the authorities in London, previous to leaving. Fee for *Visa*, 4s.

RUSSIA.—At the Consul's Office, 2, Winchester-buildings, Old Broad-street, City. Fee for Passport, 6s. 4d.; *Visa*, 1s. 7d.; but it is necessary to state that, BEFORE a *Passport* or *Visa* is granted, the *traveller* must have a recommendation from a banker, stating the purport of his or her voyage of journey, and to whom recommended in Russia. Forms of application may be had at the Consul's Office. Ambassador's residence, Chesham House, Chesham Place, Belgrave Square. For further information, see page 288.

SARDINIA.—At the Consulate, 31, Old Jewry. Fee, 3s. 6d.

SAXONY.—At the Consul's Office, 12, Copthall Court, Throgmorton Street, City, from 11½ till 3. Fee, 5s.—Chargé d'Affaire's residence, 3, Stratford Place. Passports granted by the Chargé d'Affaires to none but Saxons. Office hours from 11½ till 3. An examination of Passports and Luggage takes place at Bodenbach, between Dresden and Prague, on entering Austria. British subjects should be very particular in obtaining the *visa* of the Saxon authorities in England, if going to, or passing through Saxony, or of the Saxon Representative in any European city through which they may pass *en route*.

SPAIN.—At the Embassy, 2, Mansfield Street. Foreign-Office Passports visé *gratis*.

SWEDEN and NORWAY.—Embassy, Halkin-street, Belgrave-square. Hours from 9 till 1; delivered following day.—Fee 5s. Consul's office, 2, Crosby-square, Bishopsgate-street.

SWITZERLAND.—Consul's Office, 8, Crosby-square, Bishopsgate. A Passport from the Minister of one or other of the European States is necessary to the Traveller to Switzerland; and though a Swiss Passport or *visé* is not necessary to ensure an *entrée* into the country, and the Passport is seldom asked for, yet it should be always ready to be produced at a moment's notice. The Passports are generally demanded on entering Geneva, Berne, Lucerne, and the Capitals of the various cantons. Travellers from Switzerland to Savoy or Piedmont, the States of Austria or Bavaria, must have to their Passports the signatures of the Ministers of these States, otherwise they will not be allowed to cross the frontier. Travellers should then take care to secure their *visés* at Berne, where the Ministers accredited to the Swiss Confederation have their offices. Fee for *visa*, 2s. 6d.

TURKEY.—Turkish Embassy, 1, Bryanstone-square, *gratis*, from 12 till 3, every day, Friday and Sunday excepted.

TUSCANY.—Consul's Office, 15, Angel-court, Throgmorton-street, between 10 and 4. Fee, 5s.

URUGUAY (Monte Video).—Consul's Office, 9, New Palace Yard, Westminster; E. B. Neill, Esq., Consul.

WURTEMBERG—Consul's office, 106, Fenchurch-street. Fee, 4s.

PASSPORTS.—Parties in the country, who wish to avoid delay and trouble, can procure their Passport, by writing to our London Agent, W. J. ADAMS, 59, Fleet Street, and enclosing him a Banker's letter, containing the name and address of the person or persons recommended therein. He will also procure the *visa* of the Ambassador representing the country through which they are about to travel.

Fee for obtaining Passport........... 2s. 6d. Do. *Visa* .... 1s. each,
in addition to the charges made by the several authorities.

Passport Cases from 1s. to 4s. 6d. Travellers' Portfolios, Couriers' Bags, Continental Post Paper, and every description of Stationery useful to Travellers.

POST-OFFICE REGULATIONS BETWEEN ENGLAND AND THE CONINENT.

Foreign and Ship Letter Mails made up in London.—Letters for the Foreign Mails are received at St. Martin's-le-Grand and Lombard-street, up to *six* o'clock; from *six* till *seven*, on payment of *one penny* extra; and from *seven* till *half-past seven*, on payment of *sixpence* extra; but not at all after that time.

DESTINATION.	WHEN MADE UP.	WHEN DUE.
France.	Twice each day.	Twice each day.
Belgium.	Daily, except Sunday.	Daily, except Sunday.
Holland.	Wednesday, Saturday, and daily except Sunday (*via* Ostend).	Sunday, Thursday.
Hamburgh, Sweden and Norway	Tuesday, Friday, and daily (*via* Ostend) except Sunday.	Tuesday, Saturday, but usually arrive on the previous day.
Sweden and Norway (during the summer months (via Hull	Daily. Do. do	Tuesday.
Guernsey and Jersey.	Daily. Do. do	Monday, Thursday

Lisbon, Madeira, Vigo, Cadiz, Oporto, and Gibraltar, 7th, 17th, and 27th of each month.

Malta and Ionian Isles, via Southampton, 20th and 29th of each month.

Syria, Egypt, and India, 7th and 24th of each month; via Southampton, 20th of each month.

Brazil and Buenos Ayres, 4th of each month.

Greece, via France, morning and evening; via Marseilles, 7th and 24th; via Southampton, 20th.

Newspapers, British, Foreign, or Colonial, passing between British or Colonial and Foreign ports, and through the British post, pay 2d., if not through British post, 1d.

Belgian newspapers may be sent from Belgium at an uniform rate of 1d. each.

The postage rate to Hanover is altered to an uniform British rate of 6d. Pre-payment of the whole postage of British and Foreign rates, optional. Newspapers, 1d.

FOREIGN MONEY.

Circular notes are given by most of the principal London bankers, and form a very safe and convenient kind of letters of credit. The arrangements for cashing them in the various countries through which the traveller may have to pass are very simple and efficient, precluding almost the possibility of fraud, and as duplicates are given with them, we would caution tourists to keep the one in their pocket-book and the other in their baggage. The chief houses for transacting this continental business are the Union Bank; Herries, Farquhar, & Co.; Coutts & Co.; Sir Claude Scott, Bt., Cavendish-square; Twinings; and the London and Westminster Bank; at the Union Bank, Twinings, and Westminster Bank, they may be obtained in notes of £10 each; and in sums of £5 and upwards at Adam Spielmann's, 10, Lombard street, (corner of Post Office court), where foreign money may be obtained or exchanged to advantage. English sovereigns do not command their full value through Northern Germany, according to the exchange of the day; but the most advantageous continental gold coins that a traveller can take with him in Germany are the Prussian *Friedrichs d'Or*, as these pass current not only in Holland and Belgium, but also through all Germany. *Napoleons* are the very best coin, and may be purchased in London from 16s. to 16s. 2d.; they pass everywhere. Sovereigns are not well known in Italy, and are supposed to be pieces of 20 francs. English bank notes for £5 can be changed on the Rhine, and in Paris, Belgium, and the principal towns in Switzerland; but they are not known in other places; and even at Lyons, Florence, and Rome, they will not be taken under any circumstances; but these can be exchanged at these places at the Money Changers by paying a heavy per centage. Prussian dollars, and florins and half florins, are the most serviceable silver coins. It is scarcely necessary to hint at the advantage of being always provided with small change in the legal current coin of the country through which the traveller passes, as every exchange entails a consequent loss.

The Austrian paper gulden (Ein Gulden) passes for 1 gulden 12 kr. (72 kr.) in most parts of the Tyrol. The paper marked zehn (10) kreuzer, passes for 12 kr. The zwanziger (called in Italy lire, and marked "20,") passes for 24 kr., and in some places for 26. The pieces marked "6" pass for 7 kr., unless 10 of them are equal to a gulden. The larger kreuzer is worth 1 kr. and 1 pf. In Roveredo, Riva, and Peschiera, and in most parts of South and South-west Tyrol, they will not in general take the paper gulden; but, if they do, they will only allow for it 52 instead of 72 kr.; and, generally speaking, the other money only passes for the number marked.

GOLD AND SILVER COIN TABLE,

Showing the value at which the following Coins are now current on the Continent (varying according to the Exchange). Corrected for the present month at the Exchange and Foreign Banking Office, No. 10, Lombard Street, London, by Messrs. Adam Spielmann and Co.

Description of Coin.	France, Belgium and Switzerland.*		Prussia.			Austria in Silver		Germany.		Holland.		Hamburgh.	
	Fr.	Cts.	Thl.	Sgr.	Pf.	Fl.	Kr.	Fl.	Kr.	Guild.	Ct.	Mc.	Sh.
English Sovereign	25	0	6	20	0	10	0	11	48	11	80	16	12
English Shilling	1	25	0	10	0	0	30	0	35½	0	59	0	13¼
Ten Guilder (Dutch) not current	20	75	5	17	0	8	15	9	53	9	70	14	0
Guilder (Dutch)	2	10	0	17	0	0	48	1	0	1	0	1	6½
Five Franc Piece (French, Belg., or Swiss)	5	0	1	10	0	1	58	2	21	2	36	3	5
One Franc (French, Belgian, or Swiss)	1	0	0	8	0	0	24	0	28	0	46	0	10½
Fredricksdor (Prussian)	20	75	5	20	0	8	10	9	55	9	95	14	3½
Thaler (Prussian)	3	75	1	0	0	1	28	1	45	1	75	2	8
Louisdor (German)	20	40	5	15	0	8	14	9	45	9	70	13	14
Ducat (German)	11	81	3	5	6	4	40	5	36	5	58	8	1
Crown Dollar	5	67½	1	15	0	2	15	2	43	2	67	3	13
Florin (German)	2	10	0	17	0	0	47½	1	0	1	0	1	6
Leopold (Belgian)	25	0	6	19	0	9	50	11	32½	11	75	16	7½
Imperial (Russia)	20	35	5	16	9	8	15	9	46	9	74	14	3
Ducat (Austria)	11	82½	3	5	9	4	42	5	38	5	60	8	1½
Zwanziger (Austria)	0	85	0	7	0	0	20	0	24	0	40	0	9

** Switzerland Currency—new system—same as France and Belgium.*

Note.—The Exchanges are at present beginning to bear a slight upward tendency.

The following **Table** has also been obtained exclusively for this Work from Messrs. **Adam Spielmann** and Co., *and corrected for the current month.*

A CONCISE TABLE OF FOREIGN MONIES,

REDUCED FROM ENGLISH INTO THE CURRENCY OF VARIOUS COUNTRIES.

ENGLAND.			FRANCE, BELGIUM, AND SWITZERLAND.		PRUSSIA.			AUSTRIA. in Silver		HOLLAND.		GERMANY.		RUSSIA.		HAMBURGH	
£	s.	d.	Frs.	Cts.	Th.	Sgr.	Pf.	Fl.	Kr.	Guild.	Cts.	Fl.	Kr.	Rbl.	Kop.	Marc.	Shil.
0	0	1-10	0	1	0	0	1	0	0	0	0	0	0	0	0	0	0
0	0	0¼	0	2½	0	0	2½	0	0⅝	0	1¾	0	0¾	0	0⅝	0	0¼
0	0	0½	0	5¼	0	0	5	0	1¼	0	2⅓	0	1½	0	1¼	0	0½
0	0	1	0	10½	0	0	10	0	2½	0	5	0	3	0	2½	scarcely	1
0	0	1¼	0	13	0	1	0	0	3	0	6	0	4	0	3	,,	1¼
0	0	2	0	21	0	1	7	0	5	0	10	0	6	0	5	0	2¼
0	0	3	0	31½	0	2	5	0	7½	0	15	0	9	0	7½	0	3¼
0	0	4	0	42	0	3	2	0	10	0	20	0	12	0	10	0	4¼
0	0	5	0	52	0	4	2	0	12½	0	24¾	0	15	0	12½	0	5½
0	0	6	0	63	0	5	1	0	15	0	29¾	0	18	0	15	0	6¾
0	0	7	0	73	0	5	10	0	17½	0	34¾	0	21	0	17½	0	7¾
0	0	8	0	84	0	6	7	0	20	0	39¾	0	24	0	20	0	9
0	0	9	0	94	0	7	5	0	22½	0	44¾	0	27	0	22¼	0	10
0	0	9½	1	0	0	8	0	0	24	0	47	0	28½	0	24	0	10½
0	0	10	1	5	0	8	4	0	25	0	49½	0	30	0	25½	0	11½
0	0	11	1	15	0	9	2	0	27½	0	54½	0	33	0	28	0	12¼
0	1	0	1	25	0	10	0	0	30	0	59	0	35½	0	30½	0	13¼
0	1	2¼	1	50	0	12	0	0	36	0	70½	0	43	0	38	1	0
0	1	8¼	2	11	0	17	0	0	50	1	0	1	0	0	51	1	6¼
0	3	0	3	75	1	0	0	1	30	1	76	1	45	0	92	2	8
0	3	3½	4	10	1	2	5	1	37	1	92	1	56	1	0	2	12
0	3	4½	4	17	1	3	6	1	41	2	0	2	0	1	2	2	13
0	4	0	5	0	1	10	0	2	0	2	59	2	22	1	23	3	6
0	5	6	6	25	1	20	0	2	30	2	95	2	57	1	53	4	3
0	6	0	7	50	2	0	0	3	0	3	54	3	32	1	84	5	0
0	7	0	8	75	2	10	0	3	30	4	13	4	8	2	15	5	13½
0	8	0	10	0	2	20	0	4	0	4	72	4	43½	2	45	6	11
0	9	0	11	25	3	0	0	4	30	5	31	5	19	2	75	7	8½
0	10	0	12	50	3	10	0	5	0	5	90	5	54	3	5	8	6
0	11	0	13	75	3	20	0	5	30	6	49	6	29½	3	35	9	3
0	12	0	15	0	4	0	0	6	0	7	8	7	4½	3	66	10	0
0	13	0	16	25	4	10	0	6	30	7	67	7	40	3	96	10	13½
0	14	0	17	50	4	20	0	7	0	8	26	8	15½	4	26	11	11
0	15	0	18	75	5	0	0	7	30	8	85	8	51	4	57½	12	9
0	16	0	20	0	5	10	0	8	0	9	44	9	26½	4	88	13	6
0	17	0	21	25	5	20	0	8	30	10	3	10	2	5	18	14	3
0	18	0	22	50	6	0	0	9	0	10	62	10	37½	5	49	15	0
0	19	0	23	75	6	10	0	9	30	11	21	11	12½	5	79½	15	13

ENGLAND.			FRANCE, BELGIUM, AND SWITZERLAND.		PRUSSIA.			AUSTRIA. in Silver.		HOLLAND.		GERMANY.		RUSSIA.		HAMBURGH	
£	*s.*	*d.*	Frs.	Cts.	Th.	Sgr.	Pf.	Fl.	Kr.	Guild.	Cts.	Fl.	Kr.	Rbl.	Kop.	Marc.	Shil.
1	0	0	25	0	6	20	0	10	0	11	80	11	48	6	10	16	12
1	10	0	37	50	10	0	0	15	0	17	70	17	42	9	15	25	2
2	0	0	50	0	13	10	0	20	0	23	60	23	36	12	20	33	8
3	0	0	75	0	20	0	0	30	0	35	40	35	24	18	30	50	4
4	0	0	100	0	26	20	0	40	0	47	20	47	12	24	40	67	0
5	0	0	125	0	33	10	0	50	0	59	0	59	0	30	50	83	12
6	0	0	150	0	40	0	0	60	0	70	80	70	48	36	60	100	8
7	0	0	175	0	46	20	0	70	0	82	60	82	36	42	70	117	4
8	0	0	200	0	53	10	0	80	0	94	40	94	24	48	80	134	0
9	0	0	225	0	60	0	0	90	0	106	20	106	12	54	90	150	12
10	0	0	250	0	66	20	0	100	0	118	0	118	0	61	0	167	8
11	0	0	275	0	73	10	0	110	0	129	80	129	48	67	10	184	4
12	0	0	300	0	80	0	0	120	0	141	60	141	36	73	20	201	0
13	0	0	325	0	86	20	0	130	0	153	40	153	24	79	30	217	12
14	0	0	350	0	93	10	0	140	0	165	20	165	12	85	40	234	8
15	0	0	375	0	100	0	0	150	0	177	0	177	0	91	50	251	4
16	0	0	400	0	106	20	0	160	0	188	80	188	48	97	60	268	0
17	0	0	425	0	113	10	0	170	0	200	60	200	36	103	70	284	12
18	0	0	450	0	120	0	0	180	0	212	40	212	24	109	80	301	8
19	0	0	475	0	126	20	0	190	0	224	20	224	12	115	90	318	4
20	0	0	500	0	133	10	0	200	0	236	0	236	0	122	0	335	0
30	0	0	750	0	200	0	0	300	0	354	0	354	0	183	0	502	8
40	0	0	1000	0	266	10	0	400	0	472	0	472	0	244	0	670	0
50	0	0	1250	0	333	10	0	500	0	590	0	590	0	305	0	837	0
60	0	0	1500	0	400	0	0	600	0	708	0	708	0	366	0	1005	0
70	0	0	1750	0	466	20	0	700	0	826	0	826	0	427	0	1172	8
80	0	0	2000	0	533	10	0	800	0	944	0	944	0	488	0	1340	0
90	0	0	2250	0	600	0	0	900	0	1062	0	1062	0	549	0	1507	8
100	0	0	2500	0	666	20	0	1000	0	1180	0	1180	0	610	0	1675	0
200	0	0	5000	0	1333	10	0	2000	0	2360	0	2360	0	1220	0	3350	0
300	0	0	7500	0	2000	0	0	3000	0	3540	0	3540	0	1830	0	5025	0
500	0	0	12500	0	3333	10	0	5000	0	5900	0	5900	0	3050	0	8375	0
1000	0	0	25000	0	6666	20	0	10000	0	11800	0	11800	0	6100	0	10050	0

EXPLANATION OF THE CURRENCIES OF THE VARIOUS COUNTRIES.

FRANCE and BELGIUM, Francs, of 100 Centimes.—PRUSSIA, Thalers, of 30 Silver groschen; 1 Silver-groschen, 12 Pfennings.—AUSTRIA, Florins, of 60 Kreutzers.—HOLLAND, Guilders, of 100 Cents.—Germany, Florins of 60 Kreutzers.—HAMBURG, Marks Current, of 16 Shillings.—SWITZERLAND, Francs, new system of 100 centimes as in France or Belgium.—RUSSIA, Rubels, of 100 Kopecks.

***** For further information on distinct currency, see remarks made under the head of each Country.**

SKELETON ROUTES TO AND FROM THE PRINCIPAL CITIES IN EUROPE.

No. 1.—London to Cologne.

Via Ostend, in 21½ hours.

London ......dep.	8½ p.m.	By Railway.
Dover ....dep.	11.15 p m.	By Steamboat.
Ostend ....arr.	3 a.m.	,,
Do. ....dep.	7¼ a.m.	By Railway.
Ghent ....dep.	9 5 a.m.	,,
Brussels ......arr.	10 10 ..	,,
Cologne ......arr.	6 0 p.m.	,,

No. 2.—From Cologne to London.

Via Ostend, in 20½ hours.

	p.m.		
Cologne ..dep.	11 30	8 a.m.	By Railway.
Ostend ....arr.	11 45	6.20 p m.	,,
Do. ....dep.	..	6.30 p.m.	By Steamboat.
Dover ....dep.	..	2 0 a.m.	By Railway.
London ..arr.	..	4.30 a.m.	,,

No. 3.—London to Cologne,

via Calais, in 21½ hours.

London ..dep.	8 10 a.m.	8 30 p.m	Railway
Dover	...	11 15 ..	..
Calais ....dep.	3 0 p.m.	2 0 a.m.	Steamboat
Lille	5 15 ..	4 0 ..	
Ghent ....dep.	8 10 p.m.	9 5 a.m.	
Brussels ..arr.	10 10 ..	10 45 ..	
Do. ..dep.	..	..	
Aix'-Chap.dep.	3 0 a.m.	4 0 p.m.	
Cologne ..arr.	5 0 a.m.	6 0 p.m.	

On Sundays the Mail Packet does not sail from Dover.

No. 4.—Cologne to London,

via Ghent, Lille, and Calais, in 21 hours.

Cologne ..dep.	11 30 p.m.	8 0 a.m.
Ghent ....dep.	9 25 a.m.	
Lille ....dep.	12 35 p.m.	12 night
Calais ....arr.	3 0 p.m.	2 10 a.m.
Do. ....dep.	3 30 p.m.	2 30 ..
Dover ....dep.	7 30 ..	5 20 ..
London ..arr.	10 15 ..	8 6 ..

No. 5.—London to Vienna,

via Cologne, Magdeburg, Leipsic, Dresden, and Prague, 1,188 *miles in* 71 *hours.*

London ....dep.	8½ p.m.	By Railway and Steamboat.
Cologne ....arr.	6 p.m.	
Do. ......dep.	8 p.m.	By Railway.
Magdeburg....arr.	9 50 a.m.	,,
Do. ....dep.	10 45 a.m.	,,
Leipsic........arr.	2 5 a m.	,,
Do. ....dep.	2 30 p.m.	,,
Dresden ......arr.	5 30 p m.	,,
Do. ......dep.	9 30 p.m.	,,
Prague ....arr.	4 27 a.m.	,,
Do. ....dep.	5 15 a.m.	,,
Vienna........arr.	7 35 p.m.	,,

No. 6.—Vienna to London,

via Prague, Dresden, Leipsic, Magdeburg, and Cologne, in 70 *hours, stopping all night at Cologne.*

Vienna ....dep	6 30 a.m.
Prague........arr.	7 30 p.m.
Do. ....dep.	8 0 p.m.
Dresden ......arr.	2 0 a.m.
Do. ......dep.	4 0 a.m.
Leipsic........arr.	6 30 a.m.
Do. ....dep	7 0 a.m.
Magdeburg ....arr.	9 50 a.m.
Do. ....dep.	10 40 a.m.
Hanover .... .arr.	2 23 a.m.
Do. ......dep.	2 38 a.m.
Cologne ....arr.	10 0 p.m.
Do. ... ..dep.	7 0 a.m.
London ....arr.	4 30 a.m.

No. 7—Paris to Frankfurt.-o.-M.,

via Strasburg, in 23½ hours.

Paris ....dep.	7.30 p.m.	By Railway.
Nancy ....dep.	4.20 a.m.	,,
Strasburg ..... arr.	8.10 a.m.	,,
Do. (Kehl) ....dep.	11.18 a.m.	,,
Frankfurt ....arr.	6 57 p.m.	,,

No. 8.—Frankfurt-o.-M. to Paris,

via Strasburg, in 20 *hours.*

Frankfurt .....dep.	8.30 a.m.	By Railway.
Strasburg......arr.	1.45 p.m.	,,
Do. ......dep.	3.30 p.m.	,,
Nancy ....arr.	7.45 p.m.	,,
Paris ......arr.	4.30 a.m.	,,

No. 9.—Frankfurt-o.-M. and Vienna,

via Guntershausen and Berlin, in 59¼ *hours.*

Frankfurt....dep.	7¼ a.m.	By Railway.
Eisenach .....arr.	11.30 p.m.	,,
Berlin ......arr.	9.30 p.m.	,,
Do. ....dep.	11 p.m.	,,
Breslau ......arr.	10 a.m.	,,
Vienna ......arr.	6 a.m.	,,

No. 10.—

Vienna & Frankfurt-o.-M., *in* 69½ *hours.*

Vienna ......dep.	7 p.m.	By Railway.
Breslau......dep.	5¾ p.m.	,,
Berlin ......arr.	4¼ a.m.	,,
Do. ......dep.	7½ a m.	,,
Eisenach ....arr.	8½ p.m.	,,
Do. ......dep.	5.25 a.m.	,,
Frankfurt ....arr.	5.32 p.m.	,,

FARE—52 fl. 55 kr.

No. 11.—Frankfurt-o.-M. and Vienna,

via Guntershausen, Dresden, and Prague, in 60½, 57, and 71¾ hours.

Frankfurt ....dep.	8¼ a.m.		7¼ p.m.
Eisenach ....arr.	7¼ p.m.		11½ a.m.
Do. ......dep.	3.5 p.m.*		11½ a.m.
Leipsic ....arr	9¼ a.m.		5½ p.m.
Do. ......dep.	10 p.m.		10 p.m.
Dresden......arr.	1¼ p.m.		12½ a.m.
Dresden......dep.	9¼ p.m.	7 a.m.	1.35 p.m.
Prague ......arr.	4 a.m.	2½ p.m.	9.20 p.m.
Do. ......dep.	5½ a.m.	3¼ p.m.	5¼ a.m.
Vienna ....arr.	7½ p.m.	6 a.m.	7½ p.m.

* Stopping all night at Erfurt or Weimar.

No. 12.—Vienna and Frankfurt-o.-M.,

in 59 and 51 hours.

Vienna ......dep.	6½ a.m.	7 p.m.
Prague ....arr.	8 p.m.	9.20 a.m.
Do. ....dep.	9¼ p.m.	10¼ a.m.
Dresden ......arr.	3½ a.m.	4.50 p.m.
Do. ......dep.	4 a.m.	6 p.m.
Leipsic........arr.	6.30 a.m.	9¼ p.m.
Do. ....dep.	7 p.m.	10 p.m.†
Eisenach ......arr.	1.50 a.m.*	7.40 a.m.
Do ......dep.	1.55 a.m.	7.45 a.m.
Frankfurt .....arr.	3.45 p.m.	8.15 p.m.

*Stopping all night in Bodenbach, Erfort, or Weimar
† Stopping all night in Haile.
FARE—39 fl. 1 kr.

No. 13.—Berlin and Warsaw,

via Posen, in 46 hours.

Berlin.........dep.	6.30 a.m.	By Railway.
Posen ....arr.	4.52 p.m.	"
Do. ....dep.	12½ night.	"
Warsaw ......arr.	10 a.m.	"

No. 14.—Warsaw and Berlin,

in 47 hours.

Warsaw ......dep.	5 p.m.	By Railway.
Posen ....arr.	11 a.m.	"
Do. ....dep.	11.42 a.m.	
Berlin ....arr.	9.15 p.m.	"

FARE—14 thlr. 24½ sgr.

No. 15.—London and Marseilles,

879 Miles.

London..dep.	8 10 a.m.	11½ a.m.	8½ p.m.	By Rail.
Calais ..dep.	3 0 ..	6½ p.m.	2 a.m.	..
Paris ....arr.	10 45 ..	5½ a.m.	9 a.m.	..
Do. ..dep.	10 35 a.m.,	8 5 p.m.		..
Dijon ..dep.	7 20 p.m.,	3 1 a.m.		..
Chalons ..arr.	9 0 p.m.,	4 25 a.m.		..
Do. ..dep.	..	5 0 a.m.		By Boat
Lyons.. ..arr.	..	12 0 noon.		..
Do.. ..dep.	6 0 a.m.,	6 0 a.m.		..
Avignon..arr.	6 0 p.m.,	6 0 p.m.		..
Marseilles arr.	9 30 p.m.,	9 30 p.m.		By Rail.

FARES–First Class, £6 ; second class, £5 4s. 9d.; third class, £3 8s

No. 16.—London and Geneva,

664 Miles, *Via Dijon, in about 35½ hours.*

From London to Dijon, same as No. 13; from Dijon to Geneva, by diligence, at 3.30 a.m.; arrive at Geneva at 6 p.m. Also every other day from Chalons at 9 p.m., arriving at Geneva at 4 p.m.

No. 17,—375 Miles.

Frankfurt-o.-M. to Leipsic & Berlin

Frankfurt....dep.	8.15 a.m.	7.15 p.m.
Guntershausen, J.	3.25 p.m.	8.20 a.m.
Eisenach ....arr.	7 p.m.	11.30 a.m.
Do. ....dep.	7.5 p.m.	11½ a.m.
Erfurt ....arr. }	stopping	1.10 p.m.
Weimar.... }	all night.	1.40 p.m.
Halle ....arr.	6.35 a.m.	4.10 p.m.
Leipsic ......arr.	8¼ a.m.	5½ p.m.
Berlin.........arr.	2¼ p.m.	9½ p.m.

No. 18.—375 Miles.

Berlin & Leipsic to Frankfurt-o.-M.

Berlin ....dep.	8 a.m.	10 p.m.	...
Leipsic ..dep.	12 noon.	...	10 p.m.
Halle ....arr.	2½ p.m.	4¼ a.m.	11¼p.m.
Halle .....dep.	2¾ p.m.	4,45 a.m.	
Erfurt	6.35 p.m.	8.10 a.m.	
Eisenach ..arr	8.30 p.m.	9.50 a.m.	
Eisenach..dep.	5.25 a.m.	9.55 a.m.	
Gntershausen,J	9. 5 a.m.	2 p.m.	
Frankfurt..arr.	3.45 p.m.	8.16 p.m.	

No. 19.—Frankfurt-o.-M. to Stuttgart,

130 Miles, *via Heilbronn in 12 to 15 hours.*

Frankfurt ..dep.	6 30 a.m.	4 45 p.m.	Railway.
Heidelberg ..arr.	9 15 a.m.	7 37 p.m.	..
Do. ..dep.	10 0 a.m.	9 0 p.m.	Diligence.
Heilbronn ..arr.	4 30 p.m.	4 45 a.m.	..
Do. ..dep.	5 45 p.m.	5 30 a.m.	Railway.
Stuttgart ....arr.	7 45 p.m.	7 30 a.m.	..

No. 20.—Stuttgart to Frankfurt-o.-M

via Heilbronn in 12 or 13 hours.

Stuttgart....dep.	5 30 a.m.	8 15 p.m.	Railway.
Heilbron ....arr.	7 30 a.m.	10 5 p.m.	..
Do. ....dep.	8 15 a.m.	10 30 p.m.	Diligence.
Heidelberg ..arr.	3 0 p.m.	6 15 a.m.	..
Do. ..dep.	4 10 p.m.	7 0 a.m.	Railway.
Frankfurt ..arr.	6 57 p.m.	9 50 a.m.	..

FARES—Second Class, 7fl. 21kr.

No. 21.—Frankfurt-o.-M. to Stuttgart.

134 Miles, *via Carlsruhe in* 15 *hours.*

Frankfurt dep.	8.30 noon	1.20 p.m.	By Railway.
Carlsruhe arr.	..	6.20 p.m.	,,
Do. dep.	..	7 30 p.m.	By Diligence.
Stuttgart..arr.	8.15 a.m.	4.30 a.m.	,,

No. 22.—Stuttgart to Frankfurt-o.-M.,

via Carlsruhe, in 15 *hours.*

Stuttgart...dep.	4.30 a.m.	8.30 p.m.	By Diligence.
Carlsruhe arr.	12.30p.m.	4.45 a.m.	,,
Do. ...dep.	2. 0 p.m.	5.10 a.m.	By Railway
Frankfurt arr.	7. 0 p m.	10 0 a.m.	,,

No. 23.—Paris to Berlin,

780 Miles, *in* 41 *hours.*

Paris ...dep.	7 30 a.m.	8 p.m.	By
Brussels arr.	5 0 ,,	6 a.m.	Rail.
Do....dep.	8 0 ,,	7 and 10.15 a.m.	,,
Cologne arr.	4 0 ,,	4.15 & 6 30 p.m.	,,
Deutz ...dep.	6 30 a.m.	8 0 p.m.	,,
Berlin ...arr.	9 20 p.m.	1 10 p.m.	,,

No. 24.—Berlin to Paris,

780 Miles, *in* 33½ *hours.*

Berlin ....dep.	7.30 a.m.	By Railway.
Deutz ....arr.	10 p.m.	,,
Cologne ....dep.	11½ p.m.	,,
Brussels ....arr.	7 a.m.	,,
Do. ....dep.	8 a.m.	,,
Paris..............arr.	5 p.m.	,,

No. 25.—London and Berlin,

765 Miles, *in* 40¾ *hours.*

London ....dep.	8½ p.m.	By Railway.
Ostend...........dep	7.35 a.m.	,,
Cologne ....arr	6.30 p.m.	,,
Deutz ....dep	8. 0 p.m.	,,
Hanover ....arr.	5.10 a.m.	,,
Brunswick ......arr.	7. 5 a.m.	,,
Magdeburg ......arr	9 50 a.m	,,
Berlin ....arr.	1.10 p.m.	,,

No. 26.—Berlin to London,

in 46½ *hours.*

Stopping all night at Cologne.

Berlin ......dep.	7.30 a.m	Rail.
Magdeburg dep.	10.40 a.m.	,,
Brunswick..dep.	1.10 noon.	,,
Hanover ...dep.	2.38 p.m.	,,
Deutz ......arr.	10 p.m.	,,
Cologne .....dep.	11½ p.m., & 7. 0 a.m.	,,
Ostend ......arr.	11½ a.m., & 5.20 p.m.	,,
Ostend ......dep.	6½ p.m.	,,
London ......arr.	4½ a.m.	,,

No. 27.—Berlin to Vienna,

465 Miles, *via Prague, in* 29¾ *hours.*

Berlin.......... dep.	7 a.m.	1.45 p.m.
Dresden ....arr.	12½ noon.	8 p.m.
Do. ....dep.	1¾ p.m.	9.20 p.m.
Prague ....arr.	9.27 p.m.	4.23 a.m.
Do. .. ..dep.	,,	5½ a.m.
Vienna ....arr.	,,	7½ p.m.

No. 28.—Vienna to Berlin,

via Prague, in 39½ *hours.*

Vienna ....dep.	,,	6½ a m.
Prague ....arr.	,,	7½ p m.
Do. ....dep.	7 a.m.	9¼ p.m.
Dresden .... arr.	2¼ p.m.	3½ a.m.
Do. ....dep.	3¼ p m.	6 a m.
Berlin ....arr.	8.45 p.m.	11.45 p.m.

No. 29.—Berlin to Vienna, 509 miles,

via Breslau, in 31 *hours.*

Berlin............dep	11 p m.	
Breslau ....arr.	10 a.m.	
Do. ....dep.	1 p.m.	
Vienna ....arr.	6 a m.	

No. 30.—Vienna to Berlin, 509 miles,

via Breslau, in 33½ *hours.*

Vienna ....dep.	7 p.m.	
Breslau ....arr.	3½ p.m.	
Do. ....dep.	5¾ p.m.	
Berlin ....arr.	4½ a.m.	

No. 31.—Berlin to St Petersburg,

In 123¼ *hours.*

Berlin ....dep.	10 40 p.m.	By Railway
Dirschau..................arr.	11 10 a.m.	...
Do. ....dep.	11 48 a.m.	...
Konigsberg..............arr.	10 40 p.m.	By Diligence
Do. ....dep.	11 0 p.m.	...
Tilsit ....arr.	11 30 a.m.	...
Do. ....dep.	12 0 noon	...
Tauroggen ....arr.	3 45 p.m.	...
Do. ....dep.	7 0 p.m.	...
St. Petersburg ....arr.	2 0 a.m.	...

No. 32.—St. Petersburg to Berlin,

In 130¼ *hours.*

St. Petersburg ....dep.	7 0 p.m.	By Diligence
Tauroggen ....arr.	3 0 a.m	...
Do. ....dep.	5 0 a.m	...
Tilsit ....arr.	10 0 a.m.	...
Do. ....dep	4 30 p.m.	...
Konigsberg..............arr.	5 0 a.m.	...
Do. ....dep.	6 0 a.m.	...
Dirschau ....arr.	4 30 p.m.	By Railway
Do. ....dep.	5 23 p.m.	...
Berlin ....arr.	5 15 a.m.	...

No. 33.—THROUGH ROUTE FROM LONDON TO BASLE,

748 miles, *Via* Paris and Strasburg, in 36 Hours, stopping all night at Strasburg.

London	departure	8.10 a.m.	8½ p.m.
Paris	arrival	10.45 p.m.	9 a.m.
Paris	departure	7.30 p.m.	9½ a.m.
Commercy	arrival	2.44 a.m.	3.52 p.m.
Nancy	arrival	4.20 p.m.	5.19 p.m.
Strasburg	arrival	8.10 a.m.	9.15 p.m.
Strasburg	departure	9.30 a.m.	7. 0 a.m.
Basle	arrival	1. 5 p.m.	12. 2 p.m.

Basle	departure	5.30 a.m.
Strasburg	arrival	10.10 p.m
Strasburg	departure	10.25 a.m.
Nancy	departure	2.28 p.m.
Commercy	departure	3.59 p.m.
Paris	arrival	10. 0 p.m.
Paris	departure	11. 0 p.m.
London	arrival	10. 0 p.m

Paris to Baden-Baden, via Strasburg, in 17¾ hours. Paris to Carlsruhe, via Strasburg, in 18 hours. Paris to Mannheim, via Strasburg, in 21½ hours. Paris to Stuttgard, via Strasburg, 22½ hours. Paris to Ulm, via Strasburg, 26½ hours. Paris to Augsburg, via Strasburg, 35 hours. Paris to Munich, via Strasburg, 38 hours.

34.—Paris to Frankfort,

Via Metz, Forbach, Ludwigshafen, and Mannheim, in 20 hours.

	a.m.	p.m.	p.m.
Paris ... dep.	9 30	7 30	11 0
Metz ... arr.	7 9	5 22	12 51
Do. ... dep.	7 23	5 22	1 2
Forbach	9 30	6 57	2 45
Saarbrucken	10 15	7 45	3 47
Do. ... dep.	5 35	8 10	4 25
Ludwigshafen	10 15	12 20	9 15
Mannheim	11 0	1 0	7 0
Frankfort	2 13	3 30	9 50

35.—Frankfort-o-M. to Paris,

Via Mannheim, Ludwigshafen, Saarbrucken, Forbach, Metz, Frouard, Commercy, and Bar-le-Duc.

	a.m.	p.m.	p.m.
Frankfurt ... dep.	8 30	1 20	4 45
Mannheim	10 53	4 3	7 37
Ludwigshafen	11 35	4 50	5 30
Saarbrucken ... arr.	5 33	9 25	10 14
Do. ... dep.	4 0	3 55	10 0
Forbach	4 25	4 10	11 0
Metz	6 26	7 13	1 6
Frouard	7 51	9 0	2 31
Bar-le-Duc	10 21	1 40	4 46
Paris	4 30	8 50	10 5

No. 36.—London to Vienna,

via Paris, Strasburg, Munich, Salzburg, and Linz, 1293 *miles, in* 119 *hours.*

To Munich same as Nos. 35, 36, and 38.

	Munich (by diligence) departure	1 0 p.m.
90	Salzburg ... arrival	5 0 a.m.
	Do. ... departure	7 30 ,,
86	Linz ... arrival	9 30 p.m.
	Do. (by steam) ... departure	7 0 a.m.
125	Vienna Do. ... arrival	7 0 p.m.

No. 37.—London to Constantinople,

in 10 *days.*

London to Vienna, by rail to Cologne, Dusseldorf, Hanover, Magdeburg, Leipsic, Dresden, & Prague, in about 3 days 8 hours.

Vienna to Constantinople, by the Danube. A Steamer leaves Vienna every Friday morning at 9 for Constantinople, reaching Gelitz on the following Tuesday afternoon, distant 1160 English miles. Passengers are transhipped into a large boat, and reach Constantinople on Thursday.

No. 38.—London to Constantinople,

in 12 *days (not consecutive.)*

London, Vienna, and Trieste, by rail, in about 5 days.

Trieste to Constantinople, by steamer, in about 7 days.

No. 39.—London to Constantinople,

in 14 *days* 12½ *hours (not consecutive.)*

London to Frankfurt, by steam and rail, (*vide* No. 1,) in 1 day 20½ hours.

Frankfurt to Nuremberg & Würtzburg, by steam, on the Maine, or by diligence; and from Würtzburg to Ratisbon by diligence (193 miles), in about 1 day 8 hours.

Ratisbon to Linz and Vienna, by the Danube, in about 1 day 8 hours.

Vienna to Constantinople, by the Danube, in about 10 days.

No. 40.—London to Athens,

in 10 *days* (*not consecutive.*)

London to Trieste, by Vienna, in about 5 days.

Trieste to Patras and Athens, by steamer, in about 5 days.

No. 41.—London to Rome,

in 4 *days* (*not consecutive.*)

London to Marseilles, *via* Paris, *vide* Route No. 13, in 49 hours.

Marseilles to Civita Vecchia, by steamer, in 40 hours.

Civita Veccia to Rome, by diligence, in about 7 hours.

Fares by steamer from Marseilles to Civita Vecchia 1st class, 105 fr.; 2nd, 63 fr.; 3rd, 42 fr.

No. 42.—London to Paris, by way of Calais, in 12½ hours.

(DOUBLE POSTAL SERVICE.)

Mls.		(1) a.m.	a.m.	(1) p.m.	a.m.	a.m.	p.m.
	LONDON (2) dep.	8 10	11 30	8 30	..	..	..
88	DOVER (2)..arr.	10 35	2 15	11 0	..	..	..
..	DOVER ....dep	11 0	2 30	11* 0	..	..	..
111	CALAIS....dep.	3 0	6 30	2 0	..	8 0	6 30
176	LILLE...... ,,	5 0	9 20	3 45	6 0	10 15	9 20
221	ARRAS .... ,,	6 25	11 35	5 5	8 5	12 24	11 35
244	AMIENS .... ,,	7 40	..	6 55	10 25	1 30	..
314	CREIL ...... ,,	9 35	3 30	7 41	1 0	3 35	3 30
346¼	PARIS ...... ,,	10 45	5 30	9 0	2 40	5 0	5 30

	a.m.	(1) a.m.	p.m.	p.m.	p.m.	
PARIS ......dep.	7 30	11 45	12 15	7 30	11 0	..
CREIL ...... ,,	..	1 5	2 12	..	11 5	..
AMIENS...... ,,	..	2 30	..	9 40	4 5	..
ARRAS ...... ,,	..	..	..	11 2	6 8	..
LILLE ...... ,,	..	6 30	..	12 0	8 0	..
CALAIS......arr.	..	9 30	..	2 10	11 30	..
CALAIS .....dep.	3 50	9 40	..	2 10	..	..
DOVER (2)..dep.	7 30	2 0	..	5 20	..	..
LONDON (2)..arr.	10 0	4 30	..	7 50	..	..

* On Sundays, the Mail Packet does not sail from Dover.

(1) The direct communication between London and Paris is carried on by the French and English Packets, and the South Eastern and Continental Steam Packet Co.'s Steamers, which disembark the passengers before the departure of the corresponding train on the opposite coast. (For times of departure, see page 128.)

(2) For times of departure of all the Trains between London and Dover, and Dover and London, see page 124.

No. 43.—London to Brussels in 15 hours 10 minutes,

Via Calais, Lille, Douai, and Valenciennes.

Mls.		a.m.	p.m.	a.m.	p.m.
	LONDON (2) dep	8 10	8 30	..	..
88	DOVER (2).arr.	10 35	11 0	..	..
..	DOVER ...dep.	11 0	*11 0	..	..
111	CALAIS ..dep.	3 0	2 0	8 0	6 30
176	LILLE ....arr.	5 30	4 0	10 40	9 40
..	Ditto ..dep.	5 0	3 45	10 15	9 20
197	DOUAI....arr.	5 46	4 28	11 35	10 25
..	Ditto ..dep.		7 0	12 15	1 37
267	BRUSSELS..arr.	..	11 40	5 0	5 45

	a.m.	p.m.	p.m.	p.m.	a.m.
BRUSSELS .dep.	8 0	1 15	..	6 30	..
DOUAI ...arr.	11 50	5 50	..	10 30	7 0
Ditto ..dep.	12 10		7 30	11 35	7 5
LILLE ....arr.	1 0	..	8 55	12 20	8 0
Ditto ....dep.	12 35	..	12 0		8 0
CALAIS ..arr.	3 0	..	2 10		11 30
CALAIS ..dep.	3 50	..	2 10		
DOVER (2) dep.	7 30	..	5 20	8 0	..
LONDON (2) arr	10 0 p.m.	..	7 50	10 30	..

* On Sundays, the Mail Packet does not sail from Dover.

(2) For times of departure of all the Trains between London and Dover, and Dover and London, see page 124.

Persons going *via* Valenciennes and Mons should book only to Douai, and then re-book to Brussels.

There are two departures daily from CALAIS for COLOGNE, viz., at 2 a.m. via Ghent, and 6½ p.m., via Douai; by the latter route the train arrives at Brussels at 5.15 in the morning.

THROUGH ROUTE FROM LONDON TO BASLE,

BY RAILWAY AND STEAMBOAT,

VIA DOVER, CALAIS, OSTEND, GHENT, BRUSSELS, LIEGE, AIX-LA-CHAPELLE, COLOGNE, BONN, MAYENCE, BIEBRICH, FRANKFORT, MANNHEIM, HEIDELBERG, CARLSRUHE, STRASBURG, FREIBURG AND HALTINGEN.

Miles via Calais.	London Bridge Station.	Via Ostnd.	Via Lille and Valenciennes.				Via Lille, Ghent, and Malines.					Via Jurbise.		Fares From LONDON	
	(1) See page 124.	p.m.	a.m	p.m.	a.m.	a.m.	a.m.	a.m.	p.m.	p.m.	a.m.	p m.	p.m.	1 Cl.	2 Cl.
	LONDON ..(1)..dep.	8 30	8 0	8 30	..	11 30	..	8 10	8 30	..	..	8 30	..	s. d.	s. d.
88	DOVER.... (1) ..arr.	11 0	11 0	11 0	..	2 0	..	11 0	11 0	..	.	11 0	..	20 0	14 8
..	„ (By Packet) dep.	..	11 0	11 0	..	2 0	..	11 0	11 0	..	.	11 15	..	..	..
113	CALAIS ....arr.	..	1 0	1 0	a.m.	4 0	..	p.m.	1 0	..	..	1 0	..	..	..
..	„ (By Rail) dep.	..	3 0	2 0	8 0	6 30	8 0	3 0	2 0	6 30	..	2 0	..	..	..
178	LILLE ....arr.	..	5 15	4 0	10 40	9 40	10 40	5 15	4 0	9 40	..	4 0	..	..	..
..	„ ....dep.	..	—	4 0	10 15	9 20	11 0	5 30	6 0	—	..	6 0	..	..	..
153*	OSTEND ....dep.	7 15	..	..	..	..	..	6 10	7 15	..	..	..	..	..	..
224	GHENT .... arr.	9 0	..	..	..	..	2 10	8 30	8 45	..	..	..	..	..	..
259	MALINES....... arr	10 30	..	..	..	a.m.	4 15	—	10 30	..	..	a.m.	..	44 6	33 6
272	BRUSSELS ...... arr.	11 0	..	11 40	5 0	5 45	4 50	.	11 0	p.m.	..	11 40	..	..	..
..	„ ......dep.	10 15	..	—	—	7 0	—	..	10 15	8 0	7 0	—	..	..	..
274	ANTWERP.......dep.	10 15	..	..	..	7 0	..	..	10 15	8 15	7 0	..	..	45 0	33 0
318	LIEGE..........dep.	1 35	..	..	..	10 55	..	..	1 35	11 10	10 55	..	..	..	..
333	VERVIERS.......dep.	3 0	..	..	..	12 30	..	..	3 0	12 45	12 0	..	..	..	..
352	AIX-LA-CHAPELLE ar.	4 30	..	..	..	2 15	..	..	4 30	2 0	2 15	..	..	55 6	40 0
396	COLOGNE ...... arr.	6 30	..	..	..	4 15	..	..	6 30	4 0	4 15	..	..	62 0	45 3

* Ostend to Ghent is 41 mls., making that route about 30 mls. shorter, *i. e.*—70 mls. less of Railway, and 40 miles more of Sea Passage.

Miles	By Steamers on the Rhine.	Dusseldorf Co.'s Steamers.					Cologne Company's Steamers.						Fares FROM COLOGNE.			
		a.m.	a.m.	a.m.	p.m.	p.m.	a.m.	a.m.	a.m.	a.m.	p.m.		Ch.	Cbn.	Fre.	Cbn.
..	COLOGNE ......dep.	..	5 45	..	12 30	8 15	.	5 15	..	9 45	9 0	..	t. sg	s. d.	t. sg	s. d.
418	BONN ....dep.	..	8 0	11 0	3 5	11 0	..	7 30	..	12 30	10 30	..	..	..	..	..
463	COBLENTZ..........	..	12 0	3 15	8 30	6 30	7 0	11 30	..	4 0	5 30	..	2 6	6 5	1 3	3 2½
506	BINGEN ....dep.	1 30	4 15	8 0	—	11 0	12 0	3 30	6 15	—	10 0	..	..	..	..	..
518	BIEBRICH ......dep.	3 30	6 15	10 0	..	1 0	2 0	5 45	8 15	..	11 30	..	..	..	..	..
523	MAYENCE(Castel)arr	4 0	6 30	10 30	..	1 30	2 15	6 0	8 45	..	11 15	..	4 12	13 10	2 6	..
..	MAYENCE ......dep.	6 30	7 0	..	..	2 30	..	7 30	..	..	12 30	..	..	..	..	6 5
583	MANNHEIM .... arr.	12 30	11 30	..	..	7 0	..	12 30	..	..	5 0	..	6 0	..	3 0	..
..	STRASBURG ..... arr.	..	..	..	..	p.m.	..	..	..	..	..	..	..	17 6	..	8 9

Miles	BY RAILWAY.	a.m.	a.m.	a.m.	a.m.	a.m.	a.m.	p.m.	p.m.	p.m.	p.m.	Fares from Frankfort. s. d.	s. d.	s. d.	s. d.
..	WIESBADEN ......dep.	..	..	..	6 10	7 45	10 35	2 0	5 33	8 0	..	4 6	3 1	2 1	1 5
512	CASTEL (Mayence) dep.	..	..	..	6 20	8 0	10 50	2 30	6 0	8 20	..	4 2	3 0	2 0	1 4
533	FRANKFORT ...... arr.	..	..	..	7 30	9 15	12 0	3 35	7 5	9 30	..	—	—	—	—
..	„ ......dep.	..	5 0	..	8 30	11 5	1 20	4 45	8 45	—	..	1 Cls.	2 Cls.	3 Cls.	4 Cls.
..	DARMSTADT ...... arr.	..	6 4	..	9 15	11 51	1 51	5 16	9 31	Gds.	..	1 10	1 4	0 11	0 7
..	WEINHEIM .... arr.	..	8 5	..	..	1 14	..	7 28	—	a.m.	..	4 3	3 1	2 2	1 5
..	MANNHEIM........dep.	..	..	6 20	10 50	11 50	3 43	8 0	..	4 30	..	5 10	4 2	2 11	1 11
588	HEIDELBERG ...... arr.	..	..	6 54	11 17	12 22	4 3	7 15	..	5 0	..	5 11	4 3	2 11	2 0
..	„ ......dep.	..	..	7 4	11 23	12 30	4 30	7 50	..	5 35	..	..	..	..	..
621	CARLSRUHE ......dep.	..	5 45	9 0	12 45	2 20	5 3	—	..	10 30	..	9 7	6 9	4 9	3 2
..	BADEN............arr.	..	7 11	10 23	1 35	3 37	7 53	..	..	..	..	..	..	..	..
..	„ ....dep.	..	6 34	10 0	1 17	3 14	7 30	..	..	..	..	..	..	..	..
..	KEHL (Strasburg).. arr.	..	8 27	11 49	2 25	5 0	9 7	..	..	..	..	..	..	..	..
..	„ „ ..dep.	..	7 30	10 50	1 45	4 0	8 30	..	..	..	..	..	..	..	..
665	OFFENBURG ...... arr.	..	8 18	11 42	2 18	4 58	9 16	..	..	..	..	14 8	10 2	7 3	4 9
..	„ ......dep.	4 0	8 25	11 50	2 24	5 5	—	..	..	..	..	..	..	..	..
706	FREIBURG .... arr.	6 41	10 22	2 0	3 48	7 19	..	..	..	..	..	19 0	13 2	9 5	6 2
..	„ ...... .dep.	7 0	10 30	2 15	3 55	7 25	..	..	..	..	..	..	..	..	..
739	HALTINGEN ...... arr.	9 31	12 30	4 28	5 15	9 30	..	..	..	..	..	22 5	15 6	11 2	7 3
743	BASLE .... arr.	10 31	1 30	5 28	6 15	10 30	..	..	..	..	..	..	..	..	..

Travellers can book themselves through, and obtain *direct* tickets from London to Brussels, Malines Aix-la-Chapelle, or Cologne. Passengers by the night mail trains and boats are permitted to proceed from Calais or Ostend to any part of the Continent without waiting to have their luggage examined at either port. The direct tickets issued at the London Bridge station of the South Eastern Railway are available by any of the South Eastern and Continental Company's steamers running between Folkstone and Boulogne and Dover and Calais, as also by the Belgian, English, and French Government mail boats.

THROUGH ROUTE FROM BASLE TO LONDON,

BY RAILWAY AND STEAMBOAT

Via HALTINGEN, FREIBURG, STRASBURG, CARLSRUHE, HEIDELBERG, MANNHEIM, FRANKFORT, BIEBRICH, MAYENCE, BONN, COLOGNE, AIX-LA-CHAPELLE, LIEGE, BRUSSELS, GHENT, OSTEND, CALAIS, and DOVER

Miles fr. Basle	STATIONS.	HOURS OF ARRIVAL AND DEPARTURE OF TRAINS.									FARES.
		a.m.	a.m.	a.m.	a.m.	a.m.	p.m.	p.m.			fl. kr. fl. kr. fl. kr.
	BASLE (per Omnibus) dep	..	..	..	5 30	10 30	2 30	4 0	..	..	from Basle.
4	HALTINGEN (per Rail) dep	..	..	..	7 0	12 0	4 0	5 30	..	..	0 40..0 40..0 40
45	FREIBURG ....arr.	..	..	..	8 18	1 51	5 42	7 12	..	..	2 3..1 24..1 3
	,, ...dep.	..	..	5 45	8 25	2 0	5 48	7 18	..	..	from Freiburg.
91	OFFENBURG ....arr.	..	..	7 56	9 50	4 1	7 34	9 4	..	..	2 36..1 45..1 18
	,, ...dep.	..	6 0	8 10	10 0	4 10	7 40	9 10	..	..	from Offenburg.
	KEHL (Strasburg) ..arr.	..	6 45	..	10 31	5 0	8 20	9 42	..	..	0 51..0 33...0 24
	,, ,, ..dep.	..	5 50	..	9 50	4 0	7 25	9 0	..	..	... .
	BADEN ....arr.	..	7 41	..	11 0	5 40	8 58	10 28	..	..	1 39...! 6...0 48
	,, ...dep.	..	7 18	..	10 40	5 18	8 36	10 6	..	..	from Baden.
135	CARLSRUHE ....arr.	..	8 35	11 6	11 27	6 25	9 40	11 10	..	..	1 21...0 54..0 42
	,, ...dep.	5 10	8 45	11 40	11 35	6 35			..	..	from Carlsruhe.
191	HEIDELBERG ....arr.	6 45	10 35	1 50	12 40	8 20	..	..	..	..	2 12...1 30...1 6
	,, ...dep.	7 0	11 0	2 30	1 0	8 40	..	..	..	..	from Heidelberg.
202	MANNHEIM ....arr.	7 15	11 17	3 10	1 18	9 0	..	..	..	..	0 48...0 33...0 24
199	,, ...dep.	7 0	11 0	4 10	1 0		..	..	..	..	.. ..
223	DARMSTADT ....dep.	9 30	1 45	6 30	2 30	..	..	..	..	..	2 27...1 48...1 15
240	FRANKFORT ....arr.	9 50	2 13	6 57	3 30	a.m.	a.m.	p.m.	p.m.	..	from Dramstadt.
	,, ...dep.	11 10	2 30	..	..	6 40	8 10	8 30	6 0	..	1 6...0 48...0 33
260	CASTEL (MAYENCE) arr.	12 5	3 35	..	..	7 50	9 15	9 35	7 5	...	2 6..1 27..1 0
265	BIEBRICH ....arr.	12 30	4 0	..	..	..	..	..	..	.	from Biebrich
266	WIESBADEN ....arr	12 30	4 0	..	..	8 20	9 40	10 0	7 30	..	0 12..0 3 0 3

Miles	The Cologne Co.'s steamers sail from Mayence (Castel).	Dusseldorf Co.'s Steamers, daily.					Cologne Co.'s Steamers.					FARES FROM MANNHEIM. Chief Cabn.		Fore Cabn.	
		a.m	a.m	a.m	p.m.	p.m.	a.m.	a.m.	a.m.	a.m.	a.m.				
91	By Steamers on the Rhine. STRASBURG ....dep.	..	..	...	..	..	..	..	9 0	..	..	th. s.	s. d.	th. s.	s. d.
202	MANNHEIM....dep.	5 0	..	..	..	4 45	..	..	4 0	7 30	..	..	..	..	..
257	MAYENCE......arr.	8 30	..	..	..	8 0	..	..	8 0	11 30	..	1 18	4 8	0 24	2 4
260	MAYENCE .....dep.	9 0	12 0	7 15	4 0		..	6 15	p.m.	12 0	9 0	from Mayence			
276	BIEBRICH	9 15	12 15	7 30	4 15	..	..	6 30	..	12 15	9 15	0 8	0 10	0 4	0 5
	BINGEN	10 45	1 30	9 0	5 45	a.m.	..	8 0	..	1 30	10 30	0 18	1 9	0 9	0 11
	COBLENTZ	1 30	4 15	11 45	8 30	8 0	6 0	10 30	..	4 0	1 0	2 6	6 6	1 3	3 3
	BONN	4 30	7 0	2 30	..	10 45	9 0	1 30	..	7 0	4 0	3 28	11 6	1 29	5 9
	COLOGNE ..... arr.	5 30	8 0	3 45	..	..	10 30	3 0	..	8 30	5 30	4 12	12 10	2 6	6 6

Miles	BY RAILWAY.	*Via* Ostnd	*Via* Brussels and Valenciennes.					*Via* Malines and Ghent.				*Via* Jurbise.		
		a.m.	a.m.	a.m.	p.m.	a.m.	p.m.	p.m.	a.m.	p.m.		a.m.	p.m.	a.m.
389	COLOGNE ....dep.	7 0	7 0	11 15	5 30	..	11 30	11 30	..	..	..	..	..	7 0
433	AIX-LA-CHAPELLE ..dep.	9 15	9 15	1 45	7 30	..	1 30	1 30	..	..	..	..	..	9 15
452	VERVIERS ....dep.	11 0	11 0	3 45	..	6 30	2 45	2 45	..	..	..	..	..	11 0
430	LIEGE ....dep.	12 0	12 0	4 55	..	7 45	3 45	3 45	..	..	..	..	..	12 0
526	MALINES...............	3 15	3 5	8 5	..	10 55	6 25	6 25	..	..	..	..	..	2 50
540	ANTWERP ... .dep.	2 45	..	..	..	..	..	..	..	..	..	..	..	..
539	BRUSSELS ....arr.	3 25	3 25	8 40	..	11 30	7 0	7 0	..	..	..	..	..	3 25
	,, ...dep.	2 45	6 30	..	..	..	8 0	7 15	10 30	4 30	..	7 30	..	5 30
561	GHENT ....dep.	4 50	..	..	..	..	a.m.	9 25	1 25	6 45	..	..	..	..
602	OSTEND .... arr.	6 20	..	..	..	..	..	..	..	..	..	..	..	..
	,, (by Packet) dep.	6 30	a.m.	..	..	..	p.m.	..	..	..	..	noon	p.m.	p.m.
609	LILLE ....arr.	..	12 20	..	..	..	12 40	12 0	4 30	9 10	..	12 0	5 10	10 30
	,, ...dep.	..	12 0	..	..	..	12 35	12 35	6 30	12 0	..	12 35	6 30	12 0
674	CALAIS ....arr.	..	2 10	..	..	..	3 0	3 0	9 30	2 10	..	3 0	9 30	2 10
	,, (By Packet)..dep.	night	2 30	..	..	..	3 50	3 50	..	2 10	..	3 50	10 0	2 30
697	DOVER ....arr.	12 0	4 15	..	..	..	5 30	..	..	4 15	..	5 30	11 45	4 15
	Dover to London, p. 124	a.m.	Exp.						a.m.				a.m.	a.m.
	,, (By Rail)..dep.	2 0	5 20	..	..	..	7 30	7 30	2 6	5 20	..	7 30	5 20	5 20
785	LONDON...........arr.	4 30	7 50	..	..	..	10 0	10 0	4 30	7 50	..	10 0	7 50	7

LONDON to PARIS by way of BOULOGNE, in 10 HOURS.

Terminus] DOUBLE SERVICE DAILY. [24, Place Roubaix.

Boulogne & Amiens to Paris.

Eng. Miles.	Boulogne to Paris.	1,2,3 clss.	1,2,3 clss.	1,2,3 clss.	1—2 **Ex**	1,2,3 clss.	
		a.m.	p.m.	p.m.	p.m.	p.m.	
—	**Boulogne** ..dep.	6 30	12 30	..	5 15	8 0	..
4	Pont-de-Brique....	6 40	12 40	..	..	8 10	..
8½	Neufchatel	6 54	..	..	..	8 25	..
17	Etaples	7 16	1 8	..	..	8 55	..
24	Montreuil-Verton ..	7 40	1 25	..	5 56	9 29	..
34	Rue	8 2	1 46	..	..	9 59	..
41	Noyelle	8 17	..	..	..	10 18	..
49½	**Abbeville**	8 40	2 16	5 0	6 40	10 55	..
54	Pont-Remy	8 55	..	5 19	..	..	..
59½	Longpre	9 8	..	5 38	..	..	..
64	Hangest	9 21	..	5 55	..	..	..
68	Picquigny	9 35	..	6 12	..	..	..
..	Ailly	9 44	..	6 26	..	..	..
	arr.	10 0	3 5	6 50	7 25	12 0	..
77	**Amiens**	a.m.	p.m.		p.m.	a.m	
	(**4**) dep.	10 25	3 25	..	7 40	12 20	..
		p.m.	p.m.		p.m	a.m.	
118	Clermont	12 26	4 49	..	9 9	2 15	..
127	Creil..............	1 0	5 15	..	9 35	2 50	..
152	Pontoise	2 4	..	..	..	3 52	..
170	**Paris**	2 40	6 40	..	10 45	4 45	..

Paris & Amiens to Boulogne.

Paris to Boulogne.	1,2,3 clss.	1—2 **Ex**	1—2 clss.	1,2 3 clss.	1,2 3 clss.	
	a.m.	a.m.	a.m.	p.m.	p.m	
Paris ..dep.	..	7 30	10 0	1 0	11 0	..
Pontoise	..	..	..	1 40	12 0	..
Creil (**5**)	..	8 48	11 18	2 40	1 15	..
Clermont......	..	9 4	11 34	3 2	1 45	..
Amiens ar.	..	10 25	12 45	4 40	3 40	..
	a.m.	1 & 2	p.m.	p.m.	a.m.	..
Amiens dp.	7 0	10 45	1 5	5 0	4 5	..
Ailly	7 27	..	..	5 15	..	..
Picquigny	7 40	..	..	5 24	..	..
Hangest	8 2	..	..	5 35	..	..
Longpre	8 21	..	..	5 48	..	..
Pont-Remy ...	8 40	..	..	6 1	..	..
Abbeville ..	9 0	11 34	1 55	6 17	5 15	..
Noyelle		..	..	6 38	5 33	..
Rue	..	..	2 22	6 54	5 51	..
Montreuil-Vert.	..	12 15	2 45	7 22	6 23	..
Etaples	..	12 26	..	7 38	6 46	..
Neufchatel ...	..	..	..	7 59	7 11	..
Pont-de-Brique	..	..	..	8 12	7 27	..
Boulogne ..	..	1 0	3 30	8 25	7 40	..

For full particulars of Times of Starting, Fares, &c., on the British Railways, see Bradshaw's Railway Guide, Price 6d. To be had of all Booksellers and at every Railway Station.

Travellers change carriages for Amiens at Longeau, and at Amiens change again for Boulogne.

Carriages—Two persons may, without any additional charge, travel in carriages of two wheels, and three in those of four wheels; passengers above this number must pay second class fare.

Conveyance of Carriages —A 4-wheeled carriage from Amiens to Abbeville (27½ miles) is charged 28 frs. 80 c.; 2-wheeled, 22 frs. 50 c. Amiens to Boulogne (77 miles), 4-wheeled, 35 frs. 6 c.

(**4**) Amiens to Arras, Douai, Valenciennes, and Brussels, see pages 36 and 37.

(**5**) Creil to Compiegne, Noyon, Chauny, and St. Quentin, see page 36.

Fares—From London to Folkestone, 1st class 20s.; 2nd class 14s.; 3rd class 9s.—From Folkestone to Boulogne 1st class 8s.; 2nd and 3rd class 6s.—From Boulogne to Amiens, 1st class 10s.; 2nd class 7s. 9d.; 3rd class 5s. 9d.—From Amiens to Paris, 1st class 12s. 3d.; 2nd class 9s. 3d.; 3rd class 6s. 9d.—From London to Paris 1st class 50s 6d; 2nd class 37s.; 3rd class 27s. 6d.

Passengers should be at the Station 5 minutes before the hour of departure. Luggage should be brought at least 15 minutes before the departure of the trains, and it must be legibly directed Each passenger is allowed 60lbs. of luggage: all above this weight is charged for. There are refreshment rooms at Boulogne, Amiens, and Creil—the trains stay 10 minutes at the two last stations.

Paris time is kept on all the French railways, which is 15 minutes before London time. English money is received at the station at Boulogne.

The boats of the South Eastern and Continental Steam Packet Company perform the service daily between Folkestone and Boulogne, and *vice versa*. Passengers always walk on board and land at the piers in both ports, so as to avoid the necessity of embarking in boats out at sea.

Special Trains leave London daily, expressly to meet these Steamers. See advertisement pages 333 and 334

For full particulars of Times of Starting, Fares, &c., on the British Railways, see Bradshaw's Railway Guide, Price 6d. To be had of all Booksellers and at every Railway Station.

Direct Tickets for Paris, Brussels, Malines, Aix-la-Chapelle, Cologne, and Chalons-sur-Saone, may be obtained at the Company's Central Office, 20, Moorgate-street, City, London, where small Parcels for Paris under £10 value, and 14 lbs. weight, are received until 4½ p.m., and forwarded by the Evening Mail Train, for delivery in Paris the next morning.

Fares—CALAIS to BRUSSELS, 1st Class, 21f.; 2nd Class, 16f.—DUNKIRK to BRUSSELS, 1st Class, 19f.; 2nd Class, 14f. 50c.

* The 2 a.m. and 3 p.m. are Express, 1st and 2nd Class only. † 1st and 2nd class only.

NORTHERN OF FRANCE RAILWAY.—CALAIS TO PARIS.

Fares to Paris. A	B	C	STATIONS.	E	F	G	H	I	J	K	L	M	N	O	P	Q	R
				a.m.	a.m.	a.m.	a.m.	a.m.	a.m.	a.m.	a.m.	p.m.	p.m.	p.m.	p.m.	p.m.	p.m.
38 45	28 90	21 50	**Calais** .... Dep.	2 *0	..	..	..	..	..	8 †0	..	..	3 * 0	..	..	6 30	..
38 10	28 70	21 30	St. Pierre-les-Calais	..	..	..	..	..	..	8 6	..	..	..	..	..	6 36	..
30 40	22 90	16 85	Ardres	..	..	..	..	..	..	8 20	..	..	..	..	..	6 51	..
30 20	22 75	16 75	Audruicq	..	..	..	..	..	..	8 31	..	..	..	..	..	7 3	..
30 0	22 60	16 65	Watten	..	..	..	..	..	..	8 46	..	..	..	..	..	7 18	..
29 80	22 45	16 55	**Saint-Omer**	..	..	..	..	..	..	9 3	..	..	3 45	..	..	7 35	..
29 60	22 30	16 45	Eblinghem...........	..	..	..	..	..	..	9 17	..	..	..	..	..	7 50	..
29 40	22 15	16 45	**Hazebrouck** ....Arr.	3 3	..	..	..	..	..	9 30	..	..	4 5	..	..	8 5	..
30 40	22 90	16 85	**Dunkirk** ....Dep.	..	..	..	..	5 0	..	8 15	..	..	2 45	..	..	6 30	..
30 20	22 75	16 75	Bergues	..	..	..	..	5 19	..	8 30	..	..	3 0	..	..	6 50	..
30 0	22 60	16 65	Esquelbecq	..	..	..	..	5 39	..	8 44	..	..	3 15	..	..	7 4	..
29 80	22 45	16 55	Arneeke	..	..	..	..	5 56	..	8 55	..	..	3 27	..	..	7 17	..
29 60	22 30	16 45	Cassel	..	..	..	..	6 15	..	9 6	..	..	3 41	..	..	7 32	..
29 40	22 15	16 32	**Hazebruck** ..Arr.	..	..	..	..	6 40	..	9 20	..	..	4 0	..	..	7 50	..
..	..	..	**Hazebrouck**.... Dep	3 8	..	..	..	7 25	..	9 35	..	..	4 10	..	..	8 15	..
29 20	22 0	16 25	Strazéele	..	..	..	..	7 42	..	..	..	..	..	..	..	8 26	..
29 0	21 85	16 15	Bailleul	..	..	..	..	8 5	..	9 54	..	..	4 30	..	..	8 38	..
28 80	21 70	16 5	Steenwerck	..	..	..	..	8 18	..	..	..	..	..	..	..	8 46	..
28 60	21 55	15 95	Armentieres	..	..	..	..	8 38	..	10 9	..	..	4 47	..	..	9 0	..
28 40	21 40	15 85	Perenchies	..	..	..	..	8 57	..	..	..	..	..	..	..	9 11	..
28 20	21 25	15 75	**Lille** ....Arr.	4 0	..	..	..	9 20	..	10 40	..	..	5 15	..	..	9 40	p.m.
30 0	22 50	16 75	Mouscron ......Dep.	..	..	..	7 35	..	..	..	11 20	12 50	3 50	6 30	8 30	..	9 50
29 45	22 15	16 45	Tourcoing	..	..	..	7 50	..	..	9 10	11 35	1 15	4 5	6 45	8 45	..	10 5
29 25	22 0	16 35	Roubaix...........	..	..	..	7 57	..	..	9 35	11 42	1 30	4 12	6 52	8 52	..	10 12
28 20	21 25	15 75	**Lille** ....Arr.	..	..	..	8 15	..	..	10 0	12 0	2 0	4 30	7 10	9 10	..	10 30
..	..	..	**Lille** ....Dep.	3 45	..	6 0	..	..	..	10 15	..	..	5 0	5 35	..	9 20	..
27 15	20 45	15 20	Seclin	..	..	6 18	..	..	..	10 48	..	..	..	6 0	..	9 50	..
26 35	19 85	14 75	Carvin	..	..	6 27	..	..	..	10 59	..	..	..	6 21	..	..	..
25 60	19 30	14 30	Le Forest	..	..	6 42	..	..	..	..	..	..	..	6 41	..	..	..
24 90	18 75	13 90	**Douai**.. ....Arr.	4 28	..	6 55	..	..	..	11 25	..	..	5 46	7 0	..	10 25	..
61 85	46 55	..	**Cologne** ..Dep.	..	..	..	..	..	..	11 30	p.m.	..	p.m.	..	..	7 0	a.m.
52 35	39 20	..	Aix-la-Chapelle......	..	..	..	..	..	..	1 30	a.m.	..	..	..	..	9 15	..
35 40	26 55	..	**Brussels**	..	..	..	..	..	..	8 0	..	..	1 15	..	..	6 30	p.m.
33 0	24 75	..	Braine-le-Comte ..	..	..	..	..	..	a.m.	8 50	..	..	2 20	..	..	7 25	..
30 50	23 0	..	**Mons**	..	..	..	..	..	8 0	9 40	..	..	3 15	..	..	8 10	..
29 75	22 25	16 50	Quiévrain	..	..	..	..	..	8 40	10 0	..	..	4 0	..	..	8 50	..
29 75	22 25	16 50	Blanc-Misseron......	..	..	..	..	..	8 50	10 10	..	..	4 10	..	..	9 0	..
28 60	21 55	16 0	**Valencnns.** Arr.	..	..	a.m.	..	..	9 15	10 25	..	..	4 25	p.m.	..	9 20	..
			Valencnns. Dep	..	..	6 0	..	..	..	10 40	..	..	4 45	5 25	..	9 40	..
28 10	21 15	15 70	Raismes	..	..	6 9	..	..	..	..	..	..	..	5 38	..	..	..
27 50	20 70	15 35	Wallers	..	..	6 20	..	..	..	..	..	..	..	5 55	..	..	..
26 45	19 90	14 80	Somain	..	..	6 34	..	..	..	11 10	..	..	5 12	6 20	..	10 8	..
25 85	19 45	14 45	Montigny	..	..	6 44	..	..	..	..	..	..	..	6 35	..	..	..
24 90	18 75	13 90	**Douai** ....Arr.	..	..	6 58	..	..	..	11 35	..	..	5 35	6 55	..	10 30	..

Douai to Valenciennes, Mons, and Brussels, see page 37.

Terminus, 24, Place Roubaix, Central Office, 50 Rue Croix-des-Petits-Champs, Paris.

Carriages.—The prices are fixed at the rate of 50c. per kilometre for carriages with one seat and of two or four wheels; 64c. for carriages of two seats and four wheels. Two persons can, without any extra charge, ride in a carriage of one seat, and three in a carriage of two seats. For Horses the fare is fixed at 20c. per kilometre per horse.–The Express trains take neither Horses or Carriages.

Conveyance of Carriages.—Total cost of a four-wheeled carriage from Paris to Calais, 192 frs.; two-wheeled carriage, 151 frs.

A	B	C		D	E	F	G	J	K	L	M	N	O	P	Q	R
					a.m.		a.m.		a.m.			p.m.	p.m.		p.m.	
..	..	..	**Douai** ....Dep.	..	4 33	..	7 10	..	11 50	..	..	5 54	7 20	..	10 50	..
23 85	17 95	13 35	Vitry	..	..	..	7 28	..	..	..	..	..	7 41	..	..	..
23 25	17 50	13 0	Rœux	..	..	..	7 41	..	..	..	..	..	7 56	..	..	..
22 20	16 70	12 40	**Arras**	..	5 5	..	8 5	..	12 24	..	..	6 25	8 25	..	11 35	..
21 40	16 10	11 95	Boileux	..	..	..	8 20	..	..	..	..	..	8 46	..	..	..
20 45	15 40	11 45	Achiet	..	..	..	8 36	..	..	..	Mix.	6 48	9 10	..	..	..
18 50	13 90	10 35	**Albert**	..	..	..	9 10	..	1 6	..	4 5	7 15	9 50	..	12 32	..
16 85	12 65	9 40	Corbie	..	..	..	9 35	..	..	..	4 50	..	10 21	..	..	..
15 30	11 50	8 55	**Amiens** ....Arr.	..	6 25	..	10 5	..	2 5	..	5 35	8 10	10 45	..	1 30	..
					a.m.	a.m.	a.m.		p.m.	p.m.	p.m.	p.m.		a.m.	a.m.	
..	..	..	**Amiens** ....Dep.	..	5 55	6 30	10 25	..	1 30	3 25	5 0	7 40	..	12 20	..	..
14 35	10 80	8 5	Boves	..	..	6 46	10 47	..	..	..	5 18	..	..	..	..	..
13 35	10 5	7 45	Ailly	..	..	7 6	11 8	..	..	..	5 41	..	..	..	..	..
11 0	8 50	6 0	**Breteuil**	..	6 47	7 35	11 37	..	2 37	4 10	6 15	8 38	..	1 20	2 14	..
9 50	7 0	5 0	Saint-Just	..	..	8 0	12 2	..	..	4 29	6 45	..	..	1 45	..	..
8 0	5 50	4 0	**Clermont**	..	7 16	8 25	12 26	..	3 10	4 49	7 17	9 9	..	2 15	2 57	..
7 0	5 0	3 75	Liancourt	..	..	8 37	12 36	..	..	..	7 34	..	..	..	..	..
6 0	4 50	3 25	**Creil** ....Arrival	..	7 31	8 50	12 50	..	3 25	5 5	7 50	9 25	..	2 40	3 20	..
						a.m.		a.m.			p.m.			p.m.		
17 50	13 25	9 75	**St. Quentin**..Dep.	..	..	6 0	..	11 0	..	..	5 0	..	..	11 0	..	..
16 75	12 25	9 0	Montescourt	..	..	6 19	..	11 19	..	..	5 19	..	..	11 24	..	..
15 0	11 50	8 50	Tergnier-la-Fère	..	..	6 36	..	11 36	..	..	5 37	..	..	11 46	..	..
14 50	10 50	8 0	**Chauny**	..	..	6 54	..	11 54	..	..	5 50	..	..	12 0	..	..
13 75	10 25	7 50	Appilly	..	..	7 7	..	12 7	..	..	6 4	..	..	..	..	..
12 0	9 0	6 50	**Noyon**	..	..	7 23	..	12 23	..	..	6 20	..	..	12 39	..	..
12 0	9 0	6 50	Ourscamps	..	..	7 34	..	12 34	..	..	6 31	..	..	..	..	..
10 25	8 0	5 75	Thourette	..	..	7 48	..	12 48	..	..	6 45	..	..	1 8	..	..
9 0	7 0	5 0	**Compiegne**	..	..	8 7	..	1 7	..	..	7 4	..	..	1 30	..	..
8 0	6 0	4 50	Verberie	..	..	8 24	..	1 24	..	..	7 22	..	..	1 51	..	..
7 25	5 50	4 0	Pont-Ste. Maxence	..	..	8 39	..	1 39	..	..	7 37	..	..	2 10	..	..
6 0	4 50	3 25	**Creil** ....Arr.	..	..	8 55	..	1 55	..	..	7 55	..	..	2 32	..	..
				a.m.	a.m.	a.m.	p.m.	p.m.	p.m.	p.m.	p.m.	p.m		a.m.	a.m.	
..	..	..	**Creil** ....Departure	6 20	7 41	9 5	1 0	2 5	3 35	5 15	8 5	9 35	..	2 50	3 30	..
5 50	3 75	2 75	Saint-Leu	6 31	..	9 16	1 10	2 16	..	5 25	8 16	..	..	..	..	..
5 50	3 75	2 50	Précy	6 38	..	9 23	..	2 23	..	..	8 23	..	..	..	..	..
5 0	3 50	2 50	Boran	6 47	..	9 32	..	2 32	..	..	8 32	..	..	..	..	..
4 0	3 0	2 50	Beaumont	7 0	..	9 45	1 35	2 45	..	..	8 45	..	..	3 22	4 5	..
4 0	3 0	2 30	Isle-Adam	7 11	..	9 56	1 45	2 56	..	..	8 56	..	..	..	..	..
3 50	2 65	1 95	Auvers	7 21	..	10 6	..	3 6	..	..	9 6	..	..	..	..	..
3 0	2 25	1 65	**Pontoise**	7 35	..	10 20	2 4	3 20	..	..	9 20	..	..	3 52	4 35	..
2 15	1 65	1 20	Herblay	7 40	..	..	..	..	..	..	9 35	..	..	..	..	..
1 85	1 40	1 5	Franconville	7 57	..	..	..	..	..	..	9 41	..	..	..	..	..
1 55	1 15	0 85	Ermont	8 5	..	..	..	..	..	..	9 47	..	..	..	..	..
1 25	0 95	0 70	Enghien	8 12	..	..	..	..	..	..	9 54	..	..	..	..	..
0 70	0 55	0 40	Saint-Denis	8 23	..	..	..	..	..	..	10 5	..	..	..	..	..
—	—	—	**Paris** ....Arrival	8 35	9 0	11 5	2 40	4 5	5 0	6 40	10 15	10 45	..	4 45	5 30	..

H: Passengers are conveyed gratuitously by omnibus to and from St. Denis for each train.

I: Horses and Carriages are not taken by the Express trains.

SPECIAL SERVICE between PARIS, SAINT-DENIS, ENGHIEN,

	a.m.	a.m.	a.m.	a.m.	a.m.	a.m.	p.m.	p.m.	p.m.	p.m.	p.m.	p.m.	p.m.	p.m.	p.m.	p.m.	p.m.	p.m.
Paris	7 35	8 15	8 30	9 30	10 30	11 30	12 15	12 30	1 30	2 30	3 30	4 0	4 30	5 0	5 30	6 30	7 35	8 30
Saint-Denis	7 46	*	8 41	9 41	10 41	11 41	*	12 41	1 41	2 41	3 41	*	4 41	5 11	5 41	6 41	7 46	8 41
Enghien ..	7 58	..	8 50	9 50	10 51	11 50	12 33	12 50	1 50	2 50	3 50	..	4 51	5 20	5 51	6 50	7 55	8 51
Ermont ..	8 4	..			10 57		12 39					*	4 57		5 57			8 57
Franconvile	8 10	..	..	..	11 3	..	12 44	..	..	..	..	..	5 3	..	6 3	..	..	9 3
Herblay ..	8 16	..	..	..	11 10	..	12 50	..	..	..	..	..	5 10	..	6 10	..	..	9 10
Pontoise	8 39	9 8	..	..	11 25	..	1 4	..	..	..	..	4 37	5 25	..	6 25	..	..	9 25

Additional Trains—From Paris to Pontoise direct, at 1 and 11 p.m.

NORTHERN OF FRANCE RAILWAY.—PARIS TO CALAIS.

† The 7½ a.m. and 7½ p.m. trains are First Class Express.
‡ The 8 p.m. is a First and Second class only; all others are first, second, and third class.

English Miles.	STATIONS.	a.m.	a.m.	a.m.	a.m.	a.m.	a.m.	p.m.	p.m.	p.m.	p.m.	p.m.	p.m.	p.m.	p.m.
	Paris ....dep.	..	6 30	7†30	8 15	10 0	11 45	12 15	1 0	4 0	..	7‡30	8 ‡ 0	8 30	11 0
3¾	Saint-Denis	..	*	..	*	..	..	12 25	..	*	..		..	8 41	11 11
7	Enghien	..	..	..	..	..	..	12 33	..	*	..		..	8 51	11 21
9	Ermont	..	..	..	..	..	..	12 39	..	..	..		..	8 57	..
10¾	Franconville	..	..	..	..	..	..	12 44	..	..	..		..	9 3	..
12½	Herblay	..	..	..	..	..	..	12 50	..	..	..		..	9 10	..
17¼	**Pontoise**	..	7 18	..	8 58	*	*	1 8	1 40	4 53	..		*	9 30	12 0
20	Auvers	..	..	..	9 8	..	..	1 16	..	5 3	..		..	9 41	..
24½	Isle-Adam	..	..	..	9 19	..	..	1 26	..	5 14	..		..	9 52	..
28¾	Beaumont	..	7 47	..	9 32	..	..	1 28	2 0	5 28	..		8 59	10 6	12 30
33	Boran	..	..	..	9 43	..	..	1 48	..	5 39	..		..	10 17	..
35¾	Précy	..	..	..	9 51	..	..	1 56	..	5 48	..		..	10 24	..
37¾	Saint-Leu	..	8 10	..	9 58	..	..	2 2	..	5 55	..		..	10 30	..
42	**Creil** ....arr.	..	8 21	8 38	10 10	11 8	1 5	2 12	2 30	6 5	..		9 22	10 40	1 5
42	**Creil** ....dep.	..	..	..	10 20	..	..	2 20	..	6 15	..		..	10 50	..
48¼	P.-Ste-Maxence	..	..	..	10 40	..	..	2 40	..	6 35	..		..	11 11	..
54¾	Verberie	..	..	..	10 55	..	..	2 54	..	6 49	..		..	11 28	..
65½	**Compiegne** ..	6 40	..	..	11 15	..	..	3 15	..	7 10	..		..	11 50	..
68¼	Thourotte	7 9	..	..	11 29	..	..	3 30	..	7 25	..		..	12 6	..
73½	Ourscamps.. ...	7 37	..	..	11 42	..	..	3 44	..	7 39	..		..	..	..
77½	**Noyon**	8 10	..	..	11 55	..	..	3 57	..	7 52	..		..	12 30	..
82½	Appilly	8 32	..	..	12 8	..	..	4 10	..	8 5	..		..	..	..
87¼	**Chauny**	9 10	..	..	12 22	..	..	4 25	..	8 20	..		..	12 58	..
62¼	Tergnier-la-Fère.	9 55	..	..	12 34	..	..	4 37	..	8 32	..		..	1 10	..
93½	Montescourt	10 27	..	..	12 40	..	..	4 52	..	8 47	..		..	1 26	..
105¾	**St.Quentin** ar	11 0		..	1 10	..	..	5 15		9 10	..		..	1 50	..
			a.m.						p.m.						
42	**Creil** ....dep.	..	9 0	8 48	..	11 18	1 15	..	2 40	6 20	..		9 32	..	1 15
46¼	Liancourt	..	9 14	..	..	..	..	..	2 50	6 30	..		..	..	..
51½	**Clermont**	..	9 29	9 4	..	11 34	1 32	..	3 2	6 42	..		9 55	..	1 45
60	Saint-Just	..	9 52	..	..	..	..	..	3 22	7 2	..	..	..	..	2 17
69¼	**Breteuil**	..	10 20	9 38	..	12 0	2 10	..	3 46	7 26	..	..	10 37	..	2 45
80	Ailly	..	10 45	..	..	..	..	..	4 7	7 47	..	..	..	..	..
86¾	Boves	..	11 2	..	..	..	..	..	4 22	8 2	..	..	..	..	..
92	**Amiens** ....arr.	..	11 20	10 25	..	12 45	3 5	..	4 40	8 20	..	10 13	11 45	..	3 40
		a.m.		1 & 2			p.m.				Mix.	p.m.	p.m.		a.m.
92	**Amiens** ....dep.	8 50	..	9 55	..	..	2 30	..	..	..	4 0	9 40	11 5	..	4 5
101¾	Corbie	9 30	..	..	..	..	..	..	..	..	4 29	..	..	..	4 31
111¾	**Albert**	10 0	..	10 53	..	..	3 34	..	..	..	5 3	10 27	12 8	..	5 3
123¼	Achiet		..	11 14	..	..	..	..	..	..	5 40	..	..	..	5 33
128¾	Boileux	..	..	..	..	..	..	..	..	..	5 55	..	..	..	5 47
134¼	**Arras**	..	..	11 36	..	..	4 20	..	..	..	6 20	11 2	12 55	..	6 8
140	Rœux	..	..	..	..	..	..	..	..	..	6 38	..	..	..	6 23
144¼	Vitry	..	..	..	..	..	..	..	..	..	6 51	..	..	..	6 35
150	**Douai**	..	..	12 4	..	..	4 55	..	..	..	7 10	11 29	1 27	..	6 52
		A	B	C	D	E	F	G	H	I	J	K	L	M	N

* Stops when required, to take up or set down Passengers.

ERMONT, FRANCONVILLE, HERBLAY & PONTOISE.

	a.m.	a.m.	a.m.	a.m.	a.m.	p.m.	p.m.	p.m.	p.m.	p.m.	p.m.	p.m.	p.m.	p.m.	p.m.	p.m.	p.m.	
Pontoise dep.	6 35	7 35	..	..	10 35	..	..	..	..	3 20	3 35	..	..	..	7 35	..	9 20	..
Herblay	6 50	7 50	..	..	10 50	..	..	..	..	..	3 50	..	..	..	7 50	..	9 35	..
Franconville ..	6 57	7 57	..	..	10 57	..	..	..	..	..	3 57	..	..	..	7 57	..	9 41	..
Ermont........	7 5	8 5	..	..	11 5	..	..	..	..	..	4 5	..	..	..	8 5	..	9 47	..
Enghien	7 12	8 12	9 12	10 12	11 12	12 12	1 12	2 12	3 12	..	4 12	5 12	6 12	7 12	8 12	9 12	9 54	..
Saint-Denis § ..	7 23	8 23	9 23	10 23	11 23	12 23	1 23	2 23	3 23	..	4 23	5 23	6 23	7 23	8 23	9 23	10 5	..
Paris . ..arr.	7 35	8 35	9 35	10 35	11 35	12 35	1 35	2 35	3 35	4 5	4 35	5 35	6 35	7 35	8 35	9 35	10 15	..

Additional Trains.—From Pontoise to Paris, at 10.20 a.m., and 2 4 p.m.

Fares.—From Paris to Pontoise, first class, 3 francs; second class, 2 francs 25 centimes; third class, 1 franc, 65 centimes. § Omnibuses, gratis, meet every train to and from St. Denis.

			A	B	C	D	E	F	G	H	I	J	K	L	M	N
			a.m.	a.m.	p.m.	p.m.		p.m.				p.m.	p.m.	a.m.	a.m.	a.m.
	150	**Douai**....Dep.	..	..	12 15	..	..	5 10	..	..	..	7 25	..	1 37	..	7 5
	155¾	Montigny	..	..	..	..	..	..	..	..	..	7 45	..	..	..	7 21
	160	Somain	..	..	12 49	..	..	5 32	..	..	..	8 5	..	2 0	..	7 32
	165½	Wallers	..	..	..	..	..	..	..	..	..	8 26	..	..	..	7 45
	168¾	Raismes	..	..	..	..	..	5 46	..	..	..	8 40	..	..	..	7 56
	173	**Valenc.** Arr.	..	..	1 10	..	..	5 55	..	..	..	8 52	..	2 25	..	8 5
		Valenc. Dep	..	..	1 30	4 40	..		..	..	..		..	2 40	5 30	8 25
	180	Blanc-Misseron..	..	..	1 51	5 1	..	..	..	..	..	..	..	3 1	5 51	8 46
	180½	Quievrain	..	..	2 20	5 30	..	..	..	..	..	..	..	3 30	6 15	9 15
	192½	Mons	..	..	3 5	6 15	..	..	..	..	..	..	..	4 5	7 0	9 50
	211¾	Braine-le-Comte	..	..	4 5	7 20	..	..	..	..	..	..	..	5 0	8 5	10 50
	231¼	**Brussels** Arr.	..	..	5 0	8 20	..	..	..	..	..	..	1–2	5 45	9 0	11 40
	337	Aix-la-Chapelle	..	..	2 0	..	..	..	..	..	..	..	Class.	2 0	4 15	..
	380¾	**Cologne** Arr.	..	a.m.	4 0	..	..	..	..	..	..	p.m.	p.m.	4 15	6 30	a.m.
150		**Douai**.........Dep.	..	9 30	12 10	..	..	5 5	..	..	..	7 30	11 35	..	..	7 5
155		Le Forest	..	9 45	..	..	..	5 19	..	..	..	7 50	..	..	..	7 18
158¾		Carvin	..	10 0	..	..	..	5 30	..	..	..	8 10	..	..	..	7 29
165		Seclin	..	10 14	12 34	..	..	5 45	..	..	..	8 30	..	..	..	7 42
171¼		**Lille**...........Arr.	..	10 30	1 0	..	..	6 5	..	..	..	9 0	12 20	..	..	8 0
				a m.	p.m.	p.m.			p.m.		p.m.	p.m.	a.m.		a.m.	a.m.
	171¼	**Lille**..... Dep.	..	11 0	..	2 50	..	..	5 30	..	7 30	8 50	..	..	6 0	9 15
	177	Roubaix	..	11 16	..	3 6	..	..	5 46	..	7 46	9 6	..	..	6 16	9 45
	178¾	Tourcoing	..	11 22	..	3 12	..	..	5 52	..	7 52	9 12	..	..	6 22	9 55
	182	Mouscron ..Arr.	a.m.	11 40	..	3 30	..	..	6 10	..	8 10	9 30	..	..	6 40	10 10
171¼		**Lille**...........Dep.	10 15	..	12 35	..	..	6 30				..	12 0	..	..	8 0
176½		Perenchies...........	10 45	..	..	..	..	6 50				..	..	..	..	8 28
180		Armentieres	11 20	..	1 13	..	..	7 4				..	..	..	..	8 44
185½		Steenwerck	11 47	..	..	..	..	7 17				..	..	..	..	8 58
188		Bailleul	12 10	..	1 25	..	..	7 23				..	..	..	..	9 6
193		Strazeele	12 32	..	..	..	..	7 35				..	..	..	..	9 19
197		**Hazebrouck** ..Arr.	12 48	..	1 41	..	..	7 45				..	12 55	a.m.	..	9 30
	197	**Hazebrouck** dp	..	..	1 50	..	..	8 20				..	..	4 0	..	9 45
	203¼	Cassel..........	..	..	2 7	..	..	8 37				..	..	4 28	..	10 2
	207½	Arneeke........	..	..	2 21	..	..	8 51				..	..	4 49	..	10 16
	211¾	Esquelbecq	..	..	2 33	..	..	9 3				..	..	5 7	..	10 28
	217½	Bergues	..	..	2 48	..	..	9 20				..	..	5 35	..	10 45
	222½	**Dunkirk**..Arr.	..	..	3 0	..	..	9 35				..	a.m.	6 0	..	11 0
197		**Hazebrouck** ..Dep.	..	..	1 45	..	..	7 55				..	1 0	..	..	9 43
103¼		Eblinghem	..	..	..	..	..	8 11				..	..	..	..	9 57
210		St. Omer	..	..	2 10	..	..	8 28				..	1 22	..	..	10 18
215		Watten	..	..	..	..	..	8 43				..	..	..	..	10 33
222½		Audruicq	..	..	..	..	..	8 59				..	..	..	..	10 52
227¾		Ardres	..	..	..	..	..	9 10				..	..	..	..	11 6
234½		St. Pierre	..	..	p.m.	..	..	9 25				..	..	..	..	11 25
235¾		**Calais**.........Arr.	..	..	3 0	..	..	9 30				..	2 10	..	..	11 30
		London	..	..	10 0	..	..	4 30				..	7 50	..	..	a.m.

For Packets between London and Dunkirk, see page 132. From Calais to Dover, at 2.10 a.m. and 9.40 p.m.; also Folkestone to Boulogne, see page 128. From Calais to London, see page 127.

Conveyance of Carriages.—From Dieppe to Paris, (125½ miles), four-wheeled carriages, 135 frs. 40 c.; two-wheeled, 118 frs. From Rouen to Paris, (87½ miles), four-wheeled, 89 frs. 15 c.; two-wheeled, 68 frs. 5 c.

DIEPPE, HAVRE, ROUEN, and PARIS.

Eng. Miles.	FARES. 1st Clss.	2nd Clss.	3rd Clss.	STATIONS.	DAILY TRAINS. 1	2	3	4	5	6	7	8	9	10	11	12	13	14	15
					2, 3		1, 2, 3	1, 2, 3	1 & 2	1, 2, 3	1 & 2	2 & 3		1, 2, 3	**Ex.**	2 & 3	1, 2, 3		
Dis.	fr. c.	fr. c.	fr. c.	DIEPPE LINE.	a.m.	a.m.	a.m.	a.m.	p.m.	a.m.	p.m.	p.m.	p.m.	p.m.	p.m.	p.m	p.m.		
—	—	—	—	**Dieppe** (1) ....dep.	...	...	...	7 0	...	10 50	...	...	...	...	5 40	...	9 45	...	...
10¾	1 75	1 30	1 0	Longueville	...	...	...	7 46	...	11 20	...	...	...	...	6 9	...	10 16	...	...
16¼	2 70	2 0	1 50	Auffay	...	...	...	8 20	...	11 42	...	...	...	...	6 31	...	10 38	...	...
18¾	3 10	2 35	1 75	Saint-Victor	...	...	...	8 38	...	11 54	...	...	...	...	6 43	...	10 48	...	...
28½	4 75	3 60	2 65	Monville	...	...	...	9 24	...	12 21	...	...	...	...	7 11	...	11 15	...	...
32¼	5 25	4 5	3 0	Malaunay	...	...	...	9 54	...	12 55	...	...	...	...	7 25	...	...	...	...
34¼	6 5	4 55	3 40	Maromme	...	...	...	10 3	...	...	...	...	...	...	7 34	...	...	...	...
38	6 50	4 85	3 65	**Rouen** (right bank) ar.	...	...	...	10 15	...	1 10	...	...	...	...	7 45	...	11 45	...	...
From	Havre.			HAVRE LINE.	a.m.	a.m.	a.m.	a.m.	p.m.	a.m.	p.m.	p.m.	p.m.	p.m.	p.m.	p.m.	p.m.		
—	—	—	—	**Havre**..............dep.	...	...	...	7 0	...	10 45	...	...	...	...	6 0	6 15	10 0	...	...
4¼	0 80	0 60	0 45	Harfleur	...	...	...	7 13	...	10 55	...	...	...	...	...	6 31	10 10	...	...
11¼	2 20	1 50	1 25	Saint-Romain	...	...	...	7 40	...	...	...	...	...	...	...	7 3	...	...	
16¼	3 0	2 10	1 70	Beuzeville (Fécamp)	...	...	...	7 59	...	11 29	...	...	...	...	6 36	7 30	10 47	...	
20	3 55	2 35	1 95	Bolbec & Nointot	...	...	...	8 11	...	11 39	...	...	...	...	6 45	7 50	10 56	...	
24¾	4 60	3 20	2 60	Alvimare (Fauville)	...	...	...	8 26	...	...	...	...	...	...	...	8 8	...	...	
31¾	5 90	4 10	3 35	**Yvetot**	...	...	...	8 50	...	12 4	...	...	...	...	7 8	8 36	11 22	...	
36¾	6 80	4 75	3 85	Motteville	...		...	9 5	...	12 16	...	...	...	...	7 18	8 50	11 33	...	
43¾	8 0	5 60	4 55	Pavilly	...		...	9 25	...	...	...	...	...	...	...	9 11	...	...	
45	8 30	5 80	4 60	Barentin	...		...	9 34	...	12 36	...	...	...	...	7 37	9 20	...	...	
50	9 20	6 40	4 80	Malaunay	...		...	9 54	...	12 55	...	...	...	...	...	9 35	...	...	
51¾	9 55	6 65	4 90	Maromme	...		...	10 3	...	...	...	...	...	...	...	9 46	...	...	
55½	10 0	7 50	5 0	**Rouen** (right bank) ar.	...		...	10 15	...	1 10	...	...	...	...	8 0	10 0	12 15	...	
...	...	...	...	Do. Do. dep.	...		...	10 30	...	1 25	...	...		...	8 15		12 45	...	
				ROUEN LINE.	a.m.		a.m.	a.m.		1 & 2		p.m.		p.m.	p.m.		p.m.		
...	...	...	...	**Rouen** (left bank) dep.	...		6 45	10 35	...	1 25	...	4 15		6 0	...	...	...	...	
65	11 70	8 55	6 0	Oissel	...		7 6	11 6	...	...	...	4 42		6 21	...	...	...	...	
65½	11 80	8 70	6 10	Tourville (Elbeuf)	...		7 12	11 12	...	1 58	...	4 49		6 27	8 39	...	...	...	
68¾	12 30	9 0	6 30	Pont-de-l'Arche	...		7 22	11 22		2 7	...	5 3		6 37	...	...	...	...	
76¾	13 90	9 90	6 90	Saint-Pierre (Louviers)	...		7 44	11 44		2 27		5 42		6 58	9 4	...	...	...	
85	16 10	12 12	8 50	Gaillon (les Andelys)	...		8 4	12 4		...		6 9		7 19	...	...	...	...	
93¾	18 0	13 55	9 60	**Vernon**	...		8 25	12 25		3 1		6 35		7 40	...	...	...	...	
100½	19 25	14 80	10 60	Bonnières	...		8 43	12 43		3 15				7 58	...	...	...	...	
104¼	19 76	15 0	10 85	Rosny	...		8 55	12 55		...		...		8 10	...	...	...	...	
108	20 75	15 80	11 35	**Mantes**	6 45		9 15	1 15		3 39		...		8 30	9 59	...	...	...	
113	21 75	16 80	12 15	Epône	7 2		9 28	1 28		...		...		8 43	...	...	...	...	
118	22 75	17 60	12 80	Meulan	7 19		9 43	1 43		3 59		...		8 57	...	...	...	...	
121¾	23 75	18 80	13 25	Triel	7 33		9 55	1 55		...		...		9 9	...	...	...	...	
126¾	24 75	18 80	13 35	**Poissy**	7 55	8 30	10 11	2 11	4 10	4 20	5 20	...	9 10	9 25	...	...	...	...	
130	25 25	19 30	13 85	Conflans	8 8	...	10 22	2 22	...	...	5 30	...	9 21	9 36	...	...	...	...	...
133	25 75	19 90	14 40	**Maisons**	8 21	8 52	10 33	2 33	4 28	4 40	5 40	...	9 31	9 47	...	...	...	...	...
143	26 50	20 50	15 50	**Paris**..............arr.	9 0	9 15	11 0	3 0	4 55	5 5	6 5	...	10 0	10 15	11 5	...	5 0	...	...

Train 2: Daily, Sundays and Fêtes excepted.

Train 5: Thursdays only.

Train 7: Thursdays only.

Train 9: Sundays and Fêtes only.

(1) For Steamers from Dieppe to Newhaven, see page 128

Terminus,] **PARIS, ROUEN, HAVRE, and DIEPPE.** [15, Rue d'Amsterdam.

Eng. Miles.	FARES. 1st Clss.	2nd Clss.	3rd Clss.	STATIONS.	DAILY TRAINS. 1	2	3	4	5	6	7	8	9	10	11	12	13	14	15	16	17	18
					2&3	2 & 3	2&3	1&2	1,2,3	**Ex.**	1&2	1,2,3	1 & 2		1,2,3		1,2,3	3rd	1 & 2			
Dis.	fr. c.	fr. c.	fr. c.	ROUEN LINE.	a.m.	a.m.	a.m.	a.m.	a.m.	a.m.	a.m.	a.m.	noon	p.m.	p.m.	p.m.	p.m.	p.m.	p.m.			
—	—	—	—	**Paris** ....dep.	...	...	...	6 0	8 25	9 25	10 0	11 0	12 0	2 0	4 25	5 25	7 25	9 25	11 0	...	...	...
10¾	1 50	1 25	1 0	**Maisons**..............	...	...	...	6 25	8 53	...	...	11 34	12 28	2 28	4 53	5 46	7 51	...	...	...	...	...
13¾	1 75	1 50	1 10	Conflans	...	...	...	6 33	9 3	...	...	11 45	12 37	2 37	5 2	5 56	8 0	...	...	...	...	...
16¾	2 0	1 60	1 30	**Poissy**	...	...	...	6 40	9 15	...	10 30	12 0	12 48	2 45	5 13	6 5	8 11	...	...	...	...	...
21¾	3 0	2 25	1 75	Triel	...	...	...	☞ Thursdays only.	9 30	...	☞ Thursdays only.	12 16	1 1	☞ Sundays and Fêtes only.	5 26	☞ Daily, Sundays and Fêtes excepted.	8 23	...	...	...	...	...
25½	4 0	2 80	2 10	Meulan	...	...	...		9 42	...		12 29	1 14		5 39		8 35	...	...	...	...	...
30½	5 0	3 50	2 75	Epône	...	...	...		9 57	...		12 45	1 28		5 53		8 47	...	...	...	...	...
35½	6 0	4 50	3 25	**Mantes**	...	...	...		10 28	...		1 0	1 50		6 15		9 7	...	...	...	...	...
39½	7 50	6 0	4 75	Rosny	...	...	...		10 39	...		—	2 1		6 26		9 18	...	...	...	...	...
43	8 0	6 50	5 25	Bonnières	...	...	...		10 52	...		...	2 14		6 39		9 31	...	...	...	...	...
50	9 50	8 0	6 0	**Vernon**	...	...	7 0		11 12	10 50		...	2 34		7 0		9 50	...	...	...	...	...
58	11 0	9 50	7 25	Gaillon (les Andelys) ..	...	...	7 29		11 32	...		...	2 55		7 21		10 9	...	...	...	...	...
66¾	12 50	11 0	8 25	Saint Pierre (Louviers)	...	...	8 5		11 53	11 20		...	3 17		7 43		10 30	...	...	...	...	...
74¼	14 0	11 50	9 20	Pont-de-l'Arche.........	...	...	8 36		12 13	...		...	3 38		8 4		10 50	...	...	...	...	...
77½	15 0	12 50	9 50	Tourville (Elbeuf)	...	...	8 49		12 22	11 41		...	3 48		8 14		10 59	...	...	...	...	...
78¾	15 70	12 70	9 70	Oissel	...	...	8 55	...	12 27	...	...	...	3 53		8 19		11 4	...	...	...	...	...
85½	16 0	13 0	10 0	**Rouen** (left bnk)..ar.	...	...	9 20	...	12 55	...	...	...	4 20		8 35		11 20	...	...	...	...	...
				HAVRE LINE.	a.m.				p.m.	noon			1,2,3						1,2,3			
...	...	...	...	**Rouen** (right bk)..ar.	...	...	...	...	12 50	12 0	...	...	4 15		...		...	2 15	2 35	...	...	...
87½	16 0	13 0	10 0	,, ,, dep.	6 0	...	...	...	1 0	12 15	...	...	4 30		...		...		3 5	...	...	...
91¼	16 90	13 50	10 80	Maromme	6 15	...	...	...	1 11	...	...	...	4 40		...		...		...	...	...	...
93¼	17 25	13 70	11 0	Malaunay	6 25	...	...	...	1 20	...	...	...	4 50		...		...		...	...	...	...
98¼	18 15	14 35	11 50	Barentin	6 47	...	...	...	1 35	...	...	...	5 10	...	...		...		...	...	...	...
99¼	18 40	14 50	11 65	Pavilly	6 52	...	...	...	1 40	...	...	...	5 15	...	...		...		...	...	...	...
106¼	19 65	15 40	12 35	Motteville	7 18	...	...	...	2 0	...	...	...	5 38	...	...	...	...		...	...	...	...
111¼	20 50	16 0	12 90	**Yvetot**..............	7 42	...	...	...	2 16	1 6	...	...	5 52	...	...	...	...		...	...	...	...
118	21 85	16 90	13 60	Alvimare (Fauville) ...	8 3	...	...	...	2 31	...	...	...	6 6	...	...	...	...		...	...	...	...
123	22 60	17 35	13 95	Bolbec and Nointot ...	8 20	...	...	...	2 43	...	...	...	6 18	...	...	...	...		...	...	...	...
126¾	23 50	18 0	14 50	Beuzeville (Fécamp)...	8 40	...	...	...	2 53	...	...	...	6 29	...	...	...	...		...	...	...	...
131¾	24 35	18 70	15 0	Saint Romain	8 57	...	...	...	3 5	...	...	...	6 40	...	...	...	...		...	...	...	...
138½	25 65	19 50	15 40	Harfleur	9 15	...	...	...	3 15	...	...	...	6 51	...	...	...	...		...	...	...	...
143	26 50	20 50	15 50	**Havre** ....arr.	9 35	...	...	...	3 30	2 0	...	...	7 5	...	...	...	...		6 5	...	...	...
				DIEPPE LINE.		a.m.				p.m.			p.m.						a.m.			
87½	16 0	13 0	10 0	**Rouen** (right bank)..	...	7 15	...	...	...	12 15	...	...	4 45	...	...	...	...		3 20	...	...	...
91¼	16 90	13 50	10 80	Maromme ....[dep.	...	7 36	...	...	...	...	...	...	4 59	...	...	...	...		...	...	...	...
93¼	17 25	13 70	11 0	Malaunay	...	7 52	...	...	...	...	...	...	5 10	...	...	...	...		3 46	...	...	...
97	17 85	14 15	11 35	Monville	...	8 20	...	...	...	12 43	...	...	5 28	...	...	...	...		4 7	...	...	...
106¾	19 50	15 40	12 25	Saint-Victor	...	9 12	...	...	...	1 13	...	...	6 5	...	...	...	...		4 58	...	...	...
109¼	19 95	15 70	12 50	Auffay	...	9 30	...	...	...	1 27	...	...	6 26	...	...	...	...		5 16	...	...	...
115½	20 95	16 50	13 10	Longueville..............	...	9 50	...	...	...	1 43	...	...	6 44	...	...	...	...		5 39	...	...	...
125½	22 60	17 75	14 0	**Dieppe** ....arr.	...	10 25	...	...	...	2 15	...	...	7 15	...	...	...	...		6 15	...	...	...

LYONS, SAINT ETIENNE, AND ROANNE. [10-5-52.

English Miles.	Fares. 1st Clss	2nd Clss	3rd Clss	STATIONS.	Trains. 1	2	3	4	5	6	7	8	9	10
Dis.	fr. c.	fr. c.	fr. c.		a.m.	a.m.	a.m.	a.m.	a.m.	p.m.	p.m.	p.m.	p.m.	
—	—	—	—	**Lyons** (Perrache) dep.	..	..	6 30	8 5	10 30	2 30	..	6 30	7 30	..
2	0 50	0 35	..	Oullins	..	..	6 38	8 13	10 38	2 38	..	6 38	7 38	..
6¼	0 65	0 45	..	Irigny	..	..	6 51	8 26	10 51	2 51	..	6 51	7 51	..
8	0 75	0 50	..	Vernaison	..	..	6 58	8 33	10 58	2 58	..	6 58	7 58	..
8¾	0 80	0 60	..	La Tour	..	..	7 3	8 38	..	..	..	7 3	8 3	..
10	1 0	0 75	..	Grigny	..	..	7 8	8 43	11 8	3 8	..	7 8	8 8	..
13	1 25	1 0	..	**Givors**	..	..	7 20	8 51	11 20	3 20	..	7 20	8 16	..
18¾	2 0	1 60	.	Burel	..	..	7 41	Sundays and Fêtes only.	..	..	..	7 41		.
21¼	2 50	2 0	..	Couzon	..	..	7 51		11 51	3 51	..	7 51	..	..
21¾	2 50	2 0	..	**Rive-de-Gier**	..	7 15	7 59		11 59	3 59	..	7 59	..	..
24¼	3 15	2 50	..	Grandecroix	..	7 26	8 10		12 10	4 10	..	8 10	..	..
28	3 75	3 0	..	**St. Chamond**	..	7 44	8 28		12 28	4 28	7 15	8 28	..	..
32¼	4 40	3 50	..	Terrenoire	..	8 3	8 47		12 47	4 47	7 34	8 47	..	..
34¾	5 0	4 0	..	**St. Etienne** ... arr.	..	8 16	9 0		1 0	5 0	7 47	9 0	..	..
..	..	..	..	Do. ....dep.	6 20				1 30				..	..
46¼	6 50	5 0	..	La Renardiere	6 56	..	..		2 0	..	..	..	..	..
50	7 0	5 50	..	Saint Galmier	7 9	..	..		2 13	..	..	..	..	..
55½	7 50	6 0	..	**Montrond** (Montbrison)	7 32	.	..		2 33	..	..	..	..	..
63	8 50	7 0	..	Feurs	8 5	..	..		3 5	..	..	..	..	..
68¾	9 0	7 0	..	Balbigny	8 30	..	..	..	3 30	..	..	..	..	..
75	9 0	7 0	..	Neulize	9 13	..	..	..	4 13	..	..	..	..	..
78	9 0	7 0	..	Saint Symphorien	9 31	..	..	..	4 31	..	..	..	..	..
82½	9 0	7 0	..	L'Hopital	9 53	..	..	..	4 53	..	..	..	..	..
87½	9 0	7 0	..	**Roanne** (Coteau) arr.	10 10	..	..	..	5 10	..	..	..	..	..

ROANNE, SAINT ETIENNE, AND LYONS.

English Miles.	Fares. 1st Clss	2nd Clss	3rd Clss	STATIONS.	Trains. 1	2	3	4	5	6	7	8	9	10
Dis.	fr. c.	fr. c.	fr. c.		a.m.	a.m.	a.m.	a.m.	a.m.	p.m.	p.m.	p.m.	p.m.	p.m.
—	—	—	—	**Roanne** (Coteau) dep.	..	..	..	5 0	..	..	..	1 0		..
5	0 80	0 60	..	L'Hopital	..	..	..	5 16	..	..	..	1 16	Sundays and Fêtes only.	..
9½	1 50	1 20	..	Saint Symphorien	..	..	..	5 37	..	..	..	1 37		..
12½	2 0	1 50	..	Neulize	..	..	..	6 6	..	..	..	2 6		..
18¾	3 0	2 20	..	Balbigny	..	..	..	6 42	..	..	..	2 42		..
24¼	4 0	3 0	..	Feurs	..	..	..	7 4	..	..	..	3 4		..
31¾	5 0	4 0	..	**Montrond** (Montbrison)	..	..	..	7 32	..	..	..	3 32		..
37½	6 0	4 50	..	Saint Galmier	..	..	..	8 5	..	..	..	4 5		..
41¼	6 60	5 0	..	La Renardiere	..	..	..	8 18	..	..	..	4 18		..
50½	7 50	5 50	..	**St. Etienne** ....arr.	..	..	..	9 10	..	..	..	5 10		..
From St. Etienne.				Do. ....dep.	..	6 0	7 0	10 0	11 0	2 0	3 0	6 0		6 30
2½	0 70	0 50	..	Terrenoire	..	6 12	7 12	10 12	11 12	2 12	3 12	6 12		6 42
7½	1 25	1 0	..	**St. Chamond**	..	6 27	7 25	10 27	11 25	2 27	3 25	6 27	..	6 57
11¼	1 90	1 50	..	Grandecroix	..	6 40	..	10 40	Sunday, Thursday, & Fetes only.	2 40	Sunday, Thursday, & Fetes only.	6 40	..	7 10
13¾	2 50	2 0	..	**Rive-de-Gier**	..	6 52	..	10 52		2 52		6 52	..	7 19
14¼	2 50	2 0	..	Couzon	..	6 57	..	10 57		2 57		6 57	..	..
16¾	3 15	2 50	..	Burel	..	7 6	..	..		..		7 6	..	..
22½	3 75	3 0	..	**Givors**	6 0	7 29	..	11 29		3 29		7 29	8 45	..
24¾	4 15	3 30	..	Grigny	6 9	7 38	..	11 38		3 38		7 38	8 54	..
26	4 25	3 40	..	La Tour	6 14	7 43	..	..		..		7 43	8 59	..
27½	4 40	3 50	..	Vernaison	6 20	7 48	..	11 48		3 48		7 48	9 4	..
29¼	4 70	3 75	..	Irigny	6 27	7 55	..	11 55		3 55		7 55	9 11	..
33	4 90	3 90	..	Oullins	6 40	8 8	..	12 8		4 8		8 8	9 21	..
35	5 0	4 0	..	**Lyons** (Perrache) arr.	6 47	8 15	..	12 15		4 15		8 15	9 31	..

MONTPELLIER AND NIMES TO TARASCON. [10–10–52

English Miles.	Fares. 1st Class	2nd Class	3rd Class	4th Class	STATIONS.	Trains. 1	2	3	4	5	6
Dis.	fr. c.	fr. c.	fr. c.	fr. c.		a.m.	a.m.	a.m.	p.m.	p.m.	p.m.
—	—	—	—	—	**Montpellier** departure	6 15	...	7 50	12 45	4 45	6 0
..	0 80	0 70	0 50	0 40	Les Mazes	..	...	8 0	..	4 56	6 14
..	...	...	...	...	St. Aunès	...	...	8 7	1 2	...	6 20
..	...	...	...	...	Baillargues	...	...	8 15	...	5 6	6 28
..	1 80	1 50	1 15	0 85	St. Brès	...	...	8 21	...	...	6 34
..	...	...	...	...	Valergues	...	...	8 27	1 19	5 13	6 41
..	...	...	...	...	Lunel-Viel	..	...	8 33	...	...	6 47
..	2 85	2 45	1 85	1 35	Lunel	6 55	...	8 43	1 35	5 25	6 50
..	...	...	...	...	Gallargues	7 7	...	...	1 48	...	7 10
..	.	...	...	...	Aigues-Vives	7 12	...	...		...	7 16
..	4 10	3 50	2 60	1 90	Vergèze	7 18	...	...	1 59	...	7 21
..	...	...	...	...	Uchaud	7 29	...	...	2 8	...	7 31
..	...	...	...	...	Bernis	7 35	...	...		...	7 36
..	...	...	...	...	Milhaud	7 40	...	...	2 18	...	7 41
..	5 50	4 70	3 50	2 60	St.-Césaire	7 46	...	...		..	7 47
..	6 0	5 0	3 80	2 80	**Nimes** arrival	8 0	...	9 15	2 35	5 55	8 0
	From	Nimes.			Do. departure	—	6 35	9 25	2 45	6 15	—
2½	...	...	...	...	Marguerittes	...	6 45	...	2 55	...	...
4¼	...	...	...	...	Beaulieu	...	6 51	...	3 1	...	...
6¼	...	...	...	...	Manduel	...	6 57	...	3 7	6 30	...
9¼	...	...	...	...	Bellegarde	...	7 6	...	3 16	...	...
15½	2 25	1 75	1 25	...	Beaucaire	...	7 [illegible]2	10 2	3 32	6 52	...
..	...		...	...	**Tarascon** [1] arrival	...	7 25	10 5	3 35	6 55	...

TARASCON AND NIMES TO MONTPELLIER.

English Miles.	Fares From NIMES. 1st Class	2nd Class	3rd Class	4th Class	STATIONS.	Trains. 1	2	3	4	5	6
Dis.	fr. c.	fr. c.	fr. c.	fr. c.		a.m.	a.m.	a.m.	p.m.	p.m.	
..	...	...	...	...	**Tarascon** [1] departure	...	8 0	11 30	4 10	7 30	...
..	...	..	...	...	Beaucaire	...	8 3	11 33	4 13	7 33	...
..	...	...	...	...	Bellegarde	...	8 21	...	4 31	...	...
..	...	...	...	...	Manduel	...	8 31	...	4 41	7 56	...
..	...	...	...	...	Beaulieu	...	8 38	...	4 48	...	...
..	...	...	...	...	Marguerittes	...	8 44	...	4 54	..	...
..	...	...	...	...	**Nimes** arrival	...	8 55	12 10	5 5	8 15	...
..	—	—	—	—	Do. departure	7 0	9 10	12 20	5 15	8 25	...
..	0 70	0 60	0 45	0 30	St.-Césaire	7 9	9 19	...	5 24	...	...
..	...	...	...	...	Milhaud	7 16	9 26	12 30	5 31	...	...
..	...	...	...	...	Bernis	7 22	9 32	...	5 37	...	...
..	...	...	...	...	Uchaud	7 28	9 38	12 37	5 43	...	...
..	2 0	1 75	1 30	0 95	Vergèze	7 38	9 48	12 44	5 53	...	...
..	...	...	...	...	Aigues-Vives	7 44	9 54	...	5 59	...	...
..	...	...	...	...	Gallargues	7 48	9 58	12 50	6 3	...	...
..	3 20	2 75	2 0	1 50	Lunel	8 3	10 13	1 2	6 18	9 17	...
..	...	...	...	...	Lunel-Viel	8 10	10 20	...	6 25	...	...
..	...	...	...	...	Valergues	8 16	10 26	...	6 31	...	...
..	4 30	3 70	2 75	2 0	St. Brès	8 22	10 32	...	6 37	...	...
..	...	...	...	...	Baillargues	8 27	10 37	...	6 42	...	...
..	...	...	...	...	St. Aunès	8 35	10 45	...	6 50	...	...
..	5 10	4 40	3 30	2 40	Les Mazes	8 40	10 50	...	6 55	...	...
..	6 0	5 0	3 80	2 80	**Montpellier** arrival	8 55	11 5	1 30	7 10	10 0	...

[1] TARASCON to AVIGNON and MARSEILLES, see page 50.

PARIS TO ORLEANS, VIERZON, CHATEAUROUX, BOURGES, LE GUETIN, MOULINS, AND NEVERS. TERMINUS—No. 5, Boulevart de l'Hopital.

Eng. Miles.	Fares. 1st class.	2nd class.	3rd clss.	STATIONS.	Trains. 1,2,3 class.	1st class.	1st class.	1,2,3 clss.	1, 2, 3 class.	1,2,3 clss.	1st clss.	1st clss.	1,2,3 clss.	1,2,3 clss.
Dis.	fr. c.	fr. c.	fr. c.		a.m.	a.m.	a.m.	p.m.	p.m.	p.m.	p.m.	p.m.	p.m.	a.m.
—	—	—	—	**Paris** ....dep	7 35	9 20	10 5	12 45	4 15	5 45	7 15	7 40	11 0	..
6¼	1 0	0 60	0 40	Choisy	7 51	..	..	1 1	4 32	6 1	..	..	..	..
11¾	1 95	1 50	1 10	Juvisy	8 7	..	10 27	1 17	4 49	6 17	..	8 6	11 36	..
13¾	2 25	1 70	1 25	Savigny	8 14	..	..	1 24	4 57	6 24	..	..	..	..
15	2 45	1 85	1 40	Epernay	8 19	..	..	1 29	5 5	6 29	..	..	..	..
17½	3 0	2 25	1 65	Saint-Michel	8 30	..	10 40	1 40	5 19	6 40	7 54	8 21	11 58	..
18¾	3 20	2 40	1 80	Bretigny	8 37	..	..	1 47	5 26	6 47	..	..	..	..
22½	3 80	2 85	2 15	Marolles	8 48	..	..	1 58	5 38	6 58	..	..	..	..
25	4 15	3 10	2 30	Bouray	8 57	..	..	2 7	5 47	7 7	..	..	..	..
26¼	4 45	3 35	2 50	Lardy	9 4	..	..	2 14	5 55	7 14	..	..	..	..
30	5 5	3 80	2 80	Etrechy	9 15	..	..	2 25	6 7	7 25	..	..	..	..
35	5 80	4 35	3 25	**Etampes**	9 32	10 25	11 14	2 42	6 20	7 42	8 34	9 1	12 57	..
43¾	7 25	5 45	4 5	Monnerville	10 1	..	..	3 11		8 10	..	..	..	..
46¾	7 75	5 85	4 35	Angerville	10 11	..	..	3 21		8 21	..	..	..	..
55	9 20	6 90	5 15	Toury	10 34	11 7	11 55	3 44		8 44	9 25	9 52	2 7	..
63¾	10 55	7 95	5 90	Artena	10 55	..	..	4 5		9 5	..	..	..	..
67½	11 15	8 40	6 25	Chevilly	11 6	..	..	4 16		9 16	..	..	..	..
70	11 65	8 80	6 50	Cercottes	11 15	..	..	4 25		9 25	..	..	..	..
76¼	12 50	9 40	7 0	**Orleans** [1]...arr.	11 35	11 50	12 40	4 45		9 45	10 10	10 37	3 10	..
					a.m.		p.m.	p.m.		p.m.			a.m.	a.m.
76¼	12 50	9 40	7 0	**Orleans** ......dep.	11 50		12 20	5 0		10 50			3 35	5 30
90¾	14 95	14 25	8 35	La Ferté-St-Aubin	12 25		..	5 39		..			..	6 13
100	16 50	12 45	9 25	La Motte-Beuvron	12 52		1 20	6 9		11 42			4 48	6 45
104¼	17 25	13 0	9 65	Nouan-le-Fuselier	1 4		..	6 22		..			5 3	7 0
111⅝	18 50	13 90	10 35	Salbris	1 24		1 43	6 44		12 9			5 27	7 25
119¾	19 85	14 90	11 10	Theillay	1 43		..	7 6		..			5 51	7 49
126¼	20 85	15 70	11 65	**Vierzon** ....arr.	1 59		2 10	7 23		12 38			6 9	8 8
					p.m.					a.m.				a.m.
126¼	20 85	15 70	11 65	**Vierzon** ......dep.	2 33		..	..		12 58			..	8 20
135½	22 40	16 85	12 55	Chery	2 57		..	..		..			..	8 54
138	22 80	17 20	12 75	Reuilly	3 7		..	..		..			..	9 8
144¼	23 85	17 95	13 35	Sainte Lizaigne	3 23		..	..		..			..	9 29
148½	24 60	18 50	13 75	Issoudun	3 39		..	..		1 51			..	9 54
156	25 80	19 45	14 45	Neuvy-Pailloux	3 58		..	..		..			..	10 18
165¼	27 35	20 60	15 30	**Chateauroux** arr.	4 20		..	..		2 25			..	10 45
					p.m.		p.m.	p.m.		a.m.			a.m.	
126¼	20 85	15 70	11 65	**Vierzon** ......dep.	2 24		2 16	7 35		12 49			6 19	
132½	21 90	16 50	12 25	Foëcy	2 41		..	7 54		..			6 38	
135½	22 40	16 85	12 55	Mehun	2 51		..	8 5		..			6 49	
139¾	23 15	17 40	12 95	Marmagne	3 4		..	8 20		..			7 4	
145½	24 5	18 10	13 45	**Bourges**	3 26		2 59	8 35		1 33			7 24	
151½	25 10	18 90	14 5	Moulins	3 42		..			..			7 42	
156	25 80	19 45	14 45	Savigny	5 53		..			..			7 54	
159½	26 35	19 80	14 70	Avor	4 4		..	..		..			8 5	
164¾	27 25	20 50	15 25	Bengy	4 18		..	.		..			8 21	
167¾	27 80	20 90	15 55	**Nerondes**	4 31		3 42	..		2 26			8 35	
175¾	29 15	21 90	16 30	La Guerche	4 52		..	..		2 45			8 58	
181½	30 5	22 60	16 80	**Le Guetin** ..arr.	5 6		4 8	..		2 58			9 13	
..	..	..	..	Do. ..dep.	5 17		4 16	..		3 6			10 7	
188¼	31 20	23 50	17 45	Mars	5 37		..	..		..			10 28	
192¾	31 90	24 0	17 85	St. Pierre	5 51		4 42	..		3 32			10 46	
198¼	32 95	24 80	18 40	St. Imbert	6 10		..	..		..			11 5	
204½	33 90	25 50	18 95	Villeneuve-S.-A.	6 32		..	1,2,3	1, 2, 3	..			11 23	
213¼	35 30	26 60	19 75	**Moulins** .....arr.	6 55		5 25	clss.	class.	4 15			11 45	
					p.m.		p.m.	a.m.	p.m.	a.m.			a.m.	
181½	30 5	22 60	16 80	**Le Guetin** ..dep.	5 25		4 20	10 25	7 45	3 15			9 20	
188¼	31 20	23 50	17 45	**Nevers** ......arr.	5 45		4 35	10 55	8 5	3 35			9 35	

Additional Trains, for the conveyance of merchandise, run frequently throughout the day.

[1] Orleans to Tours, Poitiers, Angouleme and Bordeaux, see page 44.

Conveyance of Carriages.—Paris to Orleans, 4-wheeled, 82 frs.; 2-wheeled, 62 frs. Orleans to Vierzon, 4-wheeled, 53 frs. 85 c.; 2-wheeled, 42 frs. 50 c. Orleans to Chateauraux, 4-wheeled, 94 frs. 15 c.; 2-wheeled, 74 frs.

NEVERS, MOULINS, LE GUETIN, BOURGES, CHATEAUROUX, VIERZON, ORLEANS, & PARIS.

English Miles.	Fares. 1st clss.	2nd clss.	3rd clss.	Stations.	Trains. 1 1, 2, 3 c ass.	2 1, 2, 3 clsss.	3 1, 2, 3 class.	4 1, 2, 3 class.	5 1st class.	6 1, 2, 3 class.	7 1, 2, 3 class.	8 1, 2, 3 class.	9 1, 2, 3 class.
Dis.	fr. c.	fr. c.	fr. c.		a.m.	a.m.	a.m.	a.m.	a.m.	p.m.	p.m.	p.m.	p.m.
—	—	—	—	**Nevers** ......dep.	2 30	..	..	8 35	9 40	..	4 40	2 40	7 0
6¾	1 25	0 95	0 70	**Le Guetin**....arr.	2 50	..	..	8 55	9 55	..	4 55	3 10	7 20
					a.m.	a.m.	a.m.	a.m.	a.m.	p.m.	..	p.m.	p.m.
From Nevers.				**Moulins** ....dep.	..	..	..	7 40	8 55	..	..	1 45	6 10
..	..	..	..	Villeneuve-S.-A.	..	..	..	8 1	..	..	..	2 8	6 30
..	..	..	..	Saint-Imbert	..	..	..	8 17	..	..	..	2 28	6 46
..	..	..	..	Saint-Pierre	..	..	..	8 34	9 39	..	..	2 49	7 1
..	..	..	..	Mars	..	..	..	8 46	..	..	..	3 3	7 13
6¾	1 25	0 95	0 70	**Le Guetin**....arr.	..	..	..	9 3	10 4	..	..	3 21	7 30
..	..	..	..	Do. ....dep.	..	..	..	9 14	10 12	..	..	3 31	7 38
12½	2 15	1 65	1 20	La Guerche	..	..	..	9 29	..	..	..	3 47	7 53
20½	3 40	2 55	1 90	**Nerondes**........	..	..	..	9 51	10 40	..	..	4 11	8 13
24¾	4 5	3 5	2 25	Bengy	..	..	..	10 2	..	..	..	4 22	..
29¼	4 85	3 65	2 70	Avor	..	..	..	10 16	..	..	..	4 38	..
33	5 50	4 10	3 10	Savigny	..	..	..	10 27	..	..	..	4 50	..
38¾	6 10	4 60	3 40	Moulins	..	..	..	10 38	..	..	..	5 2	..
43	7 15	5 35	4 0	**Bourges**	..	..	6 20	11 0	11 26	..	..	5 24	9 4
48	8 5	6 5	4 50	Marmagne..........	..	..	6 35	11 15	..	..	..	5 40	..
53	8 90	6 70	4 95	Mehun	..	.	6 48	11 28	..	..	..	5 55	..
56¾	9 40	7 10	5 25	Foëcy	..	..	6 58	11 38	..	..	..	6 6	..
63	10 45	7 85	5 85	**Vierzon** .... arr.	..	..	7 14	11 54	12 4	..	..	6 24	9 45
					a.m.	a.m.	a.m.	a.m.	p.m.				p.m.
Fm Chateroux.				**Chateauroux** dep	..	..	5 35	9 30	..	..	..	..	8 0
9¼	1 55	1 15	0 85	Neuvy-Pailloux	..	..	5 58	9 55	..	..	..	..	8 21
16¾	2 80	2 10	1 55	Issoudun	..	..	6 23	10 25	..	..	..	..	8 43
21¼	3 50	2 65	1 95	Sainte Lizaigne	..	..	6 35	10 43	..	..	..	..	8 54
26¼	4 55	3 40	2 55	Reuilly	..	..	6 51	11 3	..	..	..	..	9 9
30	4 95	3 75	2 75	Chery	..	..	7 0	11 11	..	..	..	..	..
50	6 50	4 90	3 65	**Vierzon** ......arr.	..	..	7 24	11 14	..	..	..	..	9 35
					a.m.	a.m.	a.m.	p.m.	p.m.			p.m.	p.m.
From Nevers.				**Vierzon**......dep.	..	..	7 34	12 22	12 10	..	..	6 35	9 55
69¼	11 45	8 65	6 40	Theillay	..	..	7 51	12 39	..	..	..	6 55	..
76¾	12 80	9 65	7 15	Salbris..............	..	..	8 11	12 59	12 38	..	..	7 20	10 26
84¼	14 5	10 70	7 95	Nouan-le-Fuselier ..	..	..	8 30	1 18	..	..	..	7 44	..
88¼	14 65	11 5	8 20	La Motte-Beuvron...	..	..	8 44	1 32	1 2	..	..	8 3	10 56
98¼	16 30	12 30	9 15	La Ferté-St-Aubin ..	..	..	9 9	1 57	..	..	1st	8 33	..
113	18 70	14 5	10 45	**Orleans** ......arr.	..	..	9 47	2 35	2 0	..	Class.	9 20	11 50
						a.m.	a.m.	p.m.	p.m.	p.m.	p.m.		a.m.
From Orleans.				**Orleans** ......dep.	..	6 30	10 0	2 50	1 35	6 0	5 30	..	12 30
5½	1 5	0 80	0 60	Cercottes	..	6 45	10 15	3 5	..	6 15	..	..	..
8¾	1 45	1 10	0 80	Chevilly	..	6 54	10 24	3 14	..	6 24	..	..	..
12½	2 5	1 55	1 15	Artenay	..	7 5	10 35	3 25	..	6 35	..	..	..
21¼	3 40	2 55	1 90	Toury..	..	7 29	10 59	3 49	2 26	6 59	6 20	..	1 25
29¼	4 85	3 65	2 70	Angerville	..	7 51	11 21	4 11	..	7 21	..	..	..
32½	5 35	4 5	3 0	Monnerville	a.m.	8 0	11 30	4 20	..	7 30	..	..	..
41¼	6 80	5 15	3 80	**Etampes**	6 30	8 35	12 2	4 52	3 10	8 2	7 5	..	2 28
45½	7 55	5 70	4 20	Etrechy	6 44	8 49	12 15	5 5	..	8 15	..	..	..
49¼	8 15	6 15	4 55	Lardy	6 56	9 1	12 27	5 17	..	8 27	..	..	..
51¼	8 45	6 40	4 75	Bouray	7 5	9 10	12 34	5 24	..	8 34	..	..	..
53¾	8 90	6 70	4 95	Marolles	7 15	9 20	12 43	5 33	..	8 43	..	..	..
56¾	9 40	7 5	5 25	Bretigny	7 26	9 31	12 53	5 43	..	8 53	..	..	..
58	9 70	7 30	5 45	Saint-Michel.....	7 37	9 42	1 3	5 53	3 41	9 3	..	..	3 13
61½	10 10	7 60	5 65	Epernay............	7 48	9 53	1 12	6 2	..	9 12	..	..	..
62½	10 35	7 80	5 80	Savigny	7 55	10 0	1 17	6 7	..	9 17	..	..	..
64¼	10 65	8 0	5 95	Juvisy	8 2	10 7	1 24	6 14	3 54	9 24	..	..	..
70	11 55	8 70	6 45	Choisy	8 19	10 24	1 40	6 30	..	9 40	..	..	..
76	12 60	9 50	7 5	**Paris** ....arr.	8 40	10 45	2 0	6 50	4 20	10 0	8 10	..	4 0

Additional Trains, for the conveyance of merchandise, run frequently throughout the day.

PARIS, ORLEANS, TOURS, and BORDEAUX.

Eng Mils Dis.	Fares. 1 Cl. fr. c.	2 Cl. fr. c.	3 Cl. fr. c.	Stations.	1, 2, 3	1, 2, 3	1, 2, 3	1st.	1st.	1, 2, 3	1, 2, 3	1st.	1st.	1, 2, 3
					p.m.	a.m.	a.m	a.m.	a.m.	p.m.	p.m.	p.m.	p m.	p.m.
				PARIS ....dep.	11 0	..	7 35	9 20	10 5	12 45	5 45	7 15	7 40	..
76¼	12 60	9 50	7 5	ORLEANS ....arr.	3 10	..	11 35	11 50	12 40	4 45	9 45	10 10	10 37	..
				[1]	a.m.	a.m.	p.m.	a.m.		p.m.				..
—	—	—	—	**Orleans** ......dep.	3 25	6 50	12 0	11 30		5 15	10 25		..	..
4¼	0 75	0 55	0 40	La Chapelle	..	7 4	12 13	..	[1] PARIS to ORLEANS, see page 42.	5 29	..		..	..
8¾	1 45	1 10	0 80	Saint-Ay	..	7 17	12 25	..		5 42	..		..	..
12½	2 10	1 55	1 15	Meung	..	7 29	12 36	..		5 54	10 52		..	..
16¾	2 80	2 10	1 55	Beaugency.........	..	7 48	12 53	..		6 13	11 8		..	..
24¼	4 5	3 5	2 25	Mer..	4 12	8 10	1 13	..		6 35	11 25		..	..
31¼	5 15	3 90	2 90	Ménars	..	8 28	1 29	..		6 53	..		..	..
36¾	6 10	4 60	3 40	**Blois**	..	8 52	1 51	12 53		7 17	11 52		..	...
42¼	7 0	5 30	3 95	Chousy	5 9	9 9	2 7	..		7 34	..		..	..
46¼	7 65	5 75	4 25	Onzain	..	9 21	2 18	..		7 46	..		..	..
53	8 75	6 60	4 90	Limeray...........	..	9 41	2 36	..		8 6	..		..	..
56¾	9 40	7 5	5 25	Amboise...........	6 4	9 56	2 50	1 30		8 21	12 43		..	..
60	10 10	7 60	5 65	Noizay	6 17	10 9	3 2	..		8 34	..		..	..
62⅓	10 45	7 85	5 85	Vernou	6 25	10 17	3 9	..		8 42	..		..	..
64¼	10 75	8 10	6 0	Vouvray	6 32	10 24	3 16	..		8 49	..		..	..
65	10 85	8 15	6 5	Mont-Louis	6 36	10 28	3 20	..		8 53	..		..	..
71¼	11 85	8 95	6 65	**Tours**... ......arr.	6 58	10 50	3 40	2 0		9 15	1 18		..	..
					a.m.		p.m.	p.m.			a.m.			
71¼	11 85	8 95	6 65	**Tours** ....dep.	7 10	..	3 50	2 10		..	1 35		..	..
80	13 20	9 95	7 40	Monts	7 34	..	4 13	..	..	..	..		..	..
85½	14 15	10 65	7 90	Villeperdue	7 51	..	4 28	..	..	..	..		..	..
93¼	15 40	11 60	8 60	Sainte-Maure	8 12	..	4 51	2 57	..	..	2 20		..	..
100	16 55	12 45	9 25	Port-de-Piles	8 32	..	5 12	..	..	..	..		..	..
103	17 5	12 85	9 55	Les Ormes	8 45	..	5 25	3 18	..	..	2 45		..	..
105	17 35	13 5	9 70	Dange	8 51	..	5 35	..	..	..	..		..	..
110	18 20	13 70	10 15	Ingrandes	9 9	..	5 50	..	..	..	..		..	..
116¼	18 90	14 25	10 55	**Chatellerault** ..	9 26	..	6 6	3 43	..	..	3 14		..	..
119¼	19 75	14 85	11 5	Les Barres.........	9 42	..	6 20	..	.	..	..		..	..
122¼	20 25	15 25	11 30	La Tricherie	9 54	..	6 31	..	..	..	..		..	..
125	20 65	15 55	11 55	Dissais	10 2	..	6 38	..	..	..	..		..	..
127½	21 5	15 85	11 80	Clan	10 11	..	6 47	..	..	..	..		..	..
129¼	21 40	16 10	11 95	Chasseneuil	10 19	..	6 54	..	..	..	..		..	..
135	22 30	16 80	12 45	**Poitiers** ......arr.	10 39	..	7 12	4 25	..	..	4 1		..	..
						a.m.			p.m.		p.m.		p.m.	p.m.
—	—	—	—	**Angouleme** dep.	..	..	6 40	a.m.	..	..	12 30		..	4 4[illegible]
5	0 85	0 60	0 45	La Couronne........	..	..	6 55		..	..	..		..	5 0
9½	1 55	1 15	0 85	Manthiers	..	..	7 8		..	..	..		..	5 13
13¾	2 25	1 70	1 25	Charmant	..	..	7 21		..	..	..		..	5 27
21¾	3 60	2 70	2 0	Mont Moreau........	..	..	7 43		..	..	1 16		..	5 48
31¾	5 26	3 95	2 95	Chalais	..	..	8 12		..	..	1 42		..	6 16
40⅓	6 70	5 5	3 75	Laroche-Chalais	..	..	8 35		..	..	2 6		..	6 39
51¼	8 45	6 40	4 75	Coutras	..	..	9 2		..	..	2 31		..	7 8
56¾	9 40	7 10	5 25	Saint Denis	..	a.m.	9 17		..	..	..		p.m.	7 23
61¼	10 10	7 60	5 65	**Libourne**	..	6 30	9 37		12 0	..	3 0		4 45	7 43
66¾	11 5	8 30	6 20	Vayres	..	6 46	9 53		12 16	..	..		5 1	7 59
70½	11 65	8 80	6 55	Saint-Sulpice.......	..	6 57	10 5		12 27	..	..		5 12	8 11
72½	12 0	9 0	6 70	Saint-Loubes........	..	7 6	10 13		12 36	..	..		5 21	8 19
78¾	12 40	9 35	6 95	La Grave D'Ambares	..	7 15	10 21		12 45	..	..		5 29	8 27
80½	13 35	10 5	7 45	Lormont...........	..	7 31	10 37		1 1	..	..		5 45	8 43
83	13 75	10 35	7 70	**Bordeaux** ....arr.	..	7 45	10 52		1 15	.	3 50		6 0	8 58

MOUSCRON TO LILLE.

STATIONS.	a.m.	a.m.	a.m.	p.m.	p.m.	p.m.	p.m.	p.m.				
Mouscron [1] ....dep.	7 35	..	11 20	12 50	3 50	6 30	8 30	9 50	..	...	...	...
Tourcoing	7 50	9 10	11 35	1 15	4 5	6 45	8 45	10 5	..	...	...	...
Roubaix.	7 57	9 35	11 42	1 30	4 12	6 52	8 52	10 1	..	...	...	...
Lille [2] ....arrival	8 15	10 0	12 0	2 0	4 30	7 10	9 10	10 30	..	...	...	...

[1] *For Trains from Brussels, Malines, Ghent, and Courtray to Mouscron, see page 59.*
[2] *Lille to Calais and Dunkirk, see page 37.*

BORDEAUX, TOURS, ORLEANS, and PARIS.

Eng Mls.	Fares. 1st.	2nd.	3rd.	Stations.	1, 2, 3	1, 2, 3	1,2,3	1st	1,2,3	1,2,3	1st	1, 2, 3	1, 2, 3	1,2,3
					a.m.	a.m.	a.m.		p.m.	p.m.		p.m.	p.m	p.m.
Dis.	fr. c.	fr c.	fr. c	**Bordeaux**......dep.	6 0	9 0	11 50		3 0	5 25		..	..	8 10
3¾	0 60	0 45	0 35	Lormont	..	9 11	12 1		3 11	5 36		..	..	8 21
8¾	1 45	0 90	0 60	La Grave D'Ambares ..	..	9 27	12 17		3 27	5 52		..	..	8 37
11¼	1 85	1 40	1 0	Saint Loubes.........	..	9 35	12 25		3 35	6 0		..	..	8 45
13	2 15	1 60	1 0	Saint Sulpice.........	..	9 43	12 33		3 43	6 8		..	..	8 53
16¾	2 80	1 60	1 0	Vayres	..	9 53	12 44		3 54	6 19		..	..	9 4
22¼	3 0	1 60	1 10	**Libourne**	6 53	10 10	1 6		4 10	6 40		..	..	9 20
26¾	4 0	2 80	2 0	Saint Denis	7 5		1 20			6 53		..	..	
32¼	5 35	4 5	2 70	Coutras	7 19	..	1 36		..	7 11		..	..	..
43	7 15	5 55	3 50	Laroche-Chalais	7 44	..	2 4		..	7 34		..	..	..
51¾	8 55	6 45	4 80	Chalais	8 8	..	2 29		..	8 2		..	..	..
61¾	10 25	7 70	5 70	Montmoreau	8 33	..	2 54		..	8 28		..	..	..
70	11 55	8 70	6 45	Charmant	8 53	..	3 16		..	8 49		..	..	..
74¼	12 30	9 25	6 85	Monthiers	9 6	..	3 29		..	9 2		..	..	..
78¾	13 0	9 80	7 30	La Couronne..........	9 17	..	3 11		..	9 15		..	..	..
83	13 75	10 35	7 70	**Angouleme** ....arr.	9 35	..	3 58		..	9 32		..	..	..
							a.m.			a.m.	p.m.		p.m.	
—	—	—	—	**Poitiers**........dep.	..	..	6 50		..	10 2	1 0	..	5 30	..
5½	0 95	0 70	0 50	Chasseneuil	..	..	7 6		..	10 20	..	..	5 45	..
7½	1 25	0 95	0 70	Clan	..	..	7 14		..	10 27	..	..	5 52	..
10	1 65	1 25	0 90	Dissais	..	..	7 23		..	10 36	..	..	6 1	..
12½	2 5	1 55	1 15	La Tricherie	..	..	7 31		..	10 43	..	..	6 8	..
15½	2 60	1 95	1 40	Les Barres............	..	..	7 43		..	10 54	..	..	6 19	..
21¼	3 50	2 65	1 95	**Chatellerault**	..	..	8 3		..	11 12	1 42	..	6 37	..
24¾	4 15	3 10	2 30	Ingrandes	..	..	8 16		..	11 24	..	..	6 49	..
30	4 90	3 75	2 75	Dange................	..	..	8 31		..	11 37	..	..	7 2	..
32¼	5 35	4 5	3 0	Les Ormes............	..	..	8 43		..	11 48	2 8	..	7 13	..
34¾	5 80	4 35	3 5	Port-de-Piles..........	..	..	8 53		..	11 57	..	..	7 22	..
41¾	6 90	5 25	3 85	Sainte Maure..........	..	..	9 14		..	12 17	2 29	..	7 42	..
49¼	8 19	6 15	4 55	Villeperdue	..	..	9 34		..	12 35	..	..	8 1	..
54¾	9 10	6 85	5 10	Nonts	..	..	9 52		..	12 51	..	..	8 17	..
63	10 45	7 85	5 85	**Tours** ....arr.	..	..	10 19		..	1 16	3 10	..	8 42	..
						a.m.	a.m.			p.m.	p.m.	p.m.	p m.	
63	10 45	7 85	5 85	**Tours** ....dep.	..	5 50	10 32		..	1 30	3 30	4 50	9 7	..
70	11 55	8 70	6 45	Mont-Louis	..	6 0	..		..	1 47	..	5 8	..	..
70	11 55	8 70	6 45	Vouvray..............	..	6 10	..		..	1 52	..	5 12	..	..
71¾	11 90	8 95	6 65	Vernou	..	6 17	..		..	2 0	..	5 19	..	..
73¾	12 20	9 15	6 80	Noizay	..	6 24	..		..	2 8	..	5 27	..	..
78	12 90	9 70	7 20	Amboise..............	..	6 39	11 6		..	2 27	3 57	5 43	9 41	..
81¾	13 55	10 20	7 55	Limeray	..	6 50	..		..	2 39	..	5 55	..	..
88¾	14 65	11 5	8 20	Onzain	..	7 8	..		..	2 58	..	6 15	..	..
92½	15 30	11 50	8 55	Chousy	..	7 19	..		..	3 10	..	6 27	..	..
98¼	16 20	12 20	9 5	**Blois**	..	7 42	11 55		..	3 35	4 38	6 51	10 30	..
104¼	17 25	13 0	9 65	Ménars	..	7 57	..		..	3 51	..	7 8	..	..
110½	18 30	13 75	10 20	Mer	..	8 14	12 21		..	4 8	..	7 27	10 56	..
118	19 50	14 70	11 0	Beaugency............	..	8 36	12 41		..	4 31	..	7 52	11 16	..
122½	20 25	15 85	11 30	Meung	..	8 51	12 54		..	4 46	..	8 8	11 29	..
136¼	20 85	15 70	11 65	Saint-Ay	..	9 1	..		..	4 56	..	8 19	..	..
130½	21 60	16 25	12 5	La Chapelle	..	9 13	..		..	5 8	..	8 32	..	..
135	22 30	16 80	12 45	**Orleans** ....arr.	..	9 30	1 25		..	5 25	5 50	8 50	12 0	..
						a.m.				p.m.	p.m.		a.m.	
135	..	..	..	ORLEANS ......arr.	..	10 0	1 35	2 50	..	6 0	5 50	..	12 30	..
211¼	34 90	26 30	19 50	PARIS.........dep.	..	2 0	4 20	6 50	..	10 0	8 10	..	4 0	..

The distance from Brussels to Lille is 149 kilometres (92½ miles); from Brussels to Mouscron, 132 kilometres (82 miles); from Mouscron to Lille, 17 kilomètres (10½ English miles).

LILLE TO MOUSCRON.

STATIONS.	a.m.	a.m.	a.m.	p.m.	p.m.	p.m.	p m.					
Lille [3].......... departure	6 0	9 15	11 0	2 50	5 30	7 30	8 50	..	..	..	..	..
Roubaix	6 16	9 45	11 16	3 6	5 46	7 46	9 6	..	..	..	..	..
Tourcoing	6 22	9 55	11 22	3 12	5 52	7 52	9 12	..	..	..	..	..
Mouscron .... arrival	6 40	10 10	11 40	3 30	6 10	8 10	9 30	..	..	..	..	..

[3] *For Trains from Calais, Saint-Omer, and Dunkirk to Lille,* *see page* 34.

PARIS, TOURS, ANGERS, AND NANTES.

Eng Mls.	Fares. 1st class.	2nd clas	3rd clas	Stations.	Trains. 1	2	3	4	5	6	7	8	9
					1, 2, 3	1st	1, 2, 3	1, 2, 3	1, 2, 3	1st	1, 2, 3		
Dis.	fr. c.	fr. c.	fr. c.		p.m.	p.m.	a.m.	p.m.	noon	a.m.	a.m.		
..	—	—	—	PARIS........dep.	5 45	7 15	..	11 0	..	9 20	7 35	..	..
								a.m.		a.m.	noon		
..	12 60	9 50	7 5	ORLEANS ....dep.	10 25		..	3 25	..	11 30	12 0	..	..
..	11 85	8 95	6 65	TOURS........arr.	1 18		..	6 58	..	2 0	3 40	..	..
					a.m.		a.m.	a.m.	noon	p.m.	p.m.		
—	—	—	—	**Tours**..........dep.	1 45		..	7 25	12 0	2 20	4 5	..	
8¾	1 45	1 10	0 80	Savonnieres..........	..		..	7 49	12 24	..	4 27	..	
13	2 15	1 60	1 20	Cinq-Mars	..		..	8 2	12 37	..	4 39	..	
16¾	2 55	1 95	1 45	Langeais	2 17		..	8 13	12 48	..	4 49	..	
21¾	3 60	2 70	2 0	St. Patrice	..		..	8 30	1 5	..	5 4	..	
26	4 35	3 25	2 45	La Ch.-S.-Loire	..		..	8 45	1 20	..	5 18	..	
28½	4 75	3 60	2 65	Port-Boulet..........	2 43		..	8 56	1 31	3 9	5 28	..	
34¼	5 70	4 30	3 20	Varrennes	..		..	9 12	1 47	..	5 42	..	
40	6 60	5 0	3 70	**Saumur**..........	3 9		..	9 33	2 8	3 22	6 1	..	
45½	7 45	5 60	4 15	Saint Martin	..		..	9 48	2 23	..	6 15	..	
49¼	8 25	6 20	4 60	Les Rosiers	..		..	10 2	2 37	..	6 28	..	
53	8 90	6 70	4 95	Le Menitre	3 36		..	10 15	2 50	..	6 40	..	
54¾	9 20	6 90	5 15	Saint Mathurin	..		..	10 24	2 59	..	6 48	..	
59¾	9 90	7 45	5 55	La Bohalle	..		..	10 37	3 12	..	7 1	..	
62½	10 55	7 95	5 90	Trelaze..........	..		..	10 49	3 24	..	7 11	..	
65½	10 85	8 15	6 5	La Paperie..........	..		a.m.	..	..	..	..	..	
68	11 15	8 40	6 25	**Angers**..........	4 11		7 0	11 11	3 41	4 26	7 33	..	
71¾	11 90	8 95	6 65	Bouchemaine	..		7 13	11 24		..	7 45	..	
73	12 10	9 10	6 75	La Pointe..	..		7 19	11 30	..	..	7 51	..	
75	12 40	9 35	6 95	Les Forges	..		7 26	11 37	..	..	7 58	..	
76¾	12 70	9 55	7 10	La Poissonnier........	..		7 34	11 45	..	..	8 5	..	
80½	13 35	10 5	7 45	Chalonnes	4 36		7 47	11 58	..	..	8 17	..	
85½	14 15	10 65	7 90	Champtoce	..		8 2	12 13	..	..	8 31	..	
88¾	14 65	11 5	8 20	Ingrandes	4 54		8 13	12 21	..	..	8 41	..	
94	15 60	11 75	8 70	Varades	5 7		8 28	12 39	..	..	8 55	..	
101¾	16 85	12 65	9 40	Ancenis	5 27		8 53	1 4	..	5 26	9 18	..	
107½	17 75	13 35	6 95	Oudon	5 41		9 10	1 21	..	..	9 33	..	
110	18 20	13 70	10 15	Clermont..........	5 57		9 19	1 30	..	..	9 41	..	
113	18 70	14 5	10 45	Mauves..........	6 6		9 31	1 42	..	..	9 52	..	
116¼	19 30	14 66	10 75	Thouare	6 12		9 42	1 53	..	..	10 2	..	
118	19 50	14 70	10 90	Sainte Luce..........	6 26		9 49	2 0	..	..	10 9	..	
122¼	20 25	15 25	11 30	**Nantes** ....arr.	6 35		10 6	2 17	..	6 5	10 25	..	

Conveyance of Carriages.—Tours to Angers, 4-wheeled, 30 frs. 80 c.; 2-wheeled, 24 frs. 50 c.

TROYES TO MONTEREAU.—Terminus, Boulevart Mazas.

Eng Mls.	Fares. 1st Clss.	2nd Cls.	3rd Cls.	Stations.	Daily Trains. 1	2	3	4			
	fr. c.	f. c.	f. c.		a.m.	a.m.	p.m.	p.m.			
—	—	—	—	**Troyes** ....departure	6 30	11 45	4 20	11 32			
3¾	0 60	0 45	0 35	Barberey	6 42	..	4 34	..		..	..
7½	1 25	0 95	0 70	Payns	6 55	12 2	4 51	..		..	..
11¾	1 95	1 45	1 10	Saint-Mesmin	7 11	..	5 11	..		..	..
16½	2 65	2 0	1 50	Mesgrigny	7 28	12 22	5 30	12 10		..	..
23¾	3 90	2 95	2 20	Romilly	7 56	12 44	6 2	12 35		..	..
28¾	4 75	3 55	2 65	Pont-sur-Seine	8 19	12 59	6 28	12 52		..	..
35	5 75	4 35	3 20	Nogent	8 41	1 14	7 14	1 8		..	..
38¾	6 40	4 80	3 55	Melz	8 54	..	7 29	..		..	..
41¾	6 90	5 20	3 85	Hermé..................	9 5	..	7 42	..		..	..
47½	7 80	5 90	4 35	Les Ormes	9 37	1 46	8 12	1 43		..	..
50	8 25	6 20	4 60	Vimpelles	9 46	1 55	8 24	..		..	..
54¼	8 95	6 75	5 0	Chatenay	10 1	..	8 43	..		..	..
62½	10 30	7 75	5 75	**Montereau**......[1]..arr.	10 37	2 35	9 30	2 31		..	..
111¾	18 45	13 90	10 25	**Paris** ....arrival	1 10	5 10	..	4 30		..	..

[1] *For Trains from Montereau to Sens, Tonnerre, Dijon, Chalons, and Lyons, see page 54.*

Conveyance of Carriages.—Four-wheeled, 122 frs.; two-wheeled, 91 frs 1 c.

NANTES, ANGERS, TOURS, & PARIS.

Eng Mls.	Fares. 1st cl	2d cl.	3 cl.	Stations.	Trains. 1	2	3	4	5	6	7		
					1, 2, 3	1st	1, 2, 3	1st	1, 2, 3	1, 2, 3	1, 2, 3		
Dis.	fr. c.	fr. c.	fr. c.		1, 2, 3 a.m.		a.m.	a.m.	p.m.	p.m.	p.m.		
—	—	—	—	**Nantes**..........dep.	..		6 40	11 30	1 40	4 10	7 0	..	..
4¼	0 70	0 55	0 40	Sainte Luce	..		6 52	..	1 53	..	7 13	..	..
6¼	1 5	0 80	0 60	Thouare	..		6 59	..	2 0	..	7 20	..	..
9½	1 55	1 15	0 85	Meuves	..		7 9	..	2 11	..	7 31	..	..
13	2 15	1 65	1 20	Clermont	..		7 20	..	2 23	..	7 43	..	..
15¼	2 60	1 90	1 45	Oudon	..		7 28	..	2 32	..	7 52	..	..
21¼	3 50	2 65	1 95	Ancenis	..		7 46	12 10	2 52	4 56	8 12	..	..
28½	4 75	3 60	2 65	Varades	..		8 6	..	3 14	..	8 34	..	..
33½	5 60	4 20	3 10	Ingrandes	..		8 20	..	3 29	5 24	8 49	..	..
37½	6 20	4 65	3 45	Champtoce	..		8 30	..	3 40	..	9 0	..	..
42½	7 0	5 30	3 95	Chalonnes	..		8 45	..	3 56	5 54	9 16	..	..
46⅓	7 65	5 75	4 25	La Poissonnier	..		8 56	..	4 8	..	9 28	..	..
48	7 95	6 0	4 45	Les Forges	..		9 3	..	4 16	..	9 36	..	..
50	8 25	6 20	4 60	La Pointe	..		9 10	..	4 23	..	9 43	..	..
51¼	8 45	6 40	4 75	Bouchemaine	..		9 16	..	4 29	..	9 49	..	..
54¾	9 10	6 85	5 10	**Angers**	6 0		9 37	1 15	4 51	6 21	10 6	..	..
57¼	9 50	7 15	5 30	La Paperie	..		..	..	..	..		..	..
59¼	9 80	7 40	5 50	Trelaze	6 13		9 50	..	5 4	..	..	..	..
63	10 45	7 85	5 85	La Bohalle	6 25		10 0	..	5 16	..	..	..	..
66¾	11 5	8 30	6 20	Sainte Mathurin	6 38		10 13	..	5 29	..	..	..	..
69¼	11 45	8 65	6 40	Ma Menitre	6 48		10 22	..	5 39	6 52	..	..	..
73	12 10	9 10	6 75	Les Rosiers	7 0		10 33	..	5 51	..	..	..	..
77½	12 80	9 65	7 15	Saint Martin	7 14		10 46	..	6 5	..	..	..	..
82½	13 65	10 25	7 60	**Saumur**	7 33		11 4	2 6	6 24	7 24	..	..	..
88¼	14 55	10 95	8 15	Varrennes	7 50		11 19	..	6 41	..	..	..	..
93⅜	15 50	11 65	8 65	Port Boulet	8 7		11 34	2 26	6 58	7 49	..	..	..
96¼	15 90	11 95	8 90	La Ch.-S.-Loire	8 18		11 44	..	7 9	..	..	..	..
101¼	16 75	12 60	9 35	St. Patrice	8 32		11 57	..	7 23	..	..	..	..
106¾	17 65	13 30	9 90	Langeais	8 50		12 13	..	7 41	8 18	..	..	..
109¼	18 10	13 60	10 10	Cinq-Mars	9 0		12 22	..	7 51	..	..	..	..
113¾	18 80	14 15	10 50	Savonnieres	9 13		12 34	..	8 4	..	..	..	..
122¼	20 25	15 25	11 30	**Tours**..........arr.	9 41		1 0	3 22	8 32	8 55	..	..	..
..	..	..	..	Tours..........dep.	a.m. 10 32		p.m. 1 30	p.m. 3 30	..	p.m. 9 7	..	..	..
..	..	..	..	Orleans........dep.	2 50	1 35	p.m. 6 0	p.m. 5 50	..	a.m. 12 30	..	..	..
..	..	..	..	Paris..........arr.	6 50	4 20	10 0	8 10	..	4 0	..	..	..

MONTEREAU TO TROYES.

Eng Mls.	Fares. 1st Clss.	2nd Cls.	3rd Cls.	Stations.	Daily Trains. 1	2	3	4				
	fr. c.	f. c.	f. c.		a.m.	a.m.	p.m.	p.m.				
—	—	—	—	**Paris** ....[2]..... depart.	10 15	9 5	3 5	8 30		..	..	
49½	8 15	6 15	4 55	**Montereau**	4 20	11 34	5 42	10 53		..	..	
57¼	9 50	7 15	5 30	Chatenay	4 55	..	6 4	..		..	..	
62½	10 30	7 75	5 75	Vimpelles	5 17	12 2	6 18	..		..	..	
64½	10 60	8 0	5 95	Les Ormes	5 38	12 18	6 36	11 34		..	..	
68½	11 65	8 80	6 50	Hermé	6 3	..	6 53	..		..	..	
73	12 15	9 15	6 80	Melz	6 18	..	7 3	..		..	..	
71¼	12 80	9 65	7 15	Nogent	6 42	12 46	7 19	12 4		..	..	
83	13 70	10 35	7 65	Pont-sur-Seine	7 13	1 1	7 39	12 20		..	..	
89	14 65	11 5	8 15	Romilly	7 51	1 20	8 0	12 41		..	..	
96¼	15 85	11 95	8 85	Mesgrigny	8 31	1 39	8 28	1 2		..	..	
100	16 50	12 40	9 20	Saint-Mesmin	8 51	..	8 41	..		..	..	
104¼	17 30	13 5	9 65	Payns	9 14	1 58	8 56	..		..	..	
108¾	17 95	13 50	10 0	Barberey	9 32	..	9 8	..		..	..	
111¾	18 45	13 90	10 30	**Troyes** ....arrival	9 47	2 14	9 18	1 38		..	..	

[2] *For Stations between Paris and Montereau, see page 54.*

Conveyance of Carriages.—Montereau to Troyes, four-wheeled, 66 frs.; 2-wheeled, 52 frs.

PARIS TO CORBEIL.

Terminus, Roulevart de l'Hopital.

English Miles.	Stations.	Trains. 1	2	3	4	5	Fares. 1st clss.	2nd clss.	3rd clss.
		a.m.	a.m.	p.m.	p.m.	p.m.	fr. c.	fr. c.	fr. c.
—	**Paris**.. dep	8 0	11 0	1 45	5 5	9 0	—	—	—
$5\frac{1}{2}$	Choisy......	8 14	11 14	1 59	5 19	9 17	0 60	0 45	0 35
8	Villeneuve ..	8 22	11 22	2 7	5 27	9 26	0 70	0 55	0 40
10	Athis	8 28	11 28	2 13	5 33	9 33	1 25	0 95	0 70
$11\frac{3}{4}$	Juvisy	8 34	11 34	2 19	5 39	9 40	1 55	1 15	0 85
$14\frac{1}{4}$	Ris	8 42	11 42	2 27	5 47	9 50	1 75	1 30	1 0
$16\frac{3}{4}$	Evry	8 50	11 50	2 35	5 55	9 59	2 15	1 65	1 20
$18\frac{3}{4}$	**Corbeil**.ar	8 58	11 58	2 43	6 3	10 8	3 0	2 10	1 60

CORBEIL TO PARIS.

Stations.	Trains. 1	2	3	4	5	6
	a.m.	a.m.	p.m.	p.m.	p.m.	Sundays and Fêtes.
Corbeil.dp	7 15	11 0	3 45	7 30	9 25	
Evry	7 22	11 7	3 52	7 37	9 32	
Ris	7 30	11 15	4 0	7 45	9 40	
Juvisy......	7 38	11 23	4 9	7 53	9 49	
Athis	7 44	11 29	4 16	7 59	9 56	
Villeneuve ..	7 50	11 35	4 23	8 5	10 3	p.m.
Choisy	7 58	11 43	4 31	8 13	10 11	9 25
Paris..arr.	8 15	12 0	4 50	8 30	10 30	9 45

Conveyance of Carriages.—4-wheeled, 20 frs.; 2-wheeled, 15 frs.

PARIS AND VERSAILLES.—Left Bank.

From Paris.

8, 9, 10, and 11 a.m., 12 noon, 1, 2, 3, 4, 5, 6, 7, 8, 9, and 10 p.m., stopping at Clamart, Meudon, Bellevue, Sevres, Chaville, Viroflay, and Versailles.

From Versailles.

$7\frac{1}{2}$, $8\frac{1}{2}$, $9\frac{1}{2}$, $10\frac{1}{2}$, and $11\frac{1}{2}$ a.m., $12\frac{1}{2}$, $1\frac{1}{2}$, $2\frac{1}{2}$, $3\frac{1}{2}$, $4\frac{1}{2}$, $5\frac{1}{2}$, $7\frac{1}{2}$, $8\frac{1}{2}$, and 10 p.m., stopping at Viroflay, Chaville, Sèvres, Bellevue, Meudon, & Clamart.

Time of transit 32 minutes.

Sundays and Fetes, at $9\frac{1}{2}$ & $10\frac{1}{2}$ p.m.

Fares.—Paris to Versailles (either line) 1st class, 1fr. 50c.; 2nd class, 1fr. 25c.

NIMES & ALAIS.

English Miles.	STATIONS.	Trains. 1	2
Dis.		a.m.	p.m.
—	**Nimes** ....dep.	9 0	6 5
$6\frac{1}{4}$	Mas-de-Ponge	9 20	6 25
$11\frac{3}{4}$	Fons	9 34	6 39
15	Saint-Géniès	9 44	6 49
$17\frac{1}{2}$	Nozières................	9 52	6 57
$18\frac{3}{4}$	**Boucoiran** ....arr.	9 50	7 0
..	Do. ....dep.	9 59	7 4
$20\frac{1}{2}$	Ners	10 8	7 13
$22\frac{1}{4}$	Vézénobres	10 14	7 19
$26\frac{3}{4}$	Saint-Hilaire................	10 28	7 33
$30\frac{1}{2}$	**Alais** ....arr.	10 40	7 45

ALAIS & NIMES. [10-10-52

English Miles.	STATIONS.	Trains. 1	2
Dis.		a.m.	p.m.
$30\frac{1}{2}$	**Alais** ....dep.	7 0	4 0
$26\frac{3}{4}$	Saint-Hilaire................	7 11	4 14
$22\frac{1}{4}$	Vézénobres	7 24	4 24
$20\frac{1}{2}$	Ners	7 29	4 29
$18\frac{3}{4}$	**Boucoiran** ....arr.	7 30	4 30
..	Do. ....dep.	7 38	4 38
$17\frac{1}{2}$	Nozières................	7 42	4 42
15	Saint-Géniès	7 49	4 49
$11\frac{3}{4}$	Fons	7 59	4 59
$6\frac{1}{4}$	Mas-de-Ponge	8 16	5 16
—	**Nimes** ....arr.	8 35	5 35

Fares.—1st class, 4 fr.; 2nd class, 3 fr.; 3rd class, 2 fr. 50 c.

ALAIS & GRAND 'COMBE.

STATIONS.	Trains. 1	2	3
	a.m.	a.m.	p.m.
Alais......................dep.	5 45	11 0	3 30
Les Tamaris	6 0	11 15	3 45
La Grand 'Combe { La Pise........	6 30	11 45	4 15
La Grand 'Combe { La Levade	6 45	12 0	4 30

GRAND 'COMBE & ALAIS.

STATIONS.	Trains. 1	2	3
	a.m.	p.m.	p.m.
La Grand 'Combe { La Levade ..	7 30	12 30	5 0
La Grand 'Combe { La Pise......	8 0	1 15	5 30
Les Tamaris	8 30	1 45	6 0
Alais ....arr.	8 45	2 0	6 15

MONTPELLIER & CETTE—17 English Miles—Time of Transit, one hour.

From Montpellier to Cette, at 6 and $9\frac{3}{4}$ a.m., 1 and 5 p.m.

From Cette to Montpellier, at 6 and 9 35 a.m., $3\frac{1}{4}$ and 5 p.m.

Fares.—1st class, 2 fr. 20 c.; 2nd class, 1 fr. 50 c.

PARIS TO VERSAILLES, CHARTRES, AND LA LOUPE.

Terminus, Barrière du Maine.

English Miles.	Fares.			STATIONS.	Trains.							
	1st Class	2nd Class	3rd Class		1	2	3	4	5	6	7	8
Dis.	fr. c.	fr. c.	fr. c.		a.m.	a.m.	p.m.	p.m.	p.m.	p.m.	p.m.	p.m.
—	—	—	—	**Paris** { Gare Mont Parnas ..	7 30	11 30	4 30	7 30	8 30	..	..	..
5½	..	..	..	**Paris** { Bellevue	7 44	11 44	4 44	..	8 49	..	..	..
—	—	—	—	**Paris** { Gare St. Lazare.....	7 15	11 15	4 15	7 15	..	..	..	..
—	—	—	—	**Paris** { Saint-Cloud	7 35	11 55	4 35	..	..	..	..	..
10½	1 50	1 25	..	**Versailles**	8 2	12 2	5 2	7 59	9 13	..	..	..
13¾	2 0	1 50	1 25	Saint-Cyr	8 12	12 12	5 12	..	9 26	..	..	..
16¾	2 80	2 20	1 60	Trappes	8 23	12 23	5 23	..	9 42	..	..	..
20	3 40	2 50	1 90	Laverrière	8 34	12 34	5 34	..	9 55	..	..	..
24¼	4 10	3 0	2 30	Lartoire	8 47	12 47	5 47	..	10 13	..	..	..
30	4 50	3 50	2 75	**Rambouillet**	9 10	1 10	6 10	8 51	10 39	..	..	..
38	6 0	4 60	3 50	Epernon	9 28	1 28	6 28	..	11 6	..	..	..
43	7 0	5 0	3 95	Maintenon	9 43	1 43	6 43	9 21	11 29	..	..	..
48¾	8 0	6 0	4 50	Jouy	9 58	1 58	6 58	..	11 49	..	..	..
55	9 0	6 75	5 5	**Chartres**	10 20	2 20	7 20	9 54	12 10	..	..	..
66¼	10 95	8 25	6 5	Courville	10 48	2 48	7 48	..		..	..	..
71¼	11 80	8 85	6 50	Pontgouin	11 2	3 2	8 2	..	..	..	..	..
77½	12 80	9 65	7 10	**La Loupe**	11 20	3 27	8 20	10 45	..	..	..	..

LA LOUPE TO PARIS.

English Miles.	Fares.			STATIONS.	Trains.							
	1st Class	2nd Class	3rd Class		1	2	3	4	5	6	7	8
Dis.	fr. c.	fr. c.	fr. c.		a.m.	a.m.	a.m.	p.m.	p.m.	p.m.	p.m.	p.m.
—	—	—	—	**La Loupe**	12 20	5 50	11 20	2 20	5 50	..	..	..
6¼	1 15	0 85	0 65	Pontgouin	..	6 7	11 38	..	6 7	..	..	..
11¾	1 85	1 40	1 5	Courville	..	6 20	11 55	2 47	6 20	..	..	..
23	3 80	2 90	2 10	**Chartres** ...	1 29	6 53	12 32	3 18	6 53	..	..	..
29¼	4 85	3 65	2 70	Jouy	..	7 7	12 49	..	7 7	..	..	..
34¾	5 80	4 35	3 20	Maintenon	2 4	7 22	1 7	3 44	7 22	..	..	..
40	6 60	5 0	3 65	Epernon	..	7 37	1 24	..	7 37	..	..	..
48	7 95	6 0	4 40	**Rambouillet**	3 12	8 8	2 0	4 25	8 8	..	..	..
53	8 80	6 60	4 85	Lartoire	..	8 23	2 18	..	8 23	..	..	..
57¼	9 50	7 15	5 25	Laverrière	..	8 36	2 33	..	8 36	..	..	..
60½	10 0	7 55	5 55	Trappes	3 55	8 46	2 44	..	8 46	..	..	..
64¼	10 65	8 0	5 90	Saint-Cyr	..	8 56	2 54	..	8 56	..	..	..
67½	11 15	8 40	6 20	**Versailles**	4 22	9 8	3 7	5 10	9 8	..	..	..
72½	12 0	9 0	6 65	**Paris** { Bellevue..........	..	9 34	3 34	..	9 34	..	..	..
77½	12 80	9 65	7 10	**Paris** { Gare Mont Parnas ..	..	9 53	3 53	5 53	9 53	..	..	..
..	12 0	9 0	6 65	**Paris** { Saint-Cloud	..	9 21	3 20	..	9 21	..	..	..
..	12 80	9 65	7 10	**Paris** { Gare St. Lazare	4 55	9 35	3 35	5 35	9 35	..	..	..

Frequent communication is kept up daily between Versailles and St. Nom, Villepreux, Dreux, Jouy, St. Cyr, Chevreuse, Houdan, Montfort, and Septeuil, by omnibuses.

PARIS & VERSAILLES.—Right Bank.

From Paris.

7½, 8½, 9½, 10½, 11½ a.m., 12½, 1½, 2½, 3½, 4½, 5½, 6½, 7½, 8½, and 10 p.m., stopping at Courbevoie, Suresnes, St. Cloud, Sevres, Puteaux, and Viroflay. **On Sundays and Fetes.**—At 5 p.m., for St. Cloud, Ville-d'Avray, and Versailles.

From Versailles.

7, 8, 9, 10, and 11 a.m., 12, 1, 2, 3, 4, 5, 6, 7, 8, 9, and 10 p.m., stopping at Courbevoie, Suresnes. St. Cloud, Sevres, Puteaux, and Viroflay.

MARSEILLES TO AVIGNON. [10–52.

Eng Mls.	Fares. 1st Class	2nd Class	3rd Class	Stations.	Daily Trains. 1	2	3	4	5	6	7	8
	fr. c.	fr. c.	fr. c		a.m.	a.m.	a.m.	p.m.	p.m.			
—	—	—	—	**Marseilles** ......dep.	..	7 0	9 0	1 0	4 0	..	..	..
..	1 15	0 85	0 60	L'Estaque	..	7 16	..	1 16	4 16	..	..	..
11¾	2 0	1 50	1 0	Pas de Lanciers	..	7 31	..	1 31	4 34	..	..	..
..	2 55	1 90	1 25	Vitrolles..............	..	..	..	..	4 40	..	..	..
17½	2 95	2 20	1 50	Rognac	..	7 47	9 35	1 46	4 48	..	..	..
21¼	3 60	2 70	1 80	Berre	..	7 58	..	1 58	4 59	..	..	.
30	5 5	3 80	2 55	**Saint Chamas** ..arr.	..	8 22	10 3	2 22	5 23	..	..	..
				,, ...dep.	..	8 27	10 8	2 27	5 28	..	..	..
33	5 60	4 20	2 80	Constantine	..	8 39	..	2 39	5 39	..	..	..
36¼	6 10	4 60	3 5	Entressen	..	8 49	..	..	5 49	..	..	..
43¾	7 40	5 55	3 70	Saint-Martin...........	..	9 10	..	..	6 10	..	..	..
48¾	8 25	6 15	4 10	Raphele	..	9 23	..	..	6 23	..	..	..
53¾	9 5	6 80	4 55	**Arles** ....arrival	..	9 39	10 55	3 27	6 36	..	..	..
				,, ...departure	7 20	9 44	10 58	3 32	6 40	..	..	..
58¾	9 90	7 45	4 95	Ségonnaux	7 34	9 59	..	..	6 54	..	..	..
62½	10 55	7 90	5 30	**Tarascon**......arrival	7 45	10 10	11 17	3 53	7 5	..	..	..
				,, ...dep.	7 50	10 20	11 25	4 5	7 15	..	..	..
64¼	13 20	10 5	6 95	**Nimes** ....arrival	8 55	12 45	12 45	5 0	8 30	..	..	..
..	..	..	..	Do. ......dep.	6 30	9 45	..	2 20	6 0	..	..	..
67½	11 40	8 55	5 70	Cadillan ......departure	8 3	10 35	..	4 20	7 30	..	..	..
71¾	12 15	9 10	6 5	Rognonas	8 18	10 48	..	4 33	7 43	..	..	..
76¾	12 65	9 50	6 35	**Avignon** ......arrival	8 30	11 0	11 50	4 45	7 55	..	..	..

AVIGNON TO MARSEILLES.

Eng Mls.	Fares. 1st Class	2nd Class	3rd Class	Stations.	Daily Trains. 1	2	3	4	5	6	7
	fr. c.	fr. c.	fr. c.		a.m.	a.m.	p.m.	p.m.	p.m.		
—	—	—	—	**Avignon** ......depart.	7 0	9 50	3 10	6 0	6 50	..	..
..	..	..	..	Rognonas	7 10	..	3 20	6 10	..	..	..
..	..	..	..	Cadillan	7 20	..	3 30	6 20	..	..	..
..	..	..	..	**Tarascon** .... arrival	7 35	10 18	3 45	6 35	7 15	..	..
				,, ... dep.	7 45	10 28	3 55	6 40	7 20	..	..
..	..	..	..	**Nimes** ....arrival	8 55	12 45	5 0	8 30	8 30	..	..
..	..	..	..	Do. ......dep.	6 30	9 45	3 0	..	6 0	..	..
..	..	..	..	Ségonnaux ......depart.	7 57	..	4 7	6 52	..	..	..
..	..	..	..	**Arles** ....arrival	8 10	10 48	4 20	7 5	7 35	..	..
..	..	..	..	,, ...depart.	8 15	10 52	4 25		7 40	..	..
..	..	..	..	Raphele	8 30	..	4 40	..	..	..	..
..	..	..	..	Saint-Martin..........	8 44	..	4 54	..	..	..	..
..	..	..	..	Entressen	9 5	..	5 15	..	..	..	..
..	..	..	..	Constantine	9 16	11 37	5 26	..	..	..	..
..	..	..	..	**Saint Chamas**.. arr.	9 25	11 45	5 35	..	8 30	..	..
				,, .. dep.	9 30	11 50	5 40	..	8 35	..	..
..	..	..	..	Berre	9 51	..	6 1	..	..	..	..
..	..	..	..	Rognac	10 3	12 22	6 13	..	..	..	..
..	..	..	..	Vitrolles..............	10 12	..	..	..	..	..	..
..	..	..	..	Pas des Lanciers	10 23	..	6 33	..	..	..	..
..	..	..	..	L'Estaque	10 38	..	6 48	..	..	..	..
..	..	..	..	**Marseilles**....arrival	10 55	1 5	7 5	..	9 35	..	..

Nimes to Montpellier, see page 41.

Additional Trains on Week Days.—From MARSEILLES to L'ESTAQUE, at 6.30 & 8½ a.m., 2 and 5 p.m. From L'ESTAQUE to MARSEILLES, at 7½ and 9½ a.m., 3 and 6 p.m.

On Sundays and Fetes.—From MARSEILLES to L'ESTAQUE, at 6½, 8½, and 10 a.m. and 2, 3, and 5½ p.m. From L'ESTAQUE, at 7½, 9½, and 11 a.m., and 3, 4, and 6¼ p.m.

PARIS AND SCEAUX.

From Paris.—At 6½, 8, 9, 10, and 11 a.m.; 12, 1, 2, 3, 4, 5, 6, 7, 8, and 9½ p.m., stopping at all stations, namely, Arcueil-Cachan, Bourg-la-Reine, Fontenay, and Sceaux.

From Sceaux.—At 7, 8½, 9½, 10½, and 11½ a.m.; 12½, 1½, 2½, 3½, 4½, 5½, 6½, 7½, 8½, and 10 p.m., stopping at all stations.

SUNDAYS AND HOLIDAYS.—Supplementary Trains from Paris, 11 a.m., 3 p.m.; from Sceaux, 11½ a.m., 3½ p.m. FARES.—Paris to Sceaux, 1st class, 90c.; 2nd class, 60c.; 3rd class, 45c.; Sundays and fetes, 1st class, 1fr.; 2nd class, 80c.; 3rd class, 60c.

PARIS AND SAINT GERMAIN.

From Paris.—Every hour from 7.30 a.m. until 8.30 p.m.—Also at 10.0 p.m., stopping at Asnieres, Colombes, Nanterre, Rueil, and Chatou.

From Saint Germain.—Every hour, from 7 0 a.m. till 10.0 p.m., stopping at Chatou, Rueil, Nanterre, Colombes, and Asnieres.

FARES.—Paris to St. Germain, 1st class, 1fr. 50c.; 2nd class, 1fr. 25c.

PARIS and STRASBOURG.—NANCY to FORBACH.

[17-4-53.

Eng. Mls.	Fares. From Paris. 1st	2nd	3rd	Stations.	Trains. 1	2	3	4	5	6	7	8
					1 2 3	1 2 3	1 2 3	1 2 3	1 2 3	1 2 3	1 2 3	
Dis.	fr. c.	fr. c.	fr. c.		a.m.	a.m.	a.m.	a.m.	p.m.	p.m.	p.m.	
220	36 35	27 35	19 95	**Nancy** .... dep.	3 50	..	6 35	11 0	2 50	5 10	8 0	..
207	35 55	26 75	19 85	**Frouard**	4 6	..	6 49	11 16	3 7	5 27	8 18	..
214½	36 5	27 15	19 85	Marbache	..	..	7 0	11 27	3 18	5 38	8 32	..
218¾	36 60	27 60	19 95	Dieulouard	..	..	7 11	11 38	3 29	5 49	8 46	..
226¾	37 30	28 10	19 95	Pont-à-Mousson	4 36	..	7 26	11 53	3 44	6 4	9 3	..
232¼	37 40	28 10	19 95	Pagny-sur-Moselle	..	..	7 39	12 6	3 57	6 17	9 20	..
236	37 40	28 10	19 95	Noveant	..	..	7 49	12 16	4 7	6 27	9 33	..
239¾	37 40	28 10	19 95	Ars-sur-Moselle	..	..	7 59	12 26	4 17	6 37	9 44	..
244¾	37 40	28 10	19 95	**Metz**	5 22	6 10	8 10	12 51	4 30	7 9	10 0	..
248½	37 95	28 50	20 25	Pelter	..	6 31		1 2		7 23		..
253½	38 50	28 95	20 55	Courcelles	..	6 46	..	1 13	..	7 37	..	..
259½	39 15	29 40	20 90	Remilly	5 52	7 9	..	1 26	..	7 53	..	..
263½	39 70	29 85	21 25	Herny	..	7 35	..	1 37	..	8 7	..	..
269¼	40 60	30 50	21 75	Faulquemont	..	8 2	..	1 53	..	8 27	..	..
276¼	41 40	31 10	22 20	Saint-Avold	6 33	8 37	..	2 13	..	8 51	..	..
280½	41 95	31 55	22 50	Hombourg	..	8 54	..	2 23	..	9 4	..	..
284½	42 50	31 95	22 80	Cocheren	..	9 13	..	2 35	..	9 19	..	..
288	43 0	32 30	23 10	**Forbach** .... arr.	6 57	9 25	..	2 45	..	9 30	..	..

PARIS AND STRASBURG.—FORBACH TO NANCY.

Eng. Mls.	Fares. 1st.	2nd.	3rd.	Stations.	Trains. 1	2	3	4	5	6	7	8
					1 2 3	1 2 3	1 2 3	1 2 3	1 2 3	1 2 3		
Dis.	fr. c.	fr. c.	fr. c.		a.m.	a.m.	a.m.	p.m.	p.m.	p.m.		
				Forbach .... dep.	..	4 10	11 0	..	4 25	..	..	..
3¾	0 50	0 40	0 30	Cocheren	..	4 23	11 10	..	4 35	..	..	..
8	1 5	0 80	0 60	Hombourg	..	4 37	11 21	..	4 46	..	..	..
12½	1 60	1 20	0 90	Saint-Avold	..	5 54	11 34	..	4 59	..	..	..
18¾	2 40	1 80	1 35	Faulquemont	..	5 14	11 50	..	5 15	..	..	..
25½	3 30	2 45	1 85	Herny	..	5 35	12 6	..	5 31	..	..	..
30	3 85	2 90	2 15	Remilly	..	5 52	12 17	..	5 42	..	..	..
34¾	4 50	3 35	2 50	Courcelles	..	6 8	12 30	..	5 55	..	..	..
39½	5 5	4 0	2 80	Peltre	..	6 24	12 41	..	6 6	..	..	..
43¾	5 60	4 20	3 15	**Metz**	5 5	7 13	1 6	3 0	6 26	8 10	..	..
48¾	6 40	4 80	3 60	Ars-sur-Moselle	5 19	7 30	1 19	3 13	6 39	8 23	..	..
51¾	6 80	5 20	3 90	Noveant	5 28	7 41	1 28	3 22	6 48	8 32	..	..
55½	7 35	5 60	4 20	Pagny-sur-Moselle	5 37	7 54	1 38	3 32	6 58	8 42	..	..
61¼	8 10	6 20	4 65	Pont-à-Mousson	5 53	8 15	1 54	3 49	7 14	8 59	..	..
65½	8 70	6 70	5 5	Dieulouard	6 3	8 29	2 5	4 0	7 25	9 10	..	..
70	9 35	7 20	5 40	Marbache	6 13	8 43	2 16	4 11	7 36	9 21	..	..
73	9 70	7 50	5 60	**Frouard**	6 27	9 0	2 31	4 26	7 51	9 33	..	..
78¾	10 10	8 20	6 15	**Nancy** .... arr.	6 40	9 15	2 45	4 40	8 5	9 45	..	..

PARIS and STRASBOURG.

[17-4-53.

Eng. Mls.	Fares. 1st	2nd	3rd	Terminus, RueNeuve de Chabrol	1 2 3	1 2 3	1st.	1 2 3	1 2 3	1 2 3	1 2 3	1 2 3	1 2 3	1–2	1 2 3	1 2 3
					a.m.	a.m.	a.m.	a.m.	p.m.	p.m.	p.m.	p.m.	p.m.	p.m.	p.m.	p.m.
Dis.	fr. c.	fr. c.	fr. c.	**Paris** ....dep.	6 45	7 30	9 30	10 0	12 15	1 0	2 30	4 30	5 30	7 30	8 0	11 0
5½	0 95	0 70	0 50	Noisy-le-Sec	6 58	7 45	..	10 15	12 30	1 14	2 45	4 45	5 44	..	8 15	..
6¾	0 95	0 70	0 50	Bondy..............	7 3	7 52	..	10 21	12 37	1 18	2 52	4 51	5 48	..	8 21	..
8¾	1 45	1 10	0 80	Villemonble & Gagny	7 11	8 2	..	10 30	12 47	1 26	3 2	5 0	5 56	..	8 30	..
11¾	1 95	1 50	1 10	Chelles	7 19	8 12	..	10 39	12 57	1 34	3 12	5 9	6 4	..	8 39	..
17½	2 90	2 20	1 60	Lagny..............	7 34	8 29	10 1	10 55	1 14	1 49	3 29	5 25	6 19	8 9	8 55	11 44
23	3 75	2 90	2 0	Esbly	7 48	8 45	..	11 10	1 30	2 3	3 45	5 40	6 33	..	9 10	..
28	3 75	3 0	2 0	**Meaux**	8 5	9 0	10 26	11 25	1 45	2 20	4 0	5 55	6 50	8 36	9 25	12 24
31¾	5 25	3 95	2 95	Trilport	8 16		..			2 30			7 0	..		..
36¼	6 0	4 50	3 35	Changis	8 28	..	..	..	..	2 41			7 11	..	..	..
41¼	6 80	5 15	3 80	La Ferté-sous-Jouarre	8 44	..	10 55	..	..	2 56			7 26	9 6	..	1 4
46¼	7 65	5 75	4 25	Nanteuil...........	8 59	..	..	..	..	3 10			7 40	..	..	..
52¼	8 70	6 55	4 85	Nogent-l'Artaud	9 14	..	..	..	..	3 25			7 55	..	..	..
59¼	9 80	7 40	5 50	**Chateau-Thiery**	9 39	..	11 41	..	..	3 50			8 20	9 48	..	2 0
65	10 75	8 10	6 0	Mezy	9 53	..	..	..	..	4 4			8 34	..	..	..
66¼	10 95	8 25	6 10	Varennes	10 0	..	..	..	..	4 11			8 41	..	..	..
73	12 10	9 10	6 75	Dormans	10 17	..	..	..	..	4 27			8 57	10 18	..	2 37
78¾	13 0	9 80	7 30	Port-à-Binson	10 32	..	..	..	..	4 41			9 11	..	..	..
84¼	13 95	10 50	7 80	Damery	10 46	..	..	..	..	4 55			9 25	..	..	..
88¾	14 65	11 5	8 20	**Epernay**	11 6	..	12 40	..	..	5 15			9 45	10 58	..	3 27
92½	15 30	11 50	8 55	Oiry..............	11 16	..	..	..	..	5 25			9 55	..	..	..
99¼	16 40	12 35	9 20	Jalons-les-Vignes....	11 32	..	..	..	..	5 41			10 11	..	..	..
107½	17 75	13 35	9 95	**Chalons**	11 56	..	1 18	..	..	6 5			10 30	11 42	..	4 30
117¼	19 40	14 60	10 85	Vitry-la-Ville	12 18	..	..	..	..	6 26	..			..	..	4 51
124¾	20 55	15 45	11 50	Loisy	12 34	..	..	..	..	6 42	..		..	..	..	5 7
128	21 20	15 95	11 85	**Vitry**-le-Francois..	12 47	..	1 58	..	..	6 55	..		..	12 28	..	5 21
135½	22 40	16 85	12 55	Blesmes	1 4	..	..	..	..	7 12	..		..	..	..	5 38
140½	23 25	17 50	13 0	Pargny	1 17	..	..	..	..	7 25	..		..	..	..	5 51
144¼	23 85	17 95	13 35	Sermaize	1 28	..	..	..	..	7 36	..		..	1 3	..	6 1
148½	24 60	18 50	13 75	Revigny	1 39	..	..	..	..	7 47	..		..	..	..	6 12
158½	26 25	19 75	14 65	**Bar-le-Duc**	2 8	..	2 59	..	..	8 28	..		..	1 42	..	6 43
161	..	..	..	Longeville	..	..	..	..	..	..	..		..	..	..	..
165¼	27 35	20 60	15 30	Nancois-le-Petit	2 25	..	..	..	..	8 45	..		..	1 59	..	7 1
172	28 50	21 45	15 95	Loxeville	2 45	..	..	..	..	9 5	..		..	..	..	7 21
180¼	29 85	22 45	16 70	Lerouville	3 3	..	..	..	..	9 23	..		..	..	..	7 40
183¼	30 35	22 85	17 0	**Commercy**	3 16	..	3 52	..	..	9 36	..		..	2 44	..	7 53
188¾	31 20	23 50	17 45	Sorcy	3 28	..	..	..	..	9 48	..		..	..	..	8 6
192	31 80	23 95	17 80	Pagny-sur-Meuse....	3 38	..	..	..	..	9 58	..		..	..	..	8 16
195¼	32 35	24 35	18 10	Foug	3 47	..	..	..	..	10 7	..		..	..	..	8 25
199	32 95	24 80	18 40	Toul	4 2	..	4 24	..	..	10 22	..		..	3 21	..	8 40
204½	33 90	25 50	18 95	Fontenoy-sur-Mosel..	4 16	..	..	..	..	10 36	..		..	..	..	8 54
210¼	34 80	26 20	19 45	Liverdun	4 30	..	..	1,2,3	..	10 50	..		..	..	..	9 8
214½	35 55	26 75	19 85	**Frouard** ......arr.	4 46	..	4 57	a.m.	..	11 2	..		..	3 58	..	9 22
220	36 35	27 35	19 95	**Nancy**	5 35	..	5 19	5 30	..	11 15	..		..	4 20	..	9 48
227½	37 70	28 40	21 10	Varengeville-S-Nicola	5 58	..	..	5 52	..		..		..	..	..	10 10
230¾	..	..	..	Rosières-aux-Salines.	..	..	..	..	..	..	..	..	..	..	..	..
234½	38 85	29 25	21 70	Blainville-la-Grande .	6 18	..	..	6 12	..	..	..	..	..	..	..	10 30
240	39 75	29 95	22 25	**Luneville**	6 43	..	6 15	6 32	..	..	..	..	..	5 10	..	10 51
245	40 60	30 55	22 70	Marainviller	6 58	..	6 30	6 47	..	..	..	..	..	..	..	11 6
250	41 40	31 20	23 15	Emberménil	7 13	..	..	7 2	..	..	..	..	..	..	..	11 21
255	42 25	31 80	23 60	Avricourt	7 29	..	..	7 17	..	..	..	..	..	5 45	..	11 36
263¾	43 70	32 90	24 45	Héming	7 53	..	..	7 41	..	..	..	..	..	..	..	12 0
268¾	44 50	33 50	24 90	**Sarrebourg**	8 12	1,2,3	7 31	8 0	..	..	..	..	..	6 24	..	12 19
279½	46 30	34 85	25 85	Lützelbourg	8 41	a.m.	..	8 28	..	..	..	..	..	..	..	12 48
285	47 30	35 60	26 45	**Saverne**	9 3	5 45	8 18	8 50	..	..	..	..	..	7 13	..	1 10
288¼	47 70	35 90	26 70	Steinbourg..........	9 11	5 57	..	8 58	..	..	..	..	..	..	..	1 18
290¾	48 15	36 25	26 90	Dettwiller	9 19	6 8	..	9 6	..	..	..	..	..	..	..	1 26
295¾	48 95	36 85	27 35	Hochfelden	9 32	6 31	..	9 19	..	..	..	..	..	..	..	1 39
298¾	49 50	37 25	27 65	Mommenheim	9 41	6 44	..	9 28	..	..	..	..	..	..	..	1 48
302	50 0	37 65	27 95	Brumath	9 52	7 2	..	9 39	..	..	...	..	..	7 49	..	1 59
306¾	50 80	38 25	28 40	Vendenheim	10 5	7 21	..	9 52	..	..	..	..	..	..	..	2 12
312½	51 75	38 95	28 95	**Strasbourg**..arr.	10 20	7 40	9 15	10 5	..	..	..	..	..	8 10	..	2 25

☞ Sundays and Fêtes only. (2 30 p.m. train)

Additional Trains on Sunday and Fêtes:— From Paris to Bondy, at 9½ p.m.

PARIS and STRASBOURG.

[17-4-53.

Eng. Mls.	Fares. 1st	2nd	3rd	Stations.	1 2 3	1 2 3	1 2 3	1 2 3	1 2 3	1 2 3	1 2 3	1st.	1 2 3	1 & 2	1 2 3	1 2 3
					a.m.	a.m.	a.m.	p.m.	a.m.	p.m.	a.m.	a.m.	p.m.	p.m.	p.m.	p.m.
Dis.	fr. c.	fr. c.	fr. c.	**Strasbourg** .. dep.	..	..	..	..	..	..	5 45	10 25	12 10	3 30	6 0	6 30
6¼	0 80	0 60	0 40	Vendenheim	..	..	..	..	..	..	5 59	..	12 24	..	6 14	6 50
10¾	1 50	1 0	0 60	Brumath	..	..	..	..	..	..	6 13	..	12 37	3 54	6 27	7 13
14¼	2 40	1 80	1 20	Mommenheim	..	..	..	..	..	..	6 23	..	12 47	..	6 37	7 28
16¾	2 40	1 80	1 20	Hochfelden	..	..	..	..	..	..	6 32	..	12 56	..	6 46	7 45
22¼	3 70	2 80	2 0	Dettwiller	..	..	..	..	..	..	6 45	..	1 9	..	6 59	8 4
24¾	4 0	3 0	2 0	Steinbourg	..	..	..	..	..	..	6 53	..	1 17	..	7 7	8 15
27½	4 0	3 0	2 0	**Saverne**	..	..	..	..	..	..	7 5	11 25	1 29	4 33	7 19	8 40
33¾	4 60	3 50	2 40	Lützelbourg		..	..	..	..	..	7 23	..	1 47	..	7 37	
44¼	7 35	5 50	4 10	Sarrebourg		..	..	..	..	..	7 56	12 14	2 20	5 25	8 10	..
49¼	8 15	6 15	4 55	Heming		..	..	..	..	..	8 11	..	2 35	..	8 25	..
57¼	9 50	7 15	5 30	Avricourt		..	..	..	..	..	8 36	..	2 59	5 58	8 49	..
63	10 45	7 85	5 35	Emberménil		..	..	..	..	..	8 51	..	3 14	..	9 4	..
68	11 25	8 45	6 30	Marainviller		..	..	..	..	..	9 6	..	3 29	6 29	9 19	..
73	12 10	9 10	6 75	**Luneville**		..	..	..	..	..	9 25	1 30	3 48	6 47	9 38	..
78	12 90	9 70	7 20	Blainville-la-Grande..		..	..	..	..	..	9 42	..	4 4	..	9 55	..
82½	..	..	..	Rosieres-aux-Salines..		..	..	..	..	..	..	..	..	..	..	..
85	14 50	10 55	7 85	Varengeville-S-Nicola		..	..	..	..	..	10 9	..	4 23	..	10 18	..
93¼	15 40	11 60	8 60	**Nancy**		..	..	..	6 15	..	10 41	2 28	4 53	7 45	10 40	..
98	16 25	12 30	9 10	**Frouard** ...... dep.		..	..	..	6 32	..	10 58	2 45	5 11	8 2		..
102½	16 95	12 75	9 45	Liverdun		..	..	..	6 43	..	11 9	..	5 22	..	..	..
108¾	17 95	13 55	10 5	Fontenoy-sur-Moselle.		..	..	..	6 57	..	11 23	..	5 36	..	..	..
113¾	18 80	14 15	10 50	Toul		..	..	..	7 15	..	11 41	3 18	5 54	8 38	..	..
118	19 50	14 70	10 90	Foug		..	..	..	7 26	..	11 52	..	6 5	..	..	..
121	20 5	15 10	11 20	Fagny-Sur- Meuse		..	..	..	7 35	..	12 1	..	6 14	..	..	..
125	20 65	15 55	11 55	Sorcy		..	..	..	7 45	..	12 11	..	6 24	..	..	..
130	21 50	16 15	12 0	**Commercy**		..	..	..	8 2	..	12 28	3 50	6 41	9 15	..	..
133	22 0	16 55	12 30	Lerouville		..	..	..	8 11	..	12 37	..	6 50	..	..	..
141	23 35	17 55	13 5	Loxeville		..	..	..	8 33	..	12 59	..	7 12	..	..	..
148	24 50	18 45	13 70	Noncois-le-Petit		..	..	..	8 49	..	1 15	..	7 28	9 58	..	..
151½	..	..	..	Longeville		..	..	..	..	..	..	..	..	..	..	..
154¾	25 60	19 30	14 30	**Bar-le-Duc**		..	..	..	9 14	..	1 40	4 46	7 53	10 21	..	..
164¾	27 25	20 55	15 25	Revigny		..	..	..	9 36	..	2 2	..	8 15	..	..	..
168¾	28 0	21 5	15 65	Sermaize		..	..	..	9 47	..	2 13	..	8 27	10 51	..	..
172	28 50	21 45	15 95	Pargny		..	..	..	9 57	..	2 23	..	8 37	..	..	..
177	29 35	22 10	16 40	Blesmes		..	..	..	10 10	..	2 36	..	8 50	..	..	..
185¼	30 70	23 10	17 15	**Vitry**-le-Francois		..	..	..	10 31	..	2 57	5 42	9 11	11 29	..	..
189	31 30	23 55	17 50	Loisy		..	..	..	10 41	..	3 7	..	9 21	..	..	..
195¾	32 45	24 40	18 15	Vitry-la-Ville		..	..	..	10 57	..	3 23	..	9 37	..	..	..
205¼	34 0	25 60	19 0	**Chalons**		..	6 0	..	11 21	..	3 48	6 23	10 20	12 15	..	..
214	35 45	26 65	19 80	Jalons-les-Vignes		..	6 20	..	11 44	..	4 8	..	..	..	..	..
220½	36 55	27 50	20 45	Oiry		..	6 36	..	12 0	..	4 24	..	..	..	..	..
224½	37 20	28 0	20 80	**Epernay**		..	6 50	..	12 19	..	4 43	7 16	11 23	1 2	..	
228¾	37 90	28 55	21 20	Damery		..	7 1	..	12 30	..	4 54	..	..	..	..	
233¾	38 75	29 15	21 65	Port-à-Binson		..	7 15	..	12 44	..	5 8	..	..	..	..	
240	39 75	29 95	22 25	Dormans		..	7 30	..	12 59	..	5 23	..	12 4	1 35	..	
246¼	40 80	30 70	22 80	Varennes		..	7 45	..	1 14	..	5 38	..	..	..	..	
248¼	41 10	30 95	23 0	Mezy	..	..	7 52	..	1 21	..	5 45	..	..	..	..	
253¾	42 5	31 65	23 50	**Chateau-Thierry**	..	..	8 15	..	1 44	..	6 8	8 11	12 50	2 13	..	
260	43 10	32 40	24 10	Nogent-l'Artaud	..	..	8 31	..	2 0	..	6 24	..	..	..	..	
266¾	44 10	33 20	24 65	Nanteuil	..	..	8 46	..	2 15	..	6 39	..	..	..	..	
272	45 5	33 90	25 20	La Ferté-sous-Jouarre	..	..	9 4	..	2 33	..	6 57	8 46	1 41	2 55	..	
277	45 85	34 50	25 65	Changis	..	..	9 15	..	2 44	..	7 8	..	..	..	1,2,3	
281½	46 60	35 5	26 5	Trilport	..	..	9 26	..	2 55	..	7 19	..	..	..	p.m.	
285¼	47 20	35 55	26 40	**Meaux**	7 0	8 15	9 40	12 0	3 10	3 30	7 33	9 14	2 21	3 28	7 0	
290	48 5	36 15	26 85	Esbly	7 14	8 29	9 53	12 14	..	3 44	7 46	..	..	..	7 14	
295¾	48 95	36 85	27 35	Lagny	7 30	8 45	10 8	12 30	3 34	4 0	8 1	9 36	2 52	3 53	7 30	
301¼	49 90	37 55	27 90	Chelles	7 45	9 0	10 22	12 45	..	4 15	8 15	..	..	..	7 45	..
303¾	50 30	37 85	28 10	Villemonble & Gagny.	7 54	9 9	10 30	12 54	..	4 24	8 23	..	..	..	7 54	p.m.
306¼	50 70	38 20	28 35	Bondy	8 3	9 18	10 38	1 3	..	4 33	8 31	..	..	..	8 3	10 5
307	50 80	38 25	28 40	Noisy-le-Sec	8 9	9 24	10 42	1 9	..	4 39	8 35	..	..	..	8 9	..
312½	51 75	38 95	28 95	**Paris** .... arr.	8 25	9 40	10 55	1 25	4 10	4 55	8 50	10 5	3 30	4 30	8 25	10 25

Additional Train from Meaux to Paris at 8.5 p.m. on Sundays and Fetes only.

On Sundays and Fetes only ☞

[A slight alteration expected during the present month.]

Terminus,] **PARIS AND LYONS.** [Boulevart-Mazas.

English Miles	Fares. 1st Class	2nd Class	3rd Class	Stations.	TRAINS. 1	2	3	4	5	6	7	8	9	10	11	12
	fr. c.	fr. c.	fr. c.		a.m.	a.m.	a.m.	a.m.	a.m.	p.m.	p.m.	p.m.	p.m.	p.m.	p.m.	p.m.
—	—	—	—	**Paris**	..	7 45	9 5	10 35	11 45	3 5	4 5	5 15	8 5	8 30	9 35	10 15
9½	1 55	1 15	0 85	Villeneuve St. Grgs.	..	8 6	9 26	..	12 6	3 26	4 26	5 35	..	8 51	9 57	..
11¼	1 85	1 40	1 5	Montgeron	..	8 13	9 33	..	12 13	3 33	4 33	5 43	..	8 58	10 4	..
13¾	2 30	1 70	1 25	**Brunoy**	..	8 21	9 41	..	12 21	3 41	4 41	5 51	..	9 6	10 12	..
16¼	2 70	2 0	1 50	Combs-la-Ville	..	8 32	..	..	12 32	3 52	4 52	6 2	..	..	10 22	..
19¼	3 20	2 40	1 75	Lieusaint	..	8 42	..	..	12 42	4 2	5 2	6 12	..	9 25	..	..
23½	3 95	2 95	2 15	Cesson	..	8 54	..	..	12 54	4 14	5 14	6 24	..	..	10 41	..
28	4 65	3 50	2 55	**Melun**	..	9 5	10 16	11 29	1 5	4 25	5 25	6 35	8 55	9 45	10 51	..
31¾	5 30	3 95	2 90	Bois-le-Roi	..	9 19	..	..	1 19	4 39	5 39	6 49	..	..	11 7	..
36¾	6 10	4 60	3 35	**Fontainebleau**	..	9 32	10 41	11 52	1 32	4 52	5 55	7 2	9 17	10 10	11 21	12 37
40	6 55	5 0	3 65	Thomery	..	9 43	..	..	1 43	5 3	—	7 13	..	10 20	..	..
43	7 15	5 35	3 95	Moret-St.-Mammes	..	9 52	10 59	..	1 52	5 12	..	7 22	..	10 28	..	1 9
49¼	8 20	6 15	4 50	**Montereau** arr.	..	10 10	11 20	12 21	2 10	5 30	..	7 40	9 43	10 45	11 51	1 40
..	..	..	..	Do. dep.	6 25	10 40	—	12 46	2 20	5 40	..	—	9 48	—	12 1	2 0
56	9 35	7 0	5 15	Villeneuve la Guyd.	6 42	10 57	..	..	2 37	5 57	..	..	..	..	..	..
63¼	10 55	7 95	5 80	Pont-sur-Yonne ..	7 3	11 16	..	..	2 56	6 16	..	..	..	..	..	..
70½	11 70	8 80	6 45	**Sens**	7 24	11 35	..	1 27	3 15	6 35	..	..	10 27	..	12 49	3 22
79¼	13 15	9 85	7 25	Villeneuve-sur Yone	7 51	12 2	..	1 50	3 40	7 0		..	..	..	..	..
84¼	14 0	10 50	7 70	St.-Julien-du-Sault.	8 5	12 15	..	..	3 53	7 13		..	..	..	..	..
91¼	15 15	11 35	8 30	**Joigny**	8 27	12 33	..	2 16	4 11	7 31		..	11 8	..	1 40	4 57
97	16 5	12 5	8 85	**Laroche**	8 46	12 54	..	2 33	4 29	7 49		..	11 22	..	1 59	5 35
102½	17 0	12 75	9 35	Brienon	9 4	1 11	..	2 49	4 46	8 6		..	..	..	..	6 13
108	17 95	13 45	9 85	**St.-Florentin** ..	9 22	1 27	..	3 4	5 2	8 22		..	11 46	..	..	..
115	19 5	14 30	10 50	Flogny	9 45	1 47	..	..	5 22	8 42		..	..	..	..	..
123	20 40	15 30	11 25	**Tonnerre** ..arr.	10 10	2 5	a.m.	3 35	5 40	9 5		..	12 15	..	3 0	7 35
..	..	..	..	Do. ..dep.	—	2 25	6 5	3 45	6 10	—		..	12 25	..	3 13	—
128	21 25	15 95	11 70	Tanlay	..	2 38	6 18	..	6 23	..		..	..	..	..	
136¾	22 70	17 5	12 50	Ancy-le-Franc	..	3 1	6 41	..	6 46	..		..	..	..	..	
140½	23 30	17 50	12 80	**NuitsStRavier**	..	3 13	6 54	4 21	6 58	..		..	12 58	..	..	
145⅓	24 15	18 10	13 30	Aisy	..	3 28	7 11	..	7 13	..		..	..	..	..	
151½	25 20	18 90	13 85	**Montbard**	..	3 45	7 23	4 47	7 30	..		..	1 20	..	4 17	
160½	26 65	20 0	14 65	Les Laumes	..	4 11	7 57	5 11	7 56	..		..	..	..	..	
174	28 90	21 70	15 90	**Verrey**	..	4 48	8 34	5 44	8 33	..		..	2 9	..	5 16	
179½	29 85	22 40	16 40	Blaisy-Bas	..	5 9	8 55	6 3	8 54	..		..	..	..	5 36	
184½	30 65	23 0	16 85	Malain	..	5 24	9 9	..	9 9	..		..	..	..	5 51	
193¾	32 15	24 10	17 65	Plombieres	..	5 49	9 34	..	9 34	..		..	..	..	6 16	
196½	32 65	24 50	17 95	**Dijon** ...... arr.	p.m.	6 0	9 45	6 40	9 50	p.m.		..	2 56	..	6 28	
..	..	..	..	Do. ...... dep.	12 5	6 25	9 55	7 20	—	2 35		..	3 1	..	6 50	
203¼	33 80	25 35	18 60	Gevrey	12 22	6 42	10 12	..	..	2 52		..	..	..	7 7	
207	34 40	25 80	18 90	Vougeot	12 36	6 54	10 26	..	..	3 6		..	..	..	7 19	
210¼	34 90	26 20	19 20	**Nuits**	12 47	7 4	10 37	7 48	..	3 17		..	..	..	7 29	
214	35 55	26 65	19 55	Corgoloin	1 5	7 16	10 55	..	..	3 35		..	..	..	7 41	
219½	36 50	27 35	20 5	**Beaune**	1 20	7 30	11 10	8 9	..	3 50	..	..	3 43	..	7 55	
223¾	37 20	27 95	20 45	Meursault	1 38	7 45	11 28	..	..	4 8	..	..	..	..	8 9	
229	38 5	28 55	20 90	Chagny	1 55	8 0	11 45	8 33	..	4 25	..	..	..	..	8 24	
230¾	38 65	29 0	21 25	Fontaines	2 10	8 14	12 0	..	..	4 40	..	..	..	..	8 39	
239	39 70	29 80	21 80	**Chalon-sur-Soane**	2 30	8 35	12 20	9 0	..	5 0	..	..	4 25	..	9 0	
													a.m.		p.m.	
..	..	..	..	**Lyons** (by steamer	..	..	..	..	..	..	..	..	11 0	..	4 0	

Train 7: (Passengers are allowed 30 kilogrammes (66lbs.) of Luggage free of charge.)

Train 12: ☞ Mondays, Wednesdays, and Fridays only.

Conveyance of Carriages.—Paris to Tonnerre. Four-wheeled, 64 c. per kilom.; two-wheeled, 50 c. per kilom.

PARIS, JOIGNY, AUXERRE, AND CLAMECY.

From Paris to Joigny, Auxerre, and Clamecy, at 10.35 a.m., 1,35 and 8.5 p.m.
From Clamecy to Auxerre, Joigny, and Paris, at 9 a.m. and 5 p.m.
From Auxerre to Paris at 7½ a.m.

[A slight alteration expected during the present month.]

LYONS AND PARIS.

English Miles.	Fares. 1st Class	2nd Class	3rd Class	Stations.	TRAINS. 1	2	3	4	5	6	7	8	9	10	11	12
					a.m.	a.m.	a.m.	a.m.	a.m.	a.m.	a.m.	a.m.	p.m.	a.m.	p.m.	p.m.
Dis.	fr. c.	fr. c.	fr. c.	**Lyons** (by Steamer	..	..	..	..	..	..	..	5 0	..	9 0	..	
					a.m.	a.m.	a.m.	a.m.	a.m.	a.m.	a.m.	p.m.	p.m.	p.m.	p.m.	
—	—	—	—	**Chalon-sur-Saone** ..	..	..	..	6 5	7 35	..	10 35	1 45	3 5	6 35	8 35	Tuesdays, Thursdays, and Saturdays only.
10	1 5	0 80	0 55	Fontaines	..	..	..	..	7 50	..	10 50	..	3 20	..	8 52	
10¾	1 75	1 30	0 95	Chagny	..	..	..	6 27	8 3	..	11 3	..	3 33	6 57	9 5	
15½	2 60	1 95	1 40	Meursault	..	..	..	..	8 21	..	11 21	..	3 51	..	9 21	
20	3 30	2 50	1 80	**Beaune**	..	..	..	6 50	8 36	..	11 36	2 21	4 6	7 19	9 35	
25½	4 25	3 20	2 35	Corgoloin	..	..	..	..	8 55	..	11 55	..	4 25	..	9 56	
29¼	4 85	3 65	2 70	**Nuits**	..	..	..	7 12	9 7	..	12 7	..	4 37	7 41	10 9	
32¼	5 40	4 5	2 95	Vougeot	..	..	..	..	9 21	..	12 21	..	4 51	..	10 21	
36¼	6 0	4 50	3 30	Gevrey	..	..	..	..	9 34	..	12 34	..	5 4	..	10 34	
43	7 15	5 35	3 95	**Dijon** ....arr.	..	..	..	7 42	9 55	..	12 55	3 6	5 25	8 11	10 54	
..	..	..	..	Do. ....dep.	..	..	..	7 52	—	10 30	—	3 16	5 35	8 26	11 5	
45½	7 55	5 70	4 15	Plombières.........	..	..	..	8 1	..	10 40	..	..	5 45	8 34	..	
54¾	9 10	6 85	5 0	Malain.............	..	..	..	8 23	..	11 5	..	..	6 11	8 56	..	
59¼	9 85	7 40	5 40	Blaisy-Bas	..	..	..	8 37	..	11 20	..	..	6 28	9 10	11 49	
65½	10 90	8 15	6 0	**Verrey**	..	..	..	8 53	..	11 38	..	4 2	6 47	9 25	12 6	
78¾	13 5	9 80	7 20	Les Laumes	..	..	..	9 27	..	12 15	..	..	7 25	10 0	..	
87½	14 50	10 90	8 0	**Montbard**	..	..	..	9 47	..	12 48	..	4 49	7 51	10 21	1 3	
93¾	15 55	11 65	8 55	Aisy...............	..	..	..	10 5	..	12 57	..	..	8 11	..	..	
98	16 35	12 30	9 0	**NuitsSt.Ravier.**	..	..	..	10 18	..	1 11	..	5 13	8 27	10 49	..	
103	17 10	12 85	9 40	Ancy-Le-Franc	..	..	..	10 29	..	1 23	..	..	8 42	..	..	
111¾	18 55	13 90	10 20	Tanlay	..	..	..	10 49	..	1 45	..	..	9 7	..	..	
116¾	19 40	14 55	10 65	**Tonnerre** ....arr.	..	..	a.m.	11 1	..	1 58	p.m.	5 47	9 25	11 28	2 19	p.m.
..	..	..	..	Do. ....dep.	..	..	6 55	11 30	..	2 10	4 5	6 20	—	11 38	2 30	9
125	20 75	15 55	11 40	Flogny	..	..	7 13	..	..	2 28	4 23	..	..	..	..	..
131¾	21 85	16 40	12 0	**St.-Florentin** ..	..	..	7 32	11 59	..	2 46	4 42	..	..	12 7	..	..
137¼	22 80	17 10	12 55	Brienon	..	..	7 49	12 14	..	3 2	5 2	..	..	..	..	10 2
142¼	23 65	17 75	13 0	**Laroche**	..	..	8 4	12 27	..	3 16	5 20	7 7	..	12 32	3 28	10 4
148½	24 65	18 50	13 55	**Joigny**	..	..	8 23	12 43	..	3 34	5 40	7 22	..	12 48	3 47	11 2
155¼	25 80	19 35	14 20	St.-Julien-du-Sault...	..	..	8 44	..	..	3 55	6 3	..	..	..	..	..
159¾	26 55	19 90	14 60	Villeneuve sur Yone ..	..	..	8 57	1 11	..	4 7	6 19	..	..	..	..	..
168¾	28 10	21 5	15 45	**Sens**............	..	..	9 20	1 31	..	4 30	6 45	8 2	..	1 36	4 39	12 5
175¾	29 20	21 95	16 5	Pont-sur-Yonne	..	..	9 41	..	..	4 51	7 9	..	..	..	..	..
183¼	30 45	22 85	16 75	Villeneuve la Guyd...	..	..	10 2	..	..	5 11	7 32	..	..	..	..	..
190¼	31 60	23 70	17 40	**Montereau** ..arr.	..	..	10 21	2 15	p.m.	5 29	7 55	8 44	..	2 21	5 32	3 1
..	..	..	..	Do. ..dep.	6 0	8 0	10 35	2 20	2 35	6 5	—	8 49	..	2 31	5 45	3 3
196½	23 65	24 50	17 95	Moret-St.-Mammes..	6 17	8 17	10 52	..	2 52	6 22	..	..	..	..	..	..
199½	33 15	24 90	18 25	Thomery	6 28	8 28	11 3	..	3 3	6 32	p.m.	..	..	..	..	..
202	33 60	25 20	18 45	**Fontainebleau**..	6 38	8 38	11 13	2 45	3 13	6 41	8 0	9 13	..	2 56	6 15	4 1
207	34 40	25 80	18 90	Bois-le-Roi.........	6 55	8 55	11 30	..	3 30	6 57	8 12	..	..	..	..	..
211½	35 15	26 35	19 30	**Melun**...........	7 7	9 7	11 42	3 5	3 42	7 9	8 24	9 33	..	3 28	6 41	..
215¼	35 75	26 80	19 65	Cesson.............	7 22	9 22	11 57	..	3 57	7 24	8 39	..	..	..	..	..
220¼	36 60	27 45	20 10	Lieusaint	7 34	9 34	12 9	..	4 9	7 36	8 51	..	..	..	..	..
222½	37 0	27 75	20 35	Combs-la-Ville	7 44	9 44	12 19	..	4 19	7 45	9 0	..	..	..	..	..
225¾	37 50	28 15	20 65	**Brunoy**	7 53	9 53	12 28	..	4 28	7 54	9 9	..	..	..	..	..
228¼	37 95	28 45	20 85	Montgeron..........	8 3	10 3	12 38	..	4 38	8 3	9 18	..	..	..	..	..
230	38 25	28 70	21 5	Villeneuve St. Grgs ..	8 11	10 11	12 46	..	4 46	8 10	9 25	..	..	..	..	..
238¾	39 70	29 80	21 80	**Paris** ....arr.	8 35	10 35	1 10	4 5	5 10	8 35	9 50	10 30	..	4 30	7 55	7

SPECIAL SERVICE OF THE ARGENTEUIL RAILWAY.

From PARIS for COLOMBES and ARGENTEUIL, every hour from 7.35 a.m. till 8.35 p.m.

From ARGENTEUIL for COLOMBES, ANSIERS, PARIS, ST. GERMAIN, VERSAILLES, and Stations of the two lines, every hour from 7.25 a.m. till 9.35 p.m., and 10.35 p.m.

Fares.—From Paris to Argenteuil, 60 cents.

The latest Alterations on the Belgian Lines were received when at Press, and appear in this Issue.

BRUSSELS, LIEGE, & COLOGNE.

English Miles.	Fares. 1st Clss.	2nd Clss.	3rd Clss	Stations.	Daily Trains. 1 2 & 3	2 1, 2, 3	3 1,2, 3	4 1, 2,3	5 1st	6 1,2, 3	7 1, 2, 3	8 1, 2, 3	9 1st.
Dis.	fr. c.	fr. c.	fr. c.		a.m.	a.m.	a.m.	a.m.	a.m.	p.m.	p.m.	p.m.	p.m.
...	...	...	...	ANTWERP ....dep.	...	...	...	...	9 50	...	7 15	...	...
—	—	—	—	**Brussels** (N. S.) dep.	...	...	7 0	...	10 15	3 0	6 0	7 45	9 30
6¼	0 80	0 60	0 40	Vilvorde	...	...	7 10	...	...	..	6 10	7 55	...
12½	1 70	1 25	0 85	**Malines**	...	...	7 35	...	10 45	3 30	6 30	8 15	9 55
19¼	2 55	1 90	1 30	Haecht	...	...	7 50	...	...	3 45	6 45	8 30	...
20½	2 65	2 0	1 30	Wespelaer	...	...	7 55	...	...	3 50	...	8 35	...
27½	2 80	2 10	1 40	LOUVAIN	...	...	8 25	...	11 20	4 15	7 5	9 15	10 25
34¼	3 70	2 75	1 85	Vertryck	...	...	8 35	...	...	4 25	7 15	9 25	...
38¾	4 30	3 25	2 15	**Tirlemont**	5 15	...	8 45	...	11 45	4 45	7 35	10 0	10 50
42½	4 80	3 60	2 40	Esemael	5 30	...	...	...	...	...	...		...
46¾	5 35	4 0	2 70	LANDEN (1)...........	5 50	...	9 10	...	...	5 10	8 0	...	...
48¾	5 60	4 20	2 80	Gingelom	6 15	...	...	...	...	5 15	...	...	...
51¾	6 0	4 50	3 0	Rosoux	6 30	...	...	...	...	5 25	...	...	...
55½	6 50	4 85	3 25	WAREMME	6 45	...	9 35	...	...	5 35	8 25	...	...
62½	7 35	5 50	3 70	Fexhe	7 35	...	10 0	...	...	6 0	8 50	...	...
67½	8 0	6 0	4 0	ANS	8 5	...	10 20	...	12 55	6 20	9 10	..	12 10
71¼	8 50	6 35	4 25	**Liege** (2).........arr.	8 45	...	10 40	...	1	6 40	9 30	...	12 30
...	...	...	...	,, ...dep		6 45	10 45	11 30	1 20	6 45	9 30	...	12 35
73¾	8 70	6 55	4 35	Chênée	...	6 50	10 50	11 35	1 25	6 50	9 35	...	...
75½	9 5	6 80	4 50	Chaufontaine	...	7 0	...	11 45	1 30	7 0	9 45	...	...
78	9 35	7 0	4 70	Le Trooz	...	7 10	...	11 55	...	7 5	...	...	...
80½	9 70	7 25	4 85	Nessonvaux	...	7 20	...	12 5	...	7 15	...	...	...
83¾	10 10	7 55	5 5	Pepinster (Spa)*........	...	7 35	11 25	12 20	1 55	7 25	10 10	...	...
85½	10 30	7 75	5 15	Ensival....	...	7 40	...	12 30	...	7 30	...	...	...
86¾	10 50	7 85	5 25	**Verviers** ....arr.	...	8 0	11 45	12 45	2 15	7 50	10 30	...	1 25
					a m.	a.m.	p.m.		p.m	p.m.			a.m.
86¾	10 50	7 85	5 25	**Verviers** ....dep.	5 30	8 15	12 15	...	2 45	8 15	...	...	1 45
92	11 5	8 30	5 50	Dolhain	5 45	8 35	12 30	...	...	8 25	...	...	...
96¼	11 60	8 70	5 80	Herbesthal	6 0	9 0	12 45	...	3 5	8 40	...	...	2 20
99¼	...	...	...	Astenet...............	...	...	...	...	...	...	...	...	...
105½	15 35	11 45	7 55	**Aix-la-Chapelle**..arr	7 0	10 0	2 0	...	4 0	9 30	...	...	3 0
...	...	...	...	,, dep.	7 8	10 15	2 15	...	4 15		...	...	3 15
112½	...	...	...	Stolberg	7 18	10 33	2 33	...	...	...	...	...	...
114¼	17 10	12 70	8 55	Eschweiler	7 26	10 41	2 40	...	4 40	...	...	...	3 40
119¼	...	...	...	Langerwehe	...	...	...	...	...	...	...	...	...
125½	19 35	14 45	9 55	**Duren**	8 0	11 15	3 15	...	5 0	...	...	...	3 50
131¼	...	...	...	Buir	...	...	...	..	...	...	...	...	...
138	...	...	...	Horrem................	...	...	...	...	...	...	...	...	...
141	...	...	...	Königsdorf	...	...	...	...	...	...	...	...	...
145½	...	...	...	Müngersdorf	...	...	...	...	...	...	...	...	...
150	24 85	18 20	12 30	**Cologne** (3) ..arrival	9 5	12 15	4 15	...	6 0	...	...	...	5 0
					a.m.	a.m.			p.m.				a.m.
50	24 85	18 20	12 30	COLOGNE........dep.	11 0	...	...	...	8 0	...	...	...	6 30
174	28 60	20 70	14 17	DUSSELDORF ....arr.	12 10	...	...	...	9 0	...	...	...	7 15
155	57 60	40 7	27 92	HANOVER	10 0	...	...	...	5 10	...	...	...	1 45
352	72 62	50 7	34 17	HAMBURG.............	...	...	...	...	10 20	...	...	...	6 40
534	86 10	58 82	39 92	LEIPSIC..............	9 30	...	...	...	2 0	...	...	...	9 15
548	91 72	63 45	43 45	BERLIN...............	9 15	...	...	...	1 0	...	...	...	9 15

(1.) LANDEN to ST. TROND and HASSELT, see page 67.
(3.) COLOGNE to DUSSELDORF, HAMM, and MINDEN, see page 70.
(2) LEIGE to NAMUR, see page 64.
COLOGNE to BONN, see page 69.

* Travellers going to SPA stop at PEPINSTER.

Observations.—Trains Nos. 3 and 7 correspond, and change carriages at Landen for Hasselt, see page 67. Travellers change carriages at Verviers for Aix-la-Chapelle and Cologne. By the night train from Cologne for Berlin, at 8 p.m., the regular fare is increased by 12 francs 1st class, and 7 francs 75 cents second class. All the Trains, except No. 4, correspond direct at Pepinster for Spa. The following stations, viz., Brussels (north), Malines, Antwerp, Ghent, Bruges, Ostend, Mouscron, Louvain, Liege, Chaufontaine, Verviers, Aix-la Chapelle, and Cologne, issue tickets for Passengers and ... between Pepinster and Spa is—for the 1st and 2nd class, 1½ franc, and for the 3rd

Frame and text are truncated on the original guide

COLOGNE, LIEGE, AND BRUSSELS.

Eng. Miles.	Fares. 1st Clss.	2nd Clss.	3rd Clss.	Stations.	Daily Trains. 1 1st.	2 1,2,3	3 1,2,3	4 1, 2, 3	5 1,2,3	6 1,2,3	7 1,2,3	8 1,2,3	9 1,2,3	10
Dis.	fr. c.	fr. c.	fr. c.		a.m.	a.m.	a.m.	a.m.	a.m.	a.m.	a.m.	p.m.	p.m.	
548				Berlin ....dep.	7 30	..	..	..	..	..	..	..	10 0	
534		Fares		Leipsic	7 0	..	..	..	..	..	..	..	10 0	..
452	from	Colo	gne.	Hamburg	9 20	..	..	..	..	..	..	4 40	..	..
355				Hanover	2 40	..	..	..	..	..	..	9 50	6 45	..
174				Dusseldorf	9 10	..	..	..	..	..	..	8 0	3 0	..
150				Cologne	10 0	..	..	..	..	..	..	9 15	4 0	..
					p.m		a.m.		a.m.	a.m.	a.m.	p.m.	p.m.	p.m.
150	—	—	—	**Cologne** ....dep.	11 30	..	..	..	..	6 30	8 0	11 30	5 0	7 30
145½	1 0	1 0	0 50	Müngersdorf	..	..	..	..	..	..	..	..	..	..
141	1 88	1 38	1 0	Königsdorf	..	..	..	..	..	..	..	..	..	..
138	2 50	1 88	1 25	Horrem	12 0	..	..	..	..	..	..	..	..	..
131¼	3 75	3 0	2 0	Buir	..	..	..	..	..	..	..	..	..	..
125½	5 25	4 0	2 63	**Duren**	12 30	..	..	..	..	7 40	9 0	12 40	6 10	8 40
119¼	6 50	5 0	3 25	Langerwehe	..	..	..	..	..	..	..	..	..	..
114¼	7 50	5 75	3 75	Eschweiler	12 55	..	..	..	..	8 10	9 25	1 10	6 40	9 10
112½	8 0	6 25	4 0	Stolberg	..	..	..	..	..	8 18	..	1 18	6 48	9 18
105½	9 38	6 88	4 75	**Aix-la-Chapelle**, arr.	1 15	..	..	..	..	8 45	9 45	1 45	7 0	9 30
..	..	..	..	" " dep.	1 30	..	..	..	6 30	9 0	10 0	2 20	7 10	
99¼	..	..	..	Astenet................	..	..	..	..	7 0	..	..	..	..	..
96¼	12 82	9 63	6 50	Herbesthal	2 0	..	..	..	7 20	9 40	10 20	2 35	7 30	..
92	14 5	9 90	6 80	Dolhain	..	..	..	..	7 35	9 50	..	..	7 40	..
86¾	14 45	10 40	7 10	**Verviers** ....arr.	2 30	..	..	..	8 0	10 15	11 0	3 0	8 10	..
	From	Ver	viers		a.m.	a.m.	a.m.	a m.	a.m.	a.m.	a.m.	p.m.	p.m.	p.m.
86¾	—	—	—	**Verviers** ....dep.	3 0	..	..	6 40	8 30	10 45	11 20	3 45	8 30	..
85½	0 80	0 30	0 20	Ensival	..	..	..	6 43	8 35	10 48	..	3 48	8 35	..
83¾	0 80	0 30	0 20	Pepinster (Spa)*	..	..	..	6 48	8 40	10 53	..	3 50	8 40	..
80½	0 80	0 60	0 40	Nessonvaux	..	..	..	7 0	8 55	11 5	..	4 5	8 55	..
78	1 20	0 90	0 60	Le Trooz	..	..	..	7 10	9 5	11 15	..	4 15	9 5	..
75½	1 45	1 10	0 70	Chaufontaine	..	..	..	7 20	9 15	11 25	..	4 25	9 15	..
73¾	1 75	1 30	0 90	Chênée	..	..	..	7 30	9 25	11 35	..	4 35	9 25	..
71¼	2 10	1 55	1 5	**Liege**..(1)........arr.	3 45	..	..	7 50	9 45	11 50	12 5	4 50	9 45	..
..	..	..	..	" ....dep.	3 45	..	6 30	7 55		11 55	12 5	4 55		6 0
67½	2 55	1 90	1 30	Ans	4 0	..	6 50	8 10		12 30	..	5 15		6 20
62½	3 20	2 40	1 60	Fexhe	..	..	7 15	..	..	12 50	..	5 25	..	6 30
55½	4 10	3 5	2 5	Waremme..............	..	..	8 5	8 45	..	1 15	..	5 50	..	7 0
51¾	4 50	3 35	2 25	Rosoux................	..	..	8 15	..	..	1 25	..	..	..	7 20
48¾	4 90	3 65	2 45	Gingelom..............	..	..	8 30	..	..	1 35	..	..	..	7 35
46¾	5 10	3 85	2 55	Landen (2)..........	..	..	9 0	9 10	..	1 50	..	6 20	..	7 55
42½	5 70	4 25	2 85	Escmael	..	..		..	..	2 0	..	..	..	8 10
38¾	6 25	4 70	3 10	**Tirlemont**..........	5 10	5 0	..	9 25	..	2 10	1 40	6 40	..	9 0
34¼	6 80	5 10	3 40	Vertryck	..	5 10	..	9 35	..	2 20	..	6 50	..	
27½	7 70	5 75	3 85	Louvain................	5 35	5 40	..	9 55	..	2 45	2 5	7 10	..	
20½	8 55	6 40	4 30	Wespelaer	..	6 0	..	..	..	..	..	7 25	..	..
19¼	8 65	6 50	4 30	Haecht	..	6 5	..	10 15	..	3 10	..	7 30	..	..
12½	9 50	7 15	4 75	**Malines** (3)	6 15	6 55	..	10 45	..	3 45	2 45	8 5	..	..
6¼	10 40	7 80	5 20	Vilvorde	..	7 10	..	11 0	..	4 0	..	..	..	..
—	10 50	7 85	5 25	**Brussels** (N.Sta.) arr.	6 45	7 30	..	11 20	..	4 20	3 15	8 35	..	..
..		..	..	Antwerp ....arr.	8 35	..	12 0	..	..	4 20	9 0	..	..	..

(1) Liege to Namur, see page 64. (2) Landen to Hasselt, see page 67.
(3) Malines to Antwerp, see page 65. Malines to Ostend and Tournay, see pages 58 and 59.
* Travellers going to Spa stop at Pepinster.

Observations.—Passengers by all the Trains change carriages at Verviers. Trains Nos. 4, 6, 8, and 9 correspond direct at Pepinster for Spa. For Fares and further information, see page 56. All the Trains correspond and change carriages at Malines; for Antwerp, see page 65; for Ghent and Ostend, except No. 8, see page 58; for Tournay and Lille, except Trains No. 8, see page 62; Trains Nos. 3, 4, 6, and 10 correspond and change carriages at Landen for Hasselt, see page 67.

Spa to Pepinster, by Omnibus, at 5½ and 9.30 a.m.; 12½, 2½, 6.15, and 8.50 p.m., in 1 hour 15 minutes.

LONDON TO OSTEND, GHENT, & BRUSSELS.

Eng. Mls.	Fares. 1 Cls.	2 Cls.	3 Cls.	Stations.	1	2	3	4	5	6	7	8
					1,2,3	1,2,3	1st.	1,2,3	1,2,3	2 & 3	1 & 2	1,2,3
Dis.	fr. c.	fr. c.	fr. c.		a.m.	a.m.	p.m.	a.m.	p.m.	p.m.	p.m.	p.m
241	...	...	...	LONDON.........dep.	...	...	8 30	...	...	...	...	...
153	...	...	...	DOVER...........arr.	...	...	11 0	...	...	...	...	...
...	...	...	...	,, ...dep.	...	...	11 15	...	...	...	...	...
	From Ostend.						a.m.	a.m.	a.m.	p.m.	p.m.	p.m.
89½	—	—	—	**Ostend** ....dep.	...	6 15	7 15	...	11 20	3 0	6 45	8 0
85	0 80	0 40	0 30	Plasschendael...........	...	6 25	...	...	11 30	3 10	...	8 10
81¼	1 5	0 80	0 50	Jabbeke	...	6 35	...	...	11 35	3 20	...	8 20
75½	1 75	1 30	0 90	**Bruges**..............	...	6 55	7 40	...	11 55	3 40	7 10	8 40
71¼	2 30	1 75	1 15	Oostcamp (Fri. & Sat.).	...	7 5	...	...	...	3 50	...	8 50
68	2 70	2 5	1 35	Bloemendael............	...	7 15	...	...	12 15	4 0	...	9 0
61¾	3 50	2 65	1 75	Aeltre..................	...	7 40	...	...	12 35	4 25	...	9 25
57¼	4 10	3 5	2 5	Hansbeke................	...	7 50	...	...	12 50	4 40	...	9 35
55½	4 30	3 25	2 15	Landeghem	...	7 55	...	...	12 55	4 50	...	9 40
47½	5 35	4 0	2 70	**Ghent**..............arr.	...	8 30	8 45	...	1 30	5 30	8 15	10 15
	From Ghent.			,, ...dep.	5 30		8 55	9 30	1 40	5 55	8 20	
43	0 80	0 50	0 30	Melle....................	5 35	...	...	9 40	1 50	6 5	...	...
38¾	1 10	0 85	0 55	Wetteren................	5 45	...	9 10	9 55	2 0	6 20	...	...
34¾	1 60	1 20	0 80	Wichelen	5 55	...	...	10 10	...	6 30	...	...
30½	2 15	1 60	1 10	Audeghem	...	...	...	...	...	...	...	...
29¼	2 40	1 80	1 20	**Termonde**............	6 15	...	9 30	10 35	2 25	6 50	8 55	...
24¾	2 95	2 20	1 50	Buggenhout..............	6 25	...	...	10 55	2 35	7 5	...	...
23½	3 10	2 35	1 55	Malderen	6 30	...	...	11 0	...	7 10	...	...
20½	3 50	2 65	1 75	Londerzeel..............	6 40	...	...	11 10	2 50	7 20	...	...
17½	3 85	2 90	1 90	Cappelle	6 50	...	...	11 20	3 0	7 30	...	...
12½	4 50	3 35	2 25	**Malines**..............	7 15	...	10 15	12 15	3 25	8 25	9 40	...
6¼	5 30	3 95	2 65	Vilvorde................	7 30	...	...	12 30	3 40	8 40	...	...
—	5 30	3 95	2 65	**Brussels**.........arr.	7 50	...	10 45	12 50	4 0	9 10	10 10	...
				NORTH STATION.	p.m.		p.m.			a.m.		
...	...	..	...	COLOGNE......... arr.	4 15	...	6 0	...	...	5 0	..	...

Observations.—Trains Nos. 3, 5, 6, & 7, from Ostend, correspond at Bruges for Courtray, Tournay and Lille. See page 59. Trains Nos. 1, 3, 4, 5, 6, and 7, correspond and change carriages at Malines for Antwerp, see page 65; Nos. 1, 3, 5, and 7, for Liege, see p. 56; & also for Hasselt, except No. 6, see pages 56 & 67. No. 6 is a first, second, and third class train from Ghent

BRUSSELS, GHENT, OSTEND, & LONDON.

Eng. Mls.	Fares. 1 Cls.	2 Cls.	3 Cls.	Stations.	1	2	3	4	5	6	7	8
					1,2,3	1,2,3	1 & 2	2 & 3	1,2,3	1st.	1,2,3	1,2,3
Dis.	fr. c.	fr. c.	fr. c.	NORTH STATION.	a.m.	a.m.	a.m.	a.m.	a.m.	p.m.	p.m.	p.m.
—	—	—	—	**Brussels**.........dep.	...	6 30	8 0	...	10 30	2 45	4 30	7 45
6¼	0 80	0 60	0 40	Vilvorde................	...	6 40	...	...	10 40	...	4 40	7 55
12½	1 70	1 25	0 85	**Malines**	...	7 5	8 25	...	11 3	3 15	5 0	8 15
17½	2 30	1 75	1 15	Cappelle................	...	7 20	...	...	11 20	...	5 15	8 23
20½	2 65	2 0	1 30	Londerzeel	...	7 30	...	...	11 30	...	5 25	8 35
23½	3 5	2 30	1 50	Malderen	...	7 40	...	...	...	...	5 35	...
24¾	3 5	2 30	1 50	Buggenhout..............	...	7 45	...	...	11 40	...	5 40	...
29¼	3 5	2 30	1 50	**Termonde**............	...	8 0	9 5	...	11 55	3 50	5 55	9 0
30½	3 30	2 45	1 65	Audegham................	...	...	...	...	...	...	...	...
34¾	3 85	2 90	1 90	Wichelen................	...	8	...	...	...	...	6 10	...
38¾	4 30	3 25	2 15	Wetteren	...	8 25	...	...	12 15	...	6 20	9 15
43	4 90	3 65	2 45	Melle...................	...	8 40	...	...	12 25	...	6 35	...
47½	5 30	3 95	2 65	**Ghent**..............arr.	...	9 0	9 50	...	12 45	4 40	7 0	9 45
...	...	...	...	,, ...dep.	6 15		9 55	10 40	12 55	4 45	7 10	
55½	6 30	4 75	3 15	Landeghem	6 30	...	...	11 0	1 15	...	7 30	...
57¼	6 55	4 90	3 30	Hansbeke................	6 35	...	...	11 10	1 20	...	7 35	...
61¾	7 10	5 35	3 55	Aeltre..................	6 55	...	...	11 30	1 35	...	7 55	...
68	7 90	5 95	3 95	Bloemendael.............	7 15	...	...	12 5	1 50	,	8 10	...
71¼	8 30	6 25	4 15	Oostcamp (Fri. & Sat.).	7 20	...	...	12 15	...	...	8 20	...
75½	8 80	6 60	4 40	**Bruges**...............	7 40	...	10 50	12 30	2 10	5 40	8 35	...
81¼	9 60	7 20	4 80	Jabbeke	7 55	...	...	12 45	2 25	...	8 50	...
85	10 10	7 55	5 5	Plasschendael...........	8 10	...	...	1 0	2 30	...	9 0	...
89½	10 55	7 90	5 30	**Ostend** ....arr.	8 30	...	11 30	1 30	3 0	6 20	9 30	...
...	...	...	...	OSTEND*........dep.	...	...	...	...	...	6 30	...	...
153	...	...	...	DOVER...........dep.	...	...	...	...	...	2 0	...	...
241	57 75	39 35	...	LONDON. ....arr.	...	...	...	...	...	4 50	...	...
										a.m.		

Observations.

The first class fare between London and Dover (per Express Train), is 27 francs 50 cents.

* For the Departure of the Steam-boat, see page 134.

The Distance from Ostend to Cologne is about 212 English miles.

BRUSSELS, GHENT, TOURNAY, & CALAIS.

Eng. Mls.	Fares. 1 Cl.	2 Cl.	3 Cl.	Stations.	1 (1, 2, 3)	2 (1, 2, 3)	3 (1 & 2)	4 (1, 2, 3)	5 (1st.)	6 (1, 2, 3)	7 (1 & 2)
Dis.	fr. c.	fr. c.	fr. c.	NORTH STATION.	a.m.	a.m.	a.m.	a.m.	p.m.	p.m.	p.m.
—	..	..	..	**Brussels**....dep.	..	6 30	8 0	10 30	2 45	4 30	7 45
6¼	..	..	..	Vilvorde	..	6 40	..	10 40	..	4 40	7 55
12½	..	..	..	**Malines**	..	7 5	8 25	11 5	3 15	5 0	8 15
29¼	..	..	..	**Termonde**	..	8 0	9 5	11 55	3 50	5 55	9 0
38¾	From Ghent.			Wetteren	..	8 25	..	12 15	..	6 20	9 15
47½	—	—	—	**Ghent**........arr.	..	9 0	9 50	12 45	4 40	7 0	9 45
..	..	..	..	,, ...dep.	5 30	9 5		1 25	5 5	7 5	
54¾	1 5	0 80	0 50	Nazareth	5 50	..	..	1 45	..	7 25	..
58	1 45	1 10	0 70	Deynze	6 0	9 35	..	2 0	..	7 35	..
60½	1 75	1 30	0 90	Machelen	*6 10	..	..	†2 5	..	7 45	..
62½	2 0	1 50	1 0	Olsène	6 20	..	..	2 15	..	7 55	..
65½	2 40	1 80	1 20	Waereghem	6 30	10 0	..	2 25	..	8 5	..
71¼	3 10	2 35	1 55	Haerlebeke	6 50	10 15	..	2 40	..	8 20	..
75	3 50	2 65	1 75	**Courtray**	7 10	10 25	..	2 55	6 10	8 30	..
82½	4 50	3 35	2 25	**Mouscron**	7 40	10 55	..	4 10	6 40	8 55	..
88¾	5 30	3 95	2 65	Néchin	7 55	11 10	..	4 25	..	9 10	..
90¾	5 50	4 15	2 75	Templeuve	8 0	11 15	..	4 30	..	9 15	..
94½	6 0	4 50	3 0	**Tournay** ....arr.	8 15	11 35	..	4 45	7 10	9 30	..
					a.m.	a.m.	p.m.	p.m.	p.m.	p.m.	..
82½	4 50	3 35	2 25	MOUSCRON ..dep.	7 45	11 15	12 30	3 50	6 45	9 0	..
93¼	6 30	4 70	3 25	LILLE ......arr.	8 15	11 45	2 0	4 20	7 15	9 35	..
144¼	15 0	11 35	..	DUNKIRK	..	3 0		9 30	..	6 0	..
157¼	17 0	12 85	..	CALAIS	..	3 0	..	9 30	..	2 10	..
269	51 95	38 70	..	LONDON	..	10 15	..	4 50	..	8 6	..
..	33 75	25 35	..	PARIS ......arr.	5 0	..	..	10 45	5 30	9 0	..
					p.m.	p.m.		p.m.	a.m.	a.m.	

Observations.—All the Trains change carriages at Ghent for Tournay. Trains Nos. 1, 2, and 4 correspond at Tournay; for the line from Tournay to Jurbise, see page 63. Passengers for France change carriages at Mouscron. Train No. 2 is a first and second class, and No. 6 a first class only from Lille to Calais. Train No. 5 is a first and second class from Ghent.

* Mondays. † Fridays.

CALAIS, TOURNAY, GHENT, & BRUSSELS.

Eng. Mls.	Fares. 1 Cl.	2 Cl.	3 Cl.	Stations.	1 (1, 2, 3)	2 (2 & 3)	3 (1, 2, 3)	4 (1 & 2)	5 (1, 2, 3)	6 (1 & 2)	7 (1, 2, 3)
Dis.	fr. c.	fr. c.	fr. c.		a.m.	a.m.	p.m.	a.m.	p.m.	a.m.	a.m.
—	..	..	..	LONDON ....dep.	..	..	8 0	..	..	..	8 10
..	..	..	..	PARIS ...... ,,	..	..	a.m.	..	11 0	7 30	..
157¼	..	..	..	CALAIS ..... ,,	..	..	2 0	..	8 0	..	3 0
144¼	..	..	..	DUNKIRK ... ,,	..	..	..	..	8 15	..	2 45
93¼	..	..	..	LILLE ...... ,,	..	..	6 0	..	10 45	2 50	5 30
82½	..	..	..	MOUSCRON ..arr.	..	..	6 40	..	11 25	3 30	6 10
	From Tournay.				a.m.	a.m.	a.m.	a.m.	a.m.	p.m.	p.m.
94½	—	—	—	**Tournay** ....dep.	..	5 0	6 30	10 20	11 15	3 0	6 0
90¾	0 80	0 35	0 25	Templeuve	..	5 10	6 35	..	11 20	3 10	..
88¾	0 80	0 60	0 40	Néchin	..	5 15	6 40	..	11 25	3 15	..
82½	1 60	1 20	0 80	**Mouscron**	..	5 55	7 10	10 55	11 55	3 55	6 35
75	2 55	1 90	1 30	**Courtray**	..	6 40	7 30		12 15	4 15	6 55
71¼	2 95	2 20	1 50	Haerlebeke	..	6 50	..		12 25	4 25	7 5
65½	3 70	2 75	1 85	Waereghem	..	7 15	..		12 35	4 40	7 20
62½	4 10	3 5	2 5	Olsène	..	7 30	..		..	4 50	..
60½	4 30	3 25	2 15	Machelen	..	7 40	..		..	4 55	..
58	4 65	3 50	2 30	Deynze	..	8 0	8 10		1 0	5 10	7 40
54¾	5 5	3 80	2 50	Nazareth	..	8 25	..		..	5 20	..
47½	6 0	4 50	3 0	**Ghent** ...... arr.	..	9 15	8 45		1 35	5 50	8 15
..	..	..	..	,, ... dep.	5 30	9 30	8 55		1 40	5 55	..
38¾	7 10	5 35	3 55	Wetteren	5 45	9 55	9 10		2 0	6 20	..
29¼	8 40	6 30	4 20	**Termonde**	6 15	10 33	9 30		2 25	6 50	8 55
12½	10 50	7 85	5 25	**Malines**	7 15	12 15	10 15		3 25	8 25	9 40
6¼	11 30	8 45	5 65	Vilvorde	7 30	12 30	..		3 40	8 40	..
—	11 30	8 45	5 65	**Brussels** arr	7 50	12 50	10 45		4 0	9 10	10 10
				NORTH STATION.	p.m.		p.m.				a.m.
..	..	..	..	COLOGNE ....arr	4 15	..	6 0	..	..	..	5 0

* Mondays. † Fridays.

Observations.—Passengers for Belgium change carriages at Mouscron. Train No. 3 is a first class only from Ghent. Passengers for Brussels change carriages at Ghent. Trains Nos. 3, 5, 6, and 7, from Tournay, correspond at Courtray for Bruges and Ostend. All the Trains correspond and change carriages at Mouscron for Lille, see above, and at Malines for Antwerp, see page 65. Nos. 1, 3, 5, and 7, for Liege, see page 56; for Hasselt, except No. 5, see pages 56 and 67.

BRUSSELS, QUIEVRAIN, AND PARIS.

Eng. Mls.	Fares. 1 Cls.	2 Cls.	3 Cls.	Stations.	1 1,2,3	2 1st.	3 1,2,3	4 1,2,3	5 1,2,3	6 1& 2	
Dis.	fr. c.	fr. c.	fr. c.	SOUTH STATION.	a.m.	a.m.	a.m.	p.m.	p.m.	p.m.	
—	—	—	—	**Brussels** (1) ....dep.	5 0	8 0	..	1 15	5 15	6 30	..
2½	0 80	0 30	0 20	Forest	5 5	..	..	..	5 20	..	..
4¼	0 80	0 40	0 30	Ruysbroeck	5 10	..	..	1 20	5 25	..	..
6¼	0 80	0 60	0 40	Loth	5 15	..	..	..	5 30	..	..
8¾	1 20	0 90	0 60	Hal	5 25	..	..	1 35	5 40	..	..
10¾	1 35	1 0	0 70	Lembecq	5 30	..	..	..	5 45	..	..
12½	1 60	1 20	0 80	Tubize	5 40	..	..	1 45	5 50	..	..
18¾	2 50	1 85	1 25	**Braine-le-Comte** ar.	6 15	8 45	..	2 15	6 25	7 20	..
..	..	..	..	„ dep.	6 25	8 50	9 15	2 15	6 30	7 20	..
22¼	2 95	2 20	1 50	Soignies	6 35	..	9 25	2 25	6 35	..	..
30½	4 0	3 0	2 0	Jurbise	7 10	..	10 0	2 50	6 55	..	..
38	4 95	3 70	2 50	**Mons**	7 35	9 25	10 45	3 15	7 20	8 5	..
40½	5 30	3 95	2 65	Jemmappes	7 45	..	10 55	3 25	7 30	8 10	..
43¾	5 70	4 25	2 85	St. Ghislain...........	7 55	..	11 15	3 30	7 40	8 20	..
45	5 85	4 40	2 90	Boussu	8 0	..	11 25	3 40	7 50	..	..
47½	6 10	4 55	3 5	Thulin	8 10	..	11 40	3 45	7 55	..	..
50	6 40	4 80	3 20	**Quievrain** ......arr.	8 25	10 0	12 15	4 0	8 10	8 50	..
..	..	..	..	„ ......dep.	8 40	10 10	—	4 5	—	8 55	..
51¼	..	..	..	Blanc-Misseron	8 45	10 17	..	4 12	..	9 2	..
58	7 65	5 80	3 95	VALENCIENNES.(2)ar.	9 15	10 25	..	4 25	..	9 10	..
..	..	..	..	„ dep.	—	10 40	..	4 40	..	9 40	..
80½	11 15	8 55	6 5	DOUAI .... „	..	11 50	..	5 50	..	10 50	..
97	13 90	10 30	7 55	ARRAS .... „	..	12 24	..	6 25	..	11 35	..
139¼	20 90	15 55	11 50	AMIENS (2) .... „	..	1 30	..	7 40	..	1 30	..
231¼	35 40	26 55	20 5	PARIS (2) ......arr.	..	5 0	..	10 45	..	5 30	..
						p.m.	..	p.m.	..	a.m.	..

Observations.—Train No. 6 is a first and second class from Brussels to Quievrain, and first, second, and third class from Quievrain to Paris. Train No. 4 is a first, second, and third class as far as Quievrain, and first and second class from Quievrain.

(1) *From Ostend and Ghent to Brussels,* *see page 58.* (2) *For Trains between Paris, Amiens, and Valenciennes,* *see pages 60 and 34.*

PARIS, QUIEVRAIN, AND BRUSSELS.

Eng. Mls.	Fares. 1 Cls.	2 Cls.	3 Cls.	Stations.	1	2 1,2,3	3 1,2,3	4 1 &2	5 1,2,3	6 1 &2	
Dis.	fr. c.	fr. c.	fr. c.		p.m.	a.m.	p.m.	a.m.	a.m.	a.m.	
231¼	..	..	..	PARIS ....dep.	8 0	..	11 0	7 30	..	11 45	..
139¼	..	..	..	AMIENS .... „	11 5	..	4 0	9 55	..	2 30	..
97	..	..	.	ARRAS.......... „	12 55	..	6 8	11 36	..	4 20	..
80½	..	..	..	DOUAI .... „	1 37	..	7 0	12 15	..	5 10	..
58	..	..	..	VALENCIENNES..arr.	2 25	..	8 0	1 10	..	5 55	..
..	..	..	..	„ dep.	2 40	5 30	8 25	1 30	..	6 15	..
51¼	..	..	..	Blanc-Misseron	2 56	5 45	8 41	1 51	..	6 25	..
50	From	Quie	vrain	**Quievrain** ...... arr	3 0	6 0	8 55	2 0	..	6 40	..
..	..	..	..	„ ......dep.	3 30	6 15	9 15	2 20	4 15	7 5	..
47½	0 80	0 30	0 20	Thulin	..	6 20	9 20	2 25	4 20	..	..
45	0 80	0 50	0 30	Boussu	..	6 25	.	..	4 25	..	..
43¾	0 80	0 60	0 40	St. Ghislain...........	3*45	6 35	9 30	2 35	3 35	..	..
40½	1 20	0 90	0 60	Jemmappes	3*55	6 45	9 40	2 40	4 45	..	..
38	1 50	1 15	0 75	**Mons**..............	4 5	6 55	9 45	2 55	4 55	7 35	..
30½	2 50	1 85	1 25	Jurbise	..	7 30	10 5	3 20	5 25	7 45	..
22¼	3 50	2 65	1 75	Soignies	..	7 50	10 25	3 35	5 40	..	..
18¾	4 0	3 0	2 0	**Braine-le-Comte** ar.	4 55	8 5	10 40	3 55	6 0	8 25	..
..	..	..	..	„ dep.	4 50	8 5	10 40	3 55	6 0	8 25	..
12½	4 90	3 65	2 45	Tubize	..	8 25	11 0	4 10	..	..	..
10¾	5 10	3 85	5 55	Lembecq	..	..	11 5	..	..	..	..
8¾	5 30	3 95	2 65	Hal	..	8 30	11 10	4 20	6 25	8 45	..
6¼	5 60	4 20	2 80	Loth	..	..	..	..	..	..	..
4¼	5 85	4 40	2 90	Ruysbroeck	..	8 40	11 25	4 30	..	..	..
2½	6 10	4 55	3 5	Forest	..	..	..	..	..	..	..
—	6 40	4 80	3 20	**Brussels** ....arrival	6 0	9 0	11 45	5 0	7 0	9 15	..
				SOUTH STATION.	a.m.	a.m.	a.m.	p.m.	p.m.	p.m.	..

Observations.—Trains Nos. 1, 2, 4 & 5, correspond and change carriages at Braine-le-Comte for Charleroi and Namur.—See page 61.

* Train No. 1 will only call at these two stations when there are passengers to take up or set down.

BRUSSELS, CHARLEROI, AND NAMUR.

Eng. Mls.	Fares. 1 Cl.	2 Cl.	3 Cl.	Stations.	Trains. 1 1,2,3	2 1 & 2	3 1,2,3	4 1 & 2	5	6
Dis.	fr. c.	fr. c.	fr. c.	SOUTH STATION	a.m.	a.m.	p.m.	p.m.		..
—	—	—	—	**Brussels** ....dep.	5 0	8 15	3 15	6 30	..	..
2½	0 80	0 30	0 20	Forest	5 5	..	3 20	..	..	..
4¼	0 80	0 40	0 30	Ruysbroeck	5 10	..	3 25	..	..	..
6¼	0 80	0 60	0 40	Loth	5 15	8 25	3 30	..	..	..
8¾	1 20	0 90	0 60	Hal............	5 25	8 30	3 40	..	..	..
10¾	1 35	1 0	0 70	Lembecq	5 30	8 35	3 45	..	..	..
12½	1 60	1 20	0 80	Tubize	5 40	..	3 50	..	..	..
18¾	2 50	1 85	1 25	**Br.le-Comte**............arr.	6 15	9 5	4 25	7 20	..	..
..	..	..	..	,, (1) ....dep.	6 15	9 5	4 25	7 25	..	..
22½	2 95	2 20	1 50	Ecaussines	6 25	9 15	4 35	7 35	..	..
28	3 60	2 70	1 80	Manage...... (2)	6 50	9 25	4 55	7 45	..	..
32¼	4 15	3 10	2 10	Gouy-lez-Piéton	7 5	..	5 10	..	..	..
34¼	4 40	3 30	2 20	Pont-a-Celles	7 15	..	5 15	..	..	..
35½	4 65	3 50	2 30	Luttre	7 20	..	5 20	..	..	..
38¾	5 5	3 80	2 50	Gosselies	7 35	9 55	5 30	8 10	..	..
40½	5 5	3 80	2 50	Roux	7 40	..	5 40	..	..	..
42½	5 5	3 80	2 50	Marchiennes............	7 50	10 5	5 45	8 20	..	..
45	5 5	3 80	2 50	**Charleroi** (3)............	8 5	10 15	5 50	8 25	..	..
49¼	5 60	4 20	2 80	Chatelineau	8 15	10 25	6 5	8 35	..	..
51¼	5 75	4 30	2 90	Farciennes	8 25	..	6 10	..	..	..
54¼	6 15	4 60	3 10	Tamines	8 35	10 40	6 20	8 50	..	..
55½	6 40	4 80	3 20	Auvelais	8 45	..	6 25	..	..	..
59¼	6 80	5 10	3 40	Moustier	8 55	..	6 35	..	..	..
62½	6 90	5 15	3 45	Floreffe............	9 5	..	6 45	..	..	..
68	6 90	5 15	3 45	**Namur** (4) ....arr.	9 30	11 25	7 15	9 30	..	..
					a.m.	a.m.	p.m.	p.m.		

(1) Braine-le-Comte to Tournay, see page 62.
(2) Manage to l'Olive and Mons, see page 67.
(3) Morialme to Charleroi, see page 65.
(4) Namur to Liege, see page 64.

NAMUR, CHARLEROI, AND BRUSSELS.

Eng. Mls.	Fares. 1 Cl.	2 Cl.	3 Cl.	Stations.	Trains. 1 1,2,3	2 1 & 2	3 1,2,3	4	5	6
Dis.	fr. c.	fr. c.	fr. c.		a.m.	a.m.	p.m.	p.m.		
68	—	—	—	**Namur** ....dep.	5 30	8 15	2 30	5 15	..	..
62½	0 80	0 55	0 35	Floreffe	5 40	..	2 40	..	..	..
59¼	1 20	0 90	0 60	Moustier	5 50	..	2 50	..	..	..
55½	1 60	1 20	0 80	Auvelais............	6 5	..	3 0	..	..	..
54¼	1 85	1 40	0 90	Tamines............	6 10	8 35	3 5	5 35	..	..
51¼	2 25	1 70	1 40	Farciennes	6 20	..	3 15	..	..	..
49¼	2 50	1 85	1 25	Chatelineau	6 25	8 45	3 20	5 45	..	..
45	2 95	2 20	1 50	**Charleroi**	6 45	9 5	3 40	6 5	..	..
42½	3 30	2 45	1 65	Marchiennes............	6 50	9 10	3 45	6 10	..	..
40½	3 50	2 65	1 75	Roux	6 55	..	3 55	..	..	..
38¾	3 75	2 80	1 90	Gosselies	7 5	9 15	4 5	6 15	..	..
35½	4 15	3 10	2 10	Luttre	7 15	..	4 20	..	..	..
34¼	4 30	3 25	2 15	Pont-a-Celles	7 20	..	4 25	..	..	..
32¼	4 55	3 40	2 30	Gouy-lez-Piéton	7 25	..	4 35	..	..	..
28	5 20	3 90	2 60	Manage	7 40	9 40	4 55	6 35	..	..
22¼	5 85	4 40	2 90	Ecaussines	8 0	9 55	5 20	6 50	..	..
18¾	6 30	4 75	3 15	**Br. le Comte** ..arr.	8 25	10 15	5 45	7 10	..	..
..	..	..	..	,, (4) dep.	8 25	10 20	6 0	7 10	..	..
12½	6 90	5 15	3 45	Tubize	8 40	..	..	..	..	..
10¾	6 90	5 15	3 45	Lembecq	8 45	..	..	..	..	..
8¾	6 90	5 15	3 45	Hal............	8 55	10 40	6 25	7 30	..	..
6¼	6 90	5 15	3 45	Loth	9 5	..	..	..	..	..
4¼	6 90	5 15	3 45	Ruysbroeck	9 10	..	..	..	..	..
2½	6 90	5 15	3 45	Forest	..	..	..	..	..	..
—	6 90	5 15	3 45	**Brussels** ....arr.	9 30	11 10	7 0	8 0	..	..
					a.m.	a.m.	p.m.	p.m.		

Observations.—Trains Nos. 1, 3, and 4 correspond, and change carriages at Braine-le-Comte for Mons and Quievrain, see page 60. Trains Nos. 1 and 4 correspond at Braine-le-Comte and Jurbise for Tournay, see page 62.

(4) *Braine-le-Comte to Mons, Valenciennes, and Paris, see page 60.*

BRUSSELS, BRAINE-LE-COMTE, JURBISE, TOURNAY, LILLE, CALAIS, and LONDON.

English Miles.	Fares.			Stations.	Daily Trains.									
	1st Class	2nd Class	3rd Class		1 1,2,3 Clss	2 1,2,3 Clss	3 1 & 2 Class	4 1st Clss	5 1 & 2 Clss	6 1, 2, 3 Class	7 1, 2, 3 Class	8 1, 2, 3 Class	9 1 & 2 Clss	10 1, 2, 3 Class
Dis.	fr. c.	fr. c.	fr. c.		a.m.	a.m.	p.m.	p.m.	a.m.	p.m.	p.m.	p.m.	a.m.	a.m.
..	..	..	..	COLOGNE .... dep.	..	..	11 30	11 30	..	..	..	..	8 0	8 0
..	..	..	..	BRUSSELS (N. Sta.) arr.	..	..	6 45	6 45	..	..	..	..	3 15	3 15
	From	Bruss	els.				a.m.	a.m.	a m.	p.m.	p.m.	p.m.	p.m.	p.m.
—	—	—	—	**Brussels** (S. Sta.) dep.	..	5 0	7 30	8 0	8 15	1 15	3 15	5 15	6 30	6 45
2½	0 80	0 30	0 20	Forest	..	5 5	..	..	...	..	3 20	5 20	..	..
4¼	0 80	0 40	0 30	Ruysbroeck	..	5 10	7 35	..	...	1 20	3 25	5 25	.	6 50
6¼	0 80	0 60	0 40	Loth	..	5 15	..	..	8 25	..	3 30	5 30	..	..
8¾	1 20	0 90	0 60	**Hal**	.	5 25	7 50	..	8 30	1 35	3 40	5 40	..	7 5
10¾	1 35	1 0	0 70	Lembecq	..	5 30	..	..	8 35	..	3 45	5 45	..	..
12½	1 60	1 20	0 80	Tubize		5 40	8 0	..	...	1 45	3 50	5 50	..	7 15
18¾	2 50	1 85	1 25	**Braine-le-Comte** ..	..	6 25	8 25	8 45	9 5	2 15	4 25	6 15	7 20	7 45
22¼	2 95	2 20	1 50	Soignies	..	6 40	..			2 25		6 25		7 55
30½	4 0	3 0	2 0	**Jurbise**	..	7 25	8 55		..	3 35	For Namur.	6 35	For Paris and Namur.	8 20
33	4 80	3 30	2 20	Lens	..	7 35	..	For Paris.	..	3 40				8 25
36¼	4 80	3 55	2 35	Brugelette	..	7 45	9 5		For Namur.	3 50				8 35
37½	4 90	3 65	2 45	Attres	..	7 50	..			3 55		For Quievrain.		8 40
39½	5 10	3 85	2 55	Maffles	..	7 55	..			4 0				8 43
40½	5 30	3 95	2 65	**Ath**	..	8 0	9 20			4 10				8 55
43¾	5 70	4 25	2 85	Ligne	..	8 10	..	..		4 15	..			9 0
48	6 25	4 70	3 10	Leuze	..	8 20	9 35	..		4 25	..			9 10
51¾	6 70	5 5	3 35	Bary	..	8 35	..	..	..	4 35	..			9 20
56¾	7 35	5 50	3 70	Havinnes	a.m	8 50	..	..	..	4 50	..			9 35
60½	7 85	5 90	3 90	**Tournay**	6 30	9 15	10 20	..	..	6 0	..			10 0
72½	9 45	7 10	4 70	Mouscron	7 45		10 55	..	..	6 35	..		..	
75½	10 5	7 55	5 5	Tourcoing	8 0	..	11 10	..	..	6 50	..	..	..	..
76¾	10 30	7 70	5 15	Roubaix	8 5	..	11 17	..	..	6 57	..	..	..	..
83	11 25	8 45	5 70	LILLE ....arr.	8 15	..	11 45	..	..	7 15	..	..	..	..
								..				..		..
134¼	19 95	15 10	..	DUNKIRK ... .arr.	..	..	3 0	..	..	..	..	..	..	..
147¼	21 95	16 60	..	CALAIS * ....arr.	..	..	3 0	..	..	..	..	..	..	..
..	..	..	..	,, ...dep.	..	..	3 20	..	..	..	..	..	..	..
168¾	31 95	24 10	..	DOVER..........dep.	..	..	7 30	..	..	..	..	..	..	..
257	60 0	42 45	..	LONDON ...... arr.	..	..	10 15	..	..	..	..	..	..	..
				LONDON BRIDGE STATION.			p.m.							

* For the hours of departure of the Steam-boats from Calais for Dover, see page 127.

Observations.—All the Trains change carriages at Jurbise, for Tournay, except Nos. 3 and 10.

Train No. 3 is a Direct Train, without change of carriages, as far as Mouscron.

Travellers by all the Trains change carriages at Mouscron for Lille, and stations beyond.

Trains Nos. 3 and 6 correspond at Tournay for the line from Tournay to Ghent.

Besides the two regular services of the Steam-boats between Calais and Dover, there is also a Steam-boat service between Calais and London by the General Steam Navigation Company, see page 127.

LONDON, CALAIS, LILLE, TOURNAY, JURBISE, and BRAINE-LE-COMTE.

English Miles.	Fares. 1st Clss	2nd Clss	3rd Clss	Stations.	Daily Trains. 1 1st Class	2 1, 2, 3 Class	3 1, 2, 3 Class	4 1, 2, 3 Class	5 1 & 2 Class	6 1, 2, 3 Class	7 1 2 3 Clss.	8 1 2 3 Clss	9 1 & 2 Clss	10 1 2 3 Clss	11 1 & 2 Clss
Dis.	fr. c.	fr. c.	fr. c	London Bridge Stat.	a.m.	a.m.	a.m.	a.m.	p.m.	a.m.	a.m	p.m.	p.m.	p.m.	p.m.
—	..		..	London ......dep.	..	..	..	..	8 30	..	..	..	..	..	..
88¼	..	From Tournay.	..	Dover........dep.	..	..	..	..	11 0	..	..	..	..	..	..
110	..		..	Calais........arr.	..	..	..	..	1 0	..	..	..	..	..	..
..	..		..	Do. ......dep.	..	..	..	..	2 0	..	..	..	..	..	..
..	..		..	Dunkirk ......dep.	..	..	..	..	..	..	..	..	..	..	..
174	..		..	Lille ....dep.	..	..	..	..	6 0	..	9 15	..	..	2 50	..
180¼	..		..	Roubaix	..	..	..	..	6 16	..	9 30	..	..	3 6	..
181½	..		..	Tourcoing............	..	..	..	..	6 22	..	9 40	..	..	3 12	..
184½	..		..	Mouscron	..	..	..	..	7 40	..	10 55	..	..	4 10	..
196½	..		..	**Tournay**	..	..	5 30	..	8 25	..	12 55	..	..	4 55	..
200¼	0 80	0 40	0 30	Havinnes	..	..	..	..	..	..	1 5	From Quievrain.	..	5 10	..
205¼	1 20	0 90	0 60	Bary	..	..	5 55	..	..		1 20		..	5 25	
209	1 70	1 25	0 85	Leuze		..	6 5	From Namur.	8 55	From Paris.	1 35			5 35	From Paris.
212¾	2 15	1 60	1 10	Ligne...............	From Paris.	..	6 15		..		1 45		From Namur.	5 45	
215¾	2 55	1 90	1 30	**Ath**		..	6 30		9 15		2 0			5 55	
217¾	2 80	2 10	1 40	Maffles		..	6 35		..		2 5			6 0	
219½	2 95	2 20	1 50	Attres		..	6 45		..		2 15			6 10	
220¾	3 10	2 35	1 55	Brugelette		..	6 55		9 25		2 25			6 15	
223¾	3 50	2 65	1 75	Lens		..	7 5		..		2 35			6 25	
226¼	3 85	2 90	1 90	**Jurbise**		..	7 30		9 43	10 5	3 20	5 25		6 45	7 45
234½	4 90	3 70	2 40	Soignies	..	..	7 50	..	..	10 25	3 30	5 45		7 5	..
238¼	5 45	4 10	2 70	**Braine-le-Comte.**	4 55	6 15	8 5	8 25	10 20	10 40	3 55	6 0	7 10	7 25	8 25
245	6 25	4 70	3 10	Tubize	..	6 40	8 25	8 40	..	11 0	4 10	..	..	7 45	..
246¾	6 50	4 90	3 20	Lembecq	..	..	..	8 45	..	11 5	..	..	..	7 50	..
248¼	6 55	5 0	3 30	**Hal**	..	6 55	8 30	8 55	11 40	11 10	4 20	6 25	7 30	7 55	8 45
251¼	7 5	5 30	3 50	Loth	..	7 5	..	9 5	..	..	..	..	..	8 5	..
253	7 30	5 50	3 60	Ruysbroeck	..	7 10	8 40	9 10	..	11 25	4 30	..	..	8 10	..
255	7 45	5 60	3 70	Forest	..	7 15	..	..	..	..	..	..	..	8 15	..
257	7 85	5 90	3 90	**Brussels** (S. Sta.) ar.	6 0	7 30	9 0	9 30	11 10	11 45	5 0	7 0	8 0	8 30	9 15
					a.m.	a.m.	a.m.	a.m.	a.m.	a.m.	a.m.	p.m.	p.m.	p.m.	p.m.
..	..	..	..	Brussels (N. Sta) dep.	7 0	..	10 15	..	..	..	..	..	..	9 30	..
..	32 70	24 10	16 20	Cologne ....arr.	4 15	..	6 0	..	..	..	..	..	..	5 0	..
					p.m.		p.m.							a.m.	

Observations.—The first class fare between London and Dover by express train is 27frs. 50c.

For the time of the departure of the Steam Packets between Dover and Calais, see page 128.

Train No. 10 is a direct train between Mouscron and Brussels.

Trains Nos. 3 and 7 change carriages at Jurbise.

Train No. 7 is a first and second class only from Jurbise.

NAMUR TO LIEGE. (With MAP.)

[6-53

English Miles.	Fares. 1st Class	2nd Class	3rd Class	STATIONS.	Trains. 1	2	3	4	5	6	7	8	9	10
					1,2,3	1,2,3	3rd	1, 2, 3	1,2,3	3rd.	1,2,3			
Dis.	fr. c.	fr. c.	fr. c.		a.m.	a.m.	a.m.	a.m.	p.m.	p.m.	p.m.			
—	—	—	—	***Namur**......departure	..	6 30	8 15	11 30	1 0	4 5	7 20	..	..	..
4¼	..	..	..	Marche-les-Dames	..	6 40	..	..	..	4 15	7 30	..	..	..
6¼	..	..	..	Namèche	..	6 45	..	11 45	..	4 25	7 35	..	..	..
8¾	..	..	..	Sclaigneaux	..	6 55	8 50	..	1 45	4 35	7 40	..	..	..
11¼	1 60	1 20	0 80	Andenne	..	7 5	9 10	11 55	2 10	4 45	7 50	..	..	..
15½	..	..	..	Bas-Oha............	..	7 20	9 30	..	2 35	5 0	8 5	..	..	..
18	2 50	1 85	1 25	**Huy**..............	6 30	7 40	10 15	12 20	3 30	5 15	8 20	..	..	..
..	..	..	..	Ampsin	6 40	..	..	..	..	5 25	8 30	..	..	..
22¼	..	..	..	Amay	6 45	7 55	10 35	12 30	3 50	5 30	8 35	..	..	..
..	..	..	..	Hermalle	..	8 0	..	..	..	5 40	8 40	..	..	..
26¾	..	..	..	Engis	7 0	8 5	..	12 40	..	5 45	8 50	..	..	..
..	..	..	..	Chokier	7 5	..	..	..	..	..	..	..	..	..
29¼	..	..	..	Flémalle...............	7 10	8 10	11 15	12 50	4 30	5 50	8 55	..	..	..
31¾	..	..	..	Seraing	..	8 20	11 35	1 0	5 0	6 0	9 5	..	..	..
34¼	..	..	..	Ougrée	..	8 25	..	1 5	..	6 5	9 10	..	..	..
31¾	..	..	..	Jemeppe	7 25	..	..	1 0	..	6 0	..	..	..	..
33	..	..	..	Tilleur	7 30	..	..	..	..	6 5	..	..	..	..
36¼	..	..	..	**Liege**-Guillemins ..	7 45	..	..	1 15	..	6 15	..	..	..	..
38	4 90	3 65	2 45	†**Liege**-Longdoz	..	8 40	..	1 20	5 30	6 15	9 20	..	..	..

LIEGE TO NAMUR.

English Miles.	Fares. 1st Class	2nd Class	3rd Class	STATIONS.	Trains. 1	2	3	4	5	6	7	8	9	10
					1,2,3	3rd.	1,2,3	1, 2, 3	1,2,3	1, 2, 3	1,2,3			
Dis.	fr. c.	fr. c.	fr. c.		a.m.	a.m.	a.m.	p.m.	p.m.	p.m.	p.m.			
—	—	—	—	†**Liege**-Longdoz	6 0	7 0	11 0	3 0	3 30	6 50	..	..	..	..
2½	..	..	..	**Liege**-Guillemins ..	..	..	10 50	2 45	..	..	7 0	..	..	..
5½	..	..	..	Tilleur	..	..	..	2 55	..	..	7 10	..	..	..
6¾	..	..	..	Jemeppe	..	..	11 10	3 0	..	..	7 15	..	..	..
3¾	..	..	..	Ougrée	6 10	..	..	3 10	..	7 0	..	..	..	..
5½	0 65	0 50	0 35	Seraing	6 15	7 40	11 15	3 15	4 0	7 5	..	..	..	..
8¾	..	..	..	Flémalle	6 25	8 20	11 25	3 25	4 30	7 15	7 30	..	..	..
..	..	..	..	Chokier	..	..	..	..	..	..	7 35	..	..	..
11¼	..	..	..	Engis	6 30	..	11 30	3 30	..	7 20	7 40	..	..	..
..	..	..	..	Hermalle	6 40	..	..	3 40	..	..	7 50	..	..	..
15½	..	..	..	Amay	6 45	8 45	11 45	3 45	5 0	7 35	7 55	..	..	..
..	..	..	..	Ampsin	6 50	..	..	..	..	..	8 0	..	..	..
20	2 50	1 85	1 25	**Huy**	7 0	9 30	12 0	4 0	5 45	7 50	8 10	..	..	..
21¾	..	..	..	Bas-Oha	7 5	..	12 10	4 10	..	8 0	—	..	..	..
26¾	3 35	2 55	1 70	Andenne	7 15	10 25	12 20	4 20	6 30	8 10	..	..	..	..
29¼	..	..	..	Sclaigneaux	7 25	..	12 30	4 30	..	8 20	..	..	..	..
31¾	..	..	..	Namèche	7 35	..	12 40	4 40	7 0	8 30	..	..	..	..
33½	..	..	..	Marche-les-Dames	7 45	..	12 50	4 50	..	8 40	..	..	..	..
38	4 90	3 65	2 45	***Namur** .... arrival	8 0	11 30	1 0	5 0	7 30	8 50	..	..	..	..

* NAMUR TO BRUSSELS, see page 61. † LIEGE TO BRUSSELS, see page 57.

Observations.—Passengers should be at the Stations at least 10 minutes before the time indicated in this Table. Every information, and Time Bills, may be obtained at all the Stations.

BRUSSELS TO MALINES AND ANTWERP.

English Miles.	Fares. 1st Cls.	2nd Cls.	3rd Cls.	Stations.	Trains. 1 1,2 3 Clss	2 1—2 Clss	3 1st Class	4 1, 2, 3 Class	5 2& 3 Clss	6 1-2 Class	7 1,2 3 Clss	8 1, 2, 3 Class	9 1st Clss	10	11
Dis.	fr. c.	fr. c.	fr. c.	NORTH STATION.	a.m.	a.m.	a.m.	a.m.	p.m.	p.m.	p.m.	p.m.	p.m.		
—	—	—	—	**Brussels** ....dep.	6 45	8 30	..	10 45	..	2 30	4 0	8 0	9 30	..	..
6½	0 80	0 60	0 40	Vilvorde	6 55	..	..	..	..	2 40	4 10	..	..	..	..
12½	1 70	1 25	0 85	**Malines** (2)	7 15	8 55	10 15	11 10	12 25	2 55	4 30	8 25	9 55	..	..
17½	2 30	1 75	1 15	Duffel	7 25	..	..	11 20	12 35	..	4 40	8 35	..	..	..
20½	2 70	2 5	1 35	Contich	7 35	..	..	11 25	12 45	..	4 50	8 45	..	..	..
23½	3 5	2 30	1 50	Vieux Dieu	7 45	..	..	..	1 0	..	5 0	8 55	..	..	..
27½	3 50	2 65	1 75	**Antwerp** (1) ......arr.	8 0	9 30	11 0	11 50	1 30	3 30	5 15	9 15	10 30	..	..

ANTWERP TO MALINES AND BRUSSELS.

	Fares. 1st Cls.	2nd Cs.	3rd Cls.	Stations.	Trains. 1 1,2 3 Clss	2 1,2 3 Clss	3 1—2 Class	4 1,2,3 Clss	5 1—2 Clss	6 1,2 3 Clss	7 1, 2, 3 Class	8 1.2,3 Clss	9 1 & 2 Class	10	11
	fr. c.	fr. c.	fr. c.		a.m.	a.m.	a.m.	a.m.	p.m	p.m.	a.m.	p.m.	p.m.		
..	—	—	—	**Antwerp** (1) .... dep.	6 15	7 45	10 0	11 30	2 45	4 15	5 30	7 30	9 10	..	..
..	0 80	0 35	0 25	Vieux-Dieu	6 20	7 50	..	11 35	..	4 20	5 40	7 35	..	..	..
..	0 90	0 65	0 45	Contich................	6 25	7 55	..	11 40	..	4 25	5 50	7 40	..	..	..
..	1 30	0 95	0 65	Duffel	6 35	8 5	..	11 50	..	4 35	6 0	7 50	..	..	..
..	1 90	1 45	0 95	**Malines** (2)	6 55	8 25	10 30	12 15	3 15	4 55	6 30	8 15	9 40	..	..
..	2 80	2 10	1 40	Vilvorde	7 10	8 40	..	12 30	..	5 10	..	8 30	..	..	..
..	3 50	2 65	1 75	**Brussels** ...... arr.	7 30	9 0	11 0	12 50	3 45	5 30	..	8 45	10 10	..	..

Observations.—Trains Nos. 1, 2, & 4 correspond at Malines for Ghent and Ostend, see page 58. For Tournay and Lille, see page 59. Nos. 1, 2, 5, & 6 for Liege and Verviers. For Cologne, except by No. 5, see pages 56 and 57. Nos. 1, 2, & 5 for Hasselt, see page 67.

(1) For Steamers from Antwerp to London, see page 126. From Antwerp to Hull, see page 126. For Trains from Antwerp to Ghent (via Pays de Waes), see page 66.
(2) Malines to Liege, Verviers, and Cologne, see page 56.

SAMBRE AND MEUSE.—Length, 25 miles.

From CHARLEROI to WALCOURT, at 7.40 a.m., 2.15 and 5.35 p.m.

From CHARLEROI to MORIALME, at 7.40 a.m., and 2.15 p.m.

,, ,, to THUIN, at 5.45 and 7.25 a.m., 1.0 and 5.30 p.m.

,, ,, to ERQUELINNES, at 7.25 a.m., and 1.0 p.m.

From WALCOURT to CHARLEROI, at 6.10 & 11.15 a.m., and 4.0 p.m.

From MORIALME to CHARLEROI, at 10.20 a.m. and 3.15 p.m.

From THUIN to CHARLEROI, at 6.25 and 9.4 a.m., 4.16 and 6.10 p.m.

From ERQUELINNES to CHARLEROI, at 8.35 a.m., and 3.45 p.m.

West Flanders.—BRUGES, ROULERS, COURTRAY, & WERVICQ.

Eng Mls.	Fares.			Stations.	Trains.						
	1 Cl.	2 Cl.	3 Cl.		1	2	3	4	5	6	7
Dis.	fr. c.	fr. c.	fr. c.		a.m.	a.m.	p.m.	p.m.	p.m.		
—	—	—	—	**Bruges** .... dep.	..	8 0	12 30	3 45	7 15	..	..
..	..	..	..	Thourout	..	8 30	1 0	4 25	7 40	..	..
..	..	..	..	Lichtervelde	..	8 35	1 10	4 35	..	..	..
..	..	..	..	**Roulers**	..	9 0	1 30	5 0	8 0	..	..
..	..	..	..	Iseghem	..	9 20	1 50	5 20	8 10	..	..
..	..	..	..	Ingelmunster	..	9 30	2 0	5 30	8 15	..	..
..	4 0	3 0	2 0	**Courtray** .... arr.	..	10 0	2 30	6 0	8 25	..	..
..	..	..	..	Do. .... dep.	7 40	11 30	3 0	—	8 40	..	..
..	..	..	..	Menin	7 55	11 45	3 15	..	8 55	..	..
..	..	..	..	**Wervicq** .... arr.	8 10	11 0	3 30	..	9 10	..	..

These trains correspond with the government trains going to OSTEND, GHENT, BRUSSELS, and ANTWERP.—Tickets for Ostend, Ghent, Brussels, Liege, Mouscron, and Tournay, are delivered at Bruges Thourout, Roulers, Iseghem, and Courtray, and in the great stations tickets are delivered for Bruges Thourout Lichtervelde, Iseghem, Courtray.—Passengers arriving from PARIS by the night train, or from Calais by the 2 a.m. train, will find at Mouscron a train going direct to OSTEND.

Eng Mls.	Fares.			Stations.	Trains.						
	1 Cl.	2 Cl.	3 Cl.		1	2	3	4	5	6	7
Dis.	fr. c.	fr. c.	fr. c.		a.m.	a.m.	noon.	p.m.	p.m.		
—	—	—	—	**Wervicq** .... dep.	6 45	9 0	11 45	..	6 30	..	..
..	..	..	..	Menin	6 50	9 5	11 50	..	6 35	..	..
..	..	..	..	**Courtray** .... arr.	7 10	9 25	12 10	..	6 55	..	..
..	..	..	..	Do. .... dep.	7 40	—	12 25	4 20	7 5	..	..
..	..	..	..	Ingelmunster	8 10	..	12 50	4 40	7 20	..	..
..	..	..	..	Iseghem	8 20	..	1 0	4 45	7 25	..	..
..	..	..	..	**Roulers**	8 40	..	1 15	5 0	7 40	..	..
..	..	..	..	Lichtervelde	9 0	..	1 35	5 15	8 0	..	..
..	..	..	..	Thourout	9 10	..	1 45	5 20	8 10	..	..
..	..	..	..	**Bruges** .... arr.	9 40	..	2 5	5 40	8 30	..	..

Corresponding at Courtray with the trains for Mouscron, Tournay, Lille, and Paris, by the Northern Line

ANTWERP AND GHENT (through the Pays de Waes).

Eng Mls.	Fares.			Stations.	Trains.						
	1 Cl.	2 Cl.	3 Cl.		1	2	3	4	5	6	7
Dis.	fr. c.	fr. c.	fr. c.		a.m.	a.m.	a.m.	p.m.	p.m	p.m.	
—	—	—	—	**Antwerp** (2) .... dep.	5 30	9 0	11 0	2 30	5 0	7 0	..
2½	0 75	0 50	0 30	Zwyndrecht	5 45	..	..	..	5 15	7 15	..
5½	0 80	0 60	0 40	Beveren	5 55	9 25	11 20	2 50	5 25	7 25	..
9½	1 30	0 95	0 65	Nieukerke	6 5	..	..	..	5 35	7 35	..
11¾	1 50	1 15	0 75	**St. Nicolas**	6 15	9 40	11 45	3 5	5 45	7 45	..
15½	2 0	1 50	1 0	Mille-Pommes	6 25	..	..	3 20	5 55	7 55	..
20	2 55	1 90	1 30	Lokeren	6 40	10 5	12 5	3 40	6 10	8 10	..
25½	3 30	2 45	1 65	Beirvelde	6 50	..	..	3 50	6 20	8 25	..
31¼	4 0	3 0	2 0	**Ghent** .... (1) .... arr.	7 20	10 30	12 30	4 10	6 35	8 40	..

Eng Mls.	Fares.			Stations.	Trains.						
	1 Cl.	2	3 Cl.		1	2	3	4	5	6	7
Dis.	fr. c.	fr. c.	fr. c.		a.m.	a.m.	a.m.	p.m.	p.m.	p.m.	
—	—	—	—	**Ghent** ... (1) .... dep.	5 20	9 5	11 0	2 15	4 50	6 50	..
5½	0 80	0 60	0 40	Beirvelde	5 35	..	..	..	5 0	7 0	..
11¼	1 50	1 15	0 75	Lokeren	5 50	9 30	11 25	2 40	5 20	7 20	..
15½	2 10	1 55	1 5	Mille-Pommes	6 5	..	..	..	5 30	7 30	..
19¼	2 55	1 90	1 30	**St. Nicolas**	6 15	9 45	11 45	3 5	5 45	7 45	..
21¼	2 80	2 10	1 40	Nieukerke	6 25	..	..	..	5 50	7 50	..
24¾	3 30	2 45	1 65	Beveren	6 35	10 0	11 55	3 20	6 0	8 0	..
28½	3 70	2 75	1 85	Zwyndrecht	6 45	..	..	..	6 10	8 10	..
31¼	4 0	3 0	2 0	**Antwerp** .. (2) .... arr.	7 20	10 25	12 25	3 50	6 25	8 30	..

(1.) GHENT to OSTEND, see page 58. GHENT to TOURNAY and LILLE, see page 59.
(2.) ANTWERP to MALINES and BRUSSELS, see page 65. ANTWERP to LIEGE, see page 56.

LANDEN AND HASSELT.

Eng. Miles.	Fares.			Stations.	Trains.						
	1 Cls.	2 Cls.	3 Cls.		1	2	3	4	5	6	7
Dis.	fr. c.	fr. c.	fr. c.		a.m.	a.m.	p.m.	p.m.			
—	—	—	—	**Landen** ....dep.	..	9 15	1 55	8 5	..	..	..
3¼	0 80	0 35	0 25	Velm	..	9 20	2 5	8 15	..	..	..
6½	0 90	0 65	0 45	**St. Trond**..............	6 30	9 35	2 15	8 25	..	..	..
10¾	1 35	1 0	0 70	Cortenbosch	6 40	9 50	2 30	8 40	..	..	..
13¾	1 85	1 40	0 90	Alken	6 45	10 0	2 40	8 55	..	..	..
17¼	2 25	1 70	1 10	**Hasselt** ....arr.	7 0	10 20	3 0	9 10	..	..	..

Eng. Miles.	Fares.			Stations.	Trains.						
	1 Cls.	2 Cls.	3 Cls.		1	2	3	4	5	6	7
Dis.	fr. c.	fr. c.	fr. c.		a.m.	noon.	p.m.	p.m.			
—	—	—	—	**Hasselt** ....dep	8 0	12 30	5 0	9 30	..	..	..
..	..	..	..	Alken	8 5	12 35	5 5	9 35	..	..	..
..	..	..	..	Cortenbosch	8 15	12 45	5 15	9 45	..	..	..
10¾	1 0	0 75	0 75	**St. Trond**..............	8 30	1 0	5 30	10 0	..	..	..
..	..	..	..	Velm	8 45	1 15	5 45		..	..	..
16¾	2 25	1 75	1 25	**Landen** .....(1).....arr.	9 10	1 40	6 10	..	..	..	..

(1) LANDEN to BRUSSELS, see page 57. LANDEN to LIEGE, see page 56.

Observations.—The distance from Brussels to Hasselt is 103 kilometres (64¼ English miles). Trains Nos. 1, 2, and 3, correspond at Landen for Brussels and Antwerp, see pages 65, 57, 58, and 59 Trains Nos. 1, and 3, for Liege and Verviers, see page 56.

MONS AND MANAGE. [6-53

Eng. Miles.	Fares.			Stations.	Trains.						
	1 Cls.	2 Cls.	3 Cls.		1	2	3	4	5	6	7
Dis.					a.m.	a.m.	a.m.	p.m.	p.m.	p.m.	
—	—	—	—	**Mons** ....dep.	..	8 25	10 00	3 30	..	6 50	..
..	..	..	..	Nimy	..	8 35	10 10	3 40	..	6 55	..
..	..	..	..	Obourg	..	8 40	10 20	3 45	..	7 0	..
..	..	..	..	Havré	..	8 50	10 30	3 55	..	7 10	..
..	..	..	..	Bracquegnies	..	9 00	10 45	4 5	..	7 20	..
..	..	..	..	L'Olive	6 40	..	..	..	5 35	..	..
..	..	..	..	Mariemont..................	6 45	..	..	..	5 40	..	..
..	..	..	..	Baume	6 55	..	..	..	5 50	..	..
..	..	..	..	La Louvière	7 10	9 10	11 15	4 20	6 5	7 30	..
..	..	..	..	**Manage** ....arr.	7 30	9 20	11 35	4 40	6 25	7 40	..

Eng. Miles.	Fares,			Stations.	Trains.						
	1 Cls.	2 Cls.	3 Cls.		1	2	3	4	5	6	7
Dis					a.m.	a.m.	a.m.	p.m.	p.m.	p.m.	
—	—	—	—	**Manage**................dep.	7 50	9 40	9 50	1 45	6 40	8 0	..
..	..	..	..	La Louvière	8 5	9 55	10 10	2 0	6 55	8 15	..
..	..	..	..	Baume	..	10 5	..	..	..	8 20	..
..	..	..	..	Mariemont..................	..	10 15	..	..	..	8 30	..
..	..	..	..	L'Olive	..	10 20	..	..	..	8 35	..
..	..	..	..	Bracquegnies	8 15		10 35	2 15	7 5		..
..	..	..	..	Havré	8 25	..	10 50	2 25	7 15	..	..
..	..	..	..	Obourg	8 35	..	11 0	2 35	7 25	..	..
..	.	..	..	Nimy	8 40	..	11 10	2 40	7 30	..	..
..	..	..	..	**Mons** ....arr.	8 45	..	11 20	2 45	7 35	..	..

Fares.—1st Class, 2 frs.; 2nd Class, 1 fr. 50 cents; 3rd Class, 1 fr.

Observations.—Passengers should be at the Station at least ten minutes before the time indicated in this Table.

PRICES OF REFRESHMENTS AT THE BELGIAN RAILWAY STATIONS.

BUFFETS-RESTAURANTS

ETABLIS DANS LES STATIONS DE

MALINES, TIRLEMONT, LANDEN, LIEGE, PEPINSTER, VERVIERS, GAND, COURTRAI, MOUSCRON, BRAINE-LE-COMTE, ET QUIEVRAIN.

TARIF DES COMESTIBLES ET BOISSONS.

	fr.	c.
Bouillon	0	30
Beefsteak aux pommes de terre, avec pain	0	75
Roastbeef aux pommes de terre, avec pain	0	75
Filet de bœuf rôti	0	75
Deux côtelettes de mouton	0	75
Portion de veau chaud ou côtelettes avec pommes de terre	0	60
Portion de poulet chaud	0	90
Veau froid avec un petit pain	0	40
Jambon id. id.	0	40
Bœuf salé id. id.	0	40
Langue fumée id. id.	0	40
Poulet froid, la portion	0	75
Fromage	0	10
Id. Anglais	0	15
Un petit pain beurré	0	07
Id. sans beurre	0	05
Id. beurre et fromage	0	15
Déjeûner (café ou thé, pain et beurre)	0	50
Café, la demi-tasse	0	25
BIERES.		
Une bouteille de Faro ou de Diest	0	30
Le verre	0	10
Une bouteille ou cruch. de lambic	0	40
Une bouteille de Louvain	0	24
Le verre	0	08
Une bouteille de Bière de Bavière	0	75
Bière brune, le verre	0	08
VINS.		
Vin de Bordeaux ordinaire ...la bouteille	2	00
Id. id. ...la ½ id.	1	00
Id. de St.-Julien ...la bouteille	2	50
Id. id. ...la ½ id.	1	25
Id. de St.-Emilion ...la bouteille	2	50
Id. de St.-Estèphe ... id.	2	50
Id. de Cabarus, long bouchon, prémière qualité ...la bouteille	3	50
Vin de Cabarus, long bouchon, seconde qualité ...la bouteille	3	00
Vin de Château-Margaux ... id.	5	00
Id. de Volney ... id.	3	00
Id. de Pommard ... id.	3	00
Id. de Nuits ... id.	3	00
Id. de Châblis ... id.	3	00
Id. de Moselle ... id.	3	50
Id. de Grave, prém. qualité ... id.	3	50
Id. id. seconde id. ... id.	3	00
Id. de Tours ... id.	2	50
Id. de Rhin, prém. qualité ... id.	4	00
Id. id. seconde id. ... id.	3	50
Champagne mousseux ... id.	6	00
VINS DE LIQUEUR.		
Madère ...le verre	0	50
Malaga ... id.	0	50
Muscat ... id.	0	50
Frontignan ou Lunel ... id.	0	50
Porto ... id.	0	60
Sherry (Xérès) ... id.	0	60
LIQUEURS.		
Schiedam ...le verre	0	10
Amer de Hollande ... id.	0	10
Eau-de-Vie ... id.	0	10
Cognac, Rhum, Kirsch ... id.	0	25
Liqueurs fines de toute espèce ... id.	0	25
Marasquin ... id.	0	40
Punch à l'eau chaude ... id.	0	25
RAFRAICHISSEMENTS.		
Sirop de groseille, de mûres, de framboises, de limon, ou de punch ...le verre	0	25
Limonade ou orgeat ... id.	0	25
Grog ou orgeat ... id.	0	30
Eau sucrée avec eau de fleur d'oranger ...id.	0	20
Cigares et tabacs ...		

BELGIAN LINES.

Carriages.—Carriages of 2-wheels are charged 8 frs. from Quievrain to Mons, and 32 frs. to Brussels; those of 4wheels, 12 francs from Quievrain to Mons, and 48 frs. to Brussels; and of 2-wheels, 44 frs. from Mouscron to Brussels.

Dogs.—Dogs are charged at the rate of 3rd class fare.

Private Carriages.—Persons travelling in private carriages pay 3rd class fare, in addition to the charge for the carriage.

DUSSELDORF AND ELBERFELD.—18 English miles.

E. Mls.	Fares. 1 Cl.	2 Cl.	3 Cl.	STATIONS.	1	2	3	4	5	6			
					a.m.	a.m.	a.m.	p.m.	p.m.	p.m.			
	Sgr.	Sgr,	Sgr.	**Dusseldorf**..........departure..	5 45	8 15	11 10	3 10	6 15	9 15	..	..	..
$3\frac{1}{3}$	5	4	$2\frac{1}{2}$	Gerresheim	..	..	..	..	..	..	..	..	..
$5\frac{1}{4}$	8	6	4	Erkrath	..	..	..	..	..	..	..	..	..
$6\frac{3}{4}$	10	8	5	Hochdahl	..	..	..	..	..	..	..	..	..
$9\frac{1}{4}$	15	11	$7\frac{1}{2}$	Haan	..	..	..	..	..	..	..	..	..
$12\frac{1}{4}$	20	14	10	Vohwinkel	6 32	9 2	11 57	3 57	7 2	10 2	..	..	..
$15\frac{3}{4}$	25	18	$12\frac{1}{2}$	**Elberfeld**..Steinbeck ......arrive	6 45	9 15	12 10	4 10	7 15	10 15	..	..	..
18	27	$19\frac{1}{2}$	$13\frac{1}{2}$	,, Doppersberg ..arrive	..	..	..	..	..	..	..	..	..

ELBERFELD AND DUSSELDORF.—18 English Miles.

E. Mls.	Fares. 1 Cl.	2 Cl.	3 Cl.	STATIONS.	1	2	3	4	5	6			
					a.m.	a.m.	p.m.	p.m.	p.m.	p.m.			
—	2	$1\frac{1}{2}$	1	**Elberfeld** Doppersberg ....depart.	..	..	..	..	..	..	..	..	..
..	—	—	—	,, Steinbeck ...... depart.	6 2	9 45	1 40	3 37	5 35	7 55	..	..	..
..	5	4	$2\frac{1}{2}$	Vohwinkel	6 22	10 5	2 0	3 57	5 55	8 15	..	..	..
..	10	7	5	Haan	..	..	..	..	..	..	..	..	..
..	15	10	$7\frac{1}{2}$	Hochdahl	..	..	..	..	..	..	..	..	..
..	17	12	$8\frac{1}{2}$	Erkrath	..	..	..	..	..	..	..	..	..
..	20	14	10	Gerresheim	..	..	..	..	..	..	..	..	..
..	25	18	$12\frac{1}{2}$	**Dusseldorf** ....arrive.	7 2	10 45	2 40	4 37	6 35	8 55	..	..	..

Remarks.—LUGGAGE.—10 lbs. free; every 10 lbs. extra, 1 sgr. Four-wheeled carriage, $3\frac{1}{2}$ Prus. doll.

FRANKFURT TO HOCHST AND SODEN.—$7\frac{1}{2}$ English Miles.

From FRANKFURT to WIESBADEN, HOCHST, and SODEN, at 6.40 and 8.10 a.m.; 12, $2\frac{1}{2}$, 6, and $8\frac{1}{2}$ p.m.
From WIESBADEN to HOCHST and SODEN, at 7.45 a.m.; 2 and 5.35 p.m.
From SODEN to FRANKFURT, at 8.40 and 11.10 a.m.; 3, $6\frac{1}{2}$, and 9 p.m.
To WIESBADEN, at 8 a.m.; 5.50 and 8.20 p.m. To HOCHST, at $12\frac{1}{2}$ p.m.

FARES.—Frankfurt to Soden, 48kr., 36kr., and 24kr. Höchst to Soden, 24kr., 18kr., and 12 kr.

Remarks.—LUGGAGE.—40 lbs. are allowed free; every 10 lbs. extra, 6 kr.

BONN TO COLOGNE—$17\frac{1}{2}$ English miles.

Fares. 1 Cl.	2 Cl.	3 Cl.	4 Cl.	Stations.	Trains. 1	2		4	5	6	7
s.gr.	s.gr.	s.gr.	s.gr.		a.m.	a.m.	a.m.	p.m.	p.m.	p.m.	
..	..	..	..	**Bonn** ....dep.	6 0	8 30	11 40	2 20	5 30	8 10	..
..	3	$2\frac{1}{2}$	2	Roisdorf	..	..	..	..	..	..	..
7	5	4	3	Sechtem	..	..	..	..	..	..	..
10	6	5	4	**Bruhl**	6 20	8 50	12 0	2 40	5 50	8 30	..
12	$7\frac{1}{2}$	6	5	Kalscheuern	..	..	..	..	..	..	..
15	10	$7\frac{1}{2}$	6	**Cologne** ....arr.	6 52	9 22	12 32	3 12	6 22	9 2	..

COLOGNE TO BONN—$17\frac{1}{2}$ English miles.

Fares. 1 Cl.	2 Cl.	3 Cl.	4 Cl.	Stations.	Trains. 1	2	3	4	5	6	7
s.gr.	s.gr.	s.gr.	s.gr.		a.m.	a.m.	a.m.	p.m.	p.m.	p.m.	..
..	..	..	..	**Cologne** ....dep.	6 30	10 15	11 30	2 45	6 0	8 0	..
4	3	$2\frac{1}{2}$	2	Kalscheuern	..	..	..	..	..	..	.
$7\frac{1}{2}$	5	4	3	**Bruhl**	7 0	10 45	12 0	3 15	6 30	8 30	..
9	6	5	4	Sechtem	..	..	..	..	..	..	..
12	8	6	5	Roisdorf	..	..	..	..	..	..	..
15	10	$7\frac{1}{2}$	5	**Bonn** ....arr.	7 22	11 7	12 22	3 37	6 52	8 52	..

Remarks.—LUGGAGE.—11 lbs. free; every 10 lbs. extra, 1 sgr. Four-wheeled carriage, 3 Prus. doll.; two-wheeled, 2 Prus. doll.

For Steamers from Bonn to Coblence, Mayence & Biberich, for Frankfurt & Wiesbaden, see advertisement, page 339. From Cologne to Arnheim, see advertisement, page 337.

COLOGNE TO DUSSELDORF, HAMM, AND MINDEN. [15-11-52

English Miles.	Fares.				STATIONS.	Trains.						
	1st Class	2nd Class	3rd Class	4th Class		1	2	3	4	5	6	7
Dis.	Sgr.	Sgr.	Sgr.	Sgr.		a.m.	a.m.	a.m.	p.m.	p.m.	p.m.	
—	—	—	—	—	**Deutz (Cologne)** ......departure	...	6 30	8 0	11 0	4 0	8 0	...
2¼	4	3	2	...	Mulheim	...	...	8 9	11 9	4 9	...	...
...	...	...	...	...	Kuppersteg	...	...	8 25	11 25	4 25	...	...
11¼	16	11	8	...	Langenfeld	...	...	8 38	11 38	4 38	...	...
16	23	15	12	...	Benrath	...	...	8 53	11 53	4 53	...	...
23	30	20	15	...	**Dusseldorf**..................arrival	...	7 15	9 9	12 10	5 10	8 55	...
					" ....departure	...	7 21	9 16	12 20	5 20	9 2	...
...	...	...	...	...	Calcum	...	...	9 35	12 40	5 40	...	...
...	...	...	...	...	Groszenbaum	...	...	9 47	...	5 53	...	...
39	50	34	25	...	**Duisburg**	...	...	10 1	1 4	6 9	9 39	...
43½	56	38	28	...	Oberhausen	...	8 2	10 18	1 23	6 30	9 56	...
...	...	...	...	...	Berge-Borbeck........................	...	...	10 34	...	6 51	...	...
51	65	44	33	...	Essen	...	...	10 41	1 47	7 1	10 16	...
...	...	...	...	...	Gelsenkirchen	...	...	10 54	...	7 18	...	...
...	...	...	...	...	Herne-Bochum	...	...	11 12	2 20	7 44	...	...
...	...	...	...	...	Castrop	...	...	11 25	...	7 56	...	...
...	...	...	...	...	Mengede	...	...	11 36	2 45	8 7	...	...
73½	95	63	47	...	**Dortmund** ....departure	...	9 4	11 55	3 5	8 27	11 16	...
...	108	72	54	...	Camen	...	...	12 22	3 31	8 52	...	...
91½	120	80	60	...	**Hamm**.........[1]..............arrival	...	9 41	12 55	4 3	9 15	12 0	...
					" ....departure	...	...	...	...	...	...	...
...	...	...	...	...	Ahlen	...	...	...	4 27	...	...	...
...	...	...	...	...	Beckum	...	...	...	4 47	...	...	...
...	...	...	...	...	Oelde	...	...	...	5 6	...	...	...
116¾	152	102	76	...	Rheda	...	...	...	5 24	...	...	...
...	159	106	80	...	Gutersloh	7 30	10 48	...	5 44	...	1 22	...
...	...	...	...	...	Brackwede	8 3	...	...	6 13	...	...	...
133	173	115	87	...	**Bielefeld**	8 17	11 15	...	6 25	...	1 55	...
141½	184	123	92	...	Herford	8 47	...	...	6 49	...	...	...
150¾	197	131	99	...	Bad Oeynhausen (Rehme)...........	9 20	...	...	7 15	...	...	...
...	...	...	...	...	Porta	9 40	...	...	7 34	...	...	...
161	210	140	105	...	**Minden**......................arrival	9 52	12 9	...	7 45	...	3 5	...
...	312	207	147	...	BREMEN .... "	...	4 0	...	...	...	10 10	...
200	262	172	125	...	HANOVER .... "	...	1 45	...	10 0	...	5 10	...
...	382	255	175	...	HARBURG (Hamburg) ...... "	...	6 40	...	...	...	10 25	...
237	309	206	146	...	BRUNSWICK .... "	...	3 22	...	12 30	...	7 5	...
300½	394	261	181	...	MAGDEBURG .... "	...	6 1	...	4 50	...	9 50	...
390¾	535	362	250	...	BERLIN .... "	...	9 21	...	9 15	...	1 10	...

Remarks.—LUGGAGE: 50 lbs. free; every 10 lbs. extra, 7 sgr. Four-wheeled carriage, 41 Prus. doll. 21 sgr.; two-wheeled carriage, 27 Prus. doll. 24 sgr.

[1] HAMM to MUNSTER, see below.

For Trains from BRUSSELS, LIEGE, and AIX-LA-CHAPELLE, to COLOGNE, see pages 56 and 57.
For Trains between HANOVER, BRUNSWICK, and MAGDEBURG, see pages 84 ,85, and 86.
For Trains from BERLIN to MAGDEBURG, see page 96.

MUNSTER TO HAMM.—20¾ English Miles.

From HAMM to DRENSTEINFURT and MUNSTER, at 7½ a.m., 1¼, and 4¼ p.m.
MUNSTER to DRENSTEINFURT and HAMM, at 6 and 10½ a.m., and 2½ p.m.

Fares.—From Munster to Drensteinfurt—1st Class, 16 sgr.; 2nd Class, 11 sgr.; 3rd Class, 8 sgr.; 4th Class, 5½ sgr. Munster to Hamm, 1st Class, 30 sgr.; 2nd Class, 20 sgr.; 3rd Class, 15 sgr.; 4th Class, 10 sgr.

Luggage.—50 lbs. free; every 10 lbs. extra, 1 sgr. Four-wheeled carriage, 6 Prus. doll.; two-wheeled carriage, 4 Prus. doll.

OBERHAUSEN TO RUHRORT—5½ English Miles. [15-11-52.

From OBERHAUSEN to RUHRORT, at 7 a.m., and 2.30 and 6.40 p.m. From RUHRORT at 12 35, 5.10, and 9¼ p.m. in 20 minutes.

MINDEN, HAMM, DUSSELDORF, AND COLOGNE. [15-11-52.

English Miles.	Fares. From Berlin. 1st Class	2nd Class	3rd Class	4th Class	STATIONS.	Trains. 1	2	3	4	5	6	7
Dis.	Sgr.	Sgr.	Sgr.	Sgr.								
					BERLIN ....[2]......departure	12 0	...	10 0	...	7 30	...	...
94	140	100	70	...	MADGEBURG ...[2]...... ,,	4 15	...	1 50	...	10 40	...	...
153½	225	155	105	...	BRUNSWICK .....[2]...... ,,	7 45	...	4 50	...	1 10	...	...
190½	227½	187½	125	...	HANOVER........[2]...... ,,	9 50	...	6 45	...	2 38	...	...
231¼	325	222	145	...	MINDEN ....arrival	11 50	...	8 32	...	3 56	...	...
	FROM MINDEN.					a.m.	a.m.	a.m.	p.m.	p.m.	p.m.	
...	—	—	—	—	**Minden** ....departure	12 30	...	8 58	...	4 21	5 0	...
240½	...	...	...	...	Porta	12 41	...	...	...	...	5 13	...
249¾	12	8	6	...	Bad Oeynhausen (Rehme)	12 58	...	9 21	...	...	5 34	...
258	27	18	13	...	Herford	1 28	...	9 46	...	...	6 7	...
271	36	24	18	...	**Bielefeld**................................	1 55	...	10 13	...	...	6 38	...
...	...	...	..	...	Brackwede	2 6	...	...	...	...	6 51	...
...	37	34	25	...	Gutersloh	2 31	...	10 45	...	5 41	7 15	...
298¼	57	38	28	...	Rheda	2 46	...	...	...	...	...	...
...	...	...	...	...	Oelde	3 9	...	...	...	...	...	...
...	...	...	...	...	Beckum	3 27	...	...	...	...	...	...
...	...	...	...	...	Ahlen	3 45	...	...	...	...	...	...
...	90	60	45	...	**Hamm** .... arrival	...	...	...	...	...	...	...
					,, ...departure	4 15	7 30	12 1	3 0	6 45	...	...
316½	101	68	51	...	Camen	4 40	7 56	...	3 30	...	...	...
337½	116	77	58	...	**Dortmund** ......[3]......departure	5 10	8 30	12 48	4 2	7 22	...	...
...	...	...	...	...	Mengede	5 25	8 50	...	4 18	...	...	...
...	...	...	...	...	Castrop	5 35	9 0	...	4 30	...	...	...
...	...	...	...	...	Herne-Bochum	5 50	9 16	...	4 47	...	...	...
...	...	...	...	...	Gelsenkirchen	6 7	9 33	...	5 4	...	...	...
346½	144	96	72	...	Essen	6 20	9 47	1 40	5 19	...	...	...
...	...	...	...	...	Berge-Borbeck............................	6 27	9 55	...	5 27	...	...	...
351½	154	102	77	...	Oberhausen	6 46	10 14	2 4	5 49	8 22	...	...
367¼	160	106	80	...	**Duisburg**	7 0	10 30	2 18	6 6	8 32	...	...
...	...	...	...	..	Grozzenbaum	7 16	10 46	...	6 20	...	...	...
...	...	...	...	...	Calcum	7 34	11 0	...	6 33	...	...	...
374	180	120	90	...	**Dusseldorf**..................arrival	7 55	11 22	2 57	6 52	9 3	...	...
					,, ...departure	8 5	11 32	3 4	7 0	9 10	...	...
378¾	186	124	93	...	Benrath	8 23	11 52	...	7 18	...	...	...
...	193	129	103	...	Langenfeld	8 38	12 7	...	7 33	...	...	...
...	...	...	...	...	Kuppersteg	8 51	12 21	...	7 46	...	...	...
390¾	206	147	103	...	Mulheim	9 7	12 37	...	8 2	...	...	...
...	210	140	105	...	**Deutz (Cologne)** [4]...arrival	9 15	12 45	4 0	8 10	10 0	...	...

Remarks.—LUGGAGE: 50 lbs. free; every 10 lbs. extra, 7 sgr. Four-wheeled carriage, 41 Prus. doll. 21 sgr.; two-wheeled carriage, 27 Pruss. doll. 24 sgr.

[2] For Stations between BERLIN & MAGDEBURG, see page 96; between MAGDEBURG & BRUNSWICK, page 86; between BRUNSWICK and HANOVER, page 84; between HANOVER and MINDEN, page 87.

[3] DORTMUND to SCHWELM and ELBERFELD, see page 73.

[4] COLOGNE to AIX-LA-CHAPELLE, BRUSSELS, and OSTEND, see pages 57 and 58.

HAMM TO PADERBORN (CASSEL.) [15-11-52.

From HAMM to SOEST, LIPPSTADT, and PADERBORN (Warburg and Cassel) at 7½ a.m., 4.18 and 9½ p.m. From (Cassel and Warburg) PADERBORN to LIPPSTADT, SOEST, and HAMM, at 9.15 a.m. and 7.50 p.m. from Cassel; and 5 a.m., 12½ and 4.20 p.m. from Paderborn.

Fares.—From Hamm to Paderborn—1st Class, 66 sgr.; 2nd Class, 46 sgr.; 3rd Class, 36 sgr.

PARIS, FORBACH, HOMBURG, NEUSTADT, SPEYER, AND LUDWIGSHAFEN.

English Miles.	Fares. 1st Class	2nd Class	3rd Class	STATIONS.	Trains. 1	2	3	4	5	6	7	8
Dis.	fl. kr.	fl. kr.	fl. kr.		a.m.	a.m.	p.m.	p.m.	p.m.	p.m.	a.m.	p.m.
...	...	...	...	**Paris** departure	...	...	7 30	...	...	11 0	9 30	...
					a.m.	a.m.	a.m.	p.m.	p.m.	p.m.	p.m.	p.m.
..	—	—	—	**Forbach** departure	...	...	7 32	...	2 30	3 30	10 0	...
...	0 30	0 21	0 17	St. Johann-Saarbrucken arrival	...	...	...	...	...	...	10 15	...
				,, departure	...	5 35	8 10	...	6 25	4 25	—	...
...	...	...	...	Dudweiler	...	...	...	...	...	...	...	...
...	...	...	...	Sulzbach	...	...	...	...	...	...	...	...
...	...	...	...	Friedrichsthal	...	...	...	...	...	...	...	...
—	1 35	1 6	0 51	**Neunkirchen** arrival	...	...	...	...	...	...	...	...
				,, departure	...	6 27	9 57	...	8 0	5 17	...	...
$7\frac{1}{2}$	1 52	1 18	1 0	Bexbach	...	6 38	9 9	...	8 18	5 28	...	...
$12\frac{1}{4}$	2 13	1 30	1 9	**Homburg** arrival	...	...	...	...	...	...	...	...
				,, departure	...	6 53	9 22	...	9 25	5 42	...	...
$19\frac{1}{2}$	2 40	1 48	1 18	Bruchmuhlbach	...	7 12	...	...	9 55	6 1	...	...
...	...	...	...	Hauptstuhl	...	...	...	...	...	...	...	...
$25\frac{1}{4}$	3 7	2 3	1 30	Landstuhl	...	7 31	9 51	...	10 25	6 21	...	...
$34\frac{3}{4}$	3 49	2 27	1 45	**Kaiserslautern** arrival	...	...	...	...	...	...	...	...
				,, departure	...	8 5	10 20	12 10	11 7	6 56	...	...
...	...	...	...	Hochspeyer	...	...	...	...	...	...	...	...
...	...	...	...	Frankenstein	...	...	...	...	...	...	...	...
...	...	...	...	Weidenthal	...	...	...	...	...	...	...	...
...	...	...	...	Lambrecht	...	...	...	...	...	...	...	...
$54\frac{1}{4}$	5 19	3 21	2 21	**Neustadt** arrival	a.m.	...	...	...	...	...	...	...
				,, departure	5 15	9 22	11 28	2 25	...	8 15	...	4 35
...	...	...	...	Haszloch	...	...	...	...	...	...	...	...
...	...	...	...	Böhl	...	...	...	...	...	...	...	...
...	...	...	...	Schifferstadt arrival	...	...	...	...	...	...	...	...
				,, departure	...	...	...	...	...	...	...	...
60	6 28	4 3	2 48	**Speyer** arrival	6 13	10 13	12 18	3 40	...	9 13	...	5 50
				,, departure	5 30	9 30	12 35	2 55	...	8 30	...	4 50
...	...	...	...	Mutterstadt	...	...	...	...	...	...	...	...
$72\frac{3}{4}$	6 37	4 9	2 51	**Ludwigshafen** arrival	6 15	10 15	12 20	3 57	...	9 15	...	5 35

Remarks.—LUGGAGE: 12 lbs. of Luggage are allowed free of charge.

Additional Trains.—From SPEYER to SCHIFFERSTADT at 5.45, 9.55, and 11.10 a.m.; 12.55, 4.5, $6\frac{1}{2}$, and 8.17 p.m. SCHIFFERSTADT to SPEYER at 6.10, 10.20, and 11.35 a.m.; 1.20, $4\frac{1}{2}$, 7, and 8.42 p.m.

ELBERFELD TO DORTMUND.

English Miles.	Fares. 1st Class	2nd Class	3rd Class	STATIONS.	Trains. 1	2	3			Dortmund to Minden & Hanover, pp. 70,87.	Dortmund to Hamm, Munster, &c., p. 70.
Dis.	sgr.	sgr.	sgr.		a.m.	p.m.	p.m.				
—	—	—	—	**Elberfeld** dep.	6 30	12 30	7 25	..	..		
$2\frac{1}{3}$	4	3	2	Barmen	6 42	12 42	7 37	..	..		
4	6	$4\frac{1}{2}$	3	Rittershausen	6 48	12 48	7 43	..	..		
$6\frac{3}{4}$	10	7	5	Schwelm	7 3	1 3	7 59	..	..		
..	..	..	..	Milspe	..	..	..	..	..		
..	..	..	..	Gevelsberg	..	..	..	..	..		
..	..	..	..	Haspe	..	..	..	..	..		
16	25	18	$12\frac{1}{2}$	Hagen arr.	7 40	1 40	8 38	..	..		
..	..	..	..	Do. dep.	..	..	..	..	..		
$19\frac{1}{2}$	30	21	15	Herdecke	7 49	1 49	8 46	..	..		
..	..	..	..	Wetter	..	..	..	..	..		
$25\frac{1}{2}$	35	24	17	Witten	8 12	2 12	9 9	..	..		
$35\frac{1}{2}$	46	34	23	**Dortmund** arr.	8 45	2 44	9 38	..	..		

LUDWIGSHAFEN, SPEYER, NEUSTADT, HOMBURG, FORBACH, AND PARIS.

English Miles.	Fares.			STATIONS.	Trains.							
	1st Class	2nd Class	3rd Class		1	2	3	4	5	6	7	8
Dis.	fl. kr.	fl. kr.	fl. kr.		a.m.	a.m.	a.m.	a.m.	a.m.	p.m.	p.m.	p.m.
—	—	—	—	**Ludwigshafen** ......departure	7 45	...	...	5 30	11 35	2 50	4 50	8 25
..	...	...	...	Mutterstadt	...	...	...	...	...	...	...	...
..	...	...	...	Schifferstadt ....arrival	...	...	...	...	...	...	...	...
				" ....departure	...	...	...	...	...	...	...	...
12¼	0 57	0 36	0 21	**Speyer**........................arrival	...	...	...	6 13	12 18	3 40	5 50	9 13
				" ....departure	...	...	...	5 30	12 35	2 55	4 50	8 30
..	...	...	...	Böhl	..	...	...	...	...	...	...	..
..	...	...	...	Haszloch	...	...	...	...	...	...	...	...
18½	1 21	0 48	0 30	**Neustadt** ....arrival	9 12	...	...	...	...	3 50	...	9 25
				" ....departure		...	...	6 28	12 29		5 45	
..	...	...	...	Lambrecht	...	...	...	...	...	...	...	...
..	...	...	...	Weidenthal	...	...	...	...	...	...	...	...
..	...	...	...	Frankenstein	...	...	...	...	...	...	...	...
..	...	...	...	Hochspeyer	...	...	...	...	...	...	...	...
38	2 51	1 42	1 6	**Kaiserslautern** ....arrival	...	...	...	...	...	...	...	...
				" .....departure	...	...	...	7 55	1 48	...	7 6	...
47¼	3 30	2 6	1 24	Landstuhl	...	...	...	8 20	2 11	...	7 32	...
..	...	...	...	Hauptstuhl	...	...	...	...	...	...	...	...
53¼	3 57	2 21	1 33	Bruchmuhlbach	...	...	...	8 39	2 28	...	7 52	...
60	4 24	2 39	1 45	**Homburg** ....arrival	...	...	...	...	...	...	...	...
				" ....departure	...	...	...	8 57	2 44	...	8 11	...
65	4 45	2 51	1 51	Bexbach	...	...	...	9 11	2 56	...	8 25	...
72¾	5 3	3 4	2 1	**Neunkirchen** ....arrival	...	...	...	...	...	...	...	...
				" ....departure	...	...	5 10	2 24	3 7	...	8 37	...
..	...	...	...	Friedrichsthal	...	...	...	...	...	...	...	...
..	...	...	...	Sulzbach	...	...	...	...	...	...	...	...
..	...	...	...	Dudweiler............................	...	...	...	...	...	...	...	...
..	6 7	3 48	2 45	St. Johann-Saarbrucken ......arrival	...	...	...	...	...	...	...	...
				" ..departure	...	3 55	6 40	10 20	4 0	...	9 30	...
..	6 37	4 9	2 51	**Forbach** ....arrival	...	4 10	7 10	10 37	4 13	...	9 45	...
						p.m.		p.m.	a.m.			
..	...	...	...	**Paris** ....arrival	...	8 50	...	10 0	4 30	...	...	...

Remarks.—Luggage: 12 lbs. of Luggage are allowed free of charge.

Additional Trains.—From Speyer to Schifferstadt at 5.45, 9.55, and 11.10 a.m.; 12.55, 4.5, 6½, and 8.17 p.m. Schifferstadt to Speyer at 6.10, 10.20, and 11.35 a.m.; 1.20, 4½, 7, and 8.42 p.m.

DORTMUND TO ELBERFELD.

English Miles.	Fares.			STATIONS.	Trains.						
	1st Class	2nd Class	3rd Class		1	2	3	4			
Dis.	sgr.	sgr.	sgr.		a.m.	p.m.	p.m.				
—	—	—	—	**Dortmund** ....dep.	7 5	1 10	7 30	..	..	..	..
9½	15	10½	7½	Witten	7 41	1 42	8 3	..	..	..	..
..	..	..	..	Wetter	..	..	..	..	..	..	..
15¾	21	15	10	Herdecke	8 3	2 3	8 24	..	..	..	..
..	..	..	..	Hagen ....arr.	..	..	..	..	..	..	..
18¾	25	18	12½	Do. ....dep.	8 16	2 16	8 37	..	..	..	..
..	..	..	..	Haspe	..	..	..	..	..	..	..
..	..	..	..	Gevelsberg	..	..	..	..	..	..	..
..	..	..	..	Milspe	..	..	..	..	..	..	..
28½	38	26	19	Schwelm..........................	8 55	2 56	9 17	..	..	..	..
30	42	30	21	Rittershausen	9 5	3 6	9 27	..	..	..	..
32¾	44	32	22	Barmen	9 12	3 14	9 34	..	..	..	..
35½	46	34	23	**Elberfeld** .... arr.	9 20	3 22	9 42	..	..	..	..

Rhine Railways.

STEELE TO VOHWINKEL.

[15-11-52.

Eng. Miles.	Fares.			Stations.	Trains.						
	1 Cls.	2 Cls.	3 Cls.		1	2	3				
Dis.	s.gr.	s.gr.	s.gr.		a.m.	a.m.	p.m.				
—	—	—	—	**Steele**...............dep.	6 45	11 0	6 0	..	..	..	..
9	7	5½	3½	Laugenberg	7 30	11 45	6 45	..	..	..	..
20¾	16	12	8	**Vohwinkel** ..(1)....arr.	8 35	12 50	7 50	..	..	..	..

VOHWINKEL TO STEELE.

Eng. Miles.	Fares			Stations.	Trains.						
	1 Cls.	2 Cls.	3 Cls.		1	2	3				
Dis.	s.gr.	s.gr.	s.gr.		a.m.	p.m.	p.m.				
—	—	—	—	**Vohwinkel** ..(1) ....dep.	9 0	1 30	6 47	..	..	..	..
11¼	9	7	4½	Laugenberg	10 0	2 30	7 47	..	..	..	..
20¾	16	12	8	**Steele** ....arr.	10 35	3 5	8 22	..	..	..	..

(1) For Trains from VOHWINKEL to ELBERFELD and DUSSELDORF, see page 69.

Remarks.—LUGGAGE: 50 lbs. of Luggage are allowed free of charge.

Taunus Railway.—FRANKFURT & CASTEL TO WIESBADEN.

English Miles.	Fares.			STATIONS.	Trains.							
	1 Cl.	2 Cl.	3 Cl.		Gds. 1	2	3	4	5	6	7	8
Dis.	fl kr	fl kr	fl kr		a.m.	a.m.	a.m.	p.m.	p.m.	p.m.	p.m.	
—	—	—	—	**Frankfurt** ...... departure	6 40	8 10	11 10	..	2 30	6 0	8 30	..
5½	0 36	0 24	0 18	Höchst	6 55	8 25	11 25	..	2 45	6 15	8 45	..
9¼	1 0	0 40	0 27	Hattersheim	7 10	8 40	11 40	..	3 0	6 30	9 0	..
20¾	2 6	1 27	1 0	**Castel** ....arrival	7 50	9 15	12 15	..	3 35	7 5	9 35	..
..	..	..	..	,, ... departure	8 0	9 20	12 20	2 30	3 40	7 10	9 40	..
24¼	2 30	1 45	1 12	Biberich ....arrival	8 20	9 40	12 40	2 50	4 0	7 30	10 0	..
..	..	..	..	,, ... departure	8 0	9 20	12 20	2 30	3 40	7 10	9 40	..
26½	2 42	1 48	1 15	**Wiesbaden** ....arrival	8 20	9 40	12 40	2 50	4 0	7 30	10 0	..

WIESBADEN & CASTEL TO FRANKFURT.

English Miles.	Fares.			STATIONS.	Trains.						
	1 Cl.	2 Cl.	3 Cl.		1	2	3	4	5	6	7
Dis.	fl kr	fl kr	fl kr		a.m.	a.m.	a.m.	p.m.	p.m.	p.m.	
—	—	—	—	**Wiesbaden** ....departure	6 10	7 45	10 35	2 0	5 35	8 0	..
..	..	0 12	0 9	Biberich .... arrival	6 30	8 5	10 55	2 20	5 55	8 20	..
..	..	..	..	,, ... departure	6 10	7 45	10 35	2 0	5 35	8 0	..
5½	0 36	0 24	0 18	**Castel** ....arrival	6 30	8 5	10 55	2 20	5 55	8 20	..
..	..	..	..	,, ... departure	6 35	8 10	11 0	2 30	6 0	8 25	..
17	1 42	1 12	0 48	Hattersh	7 10	8 45	11 30	3 5	6 35	9 0	..
20¾	2 6	1 27	0 57	Höchst	7 25	9 0	11 45	3 20	6 50	9 15	..
26½	2 42	1 48	1 15	**Frankfurt** ....arrival	7 40	9 15	12 0	3 35	7 5	9 30	..

Remarks.—LUGGAGE: 40 lbs. free. Every 10 lbs. extra, 15 kr. Four-wheeled carriage, 9 fl. 12 kr. two-wheeled carriage, 7 fl.

MAYENCE TO LUDWIGSHAFEN.—Open to Oppenheim.

From MAYENCE to BODENHEIM, NIERSTEIN, and OPPENHEIM, at 6½ and 11 a.m.; 2½ and 6 p.m. From OPPENHEIM to NIERSTEIN, BODENHEIM, and MAYENCE, at 7½ a.m., 12 noon, 3½ and 7 p.m. **Fares**—1st Class, 90 kr.; 2nd Class, 42 kr.; 3rd Class, 21 kr.

Remarks—10 lbs. of luggage free.

Main-Neckar Railway.—FRANKFORT, HEIDELBERG, & MANNHEIM.

English Miles.	Fares. 1st clas.	2nd clas.	3rd clas.	4th clas.	STATIONS.	Trains. 1	2	3	4	5	6	7	8
Dis.	g. kr	g. kr	g. kr	g. kr		a.m.	a.m.	a.m.	p.m.	p.m.	p.m.		
—	—	—	—	—	**Frankfort** ....departure	6 0	8 30	10 0	1 20	4 45	8 40	..	..
..	0 33	0 24	0 15	0 9	Langen	..	..	..	..	..	..	..	..
..	0 51	0 39	0 27	0 18	Arheilgen	..	..	..	..	..	..	..	..
15¾	1 6	0 48	0 33	0 21	**Darmstadt**..........arrival	6 57	9 10	10 6	2 9	5 34	9 40	..	..
..	..	..	..	..	,, ... departure	7 7	9 15	11 30	2 17	5 40	—	..	..
..	1 21	1 0	0 42	0 27	Eberstadt	..	..	..	..	..	..	..	..
..	1 39	1 12	0 48	0 33	Bickenbach	..	..	..	..	..	..	..	..
26½	1 45	1 15	0 51	0 36	Zwingenberg........................	7 40	..	12 8	2 47	6 10	..	..	..
28	1 51	1 21	0 57	0 39	Auerbach	7 47	..	12 16	2 53	6 16	..	..	..
30	1 57	1 24	1 0	0 39	Bensheim	7 53	9 49	12 26	2 59	6 23	..	..	..
33	2 9	1 33	1 3	0 42	Heppenheim........................	8 3	..	12 39	3 7	6 32	..	..	..
..	2 21	1 42	1 12	0 48	Hemsbach........................	..	..	..	..	..	..	..	..
39¼	2 33	1 51	1 18	0 51	Weinheim	8 25	10 12	1 6	3 22	6 52	..	..	..
..	2 45	2 0	1 24	0 54	Groszsachsen	..	..	..	..	..	..	..	..
..	2 57	2 9	1 30	1 0	Ladenburg	..	..	..	..	..	..	..	..
48	3 6	2 15	1 33	1 3	Friedrichsfeld	8 59	10 38	1 50	3 48	7 22	..	..	..
54½	3 30	2 30	1 45	1 9	**Mannheim**............arrival	9 15	12 53	2 12	4 3	7 37	..	..	..
54½	3 33	2 33	1 45	1 12	**Heidelberg** .... ,,	9 15	12 53	2 10	4 3	7 37	..	..	..

HEIDELBERG, MANNHEIM, AND FRANKFORT.

English Miles.	Fares. 1st clas.	2nd clas.	3rd clas.	4th clas.	STATIONS.	Trains. 1	2	3	4	5	6	7	8
Dis.	g. kr	g. kr	g. kr	g. kr		a.m.	a.m.	a.m.	p.m.	p.m.	p.m.		
—		—	—	—	**Heidelberg** ....departure	..	7 0	11 0	1 0	4 10	6 30	..	..
11¼	8 48	0 33	0 24	..	**Mannheim** ....departure	..	7 0	11 0	1 0	4 10	6 25	..	..
6½	0 24	0 18	0 12	0 9	Friedrichsfeld	..	7 19	11 20	1 20	4 29	6 56	..	..
..	0 33	0 24	0 18	0 12	Ladenburg........................	..	..	..	..	..	..	..	..
..	0 48	0 33	0 24	0 15	Groszsachsen	..	..	..	..	..	..	..	..
14½	1 0	0 42	0 30	0 21	Weinheim	..	7 46	11 51	1 44	4 53	7 40	..	..
..	1 9	0 51	0 36	0 24	Hemsbach	..	..	..	..	..	..	..	..
21	1 24	1 0	0 42	0 27	Heppenheim........................	..	8 4	12 12	..	5 8	8 5	..	..
25	1 36	1 9	0 48	0 33	Bensheim	..	8 12	12 22	2 5	5 17	8 18	..	..
26	1 42	1 12	0 51	0 33	Auerbach	..	8 18	12 28	..	5 23	8 25	..	..
27¾	1 48	1 18	0 54	0 36	Zwingenberg........................	..	8 24	12 35	..	5 29	8 32	..	..
..	1 54	1 24	0 57	0 39	Bickenbach	..	..	..	..	..	..	..	..
..	2 12	1 36	1 6	0 45	Eberstadt	..	..	..	..	..	..	..	..
37½	2 27	1 48	1 15	0 48	**Darmstadt**..........arrival	..	9 0	1 16	2 43	6 4	9 17	..	..
..	..	..	..	..	,, ... departure	7 0	9 10	1 23	2 50	6 12	9 40	..	..
..	2 42	1 57	1 21	0 54	Arheilgen	..	..	..	..	..	..	..	..
..	3 0	2 9	1 30	1 0	Langen	..	..	..	..	..	..	..	..
54½	3 33	2 33	1 45	1 12	**Frankfort** ....arirval	7 45	9 50	2 13	3 30	6 57	10 36	..	..

From Mannheim to Carlsruhe, Baden, Offenburg, Freiburg, Efringen, & Basle, see page 78.

Remarks.—Luggage: 10 lbs. free; every 10 lbs. extra, 6 kr. Four-wheeled carriage, 19 fl. 28 kr.; two-wheeled carriage, 15 fl. 34 kr.

FRANKFURT AND OFFENBACH.—4 English Miles.

From Frankfurt to Sachsenhausen, Oberrad and Offenbach, at 6.5, 8.10, and 10.5 a.m., 12.10, 2.20, 4, 7.15, and 8.15 p.m.—From Sachsenhausen to Offenbach only, at 9.5 and 11.0 a.m.; 3.10, 5.20, and 6.20 p.m.

From Offenbach to Oberrad, Sachsenhausen, & Frankfurt, at 5.30, 7.35, 9.25, and 11.40 a.m.; 1.45, 3.30, 6.45, and 8.15 p.m.—From Offenbach to Sachenhausen only, at 8.45 and 10.35 a.m.; 2.50, 4.30, and 5.40 p.m.

Fares.—Frankfurt to Offenbach, 1st class, 24 kr.; 2nd class, 18 kr.; 3rd class, 12 kr.; 4th class, 6 kr.

Remarks.—Luggage: 10 lbs. free; every 50 lbs. extra, 3 kr.

FRANKFORT AND CASSEL.

English Miles.	Fares.			STATIONS.	Trains.							
	1st Class	2nd Class	3rd Class		1	2	3	4	5	6	7	8
Dis.	Kr.	Kr.	Kr.		a.m.	a.m.	p.m.	p.m.	p.m.			
—	—	—	—	**Frankfort** ....departure	..	8 15	12 10	4 0	7 15	..	..	..
2	8	5	3	Bockenheim	..	8 24	12 18	4 8	7 23	..	..	..
5¾	28	18	11	Bonames (Homburg)	..	8 40	12 34	4 24	7 39	..	..	..
9	40	27	16	Vilbel	..	8 52	12 44	4 36	7 49	..	..	..
..	..	.	..	Dortelweil	..	9 2	12 53	4 45	7 58	..	..	..
..	..	..	..	Groszkarben	..	9 12	1 2	4 55	8 7	..	..	..
..	..	..	..	Niederwöllstadt..............	..	9 27	1 16	5 9	8 21	..	..	..
21	95	64	39	**Friedberg**	..	9 48	1 37	5 30	8 42	..	..	..
23	106	71	44	Nauheim	..	10 0	1 49	5 43	8 54	..	..	..
29½	134	89	55	Butzbach	..	10 20	2 8	6 3	9 13	..	..	..
34¾	158	105	66	Laggöns	..	10 38	2 25	6 20	9 30	..	..	..
41½	185	123	77	Giessen	4 30	11 5	3 0	6 40	9 50	..	..	..
..	..	..	..	Lollar	4 45	11 20	3 16	—	—	.	..	..
..	..	..	..	Fronhausen	4 56	11 32	3 28	..	..	..	..	..
60	240	180	112	**Marburg**	5 26	12 5	4 0	..	..	..	..	..
69½	313	208	130	Kirchhain	5 50	12 34	4 25	..	..	..	..	..
80¾	364	243	154	**Neustadt**	6 20	1 8	4 54	..	..	..	..	..
87	394	263	166	Treisa	6 42	1 34	5 18	..	..	..	..	..
104	490	314	196	Wabern	7 35	2 35	6 10	..	..	..	..	..
116	528	352	219	Guntershausen Junc.	8 20	3 20	6 55	..	..	..	..	..
124¾	567	378	236	**Cassel**...............arrival	8 45	3 45	7 20	..	..	..	..	..
					a.m.	p.m.						
172	840	559	366	Eisenach ....arrival	11 30	7 15	..	..	..	..	..	..

CASSEL AND FRANKFORT.

English Miles.	Fares.			STATIONS.	Trains.							
	1st Class	2nd Class	3rd Class		1	2	3	4	5	6	7	8
Dis.	Sgr.	Sgr.	Sgr.		a.m.	a.m.	p.m.	a.m.	p.m.			
..	..	..	..	Eisenach ....departure	..	..	1 55	7 45	..	..	..	..
							a.m.	p.m.	p.m.			
—	—	—	—	**Cassel**........... departure	..	..	8 15	1 25	4 45	..	..	..
9	11¼	7½	4¾	Guntershausen Junc.	..	..	9 0	2 0	5 20	..	..	..
21	27¾	18½	11½	Wabern	..	..	9 45	2 40	6 4	..	..	..
38	49½	33	20½	Treisa	..	..	10 50	3 38	7 0	..	..	..
..	58	38½	24¼	**Neustadt**	..	..	11 12	3 58	7 20	..	..	..
56½	72½	48½	30¼	Kirchhain	..	..	11 45	4 28	7 50	..	..	..
66	85	56½	35½	**Marburg**	..	7 30	12 15	5 0	8 12	..	..	..
..	..	..	..	Fronhausen	..	7 54	12 40	5 25	—	..	..	..
..	..	..	..	Lollar	..	8 6	12 55	5 37	..	..	..	..
84	109	72¾	45½	Giessen	5 48	8 20	1 25	6 0	..	..	..	..
..	From Butzbach.			Laggöns	6 10	8 53	1 48	6 22	..	..	..	..
..	Kr.	Kr.	Kr.	Butzbach	6 26	9 9	2 5	6 40	..	..	..	..
..	28	18	11	Nauheim	6 43	9 26	2 22	6 58	..	..	..	..
104	39	25	16	**Friedberg**	6 57	9 40	2 36	7 12	..	..	..	..
..	..	..	..	Niederwöllstadt..............	..	9 53	2 50	7 25	..	..	..	..
..	..	..	..	Groszkarben	..	10 2	3 0	7 34	..	..	..	..
..	..	..	..	Dortelweil	..	10 8	3 7	7 40	..	..	..	..
120	94	62	39	Vilbel	7 33	10 16	3 17	7 48	..	..	..	..
..	106	71	44	Bonames (Homburg)	7 44	10 27	3 28	8 0	..	..	..	..
..	126	84	52	Bockenheim	7 55	10 38	3 40	8 11	..	..	..	..
124¾	134	89	55	**Frankfort**...........arrival	8 0	10 43	3 45	8 16	..	..	..	..

FROTTSTEDT AND WALTERSHAUSEN.—4½ English Miles.

From Frottstedt to Waltershausen in 30 minutes.
From Waltershausen to Frottstedt in 15 minutes.
Fares.—2nd Class, 3 sgr.; 3rd Class, 2 sgr.

Strasburg and Bale Railway—STRASBOURG, COLMAR, MULHOUSE, AND BALE.—89 English Miles.

Eng. Mls.	Fares. 2 Cl.	3 Cl.	4 Cl.	STATIONS.	Trains. 1	2	3	4	5	6
	fr. c.	fr. c.	fr. c.		a.m.	a.m.	a.m.	p.m.	p.m.	p.m.
—				**Strasburg** dep.	...	5 45	9 0	12 0	5 0	7 0
6¾	0 75	0 60	0 40	Geispolsheim	...	6 2	9 14	12 17	5 16	7 21
8¾	1 5	0 80	0 55	Fegersheim	...	6 9	...	12 24	5 23	7 29
11¼	1 50	1 15	0 75	Limersheim	...	6 17	...	12 32	...	7 38
13¾	2 20	1 65	1 15	Erstein	...	6 27	9 28	12 42	5 37	7 50
15¾	2 50	1 90	1 30	Matzenheim	...	6 34	...	12 49	...	7 58
18	2 95	2 20	1 50	Benfeld	...	6 43	9 38	12 58	5 50	8 10
21¼	3 45	2 60	1 75	Kogenheim	...	6 53	...	1 8	...	8 22
23¼	3 95	3 0	2 5	Ebersheim	...	7 2	...	1 17	6 6	8 33
28	4 70	3 55	2 40	**Schlestadt**	...	7 19	10 1	1 34	5 20	8 52
31¾	5 20	3 95	2 65	Saint-Hippolyte	...	7 29	...	1 44	..	9 5
34¼	5 60	4 25	2 85	Ribeauvillé	...	7 39	10 15	1 54	6 36	9 17
36¼	5 95	4 50	3 0	Ostheim	...	7 46	...	2 1	6 43	9 25
38¾	6 35	4 80	3 20	Bennwihr	a.m.	7 53	10 24	2 8	6 50	9 33
39¼	6 95	5 25	3 55	**Colmar**	5 10	8 9	10 36	2 24	7 4	9 45
45	7 40	5 55	3 75	Eguisheim	5 21	8 18	...	2 33	7 13	
46¾	7 70	5 80	3 90	Herrlisheim	5 28	8 25	...	2 40	7 19	...
50¾	8 50	6 25	4 25	Rouffach	5 43	8 37	10 53	2 52	7 31	...
53¾	8 85	6 65	4 50	Merxheim	5 55	8 47	...	3 2	7 41	...
58	9 55	7 20	4 85	Bollwiller	6 11	9 1	11 9	3 16	7 53	...
61¼	10 10	7 60	5 10	Wittelsheim	6 21	9 10	...	3 25	8 2	...
65¾	10 80	8 15	5 50	Lutterbach	6 35	9 23	11 24	3 38	8 14	...
66¾	11 0	8 30	5 60	Dornach	6 42	9 30	11 30	3 45	8 20	...
69¼	11 45	8 60	5 80	**Mulhouse**	6 58	9 43	11 40	3 58	8 31	...
72¼	11 95	9 0	6 5	Rixheim	7 10	9 53	11 48	4 8	8 41	...
73	12 5	9 10	6 10	Habsheim	7 16	9 58	11 54	4 13	8 46	...
79½	13 10	9 85	6 65	Sierentz	7 35	10 14	12 7	4 29	9 1	...
81¼	13 40	10 10	6 80	Bartenheim	7 43	10 21	...	4 36	9 8	...
86¼	14 25	10 70	7 20	Saint-Louis	8 3	10 39	12 25	4 54	9 25	...
88¼	14 65	10 95	7 35	**Bale** .... arrival	8 10	10 45	12 30	5 0	9 30	...
					a.m.	a.m.	p.m.	p.m.		
—	12 40	9 35	6 30	**Thann** ..depart	6 30	10 15	1 30	5 0	...	...
3¾	..	..	..	Cernay	6 44	10 29	1 44	5 14	...	...
9¼	10 85	8 25	5 55	Lutterbach	7 4	10 49	2 4	5 31	...	...
11¼	11 5	8 40	5 65	Dornach	7 12	10 57	2 12	5 42	...	...
13	11 45	8 60	5 80	**Mulhouse** arr.	7 20	11 5	2 20	5 50	...	...

Eng. Mls.	Fares. 2cls.	3cls.	4cls.	STATIONS.	Trains. 1	2	3	4	5	6
	fr. c.	fr. c.	fr. c.		a.m.	a.m.	a.m.	p.m.	p.m.	p.m.
—	..	..	..	**Bale** ....depart	...	6 0	9 0	11 40	4 15	6 0
2	0 40	0 25	0 15	Saint-Louis	...	6 20	9 20	12 0	4 35	6 22
6¾	1 25	0 85	0 55	Bartenheim	...	6 31	9 33	...	4 48	6 38
9½	1 45	1 10	0 70	Sierentz	...	6 37	9 40	12 14	4 55	6 46
15	2 60	1 85	1 25	Habsheim	...	6 49	9 56	12 27	5 11	7 5
16½	2 70	1 95	1 30	Rixheim	...	6 54	10 1	12 33	5 16	7 11
19¼	3 20	2 35	1 55	**Mulhouse**	...	7 6	10 16	12 45	5 31	7 31
21½	3 65	2 65	1 75	Dornach	...	7 14	10 23	12 51	5 38	7 39
23¼	3 85	2 75	1 85	Lutterbach	...	7 21	10 29	12 57	5 44	7 47
26¾	4 55	3 35	2 25	Wittelsheim	...	7 33	10 41	..	5 56	8 2
30	5 10	3 75	2 50	Bollwiller	...	7 41	10 51	1 12	6 8	8 15
34¼	5 80	4 30	2 85	Merxheim	...	7 51	11 3	...	6 18	8 30
37½	6 35	4 70	3 10	Rouffach	...	8 0	11 14	1 28	6 29	8 44
42	6 95	5 15	3 45	Herrlisheim	...	8 10	11 25	...	6 40	8 58
43	7 35	5 40	3 60	Eguisheim	...	8 17	11 31	...	6 46	9 5
46½	7 75	5 70	3 80	**Colmar**	5 0	8 28	11 44	1 48	6 59	9 15
50¼	8 30	6 15	4 25	Bennwihr	5 13	8 38	11 55	1 57	7 10	
51¾	8 70	6 45	4 35	Ostheim	5 21	...	12 2	...	7 17	...
53¾	9 15	6 70	4 50	Ribeauvillé	5 31	8 47	12 12	2 6	7 25	...
57	9 45	7 0	4 70	Saint-Hippolyte	5 41	...	12 19	...	7 34	...
60	9 95	7 40	4 95	**Schlestadt**	5 58	9 4	12 33	2 23	7 48	...
64½	10 70	7 95	5 30	Ebersheim	6 13	...	12 45	...	8 0	...
66¼	11 20	8 35	5 60	Kogenheim	6 24	...	12 54	...	8 9	...
70	11 70	8 75	5 85	Benfeld	6 38	9 25	1 5	2 43	8 20	...
72½	12 15	9 5	6 15	Matzenheim	6 48	...	1 13	...	8 28	...
74¼	12 45	9 30	6 20	Erstein	6 58	9 55	1 21	2 53	8 36	...
77½	13 15	9 85	6 60	Limersheim	7 8	...	1 29	...	8 43	...
80¼	13 60	10 15	6 80	Fegersheim	7 17	...	1 57	...	8 52	...
82	13 90	10 35	6 95	Geispolsheim	7 25	...	1 44	3 7	8 59	...
89	14 65	10 95	7 35	**Strasburg** arr.	7 45	10 0	2 0	3 20	9 15	...
					a.m.	a.m.	p.m.	p.m.		...
--	—	—	—	**Mulhouse** dep.	7 40	11 30	3 40	8 15	...	...
2½	0 35	0 25	0 20	Dornach	7 49	11 39	3 49	8 24	...	...
3¾	0 60	0 45	0 30	Lutterbach	7 57	11 47	3 57	8 32	...	...
10¼	1 65	1 25	1 0	Cernay	7 18	12 8	4 18	8 53	...	...
13	2 15	1 65	1 30	**Thann** .. arrival	8 30	12 20	4 30	9 5	...	...

First Class Fare from Strasburg to Bale, 16f. 85c.

Remarks.—Children under 7 years of age, when with their parents, go free; older Children pay the full fare.—Travelling Carriages, 4-wheeled, from Bale to Strasbourg, 75 frs.; 2-wheeled, 60 frs.; the post horses to the station are included in this rate.—Horses charged 15 cents. per kilometre.—Omnibuses to the neighbouring towns stand at all the stations; their fares differ from 1 fr. to 1 fr. 50 ct., according to distance.—Dogs pay 3rd part of the fare for 3rd places.—**Luggage.** 15 kilograms free; overweight charged for kilograms and kilometres. All the trains *to* Bale stop 5 minutes, and *from* Bale 10 minutes, at the Custom House of St. Louis.

Duke of Baden's Railway.— MANNHEIM, BADEN, FREIBURG, & BALE.

[5–53.

Eng. Miles. Dis.	Fares From Mannheim. 1 Cl fl.kr	2 Cl fl.kr	C 1 fl.kr	4 Cl fl.kr	10 lbs. of Luggage Free of Charge.	Trains. 1 a.m.	2 a.m.	3 a.m.	4 a.m.	5 a.m.	6 a.m.	7 p.m.	8 p.m.	9 p.m.
					Main-Neckar Railway.									
..	3 30	2 30	1 45	1 9	FRANKFORT ......dep.	..	..	Gds.	..	8 30	..	Gds.	1 20	4 45
..	0 48	0 33	0 24	0 15	HEIDELBERG......arr.	..	..	..	..	10 53	..	..	4 3	7 37
—	—	—	—	—	**Mannheim** ....dep.	[2] Diligences to Stuttgardt three times a day, see page 248.	..	4 30	6 20	10 50	11 50	1 25	3 45	7 15
5½	0 21	0 15	0 12	0 6	Friedrichsfeld		..	5 4	6 37	..	12 6	..	4 4	7 33
11¼	0 48	0 33	0 24	0 15	**Heidelberg**.. arr.		..	5 35	6 54	11 17	12 22	2 5	4 30	7 50
					dep.		..	6 15	7 5	11 25	12 30	2 50	4 30	8 0
..	1 6	0 45	0 33	0 21	St. Ilgen		..	..	7 19	..	12 44	..	4 44	8 14
7½	1 21	0 54	0 39	0 24	Wiesloch		..	7 0	7 32	..	12 56	3 25	4 58	8 27
9¼	1 45	1 12	0 51	0 33	Langenbrücken		..	7 52	7 50	..	1 13	..	5 17	8 44
20¾	2 9	1 27	1 3	0 42	Bruchsal		..	8 30	8 8	12 5	1 30	4 10	5 36	9 1
..	2 21	1 36	1 9	0 45	Untergrombach		..	8 52	8 19	..	1 40	..	5 47	9 12
..	2 30	1 42	1 15	0 48	Weingarten		..	9 9	8 28	..	1 48	..	5 56	9 21
32	2 48	1 54	1 24	0 54	Durlach		..	9 43	8 43	12 28	2 2	..	6 11	9 36
34	3 0	2 3	1 30	0 57	**Carlsruhe**[2] arr.		..	9 57	8 52	12 35	2 10	5 0	6 20	9 45
					dep.		5 45	10 45	9 0	12 45	2 20	5 30	6 30	[1] Strusburg to Colmar, Mulhouse, & Thann, see page 77. Stations between Frankfort & Mannheim, see page 75.
38	3 18	2 15	1 39	1 3	Ettlingen		5 58	11 17	9 14	..	2 34	..	6 44	
..	3 36	2 27	1 48	1 9	Malsch		6 12	11 45	9 29	..	2 48	..	6 59	
44¾	3 48	2 36	1 54	1 12	Muggensturm		6 20	12 3	9 38	..	2 56	..	7 8	
48½	4 0	2 42	2 0	1 15	Rastatt................		6 31	12 30	9 50	1 14	3 7	6 30	7 21	
..	4 24	3 0	2 12	1 24	Oos Junc. (for Baden) ..		6 51	1 30	10 12	1 28	3 27	..	7 43	
57	4 45	3 15	2 24	1 30	**Baden** .... arr.		7 1	..	10 22	1 37	3 37	..	7 53	
					dep.		6 38	..	10 0	1 17	3 14	..	7 30	
..	4 30	3 6	2 15	1 27	Sinzheim		6 59	..	..	..	3 35	..	7 52	
..	4 39	3 9	2 21	1 30	Steinbach..............		7 7	1 57	10 26	..	3 43	..	8 0	
61¼	4 48	3 18	2 24	1 33	Bühl		7 16	2 21	10 37	..	3 53	7 27	8 11	
..	4 57	3 24	2 30	1 36	Ottersweier		7 23	..	..	..	4 0	..	8 19	
67	5 9	3 30	2 36	1 39	Achern		7 34	2 55	10 54	..	4 11	..	8 32	
70½	5 27	3 42	2 42	1 45	Renchen		7 46	3 22	11 8	..	4 23	..	8 45	
74	5 42	3 54	2 51	1 48	Appenweier Jun for Kehl)		8 1	3 50	11 24	2 8	4 38	8 20	9 1	
82	6 12	4 12	3 6	1 57	**Kehl**(Stras)[1] arr.		8 27	..	11 49	2 25	5 0	..	9 27	
					dep.		7 30	..	10 50	1 45	4 0	..	8 30	
..	5 48	3 57	2 54	1 51	Windschläg		8 10	..	11 33	..	4 47	..	..	
79½	6 0	4 6	3 0	1 54	**Offenburg** .. arr.		8 13	4 16	11 42	2 18	4 55	8 40	9 16	
					dep.	4 0	8 25	5 10	11 50	2 24	5 5	Every **Sunday**, and 9th September, 1853. MANNHEIM to HEIDLEBERG, at 10 p.m. in 36 minutes.	Every **Monday**, and 10th September, 1853. HEIDELBERG to MANNHEIM, at 5.35 a.m., in 30 minutes.	
..	..	..	..	..	Niederschopfheim	4 19	8 40	..	12 6	..	5 21			
..	..	..	..	..	Friesenheim	4 30	..	..	12 15	..	5 30			
89¾	6 45	4 36	3 21	2 9	Dinglingen (Lahr)......	4 43	8 56	6 11	12 26	2 50	5 41			
92¼	..	..	..	..	Kippenheim	4 54	..	..	12 36	..	5 50			
..	7 6	4 51	3 33	2 15	Orschweier	5 5	9 11	6 42	12 45	..	5 59			
..	..	..	..	..	Herbolzheim	5 18	..	..	12 57	..	6 10			
..	7 27	5 6	3 45	2 24	Kenzingen	5 28	9 27	7 20	1 6	..	6 19			
104¼	7 42	5 15	3 51	2 27	Riegel	5 41	9 37	7 43	1 17	..	6 30			
..	7 57	5 24	4 0	2 33	Emmendingen	5 59	9 50	8 17	1 32	..	6 45			
..	..	..	..	..	Denzlingen	6 20	10 6	..	1 49	..	7 2			Gds.
117¼	8 36	5 51	4 18	2 45	**Freiburg** .... arr.	6 41	10 22	9 17	2 6	3 48	7 19			a.m.
					dep.	7 0	10 30		2 15	3 55	7 25			4 30
..	..	..	..	..	Schallstadt	7 19	10 47	..	2 32	..	7 41			5 2
..	9 12	6 15	4 36	2 54	Krozingen	7 33	10 58	..	2 43	..	7 51			5 25
..	..	..	..	..	Heitersheim	7 51	11 9	..	2 54	..	8 1			5 47
..	9 48	6 39	4 54	3 6	Mullheim	8 11	11 26	..	3 12	4 35	8 16			6 23
140	10 3	6 51	5 0	3 12	Schliengen	8 26	11 38	..	3 26	..	8 30			6 50
..	..	..	..	..	Bellingen	8 37	..	..	3 37	..	8 40			..
..	..	..	..	..	Rheinweiler............	8 47	11 55	..	3 46	..	8 48			7 50
..	..	..	..	..	Kleinkems	8 57	..	..	3 55	..	8 56			..
148¼	10 39	7 15	5 21	3 24	**Efringen**	9 13	12 16	..	4 11	..	9 12			8 24
..	..	..	..	..	Eimeldingen	9 25	..	..	4 22	..	9 24			..
153½	10 54	7 27	5 27	3 27	**Haltingen** ......arr.	9 31	12 30	..	4 28	5 15	9 30			8 47
157½	..	..	..	..	**Bale** (by Omnibus) arr.	10 31	1 30	..	5 28	6 15	10 30			..

... AND HANAU. Frankfort to ... Wilhelmsbad, & Hanau, at 7¾ and 9 a.m.; 12¾, 3, 5, 7, 9, & (10.40 Sun. & Fêtes only) p.m. Hanau to Wilhelmsbad, Mainkur, Frankfort, at 6¾, 8, & 10 a.m.; & 2, 4, 6, 8, & (10 Sun. & Fêtes only) p.m.

MANNHEIM AND FRIEDRICHSFELD. ...heim to Friedrichsfeld, at 7 and 11 a.m.; 1, 4.10, and 6.25 p.m. From Friedrichsfeld to Mannheim, at 9 and 10.39 a.m.; 1.46, 3.49, and 7.23 p.m.

[5–53.

Frame and text are truncated on the original guide

Duke of Baden's Railway. [5–53.

MANNHEIM, BADEN, FREIBURG, AND BALE.

Eng. M. Dis.	Fares from Haltingen. 1 Cl. fl. kr	2 Cl. fl. kr	3 Cl. fl. kr	4 Cl. fl. kr	10 lbs. of Luggage Free of Charge.	Trains. 1	2	3	4	5	6	7	8	9	10
						a.m.	a.m.	a.m.	a.m.	a.m.	a.m.	a.m.	p.m.	p.m.	p.m.
..	..	..	..	..	**Bale** (by Omnibus) dep.	..	..	Gds.	5 30	5 30	Gds.	10 30	2 30	4 0	5 30
—	—	—	—	—	**Haltingen** dep.	..	..	..	7 0	7 5	10 0	12 0	4 0	5 30	7 0
..	0 12	0 9	0 6	0 3	Eimeldingen	..	..	..	..	7 11	..	12 6	..	..	7 7
..	0 15	0 12	0 9	0 6	**Efringen**	..		..	..	7 20	10 24	12 15	4 12	5 42	7 18
..	0 20	0 21	0 15	0 9	Kleinkems	..	[1] *Mannheim to Frankfort, see page 75.*	..	..	7 30	..	12 30	..	..	7 34
..	0 36	0 24	0 18	0 12	Rheinweiler	..		..	..	7 44	11 0	12 37	4 32	6 2	7 44
..	0 45	0 30	0 21	0 15	Bellingen	..		..	..	7 51	..	12 44	..	..	7 52
13	0 51	0 36	0 27	0 18	Schliengen	..		..	..	7 59	11 36	12 52	4 44	6 14	8 1
..	1 6	0 45	0 33	0 24	Mullheim	..		..	7 40	8 13	12 4	1 2	4 54	6 24	8 17
..	1 27	1 0	0 45	0 30	Heitersheim	..		..	..	8 27	12 35	1 15	5 6	6 36	8 32
..	1 42	1 9	0 51	0 33	Krozingen	..		..	..	8 38	1 1	1 25	5 16	6 46	8 45
..	1 57	1 21	1 0	0 39	Schallstadt	..		..	..	8 49	1 37	1 35	5 26	6 56	8 58
..					**Freiburg** arr.	..		..	8 18	9 5	2 10	1 51	5 42	7 12	9 20
35	From Freiburg.				**Freiburg** dep.	5 45		..	8 25	9 12	3 0	2 0	5 48	7 18	
..	0 21	0 15	0 9	0 6	Dinzlingen	6 1		..	..	9 28	..	2 15	6 0	7 30	..
..	0 39	0 27	0 18	0 12	Emmendingen	6 17		..	..	9 44	3 48	2 29	6 11	7 41	..
49½	0 59	0 39	0 27	0 18	Riegel	6 30		..	..	9 57	4 13	2 41	6 22	7 52	..
..	1 6	0 45	0 33	0 21	Kenzingen	6 43		..	..	10 10	4 35	2 53	6 31	8 1	..
..	1 15	0 51	0 39	0 34	Herbolzheim	6 50		..	..	10 17	..	3 0	6 38	8 8	..
..	1 30	1 3	0 45	0 30	Orschweier	7 2		..	..	10 29	5 4	3 11	6 48	8 18	..
60	1 39	1 9	0 51	0 33	Kippenheim	7 10		..	..	10 37	..	3 18	6 55	8 25	..
63¾	1 51	1 15	0 57	0 36	Dinglingen (Lahr)	7 21		..	9 25	10 48	5 36	3 28	7 3	8 33	..
..	2 3	1 24	1 0	0 39	Friesenheim	7 31		..	..	10 58	..	3 38	7 12	8 42	..
..	2 12	1 30	1 6	0 42	Niederschopfheim	7 39	..	..	..	11 6	..	3 46	7 20	8 50	..
					Offenb'rg arr.	7 56	..	..	9 50	11 23	6 24	4 1	7 34	9 4	..
74	2 36	1 45	1 18	0 48	**Offenb'rg** dep.		6 0	8 10	10 0	11 30	6 50	4 10	7 40	9 10	..
..	2 45	1 54	1 24	0 54	Windschläg	..	6 9	..	..	11 38	..	4 18	..	..	..
79¼	2 54	2 0	1 27	0 57	**Appenweier**	..	6 20	8 36	10 14	11 49	7 21	4 29	7 55	9 25	..
					Kehl (Stras) arr.	..	6 45	..	10 31	12 14	..	5 0	8 20	9 42	..
87	3 24	2 21	1 42	1 6	**Kehl** (Stras) dep.	..	5 50	..	9 50	11 18	..	4 0	7 25	9 0	..
83¼	3 9	2 9	1 36	1 0	Renchen	..	6 31	..	..	11 59	7 45	4 39	8 5	9 35	..
87	3 27	2 21	1 42	1 6	Achern	..	6 44	..	..	12 10	8 21	4 50	8 16	9 46	..
..	3 39	2 30	1 48	1 9	Ottersweier	..	6 54	..	..	12 19	..	4 59	..	..	..
92	3 48	2 36	1 54	1 12	Bühl	..	7 3	9 25	..	12 26	8 55	5 6	8 29	9 59	..
..	3 57	2 42	1 57	1 15	Steinbach	..	7 12	..	..	12 34	9 11	5 14	..	..	Gds.
..	4 6	2 48	2 3	1 18	Sinzheim	..	7 19	..	..	12 40	..	5 20	..	..	a.m.
..	4 15	2 54	2 6	1 21	Oos	..	7 31	..	10 51	12 52	9 30	5 30	8 48	10 18	4 35
01¾	4 36	3 9	2 18	1 27	**Baden** arr.	..	7 41	..	11 0	1 2		5 40	8 58	10 28	..
					Baden dep.	..	7 18	..	10 40	12 39	..	5 18	8 36	10 6	..
05	4 36	3 9	2 18	1 27	Rastatt	..	7 49	10 16	11 4	1 8	..	5 45	9 3	10 33	5 10
08	4 48	3 18	2 34	1 33	Muggensturm	..	8 0	..	..	1 19	..	5 55	9 13	10 43	5 31
..	4 57	3 24	2 30	1 36	Malsch	..	8 8	..	..	1 27	..	6 2	..	..	5 48
15¾	5 18	3 39	2 39	1 42	Ettlingen	..	8 23	..	..	1 41	..	6 15	9 30	11 0	6 20
					Carlsruhe arr.	a.m.	8 35	11 6	11 27	1 51	..	6 25	9 40	11 10	6 39
..	5 36	3 48	2 48	1 48	**Carlsruhe** dep.	5 10	8 45	11 40	11 35	2 0	..	6 35			7 15
22¼	5 48	3 57	2 54	1 51	Durlach	5 19	8 55	..	11 42	2 9	..	6 45	..	..	7 40
..	..	..	..	..	Weingarten	5 32	9 9	..	..	2 22	..	6 59	..	..	8 8
..	..	..	..	..	Untergrombach	5 40	9 18	..	..	2 30	..	7 8	..	..	8 25
33	6 27	4 24	3 15	2 3	Bruchsal	5 51	9 31	12 32	12 2	2 41	..	7 20	..	..	8 51
44	6 51	4 39	3 27	2 12	Langenbrucken	6 6	9 48	..	..	2 56	..	7 35	..	..	9 22
45	..	..	..	..	Wiesloch	6 22	10 8	1 20	..	3 13	..	7 54	..	..	10 10
..	..	..	..	..	St. Ilgen	6 32	..	..	..	3 24	..	8 5	..	..	..
53½	7 51	5 21	3 54	2 30	**Heid'lb'rg** arr.	6 45	10 33	1 50	12 40	3 39	..	8 20	..	..	10 49
					Heid'lb'rg dep.	6 55	10 45	2 30	12 50	3 50	..	8 30	..	..	11 30
..	..	..	..	..	Friedrichsfeld [arr.	7 10	11 2	..	..	4 5	..	8 46	..	..	12 5
55	8 36	5 51	4 18	2 45	**Mannheim** [1].	7 25	11 17	3 10	1 18	4 20	..	9 0	..	..	12 32
.	7 51	5 21	3 54	2 30	HEIDELBERG dep.	7 0	11 0	..	1 0	4 10	..	..	..	..	..
38	11 24	7 54	5 37	3 42	FRANKFORT..arr.	9 50	2 13	..	3 30	6 57	..	..	..	..	..

KEHL AND APPENWIER.—KEHL to APPENWIER, at 5.50, 7.30, 9.50, 10 50, and 11.18 a.m.; 1.45, 4, 7.25, 8.30, and 9 p.m., in 29 minutes. From APPENWIER to KEHL, at 6.20, 8.1, 10.14, 11.24, and 11.49 a.m.; 2.8, 4.38, 7.55, 9.1, and 9.25 p m., in 25 minutes. [5–53.

BADEN AND OOS.—BADEN to OOS, at 6.38, 7.18, 10, and 10.40 a.m.; 12.39, 1.17, 3.14, 5.18, 7.30, 8.36, and 10.6 p.m., in 7 or 8 minutes. OOS to BADEN, at 6.51, 7.31, 10.12, and 10.51 a.m.; 12.52, 1.28, 3.27, 5.30, 7.43, 8.48, and 10.18 p.m., in 10 minutes. [5.53.

AMSTERDAM, The HAGUE, & ROTTERDAM.

(About 50 English miles.) [18–11–53

English Miles.	Fares. 1 cl.	2 cl.	3 cl.	Stations.	Trains. 1	2	3	4	5	6
	g. c.	g. c.	g. c.		a.m.	a.m.	a.m.	p.m.	p.m.	p.m.
—	..	..	..	**Amsterdam** ..dep	..	8 30	11 30	1 30	4 30	7 30
..	0 60	0 45	0 25	Halfweg	..	8 47	..	1 47	4 47	7 47
..	1 0	0 70	0 45	**Haarlem**	..	9 5	12 3	2 6	5 5	8 5
..	1 40	1 10	0 70	Vogelenzang	..	9 20	12 18	2 21	5 20	8 20
..	1 60	1 25	0 80	Veenenbrug	..	9 33	12 31	2 35	5 33	8 35
..	1 90	1 50	1 0	Piet Gyzenbrug	..	9 44	12 42	2 46	5 44	8 46
..	2 20	1 75	1 10	Warmond	..	9 56	..	2 58	5 56	8 58
..	2 40	1 85	1 20	**Leyden**	..	10 7	1 3	3 10	6 7	9 9
..	2 70	2 10	1 30	Voorschoten	a.m.	10 18	..	3 21	6 18	9 20
..	3 10	2 50	1 50	**Hague**	8 0	10 42	1 35	3 47	6 42	9 44
..	3 50	2 80	1 70	Delft	8 19	11 1	1 53	4 6	7 1	10 3
..	4 0	3 20	2 0	Schiedam	8 39	11 22	2 13	4 26	7 22	10 23
..	4 20	3 40	2 10	**Rotterdam** ..arr.	8 47	11 30	2 21	4 34	7 30	10 31

AMSTERDAM, UTRECHT & ARNHEIM.

[5-53.

English Miles.	Fares. 1 cl.	2 cl.	2 cl.	Stations.	Trains. 1	2	3	4
	g. c.	g. c.	g. c.		a.m.	a.m.	p.m.	p.m.
—	—	—	—	**Amsterdam**. dep	7 25	10 45	4 30	6 14
..	0 60	0 45	0 30	Abconde	7 42	11 2	4 47	6 34
..	0 90	0 70	0 50	Loenen Vreeland	7 50	11 10	4 55	6 39
..	1 0	0 80	0 50	Nieuwersluis	8 0	11 20	5 5	6 49
..	1 20	0 90	0 60	Breukelen	8 7	11 27	5 12	6 56
..	1 40	1 10	0 70	Maarssen	8 15	11 35	5 20	7 4
22	1 80	1 40	0 90	**Utrecht**	8 35	11 55	5 32	7 24
..	2 40	1 90	1 20	Leist Driebergen	8 53	12 13	5 40	7 42
..	2 90	2 30	1 50	Maarsbergen	9 10	12 30	5 58	7 59
..	3 50	2 80	1 80	Veenendaal	9 33	12 53	—	8 22
..	3 90	3 10	2 0	Ede	9 47	1 7	..	8 36
..	4 30	3 50	2 20	Wolfhezen	10 0	1 20	..	8 49
57	4 70	3 80	2 40	**Arnheim** ....arr	10 15	1 35	..	9 4

Rotterdam and the Hague to Amsterdam.

English Miles.	Fares. 1 cl.	2 cl.	3 cl.	Stations.	Trains. 1	2	3	4	5	6
	g. c.	g. c.	g. c.		a.m.	a.m.	a.m.	p.m.	p.m.	p.m.
—	..	..	..	**Rotterdam** ..dep.	6 45	9 45	11 45	3 0	5 30	7 45
..	0 40	0 30	0 20	Schiedam	6 56	9 56	11 56	3 11	5 41	7 56
..	0 90	0 70	0 40	Delft	7 16	10 16	12 16	3 31	6 1	8 16
..	1 20	1 0	0 60	**Hague**	7 37	10 37	12 36	3 52	6 17	8 37
..	1 75	1 40	0 85	Voorschoten	7 57	10 57	..	4 12	—	8 57
..	2 0	1 60	1 0	**Leyden**	8 12	11 12	1 8	4 27	..	9 12
..	2 10	1 70	1 10	Warmond	8 19	11 19	..	4 34	..	9 19
..	2 40	2 0	1 20	Piet-Gyzenbrug	8 31	11 31	1 25	4 46	..	9 31
..	2 70	2 20	1 30	Veenenbrug	8 44	11 44	1 38	4 59	..	9 44
..	3 10	2 50	1 50	Vogelenzang	8 56	11 55	1 49	5 10	..	9 55
..	3 40	2 70	1 70	**Haarlem**	9 15	12 14	2 8	5 29	..	10 14
..	3 80	3 0	1 90	Halfweg	9 29	12 28	..	5 43	..	10 28
..	4 20	3 40	2 10	**Amsterdam**..arr.	9 45	12 44	2 36	5 59	..	10 44

From Arnheim to Utrecht and Amsterdam.

English Miles.	Fares. 1 cl.	2 cl.	3cl.	Stations.	Trains. 1	2	3	4	5
	g. c.	g. c.	g. c.		a.m.	a.m.	p.m.	p.m.	p.m.
—	—	—	—	**Arnheim** ...dep	6 55	11 40	Except Sunday.	7 30	Sundays only.
..	0 50	0 40	0 25	Wolfhezen	7 10	11 55		7 45	
..	0 80	0 70	0 50	Ede	7 23	12 8		7 58	
..	1 20	1 0	0 70	Veenendaal	7 41	12 26		8 16	
..	1 80	1 50	1 0	Maarsbergen	8 0	12 45		8 35	
..	2 30	1 90	1 20	Leist Driebergen	8 17	1 2		8 52	7 6
..	2 90	2 40	1 50	**Utrecht**	8 43	1 28	6 0	9 18	7 32
..	3 40	2 70	1 70	Maarssen	8 55	1 40	6 12	9 30	7 44
..	3 50	2 90	1 80	Breukelen	9 3	1 48	6 20	9 38	7 52
..	3 70	3 0	1 90	Nieuwersluis	9 14	1 59	6 31	9 49	8 3
..	3 80	3 10	1 90	Loenen Vreeland	9 20	2 5	6 37	9 55	8 9
..	4 10	3 35	2 10	Abconde	9 28	2 13	6 45	10 3	8 17
57	4 70	3 80	2 40	**Amsterdam** arr	9 45	2 30	7 2	10 20	8 34

The Prussian quick mail travels daily from Arnheim (in conjunction with the first train from the Hague and from Amsterdam) through Emmerich, and Wesel and Duisburg, where it arrives before the first train to Dusseldorf and Cologne; so that the journey from Amsterdam to Cologne, and *vice versa*, is made in about 24 hours.—A Steamer plies from Rotterdam daily, early in the morning, to Antwerp, 10 hours to the passage, fare 1 caj. 8 fl., 2 caj. 6 fl.—A Steamer also leaves ARNHEIM for DUSSELDORF, COLOGNE, &c., at 6 a.m. and $3\frac{1}{2}$ p.m.

DENMARK.

Copenhagen to Roeskilde. Length, $17\frac{1}{2}$ miles; time of transit, 1 hour.

Frame and text are truncated on the original guide

Wurtemburg Railway.—HEILBRONN, STUTTGARDT, GEISLINGEN, ULM & FRIEDRICHSHAFEN.

Eng Mls.	STATIONS. From	1 a.m.	2 a.m.	3 a.m.	4 a.m.	5 a.m.	6 p.m	7 p.m.	8 p.m.
—	**Heilbronn** ......dep	..	..	5 30	..	11 45	..	2 0	5 45
7½	Lauffen	..	..	5 55	..	12 10	..	2 30	6 10
14⅓	Besigheim	..	..	6 15	..	12 30	..	2 55	6 30
18½	**Bietigheim**	..	..	6 30	..	12 45	..	3 15	6 45
..	Asperg	..	..	..	..	1 0	..	3 35	7 0
24¼	**Ludwigsburg**	..	..	7 0	9 0	1 15	..	3 55	7 15
..	Zuffenhausen	..	..	..	..	1 30	..	4 13	..
..	Feuerbach	..	..	..	..	1 36	..	4 20	..
33½	**Stuttgart** ... arr.	..	..	7 30	9 30	1 45	..	4 30	7 45
	dep.	5 45	..	7 45	10 0	2 0	4 0	5 45	8 0
..	**Cannstadt**	6 0	..	7 55	10 10	2 10	4 10	6 0	8 10
41½	**Esslingen** ... arr.	6 26	..	8 15	10 30	2 30	4 30	6 26	8 30
	dep.	..	..	..	—	2 37	—	..	—
..	**Plochingen**	6 58	..	8 45	..	3 0	..	6 58	..
..	Reichenbach	7 6	..	8 53	..	3 8	..	7 6	..
58¾	**Goppingen**	7 47	..	9 28	..	3 40	..	7 47	..
..	Sussen	8 10	..	9 48	..	4 0	..	8 10	..
70½	**Geislingen** .. arr.	8 46	..	10 22	..	4 33	..	8 46	..
	dep.	8 50	..	..	..	..	..	..	..
..	Amstetten	..	..	..	..	..	..	..	..
..	Lonsee	..	..	..	..	..	..	..	..
..	Beimerstetten	..	..	..	..	..	..	..	..
89¾	**Ulm** .... arr.	10 0	..	11 30	..	5 40	..	10 0	..
	dep.	—	5 45	12 0	..	6 0	..	—	..
..	Erbach	..	6 9	12 22	..	6 22	..	..	..
..	Laupheim	..	6 34	12 45	..	6 45	..	..	..
116½	**Biberach**	..	7 12	1 20	..	7 20	..	..	..
..	Ummendorf	..	..	1 28	..	7 28	..	..	..
..	Essendorf	..	7 40	1 43	..	7 43	..	..	..
..	Schussenried	..	7 58	2 0	..	8 0	..	..	..
..	Aulendorf	..	8 8	2 10	..	8 10	..	..	..
..	Durlesbach (Waldsee)	..	..	2 23	..	8 23	..	..	..
..	Mochenwangen	..	..	2 38	..	8 38	..	..	..
..	Niederbiegen	..	..	2 48	..	8 47	..	..	..
..	**Ravensburg**	..	9 5	3 0	..	9 0	..	..	..
..	Meckenbeuern	..	9 26	3 17	..	9 17	..	..	..
163	**Friedrichshafen**. ar	..	9 40	3 30	..	9 30	..	..	..

Eng Mls.	STATIONS. From	1 a.m.	2 a.m.	3 a.m.	4 a.m.	5 a.m.	6 p.m.	7 p.m	8 p.m.
—	**Friedrichshafen**. dp	..	..	..	..	6 20	5 45	..	12 25
5½	Meckenbeuern	..	..	..	..	6 36	6 3	..	12 41
11¼	**Ravensburg**	..	..	..	..	6 57	6 25	..	1 2
..	Niederbiegen	..	..	..	..	..	6 30	..	..
..	Mochenwangen	..	..	..	..	..	6 45	..	..
..	Durlesbach (Waldsee)	..	..	..	..	..	7 0	..	..
30	Aulendorf	..	..	..	..	7 48	7 20	..	1 53
32½	Schussenried	..	..	..	..	7 58	7 30	..	2 1
42½	Essendorf	..	..	..	..	8 13	7 45	..	2 18
..	Ummendorf	..	..	..	..	..	8 0	..	..
46	**Biberach**	..	..	..	..	8 36	8 15	..	2 41
54¼	Laupheim	..	..	..	..	9 5	8 45	..	3 10
66	Erbach	..	..	..	..	9 26	9 5	..	3 31
72¾	**Ulm** .... arr.	..	..	..	..	9 45	9 25	..	3 50
	dep.	..	..	5 45	..	10 10	—	2 0	4 15
..	Beimerstetten	..	..	..	..	..	..	..	..
..	Lonsee	..	..	..	..	..	..	..	..
..	Amstetten	..	..	..	..	..	..	..	..
92	**Geislingen** .. arr.	..	..	..	..	..	..	..	..
	dep.	..	..	7 8	..	11 28	..	3 22	5 34
..	Sussen	..	..	7 32	..	11 52	..	3 44	5 58
104¼	**Goppingen**	..	..	7 57	..	12 15	..	4 10	6 22
..	Reichenbach	..	..	8 26	..	12 42	..	4 42	6 50
..	**Plochingen**	..	..	8 40	..	12 57	p.m.	4 58	7 5
121	**Esslingen**	..	7 15	9 10	11 0	1 20	5 0	5 25	7 27
	Cannstadt	..	7 37	9 35	11 22	1 45	5 22	5 50	7 52
129½	**Stuttgart** ... arr.	..	7 45	9 45	11 30	1 55	5 30	6 0	8 0
	dep.	6 0	—	10 30	—	2 15	5 45	—	8 15
..	Feuerbach	..	..	..	..	2 25	5 55	..	8 25
..	Zuffenhausen	..	..	..	..	2 30	6 0	..	8 30
153½	**Ludwigsburg** arr.	..	..	..	..	2 45	6 15	..	8 45
	dep.	6 30	..	11 0	..	2 48	—	..	8 48
..	Asperg	..	..	..	..	2 55	..	..	8 55
..	**Bietigheim**	7 0	..	11 30	..	3 10	..	..	9 10
..	Besigheim	7 13	..	11 43	..	3 23	..	..	9 23
..	Lauffen	7 35	..	12 5	..	3 43	..	..	9 43
163	**Heilbronn** .....arr.	8 0	..	12 30	..	4 5	..	..	10 5

Additional Trains.—From Stuttgart to Cannstadt, 6 and 7 a.m., and 6 p.m.; Sundays, at 8-30 a.m.
From Cannstadt to Stuttgart, 6-30 and 8 a.m., and 7 p.m.; Sundays, at 9 a.m.

Fares.—From Heilbronn to Stuttgart, 1st class, 2 fl. 6kr.; 2nd class, 1fl. 21kr.; 3rd class, 54kr.
From Stuttgart to Ulm, 1st class, 3fl. 45kr; 2nd class, 2fl. 54kr.; 3rd class, 1fl. 36kr.

Remarks.—LUGGAGE.—10 lbs. free; every 10 lbs. extra, 17 kr. Four-wheeled carriage, 67 fl. 30 kr.; two-wheeled carriage, 50 fl. 39 kr.

Royal Bavarian Railway.—MUNICH, AUGSBURG, DONAUWORTH, & NUREMBERG. [5-53.

English Miles.	Fares. 1st	2nd	3rd	STATIONS.	1	2	3	4	5
	fl.kr.	fl.kr.	fl.kr.		a.m.	a.m.	a.m.	p.m.	p.m.
—				**Munich**......dep.	4 30	6 0	11 0	3 10	6 15
..	0 18	0 12	0 9	Pasing	4 50	6 14	11 14	3 30	6 29
..	0 30	0 21	0 15	Lochhausen	5 2	6 24	11 24	3 42	6 39
..	0 45	0 30	0 21	Olching	5 18	6 36	11 36	3 58	6 51
..	1 0	0 39	0 27	Maisach	5 35	6 47	11 47	4 15	7 2
..	1 15	0 51	0 33	Nanhofen	5 54	7 2	12 2	4 34	7 17
..	1 36	1 6	0 45	Althegnenberg	6 15	7 18	12 18	4 55	7 33
..	1 54	1 15	0 51	Mering	6 35	7 31	12 31	5 15	7 46
..	2 15	1 30	1 0	Stierhof	7 1	7 49	12 49	5 41	8 4
39¼	2 30	1 39	1 6	**Augsburg** ..arr.	7 15	8 0	1 0	5 55	8 15
..	..	..	..	Do. ....dep.	8 20	8 15	1 35		8 30
..	..	..	..	Gersthofen	8 37	8 29	1 49	..	8 47
..	..	..	..	Meitingen	9 13	8 55	2 15	..	9 23
..	..	..	..	Nordendorf	9 27	9 5	2 25	..	9 37
66¾	4 9	2 45	1 51	**Donauworth** arr	10 0	9 25	2 45	..	10 10
..	..	..	..	Do. dep	10 20	9 30	2 50	..	10 25
..	..	..	..	Harburg	10 57	9 53	3 13	..	11 2
..	..	..	..	Mottingen	11 20	10 10	3 30	..	11 25
82	5 21	3 33	2 24	**Nordlingen** arr	11 40	10 25	3 45	..	11 45
..	..	..	..	Do. dep	12 5	10 30	3 55	..	12 20
..	..	..	..	Durrenzimmern	12 23	10 43	4 8	..	12 36
..	5 54	3 54	2 39	**Oettingen**	12 46	10 54	4 19	..	12 56
107½	7 0	4 39	3 6	**Gunzenhausen**	2 10	11 46	5 11	..	2 11
117¾	7 39	5 6	3 27	Pleinfeld	3 0	12 17	5 42	..	2 54
..	..	..	..	Georgensgmund	3 31	12 34	5 59	..	3 22
..	..	..	..	Roth	3 58	12 49	6 14	..	3 46
135¼	8 48	5 51	3 54	Schwabach	4 34	1 10	6 35	..	4 19
144½	9 24	6 15	4 12	**Nuremberg**	5 10	1 35	7 0	..	4 50
262½	17 3	11 21	7 36	Hof ......arr.	..	9 10	5 22	..	12 42

Fares. 1st	2nd	3rd	STATIONS.	1	2	3	4	5
fl.kr	fl.kr	fl.kr		a.m.	a.m.	a.m.	p.m.	p.m.
			Nuremberg	..	7 15	7 30	1 35	9 0
0 36	0 24	0 18	Schwabach	..	7 43	8 16	2 3	9 41
..	..	..	Roth	..	8 2	8 48	2 22	10 10
..	..	..	Georgensgmund	..	8 17	9 16	2 37	10 35
1 45	1 9	0 48	Pleinfeld	..	8 37	9 47	2 57	11 3
2 30	1 39	1 6	**Gunzenhausen**	..	9 9	10 42	3 29	11 51
..	..	..	**Oettingen** ..dep	..	9 58	12 38	4 18	1 2
..	..	..	Durrenzimmern	..	10 8	12 54	4 28	1 15
4 3	2 42	1 48	**Nordlingen**..arr	..	10 20	1 11	4 40	1 30
..	..	..	Do. dep	..	10 25	1 30	4 45	2 0
..	..	..	Mottingen	..	10 41	1 51	5 1	2 21
..	..	..	Harburg	..	10 59	2 21	5 19	2 51
5 15	3 30	2 21	**Donauworth** arr	..	11 20	2 50	5 40	3 20
..	..	..	Do dep	..	11 25	3 5	5 45	3 35
..	..	..	Nordendorf	..	11 46	3 35	6 6	4 5
..	..	..	Meitingen	..	12 0	3 53	6 20	4 23
..	..	..	Gersthofen	..	12 22	4 35	6 42	5 5
6 54	4 36	3 6	**Augsburg** ..arr	..	12 35	5 0	6 55	5 30
..	..	..	Do. ..dep	8 0	1 10	5 55	7 15	6 0
..	..	..	Stierhof	8 19	1 22	6 14	7 27	6 12
..	..	..	Mering	8 45	1 41	6 40	7 46	6 31
..	..	..	Althegnenberg	9 1	1 53	6 56	7 58	6 43
..	..	..	Nanhofen	9 26	2 12	7 21	8 17	7 2
..	..	..	Maisach	9 44	2 24	7 39	8 29	7 14
..	..	..	Olching	9 58	2 35	7 53	8 40	7 25
..	..	..	Lochhausen	10 14	2 47	8 9	8 52	7 37
..	..	..	Pasing	10 29	2 58	8 24	9 3	7 48
9 24	6 15	4 12	**Munich** ....arr	10 45	3 10	8 40	9 15	8 0

6 — *Nuremberg to Bamberg, Lichtenfels, and Hof, see next page.*

NUREMBURG and FURTH.—From FURTH to NUREMBURG, every hour from 7½ a.m. to 7 (in winter 5½) p.m. From NUREMBURG to FURTH, every hour from 8 a.m. to 8 (in winter 6) p.m. Fares.—1st class, 12 kr., 2nd class, 9 kr., 3rd class, 6 kr. All the Morning trains, and last Night train, are drawn by horse power, occupying 26 minutes; the afternoon trains by steam, occupying from 10 to 12 minutes.—Distance, about 4½ miles.

BAMBERG AND SCHWEINFURT. [5-53.

Eng. Miles	Fares. 1st.	2nd.	3rd.	Stations.	1	2	3	4
	fl. kr.	fl. kr.	fl. kr.		a.m.	a.m.	p.m.	
Dis.	—	—	—	**Bamberg**.......dep.	7 45	11 0	4 30	..
20	1 18	0 51	0 36	Hassfurt	8 56	12 11	5 41	..
34½	2 12	1 27	1 0	**Schweinfurt**....arr.	9 40	12 55	6 25	..

Eng. Miles	Fares. 1st.	2nd.	3rd.	Stations.	1	2	3	4
	fl. kr.	fl. kr.	fl. kr.		a.m.	p.m.	p.m.	
Dis.	—	—	—	**Schweinfurt**..dep.	8 0	1 0	4 15	..
13½	0 54	0 36	0 24	Hassfurt	8 50	1 50	5 5	..
34½	2 12	1 27	1 0	**Bamberg** ......arr.	9 55	2 55	6 10	..

NUREMBERG, CULMBACH, NEUENMARKT, & HOF. [5–53.

Fares 1 clss	2 clss	3 clss	Stations.	1	2	3	4	5
fl. kr.	fl. kr.	fl. kr.		p.m.	p.m.	a.m.	a.m.	a.m.
..	..	..	See page 82. Munich ......dep.	6 15	3 10	6 0	4 30	11 0
..	..	..	Augsburg	8 30	5 55	8 15	8 20	1 35
..	..	..	Donauworth	10 25	—	9 30	10 20	2 50
..	..	..	Nordlingen	12 20	..	10 30	12 5	3 55
..	..	..	Gunzenhausen...	2 11	..	11 46	2 10	5 11
..	..	..	Nuremberg ..arr.	4 50	..	1 35	5 10	7 0
				a.m.	a.m.	p.m.	p.m.	p.m.
—	—	—	**Nuremberg.** ..dep	5 35	7 15	2 10	6 10	7 30
..	..	..	Kreuzung (via Fürth)	5 46	7 37	2 21	6 32	7 41
..	..	..	Poppenreuth	5 51	7 44	2 26	6 39	7 46
0 39	0 27	0 18	Eltersdorf..........	6 5	8 4	2 40	6 59	8 0
0 51	0 33	0 24	Erlangen	6 16	8 24	2 51	7 19	8 11
1 9	0 48	0 33	Baiersdorf	6 32	8 46	3 7	7 41	8 27
1 27	1 0	0 39	Forchheim	6 46	9 8	3 21	8 3	8 41
..	..	..	Eggolsheim	6 58	9 23	3 33	8 18	8 53
1 57	1 18	0 54	Hirschaid	7 10	9 43	3 45	8 38	9 5
2 24	1 36	1 6	**Bamberg** .. arr	7 27	10 5	4 2	9 0	9 22
			dep	7 40	10 40	4 10		10 0
..	..	..	Breitengüszbach.....	7 54	11 4	4 24	..	10 23
..	..	..	Bapfendorf	8 6	11 23	4 36	..	10 42
..	..	..	Ebensfeld	8 18	11 43	4 48	..	11 1
..	..	..	Staffelstein	8 29	12 5	4 59	..	11 20
3 42	2 27	1 39	**Lichtenfels.** arr	8 39	12 20	5 9	..	11 35
			dep	8 44	12 35	5 15	..	12 1
4 3	2 42	1 48	Hockstadt	8 59	1 6	5 30	..	12 28
..	..	..	Burgkundstadt	9 10	1 30	5 41	..	12 48
..	..	..	Mainleus	9 28	2 0	5 59	..	1 18
4 54	3 15	2 12	**Culmbach** .. arr	9 37	2 13	6 8	..	1 31
			dep	9 45	2 25	6 13	..	1 39
..	..	..	Untersteinach	9 57	2 49	6 25	..	1 59
5 24	2 36	2 24	**Neuenmarkt** arr	10 7	2 4	6 35	..	2 14
			dep	10 12	3 15	6 40	..	2 22
5 42	3 48	2 33	Markt Schorgast	10 40	3 48	7 8	..	2 53
..	..	..	Stambach...........	11 9	4 25	7 37	..	3 26
..	..	..	Münchberg	11 40	5 6	8 8	..	4 2
..	..	..	Schwarzenbach	12 10	5 51	8 38	..	4 40
..	..	..	Oberkotzau	12 23	6 9	8 51	..	4 56
7 39	5 6	3 24	**Hof** ....arr	12 42	6 35	9 10	p.m.	5 22
..	..	..	Hof..........dep.	2 30	..	10 0	4 15	6 0
..	..	..	Leipsic........arr.	7 30	..	3 10	9 15	11 0

Fares 1 clss	2 clss	3clss	Stations.	1	2	3	4	5
fl. kr.	fl. kr.	fl. kr.		a.m.	p.m.	a.m.	p.m.	a.m.
—	—	—	Leipsic........dep.	6 0	10 30	..	5 0	11 30
			Hof...........arr.	11 10	3 40	..	8 0	5 35
				a.m.	a.m.	a.m.	p.m.	p.m.
..	..	..	**Hof** ....dep	..	5 35	6 0	1 20	6 40
..	..	..	Oberkotzau	..	5 55	6 27	1 40	7 7
0 33	0 21	0 15	Schwarzenbach	..	6 10	6 52	1 55	7 27
..	..	..	Münchberg	..	6 42	7 37	2 27	8 6
..	..	..	Stambach...........	..	7 9	8 11	2 54	8 37
1 57	1 18	0 54	Markt Schorgast	..	7 40	8 52	3 25	9 13
2 15	1 30	1 0	**Neuenmarkt** arr	..	8 5	9 20	3 50	9 40
			dep	..	8 12	9 35	3 55	9 48
..	..	..	Untersteinach........	..	8 24	9 58	4 7	10 8
2 42	1 48	1 12	**Culmbach** .. arr	..	8 34	10 14	4 17	10 23
			dep	..	8 39	10 30	4 22	10 31
..	..	..	Mainleus	..	8 49	10 44	4 32	10 45
..	..	..	Burgkundstadt	..	9 8	11 23	4 51	11 20
3 36	2 24	1 36	Hochstadt	..	9 19	11 47	5 2	11 40
4 0	2 39	1 48	**Lichtenfels.** arr	..	9 32	12 8	5 15	12 1
			dep	..	9 37	12 30	5 23	12 15
..	..	..	Staffelstein	..	9 49	12 53	5 35	12 35
..	..	..	Ebensfeld...........	..	10 0	1 13	5 46	12 54
..	..	..	Bapfendorf	..	10 11	1 29	5 57	1 10
..	..	..	Breitengüszbach......	..	10 23	1 51	6 9	1 31
5 15	3 30	2 21	**Bamberg** .. arr	..	10 36	2 10	6 22	1 50
			dep	5 0	10 46	3 15	6 35	2 20
..	..	..	Hirschaid	5 19	11 5	3 44	6 54	2 49
..	..	..	Eggolsheim	5 30	11 16	3 58	7 5	3 3
..	..	..	Forchheim	5 43	11 29	4 19	7 18	3 24
..	..	..	Baiersdorf	5 59	11 45	4 41	7 34	3 46
6 51	4 33	3 3	Erlangen	6 14	12 0	5 6	7 49	4 11
..	..	..	Eltersdorf...........	6 23	12 9	5 19	7 58	4 24
..	..	..	Poppenreuth	6 37	12 23	5 37	8 12	4 42
..	..	..	Kreuzung (via Fürth)	6 43	12 29	5 53	8 18	4 58
7 39	5 6	3 24	**Nuremberg**....arr	6 52	12 38	6 5	8 27	5 10
..	..	..	See page 82. Nuremberg ..dep.	7 15	1 35	a.m.	9 0	7 30
9 59	6 45	4 30	Gunzenhausen...	9 9	3 29	..	11 51	10 42
11 42	7 48	5 12	Nordlingen......	10 25	4 45	..	2 0	1 30
12 54	7 36	5 45	Donauworth...	11 25	5 45	..	3 35	3 5
14 33	9 42	6 30	Augsburg.........	1 10	7 15	8 0	6 0	5 55
17 3	11 21	7 36	Munich ......arr.	3 10	9 15	10 45	8 0	8 40

Hof to Zwickau and Leipsic, page 91.

Nuremberg to Augsburg and Munich, page 82.

[5–53

Hanover & Brunswick.—MAIN LINE, HANOVER TO BRUNSWICK.

English Miles.	Fares.			STATIONS.	Trains.							
	1st Cls.	2nd Cls.	3rd Cls.		1	2	3	4	5	6	7	8
Dis.	Ggr.	Ggr.	Ggr.		a.m.	a.m.	a.m.	p.m.	p.m.	p.m.	p.m.	
—	—	—	—	**Hanover (1)** ....departure	5 30	7 45	9 30	2 0	3 0	10 30	12 0	..
..	..	..	..	Misburg	..	8 0	..	..	..	..	..	..
9½	10	7	4	Lehrte Junction	6 0	8 30	10 15	2 25	3 30	11 5	1 0	..
..	..	..	..	Hämeler Wald	..	8 50	..	..	3 50	..	..	..
..	..	..	..	Peine	6 30	9 15	11 10	..	4 15	11 40	..	..
..	..	..	..	Vechelde	6 45	9 40	11 30	..	4 40	12 0	..	..
37½	44	32	16	**Brunswick (2)**........arrival	7 5	10 15	12 15	3 22	5 15	12 30	3 0	.

English Miles.	Fares.			STATIONS.	Trains.							
	1st Cls.	2nd Cls.	3rd Cls.		1	2	3	4	5	6	7	8
Dis.	Ggr.	Ggr.	Ggr.		a.m.	a.m.	a.m.	p.m.	p.m.	p.m.	p.m.	
—	—	—	—	**Brunswick (2)** ....departure	4 50	5 0	6 45	1 10	4 15	7 45	8 0	..
..	..	..	..	Vechelde	..	..	7 10	..	4 45	8 5	..	..
15½	17	11	7	Peine	5 25	..	7 35	..	5 20	8 25	..	..
..	..	..	..	Hämeler Wald	..	..	7 45	..	5 45	..	..	..
..	35	19	12	Lehrte Junction	6 0	8 0	8 25	2 5	6 30	9 0	10 0	..
..	..	..	..	Misburg	..	..	8 35	..	6 40	..	..	..
37½	44	32	16	**Hanover (1)** ....arrival	6 20	9 0	8 50	2 23	7 0	9 25	11 0	..

Remarks.—50 lbs. of LUGGAGE free; every 10 lbs. extra, 1 ggr. (4d.) Four-wheeled Carriage, 8 Prussian dollars; two-wheeled Carriage, 5 Prussian dollars 8 ggr. **(1)** *Hanover and Minden for Cologne, see p. 87 & 70.* **(2)** *Between Brunswick and Magdeburg for Berlin. Dresden, Leipsic, Munich, and other southern routes, see pages* 86, 41, 97, 70, *&c.*

HAMBURG AND MAGDEBURG.

Magdeburg to Wittenberge, 69½ English miles. [15–11–52.

Eng. Miles.	Fares.			STATIONS.	Trains.						
	1 Cl.	2 Cl.	3 Cl.		1	2	3	4	5	6	7
Dis.	Sgr.	Sgr	Sgr.		a.m.	p.m.	p.m.				
..	..	..	..	**Hamburg** ....departure	..	..	..	..	..	..	..
—	—	—	—	**Wittenberge (1)** ..departure	5 0	1 0	6 0	..	..	..	..
6	13	8½	6⅓	Seehausen	5 25	1 15	6 25	..	..	..	..
..	..	..	..	Osterburg	5 45	1 30	6 45	..	..	..	..
..	..	..	..	Goldbeck	6 0	..	7 0	..	..	..	..
28½	48	31	24	Stendal	6 30	2 0	7 25	..	..	..	..
..	..	..	..	Demker	6 45	..	7 40	..	..	..	..
..	..	..	..	Tangerhütte	7 0	..	7 55	..	..	..	..
..	..	..	..	Mahlwinkle	7 20	2 30	8 10	..	..	..	..
..	..	..	..	Rogätz	7 40	..	8 30	..	..	..	..
60	91	58½	45½	Wollmirstedt	8 0	2 25	8 50	..	..	..	..
69½	105	67⅓	57½	**Magdeburg** ....arrrival	8 30	3 20	9 30	..	..	..	..

Eng. Miles.	Fares.			STATIONS.	Trains.			
	1 Cl.	2 Cl.	3 Cl.		1	2	3	4
Dis.	Sgr.	Sgr.	Sgr.		a.m.	a.m.	p.m.	
—	—	—	—	**Magdeburg** ....departure	7 45	10 45	5 30	..
9¼	14	9	7	Wollmirstedt	8 0	11 10	5 55	..
..	..	..	..	Rogätz	8 12	11 25	6 5	..
..	..	..	..	Mahlwinkle	8 30	11 45	6 30	..
..	..	..	..	Tangerhütte	..	11 50	6 35	..
37½	..	..	..	Demker	8 45	12 10	6 50	..
..	57½	37	29	Stendal	9 5	12 40	7 25	..
..	..	..	..	Goldbeck	9 20	1 0	7 45	..
..	..	..	..	Osterburg	9 35	1 30	8 10	..
..	92½	59⅓	46¼	Seehausen	9 50	1 45	8 30	..
60½	105	67½	57½	**Wittenberge (1)** ......arrival	10 30	2 45	9 50	..
69½	..	..	..	**Hamburg** ....arrival	3 30	8 0	10 30	..

Remarks.—50 lbs. of Luggage free; every 10 lbs. extra, 2½ sgr. Four-wheeled Carriage, 12 Prus. dollars 15 sgr.; two-wheeled Carriage, 10 Prussian dollars.

(1) *For Stations between Hamburg and Wittenberge, see page 92.*

HANOVER AND BRUNSWICK. [15-11-52.

First Intersecting Line.—LEHRTE AND HARBURG (HAMBURG).

English Miles.	Fares.			Stations.	Trains.							
	1st Class	2nd Class	3rd Class		1	2	3	4	5	6	7	8
Dis.	Ggr.	Ggr.	Ggr.		a.m.	a.m.	a.m.	a.m.	p.m.	p.m.		
—	—	—	—	**Hanover** ..(1)..dep.	..	5 30	7 45	9 30	2 0	6 0	..	
..	..	..	..	Misburg	..	..	8 0	..	..	6 10	..	
10	10	7	4	**Lehrte Junc.**	..	6 10		10 15	2 35	6 45	..	
15	14	10	6	Burgdorf	..	6 20	..	10 25	2 44	7 5	..	
..	..	..	..	Ehlershausen	..	..	..	10 40	..	7 20	..	
27	30	16	10	Celle	..	6 50	..	11 5	3 15	8 0	..	
..	..	..	..	Eschede	..	7 20	..	11 40	3 45	8 45	..	
..	..	..	..	Unterluss	..	7 35	..	12 0	4 0	9 15	..	
..	..	..	..	Suderburg	..	7 55	..	12 30	4 20	9 40	..	
60	70	44	33	Uelzen ....arrival	..	8 15	..	12 50	4 35	10 0	..	
..	..	..	..	,, ... departure	4 35	8 25	..	1 0	4 45		..	
..	..	..	..	Emmendorf	4 50	..	..	1 10	..	..	..	
..	..	..	..	Bevensen	5 10	8 45	..	1 25	5 5	..	..	
..	..	..	..	Bienenbuttell	5 40	9 0	..	1 45	5 20	..	..	
82	100	66	40	Luneburg	6 25	9 20	..	2 15	5 40	..	..	
..	..	..	..	Bardowieck	6 40	..	..	2 25	..	..	..	
..	..	..	..	Winsen	7 20	9 55	..	2 50	6 10	..	..	
..	..	..	..	Stelle	7 40	..	..	..	..	..	..	
106	120	76	46	**Harburg** ....arrival	8 10	10 25	..	3 25	6 40	..	..	

(1) *To and from Hanover or Brunswick, see page 84. To and from Hildesheim, see below.*

English Miles.	Fares.			Stations.	Trains.					
	1st Class	2nd Class	3rd Class		1	2	3	4	5	6
Dis.	Ggr.	Ggr.	Ggr.		a.m.	a.m.	a.m.	p.m.	p.m.	
—	—	—	—	**Harburg** ..departure	..	5 0	9 20	4 40	6 45	..
..	..	..	..	Stelle	..	5 20	..	..	7 10	..
..	..	..	..	Winsen	..	5 35	9 50	5 10	7 35	..
..	..	..	..	Bardowieck	..	6 0	..	..	8 5	..
24	30	16	10	Luneburg	..	6 20	10 20	5 40	8 30	..
..	..	..	..	Bienenbuttell	..	6 40	10 40	6 0	8 55	..
..	..	..	..	Bevensen	..	7 0	10 55	6 15	9 20	..
..	..	..	..	Emmendorf	..	7 10	..	..	9 35	..
45	60	38	20	Uelzen ....arrival	..	7 25	11 15	6 35	9 50	..
..	..	..	..	,, ... departure	4 40	7 35	11 25	6 45		..
..	..	..	..	Suderburg	5 5	7 55	11 40	7 0	..	..
..	..	..	..	Unterluss	5 35	8 20	12 0	7 20	..	..
..	..	..	..	Eschede	6 5	8 40	12 20	7 35	..	..
78½	90	60	36	Celle	7 0	9 15	12 45	8 5	..	..
..	..	..	..	Ehlershausen	7 25	9 35	..	8 20	..	..
90	102	68	41	Burgdorf	7 45	9 50	1 15	8 35	..	..
96	117	71	43	**Lehrte Junc**	8 25	10 30	1 40	9 0	..	..
..	..	..	..	Misburg	8 35	1 0	..	..	..	..
106	120	76	46	**Hanover** ..(1)..arr.	8 50	11 0	2 0	9 25	..	..

Remarks.—LUGGAGE: 50 lbs. free; every 10 lbs. extra, 3 ggr. (5d.) Four-wheeled Carriage, 20 Prussian dollars 12 ggr.; two-wheeled Carriage, 13 Prussian dollars 16 ggr.

HANOVER AND BRUNSWICK. [15-11-52.

Second Intersecting Line.—LEHRTE AND HILDESHEIM.

Eng. Miles.	Fares.			Stations.	Trains.				Stations.	Trains.			
	1 Cl	2 Cl.	3 Cl.		1	2	3	4		1	2	3	4
Dis.	Ggr.	Ggr.	Ggr.		a.m.	p.m.	p.m.			a.m.	p.m	p.m.	
—	—	—	—	**Lehrte Jnc**(1)dep.	8 30	2 30	6 35	..	**Hildesheim**..dep.	7 20	12 45	5 20	..
..	..	..	..	Sehnde	8 40	2 45	6 50	..	Harsum	7 30	12 55	5 30	..
..	..	..	..	Algermissen	8 55	3 5	7 5	..	Algermissen	7 40	1 5	5 45	..
..	..	..	..	Harsum	9 5	3 20	7 15	..	Sehnde	8 0	1 15	6 0	..
14	17	11	7	**Hildesheim**..arr.	9 20	3 30	7 30	..	**Lehrte Jnc**(1) ar.	8 25	1 40	6 30	..

(1) *To and from Hanover and Brunswick, see page 84. To and from Harburg (Hamburg) see above.*

MAGDEBURG, HALBERSTADT, OSCHERSLEBEN, AND BRUNSWICK. [5–53.

Fares 1 Cl.	2 Cl.	3 Cl.	Stations.	1	2	3	4	5	6
				a.m.	a.m.	a.m.	p.m.	p.m.	p.m.
			Magdeburg . . dep.	1 50	6 0	10 40	12 0	4 15	6 15
Sgr.	Sgr.	Sgr.	Dodendorf	..	6 10	..	12 10	..	6 20
..	..	..	Langenwedding	..	6 20	..	12 20	4 30	6 30
..	..	..	Blumenberg	..	6 25	..	12 25	..	6 35
..	..	..	Hadmersleben	..	6 35	..	12 35	4 45	6 45
30	20	12½	Oschersleben	3 45	7 15	11 28	2 0	5 15	8 15
..	..	..	Crottorf	..	7 20	..	..	5 20	..
..	..	..	Nienhagen	..	7 25	..	..	5 25	..
45	30	20	**Halberstadt**. arr.	4 30	8 30	12 15	..	6 15	..
..	..	..	" dep.	3 15	6 45	9 45	..	5 15	..
..	..	..	Oschersleben. dep.	2 45	7 45	11 33	3 10	5 25	5 30
..	..	..	Wegersleben	3 0	8 0	..	3 30	5 40	..
48¾	32½	21¾	Jerxheim . . . . . arr.	3 20	9 0	..	4 35	6 5	..
58¾	38¾	25½	Schoppenstedt	3 40	9 30	..	5 15	6 30	7 35
72½	48¾	31	Wolfenbuttel	4 5	10 0	12 38	5 50	6 55	8 5
85	55	35	**Brunswick** . . arr.	4 30	10 30	12 55	6 15	7 15	8 30
.	..	..	BRUNSWICK . . dep.	4 50	6 0	1 10	4 15	7 45	8 0
132½	87½	55	HANOVER . . . arr.	6 20	9 0	2 23	7 0	9 52	11 0

Fares 1 Cl.	2 Cl.	3 Cl.	Stations.	1	2	3	4	5	6
				p.m.	p.m.	a.m.	a.m.	p.m.	p.m.
			HANOVER . . dep.	10 35	12 0	5 30	9 30	2 0	3 0
Ggr.	Ggr.	Ggr.	BRUNSWICK . . arr.	12 30	3 0	7 5	12 15	3 22	5 15
..	..	..	**Brunswick** . . dep.	1 15	5 30	7 30	12 45	3 45	6 30
8	5	3	Wolfenbuttel	1 35	6 0	7 45	1 10	4 0	6 55
19	13	8	Schoppenstedt	2 10	6 45	8 10	1 45	..	7 35
27	18	11	Jerxheim	2 30	7 20	..	2 15	..	8 5
..	..	..	Wegersleben	3 0	8 0	..	2 45	..	8 35
42	28	18	Oschersleben . . . . arr.	3 15	8 20	9 0	3 0	5 10	9 0
56	36	24	**Halberstadt**. arr.	5 45	11 15	3 45	a.m.	p.m.	..
..	..	..	" dep.	2 0	6 45	8 30	10 45	2 30	4 30
..	..	..	Nienhagen	..	6 50	..	..	2 35	..
..	..	..	Crottorf	..	6 55	..	..	2 40	..
..	..	..	Oschersleben	3 45	7 15	9 5	11 28	3 15	5 15
..	..	..	Hadmersleben	..	7 30	..	..	3 20	..
..	..	..	Blumenberg	..	7 40	..	..	3 30	..
..	..	..	Langenwedding	..	7 45	..	..	3 40	..
..	..	..	Dodendorf	..	7 55	..	..	3 50	..
68	44	28	**Magdeburg** . . arr.	5 0	9 45	10 0	..	6 0	6 0

Remarks.—LUGGAGE—50 lbs. free; every 10 lbs. extra, 2½ sgr. Four-wheeled carriage, 13 P. d., 22½ sgr. Two-wheeled carriage, 9 P. d., 5 sgr. ADDITIONAL TRAINS.—OSCHERSLEBEN to MAGDEBURG, at 12 n. *Brunswick to Hanover, see p. 85. Magdeburg to Potsdam & Berlin, see p. 96.*

AUGSBURG, KAUFBEUERN, KEMPTEN, AND IMMENSTADT. [5–53.

Eng. Mls. Dis.	Fares 1 Cls. fl. kr.	2 Cls. fl. kr.	3 Cls. fl. kr.	Stations.	a.m.	a.m.	p.m.	p.m.
				Augsburg . . . . dep.	..	8 30	2 15	7 30
				Inningen	..	8 44	2 29	7 44
..	..	..	..	Bobingen	..	8 55	2 40	7 55
..	..	..	..	Grotzaitingen	..	9 10	2 55	8 10
13½	0 54	0 36	0 24	Schwabmunchen	..	9 26	3 11	8 26
..	..	..	..	Westererringen	..	9 38	3 23	8 38
24¼	1 36	1 3	0 42	Buchloe	..	10 4	3 49	9 4
..	..	..	..	Pforzen	..	10 27	4 12	9 27
36	2 24	1 36	1 6	**Kaufbeuern** . . . arr.	..	10 40	4 25	9 40
..	..	..	..	Do. . . . . dep.	..	10 45	4 30	9 45
39	2 39	1 45	1 12	Bissenhofen	..	10 59	4 46	9 59
..	..	..	..	Ruderatshofen	..	11 10	4 57	10 10
..	..	..	..	Uitrang	..	11 20	5 7	10 20
..	..	..	..	Gunzach	..	11 46	5 33	10 46
..	..	..	..	Wildpoldsried	..	12 8	5 55	11 8
..	..	..	..	Betzigau	..	12 17	6 4	11 17
64	4 9	2 45	1 51	**Kempten** . . . . . arr.	..	12 30	6 17	11 30
..	..	..	..	Do. . . . . dep.	6 40	12 35	6 25	
..	..	..	..	Waltenhofen	6 55	12 50	6 40	..
..	..	..	..	Oberdorf	7 7	1 2	6 52	..
..	..	..	..	**Immenstadt** . . arr.	7 30	1 25	7 15	..

Eng. Mls. Dis.	Fares 1 Cls. fl. kr.	2 Cls. fl. kr.	3 Cls. fl. kr.	Stations.	a.m.	a.m.	p.m.	p.m.
				Immenstadt . . dep.	..	8 0	2 20	7 40
				Oberdorf	..	8 24	2 44	8 4
..	..	..	..	Waltenhofen	..	8 36	2 56	8 16
—	—	—	—	**Kempten** . . . . . arr.	..	8 50	3 10	8 30
..	..	..	..	Do. . . . . . dep.	3 50	9 0	3 15	
..	..	..	..	Betzigau	4 4	9 14	3 29	..
..	..	..	..	Wildpoldsried	4 13	9 23	3 38	..
..	..	..	..	Gunzach	4 39	9 49	4 4	..
..	..	..	..	Uitrang	5 1	10 11	4 26	..
..	..	..	..	Ruderatshofen	5 11	10 21	4 36	..
17	1 30	1 0	0 42	Biessenhofen	5 23	10 33	4 48	..
20¼	1 45	1 9	0 48	**Kaufbeuern** . . arr.	5 35	10 45	5 0	..
..	..	..	..	Do. . . . dep.	5 40	10 50	5 5	..
..	..	..	..	Pforzen	5 54	11 4	5 19	..
38	2 33	1 42	1 9	Buchloe	6 15	11 25	5 40	..
..	..	..	..	Westererringen	6 35	11 54	6 0	..
48	3 15	2 9	1 27	Schwabmunchen	6 51	12 1	6 16	..
..	..	..	..	Grotzaitingen	7 3	12 13	6 28	..
..	..	..	..	Bobingen	7 18	12 28	6 43	..
..	..	..	..	Inningen	7 28	12 38	6 53	..
64	4 9	2 45	1 51	**Augsburg** . . . . arr.	7 40	12 50	7 5	..

BRUNSWICK AND HARZBURG. [5-53

E. Mls.	Fares.				Stations.	Trains.					
	1st Clss	2nd Clss	3rd Clss	4th Clss		1	2	3	4		
Dis	Ggr.	Ggr.	Ggr.	Ggr.		a.m.	a.m.	p.m.	p.m.		
—	..	..	..	..	**Brunswick** ....departure	5 15	7 45	1 0	7 45	..	..
$6\frac{3}{4}$	8	5	3	2	Wolfenbüttel........	5 40	8 5	1 20	8 5	..	..
$13\frac{1}{2}$	12	9	6	4	Börssum	6 5	8 25	1 40	8 25	..	..
$18\frac{1}{2}$	21	12	8	5	Schladen	6 25	8 40	1 55	8 40	..	..
23	26	15	11	7	Vienenburg	6 45	8 55	2 10	8 55	..	..
$27\frac{3}{4}$	31	17	13	8	**Harzburg**........arrive	7 5	9 15	2 30	9 15	..	..

In connexion with trains at Brunswick to Hanover, Hildesheim, and Harburg.

Additional Trains.—From BRUNSWICK to WOLFENBUTTEL, at $1\frac{1}{4}$, $5\frac{1}{4}$, 5.30, 7.30, and $7\frac{3}{4}$ a.m.; 12.45, 1, 2, $3\frac{1}{4}$, $6\frac{1}{2}$, and $7\frac{3}{4}$ p.m.

From WOLFENBUTTEL to BRUNSWICK, at 4.5, 5.55, 10, and 11.35 a.m.; $2\frac{3}{4}$, 5.50, 6.20, 6.55, and 9.20 p.m.

Remarks.—Luggage, 50 lbs., free; every 10 lbs. extra, 1 ggr. Four-wheeled Carriage, 6 Pruss. doll.; Two-wheeled Carriage, 4 Pruss. doll.

HARSBURG and BRUNSWICK.

E. Mls.	Fares.				Stations.	Trains.						
	1st Clss	2nd Clss	3rd Clss	4th Clss		1	2	3	4			
Dis	Ggr	Ggr	Ggr	Ggr		a.m.	a.m.	p.m.	p.m.			
—	—	—	—	—	**Harzburg** ....departure	4 30	10 30	5 15	8 15	..	..	..
$4\frac{1}{2}$	5	4	3	2	Vienenburg	4 50	10 45	5 30	8 30	..	..	..
$9\frac{1}{4}$	10	8	6	4	Schladen	5 10	11 0	5 45	8 45	..	..	..
..	15	11	8	5	Börssum	5 30	11 15	6 0	8 55	..	..	..
$20\frac{3}{4}$	23	14	11	7	Wolfenbüttel	5 55	11 35	6 20	9 15	..	..	..
$27\frac{3}{4}$	31	17	13	8	**Brunswick** ....arrive	6 20	11 55	6 40	9 30	..	..	..

HANOVER TO MINDEN. [15-11-52.

Eng. Miles.	Fares.			STATIONS.	Trains.							
	1st Class	2nd Class	3rd Class		1	2	3	4	5	6	7	8
Dis.	Ggr.	Ggr.	Ggr.		a.m.	a.m.	p.m.	p.m.	p.m.	p.m.		
—	—	—	—	**Hanover** ....departure	6 45	9 10	12 40	2 38	4 0	9 50	..	..
..	..	..	..	Seelze	..	9 30	..	..	4 15	..	..	..
$12\frac{1}{2}$	14	10	6	Wunstorf	7 20	9 55	1 35	3 5	4 40	10 30	..	..
$17\frac{1}{2}$	19	13	8	Haste	7 30	10 5	1 50	..		10 40	..	..
..	..	..	..	Lindhorst	..	10 20	2 10	..	..	..	..	..
$26\frac{1}{2}$	35	19	12	Stadthagen	7 55	10 40	2 35	..	..	11 5	..	..
..	..	..	..	Kirchhorsten........	..	10 55	2 55	..	..	..	..	..
34	42	30	15	Buckeburg........	8 15	11 10	3 20	3 45	..	11 30	..	..
40	47	33	17	**Minden** ....arrival	8 30	11 30	3 40	3 56	..	11 45	..	..

MINDEN TO HANOVER

Eng. Miles.	Fares.			STATIONS.	Trains.							
	1st Class	2nd Class	3rd Class		1	2	3	4	5	6	7	8
Dis.	Ggr.	Ggr.	Ggr.		a.m.	a.m.	p.m.	p.m.	p.m.			
—	—	—	—	**Minden** ....departure	3 30	6 0	12 24	2 30	8 15	..	..	..
6	5	3	2	Buckeburg........	3 45	6 25	12 35	2 50	8 30	..	..	..
..	..	..	..	Kirchhorsten	..	6 45	..	3 10	..	..	..	..
$12\frac{1}{2}$	12	8	5	Stadthagen	4 0	7 10	..	3 30	8 45	..	..	..
..	..	..	..	Lindhorst	..	7 30	..	3 50	..	..	..	..
22	22	14	9	Haste	4 20	7 50	..	4 10	9 5	..	..	..
27	33	17	11	Wunstorf	4 40	8 30	1 20	4 45	9 25	..	..	..
..	..	..	..	Seelze	..	8 45	..	5 5	..	..	..	..
40	47	33	17	**Hanover** ....arrival	5 10	9 5	1 45	5 30	10 0	..	..	..

The Luggage of Travellers from Hanover to Cologne (although booked and paid for through,) will be examined at Minden.

Minden to Hamm, Dusseldorf, & Cologne, see page 70 *Hanover to Brunswick & Madgeburg, see pages* 85, 86.

Thuringischen Railway.—HALLE, GOTHA, & EISENACH.

Eng. Mls.	Fares. 1 Cl.	2 Cl	3 Cl.	STATIONS.	Trains. 1	2	3	4	5	6	7	8
Dis.	Sgr.	Sgr.	Sgr.		a.m.	a.m.	a.m.	p.m.	p.m.			
..	..	..	..	HAMBURG .. .. .. departure	7 30	..	..	5 0	..	..	..	..
..	..	..	..	MAGDEBURG .. .. ,,	p.m.	..	6 0	10 45	..	..	..	..
..	..	..	..	BERLIN .. .. .. ,,	10 0	..	..	8 0	..	..	..	..
..	..	..	..	DRESDEN .. .. .. ,,	6 0	..	4 0	..	..	..	..	..
..	..	..	..	LEIPSIC .. .. ,,	10 0	..	7 0	12 0	5 30	..	..	..
Fr	om	Hall	e.		a.m.	a.m.	a.m.	p.m.	p.m.			
—	—	—	—	**Halle** .. .. departure	3 15	5 0	9 0	1 45	7 5	..	..	..
7½	14	8	6	Merseburg	3 35	5 35	9 20	2 5	7 30	..	..	..
..	..	..	..	Corbetha (Durrenberg)..	..	..	9 35	2 20	7 45	..	..	..
19½	34	19	15	Weissenfels	4 0	6 30	9 50	2 35	8 10	..	..	..
27¾	48	27	21	Naumburg	4 20	7 5	10 15	3 5	8 35	..	..	..
..	..	..	..	Kösen	..	..	10 25	3 15	8 50	..	..	..
..	..	..	..	Sulza	..	..	10 40	3 30	9 10	..	..	..
44¾	76	42	33	Apolda	5 0	8 30	11 5	3 55	9 35	..	..	..
53¼	92	52	40	Weimar	5 30	9 20	11 35	4 25	10 15	..	..	..
..	..	..	..	Bieselbach	..	..	11 55	4 45	10 35	..	..	..
66	115	65	50	**Erfurt**	6 5	10 30	12 10	5 0	10 55	..	..	..
74	128	72	56	Dietendorf (Arnstadt)	6 25	11 10	12 35	5 25	—	..	..	..
83¼	144	81	63	**Gotha**	6 55	12 0	1 0	5 50	..	..	..	..
89¾	155	87	68	Frottstedt (Waltershausen)	7 10	12 30	1 20	6 5	..	..	..	..
102	175	99	77	**Eisenach**	7 40	1 30	1 50	6 40	..	..	..	..
..	..	..	..	Herleshausen	..	..	..	—	..	..	..	..
116½	201	113	88	**Gerstungen** .. .. .. arrival	10 35	3 20	4 25	..	..	..	..	..
167½	278	168	126	CASSEL .. .. arrival	1 45	p.m.	7 30	p.m.	..	..	..	..
227½	324¾	258½	181¾	FRANKFURT-ON-M. .. ,,	8 15	..	..	..	..	..	..	..
..	..	..	..	HEIDELBERG & MANNHEIM ,,	9 56	..	7 11	..	..	..	..	..
..	..	..	..	KEHL (Strasburg) .. .. ,,	1 20	..	..	..	..	..	..	..
..	..	..	..	HALTINGEN (Basel) .. .. ,,	7 13	..	9 18	..	..	..	..	..

Eng. Mls.	Fares. 1 Cl.	2 Cl.	3 Cl.	STATIONS.	Trains. 1	2	3	4	5	6
Dis.	Sgr.	Sgr.	Sgr.		a.m.	a.m.	a.m.	a.m.	p m.	a.m.
..	..	..	..	HALTINGEN (Basel) .. departure	..	..	..	7 0	..	..
..	..	..	..	KEHL (Strasburg) .. ,,	..	6 10	..	11 5	..	..
..	..	..	..	HEIDELBERG & MANNHEIM ,,	..	8 0	..	4 20	..	..
..	..	..	..	FRANKFURT-ON-M. .. .. ,,	..	12 10	..	7 15	..	8 15
..	..	..	..	CASSEL .. .. ,,	..	6 30	..	8 0	..	3 0
Fro	m Ei	sena	ch.		a.m	p.m.	a.m.	a.m.	p.m.	p.m.
..	..	..	..	**Gerstungen** .. .. departure	2 30	9 15	..	11 0	..	6 30
..	..	..	..	Herleshausen	..	9 30	..	11 15	..	6 45
—	—	—	—	**Eisenach**	3 5	9 50	5 45	11 35	2 0	7 15
13¾	20	11	9	Frottstedt (Waltershausen)	..	—	6 20	12 5	2 35	7 55
15¼	31	17	14	**Gotha**	3 50	..	6 45	12 25	3 5	8 20
27¾	48	27	21	Dietendorf (Arnstadt)	4 10	..	7 15	11 55	3 35	8 50
35[illegible]	61	34	26	**Erfurt**	4 30	..	7 40	1 15	4 5	9 15
..	..	..	..	Bieselbach	..	..	7 55	..	4 20	9 30
48½	83	47	37	Weimar	5 5	..	8 25	1 50	4 50	10 0
57¾	100	56	44	Apolda	5 25	..	8 53	2 15	5 25	—
..	..	..	..	Sulza	..	..	9 20	2 35	5 45	..
..	..	..	..	Kösen	..	..	9 35	2 45	6 0	..
..	127	71	56	Naumburg	6 0	..	9 55	3 0	6 20	..
74	141	80	62	Weissenfels	6 25	..	10 25	3 25	6 50	..
..	..	..	..	Corbetha (Durrenberg)	..	..	10 45	..	7 10	.
93¼	161	91	70	Merseburg	6 50	..	11 5	3 50	7 35	..
101¾	175	99	77	**Halle** .. .. arrival	7 15	..	11 30	4 15	8 0	..
122¼	202	117	88	LEIPSIC .. .. arrival	9 30	a.m.	2 5	5 30	9 15	..
..	..	..	..	DRESDEN .. .. ,,	1 30	..	5 15	..	1 0	..
217¼	334	268	158½	BERLIN .. .. ,,	12 30	..	..	9 30	..	..
	184	145	166	MAGDEBURG .. .. ,,	9 50	..	3 15	8 45	1 15	..
	..	..	..	HAMBURG .. .. ,,	8 30	..	10 30	..	4 0	..

Remarks.—50 lbs. of luggage free; every 10 lbs. extra, 5¼ sgr. Four-wheeled carriage, 22 Prus. doll.; two-wheeled carriage, 18¼ Prus. doll.

BERLIN TO DRESDEN AND LEIPSIC (DIRECT.) [15-11-52.

There is another Route between Berlin and Leipsic, but somewhat longer, via Kothen and Halle, see p. 105.

Eng. Miles.	Fares. 1st Class	2nd Class	3rd Class	STATIONS.	Trains. 1	2	3	4	5	6
Dis.	Sgr.	Sgr.	Sgr.		a.m.	a.m.	p.m.			
—	—	—	—	**Berlin** ....departure	7 0	10 0	1 45	..	..	..
..	..	..	..	Gross Beeren..................	7 15	10 45	2 0	..	..	..
..	..	..	..	Ludwigsfelde..................	7 30	11 0	2 15	..	..	..
..	..	..	..	Trebbin	7 45	11 30	2 30	..	..	..
..	..	..	..	Luckenwalde..................	8 0	12 0	2 45	..	..	..
..	..	..	..	Juterbogk Junction............	8 30	12 45	3 15	..	..	..
..	..	..	..	Oehna	8 45	1 0	3 30	..	..	..
..	..	..	..	Linda	9 0	1 15	3 45	..	..	..
..	..	..	..	Holzdorf.......................	9 15	1 45	4 0	..	..	..
62½	88	61	47	Herzberg	9 30	2 15	4 15	..	..	..
..	..	..	..	Falkenberg	9 45	2 45	4 30	..	..	..
78	110½	76½	59½	Burxdorf	10 15	3 15	5 0	..	..	..
..	..	..	..	Jacobsthal	10 30	3 45	5 15	..	..	..
87	123½	85½	66½	Röderau	11 0	4 30	5 45	..	..	..
116½	165	110	70	**Dresden** ....arrival	12 15	..	7 30	..	..	..
129	180	120	90	**Leipsic** .... ,,	1 0	..	8 15	..	..	..

Eng. Miles.	Fares. 1st Class	2nd Class	3rd Class	STATIONS.	Trains. 1	2	3	4
Dis.	Sgr.	Sgr.	Sgr.		a.m.	a.m.	p.m.	
..	..	..	..	**Leipsic**............departure	5 15	..	2 30	..
—	—	—	—	**Dresden** .... ,,	6 0	..	3 15	..
30	39	29	20	Röderau	7 45	8 15	4 45	..
..	..	..	..	Jacobsthal	7 50	8 30	4 50	..
39	55	40	29	Burxdorf	8 0	9 0	5 0	..
..	..	..	..	Falkenberg	8 15	9 45	5 30	..
53	78	56	41	Herzberg	8 45	10 30	5 45	..
..	..	..	..	Holzdorf	9 0	11 15	6 15	..
..	..	..	..	Linda	9 15	11 30	6 30	..
..	..	..	..	Oehna..........................	9 30	12 0	6 45	..
..	..	..	..	Juterbogk Junction	9 45	1 15	6 50	..
..	..	..	..	Lockenwalde	10 15	3 0	7 15	..
..	..	..	..	Trebbin	10 30	3 45	7 30	..
..	..	..	..	Ludwigsfelde..................	10 45	4 0	7 45	..
..	..	..	..	Gross Beeren..................	11 0	4 30	8 0	..
116½	165	110	70	**Berlin** ....arrival	11 45	6 0	8 45	..

Remarks.—LUGGAGE: 50 lbs. free; every 10 lbs. extra, 5 sgr. Four-wheeled carriage, 25¼ Prus. doll.; two-wheeled carriage, 19 Prus. doll.

HANOVER TO ALFELD.

From HANOVER, at 7 a.m. and 3¼ p.m., in 1 hour 50 minutes.
From ALFELD, at 10½ a.m., and 7 p.m., in 1 hour 50 minutes.

HANOVER AND BREMEN. [15-11-52.

Eng. Miles.	Fares. 1 Cl.	2 Cl.	3 Cl.	STATIONS.	Trains. 1	2	3	4
Dis.	ggr.	ggr.	ggr.		a.m.	a.m.	p.m.	p.m.
—	—	—	—	**Hanover** ....dep.	6 45	9 10	12 40	4 0
..	..	..	..	Seelze	..	9 30	..	4 15
13½	14	10	6	Wunstorf..........	7 25		1 25	4 40
19	17	11	7	Neustadt	7 35	..	1 35	4 50
..	..	..	..	Hagen	7 50	..	..	5 5
..	..	..	..	Linsburg	8 0	..	..	5 15
34¾	38	20	13	Nienburg	8 15	..	2 15	5 30
..	..	..	..	Rohrsen	8 25	..	..	5 40
..	..	..	..	Eistrup	8 40	..	2 40	5 55
..	..	..	..	Dörverden	8 50	..	..	6 5
54¼	62	40	21	Verden	9 10	..	3 5	6 25
..	..	..	..	Langwedel	9 20	..	..	6 35
..	..	..	..	Achim	9 40	..	3 35	6 55
..	..	..	..	Sebaldsbruck	9 55	..	3 50	7 10
76¼	90	60	36	**Bremen** ..arrival	10 10	..	4 0	7 25

STATIONS.	Trains. 1	2	3	4
	a.m.	a.m.	p.m.	
Bremen ....dep.	5 20	10 10	6 25	..
Sebaldsbruck	5 30	10 15	6 30	..
Achim	5 45	10 35	6 50	..
Langwedel	6 0	..	7 10	..
Verden	6 20	11 0	7 25	..
Dörverden	6 35	..	7 35	..
Eistrup	6 50	11 25	7 50	..
Rohrsen	7 5	..	8 0	..
Nienburg	7 20	11 55	8 15	..
Linsburg	7 35	..	8 30	..
Hagen	7 50	..	8 45	..
Neustadt	8 0	12 30	8 55	..
Wunstorf..........	8 30	12 55	9 25	..
Seelze	8 45	..	..	..
Hanover ....arr.	9 5	1 25	10 0	..

Friedrich-Willheim Railway.—EISENACH TO CARLSHAFEN.

English Miles.	Fares.				Stations.	Trains.						
	1st Class	2nd Class	3rd Class	4th Class		1	2	3	4	5	6	7
Dis.	sgr.	sgr.	sgr.	sgr.		a.m.	a.m.	p.m.				
—	—	—	—	—	**Eisenach** .. .. dep.	—	10 0	3 50	—	—	—	—
14½	26	14	11	—	Gerstungen	—	10 40	4 30	—	—	—	—
—	—	—	—	—	Hönebach	—	11 0	—	—	—	—	—
28¾	43	25½	18	—	Bebra	6 0	11 25	5 25	—	—	—	—
32½	48	28½	20	—	Rotenburg	7 0	11 40	5 35	—	—	—	—
40¼	58	35	24	-	Altmorschen	7 15	12 10	6 0	—	—	—	—
—	—	—	—	—	Beiseförth	—	12 20	—	—	—	—	—
47¼	66½	41	28	—	Melsungen	8 10	12 35	6 25	—	—	—	—
—	—	—	—	—	Guxhagen	—	1 0	—	—	—	—	—
56½	89	59	43	—	Guntershausen (1) ..	8 40	1 20	7 5	—	—	—	—
—	—	—	—	—	Wahlershausen	9 0	1 40	—	—	—	—	—
66	103	69	49	—	**Cassel** .. .. .. arr	9 5	1 45	7 30	—	—	—	—
	From Cassel.				,, ... dep.	9 15		7 45	—	—	—	—
—	—	—	—	—	Mönchehof	9 35	—	—	—	—	—	—
—	18¼	12¼	7½	—	Grebenstein	9 55	—	—	—	—	—	—
15¾	21½	14½	9	—	Hofgeismar	10 5	—	8 35	—	—	—	—
19½	26½	17½	11	—	Humme	10 15	—	8 45	—	—	—	—
—	—	—	—	—	Liebenau	10 35	—	—	—	—	—	—
32½	43	28¾	18	—	**Warburg** .. .. arr.	10 55	—	9 25	—	—	—	—
					,, ... dep.	—	—	—	—	—	—	—
—	—	—	—	—	**Humme** .. .. dep.	10 25	—	9 0	—	—	—	—
—	29½	19¾	12½	—	Trendelburg	10 35	—	9 10	—	—	—	—
—	—	—	—	—	Helmarshausen	10 55	—	9 30	—	—	—	—
30	39¼	25¼	16¼	—	**Carlshafen** .. arr.	11 0	—	9 35	—	—	—	—
—	—	—	—	—	PADERBORN .. arr.	4 0	—	4 0	—	—	—	—
—	146	111	90	—	HAMM .. .. ,,	6 20	—	7 0	—	—	—	—
—	—	—	—	—	ELBERFELD .. ,,	9 42	—	2 48	—	—	—	—
—	—	—	—	—	DUSSELDORF .. ,,	9 15	—	11 10	—	—	—	—
—	—	—	—	—	COLOGNE .. .. ,,	10 15	—	12 30	—	—	—	—
—	—	—	—	—	MINDEN .. .. .. ,,	4 30	—	11 15	—	—	—	—
—	—	—	—	—	HANOVER .. ,,	6 15	—	2 40	—	—	—	—
—	—	—	—	—	BRUNSWICK .. .. ,,	8 0	—	6 5	—	—	—	—
—	—	—	—	—	BREMEN .. .. ,,	10 15	—	5 50	—	—	—	—
—	—	—	—	—	HARBURG .. .. ,,	11 20	—	—	—	—	—	—

(1) For Trains from GUNTERSHAUSEN to FRANKFORT-ON-THE-MAINE, see page 76.

Remarks.—LUGGAGE: 50 lbs. of Luggage are allowed free of charge.

Saxon-Bavarian Railway.—LEIPZIC, ZWICKAU, & HOF.

Eng. Miles.	Fares.			Stations.	Trains.					
	1st Clss	2nd Clss	3rd Clss		1	2	3	4	5	
Dis.	Ngr	Ngr	Ngr		a.m.	a.m.	a.m.	p.m.	p.m.	
..				**Leipzic** ....depart.	..	6 0	11 30	5 0	10 30	..
—	—	—	—	Kieritzsch	..	6 30	12 5	5 30	..	..
24¼	26	21	16	Altenburg................	..	7 10	12 55	6 25	11 40	..
—	39	31	23	Gosznitz	..	7 35	1 30	7 0	..	..
41½	45	36	27	Crimmitzschau	..	7 50	1 45	7 15	12 25	..
47¼	52	42	31	Werdau	..	8 20	2 15	7 45	12 50	..
53¼	59	47	35	**Zwickau**..............	..	7 50	1 45	7 15	..	..
58½	64	51	38	Reichenbach .... arr.	..	8 50	2 45	8 15	1 20	..
—	—	—	—	Do. ....dep.	..	9 30	3 0	8 25	1 30	..
—	—	—	—	Herlasgrün	..	9 10	3 15	..	..	..
74	89	76	58	Plauen	6 15	9 35	3 50	9 20	2 15	..
—	96	82	63	Mehltheuer	6 40	9 50	4 15		..	..
—	—	—	—	Reuth	..	10 20	4 45	..	..	..
103	119	100	76	**Hof** ....arr	8 0	11 10	5 35	..	3 40	..

Additional Trains.—From ZWICKAU to WERDAU, at 5 35, 7 35, and 11 35 a.m.; 1 50, 4 40, and 6 55 p.m. From WERDAU to ZWICKAU, at 8 30 a.m.; 2 15, 5 5, and 7 20 p.m.

Friedrich-Willheim Railway.—CARLSHAFEN TO EISENACH.

English Miles.	Fares. 1st Class	2nd Class	3rd Class	4th Class	Stations.	Trains. 1	2	3	4	5	6	7
Dis.	sgr.	sgr.	sgr.	sgr.		a.m.	p.m.	p.m.				
					Carlshafen .. dep.	5 35	—	4 15	—	—	—	—
—	—	—	—	—	Helmarshausen	..	—	—	—	—	—	—
—	—	—	—	—	Trendelburg	..	—	—	—	—	—	—
10¼	13	9	5½	—	**Humme** .. .. arr.	6 10	—	4 50	—	—	—	—
	From Warburg.					a.m.	p.m.	p.m.				
23	—	—	—	—	**Warburg** .. ..dep.	5 50	—	4 30	—	—	—	—
—	—	—	—	—	Liebenau	6 5	—	4 45	—	—	—	—
—	16¾	11¼	7	—	Humme	6 25	—	5 5	—	—	—	—
13½	21¾	14½	9	—	Hofgeismar	6 35	—	5 15	—	—	—	—
—	—	—	—	—	Grebenstein	6 45	—	5 25	—	—	—	—
—	—	—	—	—	Mönchehof	7 10	—	5 50	—	—	—	—
30	43	28¾	18	—	**Cassel** .. .. .. arr.	7 30	—	6 10	—	—	—	—
	From Cassel.				,, ... dep	8 0	2 45	6 30	—	—	—	—
—	—	—	—	—	Wahlershausen	8 5	—	6 35	—	—	—	—
9¼	11	7¾	4½	—	Guntershausen .. (1) ..	8 35	3 30	7 15	—	—	—	—
—	—	—	—	—	Guxhagen	8 40	—	—	—	—	—	—
18½	23¼	15½	9¾	—	Mulsungen	9 0	4 0	8 5	—	—	—	—
—	—	—	—	—	Bieseförth	9 10	—	—	—	—	—	—
25¼	32¼	21⅕	13½	—	Altmorschen	9 25	4 35	8 45	—	—	—	—
33½	42	28	17½	—	Rotenburg	9 45	5 5	9 20	—	—	—	—
37	46¾	31¼	19½	—	Bebra	10 0	5 15	9 35	—	—	—	—
—	—	—	—	—	Hönebach	10 20	—	—	—	—	—	—
51	64	42½	26½	—	Gerstungen	10 40	6 15	—	—	—	—	—
66	103	69	49	—	**Eisenach** .. .. arr.	11 30	7 10	—	—	—	—	—
						p.m.						
—	—	—	—	—	Gotha .. .. .. arr.	12 25	8 0	—	—	—	—	—
—	—	—	—	—	Erfurt .. .. ,,	1 5	8 45	—	—	—	—	—
—	—	—	—	—	Weimar .. .. ,,	1 40	9 30	—	—	—	—	—
							a.m.					
—	—	—	—	—	Halle .. .. ,,	4 10	6 35	—	—	—	—	—
187	305	186	137	—	Leipsic .. .. ,,	5 30	9 30	—	—	—	—	—
						p.m.						
—	—	—	—	—	Magdeburg .. ,,	8 48	9 15	—	—	—	—	—
						p.m.	p.m.					
283¼	437	277	207½	—	Berlin .. .. ,,	9 30	12 30	—	—	—	—	—

(1) For Trains from Guntershausen to Frankfort-on-the-Maine, see page 76.

Remarks.—Luggage: 50 lbs. of Luggage are allowed free of charge.

Saxon-Bavarian Railway.—HOF, ZWICKAU, AND LEIPZIC.

Eng. Miles.	Fares. 1st Clss	2nd Clss	3rd Clss	Stations.	Trains. 1	2	3	4	5	6
Dis.					a.m.	a.m.	a.m.	p.m.	p.m.	p.m.
..	Ngr	Ngr	Ngr	**Hof** ....dep.	..	6 0	..	2 30	4 15	10 0
—	—	—	—	Reuth	..	6 25	..	2 55	4 55	..
—	23	18	14	Mehltheuer	..	6 55	..	3 25	5 30	11 15
28¾	31	24	18	Plauen .... arr.	..	7 15	..	3 45	5 50	..
—	—	—	—	Do. ....dep.	..	7 25	..	3 55	5 55	11 35
—	—	—	—	Herlasgrün	..	7 35	..	4 5	6 20	..
43½	56	49	38	Reichenbach	..	8 0	..	4 25	6 45	12 20
—	71	62	48	**Zwickau**.........	5 35	7 55	11 30	4 40	5 35	..
53¾	67	59	45	Werdau	6 0	8 30	12 0	5 5	7 15	12 55
—	74	64	49	Crimmitzschau	6 25	8 55	12 25	5 20	..	1 10
—	80	69	53	Goszuitz	6 40	9 10	12 40	5 35	..	..
78½	93	79	61	Altenburg	7 40	9 50	1 40	6 15	..	2 5
—	—	—	—	Kieritzsch	8 20	10 20	1 55	6 45	..	..
103	119	100	76	**Leipzic** ......arr.	9 15	11 0	3 15	7 30	..	3 10

Remarks. — Luggage:—50 lbs. free; every 10lbs. extra to Zwickau, 2 ngr. (4d.) Four-wheeled carriages, 11 P. d. 10 sgr. Two-wheeled carriage, 8 P d. Hof to Bamberg, Lichtenfels, Nuremberg, Augsburg, and Munich, pages 83 and 82. Leipsic to Dresden, page 98. To Kothen and Magdeburg, page 97. To Berlin, page 89.

DRESDEN TO PRAGUE.—(118 English miles.) [1-53.

Eng. Miles. Dis.	Fares. 1st Class Ngr.	2nd Class Ngr.	3rd Class Ngr.	4th Class Ngr.	STATIONS.	Trains. 1	2	3	4	5	6
						a.m.	a.m.	p.m.	p.m.	p.m.	
—	—	—	—	—	**Dresden** departure	7 0	9 0	1 35	6 0	9 20	...
...	...	4	3	...	Nieder-Sedlitz	...	...	...	...	...	...
...	...	6	4½	...	Mugeln	...	...	...	...	...	...
11	12	10	7	...	Pirna	7 30	9 45	2 30	6 45	10 10	...
...	...	14	10	...	Pötzscha	...	...	...	...	...	...
...	...	16	11½	...	Rathen	...	...	...	...	...	...
22	24	19	14	...	Königstein	8 5	10 30	3 5	7 20	...	...
25¼	28	22	16	...	**Krippen**	8 20	10 45	3 20	7 35	10 55	...
...	...	26	19	...	Schöna	...	...	...	...	...	...
38	42	33	25	...	**Bodenbach** arrival	9 5	11 42	4 5	8 30	11 30	...
	fl. kr.	fl. kr.	fl. kr.	...	" departure	10 5	—	4 55	—	12 15	...
53¾	1 0	0 36	0 27	...	**Ausig**	10 53	...	5 39	...	1 1	...
65	1 50	1 6	0 50	...	**Lobowitz** arrival	...	...	..	...	..	...
	From Lobowitz.				" departure	11 32	...	6 18	...	1 40	...
4¼	0 18	0 11	0 8	...	Theresienstadt	...	...	...	...	...	..
11¼	0 45	0 28	0 20	...	Raudnitz	...	...	...	...	...	...
15¾	1 3	0 39	0 28	...	Wegstättl	...	...	...	...	...	...
23	1 30	0 55	0 40	...	Berkowic arrival	...	...	..	...	...	...
27¾	1 48	1 6	0 48	...	" departure	...	...	...	...	...	...
24¾	2 15	1 23	1 0	...	Weltrus	...	...	...	...	...	...
37	2 24	1 28	1 4	...	Kralup	...	...	...	...	...	...
41½	2 42	1 39	1 12	...	Lipsic	...	...	...	...	...	...
46	3 0	1 50	1 20	...	Rostok	...	...	...	...	...	...
51	3 18	2 1	1 28	...	Bubencz	...	...	...	...	...	...
53¼	3 27	2 7	1 32	...	**Prague** arrival	2 18	...	9 0	...	4 23	...
						a.m.				p.m.	
210½	13 39	8 21	6 4	...	BRUNN arrival	12 0	...	...	...	2 20	...
302¾	20 19	13 21	9 24	...	VIENNA "	5 55	...	...	...	7 35	...

Remarks.—Travellers, in going to Austria, should take their places only as far as BODENBACH, and pay with Prussian money; from BODENBACH, they can pay with Austrian paper money, which can be procured with advantage in DRESDEN. By so doing, they will save £1 between BODENBACH and VIENNA. LUGGAGE: 50 lbs. allowed free of charge.

Prague to Pardubitz, Brunn, and Vienna, see page 106.

HAMBURG TO BERLIN.—(175¾ English Miles.)

Fares. 1st Class. mk. sh	2nd Class. mk. sh	3rd Class mk sh	Stations.	Trains. 1	2	3	4	5	6
				a.m.	a.m.	a.m.	p.m.	p.m.	
—	—	—	**Hamburg** depart	...	7 30	9 0	5 0	10 30	...
0 15	0 10	0 7	Bergedorf	...	7 50	9 20	5 20	...	...
2 7	1 10	1 2	Schwarzenbeck	...	8 33	10 10	6 20	...	...
4 2	2 12	1 13	Boizenburg	...	9 25	11 5	7 20	12 0	...
6 3	4 4	2 10	Hagenow	...	10 20	12 15	8 35	12 45	...
7 8	5 3	3 2	Ludwigslust	...	10 55	12 55	9 10	1 15	...
8 0	5 8	3 5	Grabow	...	11 10	1 15	9 30	...	...
10 8	7 2	4 5	Wittenberge (1) arrivl	...	12 15	2 30	11 0	2 20	...
...	...	...	" depart	5 45	12 20	—	—	2 25	...
12 3	8 3	5 0	Glöwen	6 40	1 5	...	...	3 0	...
13 14	9 6	5 10	Neustadt	7 45	1 50	...	...	3 35	...
14 12	9 15	6 0	Friesack	8 15	2 10	...	...	...	...
16 8	11 2	6 11	Nauen	9 10	2 55	...	...	4 30	...
18 0	12 0	7 4	Spandau	9 55	3 30	...	...	5 0	...
18 12	12 8	7 8	**Berlin** arrival	10 30	4 15	...	...	5 20	...

(1) WITTEMBERG to MAGDEBURG, page 84.

Remarks.—LUGGAGE: 50 lbs. free; every 10 lbs. extra, 6¼ sgr. Four-wheeled Carriage, 38 Prussian dollars; 2-wheeled Carriage, 23⅓ Prussian dollars.

PRAGUE TO DRESDEN—(118 English miles.) [1-53.

English Miles.	Fares.				STATIONS.	Trains.					
	1st Class	2nd Class	3rd Class	4th Class		1	2	3	4	5	6
Dis.	fl. kr.	fl. kr.	fl. kr.	fl. kr.		a.m.	a.m.	a.m.	p.m.	p.m.	
—	—	—	—	—	VIENNA ....departure	6 30	...	...	7 0	...	...
92	6 40	5 0	3 20	...	BRUNN ....departure	11 45	...	...	1 0	...	...
						p.m.		a.m.	a.m.	p.m.	
249¾	16 52	11 14	7 52	...	**Prague** ....departure	9 15	...	7 0	10 50	...	...
2¼	0 9	0 6	0 4	...	Bubencz ....arrival	...	...	...	...	...	...
6¾	0 27	0 17	0 12	...	Rostok	...	...	...	...	...	...
11¼	0 45	0 28	0 20	...	Libsic	...	...	...	...	...	...
14½	1 3	0 39	0 28	...	Kralup	...	...	...	...	...	...
18½	1 12	0 44	0 32	...	Weltrus	...	...	...	...	...	...
24¼	1 39	1 1	0 44	...	Berkowic ....arrival	...	...	...	...	...	...
27¾	1 57	1 12	0 52	...	,, ...departure	...	...	...	...	...	...
37	2 24	1 28	1 4	...	Wegstädtl........	...	...	...	...	...	...
41½	2 42	1 39	1 12	...	Raudnitz	...	...	...	...	...	...
48½	3 9	1 56	1 24	...	Theresienstadt	...	...	...	...	...	...
53¼	3 27	2 7	1 32	...	**Lobowitz** ....arrival	...	...	...	12 47	...	...
					,, ...departure	11 46	...	9 34	...	...	...
65	4 40	2 48	2 6	...	**Ausig**	12 23	...	10 11	12 4	...	...
78½	5 40	3 24	2 33	...	**Bodenbach** ....arrival	1 0	...	10 49	2 0	...	...
	Ngr.	Ngr.	Ngr.		,, ...departure	1 45	5 50	12 0	2 50	6 20	...
...	...	8	6	...	Schöna	...	...	...	...	...	...
91	14	11	9	...	**Krippen**	2 15	6 35	12 40	3 30	7 5	...
94½	18	14	11	...	Königstein	...	6 50	12 50	3 40	7 20	...
...	...	17	13½	...	Rathen	...	...	...	...	...	...
...	...	19	15	...	Pötzscha	...	...	...	...	...	...
106½	30	23	18	...	Pirna	2 55	7 30	1 25	4 15	8 5	...
...	...	27	21	...	Mugeln	...	...	...	...	...	...
...	...	29	22½	...	Nieder-Sedlitz........	...	...	...	...	...	...
118	42	33	25	...	**Dresden**........	3 45	8 20	2 20	5 10	8 50	...

Remarks.—Travellers, in going to Austria, should take their places only as far as BODENBACH, and pay with Prussian money; from BODENBACH, they can pay with Austrian paper money, which can be procured with advantage in DRESDEN. By so doing, they will save £1 between BODENBACH and VIENNA. LUGGAGE: 50 lbs. allowed free of charge.

Prague to Pardubitz, Brunn, and Vienna, see page 106.

BERLIN TO HAMBURG.—(175⅝ English Miles.)

Fares.			Stations.	Trains.								
1st Clss	2nd Clss	3rd Clss		1	2	3	4	5	6	7	8	9
th sg	th sg	th sg		a.m.	a.m.	a.m.	p.m.	p m.				
...	...	...	**Berlin** ....depart.	...	7 30	...	6 0	11 0			...	...
0 9	0 6	0 3	Spandau	...	7 50	...	6 25	11 15			...	...
0 27	0 17	0 10	Nauen	...	8 25	...	7 10	11 45			...	...
1 18	1 1	0 19	Friesack	...	9 5	...	8 0	...			...	...
1 29	1 8	0 23	Neustadt	...	9 25	...	8 25	12 35			...	...
2 19	1 22	1 0	Glöwen	...	10 5	...	9 20	1 5			...	...
3 9	2 5	1 9	Wittenberge...(1)...arrival	...	10 50	...	...	1 40			...	...
...	...	...	,, ...depart	5 15	10 55	3 10	10 15	1 45			...	...
4 9	2 24	1 21	Grabow	6 20	11 50	4 15		...			...	...
4 15	2 28	1 23	Ludwigslust	6 35	1 25	4 30	...	2 45			...	...
5 1	3 9	1 29	Hagenow	7 15	12 45	5 10	...	3 10			...	...
5 26	3 27	2 9	Boizenburg	8 20	1 35	6 10	...	3 50			...	...
6 16	4 11	2 17	Schwarzenbeck	9 15	2 0	...	...	...			...	...
7 4	4 23	2 25	Bergedorf	9 55	2 45	...	...	...			...	...
7 15	5 0	3 0	**Hamburg** ......arrival	10 30	3 30	8 30	...	5 16			...	...

(1) WITTEMBERG to MAGDEBURG, see page 84.

Remarks.—LUGGAGE: 50 lbs. are allowed free of charge.

THE SAXON-SILESIAN RAILWAY.—DRESDEN TO GORLITZ, LOBAU, & ZITTAU. [8-52

Eng Mls.	Fares 1 Clss	Fares 2 Clss	Fares 3 Clss	Stations.	Train 1	Train 2	Train 3	Train 4	Train 5
	Ngr.	Ngr.	Ngr.		a.m.	a.m.	p.m.	p.m.	p.m.
—	—	—	—	**Dresden** ......dep.	6 0	10 0	2 0	5 0	11 0
..	..	..	..	Langebrück...........	6 15	..	2 15	..	..
..	10	8	6	**Radeberg**	6 30	10 30	2 30	5 30	11 25
..	..	..	..	Fischbach.............	6 40	10 40	2 40	5 40	..
..	..	..	..	Harthau	6 50	..	2 50	..	..
23	25	20	15	**Bischofswerda**	7 6	11 6	3 6	6 6	11 50
..	..	..	..	Demitz................	7 13	..	3 13	..	..
..	..	..	..	Seitschen.............	7 21	11 21	3 21	6 21	..
34¾	38	30	23	**Bautzen**...........	7 40	11 40	3 40	6 40	12 15
..	..	..	..	Kubschütz	7 49	..	3 49	..	..
..	..	..	..	Pommritz	7 55	11 55	3 55	6 55	..
48	53	42	32	**Lobau**	8 17	12 27	4 17	7 17	12 43
..	..	..	..	Zoblitz	8 26	..	4 26	..	..
..	..	..	..	**Reichenbach**.....	8 35	12 41	4 35	7 35	12 56
..	..	..	..	Markersdorf...........	8 45	..	4 45	..	..
63¾	70	56	42	**Gorlitz** ....arr.	9 0	1 0	5 0	8 0	1 15
—	..	..	..	**Lobau** ......dep.	8 15	1 45	..	7 15	..
..	..	..	..	New-Cunnersdorf	8 24	1 54	..	7 24	..
..	..	..	..	Ober-Cunnersdorf	8 31	2 1	..	7 31	..
..	62	49	37	**Herrnhut**......	8 42	2 12	..	7 42	..
..	..	..	..	Ober-Oderwitz ...	8 54	2 24	..	7 54	..
..	..	..	..	Mittle-Oderwitz...	8 57	2 27	..	7 57	..
21	68	54	41	**Zittau** ......arr.	9 15	2 45	..	8 15	..

Eng Mls.	Fares 1 Clss	Fares 2 Clss	Fares 3 Clss	Stations.	Train 1	Train 2	Train 3	Train 4	Train 5
	Ngr.	Ngr.	Ngr.		a.m.	a.m.	a.m.	p.m.	p.m.
—	—	—	—	**Zittau** ......dep.	5 45	..	11 15	4 45	..
..	..	..	..	Mittle-Oderwitz..	5 55	..	11 25	4 55	..
..	..	..	..	Ober-Oderwitz....	6 5	..	11 35	5 5	..
..	9	7	5	**Herrnhut**......	6 20	..	11 50	5 20	..
..	..	..	..	Ober-Cannersdorf	6 29	..	11 59	5 29	..
..	..	..	..	New-Cannersdorf	6 33	..	12 3	5 33	..
21	15	12	9	**Lobau** ......arr.	6 45	..	12 15	5 45	..
—	From	Gorlitz.		**Gorlitz**.........dep.	6 0	8 45	1 0	5 0	11 15
..	..	..	..	Markersdorf............	6 10	..	1 10	..	..
8	10	8	6	**Reichenbach** ...	6 22	9 7	1 22	5 22	11 32
..	..	..	..	Zoblitz	6 26	..	1 26	..	..
14½	17	14	10	**Lobau**	6 49	9 30	1 48	5 49	11 46
..	..	..	..	Pommritz................	7 2	9 43	2 0	6 2	..
..	..	..	..	Kubschütz	7 8	..	2 6	..	..
28½	32	26	19	**Bautzen**............	7 30	10 9	2 25	6 30	12 15
..	..	..	..	Seitschen	7 41	10 20	2 36	6 41	..
..	..	..	..	Demitz	7 49	..	2 44	..	..
40¼	45	36	27	**Bischofswerda**	8 8	10 47	3 3	7 8	12 45
..	..	..	..	Harthau	8 16	..	3 11	..	..
..	..	..	..	Fischbach...............	8 28	11 7	3 23	7 28	..
53	60	48	36	**Radeberg**	8 40	11 20	3 36	7 40	1 7
..	..	..	..	Langebrück............	8 45	..	3 42	..	..
63¾	70	56	42	**Dresden** ......arr.	9 0	11 45	4 0	8 0	1 30

KOHLFURT to GORLITZ, at 6¼ a.m. (for Dresden), 12 noon (for Dresden and Leipsic), 3 p.m. (for Dresden), & 9¼ p.m. GORLITZ to KOHLFURT, 5 & 11 a.m.; 2 & 8¼ p.m.

Remarks.—Travelling Carriages of all kinds pay one dollar per mile; delivering the same, costs 15 Ngr.—A horse is charged 20 Ngr. per mile: the driver or leader gets a ticket to the 3rd class.—Each traveller takes 50lbs. luggage free; overweight half Ngr. per mile for every 10lbs.; 1 lb. is charged the same as 10lbs.—One-horse Droskas, 4 Ngr., two-horse Coach, 10 and 15 Ngr. the distance.

PORTERS.—The charge in the New and Antonstadt is from 2 to 5 Ngr., in the Old Town from 4 to 6, and in the suburbs from 5 to 8.

RIESA TO DOEBELN, LIMMRITZ, & CHEMNITZ. [15-11-52

Eng Ml.	Fares 1 Cls.	Fares 2 Cls.	Fares 3 Cls.	50 lbs. of luggage free of charge.	Train 1	Train 2	Train 3	Train 4
	Ngr.	Ngr.	Ngr.		a.m.	a.m.	p.m.	p.m.
—	—	—	—	**Riesa** ....dep.	5 15	8 30	12 15	8 0
..	..	..	..	Stauchitz	5 45	8 45	12 30	8 15
9¼	11	9	7	Ostrau	6 0	9 0	12 45	8 30
15½	19	15	11	Doebeln	6 45	9 15	1 0	8 45
18½	22	18	13	**Limmritz**	..	..	..	..
21	27	22	16	Waldheim	7 15	9 45	1 30	9 15
..	36	29	21	Erlan (Rochlitz)	7 36	10 5	1 50	9 35
30	37	30	22	Mittweida	7 45	10 15	2 0	9 45
..	..	..	..	Oberlichtenau	8 0	10 45	2 30	10 15
41½	50	40	30	**Chemnitz** .....arr.	8 30	11 15	3 0	10 45

Eng Mls.	Fares 1 Cls.	Fares 2 Cls.	Fares 3 Cls.	Stations.	Train 1	Train 2	Train 3	Train 4
	Ngr.	Ngr.	Ngr.		a.m.	a.m.	p.m.	p.m.
—	—	—	—	**Chemnitz**......dep.	5 0	9 0	4 15	6 30
..	..	..	..	Oberlichtenau	5 15	9 15	4 30	6 45
11½	14	11	8	Mittweida	5 30	9 30	4 45	7 0
..	18	14	10	Erlan (Rochlitz)	5 36	9 36	4 51	7 6
18½	24	19	14	Waldheim	6 0	10 0	5 15	7 30
..	..	..	..	**Limmritz**......dep.	..	..	..	..
26	32	26	19	Doebeln	6 15	10 15	5 30	8 0
..	..	..	..	Ostrau	6 30	10 30	5 45	8 30
..	..	..	..	Stauchitz	6 45	10 45	6 0	8 45
41½	50	40	30	**Riesa** ....arr.	7 15	11 15	6 30	9 15

AIX-LA-CHAPELLE, Dusseldorf, Gladbach, Viersen, and HOMBERG.

Eng. Mls.	Fares.			Stations.	Trains.						
	1 Clss.	2 Clss.	3 Clss.		1	2	3	4	5	6	7
Dis.	Sgr.	Sgr.	Sgr.		a.m.	a.m.	a.m.	p.m.	p.m.	p.m.	p.m.
—	—	—	—	**Aix-la-Chapelle**...dep.	2 45	..	7 5	..	2 48	5 10	..
..	13	9	6	**Herzogenrath**	3 11	..	7 38	..	3 21	5 43	..
..	23	17	12	Geilenkirchen	3 27	..	8 0	..	3 39	6 4	..
..	29	21	15	Lindern	..	..	8 12	..	3 51	6 16	..
..	41	30	21	Erkelenz	3 54	..	8 36	..	4 15	6 40	..
..	53	38	27	**Rheydt**	4 12	..	9 0	..	4 39	7 4	..
..	57	41	28	**Gladbach**	4 22	6 44	9 21	1 45	4 55	7 20	..
..	73	52	36	Neuss	4 46	7 13	9 50	2 13	5 24	7 49	..
..	79	57	40	**Dusseldorf**	4 45	7 23	10 0	2 23	5 34	7 59	..
..	From Gladbach.			**Gladbach**	5 10		9 25	1 45		7 15	10 38
..	8	6	4	**Viersen**	5 25	..	9 40	2 0	..	7 30	10 51
..	22	16	11	Crefeld	5 54	..	10 9	2 29	..	7 59	11 11
..	28	20	14	Uerdingen	6 6	..	10 21	2 41	..	8 11	
..	40½	29	20½	**Homberg** (Ruhrort) arr	6 25	..	10 40	3 0	..	8 30	..
					a.m.	a.m.	p.m.	p.m.	p.m.	p.m.	
—	—	—	—	**Homberg** (Ruhrort) dep	..	8 0	12 20	3 30	..	9 30	..
7	12½	9	6½	Uerdingen	..	8 21	12 41	3 51	..	9 47	..
11¼	19½	14	9½	Crefeld	5 55	8 37	12 57	4 7	..	9 59	..
20¾	33½	24	16½	**Viersen**	6 19	9 3	1 23	4 23	..	10 21	..
25¼	40½	29	20½	**Gladbach**	6 30	9 15	1 35	4 45	..	10 32	..
..	From Dusseldorf.			**Dusseldorf**	6 51	8 32	12 56	4 6	6 26	10 0	..
..	6	5	3	Neuss	6 4	8 45	1 9	4 19	6 39	10 10	..
..	22	16	11	**Gladbach**	6 44	9 25	1 35	4 55		10 38	..
27¾	26	19	13	**Rheydt**	6 53	9 34		5 4	..	10 44	..
..	38	27	19	Erkelenz	7 18	9 59	..	5 29	..	11 2	..
..	50	36	25	Lindern	7 40	10 21	..	5 51	..	..	..
..	56	40	28	Geilenkirchen	7 55	10 33	..	6 8	..	11 30	..
..	67	48	33	**Herzogenrath**	8 51	10 56	..	6 31	..	11 47	..
..	79	57	40	**Aix-la-Chapelle** arr.	8 45	11 25	..	7 0	..	12 10	..

HAGENOW, SCHWERIN, WISMAR, AND ROSTOCK—71½ English miles.

Eng. Mls.	Fares.			Stations.	Trains.						
	1 Cls.	2 Cls.	3 Cls.		1	2	3	4	5	6	7
Dis.	th. sh.	th. sh.	th. sh.		a.m.	a.m.	p.m.	p.m.	p.m.		
—	—	—	—	**Hagenow** ...dep.	7 30	..	12 55	5 20	8 45	..	..
16	0 40	0 28	0 20	**Schwerin** ...arrival	8 12	..	1 45	6 0	9 30	..	..
..	From Schwerin.			" ...dep.	8 15	..	1 50	6 5		..	..
27	0 20	0 14	0 10	Kleinen	8 45	..	3 0	6 30	..	..	..
48	0 40	0 28	0 20	**Wismar** ...arrival	9 30	..	3 45	7 30	..	..	..
..	..		..	" ...dep.	8 0	a.m.	2 0	6 10	..	..	..
53	1 24	1 2	0 36	Bützow	10 0	7 30	5 20	7 50	..	..	..
60	1 40	1 14	0 44	Güstrow ...arrival	10 35	7 50	6 5	8 25	..	..	..
..	..	..	..	" ...dep.	9 40	..	4 45	7 30	..	..	..
62	1 44	1 16	0 46	Schwaan	10 20	..	5 45	8 15	..	..	..
71½	2 4	1 22	1 2	**Rostock** ...arrival	11 5	..	6 30	9 0	..	..	..

Eng. Miles.	Fares.			Stations.	Trains.						
	1 Cls.	2 Cls.	3 Cls.		1	2	3	4	5	6	7
Dis.	th. sh.	th. sh.	th. sh.		a.m.	a.m.	noon.	p.m.			
—	—	—	—	**Rostock** ...dep.	..	6 30	12 0	4 40	..	..	
10	0 20	0 14	0 10	Schwaan	..	6 50	12 20	5 0	..	..	
19	0 40	0 28	0 20	Bützow	..	7 20	1 0	5 30	..	..	
27	1 8	0 40	0 28	Güstrow ...arrival	..	7 50	1 40	6 5	..	..	
..	..	..	..	Güstrow ...dep.	..	7 0	12 30	4 45	..	..	
43¾	1 44	1 16	0 46	Kleinen	..	8 30	3 0	6 45	..	..	
54	2 0	1 20	1 0	**Wismar** ...arrival	..	9 30	3 45	7 30	..	..	
..	..	..	..	" ...dep.	..	8 0	2 0	6 10	..	..	
55	2 4	1 22	1 2	**Schwerin**	6 15	9 15	3 45	7 15	..	..	
71½	2 44	2 2	1 22	**Hagenow** ...arrival	7 0	10 5	4 45	8 20	..	..	

Remarks.—LUGGAGE: 50 lbs. free.

BERLIN TO MAGDEBURG. [15-11-52

Eng. Mls.	Fares. Passengers 1 cl.	2 cl.	3 cl.	Equipages. 1 class.	2 cl.	Stations.	Trains. 1	2	3	4	5	6
..	sgr.	sgr.	sgr.	dollars.	dols		a.m.	a.m.	noon	a.m.		
—	—	—	—	..	..	**Berlin** ....arr.	5 0	7 30	12 0	10 0	..	..
11¼	24	17½	12	..	..	Potsdam	5 45	8 0	12 35	10 0	..	..
—	33	24	16½	..	..	Werder	6 0	..	..	..	..	..
28¾	44	32	22	..	..	Grosskreutz......................	6 15	..	..	..	..	..
38	57	41	29	6⅞	5½	Brandenburg	7 0	8 40	1 15	11 10	..	..
—	72	51	36	..	..	Wusterwitz	7 20	..	1 30	..	..	..
56½	86	61	43	10 5-24	8⅙	Genthin	7 40	9 10	2 0	11 40	..	..
—	100	71	50	..	..	Gusen	8 0	..	2 15	..	..	..
72½	110	79	55	13⅓	10½	Burg..............................	8 30	9 40	2 40	12 10	..	..
89¾	140	100	70	16⅔	13⅓	**Magdeburg** ....arr.	11 0	10 40	4 15	1 50	..	..

MAGDEBURG TO BERLIN.

Eng. Mls.	Fares. Passengers. 1 cl.	2 cl.	3 cl.	Equipages. 1 class.	2 cl.	Stations.	Trains. 1	2	3	4	5	6
..	sgr.	sgr.	sgr.	dollars.	dols		a.m.	a.m.	p.m.	p.m.	p.m.	..
—	—	—	—	..	..	**Magdeburg** ....arr.	5 0	10 0	3 0	6 0	6 15	..
15¾	30	21	15	3 13-24	25-6	Burg	5 40	10 30	..	6 30	6 55	..
—	40	29	20	..	..	Gusen	5 55	..	..	..	7 10	..
33¼	56	40	28	6⅔	5⅓	Genthin	6 15	11 0	..	7 0	7 30	..
—	70	50	35	..	..	Wusterwitz......................	6 30	..	..	..	7 45	..
52¼	84	60	42	10	8	Brandenburg	6 50	11 30	..	7 30	8 0	..
61¼	96	69	48	..	..	Grosskreutz	7 15	..	..	..	8 20	..
—	107	76½	53½	..	..	Werder	7 30	..	..	..	8 30	..
74	115	82½	57½	13¾	11	Potsdam	7 45	12 10	..	8 10	10 0	..
89¾	140	100	70	16⅔	13⅚	**Berlin** ....arr.	9 30	1 10	9 0	9 20	11 15	..

Local Trains.—From Berlin to Potsdam at 8 and 10 a.m.; 12 noon; 2, 5, 7, and 10½ p.m. From Potsdam to Berlin at 8 and 10 a.m.; 12 noon; 2, 5, 7, 8½, and 10¼ p.m.—Transit, three quarters of an hour. FARES.—1st class, 24 sgr.; 2nd class, 17½ sgr.; 3rd class, 12 sgr. From Potsdam to Brandenburg at 5¾ p.m. From Brandenburg to Genthin at 9 p.m. From Genthin to Magdeburg at 7 a.m.

For Trains from Magdeburg to Brunswick and Hanover, see pages 86 and 85. For Trains to and from BERLIN, BRESLAU, VIENNA, and CRACOW, see pages 99 and 102.

Remarks.—LUGGAGE: 50 lbs. of Luggage free; every 10 lbs. extra, 3½ sgr. Four-wheeled carriage, 16 Prus. doll. 20 sgr.; two-wheeled carriage, 13 Prus. doll. 10 sgr.

ALTONA (HAMBURG) TO KIEL.

Eng. Miles.	Fares. 1 Clss.	2 Clss.	3 Clss.	Stations.	Trains. 1	2 gds.	3	4	5	6
Dis.	Mk. Sl	Mk. Sl	Mk. Sl		a.m.	p.m.	p.m.			
—	..	..	..	**Altona** (Hamburg) ....dep.	8 10	1 0	5 10	..	..	..
18½	2 4	1 8	0 12	**Elmshorn**......................arr.	8 50	2 0	5 50	..	..	..
28¾	..	..	..	**Gluckstadt** ....arr.	10 0	..	7 0	..	..	..
—	..	..	..	Do, ...dep.	8 15	..	5 0	..	..	..
46	5 10	3 12	1 14	**Neumunster** ....arr.	9 50	3 15	6 50	..	..	..
67¼	..	..	..	**Rendsburg** ....arr.	11 30	..	8 30	..	..	..
—	..	..	..	Do. .... dep.	6 45	..	3 45	..	..	..
65	7 8	5 0	2 8	**Kiel** .... arr.	11 0	4 30	8 0	..	..	..

Remarks.—LUGGAGE: 50 lbs. of Luggage free; every 10 lbs. extra, 4 Hamb. schill. ct. Four-wheeled carriage, 28 mk. ct.; two-wheeled carriage, 21 mk. ct.

MAGDEBURG, KOTHEN, HALLE, AND LEIPSIC RAILWAY.

[15-11-52.

English Miles.	Fares.			Stations.	Trains.						
	1st Clss.	2nd Clss.	3rd Clss		1	2	3	4	5	6	7
	Sgr.	Sgr.	Sgr.		a.m.	a.m.	a.m.	a.m.	p.m.	p.m.	
—	..	..	..	**Magdeburg** ....departure	..	6 0	7 0	10 45	6 15	7 0	..
9¼	12	8	5	Schönebeck..............................	..	6 15	7 30	11 0	..	7 30	..
12¼	17	11	7	Gnadau	..	6 30	7 45	..	..	7 45	..
17	21	14	9	Der Saale	..	6 45	8 0	11 30	..	8 0	..
31¾	40	27	17½	**Kothen** ....arrival	..	7 25	9 15	12 10	7 25	8 40	..
..	54	36	23	,, ...departure	2 5	7 30	9 30	12 15	7 30	8 45	..
40½				Stumsdorf	..	8 0	10 0	..	..	..	..
53¼	69	46	29	**Halle** ....arrival	2 55	8 25	11 10	1 10	8 25	..	..
..	84	56	35	,, ...departure	3 0	8 30	11 15	1 15	8 30	..	..
..				Schkeuditz	..	9 0	11 45	..	..	..	..
72¾	96	64	40	**Leipsic** ....arrival	4 0	9 30	12 30	2 5	9 15	..	..

LEIPSIC, HALLE, KOTHEN, AND MAGDEBURG RAILWAY.

English Miles.	Fares.			Stations.	Trains.						
	1st	2nd	3rd		1	2	3	4	5	6	7
Dis.	Sgr.	Sgr.	Sgr.		a.m.	a.m.	noon.	p.m.	p.m.	p.m.	
72¾	..	..	..	**Leipsic** ....departure	5 45	7 0	12 0	3 30	5 30	10 0	..
..	..	..	..	Schkeuditz	6 15	..	12 15	3 45	5 45	10 15	..
..	27	18	11	**Halle**	7 45	7 40	12 40	4 25	6 10	10 40	..
53¼	42	28	17	,, ...departure	7 50	7 45	12 45	4 30	6 15	10 45	..
..				Stumdorf	8 30	..	1 15	4 45	6 45	11 15	..
40½	56	37	22½	**Kothen**.......................arrival	9 25	8 30	1 55	5 30	7 25	11 40	..
31¾				,, ...departure	9 30	8 35	2 0	..	7 30	11 45	..
17	75	50	31	Der Saale	10 15	9 5	2 15	..	7 45	12 15	..
12¼	79	53	33	Gnadau	10 30	..	2 30	..	8 0	..	..
9¼	84	56	35	Schönbeck	10 45	9 20	2 45	..	8 15	12 45	..
—	96	64	40	**Magdeburg**...............arrival	11 15	9 50	3 15	..	8 45	1 15	..

Additional Trains.—(Goods and Passengers).—Halle to Leipsic, at 4½ p.m. From Kothen to Halle and Leipsic at 6 a.m. From Leipsic to Halle and Kothen, at 6½ p.m. From Kothen to Magdeburg, at 5.45 a m.

Remarks.—Luggage.—50 lbs. free; every 10 lbs. extra, 2½ sgr. Four-wheeled carriage, 16 Prus. doll.; two-wheeled carriage, 12 Prus. doll.

Munich, Augsburg, Nuremberg, Bamberg, Lichtenfels, and Hof, to Leipsic, see pages 82, 83, 90.

KIEL TO ALTONA (HAMBURG.)

Eng. Miles	Fares.			Stations.	Trains.					
	1 Clss.	2 Clss.	3 Clss.		1	2 gds.	3	4	5	6
Dis.	Mk. Sl	Mk. Sl	Mk. Sl		a.m.	a.m.	p.m.			
—	..	..	..	**Kiel**......................departure	7 0	8 45	4 0	..	..	..
18½	2 4	1 8	0 12	**Neumunster** ....arr.	7 40	10 0	4 40	..	..	..
39¼	..	..	..	**Rendsburg** ....arr.	11 30	..	8 30	..	..	..
—	..	..	..	Do. ....dep.	6 45	..	3 45	..	..	..
46	5 10	3 12	1 14	**Elmshorn**.....................arr.	8 40	..	5 40	..	..	..
56½	..	.	..	**Gluckstadt** ....arr.	10 0	..	7 0	..	..	..
—	..	..	..	Do. ....dep.	8 15	11 0	5 0	..	..	..
65	7 8	5 0	2 8	**Altona** (Hamburg) .... arr.	10 0	12 0	7 0	..	..	..

Remarks.—Luggage.—50 lbs. are allowed free of charge.

LEIPSIC TO DRESDEN.

[15-11-52.

English Miles.	Fares.				STATIONS.	Trains.									
	1st Cls.	2nd Cls.	3rd Cls.	Equipages.		1	2	3	4	5	6	7	8	9	10
Dis.	Ngr.	Ngr.	Ngr.	Rthl.		a.m.	a.m.	a.m.	a.m.	p.m.	p.m.	p.m.	p.m.	p.m.	
—	—	—	—	—	**Leipsic.** departure	5 15	6 0		10 0	2 30	2 30	.	5 30	10 0	..
..	..	..	..	..	Borsdorf	5 30	..		..	..	..		5 45	..	..
..	..	..	..	..	Machern	5 45	..	Leave Berlin at 7 a.m.	..	..	..	Leave Berlin at 1.45 p.m.	6 0	..	..
14½	20	15	10	2 5-6	Wurzen	6 0	6 30		10 30	3 0	3 0		6 15	10 10	..
..	..	..	..	..	Dornreichenbach ..	6 15	..		..	..	..		6 30	..	..
26¼	35	26	17	4 5-6	Luppe-Dahlen......	6 30	6 45		10 45	3 30	3 20		6 45	..	..
32½	42	32	21	5 5-6	Oschatz	6 45	7 0		11 0	3 45	3 35		7 0	..	..
..	..	..	..	..	Bornitz	7 0	..		..	..	..		7 15	..	..
45½	54	47	27	7⅓	Riesa Junction	7 15	7 45		11 45	4 10	4 10		7 30	11 20	..
..	..	..	..	..	Röderau	7 30	..	11 0	..	..	4 15	6 0	..	..	..
..	..	..	..	..	Zschaiten	..	8 0	..	..	..	..	6 15	..	..	..
53¾	70	52	35	9⅔	Pristewitz..........	..	8 15	11 30	12 15	4 30	..	6 30	8 0	..	..
62½	81	61	41	11⅓	Niederau	..	8 30	11 45	12 30	4 50	..	6 45	8 20	12 0	..
..	..	..	..	..	Kötschenbroda	..	8 45	..	12 45	..	..	7 0	..	..	..
..	..	..	..	..	Weintraube	..	8 55	..	12 55	..	..	7 10	..	..	..
71¾	90	68	45	13	**Dresden** ..arrival	p.m.	9 15	12 30	1 15	5 30	p.m.	8 0	9 0	12 30	..
..	..	..	..	..	BERLIN ..arrival	1 0	..	..	..	..	8 45	..	..	..	..

English Miles.	Fares.				STATIONS.	Trains.								
	1st Cls.	2nd Cls.	3rd Cls.	Equipages.		1	2	3	4	5	6	7	8	9
Dis.	Ngr.	Ngr.	Ngr.	Rthl.		a.m.	a.m.	a.m.	a.m.	a.m.	p.m.	p.m.	p.m.	p.m.
—	—	—	—	—	**Dresden**..depart.	4 0	6 0	6 30	10 30	Leave Berlin at 7 a.m.	3 15	2 30	Leave Berlin at 1¼ p.m.	6 0
..	.	..	..	..	Weintraube	..	6 10	..	10 35		..	2 35		..
..	..	..	..	..	Kötschenbroda	..	6 15	..	10 40		..	2 40		..
9¼	12	9	6	1⅔	Niederau	4 20	6 40	7 0	11 0		3 40	3 0		6 30
18½	24	18	12	3⅓	Pristewitz..........	..	7 0	7 15	11 15		3 50	3 15		6 45
..	..	..	..	..	Zschaiten	..	7 15	..	..		..	3 20		..
..	..	..	..	..	Röderau	..	7 30	..	..	11 0	4 15	..	6 0	..
30	39	29	20	5½	Riesa Junction	4 55	..	7 45	11 45	11 45	..	4 0	6 15	7 15
..	..	..	..	..	Bornitz	..	..	8 0	..	..	..	..	6 30	..
39¼	51	38	26	7⅙	Oschatz	..	..	8 15	12 15	12 15	..	4 20	7 0	7 45
44¾	59	44	29	8⅙	Luppe-Dahlen	..	..	8 30	12 30	12 30	..	4 35	7 20	8 0
..	..	..	..	..	Dornreichenbach ..	..	..	8 45	..	..	..	..	7 30	..
56½	74	55	37	10⅓	Wurzen..........	5 30	..	9 0	12 45	12 45	..	5 0	7 40	8 30
..	..	..	..	..	Machern	..	..	9 15	..	..	..	..	7 50	..
..	..	..	..	..	Borsdorf	..	..	9 30	..	..	..	..	8 0	..
71¾	90	68	45	13	**Leipsic**....arrival	6 30	..	10 0	1 30	1 30	..	6 0	8 30	9 15
..	..	..	..	..	BERLIN ..arrival	..	1 0	..	..	..	8 45	..	..	..

Remarks.—LUGGAGE: 50 lbs. are allowed free of charge.

LUBECK and BUCHEN.

Eng. Miles.	Fares.			Stations.	Trains.				
	1 Cl.	2 Cl.	3 Cl.		1	2	3	4	5
Dis.	mk. sh	mk. sh	mk. sh		a.m.	a.m.	p.m.		
—	—	—	—	**Lubeck** ....dep.	7 30	11 45	5 30	..	..
11½	1 5	1 0	0 11½	Ratzeburg	7 56	12 35	5 56	..	..
18	1 15	1 7½	1 1	Molln	8 12	1 2	6 12	..	..
29	3 3	2 6	1 12	**Buchen** ....arr.	8 40	1 45	6 40	..	..

Eng. Miles.	Fares.			Stations.	Trains.				
	1 Cl.	2 Cl.	3 Cl.		1	2	3	4	5
Dis.	mk. sh	mk. sh	mk. sh		a.m.	p.m.	p.m.		
—	—	—	—	**Buchen** ....dep.	8 50	2 15	6 50	..	..
11	0 23	0 17	0 13	Molln	9 15	2 59	7 15	..	..
16½	0 35½	0 26½	0 19½	Ratzeburg	9 33	3 27	7 33	..	..
29	1 13	0 46	0 34	**Lubeck** ....arr.	10 0	4 15	8 0	..	..

Remarks.—LUGGAGE: 50 lbs. are allowed free of charge.

BERLIN, FRANKFURT, AND BRESLAU.—219½ English miles.

English Miles.	Fares. Passengers. 1 cl.	2 cl.	3 cl.	Equipg 1cl.	2 cl	Stations.	Trains. 1	2	3	4	5
	sgr.	sgr.	sgr.	dol	dol		a.m.	a.m.	noon.	p.m.	p.m.
—	..	..	..	..	..	**Berlin**..dep	5 30	8 0	12 0	6 0	11 0
6¾	10	7½	5	5⅙	3	Cöpnick	6 0	8 15	12 30	6 15	11 15
14½	22½	7½	10	5⅙	3	Erkner	6 30	8 30	1 15	6 45	11 30
28¾	42½	32½	20	5⅙	3	Fürstenwalde	8 0	9 15	2 15	7 15	12 15
38¼	57½	42½	25	7	5	Briesen	8 30	9 45	3 0	7 45	12 30
49⅓	75	55	32½	7⅓	5⅓	**Frankfurt**	10 0	10 30	4 15	8 30	1 15
63¼	..	..	..	..	..	Fürstenburg..	11 15	11 0	5 15	..	..
68	102½	75	45	10	7	Neuzelle	11 30	11 15	5 45	..	..
79½	120	87½	52½	11⅔	9	Guben	12 30	11 45	7 30	..	2 45
95¾	147½	107½	65	14⅙	10	Sommerfeld ..	2 0	12 30	6a.m.	..	3 30
112	170	125	75	16½	12½	Sorau	3 15	1 30	7 0	..	4 30
117¾	177½	130	77½	20⅙	15⅙	Hansdorf(1)..	4 0	1 45	7 30	..	4 45
129½	..	..	..	..	..	Rauscha	..	2 15	..	..	..
137½	207½	152½	90	20⅙	15⅙	Kohlfurt arr.	..	2 45	..	..	5 45
145¾	..	..	..	..	..	Siegersdorf ..	..	3 15	..	..	..
153¾	232½	167½	100	22½	17	Bunzlau	6 45	3 30	12 15	..	6 45
169¾	257½	185	110	25	19	Hainau	8 0	4 15	1 30	..	7 30
181	275	197½	117½	26½	20	Leignitz	5¼ am	5 0	2 45	..	8 0
195	295	212½	127½	28½	21½	Maltsch	6 45	5 45	4 0	..	..
200¼	302½	217½	130	32	24	Neumarkt ..	7 15	6 0	4 30	..	9 0
205¾	312½	222½	132½	32	24	Nimkau	7 45	6 15	5 0	..	9 15
212¾	322½	230	137½	32	24	Lissa	8 30	6 30	6 0	..	9 30
219½	332½	237½	142½	32	24	**Breslau** ar.	8 45	7 0	6 30	..	10 0

English Miles.	Fares. Passengers. 1 cl.	2 cl.	3 cl.	Equipg 1cl.	2cl.	Stations.	Trains. 1	2	3	4	5
	sgr.	sgr.	sgr.	dol	dol		a.m.	a.m.	a.m.	a.m.	p.m.
—	..	..	..	..	..	**Breslau** dp	6 45	..	8 15	11 45	5 45
6¾	10	7½	5	4	3	Lissa	7 30	..	8 30	12 0	6 0
13½	20	15	10	4	3	Nimkau	8 0	..	8 45	12 45	6 15
19¼	30	20	12½	4	3	Neumarkt ...	8 15	..	9 0	1 15	6 30
25¼	37½	25	15	4	3	Maltsch	9 30	..	9 15	1 45	6 45
39½	57½	40	25	6	4½	Liegnitz	10 30	..	10 0	2 45	7 30
49⅓	75	52½	32½	7½	5¾	Hainau	11 15	..	10 15	4 15	8 0
67¼	100	70	42½	10	7½	Bunzlau	12 30	..	11 0	6 30	8 45
74¾	..	..	..	..	..	Siegersdorf ..	1 0	..	11 30	7 0	9 0
82	125	85	52½	12¼	9¼	Kohlfurt	2 45	..	12 0	7 45	9 45
89¾	..	..	..	..	..	Rauscha	3 15	..	12 15	8 30	9 45
102¾	155	107½	65	16	12	Hansdorf	4 30	..	1 0	9 30	10 30
107¾	162½	112½	67½	16	12	Sorau	5 0	..	1 15	7½ am	11 0
123½	185	130	77½	18¼	13¾	Sommerfeld..	6 0	..	2 0	8 30	11 30
141¼	212½	150	90	20	15½	Guben	7 30	..	2 45	9 45	12 30
152½	230	162½	97½	22⅓	16¼	Neuzelle	8 15	..	3 15	11 15	12 45
156	..	..	..	..	..	Furstenberg ..	8 45	..	3 30	11 30	1 0
169	257½	182½	110	24	18¾	**Frankfurt**	5 a.m	7 0	4 15	1 30	2 0
181¼	275	195	117½	28	21	Briesen	5 45	7 30	4 45	2 45	2 30
190¾	290	205	122½	28	21	Furstenwalde	6 30	8 0	5 15	3 30	3 0
204¾	310	220	132½	32	24	Erkner	7 15	8 30	6 0	4 30	3 15
212¾	322½	230	137½	32	24	Cöpnick	8 0	8 45	6 15	5 15	3 45
219½	332½	237½	142½	32	24	**Berlin** ..ar.	8 45	9 15	6 45	6 0	4 30

Hansdorf to Glogau, see page 103.

Remarks.—LUGGAGE. 50 lbs. are allowed free of charge.

KOTHEN AND BERNBURG RAILWAY.

Engl. Miles.	Fares. 1st clss.	2nd clss.	3rd clss.	Stations.	Trains. 1	2	3
	sgr.	sgr.	sgr.		a.m	p.m.	p.m
—	..	..	..	**Bernburg** ......departure..	6 30	12 30	4 30
6¾	10	7½	5	Biensdorf	7 0	1 0	5 0
12¼	17½	12½	7½	**Kothen** ....arrival..	7 15	1 15	5 15

Eng. Miles.	Fares. 1st clss.	2nd clss.	3rd clss.	Stations.	Trains. 1	2	3
	sgr.	sgr.	sgr.		a.m.	p.m.	p.m.
—	..	..	..	**Kothen** ....departure..	8 45	1 45	7 45
6¾	10	7½	5½	Biensdorf	9 0	..	7 55
12¼	17½	12½	7	**Bernburg** ....arrival..	9 30	2 30	8 30

Remarks.—LUGGAGE.—50 lbs. of Luggage are allowed free of charge.

Breslau to Freiburg and Schweidnitz, p. 104. *Kothen to Halle, Leipsic, and Berlin, p. 92, 104.*

BERLIN, STETTIN, POSEN, BROMBERG, DANTZIC, & KONIGSBERG.

English Miles.	Fares.			STATIONS.	Trains.				
	1st Class	2nd Class	3rd Class		1	2	3	4	5
Dis.	Sgr.	Sgr.	Sgr.		a.m.	a.m.	p.m.	p.m.	p.m.
—	—	—	—	**Berlin** departure	6 15	..	12 15	5 30	10 40
..	20	15	10	Bernau	6 53	..	12 53	6 8	..
..	30	22½	15	Biesenthal	7 12	..	1 12	6 27	..
27¾	40	30	20	Neustadt	7 32	..	1 32	6 48	11 45
41½	60	45	30	Angermünde	8 14	..	2 19	7 31	12 23
51	80	60	40	Passow	8 45	..	2 50	8 2	12 52
..	100	75	50	Tantow	9 19	..	3 24	8 36	..
78½	120	90	60	**Stettin** arrival	9 52	..	3 57	9 10	1 52
				„ departure	10 13	..	4 28	..	2 22
..	..	..	..	Damm	10 39	..	5 0	..	..
..	..	..	..	Carolinenhorst	10 58	..	5 27	..	..
102	127	96	65	**Stargard**	11 21	..	6 19	..	3 12
..	..	..	..	Dölitz	11 53	..	7 4	..	..
126	179	131	92	Arnswalde	12 18	..	7 49	..	3 57
..	..	..	..	Augustwalde	12 45	a.m.	8 27	..	..
143½	207	150	107	**Woldenberg**	1 11	4 47	8 52	..	4 37
157¼	227	164	118	Kreuz arrival	2 12	5 51		..	5 12
157¼	227	164	118	Kreuz departure	2 36	..	..	..	5 47
..	..	..	..	Wronke	3 35	..	..	..	6 42
..	..	..	.	Samter	4 6	..	..	..	7 12
..	..	..	..	Rokietnice	4 30	..	..	..	7 34
206	297	212	155	**Posen** arrival	4 52	..	..	..	7 56
..	..	..	..	Filehne	2 31	6 27	..	..	..
..	..	..	..	Schönlanke	3 9	7 25	..	..	..
193	277	1:9	145	Schneidemuhl	3 46	8 23	..	..	6 23
..	..	..	..	Miasteczko	4 16	9 5	..	..	..
..	..	..	..	Bialosliwe	4 27	9 33	..	..	6 56
..	..	..	..	Osiek	4 46	9 59	..	..	.
226½	329	235	173	Nakel	5 21	10 54	..	..	7 39
246	352	251	185	**Bromberg**	6 8	12 10	..	..	8 19
..	..	..	..	Kotomiers	6 41	12 55	..	..	..
269½	387	275	204	Terespol	7 16	1 53	..	..	9 14
..	..	..	..	Laskowitz	7 33	2 23	..	..	..
289	411	291	217	Warlubien	8 1	3 0	..	..	9 54
300½	427	393	225	Czerwinsk	8 30	3 42	..	..	10 18
311	455	315	235	Pelplin	8 59	4 22	..	..	10 46
325	462	327	244	Dirschau arrival	9 57	4 57	..	..	11 48
							a.m.		a.m.
325	462	327	244	Dirschau departure	9 47	5 57	7 7	..	11 25
..	..	..	..	Hohenstein	10 3	6 21	7 26	..	..
..	..	..	..	Praust	10 18	6 42	7 43	..	..
344½	489	346	259	**Dantzic**	10 33	7 1	7 59	..	12 1
								a.m	
325	462	327	244	Dirschau departure	..	..	..	7 12	..
332	..	..	..	Marienburg	12 27	..	..	9 48	2 18
..	..	..	..	Altfelde	12 56	..	..	10 20	2 39
..	..	..	..	Grunau	1 16	..	..	10 43	2 53
356	..	..	..	Elbing	1 44	..	..	11 12	3 14
..	..	..	..	Guldenboden	2 20	..	..	11 45	3 36
..	..	..	..	Schlobitten	2 50	..	..	12 15	4 4
..	..	..	..	Muhlhausen	3 12	..	..	12 38	4 20
389	..	..	..	Braunsberg	3 56	..	..	1 20	4 55
420	..	..	..	**Konigsberg** arrival	..	..	..	..	..

Remarks.—Children under 2 years of age go free; up to 12 years of age, two for the price of one ticket. LUGGAGE: 50 lbs. free; for every 25 lbs. overweight 1 silbergroschen is charged from one station to another. Droskas from the station to the town for 5 sgr.

Travelling carriages from Stettin to Stargard, 1st class 3 dollars 22½ sgr., 2nd class 3 dollars, 3rd class, 5 sgr.

N.B.—Finkenwalde lies between Damm and Carolinenhorst, and passengers are taken up and set down there. 1st class 7½ sgr.

KONIGSBERG, DANTZIC, BROMBERG, POSEN, STETTIN, & BERLIN.

English Miles.	Fares.			STATIONS.	Trains.				
	1st Class	2nd Class	3rd Class		1	2	3	4	5
Dis.	Sgr.	Sgr.	Sgr.		a.m.	a.m.	p.m.	p.m.	
—	—	—	—	**Konigsberg** ....departure	..	..	..	..	..
..	..	..	..	Braunsberg	11 47	12 31	2 46	..	..
..	..	..	..	Muhlhausen	12 30	1 17	3 36	..	..
..	..	..	..	Schlobitten	12 44	1 37	3 59	..	..
..	..	..	..	Guldenboden	1 5	2 12	4 30	..	..
..	..	..	..	Elbing	1 27	2 41	5 1	..	..
..	..	..	..	Grunau	1 44	3 8	5 28	..	..
..	..	..	..	Altfelde	1 58	3 30	5 51	..	..
..	..	..	..	Marienburg	2 45	4 22	6 59	..	..
..	..	..	..	Dirschau ....arrival	5 23	6 54	8 59	..	..
					p.m.	a.m.	a.m.	p.m.	
..	Frm.	Dant	zic.	**Dantzic** ....departure	4 14	5 45	10 6	8 16	..
..	..	..	..	Praust	4 33	6 2	10 25	8 35	..
..	..	..	..	Hohenstein	4 50	6 17	10 42	8 52	..
..	28	19	15	Dirschau..................arrival	5 8	6 33	11 0	9 10	..
							a.m.		
..	Frm.	Dirsc	hau	Dirschau ....departure	..	..	8 45	..	..
..	18	12	10	Pelplin	5 48	7 22	9 25	..	..
..	35	25	19	Czerwinsk	6 15	7 52	10 17	..	..
..	55	36	28	Warlubien	6 43	8 23	11 4	..	..
..	..	..	..	Laskowitz	..	8 45	11 37	..	..
..	75	55	41	Terespol	7 18	9 12	12 15	..	..
..	..	..	..	Kotomiers	..	9 41	1 11	..	..
..	110	77	60	**Bromberg**	8 19	10 16	2 14	..	..
..	134	99	72	Nakel	8 53	10 58	3 20	..	..
..	..	..	..	Osiek	..	11 27	3 59	..	..
..	..	..	..	Bialosliwe	9 28	11 44	4 40	..	..
..	..	..	..	Miasteczko	..	11 55	5 5	..	..
..	186	129	100	Schneidemuhl	10 3	12 28	5 59	..	..
..	..	..	..	Schönlanke	..	1 0	6 52	..	..
..	..	..	..	Filehne	..	1 33	7 48	..	..
					p.m.	a.m.			
..	307	212	165	**Posen**..............departure	8 55	11 42	..	..	..
..	..	..	..	Rokietnice	9 17	12 6	..	..	..
..	..	..	..	Samter	9 42	12 32	..	..	..
..	..	..	..	Wronke	10 11	1 5	..	..	..
..	..	..	..	Kreuz ....arrival	10 58	1 51	..	..	..
								a.m.	
..	236	163	127	Kreuz ....departure	11 10	2 9	8 7	5 57	..
..	255	177	138	**Woldenberg**	11 37	2 44	..	6 55	..
..	..	..	.	Augustwalde.....................	..	3 4	..	7 23	..
..	283	196	153	Arnswalde.....................	12 17	3 32	..	8 14	..
..	..	..	..	Dölitz	..	3 54	..	8 49	..
..	313	217	159	**Stargard**	12 56	4 26	..	9 47	..
..	..	..	..	Carolinenhorst	..	4 43	..	10 12	..
..	..	..	..	Damm	..	5 1	..	10 43	..
..	342	237	184	**Stettin** ....arrival	1 42	5 25	..	11 8	..
					a.m.	p.m.	a.m.	p.m.	
	Frm.	Stet	tin.	,, ...departure	2 12	5 45	6 30	12 35	..
..	20	15	10	Tantow	..	6 22	7 7	1 12	..
..	40	30	20	Passow	3 16	6 54	7 39	1 44	..
..	60	45	30	Angermunde	3 44	7 27	8 12	2 22	..
..	80	60	40	Neustadt	4 23	8 6	8 49	2 59	..
..	..	..	..	Biesenthal	..	8 24	9 7	3 18	..
..	..	..	..	Bernau	..	8 44	2 26	3 37	..
..	120	90	60	**Berlin** ....arrival	5 20	9 15	9 57	4 8	..

Remarks.—Children under 2 years of age go free; up to 12 years of age, two for the price of one ticket.

LUGGAGE: 50 lbs. free; for every 25 lbs. overweight 1 silbergroschen is charged from one station to another. Droskus from the station to the town for 5 sgr.

Travelling carriages from Stettin to Stargard, 1st class 3 dollars $22\frac{1}{2}$ sgr., 2nd class 3 dollars.

N.B.—Finkenwalde lies between Damm and Carolinenhorst, and passengers are taken up and set down there. 1st class $7\frac{1}{2}$ sgr., 3rd class 5 sgr.

BRESLAU, OPPELN, VIENNA, KONIGSHUTTE, AND CRACOW.

[12-52.

(Breslau to Vienna, 290 English miles.)

Eng. Miles.	Fares. 1st Clss	2nd Clss	3rd Clss	STATIONS.	Trains. 1	2	3	4
Dis.	Sgr.	Sgr.	Sgr.		a.m.	a.m.	p.m.	p.m.
—	—	—	—	**Breslau**...... dep.	7 0	6 0	1 0	2 0
18½	21	16	10	Ohlau	7 52	7 6	1 46	3 10
27¾	33	25	15	Brieg................	8 26	7 47	2 18	3 50
..	46	34	21	Löwen	9 0	8 36	2 49	4 32
51	66	49	30	**Oppeln** .... arr.	9 50	9 40	3 30	5 40
..	..	..	..	,, ...dep.	9 54	9 48	3 35	5 45
..	81	61	37	Gogolin	10 35	10 45	4 10	6 37
78½	99	74	45	Kandrzin (Kosel)..arr.	11 15	11 45	4 40	7 30
..	..	..	..	Kandrzin ....dep.	11 15	..	4 45	
..	125	93	58	Ratibor ......arr.	12 15	..	5 30	..
..	..	..	..	,, ... dep.	..	..	5 30	..
..	144	107	67	Annaberg.... arr.	..	..	7 45	..
							a.m.	
290	416½	314	208½	**Vienna** ....arr.	..	..	6 0	..
					a.m.		p.m.	
..	99	74	45	Kandrzin (Kosel). dep.	11 20	11 50	5 5	..
..	111	83	50	Rudzinitz ....arr.	11 54	12 50	5 38	..
					p.m.		p.m.	
101¾	129	96	58	Gleiwitz.......... ,,	12 38	1 57	6 26	..
111	144	107	65	**Konigshutte**	1 22	3 10	7 15	..
124½	159	119	73	**Myslowitz** ..arr.	1 54	3 55	7 45	..
					p.m.		a.m.	
..	..	..	..	,, ..dep.	2 30	..	6 0	..
..	170	127¼	78½	Szczakowa ...... ,,	3 23	..	7 0	..
..	..	..	..	Cieszkowice..........	3 34	..	7 13	..
..	..	..	..	Trzebinia............	4 1	..	7 48	..
..	..	..	..	Krzeszowice	4 51	..	8 21	..
..	..	..	..	Zabierzow	5 10	..	8 42	..
..	218½	162¾	99¼	**Cracow** ......arr.	5 32	..	9 7	..

Eng. Miles.	Fares. 1st Clss	2nd Clss	3rd Clss	STATIONS.	Trains. 1	2	3	4
Dis.	Sgr.	Sgr.	Sgr.		a.m.	a.m.	p.m.	p.m.
—	—	—	—	**Cracow** ......dep.	..	10 0	4 0	..
..	..	..	..	Zabierzow	..	10 23	4 26	..
..	..	..	..	Krzeszowice	..	10 49	4 58	..
..	..	..	..	Trzebinia	..	11 20	5 39	..
..	..	..	..	Cieszkowice	..	11 41	6 6	..
..	48½	34½	20½	Szczakowa	..	12 14	6 45	..
..	59½	43	26	**Myslowitz** ..arr.	..	12 32	7 8	..
						p.m.	a.m.	
..	..	..	..	,, ..dep.	6 0	1 15	8 30	2 15
13½	87	55	34	**Konigshutte**	7 0	1 56	9 5	3 20
23	95½	66	41	Gleiwitz	8 15	2 40	9 48	4 25
..	107½	79	49	Rudzinitz...........	9 15	3 26	10 30	5 57
46	119½	88	54	Kandrzin (Kosel) arr.	10 0	4 8	11 15	6 35
..	..	..	..	Kandrzin ....dep.	..	4 45	11 15	..
..	..	..	..	Ratibor........arr	..	5 30	12 15	..
..	..	..	.	**Vienna** .... arr.	..	6 0	..	..
						p.m.	a.m.	
..	145½	107¾	67¼	Ratibor ......dep.	..	2 45	10 0	..
46	119½	88	54	Kandrzin......arr.	..	4 0	11 15	p.m.
..	..	..	..	Kandrzin (Kosel) dep.	10 8	4 8	11 30	6 40
..	137½	101¾	80¼	Gogolin	11 0	4 51	12 10	7 35
74	152½	113¾	69¼	**Oppeln** ....arr.	12 0	5 30	12 50	8 25
							p.m.	
..	..	..	..	,, ...dep.	12 6	5 37	12 53	..
..	173½	158¾	79¼	Löwen .... ,,	1 5	6 26	1 39	..
97	185½	137¾	84¼	Brieg............ ,,	2 30	7 5	2 15	..
106½	197½	146¾	89¼	Ohlau .... ,,	3 15	7 35	2 45	..
124¼	218½	162¾	99¼	**Breslau** ....arrival	4 15	8 20	3 30	..
..	551	400¼	241¾	**Berlin** .... ,,	..	..	4½ a.m	..
..	776	570¼	366¾	**Hamburg** .... ,,	..	..	3½ p.m	..

Extra.—From Breslau to Oppeln at 5.40 p.m. in 2¾ hours; Oppeln to Breslau at 7 a.m. in 2¾ hours.

Remarks.—Children under 2 years free; under 10 years of age, two for price of one ticket; a child 10 years of age, with a ticket, can ride in the next higher class carriage.—Dogs 1 sgr. each per mile.——LUGGAGE.—50lbs. are allowed free of charge.

Riederschlesische Railway.—GLOGAU AND HANSDORF. [10-52.

English Miles.	Fares.			STATIONS.	Trains.			STATIONS.	Trains.		
	1st Clss	2nd Clss	3rd Clss		1	2	3		1	2	3
Dis.	sgr.	sgr.	sgr.		a.m.	p.m.			a.m.	p.m.	
—	—	—	—	**Glogau** ....dep.	10 0	7 0	...	**Hansdorf** ....dep.	5 15	2 0	...
$9\frac{1}{4}$	15	9	7	Klopschen	10 30	7 30	...	**Sagan**	5 30	2 20	...
$11\frac{1}{4}$	...	...	...	Quaritz	10 45	7 45	...	Buchwald	5 45	2 30	...
$18\frac{1}{2}$	...	...	...	Waltersdorf	11 0	8 0	...	Sprottau	6 0	2 55	...
$27\frac{3}{4}$	45	27	21	Sprottau	11 30	8 30	...	Waltersdorf	6 15	3 15	...
32	...	...	...	Buchwald	11 45	8 45	...	Quaritz	6 45	3 30	...
37	60	36	28	**Sagan**	12 0	9 0	...	Klopschen	7 0	3 45	...
44	72	$42\frac{1}{2}$	33	**Hansdorf** ....arr.	12 30	9 30	...	**Glogau** ....arr.	7 30	4 20	...
					p.m.	a.m.			p.m.	a.m.	
$113\frac{1}{4}$	$174\frac{1}{2}$	$108\frac{1}{2}$	$84\frac{1}{2}$	Frankf rt-on-Oder. ar.	4 15	2 0	...	Berlin ....arr.	11 0	8 0	...
162	$249\frac{1}{2}$	157	122	Berlin .... ,,	6 45	4 30	...	Frankf rt-on-Oder. ,,	1 15	10 30	...
$80\frac{3}{4}$	127	62	48	Bunzlau .... ,,	3 30	6 45	...	Breslau .... ,,	5 45	8 15	...
92	...	...	...	Hainau .... ,,	4 15	7 15	...	Liegnitz .... ,,	7 30	10 0	...
106	$169\frac{1}{4}$	$104\frac{1}{2}$	81	Liegnitz .... ,,	5 0	8 0	...	Hainau .... ,,	8 0	10 15	...
144	227	143	$111\frac{1}{2}$	Breslau .... ,,	7 0	10 0	...	Bunzlau .... ,,	8 45	11 0	...
80	$129\frac{1}{2}$	79	61	Gorlitz .... ,,	4 0	7 0	...	Leipsic .... ,,	12 30	a.m.	...
144	$199\frac{1}{4}$	135	103	Dresden .... ,,	8 0	11 45	...	Dresden .... ,,	5 0	6 0	...
$217\frac{1}{4}$	$289\frac{1}{2}$	203	148	Leipsic .... ,,	5 0	4 0	...	Gorlitz .... ,,	8 45	11 0	..

Remarks.—Luggage: 50 lbs. of Luggage are allowed free of charge; for every additional 10 lbs $2\frac{1}{2}$ pfennings per German mile will have to be paid.

WARSAW TO SZCZAKOWA.—$190\frac{1}{2}$ English Miles.

Eng. Miles.	Fares.			STATIONS.	Trains.						
	1st Clss	2nd Clss	3rd Clss		1	2	3 Goods.	4 Goods.	5	6	7
Dis.	Kop	Kop	Kop		a.m.	a.m.	p.m.	p.m.			
—	—	—	—	**Warsaw** ....dep	7 30	..	1 20	5 0	..	..	..
$41\frac{1}{2}$	135	$101\frac{1}{2}$	$67\frac{1}{2}$	Skierniewice	9 50	..	3 45	7 25	..	..	..
..	180	$135\frac{1}{2}$	90	Lowicz	10 45	..	..	8 0	..	..	..
$89\frac{3}{4}$	$292\frac{1}{2}$	$218\frac{1}{2}$	$146\frac{1}{2}$	Petrikau	1 5	..	6 30	..	..	..	..
$143\frac{1}{2}$	465	$348\frac{3}{4}$	$232\frac{1}{2}$	Czenstochau	3 50	7 0	9 0	..	..	..	..
$190\frac{1}{2}$	615	$461\frac{1}{2}$	$307\frac{1}{2}$	**Szczakowa** ....arr.	6 15	10 20	..	..	..	..	..

SZCZAKOWA TO WARSAW.

Eng. Miles.	Fares.			STATIONS.	Trains.						
	1st Clss	2nd Clss	3rd Clss		1	2	3 Goods.	4 Goods.	5	6	7
Dis.	Kop	Kop	Kop		a.m	a.m.	p.m.	a.m.			
—	—	—	—	**Szczakowa** ....dep.	9 15	..	5 5	..	..	..	..
$47\frac{1}{4}$	150	113	75	Czenstochau	11 50	..	8 35	7 45	..	..	..
$100\frac{3}{4}$	$322\frac{1}{2}$	243	161	Petrikau	3 0	..	..	10 30	..	..	..
..	..	..	..	Lowicz	4 55	7 0	..	..	..	..	..
149	480	360	240	Skierniewice	5 40	7 55	..	1 10	..	..	..
$190\frac{1}{2}$	615	$461\frac{1}{2}$	307	**Warsaw** ....arr.	7 50	10 10	..	3 15	..	..	..

BRESLAU AND SCHWEIDNITZ TO FREIBURG.

English Miles.	Fares. 1st Clss	2nd Clss	3rd Clss	STATIONS.	Trains. In Summer. 1 Mixd	2 Mixd	3 Mixd	In Winter. 4	5	6	7
	Sgr.	Sgr.	Sgr.		a.m.	p.m.	p.m.	a.m.	p.m		
—	..	..	..	**Breslau** ....departure	6 30	1 0	5 30	8 0	5 15	..	..
9¼	..	8	4	Schmolz..............................	..	..	..	..	..	..	..
12¼	16	11	7	Kanth	..	..	..	..	..	..	..
..	..	..	..	Mettkau	..	..	..	..	..	..	..
22	28	19	12	Ingramsdorf..........................	..	..	..	..	..	..	..
31	39	26	19	Königszelt...........................	8 9	2 39	7 9	9 39	6 54	..	..
35¼	45	30	22	**Schweidnitz** ....arrival	8 25	2 55	7 25	9 55	7 10	..	..
35¾	45	30	22	**Freiburg**................. ,,	8 25	2 55	7 25	9 55	7 20	..	..

FREIBURG AND SCHWEIDNITZ TO BRESLAU.

English Miles	Fares. 1st Clss	2nd Clss	3rd Clss	STATIONS.	Trains. In Summer. 1 Mixd	2 Mixd	3 Mixd	In Winter. 4	5	6	7
	Sgr.	Sgr.	Sgr.		a.m.	p.m.	p.m.	a.m.	p.m.		
—	..	..	..	**Freiburg**.................depart.	5 45	1 18	8 0	7 10	3 15	..	..
..	15	10	6	**Schweidnitz** .... ,,	5 40	1 15	7 50	7 0	3 5	..	..
4½	8	6	4	Königszelt............................	6 5	1 39	8 21	7 30	3 35	..	..
13	18	12	8	Ingramsdorf..........................	..	..	..	..	..	..	..
..	..	..	..	Mettkau	..	..	..	..	..	..	..
22½	30	20	13	Kanth	..	..	..	..	..	..	..
26½		..	..	Schmolz...............................	..	..	..	..	..	..	..
35¾	45	30	22	**Breslau** ....arrival	7 39	3 13	9 55	9 4	5 9	..	..

Additional Trains.—From Freiburg at 5.45 a.m., 1.18 and 8 p.m.; arrive in Schweidnitz at 8.25 a.m., 2.55 and 8.37 p.m. From Schweidnitz at 5.40 a.m., 1.15 and 6.40 p.m.; arrive in Freiburg at 8.25 a.m., 2.55 and 7.25 p.m.

Remarks.—Children under 2 years of age, free; tickets must be procured for older children, but one ticket will procure two seats for children under 10 years of age.

Luggage.—50lbs. free; for 20lbs. overweight, 2½ sgr. as far as Kanth, 4 sgr. to Ingramsdorf, 5 sgr. to Königszelt, and 6 sgr. to Schweidnitz or Freiburg; for every 20lbs. above 70lbs., ½ sgr. in addition; also for 90lbs. to Freiburg, 6½ sgr.; for 150lbs., 8 sgr.

Breslau to Oppeln, Kosel, Ratibor, Vienna, and Cracow, see page 102.
Breslau to Bunzlau, Guben, Frankfurt, and Berlin, see page 99.

BERLIN, KOTHEN HALLE, AND LEIPSIC.—134 English miles.

There is a shorter route between Berlin and Leipzic, see page 89. [15-11-52.

Eng. Miles.	Fares.			STATIONS.	Trains.							
	1st Class	2nd Class	3rd Class		1	2	3	4	5	6	7	8
Dis.	Sgr.	Sgr.	Sgr.		a.m.	noon.	p.m.					
—	—	—	—	**Berlin** dep.	8 0	12 0	10 0	..	..	..	..	..
..	..	..	..	Grossbeeren	8 15	12 30	10 15	..	..	..	..	..
..	..	..	..	Ludwigsfelde	8 30	12 45	10 30	..	..	..	..	..
20¾	30	20	12	Trebbin	8 45	1 30	10 45	..	..	..	..	..
30	40	27	17	Luckenwalde	9 0	2 0	11 0	..	..	..	..	..
38	55	35	22	Jüterbogk	9 30	2 45	11 15	..	..	..	..	..
..	..	..	..	Seehausen	9 45	3 15	11 30	..	..	..	..	..
51	70	45	28	Zahna	10 0	3 30	12 0	..	..	..	..	...
58¾	84½	58½	45½	Wittenberg	10 15	3 45	12 15	..	..	..	..	..
66	90	..	..	Koswig	10 45	4 30	12 30	..	..	..	..	..
..	..	..	..	Kliecken	10 50	4 45	..	..	..	..	..	..
76¼	100	..	..	Rosslau	11 0	5 15	1 0	..	..	..	..	..
79½	114	79	61	Dessau	11 15	5 45	1 15	..	..	..	..	..
93	130	90	70	**Kothen** Junc.	12 0	7 0	2 0	..	..	..	..	..
..	..	..	..	Stumsdorf	..	..	..	..	..	..	..	..
115	159	109	81½	**Halle**	1 15	8 30	3 0	..	..	..	..	..
..	..	..	..	Schkeuditz	..	..	..	..	..	..	..	..
134	180	120	90	**Leipsic** arr.	2 0	9 15	4 0	..	..	..	..	..

LEIPSIC, HALLE, KOTHEN, AND BERLIN.—134 English miles.

Eng. Miles.	Fares.			STATIONS.	Trains.							
	1st Class	2nd Class	3rd Class		1	2	3	4	5	6	7	8
Dis.	Sgr.	Sgr.	Sgr.		a.m.	p.m.	p.m.	a.m.				
—	—	—	—	**Leipsic** dep.	7 0	3 30	5 30	..	..	..	..	..
..	..	..	..	Schkeuditz	..	..	..	..	..	..	..	..
..	27	18	11	**Halle**	7 45	4 30	6 15	..	..	..	..	..
..	..	..	..	Stumsdorf	..	..	..	..	..	..	..	..
—	56	37	22½	**Kothen** Junc.	8 45	5 30	7 45	..	..	..	..	..
13	74	50	31½	Dessau	9 0	5 45	8 30	..	..	..	..	..
17½	..	..	..	Rosslau	9 15	6 0	8 45	..	..	..	..	..
..	..	..	..	Kliecken	9 20	6 15	9 15	..	..	..	..	..
27	..	..	..	Koswig	9 30	6 30	9 30	..	..	..	..	..
36	105	71	48½	Wittenberg	9 45	6 45	10 15	5 0	..	..	..	..
42½	..	..	..	Zahna	10 15	7 0	—	5 30	..	..	..	..
..	..	..	..	Seehausen	..	7 15	..	5 45	..	..	..	..
55	134	91	64½	Jüterbogk	10 45	7 30	..	6 15	..	..	..	..
64	..	..	..	Luckenwalde	11 0	8 0	..	7 0	..	..	..	..
73	..	..	..	Trebbin	11 15	8 15	..	7 30	..	..	..	..
..	..	..	..	Ludwigsfelde	..	8 30	..	8 0	..	..	..	..
..	..	..	..	Grossbeeren	..	8 45	..	8 30	..	..	..	..
93	180	120	90	**Berlin** arrival	12 30	9 30	..	9 30	..	..	..	..

Remarks.—LUGGAGE.—50 lbs. free; every 10 lbs. extra, 5 sgr. Four-wheeled carriages, 25½ Prus. doll.; two-wheeled carriage, 19 Prus. doll.

Leipsic to Altenberg, Hof, Bamberg, Nuremberg, Augsburg, and Munich, pages 90, 83, 82.

Halle to Weimar, Erfurt, Gotha, and Eisenach, page 88.

Hamburg to Berlin, page 92. *Posen, Woldenberg, Stargard, Stettin, andNeustad to Berlin, see page* 100.

Dresden to Leipsic, page 98.

NORTHERN STATES RAILWAY.] [250 ENGLISH MILES.

VIENNA, BRUNN AND TRUBAU, TO PRAGUE.

English Miles.	Fares.				STATIONS.	Trains.				
	1st Class	2nd Class	3rd Class	4th Class		1	2	3	4	5
Dis.	fl. kr.	fl kr.	fl kr.	fl. kr.		a.m.	a.m.	p.m.		
—	—	—	—	—	**Vienna** ....dep.	...	6 30	7 0	...	...
4½	0 20	0 15	0 10	0 6	Floridsdorf........	...	6 43	7 12	...	...
9¼	0 40	0 30	0 20	0 12	Sussenbrunn	...	...	7 30	...	...
11¼	0 50	0 38	0 25	0 15	Wagram	...	7 6	7 42	...	...
18½	1 20	1 0	0 40	0 24	**Ganserndorf** ....arr.	...	7 25	8 6	...	...
					" ....dep.	...	7 35	8 16	...	...
23	1 40	1 15	0 50	0 30	Angern	...	7 51	8 35	...	...
32½	2 20	1 45	1 10	0 42	Durnkrut	...	8 10	8 58	...	...
37	2 40	2 0	1 20	0 48	Drösing	...	...	9 13	...	...
41½	3 0	2 15	1 30	0 54	Hohenau........	...	8 37	9 32	...	...
51	3 40	2 45	1 50	1 6	**Lundenburg** ....arr.	...	9 6	10 7	...	...
					" ....dep.	3 30	9 21	10 23	...	...
60	4 20	3 15	2 10	1 18	Saitz	4 36	9 58	11 6	...	...
74	5 20	4 0	2 40	1 36	Branowitz	5 33	10 28	11 45	...	...
83¼	6 0	4 30	3 0	1 48	Raigern	6 25	10 54	12 17	...	...
92	6 40	5 0	3 20	2 0	**Brunn** ....arr.	6 56	11 13	12 42	...	...
	From Brunn.				" ....dep.		11 45	1 0	...	...
9¼	0 36	0 22	0 16	...	Adamsthal........	...	...	...	...	...
13½	0 54	0 33	0 24	...	Blansko	...	...	...	...	...
18½	1 12	0 44	0 32	...	Raitz	...	...	...	...	...
23	1 30	0 55	0 40	...	Skalitz........	...	...	...	...	...
27¾	1 48	1 6	0 48	...	Lettowitz	...	...	...	...	...
32½	2 6	1 17	0 56	...	Brusau	...	...	...	...	...
39¼	2 33	1 34	1 8	...	Greifendorf........	...	...	...	...	...
43¾	2 51	1 45	1 16	...	Zwittau	...	2 19	3 34	...	...
46	3 0	1 50	1 20	...	Abtsdorf........	...	...	...	...	...
55½	3 36	2 12	1 36	...	**Bohm-Trubau** ....arr.	...	2 45	4 15	...	...
	From Trubau.				" ....dep.	...	3 0	4 20	...	...
4½	0 18	0 11	0 8	...	Wildenschwert	...	...	...	...	...
11¼	0 45	0 28	0 20	...	Brandeis........	...	...	...	...	...
13½	0 54	0 33	0 24	...	Chotzen	...	...	...	...	...
18½	1 12	0 44	0 32	...	Zamersk	...	...	...	...	...
23	1 30	0 55	0 40	...	Uhersko	...	...	...	...	...
27¾	1 48	1 6	0 48	...	Morawan........	...	...	...	...	...
37	2 24	1 28	1 4	...	Pardubitz	...	4 46	6 10	...	...
46	3 0	1 50	1 20	...	Przelautsch	...	...	...	...	...
57¾	3 45	2 18	1 40	...	Elbeteinitz........	...	...	...	...	...
62½	4 3	2 29	1 48	...	Kolin	...	6 1	7 25	...	...
71¾	4 39	2 51	2 4	...	Podiebrad	...	6 27	7 52	...	...
80¾	5 15	3 13	2 20	...	Böhm. Brod	...	...	...	...	...
87¾	5 32	3 29	2 32	...	Auwal	...	...	...	...	...
92	6 0	3 40	2 40	...	Biechowitz........	...	...	...	...	...
101¾	6 36	4 2	2 56	...	**Prague**........arr.	...	7 55	10 6	...	...
							a.m	p.m.		
...	...	...	...	...	DRESDEN ....arr.	...	3 30	4 55	...	...

Remarks.—A great saving of distance has been effected since the opening of the portion of this line from Brunn to Böhm-Trubau direct.

LUGGAGE: 50 lbs. of Luggage free, every extra 20 lbs. 54 kr. c.m.; four-wheeled Carriage, 87 fl. 36 kr.; two-wheeled Carriage, 70 fl. 48 kr.

NORTHERN STATES RAILWAY.] [250 ENGLISH MILES.

PRAGUE, TRUBAU, AND BRUNN, TO VIENNA.

English Miles.	Fares.				STATIONS.	Trains.				
	1st Class	2nd Class	3rd Class	4th Class		1	2	3	4	5
Dis.	fl. kr.	fl. kr.	fl. kr.	fl. kr.		p.m.	a.m			
...	...	...	...	...	DRESDEN ....dep.	9 20	7 0	...	...	...
						a.m.	p.m.	p.m.		
—	—	—	—	—	**Prague** ....dep.	5 30	3 15	...	...	...
9¼	0 36	0 22	0 16	...	Biechowitz	...	...	...	...	...
13½	0 54	0 33	0 24	...	Auwal	...	...	...	...	...
20¾	1 21	0 50	0 36	...	Böhm-Brod	...	...	...	...	...
30	1 57	1 12	0 52	...	Podiebrad	7 2	4 47	...	...	...
39¼	2 33	1 34	1 8	...	Kolin	7 30	5 14	...	...	...
43¾	2 51	1 45	1 16	...	Elbeteinitz..........	...	...	...	...	...
55½	3 36	2 12	1 36	...	Przelautsch	...	...	...	...	...
65	4 12	2 34	1 52	...	Pardubitz...	8 49	6 30	...	...	...
74	4 48	2 56	2 8	...	Morawan..........	...	...	...	...	...
78½	5 6	3 7	2 16	...	Uhersko	...	...	...	...	...
83¼	5 24	3 18	2 24	...	Zamersk	...	...	...	...	...
87¾	5 42	3 29	2 32	...	Chotzen	...	...	...	...	...
89¾	5 51	3 35	2 36	...	Brandeis	...	...	...	...	...
97	6 18	3 51	2 48	...	Wildenschwert	...	...	...	...	...
101¾	6 36	4 2	2 56	...	**Bohm-Trubau** ....arr.	...	...	...	...	...
	From Trubau.				" ....dep.	11 7	8 45	...	...	...
9¼	0 36	0 22	0 16	...	Abtsdorf..........	...	...	...	...	...
11¾	0 45	0 28	0 20	...	Zwittau	11 48	9 29	...	...	...
15¾	1 3	0 39	0 28	...	Griefendorf	...	...	...	...	...
23	1 30	0 55	0 40	...	Brüsau	...	...	...	...	...
27¾	1 48	1 6	0 48	...	Lettowitz	...	...	...	...	...
32½	2 6	1 17	0 56	...	Skalitz..........	...	...	...	...	...
37	2 24	1 28	1 4	...	Raitz..........	...	...	...	...	...
41½	2 42	1 39	1 12	...	Blansko	...	...	...	...	...
46	3 0	1 50	1 20	...	Adamsthal	...	...	...	...	...
55½	3 36	2 12	1 36	...	**Brunn** ....arr.	2 20	11 58	...	...	...
	From Brunn.				" ....dep.	2 55	12 42	6 15	...	...
9¼	0 40	0 30	0 20	...	Raigern	3 18	1 8	7 1	...	...
18½	1 20	1 0	0 40	...	Branowitz	3 44	1 37	7 53	...	...
32¾	2 20	1 45	1 10	...	Saitz	4 13	2 8	8 44	...	...
41½	3 0	2 15	1 30	...	**Lundenburg** ....arr.	4 44	2 41	9 34	...	...
					" ....dep.	4 56	3 10		...	...
51	3 40	2 45	1 50	...	Hohenau..........	5 29	3 43	...	...	...
55½	4 0	3 0	2 0	...	Drösing	...	3 57	...	...	...
60	4 20	3 15	2 10	...	Dürnkrut..........	5 56	4 12	...	...	...
69½	5 0	3 45	2 30	...	Angern	6 15	4 31	...	...	...
74	5 20	4 0	2 40	...	**Ganserndorf** ....arr.	6 29	4 45	...	...	...
					" ....dep.	6 39	4 55	...	..	...
80¾	5 50	4 23	2 55	...	Wagram..........	7 2	5 19	...	...	...
83¼	6 0	4 30	3 0	...	Süssenbrunn	...	5 27	...	...	...
87¾	6 20	4 45	3 10	...	Floridsdorf	7 26	5 46	...	...	...
92	6 40	5 0	3 20	...	**Vienna**..........arr.	7 35	5 55	...	...	...

Remarks.—A great saving of distance has been effected since the opening of the portion of this line from Brunn to Böhm-Trubau direct.

LUGGAGE: 50 lbs. of Luggage are allowed free of charge.

VIENNA TO BRUCK.

[5-53—9-53.

English Miles.	Fares.				STATIONS.	Trains.				
	1st Class	2nd Class	3rd Class	4th Class		1	2	3	4	5
Dis.	fl. kr.	fl. kr.	fl. kr.	fl. kr.		a.m.	p.m.			
—	—	—	—	—	**Vienna** ....dep.	8 0	4 0	..	..	..
4½	..	0 15	0 10	..	Simmering	8 7	4 7	..	..	..
..	..	..	..	..	Schwechat	8 17	4 17	..	..	..
6½	..	0 21	0 14	..	Lanzendorf	8 26	4 26	..	..	..
7½	..	0 27	0 18	..	Himberg	8 33	4 33	..	..	..
10¼	..	0 33	0 22	..	Gutenhof-Velm	8 40	4 40	..	..	..
11½	..	0 39	0 26	..	Grammat Neusiedel	8 52	4 52	..	..	..
15¾	..	0 53	0 35	..	Götzendorf	9 9	5 9	..	..	..
19	..	1 2	0 41	..	Trantmannsdorf	9 18	5 18	..	..	..
22¾	..	1 12	0 48	..	Wilfleinsdorf	9 30	5 30	..	..	..
25¼	1 50	1 23	0 55	0 33	**Bruck** ....arr.	9 38	5 38	..	..	..

English Miles	Fares.				STATIONS.	Trains.				
	1st Class	2nd Class	3rd Class	4th Class		1	2	*3	4	5
Dis.	fl. kr.	fl. kr.	fl. kr.	fl. kr.		a.m.	p.m.	p.m.		
—	—	—	-	—	**Bruck** ....dep.	6 0	4 0	7 0	..	
4	..	0 15	0 10	..	Wilfleinsdorf	6 10	4 10	7 10	..	
6½	..	0 21	0 14	..	Trantmannsdorf	6 22	4 22	7 22	..	
9¼	..	0 29	0 19	..	Götzendorf	6 33	4 33	7 31	..	
12½	..	0 44	0 29	..	Grammat Neusiedel	6 52	4 52	7 50	..	
14½	..	0 51	0 34	..	Gutenhof-Velm	7 0	5 0	7 58	..	
17	..	0 57	0 38	..	Himberg	7 8	5 8	8 5	..	
19	..	1 0	0 40	..	Lanzendorf	7 15	5 15	8 11	..	
20¾	..	1 8	0 45	..	Schwechat	7 23	5 23	8 19	..	
24	..	1 17	0 51	..	Simmering	7 36	5 36	8 29	..	
25¼	1 50	1 23	0 55	0 33	**Vienna** ....arr.	7 44	5 44	8 35	..	

* Sundays and Festivals only.

Remarks.—LUGGAGE: 20 lbs. of Luggage are allowed free of charge.

VIENNA TO STOCKERAU.

[8-52

English Miles.	Fares.				STATIONS.	Trains.						
	1st Clss.	2nd Clss.	3rd Clss.	4th Clss.		1	2	3	4	5	6	7
Dis.	fl. kr.	fl. kr.	fl. kr.	fl kr.		a.m.	a.m.	p.m.	p.m.			
—	..	..	..	..	**Vienna** ....dep.	5 30	10 0	3 30	7 30	..	..	..
4½	0 20	0 15	0 10	0 6	Floridsdorf	5 41	10 11	3 41	7 44	..	..	..
5½	0 25	0 18	0 12	0 8	Jedlersee	5 46	10 17	3 47	7 52	..	..	..
6¾	0 30	0 24	0 15	0 10	Enzersdorf	5 57	10 29	3 59	8 8	..	..	..
9¼	0 40	0 30	0 20	0 12	Korneuburg	6 7	10 39	4 9	8 23	..	..	..
13½	1 0	0 45	0 30	0 18	**Stockerau** ....arr.	6 27	10 59	4 29	8 45	..	..	..

English Miles.	Fares.				STATIONS.	Trains.						
	1st Class	2nd Class	3rd Class	4th Class		1	2	3	4	5	6	7
Dis.	fl. kr.	fl. kr.	fl. kr.	fl. kr.		a.m.	a.m.	p.m.	p.m.			
—	..	..	..	..	**Stockerau**	5 30	8 0	2 15	8 0	..	..	..
4½	0 24	0 15	0 10	0 6	Korneuburg	6 5	8 22	2 37	8 23	..	..	..
6¾	0 36	0 21	0 15	0 8	Enzersdorf	6 15	8 32	2 47	8 33	..	..	..
7½	0 42	0 27	0 18	0 10	Jedlersee	6 27	8 44	2 59	8 45	..	..	..
9¼	0 48	0 30	0 20	0 12	Floridsdorf	6 33	8 50	3 5	8 51	..	..	..
13½	1 0	0 45	0 30	0 18	**Vienna** ....arr.	6 42	8 59	3 14	9 0	..	..	..

PRESSBURG AND TYRNAU, TO SZERED.

Eng. Miles.	Fares. 1st Class	2nd Class	3rd Class	4th Class	STATIONS.	Trains. 1	2	3	4	5
Dis.	fl kr.	fl. kr.	fl. kr.	fl. kr.		a.m.	p.m.	p.m.		
—	—	—	—	—	**Pressburg** dep.	7 0	3 0	5 30	...	...
...	0 5	0 3	..	...	Pressburger-Bahnhof	...	...	...	...	...
..	0 15	0 10	0 6	...	Ratzersdorf	...	...	...	...	...
...	0 22	0 15	0 10	...	Wajnor	...	...	...	...	...
...	0 25	0 16	0 12	...	St. Georgen	...	...	...	...	..
...	0 30	0 22	0 14	...	Grunau	...	...	...	...	...
...	0 35	0 24	0 15	...	Pösing	...	...	...	...	...
16	0 45	0 30	0 20	...	**Schenkwitz**	...	...	...	...	...
...	0 58	0 40	0 25	...	Báhony	...	...	...	...	...
...	1 4	0 48	0 30	...	Cziffer	...	...	...	...	...
30	1 20	1 0	0 36	...	**Tyrnau**	11 15	7 15	9 45	...	...
38	...	...	...	...	**Szered** arr.	12 30	8 30	...	...	...
						a.m.	a.m.	p.m.		
...	...	...	...	...	**Szered** dep.	...	5 15	1 30	...	...
—	—	—	—	—	**Tyrnau**	4 0	6 45	2 50	...	...
...	0 16	0 12	0 6	...	Cziffer	...	...	...	...	...
...	0 22	0 20	0 11	...	Ráhony	...	...	...	...	...
12½	0 35	0 30	0 16	...	**Schenkwitz**	...	...	...	...	...
...	0 45	0 36	0 21	...	Pösing	...	...	...	...	...
...	0 50	0 48	0 22	...	Grunau	...	...	...	...	...
...	0 55	0 44	0 24	...	St. Georgen	...	...	..	...	...
...	0 58	0 45	0 26	...	Wajnor	...	...	...	...	...
...	1 5	0 50	0 30	...	Ratzersdorf	...	...	...	...	...
...	1 15	0 57	0 36	...	Pressburger-Bahnhof	...	...	...	...	...
28¾	1 20	1 0	0 36	...	**Pressburg** arr.	8 15	10 45	7 15	...	...

Remarks.—LUGGAGE: 20 lbs. are allowed to 1st and 2nd class passengers, and 19 lbs. to the 3rd class.

OLMUTZ TO TRUBAU.

Eng. Miles.	Fares. 1st Class	2nd Class	3rd Class	4th Class	STATIONS.	Trains. 1	2	3	4	5
Dis.	fl. kr.	fl. kr.	fl kr.	fl kr.		p.m.	a.m.			
—	—	—	—	—	**Prerau** departure	11 40	...	...	...	...
6¾	0 30	0 23	0 15	...	Brodek	11 59	...	...	...	...
13½	1 0	0 45	0 30	...	**Olmutz**	12 40	6 0	...	...	...
4½	0 18	0 11	0 8	...	Stefanau	12 45	6 15	...	...	...
11¼	0 45	0 28	0 20	...	Littau	1 15	6 45	...	...	...
18¾	1 12	0 44	0 32	...	Müglitz	1 30	7 15	...	...	...
20¾	1 21	0 50	0 36	...	Lukawetz	1 45	7 45	...	...	...
25¼	1 39	1 1	0 44	...	**Hohenstadt**	2 15	8 14	...	...	...
34¾	2 15	1 23	1 0	...	Budigsdorf	2 45	8 45	...	...	...
37	2 24	1 28	1 4	...	Landskron	2 50	9 0	...	...	...
46	3 0	1 50	1 20	...	Triebitz	3 15	10 0	...	...	...
51	3 18	2 0	1 28	...	**Trubau** arrival	3 45	10 12	...	...	...
						p.m.	p.m.			
—	—	—	—	—	**Trubau** departure	9 5	3 10	...	...	...
4½	0 18	0 11	0 8	...	Triebitz	9 25	3 30	...	...	...
13½	0 54	0 33	0 24	...	Landskron	9 45	4 0	...	...	...
15¾	1 3	0 39	0 28	...	Budigsdorf	10 0	4 15	...	...	...
25¼	1 30	1 1	0 44	...	**Hohenstadt**	10 30	4 45	...	...	...
30	1 57	1 12	0 52	...	Lukawetz	10 45	5 30	...	...	...
32½	2 6	1 17	0 56	...	Müglitz	11 0	5 45	...	...	...
39¼	2 33	1 34	1 8	...	Littau	11 15	6 15	...	...	...
46	3 0	1 50	1 20	...	Stefanau	11 45	6 45	...	...	..
51	3 18	2 1	1 28	...	**Olmutz**	12 1	7 23	...	...	...
57¾	3 48	2 24	1 43	...	Brodek	12 52	...	...	...	...
65	4 18	2 46	1 58	...	**Prerau** arrival	1 10	...	...	...	...

Remarks.—LUGGAGE: 40 lbs. of luggage are allowed free of charge.

VIENNA TO PRESSBURG, PESTH, AND SZOLNOK.

English Miles.	Fares.				STATIONS.	Trains.				
	1st Class	2nd Class	3rd Class	4th Class		1	2	3	4	5
Dis.	fl. kr.	fl. kr.	fl. kr.	fl. kr.		a.m.	p.m.	p.m.	...	...
—	—	—	—	—	**Vienna** ....departure	7 0	2 30	6 30	...	...
$4\frac{1}{3}$	0 20	0 15	0 10	...	Floridsdorf	7 12	2 45	6 45	...	...
$9\frac{1}{4}$	0 40	0 30	0 20	...	Sussenbrunn	...	...		...	...
$11\frac{1}{4}$	0 50	0 38	0 25	...	Wagram	7 37	3 19	7 14	...	...
$18\frac{1}{2}$	1 20	1 0	0 40	0 24	**Ganserndorf** ....arrival	7 57	3 46	7 38	...	...
					,, ... departure	8 8	4 0	7 53	...	...
23	...	1 15	0 30	...	Ob. Waiden	...	...	...	...	...
30	2 10	1 38	1 5	...	Marchegg	8 40	4 43	8 29	...	...
$32\frac{1}{2}$	2 16	1 43	1 9	...	Neudorf	8 55	5 2	8 48	...	...
$41\frac{1}{2}$	3 0	2 8	1 28	...	**Pressburg**	9 53	5 38	9 53	...	...
..	...	...	...	...	Weinern	10 6		10 16	...	...
..	...	...	...	...	Lanschutz	10 15	...	10 29	...	...
..	...	...	...	...	Wartberg	10 33	...	10 47	...	...
..	...	...	...	...	Diószeg	10 55	...	11 17	...	...
..	...	...	...	...	Galantha	11 5	...	11 35	...	...
..	...	...	...	...	Sellye	11 28	...	12 3	...	...
..	...	..	...	...	Tornócz	11 36	...	12 20	...	...
..	...	...	...	..	Tardosked	11 50	...	12 44	...	...
..	...	...	...	...	Tot-Megyer	11 56	...	12 55	...	...
..	...	...	...	...	**Neuhausel**	12 39	..	1 26	...	...
..	...	...	...	...	Sz. Miklós	12 58	...	1 52	...	...
..	...	...	...	...	Köbölkut	1 22	...	2 32	...	...
..	...	...	...	...	**Gran Nana**	1 47	...	3 2	...	...
..	..	...	...	...	Szobb	2 7	...	3 29	...	...
..	...	...	...	...	Gross Maros	2 28	...	3 54	...	...
..	...	...	...	...	Veröcze	2 40	...	4 11	...	...
	From Waitzen.				**Waitzen**	3 0	...	4 39	...	...
$10\frac{1}{4}$	0 27	0 23	0 18	...	Dunakesz	3 25	...	5 12	...	...
$14\frac{1}{2}$	0 39	0 33	0 26	...	Palota	3 36	...	5 25	...	...
$20\frac{3}{4}$	0 54	0 45	0 30	...	**Pesth** ....arrival	3 47	...	5 39	...	...
	From Pesth.				,, ... departure	4 37	...	6 40	...	...
$5\frac{1}{2}$	0 15	0 13	0 10	...	Steinbruch	4 59	...	6 56	...	...
$13\frac{1}{2}$	0 36	0 30	0 24	...	Vecsés	5 35	...	7 27	...	...
$19\frac{1}{2}$	0 51	0 43	0 34	...	Ullö	5 55	...	7 49	...	...
$24\frac{1}{4}$	1 3	0 53	0 42	...	Monor	6 21	...	8 6	...	...
$31\frac{1}{4}$	1 21	1 8	0 54	...	Pilis	6 46	...	8 25	...	...
$35\frac{3}{4}$	1 33	1 18	1 2	...	Alberti Irsa	7 6	...	8 41	...	...
$47\frac{1}{4}$	2 3	1 43	1 22	...	Czegléd	7 45	...	9 12	...	...
$57\frac{1}{4}$	2 30	2 5	1 40	...	Abony	8 19	...	9 42	...	...
65	2 48	2 20	1 54	...	**Szolnok** ....arrival	8 38	...	10 0	...	...

Remarks.—Luggage: 50 lbs. of Luggage allowed free of charge.

Pesth to Waitzen and Waitzen to Pesth twice each day.

NEISSE TO BRIEG—30 English miles.

Eng. Miles.	Fares.			STATIONS.	Trains.				
	1 Cls.	2 Cls.	3 Cls.		1	2	3	4	5
	s.gr.	s.gr.	s.gr.		a.m.	p.m.			
—	—	—	—	**Neisse** ....dep.	6 40	5 15	..	..	..
5	10	7	4	Bösdorf	7 0	5 34	..	..	..
$15\frac{1}{2}$	20	15	10	Grottkau	7 34	6 9	..	..	..
30	40	30	20	**Brieg** ....arr.	8 10	6 45	..	..	..

SZOLNOK TO PESTH, PRESSBURG, AND VIENNA.

English Miles.	Fares.				STATIONS.	Trains.				
	1st Class	2nd Class	3rd Class	4th Class.		1	2	3	4	5
Dis.	fl. kr.	fl. kr.	fl. kr.	fl. kr.		a.m.	a.m.	p.m.		
—	—	—	—	—	**Szolnok** .... departure	5 30	...	12 30	...	...
$6\frac{3}{4}$	0 18	0 15	0 12	...	Abony	5 54	...	1 4	...	...
17	0 45	0 38	0 30	...	Czegléd	6 27	...	1 52	...	...
$28\frac{3}{4}$	1 15	1 3	0 50	...	Alberti Irsa	7 3	...	2 43	...	...
$33\frac{1}{3}$	1 27	1 13	0 58	...	Pilis	7 15	...	3 5	...	...
$40\frac{1}{4}$	1 45	1 28	1 10	...	Monor	7 36	...	3 34	...	...
$44\frac{3}{4}$	1 57	1 38	1 18	...	Üllö	7 49	...	3 53	...	..
51	2 12	1 50	1 28	...	Vecsés	8 6	...	4 19	...	...
$58\frac{3}{4}$	2 33	2 8	1 42	...	Steinbruch	8 28	...	4 56	...	...
65	2 48	2 20	1 52	...	**Pesth** .... arrival	8 40	...	5 11	...	...
	From Pesth.				" .... departure	9 30	...	6 15	...	...
$5\frac{1}{3}$	0 15	0 12	0 10	...	Palota	9 42	...	6 33	...	...
$10\frac{1}{4}$	0 27	0 23	0 18	...	Dunakesz	9 52	...	6 51	...	...
$20\frac{3}{4}$	0 54	0 45	0 30	...	**Waitzen**	10 22	...	7 28	...	...
..	...	...	...	...	Veröcze	10 34	...	7 47	...	...
..	...	...	..	...	Gross Maros	10 51	...	8 8	...	...
..	...	...	...	...	Szobb	11 8	...	8 34	...	...
..	...	...	...	...	**Gran Nana**	11 35	...	9 8	...	...
..	...	...	...	...	Köbölkut	11 54	...	9 35	...	...
..	...	...	...	...	Sz. Milkós	12 20	...	10 13	...	...
..	...	...	...	...	**Neuhausel**	1 2	...	10 48	...	...
..	...	...	..	...	Tot-Megyer	1 14	...	11 4	...	...
..	...	...	...	...	Tardesked	1 20	..	11 18	...	...
..	...	...	...	...	Tornócz	1 35	...	11 44	...	...
..	...	...	..	...	Sellye	1 50	...	11 59	...	...
..	...	...	...	...	Galantha	2 6	...	12 25	...	...
..	...	...	...	...	Diószeg	2 16	...	12 43	...	...
.	...	...	...	...	Wartberg	2 44	...	1 17	...	...
..	...	...	...	...	Lanschutz	2 55	...	1 32	...	...
..	...	...	...	...	Weinern	3 9	a.m.	1 49	...	...
	From Pressburg.				**Pressburg**	4 0	10 0	2 44	...	...
$9\frac{1}{4}$	0 24	0 20	0 10	...	Neudorf	4 31	10 40	3 20	...	...
$11\frac{1}{4}$	0 40	0 33	0 25	...	Marchegg	4 42	10 55	3 34	...	...
$18\frac{1}{2}$	...	0 48	0 35	...	Ob. Waiden	...	...	...	...	...
23	1 20	1 3	0 45	...	**Ganserndorf** .... arrival	5 15	11 32	4 10	...	...
			...		" .... departure	5 22	11 47	4 30	...	...
30	1 50	1 25	1 0	...	Wagram	5 45	12 20	4 58	...	...
$32\frac{1}{2}$	2 0	1 33	1 5	...	Sussenbrunn	...	..	...	...	...
37	2 20	1 48	1 15	...	Floridsdorf	6 10	12 56	5 28	...	...
$41\frac{1}{2}$	2 40	2 3	1 25	...	**Vienna** .... arrival	6 19	1 6	5 38	...	...

Remarks.—LUGGAGE: 50 lbs. of Luggage are allowed free of charge.

PESTH to WAITZEN and WAITZEN to PESTH twice each day

BRIEG TO NEISSE.

Eng. Miles.	Fares.			Stations.	Trains.				
	1 Cls.	2 Cls.	3 Cls.		1	2	3	4	5
	s.gr.	s.gr.	s.gr.		a.m.	p.m.			
—	—	—	—	**Brieg** .... dep.	8 40	7 15	..	..	..
$14\frac{1}{2}$	20	15	10	Grottkau	9 21	7 56	..	..	..
24	30	23	16	Bösdorf	9 56	8 30	..	..	..
30	40	30	20	**Neisse** .... arr.	10 10	8 45	..	..	..

PRERAU TO ODERBERG.

Eng. Miles.	Fares. 1st Class	2nd Class	3rd Class	4th Class	STATIONS.	Trains. 1	2	3	4	5
Dis.	fl.kr.	fl.kr.	fl.kr.	fl.kr.		a.m.	p.m.			
...	...	...	...	...	VIENNA ....dep.	6 30	7 0	...	...	...
							a.m.			
—	—	—	—	—	**Prerau** ....dep.	12 27	3 0	...	...	...
9¼	0 40	0 30	0 20	...	Leipnik	...	3 38	...	...	...
15¾	1 10	0 53	0 35	...	Weisskirchen..........	...	4 16	...	...	...
23	1 40	1 15	0 50	...	Pohl..........	..	4 43	...	...	...
30	2 10	1 38	1 5	...	Zanchtl	...	5 7	...	...	...
37	2 40	2 0	1 20	...	Stauding	...	5 33	...	...	...
48½	3 30	2 38	1 45	...	Schönbrunn	...	6 7	...	...	...
51	3 40	2 45	1 50	...	Mahr. Ostrau..........	...	6 25	...	...	...
57¾	4 10	3 8	2 5	...	**Oderberg** ....arr.	...	6 41	...	...	...
						p.m.	p.m.			
—	—	—	—	—	**Oderberg** ....dep.	...	7 45	...	...	...
6¾	0 30	0 23	0 15	...	Mahr. Ostrau	...	8 8	...	...	...
9¼	0 40	0 30	0 20	...	Schönbrunn	...	8 22	...	...	...
20¾	1 30	1 8	0 45	...	Stauding..........	...	8 59	...	...	...
27¾	2 0	1 30	1 0	...	Zanchtl	...	9 24	...	...	...
34¾	2 30	1 53	1 15	...	Pohl..........	...	9 51	...	..	...
41½	3 0	2 15	1 30	...	Weisskirchen..........	...	10 21	...	...	...
48½	3 30	2 38	1 45	...	Leipnik	...	10 53	...	...	...
57¾	4 10	3 8	2 5	..	**Prerau** ....arrival	1 27	11 19	...	...	...
							a.m.			
173½	12 30	9 23	6 15	...	VIENNA..........arr.	7 35	5 55	...	...	...

Remarks.—Passengers from ODERBERG for VIENNA change carriages at Lundenberg, and also wait for the Mail train up the other line.

Luggage.—40 lbs. of Luggage are allowed free of charge.

LUNDENBURG TO PRERAU AND OLLMUTZ.

Eng. Miles.	Fares. 1st Class	2nd Class	3rd Class	4th Class	STATIONS.	Trains. 1	2	3	4	5
Dis	fl.kr	fl.kr.	fl.kr.	fl.kr.		a.m.	p.m.	p.m.		
—	—	—	—	—	VIENNA ....departure	6 30	7 0	...	...	...
51	3 40	2 45	1 50	...	**Lundenburg** ....departure	9 22	10 32	...	...	...
57¾	4 10	3 8	2 5	...	Mahr Neudorf	9 45	11 5	...	...	...
65	4 40	3 30	2 20	...	Göding	10 4	11 29	...	...	...
78½	5 40	4 15	2 50	...	Bisenz..........	10 41	12 16	...	...	...
87¾	6 20	4 45	3 10	...	Hradisch	11 7	1 1	...	...	...
97	7 0	5 15	3 30	...	Napajedl..........	11 30	1 29	...	...	...
106½	7 40	5 45	3 50	...	Hullein..........	12 3	2 10	...	...	...
115½	8 20	6 15	4 10	...	**Prerau**	1 12	3 1	11 40	...	...
122¼	8 50	6 38	4 25	...	Brodek	1 32	3 22	11 59	...	...
129½	9 20	7 0	4 40	...	**Ollmutz**.......... arrival	1 59	3 49	12 25	...	...
						a.m.	noon	p.m.		
—	—	—	—	—	**Ollmutz** ....departue	12 25	12 0	10 15	...	...
6¾	0 30	0 23	0 15	...	Brodek	12 52	12 28	10 44	...	...
13½	1 0	0 45	0 30	...	**Prerau**	1 10	1 27	11 37	...	...
23	1 40	1 15	0 45	...	Hullein	...	1 55	12 6	...	...
32½	2 20	1 45	1 10	...	Napajedl	...	2 28	12 41	...	...
41½	3 0	2 15	1 30	...	Hradisch	...	2 51	1 5	...	...
51	3 40	2 45	1 50	...	Bisenz..........	...	3 17	1 32	...	...
65	4 40	3 30	2 20	...	Göding	..	3 54	2 14	...	...
71¾	5 10	3 53	2 35	...	Mahr Neudorf	...	4 10	2 34	...	...
78½	5 40	4 15	2 50	...	**Lundenburg**	...	4 30	2 54	...	...
129½	9 20	7 0	4 40	...	VIENNA ....arrival	...	7 35	5 55	...	...

Remarks.—LUGGAGE: 40 lbs. of Luggage are allowed free of charge.

BUDWEIS TO GMUNDEN (Horse Railway.)

English Miles.	Fares. 1 Cl.	Fares. 2 Cl.	STATIONS.	Trains. 1	2	3	4	5	6	7
Dis.	fl kr.	fl.kr.		a.m.	a.m.	p.m.	p.m.			
—	—	—	**Budweis** ....departure	5 0	...	...	...	...	...	...
..	0 30	0 20	Holkau	...	...	...	...	...	...	...
..	1 0	0 40	Angern	...	...	..	...	...	...	...
..	1 30	1 0	Kerschbaum	...	...	...	...	...	...	...
..	2 0	1 20	Lest	..	...	...	...	...	...	...
..	2 30	1 40	Oberndorf	p.m.	...	...	...	...	...	...
..	3 0	2 0	**Linz** ....arrival	6 45	...	...	...	...	...	...
				a.m.						
	Frm.	Linz	Do. ....departure	5 0	6 0	2 0	5 0	...	...	...
..	0 15	0 10	Neubau	...	...	...	...	...	...	...
..	0 30	0 20	Wels	a.m.	a.m.	...	...	...	...	...
..	0 45	0 30	Lambach	10 0	11 0	7 0	10 0	...	...	...
41½	1 20	0 50	**Gmunden**........................arrival	...	1 45	...	...	...	...	...

GMUNDEN TO BUDWEIS (Horse Railway.)

English Miles.	Fares. 1Cl.	Fares. 2 Cl.	STATIONS.	Trains. 1	2	3	4	5	6	7
fl.kr	fl.kr.	fl.kr.		a.m.	a.m.	p.m.	p.m.			
—	—	—	**Gmunden** ....departure	..	6 0		...	...	...	...
..	0 35	0 20	Lambach	4 30	8 30	12 45	5 0	...	...	...
..	0 50	0 30	Wels	...	...	...	...	...	...	...
..	1 5	0 40	Neubau	...	...	...	...	...	...	...
41½	1 20	0 50	**Linz** ....arrival	8 15	12 15	4 30	8 30	...	...	...
							a.m.			
..	Frm.	Linz	Do. ....departure	...	...	...	5 0	...	...	...
..	0 30	0 20	Oberndorf	...	...	...	...	...	...	...
..	1 0	0 40	Lest	...	...	...	...	...	...	...
..	1 30	1 0	Kerschbaum	...	. .	...	...	...	...	...
..	2 0	1 20	Angern	...	...	...	...	...	...	...
..	2 30	1 40	Holkau	...	...	...	p.m.	. .	...	...
..	3 0	2 0	**Budweis** ....arrival	...	...	...	6 45	...	...	...

Remarks.—TRAVELLING CARRIAGES.—From Budweis to Linz, 2-Horse 17, 3-Horse 21, 4-Horse 25, florins, From Linz to Budweis, 2-Horse 17, 3-Horse 21, 4-Horse 25, florins. From Linz to Gmunden, 2-Horse 9, 3-Horse 12, 4 Horse 15, florins. From Gmunden to Linz, 2-Horse 9, 3-Horse 12, 4-Horse 15, florins. The conveyance of Passengers by means of the Travelling Carriages is not allowed on the line from Linz to Budweis. On the railway from Linz to Gmunden, every person making use of the above conveyance pays the 1st class fare charged in the open carriages. SEPARATE CARRIAGES are only to be had on the line to Gmunden, and then only as they become disengaged. CHARGE FOR A SEPARATE CARRIAGE:—From Linz to Neubau and back, 1fl. 45kr.; to Wells, 3fl. 30kr.; to Lambach, 5fl. 15kr.; and to Gmunden, 7fl. From Wells to Neubau, 1fl. 45kr.; to Lambach, 1fl. 45kr.; to Gmunden, 4fl. 20kr.; and from Lambach to Gmunden, 2fl. 35kr.; and to pay likewise the first class fare charged in the open carriage. Travellers who make use of the separate carriages, are bound to the hours prescribed for the departure of the open carriage trains, for, on account of the necessary and unavoidable delays of these and the goods trains, it would not be allowed to run the separate carriages at any other times.

Luggage.—20 lbs. are allowed free of charge.

VIENNA TO MODLING, LAXENBURG, NEUSTADT, OEDENBURG, GLOGGNITZ, GRATZ, CILLY, AND LAIBACH.—(264 English Miles.) [5-53.

Eng. Miles.	Fares. 1st Class	2nd Class	3rd Class	4th Class	STATIONS.	Trains. 1	2	3	4	5	6	7	8	9	10	11	12
Dis.	fl. kr.	fl. kr.	fl. kr.	fl. kr.	DOWN TRAINS.	a.m.	a.m.	a.m.	a.m.	p.m.	p.m.	p.m.	p.m.	p.m.	a.m.		
—	—	—	—	—	**Vienna** ....departure	7 15	8 30	10 0	11 30	2 0	3 0	4 0	5 30	9 0	...	...	...
..	...	...	..	...	Matzleinsdorf	...	...	...	11 35	...	...	4 5	...	...	...	...	...
..	0 20	0 15	0 10	...	Meidling	7 25	8 40	10 10	11 41	2 10	3 10	4 10	5 40	9 10	...	...	...
..	0 20	0 15	0 10	...	Hetzendorf	7 30	8 45	10 15	11 46	2 15	3 15	4 15	5 45	...	...	...	...
..	0 20	0 15	0 10	...	Atzgersdorf	7 36	8 51	10 21	11 52	2 21	3 21	4 21	5 51	9 20	...	...	...
..	0 30	0 23	0 15	...	Liesing	7 40	8 55	10 25	11 56	2 25	3 26	4 25	5 55	9 25	...	...	...
..	0 30	0 23	0 15	...	Perchtoldsdorf	...	8 59	...	12 0	...	3 30	4 29	...	...	...	...	...
..	0 40	0 30	0 20	...	Brunn	7 47	9 4	10 32	12 5	2 32	3 35	4 34	6 2	9 32	...	...	...
..	0 40	0 30	0 20	...	**Modling**	7 53	9 10	10 38	12 11	2 38	3 43	4 40	6 8	9 38	...	...	...
..	0 50	0 38	0 25	...	**Laxenburg** ....arrival	8 2	...	10 47	...	2 47	...	4 49	...	...	...	...	...
..	0 50	0 38	0 25	...	Guntramsdorf	...	...	...	12 18	...	...	4 47	...	...	...	...	...
..	1 0	0 45	0 30	...	Gumpoldskirchen	8 4	9 21	10 49	12 23	2 49	3 54	4 52	6 19	9 49	...	...	...
..	1 0	0 45	0 30	...	Pfaffstätten	...	...	...	12 29	...	...	4 58	...	...	...	...	...
14½	1 10	0 53	0 35	...	Baden	8 18	9 30	11 3	12 33	3 3	4 3	5 7	6 33	10 4	...	...	...
..	1 20	1 0	0 40	...	Böslau	8 27	...	11 12		3 12	..	5 15	6 42	10 13	...	...	...
..	1 30	1 8	0 45	...	Kottingbrunn	...	Sundays and Festivals only.	11 17	...	3 17	...		...	...	...	...	...
..	1 30	1 8	0 45	...	Leobersdorf	8 36		11 21	...	3 21	...	...	6 50	10 22	...	...	...
..	1 40	1 15	0 50	...	Solenau	...		11 28	...	3 28	Sundays and Festivals only.	...	...	...	...	...	...
..	1 50	1 23	0 55	...	Felixdorf	8 46		11 32	...	3 32		...	7 0	10 33	...	...	...
..	1 50	1 23	0 55	...	Therestenfeld	8 52		11 38	...	3 38		...	7 6	...	...	...	...
30	2 10	1 38	1 5	...	**Wiener Neustadt**....arr.	9 9		11 47	...	4 0		...	7 15	10 57	...	...	...
..	2 10	1 38	1 5	...	**Wiener Neustadt**....dep.	9 20		...	...	...		...	7 30	...	...	...	...
..	2 20	1 45	1 10	...	Katzelsdorf	9 30		...	...	...		...	7 40	...	...	...	...
..	2 34	1 56	1 17	...	Neudorfl	9 35		...	..	...		...	7 45	...	...	...	...
..	2 40	2 1	1 20	...	Sauerbrunnen	9 43		...	...	...		...	7 53	...	...	...	...
..	2 50	2 8	1 25	...	Wiesen-Sigletz	9 53		...	...	...		...	8 3	...	...	...	...
..	3 2	2 17	1 31	...	Mattersdorf	10 6		...	...	...		...	8 16	...	...	...	...
..	3 11	2 23	1 36	...	Marz-Rohrbach	10 14		...	...	...		...	8 24	...	...	...	...
..	3 29	2 37	1 45	...	Schadendorf	10 32		...	...	...		...	8 42	...	...	...	...
..	3 38	2 44	1 49	...	Agendorf	10 38	...	...	...	...		...	8 48	...	...	...	...
..	3 50	2 53	1 55	...	**Oedenburg** ....arrival	10 45	...	...	...	...	...	...	8 55	...	...	...	...
..	2 30	1 53	1 15	...	St. Egiden	9 30	...	...	...	4 21	...	...	...	...	...	...	...
..	2 50	2 8	1 25	...	Neunkirchen	9 45	...	...	...	4 36	...	...	...	11 32	...	...	...
..	3 0	2 15	1 30	...	Ternitz	9 55	...	...	...	4 46	...	...	...	...	...	...	...
..	3 10	2 23	1 35	..	Pottschach	10 2	...	...	...	4 53	...	...	...	...	...	...	...
..	3 20	2 30	1 40	...	**Gloggnitz** ....arrival	10 12	...	...	...	5 3	...	...	...	11 57	...	...	...
					" ....departure	11 0	...	...	...	...	...	...	...	12 0	...	...	...
A	B	C	D	E		F	G	H	I	J	K	L	M	N	O	P	Q

Remarks.—The distance between GLOGGNITZ and MURZZUSCHLAG is performed by Omnibus at a charge of 1 fl. 20 kr., and 1 fl.

LUGGAGE: 40 lbs. of Luggage are allowed free of charge.

Fares.—MURZZUSCHLAG to LAIBACH—1st class, 12fl. 54kr.; 2nd class, 7fl. 53kr.; 3rd class, 5fl. 44kr.

[1] Marburg to Warasdin by Postzig in 8 hours; to Klagenfurt in 16 hours.

[15-5-51.

Remarks.—The distance between Gloggnitz and Murzzuschlag is performed by Omnibus at a charge of 1 fl. 20 kr., and 1 fl.—Luggage: 40 lbs. of Luggage are allowed free of charge.

Fares.—Murzzuschlag to Laibach—1st class, 12 fl. 54 kr.; 2nd class, 7 fl. 53 kr; 3rd class, 5 fl. 44 kr.

[1] Marburg to Warasdin by Postzig in 8 hours; to Klagenfurt in 16 hours.

A	B	C	D	E		F	G	H	I	J	K	L	M	N	O	P	Q
	From Murzzuschlag.					p.m.			p.m.					a.m.	a.m.		
—	—	—	—	—	**Murzzuschlag** ..departure	3 0	...	...	3 30	...	...	...	...	4 45	5 15	...	...
4½	0 18	0 11	0 8	...	Langenwang	3 13	...	...	3 48	...	...	...	...	4 58	5 36	...	...
7	0 29	0 18	0 13	...	Krieglach	3 24	...	...	4 1	...	...	...	...	5 9	5 57	...	...
14¼	0 56	0 34	0 25	...	Kindberg	3 48	...	...	4 35	...	...	...	...	5 31	6 34	...	...
18½	1 12	0 44	0 32	...	Marein	4 5	...	...	4 56	...	...	...	...	5 47	7 0	...	...
22½	1 28	0 54	0 39	...	Kapfenberg	4 22	...	...	5 18	...	...	...	...	6 4	7 27	...	...
25	1 37	0 59	0 43	...	**Bruck**	4 40	...	...	5 40	...	...	...	...	6 20	8 16	...	...
30½	1 59	1 13	0 53	...	Pernegg	4 59	...	...	6 0	...	...	...	...	6 39	8 40	...	...
33	2 8	1 18	0 57	...	Mirnitz	5 11	...	...	6 13	...	...	...	...	6 50	8 57	...	...
40	2 38	1 36	1 10	...	Frohnleiten	5 34	...	...	6 46	...	...	...	...	7 18	9 30	...	...
44	2 56	1 47	1 18	...	Peggau	5 52	...	...	7 10	...	...	...	...	7 35	9 56	...	...
47¼	3 5	1 53	1 22	...	Stübing	6 8	...	...	7 19	...	...	...	...	7 43	10 10	...	...
49	3 14	1 58	1 26	...	Gradwein	6 20	...	...	7 32	...	...	...	...	7 55	10 26	...	...
53	3 25	2 5	1 31	...	Judendorf	6 26	...	...	7 38	...	...	...	...	8 1	10 37	...	...
58	3 45	2 18	1 40	...	**Gratz** ....arrival	p.m.	...	...	p.m.	...	...	...	...	a.m.	a.m.	...	...
	From Gratz.				" ....departure	6 55	...	...	8 30	...	...	...	...	8 35	11 40	...	...
7	0 29	0 18	0 13	...	Kalsdorf	7 18	...	...	8 56	...	...	...	...	8 56	12 10	...	...
14½	0 59	0 36	0 26	...	**Wildon**	7 41	...	...	9 22	...	...	...	...	9 16	12 40	...	...
16	1 8	0 41	0 30	...	Lebring	7 49	...	...	9 31	...	...	...	...	9 23	12 52	...	...
24	1 32	0 56	0 41	...	**Leibnitz**	8 6	...	...	9 49	...	...	...	...	9 38	1 20	...	...
28¾	1 53	1 9	0 50	...	Ehrenhausen	8 21	...	...	10 5	...	...	...	...	9 51	1 41	...	...
32	2 4	1 16	0 55	...	Spielfeld	8 35	...	...	10 25	...	...	...	...	10 5	2 15	...	...
41	2 40	1 38	1 11	...	Pessnitzhofen	9 2	...	...	10 58	...	...	...	...	10 31	3 0	...	...
45	2 56	1 47	1 18	...	**Marburg** ...[1]	9 27	...	...	11 30	...	...	...	...	10 55	3 50	...	...
53	3 25	2 5	1 31	...	Kranichsfeld	9 53	...	...	12 1	...	...	...	...	11 17	4 30	...	...
56½	3 41	2 15	1 38	...	Pragerhof	10 12	...	...	12 22	...	...	...	...	11 30	4 56	...	...
65	4 14	2 35	1 53	...	Pöltschach	10 53	...	...	1 30	...	...	...	...	12 3	5 55	...	...
75	4 53	2 59	2 10	...	Ponigl	11 36	...	...	2 25	...	...	...	...	12 42	6 55	...	...
80¾	5 15	3 13	2 20	...	St. Georgen	12 5	...	...	2 42	...	...	...	...	12 57	7 18	...	...
86	5 38	3 26	2 30	...	**Cilly** ....arrival	p.m.	...	...	a.m.	...	...	...	...	p.m.	p.m	...	...
	From Cilly.				" ....departure	12 50	...	...	3 20	...	...	...	...	1 45	8 10	...	...
6½	0 25	0 15	0 11	...	Markt-Tüffer	1 18	...	...	3 45	...	...	...	...	2 7	8 43	...	...
10¼	0 41	0 25	0 18	...	Römerbad	1 35	...	...	4 2	...	...	...	...	2 23	9 5	...	...
15¾	0 59	0 36	0 26	...	Steinbruck	2 0	...	...	4 30	...	...	...	...	2 44	10 0	...	...
19½	1 17	0 47	0 34	...	Hrastnigg	2 18	...	...	4 54	...	...	...	...	3 0	10 40	...	...
23	1 30	0 55	0 40	...	Triffail	2 30	...	...	5 10	...	...	...	...	3 10	11 4	...	...
25½	1 41	1 2	0 45	...	Sagor	2 45	...	...	5 29	...	...	...	...	3 22	11 30	...	...
30½	2 2	1 14	0 54	...	Sava	3 5	...	...	5 56	...	...	...	...	3 39	12 2	...	...
35	2 17	1 24	1 1	...	Littai	3 25	...	...	6 22	...	...	...	...	3 55	12 40	...	...
39¼	2 33	1 34	1 8	...	Kressnitz	3 42	...	...	6 46	...	...	...	...	4 9	1 10	...	...
44¼	2 56	1 47	1 18	...	Laase	4 7	...	...	7 21	...	...	...	...	4 30	1 50	...	...
49	3 11	1 57	1 25	...	Salloch	4 23	...	...	7 43	...	...	...	...	4 44	2 20	...	...
54	3 32	2 9	1 34	...	**Laibach** ....arrival	4 41	...	...	8 14	...	...	...	...	5 0	2 51	...	...
						p.m.								a.m.			
..	...	...	...	...	**Trieste** (by Post)....arrival	7 0	...	...	...	...	...	...	...	4 0	...	...	...

LAIBACH, CILLY, GRATZ, GLOGGNITZ, OEDENBURG, NEUSTADT, LAXENBURG, AND MODLING TO VIENNA.—(264 English Miles.) [15-5-51

English Miles.	Fares.				STATIONS.	TRAINS.												
	1st Class	2nd Class	3rd Class	4th Clas		1	2	3	4	5	6	7	8	9	10	11	12	13
Dis.	fl. kr.	fl. kr.	fl. kr.	fl. kr.	**Up Trains.**	p.m.		p.m.	a.m.		a.m.		p.m.	p.m.				
..	...	...	...	...	**Trieste** (by Post)..departure	8 0	...	...	...	...	3 0	...	...	...	...	..	...	..
						a.m.		p.m.	a.m.		p.m.		p.m.	p.m.				
—	—	—	—	—	**Laibach** .... departure	8 15	...	3 45	...	...	7 30	...	7 45	...	...	...	...	..
10¼	0 20	0 12	0 9	...	Salloch	8 31	...	4 2	...	...	7 47	...	8 5	...	...	...	...	..
13½	0 36	0 22	0 16	...	Laase	8 47	...	4 30	...	...	8 5	...	8 25	...	...	...	...	..
14½	0 59	0 36	0 26	...	Kressnitz	9 5	...	4 49	..	...	8 23	...	8 47	...	...	...	...	..
19	1 14	0 45	0 33	...	Littai........................	9 23	...	5 10	...	...	8 43	...	9 11	...	...	...	...	..
23	1 30	0 55	0 40	...	Sava	9 37	...	5 25	...	...	8 58	...	9 29	...	...	...	...	..
28¼	1 50	1 7	0 49	...	Sagor.........................	9 59	...	5 50	...	...	9 20	...	9 57	...	...	...	...	..
30½	2 2	1 14	0 54	...	Triffail	10 9	...	6 0	...	...	9 30	...	10 12	...	...	...	...	..
34½	2 15	1 23	1 0	...	Hrastnigg	10 20	...	6 11	...	...	9 41	...	10 30	...	...	...	...	..
39¼	2 33	1 34	1 8	...	Steinbruck	10 40	...	6 40	...	...	10 4	...	11 10	...	.	...	...	..
43¾	2 51	1 45	1 16	...	Bad Tuffer	10 56	...	7 4	..	...	10 22	...	11 39	...	...	...	...	..
48	3 7	1 54	1 23	...	Markt-Tuffer	11 14	...	7 32	...	...	10 43	...	12 10	...	...	...	...	..
53½	3 32	2 9	1 34	...	**Cilly** ....arrival	p.m.	...	p.m.	...	...	p.m.	...	a.m.	...	...	...	...	..
	From Cilly.				,, ... departure	12 5	...	8 45	...	...	11 40	...	1 15	...	...	...	...	..
5½	0 23	0 14	0 10	...	St. Georgen	12 26	...	9 17	...	...	12 6	...	1 52	...	...	...	...	..
11¼	0 45	0 28	0 20	...	Ponigl	12 45	...	9 59	...	...	12 28	...	2 30	...	...	...	...	..
21	1 23	0 51	0 37	...	Poitschach	1 22	...	10 48	...	...	1 18	...	3 35	...	...	...	...	..
30	1 57	1 12	0 52	...	Pragerhof.....................	1 55	..	11 37	...	...	2 0	...	4 29	...	...	...	...	..
34½	2 13	1 21	0 59	...	Kranichsfeld	2 11	...	12 5	...	...	2 19	...	4 59	...	...	...	...	..
41½	2 42	1 39	1 12	...	**Marburg**...................	2 40	...	1 0	...	...	2 57	...	6 0	...	...	..	...	..
45	2 58	1 49	1 19	...	Pössnitz	2 59	...	1 20	...	...	3 15	...	6 25	...	...	...	...	..
55	3 34	2 11	1 35	...	Spielfeld	3 30	...	2 8	...	...	3 55	...	7 20	...	...	...	...	..
57¾	3 45	2 18	1 40	...	Ehrenhausen	3 39	...	2 19	...	...	4 5	...	7 36	...	...	...	...	..
62½	4 5	2 30	1 49	...	**Liebnitz**	3 56	...	2 48	...	...	4 24	...	8 10	...	...	...	...	..
69½	4 30	2 45	2 0	...	Lebring	4 14	...	3 15	...	...	4 45	...	8 42	...	...	...	...	..
71¾	4 39	2 51	2 4	...	**Wildon**	4 25	...	3 30	...	...	4 58	...	9 15	...	...	...	..	..
79¼	5 8	3 8	2 17	...	Kabsdorf	4 47	...	4 11	...	...	5 24	...	9 58	...	...	...	...	..
87	5 38	3 26	2 30	...	**Gratz** ....arrival	5 23	...	a.m.	...	...	6 0	...	a.m.	...	...	...	...	..
	From Gratz.				,, ... departure	5 30	...	5 20	...	...	6 15	...	11 10	...	...	...	...	..
5¼	0 20	0 12	0 9	...	Judendorf	5 48	...	5 48	...	...	6 31	...	11 41		...	...	...	..
6¼	0 32	0 19	0 14	...	Gratwein	5 54	...	5 56	..	...	6 37	...	11 53	Sundays and	...	...	...	..
10¼	0 41	0 25	0 18	...	Stubing.......................	6 10	...	6 16	...	...	6 50	...	12 18		...	...	...	..
12½	0 50	0 30	0 22	...	Peggau	6 27	...	6 33	...	...	7 1	...	12 40		...	...	..	..
17½	1 8	0 41	0 30	...	Frohnleiten	6 45	...	7 32	...	...	7 17	...	1 15		...	...	...	..
25	1 37	0 59	0 43	...	Mirnitz	7 12	...	8 10	...	...	7 43	...	1 55		...	...	...	..
26¾	1 46	1 5	0 47	...	Pernegg	7 22	..	8 40	...	...	7 53	...	2 11		...	...	..	..
A	B	C	D	E		F	G	H	I	J	K	L	M	N	O	P	Q	R

Remarks.—The distance between MURZZUSCHLAG and GLOGGNITZ is performed by Omnibus, at a charge of 1 fl. 20 kr. and 1 fl.

LUGGAGE: 40 lbs. of Luggage are allowed free of charge.

[5-53

Fares.—From Laibach to Murzzuschlag: 1st class, 12 fl. 54 kr.; 2nd class, 7 fl. 53 kr.; 3rd class, 5 fl. 44 kr.

[1] Vienna to Oderberg, Prague, Ollmutz, Bruck, Pressburg, and Stockerau, see pages 112, 106, 108, and 109.

A	B	C	D	E		F	G	H	I	J	K	L	M	N	O	P	Q	R
33	2 8	1 18	0 57	...	**Bruck**	7 50	...	9 30	...	...	8 20	...	3 10	Festivals only.	...	...	...	..
35	2 17	1 24	1 1	...	Kapfenberg	8 1	...	9 44	...	...	8 31	...	3 30		...	...	...	..
39¼	2 33	1 34	1 8	...	Marein	8 20	...	10 8	...	...	8 50	...	4 7		...	...	...	..
43½	2 49	1 43	1 15	...	Kindberg	8 40	...	10 40	...	...	9 10	...	4 50		...	...	...	..
49	3 16	2 0	1 27	...	Krieglach	9 7	...	11 30	...	...	9 34	...	5 45		...	...	...	..
53¼	3 27	2 7	1 32	...	Langenwang	9 19	...	11 50	...	...	9 46	...	6 15		...	...	...	..
57¾	3 45	2 18	1 40	...	**Murzzuschlag** ....arrival	9 36	...	12 18	..	...	10 2	...	6 48		...	...	...	..
..	...	...	...	...	" ..departure	10 0	...	...	...	...	10 5	...		...	...	...		..
	From Gloggnitz.							a.m.						p.m.				
—	—	—	—	—	**Gloggnitz** ....arrival	2 0	...	...	...	...	2 15	...	...	...	...	...	...	..
..	...	...	...	...	" .... departure	2 15	...	6 10	Sundays and Festivals only.	...	2 30	...	...	6 30	...	...	...	..
..	0 20	0 15	0 10	...	Pottschach	...	...	6 24		...	2 41	...	...	6 41	...	...	...	..
..	0 20	0 15	0 10	...	Ternitz	...	...	6 34		...	2 48	...	...	6 48	...	...	...	..
..	0 30	0 23	0 15	...	Neunkirchen	2 42	...	6 50		...	2 59	...	...	6 59	...	...	...	..
..	0 50	0 38	0 25	...	St. Egiden	...	...	7 9		...	3 11	...	...	7 11	...	..	...	..
	From Oedenburg.																	
—	—	—	—	—	**Oedenburg** ......departure	...	...	5 45		...	1 45	...	...	...	...	...	...	..
..	0 20	0 15	0 10	...	Agendorf	...	...	5 59		...	1 59	...	...	...	...	...	...	..
..	0 20	0 15	0 10	...	Schadendorf	...	...	6 9		...	2 9	...	...	...	...	...	...	..
..	0 39	0 29	0 20	...	Marz-Rohrbach	...	...	6 22		...	2 22	...	...	...	...	...	...	..
..	0 48	0 36	0 24	...	Mattersdorf	...	...	6 32		...	2 32	...	...	...	...	...	...	..
..	1 0	0 45	0 30	...	Wiesen-Sigletz	...	...	6 45		...	2 45	...	...	...	...	...	...	..
..	1 12	0 54	0 36	...	Sanerbrunnen	...	...	6 55		...	2 58	...	...	...	...	...	...	..
..	1 21	1 0	0 40	...	Neudorfl	...	...	7 5		...	3 5	...	...	...	...	...	...	..
..	1 30	1 8	0 45	...	Katzelsdorf	...	...	7 10		...	3 10	...	...	...	...	...	...	..
..	1 42	1 17	0 51	...	**Wiener Neustadt** .. arr.	...	...	7 18	...	...	3 18	...	...	...	...	...	...	..
..	1 42	1 17	0 51	...	**Wiener Neustadt** .. dep.	3 24	5 45	7 40	...	1 30	3 36	...	...	7 36	...	...	...	..
..	2 0	1 31	1 0	...	Therestenfeld	...	5 56	7 51	...	1 41	3 47	...	...	7 47	...	...	...	..
..	2 0	1 31	1 0	...	Felixdorf	3 43	6 2	7 57	...	1 47	3 53	...	...	7 53	...	...	...	..
..	2 10	1 38	1 5	...	Solenau	...	6 6	...	...	1 51	...	..	...	7 57	...	...	...	..
..	2 20	1 46	1 10	...	Leobersdorf	3 54	6 14	8 8	...	1 59	4 3	...	...	8 5	...	...	...	..
..	2 20	1 46	1 10	...	Kottingbrunn	...	6 18	...	...	2 3	...	...	p.m.	8 9	...	...	...	..
..	2 30	1 53	1 15	...	Böslau	...	6 22	8 15	a.m.	2 7	4 10	...	7 18	8 13	...	...	...	..
..	2 40	2 1	1 20	...	Baden	4 15	6 34	8 30	11 0	2 19	4 22	6 30	7 30	8 30	...	...	...	..
..	2 40	2 1	1 20	...	Pfaffstätten	...	6 38	...	14 4	2 23	...	6 34	...	...	...	...	...	..
..	2 50	2 8	1 25	...	Gumpoldskirchen	4 24	6 43	8 38	11 9	2 28	4 30	6 39	7 38	8 38	...	...	...	..
..	3 0	2 16	1 30	...	Guntramsdorf	...	6 47	...	11 13	2 32	...	6 43	...	...	...	...	...	..
.	3 20	2 31	1 40	...	**Laxenburg** ......departure	...	...	8 30	...	2 20	4 22	...	7 34	...	...	...	...	..
..	3 10	2 23	1 35	...	**Modling**	4 35	6 55	8 48	11 24	2 40	4 40	6 54	7 52	8 52	...	...	...	..
..	3 10	2 23	1 35	...	Brunn	...	7 1	8 54	11 30	2 46	4 47	7 1	7 59	8 59	...	...	...	..
..	3 20	2 31	1 40	...	Perchtoldsdorf	...	7 6	...	11 35	2 51	...	7 6	...	...	...	...	...	..
..	3 20	2 31	1 40	...	Liesing	4 48	7 10	9 1	11 39	2 55	4 54	7 11	8 8	9 8	...	...	...	..
..	3 30	2 38	1 45	...	Atzgersdorf	...	7 14	9 5	11 43	2 59	...	7 15	8 12	9 12	...	...	...	..
..	3 30	2 38	1 45	...	Hetzendorf	...	7 20	9 11	11 49	3 5	5 3	7 21	8 18	9 18	...	...	...	..
..	3 40	2 46	1 50	...	Meidling	5 1	7 25	9 17	11 54	3 10	5 8	7 26	8 24	9 24	...	...	...	..
..	...	...	...	...	Matzleinsdorf	...	7 29	...	11 58	3 14	...	7 30	...	...	...	...	...	..
..	3 50	2 53	1 55	...	**Vienna** .....[1].... arrival	5 7	7 33	9 23	12 2	3 18	5 14	7 34	8 31	9 31	...	...	...	..

ST. PETERSBURG & MOSCOW.—(400 English Miles.)

Fares 1st Class	Fares 2nd Class	Fares 3rd Class	Stations.	Trains.	Goods Train.	Stations.	Trains.	Goods Train.
				a.m.	a.m.		a.m.	a.m.
—	—	—	**St. Petersburgh**...dep.	11 0	8 0	**Moscow** ...dep.	11 0	8 0
...	...	...	Calpinskoy	11 55	9 45	Chimskoy	11 40	9 20
...	...	...	Tosnenskoy	12 45	11 35	Crukovskoy	12 25	10 45
...	...	...	Lubanskoy	1 45	2 30	Podsolnetchnoy	1 20	1 25
...	...	...	Pomeranskoy	2 0	2 55	Clinskoy	2 10	3 10
...	...	...	Tchudovskoy	3 0	5 10	Zavidovskoy	3 10	5 25
...	...	...	Volhovskoy	3 20	5 45	Tverskoy	5 0	8 45
...	...	...	Malo Veshuskoy	4 55	8 20	Ostashkovskoy	6 20	11 40
...	...	...	Oealovskoy	7 40	2 55	Sperovskoy	7 40	2 45
...	...	...	Valiaskoy	8 55	5 40	Veshnevolstchok	8 50	5 15
...	...	...	Bologovskoy	10 15	8 20	Bologovskoy	10 35	8 40
...	...	...	Veshnevolstchok	11 40	11 25	Valiaskoy	11 35	11 0
...	...	...	Sperovskoy	12 50	1 35	Oealovskoy	12 50	1 45
...	...	...	Ostashkovskoy	2 10	5 0	Malo Veshuskoy	3 25	7 55
...	...	...	Tverskoy	3 30	7 55	Valhovskoy	4 45	11 25
...	...	...	Zavidovskoy	5 0	11 15	Tchudovskoy	5 10	11 5
...	...	...	Clinskoy	6 0	1 30	Pomeranskoy	6 5	1 15
...	...	...	Podsolnetchnoy	6 50	3 15	Lubanskoy	6 25	1 45
...	...	...	Crukovskoy	7 45	5 5	Tosnenskoy	7 20	4 0
...	...	...	Chimskoy	8 30	6 30	Calpinskoy	8 15	5 55
...	...	...	**Moscow**...arr.	9 10	7 50	**St. Petersburgh**...arr.	9 10	6 40

Fares.—About 19 Rupels from Moscow to St. Petersburgh—about £2 18s. in English money.

Luggage.—A trifle is charged for Luggage, and a Ticket given for the same, as in other parts of the Continent.

RAILWAYS IN ITALY. [10-2-53

The Charge for Luggage upon all the Italian railways is very high.

TURIN AND GENOA RAILWAY, open to BUSALLA.

Length—130 Kilometres, about 80 English miles.

STATIONS.	1	2	3	4	STATIONS.	1	2	3	4
	a.m.	a.m.	p.m.			a.m.	a.m.	p.m.	
Turin....departure	6 0	10 0	4 0	..	**Busalla** ....dep.	4 30	11 30	3 30	..
Moncalieri	6 14	10 14	4 14	..	Ronco	4 42	11 42	3 42	..
Truffarello	6 24	10 24	4 24	..	Isola del Contone	4 55	11 55	3 55	..
Cambiano	6 30	10 30	4 30	..	**Arquata**	5 16	12 16	4 16	..
Pessione	6 39	10 39	4 39	..	Serravalle	5 24	12 24	4 24	..
Valdichiesa	6 48	10 48	4 48	..	**Novi**	5 36	12 36	4 36	..
Dusino	7 2	11 2	5 2	..	Frugarolo	5 51	12 51	4 51	..
Villafranca	7 16	11 16	5 16	..	Alessandria	6 7	1 7	5 7	..
Baldichieri	7 22	..	..	..	Solero	6 19	1 19	5 19	..
San Damiano	7 27	11 27	5 27	..	Felizzano	6 30	1 30	5 30	..
Asti	7 41	11 41	5 41	..	Cerro	6 40	..	5 40	..
Annone	7 55	11 55	5 55	..	Annone	6 46	1 46	5 46	..
Cerro	8 0	..	6 0	..	**Asti**	7 2	2 2	6 2	..
Felizzano	8 13	12 13	6 13	..	San Damiano	7 13	2 13	6 13	..
Solero	8 23	12 23	6 23	..	Baldichieri	..	2 18	..	..
Alessandria	8 39	12 39	6 39	..	Villafranca	7 26	2 26	6 26	..
Frugarolo	8 53	12 53	6 53	..	Dusino	7 39	2 39	6 39	..
Novi	9 18	1 18	7 18	..	Valdichiesa	7 52	2 52	6 52	..
Serravalle	9 29	1 29	7 29	..	Pessione	8 1	3 1	7 1	..
Arquata	9 39	1 39	7 39	..	Cambiano	8 10	3 10	7 10	..
Isola del Cantone	10 1	2 1	8 1	..	Truffarello	8 16	3 16	7 16	..
Ronco	10 13	2 13	8 13	..	Moncalieri	8 25	3 25	7 25	..
Busalla ......arr.	10 24	2 24	8 24	..	**Turin**......arrival	8 37	3 37	7 37	..

Between Busalla and Genoa passengers are conveyed in Diligences provided by the Government, occupying about 4 hours. Fares—4 francs, outside; 5 francs, inside.

Passengers can also book their places at the various Diligence Offices in Turin and Genoa.

Fares.—Turin to Busalla, 1st Class, 14f. 40c.; 2nd Class, 10f. 10c.; 3rd Class, 5f. 75c.

SWISS NORTHERN RAILWAY.—13½ English miles.

ZURICH to DIETIKON & BADEN, at 5½ & 8 a.m.; 2, & 7 p.m.; also 10½ a.m. on Sundays Festivals only.
From BADEN to DIETIKON and ZURICH, at 5½ & 9¼ a.m.; 5, & 8 p.m.; 11½ a.m. Sundays & Festivals only.
Fares, from Zurich to Baden, first class, 1 fr. 40 rappen; second, 1 fr.; third 60 rp.
Forty-five minutes are occupied in the transit.
Remarks.—10lbs. of Luggage are allowed free of charge.

MILAN, MONZA, and CAMERLATA—28 English Miles.

STATIONS.	Trains. 1	2	3	4	5	6
	a.m.	a.m.	a.m.	pm.	p.m.	p.m.
Milan........dep.	6 0	7 30	9 30	3 15	5 0	6 30
Sesto S. Gio	6 11	7 41	9 41	3 26	5 11	6 41
Monza	6 23	7 51	9 53	3 38	5 21	6 53
Desio	6 36	—	10 6	4 51	—	7 7
Seregno............	6 44	..	10 14	3 39	..	7 14
Camnago	6 55	..	10 25	4 10	..	7 25
Cucciago	7 11	..	10 41	4 26	..	7 41
Camerlata ..arr.	7 21	..	10 51	4 36	..	7 51

STATIONS.	Trains. 1	2	3	4	5	6
	a.m.	a.m.	a.m.	p.m.	p.m.	p.m.
Camerlata ..dep.	..	7 21	9 40	3 22	..	6 40
Camnago	..	7 31	9 50	3 32	..	6 50
Cucciago	..	7 46	10 5	3 47	..	7 5
Seregno............	..	7 56	10 16	3 59	..	7 16
Desio	..	8 4	10 24	4 6	..	7 24
Monza	6 45	8 17	10 37	4 19	5 40	7 37
Sesto S. Gio	6 56	8 28	10 48	4 30	5 51	7 48
Milan ....arr.	7 6	8 38	10 58	4 40	6 1	7 58

Fares—From Milan to Monza, 1st class, 2l. 40c.; 2nd class, 2l.; 3rd class, 1l. 40c.
To Comnago, 1st class, 4l. 50c.; 2nd class, 3l. 50c.; 3rd class, 2l. 75c.

VENICE AND TREVISO. [15-10-52

STATIONS.	Trains. 1	2	3	4
	a.m.	a.m.	p.m.	p.m.
Venice ....dep.	8 15	10 26	2 46	6 35
Mestre	8 31	10 42	3 2	6 54
Mogliano	8 46	10 57	3 17	7 9
Preganziol............	8 56	11 7	3 25	7 17
Treviso.......arr.	9 5	11 16	3 35	7 27

STATIONS.	Trains. 1	2	3	4
	a.m.	a.m.	p.m.	p.m.
Treviso ......dep.	6 55	10 5	2 25	5 7
Preganziol	7 6	10 16	2 36	5 18
Mogliano	7 14	10 24	2 44	5 26
Mestre	7 32	10 40	3 0	5 42
Venice.........arr.	7 46	10 54	3 14	5 56

MILAN TO TREVIGLIO. [12-5-53

English Miles.	Fares. 1st Class	2nd Class	3rd Class		STATIONS.	Trains. 1	2	3	4	5
Dis.	l. c.	l. c.	l. c			a.m.	a.m.	p.m.	p.m.	
—	—	—	—	...	**Milan** ....departure	5 50	9 45	3 0	6 0	...
..	1 50	1 0	0 75	...	Limito	6 5	10 0	3 15	6 15	...
..	2 25	1 75	1 25	...	Melzo	6 16	10 11	3 26	6 26	...
..	3 0	3 25	1 75	...	Cassano	6 27	10 22	3 37	6 37	...
15	3 50	2 70	2 0	...	**Treviglio** ....arrival	6 36	10 31	3 46	6 46	...

TREVIGLIO TO MILAN.

English Miles.	Fares. 1st Class	2nd Class	3rd Class		STATIONS.	Trains. 1	2	3	4	5
Dis.	l. c.	l. c.	l. c.			a.m.	a.m.	p.m	p.m.	
—	—	—	—	—	**Treviglio** ....departure	7 0	11 0	4 15	7 15	...
..	1 0	0 75	0 50	...	Cassano	7 10	11 10	4 25	7 25	...
..	2 0	1 50	1 0	...	Melzo	7 21	11 21	4 36	7 36	...
..	3 25	2 25	1 50	...	Limito	7 32	11 32	4 47	7 47	...
15	3 50	2 70	2 0	...	**Milan** ....arrival	7 46	11 46	5 1	8 1	...

Remarks.—LUGGAGE: 10 lbs. of Luggage are allowed to 1st class passengers, 8 lbs. to 2nd class, and 5 lbs, to 3rd class, free of charge.

VENICE AND VERONA.—75 English Miles. [15-10-52

English Miles.	Fares.			STATIONS.	Trains.						
	1st Class	2nd Class	3rd Class		1	2	3	4	5	6	7
Dis.	l. c.	l. c.	l. c.		a.m.	a.m.	a.m.	p m.	p.m.		
—	—	—	—	**Venice** departure	..	7 18	10 38	3 4	5 10	..	..
..	1 25	1 0	0 50	Mestre	..	7 37	10 57	3 23	5 42	..	..
..	2 25	1 25	1 0	Marano	..	7 52	11 12	3 38	6 9	..	..
..	2 75	1 75	1 25	Dolo	..	7 58	11 20	3 46	6 26	..	..
..	4 0	3 0	1 75	Ponte di Brenta	..	8 16	11 36	4 2	6 49	..	..
..	4 50	3 50	2 0	**Padau**	..	8 34	11 54	4 20	7 35	..	..
..	6 25	5 0	3 0	Pojana	..	8 59	12 17	4 43	8 14	..	..
..	8 50	6 50	3 75	**Vicenza**	6 45	9 30	12 48	5 14	8 48	..	..
..	9 25	7 25	4 25	Tavernelle	..	9 43	1 1	5 27		..	..
..	10 50	8 0	4 75	Montebello	7 25	9 58	1 16	5 42	..	..	..
..	11 0	8 75	5 0	Lonigo	7 48	10 9	1 27	5 53	..	..	..
..	11 75	9 25	5 50	S. Bonifacio	8 5	10 20	1 38	6 4	..	..	..
..	12 75	10 0	5 75	Caldiero	8 26	10 35	1 53	6 19		..	..
..	13 75	10 50	6 25	S. Martino	8 41	10 47	2 5	6 31	..	..	..
..	14 50	11 25	6 50	**Verona** arrived	8 55	10 58	2 16	6 42	..	..	..

VERONA TO VENICE.

English Miles.	Fares.			STATIONS.	Trains.						
	1st Class	2nd Class	3rd Class		1	2	3	4	5	6	7
Dis.	l. c.	l. c.	l. c.		a.m.	a.m.	a.m.	p.m.	p.m.		
—	—	—	—	**Verona** departure	..	7 0	11 20	3 30	5 5	..	..
..	1 0	0 75	0 50	S. Martino	..	7 12	11 32	3 42	5 20	..	..
..	1 50	1 25	0 75	Caldiero	..	7 24	11 44	3 54	5 35	..	..
..	2 50	2 0	1 25	S. Bonifacio	..	7 38	11 58	4 8	6 3	..	..
..	3 25	2 50	1 50	Lonigo	..	7 49	12 9	4 19	6 22	..	..
..	4 0	3 0	1 75	Montebello	..	8 2	12 22	4 32	6 40	..	..
..	5 0	4 0	2 25	Tavernelle	..	8 16	12 36	4 46	..	..	..
..	6 0	4 75	2 75	**Vicenza**	..	8 36	12 56	5 6	7 40	..	..
..	8 0	6 25	3 75	Pojana	..	9 0	1 20	5 30	8 15	..	..
..	9 75	7 50	4 50	**Padua**	6 55	9 30	1 50	6 0	8 47	..	..
..	10 50	8 25	4 75	Ponte di Brenta	7 10	9 41	2 1	6 11		..	..
..	11 75	9 25	5 25	Dolo	7 32	9 57	2 17	6 27	..	..	..
..	12 25	9 50	5 50	Marano	7 51	10 5	2 25	6 35	..	..	..
..	13 50	10 50	6 0	Mestre	8 20	10 24	2 44	6 54	..	..	..
..	14 50	11 25	6 50	**Venice** arrival	8 40	10 38	2 58	7 8	..	..	.

Remarks.– There is a diligence between Treviglio and Verona, occupying about 17 to 19 hours. The Posting is very good, and occupies about 12 hours; the Courier about 18 hours. The distance is about 85 English miles. VENICE to MILAN—Fares—2nd class by Rail to Verona, and any part of Diligence, 36 Aust. Lire.—in $22\frac{1}{2}$ hours.

NAPLES, CASERTA & CAPUA.

NAPLES to CASERTA and CAPUA, at $6\frac{1}{2}$, $8\frac{1}{2}$, $10\frac{1}{2}$, and $12\frac{1}{2}$ a.m., $2\frac{1}{2}$, $4\frac{1}{2}$, and $5\frac{1}{2}$ p.m.
CAPUA to CASERTA and NAPLES, at $6\frac{1}{4}$, $8\frac{1}{4}$, and $10\frac{1}{4}$ a.m.; $12\frac{1}{4}$, $2\frac{1}{4}$, $4\frac{1}{4}$, and $6\frac{1}{4}$ p.m.
The trains stop at Casalnuova, Acerra, Cancello, Nola, Maddaloni, Caserta, and Santa Maria.

VERONA AND MANTUA. [15-12-52

STATIONS.	Trains. 1	2	3	4	5
	a.m.	a.m.	p.m.		
Verona.......dep.	7 5	11 20	3 40	..	..
Dossobuono	7 28	11 43	4 3	..	..
Villafranca	7 41	11 56	4 16	..	..
Mozzecane............	7 51	12 6	4 26	..	..
Roverbella	8 3	12 18	4 38	..	..
Mantua ......arr.	8 15	12 30	4 50	..	..

STATIONS.	Trains. 1	2	3	4	5
	a.m.	p.m.	p.m.		
Mantua......dep.	8 35	1 40	5 10	..	..
Roverbella	8 48	1 53	5 23	..	..
Mozzecane	9 0	2 5	5 35	..	..
Villafranca	9 10	2 15	5 45	..	..
Dossobuono	9 23	2 28	5 58	..	..
Verona ....arr.	9 45	2 50	6 20	..	..

(11–51.

NAPLES, POMPEII, NOCERA, with Branch to CASTELLAMARE.

From Naples to Portici, Torre del Greco, Torre Annunziata, & Castellamare, at 7, 8, 9, and 10½ a.m., 12 noon, 1½, 3, 4, and 5 p.m.; to Pompeii, Scafati, Angri, Pagani, Nocera, &c., at 7 and 9 a.m. 12 noon, 3 and 5 p.m.

From Castellamare to Pompeii, Scafati, Angri, Pagani, Nocera, &c. at 7 25 and 9 25 a.m.: 12 25, 3 25, and 5 25 p.m.; to Torre Annunziata, Torre del Greco, Portici, and Naples, at 7 25, 8 25, 9 25 and 11 a.m.; 12 25, 2, 3 25, 4 25, and 5 25 p.m.

Fares.—From Naples to Castellamare, 1st Class, 50; 2nd Class, 35; 3rd Class, 25 grana. To Nocera, 1st Class, 75; 2nd Class, 50; 3rd Class, 32 grana.

LEOPOLDA RAILWAY.—LEGHORN to FLORENCE. [5–53.

STATIONS.	1	2	3	4	5	6	7
	a.m.	a.m.	p.m.	p.m.	p.m.	p.m.	
Leghorn ..dep.	6 20	10 30	1 0	3 45	6 0	7 45	..
Pisa............	6 50	11 0	1 30	4 15	6 30	8 15	..
Navacchio........	7 10	11 20	1 50	4 35	..	8 35	..
Cascina	7 15	11 25	1 55	4 45	..	8 45	..
Pontedera	7 30	11 40	2 10	5 0	7 5	9 0	..
La Ratta	7 40	11 50	—	5 10	7 15	—	..
S. Romano	7 55	12 5	..	5 25	7 30	..	..
S. Pierino........	8 5	12 15	..	5 35	7 40	..	..
Empoli	8 20	12 30	..	5 50	8 0	..	..
Montelupo...... .	8 35	12 45	..	6 0	8 15	..	..
Signa	8 55	1 5	..	6 20	8 35	..	..
Brazzi..	9 5	1 15	..	6 30	8 45	..	..
Florence ..arr.	9 20	1 30	..	6 45	9 0	..	..

STATIONS.	1	2	3	4	5	6
	a.m	a.m.	a.m	p.m.	p.m.	p.m
Florence. .dep.	..	7 0	10 30	..	3 0	5 30
Brazzi	..	7 15	10 45	..	3 15	5 45
Signa	..	7 20	10 50	..	3 20	5 50
Montelupo	..	7 40	11 10	..	3 40	6 10
Empoli	..	7 50	11 20	..	3 50	6 20
S. Pierino	..	8 10	11 40	..	4 10	6 40
S. Romano......	..	8 20	11 50	..	4 20	6 50
La. Ratta.........	..	8 40	12 10	..	4 40	7 10
Pontedera....	6 0	8 45	12 15	2 45	4 45	7 15
Cascina	6 15	9 0	12 30	3 0	..	7 30
Navacchio	6 25	9 10	12 40	3 10	..	7 40
Pisa	6 35	9 20	12 50	3 20	5 15	7 50
Leghorn ..arr.	7 15	10 0	1 30	4 0	6 0	8 30

Fares.—1st Class, about 7s.; 2nd Class, 4s. 6d.; 3rd Class, 3s.

SIENNA AND EMPOLI. [5-53.

STATIONS.	1	2	3
	a.m.	a.m.	p.m.
Sienna ....dep.	6 0	10 50	4 0
Poggibonsi	6 45	11 30	4 45
Certaldo	7 5	12 50	5 5
Castel-Fiorentino	7 20	12 5	5 20
Granajolo	7 30	12 15	5 30
Empoli ....arr.	7 50	12 30	5 50

STATIONS.	1	2	3
	a.m.	p.m.	p.m.
Empoli ....dep.	8 30	12 40	6 25
Granajolo	8 45	12 55	6 45
Castel-Fiorentino.............	8 55	1 5	6 55
Certaldo	9 20	1 20	7 15
Poggibonsi..................	9 40	1 50	7 45
Sienna.. ....arr.	10 40	2 35	8 45

This Line being now extended from Empoli to Sienna, on the road towards Rome, reduces the distance to that City to twenty four hours posting.

PESCIA, LUCCA, AND PISA. (3-53.

STATIONS.	1	2	3	4
	a.m.	a.m.	p.m.	
Pescia ....dep.	..	7 30	2 15	..
St. Salvadore...............	..	7 40	2 25	..
Dall 'Altopascio	..	7 50	2 35	..
Lucca	5 45	8 30	3 50	..
Ripafratta	6 0	8 45	4 5	..
Giuliano	6 15	9 0	4 20	..
Pisa ....arr.	6 25	9 10	4 30	..

STATIONS.	1	2	3	4
	a.m.	p.m.	p.m.	
Pisa ....dep.	7 45	2 0	6 10	..
Giuliano	8 0	2 15	6 25	..
Ripafratta	8 15	2 30	6 40	..
Lucca	8 45	3 15		..
Dall' Altopascio	9 5	3 35	..	..
St. Salvadore	9 15	3 45	..	..
Pescia ....arr.	9 25	3 55	..	..

The Stations of the Leopolda and the Lucca and Pisa Railways are outside the town of Pisa, about one English mile distance from each other.

MARIA ANTONIA RAILWAY.—Length about 21 miles. [10-52.

FLORENCE to PRATO and PISTOJA.

Eng. Miles.	STATIONS.	1	2	3	4	
		a.m.	a.m.	p.m.	p.m.	
..	**Florence** ......dep.	7 0	10 0	2 0	5 0	..
..	Rifredi	7 7	10 7	2 7	5 7	..
..	Castello	7 15	10 15	2 15	5 15	..
..	Sesto	7 23	10 23	2 23	5 23	..
11	**Prato**	7 40	10 40	2 40	5 40	..
..	S. Piero	7 55	10 25	2 55	5 55	..
21	**Pistoja** ....arr.	8 10	11 10	3 10	6 10	..

PISTOJA to PRATO & FLORENCE

STATIONS.	1	2	3	4	
	a.m.	a.m.	p.m.	p m.	
Pistoja ....dep.	7 5	10 5	2 5	5 5	..
S. Piero	7 20	10 20	2 20	5 20	..
Prato	7 35	10 35	2 35	5 35	..
Sesto	7 50	10 50	2 50	5 50	..
Castello	7 57	10 57	2 57	5 57	..
Rifredi	8 4	11 4	3 4	6 4	..
Florence .....arr.	8 10	11 10	3 10	6 10	..

Fares.—From Florence to Pistoja—1st class, 40 crazia; 2nd class, 28 crazia; 3rd class, 20 crazia. 1 crazia is equal to two-thirds of a penny.

SPAIN.

BARCELONA AND MATARO.—Length, 17¾ miles.

Stations.	Trains. 1	2	3	4	5	6
	a.m.	a.m.	a.m.	p.m.	p.m.	p.m.
Barcelona.	7 0	8 30	10 0	12 30	2 30	4 0
Badalona	7 15	8 45	10 15	12 45	2 45	4 15
Mongat	7 22	8 52	10 22	12 52	2 52	4 22
Masnou	7 30	9 0	10 30	1 0	3 0	4 30
Premia	7 39	9 9	10 39	1 9	3 9	4 39
Vilasar	7 46	9 16	10 46	1 16	3 16	4 46
Mataro	8 0	9 30	11 0	1 30	3 30	5 0

Stations.	Trains. 1	2	3	4	5	6
	a.m.	a.m.	a.m.	p.m.	p.m.	p.m.
Mataro	7 0	8 30	10 0	12 30	2 30	4 0
Vilasar	7 10	8 40	10 10	12 40	2 40	4 10
Premia	7 18	8 48	10 18	12 48	2 48	4 18
Masnou	7 27	8 57	10 27	12 57	2 57	4 27
Mongat	7 35	9 5	10 35	1 5	3 5	4 35
Badalona ...	7 42	9 12	10 42	1 12	3 12	4 42
Barcelona.	8 0	9 30	11 0	1 30	3 30	5 0

Fares.—From Barcelona to Mataro, 1st class, 10 reals (2s. 1d.); 2d class, 8 reals (1s. 8d.); 3d class, 6 reals (1s. 3d.)

MADRID and ARANJUEZ.—In about 1½ hours.

From **Madrid** to **Aranjuez,** at 7.30 and 11.30 a.m.; and 5.30 p.m.
From **Aranjuez** to **Madrid,** at 6 and 10 a.m.; and 4 p.m.

Fares.—From **Madrid** to **Aranjuez,** 1st class, 20 reals, (4s. 2d.); 2nd class, 14 reals, (2s. 11d.) 3rd class, 8 reals, (1s. 8d.)

RAILWAYS IN ENGLAND.

LONDON AND NORTH WESTERN RAILWAY.—STATION—EUSTON SQUARE.

From LONDON to COVENTRY and BIRMINGHAM, at 6, $6\frac{1}{2}$, 7, $7\frac{1}{2}$, $9\frac{1}{2}$, (to Birmingham only), and 10 a.m.; 12 noon, 2, $5\frac{1}{4}$, $5\frac{3}{4}$, and 9 p.m. On SUNDAYS at 7, $7\frac{1}{2}$, and 10 a.m.; and 9 p m.

From BIRMINGHAM to COVENTRY and LONDON, at $12\frac{1}{4}$, $7\frac{1}{2}$, 8, 9, and $10\frac{1}{2}$ a.m.; 12, 1, 4, 5.20, and 7.25 p.m. On SUNDAYS at $12\frac{1}{4}$, 7.30, and 8 a.m.; and 1 p.m.

From LONDON to STAFFORD, at 6, $6\frac{1}{2}$, 7, $7\frac{1}{2}$, $9\frac{1}{4}$, and 10 a.m.; 12 noon, 2, 5, and $8\frac{3}{4}$ p.m. On SUNDAYS at 7 and 10 a.m.; and $8\frac{3}{4}$ p.m.

From STAFFORD to LONDON, at 6.26, 7.50, and 11.46 a.m.; 12 noon, 2.3, 4.10, 7.2, $7\frac{1}{2}$, and 11.49 p.m On SUNDAYS at 6.26 a.m.; 12.5 and 11.49 p.m.

From LONDON to CHESTER, at 6, $6\frac{1}{2}$, 7, $9\frac{1}{4}$, and 10 a.m.; 12 noon, 5 and $8\frac{3}{4}$ p.m. On SUNDAYS at 10 a.m.; and $8\frac{3}{4}$ p.m.

From CHESTER to LONDON, at $4\frac{3}{4}$, 7.30, $9\frac{3}{4}$, and 11.45 a.m.; 1.50, 5.40, and 9.50 p.m. On SUNDAYS at 4 45 a.m., and 9.50 p.m.

From LONDON to LIVERPOOL, at 6, $6\frac{1}{2}$, 7, $9\frac{1}{4}$, and 10 a.m.; 12 noon, 5 and $8\frac{3}{4}$ p.m. On SUNDAYS at 7 and 10 a.m.; and $8\frac{3}{4}$ p.m.

From LIVERPOOL to LONDON, at $4\frac{1}{4}$, $7\frac{1}{2}$, $9\frac{1}{2}$, and $11\frac{1}{4}$ a.m.; 1, 5, and 8.52 p.m. On SUNDAYS at $4\frac{1}{4}$ and $9\frac{1}{2}$ a.m.; and 8.52 p.m.

From LONDON to MANCHESTER, at 6, $6\frac{1}{2}$, 7, $9\frac{1}{4}$, and 10 a.m.; 12 noon, 5 and $8\frac{3}{4}$ p.m. On SUNDAYS at 7 and 10 a.m.; and $8\frac{3}{4}$ p.m.

From MANCHESTER to LONDON, at 4.24, $8\frac{1}{4}$, $9\frac{3}{4}$, and 11.35 a.m.; $1\frac{1}{4}$, 5.20 and 9.12 p.m. On SUNDAYS 4.24 and $9\frac{1}{2}$ a.m.; and 9 12 p.m.

From LONDON to LEEDS, at 6, $6\frac{1}{2}$, 7, $9\frac{1}{4}$, and 10 a.m.; and 12 noon.

From LEEDS to LONDON, at 5.50, 7.20, $9\frac{1}{2}$, & $10\frac{1}{2}$ a.m.; 3.40 & $6\frac{1}{4}$ p.m. On SUNDAYS at $6\frac{3}{4}$ p.m.

From LONDON to PRESTON and the NORTH, at 6, $6\frac{1}{2}$, $9\frac{1}{4}$, and 10 a.m.; 5 and $8\frac{3}{4}$ p.m. On SUNDAYS at 10 a.m. and $8\frac{3}{4}$ p.m.

From PRESTON, at 3.44, and 8.45 a.m., 12.15, 4.50 and 8.33 p.m. On SUNDAYS at 3.44 a.m. and 8.33 p.m.

FARES:—London to Birmingham, express, 25s.; 1st class, 20s.; second class, 15s.; third class, 9s. $4\frac{1}{2}$d. To Stafford, express, 30s. 6d.; 1st class, 25s.; 2nd class, 18s.; third class, (by Birmingham), 11s. $9\frac{1}{2}$d.; (by Trent Valley), 11s. $0\frac{1}{2}$. To Chester, express, 40s. 6d.; 1st class, 33s.; 2nd class, 24s.; 3rd class, (by Birmingham), 15s. $7\frac{1}{2}$d.; (by Trent Valley), 14s. $10\frac{1}{2}$d. To Liverpool, express, 45s.; 1st class, 37s.; 2nd class, 27s.; 3rd class (by Birmingham), 17s. 6d.; (by Trent Valley), 16s. 9d. To Manchester, express, 42s. 6d.; 1st class, 35s.; 2nd class, 25s.; 3rd class, (by Birmingham), 16s. $5\frac{1}{2}$d.; (by Trent Valley), 15s. 8d. Liverpool to Manchester, 1st class, 5s. 6d.; 2nd, 4s.: 3rd, 2s. $7\frac{1}{2}$d.

GREAT NORTHERN RAILWAY.

From LONDON to YORK, PETERBOROUGH, HUNTINGDON, BOSTON, LINCOLN, SHEFFIELD, MANCHESTER, WAKEFIELD, LEEDS, GREAT GRIMSBY, HULL, and DONCASTER, Trains leave King's Cross Station at 7, (Parl.) $9\frac{1}{2}$ (exp.) $10\frac{1}{2}$ a.m.; 5 p.m. On SUNDAYS at $7\frac{1}{2}$ a.m. (Parl.)

From YORK, LEEDS, WAKEFIELD, HULL, SHEFFIELD, to DONCASTER, LINCOLN, BOSTON, PETERBOROUGH, HUNTINGDON & LONDON at 7.20 (Parl.), 9.50 (fast), 11 a.m.; 12 30, 4 10, (Express) and 8 40 (mail) p.m. On SUNDAYS at 9.45 a.m. (Parl.) and 8 40 p.m. (mail.)

FARES:—To York, express, 52s. 6d.; 1st class, 39s. 6d.; 2nd class, 29s.; 3rd class, 17s. 6d. To Peterborough, express, 20s.; 1st class, 13s. 6d.; 2nd class, 10s. 6d.; 3rd class, 6s. 4d. To Boston, express, 28s. 6d.; 1st class, 18s. 10d.; 2nd class, 14s. 2d.; 3rd class, 8s. $10\frac{1}{2}$d. To Lincoln, express, 36s.; 1st class, 24s. 8d.; 2nd class, 18s. 4d.; 3rd class, 11s. 6d. To Doncaster, express, 46s.; 1st class, 30s. 11d.; 2nd class, 23s. 1d.; 3rd class 14s. $7\frac{1}{2}$d. The distance from London to York is 210 miles.

SOUTH EASTERN, OR LONDON AND DOVER.

From LONDON to FOLKESTONE & DOVER, at 6.45, 8.10, 9½, & 11½ a.m.; 1½, 4½, 5½, 6.10, & 8½ p.m.
On SUNDAYS at 6½, 8.10, and 10½ a.m.; 5½ and 8½ p.m.
From DOVER and FOLKESTONE to LONDON at 2, 5.20, 6.45, 8, 9¼ and 11½ a.m.; 2, 5¼ & 7½ p.m.
On SUNDAYS at 2, 6¼, and 10 a.m.; 5¾ and 7¼ p.m.
From MARGATE to LONDON at 6, 7.10, and 10¼ a.m., 1.10, 3.10, 4.25, and 6½ p.m.
On SUNDAYS at 5.30 and 9.10 a m., 4.55 and 7 p.m.
From RAMSGATE to LONDON at 6.10, 7.25, and 10 27 a.m., 1.20, 3.25, 4.35, and 6¾ p.m.
On SUNDAYS at 5.42 and 9.22 a.m.; 5.6 and 7.10 p.m.

FARES:—London to Folkestone, 1st class express, 21s. 0d.; 2nd class express, 17s. 3d. ordinary 1st class, 20s.; 2nd, 14s; 3rd, 9s.; Parl. 6s. 10d. To Dover, 1st class express, 22s.; 2nd class express, 18s. 4d.; ordinary 1st class, 20s.; 2nd, 14s. 8d.; 3rd, 9s. 2d.; Parl. 7s. 3d.

Distance from London to Folkestone, 82 miles—to Dover, 88 miles.

EASTERN COUNTIES AND NORFOLK.

From YARMOUTH to LONDON at 5¾, 7, and 9¾ a.m.; 3, 4 30, and 9 10 p.m.
On SUNDAYS at 1½ and 9 10 p.m.
From LONDON to YARMOUTH at 7, 8, 10 40, and 11½ a.m.; 3 20, 4, 5, and 9 p.m.
On SUNDAYS at 7 a.m.; 1½ and 8¾ p.m.

FARES:—London to Yarmouth, 1st class, 30s.; 2nd, 23s. 6d.; 3rd, 17s.

Distance from London to Yarmouth, 146 miles.

GREAT WESTERN.

From LONDON to BRISTOL at 6 15, 6 50, 7 40, 9¾, and 10¼ a.m.; 12 40, 2¾, 4 50, 5 30 and 8 55 p m.
On SUNDAYS at 8 a.m.; 2 and 8 55 p.m.
From BRISTOL to LONDON at 8 20, 8 35, and 10 50 a.m.; 12 45, 2 45, 3, 3 40, 5 50, and 11 50 p m.
On SUNDAYS at 10 a.m.; 5½ and 11 50 p.m.

FARES:—London to Bristol, 1st class express, 30s.; 2nd class express, 25s.: ordinary 1st class, 27s.; 2nd class, 18s. 6d.; 3rd class, 1d. per mile..

Distance between London and Bristol, 118¼ miles.

LONDON AND SOUTH WESTERN.

From LONDON to SOUTHAMPTON & GOSPORT at 6¾, 7, 7½, 9 40, 10¼, and 11 a.m.; 12½, 3, 4, 5, and 8½ p.m.
On SUNDAYS at 9 and 10 a.m.; 5 and 8½ p.m.
From GOSPORT to LONDON at 6 10, 8 15, 11 5, and 11 45 a.m.; 2 25 and 6 25 p.m.
On SUNDAYS at 8 55 a.m. and 5 25 p.m.
From SOUTHAMPTON to LONDON at 1½, 6¾, 8 50, 9, and 11½ a.m.; 12½, 3 and 7 p.m.
On SUNDAYS at 1½ and 9½ a.m. 6, and 7 p.m.

FARES:—London to Southampton or Gosport, 1st class express, 20s.; 2nd express, 14s.: ordinary 1st class, 14s.; 2nd, 10s.; 3rd, 6s. 6d.

Distance between London and Southampton, 80 miles—Gosport, 90 miles.

LONDON, BRIGHTON, AND SOUTH COAST.

From LONDON to BRIGHTON at 6, 9, and 10 a.m.; 12 noon, 2, 3, 4, 5, 5.10, 7 & 10 p.m.
On SUNDAYS at 7, and 10¾ a.m.; and 6 p.m.
From BRIGHTON to LONDON at 6½, 8, 8¾, 9, 10, and 11 a.m.; 1¾, 3½, 5, 6 and 8 p.m.
On SUNDAYS at 8½ a.m.; 2¾, and 6½, p.m.

FARES—London to Brighton, express, 1st class, 13s.; express, 2nd class, 10s. 6d.; ordinary 1st class, 10s 6d.: 2nd class, 8s; third class, 5s. 4d.; Parl., 4s. 2d

Distance between London and Brighton, 50½ miles.

For further information, See "BRADSHAW'S RAILWAY GUIDE *for Great Britain and Ireland.*"

BI-MONTHLY ALMANAC & TIDE TABLE.

5th Mo. (May) 1853.

Day.	Sun Rises.	Sun Sets.	Moon's Age.	Moon Rises.	Moon Sets.	High Water London Bridge Morn.	High Water London Bridge Aftern.
	h.m.	h.m.		h.m.	h.m.	h.m.	h.m.
1 **S**	4 34	7 21	23·0	2m47	11m45	7 57	8 39
2 M	4 32	7 22	24·0	3 10	0a59	9 24	10 6
3 Tu	4 30	7 24	25·0	3 29	2 12	10 44	11 20
4 W	4 28	7 26	26·0	3 45	3 22	11 46	— —
5 Th	4 27	7 27	27·0	4 0	4 30	0 13	0 36
6 F	4 25	7 29	28·0	4 14	5 39	0 54	1 14
7 S	4 23	7 30	29.0	4 30	6 47	1 33	1 50
8 **S**	4 21	7 32	●	4 47	7 55	2 5	2 22
9 M	4 20	7 34	1.3	5 8	9 3	2 37	2 54
10 Tu	4 18	7 35	2·3	5 34	10 9	3 8	3 22
11 W	4 17	7 37	3·3	6 6	11 13	3 38	3 53
12 Th	4 15	7 38	4·3	6 48	morn	4 9	4 26
13 F	4 13	7 40	5·3	7 40	0 2	4 42	5 2
14 S	4 12	7 41	6·3	8 42	0 45	5 23	5 44
15 **S**	4 10	7 43	7·3	9 51	1 20	6 7	6 33
16 M	4 9	7 44	☽	11 6	1 48	7 2	7 34
17 Tu	4 7	7 46	9·3	0a24	2 11	8 11	8 49
18 W	4 6	7 47	10·3	1 44	2 31	9 29	10 5
19 Th	4 5	7 49	11·3	3 7	2 50	10 39	11 10
20 F	4 3	7 50	12·3	4 32	3 8	11 37	— —
21 S	4 2	7 51	13·3	6 1	3 27	0 4	0 27
22 **S**	4 1	7 53	○	7 32	3 51	0 50	1 12
23 M	4 0	7 54	15·3	9 1	4 26	1 36	1 59
24 Tu	3 58	7 56	16·3	10 21	4 58	2 24	2 49
25 W	3 57	7 57	17·3	11 26	5 50	3 13	3 35
26 Th	3 56	7 58	18·3	morn	6 55	3 57	4 22
27 F	3 55	7 59	19·3	0 15	8 10	4 48	5 16
28 S	3 54	8 1	20·3	0 50	9 28	5 41	6 9
29 **S**	3 53	8 2	☾	1 16	10 46	6 37	7 8
30 M	3 52	8 3	22·3	1 36	12 0	7 41	8 15
31 Tu	3 51	8 4	23·3	1 53	1a12	8 50	9 25

6th Mo. (June) 1853.

Day.	Sun Rises.	Sun Sets.	Moon's Age.	Moon Rises.	Moon Sets.	High Water. London Bridge Morn.	High Water. London Bridge Aftern
	h.m.	h.m.		h.m.	h.m.	h.m.	h.m.
1 W	3 52	8 5	24·3	2m 8	2a21	9 58	10 31
2 Th	3 50	8 6	25·3	2 24	3 29	11 1	11 28
3 F	3 49	8 7	26·3	2 38	4 37	11 54	— —
4 S	3 48	8 8	27·3	2 54	5 46	0 17	0 36
5 **S**	3 48	8 9	28·3	3 14	6 52	0 56	1 14
6 M	3 47	8 10	●	3 37	8 0	1 35	1 53
7 Tu	3 47	8 11	0·7	4 7	9 3	2 10	2 28
8 W	3 46	8 12	1·7	4 46	5 59	2 45	3 2
9 Th	3 46	8 12	2·7	5 35	10 46	3 19	3 35
10 F	3 45	8 13	3.7	6 34	11 22	3 53	4 11
11 S	3 45	8 14	4·7	7 41	11 53	4 29	4 49
12 **S**	3 45	8 14	5·7	8 53	morn	5 8	5 31
13 M	3 44	8 15	6 7	10 8	0 17	5 54	6 20
14 Tu	3 44	8 16	☽	11 26	0 37	6 46	7 12
15 W	3 44	8 16	8·7	0a44	0 55	7 45	8 16
16 Th	3 44	8 17	9·7	2 6	1 12	8 48	9 22
17 F	3 44	8 17	10·7	3 30	1 30	9 53	10 25
18 S	3 44	8 17	11·7	4 58	1 31	10 57	11 25
19 **S**	3 44	8 18	12·7	6 27	2 16	11 54	— —
20 M	3 44	8 18	13·7	7 52	2 48	0 22	0 49
21 Tu	3 44	8 18	○	9 7	3 33	1 15	1 43
22 W	3 45	8 18	15·7	10 5	4 32	2 8	2 35
23 Th	3 45	8 19	16·7	10 47	5 44	3 1	3 26
24 F	3 45	8 19	17·7	11 18	7 4	3 50	4 15
25 S	3 46	8 19	18·7	11 41	8 25	4 40	5 5
26 **S**	3 46	8 19	19·7	11 59	9 43	5 29	5 55
27 M	3 47	8 19	20·7	morn	10 58	6 19	6 42
28 Tu	3 47	8 19	☾	0 15	0 a 9	7 7	7 35
29 W	3 48	8 18	22·7	0 30	1 18	8 3	8 34
30 Th	3 48	8 18	23·7	0 45	2 26	9 3	9 32

The following List, showing the difference of Time between London and the principal Continental and British Ports, is derived from Local Tide Tables, and the best books on Navigation.

		H. M.
Aberdeen	sub.	0 55
Antwerp	add	3 36
Berwick	—	0 12
Boulogne	sub.	2 40
Brest Harbour	add	1 40
Brielle	—	0 54
Brighton	sub.	2 28
Bristol	add	5 10
Calais	sub.	2 36
Cape Clear	add	1 54
Cardigan Bar	—	4 39
Cork Harbour (Cove)	—	2 24
Cowes	sub.	3 21
Cuxhaven	—	1 6
Dieppe	—	2 59
Douglas Harbour (Isle of Man)	—	2 56
Dover Harbour	sub.	2 56
Dublin	—	2 54
Dunkirk	—	2 26
Folkestone	—	3 7
Gravelines	—	2 26
Guernsey Pier	add	4 24
Havre-de-Grace	sub.	4 14
Heligoland	—	3 6
Hellevoet Sluys	add	0 9
Holyhead Harbour	sub.	3 42
Hull	add	3 54
Hythe	sub.	3 21
Jersey (St. Aubyn)	add	4 4
Leith	sub.	0 16
Liverpool	—	2 44
Margate	—	2 2
Milford Haven, entrnc.	add	3 39
Morlaix	add	2 59
Newhaven	sub.	2 15
Newport (Isle of Wight)	—	3 10
NewShoreham Harbour	—	2 17
Ostend	—	1 56
Port Glasgow	—	2 41
Portsmouth Harbour	—	2 27
Ramsgate Harbour	—	2 46
Scilly Islands	add	2 24
Southampton	sub.	3 26
Southend & Sheerness	—	1 27
St. Malo	add	3 34
Stromness	sub.	5 6
Texel Road	—	5 6
Torbay	add	3 54
West Scheldt, entrance	sub.	1 36
Wranger Oog	—	2 1

Explanation.—To find the time of High Water at the above Places, it will be necessary to add or subtract the numbers in the above Table, according to the directions here given, to or from the time of High Water at London, as given in the Calendar for the day required.

ALPHABETICAL LIST OF STEAMERS TO & FROM FOREIGN PORTS.

ADDRESSES OF THE VARIOUS COMPANIES.

ANGLO-ITALIAN STEAM NAVIGATION CO., 31, Water-street, Liverpool.
ANTWERP STEAM CO., 123, Fenchurch-street, London.
AUSTRIAN LLOYDS MAIL STEAM PACKET CO., 127, Leadenhall-street, London.
BRIGHTON STEAM PACKET CO.—Agent: H. P. Maples, 5, Arthur-st. East, London Bridge, London.
COLOGNE STEAM NAVIGATION CO., 52, Gracechurch-street, London.
COMMERCIAL STEAM NAVIGATION CO., 4, Arthur-street East, London.
ENGLISH AND BELGIAN GOVERNMENT STEAM CO., 52, Gracechurch-street, London.
GENERAL SCREW STEAM SHIPPING CO., 2, Royal Exchange Buildings, London.
GENERAL STEAM NAVIGATION CO., 71, Lombard-street, London.
HULL STEAM PACKET CO. (Brownlow, Pearson & Co., Agents, Hull.)
LIVERPOOL AND PHILADELPHIA STEAM SHIP CO., 12, Tower Buildings, Liverpool.
LONDON AND SOUTH WESTERN RAILWAY STEAM PACKET CO., York-road, Waterloo-road, London.
MEDITERRANEAN STEAM PACKET CO., 1, Place Royale, Marseilles.
NETHERLAND STEAM PACKET CO., 11, Rood Lane, City, London.
NORTHERN STEAM PACKET CO.—Agents: Small and Frey, Lowestoft,
PENINSULAR AND ORIENTAL STEAM NAVIGATION CO., 122, Leadenhall-street, London.
ROYAL MAIL STEAM PACKET CO., 55, Moorgate-street, London.
SOUTH EASTERN RAILWAY STEAM PACKET CO., Station, London Bridge, London.

Ajaccio to Marseilles—By the French Government Steamers, every Tuesday at 9 a.m. Fares—30, 20, and 15 francs. See page 332.
Alexandria to Cairo—In 20 hours.
Alexandria to Corfu and Trieste.—To Corfu in 126 hours. Fares 80fl., 56fl., and 40fl. —To Trieste in 186 hours. Fares 120fl., 80fl., and 60fl.
Alexandria to Malta, by her Majesty's packets, about the 20th of each month.
Alexandria to Malta, Gibraltar, and Southampton.—By the Peninsular and Oriental Steam Navigation Co.'s Steamers, on the 6th and 20th.
Alexandria to Marseilles—French Government steamers, with the Indian mail, 8th and 21st of each month.
Alexandria to Smyrna and Constantinople.—To Smyrna in 96 hours. Fares 60fl., 40fl., and 26fl.—To Constantinople in 132 hours. Fares 80fl., 50fl., and 30fl.
Alexandria to Syra in 72 hours. Fares 54fl., 36fl., and 24fl.
Alexandria to Trieste.—By the Austrian Lloyd's Mail Steamer, "Direct," in connection with the Bombay and Calcutta Steamers, or the "Indirect," via Smyrna and Syra, every alternate Thursday.
Algiers to Cette.—On the 5th, 15th, and 20th of each month.
Alicante to Marseilles—See Marseilles.
Amsterdam to Hamburg—On the 5th, 10th, 15th, 20th, 25th, and 30th of every month, in the morning very early, in 33 and 36 hours. Fares, 1st Class, 20½ fl.; 2nd Class, 14½ fl.
Amsterdam to Harlingen—Every Tuesday, Thursday, and Saturday, at 7 a.m.
Amsterdam to Lemmer—On Mondays, Wednesdays, and Fridays, at 7 a.m.
Amsterdam to Zaandam—Daily at 7, and 9½ a.m., 3 and 5 p.m., in about an hour.
Ancona to Trieste—Four times a-week, in 16 hours. Fares, 15f. and 10 fl.
Ancona to Venice—in 20 hours. Fares, 15 fl. and 10 fl.
Angers to Nantes,—6 and 9 a.m., and 2 and 5 p.m. Fares, 6 francs, and 4 francs.
Antwerp to Flessingue.—Every Thursday at 9 a.m. Fares—9frs. 50c., and 5frs. 92c.
Antwerp to Goole, (Calling at Hull).—The "Schelde," every Tuesday. Fares 15s, and 10s.; Return Tickets, 20s.
Antwerp to Hull—Hull Steam Packet Company's Steamers, every Wednesday, Fares, 21s. and 12s. 6d, see page 344.
Gee and Co.'s steamer, Emerald Isle, every Saturday evening.
Antwerp to London and the Rhine—By the General Steam Navigation Company's Steamers every Sunday, at 3 p.m. Fares chief cabin £1 4s.; fore cabin 16s; children under 10 years half price. Also by the Baron Osy, from St. Katharine's Wharf, every Wednesday, at 11 a.m. Fares—£1 4s. and 16s. See page 344.
Antwerp to Rotterdam—Every Wednesday and Saturday during winter, and daily in summer. Fares, 17f., 12f. 70c., and 8f. 50c.
Antwerp to Tamise.—3 p.m., Sundays excepted.
Athens to Constantinople.—Fares, 42 fl., 28 fl., and 14 fl.
Athens to Dardanelles.—Fares, 30 fl., 20 fl., and 10 fl.
Athens to Smyrna—in 24 hours. Fares, 24 fl., 16 fl., and 8 fl.
Avignon to Valence and **Lyons** at 4 a.m.
Barcelona to Marseilles—About four times a-month. Fares, 88f. and 70f.—To **Valencia, Alicante, Carthagena, Gibraltar, and Cadiz.**—For fares, see page 133.

Bastia to Marseilles—French Government steamers, every Friday.

Beyrout to Jaffa in 2 days. Jaffa is 36 miles, or 12 hours, from Jerusalem. (See page 330.)

Bingen to Mayence and Frankfort.—Daily at 5¼ p.m.

Bombay to Galle (Ceylon), Penang, Singapore, and Hong Kong.—By the Peninsular and Oriental Steam Navigation Company's Steamers, on the 3rd and 19th.

Bordeaux to Rotterdam—By the Steamers "Bordeaux" and "Gironde," June 10th. Fares—1st cabin, 80 frs., provisions included.

Boston, U.S., to Liverpool—By the British and North American Royal Mail Steam Ships, (Calling at Halifax). Europa, June 8th. Fares, £25 and £15.

Boulogne to Folkestone—The South Eastern and Continental Company's Steam Ships—during the present month according to tide. Average passage, 2 hours. (Full particulars, see pages 333 & 334.)

Boulogne to London.—By the General Steam Navigation Company's Steamers.—June 1st, 5 a.m.; 3d, 11 p.m.; 8th, 1 a.m.; 10th, midnight; 15th, 6 a.m.; 17th, 9½ p.m.; 22nd, 1 a.m.; 24th, midnight; 29th, 6 a.m. Fares—chief cabin, 12s.; fore cabin, 8s.; children under 10 years half price.

The Commercial Steam Company's Steamers, City of Boulogne, or City of Paris—June 2nd, 10 p.m.; 5th, midnight; 10th, 2 a.m.; 13th, 4 a.m.; 17th, 5 a.m.; 19th, 11 p.m.; 24th, 2 a.m.; 27th 5 a.m. Fares, 12s. and 8s.

Bregenz to Constance.—Sunday and Friday, 6 a.m.

Bregenz to Friedrichshafen.—Monday, 10 a.m.; Friday, 7 a.m.; Wednesday and Saturday, 12½ noon; Sunday, 6 a.m.

Bregenz to Lindau.—Monday, 10 a.m.; Wednesday and Saturday, 12½ noon; Friday, 7 a.m.

Bregenz to Rorschach.—Monday, 10 a.m.; Wednesday and Saturday, 12½ noon; Sunday and Friday, 6 a.m.

Bremen to Bremerhafen.—Three times a day, in 6 hours.

Bremen (by the Weser) to Minden, and Hameln to Minden. Fares, 2 th. 12 gr., and 1 th. 10 gr.—From Minden to Hameln. Fares, 1 th, and 14 gr.—From Hameln to Minden. Fares, 2 th. 12 gr., and 1 th. 10 gr.

Bremen to Oldenburg.—Daily, in the afternoon.

Bremen to Vegesack.—Three times a day.

Bremerhafen to Bremen.—Twice a day, in 6 hours

Brientz to Interlaken.—Twice a day in summer.

Brighton (Newhaven) to Dieppe.—By the Brighton Steam Packet Company's Steamers, in connexion with London, Brighton, and South Coast, and Paris, Rouen, and Dieppe Railway Trains, see page 335.

Brighton (Newhaven) to Jersey—By the Brighton Steam Packet Co.'s Steamers, in connexion with London, Brighton, and South Coast Railway Trains—see page 335.

Caglaire to Genoa—By the Sardinian Royal Mail Steamers, on the 5th, 15th, and 25th of every month. Fares—70 and 45 francs (provisions included), See page 329.

Cairo to Alexandria—In 15 hours.

Calais to Dover—The South Eastern and Continental Steam Packet Company's ships, daily, see pages 333 and 334.

By the English Government Mail Steamers—Every day (except Sunday), at 2 10 a.m.; and by the French Government Boat every night, at 9.40 p.m.—(Average passage, 1½ hour). Fares—chief cabin, 8s.; fore cabin, 6s.; four-wheeled carriages, £2 2s.; two-wheeled, £1 1s.; horses, £1 5s.; dogs, 2s. 6d.

Calais to London—By the General Steam Navigation Company's Steamers—June 1st, 10 p.m.; 5th, 2½ a.m.; 9th, 3 a.m.; 12th, 3 a.m.; 16th, 5 a.m.; 18th, 11 p.m.; 23rd, 2¼ a.m.; 26th, 3 a.m.; 30th, 5 a.m. Fares, 12s. and 8s.; children under ten years, half-price.

Calcutta to Madras, Ceylon (Galle), Aden, and Suez.—By the Peninsular and Oriental Steam Navigation Company's Steamers, on the 6th and 20th. Note.— In June and July, the steamer leaves Calcutta 5 days earlier. (Sixty hours from Suez to Alexandria.)

Calcutta to Penang, Singapore, Hong Kong, and Shanghai.—By the Peninsular and Oriental Steam Navigation Company's Steamers, on the 15th.

Calvi to Marseilles—By the French Government Steamers, every Saturday at Mid-day. Fares —30, 20, and 15 francs. See page 332.

Cette to Algiers—On the 10th, 20th, and 30th of each month.

Chalons-sur-Saone to Lyons, by the Saone, (86½ English miles, or 136 kilometres), in 6 hours daily—at 5 and 10 a.m. Fares, 8 fr., and 6 fr.

Cherbourg to Weymouth.—Twice a week in summer.

Civita Vecchia to Naples—By the Sardinian Royal Mail Steamers, on the 7th, 17th, and 27th of every month. See page 329.

Coblentz to Treves—Tuesday and Fridays, at 6 a.m. Fares, 47 h., and 27 h. 20 sgr.

Colico to Como.—Every afternoon.

Cologne to Dusseldorf, Wesel, Emmerich, Arnheim, Doesborgh, Zutphen, Deventer, Zwolle, Kampen, and Amsterdam, (Bremen, Hamburg, Hull.) every Sunday, Tuesday, and Friday, at 10 a.m.

Cologne to Mannheim, see pages 337 and 339.

Como to Colico.—Every morning.

Cologne to Rotterdam, by the Netherland steamers, every Monday and Thursday, at 6 a.m.
Constance to Bregenz.—Wednesday and Saturday, 7 a.m.
Constance to Friedrichshafen.—Every day 9¾ a.m. and 2 p.m.
Constance to Lindau and Rorschach.—Every day at 1 p.m.
Constance to Meersburg.—Every day at 6 or 8 a.m. and 2 p.m.
Constance to Schaffhausen.—Every day at 1 p.m.
Constantinople to Beyrout in 136 hours. Fares 96fl., 64fl., and 35fl.
Constantinople to Larnaca in 120 hours. Fares 84fl., 56fl., and 30fl.
Constantinople to Marseilles, by way of the Dardanelles, Smyrna, Athens and Malta—French Government steamers, the 5th, 15th, and 25th of each month.
Constantinople to Odessa—also to **Samsoun, Sinope, & Trebizonde.**—To Odessa, 125 French leagues; to Trebizonde, 190 ditto.
Constantinople to Rhodes in 78 hours. Fares 54fl., 36fl., and 20fl.
Constantinople to Smyrna—19th of every month, in 36 hours. Fares, 30 fl., 20 fl., and 10 fl.
Constantinople to Smyrna, Malta, Gibraltar, and Southampton.—By the Peninsular and Oriental Steam Navigation Company's Steamers, on the 17th.
Constantinople to Smyrna, Rhodes, Messina, Alexandretta, Latakia, Beyrout, Jaffa, and Alexandria.—See Advertisement of the Marine Service of the Messageries National, pages 330 and 331.
Constantinople to Varna, Tulsia, Galatz, and Ibraila—in connexion with river boats to Vienna—weekly, in about 18 days. Fares, 89 fl. 30 kr., and 63 fl.
Copenhagen to Christiania—in 60 hours.
Copenhagen to Flensburg.—Twice a week, by the Iron Steamer, Caroline Amalie.
Copenhagen to Gothenburg—Once a-week, in 24 hours. Fares, 9 spec. th. and 4¼ spec. th.
Copenhagen to Kiel.—(Vide Kiel.)
Copenhagen to Lubeck.—(Vide Lubeck.)
Dieppe to Newhaven (Brighton).—By the Brighton Steam Packet Co.'s Steamers, in connection with the London, Brighton and South Coast, and Paris, Rouen and Havre Railway trains. See page 335.
Dinant to Namur.—6 a.m. Fares—1 fr. 75 c., or 1 fr. 25 c.
Donauworth to Regensburg—At 11½ a.m., in 8 hours.
Dover to Calais.—By the South Eastern and Continental Steam Packet Co.'s Ships. See p. 333, 334. By the French Government Mail Steamers, daily, Sunday excepted, at 2 p.m., and the English every day, except Sunday, at 11 p.m. Fares, 8s. and 6s.; Children, 4s. and 3s.
Dover to Ostend.—The English and Belgian Government Mail Steamers, every night, except Sunday, at 11.15 p.m. Fares—15s. and 10s.; Children, 7s. 6d. and 5s. See page 340.
Dresden to Prague (by the Elbe.)—Fares 7fl. and 5fl.
Dunkirk to Amsterdam—Every Saturday morning.
Dunkirk to Hamburgh—Once a week.
Dunkirk to Havre—Once a week. Fares, cabin 25f, fore cabin 15f.
Dunkirk to London—By the General Screw Steam Shipping Co.'s Steamers, City of Rotterdam and City of London, June 1st, 8 a.m.; 2nd, 10 p.m; 4th, 11 p.m.; 7th, midnight; 10th, 1 am.; 12th, 3 a.m; 15th, 6 a.m.; 17th, 8 a.m.; 18th, 10 p.m.; 21st, midnight; 24th, 1 p.m.; 26th, 3 a.m.; 29th, 6 a.m. Fares, 10s. and 7s.; children under ten years, half price. Steward's fee, 1s.
Dunkirk to St. Petersburgh—1st and 15th of the month.
Ebensee to Gmunden.—Across the lake several times a day in summer Fares, 50 kreutzers.
Edinburgh to Rotterdam.—The Ivanhoe or Balmoral, every Saturday afternoon.
Elbing to Konigsberg.—Daily. Fares, 1⅔ th. and 1⅙ th.
Elbing to Pillau.—Fares, 1 th. 10 sgr., and 25 sgr
Flensburg to Copenhagen.—On Tuesdays and Thursdays, at 12 noon, passing the Danish Islands. The whole voyage performed in about 24 hours. Fares, 4, 3. and 2 species dollars.
Flessingue to Antwerp.—Every Wednesday in the morning. Fares, 9frs. 50c., and 5 frs. 22c.
Fluelen to Luzern.—8 a.m. and 4 p.m.
Folkestone to Boulogne—The South Eastern and Continental Steam Packet Co.'s Ships. During the present month, according to tide. Average passage, 2 hours. For full particulars, see pages 333 and 334.
Fankforrt to Mayence and Bingen.—Daily at 3 p.m. Fares to Mayence, 1st Class, 48 kr.; 2nd Class, 30 kr.
Frankfort to Offenbach, Hanau, Aschaffenburg, Miltenburg, and Wertheim—Daily, at 5.30 p.m., in 14½ hours. Fares to Wertheim, 2 fl. 12 kr., and 1 fl. 48 kr.
Frankfurt-on-the-Oder to Stettin.—Daily, at 6 a.m.
Friedrichshafen to Bregenz.—Monday, Wednesday, and Saturday, 6 a.m. (per Rorschach).
Friedrichshafen to Constance.—Sunday, Monday, Thursday, and Friday, 6 a.m. (per Romanshorn); Tuesday and Friday, 11½ a.m.; Monday and Saturday, 4 p.m.
Friedrichshafen to Lindau.—Sunday, 11 a.m.; Friday, 5 a.m.; and Daily, at 6 p.m. (per Rorschach).
Friedrichshafen to Meersburg.—Tuesday and Friday, 11½ a.m. (per Constance); Monday and Saturday, 4 p.m. (direct).

Friedrichshafen to Romanshorn.—Daily, at 6 a.m. (direct); Tuesday and Friday, 11½ a.m. (per Constance).

Friedrichshafen to Rorschach.—Daily, 6 a.m. (per Romanshorn), in 2½ hours; and 4 p.m. (direct), in 1½ hours.

Friedrichshafen to Schaffhausen.—Monday and Tuesday, 6 a.m. (per Romanshorn).

Geneva to Nyon, Rolle, Lausanne, Morges, Vevay, & Villeneuve.—Daily, at 8 a.m.

Geneva to Villeneuve.—Daily at 8 a.m. and 2 p.m., calling at Lausanne and Vevay.

Genoa to Caglaire—By the Sardinian Royal Mail Steamers, on the 1st, 10th, and 20th of every month. Fares—70 and 45 francs (provisions included). See page 329.

Genoa to Leghorn, Civita Vecchia, and Naples—By the Sardinian Royal Mail Steamers, on the 5th, 15th, and 25th of every month. See page 329.

Genoa to Marseilles—By the Sardinian Royal Mail Steamers, on the 9th, 19th, and 29th of every month. See page 329.

Genoa to Nice—By the Sardinian Royal Mail Steamers, every Saturday, in 12 hours. Fares—25 and 15 francs. See page 329.

Genoa to Portotorres—By the Sardinian Royal Mail Steamers, on the 5th, 15th, and 25th of every month. Fares—55 and 35 francs (provisions included). See page 329.

Genoa to Tunis (*viâ* Caglaire)—By the Sardinian Royal Mail Steamers, on the 10th and 20th of every month. Fares—115 and 75 francs (provisions included). See page 329.

Gibraltar to Cadiz, Lisbon, off Oporto, Vigo, & Southampton.—By the Peninsular and Oriental Steam Navigation Company's Steamers, on the 5th, 16th, and 26th.

Gibraltar to Italy and Liverpool—By the Anglo Italian Co.'s Steamers. See page 346.

Gibraltar to Malaga—in 10 hours.

Gibraltar to Malta—in four days.

Gmunden to Ebensee.—Several times a day in Summer. Fare—50 kreutzers.

Goole to Antwerp (calling at Hull.)—The De Schelde, every Tuesday. Fares, 15s., and 10s; Return Tickets, 20s.; fore cabin, 10s.

Goole to Rotterdam—The Norfolk (calling at Hull).—June 4th, 5 p.m.; 11th, 9 p.m.; 18th, 4 p.m.; 25th, 10 a.m. The Corkscrew, June 1st, 3 p.m; 8th, 7 p.m.; 15th, noon; 22nd, 7 p.m.; 29th, 1 p.m. Sea passage, 17 hours. Fares, 15s. and 10s. Out and Home, £1.

Gothenburg to Christiania.—Fares, first place, 8 spec. th.

Gothenburg to Hull—Every Friday afternoon, for Hull direct.

Grimsby to Hamburg.—The Hamburg, Leipsic, City of Norwich, Cumberland, or Jupiter, every Saturday evening. Fares, £2, £1, & 10s. See page 345.

Grimsby to Rotterdam.—The Swanland, average passage, 18 to 20 hours.—Every Wednesday during the Season.

Guernsey to London.—The Foyle, from Custom House Quay, every ten days during the month of June. Fares, Deck, 5s.; Fore Cabin, 7s. 6d.; Saloon, 10s. See page 338.

Guernsey to Plymouth.—The Sir Francis Drake.—Every Friday at 5 p.m. Fares—to Torquay, 20s., 14s., and 9s.—to Plymouth, 18s., 12s, and 7s.

Guernsey and Jersey to Southampton.—The London and South Western Royal Mail Steam Packet, every Monday, Wednesday, and Friday; Transit, every Thursday. Fares, 20s. and 13s.; Children under two, free; above two, and under twelve, half-price.

Gulnar (Kelendri in Asia Minor.—By sailing-boat to Cyprus, at 6 a.m.

Hamburgh to Amsterdam—Same as Amsterdam to Hamburg.

Hamburg to Harburg.—6¾, 9, and 10¼, a.m.; 12, 2, 3½, 4½, 6 and 7½ p.m., in about 1¼ hours.

Hamburg to Hoopte.—Monday, Thursday, and Saturday, at 3 p.m.

Hamburgh to Hull—By the Hull Steam Packet Co.'s vessels. Fares £1 and 10s. See page 344. Gee and Company's Steamers, Queen of Scotland, or Rob Roy, every Saturday evening.

Hamburg to Leith.—June 4th, 11th, 18th, and 25th.

Hamburgh to London—By the General Steam Navigation Company's Steamers—June 3rd, midnight; 8th, 3 a.m.; 11th, 4 a.m.; 15th, 7 a.m.; 17th, 11 p.m.; 22nd, 2 a.m.; 25th, 4 a.m.; 29th, 7 a.m. Fares—Chief Cabin, £2, Fore Cabin, £1 5s.

Hamburgh to Newcastle.—The Chevy Chase or Earl Percy—See page 345.

Hamburg to Stade.—Daily, except Sundays, at 2 and 3 p.m., in 2½ hours.

Harburg to Hamburg.—6¼, 7½, 9, 11, and 11½ a.m.; 1½, 3¼, 5, and 7 p.m., in about 1¼ hours.

Harlingen to Amsterdam—8 a.m. on Sundays, Wednesday, and Friday.

Harlingen to London.—By the Lord John Russel, every Wednesday morning.

Havre to Caen—daily, in 4 hours. Fares, 6f. and 5f.

Havre to Cherbourg in 10 hours. Fares, 12f. and 10f.

Havre to Liverpool—By the Commodore or Margaret, or other suitable vessels—No Information. Fares, Cabin, 25s. Steerage, 12s. 6d.

Havre to London—By the General Steam Navigation Company's Steamers—June 5th, 9 a.m.;

10th, noon; 15th, 3 p.m.; 19th, 8 a.m.; 22nd, $10\frac{1}{2}$ a.m.; 26th, noon; 29th, 4 p.m. Fares—Chief Cabin, 12s.; Fore Cabin, 8s. Children under 10 years, half-price.

Havre to Southampton—The London and South Western Railway Company's Steamers, calling off Portsmouth, every Monday, Wednesday, and Friday, viz.:—June 1st, $8\frac{1}{2}$ p.m.; 3rd, $8\frac{1}{2}$ p.m.; 6th, $8\frac{1}{2}$ p.m.; 8th, $8\frac{1}{2}$ p.m.; 10th, 10 p.m.; 13th, midnight; 15th, 6 p.m.; 17th, $8\frac{1}{2}$ p.m.; 20th, $8\frac{1}{2}$ p.m.; 22nd, $8\frac{1}{2}$ p.m.; 24th, 10 p.m.; 27th, midnight; 29th, $6\frac{1}{2}$ p.m. Fares—Main Cabin, 18s.; Fore Cabin, 12s.; Children, under two years of age, free; above two and under twelve, half-fare.

Havre to Spain—Once a month. Fares to San Sebastian 120f., Santander 150f., Corunna 253f. Cadiz 360f., Malaga 400f.

Havre to St. Petersburg, calling at Copenhagen—Monthly.

Heidelberg to Heilbronn—Daily, at 6 a.m., in 12 or 13 hours. Fares, 1 class, 3 fl.; 2nd class, 2 fl.

Heilbronn to Heidelberg—Daily, at 8 a.m., after arrival of first train from Stuttgart.

Heilbronn to Mannheim. Fares, 3 fl. 24 kr., and2 fl. 16 kr

Helsingborg and Helsigor to Copenhagen—Twice a-week, in 4 to 5 hours.

Hong Kong to Singapore, Penang, Galle (Ceylon), and Bombay.—By the Peninsular and Oriental Steam Navigation Company's Steamers, on the 11th, and 27th.

Hoopte to Hamburg.—Monday, Thursday, and Saturday, at $7\frac{1}{2}$ a.m.

Hull to Antwerp.—The Hull Steam Packet Company's Steamers (carrying Post Office letter-bags) every Saturday. Fares, 21s., and 12s. 6d. See page 344.

The Emerald Isle, every Wednesday, as soon after 4 p.m. as the tide permits.

Hull to Bremen.—The Hull Steam Packet Company's Steamers, monthly, or oftener if required. See page 344.

Hull to Christiansand & Christiania.—From the Humber Dock, 3rd June, and every alternate Friday evening.

Hull to Copenhagen and St. Petersburg.—Hull Steam Packet Company's Steamers. See page 344.

The Helen Macgregor, Wednesday Evening, June 1st.

Hull to Gothenburg.—From the Humber Dock every Friday evening.

Hull to Hamburgh.—The Hull Steam Packet Co.'s vessels (carrying the Royal Mails).—Fares —£2, £1, and 10s. See page 344.

Gee & Co.'s Hamburgh Steamers, Helen Macgregor, Rob Roy, or Queen of Scotland, June 4th, 11th, 18th, 25th, and 28th, as soon after 6 p.m. as the tide permits.

The Elbe-Humber Steam Navigation Company's Steamers—from Junction Dock Quay—every Wednesday and Saturday, as soon after 6 as the tide permits. Fares—£1, and 10s.

Hull to London.—The Hull Steam Packet Company's Steamers, every Monday, Wednesday, and Friday at or after 1 p m. Fares—6s. 6d., and 4s. See page 344.

By the General Steam Navigation Company's steamers, every Tuesday and Saturday at 1 p.m. Fares, 8s. and 5s.

Hull to Norway and Sweden—Every Friday. (See page 345.)

Hull to Rotterdam.—The Sea Gull, June 8th, 6 p.m.; 15th, 10 p.m.; 22nd, 5 p.m.; 29th, 9 p.m. Fares—23s. 6d. and 10s. 6d. Out and home, 30s.

Hull to St. Petersburg.—The Hull Steam Packet Company's Steamer. See page 344.

Gee & Co.'s Steamer, June 1st.

Interlachen to Brientz.—Twice a day in summer.

Interlachen (Neuhaus) **to Thun.**—Two or three times a day in summer

Jaffa to Alexandria in 2 days. (See page 330 & 331.)

Jersey to (Newhaven) Brighton—The Brighton Steam Packet Company's steamers, in connexion with the London, Brighton, and South Coast trains. See page 335 and Cover.

Jersey to Granville.—By the Jersey Steam Packet Company's Steamer, Rose, in connection with the Royal Mail Steamers from Southampton.—June 7th, noon; 14th, 7 a.m.; 21st, noon; 28th, 7 a.m.

Jersey (*via* Guernsey) to Plymouth—The Sir Francis Drake. Fares from Jersey, 21s., 14s., 8s.; from Guernsey, 18s., 12s., 7s.—Every Friday at noon; from Guernsey at 5 p.m.

The Brunswick (calling at Torquay). Fares, same as the Sir Francis Drake.—No Information.

Jersey & Guernsey to Southampton.—The London and South Western Royal Mail Steam Packets—From Jersey, every Monday, Wednesday, and Friday, at 7 a.m. Fares, 20s. and 13s. The Transit, every Thursday. Fares, 15s. and 10s.

Jersey to London.—(See page 338.)

Jersey to St. Malo.—The Jersey Steam Packet Company's Steamer. The Rose, June 1st, 10 a.m.; 8th, 6 a.m.; 15th, 9 a.m.; 22nd, 6 a.m.; 29th, 9 a.m.; and every Saturday at 7 a.m. Fares, 7s. 6d. and 5s. Return Tickets, available for ten days, 10s. and 8s.

Kiel to Copenhagen—Twice a-week at 12 noon, in 20 to 24 hours. Fares 12 rth. and 7 rth.

Konigsberg to Elbing—Daily.

Konigsberg to Memel—in 24 hours. Morning early. Fares, 3 th. 10 sgr., and 2 th.

Konigsberg to Pillau and Danzig—Three times a-week.

Lago di Como.—Steam-boats daily from Como to Domaso. Fares 2 fl. and 1 fl.

Lago di Garda.—Steam-boats daily from Riva, at half-past 6 a.m., to Peschiera, stopping at Garda and several other places; arrives at half-past 10, returns at 2, and arrives at Riva at 5. Fares each way, 4 Austrian lire, and 2 ditto.

Lago Maggiore.—Steam-boats daily, at 6 a.m., from Magadino to Sesto Calande and Arona. Fares to Arona, 1 fr. 20 c.

Leghorn to Bastia in 6 hours. Fares 15 fr., 12 fr., and 6 fr.

Leghorn to Civita Vecchia and Naples—By the Sardinian Royal Mail Steamers, on the 6th, 16th, and 26th of every month. See page 329.

Leghorn to Genoa and Marseilles—By the Sardinian Royal Mail Steamers, on the 8th, 18th, and 28th of every month. See page 329.

Leghorn to Liverpool (calling at Marseilles and Gibraltar)—By the Anglo-Italian Co.'s Steamers. See page 346.

Leghorn to Marseilles (*viâ* Bastia)—By the French Government Steamers, every Wednesday afternoon. Fares—60, 40, and 21 francs (meals 9 and 6 francs). See page 332.

Leith to Hamburg.—June 4th, 10 p.m.; 11th, 4 p.m.; 18th, 10 p.m.; 25th, 4 p.m.

Lemmer to Amsterdam—At 10 a.m., Tuesdays, Thursdays, and Saturdays.

Liege to Maestricht.—6½ a.m., and 3 p.m.

Liege to Namur.—6 a.m. and 12 noon. Fares, 2 frs. and 1 fr.

Lindau to Bregenz.—Wednesday and Saturday, at 11 a.m., and 1 p.m.

Lindau to Constance.—Sunday, Monday, Thursday, and Friday, at 6 a.m. (per Rorschach); Tuesday and Saturday, at 6 a.m. (per Rorschach and Friedrichshafen).

Lindau to Friedrichshafen.—Daily, at 6 a.m.; Monday, 12 noon (per Rorschach); Sunday and Saturday, 2 p.m. (per Romanshorn); Friday, 9 a.m. (direct).

Lindau to Meersburg.—Sunday, Thursday, and Friday, at 6 a.m. (per Rorschach & Constance); Monday, Tuesday, and Saturday, at 6 a.m. (per Rorschach and Friedrichshafen).

Lindau to Romanshorn.—Daily, at 6 a.m.; Saturday and Sunday, 2 p.m.; in 1½ hours.

Lindau to Rorschach.—Daily, at 6 a.m. and 2 p.m.; Saturday, 2½ p.m.; in 1¼ hours.

Lindau to Schaffhausen.—Monday and Thursday, 6 a.m.

Linz to Passau.—Every day, at 4 a.m. Fares—first class, 3fl. 3kr.; second class, 2fl. 12kr.

Linz to Ratisbon—At 7 a.m. Fares, 9 fl. and 6 fl.

Linz to Vienna—Every other day, at 7 a.m., in 12 hours. Fares, 8 fl. and 5 fl. 20 kr.

Liverpool to Ancona, Venice, and Trieste, calling at **Gibraltar, Sicily,** and **Brindisi.**—The Liverpool and Mediterranean Steam Ship Company's Screw Steamer.—No Information.

Liverpool to Alexandretta, Beyrout, and Alexandria, calling at **Gibraltar and Malta.**—No information.

Liverpool to Alexandria.—By the Teneriffe—No information.

Liverpool to Boston (calling at Halifax).—The British and North American Royal Mail Steam Ships.—Niagara, June 11th; America, June 25th Fares, £25 and £15.

Liverpool to Gibraltar, Malta, Syra, Constantinople, and Smyrna.—The Taurus, June 18th. Fares—Cabin (including provisions), to Gibraltar,, £10; to Malta, £15; to Syra, £18; to Constantinople, £20; to Smyrna, £23. For the round out and home, £30. These vessels carry Stewardesses.

Liverpool to Havre—The Balbec, Margaret, or Commodore, from Coburg Dock, June 6th, 10 a.m.; 13th, 2 p.m.; 20th, 9 a.m.; 27th, 3 p.m. Fares—25s., and 12s. 6d.

Liverpool to Italy & Sicily—The Livorno, for Genoa, Leghorn, Civita Vecchia (for Rome), Naples, Messina, and Palermo, calling at Gibraltar and Marseilles, June 7th. Fares—to Gibraltar, 10 guineas; to Marseilles, 12 guineas; to Genoa, 13 guineas; to Leghorn, 14 guineas; to Civita Vecchia, 15 guineas; to Naples, 16 guineas; to Messina, 17 guineas; to Palermo, 18 guineas; for the round, 30 guineas. See page 346.

Liverpool to Lisbon.—The Albatross, June 1st, 9 a.m. Cabin fare, £7.

Liverpool to New York.—By the British and North American Royal Mail Steam Ships.—The Asia, June 4th; Africa, June 18th. Fares, £30, (including Steward's fee,) and £20.

By the United States Mail Steamers—The Pacific, 1st June; Baltic, 15th June; Atlantic, 29th June; and every alternate Wednesday to the end of 1853. Fares, £30 and £20.

Liverpool to New York, and (via Jamaica) **to Chagres.**—The Alps will sail for Boston and New York, on July 6th. Fares, £20 and £15.

Liverpool to Oporto.—The Rattler—every fortnight.

Liverpool to Philadelphia.—The Liverpool and Philadelphia Steam Ship Company's Steamers, City of Manchester and City of Glasgow. See page 341.

Liverpool to Quebec.—The Lady Eglinton, June 16th—see page 346.

Liverpool to Rotterdam.—The Pelican—Saturday, June 4th, 8 a.m.; June 18th, 7 a.m. Cabin fare—£1 7s. 6d.

Liverpool to Sydney, calling at the **Cape of Good Hope, Melbourne, and Port Philip.**—No Information.

London to Amsterdam.—The Diana, from off the Tower, every Sunday.

London and Antwerp.—The Antwerp Company's steam ship the Baron Osy, from St. Katherine's Wharf, every Sunday at 12 noon. Sea passage 5 hours. Fares, £1 4s. and 16s. Children under 10 years, half price.—See page 344.

The General Steam Navigation Company's steamers from St. Katharine's Steam Wharf, every Thursday at 12 noon. Fares—Chief Cabin, £1 4s; Fore Cabin, 16s.

London to Bordeaux.—The Sylph, from off the Tower, once a fortnight.

London and Boulogne.—The General Steam Navigation Co.'s Steamers, from London Bridge Wharf, June 1st, 9 a.m.; 5th, noon; 8th, 1 a.m.; 12th, 4 a.m.; 15th, 6 a.m.; 19th, 11 a.m.; 22nd, 1 a.m.; 26th, 4 a.m.; 29th, 7 a.m. Fares—chief cabin, 12s.; fore cabin, 8s. Children under 10 years, half-price.

The Commercial Steam Company's steamers, City of Boulogne, or City of Paris from London Bridge Wharf, June 3rd, 11 a.m.; 7th, 11 a.m.; 10th, 3 a.m; 14th, 4 a.m.; 17th, 9 a.m.; 21st, 11 a.m.; 24th, 3 a.m.; 28th, 5 a.m. Fares—12s. and 8s. Children under 10 years, half-price.

London to Bremen.—The Adonis, from off the Tower, every 10 days.

London to Cadiz.—From Irongate Wharf, about the 10th of every month.

London to Calais.—By the General Steam Navigation Company's steamers, from London Bridge Wharf, June 1st, 9 a.m.; 4th, 11 a.m.; 8th, 2 p.m.: 11th, 4 a.m.; 15th, 7 a.m.; 18th, 10 a.m.; 22nd, 1 p.m.; 25th, 4 a.m.; 29th, 7 a.m. Fares, 12s. and 8s. Children, under 10 years, half-price.

London to Cape of Good Hope, via St. Vincent (Cape de Verds) **and Sierra Leone.**—The Royal Mail Screw Steamer. Fares to St. Vincent, 35 guineas, and 30 guineas: Sierra Leone, 40 guineas, and 35 guineas; Cape of Good Hope, 50 guineas, and 40 guineas. Steward's fee, 1 guinea. No Information.

London to Copenhagen and St. Petersburg—Neptune from the British and Foreign (late Dublin) Steam Wharf, Lower East Smithfield. About the 1st June.

London to Dunkirk, Lille, and Paris.—The City of London, or City of Rotterdam, from Irongate Wharf, June 1st, 8 a.m.; 2nd, 10 p.m.; 4th, 11 p.m.; 7th, midnight; 10th, 2 a.m.; 12th, 3 a.m.; 15th, 6 a.m.: 17th, 8 a.m.; 18th, 10 p.m.; 21st, midnight; 24th, 2 a.m.; 26th, 4 a.m., 29th, 6 a.m. Fares to Dunkirk, 10s. and 7s. Children under 10 years, half fare. Steward's Fee, 1s. To Paris, 18s. 5d. and 13s. 8d. Return Tickets, available for a month, 29s. 8d. and 22s. 5d.

London to Guernsey and Jersey.—The Foyle, from Custom House Quay Fares, Deck, 5s.; Fore Cabin, 7s. 6d.; Saloon, 10s. See page 338.

London to Hamburg—By the General Steam Navigation Co.'s Steamers from St Katherine's Wharf, June 3rd, 10 p.m.; 7th, 11 p.m.; 11th, 1 a.m.; 15th, 3 a.m.; 17th, 10 p.m.; 21st, 10 p.m.; 25th, 1 a.m.; 29th, 3 a.m. Fares, chief cabin, £2; fore cabin, £15s.

London to Harlingen—By the Magnet, from off the Tower, every Wednesday.

By the Lord John Russell, from off the Tower, every Sunday morning.

London to Havre.—By the General Steam Navigation Company's Steamers from St Katherine's Steam Wharf—June 5th, 10th, 15th, 19th, 23rd, 26th, and 30th, at 8 a.m. Fares, 12s. and 8s. Children under 10 years, half-price.

London to Hull.—The Hull Steam Packet Company's steamers, from Custom House Quay, every Tuesday, Thursday, and Saturday, at 8 a.m. Fares—6s. 6d. and 4s. See page 344.

Also by the General Steam Navigation Company's steamers, from London Bridge Wharf, every Tuesday and Friday, at 8 a.m. Fares, 8s. and 5s.

London to Madeira—From the British and Foreign Steam Wharf, Lower East Smithfield.—No Information.

London to Nieu Diep.—The Magnet, from off the Tower every Wednesday, and Diana every Sunday.

London to Ostend—By the General Steam Navigation Company's Steamers from St. Katherine's Steam Wharf—June 1st, 9 a.m.; 4th, 11 a.m.; 8th, 2 a.m.; 11th, 3 a.m.; 15th, 7 a.m.; 18th, 10 a.m.; 22nd, noon; 25th, 3 a.m.; 29th, 7 a.m. Fares—chief cabin, 15s.; fore cabin, 12s.; Children under 10 years, half price.

London to Rotterdam.—The General Steam Navigation Co.'s Steamers, from St. Katharine's Steam Wharf, every Wednesday and Saturday, at 10 a.m. Fares—30s. and 17s. 6d.

By the Netherlands Steam Packet Co.'s Steamers, The Batavier and Fyenoord, from St. Katharine's Steam Wharf. Fares—£2 2s., £1 10s., 17s. 6d., and 14s. See page 336.

By the Ceres from off the Tower, every Wednesday.

The Earl of Auckland, from off the Tower, every Sunday morning.

London to Santander.—From Irongate Wharf, about the 10th of every month.

London to Teneriffe.—From the British and Foreign Steam Wharf, Lower East Smithfield. No information.

London to Vigo.—From Irongate Wharf, about the 10th of every month.

London to the West Coast of Africa.—From the British and Foreign Steam Wharf, Lower East Smithfield.—No information.

Lowestoft to Tonning on the Eider.—The Northern Steam Packet Company's vessels, The City of Norwich, or Cumberland.—Not running at present. Fares—30s., 25s., and 10s. Children above two and under twelve, half fare. Steward's fee, 2s. 6d.

Lubeck to Copenhagen—Every Friday at 3 p.m., during the Summer.

Lubeck (Travemunde) to Kronstadt direct, every Saturday during the summer, at 3 p.m. Fares, 54 rth. and 22 rth.

Lubeck to Ystadt, Calmar, Stockholm, Revel, Kronstadt, (St. Petersburg) to Ystadt. Fares, 33 th. and 25 th. To Stockholm in 2½ to 3 days. Fares, 62 th. and 50 th. To Kronstadt. Fares, 20 duc. and 15 duc.

Ludwigshafen to Mannheim and Mayence.—Daily at 4 p.m. Fares, 2 fl. and 1 fl.

Luzern to Fluelen.—6 a.m., and 1¾ p.m.

Lyons to Avignon—in 9 hours—daily, at 6 a.m. Fares, 12f. and 8f.

Lyons to Beaucaire—in 14 hours—daily, at 4 a.m. Fares, 22f. and 17f.

Lyons to Chalons—in 8½ hours—daily, at 5, and 9 a.m. Fares, 8f. and 6f.

Lyons to Valence—in 6 hour—daily, at 4, 6 and 11 a.m. Fares, 10f. and 7f. 50c.

Maestricht to Liege.—6½ a.m , and 3 p.m.
Maestricht to Rotterdam.—Fares, 6frs. 80c,, and 4frs. 70c.
Maestricht to Venlo.—Daily.
Magadino to Sesto Calende on the Lago Maggiore, every morning at 6, calling at Baveno, the Borromean Islands and Arona.
Malta to Alexandria—in 4 days—on the 12th of every month, by her Britannic Majesty's packets. Fares—1st class, £12 10s.; 2nd class, £7 2s.; 3rd class, £3 16s., including a liberal table and every charge.—Also on the 1st of each month, by the Peninsular and Oriental Company's steamers.
Malta to Alexandria & Beyrout—7th & 27th of every month, by French Government Steamers.
Malta to Athens, Smyrna, and Constantinople—5th, 15th, and 25th of every month, by French Government steamers; also once a month by Rostand's French steamers, and likewise once a month by English screw steamers to Athens in 60 hours.
Malta to the Ionian Isles and Greece—12th & 31st of every month, by her Britannic Majesty's packets.
Malta to Marseilles.—By the Peninsular and Oriental Steam Navigation Company's Steamers, on the 9th and 23rd. These Steamers leave with the Mails dispatched *via* Marseilles from Caleutta on the 6th and 20th of the previous month.
Malta to Marseilles—On the 9th, and 23rd, and about the 11th and 26th, by the French Government steamers direct.
Malta to Sicily Italy, and Marseilles—By French Government steamers, 2nd, 12th, and 22nd of every month. Also, by the Neapolitan Company, to Syracuse, 44f., servants, 13f. To Catania, 60f., servants, 15f. To Messina, 66f., servants, 18f. To Naples, 106f., servants, 29f. To Civita Vecchia, 145f., servants, 43f. To Leghorn, 185f., servants, 51f. To Genoa, 210f., servants, 56f.
Mannheim to Heilbron.—Fares, 2 fl. 6 kr. and 1 fl. 24 kr
Marseilles to Ajaccio—French Government steamers every Friday at 9 a.m. Fares—30, 20, and 15 francs (meals 6 and 4 francs). See page 332.
Marseilles to the different port in the Mediterranean.—See Advertisement of the Marine Service of the Messageries Nationales, pages 330 and 331.
Marseilles to Algiers, Boue, Bougie, and Mihanah—The 5th, 10th, 15th, 20th 25th, and 30th of every month, at noon, to Angiers in 48 hours. Fares, 103 fr. and 80 fr.

Marseilles to Barcelona, Valencia, Alicante, Carthagena, Malaga, Gibraltar, and Cadiz—1st, 8th, 15th, and 23rd of every month. Fares, to Barcelona, 88 fr., 70 fr., and 42 fr.; to Valencia, 146 fr., 112 fr., and 55 fr.; to Alicante, 177 fr., 135 fr., and 73 fr.; to Carthagena, 205 fr., 159 fr., and 81 fr.; to Malaga, 260 fr., 192 fr., and 107 fr.; to Gibraltar, 286 fr., 205 fr., and 120 fr.; to Cadiz, 317 fr., 234 fr., and 133 fr.
Marseilles to Bastia—French Government steamers every Tuesday, in 18 hours. Fares 30 fr., 20 fr., and 15 fr.
Marseilles to Calvi and L'Ile Rousse—By the French Government Steamers, every Tuesday at 9 a m. Fares—30, 20, and 15 francs (meals 6 and 4 francs). See page 332.
Marseilles to Cette—in 11 hours--daily.

Marseilles to Genoa, Leghorn, Civita Vecchia, and Naples—By the Sardinian Royal Mail Steamers, on the 4th, 14th, and 24th of every month. See page 329.

Marseilles to Genoa, Leghorn, Civita Vecchia, Naples, Messina, & Malta.—By the Mediterranean Steam Packet Company's Steamers. See pages 330 and 331.

Marseilles to Leghorn (*vid* Bastia)—By the French Government Steamers, every Sunday at 9 a.m. Fares—60, 40, and 21 francs (meals 9 and 6 francs). See page 332.

Marseilles to Malta and Alexandria.—See the Advertisement of the Marine Service of the Messageries Nationales, pages 330 and 331.

Marseilles to Malta, Alexandria, and Beyrout.—English Steamers, well appointed in every respect, leave Malta on the 8th and 26th of each month—when the 8th and 26th fall on Sunday, they leave Marseilles one day later. Fare to Malta, £8 2s., everything included.

Marseilles to Malta, Syra, Smyrna, Metelin, the Dardanelles, Gallipoli & Constantinople.—See advertisement of the Marine Service of the Messageries Nationales, pages 330 and 331.

Marseilles to Malta.—By the Peninsular and Oriental Steam Navigation Company's Steamers, on the 10th and 26th. *Note*—These steamers arrive at Malta with the Mail, which leaves London *vid* Marseilles on the 8th and 24th of the month.

Marseilles to Nice—in 12 hours—Twice a-week. Fares, 31 fr. and 21 fr.

Marseilles to Stora and Tunis—Government packets leave on the 8th and 23rd of each month, arriving at Stora on the 12th and 27th, and at Tunis on the 15th and 30th.

Marseilles to Syra, Piræus, Salonica, Nauplia, Calamata, and Chalcis.—See Advertisement of the Marine Service of the Messageries Nationales, pages 330 and 331.

Mayence to Frankfort.—Daily.

Mayence to Ludwigshafen and Mannheim.—Daily, at 5 a.m. Fares, 2fl. and 1fl.

Mayence to Rotterdam, see page 337 and 339.

Megara to Athens—in 6½ hours.

Metz to Treves—daily, in Summer at 7.30 a.m

Namur to Dinant.—4½ p.m. Fares, 1 fr. 75 c., and 1 fr. 25 c.

Namur to Liege.—7 a.m. Fares—2 frs. and 1 fr.

Nantes to Bordeaux—Sunday, Wednes., & Friday, at 7 a.m., in 26 hours. Fares, 15frs. & 12frs.

Nantes to Brest and L'Orient—Every Sunday, in 20 hours.

Nantes to Paimbeuf.—7½ a.m. and 2 p.m Fares—first class, 1fr. 70c.; second class, 1fr. 20c.

Naples to Civita Vecchia, Leghorn, Genoa, and Marseilles—By the Sardinian Royal Mail Steamers, on the 6th, 16th, and 26th of every month. See page 329.

Naples to Malta—French Government steamers, on the 3rd, 13th, and 23d of each month.

Naples to Messina and Palermo—About twice a week.

Neuburg to Donauworth.—Daily, at 4 a.m.

Neuchatel (on Lake of) to Yverdun—7½ a.m.,—in 2½ hours. Fares, 20 batz and 15 batz.

Newcastle to Hamburgh.—The Chevy Chase, or Earl Percy.—June 7th, 3 p.m.; 14th, 6 p.m.; 21st, 3 p.m.; 28th, 4 p.m. Fares, £2 and £1. Return Tickets, £3 and £1 10s.

Newcastle to Rotterdam.—Earl Douglas—June 7th, 3 p.m.; 14th, 4 p.m.; 21st, 6 p.m.; 28th, 4 p.m. Fares, £1 10s., and 15s. There and back, £2, 5s., and £1, 2s. 6d.

Newhaven (Brighton) to Dieppe.—The Brighton Steam Packet Company's Steamers, in connection with the London, Brighton, and South Coast, and Paris, Rouen, and Dieppe Trains. See page 335, and Cover.

Newhaven (Brighton) to Jersey—The Brighton Steam Packet Company's Steamers, in connexion with the London, Brighton, and South Coast Trains. See page 335.

New York to Liverpool.—British and North American Royal Mail Steam Ships — Africa, June 1st; Arabia, June 15th. Fares, £30 and £20.

United States Mail Steamers—Atlantic, June 11th; Arctic, June 25th, & every alternate Saturday to the end of 1853.

New York to Southampton.—By the United States Mail Steam Packet Company's steamers. No information.

Nice to Genoa—By the Sardinian Royal Mail Steamers, every Monday, in 12 hours. Fares—25 and 15 francs. See page 329.

Oldenburg to Bremen.—Daily, in the morning.

Orleans to Nantes—daily, in 24 hours Fares, 29f. and 20f.

Ostend to Dover—Every evening (except Saturday), by the British and Belgian Government Mail packets, at 6.30. See page 340.

Ostend to London—The General Steam Navigation Company's Steamers. June 3rd, 11 p.m.; 7th, 11 p.m.; 10th, midnight; 14th, 9 p.m.; 17th, 10 p.m.; 21st, 11 p.m.; 24th, midnight; 28th, 8 p.m. Fares, Chief Cabin, 15s.; Fore Cabin, 12s. Children under 10, half-price.

Otranto to Corfu in 12 hours. Fares, 5 Sp. dols. (£1, 8s.)

Passau to Regensburg.—Every day, at 5 a.m. Fares—1st class, 4fl. 48kr.; 2nd class, 3fl. 27kr.

Patras to Missolonghi—in 2 or 3 hours.

Philadelphia to Liverpool.—The Liverpool and Philadelphia Steam Ship Company's steamers, City of Manchester and City of Glasgow. See page 341.

Plymouth to Calcutta.—The General Screw Steam Shipping Company's steamers (with Her Majesty's Mails). No information. Fares, in general cabin, £100; one person in a cabin for two, £125 (with a w.c., £135); two persons in a cabin for three, £240 (with a w.c., 250); two persons in a cabin for two, with a w.c., £210. Steward's fee, £2.

Plymouth to the Cape of Good Hope, and Natal, *Viâ* St. Vincent (Cape de Verds), & Ascension.—The General Screw Steam Shipping Company's steamers (with H. M. Mails). No information. Fares, to St. Vincent, in general cabin, £40; to Ascension, and the Cape, in general cabin, £58; one person in a cabin for two, £80 (with a w.c., £90); two persons in a cabin for three, £148 (with a w.c., £158); two persons in a cabin for two, with a w.c., £126. Steward's fee, £1.

Plymouth to Ceylon (Point de Galle).—The General Screw Steam Shipping Company's steamers, with Her Majesty's Mails.—No information. Fares, in general cabin, £90; one person in a cabin for two, £110 (with a w.c., £120); two persons in a cabin for three, £210 (with a w.c., £220); two persons in a cabin for two, with a w.c., £190. Steward's fee, £2.

Plymouth to Guernsey and Jersey—The Sir Francis Drake—Every Thursday at 5½ p.m. Fares to Guernsey, 18s., 12s., and 7s.; to Jersey, 21s., 14s., and 8s. Children under 10 years, half fare.

The Brunswick — average passage, 7 or 8 hours — Fares the same as by the Sir Francis Drake. Ceased running for the season.

Plymouth to Madras.—The General Screw Steam Shipping Company's Steamers, with H. M. Mails—No information. Fares—in general cabin, £92, 10s.; one person in a cabin for two, £112, 10s. (with a w.c., £122, 10s.); two persons in a cabin for three, £225 (with a w.c., £235); two persons in a cabin for two, with a w.c., £195. Steward's fee. £2.

Plymouth to Mauritius.—The General Screw Steam Shipping Company's Steamers, with H. M. Mails—No information. Fares—in general cabin, £80; one person in a cabin for two, £100 (with a w.c., £110); two persons in a cabin for three, £190—with a w.c., £200; two persons in a cabin for two, with a w.c., £170. Steward's fee, £1, 10s.

Portotorres to Genoa—By the Sardinian Royal Mail Steamers, on the 1st, 10th, and 20th of every month. Fares—55 and 35 francs (provisions included). See page 329.

Prague to Dresden, by the Elbe.—Fares, 9 fl. and 6 fl.

Ratisbon to Donauworth—Daily.

Ratisbon to Linz—at 5 a.m., in 14½ hours. Fares—12 fl. and 8 fl.

Ratisbon to Neuburg.—Daily, at 5½ a.m. Fares—

Rendsburg to Friedrichstadt and Tonning.—Mondays, Tuesdays, Thursdays & Saturdays, at 1 p.m., in 6 or 8 hours.

Rhodes to Cyprus in about two days.

Romanshorn to Bregenz.—Monday, Wednesday and Saturday, at 7 a.m.

Romanshorn to Constance.—Sunday, Monday, Thursday and Friday, at 9 a.m.

Romanshorn to Friedrichshafen.—Daily (except Thursday), 7 a.m. and 4 p.m. (direct)

Romanshorn to Lindau.—Daily, 7 a.m. (per Rorschach); 4 p.m. (direct); also on Saturdays, at 7½ a.m. (direct); Sunday, 9 a.m.

Romanshorn to Meersburg.—Sunday, Thursday and Friday, 9 a.m. (per Constance).

Romanshorn to Rorschach.—Daily, at 7 a.m.; Tuesday and Friday, at 3 p.m.

Romanshorn to Schaffhausen.—Monday and Thursday, at 9 a.m.

Rorschach to Bregenz.—Monday, 8½ a.m.; Wednesday and Saturday, 9 and 10 a.m.

Rorschach to Constance.—Sunday, Monday, Thursday, and Friday, at 8 a.m.; Tuesday and Saturday, at 9½ a.m. (per Friedrichshafen).

Rorschach to Friedrichshafen.—Daily, at 9½ a.m. and 6 p.m.

Rorschach to Lindau.—Daily, at 9 a.m. and 6 p.m.

Rorschach to Romanshorn.—Sunday, Monday, Thursday, and Friday, at 8 a.m.; Sunday, Monday, Wednesday, Thursday, and Saturday, at 2 p.m.

Rorschach to Schaffhausen.—Monday and Thursday, at 8 a.m.

Rostock to Copenhagen in 14 hours.

Rotterdam to Antwerp.—Every Wednesday and Saturday during winter, and daily in summer. Fares—13s. 4d., 10s., and 6s. 8d. (in guilders.)

Rotterdam to Bordeaux.—By the Steamers "Bordeaux" and "Gironde"—June 20th. Fares—1st cabin, 80 frs. (provisions included.)

Rotterdam to Copenhagen and St. Petersburg.—By the Steamer Gironde—June 1st July 1st, August 1st, September 1st. Fares—1st class, £6 6s.; 2nd class, £4 4s.

Rotterdam to Dunkirk—Every Saturday morning.

Rotterdam to Edinburgh.—The Ivanhoe, or Balmoral, every Saturday morning.

Rotterdam to Goole.—The Norfolk. No information. Fares—15s. and 10s. Return Tickets, £1.

Rotterdam to Havre.—By the Steamers "Rotterdam" and "Hamburg," weekly. Fares—1st class, 30 frs.; 2nd class, 18 frs. (provisions included.)

Rotterdam to Hull.—The Sea Gull (ceased running for the season). Fares—23s. 6d., and 10s. 6d

Rotterdam to Liverpool—By the Pelican or Albatross—Every Saturday morning. Cabin Fare, (including Steward's fee), £1 7s. 6d.

Rotterdam to London—By the General Steam Navigation Company's Steamers—June 1st, 7 a.m.; 4th, 9 a.m.; 8th, noon; 11th, 2 p.m.; 15th, 7 a.m; 18th, 9 a.m; 22nd, noon; 25th, 2 p.m.; 29th, 7 a.m. Fares—Chief Cabin, £1, 10s.; Fore Cabin, 17s. 6d. Children under 10, half price.

By the Netherland Steam Packet Company's steamers, Batavier and Fyenoord, see page 336.

By the Earl of Auckland—Every Wednesday morning.

Rotterdam to Maestricht.—Fares, 6frs. 8c.; and 4frs. 70c.

Rotterdam to Newcastle—see page 345.

Rotterdam to places on the Rhine, by the Dusseldorf Co.'s steamers, see pages 337 and 339.

Rotterdam to Venlo.—Daily, at 12 night.

Schaffhausen to Constance, every morning at 6.

Schaffhausen to Friedrichshafen, Lindau, Rorschach, & Romanshorn.—Tuesday and Friday, at 8 a.m.

Sesto Calende to Magadino—On Lago Maggiore, every day about 12.

Shalsund to Ystadt—weekly, in 8 to 12 hours.

Shanghai to Hong Kong, Singapore, Penang, and Calcutta.—By the Peninsular and Oriental Steam Navigation Company's Steamer, on the 4th and 19th.

Sierk to Treves—Daily at 12 noon.

Singapore to Batavia, King George's Sound, Adelaide, Port Philip, and Sydney.—By the Peninsular and Oriental Steam Navigation Company's Steamers, on the 16th.

NOTE.—These Steamers sail 16th August, and every alternate month, with the Mails which leave England on the 4th July, and 4th of every alternate month thereafter.

Sissek, by the "Theiss" and "Save," to **Semlin, Neusatz,** and **Szegedin** to **Semlin.** Fares, 14 fl., 9 fl. 20 kr. and 4 fl. 40 kr. To Neusatz, 16 fl. 30 kr., 11 fl., and 5 fl. 30 kr. To Szegedin, 21. fl. 20 kr., 14 fl. 10 kr., and 7 fl. 5 kr.

Smyrna to Constantinople—in 32 hours. Fares 30 fl., 20 fl., and 15 fl.

Smyrna to Rhodes—in 3 days.

Southampton to Aden, (Aden for Bombay) **Ceylon, Madras, Calcutta, Penang, Singapore, and Hong Kong.**—By the Peninsular and Oriental Company's Steamers—4th and 20th of every month, at 1 p.m.

Southampton to Batavia, King George's Sound, Adelaide, Port Philip, Sydney.—The Peninsular and Oriental Company's Steamers, on the 4th July, and the 4th of every alternate month thereafter, at 1 p.m.

Southampton to Calcutta—The General Screw Steam Shipping Co.'s steamer, with H. M. Mails.—The Propontis, June 13th. Fares—one passenger in general cabin, £90; one passenger occupying a double cabin, £115; ditto, with a w. c., £125; two persons occupying a treble cabin, £220; ditto, with a w. c., £230; two persons occupying a treble cabin with a w. c., £190. Steward's fee, £2. Return tickets available for a year, 10 per cent. less.

Southampton to the Cape of Good Hope and Natal.—The General Screw Steam Shipping Co.'s steamer, with Her Majesty's Mails.—The Propontis, June 13th. Fares—one passenger in general Cabin, £53; one passenger occupying a double cabin, £75; ditto with a w. c. £85; two persons occupying a treble cabin, £138; do with a w. c., £153; two persons in a double cabin with a w. c., £121. Seward's fee, £1.

Southampton to Carthagena, Grey Town, and Santa Martha.—The Royal Mail Steam Company's ships on the 2nd and 17th of every month at 2 p.m., unless these dates fall on Sunday, then on the day following. Fares—after cabin, single, £60; double, each berth, £4., Fore cabin, single, £50.; double, each berth, £35. Children of cabin passengers under 3 years, free; 3 and under 8, quarter fare; 8 and under 12, half fares. Return Tickets, available for six months, 25 per cent. less.

Southampton to Ceylon (Point de Galle)—The General Screw Steam Shipping Co.'s steamers with Her Majesty's Mails.—The Propontis, June 13th. Fares—one passenger in general cabin, £81; one passenger in a double cabin, £101; ditto, with a w. c., £111; two passengers in a treble Cabin, £192; ditto, with a w.c., £202; two passengers in a double cabin, with a w. c., £172. Steward's fee, £2.

Southampton to Chagres.—The Royal Mail Steam Packet Company's ships. On the 2nd and 17th of every Month, at 2 p.m., unless these dates fall on Sunday, and then on the day following.

Fares, After Cabin, single berth, £60; double, each berth £40; Fore Cabin, single berth, £50; double, each berth, £35. Children of Cabin passengers under 3 years free; 3 and under 8 quarter fare; 8 and under 12, half fares. Return Tickets, available for six months, 25 per cent less; a limited number, finding their own hammocks and bedding, at £20.

Southampton to Constantinople, and Smyrna.—The Peninsular and Oriental Company's Steamer, on the 27th of every month, at 1 p.m.; when the 27th falls on Sunday, the departure is at 9 a.m.

Southampton to Gibraltar, Malta, and Constantinople.—By the Peninsular and Oriental Steam Navigation Co.'s Steamer on the 27th. When the 27th falls on Sunday, the Steamers leave at 9 a.m. on that day.

Southampton to Gibraltar, Malta, and Alexandria.—By the Peninsular and Oriental Steam Navigation Co.'s Steamers on the the 4th and 20th. (60 hours are required for the journey from Alexandria to Suez.)

Southampton to Guernsey and Jersey—By the London and South Western Royal Mail Steam Packets. Every Monday, Wednesday, and Friday, at a quarter to 12 night, or immediately on the arrival of the 8½ p.m. mail train from London. Fares from London, 30s. and 20s.; from Southampton, 20s. and 13s. The Transit, every Tuesday at 5½ p.m. Fares—from London, 21s., 12s. 6d., and 10s.; from Southampton, 15s.and 10s.

Southampton to Havana.—The Royal Mail Steam Packet Company's Ship, on the 2nd of every every month, at 2 p.m.; if this date falls on Sunday, then on the day following. Fares, after cabin, single berth, £60; double, each berth, £40; fore cabin, £45; double, each berth, £35; children of Cabin Passengers under 3 years, free; 3 and under 8, quarter fare; 8 and under 12, half fare. Return Tickets, available for six months, 25 per cent less.

Southampton to Havre—calling off Portsmouth.—The London and South Western Railway Company's Steam Ships, every Monday, Wednesday, and Friday, viz.:—June 1st, 6½ p.m.; 3rd, 8½ p.m.; 6th, 10 p.m.; 8th, 10½ p.m.; 10th, midnight; 13th, 2½ p.m.; 15th, 4½ p.m.; 17th, 6½ p.m.; 20th, 9½ p.m.; 22nd, 10½ p.m.; 24th, midnight; 27th, 2½ p.m.; 29th, 4½ p.m. Fares, 18s. and 12s. Children under 2 years, free; 2 and under 12, half fare. Carriages, £3; Horses, £3; Dogs, 5s.

Southampton to Honduras,—The Royal Mail Steam Packet Company's Ship, on the 17th of each month; if this date fall on Sunday, then on the following day at 2 p.m. Fares, after cabin, single, £60; double, each berth, £40. Fore cabin, single, £45; double, each berth, £35. Children of cabin passengers under 3 years, free; 3 and under 8, quarter fare; 8 and under 12, half fare Return Tickets, available for six months, 25 per cent less.

Southampton to Jacmel (Hayti).—The Royal Mail Steam Packet Company's ships—On the 2nd and 17th of every month, at 2 p.m., unless these dates fall on Sunday, and then on the day following. Fares, after cabin, single berth, £55; double, each berth, £35. Fore cabin, £40 and £30. Children of cabin passengers under 3 years, free; 3 and under 8, quarter fare; 8 and under 12, half fare. Return Tickets, available for six months, 25 per cent. less.

Southampton to Lisbon, Madeira, the Brazils, and River Plate.—The Royal Mail Steam Packet Company's Ships on the 9th of each month, unless that date should fall on a Sunday, and then on the day following. Fares, to Madeira, after Cabin, single berth, £26; double, each berth, £18; fore cabin single berth, £21; double, each berth, £16; to Teneriffe, after cabin, £35 and £25; fore cabin, £30 and £22; to St. Vincent (Cape de Verds), after cabin, £45 and £30; fore cabin, £35 and £25; to Pernambuco, after cabin, £50 and £35; fore cabin, £45 and £30; to Bahia, after cabin, £52 and £37; fore cabin, £47 and £32; to Rio Janeiro, after cabin, £60 and £45; fore cabin, £50 and £35; to Monte Video or Buenos Ayres, after cabin, £70 and £50; fore cabin, £60 and £45. Children of cabin passengers under 3 years, free; 3 and under 8, quarter fare; 8 and under 12, half fare. Return Tickets available for six months, 25 per cent. less. A limited number to the Brazils, finding their own hammocks and bedding, at £20 each.

Southampton to Madras.—The General Screw Steam Shipping Company's Steamer, with her Majesty's Mails, The Propontis, June 13th. Fares, in general cabin, £82, 10s.; one passenger in a double cabin, £102 10s., ditto, with a w.c., £112 10s.; two passengers in a treble cabin £205, ditto, with a w.c., £215; two passengers in a double cabin with a w.c., £175. Steward's fee, £2. Return Tickets, available for a year, 10 per cent. less.

Southampton to Malta and Alexandria.—The Peninsular and Oriental Company's Steamers—On the 4th, 20th, and 27th of every month, at 1 p.m.

Southampton to Mauritius.—The General Screw Steam Ship Co.'s Steamer, with H.M. Mails—The Propontis, June 13th. Fares in general Cabin, £73; one passenger in a double Cabin, £93, ditto, with a w.c., £103; two passengers in a treble Cabin, £176, ditto, with a w.c., £186; two passengers in a double Cabin, with a w. c., £150. Steward's fee, £1 10s. Return Tickets, available for a year, 10 per cent. less.

Southampton to Nassau.—By the Royal Mail Steam Packet Company's Ships.—On the 2nd of each month, at 2 p.m., unless that date should fall on Sunday, then on the day following. Fares; After Cabin, single berth, £55; double, each berth, £40; Fore Cabin, £45 and £35. Children of Cabin passengers under three years, free; three years, and under 8 years, quarter fare; eight, and under 12, half fare. Return Tickets, available for Six Months, 25 per cent. less.

Southampton to New York.—The Humboldt, June 8th; the Hermann, June 22nd. Fares, £30 and £20, when second class are taken; second class, forward, £15. Children under ten years, half fare.

Southampton to St. Vincent (**Cape de Verds**)—The General Screw Steam Ship Company's Steamer, with Her Majesty's mails. The Propontis, June 13th. Fares, £38 10s.

Southampton to Tampico and Vera Cruz.—The Royal Mail Steam Packet Company's Steamers—On the 2nd of every month, at 2 p.m., unless that date falls on Sunday, then on the following day. Fares—after cabin, single berth, £65; double, each berth, £45; fore cabin, single berth, £50; double, each berth, £40. Children of Cabin Passengers under three years, free; three years, and under eight, quarter fare; eight, and under twelve, half fare. Return Tickets, available for six months, 25 per cent. less. A limited number, finding their own hammocks and bedding, at £20 each.

Southampton to Vigo, off Oporto, Lisbon, Cadiz, & Gibraltar. —By the Peninsular and Oriental Company's Steamers—7th, 17th, and 27th of every month, at 1 p.m. When the above dates fall on Sunday, then on Monday at 1 p.m.

Southampton to the West Indies—The Royal Mail Steam Packet Company's ships on the 2nd and 17th of every month, at 2 p.m.—if the 2nd or 17th fall on a Sunday, then on the following day. Fares to Jamaica—After cabin, single berth, £55; double, each berth, £35; fore cabin, single berth, £40; double, each berth, £30. To Antigua, Barbadoes, Carriacou, Demerara, Dominica, Granada, Guadaloupe, Martinique, Porto Rico, St. Kitts, St. Lucia, St. Thomas, St. Vincent, Tobago, and Trinadad, after cabin, £50 and £35; fore cabin, £40 and £30. Children of Cabin passengers under three years, free; three, and under eight, quarter fare; eight, and under twelve, half fare. Return Tickets available for six months, 25 per cent. less. A limited number, finding their own hammocks and bedding, at £20. each. From *West Indies* arrive at Southampton on the 2nd and 17th of each month.

Stade to Hamburg.—7¼ and 8 a.m., in 2½ hours.

Stettin to Cronstatt—Every Saturday, at 12 noon, in from 65 to 70 hours.

Stettin to Frankfurt-on-the-Oder.—Daily, at 4½ p.m.

Stettin and Swinemunde to Copenhagen—weekly. Fares, 10 rth., 6 rth. and 3 rth.

Stettin and Swinemunde to Petersburg—every fortnight, in 72 to 80 hours. Fares, 6 rth. and 40 rth.

St. Malo to Jersey.—By the Jersey Steam Packet Company's Steamer, Rose, in correspondence with the London and South Western Royal Mail Steamers.

St. Petersburgh to Hull—Gee and Company's Steamer.—The "Emperor," or "Helen Macgregor," about the 15th of each month during the season.

St. Petersburgh to Rotterdam—By the steamer Gironde, June 15th, July 15th, August 15th, September 15th. Fares—1st class, £6 6s.; 2nd class, £4 4s.

Suez to Aden, Galle (Ceylon), **Madras, and Calcutta.**—By the Peninsular and Oriental Steam Navigation Co.'s Steamers, on the 6th and 21st. The steamer of the 21st corresponds with that which leaves Southampton on the 4th.

Sydney to Port-Philip, Adelaide, King George's Sound, Batavia & Singapore. —By the Peninsular and Oriental Steam Navigation Co.'s Steamers, on the 20th. These vessels transfer mails and passengers at Singapore to the steamer for Galle of 17th. The steamers will leave Sydney on the 20th May, and 20th of every alternate month; and the mails are due in London on the 4th August, and 4th of every alternate month thereafter.

Tamise to Antwerp.—Daily, at 7½ a.m., Sundays excepted.

Thun to Neuhaus for Intertaken—two or three times a day in summer.

Tonning to Rendsburg.—Sundays, Tuesdays, Wednesdays and Fridays.

Traunsee.—In summer daily, four to five times from Gmunden to Ebensee. Fares, 40 kr. Omnibus to Ischl. Fare, 30 kr.

Treves to Coblentz—(25¾ German miles,) Mondays and Thursdays at 5 a.m., in 12 hours.

Treves to Metz—Daily in summer. Fares, 10 frs. and 8 frs.

Treves to Sierk, daily, at 6½ a.m.

Trieste to Alexandria, direct.—By the the Austrian Lloyd's Mail Steamers.—On the 10th of every month, at 8 a.m., in correspondence with the Bombay line of steamers; the 27th of every month, at 8 a.m., in correspondence with the Calcutta and Bombay line of steamers; Fares—1st cabin, £18; 2nd cabin, £12; deck fare, £8.——In addition to which, there are steamers, via **Smyrna,** every alternate Thursday.

Trieste to Ancona.—*Vide* latter.

Trieste to Dalmatia.—By the Austrian Lloyd's Mail Steamers.—every Tuesday, at 4 p.m.

Trieste to Greece.—By the Austrian Lloyd's Mail Steamers.—Every Tuesday at 4 p.m.; also, every alternate Monday, at 4 p.m. Fares to Syra, 80 fl., 60 fl., and 40 fl.; to Athens, 85 fl., 63 fl., and 42 fl.; to Athens by Patras and Isthmus of Corinth, 80 fl., 60 fl., and 40 fl.; to Patras, 65 fl., 50 fl., and 34 fl.

Trieste to Istria.—By the Austrian Lloyd's Mail Steamers.—Every Wednesday and Saturday, at 6 a.m.

Trieste to the Levant--The Austrian Lloyds' Mail Steamers—calling at Corfu, Syra, Smyrna, the Dardanelles, and Constantinople—every Friday, 4 p.m. Fares to Salonica, 90 fl., 70 fl., and 45 fl.

Trieste to Venice.—The Austrian Lloyds' Mail Steamers, daily, at 6 a.m. Average passage 8 hours. Fares, 7 fl., 5 fl., and 4 fl.

Tunis to Genoa (*viâ* Caglaire)—By the Sardinian Royal Mail Steamers, on the 20th and 30th of every month. Fares—115 and 75 francs (provisions included). See page 329.

Tunis to Stora and Marseilles—Government packets leave on the 4th and 19th, arriving at Stora on the 7th and 22nd, and at Marseilles on the 10th and 25th.

Valence to Avignon—daily, at 7 a.m., in six hours.

Vegesack to Bremen.—Daily, in the morning.

Venice to Trieste—The Austrian Lloyds' Mail Steamers—daily, at midnight. Average passage 8 hours. Fares—1st cabin, 7 guilders 20 kreutz; 2nd cabin, 5 guilders.

Venlo to Maestricht.—Daily.

Venlo to Rotterdam.—Daily, at 12 night.

Vevay to Geneva.—2 p.m., in 4 hours.

Vienna to Constantinople—By the Danube about 2 or 3 times a month from April to November inclusive in about 10 days. Fares, 94 fl., and 66 fl.

Vienna to Komorn—6 fl. 30 kr., and 4 fl. 20 kr

Vienna to Linz—Every other day, at 7 a m. Fares, 16s. and 10s. 8d.

Vienna to Pesth—daily, at 6 a.m. Fares, 7 fl. 30 kr. and 5 fl. down to Pesth, and 5 fl. 30 kr. and fl3. up from Pesth.

Vienna to Presburg—daily, at 6 a.m. Fares, 2 fl. 20 kr. and 1 fl. 30 kr.

Wertheim to Lohr, Gemunden, Karlstadt, and Wurzburg—daily, at 5.30 a.m., in 10½ hours. Fares, 1 fl. 42 kr., and 52 kr.

Wurtzburg to Karlstadt, Gemunden, Lohr, Wertheim, Miltenberg, Aschaffenburg Hanau, Offenbach, and Frankfort—daily, at 5½ a.m.; in 14 hours. Fares to Frankfurt, 6 fl. and 4 fl.

Yverdun to Neuchatel.—10½ a.m., in 2½ hours.

Zaandam to Amsterdam—Daily at 8½, 10½ a.m., 4 and 7½ p.m., in about an hour.

Zurich to Italy, by **Splugen.**—Down the Lake at 8 a.m., in connection with diligences and steamers on Lake Wallenstadt.

Zurich to Wallenstadt and Wesen,—9½ a.m. and 6¼ p.m., in 1½ hours.

FRANCE.

(WITH MAP IN SPECIAL EDITION.)

France extends from the foot of the Eastern Pyrenees in the lat. of 42·25, in almost a perpendicular line, to Dunkirk, in the department of Nord, in the lat. of 51·2 N. The superficies is equal to 128 millions of acres, 92 millions of which are in a state of cultivation, and 32 millions unproductive. The historical records of monarchical, imperial, and revolutionary France, are so well known to every reader, as to render unnecessary a lengthened notice of its history. France could boast of an unbroken dynasty up to the close of the eighteenth century, at which period the social grievances endured by the people, produced an internal convulsion, that ended in that sanguinary event called the "French Revolution." The productive industry of France, which first began to be developed after the accession of Charlemagne, is now important and extensive. The above monarch was the first to encourage industrial development, by establishing friendly relations with Persia; receiving into his dominions Italian workmen; repressing the Norman pirates; and drawing manufactures from the cloisters to spread them throughout the land. Philip Augustus also imparted a stimulus to industry, by relieving the artisans from baronial oppression; and the crusaders who returned from the Holy Land, introduced many arts until then unknown to the people, such as distilling wine, making perfumes, and manufacturing various kinds of cloth. Saint Louis seconded this movement by the enactment of salutary laws; and Charles VII. added considerable zest to it, by repressing monopolies. The silk manufactures of France were given birth to by the luxury of the court of Francis I. In the reign of Louis XIV., and under the premiership of Colbert, new roads were made into the interior, and new markets were thrown open for foreign commerce. The workmen of Venice and Flanders filled the workshops of France; and during a period of 20 years, productive industry in that country bid fair to attain the highest pinnacle of success; but in 1685 all these brilliant prospects were destroyed by the death of Colbert and the revocation of the edict of Nantes. The revolution of 1798 removed the gloom; and science coming to the aid of industry, with intelligence governing physical labour, soon gave it a strong and lasting impulse, which, since 1814, has been steady and sure. France has rapidly improved in her agricultural system of late years, and has become eminent for its cultivation of beet-root, which crop produces annually 45,484 tons of raw sugar, in the manufacture of which about 12,000 men are employed, and a capital of £2,400,000 circulated. In her Arts and Manufactures she has also been signally and successfully progressive; she has over 3,000 steam-engines at work in her workshops, and of forges and great furnaces 4,412. The digging of coal has also been much extended, but is not yet sufficient to supply the demand of 300.000 tons which are consumed annually. The iron trade in France is also flourishing; and the glass and crystal manufactured yield an annual produce of £1,200,000. Paper is also manufactured with great perfection, and the annual produce is over one million pounds sterling. The woollen, cotton, and linen manufactures, are carried on in France with great success; and in the manufacture of silk she possesses a decided superiority over any other country in Europe. As regards commerce, France cultivates an extensive inland and foreign trade, from both of which she enjoys much advantage. In France there is only one privileged Bank, that of Paris; it is under the direction of a governor, nominated by the chief of the State, at a salary of £4,000 per annum.

DIFFERENT ROUTES TO PARIS.

1. Calais Route.—LONDON TO PARIS DIRECT, *via* DOVER AND CALAIS, IN 12½ HOURS, VIZ.:—Departure from London for Dover, 8½ p.m.; arrival at Dover, 11 p.m.; departure from Dover, 11½ p.m.; arrival at Calais, 1 a.m.; departure from Calais, 2 a.m.; arrival in Paris, 9 a.m. By this direct train the luggage is only examined on the arrival in Paris. There is also a train at 8.10 a.m.; for particulars of time, &c., see pages 333 and 334. Travellers for Marseilles, on landing at Boulogne and Calais, should require their passports to be vised for that place direct, which will save them several days' delay in Paris. They will receive a provisionary passport, which will cost 2 francs. The railroad station at Calais is close to the quay where the steam-packets land their passengers, and every facility is given them for departure. The Passport-office is at the Station, and there is a good refreshment room also. The steam-boats can enter and leave Calais except for about 1½ hour before and after low water. The French mail boat leaves Dover at 2½ p.m.; the English mail boat at 11½ p.m.; and one of the steamers of the South Eastern Company every day at 11 a.m., (see pages 333 and 334.) There are also three departures from Calais for Dover, every day.

2. Boulogne Route.—London to Paris, direct, in about eleven hours, by the South Eastern Railway and their Packets from Folkestone. See special service, pages 333 and 334.

3. London to Paris, direct by London and Brighton Railway and Steamers from Newhaven to Dieppe, and from thence to Paris by Railway. For fares, times of sailings, &c., see page 335.

4. London and Calais.—By Steam direct from London Bridge Wharf, twice a week, by the General Steam Navigation Co.'s Packets. Voyage performed in about 9 hrs.—Fares 12s. & 8s.—See p. 132.

5. London and Boulogne.—By Steam direct from London Bridge Wharf, four times a week; twice by the General Steam Navigation Co.'s Packets; and twice by those of the Commercial Steam Co.'s. Voyage performed in about 9 hours.—Fare 12s. and 8s. (See page 132.)

6. By South Western Railway (*via* Southampton and Havre) the route, though interesting, is somewhat longer, owing to the sea passage to Havre. (For hours of departure from Southampton and Havre, see Alphabetical Steamers, page 137.)

By an arrangement entered into between the London and South Western, the Rouen and Havre, and Havre and Paris Railways, in conjunction with the New South Western Steam Navigation Company's boats, passengers may pay their passage-money throughout to Paris at the Waterloo Station.—First class, 22s.; second class, 17s.

7. London and Dunkirk.—By Steam direct from Irongate Wharf two or three times a week. Fares 10s. and 7s. See List of Sailings, page 132.

Money.—Accounts in France are kept by francs and centimes; the modern gold coins are pieces of 10fr., 20fr., and 40fr. The decimal system being adopted in reckoning throughout France, all calculations are made on that principle. The chief coins are *centime*, a copper coin, equivalent to about a fifth part of an English halfpenny; *sou*, of the value of 5 centimes, equal to 1 halfpenny English; silver coins, 20 centimes, a quarter of a franc or 25 centimes, a half franc, a franc equal to 9½d. English, 2 francs, 5 francs; gold coin, a *Napoleon*, equivalent to 20 francs, or 15s. 11d. of our English money. An English sovereign realizes 25 francs, varying according to the rate of exchange. English and foreign money may be exchanged to advantage at Spielmann's Office, 26, Rue Neuve Vivienne.

Passports.—See pages 19 to 22.

Explanation.—Five furlongs, or 1094 yards English, are equal to 1 kilometre; 4 kilometres are equal to 1 French league.

DESCRIPTIONS, &c., OF TOWNS.

Abbeville.—Hotels:—
D'Angleterre and La Tête de Bœuf—both good.

A fortified town, on the Boulogne and Amiens Railway, containing about 18,000 inhabitants, and situated on the river Somme, twelve miles from the beautiful and picturesque town of St. Valery sur Somme. A few miles from Crotoi the Chateau D'Eu is situated, and Treport about four miles further. The scenery is lovely, and well worthy the attention of travellers.

Conveyances.—Railway Trains to Amiens, Paris, and Boulogne, see Time Table, page 33.—Passage Boat to St. Valery, daily, and return.

Aix.—Hotels:—
Hotel de Princes.
Hotel du Mule Blanc.

An ancient city of France, formerly the capital of Provence, but now in the department of the Mouths of the Rhone. Population about 22,000; 530 English miles from Paris, and 18 from Marseilles. It was founded by Caius Sextius Calvinus, a Roman general, 128 years before the Christian era, and received the name of *Aquæ Sextiæ*, from its famous springs. It is a well-built town, and the streets are in general well paved, as well as wide and clean. The number of its gates is eight, and it has a charming public promenade, and an elegant square, one side of which is formed by what is called the Palais, an old building containing some spacious halls, formerly occupied by the Parliament and other public bodies. It has also a town-hall, and a cathedral which is not without some striking beauties. The chapel of Notre Dame de l'Esperance is much frequented by pious Catholics. The monastery of Jacobins, or Dominicans, would be one of the finest structures in Provence were it completed. The mineral springs were accidentally re-discovered in 1704, when the medals, inscriptions, &c., which were dug up, confirmed the opinions of antiquaries as to their being the springs known to the Romans.

Alais is situated in Lower Languedoc, on the Gardon; 13½ leagues north of Montpellier, and 30

English miles; population 15,884. It carries on some trade in grain, olives, oil, wine, and silk.

Amiens.—HOTELS:—

HOTEL DE FRANCE ET D'ANGLETERRE—first-rate, and highly recommended.

HOTEL DU RHIN, Place St. Denis, close to the railway—highly recommended.

HOTEL DE LONDRES AND DU NORD, opposite the railway station, and very good.

Population 47,000. 92 miles N. of Paris, on the Northern of France Railway. An ancient, handsome, fortified city on the Somme, which is navigable here for vessels of considerable burden. The town is well built, and being intersected by canals, resembles some of the Dutch cities. The ramparts, which surround it, furnish a beautiful walk, and in the neighbourhood there are delightful promenades.

OBJECTS OF ATTRACTION.—The Chateau d'Eau, the Palais de Justice, the Hotel de Ville, built by Henry IV., the Corn Market, and particularly the Cathedral, the nave of which is considered a masterpiece of architecture. This town is noted in history for the treaty of peace concluded here in 1802 between France and England.

CONVEYANCE.—Railway trains to Abbeville, Boulogne, and Paris, see page 33. — To Arras, and Belgium, several times daily.—See Time Table, pages 36, 37, and 60.

Angers.—HOTELS:—

Cheval Blanc—good.

De Londres.

Population, 33,400. 216 E. miles S. W. of Paris, on the river Sarthe, in the department of Lower Loire. It contains a public library, museum of paintings, cabinet of natural history and medicine, botanical gardens, public baths, &c. The principal articles of manufacture and commerce are linen, cotton, sugar, corn, oil, wax, honey, wine, spirits, vinegar, marble, slate, and silk handkerchiefs.

CONVEYANCE.—Railway to Tours, Orleans, and Paris, also to Nantes, see pages 46 and 47.

Angouleme.—HOTELS:—

The Post, Royal Table, Golden Cross, and Grand Stag.

This town is situated on the Charente, 275½ English miles from Paris, and 73¾ from Bourdeaux, containing a population of about 18,000. It is a very old town, built on a hill bristling with rocks, and surrounded by an extensive and beautiful terraced promenade. The air is very pure and bracing, yet does not agree with delicate constitutions. The streets are narrow, dull, and steep; but some years ago a wide and spacious road was constructed, 860 metres long, with an agreeable slope, planted the whole way with trees, from the Place of St. Peter to the road from Paris to Bourdeaux; in the centre is a column about 50 feet high, surmounted by a globe.

Angoulême has few objects worth noticing except the cathedral, re-built in 1816, topped by a gothic steeple, a theatre, a cabinet of natural and physical history, a library containing 18,000 vols. In the environs are some paper mills, which produce an excellent article. The trade consists in corn, wine, ardent spirits, hemp, flax, chestnuts, saffron, cork, and paper.

CONVEYANCE.—Railway to Libourne and Bordeaux, see page 44.

Arles.—HOTELS:—

Du Nord and Forum.

An irregularly-built town, situated on one of the embouchures of the Rhone and a station of the Marseilles and Avignon Railway, contains about 20,000 inhabitants, and is alike celebrated for the beauty of the women, which is heightened by their picturesque costume, and for its Roman remains, of which the principal is an amphitheatre in a tolerable state of preservation. Adjoining the cathedral are the cloisters, of which the Gothic arches, supported by finely-sculptured pillars, are good specimens of architectural skill in the earlier periods of Christianity.

The remains of the Roman Theatre, the Museum, where many early Christian tombstones, statues, &c., are preserved, and Les Champs Elysées, converted by the Christians into a burial-grouud, where numbers of their tombs still remain, and where is a chapel dedicated to St. Honorius. The Cathedral, a building of the 6th century, by B. Vigilius, has a splendidly ornamented doorway.

CONVEYANCES.—Railway to Marseilles, Avignon, Nimes, & Montpellier, see Time Table, pages 50 & 41.

Arras.—HOTELS:—

Hotel de l'Europe—good.

Hotel St. Paul.

Population 24,000. 134 miles N. of Paris, on the Northern of France Railway. A place of considerable trade, on the Scarpe, which divides it, and is here joined by the Crinchon. The town is built partly on an eminence, and partly on the plain, and consists of four distinct divisions—the City, the Upper Town, the Lower Town, and the Citadel, besides several suburbs. The Esplanade, in the centre, is a fine promenade. The city is on the site of Nemetocenna, the capital of the Atrebates, which Cæsar took about 50 B.C.. This part of Arras is very beautiful, formed of houses of hewn stone. The public squares are surrounded by buildings in the Gothic style. The Cathedral, dedicated to Our Lady, is a large Grecian building, finished in 1832, the ancient one having been destroyed in the great Revolution. Robespierre was born here. Manufactures of linen and tapestry.

CONVEYANCES.—Railway to Douai, Valenciennes, Mons, Braine-le-Comte, Charleroi, Namur, and Brussels, see Time Table, pages 36, 37, and 61. To Lille, Dunkirk, and Calais, page 37. To Amiens and Paris, page 35.

Auch.—HOTELS:—

De France, and De la Paix.

Population 10,700; 421 English miles from Paris 68 from Pau, and 11¼ from Montastruc. The town is built in the form of an amphitheatre on the top of a hill, watered by the river Gers; the streets are narrow and ill-built, with the exception of some in the upper quarter. The traveller will not fail to notice the church of Notre Dame, built in the reign of Clovis, with its superb portals, surmounted by two square towers; also the archbishop's palace, the statue of d'Estigny in the Place Royal, and the promenade at the extremity of the place, where one has a splendid view of the Pyrenees. A considerable trade is carried on in woollens, stuffs, thread, cotton, wines, ardent spirits, goose' feathers, and cattle.

Autun.—Hotel:—

De la Poste.

An ancient town, with about 10,500 inhabitants. It is 26 miles N.W. of Chalons-sur-Saone, and was strongly fortified by the Romans. Portions of the wall are still standing, and two of the gates are in a pretty good state of preservation. There is a Cathedral and a Museum; the neighbourhood is picturesque.

Avignon.—

The chief city of the department of the Vaucluse, on the Rhone, 77 English miles North of Marseilles, containing more than 32,000 inhabitants. It contains a great number of churches and sacred buildings. The once celebrated Church of the Franciscans, however, is now destroyed. The most attractive object, perhaps, is the old Palace of the Popes, now converted into barracks. Petrarch resided in this city several years, and here he saw his Laura, whose tomb was in the Franciscan Church. The Fountain of Vaucluse is about seventeen English miles distant from Avignon. A Calèche may be hired to take a party there and back for 22 francs, including the driver's gratuity. Besides the Fountain itself, an object of greater curiosity, the house where Petrarch resided is shown. Avignon is the centre of the Madder districts of France, the cultivation of which is very general in the neighbourhood. Near the Cathedral is a statue to the memory of the first introducer into France of that valuable root. The Pont du Gard is distant about 15 miles, and is in fine preservation. The railway from hence to Marseilles adds much to the importance of this town.

The News-room of Avignon is also well worth a visit; it contains a variety of Roman sculpture, pottery, glass, coins, &c., found from time to time in the neighbourhood, also a very good collection of modern French paintings, among which are a few by Horace Vernet, who was born there, and his father Joseph.

Conveyances.—Railway to Nimes, Arles, and Marseilles, page 50. Steamers and diligences daily to Lyons and Valence. The new road from Avignon to Geneva, by the beautiful plains of the Bresse, is now open.

Bayonne.—Hotels:—

St. Etienne, Du Commerce, and St. Martin.

Population 16,000; 492½ English miles from Paris. A well-built, opulent, and commercial town of France, in Gascony, department of the Lower Pyrenees, situated at the confluence of the Nive and Adour. These rivers here form a commodious harbour, two miles from the Bay of Biscay, and divide the city into three parts. A citadel, constructed by Vauban on an eminence in the suburb, commands both the harbour and the town, which are farther defended by small redoubts. The cathedral is a venerable structure, and the quay is a superb, much-frequented promenade; but the most beautiful part of the city is the Place de Grammont. A wooden drawbridge, which allows vessels to pass, and where a small toll is levied, connects the suburb with the town. A considerable commerce is carried on at Bayonne with Spain; French and foreign goods being given in exchange for wood, iron, fruit, gold, and silver. The hams of Bayonne have long been famous, and its wines and chocolate are exported in great quantities to the north of Europe. The military weapon called the bayonet takes its name from this city, where it was invented in the seventeenth century.

Conveyances.—Diligences to Spain; also to Bordeaux, in 25 hours.

Beauvais.—Hotel:—

Hotel d' Angleterre.

The chief town of the Department de l'Oise, having a population of about 14,000. The central portion of the town is very ancient, and is still partly enclosed by its old walls, the eastern portion of which has been removed and its place supplied by spacious boulevards tastefully planted, having many wooden houses erected about. A boulevard elegantly studded with trees, surrounds the modern quarter, built on the site of the old fortifications. Its principal object of attraction is the Cathedral; seen from a distance it appears a dull and unimposing mass, divested of architectural beauty of site and construction. The roof rests on three rows of flying buttresses, topped by double ranges of pinnacles. It was commenced in 1225, and intended to have been one of the largest and most magnificent Gothic churches in the world; but the resources were not equal to the design, and the edifice now remains as it was when half finished—a mere stupendous choir and transept. The choir is no doubt the loftiest in the world, the elevation of the roof above the pavement being 153 feet high. In the interior the effect of the beautifully painted glass is exceedingly rich.

St. Stephen's Church, a church of no great beauty, and only remarkable for its painted glass windows. Beauvais is rendered particularly remarkable on account of the siege it withstood against Charles the Bold. Though without a garrison, its citizens closed their gates against 80,000 Burgundians, and resisted his assault until succour arrived from Paris. The wives and daughters of the burghers aided nobly in defending the city. They were led on by Jeanne Hachette, who appeared upon the breach the moment of the most desperate struggles, seized a Burgundian standard that a soldier was endeavouring to plant on the ramparts, and, after hurling off the bearer, bore the standard in triumph to the town. The valour of the citizens was rewarded by Louis XI., who exempted them from all taxes, and decreed precedence to the ladies in the procession of the Augadrémme, commemorative of the raising of the siege. The banner taken by Jeanne Hachette is still preserved in the Hotel de Ville.

Besançon.—Population about 30,000. 251¼ E. miles S. E. of Paris, and 60 miles from Dijon A large, ancient, and well-built city of France situated on the river Daubs, which nearly surrounds it, dividing it into two parts, joined together by a bridge. It has six gates, and is strong both by nature and art, having been fortified by Louis XIV., and being, besides, protected by a citadel standing on a sharp rock. Its chief manufactures are arms, woollen stuffs, silk stockings, linen, calico, leather, hats, clocks, and watches. The trade consists in corn, wine, cattle, cheese, iron, pins, &c. The library here contains some rare manuscripts, and a valuable collection of coins and medals.

Blois.—HOTELS:—

D'Angleterre, de l'Europe, and la Tete-Noire.

Population about 14,500; 113 E. miles S. of Paris, on the Orleans and Tours railway. This is an ancient town of France, in the Orleannois, department of the Loire and Cher, on the Loire, which is here crossed by an elegant stone bridge. The streets are narrow, and many of the houses low. The castle stands on a rock overhanging the river. The principal public buildings are the cathedral, the Jesuits' college, (now a provincial school,) and the Episcopal palace, the terrace of which affords a very pleasing walk. The trade of the town consists in wine, brandy, corn, wood, and fruit; there are manufactures of serge, stamin, and other cloths, as well as of hardware and glass.

CONVEYANCES.—Railway to Tours; also to Orleans, see page 44.

Bordeaux.—HOTELS:—

De France, de la Paix, des Princes, de Paris, de Richelieu, and du Midi.

The second sea-port of France, on the bank of the Garonne. Population 110,000. Bordeaux has nearly 1,000 merchant vessels, and exports annually more than 100,000 hogsheads of wine, and 20,000 of French brandy, as also vinegar, dried fruits, hams, turpentine, glass, cork, honey, &c. Bordeaux possesses a chamber of commerce, a commercial court, a university, established in 1441; an academy of sciences, instituted in 1712, which has a library of more than 55,000 volumes; an academy of fine arts, founded in 1670, and renewed in 1768; a museum, a lyceum, a Linnæan society, an institution for the education of the deaf and dumb, a school of trade and navigation, &c. Bordeaux is the ancient *Burdigala* of the Romans.

OBJECTS OF ATTRACTION.—The cathedral and churches; the grand theatre; the Grand Hospital; the Courts of Justice; Hotel de Ville; the Exchange; the Custom House; the bridge over the Gironde; the Barracks; the New Gaol; the Lunatic Asylum; the Military Hospital; the Slaughter-house; the Museum; the Gallery of Paintings; the Public Library; the Botanical Gardens, &c. &c.

ENGLISH BANKERS.—Barton and Guestur, Quay des Chartrons, 35; Natl. Johnston and Sons, Rue Foy, 21.

BRITISH CHAPEL.—Service, morning and evening; chaplains, the Rev. Thomas and John Quin and the Rev. Colin Campbell.

CONVEYANCES.—Railway to Libourne and Angouleme, see page 45. Steamers to Agen, via Langon, La Reole, Marmande, Tonneins, and Thouars, every morning at 4 o'clock. Fares, 10 frs. and 7 frs. To Nantes, six times a month, in 26 hours. Fares 26 frs., 20 frs., and 15 frs. There is a railway to Teste.

Boulogne-Sur-Mer.—HOTELS:—

HOTEL DE L'EUROPE, close to the railway and steam packet stations, highly recommended.

HOTEL BRIGHTON—very good, and in a fine situation.

The BEDFORD HOTEL is an excellent house, and is strongly recommended.

MRS. LEA'S BOARDING HOUSE is good, and highly spoken of.

One of the chief ports of France, in the Channel, 29 miles from Folkestone, 112 miles distant from London, and 140 from Paris. As a watering-place it is much resorted to by parties chiefly from England. It is situated at the mouth of the Liane, in the department of the Pas de Calais. The town is divided into "the high and low town," connected by means of a steep street called La Grande Rue. The favourite locality of the English is in the modern part called the Tintelleries, which lies in a valley towards the north. The railway station is on the opposite side of the river, near to the Place Bellevue. Boulogne is of great antiquity: 2000 years ago the Roman emperor Caligula visited it, and ordered a lighthouse to be constructed, some small remains of which are still in existence. The present population is about 31,000. The objects of interest are numerous and worthy of notice. We can only find space to enumerate some of them. The nucleus of the New Town was a small oratory erected by St. Waast, in the 6th century, which, under one of the sons of Clovis, was expanded into an abbey. The Lower Town is modern and regularly built. It extends to the glacis of the Citadel, erected under Louis XIV. by the celebrated Vauban. Without entering into details:—The Church of St. Nicholas, in the Place de Alton, has very frequently festivals, in the celebration of which the traveller might find something to interest him; the church, however, has no pretensions to architectural elegance. The Hotel de Ville is interesting, as having been built on the ancient site of the Palace of the Counts of Boulogne. The hall contains several portraits of distinguished persons.

The Museum in the Grand Rue is well worth visiting, and contains some paintings deserving of notice, besides many curiosities. The Baths is a splendid establishment. The Belfry, behind the Hotel de Ville, is one of the most ancient buildings in Boulogne; the tower, 140 feet high, should be ascended, from which a magnificent view of the town and its beautiful environs may be obtained. The chief architectural attraction of Boulogne, however, is the Monument, an exceedingly handsome structure; it was intended to commemorate the invasion of England by Napoleon. The first stone was laid in November, 1804, by Marshal Soult. It was finished by Louis XVIII., to commemorate so says the inscription placed on the keystone, "his happy return to his country" in 1814: there is a colossal bronze statue of Napoleon at the top. The ramparts surrounding the high town are laid out as a promenade; from their commanding elevation a fine view of the country is obtained. There is also another promenade on the outside of the walls of the old town, shaded with trees, known as the Promenade des Petits Arbres. The Jetty is, however, the favourite walk, extending about 2000 feet from the end of the quay, and commanding a fine view of the harbour and part of the coast; it presents, on a fine summer evening, with its numerous visitors, a very gay and lively appearance. To the literary man we would recommend a visit to the Public Library; it is situated in the Grand Rue, and is open for the free admission of the public every day from 10 till 3, except Tuesdays and Thursdays; but by application to the librarian, permission to inspect it may be obtained at almost any time. The environs of Boulogne are exceedingly interesting, and among the places of celebrity we may point out the following:—Mont St. Etienne, a quaint little village, about five miles distant from Boulogne; Mont Outreau, within a short distance, will interest the visitor by its antiquarian remains, intimately associated with historical events; Mont Lambert, from the summit of which is obtained a rare and beautiful view, diversified with hill and dale, sea and land, and far in the distance the white cliffs of "rare old England." There are some remains still existing of the Roman road, some fourteen miles from Boulogne. To the geologist the singular range of stones near the village of Ferques, about the same distance, present something worthy of notice. The Valley of Denacre is the resort of the inhabitants to celebrate their fêtes. The Castle of Cregni is surroundid by neatly laid-out gardens, and are much resorted to by pleasure parties. The Chateau de Colembert, as also the Chateau de la Cocherie, celebrated for its gardens, will well repay a visit. The Botanic Gardens, at Mount Pelé, fourteen miles distant, are open to the public twice a week.

PROTESTANT FRENCH CHAPEL.—Service by the Rev. — Poulain. ENGLISH EPISCOPAL CHAPELS.—Upper Town, Rev. George Brooks; Lower Town, Rev. W. K. Groves; Rue Royale, Rev. J. Bewsher; Rue de la Lampe, Rev. C. J. Furlong. WESLEYAN CHAPEL.—Rev. — Chapman. SCOTCH CHAPEL.—Rev. — Stewart.

MONEY CHANGERS AND HOUSE AGENTS.—Messrs. Packman and Pay, 28, Quai des Paquebots, give the highest rate of exchange; and we recommend the firm for the civility and politeness invariably shown to strangers. A list of new arrivals and residents is kept at this office. Messrs. Packman and Pay are also Licensed Custom-house Agents, and are always in attendance on the arrival of the steam boats, to offer their services for clearing travellers luggage, horses and carriages, or goods. Parties having deposited money at the Custom-house on carriages, horses, or plate, can have the same returned at this office, the day before they leave for England.

BRITISH LIBRARY AND READING ROOM.—Merridew, 60, Rue de l'Ecu.

CONVEYANCES.—Railway Trains to Abbeville, Amiens, and Paris, see Time Table, page 33; steamers to Folkestone daily, according to tide, in two hours, see page 128; to London, twice a week, see page 127, in from 12 to 14 hours.

Bourges.—HOTELS:—

De la Poste, Du Bœut-Couronne, de la Boule d'Or, du Cheval-Blanc, and de France.

Population 21,000; 146¾ E. miles S. of Paris, and a principal station on the Orleans and Nevers railway. This is a large town, in the department of the Cher, and stands on a rising ground between the rivers Evre and Auron, which here unite their streams. The only public buildings of note are the fine gothic cathedral, the great tower, formerly used as a state prison, and the Hotel de Ville, formerly the house of Jacques Cœur. It has manufactures of silk, woollen, and cotton stuffs, as well as of stockings, caps, and other articles of clothing. The chief objects of trade are corn, wine, cattle, wool, hemp, and cloth.

CONVEYANCES.—Railway to Vierzon and Orleans see page 43.

Brest.—HOTELS:—

De Provence, Grand Monarque, de Nantes, and Tour d'Argent.

One of the principal seaports and arsenals of France. Population 33,000. No English banker, physician, or clergyman. French Protestant service twice on Sunday. Principal bankers, H. Guilhem; Sh. Boëlle; —— Monge.

CONVEYANCES.—Malle Poste daily to Paris, in 42 hours, at 10 a.m. during summer, 7 a.m. during winter. Fare 103.80.—Diligences to Paris every day about noon, through Tours; from Tours by railway. Fares: Coupé, 70 fr.; Interieur, 60 fr.; Rotonde, 50 fr.; Banquette, 60 fr.

Breteuil.—HOTEL:—

Hotel d'Angleterre.

Population 2,400. Situated on the river Noye; and a station of the Great Northern Railway. The air is salubrious, but the town, for the most part, is ill built. There are some fine edifices particularly the Abbey of St. Marie, and the church of St. Maur. The station is at some distance from the town, in the village of Baconei, where the road from Montdidier crosses the line. Near Breteuil a great number of antiquities have been found. At this station there are conveyances to Amale, Eu, Beauvais, Crèvecœur, and Montdidier.

Caen.—Population 44,000. 139½ English miles W. of Paris. A large, well-built, and populous town, in the department of Calvadas. It contains 12 parish churches, several hospitals, a public library containing 25,000 volumes, public garden, cabinet of natural history, &c. Caen is situated at the influx of the small river Odon into the larger stream of the Orne. An active trade is carried on in linen, serges, lace, stockings, caps, cider, dye-stuffs, skins, &c.

CONVEYANCE.—Steamers from Havre in 4 hours.

Calais.—HOTELS.:—

HOTEL QUILLACQ, a first-rate and comfortable house

HOTEL DESSIN, one of the oldest and most respectable establishments on the continent; it is highly and deservedly recommended.

Calais is situated in the department of the Pas de Calais, opposite to Dover. It is surrounded by a moat and wall, and defended by a very large citadel. The streets are wide and regular. Its form is that of an oblong square, with the longer side parallel to the sea; and has two gates, one towards the sea, the other towards the land. Most of the houses are built of brick. The harbour is defended by several small forts, and consist of a large quay, terminated by two long wooden piers, which stretch into the sea. Its inhabitants are much engaged in the herring and cod fishery, and carry on a considerable traffic in Dutch spirits. Good drinking water is very scarce, and living is very high.

Population about 13,000, with a commodious harbour. The railway, being now open from hence to Lille, enables passengers to proceed direct by rail to Brussels and all parts of Belgium; also to Douai and Paris (see Time Tables, pages 34 and 35). Travellers proceeding to Belgium or Germany will avoid much trouble by informing the authorities of their place of destination and by what train they intend to proceed; their luggage will then be duly marked for transit, and they will avoid the annoyance of a Custom-house search in France. Travellers with a Foreign passport are subject to a *visa*, the expense of which is two francs. The British Minister's passport is an exception, no charge being made for the *visa*.

Cassel.—A neat little town, on the line of railway from Dunkirk to Lille. It stands on a considerable eminence in the midst of a vast plain, and commands a fine view of Flanders and Belgium, with a horizon of immense extent. Distance from Dunkirk 19¼ English miles.

Cette.—Population about 15,000. An important seaport town of France, 17 miles west of Montpellier, being the chief place for the export of the productions of Languedoc. M. Balard, a Member of the Institute, has here an establishment for the production of the sulphates of soda, magnesia, and potash, by the direct method. By the excellent process adopted, he is enabled to procure these salts by evaporation from sea-water, at a trifling expense, thus saving the duty at present paid to Sicily for the sulphur, and to America for the potash.

CONVEYANCES.—Steam-boats daily to Marseilles, (which sometimes stop at Agde). To Cannes and Grasse every three days; to Oran every ten days; and to Marseillan once a day. Railroad to Montpellier, see page 48.

Chalons-sur-Marne.—HOTELS:—

Du Palais Royal, de la Ville-de-Paris, de la Ville-de-Nancy, and de la Croix d'Or.

Population about 13,000; 107½ English miles from Paris, and 25 from Rheims, on the Paris and Strasburg line of Railway. A large town in Champagne, on the Marne, which divides it into three parts, and is crossed by several bridges, one of which, erected in 1787, is admired for its boldness and elegance. There are a handsome town-house, a gothic cathedral, built in the thirteenth century, eleven parish churches, three secularized abbeys, several convents, and a fine public walk.

CONVEYANCES.—Railway to Paris, Vitry, Bar-le-Duc, Commercy, and Strasburg, see page 52.

Chalon-sur-Saone.—HOTEL:—

HOTEL DU PARC; this Hotel being first-rate, we strongly recommend it.

HOTEL DES DILIGENCES, a very good house, and well situated.

A neat town, 239 English miles south-east of Paris, containing about 12,500 inhabitants. It is pleasantly situated on the banks of the Saone, with a broad quay, which is used as a promenade. Five steamers descend the Saone daily to Lyons, making the transit in six or seven hours. The banks of the river are, for the most part, flat, but well cultivated. Beyond Macon, celebrated for its wine, the scenery is extremely pleasing, and increases in interest on approaching Lyons. The road, which runs in great part parallel with the river, passes over Mont d'Or, so called from the rich colour of its vineyards in autumn, and from the summit of which a charming and extensive prospect may be enjoyed of the rich plains of Burgundy on the one side, of the Lyonnois on the other, and of the snow-clad Alps of Dauphiné in the distance. The descent to Lyons is through a succession of meadow-lands, orchards, and vineyards. At about 25 English miles from the town (part by railway), are the extensive iron works, called Le Creusot, the glass bottle works of Blanzy and of Epinac, Collieries, &c. The town has large beet-root sugar factories, breweries, flour and seed crushing mills, iron steam-ship building yards, &c.

CONVEYANCES.—Railway trains to Dijon and Paris several times a day, see page 55. Steamers also to Lyons daily, see page 127. Chalons to Lyons is performed by diligence when the Saone is not navigable, occupying much longer time. Diligence to Genoa every other day.

Chantilly.—HOTEL:—

Hotel de Bourbon.

Population 2500. The beautiful domain of Chantilly, one of the most remarkable ornaments of France, was enriched and adorned under a long succession of wealthy and noble proprietors; but owes most of its splendour to the Princes of Condé. It possesses an European celebrity, and attracts a never-ceasing crowd of visitors.

Chartres.—Population 15,000. 57¼ English miles W. of Paris. An ancient town in the department of the Eure and Loire, on the Eure, which divides it into two parts, across which there is a bridge planned by the celebrated Vauban. Most of the streets are narrow and crowded, but some of the comparatively modern buildings are very neat. The cathedral is one of the finest in France.

CONVEYANCE.—Rail to Versailles and Paris, and also to La Loupe, see page 49.

Chateauroux (Chateau of Raoul de Dols.)—HOTELS:—

De la Promenade, du Dauphin, and de St. Catherine.

Population 14,000; 166¼ English miles from Paris. This town is situated on the Indre, and has a large woollen manufactory. Near this place is found some of the best iron in France.

CONVEYANCES.—Railway to Vierzon, Bourges, and Orleans, see page 43.

Clermont Ferrand.—HOTELS:—

De l'Ecu, de la Paix, and des Messageries.

Capital town of, and situated in the department of the Puy de Dôme, between two small rivers. It has rather a gloomy appearance. The cathedral, which is in the centre of the town, is one of the finest in France, though in an imperfect state. Here are also a cabinet of natural history, a public library, a botanic garden, a neat theatre, and several hospitals. There are four public squares. In one of them is an obelisk, erected by the town to the memory of General Desaix, who was born in the neighbourhood. Its trade is considerable, and it has manufactures of paper, hats, leather, pottery, linen, serge, ratteens, druggets, and other woollen stuffs. It is 78 miles west of Lyons, and contains a population of 33,000 The geologist or the admirer of mountain scenery will be amply repaid the trouble of ascending the mountain called the Puy de Dôme. The singular strata of the district will also interest. Clermont is the name of several other small towns in France.

Corbeil.—Population 4,000: 18¾ miles south of Paris; in the department of Seine and Oise; seated on the Seine, at the influx of the Juino.

Creil.—Population 1600. Noted for its manufactures of earthenware. Communication hence by steam-boats with Compeigne and Soissons.

CONVEYANCES.—Railway to St. Quentin, Chauny, Noyon, Compiegne, Pontoise, and Paris, see page 35. To Amiens, Douai, Valenciennes, Brussels, Cologne, Dunkirk, and Calais see pages 36 and 37.

Dieppe.—HOTELS:—

GOSSER'S HOTEL DE L'EUROPE, a first-rate old established house.

A watering place of France, easy of access from London, Brighton, and Paris. Population 17,000. The town itself is neat; the principal street (Grande Rue), running through to the port, contains the best hotels, and in the season has a cheerful and animated appearance. The port is spacious, and is commanded by a citadel and castle. The baths here, as at the other sea and mineral bathing places in France, are under the superintendence of a physician inspector. This is the nearest sea-bathing establishment to Paris—distant about 125 miles.

ENGLISH PHYSICIANS.—Dr. Tabois, & Dr. Moriaty.

BANKERS.—Osmont Dufaur and Co., D. Destandes, Vincent Sanchon, Ferdinand Segrial. MONEY CHANGERS.—M. Segrial, Delaport, & Reville Bremer.

CONVEYANCES.—Railway to Rouen, Havre, Paris, &c, see Time Tables, pages 38 and 39. Steamers to Newhaven during the season, see page 128.

Dijon.—HOTEL:—

HOTEL DU PARC, a first-rate house, and highly recommended.

Population 27,000; 196 E. miles S. of Paris, and a principal station on the Paris and Lyons railway. An ancient and well-built city, the chief town in the department of the Côte d'Or, and formerly the capital of Burgundy, situate between the river. Ouche and Suzon and on the canal of Burgogne. The streets are regular and well-paved, and the houses in general neat and commodious. The principal square, called Place d' Armes, or Place Royale, is in the form of a horse shoe, and in front of the ancient palace of the Dukes of Burgundy, also used as the house of assembly of the ancient parliament of Burgundy. It has four churches, remarkable for the richness of their architectural decorations, and also a university, deservedly celebrated. A French Protestant Chapel; service by the Rev. Mr. Pertuzon. At the gates of the town is the Chartreuse, where some of the members of the ducal family are interred. It has a few small manufacturies of woollens, cotton, and silk.

The Museum here, which is in the ancient ducal palace, should not be omitted to be visited by any traveller. It contains two most splendid marble tombs of Philippe le Hardi, and Jean his son, Duke of Burgundy, which is reckoned quite a *chef d-œuvre;* also a gallery of paintings, and especially a variety of curious and beautiful ecclesiastical relics. The cathedral will also repay a visit.

PRINCIPAL BANKERS.—Messrs. Dunoyer and Co.; Marion & Co.

The town has a rich and extensive museum, a picture gallery, a cabinet of natural history, botanic gardens, a fine theatre, and a public park designed by Le Notre, under Louis XIV. The renowned wines of Chambertin, Vougeot, Romanee, and Beaune, are grown in the immediate neighbourhood.

CONVEYANCES—Railway to Tonnerre and Paris, see page 55. Railway to Chalons, see page 54, thence by Steamer to Lyons, see page 127. Diligence to and from Geneva, see page 250.

Douai.—HOTEL:—

Hotel de Flandre.

Douai—Population 18,000—of very remote origin; conveniently situated for its extensive trade on the river Scarpe, which communicates with the canal of Sensée. The railway station here is quite within the walls, and the line twice crosses the fortifications. It is pleasant to see in this city of industry and the arts the triumph of the modern ideas of free and peaceful communication over the feudal and exclusive military spirit. The ramparts afford very agreeable promenades. Conveyance hence to Cambrai, Bouchen, and Hénin-Lietaud. The Northern Railway, at this point, divides into two branches, the one proceeding to join the Belgian railways by Lille and Mouscron, the other by Valenciennes and Quiverain to Brussels and Cologne.

CONVEYANCES.—Railway to Arras, Amiens, and Paris, see Time Tables, page 35. To Valenciennes, Mons, and Brussels, page 37. To Lille, Dunkirk, and Calais, page 37. To Lille, Mouscron, Courtray, and Ghent, pages 37 and 59.

Dunkirk.—(*Dunkerque* in French)—HOTEL:—

Hotel de Flandre.

(The Church on the Downs, so called from sandbanks on the coast), a seaport of French Flanders, It is in general well built; the houses are of white brick, but seldom exceed two stories in height. It is a place of considerable trade in corn, fish, and home manufactures; also in colonial produce. One of its chief inconveniences is a scarcity of fresh water The barracks are extensive and elegant; the churches are less remarkable for architecture than for the paintings they contain. Large sums were expended by the French government on its harbour and docks; these it was agreed to demolish at the peace of Utrecht; but their dilapidation was never complied with; and at the peace of 1783 they were abandoned. Dunkirk has since been the unmolested resort of armed ships during war, and of smuggling vessels at all times. The English army, under the Duke of York, in 1793, sustained a considerable defeat before Dunkirk. Population 25,000; 25 English miles from Calais. The services of the Protestant Church in this town are performed by the Rev. —— Thompson.

CONVEYANCES.—By means of the branch of the Northern Railway, now open to this town, Calais, Lille, Ostend, Valenciennes, Brussels, Antwerp, Paris, &c., are easily accessible.

Enghien-les-Bains.—A village 7 miles N. of Paris, situated in the valley of Montmorency, with an establishment of baths. The large lake is surrounded by plantations and picturesque villas. The opening of the railway has added considerably to the importance of this village, which is one of the prettiest places near Paris, and attracts good society. The town of Montmorency, which is close at hand, will be found of great interest. The church, situated on an eminence above the lake of Enghien, is a master-piece of Gothic architecture of the 14th century. The Chateau de Luxembourg, built in the reign of Louis XIV., presents some magnificent prospects. The Hermitage, in which J. J. Rousseau lived, and the house called Mont-Louis, to which he afterwards removed, are much visited.

CONVEYANCES.—Railway to Paris, see pages 35 and 37. To Pontoise, Amiens, Douai, Brussels, Lille, Dunkirk, and Calais, see pages 36 and 37.

Epernay.—HOTELS:—

De l'Europe, de l'Ecu, and du Buisson.

Population 5,500; 88¾ E. miles E. of Paris, and 14 from Rheims, on the Paris and Strasburg Railway. This is a town in Champagne, noted for its wine. It is situated in the department of Marne, on the river Marne.

CONVEYANCES.—Railway to Paris, see pages 43 and 53.

Fontainbleau.—HOTEL:—

Hotel de l'Aigle Noir.

May be reached by rail, or per steam from the Quay de Greve, Paris.

An important and populous town, situated in the centre of a forest, from whence it derives its name. It was but a little hamlet in the days of Louis VII., but owing to the royal favours showered upon it, it soon rose to be a place of importance. Its chief object of attraction is its Château Royal, a palace whose historical interest cannot fail to recommend it to the visiter. The building itself is not at all imposing as an edifice, and time, decay, and ill-usage, have considerably dimmed its splendours. The buildings, decorations, &c., have been much improved by the late Louis Philippe. The château is entered by the "Cour de Cheval Blanc," called after a plaster cast of the equestrian statue of Marcus Aurelius at Rome, which Catherine de Medici caused to be placed in it. It was in this court, near the foot of the Horse-shoe Stairs, that Napoleon bade adieu to the remnant of the Old Guard previous to his departure for Elba, in 1814. The event has been commemorated by the well-known painting, "Les Adieux de Fontainbleau." The apartments first entered are those recently fitted up for the late Duc d' Orleans at the time of his marriage. Catherine de Medici, and Ann of Austria originally occupied them, and hence the title Reines Mères applied to the apartments. They afterwards were occupied by Pius VII. when Napoleon's prisoner. The gorgeous grandeur of the ceiling will attract notice. The Chapelle de la Trinite in the palace is eminently attractive, though its paintings are now faded and worn. In it, in the year 1725, Louis XV. was married to Maria Leckzinska; the marriage of the late Duc d' Orleans was also celebrated there in 1837. The Galerie de François I. is very attractive. In it are some specimens of the Italian style of painting. Its roof is of walnut-wood, and its sides and walls are magnificently panelled, stuccoed, and beautified with scroll-work, carvings, tapestries, and devices, among which the Salamander of Francis I. is often repeated. In it there are fourteen pictures in fresco, the work of Rossi Maitre Roux, a Florentine, and his scholars. Primacticcio is said to have designed the ornaments seen all round; and one of Danæ is also attributed to him.

The paintings have all been chosen for their allegorical reference to the life of Francis. Within the Cabinet de Travail is to be seen the mahogany table at which Napoleon signed his abdication in 1814. His bedroom remains almost the same as he left it. The Salle de Trône, and the Boudoir de la Reine, fitted up for the unfortunate Maria Antoinette by Louis X., who is said to have wrought with his own hand the metal window bolts seen therein. The Galerie di Diania, a long corridor of the 17th century, decorated with paintings, is also worth notice, as is also the Galerie des Cerfs, built in 1657, and painfully interesting, as being the scene of the assassination of the Italian Marquis Monaldischi, by three wretches engaged for the service by Christina of Sweden, then a guest of Louis XIII., resident in the Chateau. This gallery is not shown. The Salons de reception—one called de Francois I. contains gobelins tapestries, and a mantelpiece ornamented with Sevres china; the second is called after Louis XIII., he being born in it. The Salle de St. Louis, having over the fire-place a high relief of Henry IV. on horseback. The Salle des Gardes is beautifully ornamented with paintings on the walls in the style of the Loggie of Raphael. Two figures of Strength and Peace, with a bust of Henry VI. in the centre, support the mantle-piece. The Salle de Balle, or Galerie de Henri II., is one of the finest things in the Palace. The Chapelle St. Saturnin and the Porte Dorée are also worth notice. The gardens, though not remarkable, will repay a visit. Fonutenbleau is remarkable as having been the birthplace of Philippe le Belle; the place where Francis I., in 1539, entertained Charles V.; as the refuge of Henrietta Maria, when Charles I.'s cause became hopeless; here a so the Maréchal de Biron, betrayed by his agent Mafin, was arrested and sent to the Bastile for conspiracy against Henry IV.; the great Condé died here in 1686; and here the revocation of the Edict of Nantes was signed by Louis XIV. in 1685.

Granville.—HOTELS:—

Trois Couronnes, Hotel du Nord, & Hotel de Paris.

A small seaport town. Population 8000. Much resorted to for sea-bathing.

BRITISH CONSUL.—John Turnbull.

BANKERS.—Coussel and Co.; Jouet and Gannier.

CONVEYANCES.—Steam-packet to Jersey once a week, during the summer season. Diligences.—For Paris three times daily; for Avranches, St. Malo, Dinian, Nantes, and Bordeaux, daily.

Grenoble.—HOTELS:—

Des Ambassadeurs and des Trois Dauphins.

This town contains a population of 29,000, situated about 70 miles south of Lyons, in the department of the Isere, and is divided by the river Isere into two parts, which are joined by two bridges. Grenoble, though not a fine town, has several spacious squares; the streets are tolerably wide and regular, but the houses ill-built, and part of the town is exposed to inundation from the Isere. It is surrounded with ramparts. The public buildings are the ancient Hotel de Lesdiguieres, now the town house, with its spacious gardens, used as a public promenade; the court-house, an elegant gothic building, situate in a square; the cathedral, a heavy edifice, also in the gothic style; a university a great provincial school, an academy of arts and sciences, societies of medicine and agriculture, an artillery school, and on an eminence, near the middle of the town, stand the ruins of a once strong citadel, called the bastile. The town also contains a library of 70,000 volumes, a museum, a botanical garden, a cabinet of natural history, and a small cabinet of antiquities. The principal manufactures are gloves, cotton articles, and different kinds of liquors.

Havre.—HOTEL:—

WHEELER'S HOTEL—a comfortable and highly respectable house, strongly recommended to travellers.

Havre is one of the most important maritime towns of France, at the mouth of the Seine, a prosperous packet station, with ready access to the capital by the river and railway. Population 30,000. English church service on Sundays. The American Church, Rue de la Paix, is very generally attended by English and Americans, Rev. E. E. Adams, chaplain. Service 11 a.m. and 7 p.m.

WINE AND COMMISSION MERCHANT.—Mr. L. Hyman, the Agent of the Royal Western Yacht Club of England, forwards Goods to all parts of the world.

CONVEYANCES.—Numerous steamers coastwise, inland, and to foreign ports, see "Packets on Foreign Stations." Railway trains several times a day to Paris, Rouen, Dieppe, Mantes, and Poissy, see Time Tables, pages 38 and 39.

Hieres.—(Isles d'Hyers.)—HOTEL:—

The newly-built hotel, DES ISLES D'OR, is one of the finest establishments in Europe. Mr. Brun, the landlord, is well known for his urbanity of manners and attention to his visitors—the prices are also moderate. Hieres, about four miles from Toulon, and is built on a hill in the form of an amphitheatre. The climate is milder, and reputed more salubrious even than that of Nice. Hieres is a delightful place—the country of flowers, vineyards, fruit, orange and palm trees; and Nature has omitted nothing to render it one of the most delightful winter residences, from its being free from rain and sheltered from the north winds. It contains a population of 4,246 souls.

Honfleur.—HOTEL:—

Hotel d'Angleterre.

A seaport town, situated at the mouth of the Seine, containing about 10,000 or 11,000 inhabitans. The river is seven miles wide; steam-boats keep up a daily communication between Honfleur and the opposite coast, on which is situated Havre. Though the situation of the town is very pleasant, yet it is dirty, and utterly barren of interest for the traveller. A magnificent view of the Seine can be had from the church of Notre Dame de Grace to the west above the town.

Lille.—HOTEL:—

HOTEL DE L'EUROPE—the first in the town, and highly recommended.

Population 64,000. A very fine city, and one of the most considerable of France. It communicates by canal with Sensée and the sea; and the river Deûle, which runs through it, is navigable. The fortifications are reckoned Vauban's chef d'œuvres. The streets are wide, and well formed; the houses mostly in the modern taste and well built.

OBJECTS OF ATTRACTION.—The Bourse, the Theatre, the Palace of Richebourg, built in 1430, now the Hotel de Ville, the church of St. Maurice, the Hospital, founded in 1739, the Museum, the Bridge, the Concert Hall, the Gaol, the Botanical Garden, the Triumphal Arch, erected in 1782, in honor of Louis XIV., and the Column raised in memory of the siege sustained by the city in 1792.

CONVEYANCES.—Railway to Arras, Amiens, and Paris, see Time Table, pages 35 and 36.—To Mouscron, Courtray, Ghent, and Brussels, page 59. Also to Dunkirk and Calais, page 37.

Limoges.—HOTELS:—

De l'Aigle-d'Argent, de la Boule-d'Or, du Perigord, and des Pyramides.

Population 28,000; 256 E. miles from Paris, 255 from Pau, and 66 from Poitiers. It is situated in the department of Upper Vienne, of which it is the capital, on the Vienne. Limoges contains several fine squares and fountains, also a cathedral, said to have been built by the English. The town carries on a brisk trade, and its manufactures are of cotton and woollen cloths, glass, porcelain, pottery paper, &c.

Lyons.—HOTELS:—

HOTEL DE L'UNIVERS, near the Post-Office and Steam-boats, is a first-class Hotel, and highly spoken of. Mr. Glover is English.

HOTEL DE L'EUROPE, highly respectable, and commanding a delightful view of the most picturesque scenery, including the Fourviers Hills, and the Saone.

The journey from Paris to Chalons by Railway occupies from 10 to 11 hours. The traveller should sleep at Chalons, from which place Steamers start for Lyons every morning, from 7 to 10 a.m., according to the season. Diligences from Lyons to Geneva in 13 hours every day, morning and evening. Lyons to Avignon by Steamboat in 12 hours every day. The journey from Avignon to Marseilles by Railway occupies about 3 hours Diligences from Lyons to Aix les Bains every day in about 11 hours.

Lyons is the chief manufacturing city of France. Population, including suburbs, 200,000. Well situated at the junction of the two great rivers the Saône and the Rhone. The Rhone is crossed by 8 bridges, and the Saône by 9. Lyons contains many public squares, among which is that of Louis le Grand, or Bellecour, one of the most magnificent in Europe, adorned with beautiful lime-trees and an equestrian statue of Louis XIV. The interior of the city presents the aspect of an old town, with narrow and dark streets, and houses seven or eight stories high, solidly built of stone: the rivers are lined with wharfs, and resound with the hum of mills and water-works. This city contains one of the finest libraries in France consisting of nearly 100,000 volumes, and scientific and benevolent institutions are numerous. The commerce and manufactures of Lyons are very extensive, consisting chiefly of silks, woollens, and cotton stuffs, shawls, crape, gold and silver lace, &c Within the walls of the city there are upwards of 7,000 establishments for the manufacture of silk, employing nearly 20,000 looms. No traveller should omit ascending the height of Fouvier, on account of the magnificent view to be obtained therefrom. On a clear day, the Alps and Mount Blanc can be seen in the distance It is 326 miles S.E. of Paris, and 190 N.W. of Marseilles. For climate, &c., see Bradshaw's Companion to the Continent, (price 7s. 6d.)

The descent of the Saone from Chalons to Lyons, and of the Rhone from the latter town, in many respects resemble that of the Rhine. In fine weather it may be doubted whether the scenery is not equal in beauty and variety. The cities on the Rhone are, generally speaking, of very remote antiquity, much more so than those on the Rhine. The historical associations are, at least, of equal interest, whether considered with reference to the period of classical antiquity, of that of the feudal ages, or of the more recent one of the French revolution. Ruins of ancient castles and fortresses frequently occur, whilst the *bon vivant* is gratified by observing, as he passes, the vineyards which produce Côte Roti, Hermitage, and St. Peray.

Objects of Attraction.—The Cathedral, the Churches, the Hotel de Ville, the Museum, the Place Bellecour, the numerous bridges, the Observatory, from which Mont Blanc may be distinctly seen on a fine evening, &c.

Malle Poste.—To Paris, by Chalons and Auxerre, in 33½ hours, at 9 p.m. Fare, 84 fr. 35 c.—To Mulhouse, in 23 hours, at 11 a.m. Fare 64 fr. 30 c.—To Marseilles, in 20 hours, at noon. Fare, 60 fr. 55 c. —To Bordeaux, in 38 hours, at 2 p.m. Fare 97 fr. 10 c.—To Geneva, in 13 hours, at 6 a.m. and 4 p.m.

Conveyances.—Lyons to Paris in 18 hours.—By Steam from Lyons to Chalons; from thence to Paris by Railway, see page 55. Railroad to St. Etienne, see Time Table, page 40. Courier for Turin every morning at six; in 15 hours to Chambery; 39 hours to Turin; and by correspondence, in 72 hours for Genoa and Milan, and 116 hours to Florence, including stoppages. Fares—to Turin, coupé, 50 francs; interieur, 42 francs; bauguette and rotonda, 36 francs; change carriages, for sledges, near summit of Mont Cenis in winter. Steamers to Valence in 6 hours, at 11 a.m., and to Avignon in 12 hours—start about 4 a.m.; all daily, and very uncomfortable—the entire deck being covered with heavy merchandise.

Diligences.—Bonafous' Diligence to Turin daily, at 8 p.m., without changing carriages, by the Mont Cenis. Fares: Coupè 66 francs, Interior 63 francs. Diligence to Chambery at 6 a.m. and 9½ a.m. Diligences to Paris in 38 hours, by the Bourbonnais, Orleans, and the Railroad, at 8 p.m.; by Moulins, Orleans, and the Railroad, at Noon; by Burgundy, Macon, and Chalon, at 10 p.m.; by Amay and the Steamers to Chalons, at 8 and 11 a.m.—Diligence to Marseilles, Toulon, and Avignon, at 7 a.m.; Nismes and Valence at noon; to Grenoble at 6 a.m. and 5 p.m.: to Geneva at 6½ p.m.; to Bordeaux, in 60 hours, at 6¾ a.m.; to Mulhouse, in 36 hours, at 7 p.m.

Marseilles.—Hotels.—

Hotel des Colonies, a first-rate house, and highly recommended.

Hotel Bristol.—very comfortable, and the host intelligent and obliging.

Hotel des Ambassadeurs, pleasantly situated, very comfortable, and moderate.

Chief port of the Mediterranean, and Steam Packet station for Italy, the Peninsula, and the East. Population about 190,000. The ports of Marseilles afford accommodation to nearly 2,000 vessels, of all classes. The city was founded 600 years before the Christian era, by a colony of Phœcians. Marseilles was ravaged by a dreadful plague in the year 1720; and, during the temporary triumph of the Jacobin party, at the time of the revolution, this city was the scene of the most frightful and tumultuous massacres. Marseilles is considered by many as the finest city of France, and the various approaches to it are lined with trees and well built houses: the city itself is composed of the old and new towns, the latter portion especially being elegantly built. The manufactures consist chiefly of tobacco, printed goods, hats, glass, porcelain, china, soap, coral, &c. It is 224 miles south by east of Lyons, 300 east-south-east of Bordeaux, and 550 from Paris.

Conveyances.—Railway to Avignon, see page 50. Her Britannic Majesty's packets leave Marseilles for Malta (Ionian Isles and India), on the 8th and 26th of each month, The voyage occupies about 60 hours. The Anglo Italian Co.'s Screw Steamers join from Italy on the 15th-17th each month, and proceed to Liverpool, calling at Gibraltar on the 17th-20th. Office, 12, rue jeune Anacharsis. French Government steamers leave Marseilles *en route* for Greece, Egypt, and Turkey, on the 9th, 19th, and 29th, calling at the ports of Italy and Sicily, and arrive at Malta on the 5th, 15th, and 25th; packets also leave Marseilles for Malta *direct* on the 1st, 11th, and 21st, arriving on the 5th, 15th, and 25th; and also on the 2nd, and 22nd, *en route* to Egypt and Syria, arriving on the 6th, and 26th of each month. Rostand's French Company's Steamers arrive at Malta once a-month from Marseilles and Leghorn—dates uncertain. For the Sailings of Steamers from this Port, see the Alphabetical List, p. 133 & 134. The United French, Sardinian, and Neapolitan Steamers, start for Geneva, Leghorn, Civitta Vecchia, and Naples, every other evening about 4 o'clock.—They are all managed by English Engineers, but the Neapolitan boats are cleanest and best; the fare, however, is very high.—They go from Port at night arriving early in the morning, and remaining to take in goods till about 4 p.m. —a most inconvenient arrangement. The usual time of voyage is as follows:—From Marseilles to Genoa, 18 hours; Genoa to Leghorn, 10 hours; Leghorn to Civita Vecchia, 12 hours; Civita Vecchia, to Naples, 14 hours. Enquiries should be made, before paying for your Passage, as to whether any quarantine exists in the Italian Ports, otherwise you may find yourself shut up in the vessel for 6 days. London by way of Paris may now be reached in 49 hrs. Fare, £6. Steamboats to Cette 3 times a week. Fares, 18 frs. and 13 frs. There is also a railway. Steamers to Barcelona (67 French leagues), Valencia. (114 French leagues), Alicante, Carthagena, Malaga, Gibraltar, and Cadiz, see page 133.

English Church, 100, Rue Silvabelle. Service performed by the Rev. M. John Mayers; in the morning at half-past 10, and in the afternoon at half-past three.

Melun.—Hotels.—

Du Commerce, de France, du Grand Monarque.

Population 6,700; 27½ English miles from Paris, on the Paris and Lyons Railway, capital of the department of Seine and Marne, on the Seine. It has a trade with Paris in corn, meal, wine, and cheese.

Metz.—Hotels.—

Du Commerce, de la Croix-d'Or, de l'Europe, du Grand St. Christophe, du Lion-d'Or, de la Ville-de-Londres, de la Ville-de-Thionville.

Population 44,500; 198¾ English miles E. of Paris. The ancient Divodurum, a strongly fortified town, capital of the department of the Moselle, at the confluence of the Seille and Moselle. The circumference of the whole town and fortifications is between three and four miles; the breadth is nearly equal to its length. Two quarters, the east and north, are insulated by intersections of the rivers; the latter are bordered in some parts with quays, and crossed by a number of small bridges. The public squares are small; the principal are the Place d'Armes, near the centre of the town, the Place de la Comedie, and the Place Mazelle. The esplanade is a fine walk, planted with trees, and separating the town from the old citadel. The principal public buildings are the governor's residence on the esplanade; the cathedral, forming one of the sides of the Place d'Armes, which is much admired; the theatre, the town-hall, the residence of the intendant, the hospitals, and a number of churches and religious houses, and likewise extensive barracks. The chief establishments for education are a college royal, or provincial school, and an artillery and engineer's school. There is an extensive public library. The manufactures are cotton, linen, muslin, gauze, fustian, chintz, calico, and different kinds of woollens. The leather trade is considerable.

Conveyances.—Railway to Nancy and Bexbach, see pages 52 and 53.

Montbrison.—Hotels.—

Du Centre, du Midi, du Nord.

Population 6,300; 320 English miles S. of Paris. It is the capital of the department of the Loire, on the Vigez.

Conveyances.—Railway to St. Etienne, Lyons, and Roanne, see page 40.

Montpellier.—A very ancient city, the capital of the department of the Herault, containing a population of about 41,000. It is highly celebrated for the salubrity of its air, aud for its extensive and interesting prospects, which on the one hand embrace the Pyrenees, and on the other the Alps, and is much visited by invalids from foreign countries. The town is situated on a declivity between the rivers Masson and Lez, about five miles from the sea, with which it communicates by means of the Canal de Grave. Some of the streets are steep and irregular, in the interior of the town they are winding, narrow, and dark, the most regular streets and best houses being in the suburbs. The public promenade, called Peyroun, is one of the finest in Europe; an equestrian statue of Louis XIV. was erected in it in 1829. Montpellier is the seat of a celebrated university, famous for its school of medicine: the anatomical theatre alone is capable of accommodating about 2000 persons. The town also contains a botanical garden, museum, cabinet of natural history and anatomy, an observatory, and a public library of 35,000 volumes and many valuable manuscripts. The principal manufactures are in verdigris, wool, wine, aqua vitæ, woollen carpets, fustians, and silk stockings. It is 375 miles distant from Paris, and 115 miles west of Marseilles by rail.

Conveyances.—Railway to Nimes, see page 41.

Mulhausen.—Hotels.—

De l'Ange, du Bouc, de la Cigogne, de la Couronne, de Paris, du Lion Rouge, du Sauvage.

Population 20,500; 295½ English miles from Paris, and 19 E. miles from Bale, situated between two arms of the river Ille, and on the canal of Monsieur. It is well built, and contains some fine edifices, of which the chief are the church of St. Stephen, belonging to the Reformed church, the Catholic church, the town-hall, the college, hospital, &c. There are numerous manufactures of printed silks, cottons, ribbons, wool and cotton yarns, laces, watchwork, sugar from beet-root, and chemical products. Among the manufacturing establishments, that of the brothers Koechlin is remarkable. The trade consists of corn, wines, ardent spirits, and its native manufactures.

Conveyances.—Railway to Bale and Strasburg, see page 77.

Nancy.—Hotels.—

Hotel de L'Europe.—The best, strongly recommended.

Population 36,000; 220 E. miles from Paris, and 93 from Strasbourg by rail. It is the capital of the department of Meurthe, on the river of that name. It is divided into the old and new towns; the latter being by far the larger as well as more handsome of the two. The gates of Nancy are particularly fine, and are more like triumphal arches than the mere entrance to a city. The royal square, built by Stanislaus, is surrounded by an iron railing, and by some of the finest buildings in the town. The streets of the old town are narrow and crooked; but it contains two elegant squares. Besides the old and new town, Nancy has two well built suburbs. Of its public edifices the chief are the elegant town-hall, the cathedral, a large modern edifice, the church of

St. Sebastian, the church of Notre Dame, and the theatre, all situated in the new town; the palais de justice, the exchange, the arsenal, the barracks, and churches. Nancy has no manufactures of consequence, with the exception of linen and woollen.

CONVEYANCES.—Railway to Paris, and Strasburg, see page 53; to Metz, St. Avold, Forbach, and Bexbach, see pages 52 and 53.

Nantes.—HOTEL.—

Hotel de France.

One of the largest and richest commercial cities in France, capital of the department of Lower Loire, seated on the Loire. It was formerly the residence of the Dukes of Bretagne, who built a strong castle on the side of the river, which still exists. The cathedral contains the tombs of the ancient dukes, besides which there are a collegiate church and 11 parish churches. The bridges over the Loire, in which are some islands, are almost a league in length. The city contains 20 squares, 17 churches, and many handsome buildings, together with scientific and literary establishments. The suburbs exceed the city in extent. A great quantity of salt is made in the territory of Nantes, both at the bay of Bourgneuf and in the salt marshes of Guerande and Croisic. Large vessels can come no higher than Paimbœuf, which is 12 miles from Nantes; but its quays are crowded with those of less burden than 200 tons. It has some building-yards for Steam vessels, and also large naval store-houses. The inhabitants in 1836 were computed at 75,150. Present population 80,000, principally engaged in fishing, and in the manufacture of cotton goods, glass, &c. It was here that Henry IV. promulgated the famous edict, in 1598, in favour of the Protestants, which was revoked by Louis XIV. in 1685. It is 269 miles W. of Paris by rail, and 58 from Rennes.

CONVEYANCES. — Railway to Paris, see page 47. Steamboats to Angers, Tours, Orleans, and Bordeaux in 14 hours. Fares, 20 frs.

Nevers.—HOTELS.—

De France, du Lion d'Or, de la Belle-Image.

Population 17,185; 189 English miles S. of Paris, and 116 from Lyons. This is a considerable but ill built town on the Loire, with narrow and winding streets. The cavalry barracks is a large building. The Loire is here crossed by a fine bridge of 20 arches. The town contains manufactures of iron wares of massive character, glass, plate, earthenware, and enamel.

CONVEYANCES.—Railway to Bourges and Orleans, see pages 42 and 43.

Nismes.—Nismes is the capital of the department of Gard, and a bishop's see. Here are numerous monuments of antiquity, of which the amphitheatre, built by the Romans, is the principal. There are likewise the ruins of a temple of Diana, and a grand tower. It is much and deservedly celebrated for the number and interest of its antiquarian remains. The Maison Quarrée, or the Square House, is one of the finest pieces of architecture of the Corinthian order in the world. Here are manufactures of silk, stockings, cloth, leather, &c., and a considerable trade in silk, corn, dried fruits, oil, and wine. It is seated in a plain, abounding in wine and oil; population, 44,500, 79 miles N. of Marseilles.

Besides the antiquities mentioned, the public gardens, in which the remains of the temple of Diana are situated, and from which the Tour Magne is reached, are worthy of notice for their extent and arrangement. A band plays here on Sunday afternoons. The view from the Tour Magne is one of the most extensive in France. In the "Grande Place" there is a magnificent marble fountain by the great sculptor Pradier, which cost 250,000 francs, and is probably the finest in France; when viewed by moonlight the effect is admirable.

CONVEYANCES.—Railroad to Alais, Beaucaire, Montpellier, and Cette, see pages 48 and 41. Malles Postes for Paris at 9 p.m.; for Lyons, at 9 a.m.

Noyon.—HOTELS.—

Du Chevalet, du Nord, and la Tete-Noire.

Population 6,500; 77⅝ English miles from Paris, and 28¼ from St. Quentin, on the Great Northern of France Railway. It has manufactures of linen, leather, hats and stockings.

CONVEYANCES.—Railway to Paris and St. Quentin, see pages 35 and 36.

Orleans.—HOTEL.—

Hotel des Trois Empereurs.

The capital of the department of Loiret, is situated on the right bank of the Loire, 76 miles south-west of Paris, and 71 north-west of Tours, and contains about 46,000 inhabitants. Many of the houses are built of wood, and the streets are very irregular. Under the sons of Clovis it was the capital of a kingdom. In 1428 it stood a memorable siege against the English, which was raised by the celebrated Joan of Arc, called the Maid of Orleans. It is now considered one of the largest and most pleasant cities of France, and a bishop's see. The principal public buildings are the fine cathedral, town-house, court of Justice, mint, and theatre. The trade consists in stockings, sheep skins, wine, brandy, corn, grocery, and particularly sugar, which is brought raw from Nantes and Rochelle. The faubourg of Paris is of a prodigious length, and that of Olivet, on the left side of the Loire, has a communication with the city by a bridge of nine arches. Near the city is a forest, containing 94,000 acres planted with oak & other valuable trees.

OBJECTS OF ATTRACTION.—The Botanic Garden and Museum; Cathedral, with its two lofty towers, upwards of 250 feet in height, and regarded as the finest Gothic edifice in France; Monument of the Maid of Orleans; Belfry Tower; the Hotel de Ville, &c. The Public Library contains about 30,000 volumes.

CONVEYANCES.—Railway to Etampes, Epernay, and Paris, see page 43.—To Blois, Tours, Angers, and Nantes, pages 44 and 46.—To Vierzon, Issoudon Chateauroux, Bourges, and Nevers, see page 42.

Paris (*With Map in Special Edition.*)—HOTELS—There are a great many hotels in Paris, some magnificent in appearance, but dear and uncomfortable; others cheap, but questionable. The following are carefully selected as deserving our recommendation:

HOTEL BEDFORD, 11, Place de l'Arcade, near the Madeleine, excellent in every respect.

GRAND HOTEL D'ANGLETERRE, 10, Rue des Filles St. Thomas, between the Rue Richelieu, and the Place de la Bourse, a first-rate house, and highly recommended.

HOTEL WAGRAM—good, very clean, and well conducted.

Hotel Victoria—very good, comfortable, and reasonable.

Hotel de Normandie, 240, Rue St. Honoré, good and moderate.

Hotel de Lille et Albion, 323, Rue St. Honoré, a well-conducted, good house.

Hotel Folkestone, 9, Rue Castellane, very comfortable, and charges moderate.

Hotel des Etrangers 3, Rue Vivienne, very comfortable and reasonable.

Grand Hotel de Lyon, 12, Rue des Filles St. Thomas, with a large frontage in the Rue Richelieu, very comfortable, and charges moderate.

Brown's Albion Hotel and Commercial Tavern, 30, Faubourg St. Honore, is respectable and well conducted.

Restaurant—British Tavern, (Tavern Britannique), Rue Richelieu, 104, near the Boulevard. This restaurant commands a greater assemblage of Persons of Distinction of all nations than is to be found in any other restaurant in Paris. The elegance of the establishment, its excellent cellar of wines, and its pure English cookery, constitute its recommendation.

We recommend to such of our readers as may be desirous of attaining that desideratum, a pure French pronunciation, Mr. Emile, an energetic little gentleman of some five and thirty years of age, with a highly cultivated voice, and, so far as we can judge, of solid professional attainments. His assistance will be found especially valuable to medical men who purpose walking the Paris hospitals, and to military candidates preparing for the Sandhurst examination. He speaks English well. His address is No. 320, Rue St. Honoré, Paris.

Teachers of Modern Languages in Paris.—In answer to the frequent enquiries addressed to us on this subject, we insert the following list, furnished by our Paris Correspondent, to whom the gentlemen, whose morality and ability he guarantees, are personally known:—Spanish, Mr. Florez; Italian, Dr. Monti; German, M. Eichendoff; Portuguese, Mr. S. de Vasco; Russian, Mr. Kednoff; Turkish and Arabic, Mr. Beuna; Modern Greek, Mr. Posri. Cards may be had at Messrs. Galignani's Library; and of Mr. Hogg, Chemist to the British Embassy, 2, Rue Castiglione, three doors from the Rue Rivoli.

Paris is situated on the Seine, in the same manner as London on the Thames, the river running from east to west; its circumference is 15 English miles. Population about 1,200,000; number of houses about 50,000. Viewed from any eminence, the form of the city is nearly circular. Paris contains about 1,350 streets, 204 covered avenues, 30 boulevards, 99 public establishments, 58 barriers, 28 bridges, and 38 quays. The city is divided into 12 parishes, each containing its church, and two or three chapels of ease. There are two islands formed in the Seine—one called the Palace Island, the other the Island of St. Louis. The numbers of the houses in the streets parallel with the river are arranged according to the course of the stream, and in the streets at right angles with the Seine the numbers begin at the end nearest the river: in both cases the numbers on the right side of the street being even, and on the left odd. The locality of the Chaussée d'Antin, and the suburb St. Germain are the handsomest, the former containing the residences of the bankers, the latter most of the nobility, ambassadors and consuls.

The most lively streets are the Rue St. Honoré, Vivienne, Richelieu, Neuve-des-Petits-Champs, &c. The streets, squares, and bridges are lighted by upwards of 6,600 gas lamps, and the city is fortified with a strong wall, taking in all the town, as far as St. Denis and Mont Valerien. On passing the barrier, the passport is asked for, but immediately returned, and the luggage examined. Commissioners (or porters) ply at every railway station or coach office, who will convey the traveller and his luggage to any of the hotels, at a charge of 1 franc. Having arrived at the hotel, it is necessary to arrange the charge for lodging from one mid-day to another.

The Second Great European Peace Congress was held in Paris on the 22nd, 23rd, and 24th of Aug., 1849. About 700 delegates from Britain, America, and various parts of the European Continent, assembled on this occasion in the Salle de Sainte Cecile, and unanimously passed resolutions condemnatory of recourse to arms, as being a usage condemned alike by religion, morality, reason, and humanity—recommending international arbitration as a practical substitute—urging the necessity of a general disarmament—calling on the friends of peace to prepare the minds of all people for a Congress and a High Court of Nations—and condemning all loans and taxes for wars of ambition and conquest. The full results of this Congress are yet in the future; but the promoters of it express their devout gratitude to the source of all good for the evident blessing that has attended their labours. To the English and American delegates and visitors, numbering about 650, every kindness and facility was cheerfully granted by the French Government. They went from London in a body by special trains and steamers, and were courteously permitted to proceed direct to Paris without passports, and without examination of baggage either at Boulogne or Paris. All the public places and exhibitions were free on presentation of their Peace Congress admission cards; and the Minister of Foreign Affairs, (M. de Tocqueville,) invited the whole company to a *soirée* at his official residence, on the evening of the 25th. On the afternoon and evening of the 27th, the splendid waterworks at Versailles and St. Cloud "played in honour of the foreign visitors," the latter being gorgeously illuminated. We believe it is the only occasion on which these works have been specially exhibited, except "in honour of sovereigns." This peaceful act of "foreign intervention" will, we trust, not be soon forgotten by the French; and we are sure the English and Americans will long retain a lively sense of the "courteous and cordial welcome with which they were everywhere received." —[See notice of First Congress under "Brussels," page 168.]

Post-office.—The General Post-office is situated in the Rues Jean-Jacques Rousseau and Coq-Heron.

There are also 16 auxiliary Bureaux, called Bureaux d'Arrondissement, and 268 smaller offices, called Boites aux Lettres. The charge for a letter within Paris, not exceeding the weight allowed, is three sous. The system of postage stamps is now adopted in France, at a universal rate of 25 centimes, or 2½d. Letters for England, foreign countries, and the departments, are in time at the boites till half-past three o'clock; at the bureaux d'arrondissement, till four; and at the general post-office till five, except on Sundays and holidays, when the Exchange is shut —the general post-office then closes at three o'clock. Letters may be directed to a traveller, *Poste Restante*, Paris, or any other town where he intends to go. The *Poste Restante* is open daily from 8 a.m. to 7 p.m., Sundays excepted, when it closes at 5 p.m.

CONVEYANCES.—*Diligences.*—These vehicles convey eighteen passengers, and contain four compartments. The *Coupé* holds three, and is the dearest but most comfortable place; the *Interieur* six; the *Rotonde* six, and the *Banquette* three. The latter being on the top of the vehicle is chiefly to be recommended in summer, as it affords an opportunity of seeing the surrounding country. 50lb. of luggage is allowed to each passenger; all above is charged by weight. Some of these vehicles. are much accelerated in speed, travelling 9 miles an hour.

Omnibuses.—In addition to cabriolets, fiacres, voitures, and similar vehicles that ply in the streets of Paris, numerous sets of Omnibuses are established. Their uniform price for all distances is *six sous*, and as each of them corresponds with a similar one that intersects their line, a person may, without any extra charge, change from one to another, merely by asking for a ticket called *cachet de correspondance.*

Hackney Coach and Cabriolet Fares.—In Paris Hackney Coach and Cab Fares are regulated by the *course*, or by time, at the option of the traveller, who is required to signify to the driver before starting which he selects. A Course is any given distance within the limits of Paris, whether long or short, and *without* stoppage. There is a better class of public vehicles called Voitures de Remise; these must be looked for at certain stations, and not on the public stands; the carriages are cleaner, and the cattle somewhat better.

Mail Coaches leave the General Post-office, Paris, Rue Jean-Jacques Rousseau, daily, at 6 p.m., for the conveyance of letters and passengers. Each Malle Poste conveys from one to four passengers. Places must be booked some time beforehand, the full fare paid at the time and the passport produced. Each passenger is allowed 25 kilogrammes of luggage; but provided the excess is not very great, and the packages are within the size allowed, great indulgence is shown. No trunk or box is admitted in the malles postes exceeding the following dimensions:—length, 27 inches; breadth, 15 inches; depth, 13 inches.

Railway Routes from Paris.—To Pontoise, Creil, Compiegne, Noyon, Chauny, St. Quentin, Clermont, Breteuil, Amiens, Abbeville, Boulogne, and Arras, see pages 36 and 33; to Douai, Valenciennes, Mons, Brussels, Mouseron (for Ghent,) Dunkirk, and Calais see pages 37 and 59; to Poissy, Mantes, Rouen, Havre, and Dieppe, see pages 39 and 33; to Epernay, Etampes, Orleans Blois ,Tours, Angers ,and Nantes, see pages 42, 44, and 46; to Choisy and Corbeil, see page 48; to Versailles (left bank,) Rambouillet, and Chartres, page 49; to Versailles (right bank,) page 49: to St. Germain, page 51, and to Sceaux, page 51; Meaux, Epernay, Chalon-sur-Marne, Bar-le-Duc, Commercy, Nancy, and Strasburgh, see pages 52 and 53; from Nancy to Metz, St. Avold, and Forbach, see page 51; to Montereau, Nogent, and Troyes, pages 46 and 47; to Fontainebleau, Montereau, Joigny, Tonnerre, Dijon, and Chalon-sur-Soane, see pages 54 and 55.

PLACES OF WORSHIP.—The British Episcopal Church. Rue d'Agesseau, Faubourg St. Honoré, service 11½ and 3 during winter months, and half-past during summer. Holy Communion on Christmas day, Easter day, Ascension day, Whitsunday, Trinity Sunday, and the first Sunday of every month; Episcopal Chapel, Avenue Marbeuf, service 11 and 3; French Independents, 44, Rue de Provence, service in English and French; Wesleyan Chapel, 21, Rue Royal St. Honoré, service in French and English; British and American Church, Rue Chauchat, near the Italian Boulevard, service every Sunday afternoon, at four o'clock. Friends Meeting-room and Library, at R. Develay's Boarding House, 19, Rue Neuve des Mathurin, (near the Madeleine,) ground floor. Apply to the porter.

PRINCIPAL SQUARES AND PLACES.—Place Royale, or des Vosges, a square with 39 regularly built houses, ornamented with an equestrian statue of Louis XIII., and four fountains.-The Place des Victoires, containing in the centre the equestrian statue of Louis XIV. The Place Vendome, near the Tuilleries, in the midst of the most beautiful part of the city, and ornamented with a splendid pillar called the Vendome Pillar, 134 feet high and 12 feet in diameter, surmounted on its summit by the statue of Napoleon.—Place de la Bastile, in the centre of which is the memorable pillar of July 1830.—Place de la Concorde, or Louis XV., the most beautifully situated of all the squares, in the form of an octagon, tastefully ornamented with statues, fountains, and an obelisk of red granite (the Obelisk of Luxor,) a curious memorial of the ancient grandeur of Egypt. It is one of the two pillars that stood at the gate of the Temple of Thebes (the modern Luxor,) where it was erected by Sesostris, King of Egypt, 1,550 years before the birth of Christ, and whence it was brought to Paris at great expense. It is formed from a single block of red syenite, 72 feet in height, and covered from its base to the summit with hieroglyphics. It was here that the unfortunate Louis XVI was guillotined; and between January 1793, and May 1795, upwards of 2,800 other victims of the revolution.—Place du Chatelet, adorned in its centre with a basin of water, out of which towers a pillar, surmounted by the gilt statue of Victory, and four symbolical figures adorn the basement of the column. The Place Dauphine, on the west point of the City Island, ornamented by a monumental fountain, in honour of General Desaix. Marché des Innocens, in the Rue St. Denis, a large square adorned with a splendid fountain.—Place Richelieu, in the Rue Richelieu, likewise containing a fountain, erected in 1835. —Place de la Bourse, brilliant and lively, surrounding the Exchange, with elegant shops and taverns, &c.

Bridges.—The Bridge d'Austerlitz, joining the Jardin des Plantes, and the suburb St. Antoine.—The Bridge de Damiette, a suspension bridge from the Quai St Bernard to the Quay Bethune, branching on to the Island of St. Louis.—The Bridge de Constantine (which, as well as the last-mentioned, is only for foot passengers,) joins the Quai d'Anjou with the Quai Celestins; charge for crossing, 5 cents.—The Bridge Marie, over the right arm of the Seine, from the Quai des Ormes to the Island St Louis.—The Bridge de la Tournelle, over the left arm of the Seine, leading from the Island St. Louis to the Quai St. Bernard.—The Bridge de l'Archevéché, on the Quai de la Tournelle, opposite the Rue des Bernardins, built 1827.—Bridge (formerly Louis Philippe) a beautiful suspension bridge, built in 1834, leading from the Quai de la Cité to the Port au Blé.—The Bridge d'Arcole (for foot passengers only) joins the Rue d'Arcole to the Place of the Hotel de Ville, and is supported by a single buttress formed in the bed of the river.—The Bridge de la Cité joins the west point of the St. Louis Island with the city, a beautiful suspension bridge, ornamented at each end with a gothic gate, to which the chains that support the bridge are attached.—The Bridge Notre Dame, over the right arm of the Seine, between the Rue de la Planche Mibray and the Rue de la Cité, resting on seven arches. The Exchange Bridge, over the right arm of the Seine, leading from the Place du Chatelet to the Palais de Justice.—The Pont Neuf is the largest and most frequented in Paris, at the junction of the two arms of the Seine, supported in the centre on a point of the City Island; it rests on 12 arches, and is 1,020ft. long. The equestrian statue of Henry IV. stands in the centre of this bridge, from which a fine view of the town is obtained. The Bridge des Arts, for foot passengers, between the Louvre and the Palais de l'Institute, resting on nine iron arches.—The Bridge du Carousel.—The National Bridge, joining the Tuilleries and the Rue du Bac.—The Bridge de la Concorde joins the Place de la Concorde, to the Palais Bourbon. The Bridge d'Iena from the Champ de Mars to the Bas de Chaillot, was finished in 1813; its abutments are built after the style of the Temple of Mars at Rome. Its name was changed by order of Blucher in 1814. The Bridge d'Antin, or des Invalides, joins the Quai de la Conference and the Quai d'Orsay.

Fountains and Waterworks.—The Reservoir opposite St. Gervais, or Romainville Fountains, for the suburbs of St. Martin and St. Denis. The Reservoire de Belleville serves the Hospital St. Louis.—The Reservoir d'Arcueil is 592 metres long, and supplies 13 fountains and many houses in the town.—The Reservoir de Ceinture forces the water out of the Ourcq Canal into the town at the north side of the Seine, in a direct line through the Boulevards from the Barrier St. Martin to Monceaux; it is 9,500 metres in length.—The Basin de la Villette, at the Barrier de la Villette, forms the harbour of the Ourcq Canal.—The Basin of the Arsenal, capable of holding 70 to 80 large vessels, at the canal of St. Denis. Amongst the various hydraulic machines in the town, the one at the Bridge of Notre Dame is most worthy of notice.—Among the Public fountains in Paris, the best are those on the Place de la Concorde, the Boulevard du Temple, in the Richelieu Place, and at the end of the Rues Richelieu and Traversiere.—The Artesian Well de Grenelle, made from 1834 to 1841, is 1650 feet in depth, and throw up 1,700 cubic feet of water per hour.—The Water Filtering Establishment, No. 24, Quai des Celestins, is well worth seeing.

The Quays are formed on both sides of the Seine, and have thirty-three different names.

Churches.—The Cathedral of Notre Dame is a very noble pile of building, erected in the 12th century. It has two majestic towers. The three principal entrances are finely carved, from subjects out of the New Testament. The colossal bell in the north tower, called Le Bourdon, weighs 322 cwt. It is only rang on state occasions, requiring the labour of eight men. There are some most beautiful paintings and magnificent carvings in the choir, which is supported by 120 massive pillars, and the gallery by 297 pillars. The floor is of marble. The altar is most magnificently carved, and here are placed the statues of Louis XIII. and XIV. In a niche there is a beautiful marble group, representing the Descent from the Cross. There are also forty-five chapels filled with monuments, in the same manner as at Westminster Abbey. The charge for ascending the tower is 20 cents., from which there is a delightful prospect.—The New Church of the Madeleine, situated on the place of the same name, opposite the Rue Nationale. The first stone was laid in 1764, and it was finished by Louis Philippe. It is surrounded by 52 Corinthian pillars, ornamented by a splendid façade. This building was intended by Napoleon to represent the Temple of Fame. The bas-relief over the portico is worthy of particular attention. The interior is most magnificently ornamented with rich gilding, paintings, and statuary, and is lighted by its three domes, which are most beautifully painted.—The Church Notre Dame de Lorette, at the end of the Rue Lafitte, was completed in 1823, and is fitted up in the most costly manner with paintings by the best French artists.—The Church St. Etienne du Mont, in the square of the same name, behind the Pantheon, celebrated for its choir, pulpit, and the grave of the holy Genoveva.—The Church St. Eustache, in the Rue Trainée, is one of the largest and most handsome in Paris.—The Church of St. Germain des Prés, in the square of the same name, is the oldest in Paris, containing the monument to King Casimir of Poland, and the remains of Descartes and Boileau.—The Church of St. Germain l'Auxerrois, in the place of the same name, opposite the colonnade of the Louvre, is remarkable for its antique architecture.—Also the Gothic Church of St. Merry, in the Rue St. Martin, and the Church of St. Roch, in the Rue St. Honoré, containing monuments of Crequi, Corneille, and Lenôtres, and a splendid pulpit.—The Church of St. Sulpice, in the place of the same name, has a beautiful portico, baptismal fonts of colossal shells, and a beautiful pulpit.—The Pantheon, (formerly the Church of Geneviève) may be classed among the most beautiful buildings in Paris. It is intended to place the remains of celebrated men in its tombs: those of Voltaire and Rousseau are interred here.—The Synagogue of the

Jews, in the Rue Notre Dame de Nazareth, is a beautiful temple, resting on thirty Doric pillars.

PALACES AND OTHER PUBLIC BUILDINGS.—The Palace of the Tuilleries (formerly the residence of the Kings of France) claims attention for its magnificent garden, adorned with statues, vases, and fountains.—The Louvre may be classed among the most beautiful of the Parisian palaces; its splendid picture gallery reaches to the Tuilleries. The colonnade, opposite the Church St. Germain l'Auxerrois, is worthy notice.—The Palace of the Luxembourg, Rue de Vaugirard, was formerly used as the House of Peers, and has a beautiful garden. The splendid steps, the Hercules Saloon, the Saloon de la Reunion and des Seances, with its amphitheatrical arrangement for its members; la Salle de Trone, the Library next to the Chapel, a saloon adorned with panel paintings by Rubens; a gallery studded with sculpture and paintings, and the Observatory, claim the visitor's inspection.—The Palace Nationale (formerly the Palais Royal), Rue St. Honoré, contains innumerable courts, galleries, arcades, and a garden planned by Cardinal Richelieu in 1629. The father of Louis Philippe converted the whole of this superb mass of building into mercantile purposes. Louis Philippe finished a part of the square which had been left incomplete. The principal entrance is from the Rue St. Honoré. The shops consist mostly of libraries, booksellers, jewellers, bazaars, coffee-houses, taverns, confectioners, &c.—The Palace de Justice, situated in the Place of the same name, contains an enormous saloon called the Salle des Pas-Perdus, and the Monument Malesherbes. On the south side is the chapel, a gothic building, erected by St. Louis. Those who wish to view the interior must apply to the porter, behind the chapel.—The Palace des Beaux Arts, in the Rue des Petits Augustins, is principally used for the exhibition of works of art, manufactures, and architectural models. In the large court-yard is a portico of the Palace of Gaillon.—The Hotel des Invalides is situated between the Suburb St. Germain and Le Gros Caillou, and is open to public inspection on Tuesdays and Fridays from 12 to 3. Under the beautiful dome of the church rest the remains of Napoleon. The Entrance Gate, the Royal Court, the Library, and the Kitchens, are well worthy inspection.—The Palace Bourbon, (now the National Assembly, where the members hold their sittings), is situated in the Rue de l'Université. The Military School (now used as barracks) is on the Champ de Mars. The Hotel des Monnaies (containing a rich collection of coins and medals), is on the Quai de Conti.—The Hotel de Ville (Town Hall), and residence of the Prefet de la Seine, is situated in the place of the same name. It is adorned with sixteen statues of celebrated men. —The Exchange (La Bourse), is situated in the square of the same name, the buildings composing it forming a parallelogram, supported externally by 66 Corinthian columns. The principal saloon will contain two thousand persons, and is handsomely decorated with cartoons.—The Halle au Blé, in the Rue de Viarmes, is a most beautiful structure, in which there is a most astonishing echo, and near to this building stands the Pillar built by Catharine de Medicis, and on which she was accustomed to make her astronomical observations. This building is the grain market and granary of Paris, and is capable of containing 30,000 sacks of corn. The hall is 126 feet in diameter.—The Halle aux Vins (Wine Market,) on the Quai St. Bernard, is well worth a visit. It covers a vast surface, and is portioned off into streets, named according to the kind of wine contained in the warehouses that form them. Open daily.

EXHIBITIONS, MUSEUMS, AND LIBRARIES.—The National Library, in the Rue Richelieu, contains 800,000 volumes, 72,000 manuscripts, 5,000 portfolios of engravings, and a most complete collection of coins and medals.—The Library of the Arsenal, in the Rue de Sully, contains 170,000 volumes, and 6,000 manuscripts.—The Library of St. Genevieve in the upper story of the Abbey of St. Genevieve, in the Square of the Pantheon, contains 110,000 vols., and 2,000 manuscripts, besides several other collections of rare books.—The Museum of the Jardin des Plantes has three entrances, one in the Rue du Jardin, the second in the Rue Cuvier, and the third opposite the Bridge of Austerlitz. This is a most astonishing exhibition somewhat like the Zoological Gardens, Regent's Park, London. The zoological collection is in the Swiss Valley. The museum contains a magnificent collection of mineralogical, botanical, and zoological specimens; also a splendid anatomical collection.—The Conservatoire des Arts et Metiers, Rue St. Martin, contains a good collection of mechanical and industrial models, &c.—The Museum of the Louvre is divided in the following manner:—1. Collection of Antiquities. 2. Museum of French Sculpture. 3. Gallery of Drawings. 4. Gallery of Paintings of the Italian, Flemish, and French Schools. 5. Collections of Spanish Paintings. 6. Collection of Greek, Roman, and Egyptian Antiquities, Vases, Statues &c. 7. Models of Shipping, highly interesting; far surpassing any thing of the kind in England.—[We recommend the visitor to purchase a catalogue at the entrance, costing but a trifle.] Admission (on production of passport and writing down your name) 10 till 4 daily, except Monday.—The Museum of the Luxembourg contains the best collection of paintings by modern artists; and the Artillery Museum, in the Place St. Thomas d'Aquin, a fine collection of armour and accoutrements, from the most remote ages to the present time. Admission, same as the Louvre.—The Museum de l'Hotel de Cluny and du Palais des Thermes, in the Rue de la Harpe, joined to each other by a passage, contain surprising collections of rare mediæval productions. The former is open Wednesdays, Thursdays, and Fridays, 12 till 4.—The National Institute of France is on the Quai Conti, and the College of France in the Place Cambrai, and various literary and scientific societies hold their meetings in the Town Hall, &c.

The attention of visiters to Paris should be directed to the Chapelle St. Ferdinand, erected on the spot where the Duke of Orleans died in 1842; and to the Chapelle Expiatoire, on the spot where the remains of Louis XVI. and Marie Antoinette were interred, after being guillotined.

GATES AND ARCHWAYS.—The Porte St. Denis, 73 feet high, erected by Louis XIV., and ornamented with a variety of bas reliefs.—The Arc de Triomphe de l'Etoile (at the barrier of that name), commenced by Napoleon in August 1806, and finished only in 1832. It is 133 feet high and 138 feet broad, ornamented with bas reliefs of the various victories of Napoleon.—The Triumphal Arch at the entrance of the Tuilleries, adorned with bas reliefs and an equestrian figure of Victory.

PERE LA CHAISE.—This celebrated cemetry, situated at the end of the Rue de la Roquette, is well worth a visit, containing as it does the celebrated monuments to Abelard and Heloise, to Fontaine, Molière, Talma, Rancourt, De Lille, Kellermann, Davoust, and many others, as well as the beautiful mausoleum of Demidof. Prince Demidof's mausoleum is being rebuilt.

THE CATACOMBS, at the Barrier d'Enfer, is the most remarkable place of the kind in Europe, its immense subterranean passages containing upwards of three million human remains, and traversing a great part of the city.

PASSPORT OFFICES IN PARIS.—The following is a detailed list of the Ambassadors' Residences at Paris. The circumstances under which a visé to a passport is necessary, will be found given in the observations at pages 19 to 22. The hours of business are from 11 to 1.

Argentine Confederation.—Charge d'Affaires, 35, St. George's.

Austria and Parma.—Envoy Extraordinary and Minister Plenipotentiary, 134, Rue de Grenelle, St. Germain.

Baden, Resident Minister, 26, Rue de la Ville l'Evêque.

Bavaria.—Envoy Extraordinary & Minister Plenipotentiary, 15, Rue d'Aguesseau.

Belgium.—Envoy Extraordinary & Minister Plenipotentiary, 97, Rue de la Pépinière.

Brazil.—Charge d'Affaires, 36, Rue de la Ferme; Consul, 11, Rue Joubert.

Chili, Charge d'Affaires, 69, Rue de l'Université.

Costa-Rica.—Charge d'Affaires, 4, Place de la Bourse.

Denmark.—Envoy Extraordinary and Minister Plenipotentiary, 88, Rue de la Pépinière; Consul, 29, Rue de Trevise.

Free Towns, Resident Minister, 6, Rue Trudon.

Germanic Confederation.—

Great Britain, Ambassador Extraordinary and Minister Plenipotentiary, 39, Rue de Faubourg St. Honoré; Consul, same address.

Greece.—Envoy Extraordinary & Minister Plenipotentiary, 70, Faubourg St. Honoré; Consul, 30, Rue Basse du Rempart.

Hanover.—Resident Minister, 16, Rue Miromesnil.

Hesse-Electorale.—Charge d'Affaires, 4 Menars.

Hesse, Grand Duchy.—See Baden.

Holland.—Envoy Extraordinary & Minister Plenipotentiary, 28, Rue de Suresnes.

Lucca.—Charge d'Affaires, 3 Rue Caumartin.

Mecklenburg-Schwerin.—Resident Minister, 35, Rue Faubourg St. Honoré

Mecklenburg-Strelitz.—Charge d'Affaires, 7, Rue Caumartin.

Mexico.—Charge d'Affaires, 4, Rue d'Isly.

Nassau.—Charge d'Affaires, 28, Rue de Suresnes.

Nicaragua.—Charge de Affaires, 13, Rue de la Ferme.

New Grenada.—Charge d'Affaires, 35, Rue de la Madeleine.

Oldenburg, Resident Minister, 7, Rue Caumartin.

Pays-Bas.—Envoy Extraordinary and Minister Plenipotentiary, 28, Rue Suresnes.

Portugal.—Envoy Extraordinary and Minister Plenipotentiary, 12, Rue d'Astorg. — Consul, 44, Rue Blanche.

Prussia.—Envoy Extraordinary and Minister Plenipotentiary, 78, Rue de Lille.

Roman States.—Charge d'Affaires, 69, Rue de l'Université.

Russia.—Charge d'Affaires, 33, Faubourg St. Honoré.—Consul, same Address.

Sardinia.—Envoy Extraordinary and Minister Plenipotentiary. 133, Rue St. Dominique, St. Germain.

Saxony.—Envoy Extraordinary and Minister Plenipotentiary, 2, Place de la Madeleine.

Saxe Weimar.—See Saxony.

Spain.—Envoy Extraordinary and Minister Plenipotentiary, 29, Rue de Courcelles.—Consul, 27, Rue Trouchet.

Sweden and *Norway.*—Envoy Extraordinary and Minister Plenipotentiary, 74, Rue d'Anjou, St. Honoré.—Consul, 29, Rue Lafitte.

Switzerland.—Charged'Affaires, 9, Rue Chauchat.

Tuscany.—Minister Plenipotentiary, 3, Rue Caumartin.

Turkey.—Envoy Extraordinary and Minister Plenipotentiary, 5, Rue des Champs Elysées.

Two Sicilies.—Envoy Extraordinary and Minister Plenipotentiary, 47, Rue de Foubourg, St. Honoré.

United States.—Envoy Extraordinary and Minister Plenipotentiary, 19, Rue de Matignon.—Consul, 27, Boulevard de Italiens.

Uruguay.—Envoy Extraordinary and Minister Plenipotentiary, 17, Rue Notre Dame de Lorette, and 9, Provence.

Wurtemberg.—Resident Minister, 13, Rue d'Aguesseau.

ENGLISH DIRECTORY OF PARIS.

Apartment, House, and Commission Agent.—A. Webb, 36, Rue di Rivoli. Persons intending to reside in Paris, or wishing to forward goods to England, will find Mr. Webb's services of great advantage.

Chemist and Druggist.—T. P. Hogg, English Chemist to the Embassy, 2, Rue Castiglione, (three doors from Rue Rivoli), highly deserving our best recommendation.

Dancing and Waltzing.—Mademoiselle Victorine, and the veteran Coulon, of the Paris opera, give lessons at 320, Rue St. Honoré; just opposite the Hotel de Lille et d'Albion.

Dentist.—Mr. W. Rogers, 270, Rue Saint Honoré, author of several important medical and surgical works on Dentistry. Mr. Rogers also enjoys a first reputation as a practical dentist.

English Ale and Porter Stores.—B. Harris & Co., 17, Boulevard de la Madeleine, we need only refer to the advertisement, page 368, to the respectability and importance of this establishment.

Furnished Apartments. combining English comfort with economy, may be had at 19, Boulevard Montmartre. We can recommend this as being a highly respectable house, and well situated.

Jewellery—Goldsmiths and Jewellers.—Paris being so distinguished in the fine arts, it requires some judgment and care to select the best establishments connected therewith. Duponchel & Co., Orfevre, Bijoutier, Joallier, 47, Rue Neuve St. Augustin, are recommended as having an unrivalled stock of Jewellery, and as being highly respectable.

Lace.—A visit to the "French and Belgian Manufactory," 57, Rue Neuve Vivienne, 15, Boulevart Montmartre, will convince our fair readers that we have selected a house deserving our best recommendation.

Money Changers and Foreign Bankers.—Messrs. Meyer, Spielmann, & Co., of 26 Rue neuve Vivienne, are well known, and deserving our best recommendation. English and all foreign monies can be exchanged at this establishment to the best advantage. They grant drafts on London and the principal cities of Europe and America.

Nouveautes.—We have exercised our usual care in choosing the best firm in Paris for these "articles," and in recommending the first-rate establishment, the Trois Quartiers, of Messrs. Gallois, Gignaux, & Co., 21, and 23, Boulevard de Madeleine, and 26, Rue Duphot, near the Madeleine, we are confident our selection will be approved.

Pau.—HOTELS:—

Hotel de France and Hotel de l'Europe.

In the Basses Pyrenees, formerly the capital of Navarre, and a place of great resort of the English. It possesses an English church, well supported; a good circulating library; excellent hotels; and physicians of reputation. Population, 13,000.

BANKERS.—Messrs. Davantes Brothers do business with England; M. Merrillon, senior.

ENGLISH CLERGYMAN.—Rev. Edw. Hedges, M.A., of Queen's College, Cambridge. French Service twice a day on Sundays at the English Church.—Rev. M. Buscarlet, Minister.

ENGLISH PHYSICIANS,—Alex. Taylor, M.D., A. Smythe, M.D., N. Hill, M.D., and D. Ottley.

VICE-CONSUL.—Mr. G. P. Hodgson, who also banks for the English at Pau.

CONVEYANCES.—Diligences daily to Bordeaux, in twenty to twenty-two hours, according to season; to Bayonne, in 10 hours and to all the neighbouring towns.

Poitiers.—HOTELS.—

De la Poste, de France-de l'Europe, de la Tête Noire, des Trois Piliers.

Population 23,500, 221 English miles from Paris, capital of the department of Vienne, near the river Clain. It is divided into four quarters, all built in a mean and antiquated style. The streets are for the most part steep, winding, and ill paved. It has several squares, the finest of which is the Place Royal. The cathedral is in the gothic style, and wants only a little more elevation. Of the other churches the most interesting is that of St. Hilaire. The town has several Roman antiquities. Its manufactures consists of woollen stuffs, leather, and gloves. The Tours and Bordeaux Railway when completed will pass through this town.

Pontoise.—Population 5,500; 17¾ miles E. from Paris, and a Station on the Great Northern Railway Derives its name from the bridge over the river Oise. It is in general well built, but the streets are steep and narrow. From the higher part of the town there is a magnificent prospect. The remains of the ancient castle still exist. Remark the Hospital, the fine promenade, and the church of St. Mailon: in the neighbourhood, the Chateau St. Martin. From the station to Creil the Oise is on the right of the Railway, sometimes visible, sometimes its course only indicated by the luxuriant vegetation, and the trees which skirt its banks.

Rennes.—HOTELS.—

De France, de l'Europe, du Commerce, and de la Corne-de-Cerf.

Population 38,000; 220¾ English miles W. of Paris. It is the capital of the department of the Ille and Vilaine, situated at the confluence of these two rivers, the latter dividing the town into two parts, connected by bridges. The part built on the left bank is called the lower town; that on the right, called the upper town, stands on an eminence, and forms the finest and most considerable part of the city. It has several fine squares and promenades. The principal public edifices are the cathedral, dedicated to St. Peter, with its lofty towers and its relics; the building formerly the house of meeting for the Parliament of Brittany; the town-hall, and the college formerly belonging to the Jesuits; also, a public library containing 30,000 volumes. Rennes is the seat of a small university. The manufactures consist of sail-cloth, blankets, hats, thread, stockings, gloves, hardware, all of which are exported.

Rheims.—HOTELS.—

Du Palais, de la Maison Rouge, and du Commerce.

This town contains a population of about 40,000, and is the chief town in the department of the Marne, and formerly capital of the province of Champagne. It presents great attractions to tourists. The town has a fine cathedral, wherein the former kings of France were crowned. There is also the church of Saint Remy, together with extensive manufactories of spinners. Omnibuses meet all trains at Epernay, (distance, 14 miles) on the Paris and Strasbourg Railway.

Roanne.—HOTELS.—

De Flandre, du Parc, du Renard, and De Centre.

Population 12,000; 238$\frac{1}{4}$ English miles from Paris and 52 N.W. of Lyons. It is situated on the Loire, and has the appearance of a village; the streets stretching out in various directions into the open country, and the most remote houses being intermixed with trees.

CONVEYANCES.—Railway trains to St. Etienne and Lyons, see page 40. Railway very slow, and badly conducted; horses employed to draw the carriages on some portions of the line. Diligence to Nevers.

Roubaix.—A manufacturing town, which has of late risen into great importance, and is still increasing in population, which now exceeds 24,200, besides a large number of foreign workmen, when the factories are in full operation. It lies six miles north of Lile.

Rouen.—HOTELS.—

HOTEL D'ANGLETERRE, kept by Mr. Dalafosse, good, and highly recommended.

HOTEL D'ALBION, deserving our best recommendation.

The fine old Gothic town of Rouen, situated on the river Seine, the ancient capital of Normandy, is replete with picturesque attractions to the English tourist. The population is nearly 94,000, Some relic of antiquity here meets the traveller at every turn, either in the form of a pointed arch, the mutilated statue of some saint, or a gothic fountain; the door-posts, window-frames. beam-ends, and wood work of almost every building are chequered, intersected, and ornamented with rich carving, grotesque heads, flowers, and other fanciful devices; while the mouldering magnificence of the cathedral, churches, palais de justice, and other public edifices, carries the traveller in imagination half-a-dozen centuries backward. The cathedral, among the public edifices of Rouen, stands preeminent, and is said to have been founded as early as 260. Some splendid monuments are found within its walls; and its churches are equally rich in this respect. St. Ouen is a magnificent church. Joan of Arc's statue ornaments the Market-place, which is situated in the Place de la Pucelli. The Jardin de Plantes, rue d' Elbœuf, Faubourg St. Serer, is well worth seeing.

ENGLISH VICE-CONSUL, Mr. Bréard, 47, Rue de la Viscomté.

ENGLISH PHYSICIAN, Dr. Murphy, 46, Rue des Charrettes, chemen de Fer.

CONVEYANCES.—Railway to Paris, Havre, and Dieppe, several times daily, see pages 38, 39. Steamers to Elbeuf and Lahonelle four times daily. Diligence to Caen, at 7 a.m. and 5 p.m. For Abbeville, at 1 p.m.

St. Cloud, with its beautiful palace, park, saloons, chapel, and reception room, in which is placed the Gobelin Tapestry, and paintings by Mignard. The fountains only play three or four times a year. About 5 miles from Paris.

St, Denis.—A town four miles from Paris, and a Station on the G. N. Rail. Population 8,600. It is of very ancient origin, celebrated for its abbey. The church is a structure of great beauty and interest, highly ornamented, and rich in sculpture and paintings. It is the burial place of the kings of France. During the revolution more than fifty of the tombs were demolished, in consequence of the decree of 1793, for the destruction of all mausoleums of kings erected in the church of St Denis, and throughout the territory of the republic. Bonaparte made considerable additions to the church, and was careful to restore the injuries it had received. He intended it should be the last resting place for the emperors of his own dynasty. Napoleon founded here an institution for the gratuitous education of relatives of members of the Legion of Honour, in which 500 pupils (girls) are educated. The town of St. Denis is well built; there are numerous manufactures; and its confectionery is much in request.

St. Etienne.—HOTELS.—

De l'Europe, du Nord, de la Paix, de la Poste.

Population 72,000; 361 E. miles from Paris, 302$\frac{1}{4}$ from Marseilles, and 25 S. of Lyons; situated on the small rivulet of Furens. It has coal and iron mines, and the greatest manufactures of fire-arms and hardware in France; stones for grindstones are found in the neighbourhood.

CONVEYANCES.—Railway to Lyons, Roanne, and Montbrison, see page 40. Very slow, and badly conducted; that to Roanne is the worst.

St Germain may be reached by rail from Paris in half an hour. The Terrace is on the borders of the Seine, and will well repay a visit

St. Omer.—HOTEL.—

HOTEL DE L'ANCIENNE Poste an old-established good house.

Population 20,000. Situated in a marshy district on the Aa, well built and strongly fortified; streets wide and well made. A plentiful supply of refreshing water is afforded from 12 fountains in different quarters. The Hotel de Ville is situated on the Place d'Armes. Beyond the walls are two considerable suburbs, between which and Clairmarais are situated, amid extensive marshes, several floating islands, covered with trees and excellent pasture. The proprietors row them like a boat to land their cattle or take them up. The town is on the line of railway from Calais to Lille. Living is said to be cheap. The distance from Calais is about 41 kilometres, or 25$\frac{1}{2}$ E. miles.

CONVEYANCES.—Railway to Calais, see page 37. To Lille, Douai, Arras, Amiens, and Paris, see pages 34 and 35.

St. Quentin.—HOTELS.—

De l'Ange, d'Angleterre, du Commerce, du Cornet-d'Or, du Cygne, du Pot-d'Etain, de St. Nicholas.

Population 25,000; 105$\frac{1}{4}$ from Paris, and 44$\frac{1}{4}$ from Valenciennes, on the Great Northern Railway. This town is built on the brow of a hill, whose base is watered by the Somme; its streets are spacious, and its houses well built. The traveller will remark here the principal church, a gothic building, situated in the high part of the town, of a bold and beautiful style of architecture; its vault is 131 feet high, and its windows (of which there are 110) 43 feet high. The Hotel-de-Ville, in the Grand Place, is surrounded with a gallery which exhibits numerous arcades in ogee, and of which the capitals and frizes are adorned with sculptures of a whimsical description; the turret which surmounts the façade contains a beautiful chime of bells. The church of St. James, the palace of justice, the belfry, the theatre, the garden of the arquebuse, the hotel Dieu, the orphan hospital, the public promenades, on the site of the ancient ramparts, the subterranean vaults of the canal, which bears the name of the town, and joins the Somme at Escaut, are all worthy of notice. The principal occupation of the inhabitants is afforded by numerous manufactories for shawls, muslins, table linen, &c.; cotton yarn and coloured wool; iron and copper foundries, and sugar refineries.

CONVEYANCES.—Railway to Chauny, Noyon, Compiegne, Creil, Pontoise, and Paris, see page 35.

Strasbourg.—HOTELS :—

The HOTEL DE PARIS deserves our best recommendation.

HOTEL DE LA MAISON ROUGE, comfortable and moderate.

Population 70,300, with a garrison of 6000 men. Strongly fortified town on the French frontier. The spire of Strasbourg Cathedral is 474 feet above the pavement, being 112 feet higher than St. Paul's in London, and 24 feet higher than the great Pyramid. It is considered a masterpiece of architecture, being built of hewn stone, cut with such precision, as to give it, at a distance, a strong resemblance to lace. The tower was planned by Erwin of Steinbach, by whom it was commenced, but it was completed by his brother John, on the death of the former, in 1318. The clock, however, is the most remarkable thing connected with this Cathedral. It is a complete astronomical Almanac, from which you can read the revolutions of the heavenly bodies, and the various phenomena which they exhibit. It has three departments; the first is astronomical, the second ecclesiastical, indicating the fasts and holydays of the Roman Catholic church, and the third office of the automaton is a moral and religious one. Strasbourg claims the honour of the discovery of the art of printing, by Guttenburg, in 1436. It is favourably situated for commerce, the Rhine connecting it with Switzerland, Holland, and Belgium: its chief exports are corn, flax, hemp, wine and spirits, linen, sail-cloth, blankets, carpets, hardware, leather, cotton, lace, tobacco, and snuff. Steamers descend the Rhine from Strasbourg to Mayence (150 miles) daily, performing the voyage in nine hours. The ascent of the Rhine from Mayence to Strasbourg requires, on the contrary, two days. By making the best use of the railways now in operation, a traveller returning from Switzerland may go from Basle to London in 36 hours,

CONVEYANCES.—Railway to Schledstadt, Colmar Mulhouse, Thann, and Bâle, see page 77; to Kehl, Baden, Carlsruhe, Heidelberg, Mannheim, & Frankfort, see page 79; *fast* train to Paris in 11¾ hours, *1st Class only;* 1st and 2nd Class train in 12½ hours; ordinary train in 15½ hours. Fares, 1st Class 51 fr. 75 c.; 2nd Class, 38 fr. 95 c.; and 3rd Class, 28 fr. 95 c., see page 53.—DILIGENCES to Lyons, Nancy, and Paris, see page 261.

Thann, in Alsace, on the river Thuron. Population 3,937, on the Strasburg and Basle Railway.

Toulon.—HOTEL.—

HOTEL DE LA CROIX-DE-MALTE, a very good house.

Population 39,500; 580 English miles from Paris, and 30 from Marseilles. Toulon is a well-known seaport in the south-east of France, department of the Var, in a bay of the Mediterranean. It is built at the foot of a ridge of lofty mountains, which shelter it from the north; and is surrounded with ramparts, ditches, and bastions, and defended by a fine citadel, and a number of forts and batteries distributed on the neighbouring eminences. The town is divided into two parts, the old and the new. The former is ill built, but the new town is better, containing the public structures erected by Louis XIV., several straight streets and a square, or rather oblong, called the Champ de Cataille, and used for exercising the garrison. Toulon has no river; but several streamlets descending from the neighbouring mountains supply the fountains constructed in different parts of the town. The principal public buildings are the town-hall, the hotel de l'Intendance, and the churches and hospitals. Toulon has long been one of the chief stations of the French navy, being on the Mediterranean what Brest is on the Atlantic. It has two ports. The old one is a basin, not large but commodious, surrounded with a handsome quay; the new port is one of the finest in Europe, and is said to be capable of containing 200 sail of the line. The roadstead is spacious, and communicates with the outer port by a narrow passage. The passage by which the two ports communicate with each other is also narrow. Here are docks for ship-building, storehouses for timber, manufactures for canvas, cordage, ship anchors, &c. Toulon has some trade in wine, oil, silk, and fruit of different kinds. The manufactures are limited to soap, glass, hats, and caps. The tunny fishery is extensive.

CONVEYANCE.—Diligence to Marseilles and Nice.

Toulouse.—This town is situated in the department of the Upper Garonne, and over the river of that name there is a fine bridge. The town also possesses a magnificent cathedral and forty Catholic churches. Population about 77,500.

Tours.—HOTELS.—

Hôtel de L'Univers, close to the Railway Station.
Hotel Faisan, both good.

A considerable town on the Loire, containing about 25,000 inhabitants, who were formerly actively engaged in the silk manufacture, which however, has much declined of late years. It is 147 miles south-west of Paris, and the surrounding country is delightful. There is a handsome bridge here, 1300 feet long. A few miles from Tours, at Mettray, is the very interesting establishment for reclaiming delinquents, which will well repay a visit. A large number of English constantly reside at Tours.

CONVEYANCES.—Railway to Cinq Mars, Saumur, Angers and Nantes, see page 46. To Blois, Orleans, Paris, and Poitiers, pages 44 and 45.

Troyes.—HOTELS.—

De la Croix-d'Or, de la Fontaine.

Population 26,000; 113¾ English miles from Paris, 152¼ from Besançon, and 70 from Rheims. Troyes is a large town in Champagne, the capital of the department of the Aube, situated between two fine meadows on the Seine. It is ill built, the chief material being wood. It has considerable manufactures, particularly in cotton and cotton stockings. Woollen, linen, leather, and thread, are all made here, but on a smaller scale. Its chief edifices are the churches; in particular the cathedral, and the churches of St. Etienne and St. Urban. Its castle, now antiquated, was long the residence of the Counts of Champagne. A public mall, or walk, extends along the ramparts, and is of great length. Here are also a town-hall, a central school, a public library, and a society of arts.

CONVEYANCES.—Railway to Montereau and Paris see pages 46 and 47.

Valence.—Hotel.—

HOTEL DE LA POSTE, an excellent house.

Population 11,000; 396 English miles from Paris, 154 from Marseilles, and 45 from Grenoble. Valence is situated in the department of the Drome, on the Rhone. It is old, ill built, and irregular, with narrow, winding, and dirty streets. The cathedral is an ancient building; but neither it nor the episcopal palace are distinguished for their architecture. The case is otherwise with the gothic façade of an old castle at this place, which is said to be one of the finest specimens of that style in France. Its manufactures comprise silk, cotton, and leather: and an extensive trade is carried on in wine.

The well-known St. Peray wine is produced from a small mountainous district, about 2 miles distant on the opposite side of the Rhone. Valence is about half way between Lyons and Avignon, so that persons who have an objection to a 12 hours journey from the former to the latter town, would do well to take their places by the boat, which they may do at Lyons, and then start from thence at about 11 a.m., by the steamer to Valence, remain there the night, and proceed by the Lyons steamer the next day, which reaches Valence at about 10½ a.m. Enquiry should of course be made at Lyons, as arrangements may vary.

CONVEYANCE.-Steamers to Lyons & Avignon daily, see Alphabetical List, page 139.

Valenciennes—Hotels:—

HOTEL DU GRAND CANARD, on the Grande Place, an excellent house and obliging landlord.

Population 22,600. A place of considerable trade and wealth; situated on the Great Northern Railway; also strongly fortified by its position on the Scheldt, at its confluence with the Rhendelle, by which it may be surrounded for three-fourths of its circumference by water, retained by means of sluices in the fortifications. The town is well built; the houses are generally of brick and white stone. The Hotel de Ville, in which the Gothic style is mingled with several orders of architecture, will claim attention; it is highly decorated; the handsome façade, surmounted by an attic, adorned with Cariatide figures, representing the four seasons. The Hospital and the Theatre are also remarkable. Many agreeable promenades will be found the Cours-Bourbon, the Place-Verte, the Embankment between the city and the suburbs, the circuit of the outer fortifications from the Mons Gate to the Quesnoy Gate, the Faubourg Cambrai. From the Citadel the valley of the Scheldt is seen to advantage. Froissart, the historian of the 14th century, was born here.

CONVEYANCES —Railway to Brussels and to Paris, see pages 34, 35, 36, 37, and 60.

Versailles.—Reached by Railways from Paris on both sides f the Seine in half an hour (see pages 48) & 49).

It would require a volume to explain the beanties and remarkable productions of this palace, its pleasure-grounds, galleries, and noble saloons, containing the Historical Museum, a magnificent collection of paintings, representing the History of France or rather the wars of France, from the earliest period to the present time. Louis Philippe caused the interior of this magnificent building to be entirely redecorated, in keeping with the splendid collection of paintings. The whole is arranged to show the progress of time; and some future day, not far in the distance we would hope, will surely give way to a history of the peace of France, and its attendant blessings. The floors throughout are studded with statuary. It requires fully four hours merely to wander through the various apartments and gardens. The principal masters who have contributed to its adornment are Horace Vernet, Paul Delaroche, Johannot, and many others. The Cabinet of Natural History, the Opera Saloon, the Chapel, and the Park, with its splendid statues, fountains, and cascades, as planned by Louis XIV., will each in succession excite the admiration of the beholder.—A Catalogue may be bought at the Palace, explaining everything worth seeing in it.—The Museum is shown on Saturdays, Sundays, Mondays, and Tuesdays, from ten till four. The various small fountains play the first Sunday in every month—the larger ones only a few days in the year, of which notice is given in all the Parisian newspapers.—The railway on the left bank of the Seine passes Sevres, where the national china manufactories are carried on.

CONVEYANCES.—Railway trains to Lartoire and Chartres, also to Paris, on the right and left banks of the Seine, see pages 48 and 49.

Vierzon.—Hotel.—

De la Croix-Blanche.

Population 4,980; 126¾ English miles from Paris, 8¾ from La Doge, and 50 from Orleans. In the department of Cher, at the influx of the Eure into the Cher. It has manufactures of woollen and silk stuffs, and also a cannon foundry.

CONVEYANCES.—Railway to Chateauroux, Bourges, and Orleans, see pages 42 and 43.

BELGIUM.

BELGIUM is situated between 49°27 and 57°31 north latitude, and 2°37 and 6°0 east longitude. Its greatest length from N.W. to S.E. is about 175 English miles, and its greatest breadth from N.E. to S.W. about 127 English miles. Its superficial area is about 7,279,448 English acres, or 11,375 square miles. The general aspect of Belgium is level, indeed it contains no ridge that could be properly called a mountain. The southern portion is high and rugged, but towards the north it sinks into a flat plain. The country in the northern provinces, along the rivers and estuaries is, like that of Holland, protected from inundation by dykes; and along the open sea by sand hills or downs, which vary in breadth from one to three miles, rise to a height of fifty or sixty feet, and are in most cases thickly covered with pine trees. The sea itself, to a great distance from the shore, is filled along the whole coast with sand banks, which render the navigation very intricate, and very dangerous to large vessels.

In climate the Belgian provinces differ much; for whilst in Luxembourg the climate is temperate and healthy, in Liege it is often hazy and damp. In Namur the air is sharp and agreeable, and in Hainault the climate is mild and temperate. East and West Flanders enjoy a moist climate, and in some places are subject to malaria. The summer here is warm and rainy, and the winter cold.

The Belgian people consist of two distinct stocks—the *Germanic* and the *Græco-Latin*. To the former belong the proper Belgians or Netherlanders, who speak the Flemish tongue, and a small number of German-Dutch—mostly in Limburg and Luxembourg. To the latter belong the Wallons, who inhabit the higher or southern portion of the country, and speak the French-Flemish and the Wallon—two dialects of the French language. Productive industry has long characterised the Belgians, the principal productions of which are Brussels, Mechlin, Bruges, Ghent, and St. Tron laces, the clothes of Flanders, Brabant, and Hainault, the printed cottons of Ghent, Brussels, and other places, the bleaching establishments of Courtray, which rival those of Haarlem, the carpets of Tournay, the papers of Liege, with its military arms and cutlery. The industry of the Flemings has within two hundred years converted a tract of land, once a sandy and barren heath, into a beautiful garden; and the product of its wheat is often not less than sixteen to one, and oats ten to one; whilst scarcely in any part of Britain does wheat give more than eight to ten for one. East and West Flanders alone produce annually flax to the amount of £1,600,000. The Coal Mines of Hainault produce more than those of the whole of France; and the annual quantity raised in Belgium is 2,000,000 chaldrons. More than 150,000 tons of iron are annually founded. The cloth manufactures at Verviers employ 4000 men; and the cotton manufactures, notwithstanding the loss of the Dutch colonial markets, has improved steadily since 1830, and now represents a capital of £3,000,000 sterling. Commerce has greatly increased in Belgium lately. The principal exports are the productions of its flourishing agriculture and numerous manufactures, such as corn, bran, coal, oil, lace, woollen and cotton cloths, linen, canvass, arms, cutlery, and ironmongery.

The Administrative divisions of Belgium consist of nine provinces, subdivided into arrondisements, communes, and cantons, after the French models.

Railways in Belgium.—Believing the following to be well worth our reader's attention, we extract it from an article in *Chambers's Edinburgh Journal* of August 28th, entitled—

"THE CONTINENTAL BRADSHAW IN 1852.—Belgium was the first continental country to follow the railway example of England. Very soon after King Leopold was seated securely on his throne, he instituted measures for the construction of railways in Belgium; and a law was passed in 1834, sanctioning that compact system, which, having Mechlin as a centre, branches out in four directions—to Liege, Antwerp, Brussels, and Ostend; and there were also lines sanctioned to the Prussian frontier, and the French frontier—the whole giving a length of about 247 English miles. Three years afterwards, a law was passed for the construction of ninety-four additional miles of railway—to Courtrai, Tournay, Namur, and other towns. In the western part of Belgium, the engineering difficulties were not of a formidable character; but towards the Prussian frontier, the bridges, cuttings, and embankments are so extensive, as to have rendered the works far more costly than in the average of continental railways. The Belgian Chambers provided the money, or rather, authorised the government to borrow it, year after year. The first portion of railway was opened in 1835; and every year from thence till 1843, witnessed the opening of additional portions, until at length, in this last-named year, all the 341 miles mentioned above were opened for traffic. The cost varied from £6140 per mile (near Courtrai), to £38,700 per mile (near Liege.) The entire cost of the whole, including working plant, was within £17,000 per average mile. While these railways were progressing, private companies were formed for the construction of other lines, to the extent of about 200 additional miles, most of which are now open—the Namur and Liege being opened in 1851. These various railways are said to have yielded, on an average, about 3½ per cent. on the outlay.

Passports.—See pages 19 to 22.

Money.—Although in some places accounts are still kept in Guilders and Cents (as in Holland, p. 180,) French money is so generally current, that a traveller who confines himself to Belgium need not provide himself with any other. At all the large towns English sovereigns will be readily exchanged, and should command the full equivalent of 25 fr. 50 cts., or as near as possible, according to the rate of exchange. A new gold coin, 25 francs value, has recently been issued. The Belgian bank issues notes of the value of 1000, 500, 100, 50, 20, and 5 francs.—See Money, under the head of France, page 141.

Posting is now nearly obsolete, but a post is equivalent to 5 English, or about 1 German mile, or to two Belgian or French leagues. The charge, per post, for each horse is 1 fr. 30 cts. and for each postillion that distance, 15 sous. Half a post extra is charged for post-horses arriving at Brussels or quitting it, and a fourth extra on quitting Ghent, Liege, Namur, and Mons.

ELECTRIC TELEGRAPH.—The lines were opened on the 15th of March, 1851, and extend from Ostend to Verviers, where they are in connection with the Prussian, Austrian, Saxon and Bavarian lines to Brussels, and from thence to Paris. These lines are also in connexion with the Submarine Telegraph.

DIFFERENT ROUTES.

1.—By Railway from London to Dover, and thence by Steam-packets to **Calais,** see advertisement page; and by Northern of France Railway to **Lille** and **Ghent,** or **Lille** to **Douai, Valenciennes,** and **Mons,** to **Brussels.** Also by **Lille, Mouscron, Tournay,** and **Jurbise,** to **Brussels.**

2.—By South Eastern Railway to Dover every night at 8½, and thence by Steam-packet at 11.15 to OSTEND, every night except Sunday. See Advertisement, page 340.

3.—By Steam to **Ostend** every Wednesday and Saturday morning, direct from St. Katherine's Wharf. See page 132. The "Panther" and "Triton" are splendid new packets, and perform the passage in ten hours.

4.—By Steam to **Antwerp,** direct from St. Katherine's Wharf. See page 132. The packets on this station are now of a very superior description. The General Steam Navigation Company's new ship "Ravensbourne," is a magnificent vessel. The Belgian Company's new ship "Baron Osy," is also a very fine vessel. They perform the passage in about 15 to 15½ hours, and reach Antwerp on the day after leaving London, in ample time to enable the passengers to proceed, if they wish, by the first or second train to Cologne. But few persons do this, as the "glorious works of art" in Antwerp are objects of too much interest to be passed unvisited,

5.—By Steam to **Calais** every Sunday and Thursday morning, direct from London Bridge Wharf. See page 132.

ROUTE 1.

In order to facilitate travellers in their Belgian tour, we arrange in consecutive order the principal railway routes at present existing in that country. We are the better enabled to do so in consequence of much practical information derived by us from a long tour which we have just completed through Belgium. We may also observe, that we have pointed to such places of note worth the excursionist's attention, which, though not immediately on the direct route, yet branch off at intervals and admit of a short visit by a little delay. The first route we give is from

OSTEND TO BRUSSELS.

Ostend (*With Map in Special Edition.*)—HOTEL:—

HOTEL DES BAINS—an old-established, good house.

BOOKSELLERS.—Kiesling & Co., German Booksellers, 7, Rue des Capucins.

Ostend is a most convenient port for receiving imports destined for the north of Europe, from its being connected by an almost continuous line of railway with the principal cities of Germany, Austria, and several ports of the Mediterranean.

At present it is principally known as a favourite watering-place, much patronized by the elite of the neighbouring states, who resort here in great numbers during the summer. The town itself has no particular object deserving of notice beyond its ramparts and fortifications, but it possesses one of the finest marine parades in Europe. The Digue of Ostend is a celebrated walk along the shore, upon an elevated mole built parallel with the sea-ward rampart of the town, and so constructed, that while it serves as a barrier against the encroaching and formidable attacks of the sea, it forms one of the most agreeable promenades imaginable.

By recent arrangements, travellers proceeding to or returning from Germany, by declaring the same at the Ostend or frontier Custom-house, their luggage is not examined in Belgium, but entered *in transit,* thus avoiding the annoyance of a search of luggage until the end of the journey. By an order of the Board of Customs, luggage of travellers arriving by the mails at Dover or Ostend is examined at any hour of the day or night.

AGENT for the sale of J. A. Farina's *Eau de Cologne*—Mr. Wm. Phillips.

CONVEYANCES. — Railway trains to Bruges, Ghent, and Brussels, page 58.—To Tirlemont, Liege, Verviers, Aix-la-Chapelle, and Cologne, pages 56 and 57. Steamer from Ostend to Dover, see page 134. To London direct, by the General Steam Navigation Company's new ships, "Panther" or "Rhine," according to tide, see page 134, viz., Ostend to London.

Bruges—Hotels:—

Hotel de la Fleur Ble, has always enjoyed a good reputation; it has been recently newly furnished, and the new landlord appears desirous to deserve the patronage of English travellers.

Hotel de Flandre—an old established house, famous for its fine wines and good dinners.

Hotel de Commerce, an obliging landlord, and decidedly a good house.

Distance from Ostend, 22 kilometres (14 miles); time occupied in transit 30 to 35 minutes. Six canals here meet, from Ghent, Ostend, Dunkirk, Sluys, Furnes, and Ypres, in the large dock or basin, which is the finest in Belgium. *Fares of Vigilantes*, 1 franc per drive; or for the first hour, 1 fr. 50 c.; for the others 1 fr. The rail way station at Bruges is on the Vrydags Markt. The West Flanders Railway is now open to Courtray, making a direct railway from Ostend and Bruges to Paris, *via* Lille, Amiens, &c. It is 23 miles shorter than by Ghent.

On leaving Ostend, it is a very general custom for travellers going to Germany to take a railway ticket for the whole distance to Cologne, for the purpose of reaching the Rhine with the least possible delay. In so doing they deprive themselves of the opportunity of visiting the cities in Belgium which possess more objects of interest to the lover of the fine arts, more pure and perfect specimens of florid gothic architecture, a richer collection of rare and beautiful paintings, by the old Flemish masters, that can probably be found in the whole of Germany. If, instead of hurrying in this hot-haste through a country which presents so many points of interest to travellers in general, and to Englishmen in particular, our countrymen were to devote a part of their time to Belgium, they would never regret becoming acquainted with its peculiarities, its fine old cities, its glorious monuments, its arts and sciences, the people and their institutions.

Commencing with Bruges, which occupies so prominent a place in the history of Flanders, the traveller will find this town especially worthy of notice —not that it presents the aspect of a populous modern city, but because it has preserved the peculiarities which distinguished its appearance during the middle ages, when it was the emporium of European commerce, the residence of merchant princes, occasionally that of the reigning sovereign, and when its population is said to have exceeded two hundred thousand. The mailed warrior or the glaived artisan meet no more upon the fortifications, the commerce which animated its quays and canals is dispersed over Europe, its merchants are no longer opulent as princes, the city is no longer the capital of Western Flanders. Yet though these things have passed away, we cannot infer that it was in vain that Providence raised up this town to such a remarkable point of grandeur and importance in a remote age. The characteristic intrepidity, activity, and proverbial turbulence of its artisans, the inflexible will and sturdiness of its burghers, the associations of its merchants and traders, which led to that interchange of opinion, that communion and unity of sentiment so fatal to despotism and feudal oppression, created and fostered that honest love of individual liberty, that regard and attachment for corporative and communal privileges, for which the men of Ghent and Bruges struggled during several centuries. This deep attachment to local institutions has been merged into that of national patriotism; and if the traveller, in conversing with an intelligent inhabitant of Bruges, deplores its depopulated streets, he will be told that if Bruges is not the great and important city it was formerly, it has still much to be thankful for; its citizens, instead of being at continual variance with their sovereign or the neighbouring towns, are now members of an independent kingdom, governed by a Prince of their own choice, with one of the most liberal constitutions in the world—that Bruges is no longer isolated in its splendour and solitude, but that it forms a component part of the nation, and, confident in the resources of the country for the gradual development of all branches of industry, it anticipates a return of comparative prosperity. His informant will add, that indications of a more flourishing state of things is already apparent in the increasing activity of its manufactures, and the decrease in the number of persons dependent upon public charity.

The population of Bruges is about 49,000, and on fete days the fine old city wears a gay and animated appearance. The beauty of the women of Bruges is of ancient repute, and the present generation by no means dishonour the proverb "*Formosis Bruga puellis.*" When they are seen enveloped in the mantilla of Spanish origin, their brunette complexions and dark eyes render them most picturesque and pleasing objects among the many splendid and exquisite specimens of architecture with which their dwellings are adorned and embellished.

The churches and other public edifices of Bruges contain several rare paintings. The church of Notre Dame has many works of art worthy of an attentive examination. A statue of the Virgin and the infant Jesus, supposed to be by Michael Angelo, is greatly admired by connoisseurs for the classical beauty of feature and delicate form of the hands which characterises the two figures. Among the paintings we need only direct attention to a picture of the Virgin and Child, surrounded by Saints, reputed to be by Van Dyck, the "Adoration of the Shepherds," and the "Adoration of the Magi." Before quitting the church the traveller should inspect the pulpit, one of the most beautiful and highly finished pieces of carving in wood to be seen in Belgium. Instead of visiting the neighbouring churches, the traveller will do well to go to the Hospital of St. John, which is close to the church of Notre Dame, as this institution is celebrated for possessing several beautiful pictures, painted by *Hans Hemling*, so remarkable for purity of colouring and brightness of tone, that the most indifferent spectator will find himself an admirer and a describer of their prominent beauties.

Agent for the Sale of J. A. Farina's *Eau de Cologne*—Mr. J. B Molhant.

Conveyances.— For railway conveyance, see Time Table, pages 58 and 66.

Ghent *(With Map in Special Edition.)* HOTELS:—

HOTEL DE VIENNE, recommended for its moderate charges and good accommodation.

HOTEL ROYAL, Place d'Armes, in the centre of the town, and nearest to the railway station—highly recommended to English travellers.

HOTEL DE LA POSTE, Place d'Armes, highly recommended to English Families.

HOTEL DE FLANDRE -a very good house, and charges moderate.

TAILORS.—Travellers will find a large stock of ready-made wearing-apparel of the best fashion at Mr. T. B. Collards, 16, Rue des Champs, and at very reasonable prices. Orders are promptly executed, which is a great consideration for Tourists.

Distance from Bruges, 44 kilometres=28 miles; time 1h. 25m.—The stations between this place and Bruges are Blœmendæl, Æltre, Hansbeke, and Landeghem. The station of the Direct railway to Antwerp is at the Porte d'Anvers. This direct line, worked by a private company, runs through the Pays de Waes, the finest garden-like and most densely populated district in Belgium; it passes the important towns of Lokeren with 18,000, and St. Nicholas with 21,000 inhabitants. Post-Office in Rue de l'Université. *Vigilantes* as at Bruges.

After leaving Ostend and Bruges, the traveller will be most agreeably surprised, on entering this rich and populous city, to observe the animation and activity imparted by the flourishing state of its manufactories. Its population of 90,000 persons is chiefly engaged in the manufacturing of linen and cotton threads by machinery, and the bleaching and printing of calicoes. During the annexation of this country to Holland, Ghent increased in opulence and prosperity under the patronage of William I., who protected and assisted its commercial and manufacturing interests. On the accession of the present dynasty, the good folks of Ghent predicted an immediate declension of their trade, and a general reverse of prosperity, as the inevitable results of the separation from Holland. We are happy to learn that the prophecy has proved false in every respect, and that its trade is increasing and flourishing now more than ever. This circumstance is explained by a consideration of the fact, that the reigning king is not the patron and protector of particular interests, but the promoter of good to the whole nation, governing constitutionally by a Cabinet possessing the confidence of its Parliament, and composed of men representing the interests, and conversant with the wants and necessities of the agricultural, commercial, manufacturing, and mineral branches of Belgian industry; hence there is a more general prosperity throughout the land—and, if the city of Ghent no longer monopolizes the manufacturing trade of Belgium, it is satisfactory to know, that the great centres of population, Antwerp, Liege, Brussels, Namur, and Verviers, were never in a more flourishing state than at present; and there can be no doubt, if the enlightened men now in office pursue the further development of a truly national policy-the gradual abolition of the differential system—they will find it conducive to increased exports, to a participation in the commerce of the world, and a reciprocation of trade with their most profitable customers, the English.

The political history of Ghent is various and interesting, but too voluminous for the pages of a Monthly Guide. We can only observe, as Englishmen, that, notwithstanding the severe strictures of the historian Hallam, it calls up to the recollection many scenes which inspire us with every sentiment of sympathy and good will towards the descendants of many a name illustrated in centuries past by deeds of patriotism and domestic virtue, which still do honour to the Flemish character. Among the names recorded in its history none deserve the passing tribute of notice more than that of the brewer of Ghent, James Van Arteveldt, the popular leader who restrained the excesses of an impetuous people, and who contributed more than any other man to secure the communal liberties and corporative privileges of the country. He perished by the hand of an ungrateful fellow-citizen, but his memory is still revered four centuries after his untimely death.

Ghent is one of the handsomest towns on the Continent; its streets and public squares are wide and spacious; it has more the appearance of a modern city than Bruges; and there are a number of elegant and dashing equipages constantly rolling through its busy thoroughfares. The Town Hall of Ghent is apparently an unfinished structure; and in admiring this exquisite specimen of florid gothic architecture of the right wing and corner, the traveller will regret that the architect who executed this part of the edifice did not complete the other side in the same style of elegance and beauty of design, which is probably unequalled by any other specimen in Europe. The cathedral church of St. Bavon is not remarkable for external beauty, but the interior presents a singular appearance, from its being lined with black marble, and from its having 24 chapels containing ornaments and paintings of great value.

It would occupy too much of our limited space to describe each oratory, but we would direct attention to the eleventh, which is embellished by one of the most remarkable works of the early Flemish school. A painting, representing "The Adoration of the Lamb," by the brothers Van Eyck, is considered an extraordinary *chef d'œuvre.* The colouring is as brilliant and as pure as the first day it left the hands of the painters. The composition combines the breadth and power of the Flemish school, with the grace and delicacy of the Italian. No person should quit this chapel without having the details of the picture described to him. In another part of the church (in chapel fourteenth) there is a painting by Rubens equally admired. It is a picture representing a religious ceremony—St. Bavon renouncing the military profession to become a monk. Sir Joshua Reynolds says of this painting, that "for composition, colouring, richness of effect, and all those qualities in which Rubens more particularly excelled, it claims a rank among his greatest and best works." The pictures in the church of St. Michael have been shamefully treated by the vandalism of ruthless depredators and modern restorers or picture cleaners. The once beautiful work representing the Crucifixion, by Van Dyck, is so disfigured as not to be worth examination! The Museum of Ghent is by no means worthy of such a city; but the florist will be much gratified by a visit to the Botanical Gardens, which contain some of the choicest exotics and rarest plants acclimated in Europe.

AGENT for the Sale of J. A. Farina's *Eau de Cologne*—Mr. J. Poitie, Coiffeur.

CONVEYANCES.—Railway to Malines, Brussels, Bruges, and Ostend, see page 58.—To Courtray, Tournay, and Mouscron, page 59. Also to Antwerp direct, page 66; to Louvain, Tirlemont, Liege, Verviers, Aix-la-Chapelle, and Cologne, see pages 56 and 57.

GHENT TO ANTWERP, *via* ST. NICHOLAS AND LOKEREN.

Parties entering Belgium at Ostend, and who, proceeding to Ghent, wish to visit Antwerp, might make a very expeditious tour by proceeding direct from Ghent, and they will arrive at Antwerp in about one hour and a half. If it be so wished a visit can be made to

Lokeren.—HOTELS.—

De la Poste and Des Quatre Sceaux.

A considerable manufacturing town, on the direct railway from Ghent to Antwerp, containing 17,000 inhabitants. It is situated on the river Durme, by which it communicates with the Scheldt. The market-place and the quay are remarkable. The church, the construction of which dates as far back as the seventeenth century, is adorned with an elevated tower, and contains one of the finest pulpits in Belgium, magnificently carved, and representing, in a group of ten figures, "Jesus among the Doctors." There are also some fine pictures: one especially should be examined, the Circumcision, by Veraeghen. A fine picture, representing "Abigail going to meet David," by Otto Venius, is the property of a baker of the town.

CONVEYANCE.—Railway trains to Antwerp and Ghent, see page 66.

A visit may also be paid to

St. Nicholas.—HOTELS:—

Des Quatre Sceaux and Pomme d'Or.

The chief town of a district of East Flanders, on the road from Ghent to Antwerp. A flourishing trade is carried on in all sorts of stuffs, which are here manufactured. The population numbers upwards of 18,000. The principal church contains some fine pictures, and the Town Hall is a splendid specimen of art, by Smeyers.

CONVEYANCE.—Railway to Antwerp and Ghent. See Time Table, page 66.

Passing Nieukerke, Beveren, Zwyndrecht, we arrive at

Antwerp.—See page 170.

Audeghem.—Tourists wishing to visit Alost, about 8 miles distant from here, will find Omnibuses at this station ready to convey them.

Alost, on the river Dendre, the chief town of the district of East Flanders, is said to owe its origin to a fortress built by the Goths in 411. It was formerly the capital of what was called Imperial Flanders, and was reduced to ashes by a conflagration in 1360, and in 1667 the celebrated Marshal Turenne took and dismantled it. The town hall is a fine gothic edifice, built in 1210, and is in excellent preservation. The collegiate church of St. Martin was built by the same architect as the cathedral of Amiens, and contains a fine picture by Rubens, representing the "Plague of Alost." The population is about 15,000, chiefly engaged in linen, soap, and thread-lace manufactures.

CONVEYANCES.—Omnibuses to Audeghem station; from thence by railway to Ghent, Malines, and Brussels.

Having paid a visit to Alost, the tourist, continuing his journey, arrives at

Termonde, an ancient town, said to be earlier than the time of Charlemagne. It is situated at the mouth of the river Dendre, at its confluence with the Scheldt. The inhabitants have a taste for the fine arts, and the traveller may readily obtain access to several private collections, among which we may name those of M. Schellekin and Madame Terlinden. David Teniers married in this town, and resided here several years. The population is about 8,000, chiefly engaged in the hemp and flax trade. It is 16 miles, by railway, west of Malines, and 19 from Ghent.

CONVEYANCES.—Coaches leave for St. Nicholas and Lokeren several times a day. For trains, see Time Table, pages 58 and 59.

Mechlin.—(In French, **Malines.**)—HOTEL: Hotel de la Grue, is an excellent house, well situated in the Grand Place facing the Cathedral. The landlord and waiters speak English.

A large town, in the province of Antwerp, divided by the Dyle into two parts. It is equidistant from Brussels, Antwerp, and Louvain, and contains a population of 25,000. The Malines station is about five minutes' walk from the town, which is one of the most picturesque Flemish cities. An obelisk is here erected, to mark the point where the various Belgic lines of railway diverge.

The entrance from the railway station is very fine. The streets are broad, and bordered in many places by good buildings. The public square and the market-place are spacious, and regularly built. The cathedral has a tower 350 feet high, of massive Gothic construction. Although unfinished, it is worthy of attention, especially the interior, which is elegant. The other buildings of interest are the arsenal, the town-house, a Franciscan monastery, and an asylum for 800 widows and elderly women. The town also contains many curious old buildings. It has manufactures of fine Brabant lace and linen, damask and silk, and woollen stuffs, besides a thread lace, known and celebrated as the Mechlin lace. It contains, likewise, some breweries.

WORKS OF ART IN THE CHURCHES AT MALINES:—The Church of St. Romband—in the chapel on he left there is a fine painting, "Christ crucified between the two thieves," by Van Dyke. The Church of Notre Dame contains a picture by Rubens, "The miraculous draught of fishes." The Church of St. John possesses several of Rubens finest paintings, "The Worshipping of the Magi," two painted shutters, and three other small pictures. The receipt is shown in the vestry, dated March 12, 1624, stating that Rubens painted these eight paintings, in eighteen days, and received 1800 florins for them.

CONVEYANCES.—The railway from Antwerp to Cologne and the Rhine, proceeds east from Malines to Louvain and Liege, see page 56. West to Ostend and Ghent, see page 58. South to Brussels, see page

65. To Ghent, Courtray, Tournay, Mouscron, Lille, and Calais, page 59.

Continuing his journey, he next arrives at

Vilvorde.—A small, healthy town, of 6,500 inhabitants, situated between Malines and Brussels. It is one of the most ancient in Belgium, and is much visited by philanthropists desirous of inspecting the great prison or penitentiary, situated in the suburbs of the town. The church of Vilvorde contains some exquisite carvings in wood. In this town Tindal, the first English translator of the Bible, suffered martyrdom in 1536. At present this little town has acquired considerable reputation from its possessing an excellent Boarding-School for the education of young ladies; this establishment is conducted by Madame Flasschoen Michaux, and the concurrent testimony of innumerable Protestant families represent it as being one of the best and most irreproachable institutions on the continent. From here he passes through a very agreeable country until he enters Brussels.

Brussels (*With Map in Special Edition.*)—CAUTION.—Travellers are recommended not to believe cab drivers and omnibus conductors, when they represent certain hotels as being full, but to insist upon being put down at the house they wish to go to.

HOTELS:—

HOTEL DE BELLE VUE, one of the most highly recommended hotels on the Continent.

HOTEL DE FRANCE, fronting the Park, most comfortable and much commended.

HOTEL DE L'UNIVERS, one of the best in Belgium.

HOTEL DE SAXE, exceedingly good in every respect and close to the railway.

HOTEL DE FLANDRE.—This old-established and highly-recommended hotel is still conducted by Madame Basten.

HOTEL DE L'EUROPE, a first-rate old established house, enjoying an excellent reputation.

GRANDE BRETAGNE.—Well situated, in the Place Royale, and charges moderate.

HOTEL WINDSOR, a comfortable and reasonable family hotel.

HOTEL DE HOLLANDE, a very clean, well-conducted. quiet, good house.

CALLOS' HOTEL DES CHATELER moderate, and obliging host.

BAILY'S COMMERCIAL TAVERN, rue du Musee. Ale and Porter on draft. Board and Lodging on reasonable terms.

BOARDING & LODGING-HOUSE.—Mrs. Haydon's, 27, Quartier Louise, is most respectable, and deserves our best recommendations.

This, the capital of the kingdom, and seat of Government, is 88 miles from Ostend, 27¼ from Antwerp, 48 from Ghent, 71¼ from Liege, 92½ from Lille, 149¾ from Cologne, and 150 from Paris. Population (including suburbs) 145,000. The local attractions are numerous.

We have now to introduce this fair city to our readers, a city which has formed the subject of the warmest eulogiums from three of our greatest modern poets, Byron, Scott, and Southey; and no person who visits it in the present day will say that their praises are exaggerated or undeserved. No traveller who visits the lower town, observes its noble streets and mansions, inhabited by the mercantile part of the community, and then proceeds to the upper or "west end" of the city, commencing with the Place Royale, embellished by the church of St. Jaques sur Caudenberg, and the statue of the Crusader, Godfrey of Bouillon, thence to the Place des Palais, and there admires the pleasing coup d'œil formed by the King's Palece, the Palace of the Prince of Orange, the beautiful and umbrageous Park, the magnificent Rue Royale, the noble buildings in the Rue de la Loi, the splendid view from the Place du Congrès, but what will exclaim that the beauty of the tout ensemble, the neatness and cleanliness of this part of Brussels, render it one of the most charming cities in Europe, and impart a becoming dignity to the seat of the Belgian government.

Its history is replete with a succession of eventful scenes and tragical dramas of the most harrowing description. At one period depopulated by the plague, produced by thirteen months of consecutive rain; at another epoch its citizens decimated by the atrocious cruelties of the Duke of Alva, the Spanish Regent; by civil wars and revolutions, religious persecutions of the Protestants by the Catholics, of the Hebrews by the Christians. The successive dominion of the house of Austria, of Spain, of France, and of Holland, render its history one unvarying repetition of deeds of cruelty, bigotry, and intolerance.

If the cities of Antwerp, Bruges, and Ghent, are objects of reverence to the antiquarian, the historian, the lover of the fine arts, the fair capital of Belgium is peculiarly the property of the ladies. It is Paris in miniature—Parisian toilettes, ganteries, chaussseries, and, above all, the genuine lace of Mechlin and Brussels' manufacture are to be had here on *advantageous terms!* The Montagne de la Cour, the Rue de la Madeleine, and the beautiful Arcade of St. Hubert, should be the special objects of their attention, and whilst they are making acquisitions at these marts, we will invite the messieurs to accompany us to the Grande Place, to admire the beautiful Gothic spire of the Hotel de Ville, and the various architectural designs of the surrounding buildings. Then crossing the *Place* to the Rue de l'Etuve, and proceeding to the corner of the Rue du Chene, the traveller will suddenly find himself in the presence of the oldest citizen of Brussels, the celebrated "Manniken" fountain. *Honi soit qui mal y pense!* Diminutive as this personage is, he is nevertheless of great importance to the bourgoisie of Brussels. Legends and traditions invest him with a halo and dignity which is peculiarly manifested upon holidays or gala days, fêtes and kermesses, when the Manniken is attired in the field-day uniform of a *garde civique,* and decorated *with the order of St. Louis.*

The traveller next visits the Cathedral Church of Saint Gudule, and is stricken by the beautiful painted glass in its windows, particularly that of the St. Sacrement chapel, which is deemed the most exquisitely painted window in Europe. The carved pulpit, by Verbruggen, representing the expulsion of Adam and Eve from the garden of Eden, is also an object of admiration, and we would likewise direct attention to a monument recently placed in this cathedral, to the memory of a Belgian philanthropist, the late Chanoine Triste. This piece of sculpture is by the same artist that executed the statue of Godfrey de Bouillon, in the Place Royale, and is considered one of the purest and most classical works of modern times.

The amateur of paintings will be gratified by paying a visit to the Museum, which we have not space to describe, to the gallery of the Duke D'Aremberg, in the Petit Sablon, and to the collection of Monsieur Rochard, an eminent portrait painter, in the Rue des Douze Apôtres, who possesses some specimens of the best masters, and who receives our countrymen with gentlemanly urbanity and attention.

September, 1848, will be memorable in the history of this fine old city as the days on which the First Peace Congress, consisting of 150 gentlemen from England, Scotland, and Wales, together with delegates from various parts of the Continent, assembled therein, to enunciate their principles—for the promotion of universal peace—for the settlement of international differences by arbitration—and to call the attention of governments to the advantages of a measure of general disarmament, as conducive to a friendly understanding among the nations, and tending directly to prepare the way for the formation of a general Congress of Nations. The proceedings of the Convention, from their novelty, and the influential and talented character of the assembled representatives, excited the greatest interest. The reception given to the delegates, both at Ostend and Brussels, was extremely gratifying; and we can but hope that this exposition of the principles of peace before the world may be the herald of that day "when nation shall not lift up sword against nation, neither shall they learn war any more." [For notice of Second Great Peace Congress, see under the head of Paris, at page 153.]

A valet-de place may be hired for 5fr. per day. The Post-office at the top of Rue de la Montagne, is open from 5 till 9. Postage stamps are in use throughout the kingdom: single rate for one-third of an oz. 10 centimes, for 30 kilometres (about 18¾ miles,) 20 centimes for all distances above; prepayment optional. Between Belgium and all France the stamp is 40 centimes. The following is a list of the offices for obtaining passports:—France, 146, Rue Royale Neuve: Austria, 9, Rue Belliard, Quartier Leopold: English Embassy, Rue Belliard, Quartier Leopold. Prussian Embassy in Brussels, 37, Rue des Petit Carmes.

The King's Palaces may be viewed during his Majesty's absence. The Museum is open every Sunday, Monday, and Thursday, from 10 till 3, and every other day to strangers on producing their passports. The Duke d'Arenberg's Palace daily, by applying to the porter, and producing a passport. The Town Hall daily, from 10 till 5, (gratis.) The two Houses of Parliament daily, from 10 till 3. The Botanical Gardens, (gratis) every Tuesday, Thursday, and Saturday, from 9 till 5. The Passport Office is at the Hotel de Ville, and is open daily from 10 till 4. The London mail arrives in Brussels every day, except Monday, and departs from Brussels every day, except Saturday, in the afternoon. Letters for England must be posted at the Chief Office, Rue de la Montangne, before 2 p.m. for the first dispatch, and before 5.45 p.m. for the second, *via* France. Letters, &c., forwarded by the former are delivered in London by 9 in the morning, and by the latter by 12 the day after their leaving Brussels. Theatre Royal de la Mormaie.—Performances every evening. Theatre des Galeries Saint Hubert.—Performances every evening. Concert in the Park every evening during the summer.

The "Brussels Herald" English Newspaper, the only English journal in Belgium, is published every Monday, at the office, 4, Rue de la Paille, and will be found to contain much useful local information. Terms of subscription 5 francs per quarter. Single papers can be had at the office, at 40 centimes each, or of Mr. Froments, Library, Montague de la Cour.

In conclusion we may remark, that it is customary for travellers passing through Belgium, to sojourn and rest during the Sabbath in Brussels, as it offers the advantages of possessing several Protestant places of worship:—

Church of England Service:—On Sundays, at the Chapel Royal, Rue du Musèe, at 9 a m. and half past 2. by the Rev. M. J. Blacker, B.A.; in the chapel, on the Boulevard de l'Observatoire, at a quarter to 1, and half past three in the afternoon, by the Rev. W. Drury, M.A.; and at the Evangelical Chapel, Rue Belliard, by the Rev. G. P. Keogh, at 9.30 a.m. and 3 p.m. **Independent**:—by Mr. Tiddy, 21, Rue Belliard, Quartier Leopold, at 11 morn and 6 evening.

CONVEYANCES.—*Excursion to Waterloo*—See next page.—Railroad to Malines & Antwerp, see page 65. —To Ghent, Bruges, and Ostend, see page 58. —To Louvain, Tirlemont Liege, Aix-la-Chapelle, and Cologne, see page 56. To Mons, Valenciennes, Douai, Arras, Amiens, & Paris, see pages 34, 35, & 36.—To Braine-le-Comte, Charleroi, & Namur, see page 61. — To Malines, Ghent, Courtray, Mouscron, Lille, Calais, and Dunkirk, see page 59.—To Jurbise, Ath, and Tournay see page 62.—Steamers from Ostend to Dover every night. To London direct, every Tuesday and Friday night, according to the tide, see page 134.—From Antwerp to London, see page 126.

ENGLISH DIRECTORY OF BRUSSELS.

Railway Termini.—The terminus of the Northern line communicating with Antwerp. Ostend, Ghent, Bruges, Lille, Malines, Louvain, Liege, Verviers, Aix-la-Chapelle, and Cologne, is outside the Porte de Cologne. That of the Southern line for Mons, Namur, Valenciennes, and Paris, is designated the Station du Midi.

Professional Gentlemen recommended by the Editors.

PHYSICIAN.—Dr. Parkinson, F.R.C.S.I., 15, Rue de la Pepiniere; is highly esteemed by the English residing in Brussels, and we strongly recommend him from our own experience.

DENTIST.—Mr. J. Alex, 3, Place Belliard, opposite the Park, Surgeon-dentist to his Majesty King Leopold. Mr. Alex having been established in Brussels during the last 16 years, has acquired the confidence of the English and Belgian Medical profession, and his recent appointment as honorary Dentist to the King of the Belgians, proves the high estimation in which his talents are held in this country.

CHEMISTRY.—J. B. Fierens, 86, Montagne de la Cour.—SOLICITOR—T. J. Maltby, 4, Rue de la Paille. AGENT for the Sale of J. A. Farina's *Eau de Cologne*—Maison St. Leger.

Boot and Shoemaker—As few travellers visit Brussels without purchasing these articles, we recommend J. Schott, 41, Montagne de la Cour, as being the best manufacturer of ladies and gentlemens boots and shoes.

Booksellers.—We can recommend, with confidence, the establishment of Kiesling & Co., 26, Montagne de la Cour, as having an excellent and extensive stock of books in English and all the Continental languages - Guides, Maps, &c.; Murray's Hand Books, Bradshaw's Monthly Guides, German and French Circulating Library.

Carriages and Saddle Horses.—Travellers wishing to go to Waterloo, can do so by the Mail Coaches, see particulars next column, or if they wish to visit different objects of interest in Brussels and the environs, Lacken or Boitsfort, may obtain good vehicles or saddle horses at reasonable rates, of J. Suffells, 17, Rue Villa Hermosa, Montagne de la Cour, and of J. Copper, 23, Esplanade, Porte de Namur.

Chemist and Druggist.—As it is somewhat difficult to have English prescriptions carefully prepared on the Continent, we have found Mr. J. B. Fierens, 86, Montagne de la Cour. deserving all confidence, from the attention he pays to his customers and the moderateness of his prices.

Daily Express Office for the daily conveyance of small parcels, samples, law papers, &c., simultaneously with the mails, 74, Montagne de la Cour.

English Bankers.—The old English Bank and Exchange Office are now at No. 8, Rue Royale. Messrs. Salter and Bigwood corres ond with the Union Bank of London; the Firms of Messrs. Chas. Hoare and Co., and Messrs. Martin & Co., London; Oriental Bank Corporation; Messrs. Duncan & Co., New York.

Gloves.—There are so many shops for this article that we can scarcely expect ladies to abide implicitly by our recommendation; but, from personal experience, confirmed by general repute, we advise them not to purchase until they have seen the gloves of Mr. Auvray, 9, Passage des Princes, Galeries St. Hubert.

Lace.—We recommend with all confidence the establishment of M. Vanderkelen Bresson, No. 248, or 1, Rue du Marquis, near the Cathedral of St. Gudule; and we advise the ladies to postpone making any purchases until they have seen the above stock. Awarded the Prize Medal by the Commissioners of the Great Exhibition, and a Gold Medal by the Belgian Government. Visitors should be particular in not mistaking the house, or confounding this establishment with others, which may be easily avoided, *as the name is on the door.*

Library and Reading Rooms.—Froment's, No. 84, Montagne de la Cour; well supplied in every respect, as regards an extensive library and variety of newspapers and periodicals. It is also the depôt for the sale of BRADSHAW'S RAILWAY GUIDES

Millinery, Flowers, Head-dresses, Lace Caps, Handkerchiefs, &c—We recommend, in full confidence for all these articles, the establishment of Miss Marie Serraris, 73, Rue de la Montagne, near the General Post Office, as this person enjoys an excellent renommée among the highest classes of society in Brussels.

Nouveautes.—A visit to the extensive *Fabrique Européene et des Indes* of M. Gluzeau, Ainé, 86, Rue de la Montagne, facing the General Post Office, will remind the ladies of the best houses in London.

Piano-fortes—English families residing in Brussels, or any other part of Belgium, can always hire or purchase excellent pianos of Mr. F. Jastrzebski, at his establishment, 23, Rue de Ruysbroeck, near the Palais de Justice. Awarded the Prize Medal by the Commissioners of the Great Exhibition.

Tailor.—Travellers will find a large stock of ready made wearing apparel, of the best fashion, at T. B Collard's, 42, Rue de la Madeleine, and at most reasonable prices. Orders are promptly executed, which is a great consideration for tourists.

Mr. Collard has also several branch establishments in the provincial towns, *i. e*, a splendid one at Ghent, and others at Namur and Charleroi.

Watchmaker—H. Plet, 52, Rue de la Madeleine. Persons desirous of buying good Geneva watches, time-pieces, or exquisite small watches for ladies, are recommended to this manufacturer, as his prices are reasonable and the articles warranted.

Waterloo.—HOTEL:—Brassine.

The best Guides, to conduct travellers over the field, are Martin Viseur and Joseph Dehaze.

The expense of a party going to Waterloo was formerly 27 francs, but this has been reduced to a more reasonable price by the spirit of English enterprise. Instead of the close *vigilante*, or lumbering carriage, there are now *two* English four-horse Mail Coaches, belonging to Messrs. Copper and Suffell, which run daily between Brussels and Mount St. Jean on he field of Waterloo. Fares—5 francs there and back. The "Warrior" starts from the Hotel de l' nivers, at 9 o'clock, and the "Victoria," from the Hotel de Saxe, at 10 o'clock, both taking up passengers, a short time after, at the Hotel "Grande Bretagne," on the Place Royale, returning to Brussels in time for the Table d'Hôte. And we strongly recommend travellers to secure their places. for the day they wish to go, immediately on their arrival in Brussels, at Suffell's, No. 17, Rue Villa Hermosa, Montagne de la Cour, or of J. Copper, 23, Esplanade, Port de Namur.

These conveyances render a visit to Waterloo an agreeable and cheap excursion, but as they interfere with the parties who formerly let out vehicles for Waterloo, these coaches are opposed by hotel-keepers, waiters, commissioners, &c. We therefore think it right to warn our readers, that if they mention "Waterloo," attempts will be made to dissuade them from going by the "Mail Coaches," though we hope unsuccessfully, as these conveyances are decidedly the best, being respectably conducted by steady English coachmen; and considering that the proprietors are two industrious Englishmen, who have established these coaches for the conveyance of travellers, we think they are entitled to the support of their fellow-countrymen.

N.B.—These coaches ceased running on the 30th of October for the Winter months; but the 10 o'clock Coach re-commences running, April 25th; and the 9 o'clock, June 1st.

The excursion to Waterloo is a very pleasant one indeed—through the forest of Soignies. Few English or American travellers who visit Brussels, can refrain from going to Waterloo and Mount St. Jean; the Chateau of Hougoumont, La Haie Sainte, Quartre Bras, &c., with their exciting associations, are as attractive as ever, though seven and thirty years have elapsed since this field was the scene of that international conflict and carnage, in which 70 thousand men were slain. The Lion Mount commemorates the victories of the allies over their common enemy. But we hope it may not be illusory to anticipate that the day will come when the Lion Mount shall have disappeared, and the Gaul meet the Anglo-Saxon in peaceful amity, midst these quiet, fertile scenes, in a better and more enobling spirit, produced by that commercial rivalry, and glorious emulation in the civilising arts of peace, which give these two races so prominent a part to play for the general good of mankind.

If travellers wish to possess correct information concerning this event, we recommend them to purchase at Cotton's Waterloo Museum, a small book intitled " A Voice from Waterloo."

The chapel of Waterloo is worth a visit by those anxious to see the many monuments erected by the families of the brave fellows who fell at the battle.

ROUTE 2.

Brussels, Antwerp, Liege, Verviers, Aix-la-Chapelle, and Cologne.

Brussels.—See page 167.

Brussels to Cologne, *via* Malines, Louvain. Liége, Verviers, and Aix-la-Chapelle. The journey is particularly interesting, and interspersed with very many agreeable associations. The traveller, on leaving by the North Station, finds himself carried along a very flat but highly cultivated country, until he arrives at

Vilvorde.—See page 166.

Malines.—See page 166.

Antwerp (*With Map in Special Edition.*)—(In French, *Anvers.*)—Hotels:—

The Hotel St. Antoine, one of the best in Europe; much frequented by the English for the excellent accommodation it affords, and its table d'hote, which is deservedly celebrated.

The Hotel du Parc is an excellent house. The proprietor speaks English fluently, is attentive and obliging, and extremely popular with English travellers.

Ship Broker.—Mr. B. Kennedy, Agent of the General Steam Navigation Company.

It is 60 miles from the sea, 27¼ from Brussels, 32 from Ghent, 150½ from Cologne, and 258¼ from Paris. The Post-Office is in the Place Verte. A British Consul is resident. On the Quay Van Dyck, on the opposite bank of the river, is the station of the Direct railway to Ghent, through St. Nicholas, Lockeren, and the fine country called the Pays de Waes, shortening the distance by more than one-third (52 kilometres or 32 miles, instead of 80 kiloms. or 50 miles), and saving about 1 hour's time; the fares also are less than those of the State line. Omnibuses call at the hotels to convey passengers. The stand for Vigilantes is by the Post-Office and Place de Meir.

" Astonished I beheld th' adjoining port,
Belgium's emporium, and the fam'd repute
Of riches maritime; a wondrous sight."

The commercial capital of Belgium is situated on the banks of the Scheldt. It is celebrated for its magnificent docks, constructed under the direction of Napoleon, which are capable of receiving two thousand ships. At a former period of its history Antwerp contained a population of 200,000 souls, and at this instant it still appears a bustling, thriving city, with only 80,000 persons, who find employment in the occupations afforded by its maritime commerce, and its manufactories of black silk, its sugar refineries, its manufacture, bleaching, and embroidery of lace. Antwerp possesses several large and spacious streets, with more splendid mansions than there are suitable inhabitants for. But although it is still a comparatively flourishing city, and carries on a maritime trade with the whole world, and the Bourse or Change is still filled with the modern merchant or shipowner, yet its ancient greatness has departed, though the mansions of its once merchant princes still remain as memorials of its former greatness.

In many parts of this otherwise fine city the habitations of the poor would be greatly benefited by the effect of a sanitary act—such as that which is now in operation in England.

Probably there is no place in Europe so rich in magnificent churches, embellished by the most remarkable works of art, as the town of Antwerp—enriched by the best productions of Rubens and Van Dyck, and other great masters of painting, who were natives of the city. Commencing with the Cathedral of Notre Dame, the traveller must first examine the architecture of the spire—a Gothic structure of exceeding beauty. It is 466 feet high, and runs up tapering into the clouds, with a gradual, yet correct mathematical precision which is unequalled in any other edifice on the Continent. Entering the Cathedral, the first object of attraction is the celebrated painting—with engraved copies of which most people are familiar—viz., *The Descent from the Cross*—reputed to be the *chef d'œuvre* of Rubens. Most persons, however, feel disappointed — it scarcely answers the general expectation. The fact is that the composition is very fine, but the colouring seems to have lost that peculiar brilliancy of tone which distinguishes the works of Rubens. We fear the damp and saline properties of the atmosphere in which it hangs will gradually destroy the colouring entirely. To our mind the helpless heaviness of the dead body of the Saviour—suspended and supported by the Apostles, and being gradually lowered—is represented with inimitable truth.

On the other side is another painting—the pendant, as the French express it—representing the " Elevation of the Cross," which Sir Joshua Reynolds describes as one of the best and most animated compositions painted by Rubens. " The Assumption of the Virgin " and " The Resurrection of the Saviour," two other admirable paintings by the same master, should lso be inspected; as also the pulpit in carved wood, and the newly-erected sculptured gothic stalls in the principal Choir, which will remind the traveller of those in St. George's chapel, at Windsor.

In front of the west door of the cathedral is a remarkable *chef d'oeuvre* in iron, executed by the celebrated Antwerp blacksmith, Quentin Matsys, who subsequently became a great painter.

The church of St. Jaques is an imposing-looking edifice, which contains many precious and rare works in painting and sculpture; and the interior of the church is embellished with a degree of splendour and richness of decoration quite dazzling. The tomb of Rubens is, however, the principal object of attraction. The altar-piece is also by Rubens, and the beautiful picture of the Saviour crucified is by Van Dyck. The marble statue of the Virgin is greatly admired; it is by Duquesnoy.

On entering the church of St. Paul, the visitor will be struck by a representation of Mount Calvary, —the Crucifixion—and the Ordeal of Purgatory The coarse and rough manner in which these scenes are represented, form a singular contrast to the numerous works of Art executed in the highest perfection within the church. The "Adoration of the Shepherds" is said to be—but not generally considered to be—the production of Rubens. "The Descent from the Cross"—A magnificent altar-piece—"The Works of Mercy"—and last, though not the least worthy of notice, the thrilling picture designated "The Scourging of Christ," by Rubens. No person can behold this extraordinary painting with unmoved feelings of admiration of the painter who could delineate the person of the Saviour undergoing the "flagellation" from the hands of the public executioner—and indignant sympathy with the suffering Saviour and author of Christianity.

The churches of St. Augustine and that of the Jesuits also contain several good paintings. The collection of pictures at the Museum should likewise be visited. Quentin Matsys has several works here of merit—his "Descent from the Cross" is one of the best; No. 82, "The Dead Christ"; 84, "The Virgin holding the infant Redeemer;" 83, "St John;" 85, "A Holy Family;" 86, "Our Saviour on the Cross." 72, "The Crucifixion of Christ between the two Thieves;" 73, 77, 75, 76, and 79, are the Works of Rubens. 111, 112, 113, are admirable specimens of the productions of Van Dyck.

Before quitting Antwerp, the traveller should visit the Exchange or Bourse, which is a curious specimen of Spanish or Moorish architecture, reminding one strongly of the Piazzas of the Alhambra at Grenada. The Zoological gardens are also worth visiting; the collection of beautiful birds, and various specimens of animals, will even be found worthy of a visit from a subscriber to the aristocratic gardens in London. There are several private collections of paintings which are shown to strangers. We give the address of a few of them:—M. Henry, Rue de la Digue d'Ever; M. Van Comp, Rue d'Hoboken; M. Traché, Rue de Couvent.

CONVEYANCES. — Railway trains to Ghent direct, see page 66.—To Malines and Brussels, page 65.—To Malines, Liege, Verviers, Aix-la-Chapelle, and Cologne, pages 65 and 56. The passage from Antwerp direct to London is now performed in 15 hours by the General Steam Navigation Companys New Ship, "Ravensbourne," see page 126; or by the Belgian Company's New Ship, "Baron Osy." These vessels have the best of accommodation for passengers; and from the sea passage only occupying a few hours, the route, *via* the Scheld and Thames, or *vice versa*, is one of the most agreeable and particularly convenient for families going to or returning from the Rhine. Steamers from Antwerp to Hull, see page 126. Steamers from Antwerp to Rotterdam by the Scheld, daily, see page 126.

Louvain.—HOTEL:—

Hotel de Suede, an excellent house, highly recommended.

This town is situated on the river Dyle, 27 miles from Brussels by the railroad, and 44 from Liége. The Town-hall is a splendid specimen of gothic architecture, and contains a fine gallery of paintings, the greater part by the first masters of the Flemish school. Travellers should also pay a visit to the Church of St. Peter, and its celebrated chapel of "Magrietge." The Church of St. Peter has several fine pictures; the one representing "Jesus giving the Keys to St. Peter," was taken by the French to Paris, and afterwards returned. The stalls in the choir of the Church St. Gertrude are considered remarkably beautiful. In the 14th century Louvain contained 140,000 inhabitants: now less than 30,000. The most important article of industry is beer, of which large quantities are annually exported. It also carries on considerable traffic in lace, corn, and hops.

The country through which the tourist passes from Malines to Louvain is very picturesque and well cultivated.

The country from Louvain to Tirlemont is rather uninteresting in its general appearance, taking in one or two villages of no very great importance. The railroad from Louvain passes through a short tunnel, and then leaves the Abbey of Parc on the right. The Abbey is still inhabited by the monks, and furnished with three fish ponds. Passing through a tunnel we arrive at

Tirlemont, the chief city of a canton in the Louvaine district and province of Brabant. It contains 8,500 inhabitants. The space within its walls south of the railway contains at present very few houses, but has very old gates. Among the chief objects of its attractions may be enumerated the old Church of St. Germain, built upon an eminence overhanging the town. It can be seen from the railway, and is an erection of the ninth century, containing an altar-piece by Wappes. Outside the gate leading to Maestricht are three large burrows, supposed to be the graves of some Barbarians of a very remote age. They can be seen from the railway, on the left. The railroad, after leaving the station, looks down from an embankment on the town. On nearing Landen, it runs through the plain of Neirweiden, celebrated for two great battles crossing the windings of the stream all the way to fought there in 1693, when our countrymen, under the third William, were beaten by the French under Marshal Luxembourg; and in 1793, when the Austrians defeated the revolutionary army, and drove them from Belgium The town itself is seated on the river Beck, 19 miles south-east of Louvaine.

Landen.—A small place containing about 700 inhabitants. It is seated on the river Beck, 19 miles south east of Louvain, and is remarkable as having been the birth-place of Pepin of Landen, the founder of the race of Charlemagne. It was once a large town, and the ruins of its ancient walls still remain to attest its former importance.

A branch railway from Landen leads to St. Trond and Hasselt, the former a very ancient city of 9000 inhabitants, and called after St. Trudon, who built a monastery here. At Brustem, near this, a great battle was fought in 14 7, between Charles the Bold and his rebellious subjects at Liege. In this war all the gates and ramparts were destroyed; the city is situated in the province of Liege, 15 miles W.N W. of Maestricht.

The direct route of line from Landen. after leaving that station, passes

Waremme—chief town of a district in the province of Leige, formerly capital of the Herbaic, and now containing 1,500 inhabitants. Its church, an ancient foundation, by the Ganthier, of the 12th century, is worth a visit.

Fexhe is next met.

On approaching Liége the traveller should be particular in watching the as cent of the train, from the station at Ans to the stationary engine-house on the summit of the hill, and then prepare himself to behold, during the descent on the inclined plane, one of the most splendid panoramic views in the world, which will burst upon his sight with instantaneous grandeur. The whole city of Liége, with its cupola domes, its innumerable manufactories, and its palace, extended over the valley, or plain—at the junction of the Meuse and Ourthe—is one of those sights never to be forgotten. The traveller, however, should linger over the scene, and, if possible, stay a day or two at

Liege.–Hotels –The best Hotels are in the town.

The Hotel de l'Europe we can strongly recommend.

Hotel d'Angleterre, an old established and very good house.

Hotel de Belle Vue—a first-rate house, in a good situation, and well conducted.

Hotel de Suede, exceedingly good in every respect.

Distance from Malines, 58½ miles.

The Liége terminus lies on the south bank of the Meuse, close to the Quai d'Avroy. The railway crosses the river by the bridge of Val St. Benoit. This thriving town is situated in the middle of a plain, girt by mountains, at the junction of the Meuse and Ourthe, 71¼ miles from Brussels, and 34¾ from Aix-la-Chapelle. Population 62,000. Post-Office, Rue de la Regence. Excursions to Spa and the hot springs are recommended. Liége, from its extensive iron works, has acquired the title of the Birmingham of Belgium. It presents many historical reminiscences and associations to interest the antiquarian, many splendid churches to attract the curious; and an active, hardy, and industrious population, to amuse the observant man of commercial acquirements. Its history is connected with the celebrated bishops of Liége—the repeated conflicts between the citizens and their bishops—the bishops against their allies, the Dukes of Burgundy—and there is probably no better historical narrative of these events than that given by Scott in Quentin Durward; even the town and palace of Liége are so graphically described, that the details are correct even at the present day. The church of St. Jaques is remarkable for a similarity existing between the style of its architecture and that of the Bourse at Antwerp: both are distinguished by the piazzas, or pillars of Gothic Moorish art—each of different pattern—and each characterized by the same beautiful elegance of design and finish. If a traveller, undeterred by the unprepossessing appearance of the old part of the town, will venture to penetrate into the narrow streets leading to the banks of the Meuse, he will see the hardy, industrious Walloon population in all their peculiar attributes, provident, self-denying, hard working, cheerful, and even joyous at their labours, they work at home, every member of the family performing his or her part; every house has its own smith's fire and anvil, and a person must remain very late at night, and visit this scene very early in the morning to find the industrious artizan absent from his work. The view from the citadel is magnificent.

Pursuing his route onwards, by railway, from Liége to Verviers, the traveller will pass through the most picturesque portion of the line to Cologne. The beautiful railway bridge over the Meuse, undulating hills and valleys, rivulets and waterfalls, tunnels and aqueducts, the varying landscape, and the changing scenery, render this a panoramic view of so uncommon a description, as the traveller glides along, with almost silent velocity, behind the fiery pegasus, that many persons perform the journey, to and from, several times, in order to retain a vivid and lively recollection of the scene.

Conveyances.—Railway to Verviers, Aix-la-Chapelle and Cologne, see page 56; to Tirlemont, Malines, and Brussels, see page 57; to Namur, see page 64. Steamers—see alphabetical l st, page 131.

Leaving Liege, the traveller proceeds on his route to Aix-la-Chapelle, and crosses the Meuse by a fine bridge of seven arches, 469 feet long. There are nineteen tunnels on the Belgian part of the line alone. It follows close to the same course as the high road as far as Limbourg, crossing the bridge by seventeen arches, and frequently piercing the rock. The Ourthe is crossed by a bridge of three arches at

Chenee, a manufacturing place, situated at the junction of the Ourthe with the Visdre. The railway passes the beautiful vale of the Visdre-Limbourg. The scenery along is interspersed with orchards, villas, gardens, and rich pasturage, at times varied by large manufactories, principally of cloth, all along to

Chaufontaine (Warm Fountain).

The HOTEL DES BAINS is an excellent house, and the warm mineral bath will be found a great luxury to the tired traveller. This establishment belongs to Mr. Henrard, proprietor of the Hotel de l'Europe, at Liege, who has several furnished houses at Chaufontaine, always ready to receive families.

A beautiful village, five miles distant from Liége on the Cologne railway. Delightfully situated in the valley de la Vesdre, it is much frequented by travellers on account of its picturesque promenades and warm mineral springs, as also from its proximity to Spa and Verviers. The season for taking the baths commences on the 1st of May, and travellers going to the Rhine, or returning from Germany, find it most refreshing to take a few hours' rest at this charming place, and in so doing they obviate the expenses incidental to the removal of luggage to and from the stations of larger towns.

Le Trooz.—A place of no importance.

Nessonvaux.

Pepinster.—Here is the station for Spa—distance about 5 English miles. Omnibuses and conveyances effect the journey in 1½ hours. Fares: see page 56; 6 or 7 francs, and even 12 francs, are charged at the hotels at the Spa for two-horse carriages.

Spa.—HOTELS:—

HOTEL DE FLANDRE, highly recommended.

GRAND HOTEL BRITANNIQUE—a very good house, and well conducted.

This celebrated watering-place is situated in a romantic valley, about seventeen miles from Aix-la-Chapelle. The springs are all chalybeate, and a considerable trade is carried on in bottling the water for exportation. This town has enjoyed a perfect neutrality during some of the hottest wars, chiefly on account of its being a place of medical resort for invalids from all parts of the world. The waters are highly beneficial in liver complaints. It contains a resident population of about 4000.

The fountains of Spa are distinguished by the following names. viz.:—The Pouhon, situate in the centre of the town, is the most celebrated; the Geronstere is about two miles from Spa, in a charming spot in the middle of a wood; the Sauveniere and the Groosbeck are at about the same distance, in a wood containing most delightful walks. The Redonte of Spa is situate in the centre of the town; and during the season, which generally commences in June, is one of the most frequented establishments in Europe. The articles of Spa wood made here, are most beautiful, and few ladies leave Spa without taking some of these with them. The Cascade of Coo, and the Grotto of Remouchamp, should be visited by every admirer of picturesque scenery.

AGENT for the Sale of J. A. Farina's *Eau de Cologne*—Mr. Richard Schwaiger.

CONVEYANCES.—Railway from Brussels to Pepinster, see page 56.

The railway from Pepinster passes a valley containing large cloth manufactories, and handsome villas with neat gardens, until it arrives at

Ensival.—A considerable place, possessing some important manufactories, and looked upon as a suburb of Verviers.

Verviers.—HOTEL:—

Hotel de Flandre.

Situated in the valley of the Vesdre, about sixteen miles from Liége, the seat of the cloth trade, and may justly be termed the Leeds of Belgium. Population about 23,000, happy and thriving. It is rarely that a complaint is heard from Verviers of want of employment; the manufacturers, instead of distracting the government with demands which it cannot satisfy, quietly pursue their vocation, and study to improve their productions: many of them are very wealthy. The town contains nothing remarkable, but the site is extremely picturesque. The railway station is very convenient for the examination of the luggage and passports by the Belgian authorities, which takes place here, in returning from Germany.

Here travellers entering Belgium from Prussia have their luggage subject to a long and tedious examination. Carriages are also changed here, in both going and returning.

CONVEYANCES.—Railway trains to Aix-la-Chapelle and Cologne, page 56.—To Liége, Tirlemont, Louvain, Malines, Brussels, Ghent Bruges, and Ostend, pages 57 and 58.

Dolhain.—Passengers are sometimes required to alight here, that it may be ascertained that the carriage contains no small luggage. This once flourishing town is now nearly in ruins. The view into the valley is agreeable, but there is nothing worth stopping to see. The railway here quits the valley of the Visdre. The first Prussian station met with is

Herbesthal.—Passports are called for at this station, and taken away. If not *visé* and returned, they must be reclaimed at the Bureau des Passports at the Aix-la-Chapelle station, where the luggage is all examined and declared for transit The railway is carried over a bridge of seventeen arches 120 feet high in the centre over the valley of the Guile, passing through two tunnels, the second of which is 2,220 feet long, pierced through a sand hill. It finally terminates at Aix-la-Chapelle, down an inclined plane, up which carriages are drawn by a stationery engine in coming from

Aix-la-Chapelle, see page 203.

From Aix the traveller proceeds per rail to Cologne, a distance of 43¼ English miles, and to Dusseldorf direct. Close by the side of the line is the Castle of Frakenburg. Charlemagne is reported to have founded a Castle on this spot, in which he dwelt, and there died his Queen Fastrado.

Nirem.—This village is seen just previous to entering the cutting leading to the Nirem Tunnel, 327 yards long, and carrying the railway through the basin of hills which surround Aix. Passing through the beautiful wood of Reichswald,

Stolberg is reached. The town, a manufacturing one, with about 3000 inhabitants, is built about three miles south of the station, up a valley studded with mills, forges, &c. The town is surmounted by a picturesque old castle.

Escheweiler—An industrious little town, of 3,600 inhabitants, built on the Jude, and having silk, iron and wire manufactories, and also an old picturesque castle close to the line. The old Castle of Nothberg is next passed, it is flanked with four towers.

Langerwehe.—Beyond this, through the Vale of the Wehe, a viaduct of seven arches conveys the railway, which, after emerging from the cutting, looks by the village and castle of Merode, and again pursuing its course through the village of Dhorn; crossing the Rhine immediately after by a bridge of six arches, we enter the station of

Duren, a town of 8000 inhabitants. It is no way remarkable. From here a pleasant excursion may be made up the Valley of the Rhur to the beautiful village Niedhegan, eight miles south of Duren, built on a hill, on which are the ruins of a castle, where Engelbert, Archbishop of Cologne, was imprisoned in the thirteenth century; the Meuse and Rhine, terminating a little way short of

Buir, from which it proceeds by a high embankment, over the lowlands of the Valley of the Erft; crossing that river by three bridges before reaching

Horrem, beyond whose village is the fine old Castle of Frenz. Passing from the Erft into the Valley of the Rhine, through Königsdorf Tunnel, a mile long, carried through a hill of sand 136 feet below the summit, we arrive at

Konigsdorf; from here we proceed to

Mugernsdorf, crossing the road from Cologne to Julich. Here a very fine view can be had of Cologne, with its myriad towers and steeples, towering far above which rises the octagon of St. Gereon, with its detached forts and half-buried towers surrounded with trees. This brings us to the

Cologne Terminus—For description of Cologne see page 185.

ROUTE 3.

London to Brussels, via Dover and Calais.

The tourist, on leaving London Bridge, finds himself whirled over a beautiful country; and at about six and a quarter miles he finds himself at Sydenham. To the right of the line the Crystal Palace of 1851 has found a permanent home, and stands forth as a grand and splendid monument representing the combined elements of universal industry, and ornamenting the picturesque locality in which it is situated. Very little of interest surrounds the remaining part of the journey to Dover, where the traveller takes the steam-boat, and leaving the old cliffs of England, finds himself after a delightful sea trip of two hours at Calais, in France. On arrival here tourists should proceed direct to the passport office, on the railway station, and get their passport properly *vised*, after which they should proceed to an adjoining room for the purpose of having their baggage examined. This, however, can be avoided by declaring them for transit.

Calais.—See page 145.

The journey between Calais and Brussels is performed by rail. The first place of interest to be met with is Lille, where carriages are changed.

Lille.—See page 149.

Passengers who take this route change carriages at Mouscron. It being a frontier town, the Passports are strictly examined, and the luggage looked after.

Roubaix.—See page 159.

Tourcoing.

Mouscron is seen on an eminence to the right, with its beautiful church built of bricks. Its chief importance arises from the fact of its being situated on the frontier. It is the chief place of its commune, which contains a population of 5536 souls. The country about is rich and well cultivated, producing wheat and rich pastures. Facing Mouscron to the left is the village of Luingues.

From Mouscron the traveller can proceed to Brussels by either of two routes. By that leading to Ghent, Malines, and thence to Brussels, or by the one leading from Tournay to Ath, Jurbise, &c.

MOUSCRON TO BRUSSELS, *via* COURTRAY, GHENT, AND TERMONDE.

Courtray, which is a fortified town of West Flanders, situated on the river Lys. The town is much celebrated for its manufactures of linen and lace. Population about 20,000. It is 32 miles south of Bruges, and 27 miles south-west of Ghent.

The Town Hall deserves to be seen, on account of two chimneys, the sculpture of which are of the greatest beauty, and most highly finished. One is placed in a sort of ante-chamber, which leads to the council hall, the other is in the hall, which it wonderfully beautifies. The Church of St. Martin, founded about 650 by St. Eloi, apostle of Flanders, is remarkable for its tower, which surmounts the front portal, commands a splendid view of the surrounding country and adds much to the majestic appearance of the building. The multitude and richness of the ornaments in the interior attracts attention. The Tabernacle of brown stone of Avernus is worth notice. The church also contains a very valuable painting—"The Scene of Martyrdom at Rome," by Van Manderen, who was a poet and historian rather than a painter. It also contains a picture representing the "Descent of the Holy Spirit upon the Apostles;" and the two shutters, the "Sleep of Adam in Paradise;" and the "Baptism of Christ." The Church of Notre Dame possesses a Vandyke, it is in Baldwin's Chapel, and represents the "Crucifixion;" this painting is greatly admired. It was erected by Baldwin, Count of Flanders, and Emperor of Constantine. It deserves to be visited both on account of the splendour of its ornaments as also for the richness of its paintings. In the Chapel of St. Catherine, surnamed the Baldwin Chapel, is the "Elevation on the Cross," by Vandyke; two bas-reliefs by Godecharles, and a "Christ in the Tomb," by Van Reable, deserve attention also; the Church of St. Michael has a small picture of the celebrated "Battle of the Spurs." The Tabernacle will attract the visitor's attention. The Academy, Museum, and Library together with the Market Hall are the only other places worth visiting.

CONVEYANCES.—Railway to Ghent, Malines, and Brussels, see page 59.

Haerlebeke.

Olsene.

Nazareth.

Ghent.—see page 165.

Wetteren.

Termonde.—See page 166.

Malines.—See page 166.

Vilvorde.—See page 166.

Brussels.—See page 167.

MOUSCRON TO BRUSSELS, BY TOURNAY, ATH, AND JURBISE.

Mouscron.—See page 174.

Tournay.—HOTEL:—L'Imperature.

A Belgian city, in the province of Hainault. The town itself is indifferently built, and has a gloomy aspect: it contains a population of nearly 40,000, who are engaged in the manufacture of cotton and woollen stuffs. Tournay contains the most ancient cathedral in the country, in which are several celebrated pictures by Rubens and some marble groupings by Dufresnoy, a library, in which are 22,000 volumes; and a Museum (at the Hotel de Ville), containing some interesting curiosities, a cabinet of natural history, &c.

CONVEYANCES. — Railway to Mouscron, Courtray, Ghent, Malines, and Brussels, see page 59.—To Ath, Jurbise, Braine-le-Comte, & Brussels, see p. 63.

Ath, a fortified town on the Dendresee, 21 miles from Tournay. A terrible fire in 1433, a hurricane in 1600, and an earthquake in 1691. and other disastrous events dismantled Ath of all her monuments, &c. St. Julien's Tower and the Parish Church alone escaped the conflagration. Ath sustained many deadly sieges. The fortifications constructed in 1815 are strengthened with great care. The population is about 9000.

Maffles.

Attres.

Brugelette.

Lens.

Jurbise, a small commune with a population of 700 souls. It is about eight miles from Mons by railway. The country along from Jurbise to Braine-le-Comte is rather interesting.

Soignies, the chief town of a district in the province of Hainaut, is a pretty and neat town, agreeably situated on the Senne, and passed by the railway. Its churches and tombstones are very old, and cannot fail to interest the antiquarian.

Braine-le-Comte.—This town was formerly in the department of Jemappe, and derived its name from the celebrated Brennus, in the time of Julius Cæsar, who built the town, and strongly fortified it with a castle, &c. Both castle and town, however, were destroyed by the Spaniards about the year 1677. The district around furnishes some of the finest flax in the world. A few miles to the north-west is Steenkerke, remarkable as being the spot where the Duke of Luxembourg defeated William III., in 1692, with a loss of 7000 men. From here a railway branches off to Charleroi and Namur.

CONVEYANCES.—Railway trains to Charleroi and Namur, page 61.—To Jurbise, Ath, and Tournai, see Time Table, page 62.—To Mons, Valenciennes, Douai, Arras, Amiens, and Paris, see pages 60, 34, and 35. To Brussels, see pages 60 and 61.

A tunnel precedes our entry to

Tubise, which possesses no interest for the traveller.

Lembecq—A town containing 2300 inhabitants, with no objects of interests save its old chateau and its numerous distilleries. Nothing worth notice presents itself after leaving the Turbise station.

Hal.—A small but pretty village of 5000 inhabitants, built partly on the Senne, and partly on the canal Charleroi. It has no objects of particular interest, save the Church of St. Mary, celebrated as possessing a miracle-working image of the Virgin. It is of wood, 2 feet high, and has acquired immense wealth by pious offerings, including gold plate given by Charles V., Maximillan I., Pope Julius II., &c.

Loth — Where we halt to take on some carriages.

Ruysbroeck.—A little village of 500 inhabitants, deserving no special notice.

Forest.

Brussels.—See page 167.

ROUTE 4.

Brussels to Paris.

(Distance—231¼ miles; time—10½ hours.)

Terminus at Brussels on the south side of the town, between the Rue d'Anderlecht and Rue de Terre Neuve. There are many cuttings on the line.

On leaving the Station, we cross the Boulevard, getting a view of the Port de Hal on the left, and traversing the river Senne near Forest. On quitting this latter place we see the Senne again, and for some moments behold highly cultivated fields, and immediately arrive at

Ruysbroeck.—See above.

Between Ruysbruck and Hal stations the railway runs side by side with the Canal de Charleroi.

Loth.—See above.

Hal.—See above.

Lembecq.—See above

Tubise.—See page 175.

Braine-le-Comte.—See page 175.

At Braine-le-Comte a branch line diverges to Charleroi and Namur, 49 miles.

Soignies.—See page 175.

Jurbise.—See page 175.

At Jurbise the line branches off to Ath and Tournay.

Mons (Bergen in German).—HOTEL:—
HOTEL DE LA COURONNE, highly recommended.

This important town is divided into two sections by the river Trouille. It is surrounded by an earth-work and ditch, and was considerably strengthened in 1820. The Hotel de Ville is a fine old structure, richly ornamented with sculpture; and the old church of St. Elizabeth is said to have been erected on the site of a fortress erected by Julius Cæsar. It has suffered considerably at times from the ravages of war. The chief manufactures of Mons are woollen stuffs, linen, lace, and earthenware, carried on by a population of about 30,000. The surrounding district abounds with coal-mines. There are also in the neighbourhood extensive bleaching grounds. The principal building is the Church of St. Naudru, built in the Gothic style, commenced in 1460, but not finished until 1580. It stands on the left hand side as we enter Mons from the railway. The interior of the church is well worth a visit; its rude piers without capitals, net-work of ribs, and high altar decorated with bas-reliefs from the New Testament, and cut by an Italian artist, commands attention.

Mons was the natal town of Orlando Lassus, the celebrated musician of the sixteenth century. Ten miles south of Mons, within the French territories, is the spot where was fought the sanguinary battle of Malplaquet, at which the Duke of Marlborough and Prince Eugene conquered the French, and lost on the battle field 20,000 men.

Mons has a communication with the Scheldt by the Canal de Condé, and also, by railway, with Jurbise, Ath, Tournai, Lille, and Calais.

CONVEYANCES.—Railway to Valenciennes, Douai, Lille, Dunkirk, and Calais, see pages 60 and 34. To Valenciennes, Arras, Amiens, and Paris, see pages 34 and 35.

At Mons a branch railway ensures a direct communication from Paris to Charleroi, Namur, and Cologne. This route avoids the detour to Braine-le-Comte. On leaving Mons, the Railway crosses the river Trouille, and passes not very far from the Canal de Conde and the Sluices of St. Ghislain, after which it reaches Jemmappes Station.

Jemmappes.—The village is only remarkable for the defeat of the Austrians by the French, under General Dumouriaz, afterwards Louis Philippe. As we approach St. Ghislain to the left are seen the magnificent establishments of Hornu, after which we arrive at

St. Ghislain.—The country about here has a great resemblance to the neighbourhood of Manchester and Bolton, the roads being black with coal dust and studded with cottages. From this Station there is nothing remarkable to be seen until we reach

Bousu.

Thulin.

Quievrain.—A town containing 2000 inhabitants, carrying on an active commerce with France. It does not absolutely contain any thing worth notice. This is the frontier station of the Southern Line, and the point of junction with the Great Northern of France Railway. At Quievrain is the Belgian custom-house, where the examination of the Passport and Luggage take place on entering Belgium; and one half mile further, the small river Annelle marks the boundary of France. The neighbourhood abounds in coal and other minerals.

Blanc Misseron is next met with, after which we enter

Valenciennes.—See page 161.

The delay during the examination of luggage, which takes place at Valenciennes, is considerable.

The next station of importance met with is Douai after passing St. Raismes, St. Uallars, Louvain, and Martigny, all places of small note, and not requiring a special notice at our hands; we arrive at

Douai.—See page 147.

Meeting St. Vitry and Roux we reach Arras, which is described at page 142.

We meet Amiens next, for description of which see page 142.

From this place the traveller is carried on, passing Claremont, Creil, and St. Denis, and immediately after enters

Paris, described at page 153.

ROUTE 5.

Brussels to Namur.

The railway branches off at Braine-le-Comte. The route becomes most interesting between Marchienne-au-Pont and Charleroi, traversing a country rendered picturesque by nature, and interesting by art. Villages, iron works, coal mines, and manufactories skirt the line.

Charleroi.—HOTEL:
Pays Bas.

Has not more than 5,000 inhabitants, and is of little consequence, the fortifications having prevented its becoming what it otherwise would have been—one of the most flourishing towns on the Continent; but the surrounding neighbourhood has a population of 80,000, and presents a scene of extraordinary activity. The Charleroi coal-field is the most extensive in Belgium, giving employment to 10,000 miners, and yielding annually 3,000,000 tons of coal; the glass trade is also carried on to a very great extent, and these numerous and extensive iron works, which derive their supplies of iron ore from the Sambre and Meuse district,—one of the most picturesque and interesting countries in Belgium, but, with the exception of a few eminent geologists, totally unknown to travellers. It extends about 40 miles south of Charleroi to the French Ardennes. The Sambre and Meuse Railway, which commences at Marchiennes-au-Pont, about a mile from Charleroi, will shortly traverse it in its entire length, terminating on the Meuse, near Givet Twenty-five miles are already open for traffic—from Marchienne to Morialmé, &c. See page 65.

Tailors.—Travellers will find a large stock of ready-made wearing apparel, of the best fashion, at Mr. T. B. Collard's, Rue des Chaudronniers, and at very reasonable prices. Orders are promptly executed, which is a great consideration for Tourists.

Conveyances.-Railway to Namur, Liege, Braine-le-Comte, and Brussels, see Time Table, page 61. To Morialme and Laneffe, page 65.

At two leagues' distance from Charleroi, in the picturesque valley of the Sambre, are the ruins of the Abbaye d'Alne, the most ancient monastery perhaps in Europe, built in the year 656.

The Railway crosses the river Sambre many times between Charleroi and Namur. The scenery is most charming. At Charleroi the line branches off, and leads to Walcourt, and having offshoots to Laneffe, Morialme, and Florenne.

Namur.—Hotel.—

Hotel d'Harscamp, highly recommended.

The capital of the province of Namur, at the conflux of the Sambre and the Maese, a well-built city, with wide and clean streets. It contains a population of 25,000, who are chiefly employed in the cutlery business. It is defended by a citadel, built on the summit of a craggy rock. The cathedral and the church of the Jesuits are both worthy attention: the former is a fine specimen of modern, the latter of ancient, architecture. Here are extensive manufactures of fire-arms, swords, knives, scissors, and other articles of iron, copper, and brass. Quantities of leather, paper, thread, and tobacco are also prepared here. Namur has often changed masters, and is noted for the many sieges which it has sustained. It is the strongest fortress in Belgium.

The environs of Dinant offer much scenery, worthy the notice of amateurs—La Petite Suisse, the Grotto of Hans, the Chateau of King Leopold, &c.

Tailors.—Travellers will find a large stock of ready-made wearing apparel, of the best fashion, at Mr. T. B. Collard's, 739, Rue de l'Auge, and at very reasonable prices. Orders are promptly executed, which is a great consideration for Tourists.

Conveyances.—Railway trains to Charleroi, Braine-le-Comte, and Brussels, see p. 61. Post-horses are kept in readiness at all the principal stations. Steamers to Dinant

Dinant.—Hotel:—

Hotel de la Tete D'Or, highly recommended.

A romantically-situated town on the banks of the Meuse, containing about 6000 inhabitants. The town is rich in historical recollections, having been the scene of one of the bad acts of Philip the Good, who entirely destroyed the town, under circumstances of great cruelty. Some highly interesting natural curiosities may be visited in the neighbourhood.

ROUTE 6.

Namur and Liege Line.—(with Map.)

This line, (belonging to an English Company), which was opened throughout at the latter end of 1851, offers inducements rarely surpassed to those travellers whose object is the enjoyment of the picturesque. The journey from Brussels to either extremity of the line is easy, (see pages 56 and 61), and corresponding trains will be found either at Namur or Liege, the stations occupied by the Government and Company being the same. It is, however, advisable that Namur should be taken as the starting point, the scenery on the river presenting more agreeable points of view when going down the valley.

This is the first line which has adopted, during the summer season, (1st April to 1st October), the system of open first-class carriages with saloons at either end. They afford a most agreeable means of enjoying the scenery, and much more advantageously than by the river boats, which are very slow and irregular in their times in consequence of the shallow state of the river and the many shoals which exist.

The following are the stations on the line, and the chief objects of attraction or of notice which they present:—

Namur.—(See above.)

Marche-les-Dames.—The scenery in the vicinity of this station is of a bold and singularly romantic description. The lofty rocks, which rise as it were from the water's edge, and which have obliged the railway to encroach considerably upon the river, are some of the finest to be found on the line.

Nameche.—At this station the views of the opposite side of the river from that on which the railway runs are very picturesque, the dislocation of the strata giving them a grotesque and castellated appearance.

Sclaigneaux.—This village in particular, as well as all those in general, between Namur and Huy, supplies large quantities of iron ore for the smelting furnaces near Liege, forming a lucrative traffic for the line.

Andenne.—An important town on the right bank of the river. A bridge is now constructing for uniting the two banks, and affording to the town all the advantages which the railway affords. The population is 6000, of which a large number is employed in the paper mills, pottery works, and iron mines, which the town and its vicinity possess.

Bas-Oha.—A picturesque village on the left bank of the Meuse. On the opposite side will be observed the ruins of Beaufort and of Moha, which are rapidly disappearing under the hand of time. It was here that the two brothers, Beaufort, while imitating the evolutions of a tournament which they had visited at Andenne, not being able to hold in their horses, charged with such impetuosity that they killed each other on the spot.

Huy.—This is the most flourishing and remarkable town between Namur and Liege. The fort may be distinguished in the distance shortly after leaving Bas-Oha; but a sharp bend of the river prevents the town from being seen, till the Statte tunnel has been passed and the station entered. The fort and church are very striking; the latter possesses a fine oriel window and carved gateway. The number of establishments of all descriptions in Huy and its vicinity, exceeds one hundred. The population of the town itself is 10,000, but the suburbs are very considerable and thickly populated. A day's stay at this town will be amply repaid; and an excursion up the valley of the Hoyoux as far as Modave is strongly recommended. The trout fishing in the neighbourhood is excellent.

Amay.—Shortly after leaving Huy, the Corphalie Zinc Works are passed, after which the Amay Station is reached. This is a pretty village, situated at the foot of the hills, and is the principal locality for the manufacture of the wines made from the vineyards of the Meuse.

Engis.—There are many châteaus in the neighbourhood, of which the two principal may be observed on the left, shortly after leaving the station: the first, called the Château d'Aigremont, was the residence of the celebrated William de la Marcke, the "Wild Boar of the Ardennes;" the second, called the Château de Chokier, is situated on the summit of a wild and rugged rock, and though not possessing any historical claim to consideration, is remarkable for the striking eminence it occupies.

Flemalle.—It is at this station that the branch line leaves for the Government Station at Liége. The main line crosses the Meuse, and proceeds towards Liége on the other side of the river to that which it has followed since leaving Namur. Travellers desirous of continuing direct towards Germany must change carriages; but those who make a stay at Liége should continue on the main line, as the Company's Station at Liége is much more central and nearer to the town than that of Government.

Seraing.—This village is celebrated as being the centre of numerous manufactories, smelting furnaces, rolling mills, and collieries. The chief establishment is that originally founded by an Englishman, John Cockerill, which employs alone five thousand men, and is of an extent probably unsurpassed even in England, Scotland, or Wales. It may be seen immediately on the left of the station.

Ougree.—Here, also, rolling mills, furnaces, and collieries are the prevailing characteristies. After passing Ougrée the line runs along the side of a picturesque hill, and, on nearing Liége, crosses the Government line from Liége to Cologne, with which it has junction curves in the four directions. A mile and a half beyond this point the train arrives at the Longdoz Station, **Liege.** (See page 172.)

The branch line which leaves at Flémalle runs through a populous and thriving district, on the left bank of the Meuse, possessing many establishments and collieries. The two stations are those of Jemeppe and Tilleur. The branch terminates at the Guillemins Station, which is conjointly worked by the Government and Company, and where trains must be changed by those passengers going through to Verviers, Aix-la-Chapelle, and Cologne, in the one direction, or to Brussels, Antwerp, and Ostend in the other.

Direct Communication by the Namur and Liege Line between Calais and Cologne, and between Paris and Cologne.—Travellers wishing to avail themselves of the speed and economy offered by the direct communication *viâ* Namur and Liége, should, when leaving Calais or Paris for Aix la Chapelle and Cologne, take their tickets *to Namur*, where they will find a train in direct correspondence, ready to take them on to Liége. At this latter town they will meet trains going on to their destination. In the same way, travellers coming from Cologne should take tickets simply *to Liége*, and proceed to Namur by following train, where they will find trains in correspondence towards France.

HOLLAND.

HOLLAND is situated along the south-eastern coast of the North Sea, and extends in its greatest length, from N.E. to S.W., about 190 English miles. Its greatest breadth, from E. to W., is about 123 English miles. The superficial area is 7,614,252 English acres, or 11,897 English square miles. All accounts of Holland represent it as an extended swamp, alternately covered with and abandoned by the waters of the ocean. Holland has had a severe contest with the ocean, which has ended as a great, almost omnipotent, triumph for human industry, and in the country being brought into a high state of cultivation and comparative safety. The canals are indeed very numerous, and of the greatest utility in facilitating the internal trade. They are lined with trees, which tend greatly to beautify the country, in itself so flat, that to those approaching it along the rivers, and some part of the coast, the trees and spires seem to rise out of the water. Along the coast of the North Sea there is a line of broad sand-hills and downs, in some parts so very high as to shut out the view of the sea even from the tops of the spires. The industry of the people has multiplied cattle and pasture-grounds. Vast meadows, dazzling with the richest verdure, are, during eight months of the year, covered with cattle, whose high condition attests an abundant and wholesome nutriment. In the North, wheat, flax, and madder are raised; and in the South, where agriculture has made the greatest progress, tobacco and different kinds of fruit-trees cover the field.

The Dutch possess an excellent system of elementary education. The last act of the Batavian Republic was the law ordaining the institution and regulation of primary schools. This law is most complete in all its details and provisions, which ensure that *every* child in the country shall receive an education in the simple branches of secular knowledge. The law does not compel parents to send their children to school, but refuses *all* relief from the public funds unless they do so; and the result is, there are *none* without education.

The **Government** is a Constitutional Monarchy. The King shares the legislative power with the States-general, which is divided into two Chambers. The *first* consists of 60 members, nominated for life by the King; the *second* is composed of 116 Deputies, elected by the people. Each province has also its own States, composed of members chosen by three orders—the nobility, the citizens, and the rural population. The Provincial States assemble at least once a year, and are convoked by the King. The Colonial Government is vested exclusively in the Throne.

Productive Industry.—At present the manufactures of Holland are upon a narrow scale. Linen, tapes, and other smallware are partially manufactured, principally for domestic consumption. The sugar-refining trade is extensively cultivated; and the manufacture of tobacco and snuff gives employment to a large number of persons. The breweries are also extensive; but the building of ships, barges, and boats, at present form the staple industry of the country.

The **Fisheries** on the Dutch coasts, as also on those of Great Britain, and the Greenland Whale Fishery, employ many seamen; but this is chiefly a summer labour. There are altogether about eighty vessels employed in the herring fishery. The agriculture of Holland is well attended to.

The Kingdom of Holland is divided into ten provinces, which are sub-divided into districts and these latter into cantons.

LONDON TO ROTTERDAM.—Distance about 200 miles. Steamers thrice a week, in summer, in from twenty to twenty-four hours. By the General Steam Navigation Company's vessels, from St. Katherine's Steam Wharf, at 10 a.m. every Wednesday and Saturday, returning on the same day. Also by the Netherlands Steam Boat Company's vessel, the "Batavier," on Sunday, returning on Tuesday. Fares, 30s. and 17s. 6d., see page 132.

HULL TO ROTTERDAM.—Steamers, in about twenty hours, every Wednesday and Saturday, returning on the same days. Fares, 21s. and 10s. 6d., see page 131.

LEITH TO ROTTERDAM.—See page 131.

ROTTERDAM TO ANTWERP.—See page 135.

PASSPORTS.—See pages 19 to 22.

MONEY.—Guilders (or Florins) and cents, are the chief current coins throughout Holland. The Dutch Florin is equal to 100 cents, or 20 stivers=1s. 8d. English money; 1 stiver=5 Dutch cents, is equivalent to 1d. English. French coins are not taken here as in Belgium, therefore the traveller should, as soon as possible, provide himself with Dutch money, which will be received in Belgium, and up the Rhine to Cologne. The William (Willem) gold coin equals 10 guilders, or about 16s. 8d. British. The guilder is worth 2 francs 12½ centimes French

RAILWAY.—The Railway is now open from Rotterdam to the Hague, Leyden, Haarlem, and Amsterdam, and from thence to Utrecht and Arnheim.—*See page* 80.

CANALS.—These afford abundant modes of conveyance, several times a day, to all the larger towns. Barges (*Trekschuiten*) are very convenient, and not fatiguing for night travelling. The fares are about 1 stiver per mile. Rate of travelling five miles per hour. A trip by Canal would give the best notion of Holland.

INNS.—The average charges are—bed 1 guilder; breakfast 12 stivers; tea ditto; dinner, with wine, 2 guilders; table d'hôte at 4 o'clock. Throughout Holland the waiter is called "*Jan.*" The only water fit for table use is the effervescing water from the Nassau springs, which is generally adopted for drinking by travellers.

COUNTRY.—Travellers should observe the admirable and perfect system of canal inter-communication, forming not only the high roads but almost the streets of Holland. Also the stupendous dykes, (the annual repair of which costs upwards of £500,000,) the sole protection from the sea, which is at a higher level than much of the land. The number of windmills presents a curious feature; their use is, however, much more general than in England. In the towns, beyond the complete collections of Dutch Paintings at the Hague and Amsterdam, (and the Japanese Collections, which circumstances render peculiar to Holland,) there is little to attract. Holland, however, presents the picture of a people owing not only their wealth and high commercial position, but even the very land, to their own labour and enterprise

---

Rotterdam.—Hotels:—

Grand Hotel des Pays-Bas, one of the best in Holland.

New Bath Hotel—a first-rate house, offering excellent accommodation.

Persons in want of a Courier will find James Druff, at the Grand Hotel des Pays Bas, an active, tntelligent, and trustworthy man, highly recommended by Mrs. Walter, the landlady.

A large commercial city of Holland, being the second in the kingdom. It is in the province of South Holland, delightfully situated on the north bank of the river Maas, which here resembles an arm of the sea, although nearly 20 miles from its mouth. The steam packets arrive and land their Passengers at the Quay, (Boompjes). Luggage is examined near the landing place. The form of Rotterdam is triangular, its longest side (above a mile and a half in extent) stretching along the bank of the Maas. The town is surrounded by a moat, and entered by six gates towards the land and four towards the water. It is traversed by the Rotte, which here joins the Maas and is intersected, even more than other Dutch towns, by canals, which divide the half of the town near the river into several insulated spots, connected by draw-bridges. These canals are almost all bordered with trees. The row called the Boompjes is the finest,as well in regard to buildings as for its pleasant prospect across the Maas. Next to it comes the Having-vliet. The other streets are in general long, but narrow. The houses of Rotterdam are more convenient than elegant; their height is from four and five to six stories. Of the public buildings, the principal are the Exchange, finished in 1736; the great church of St. Lawrence, from the top of which there is an extensive prospect; besides several other churches; the Town House, an old edifice; the Admiralty, the Academy, the Theatre, and the extensive buildings of the East India Company. Rotterdam contains both an English Episcopal chapel and a Scotch Presbyterian church. It became a privileged town, and was surrounded with walls, in the thirteenth century. Its commerce extends to all parts of the world, and embraces almost every kind of produce and manufacture. Population in 1840, 78,098, having increased 10,000 during the previous ten years; 14 miles from the Hague. English and French universally spoken. Post-office, Wine-street.

Conveyances. — Railway to Hague, Leyden, Haarlem, Amsterdam, Utrecht, and Arnheim, see page 80. For travelling to the interior, canal boats hourly to Delft and Hague; fare to the latter place 75 cents. Diligences to Utrecht, Arnheim, and Nymegen, twice daily. Also to Antwerp daily, in twelve hours, distance 63 miles. Steamer to Antwerp in 8 hours by Dort and the Sheldt; also to London, see page 135.

The diligences (through Gonda) to Utrecht leave (Sundays excepted) at 6.15 a.m., and 3.30 p.m., arriving respectively at 11 30 a.m., (in time for the 11.55 train to Arnheim, thus avoiding the journey round by Amsterdam,) and 9 p.m. A boat leaves at 2 p.m. for Vreeswijk, whence there is an omnibus to Utrecht.

Gonda.—Hotel.—
Hotel "Hertheus."

A country town, containing about 18 or 20,000 inhabitants, about 13 English miles from Rotterdam, on the road to Utrecht. There is no particular object of attraction, excepting 20 or 30 very fine painted windows in the large Presbyterian Church, principally scriptural subjects. Should the traveller have time, these will repay a visit.

Delft.—Hotel.—
Gouden Moulen.

17,000 inhabitants. In the new church in the great square is the pompous monument erected by the States in memory of William I., Prince of Orange, who was assassinated here in 1584. Here also lie the remains of Grotius, who was a native of Delft; his tomb, however, is very simple. The pottery trade, for which this town was so famous, does not now employ more than 200 persons. In the old church, distinguished by its leaning tower, is the monument of Admiral Tromp, with a bas-relief representing the engagement in which he was killed. On an island near the entrance of the town is the State arsenal, formerly the Dutch East India House. A pleasant excursion may be made from here to the Hague, 4¾ miles, on the Treckschuite.

CONVEYANCES.—Railway to the Hague, Leyden, Haarlem, and Amsterdam; also to Rotterdam, see page 80.

The Hague—with Map in Special Edition—*(La Haye*, French; *s'Gravenhage*, Dutch).—HOTELS.—

HOTEL BELLE VUE, is not only one of the best in Holland, but in Europe, and will be found deserving our highest recommendation.

HOTEL PAULEZ.—A capital house, well situated, and good in every respect.

Distance from Rotterdam, 13 miles. Residence of the King of Holland. The chief attraction is an unrivalled collection of paintings by Dutch Masters in the Maurits Huis, open daily, except Sunday, from 9 till 3; on Saturday from 10 till 1. Among these may be mentioned Paul Potter's Bull, Rembrandt's Surgeon Dissecting, and Vandyke's portrait of Simon. The Razaar Royal de D. Boer is a collection of curiosities, consisting of historical relics, Chinese and Japanese costumes, &c., the last well deserving inspection, being extremely rare. The post-office lies at the back of St. James' Church. Population, 64,000.

Leyden.—(*LugdunumBatavorum.*)—HOTEL.—Golden Sun.

Distance from the Hague, 10 miles; time of transit half an hour: intermediate stations, Nieuw Oosteinde Voorschoten. The Rhine is crossed before reaching Leyden, on which the town is situated. Population, 36,000. It is 23 miles from Rotterdam, and 30 from Amsterdam. The University of this city ranks as the first in Holland, and was one of the most celebrated on the Continent. The Museums, &c., connected with the University, the Japanese Collection of Dr. Siebold, and the Botanical Garden, form the chief objects of interest.

Eight miles from Leyden is Katwyk, where the Rhine discharges its narrowed stream into the sea.

Haarlem.—HOTEL.—
Lion d'Or.

Distance from Leiden, eighteen miles; time, 1 hour; intermediate stations, Warmond, Piet, Gigzenbrug, Veenenburg. This part of the line is chiefly cut through the *Dunes*, or Sandhills. At Haarlem station refreshments may be obtained, and luggage left, at a large coffee-house adjoining. *Haarlem* is remarkable for its powerful organ, containing 5,000 pipes. To hear the organ a fee of 12 guilders (£1) must be paid to the organist; this will, however admit a party, which can be easily formed at the traveller's hotel. Population, 24,000. Omnibuses convey passengers to and from the station for 15c.=3d. The three straight lines of the Railway, the high road, and a long row of willows, all running parallel to each other, give a strikingly singular effect to the prospect.

CONVEYANCES.—Railway trains to Amsterdam, Utrecht, Arnheim, the Hague, and Rotterdam, see page 80.

Amsterdam.—HOTEL.—

BRACK'S DOELEN HOTEL, one of the best in Holland, and recommended in confidence.

Distance from Haarlem 12 miles; time 30 minutes. *Halfweg*, the station half way, is famed for the Dutch delicacy, *Water Sootjie;* and here the sluices, to protect the country from inundation, may be seen to advantage. The terminus is some way from the city. Vigilantes may be had for 15 stivers, or 1 guilder the hour. The twenty-six windmills which surround the town are very conspicuous. Population, 212,000. Circumference of city walls, 9 miles. This singular city, the capital of Holland, is entirely built upon piles driven into the bog beneath. Its numerous canals are spanned by nearly 300 bridges. The palace is a vast stone structure, built upon 13,695 piles. There is a fine gallery of Dutch paintings in the Trippenhuis open to the public on Thursdays and on Fridays, and on other days by payment. The harbour and Quay along the estuary of the Y. form a scene of much interest. The passport office is on the Staal Straat. The post-office on the Voorburghwal, behind the palace. A great fair is held in September. The great ship canal, the most stupendous undertaking of the kind ever executed, commences opposite Amsterdam, and extends to Helder and the Texel, a distance of 50 miles It required 6 years, and 12 million guilders to complete it.

AGENT for the sale of J. A. Farina's *Eau de Cologne*—Mad-la-Vve, Verhulst & Fils.

CONVEYANCES.—Railway trains to Haarlem, Leyden, the Hague, and Rotterdam, as also to Utrecht and Arnheim, see page 80. The railway terminus to Haarlem, Leyden, The Hague, and Rotterdam, is outside the Haarlem Gate; that to Utrecht and Arnheim outside the Weesp Gate. Diligences start several times daily to Groningen. Steamers to Hamburgh, six times a month, from April until November:—Fares 44 guilders. A Steamer runs 2 or 3 times a day to Zaardam in about 1 hour.

Utrecht.—HOTEL.—
Pays Bas.

Distance from Amsterdam 23 miles; time 1 hour; intermediate stations, Abcoude, Vreeland, Nieuwerslius, Breukelen, Maarsen. The scenery consists of villages and gardens. *Utrecht* contains 50,000 inhabitants. The cathedral tower, 321 feet high, commands an extensive view. The mint, University, and Museums, are the remaining attractions. An omnibus to Vreeswyck, to meet the Rhine steamers, leaves every Monday, Wednesday, Friday, and Saturday, and accomplishes the distance in one hour.

The town walks round the old fortifications, and a very fine avenue called the Maliebeaú, we recommend to the attention of travellers.

From Utrecht the traveller may make a very delightful excursion to the woods of Zeist, and the trip will give him a good idea of the character of Dutch country-houses. The palace of Soestdijk is about twelve miles from Utrecht.

CONVEYANCES.—Railway trains to Amsterdam, the Hague, and Rotterdam, and likewise to Arnheim, see page 80.

A diligence leaves early every morning (Sundays excepted) for Antwerp, by way of Bois-le-Duc (Den Bosch).

The omnibus to Vreeswijk, to meet the Rhine steamers, leaves *every* day (Sundays excepted), at 7.30 a.m., with the exception of Monday, when it leaves at 4.30 a.m. The arrival at Rotterdam on Mondays is at 9 a.m., and on other days at 11.30 a.m.

Diligences also leave Utrecht for Rotterdam (*via* Gonda), at 6.15 a.m. and 2 p.m., arriving at 12 and 7.30 p.m.

For the Hague (*via* Leiden), at 2 p.m.

Dortrecht (Dort).—HOTEL.—
Hotel Valk.

21,000 inhabitants. One of the oldest towns in Holland, and the first place where an Assembly of the States was held after casting off the Spanish yoke. It is situated on an island formed by the awful inundation of 1421. East-Indiamen heavily laden can come up to the town; the huge rafts of timber brought down by the Rhine from the Swiss and German forests also come in here to be broken up and stored. The famous Protestant Synod of 1618 was held in an old gothic edifice, now a public-house. There is a pulpit of white marble finely carved in the old church, whose tall square tower is seen from a great distance; there are also numerous monuments in it, and its plate is of massive gold, the gift of an East-India merchant.

Arnheim.—HOTEL.—
The Boar's Head.

Distance from Utrecht 33 miles; time 1½ hour; intermediate stations, Driebergen (near Zeist), Maarsberg, Veenendael, Ede, Wolfex. Arnheim, situated on the Rhine, is the chief town of Guelderland. Population, 15,000

CONVEYANCES.—Steamers daily to Cologne and to Rotterdam. There are Diligences four times daily to Nymegen, and also to Dusseldorf (in 12 hours), from which place Cologne can be reached in one hour.

Nymegen.—HOTEL.—
Pays Bas.

Population 24,000. Nymegen being a frontier town, passports are demanded of strangers on their arrival. On the arrival of the steamer no time should be lost in securing an inn, as the concourse of travellers is here very great. It is situated on the left bank of the Waal, and strongly fortified. The buildings chiefly worth seeing are the Town-hall, with its two rows of statues of German Emperors in front, containing some portraits and a few Roman antiquities found in the neighbourhood the Cathedral, commenced in the thirteenth century, a gothic edifice of brick; and the ruins of Schloss Falkenhof, on a height, the building of which is attributed to Julius Cæsar, and said to have been at one time inhabited by Charlemagne. Above these ruins stands the Belvedere, commanding a fine view over the Rhine, Waal, and Yssel, as they branch off at the delta, while the Maas is seen stretching to the south; there are pleasing views also from Berg-en-dal, Beek, and Upbergen, in the vicinity of the town.

Emmerich.—HOTEL.—
Pays Bas.

The first Prussian town on the left bank of the Rhine. Population 5000. Passports are visé́d here and luggage examined.

In the ascent of the Rhine, the traveller would do well to spend the night here.

Dusseldorf, for account of, see page 184.

THE RHINE.

(WITH MAP IN SPECIAL EDITION.)

The following are the routes from England to the Rhine:—

1st. London to Dover, rail; Dover to Ostend, steam-boat; Ostend to Ghent, Malines, Liege, to Cologne, by railway. 2nd. London to Dover, rail; Dover to Calais, steam-boat; Calais to Lille, Mouscron, Ghent, Malines, Liege, and Cologne, by rail. 3rd. London to Ostend direct by steam-boat; from thence to Cologne by rail. 4th. London to Antwerp, by steam-boat; from thence to Cologne by rail. 5th. London to Rotterdam, by steam-boat; from thence by the Rhine, steamers; or from Rotterdam, Hague, Amsterdam, Utrecht, and Arnheim by railway, and by steam from thence to Dusseldorf, where the Traveller can take the Railway to Cologne. By the two first routes the Rhine is reached from London in 22½ hours. Also Steamers from Hull to Antwerp, see page 130, and from Hull to Rotterdam, see page 130. The voyage down the Rhine, from (Kehl) Strasburg to London, may be performed by steam-boat in 82 hours, at an expense of £2 17s. 10d., and by railway and steam-boat in 42 hours.

STEAMERS ON THE RHINE.—There are three Companies of Steamers navigating the Rhine, viz. the Dusseldorf, which may be distinguished by having the funnels of their vessels marked with black and white stripes; the Cologne, distinguished by their black funnels; the Netherlands, by having the funnels painted half black and half white: the Cologne Company's boats do not go lower down the stream than Arnheim (see advertisement pages, 337 and 339), passengers proceeding further are taken by the Netherland Company's boats. The Steamers are divided into three cabins—the Pavilion, the Chief Cabin, and the Fore Cabin. Refreshments are provided on board at a moderate rate, fixed by a printed tariff. In going up or down the Rhine, in the river boats, if a person wishes, or has necessity, to travel with economy, he may take a second class ticket, and dine at the table d'hôte in the main cabin by paying the difference of fare between the two places for such time as he is at dinner; or, in other words, he will pay 3s. instead of 2s. for his dinner; they permit this when not too crowded. The quickest boats go in one day down the Rhine, from Mannheim to Cologne and Dusseldorf; Mayence to Dusseldorf; Dusseldorf to Rotterdam. Up the stream in one day from Cologne to Mannheim (see advertisement pages, 337 and 339), in summer, and to Coblentz in winter; Coblentz to Mannheim. The following will be found the average time occupied on the voyage between

	MILES.	DOWN.	UP.
Rotterdam and Emmerich	111	8 hrs.	12 hrs.
Emmerich and Dusseldorf	73½	,,	10 ,,
Dusseldorf and Cologne	31½	3 hrs.	5 hrs.
Cologne and Mayence	127	9 ,,	13½ ,,
Mayence and Mannheim	46½	3½ ,,	5½ ,,

In addition to the above stations, there are 38 small towns and 21 landing-places at which the steamers touch, some of them being the most picturesque points on the Rhine. At any of them, without exception, the tourist may land, and continue his journey when he pleases, up or down the river, by any of the company's steamers: he has only to take care to have his ticket marked by the conductor of the boat before leaving it. For landing or embarking at any of these points the charge is three halfpence.

For Dusseldorf and Cologne Company's Rhine Steamers, see advertisements, pages 337 and 339.

PASSPORTS.—See pages 19 to 22.

MONEY.—The Prussian currency is available on the Rhine as far as Nassau, where Florins and Kreutzers supersede the Dollars and Groschen. French being generally spoken all through Rhenish Prussia, the traveller, who restricts himself to the Rhine and the roads leading therefrom, will scarcely require the knowledge of any other language, as was hitherto required.

SCENERY of the RHINE.—Below Bonn, in the direction of Cologne, or above Mayence, there is scarcely any object striking enough to merit admiration. About 20 miles above Cologne the scenery of the Rhine may be said to begin with the Seven Mountains, and thence to Coblentz; and from Coblentz to Mayence the turreted towns, castellated ruins, and vine-terraced hills, succeed each other in picturesque profusion. The most appropriate starting places to explore the inland glories of the Rhine are Bonn, Godesberg, Coblentz, St. Goar, Bingen, and Mayence. We trace in the elevated Alps, in Switzerland, and near Mount St. Gothard, the sources of the Rhône, the Tessin, and the *Rhine*, or the king of the German—nay, of the West European rivers. The visitor, on ascending the Rhine, or on his arrival at Strasbourg, calls to his recollection how this stream has hastened his course through the Lakes of Constance and Zellern; how he precipitated himself over the rocky ramparts at Schaffhausen, then, strengthened by the collected waters of Switzerland—the influx of 370 glaciers and upwards of 270 rivers of various sizes—he commences his majestic course near the ancient Roman city of Bale; how he expands between the upper Black Forest, amidst ranges of mountains encircling a valley of nearly thirty miles in breadth, through which he playfully winds, and receiving, besides other streams, the important Neckar and Maine, until a rocky gate at Bingen seems to arrest his further career, but which he powerfully bursts, and strengthened by the Nahe and Moselle, overcomes a similar obstacle at Andernach, when he continues his victorious course towards the sea.

COLOGNE TO BONN.—(Railway, 17 miles; time 1 hour.)—Trains six times daily. Stations, Kalscheuren, Brühl, Sechtem, and Roisdorf. Terminus at Cologne outside St. Pantaleon's Gate; at Bonn, adjoining the Horse-Chesnut Avenue, leading to Poppelsdorf.

ROUTE UP THE RHINE.

Among other sources of information, we have referred, in drawing up these brief notices of the Towns and Scenery of the Rhine, to the "Nouveau Guide des Voyageurs du Rhin," and to an excellent work by E. Lee, Esq., entitled "Bradshaw's Companion to the Continent."

Duisburg.—INNS.—
Post, Rheinischer Hof.

38 miles from Cologne; population 7,000; a manufacturing town near the Ruhr, three miles from its influx into the Rhine, and connected with Cologne by the Minden and Cologne Railway. The valley of the Ruhr is distinguished not only for picturesque scenery, but also for its coal-mines and the industry of its inhabitants. This is the best landing point for North Germany, and in ascending the Rhine it would be well to take the train to Cologne, the river presenting no object of attraction.—Omnibuses meet the steamers.

CONVEYANCES.—Railway to Dusseldorf, Cologne, Hamm, Minden, and Hanover, see page 70.

Dusseldorf.—HOTEL:—

HOTEL DE L'EUROPE, near the Railway Station, Post-Office, and Landing-place of the Rhine Steamers, an excellent house, and highly recommended.

Dusseldorf is one of the nicest and most regular towns on the Rhine, containing 31,000 inhabitants, In the Market Place, a bronze statue on a pedestal of grey marble is erected to the Elector, John William, by Grepello, to whom Dusseldorf owes much of its splendour. The principal buildings are the barracks; the church of Lambert, the Jesuits, and of the Cordeliers; the ancient castle, the residence of the Electors; the Hotel de Ville, &c. The celebrated gallery of paintings was removed to Munich in 1805; the present gallery is inferior, but the School of Painting here is very celebrated, and there is an exhibition of modern pictures every summer. There is also an interesting collection of drawings by the old masters. There is here a bridge of boats across the Rhine. Steamboats leave Mayence for Dusseldorf daily, at 7¾ and 10½ a.m.; and start from Dusseldorf for Rotterdam at midnight.

The distance by railway to Berlin is 371¾ miles, to Hamburgh 275, to Leipsic 355¾, to Paris 401 miles.

ENGLISH CHURCH SERVICE.—At the German Protestant Temple, Berger Strasse, at 11.45 and 3.30 on Sundays.

CONVEYANCES.—Steamers daily to Cologne, Bonn, Mayence, and Mannheim, also to Arnheim and Rotterdam, see advertisement.—Railway to Elberfeld, page 69. — To Langennfeld, Dortmund, Hamm, Minden, Hanover, Bremen, and Berlin, as also to Cologne, see page 70.

Elberfeld.—HOTEL:—

Hotel Palatine.

Elberfeld, in the Wupperthal; 85,000 inhabitants, with the adjoining town of Barmen; a considerable manufacturing town, being the capital of the district of Dusseldorf. Two centuries since the population of Elberfeld was scarcely a thousand. The pure mountain stream of the Wupper, particularly adapted for bleaching, first led to the establishment of linen works here. The undressed yarn comes from Hesse, Brunswick, Hildesheim, and Hanover. The manufactures of linen and woollen cloth were the first established. France, Italy, Spain, Russia, America, &c., consume vast quantities of these goods. Fringes, bed-tickings, thread, thread-lace, &c., also employ a large number of workmen. When the English process of spinning yarn became known, the manufacture of cotton articles was highly improved. Dyeing with Turkish red has been another very important branch of business in Elberfeld since 1780; and the silk manufacture, since 1760, has been of great importance, large quantities being exported annually.

CONVEYANCES.—Railway trains to Dusseldorf and Cologne, see pages 69 and 70.—To Schwelm, Dortmund Hamm, Minden and Hanover, see pages 72 and 70.

Cologne.—HOTELS:—

HOTEL DISCH, situated in Bridge-street, very highly recommended, as combining good accommodation with moderate charges. The proprietors, Messrs, Disch and Capellen, also have a large assortment of the best Rhin and Moselle Wines for wholesale.

HOTEL DE HOLLANDE, a first-rate establishment, overlooking the Rhine.

HOTEL ROYAL, excellent in every respect, and commanding a fine view of the Rhine.

HOTEL DE GERMANIE, (Germanischer Hof,) close to the cathedral, and centrally situated between the Paris and Berlin Railway stations, combines comfort and economy.

HOTEL DE BRUSSELS, near the railway station,

EAU DE COLOGNE.—Travellers are frequently importuned by officious persons offering to direct or accompany them to this or that vendor of the celebrated perfume; and as there are upwards of sixty manufacturers of this article, we have deemed it right to try the qualities of several samples, and having submitted them to good connoisseurs, we recommend, in full confidence, the establishment of JOHANN ANTON FARINA, known by the name of the City of Milan, 129, High-street, Hohe Strass—a descendant of the original Farina family, and purveyor to most of the reigning monarchs in Europe, to whom the Commissioners of the Rhine and Westphalian Exhibition recently awarded the *first and exclusive prize* as manufacturer *of the best Eau de Cologne produced in the present day.*

Mr. J. A. Farina has recently appointed Agents in the principal towns on the continent to enable English travellers to obtain the Eau de Cologne manufactured by him; but he recommends purchasers to be particular in observing that the labels on the bottles bear the words "Zum Stadt Mailand," without which the article cannot be genuine.

Cologne, city and fortress of Prussia, on the Rhine, with a population of 90,000. It has 20 churches, 7,900 houses, 19 gates, 33 squares, 270 streets, is strongly fortified, and possesses a bridge upon 39 boats across the Rhine, 1250 feet in length. It carries on a brisk trade by means of its connection by railways with all the chief cities of the continent.

This city was originally founded by the Ubii. The Roman Empress Agrippina, whose birth-place it was, introduced a colony of veterans, made it a municipality, and named it Colonia Agrippina. As capital of lower Germany, upon the revolt of the Batavians in 69 it passed over to the party of Civilis. Here it was that Vitellius had himself proclaimed emperor, and Trajan, during his lieutenancy, erected many buildings, extended to the city the freedom of Rome, and conferred upon it other privileges. Constantine began the construction of a stone bridge, the ruined piers of which may still be seen at low water, and shortly after his time Cologne became a bishop's see. It had the misfortune however of falling into the hands of the terrible Attila, was afterwards the scene of Childeric's coronation in 486, and continued from thenceforward an appanage of the Frankish kings, without however, losing its old Roman constitution. About the beginning of the 7th century it was conquered by Theodric of Burgundy, and, in 881, suffered severely from the violence of the Normans.

During the early part of the middle ages, Cologne continued to increase in wealth and importance, so that in 1201 it was looked upon as one of the most considerable members of the Hanseatic League, but was subsequently one of the first to separate from that confederacy. In 1259, the free city of Cologne obtained for itself the "Stapelrecht" (staple laws); all goods arriving at this port were transferred to Cologne bottoms, and made to pay a high rate of duty for further transit. The dignity and importance of the city had by this time become acknowledged all over Europe; it was called the "heilige stadt" (holy city), and numbered within its walls 363 churches. Its University was founded in 1388, by the archbishop, Frederick III. In 1396, an unsuccessful struggle was maintained by the citizens against their archbishop; many were in consequence beheaded or banished and a constitution settled; but the strife with the clerical authorities continued without intermission, until in 1618 a persecution of the Protestants left 1400 houses untenanted. By the peace of Luinville, Cologne was ceded to France, the archbishopric secularized, and trial by jury introduced; but by the treaty of Paris, 1814, it passed into the hands of Prussia, was again submitted to an archbishop, and strongly fortified. Since 1814, the town and trade of Cologne has increased rapidly, many of the streets have been widened, and new ones formed.

Objects of Attraction.—The cathedral of Cologne merits the traveller's first notice. It was commenced in 1248, and is not yet finished, but its colossal proportions and magnificent architecture are calculated to inspire feelings of the deepest admiration. A well executed model of the Cathedral, as it will be when completed, and which we recommend to the inspection of all strangers visiting Cologne, is to be seen every day from morning till night at 129 High Street, near the Cathedral. A beautiful engraving, representing the edifice, has also been published by Mr. Zwirner, the architect, who is now executing the work, which print may be had at Eisen's Library, 2 Frederick Wilhelm street. Among the objects of interest may be noted the chapel of the Holy Three Kings, sepulchre of Maria of Medicis, of Conrad of Hochstetten, and of the Count of Schaumberg, &c.—St. Peter's church, with the celebrated "Crucifixion of Peter," by Rubens, the original of which is shown on all days, by paying a fixed fee; the church of St. Ursula, with eleven thousand damsels, whose relics are to be seen in the walls of the church; the Jesuits' church, the clocks of which are cast out of the cannons which Tilly took in Magdeburg; the houses in which Maria of Medicis died, and in which Rubens was born, 1577, in the Sternengasse, No. 10; the Apostle's church, in the new market, built 1200; the museum in the Frankgasse, No. 7, near the cathedral, admission 5 sgr.; it contains many valuable relics, besides a good collection of Roman antiquities; the Senate House, with the Hansaroom; the Gurzenich or the Company's hall, completed 1474; the toy-house, in the Rheingasse, No. 8; the casino, with a good reading-room; the exchange, &c.

Conveyances.—Railway to Bonn six times daily, in one hour, see page 69; to Berlin, Dusseldorf, &c.; as also to Aix-la-Chapelle, Antwerp, and Brussels, pages 70, 57, & 65. Schnellposts, morning and evening, to Coblentz. Steamers leave Cologne several times daily to Coblentz in 10 hours, and down the Rhine to Dusseldorf and Nymegen in 14 hours. To Bonn in 3 hours. Cologne, on account of steam navigation and railways, stands in the most intimate connection with Belgium, Holland, England, France, and the German states. The steam-boat usually stops at the following places between Cologne and Coblenz, viz., Wessling, Widdig, Bonn, Plittersdorf, Königswinter, Rolandseck, Unkel, Remagen, Linz, Breisig, Brohl, Andernach, Neuwied, and Eugers.

On leaving Cologne to sail up the Rhine, the traveller sees nothing as yet of that surpassing beauty for which this magnificent river is so justly famed; still the banks, even here, are by no means devoid of interest. The country is not altogether flat; its spect is enlivened by villages and well cultivated fields. As we approach Bonn, the summits of the famous Siebengebirge (seven mountains) rise gradually into view, sometimes to the right and at other times to the left, according as the direction of the boat's head is changed to suit the windings of the stream. These, with their rugged sides and ruined castles, on a nearer approach, produce an imposing effect, and mark, as it were, the entrance into the "Paradise of Germany," as that portion of the Rhine is called which lies between Bonn and Mayence.

Return from the Rhine. Routes to England.—The following are the different **Routes from Cologne to England:—**

1. From Cologne to Rotterdam down the Rhine, and thence by Steam Packet to London. See p. 136.
2. From Cologne by railway to Ostend, thence to Dover by Steam Packet; and from Dover to London by South Eastern Railway. The Mail Packets leave Ostend for Dover every evening at half-past 6, except Saturday, *when there is no departure.*
3. Or from Ostend direct to London by the General Steam Navigation Company's Packets, which leave Ostend every Tuesday and Friday, according to the tide.
4. From Cologne to Antwerp by railway, and thence direct to London by the General Steam Navigation Company's steam ship "Ravensbourne," every Sunday, at 3 afternoon; or by the Antwerp Company's steam ship "Baron Osy," every Wednesday, at 1 afternoon.
5. From Cologne to Calais by railway, thence by Steam Packet to Dover, and from Dover by South Eastern Railway to London. See page 127.

By consulting the information respecting steamers to and from Foreign Ports—which commences at page 126—the different fares can be ascertained, and a reference to the railway tables will give the railway fares, the traveller can then choose his route, and decide as he thinks proper. But whichever route it may be, he can have his luggage conveyed in transit from Cologne through Belgium. We must caution the traveller, however, against the practises of the clerks at the railway station for Belgium, who seem to have a strong interest in sending or booking passengers by one particular route, and in putting obstacles in the way of their going by the others. Our readers will do well to be on their guard; and if there is any unfair bias, they should report the circumstance to the superintendent of the station.

Bonn.—Hotels:—

Hotel de Belle Vue, pleasantly situated on the banks of the Rhine, and good in every respect.

The Grand Hotel Royal, overlooking the Rhine and facing the Park, is a good house, commanding a delightful view of the Seven Mountains.

The Golden Star Hotel, patronised by the English Royal Family, is an admirably conducted house; the landlord, Mr. Schmidt, is attentive and obliging, and we recommend travellers to this hotel with great pleasure.

Population 15,000, including the students and garrison. A university town in Rhenish-Prussia, of Roman origin, and formerly the residence of the Electors of Cologne. Its best edifices are the university, formerly the electoral palace, in which, besides lecture rooms, are a library of 150,000 volumes; the academical and Rhenish museums; a fine collection of Roman antiquities, including an altar to victory; and the aula, or academical hall, decorated with fresco paintings. The minster, in which there is a bronze statue of the Empress Helena, mother of Constantine, by whom it was founded in 320, and built in the Byzantine style; the collegiate church; that of the Jesuits; of St. Remi, in which is a fine painting by Spielberg; and the schlosskirche. The house of Beethoven is pointed out in the Rhelngasse, and his monument in the minster-platz. There are many beautiful walks, especially to the Hofgarten, with a fine terrace on the Rhine called "der alte Zoll," which gives a magnificent view of the river and Siebengebirge; of greater extent is that by the Poppelsdorf avenue, with its double rows of chestnut trees, to the castle of Poppelsdorf, and to the Kreutzberg, with its picturesque grounds.

From Bonn, which is connected with Cologne by a railway, the Siebengebirge are generally visited.

Agent for the sale of J. A. Farina's *Eau de Cologne*—Messrs. Henry and Cohen.

Omnibuses ply daily to Godesberg; steamboats up and down the Rhine, see advertisement, pages 275 and 276; railway trains to Cologne, page 69.

Konigswinter.—Hotel:—

Hotel de l'Europe.

The beauties of the Rhine begin at this town, situated at the foot of the Drachenfels, the nearest of the seven mountains to the river. No traveller ought on any account to omit ascending this hill, even if he have to lose a day by doing so, as the view from its summit is one of the most lovely on the whole course of the Rhine. The walk from the pier to the top is not more than half an hour, and mules are always in waiting at the foot of the ascent for those who prefer to ride. The principal inn affords very tolerable accommodation. The best way of reaching Konigswinter from Cologne is, not by the steamers, which occupy nearly four hours, but by rail to Bonn, and thence in a carriage (about three quarters of an hour's drive) to the ferry opposite Konigswinter, where boats are always waiting. By leaving Cologne by the first train, and proceeding immediately by a car from the station at Bonn, the traveller may easily reach Konigswinter, ascend the Drachenfels, and proceed by steamer to Coblentz about noon. But should he be obliged to spend the day at Konigswinter, he will not repent the delay, as he may find a delightful and picturesque walk, turn which way he will.

In passing the Siebengebirge, we have a view of "the castled crag of Drachenfels," which is, in fact, one of the seven hills, and afterwards leave on the other side the ruins of Rolandseck, a castle said to have been built by Roland, nephew of Charlemagne; opposite is the charming island of Nonnenswerth, with its ancient nunnery, now a farm house and inn. (The legend of Roland and the fair Hildegard of Drachenfels, forms the subject of Schiller's romantic ballad "Ritter Toggenburg.")

Oberwinter, also on the right bank, farther on, is an ancient borough, agreeably situated in a semi-circle of mountains.

Rheinbreitbach, on the left bank, is a large village, with castles and towers, at the entrance of a valley, in which are the copper mines of Birnberg and Marienberg, now no longer worked, the largest having been inundated by the river.

At **Unkel** the cliffs encroach on the bed of the stream, so as to produce a slight rapid on one side.

Just above this, and on the opposite bank, **Apollinarisberg** stands conspicuous, with its splendid gothic church and convent.

A little below **Erpel,** on the left bank, is a basaltic mountain, 700 feet high, called the Erpeler Ley. The vines planted on its slopes are rooted in baskets forced into the clefts of the rock.

Near **Sinzig,** a small old town on the road between Bonn and Coblentz, about 1½ mile from the Rhine, commences the valley of the Ahr, which is full of wild and picturesque scenery, well worth visiting.

Close to the confluence of the Ahr is the village of **Unterkrippe,** communicating by a flying bridge with **Linz,** a commercial town, at which the steam vessels put in. Charles the Bold took this town in 1476; in 1632 it was taken by the Swedes, and in 1688 it was garrisoned by the French. The castle, as well as the town walls of Linz, are built of basalt, and the streets are paved with the same material. The surrounding country produces copper, iron, lead, &c., which are exported from this town, and render it a thriving and commercial community.

Andernach.

An ancient town, founded by the Romans, and, in the middle ages, a free city of the empire. Enclosed with lofty old walls, it contrasts strikingly with Neuwied, further on, which lies quite open. Its Roman gate, and the ruins of the Pfalz or Episcopal palace, its ancient church and tower, with the town arms, at least 1000 years old, are well worthy of notice.

The Laacher lake may be visited either from this

place or from Brohl. It is a singular sheet of deep blue water, of almost circular form, occupying what would seem the crater of an extinct volcano, 666 feet above the Rhine, about $1\frac{3}{4}$ mile long, and $1\frac{1}{2}$ broad, depth in the centre 214 feet, surrounded by hills richly wooded to the water's edge. A jet of carbonic acid gas issues from a little opening on the N. E. side, and this, together with the scoriæ ashes, pumice, &c., found on the banks, gives evidence of its volcanic origin. The deserted abbey of Laach, with its five towers, forms a picturesque object in the view.

The great millstone quarries of Nieder Mendig, 2 miles S. E. of the abbey, are also well worthy of a visit. The distance from Andernach to the Laacher sea is about 6 miles.

Beyond this town the mountains again approach the river, forming a magnificent defile, and having, at the water's edge on the left bank, the ruined castle of Friedrichstein, the building of which was begun in the 17th century, but never finished. On the same side lies the village of Irrlich, connected by an avenue of poplars with the town of

Neuwied.—HOTEL.—

Hotel du Rhin.

Population 5,200. Capital of the mediatized principality of Wied. Overlooking the river is the Prince's palace, which contains a collection of very interesting Roman antiquities, chiefly from the buried city of Victoria, near Niederbiber, a village 2 miles to the N. The museum of natural history is in the Pheasantry, (Fasanerie Gebaude,) and consists for the most part of collections made by Prince Maximilian of Neuwied, during his travels in Brazil and North America. A distinct quarter of the town is occupied by Moravian brethren, whose schools and workshops are worth visiting.

The chateau of Monrepos, with its park and gardens, 6 miles N.N.E., is the object of a very pleasant excursion. Neuwied has also a flying bridge over the Rhine.

Weissenthurm, (White Tower) on the right bank, so called from the old watch-tower which stands at the extremity of the village; on an eminence to the left of which is the monument of General Hoche, who crossed the Rhine at this place. Here it is asserted that Julius Cæsar constructed the famous bridge described in his commentaries; but this is very improbable, as he makes no mention of the island in mid-channel of which Hoche availed himself in his passage.

Further on to the right is **Muhlhofen,** a village at the mouth of the Sayn, from which pleasant excursions may be made through the beautifully wooded valley traversed by that stream.

Kesselheim.—Near this are the ruins of Schönbornlust, once a palace of the Elector of Treves; famous also as the residence of the exiled Bourbon princes, and head-quarters of the army of refugees during the revolution.

Near the junction of the Moselle and Rhine stands the monument of General Marceau.

Neuendorf.—Here the smaller timber-rafts from the Upper Rhine and its branches, as also from the Moselle, are formed into the great rafts which go down to Holland.

Long before the steamer approaches Coblenz, the fortress of Ehrenbreitstein is visible, while, as she reaches her moorings at that city, one of the most conspicuous objects is the stately palace of the King of Prussia, formerly belonging to the Electors of Treves, stretching along the bank of the river.

Coblenz.—HOTEL:—

Hotel des Trois Suisses.

Coblenz, the "Confluentes" of the Romans, is a strongly fortified town on the right bank of the Rhine, and left of the Moselle; capital of Rhenish Prussia, with a population of 26,000, including 4,000 military. It occupies a large triangle, formed by the influx of the Moselle into the Rhine, and has a stone bridge over the Moselle: from this bridge there is a magnificent view. On the opposite bank of the Rhine is the rocky fortress of Ehrenbreitstein, with the town at its foot, containing 2,800 inhabitants, and communicating with Coblenz by a bridge of boats, 485 paces in length. The view from the summit of the fortress extends as far as the mountains of Lorraine, and will amply repay the fatigue of ascending. There is a road thence to Ems, 6 miles distant, and to Frankfort. Coblenz is adorned with many fine buildings, squares, and avenues of trees. The old castle, near the Moselle bridge, possesses historical interest, having been the sojourn of several emperors. The church of St. Castor, at the very confluence of the two rivers, and distinguished by its four towers, dates from 836; here met the grandsons of Charlemagne, to divide amongst them his mighty empire into Germany, France, and Italy. On the left of the chancel stands the beautiful tomb of Cuno of Falkenstein, archbishop of Treves, with a painting of the Crucifixion, attributed to the old German master, William of Cologne. Here, also, Edward III. of England was installed Vicar of the Empire, by Lewis of Bavaria. The cellars under the grammar school, formerly a Jesuits' convent, are worth visiting from their great extent, containing about 300 vats, or 400,000 bottles of Rhine and Moselle wines. From the vicinity of this town to the wine districts, it forms the great depôt for the export of their produce, as also of the seltzer waters of Nassau, and the various volcanic productions of the neighbourhood.

The fortifications of Coblenz are of vast extent; of these Ehrenbreitstein is the most remarkable, having cost, it is said, 5,000,000 dollars.

In the environs of Coblenz are Mosselweiss, a pretty village, much resorted to for recreation; Metternich, 8 miles distant, at the foot of the Krümmelberg. Here are the sources which supply Coblenz with water by pipes which pass over the bridge of the Moselle. This river is navigable to a great distance beyond Treves; during the whole of its course from that city to its mouth, 147 miles, (72 by land) it is closed in by mountains, which form a continued series of the most diversified landscapes, in consequence of the sinuosities of the stream. German steamers ply between Coblenz and Treves, from which place to Metz is navigated by a French company. Besides the beautiful valley of the Moselle itself, which contains some of the most picturesque river scenery in Germany, many of the adjacent valleys are well worth a visit.

Coblenz being one of those points on the Rhine from whence so many interesting excursions may be made, it is well, if possible, to make it a halting place for some days. Among the places most worth visiting are the following:—the Pfaffendorfer Hohe, a hill on the same side with Ehrenbreitstein, and commanding almost as fine a view; the hill of the Chartreuse; the castle of Stolzenfels, 3 miles up, on the right bank of the Rhine—vehicles there and back 1 dollar; to the top of the Kuhkopf, the highest hill near the town; Lahnstein, on the left bank; Sayn and the abbey of Rommersdorf; abbey and lake of Laach; castle of Elz; Neuwied and Marksburg; more distant, Ems and Nassau. The neighbouring forests abound in game.

AGENT for the sale of J. A. Farina's *Eau de Cologne*—Mr. Gust. Dorset.

CONVEYANCES.—Eilwagen to Ems, Kreuznach, Treves, and Wiesbaden. Steamers several times daily to Biebrich, Mayence, and Mannheim; as also to Bonn, Cologne, Dusseldorf, and Rotterdam, see advertisement, pages 337 and 339. Steamers ascend the Moselle as far as Treves and Metz.

Ems.—HOTEL:—

Hotel de Russie, good.

This celebrated watering place is a few miles from Coblenz.

AGENT for the sale of J. A. Farina's *Eau de Cologne*—Mr. Charles Vogelsberger.

CONVEYANCES.—Omnibuses several times daily.

Schwalbach and Schlangenbad, rendered famous and much frequented watering places by Head's "Bubbles from the Brunnens of Nassau," are situated on the road from Coblenz to Wiesbaden. The scenery alone will repay the tourist.

CONVEYANCES.—Eilwagen to Coblenz and Wiesbaden, and omnibus to Bieberich.

Horchheim, on the left bank, is the last Prussian village. The island opposite is Oberwerth, on which was formerly a nunnery, now the country house of Count Pfaffenhofen.

Stolzenfels, a fine castle of the middle ages, on a projecting rock overlooking the Rhine and the village of Kapellan. This grand edifice belongs to the king of Prussia, by whom it was restored and fitted up for a summer residence; it was here he entertained Queen Victoria in a most splendid manner in 1845. It is the most beautifully situated of all the Rhine castles, commanding a prospect up the river as far as the valley of the Drinkholder spring, with Rhense, Oberlahnstein and Marksburg included. Opposite is the lovely valley of the Lahn, and the confluence of that river with the Rhine; while down the stream the view embraces Coblenz, with its fortifications, and the mountains of Andernach in the distance.

Both banks of the Lahn, and the left bank of the Rhine, almost the whole way to Mayence, belong to Nassau.

There is a ferry from Stolzenfels to Lahnstein, and another over the mouth of the Lahn; a carriage road leads to Ems, up the left bank of this river. Above the mouth of the Lahn are the ruins of Lahneck castle, on the summit of a rock.

Oberlahnstein, an old walled town, with a conspicuous red building at the edge of the Rhine, once a castle of the electors of Mayence; near it is a small white chapel among trees, where, in 1400, the deposition of the emperor Wenceslaus, and the election of Rupert were pronounced by the electors.

Rhense.

A very antique town, scarcely altered since the middle ages. Near it is the Königsstuhl (King's seat), an open vaulted hall, with seven stone seats for the seven electors who used to meet in it to discuss affairs of state.

Braubach.

Another ancient little town, at the entrance of the valley that winds round the Marksburg. There are copper and silver mines in the neighbourhood; there is also a road to Ems from this place.

Marksburg, a fortress of the middle ages, in perfect preservation, being the only one of the Rhine castles which has escaped destruction. It is situated on a lofty rock, was used as a state prison, but recently as an infirmary, or rather it is garrisoned by invalids. It is well worth visiting, as a remarkable specimen of those terrible strongholds where "power dwelt amidst her passions;" narrow and mysterious passages, dungeons cut in the living rock, are here to be seen; among these is one called the Hundloch (dog hole,) into which prisoners were let down by a windlass, and another the horrible Folterkammer (chamber of torture). A cell is pointed out as the one in which the emperor Henry IV. was confined. After viewing these dismal records of human folly, the tourist may ascend the donjon keep and take a view of the surrounding scenery, which is picturesque in the extreme.

Boppart.—HOTEL:—

Hotel du Rhin.

An ancient walled town, population 4,000. This is a gloomy but interesting place, of Roman origin, having been one of the 50 castles of Drusus on the Rhine. In it are the remains of the palace of the Frankish kings, and the ruins of a fine chapel. Behind the town is the ancient nunnery of Marienberg, now an establishment for the water-cure.

The walls of the Roman castrum, a quadrangle of strong masonry, still exists in the heart of the town. The situation of Boppart is remarkably beautiful. The Rhine here makes one of its most considerable curves, and at some distance further the mountains recede a little from the river, giving way to meadows and corn fields. The streets of Boppart are very narrow and dark, but possess many attractions for the architect and antiquary, many of the buildings presenting great peculiarities of architecture.

Salzig, an agreeable village, with large plantations of cherry trees. Opposite, on the twin peaks of a lofty rock, are the ruins of Sternberg and Liebenstein, called the two brothers, and the subject of a legend. At the foot of the steep mountain, in a narrow valley, is the village and ancient convent of Bornhofen.

In **Ehrenthal** are silver, lead, and copper works, whose annual produce is 100,000 florins.

Welmich, a little village with a fine old church, at the foot of the mountain on which stands the castle of Thurnberg, or Kunoberg, called "the Mouse," now fast falling into ruin; the walls are, however, still perfect. The castle called "the Cat" is above St. Goarhausen.

Marienberg—Formerly a convent and place of education; now an establishment for the cold water cure. The position of St. Goar is eminently beautiful. On the hill are the ruins of Rheinfels, formerly one of the most extensive fortresses; now a picture of desolation. Opposite is the pretty village of St. Goarhausen, and the ruins of Thurnberg or Katz. Above this point a narrow defile confines the river, which is precipitated over a rocky channel; on the left is the enormous rock of Lurley, and a little higher are discovered the rocks called the Seven Sisters (Sieben Jungfrauen), the subject of a legend.

Below St. Goar we meet with the most extensive ruin on the Rhine, namely, the fortress of Rheinfels. This immense stronghold was built in 1245 by a count of Katzenellnbogen, to levy duties on the passing merchandise; but, pushing his extortions too far, he was besieged by the people of the adjacent towns, who, for fifteen months, endeavoured to reduce the castle, but without success: it fell afterwards, however, with most of the other robber-dens, before the confederacy of the German and Rhine towns. It became afterwards, in the hands of the Landgrave of Hesse, a modern fortress, which baffled the French in 1692, but was taken and blown up by them in 1794. An inn has been built in the midst of the ruins, from whence is a magnificent view.

St. Goar.

Population, 1500 inhabitants. A cheerful little town, and very desirable as a sojourn for the purpose of making excursions in the vicinity, as it lies in the midst of some of the finest of the Rhine scenery. This town is also famous for its extensive salmon fishery. Near it is a dangerous rapid called the Bank, and below this the whirlpool Gewirr. A very fine view is to be had from the heights above St. Goar, rising directly in face of the Lurleiberg. On the opposite side of the river is

St. Goarhausen, 800 inhabitants, still partly surrounded with its old walls. Here begins the Forstbach, or Swiss Valley, celebrated for its beauty, being traversed by a clear stream, forming numerous cascades between precipitous masses of rock. At the entrance of this valley stands the castle of the Cat, a very picturesque object in the landscape. An excursion well worth taking is that to the ruined castle of Reichenberg, at a distance of a mile and a half inland.

On the same side, but a little above St. Goarhausen, the black perpendicular precipice of the Lurleiberg rises abruptly from the water's edge, opposite to which on the road side, is a grotto, in which is stationed a man who, with a bugle or by firing a pistol, awakens the echo of the Lurlei, which is said to repeat sounds fifteen times. Above this, in mid-channel, and visible at low water, are the rocks called the Seven Sisters, the subject of a legend.

Oberwesel.

The Vesalia of the Romans. A small town of 2500 inhabitants; very interesting to visit, and delightfully situated. The whole course of the river from Bonn, where it becomes narrower and more rapid, and onwards to Bingen, is through scenery of surpassing beauty, rocks crowned with castellated ruins, and hills cut in terraces for the cultivation of the vine, rising above the towns and villages on either bank. The church of Our Lady in Oberwesel is considered a model of the gothic style; in St. Martin's is a "Descent from the Cross," by Diepenbrock. The picturesque appearance of this town is much increased by its turreted walls and the lofty round tower called the Ox Tower, by the water side. The village of Engehölle is well worth a visit, as also the ruins of Schönberg Castle, known for the tradition of the Seven Sisters.

Caub, a small town on the right bank, above which, on a steep rock, rise the ruins of the castle of Gutenfels. In the middle of the river, between Bacherach and Caub, is a well-preserved old castle, called the Pfatz, built by the Emperor Lewis of Bavaria for a toll-house; there are dungeons under it below the level of the river; it is accessible only by a ladder through a single entrance closed by a port-cullis. The well for its supply of water is much leeper than the bed of the Rhine. In the lateral valleys are extensive slate-quarries.

Bacharach.

With the ruins of the chapel of Werner, a master-piece of old German architecture, destroyed by the Swedes in the Thirty-years' War. A busy town of 1800 inhabitants; formerly the entrepôt for the fine Rhenish wines, which were named on this account "the wines of Bacharach." In the Rhine, when the water is low, a large stone appears, called the Altar of Bacchus (Bacchiara)—hence the name. The sight of this rock is hailed with joy, as a good omen for the vintage; it is usually covered with water.

OBJECTS OF ATTRACTION.—The Church of St. Peter, dating from the 12th century; the ruins of the castle of Slahleck, with its truncated walls, on a high hill behind the town, from whence there is a fine view; and the town walls, with twelve towers of peculiar construction.

Lorch.

On the opposite bank; 1800 inhabitants. One of the oldest towns on the Rhine, situated at the embouchure of the Wisperbach, and entrance of its picturesque valley. On the right bank of the Wisper is a rocky eminence, called the Devil's Ladder, with the ruins of Nollingen castle on its summit. Above the village of Rheindiebach stand the round tower and broken walls of Fürstenburg, devastated by the French in 1687. The church is a handsome relic of the 12th century; in front of it is a carved stone cross dated 1491.

Here commences that region of castles and vineyards called the Rheingau, which extends up the right bank as far as Walluf.

Close by the water's edge is the village of Nieder Heimbach, above which appear the remains of the castle of Heimburg, and higher up the turreted ruin of Sonneck.

As we approach Bingen and Assmanshausen, those picturesque monuments of the old iron times become still more numerous.

One of them called the Rheinstein, which has been restored and fitted up in the antique style for a summer residence of Prince Frederick of Prussia, is well worth visiting. It stands upon a projecting cliff, rising almost perpendicularly from the water side. Opposite to this is the village of

Assmanshausen.

On the left bank, with a warm mineral spring. The fine red wine of that name is produced from the vines in the neighbourhood, which are cultivated on such steep heights as to require baskets and other contrivances to secure them in their places; some of the terraced heights are one thousand feet above the river.

One of the finest views in the whole course of the river may be obtained by ascending to the Rossel a little tower on the edge of the heights above Assmanshausen. From this village also may be made the ascent of the Niederwald.

The great gorge of the Rhine, the commencement of which is about Boppart, terminates here. It is formed by a range of mountains crossing the river's course, nearly at right angles. It is supposed that at some very remote period its passage was completely barred by this impediment, and that its arrested waters spread themselves into a vast lake, some fifty miles in breadth, and extending as far as Basle: shells and other deposits found in the great Rhine Valley above Mayence favour this opinion. The Bingerloch, formed by a ledge of rock supposed to be a remnant of that primeval barrier, obstructed for a long time the navigation of the Rhine; but this passage was widened to 210, being ten times its former breadth, by the Prussians, in 1830–32, and the fragments, taken from the river bed by blasting, were formed into a monument on the road side to commemorate the work. This channel is near the left bank, and overlooked by the ruins of the fortress of Ehrenfels.

Near the right bank, and adjacent to the influx of the Nahe, is an islet with a ruin called the Mäusethurm (Mice Tower), the scene of a strange tradition, which Southey gives in his ballad of Bishop Hatto. Opposite to the mouth of the Nahe, on the left bank, rises a rock called Mühlstein, wherein lie buried according to his will, the brain and heart of Alderman Vogt of Frankfort, whose works on the Rhine and its traditions are well known.

Bingen.—HOTEL.—

Victoria.

In an angle of the beautiful valley of the Nahe the frontier town of the Rheno-Hessian territory, 5000 inhabitants. A considerable entrepôt for trade in corn and wines. The town is much frequented by strangers. The Rhine here makes a considerable curve, and the scenery around is in the highest degree attractive. The ruins of Klopp, on the Drususberg (once a Roman castle) afford a favourite promenade and a view from the tower of the celebrated Nahethal, and the environs as far as the Donnersberg.

An agreeable tour may be made to the Rochusberg and its chapel, from whence there is a prospect of extraordinary beauty; as also up the Nahe to Kreuznach and Oberstein. Opposite Bingen, on the left bank of the Nahe, stands the Rupertsberg, and, about a mile and a half distance, the Elisenhöhe, from the moss-house of which there is another magnificent view. An excursion to Rüdesheim, and to the heights of the Niederwald is also recommended.

Kreuznach.—HOTEL.—

Adler.

A town of 9000 inhabitants, beautifully situated in the lovely valley of the Nahe. It has lately risen into great repute as a watering-place.

CONVEYANCES.—Omnibuses to and from Bingen, to meet the steam-vessels on the Rhine.

Rudesheim.—HOTEL :—

Hotel Darmstadter Hoff, good.

Duchy of Nassau. A borough at the foot of the mountain of same name, which is covered with vineyards. At the further end is an old tower, remarkable for the elegant style of its architecture. there are also four ancient castles in this town, well worthy of notice.

Geissenheim.—A large town in the same duchy, noted as well as Rüdesheim for its wines; one of the most beautiful places in the Rheingau, situated at the widest part of the stream, which here measures 2000 feet; there are many handsome country seats, among which the villa of Baron V. Zwierlein is worth visiting, for its collection of painted glass.

Johannisberg, on its vine-clad hill, is a prominent object here. The castle belongs to Prince Metternich, who has laid out the grounds with much taste. The vines cover a space of 65 acres; those most esteemed grow round the castle, and indeed partly over the cellars.

In the middle of the Rhine channel, on to Mayence, are numerous islands.

Bieberich.—HOTEL:—

HOTEL DE L'EUROPE, good and reasonable.

The Albert House—Boarding and Lodging-House, very respectable, and highly recommended.

Near the Rhine, the summer residence of the Duke of Nassau; his palace looks well from the river. The gardens attached are very extensive and much admired. A beautiful statue has recently been added. Travellers wishing to proceed direct to Frankfort-on-the-Maine, will leave the steamboat here, and proceed by railway.

CONVEYANCES.—Railway trains to Wiesbaden and Frankfort, see page 74. Steamers up and down the Rhine several times a day, see advertisement, pages 337 and 339.

Wiesbaden.—HOTELS.—

ROSE HOTEL AND BATH-HOUSE, first rate and reasonable, kept by Mr. Schmitt, formerly of Meurices Hotel, Paris.

HOTEL DE L'AIGLE AND POSTE, deserving our best recommendation.

HOTEL D'ANGLETERRE, an excellent house, highly recommended.

Considered the first watering-place of Germany, is situated in a beautiful valley, surrounded by the hills of the Taunus, containing about 15,000 inhabitants, and is rich in public saloons and garden. It is reached from the Rhine by railway in a quarter of an hour (distance from Frankfort 26½ English miles), and trains run each way six times a-day.

Dr. Edwin Lee (of Brighton), author of "The Baths of Germany," "Continental Travel," &c., usually passes the season here.

ENGLISH PHYSICIAN.—Dr. John R. Robertson attends weekly on certain days from Frankfort.

AGENT for the sale of J. A. Farina's *Eau de Cologne*—Schroder, Coiffeur de la Cour.

Castel.—A town and fortress on the right bank, almost a suburb of Mayence, 2,500 inhabitants, and connected with it by a bridge of boats. Here is the terminus of the Wiesbaden and Frankfort Railway. The Cologne Company have established here a commodious landing jetty, to spare travellers the *detour* by the Bridge.

Mayence—(*with Map in Special Edition*).—HOTELS:—

HOTEL DE HOLLANDE, an old-established excellent house.

HOTEL D'ANGLETERRE, recommended with great confidence.

(German, *Mainz*) is a fortress of the Confederation and strongly garrisoned by the Austrians and Prussians; 36,000 inhabitants; 8,000 garrison. It looks well from a distance; but, except the Cathedral, contains few public buildings of much interest. At a short distance is the new park, overlooking the Rhine, and commanding a good view of its junction with the Maine, the bridge of boats and part of the Rheingau, with the Taunus in the back ground. Travellers can now go the whole distance to Bale in one day. Gutemberg, the inventor of printing, was born here, and here is a fine statue to his memory, modelled by Thorwaldsen. There is also the Chateau of the old Prince Electoral of Mayence, containing a collection of paintings. Steamers run four or five times a-day to Frankfort, distant about 30 miles. From Hoechst is a private railway to Soden, a famous watering-place, celebrated for its cold springs. Warm and cold baths can be had on the banks of the river. Warm bath, 30 kr.

CONVEYANCES. — Steamers to Coblentz, Bonn, Cologne, Dusseldorf, and Rotterdam, daily, as also to Mannheim, see advertisement, pages 337 & 339. The steamers usually stop at the following places between Mayence and Mannheim, viz., Oppenheim, Gornsheim, Rheindürkheim, and Worms.

Oppenheim.—2,500 inhabitants. The Church of St. Catherine, in the purest gothic style, (built 1262—1317), contains several superb sculptures and tombs, and some stained glass in a good state of preservation.

Gernsheim. — Population 3,000; the birthplace of Pierre Shoeffer, an early printer, in whose honour there is a handsome monument.

Frankfort-on-the-Maine—(*with Map in Special Edition*).—HOTELS: —

The HOTEL DE L'EMPEREUR ROMAN, a first-rate Family Hotel.

HOTEL WEIDENSBUSCH, well known, good, and reasonable.

HOTEL DE RUSSIE, one of the best in Europe, conducted by Mr. Reid, well known to English travellers for his obliging civility and attention.

LANDSBERG HOTEL, an excellent and comfortable Hotel.

Free town, with 70,000 inhabitants, and seat of the German Diet. Amid a great variety of objects to interest the traveller in this place may be mentioned as worthy of inspection the Hotel de Ville (Roemer) with a large saloon, containing portraits of all the German emperors, who were formerly crowned in this city. The town library, with more than 60,000 volumes, is open every Tuesday and Thursday, from 10 to 12, Mondays, Wednesdays, and Fridays, from 2 to 4 o'clock; a gallery of paintings, with more than 900 original paintings, is open on Tuesdays and Thursdays, from 11 to 12 o'clock; the Städel Museum of Paintings, open daily, (except Saturdays) from 10 to 1; the natural history museum, open every Wednesday, from 2 to 4 o'clock, on Fridays, from 11 to 1; the Bethmann museum, with Danneker's Ariadne, open daily from 11 to 1 o'clock; the monument of Goethe, in the square before the theatre; the house in which Goethe was born, in the Great Hirschgraben, No. 74; the new cemetry, with several beautiful monuments. In the neighbourhood: the Mainlust, with a beautiful distant prospect. The Taunus Mountains can be reached by railway as far as Höchst.

Frankfort to Kissengen.—To avoid the Lohr road, which is cut up by the railway works, the road by rail to Hanau, to Schlucteren, and Bruckenan, is recommended.

Eibingen (office *Zeil*, next to the post-office and Hotel de Russie) to Leipsic, *via* Cassel and Eisenach (the railway being open to Marburg), daily (see page 75); to Basle, by railway, in 14 hours; by railway, through Wurzberg and Nuremberg—Hanover, Hamburg, Darmstadt, &c.; and to Paris in less than 24 hours, by steam-boat and railway, *via* Brussels. At a cost of £3 18s. a traveller may reach London from Frankfurt, *via* Ostend, in 56 hours. As ministers from Great Britain, America, and most of the European states reside in Frankfort, travellers proceeding to Italy or Austria should have their passports signed. Two large fairs are held here, in spring and autumn, when merchandise is brought from all parts of Europe.

The third Continental Peace Congress was held at Frankfort on the 22nd August, 1850, and the two following days. The special train from London, *via* Calais and Cologne and thence up the Rhine, contained about 500 delegates and visitors. The place of meeting was St. Paul's church. This magnificent building, capable of holding more than 2000 persons, was thronged each day. The proceedings were similar in character to those at Brussels and Paris in 1848 and 1849; and the effect of this Congress on the public mind is understood to have been very satisfactory to its promoters.

BANKERS, EXCHANGE OFFICE. — L. A. Hahn, banker and money changer, Zeil, No. 35.—Purchases and sales of all sorts of English and foreign bonds effected. Coupons of all foreign stocks and railway shares cashed. Bank notes, all foreign notes, approved bills of exchange, and circular notes exchanged. Gold and silver bullion, in bars or otherwise, and old plate purchased.

BRITISH CONSUL, BANKER, AND WINE MERCHANT.—Mr. Koch, near the Hotel d'Angletérre.

PHYSICIANS.—Dr. Funche, Physician to Her Majesty's Mission, and Dr. John R. Robertson.

ENGLISH AND FOREIGN BOOKSELLERS.—C Jugal, and M. L. St. Goar, Zeil.

AGENT for the sale of J. A, Farina's *Eau de Cologne*—Antbocher, Coiffeur.

CONVEYANCES.—Railway trains to Darmstadt, Mannheim, Heidelberg, Carlsruhe, Baden, Strasburg, Freiburg, and Basle, see pages 75 and 78.—To Offenbach, Castel, Biebrich, and Wiesbaden, see page 74. Eilwagen to Augsburg, Bamberg, Kissingen, Leipzig, Munich, Nuremberg, Ratisbon, & Wurtzburg, see page 251.

Homburg.—HOTELS:—

Hotel des Quatre Saisons—decidedly the best.

About nine miles from Frankfort, as a watering-place rivalling Wiesbaden and Baden in the number of visitors; the view of the Taunus mountains is the chief attraction in point of scenery. We refer with confidence those who really desire to become acquainted with the resources and virtues of these justly celebrated waters, to the "Observations on the Mineral Waters of Homburg, by F. H. Prytherch, M.D., &c. &c. &c.," who is the authorised English resident physician. The third edition of this work is now published, and may be had of John Churchill, Prince's-street, Soho, London; Louis Schick, Homburg; or through them, of the principal continental booksellers. Population 4000.

ENGLISH PHYSICIAN.—Dr. John R. Robertson attends weekly on certain days from Frankfort.

AGENT for the sale of J. A. Farina's *Eau de Cologne*—Privart.

CONVEYANCES.—Omnibuses correspond with the trains to and from Frankfort almost every hour.

Wilhemsbad.—HOTELS:—

The Ducal Palace, Bath House and Kursaal.

This charming watering place is situated in one of the most picturesque scenes imaginable, within fifteen minutes railway distance from Frankfort-on-the-Maine. The attractions to this interesting place are so remarkable that Wilhemsbad has become a rival to Hombourg, and promises to eclipse some of the more important bathing places in Germany.

Worms.—HOTEL:—

Hotel de la Poste.

Population 8360, besides the garrison. The Cathedral is a venerable monument of the eighth century, completed in 1016, and inaugurated in the presence of the Emperor, Henry II. The memorable diet at which Luther appeared was held here by Charles V, in 1521. Rosenwald, on an island where the valiant Siegfried killed the dragon, is the scene of the romantic poem, the *Niebelungen Lied*. Public Places—the Markets, the Place St. Andre, St. Martin, and St. Paul, Hotel de Ville, &c. In the ancient city of Worms on he Rhine, there existed a convent of Capucines, the church adjoining is called the Liebfrau Kirche, erected in the 9th century. The edifice is constructed in the gothic style, and is very well worth a visit on account of its architectural merits. Immediately on the south and south-eastern sides of the church lie the celebrated vineyards, where the Liebfraumilch is grown, the best quality of the wine is produced nearest the walls of the church, and the estate, which is enclosed by a wall, is called the garden of the Capucines, it is the property of the house of P. J. Valckenberg. The grapes which yield this fine Rhine wine are of the Riesling kind.

Mannheim.—HOTEL:—

HOTEL DE L'EUROPE, situated opposite the landing-place of the Rhine Steamers, the Railway Station, &c., is an excellent house in every respect.

At the influx of the Neckar into the Rhine, with 25,000 inhabitants. It is a clean and well built town, but monotonous on account of the regularity of the buildings. The largest building in the town is the Grand Duke's palace, wherein is a picture gallery and a cabinet of natural history; the pleasantest walks are, the garden behind the palace and the Plankenstrasse. In the neighbourhood lies Schwetzingen, with its beautiful garden. At Mannheim the extensive and superiorly constructed Grand Ducal Baden Railway commences, which is now open nearly to Bale. Trains run six or seven times a day (see page 78, 79), and the journey from Mannheim to Heidelberg is performed in 36 minutes; to Carlsruhe, 2 hours 34 minutes; to Baden, 4 hours; to Kehl, 5 hours 34 minutes; to Efringen (Bale), in about $9\frac{1}{4}$ hours.

CONVEYANCES.—Railway trains to Heidelberg, Carlsruhe, Baden; Kehl (for Strasburg), Freiburg, and Basle, see page 78; to Darmstadt and Frankfort, page 75. Steamers to Cologne, see advertisement, pages 337 and 339.

Heidelberg.—HOTELS:—

HOTEL ADLER, or Eagle, near to and opposite the Castle, very comfortable and moderate.

GOLDEN FALCON, in the market-place, good and moderate prices.

HOTEL PRINCE CHARLES, first-rate and excellent, near the Castle.

HOTEL DE LA COUR DE BADEN, first rate, one of the best in Germany.

HOTEL DE HOLLANDE, a good and highly respectable Hotel.

On the Neckar, is an old and cheerful looking town, of 16,000 inhabitants, and a pleasant place of sojourn for a time in summer. The picturesque ruins of the castle, one of the most interesting objects in Rhenish Germany, formerly the residence of the Electors-Palatine, occupy the hill behind the town. The University is attended by about 500 students. The environs of Heidelberg are a perfect garden, producing abundance of grain and fruit.

PIANOFORTES.—Persons wishing to hire or purchase excellent Pianos are recommended to Mr. George Trau, 7, Hauptstrasse, opposite the Hotel de Baden.

CONVEYANCES.—Railway to Carlsruhe and Baden, page 78, and steamers ascend the Neckar daily to Heilbronn.

Speyer, or **Spire** (SPEIER, German).—Population 9500. One of the oldest towns of Rhenish Germany.—Remarkable Buildings—the Cathedral, the Church of the Trinity, the Altportel.

Leopoldhofen.—A little village where passengers are landed to go to

Carlsruhe.—HOTEL.—

The Golden Cross Hotel, good and reasonable.

Capital of the Grand Duchy of Baden, with 24,000 inhabitants. Amongst the edifices are to be observed the Palace, the Protestant and Catholic churches, built by Weinbrenner: the Palace of the Count Palatine of Baden, and the Polytechnic School, the latter in the architectural style of the middle centuries. Before the castle is a bronze statue of the deceased Grand Duke of Baden by Schwanthaler; a pyramid of red sandstone in the interior of the town points out the grave of the founder and builder of the town.

CONVEYANCES.—Railway trains to Heidelberg, Mannheim, and Frankfort, see page 79, to Baden, Kehl, Offenburg, Freiburg, Haltingen and Bale, see page 78. Eilwagens daily to Landau, Pforzheim, Stuttgardt, Wildbad, and Zweibrucken. To Stuttgardt in about 9 hours. Fare, 4 fl. 10 kr. The Post station adjoins the Railway.

Baden-Baden.—HOTELS:—

HOTEL DU RHIN, good and comfortable.

The HOTEL DE HOLLANDE, near the Kursaal; table d'hôte at 1 and 5 o'clock; highly recommended.

HOTEL DE RUSSIE, first-rate; every thing good, clean, and comfortable.

Baden-Baden is invested with peculiar attraction by the picturesque beauty of its situation, being romantically seated on the banks of the Oos, and embosomed among majestic hills—the children of the Black Forest. The town has about 6000 permanent residents, and is chiefly built on the slope of a hill, owing to the narrowness of the valley, which consists for the most part of charming prairies, whose light green forms a pleasant contrast to the dark fir-trees that cover the surrounding hills. This excellent site of the town is added to by the mild climate, inasmuch as the neighbouring mountains check the north and east winds, and the hot-wells concealed in the bosom of the earth impart warmth to the soil. These springs were known to, and appreciated by, the Romans, who colonised the spot, and named it *Civitas Aurelia Aquensis.* Within its palaces the Margraves of Baden resided for more than six centuries, and only left their favoured retreat when the fierce fury of war, and the barbarous devastation of the Palatinate by the French, forced them to remove to Rastadt, in the flat plain of the Rhine. At present there exists here a villa of the Duke of Baden, to which he makes occasional visits, but his principal summer residence is the Castle of Eberstein. At one period, Baden was considered the most fashionable watering-place in Germany, and is to-day by far the most beautiful of the baths of North Germany, not even excepting that of the Brunnen of Nassau but it is much gone down in respectability, owing to the gambling system so unhappily prevalent there. As a consequence, the credit of the society met with there is much deteriorated, and the number of visiters considerably decreased; but even now, princes and nobles are met with there in the season. Prospects—vivid, brilliant, and commandingly attractive; walks—shady, retired, and gorgeous in their floral and sylvan foliage—distinguish and characterise each spot of the neighbourhood; whilst the ball-rooms and salons, the concert halls and gaming-tables, minister to an unwholesome luxury, sufficient even for the most effeminate. The invalid will also find retirement and solitude, even amid the surrounding din of mirth—it may be of revelry and dissipation. The numerous agreeable promenades, cutting through the woods, will furnish him with means of quiet recreation and healthful walking, even in the fierce glow of a midsummer sunshine. July and August are the *Season;* but from May to October a succession of visiters continue to arrive and depart. So many as 32,000 have visited Baden in a year, of whom 10,000 repaired thither to take the baths. The springs are thirteen in number, bursting out from rocks behind the parish church, at the foot of the castle terrace, called "Schneckengarten," and preserving an unvaried temperature in summer and winter, viz.—the hottest, 54° Réaum; the coldest, 37°. This portion of the town is called "Hell," and snow never rests upon it, even in the most severe atmosphere. The water of these springs is carried through the town by means of pipes, and a beautiful temple covers the principal well, called the "Ursprung." The various, and indeed very interesting, monuments of the Romans, found and seen about Baden, will deeply interest the antiquarian. The "Neue Trinkhalle," or pump-room, situated on the public walks, close to the "Conversationshaus," will interest, both by reason of its architectural beauty, and frescoes representing legends of the Black Forest. The design was by Hübsch, and reflects on him much credit. The time for assembling to drink the waters, is between 6½ and 7½ a.m., when the band plays from a kind of pavilion. On the left bank of the Oosbach, we see the "Promenade" and "Conversationshaus" — a magnificent building, adorned by a Corinthian portico, and surrounded by tastefully laid out gardens and pleasure-grounds. It consists of a large assembly room, in which there is dancing three times a week. Except on Saturday, the gaming-tables are occupied day and night. There is a theatre on the right wing, and on the left a restaurant, and attached to it a library and reading room. The *rouge-et-noir* tables are much frequented in the evening; the stakes are generally heavy, and the victims of this degrading passion numerous. Many a heart broken, many a fortune ruined, many a reputation blasted, and many a young and innocent victim driven to suicide, attest the ruinous consequences of indulgence in it. To all who visit Baden, we would say—"avoid the gaming-table, in order to avoid the gambler's fate." This "Conversationshaus" is rented by a company of gambling speculators, who pay to the Baden government £6000 a year for the *exclusive* privilege of having the gaming-tables. Besides this, they are bound to spend about £18,000 per annum on the walks and buildings. From this fact may be gleaned the immense sums lost by the blind dupes visiting the place.

Above the town we see the das Neue Schloss, or new castle, so called to distinguish it from the old one, on the top of the hill. The halls, judgment seat, and horrible dungeons in this castle, ought to be visited. Their appearance will freeze and chill the very life's blood of the spectator who looks on them for the first time, and reads in their iron rings, racks, knives, and instruments of torture—the awful punishment inflicted on the victims of man's barbarism and society's cruelty. Baden is also memorable as being the seat of the Secret Tribunal (vehmgericht), similar to that described by Scott in *Anne of Geierstein*. The parish church is worth notice, chiefly on account of being the burial-place of the Margraves of Baden, and as containing many of their monuments.

English church service in Spital Kirche on Sundays, at 11 a.m.

Delightful excursions can be made from here to das Alte Schloss, an hour's walk; to Eberstein-burg; the Jagdhaus, or hunting-lodge, near the Lichenthal, &c.

AGENT for the sale of J. A. Farina's *Eau de Cologne*—Mr. Alois Grosholz.

CONVEYANCES. — Railway trains to Carlsruhe, Heidelberg, Mannheim, and Frankfort, see pages 79 and 75; to Strasburg, Freiburg, and Basle, see page 75.

Kehl.—HOTEL:—

HOTEL DU PIED DE CHEVREUIL, very good, comfortable, and reasonable.

Persons wishing to visit Strasbourg will find an Omnibus at the Station on arrival of each train, to convey them to the Hotel de la Poste, where they will be as well lodged as at Strasburg. Carriages are always ready to take them to Strasburg and back, thus avoiding the inspection of luggage, which takes place each time of crossing the Rhine.

Friburg.—HOTELS:—

HOTEL DE'ALLEMAGNE, an excellent house, and the landlord speaks English.

ZAHRINGER HOF; very good; the nearest to the Cathedral and Railway Station.

The ancient capital of the Breisgau, situated on the Triesau, at the entrance into the Höllenthal. The minster is worth seeing, a large gothic church; it was begun under Conrad III., of Zähringen, 1122 to 1152; the tower is 380 feet high. The university, with its collection; the company's hall; the St. Ludwig's church. In the neighbourhood: the Schlossberg, Alt Breisch, the Glacis, the coffee-house on the top; the Carthusian monastry, Bad-Pfersich, Allee-graten, Renngarf, the small castle.

CONVEYANCES.—Railway trains to Haltingen, for Basle, see page 78; also to Offenburg, Kehl (Strasburg), Baden, Carlsruhe, Heidelberg, and Frankfort, see page 79. EILWAGEN to Schaffhausen and Constance, through the Black Forest, passing through the grand scenery of the Hollenthal, and affording, perhaps, the finest distant view of the Alps. On this road is

Lenzkirch, a most romantic town, occupying about 10 hours to Schaffhausen, and 14½ hours to Constance.

Bale, or **Basle.**—HOTELS:—

HOTEL OF THE THREE KINGS (Trois Rois)—highly recommended. Good rooms and clean, excellent cuisine, and attentive servants.

HOTEL DU SAVAGE, very good and moderate.

The capital of Bale Canton and the largest town in Switzerland, lies on the Rhine, which divides it into two unequal parts, joined together by a bridge of 690 feet in length. The minster, or cathedral church, the town-house, and the arsenal, are objects worthy of attention. The university, founded here in 1459, has an excellent library, a cabinet of medals, and botanic garden. It has manufactures of silk ribbons, silk stuffs, cotton, paper, linen, and gloves; there are also considerable bleachfields and dye-houses.

BANKERS.—M. Passavant & Co. cash English Bank Notes and the Circular Notes of all the Banks and Banking Houses of London, Dublin, Edinburgh, and New York. The Offices of the Bank are close to the Post-office and principal hotels.

CONVEYANCES.—Diligence to Haltingen, thence by railway to Efringen, Kehl (Strasburg), Heidelberg, Mannheim, and Frankfort, see page 79. There is also a railway on the French side of the Rhine to Strasburg, see page 77.

GERMANY.

London to Hamburgh.—Steamers leave the Tower two or three times a-week for Hamburgh early in the morning. (See page 132.) The average passage is 55 hours. Much time, however, will be saved by adopting the route *via* Dover and Ostend to Malines, thence to Cologne, from which place Hamburgh may be reached in 19 hours, making the whole time from London about 37 hours.

Hull to Hamburgh.—By the Hull Steam Packet Company's Vessels, Gee & Co.'s Steamers, and Sanderson & Co.'s Steamers. See page 130.

Altenburg on the Pleisse, capital of the Duchy of Saxon-Altenburg: 14,200 inhabitants. The castle is remarkable; it consists of two parts, the older portion built in the 13th, and the newer part in the 17th century.

Conveyances.—Railway to Leipsic and Hof, p.90.

Altona.—After Copenhagen, the largest city of Denmark, containing about 30,000 inhabitants. It is built on the side of a steep hill, which gives it the appearance of an amphitheatre, when viewed from the side of the Elbe. The commerce of Altona, both inland and foreign, is considerable. It is connected by railway with Kiel, on the Baltic. (See pages 96 and 97.)

Conveyances.—For railway trains from Hamburgh to Berlin, see pages 92 and 93.

Aschaffenburg.—Hotel:—

Hotel Freihof.

Aschaffenburg, situated prettily on the right bank of the Maine, not far from the forest of Spessart, the largest in Germany. The ancient Hercyinia of Cæsar and Tacitus; population 10,000. This town was the station for the 10th and 23rd Roman Legions. The Frankish kings had a palace built on the ruins of a Roman castle. The late King of Bavaria, Ludwig, caused an exact model of a Roman villa to be built on the banks of the Maine, after the plan of one in the ruins of Pompeii; the paintings on the walls are executed by the first artists, and it is interesting to see the private dwellings of a Roman citizen brought within our understanding. The present royal residence is a handsome palace, built in 1606. The church is worthy of attention, built in 974. There is a monument in bronze of Cardinal Albert of Brandenburg, by Peter Vischer, a bronze Virgin by his son Hermann, and another monument in bronze, by Hack. The road from Aschaffenburg to Gemunden is very much cut up by the carriage of heavy stones, used for the railroad viaducts of the line now being constructed between Frankfort and Wurtzburg. The line is to be open in 1854.

The other road to Kissengen recommended to travellers is by Rail to Hanan, and by Post to Schlicterne and Brukanau.

Augsburg.—Inns.—

Drei Mohren (Three Moors)—good—Goldene Traube (Golden Grapes), Moor's Head, Hotel Lutz, and Die Weisse Lamm (the White Lamb).

Augsburg, at the influx of the Wertha, in the Lech; considerable manufacturing town, with 36,000 inhabitants. Great trade in money and exchange.

Objects of Attraction.—The Maximilian street, with its bronze fountains, by Adrian de Vries, 1599, and the well of Augustus, by Hubert Gerhard, 1590; the town-hall, a beautiful building in the Italian style of architecture, by Elias Hole, 1620; the cathedral, an irregular building in the Byzantine style; the castle or palace in which the Emperor Charles the Fifth resided when the Augsburg confession was presented to him, 1635; the St. Ulrich and Alfra church, with many monuments of the family of Fugger; the so-called Fuggerei; the inn of the Three Moors, of which mention was made in the year 1364, and no doubt one of the oldest in the world; the store-house; the poor-house; the industrial school, and the academy for the study of painting. In the neighbourhood,—Park, Bavarian and Schwabian Himmelreich, Tivoli, Rosenau, Göginan,' Schatzler's villa.

Omnibuses run between the railway stations and the following places, calling at the different inns in their route,—St. Ulrich's kirche, St. Margaretha, Gasthofe, and St. Jacob's kirche.

Agent for the sale of J. A. Farina's *Eau de Cologne*—Mr. Ant. Nägelli, Coiffeur.

Conveyances.—Railway trains to Munich, Donauworth, Nordlingen, Oettingen, Gunzenhausen, & Nuremberg, see page 82; to Kaufbeurn & Kempten, see page 86. Diligences to Ulm, see page 245.

Bamberg.—Inns.—

Bamberger-hof, Deutschehaus, and the Drei Kronen.

Bamberg, on the Regnitz and on the Ludwig canal, is a beautiful town, with 21,000 inhabitants. The chief objects of attraction are the cathedral, which is one of the finest in Germany; the Palace; the Pfarrkirche; the Rathaus, and the view from the ruined Castle of Altenberg, situated about half a mile from the town; this view is considered one of the finest in Franconia.

Conveyances.—Railway trains to Nuremberg, Nordlingen, Augsburg, Kaufbeurn, and Munich, as also to Lichtenfels, see page 82, 83. Eilwagen to Bayreuth, Frankfort-on-the-Maine, Kissingen, and Wurtzburg.

Berncastel.—A town on the Moselle, with 2000 inhabitants. The steam-vessels ascending the river from Coblentz to Treves stop here for the night, and leave for Treves at 6 a.m.

Bremen.—Hotel.—

Hotel de l'Europe, a first-class house, highly recommended.

Situated on the Weser, and containing in the city and suburbs upwards of 75,000 inhabitants. It is divided by the Weser into the old and new towns. The fortifications of the city having been destroyed, the ground on which they stood has been laid out as public gardens, in the English style, with running water, sheltered walks, &c. The principal buildings, besides its churches, are the City Hall the Exchange, Museum, Theatre, and Hospital. Olbers and Heeren were born at Bremen. Bremen does an immense trade in tobacco, and has the largest cigar manufactories in the world; ship-building is carried on to a considerable extent, and there is a large trade between this important port and America, as well as with almost all parts of the globe. Connected with Hanover by railway. (See page 89.)

Brunswick.—HOTEL.—

Hotel d'Angleterre—an excellent house.

Brunswick on the Otter, 38,000 inhabitants, a town with clean streets, much picturesque architecture in the old buildings, and surrounded with walks and parks, beautifully laid out; the new palace is a neat edifice, built after the plan of Ottmar, the permission to inspect it costs two dollars!! The museum in the arsenal has the usual attractions, and is only open on each Wednesday and Saturday, from 11 to 1 o'clock; a visit to it at other times costs 2½ dollars. The cathedral, or the church of the Holy Blasius in the gothic-Norman style, was completed in the year 1194, by Heinrich der Löwe who lies buried here, as also his wife; the Duke of Brunswick, who was slain at the battle of Waterloo, and the unfortunate wife of George IV., Caroline of Brunswick, also lie buried here. Near the church stands a large bronze lion, which Heinrich der Löwe (Henry the Lion) brought from Constantinople. In the promenades is the large and beautiful monument erected to the memory of the two Dukes of Brunswick, who fell at Jena and Waterloo; before the gate Steinthor, is the monument of the valiant and unfortunate Schill, who died in 1808.

AGENT for the sale of J. A. Farina's *Eau de Cologne*—Mr. Wm. Sprung & Co.

CONVEYANCES.—Railway trains to Schladen and Harzburg, and also to Wolfenbuttel, page 87.—To Hanover, Minden, and Cologne, pages 84, 87 and 70. —To Magdeburg and Berlin, pages 88 and 97.—To Magdeburg, Kothen, Halle, & Leipsic, pages 86 & 97.

Cannstadt.—INN—

Hermann's and Formis's.

Cannstadt is situated on the fertile shores of the Neckar, containing 4000 inhabitants, celebrated for its mineral springs, and the beauty of the situation, besides its salubrity. The Kursaal is very elegant, and distinguished for its fresco paintings; three quarters of an hour from Stuttgardt, a pleasant walk through the Royal Park, or 10 minutes by Railway. Travellers would do well not to remain in the unhealthy town of Stuttgardt, but continue their journey 10 minutes longer to Cannstadt, from which place they can visit every thing worth seeing. It is recommended to tourists on account of its mild climate during winter. It has an Institution for the cure of all distortions of the human frame.

ENGLISH PHYSICIAN—Dr. Buckhart.

CONVEYANCES.——Railway to Stuttgardt, Esslingen, Plochingen, Sussen, Geislingen, Ulm, Biberach, and Friedrichshafen, page 81.

Cassel.—HOTEL:—

Koning Von Preussen

Is the capital of Lower Hesse, and seat of the Electorate, containing about 33,000 inhabitants. It is divided into the Old Town, the Lower New Town, and the Upper New Town, and is situated on the Fulda. It enjoys a fair manufacturing trade in linen cloth, hats, and porcelain. Its objects of attraction are rather few. In the Friedrich's Platz, one of the largest squares in Germany, is the Elector's Palace, a building devoid of any imposing effect, and far surpassed by very many of the hotels inhabited by the bankers in Frankfort. Near it stands the Museum, one of the prettiest buildings in Cassel; and immediately to the rear are the Government Offices. A very fine view of the valley and windings of the Fulda, as also of the remote Mount Meissner, can be enjoyed from an open side of the square on the brow of the hill. In the middle of the square there is a statue of Frederick II., the founder and patron of the principal establishments and collections of art in Cassel. The wealth of this Prince was accumulated by his traffic in the lives of his subjects, by hiring them out to the King of England to fight against the Pretender in Scotland, and against the Americans for their war of independence; for the latter job he received 22,000,000 dollars!!

THE MUSEUM is open daily, from 11 to 1: it contains a library of 90,000 volumes, a cabinet of curiosities well worth attention, the collection of natural philosophy, and the picture gallery, in which are some very rare and valuable paintings.

The THEATRE is also worth notice. It was built by King Jerome Buonaparte. The conservatories and fountains behind it are the highest in Europe, except that at Chatsworth. The famous gardens of Wilhelmshohe, the Versailles of Germany; in them is the Elector's summer palace, about three or four miles from Cassel. Wednesday and Sunday are the best days for a visit.

The Cascade of the Karlsburg is worth a visit. At the top is a colossal statue, over which falls, at intervals, a stream of water. The statue is led up to by a flight of stone steps 900 feet long. The hill can be ascended by means of a carriage road. On a sort of landing, half-way up the stairs, the Giant Euceladus, rudely carved, is represented in a horizontal position, a mountain of rocks covering his bosom. An eight-sided figure, 1,312 feet over the Fulda, topped by a pyramid supporting the colossal figure of Hercules (31 feet high) manufactured of beaten copper, surmounts the Chateau d'Eau: within the hollow of the club eight persons can be accommodated, and enjoy a very fine view of the surrounding country from a small window constructed therein. The Aquatic Staircase and Temple of the Winds employed 2000 men for fourteen years.

Lowenburg Foy Castle, met with in the descent, is worth notice. Its contents are—armour, belonging to the Great Condé; a curious collection of drinking glasses; some portraits of the Tudors and Stuarts, and a library of romances. The chapel contains the remains of the Elector who built it.

AGENT for the sale of J. A. Farina's *Eau de Cologne*—Messrs. G. Franche & Ponnaz.

Coburg, is the capital of a principality of the same name, situated on the river Itz or Itsch. The market-place is a fine square, and contains the government offices and town-house. Here is a celebrated academy, founded in 1597, and also a castle. Leopold, who married Princess Charlotte of England, and afterwards became King of Belgium, is a descendant of the Coburg family. Prince Albert, who married the Queen of England, is of the same family. The inhabitants carry on some traffic in wool. Population 7000. 100 miles from Frankfort-on-the-Maine.

Darmstadt.—HOTEL.—

Hotel de Köhler, near the Railway Station.

Darmstadt, the capital of the grand duchy of Hesse Darmstadt, and residence of the Grand Duke. Population 22,000, principally Protestants. In the new town the streets are wide and regularly built. There is one good square, called the Louisenplatz, in which is a fine monument in memory of the last duke. The railway station is outside the Rheinthor.

Donauworth, a well-built town of Bavaria, seated on the north bank of the Danube, at the influx of the Wernitz; 25 miles from Augsburg; here is a bridge over the Danube. Population 25,000.

CONVEYANCES.—Steamboats down the Danube to Ratisbon, and from thence to Lintz and Vienna.

Dresden.—HOTELS—

HOTEL DE SAXE, a first-rate, capital house, highly recommended.

BRITISH HOTEL, an excellent house, deserving our strong recommendation.

HOTEL DE POLOGNE, situated in a central and most convenient position, is an old established fashionable house.

VICTORIA HOTEL.—This magnificent, first-rate, and highly recommended house, is kept by Mr. Edward Dremel, son of the well-known Mr. Dremel of the Grand Monarque Hotel, at Aix-la-Chapelle.

HOTEL DE L'EUROPE well situated and a good house.

Capital of the kingdom of Saxony, celebrated on account of its charming environs and the extraordinary richness of its works of art; situated on both shores of the Elbe, which are united by a beautiful bridge, 552 yards long; 90,000 inhabitants. The terminus of the Leipsic and Dresden Railway is in the Neustadt, on the right bank of the Elbe. Trains to Leipsic five times a-day (see page 97). Fiacres and omnibuses convey passengers to all parts of the town, for 10 and 5 neu groschen.—*Eilposten* daily to Prague, Carlsbad, and Vienna. By way of Ostend and Cologne, Dresden may be reached in 60½ hours. The traveller should, by all means, visit The Saxon Switzerland. There is a railroad to Konigstein, from whence he may visit that fortress, and take a boat down the river to the Basti, a most delightful place.

Exquisitely finished miniatures for broaches, bracelets, or pictures, are taken here for moderate prices; also, copies on enamel of the celebrated pictures in the gallery. The prices of these latter range from 5s. upwards.

OBJECTS OF ATTRACTION.—The celebrated Dresden Gallery; the Grüne Gewölbe, or Green Vaults, a collection of precious stones, gold and silver ornaments, and articles of vertu, valued at several millions sterling; the Frauen Kirche, with a a beautiful dome, altar, and organ; Catholic church; Synagogue; Zwinger and Japanese Palaces, and Brühl Terrace, where there is a most excellent coffee-house; Academy of Arts, Catholic churchyard, Bath of Link (tea-gardens), &c.

BRITISH ENVOY—Hon. Mr. Forbes. CHAPLAIN —Rev. C. Lindsay.

JEWELLER—M. Elimeyer. (See advertisement, end of book.)

ENGLISH PHYSICIAN—Dr. Pincoffs.

CONVEYANCES.—Railway to Burxdorf, Herzberg, and Berlin, page 89.—From Riesa to Limmritz and Chemnitz, page 94.—To Zittau and Gorlitz, page 94. —EILWAGEN to Marienburg, Prague, and Zwickau &c. See page 250. Steamers ascend the Elbe to Lobowitz, (whence there is a Railway to Prague) passing through the Saxon Switzerland. Railway from Dresden to Prague. See page 92.

The easiest and most profitable way of visiting Saxon Switzerland, particularly for those who cannot devote much time to it, is, to set out from Dresden at 11 o'clock, morn., by Railway, with a ticket for the station "Potscha," there to leave the train, cross the river Elbe to Wehlen, ascend to the Bastei rock and go on as far as the little town of Schandau, and sleep there. The next day the traveller goes by the Kuhstall, the Winterberg, and the Prebischthor, to Herniskretschen, where he meets the steamer for Dresden at 5 o;clock, and reaches that city at 8 in the evening.

CABS are stationed in a great many public places. Fares, 6 groschen for half an hour.

Carriages with 2 horses—charge, 4 thalers a whole day, 3 thalers half a day, and 20 grochen one hour.

Steamers go up the river to Saxon-Switzerland at 6, 10, and 2 o'clock. Coming down the river to Dresden, they leave Aussig at 10, Tetschen at 5 and 11½, and Herniskretschen at 11½ in the morning, and 5 o'clock in the evening Pillnitz at 3½, 7½, and 8½, evening.

Railroad travellers coming down from Prague will do well to leave the railroad at Aussig, and to go at this place on the steamer, the trifling sacrifice of time being richly repaid by the charming beauty of the scenery brought before the eyes of the traveller on the river.

POST OFFICE.—All letters posted before 3 o'clock in the afternoon, will invariably be forwarded the same day.

Daily post of letters from England, France, Russia. Delivery of letters after arrival of respective trains.

Letters to and from London commonly take 3 days.

Electric telegraph in operation between Dresden, Belgium, France, Vienna, Berlin, Breslau.

English Divine Service--Sunday at 11 & 3 o'clock.

Roman Catholic Church—Musical Mass—Saturday, at 4 afternoon; Sunday, at 11 in the morning. Protestant Churches.—Divine Service.—Sunday, at 9 and 10 in the morning.

Picture Gallery—Admission free every day from 9 till 5 afternoon, except on Saturday. French catalogues, at 20 groschen, to got at the doors.

The Green Vaults, engravings, China Collection, and Armoury, are to be seen only by tickets at 2 thalers, and good for six persons.

The Royal Library, admission free, open daily for public use till 1 o'clock.

Royal Opera or Theatre daily. Doors open at 5, performance commence at 6 o'clock.

Eisenach.—A well-built town on the Nesse, forty miles west of Weimar, and twenty-six west of Erfurt, with which places, as well as Halle, &c., it is connected by railway (see page 88). It contains about 10,000 inhabitants, chiefly engaged in woollen manufactures. It contains five churches, a gymnasium, and a library.

Erfurt.—An important town, situated on the great road which leads from Frankfort-on-the-Maine to the north of Germany, twelve miles west of Weimar. Erfurt, according to tradition, was founded as early as the fifth century, by a noble named Erpes. It contains about 30,000 inhabitants, who are partly employed in the manufacture of woollens and silks. Among the objects of attraction in Erfurt may be mentioned the cell in which Luther lived from 1505 to 1512, and the large bell, weighing 275 cwt. The town also contains many scientific and other institutions.

Erlangen.—INNS.—

Golden Swan, Golden Wallfish, and Blue Clock.

Erlangen, University town, on the Regnitz, 10,000 inhabitants. Half an hour's ride, by railway, from Nuremberg, see page 83.

Esslingen.—INNS.—

Reichsadler, and Crown.

Esslingen, on the Neckar; manufacturing town, with 6,500 inhabitants. Here is the establishment of Dr. Stummel for the cure of nervous affections. —In the neighbourhood, on the Rothenberg, is situated the Russian chapel; important on account of the statue of the Four Evangelists, by Dannecker and Thorwaldsen.

CONVEYANCES.—Railway to Ulm, Friedrichshafen, Stutgart, and Heilbronn, see page 81.

Furth.—INN.—

Crown Prince of Prussia.

Furth, near Nuremberg, is a manufacturing town, with 16,000 inhabitants.

Gotha.—This town is built on an eminence, at the foot of which flows the Sale, and contains about 15,000 inhabitants. The Lutheran is the prevalent religion. The town contains a great number of ancient buildings, the principal of which is the Castle. The Museum contains 150,000 volumes and many valuable manuscripts, one of the best cabinets of coins in Europe, a fine numismatic library, an Oriental museum, a museum of curiosities of nature and art, and a gallery of paintings, rich in the productions of the old German school. The seminary for teachers is the oldest in Germany. There is also a gymnasium, and considerable manufactures and commerce. Near Gotha is situated the celebrated observatory on the Seeberg, erected and endowed by Ernest II.

CONVEYANCES.—Railway trains to Eisenach, Erfurt, Weimar, Merseburg, Halle, Magdeburg, Leipsic, and Berlin, see page 88.

Gottingen.—Situated on the Leine, distant from Cassel about 38 miles. The University is the chief point of attraction. It is conveniently situated for visiting the Hartz mountains.

Hamburgh.—HOTEL.—

HOTEL DE L'EUROPE, one of the best in Germany for civility, good fare, &c. Baths in the house.

The ENGLISH HOTEL is in a central situation; it is comfortable and moderate.

Hamburg.—Population 145,000. 80 miles from the mouth of the Elbe. Steamboats once a week to Amsterdam, in 40 hours; to London every Tuesday and Friday; to Hull weekly in 44 hours. By the way of Ostend, Dover, &c., London may now be reached in the same time daily. See advertisement, page 340. Steamers ascend the Elbe to Magdeburg daily, in 40 hours. Schnellposts twice weekly to Rostock; daily to Lubeck, Bremen, and Frankfort.

OBJECTS OF ATTRACTION.—Since the terrible fire which occurred in 1842, which burned down 1749 houses and 61 streets, the city has been wonderfully improved, rows of superb houses have been as quickly as they have been tastefully built up again; those along the Alster Bason, on the Three Jungferstiege, and the streets adjoining, particularly. Of public buildings, on the contrary, which distinguish themselves by their fine architectural beauties, there are none, with the exception of the Exchange. The only church that distinguishes itself is St. Michael's, with its steeple 456 feet high. The city, however, has many noble private houses and excellent benevolent institutions, amongst which may be particularly noticed the Orphan Asylum, and the large hospital with from 4,000 to 5,000 beds; they are remarkably well directed. Klopstock's house, in which the poet lived thirty years, and wherein he died, is No. 232, in the Konigstrasse, Of the coffee-houses, the Elbe and Alster Pavilions are very much resorted to; the stranger should not omit to visit the Exchange-hall. The environs of Hamburg are very alluring, particularly on the right shore of the Elbe, from Altona to Blankenese. Near to Altona lies the suburb Ottensen, where is to be seen the tomb of Klopstock and the monument erected to the memory of 1138 Hamburgers, who were starved to death by Davoust in the winter of 1813 and 1814. A little further on is Rainvilles, an hotel, assembly-room, and garden, with a beautiful prospect of the river Elbe. The stranger should not neglect to visit the village of Wansbeck, where the astronomer Tycho de Brahe and the poet Voss lived a long time, and which is become noted as the dwelling-place of Claudius, who wrote under the name of the Wansbeck-messenger (wansbecker-boten); near to Flottbeck, on the Elbe, five miles from Hamburgh, lies Booth's flower-garden, one of the most beautiful in Germany. The places most frequented are Elbhöhe, with a beautiful prospect, and the Esplanade, situated in the town itself, and Appendorf, Flottbeck, Eimsbüttel, Ham, and Horn, and about half a German mile from the town; the more distant places of resort are Bauer's Park, near Blankenese, the Vierlande, and Helgoland, the flower, fruit, and kitchen gardens of Hamburg.

CONVEYANCES.—Railway trains from Altona to Gluckstadt, Neumunster, Rendsburg, and Kiel, see page 96.—Hamburgh to Berlin, page 92.

Hamm.--HOTEL:—

HOTEL STADT LONDON.

The capital of the Earldom of Mark contains 8,000 inhabitants, and some manufactories in metals. At a short distance from it, at the confluence of the rivers Lippe and Aass, about ten minutes walk to the westward, there are yet existing the remains of the strong Castle of Aliso, mentioned by Tacitus in his work upon the battles of the Romans. Farther to the westward, upon the Lippe, there are still to be seen the constructions of Roman encampments. In the year 1790, during their banishment, the French Princes of the house of Bourbon, the King, afterwards Charles X., and his descendants, resided at Hamm. Their place of residence is still in existence, and is called "Nassauer Hof." The town is the point of intersection of four lines of railway, viz. :—To Cologne, Minden, Munster, Cassel. Distance from Hanover 111, and from Cologne 92 English miles. It possesses two Evangelical and one Catholic Church. The town is situate on a plain, has wide, and at all times cleanly streets, and the surrounding country is beautiful.

There is a Court of Appeal (Appellhof), an Assize Court (Assisenhof), a High School (Gymnasium illustre), a garrison of Cuirassiers, and excellent wave and river Baths. The water of the river Lippy has medicinal qualities for the cure of inflammation in the eyes.

Hanover.—Hotel:—

The Union Hotel, an excellent house; we can recommend it with confidence.

Hotel Royal, a first-rate house, near the Railway Station.

Hanover, on the Leine; residence of the King of Hanover; has 40,000 inhabitants. It possesses little that would gratify a stranger, and its commerce is not very considerable, but still, since the king has made the town his permanent residence, it has very much increased in beauty. The best streets are the George, Frederick, and Adolph-streets. The old royal palace, outwardly pretty, has its interior adorned in a moderately sumptuous manner; the Rittersaal in this palace contains a large collection of family portraits, amongst which, the most remarkable is that of Elizabeth, Queen of Bohemia. The old gothic Town-hall is perhaps the most remarkable building in the city; and the Kaserne (Barracks) the Industrial School, the Royal Riding School, and the Harstall (Royal Stables), are all worthy of inspection. Leibnitz's house is in the Schmiedegrasse, and there is likewise a monument to his memory in Hanover. The Schloss kirche is the prettiest in the town; it contains relics which were brought from Italy by Heinrich der Löwe. Herschel, the astronomer, was born here; he was originally a musician in the military service. In the neighbourhood is the Lindenberg, with a beautiful prospect. The establishment containing the royal stud (admission to which is free) is well worth a visit. Hanover may be reached from London, by way of Dover, Ostend, and Cologne, in 37 hours.

Conveyances.—Railway Trains to Minden, Hamm, Dortmund, Dusseldorf, and Cologne, see pages 87 and 70. —To Bremen, page 89.—To Brunswick, Magdedurg, Kothen Halle, and Leipsic, see pages 84, 86, and 97.—To Brunswick, Magdeburg, and Berlin, pages 84, 86, and 96.

Harzburg, 27 English miles from Brunswick, one of the most favoured points for the commencement of a tour in the Hartz. In the environs is situated the Harzburg-on-the-Burgberg, a beautiful ruin, with a delicious prospect and good accommodation; the ascent takes up a good half hour.

Heilbronn.—Hotels:—

The Lion, the Sun, the Rose, and the Railway Hotel close to the station, a small new house.

Situated on the Neckar, with 11,000 inhabitants. It formerly had the privileges of a free city, given by the Emperor Barbarossa; was a frontier town, and place of commerce.

Public attractions.—The Church and Gothic town of St. Killian, remarkable for its architecture in the Byzantine style. In its archives are preserved the letters of Francis of Sickingen, and Gotz of Berlichingen. The tower in which the latter was imprisoned, the covered bridge, the Penitentiary, great fountain of limpid water, the beautiful promenade before the gates of the town, the Rathaus, an ancient edifice with a curious clock, several imperial charters and papal bulls, are all worthy special notice. A very good trade in brandy, oil, and snuff. Paper and polishing mills are carried on at Heilbronn, which also boasts of a very healthy climate. Three miles from Heilbronn stands the ruined castle of Winsberg, called Weiber treue.

Hof.—This town contains about 8000 inhabitants. It was entirely destroyed by fire, but rebuilt in 1823. From hence the road continues for twelve miles to Kirchenhamitz, and ten miles further is the friendly town of Wunsiedel, the birthplace of the celebrated Jean Paul. Near this town are the Fichtel Mountains, on which is situated Alexanderbad. From Hof there are eilwagens (diligences) twice a-day to Franzensbrunn, Carlsbad, &c., giving ready access to all the celebrated Bohemian springs of Toeplitz, Marienbad, &c. Diligences proceed through Wurtzburg to Bamberg occupying twenty hours; and from Bamberg, Hof is gained in six hours by railway.

Conveyances.—Railway trains to Neuenmarkt, Culmbach, Lichtenfels, Bamberg, Nuremberg, Donauworth, Augsburg, and Munich, pages 83 and 82.—To Zwickau and Leipsic, page 90.

Kiel.—An important city on the Baltic, formerly in the duchy of Holstein. Its university was established in 1665, by Christian Albert, after whom it is named, and contains a library of 100,000 volumes, an observatory, and a museum of natural history. Kiel also contains a seminary for teachers, and other valuable institutions. Altona is reached by means of railway. (See pages 96 and 97.) Steamers to Copenhagen, Stockholm, and St. Petersburg.

Kissingen.—Hotels.—

Kurhans, Hotel de Russie, Hotel de Baviere, Schlatter's Family Hotel. Table de Hote 1 o'clock at all—1 florin a head.

Kissingen in Bavaria, a much-frequented watering-place—the visitors in 1850 amounting to upwards of 4,000, including a great number of English families.

English Physicians: Dr. Granville, Dr. Travis, and Dr. Welsche. Season: May to August.

Conveyances.—Diligence from Frankfort daily in 14 hours, at 6 a.m.; from Courtzburg, twice daily. Steamers on the Main from Frankfort as far as Germenden, thence by Diligence or Omnibus.

Krimmitzschau on the Pleisse, a manufacturing town, with 3,800 inhabitants; church, with remarkable altar painting.

Leipsic.—Hotels:—

Hotel de Russie, an excellent house, highly spoken of.

HOTEL DE POLOGNE, Hainstrasse — a first-rate hotel; frequented and recommended by most English travellers for comfort, attention, and moderate charges. The "*Times*" taken in.—See advertisement.

HOTEL DE BAVIERE, a first-rate house, highly recommended.

Distance from Dresden, 71 miles; time, 3 hours. Trains go five times a-day; (see page 97). The Leipsic terminus is between the Halle and Grimma Gates. The only tunnel on the line, 500 yards long, is passed through at Oberau.—Leipsic is of great historical note and commercial celebrity: population 60,000. It has no very particular attractions, except at the fair-time, when it is particularly lively, and strangers are to be found there from all parts of the world. The number of visitors. amounts generally to more than 50,000, and the market-wares to 80,000,000 dollars yearly. Leipsic is the centre of the German book trade; has 120 depôts, 14 steam-presses, and above 200 hand presses; Booksellers' Exchange, University, founded 1409, containing three colleges, viz., the Augusteum, the Paulinum, with the museum of natural history and anatomy, and the Fûrsten Collegium; the town library, with a collection of eastern manuscripts; the St.Nicolas' church; the large market-place, where is situated the Town-hall and the so-called King's-hall (Konig's-haus): in the latter lived Napoleon, during the battle near Leipsic, and General Field-marshal Schwarzenberg died in it; near it is Auerbach's keller (cellar), celebrated on account of Goethe's Faust,—there is now a good ordinary in it. The post-office; the Sternwarte (Observatory), on the Pleissenburg; Gerhard's garden, in which is placed the monument of Poniatowsky; Gellert's grave, in the Friedhof; the Rosenthal (park); and round about the town, many public gardens, are all well worth seeing.

The traveller should not omit to ascend the tower of the Pleisenburg, whence a magnificent view of the city and country is obtained, including the whole of the field of the celebrated battle.

AGENT for the sale of J. A. Farina's *Eau de Cologne*—Mr. Fred. Fleischer, Library.

CONVEYANCES.—From Leipsic to Frankfort-on-the-Maine take railway to Eisenach, where the mail joins the trains twice a-day.—Railway trains to Altenburg, Zwickau. Hof, Lichtenfels, Bamberg, Nuremberg, Donauworth, Augsburg, Kaufbeurn, and Munich; see pages 90, 83, and 82.—To Halle, Kothen, and Magdeburg, page 97.—To Dresden, page 89.—To Kothen, Juterbogk, and Berlin, page 105.—To Halle, Merseburg, Weimar, Erfurt, Gotha, Eisenach, and Cassel, pages 90 and 91.

Lubeck. — One of the Hanse towns, with 27,000 inhabitants, is situated on a ridge between the rivers Trave and Wackenitz, by whose waters it is completely surrounded; the situation is much admired, and the town itself is highly interesting for its historical vicissitudes: from having been once the most eminent in the Hanseatic League, it is now stamped with the marks of commercial decay—grass-grown streets and empty houses. The last blow it received was after the battle of Jena, when Blucher in his retreat took refuge in it, and being driven out by the victorious French, a pillage of three days ensued, leaving the already time-stricken town a scene of deplorable misery and ruin. The enormous size of its ramparts bear witness to its former importance; they are planted with trees, and serve as drives and promenades. The quaint architecture of its buildings also tell of the magnificence of its olden days; among these the Cathedral is remarkable for its wood-carvings and paintings, some of which are highly prized as specimens of ancient art. The Marienkirche is also well worth seeing. Sir Godfrey Kneller and the brothers Van Ostade were born in Lubeck, where their houses are still shown. In the Rathhaus is the famous aud beautiful Hall of the Hansa, in which the deputies from 85 cities used to meet and hold council together on the affairs of the Confederation. The Holstein-gate is a peculiar specimen of old fortification; the Burg-gate is also a very singular building.

CONVEYANCES.—Steamers to Copenhagen, Stockholm, and St. Petersburg.

Munich (*With Map in Special Edition*)—HOTEL:—

HOTEL DU CERF D'OR, or Golden Stag. This Hotel is greatly improved. It is well conducted and comfortable.

Munich on the Isar, with its suburbs, has more than 100,000 inhabitants and is one of the most beautiful towns in Germany. The most important churches are the Frauen kirche, or the cathedral, built of bricks, in the year 1488; the Jesuit church a beautiful structure in the Italian style, with the tomb of Prince Eugene Beauharnois, by Thorwaldsen—on each Sunday is to be heard classical music; the St. Peter's church, the oldest in Munich; the Theatiner kirche, in the cumbersome Italian style, with the vault of the royal family; the Ludwig's kirche, completed 1842; the All Saints' chapel, in the royal palace; the Mariahilf kirche, in the suburb, in pure gothic style, with nineteen beautifully painted glass windows; the Basalica of Holy Boniface, in the Carlstrasse, without exception, the most beautiful church in Germany, in the Byzantine style,—the frescos which adorn the interior undoubtedly surpass in beauty and richness all other works of living artists The Royal Palace consists of two parts, the old and new, a beautiful edifice, after the model of the Pitti-palace in Florence. It is, without exception, the most tasteful and the most beautiful in Europe; it is open on certain days to the public, and is rich in fresco paintings, The glyptotheck, a sculpture gallery, is a very noble and classical building; admission gratis, on Sunday, Monday, Tuesday, and Thursday, by ticket, which may be obtained from the gallery director, in the Pinakothek; each Friday, from 9 to 12 and from 2 to 4, admission without ticket. When the king is not in town the gallery is only open on the Wednesday and Saturday. This museum is one of the most beautiful and richest of the kind in Germany; the Pinakothek, or painting gallery, is also one of the most beautiful buildings of the kind in Europe. Admission to the picture gallery is free, open daily, from 9 to 2 o'clock, with the exception of Sundays. The picture gallery of the Duke of Leuchtenberg is only a small one, but has a good collection of masterpieces; admission free, every Thursday, from 10 to 11 o'clock. The collection of painted glass, formerly belonging to Messrs. Boiserie and Bertran, is now in the Pinakothek. The Jesuits' college, with the cabinet of coins and the natural history museum; the royal library, a superb edifice, in the Ludwigstrasse, with room enough to hold two millions of volumes, and in richness the second in the world; the reading-room is open Monday, Wednesday, and Friday, from 8 to 1 o'clock. The university, a new building, in the Ludwigstrasse, has also a good library, consisting of 500,000 volumes, the largest after Paris; the Isarthor, newly renovated by King Ludwig, and adorned with beautiful frescos. The Odeon, a beautiful building allotted to musical soirèes. In the story underneath is the literary Verein, in which the stranger finds a rich collection of newspapers, and the charge of admission for a whole month is only 1 florin.

Hired Servants (valet de place) are, to the stranger visiting Munich, indispensable; the charge for a day's hire is from 3 to 4 zwanzigern.—Fiacres stand in all public places, and have fixed rates; a quarter of an hour or a single drive costs 18 kreutzers, half an hour 36 kreutzers, a full hour 1 florin, for one person; for two persons the fare is $\frac{1}{4}$ more. Passes are required from strangers, but it is not necessary to appear personally at the pass-office, as they can be procured through the medium of the valet de place.

Omnibuses are stationed at the following places; —In the Schrannen-platz, passing through the Sendlinger, Sonnen, and Bayerstrasse; in the Hof-garten, passing through Ludwig's, Theresien, Fürsten, Brimnenstrasse, the Carolinen-platz, the Ottostrasse, &c.; at the Isarthor; and Max Joseph's-platz. The Omnibuses call at the various appointed inns lying in their route. Drivers are responsible for the loss of luggage or for damage done to it. The charge by omnibuses, if without luggage, 6 kreutzers; with luggage, 12 kreutzers; with two or more trunks or boxes, 18 kreutzers. Cabs await the trains at the various stations.

Conveyances.—Railway trains to Augsburg, Kaufbeuern, Kempten, Donauworth, Nordlingen, Gunzenhausen, Nuremberg, Bamberg, Lichtenfels, Culmbach, Neuenmarkt, Hof, Zwickau, and Leipsic, see pages 82, 83, 86, and 90. Eilwagen to Berchtesgad, Innsbruck, Kreuth, Linz, Ratisbon, Salzburg, Vienna, and Wurtzburg, see page 257.

Nurnberg. Inns.—

The Wittelsbacher, Bavarian Court, Red Horse, and Strauss's.

Nurnberg, one of the oldest and most noted towns of Germany; centre of the trade between South and North Germany. The appearance of St. Sebald's church from the river is most romantic. This church and the ancient castle, the residence of the emperors in the middle ages, and afterwards of the mayors of the town, are the most attractive of its public edifices. The church of St. Œgidien (rebuilt in 1718, and called the new church) contains an altar-piece by Vandyck It was here that Caspar Hauser was discovered. Population upwards of 40,000 Protestants and 3,000 Catholics.

Objects of Attraction.—The town-hall, with paintings by Albrecht Dürer, and also the old prison-hole; the Reichsfeilte, where formerly the regalia were kept; Albrecht Dürer's house in the Dürerstrasse, No.376; Dürer's statue in the Milk-market (Milch-markt); the St. Sebaldus church, a very beautiful gothic building: the Aegide church; the Lindauer picture gallery; the Catholic church; the beautiful well; the Gänse-markt (Goose-market), with a singular statue in bronze of Labenwolf; the house of Hans Sachs; the St. Lawrence church, built 1274, completed 1477; the German Haus kirche, in the new Italian style; the churchyard of St. John, where are the tombs of Albrecht Dürer and Hans Sachs, the vaults of the family Behein and Holzschuher; many private collections.

Omnibuses run to and from the new Thor, Guttenhof in the suburbs, and the Lauferthor. The fare to or from the station, without portable luggage, 6 kreutzers; with a box or trunk, 12 kreutzers; with two or more trunks, 15 kreutzers; children under four years of age pass free, but they must sit on the knees of those accompanying them, otherwise a charge of 3 kreutzers will be made. For a hired chaise with four seats, including luggage, 48 kreutzers.

Offenburg.—Hotels.—

Die Fortuna and La Poste.

A town containing about 4000 inhabitants, 17 German miles from Carlsruhe by railway, on the route to Basle. The country in the neighbourhood is interesting.

Conveyances.—Railway trains to Freiburg and Basle, page 78.—To Kehl (Strasburg), Baden, Carlsruhe, Heidelberg, Mannheim, and Frankfort, see pages 79 and 75.

Passau, also on the banks of the Danube; the situation of which, from the river, in all points most beautiful and singular, at the junction of the River Inn and Ilz; contains 12,000 inhabitants. This town resembles Coblentz, and is the Coblentz of the Danube. The most remarkable objects are the cathedral, Jesuits college, the convent of our Lady of good aid, from which there is a splendid view. The sands of the Inn are washed for gold, and pearls are found in a mussel found in the Ilz.

Conveyances.—Steamers to Linz, Vienna, and to Ratisbon and Ulm.

Pforzheim, a town of about 7000 inhabitants, situated on the borders of the Black Forest, on the road between Carlsruhe and Stuttgart, containing several iron and copper works. A considerable trade in jewellery is likewise carried on here.

Conveyances.—Diligences to Carlsruhe and Stuttgardt.

Pilsen.—The chief town in a circle of the same name in Bohemia, at the angle formed by the Misa and Radbusa. Its manufactures are woollens, cottons, and leather. Population about 9,000.

Ratisbon, (in German, Regensburg.)—Hotel. Drei Helman.

Situated beautifully on the banks of the Danube, where it is joined by the river Regen, from whence steamers start every day from the month of May to September; and every other day from September to May, carrying goods and passengers up the Danube to Donauworth and Ulm; down the Danube to Passau, Linz, and Vienna. Ratisbon contains 23,000 inhabitants. The Walhalla is three miles to the north-east, near to the village of Donaustauf. A considerable fortress in ruins, blown up in the 30 years' war after a siege of two months, stands on the hill above the village, and the country seat of the Prince of Tour and Taxis below it, on the banks of the Danube. In Ratisbon are to be seen, at the Rathhaus, many curiosities—among them the dungeons of former days, the torture chamber, with the instruments of torture, just as they were used as late as 1784—the cathedral, and an old church behind it of great antiquity and preservation, said to be 1200 years built, and the cabinet of antiquities of Mr. Koch, with many other interesting things.

Schweinfurth.—HOTELS:—

HOTEL RUHE AND GOLDEN KRONE.

Schweinfurth contains 7,000 inhabitants, situated on the Maine; a place of great antiquity, and an imperial city, with some manufactures. The Bastions are planted, and form an agreeable promenade. Steam-boats every day to and from Frankfort. The Railroad is now open from Bamberg to Schweinfurth, and will be finished to Hanau in 1854. The Château of Mainberg, half an hour's drive, is worth visiting, being restored by its present proprietor.

Stuttgardt.—HOTELS.—

HOTEL DE RUSSIE, a capital house.

Capital of Wirtemberg, residence of the court and seat of the exchequer; has 40,000 inhabitants. The Konigstrasse cuts through the town in a direct line, leading to the palaces, the theatres, and most places of amusement and resort. Persons proceeding from Stuttgart to Munich or Nuremberg proceed by railway to Ulm, by diligence to Augsburg, and thence to Munich by railway. (See page 81.) In the neighbourhood of Stuttgardt is to be seen the elegant modern Grecian villa of Rosenstein, which contains some capital sculptures.

AGENT for the sale of J. A. Farina's *Eau de Cologne*—Mr. C. F. Autenrieth.

CONVEYANCES.—Railway trains to Ludwigsburg and Heilbronn, Esslingen, and Geislingen, see page 81.—Coaches travel daily to Augsburg, Carlsruhe, Hall, Nüremberg, Würzburg, Schaffhausen, and Wildbad. See page 261.

Ulm, a town of Wurtemburgh, situated on the left bank of the Danube, at the confluence of that river with the Iller and Blau. The streets are narrow and the houses are old fashioned. The cathedral is a fine gothic building, being upwards of 500 feet long by 200 broad. Originally belonging to the Catholics, it is now a Protestant place of worship. Ulm contains a population of some 16,000 inhabitants, and is forty miles west of Augsburg.

CONVEYANCES.—Railway trains to Stuttgart and Heilbronn, also Biberach and Frederickshafen, see Time Table, page 81.—Diligences to Augsburg, see page 262; and from thence to Munich by railway, page 82; also to Kempten and Füssen in about 17 hours. Fares—to Kempten, 4 fl. 48 kr; to Füssen, 6 fl. 54 kr. Füssen is a good starting point for the Tyrol, being *en route* to Innsbruck.

Weimar.—HOTEL—

De Russie.

This town, on the line of railway from Eisenach to Halle (page 88), stands on the banks of the river Hun, and contains about 10,000 inhabitants. It is built in a plain but antique style, and is fifty miles west-south-west of Leipsic.

CONVEYANCES.—Railway trains to Erfurt, Gotha, and Eisenach, as also to Merseburg, Halle, Magdeburg, Leipsic, and Berlin, see page 88.

Wittenburg, a city of Prussian Saxony, of considerable antiquity, situated on the banks of the Elbe. It is celebrated as the city from whence Luther first commenced his exposition of the abuses of the Roman Catholic church, which led to the Reformation. A colossal statue of the great Reformer was erected in 1821. It is about 70 miles north-west of Dresden, and forty north north-east of Leipsic. Population about 7,000.

Wolfenbuttel.—INNS.—

Golden Lion, Golden Angel, and Hereditary Prince.

A town with 10,000 inhabitants; noted on account of its large library. Amongst its books is to be found the Bible belonging to Luther, with notes attached to it in his own handwriting, his wedding and doctor ring, spoon, drinking glass, and likeness by Cranach. Lessing lived a long time here as librarian.

CONVEYANCES.—Railway trains to Brunswick and Harzburg, see page 87.

Wurtzburg.—INNS.—

Kronpinz, Post, and Russischer-hof.

A town containing 25,000 inhabitants, beautifully situated on the Maine. It was formerly the capital of an ecclesiastical principality, and was governed by a bishop, who was a primate of the German empire.

OBJECTS OF ATTRACTION.—The cathedral, the royal (formerly episcopal) palace; Julius Spital; Marienkirche, and the citadel.

EILWAGEN to Augsburg, Bamberg, Frankfort-on-the-Maine, Nuremberg, and Ratisbon, (on the Danube.) Wurtzburg to Nuremberg, 13 German miles; to Ratisbon, 26½ German miles; to Carlsbad, through Baireuth and Egra, 44½ German miles, or 294 English miles. Omnibus to Heilbronn on the Wekar. Steamers in summer to Frankfurt daily.

Zwickau.—INNS.—

Post-office, Tanne (Fir tree), Anchor.

Zwickau on the Mulde; 5,300 inhabitants. The Marien kirche is worth seeing; it is a beautiful gothic building, built in the years 1453 to 1536; there is in the church a superb altar-piece, by M. Wohlgemuth (1479). Luther often ascended the high steeple that he might enjoy the beautiful prospect which it afforded.

CONVEYANCE.—Railway to Leipsic and Hof, see page 90.

PRUSSIA.

PRUSSIA—formerly a duchy, but now an extensive kingdom, of second rank—was formed on the ancient electoral possessions, as a nucleus, by means of successive territorial acquisitions, particularly in Poland, Westphalia, and the Rhine. It had for its original inhabitants the Slavi, or Sarmatiæ, on the E. and N.E.,—the Vandals on the shores of the Baltic, to the N. of Pomerania—and the Suevi in the remainder of the kingdom. Prussia has been engaged, during a succession of ages, in very many wars—the particulars of which we do not require to notice here, as they are known to every student of history. Her part in the campaigns of the earlier portion of this century is well known, particularly in the campaigns of 1814 and 1815. At the Congress of Vienna, Prussia had secured her the restitution of the provinces formerly wrested from her, excepting part of Poland, united to the Duchy of Warsaw; and for this small sacrifice she was amply indemnified by the concession of such territories in Saxony and the Lower Rhine, as were deemed consistent with the stability and security of the balance of power in Europe. In this year also, Prussia, partly by exchange and partly by purchase, obtained from Denmark that part of Western which is commonly called Swedish Pomerania, together with the island of Rugen. And thus, after experiencing violent shocks and vicissitudes, by which the kingdom had been broken into pieces, and little more than the name of the monarchy saved from the wreck, we behold Prussia, after a series of unparalleled changes in another direction, again taking her station among the first sovereign states of Europe, as firm and able as in the days of Frederick the Great—and with a territory and population far exceeding any thing he could boast of.

The Kingdom of Prussia is situated in the northern part of Germany. It is bounded on the N. by the Baltic Sea, and a small portion of the Duchy of Mecklenburg; on the E. by Russia and Poland; on the S.E. by Austria; on the S. by Saxony and the Saxon Duchies; on the S.W. by Bavaria and part of France; and on the W. by France and the Netherlands. In describing these boundaries, we must observe that some parts of the kingdom are small detached portions, entirely insulated by the dominions of other powers—such as Neuchatel in Switzerland, Saxe in Saxony, and Rahnis in Saxe-Weimar. There is no communication between the eastern and western provinces of Prussia, without passing through the states of other princes. Hanover, on the N., is interspersed between its eastern and western provinces; and the territories of the sovereigns of Brunswick, Waldeck, Hesse-Cassel, Hesse-Darmstadt, and Saxe-Gotha, intercept a direct communication between its southern parts. The Prussian monarchy is divided into eight provinces, as follows:—Prussia, Posen, Brandenburg, Pomerania, Silesia, Saxony, Westphalia, and the Rhine province; and these are divided into 25 regencies, which are further divided into 335 circles. The population is 14,157,573; and the area in English square miles is 107,937, or, in geographical square miles, 509,136, with a population of 2781 persons to each latter mile. The surface of the Prussian States is generally flat, except a part of the Hartz Mountains, in the province of Saxony. The volcanic districts in it and the Lower Rhine are Riesengegebirge, on the S.W. confines of Silesia, and some other mountains in Westphalia. The quality of the soil is very various, and the country is very well watered. The climate of Prussia is not less varied than its soil. Along the Baltic it is worst; and in Ducal Prussia especially, the winter is long. It is also severe in the south parts of Silesia, contiguous to the Carpathian Mountains.

Commerce.—The exports from Prussia consist principally of corn, wool, timber, Westphalian hams, zinc, flax, bristles, salted provisions, with other articles of raw produce; with linen and woollen cloth, silk wares, iron and hardware, jewellery, watches, and wooden clocks; Prussian blue, spirits, beer, &c. The imports consist chiefly of sugar, coffee, and other coloured products; raw cotton, and cotton twist and stuffs, indigo and other dye-stuffs, &c.

The **Government** of Prussia is monarchical, the King being assisted by a Council of State, each Department having nine Ministers. The established religion is Protestant—comprehending Lutherans, Calvinists, Moravians, and Hussites.

Education.—In Prussia, the State imposes on all parents the strict obligation of sending their children to school, unless they can prove that they are giving them a competent education at home. Neglect of this duty exposes the parents or guardians to imprisonment or fine.

Language.—German spoken at Court, and by all the respectable classes.

English Passports may be had at the Foreign Office, for 7s. 6d. For further information, see pages 19 to 22.

Custom-House.—*(Zollhaus.)*—The *Douaniers* are strict in their examination, but also unexceptionably civil. Every precaution is taken to prevent unnecessary delay.

Money.—The copper coin is a *Pfenning;* 12=1 Silber Groschen, equivalent to 1d. 1-5th English. The *Thaler* (silver coin) contains 30 silver groschen=3s. English. The *Friedrich d'Or* (gold coin) contains 5 dollars=5 thalers 20 s. gr.=16s. 6½d. English. One-third thaler coin, 10 s. gr.=11¾d.; one-sixth thaler, 5 s. gr.=5¾d.; one-twelfth thaler, 2½ s. gr.=2¾d. Paper money, in notes of 1, 5, 10, 25, or 50 thalers, is freely issued. An English sovereign is equal to 6 dollars 25 s. gr. 8 pf. An English shilling=10 s. gr. Prussian coins are current along the Rhine, south as far as Nassau, and through the whole of Northern Germany. Napoleons are taken universally.

Schnellposts.—*(Eilwagen,* Aust.)—These are the mail coaches, conducted by government officials. All the seats are numbered. Fares about 10 s. gr. per German mile. Rate of travelling 8 miles per hour. 30 lbs. of luggage may be taken free of charge, and 20 lbs. more if paid for. Every package must be distinctly inscribed with name of owner, and place to which he is going. Prussian coaches take no outside passengers.

Inns.—The average charges are,—bed 12 s. gr.; table d'hote, 20 s. gr.; tea or coffee, 6 s. gr.; breakfast, 15 s. gr.

Forwarding Luggage.—Travellers are strongly recommended to avoid altogether entrusting *to any one*, their Luggage to be sent on before or after them. On the Continent, Luggage once separated from the Traveller, becomes *Merchandize*, and is subjected to endless formalities and delays resulting in disappointment and increased expense to the owner, very frequently loss.

THE ELECTRIC TELEGRAPH.—The Electric Telegraph is in operation throughout the principal parts of Prussia and Germany—on the same plan as that recommended by Mr. Wishhaw for India, the principle consisting of a single wire two feet under ground, coated with gutta percha—connecting Berlin with Aix-la-Chapelle, also with Frankfort-on-the-Maine, Hamburgh, Stettin, Breslau, and Oderberg, where the Austrian system is taken up; by means of which continuous lines exists between Trieste and Hamburgh, and Triest e,Verviers, Ostend, Brussels, Calsia, and Paris; and with London by Submarine Telegraph

Explanation.—The German Mile is equal to 4 miles 1056 yards English, or 8096 yards.

Aix-la-Chapelle (in German Aachen).—HOTELS:—

HOTEL DU GRAND MONARQUE, or Dremel's Hotel. First-rate. We confirm the great reputation this magnificent house has enjoyed for the last thirty years. An excellent bath-house is attached to it.

HOTEL DES QUATRE SAISON has good accommodation, and the landlord is also proprietor of the Hotel des Bains de la Rose at Bourcette.

HOTEL NUELLENS, first-rate, in a good situation facing the Eliza Fountain—is one we can recommend very highly.

At Herbesthal the station, previous to arriving at Aix-la-Chapelle from Ostend, the luggage and passports are taken away by the Prussian authorities. The *passport* must be reclaimed at the station at *Aix*, where the luggage, for *that* city only, is also searched; but the luggage for *Cologne* is searched on arriving *there*. Without this information the traveller may be looking for his luggage at *Aix*, while the train is starting with it for *Cologne*.

Among the many peculiarities of travelling by railway, we have often experienced the inconvenience of being conveyed in that arbitrary manner, *bon gré mal gré*, from the threshold of one country to the frontier of another. Unthinkingly taking tickets *throughout*, the traveller is carried over a country, deprived of the power of stopping at any of the attractive scenes he may observe on the journey. Booked for a certain point, to that destination he must go; and though he beheld the auriferous California on the one side, or heard the dulcet notes of the Swedish Nightingale from the groves on the other, the traveller must imitate the self-denial of Ulysses—close his eyes to the tempting land of the "*diggins*," and turn away his ear from the melody of the Syren, for the obdurate bye-laws which regulate modern locomotion admit of no stoppage on the road—no loitering behind—unless at the sacrifice of one's fare, or the probable loss of one's baggage. This will explain the reason of so few English visiting Aix-la-Chapelle.

Aix-la-Chapelle is a pleasant and convenient break in the journey between Ostend and Cologne, and *vice versâ*, and many make it a resting place for the night on that account. There is an English church here, in the Anna Strasse, and the services on Sundays are at 12 and 6 o'clock.

Historically it is associated with the grandeur and the celebrity of Charlemagne, who died there. The emperors of Germany were formerly crowned within its walls, and its citizens possessed, during the middle ages, so many important privileges and immunities, that it was said the very air of Aix-la-Chapelle enfranchised even the outlaw! During the earlier progress of the Reformation, this city was the scene of civil dissensions and religious conflicts between the Catholics and Protestants, until the latter were compelled to emigrate to other countries; and as they were principally the most wealthy and influential merchants, their emigration proved highly prejudicial to the prosperity of the town, which declined for centuries. Latterly it has acquired an adventitious importance in history, from its having had several European Congresses held within its walls. This invested it with a temporary dignity, emanating, as it were, in a graceful act of filial piety from the sovereigns of modern Europe towards the favourite city of Charlemagne.

Commercially, Aix-la-Chapelle was renowned in former ages for the excellency of its woollen manufactures. Its cloths, in particular, were highly esteemed in the maritime cities of the Continent; and, even at the present day, the manufacturers of Aix are still enabled to produce, from some remarkable properties in the mineral waters of the town, a peculiar light blue cloth, the dye of which wears to the last, and of which they export a great quantity to North and South America. There are also considerable establishments for manufacturing needles and pins, which are largely exported. Also extensive iron foundries, machine shops, coach makers, &c. Aix-la-Chapelle has also become celebrated for its warm medicinal springs, which break forth in all parts of the city, and afford a great source of revenue and attraction. These waters are very efficacious, but may be injurious when taken improperly or without medical advice. We refer those who wish to obtain information on their composition and medical virtues to a book written by an experienced physician living at Aix-la-Chapelle. "The Mineral Waters of Aix-la-Chapelle," by L. Wetzlar, M.D., Physician at Aix-la-Chapelle. London, John Churchill, 1852.

In addition to the baths, there is an equally powerful object of attraction, namely, the Kursaal, or Gaming-house, to which visitors resort to pass their time at roulette or rouge et noir; and thus, after submitting to the depressing effect of the aperient waters, the hypocondriac is stimulated under the exciting scenes and chances of the gambling-table! We do not conceive this alternate course can be conducive to health—*mais ce n'est pas notre affaire.*

OBJECTS OF ATTRACTION.—The Town Hall, an edifice no ways remarkable, is now undergoing a thorough restoration. It bears the stamp of antiquity, and in it are now being executed, by Alfred Rethel, a number of fresco paintings from scenes in the history of Charlemagne. The Cathedral, begun under Charlemagne in 796, is one of the most important in Germany, and here repose the remains of this great Emperor. The choir of the Cathedral is now being restored. There are also an almost innumerable number of precious relics of various authenticity and value; there are sculls and bones of questionable anatomy, and sacred relics that would make a sceptic of the credulous; but we are told these are all exhibited once in seven years, and that pilgrims flock to see them from all parts of Europe. We need not indulge in a comment upon this fact; but if the traveller makes a minute from a list of the relics, it may afford him and his friends a subject of conversation for many evenings, to determine the possibility of their being what they are described. The hot water fountain of Eliza. The Kurhause or assembly rooms for strangers; subscription for the season for one person, 4 thalers; for two persons, if of the same family, 6 thalers; for each person above, 2 thalers. The new government building, in the court of which is deposited the ponderous Aerolite, said to weigh seven thousand pounds. The monument erected in memory of the Congress of Aix-la-Chapelle, in 1818. The Belvedere in the Louisberg, and the hill itself. The new hospital now building outside the town, between Sandkam and Cologne gates.

The suburbs and environs of Aix-la-Chapelle are both pleasant and interesting. A charming view of the whole city and surrounding country is obtained from the hill of Louisberg, a favourite resort of the good citizens on Sundays and holidays. The valley of Burtscheid is also worth visiting. It extends from east to west, and is celebrated for the numerous warm springs and brooks that run through it. These hot wells supply several large bathing-houses, in opposition to the more aristocratic establishments in the city. There are also manufactories of cloth and cachmeres in the valley, established by Protestants, who were formerly not permitted to have an independent place of worship at Aix; but we are happy to add that the spirit of intolerance in Prussia has been greatly subdued since the events of the last two years, and we anticipate a further modification in this respect, in accordance with the development of liberal institutions and the *spirit of the age.*

A short distance from the town is situated Frankenberg, an old castle, said to have been a hunting lodge of Charlemagne; a moat surrounds it, into which the legend says Frastrada threw her ring.

AGENT for the sale of J. A. Farina's *Eau de Cologne*—Mr. Auguste Allard.

CONVEYANCES.—Railway trains to Cologne, also to Verviers, Brussels, Ostend, and Calais.

Berlin.—(*With Map in Special Edition.*)—HOTELS:—

HOTEL DU NORD, a good first-rate house, and highly recommended.

HOTEL DE RUSSIE, near the Schlossbrücke, within five minutes walk of the Royal and public buildings; a first rate house, which deserves in every respect its European reputation. The Landlord is very attentive and obliging.

ENGLISH EPISCOPAL CHAPEL.—This is held in the large room of the Hotel du Nord, which is situated in the Unter den Linden.

Capital of Prussia, situated on the river Spree, 127 feet above the level of the sea. It is one of the largest and handsomest cities of Europe, being about twelve miles in circumference, with 27 parish churches, 37 bridges, &c., and containing a population of 350,000. Berlin contains upwards of 100 public schools, and as many of a private description; its charitable and scientific institutions are very numerous; and its manufactures consist of wool, cotton, silk, ribbons, porcelain and stoneware, bronze, gold and silver ware, straw-hats, artificial flowers, &c. &c.

POST-OFFICE, 60, Konigsstrasse; open from 7 a.m. to 8 p.m. Letters reach England on the third day (postage 1s.) *via* Ostend.

GUIDE—Rading, No. 18, Unter den Linden, speaks English, and is a good guide.

AGENT for the sale of J. A. Farina's *Eau de Cologne*—Mr. Edward Hoff.

THE RAILROAD TERMINI are—to Potsdam (in 40 minutes), outside the Potsdam Gate; to Anhalt and Leipsig, Magdeburg, and Hanover (reached in 12 hours), outside the Anhalt Gate; to Stettin, outside the Oranienburg Gate; to Frankfurt-on-the-Oder, near the Stralauer Platz.

OPEN DROSKIES, drawn by one horse, stand in the streets. Fare for a drive into the town, 5 silbergroschen. The regulations, as to charges, are hung up in every vehicle.—A servant serving for hire receives generally 1 dollar a day, 15 sgr. for half a day, and 5 sgr. for the hour.—The best Baths are No. 1, New Packhof, and No. 19, New Friedrichstrasse.

OBJECTS OF ATTRACTION.—The street called Unter-den-Linden (Under the Linden-trees,) reaching in a direct line from the royal palace to the Brandenburg-gate, with many public and private edifices. The castle, or royal palace, is large but not beautiful; the hall of arts (Kunst kammer), which is to be seen on Tuesdays, Wednesdays, Thursdays, and Fridays, by means of tickets of admission, which are most readily procured through the medium of the person who serves for hire, contains a multitude of Chinese, Japanese, and American curiosities, and the very large ale-cup belonging to Luther; the new museum, a very chaste edifice, built after the plan of the architect Schinkel,—the foundation is laid upon stakes. Before the museum stands a gigantic basin, cut out of one solid piece of granite, 22 feet in diameter; the fore colonade is adorned with beautiful designs in fresco, by Cornelius. The interior of the museum has its usual attractions. The sculpture and picture galleries are open daily to the public (Sundays excepted),—in the summer, from 10 to 4, in the winter season, from 10 to 3 o'clock. The collection of vases and bronzes can only be visited on the Wednesdays; the entrance is at the back part of the museum. The King has lately added a new building to the Museum, in extent twice its size, and most beautifully decorated, into which the Egyptian Museum, recently enriched by the acquisitions of Lepsius, has been removed, and to which it is intended to remove other works of antiquity, now scattered in various royal palaces. The picture gallery is very good, of which a catalogue may be obtained. The royal library is a very tasteless building, with 500,000 volumes and 500 manuscripts, the most interesting of which are an album with six very beautiful miniature portraits, by Lucas Cranach, and Guttenberg's Bible, the first book printed with moveable types. The reading-room is daily open; the apartments, however, in which are kept the periodical publications, are only open from 10 to 12, and admission by ticket from the principal librarian. The university is a large beautiful building, with the natural history museum, and zoological cabinet, open every Tuesday and Friday, from 12 to 2, admission only by ticket, which is given out by the director; the minerological cabinet; the anatomical museum, open every Wednesday and Saturday, from 4 to 6 in the summer, and from 2 to 4 o'clock in the winter, admission by ticket only. The arsenal, built 1695, by Schlitter, is considered a master-work, in the pure style; tickets of admission are to be procured at No. 1, Mollars-gasse; the new Opera-House; the picture gallery of Prince Raczinsky is well worth visiting; the palace of Prince Charles, No. 9, Wilhelms-platz; the palace of Prince William of Prussia, Under the Linden trees; the palace of Prince Albert, 102, Wilhelms-strasse, built by Schinkel. Kroll's winter-garden is also worthy a visit.

Bielefeld.—Inns.—

Ravensberger Hof, Three Crowns, German House.

7,000 inhabitants. Its best buildings are the St. Maria and St. Nicholas churches, the Frangiskaner-kloster, and its ancient castle, now a prison. The town is famous for its trade in linen and thread; the best linen comes from Jöllenbeck, the best thread from Isselhorst. The environs are delightful, rich in gardens and promenades, especially Sparenberg with its ruins, Johannisberg and its grounds, &c. At the upper gate are some fine premises belonging to the merchants Laer, Weber, and Wittgenstein.

Conveyances.—Railway to Minden, Hanover, and Berlin, see pages 70 & 87; to Hamm, Munster, and Cologne, see pages 70 & 71.

Brandenburg.—Inns.—

Hotel de Brandenburg (good), Black Eagle, Golden Eagle, White Swan, Golden Ball.

Chief town of the electorate, with 14,000 inhabitants, 38 miles from Berlin. The Katharinenkirche, built in 1410, contains an antique font and a library. The Cathedral, which is in the Burg, on an island in the river Havel, possesses some paintings by Cranach, a subterranean chapel, tombs of three Margraves, and some remarkable statues. There is a fine prospect from the Marienberg, in which appear the towers of Potsdam.

Conveyances.—Railway to Potsdam, Berlin, and Magdeburg, see page 96.

Breslau.—Hotel.—

Breslau, on the Oder, capital of the province of Silesia, with 110,000 inhabitants.

Objects of Attraction.—The cathedral, erected 1170, out of bricks, and not in a tasteful style; the Kreuzkirche, built upon the site of a much older church, with a remarkable monument of Duke Henry the Fourth, and a bronze relief of John of Breslau, 1496, by Peter Vischer; the St. Elizabeth church, with the highest tower in Prussia (364 feet), was built in the 9th century; the church of Our Blessed Lady, on the sand, has in the interior very beautiful proportions; the great Ring, with town hall; the Blucher-platz, with a bronze statue of Blucher; the Tauenzien-platz, with the statue of General Tauenzien; the university, brought hither in the year 1811, from Frankfort-on-the-Oder; the museum of natural history; and the library. In the environs are Liebiech's garden, Morgenau, Oswitz, Pögelwitz, Lissa.

Conveyances.—Railway to Dresden, Berlin, Prague, Olmutz, Vienna, Cracow, and Warsaw.

Brieg.—Inn.—

Golden Cross.

Population 12,600. The church of St. Nicholas has a fine organ and an altar-piece by Rode Among other buildings here, are the gymnasium and the old ducal palace. Near this town is Mollwitz, where the Austrians were defeated by Frederick the Great in 1741.

Conveyances.—Railway to Neisse, see pages 110 and 111; to Breslau, Cracow, and Vienna, see page 102.

Cleves.—Inns.—

Prinz Mauritz von Nassau, an excellent house, with a fine view; Hotel zum Thiergarten, also good; König von Preussen.

Capital of the Duchy of Cleves, with 8,000 inhabitants, connected with the Rhine by a canal about 2½ miles in length. It is situated upon gently sloping hills, three in number, in the midst of a lovely and fertile country, well diversified with hills, vales, and woodland. The ancient castle of Schwanenburg, formerly the residence of the Dukes of Cleves, was the birth-place of Anne, wife of Henry VIII., also the scene of a legend which is the subject of one of Southey's poems. Its tower, 180 feet high, built on the summit of a rock, commands a view of all the country round; there is also a fine prospect from Clevesburg near the Thiergarten, and another from the Prinzenhof, which is a fine building. There is a mineral spring and pleasant walks in the Thiergarten. The remains of Prince Maurice of Nassau lie in an iron sarcophagus, in a little wood half a mile from the town. Cleves is the birth-place of the celebrated Seydlitz.

Dantzic.—Hotels.—

Nord, Hotel de Berlin, Englischer Hof.

A highly interesting city, on account of its ancient architecture. Population 70,000. It is one of the most important Prussian ports.

CONSULS, England—**H. R. Peaw, A. Gibson, V. C.** French—E. Dommerc. Belgium—Watley. Holland—Forking.

ENGLISH CLERGYMAN, Rev. H. Lawrence.

BANKERS, Messsrs. Normann, S. H. Goldschmidt and Sons.

MONEY.—30 Silver groschen, 1 Thaler, 10 silver groschen, 1 Guilder: the Guilder is about 1s. sterling.

CONVEYANCES.—Steamers daily in Summer to and from Konigsberg; Post Office Carriages, to Berlin 61½ German miles, 4 times daily; to Konigsberg 24¼ German miles, 4 times daily; Fares 6 & 8 silver groschen per mile.

Dessau.—HOTELS.—

Der Goldene Beutel, Ring, and Hirsch.

Capital of the Dukedom of Anhault Dessau, with a population of 12,000, on the Mulde, near its junction with the Elbe. The edifices are of modern date, of which the princinal is the ducal palace, containing a library, cabinet of curiosities, and picture gallery. There is an elegant theatre here, to which is attached a spacious concert room; and the orchestra, under the direction of Dr. Fr. Schneider, capelmeister to his highness the Duke of Anhalt, Dessau, and numbering among its members many artists of the first ability, is justly celebrated for its excellence. From October until May, the theatre is open three times a week for operas or concerts; and visitors should embrace the opportunity here afforded them, of hearing the works of the great composers executed in the best style. During the remainder of the year, except in the month of July, the orchestra meets for practice three times a week; and strangers visiting Dessau in the month during which the theatre is closed, will find their practising a rich treat; and permission to attend is at once granted on application to Dr. Schnieder. In the Schlosskirche is the famous "Last Supper" by Cranach, in which he introduced portraits of some of the chief actors in the Reformation. Dessau is the birth-place of Mendelssohn. The gardens in the neighbourhood are much admired, especially the garden of Wörlitz, about six English miles from Dessau, which is well worthy of a visit.

CONVEYANCES.—Railway to Cothen, Halle, and Leipsic; also to Berlin, see page 105.

Frankfurt on the Oder.—HOTEL:—Adler.

A city, with 26,000 inhabitants. A wooden bridge laden with stones, so that the stream may not carry it away, joins the old town on the left shore of the Oder, with the suburbs on the right. The prosperity of the town is owing to its being situated on the principal road or thoroughfare to Silesia and to its navigable river, which is connected by canals to the Weichsel and the Elbe; three fairs are annually held here. The university was removed in the year 1810 to Breslau. Near to the bridge stands a monument to the memory of Prince Leopold of Brunswick, who was drowned at that spot, in the year 1785, in his endeavours to save an unfortunate family from the waters. In the neighbourhood of the town is the battle-field of Kunnersdorf, where Frederick the Great was beaten, in the year 1759, by the combined armies of Russia and Austria.

CONVEYANCES. — Railway to Berlin, Dresden, Prague, Breslau, Vienna, &c.

Glogau.—INNS.—

German House, White House (good), Tscharmer Hof.

A strongly fortified town on the left bank of the Oder, with 13,000 inhabitants. The Cathedral stands on the right bank of the river, and is well worth seeing; as also the former ducal castle, the two gymnasia, the town-hall, two sugar refineries, &c. The Citadel and Brückenkopf are deserving of notice. Its promenades are much admired, and among the places in the vicinity, Friedensthal, Lindenruh, Rauschwitz, Zarkau, Brostau, and Hermsdorf are most frequented.

CONVEYANCES.—Railway to Hansdorf, Frankfurt, Berlin, and Breslau, see page 99.

Gorlitz, a town in Upper Lusatia, on the Neisse, noted for its woollen and linen manufactures. It contains six churches, the chief of which has an excellent organ. Here also is a spire of great height. Population 14,000; 50 miles from Dresden.

CONVEYANCE.—Railway to Kohlfurt, see page 94.

Halberstadt.—INNS.—

Prince Eugene, and the Prussian Court.

An old town, with 20,000 inhabitants, built on an arm of the Holtemme, twenty-five miles West of Magdeburgh. The cathedral is a remarkable gothic edifice, erected in the middle of the 13th century; the western front is however of more ancient date. The church of Our Dear Lady, after the Byzantine style, is very ancient, it was finished in the year 1005; the Rolandssäule; the Lägenstein; many houses are curiously adorned with wood. In the neighbourhood are worth visiting the Spiegelberg, Langenstein, Bullenberg, from whence you have the best prospect of the town; Ströbeck, notorious for its chessplayer. A tour can be made from Halberstadt to Rosstrappe, in the Hartz.

CONVEYANCES.—Railway to Oschersleben & Magdeburg, see page 86.

Halle.—HOTELS—

KRON PRINZ (Crown Prince), highly recommended.

A large town, built in the form of an irregular square, on the river Sale. It contains scientific institutions of almost every description, and is celebrated as the birthplace of a number of distinguished individuals. In the immediate vicinity are two interesting institutions—an orphan asylum and an establishment for printing the Scriptures, erected in 1712, which is said to have issued since its foundation more than two millions of Bibles, and half that number of New Testaments. Halle contains two public libraries, that of the University and that of the Town, besides a number of other institutions. The principal manufactures are woollens, stockings, silk, leather, buttons, hardware, and starch. Coal and salt-springs are met with in the neighbourhood. The ruins of the castle, as well as the Markt-kirche (Market-church), which is a beautiful gothic building, with a superb painting by Lucas Cranach, are worth seeing. Population, about 30,000

CONVEYANCES.—Railway three or four times a-day to Eisenach (page 88), (from thence to Cassel, Carlshafen, and Frankfort-on-the-Maine), and to the Rhine and Cologne *via* Magdeburg.

Herford.—INNS.—
Preussischer Hof, Stadt Berlin.
7,56 miles from Hanover, on the Werre, with k000 inhabitants. The ancient abbey of Mönchtirche, and the church of St. John Baptist, with the ower 400 feet high, are worth visiting; here are shewn the crucifix and cup of Duke Wedekind—his tomb is at Engern, 5 miles eastward. In the neighbourhood of this place it is supposed that the army of Varus was cut off by Arminius.

CONVEYANCES.—Railway to Minden, Hanover, Hamm, and Cologne, see page 70.

Iserlohn.—INN.—
Quinke's Hotel.
11,000 inhabitants; remarkable for its manufactures in iron, steel, and bronze. In its neighbourhood is the famous Felsenmeer (sea of rocks), and the remarkable sounding cave containing fossil-bones. The country all around is finely diversified with picturesque ruins, rocks, glens, and valleys, among which are interspersed workshops, forges, paper-mills, &c.

Kothen.—INNS.—
Grosser Gasthof, Prinz von Preussen.
6,000 inhabitants; remarkable only for the magnificence of its railway station.

CONVEYANCES.—Railway to Wittenberg and Berlin, see page 105; to Leipsic, Dresden, and Magdeburg, see page 97; to Bernburg, see page 99.

Leignitz.—INNS.—
Rautenkranz, Black Eagle, Prussian Hof.
Population 14,000. A handsome town, well situated at the junction of the Katsbach and Schwarzwasser. Its castle, which was burned down in 1834, has been rebuilt. The Fürstencapelle contains the tombs of the Piast family, 24 of whose members were Kings of Poland, and 123 Dukes of Leignitz. Some suits of antique mail are shown in the town-hall. The Kloster Wahlstadt, built upon the spot where, in 1241, the Tartar hordes were routed, contains some pictures, and affords a fine prospect from its walls. The new cemetery is also worth seeing.

CONVEYANCES.—Railway to Breslau and Berlin, see page 99; to Lobau and Dresden, see page 94.

Magdeburg.—HOTELS:—
HOTEL STADT LONDON (LONDON HOTEL)—the best in the town. The landlord is obliging and attentive.

On both sides of the Elbe, a strong fortress; with the military included, has 55,000 inhabitants; is a noted commercial and manufacturing town—90 E. miles S.W. of Berlin, and 72 N. of Leipsic.

OBJECTS OF ATTRACTION.—The cathedral, erected in the years 1211 to 1363, in the latter time restored again; the tomb of the Emperor Otto and Editha; the monument of Archbishop Ernest (1495); a splendid pulpit, a work by Caput of Nordh, 1594; a monument of Bake, canon, who saved the cathedral before its demolition by Tilly; a monument of the woman of Asseburg, who returned home the night after her burial, and lived nine years after; the St. Sebastian's kirche, with the tomb of Otto of Guerike; the old market, with an equestrian statue of the Emperor Otto, in the year 979; in the Friedhof (churchyard) before the Krökenthor, lies buried the celebrated republican general Carnot. A canal joins here the Elbe to the Havel.

CONVEYANCES.—Rail to the Rhine, *via* Hanover; to Hamburgh, *via* Hanover and Harburg, and direct, joining the Hamburgh and Berlin line at Wittenberge. Steamboats also ply daily to Hamburg and run the distance in 15 hours.

Minden.—INNS.—
German House, Stadt London, Stadt Bremen.
Population 9,000; a Prussian fortress. The Cathedral is a fine structure in the pointed style. The Weser is here crossed by a bridge 600 feet long. The best things to be seen here are Herr Kruger's collection of pictures, in which are to be found some curious specimens of ancient German masters, and the Westphalian Museum. Several Diets were held in this place, and some of the early German Emperors made it their residence.

CONVEYANCE.—Railway to Hanover and Bremen, see page 89; to Hamm, Munster, and Cologne, see page 70.

Munster.—INNS.—
Münsterischer Hof, König von England.
Population 21,000; capital of Westphalia; is a well-built and flourishing town, antique and curious, with some gothic buildings of great beauty, among which are conspicuous the Rath-haus, where the Peace of Westphalia was signed at the end of the 30 years' war (in the Frieden Saal, as it is called, are preserved the portraits of the great contracting parties, with the seats on which they sat); the Cathedral, with the tomb of Bishop Galen, famous for his warlike tastes, his immense standing army, with which he bombarded his own town when in a fit of ill-humour, and for the citadel he built; the Oberwasser Kirche; St. Lambert's church, with its tower, on which are still hanging the three iron cages wherein John of Leyden and his two friends were fixed to be tortured with red-hot pincers previous to their execution; the Ludgeri Kirche, a peculiarly fine specimen of the Romanesque; the Schloss, formerly the Bishop's palace, a handsome but somewhat ruinous building, with its gardens on the site of the ancient citadel. The old fortifications have been levelled, and converted into pleasant promenades. John of Leyden's house is still shewn in the market place; it is marked with quaint carving. The main street is remarkable for its arcades running along the ground floor.

CONVEYANCES.—Railway to Hamm, Paderborn, Hanover, and Cologne, see page 71.

Nordhausen.—INNS.—
Berliner Hof, Englischer Hof, German House, outside the town (good).
39 miles N. of Erfurt; population 13,500; situate in a fertile country south of the Hartz mountains. In the church of St. Blasius are two pictures by Luke Cranach. In the neighbourhood are the ruins of Hohenstein and Ebersburg; there are many beautiful walks and points of view, such as the Kohnstein, Geiersberg, and the alabaster grotto.

Oeynhausen.—HOTELS:—
Hotel Vogeler.
Hans Westphalen.
Hotel Hennjes.
Hotel Polkening.
Sultemeyer's Family Hotel.

Oeynhausen, near Rehme on Weser, the most delightful flourishing bathing and watering place in the North of Germany. A charming view is here obtained of the surrounding country, including the pleasant chain of the Weser mountains. In addition to the bath, there are manifold points of attraction, viz., the Porta Wesphalica, (gate of Westphalia,) formed by the mountains Wittekind and St. Jacob, the delightful vale of the river Weser, with different ruins and castles. Historically, these environs are famed as those where, in the year 9 before Christ, Arminius began the great victorious battle against the Romans. This part of the country is said to have been a favourite resorting place of Charlemagne.

CONVEYANCES.—Railway to Minden, Bremen, Berlin, Hamm, and Cologne; Steamboats upwards to Plotho, Rinteln, Hameln, downwards to Minden, and Bremen. Diligences and Omnibuses to all directions in the neighbourhood.

Posen.—INNS.—

Bazaar, Hotel de Bavière, de Berlin, de Cracow, de Vienne (good), Black Eagle.

A strongly fortified town on the Russian frontier, with a population of 40,000, of whom 9,000 are Jews. Of its 23 churches that of St. Stanislaus is distinguished as a masterpiece of Italian architecture. The Cathedral is remarkable for the noble simplicity of its style; the Golden Chapel, painted in the byzantine style, contains two bronze statues of Polish kings; the Rath-haus is a splendid gothic edifice, with a tower which is the loftiest in the town; what was formerly a Jesuits' College is now the seat of government; there is also a very magnificent palace, with a library of 20,000 volumes, presented to the town by Count Raczynski; also many other good buildings. Posen has a considerable trade in corn, cloth, linen, leather, and tobacco, and a wool fair in June. It possesses many places of public amusement—theatre, casino, coffee-houses with gardens, promenades, &c.

CONVEYANCES.—Railway to Stargard, Stettin, and Berlin, see page 101.

Potsdam.—HOTEL.—

HOTEL EINSIEDLER, an excellent house, one of the best in Germany. Mr. Kast is civil and obliging.

If you wish for a guide through Potsdam and its neighbourhood, Wrowell is to be heard of at the Einsiedler.

This Prussian Versailles lies on the right shore of the Havel, which, at this part, flows into a lake. It has 26,000 inhabitants, without the military, founded by the Electoral Prince of Brandenburg. It was, when Fortune favoured the royal house, the residence of the Prussian princes; it owes, however, its prosperity to Frederick the Great. It may be termed a city of palaces, not alone on account of the four royal residences which it is in possession of, but also on account of its private houses, which, for the most part, are built in a princely style; the deserted streets however contrast badly with the splendour of the architecture. The principal buildings are: the Garnison kirche, with the tomb of Frederick the Great; the St. Nicolas church; the Royal Palace, with the rooms of Frederick the Great; the house on the basin, where Frederick's father used to hold his tobacco lectures; Sans Souci, before the Brandenburg-gate; the garden is laid out in the insipid French style; the palace usually inhabited by the present king. There is to be seen here the room in which Frederick the Great died, and also the room in which Voltaire lived. The Russian colony is deserving a visit.

CONVEYANCES.—Railway to Berlin and Magdeburg, see page 96.

Prenzlau.—INN.—

Hotel de Prusse.

Situated on the Unter Uckerlake, with 11,000 inhabitants In its gothic Hauptkirche is a beautiful altar and picture by Rode. It possesses a gymnasium, library, and baths, with pleasing gardens and grounds. An organ has lately been erected here, said to rival those of Haarlem and Fribourg. The neighbouring lake abounds in fish.

Rostock.—INNS.—

Hotel de Russie, Swa, Stadt London, Stadt Stettin, Stadt Amsterdam.

The largest town in Mecklenburg, with 20,000 inhabitants, on the Warnow; birth-place of Blucher, whose statue in bronze stands in the square called after him the Blucher-platz The Marienkirche has a magnificent altar and altar-piece by Rhode, an astronomical clock behind the altar, and the tomb of the renowned Hugo Grotius. Peter's church, in the Altstadt, is surmounted by a tower 380 feet high. This town contains a great number of other fine edifices, and altogether wears an aspect of great antiquity. It carries on a considerable trade with its own ships to the number of 150, and has considerable factories. The famous Keppler was for a while professor in the university of Rostock. The port and bathing-place is Warnemünde, at 9 miles distance on the Baltic, and on the mouth of the Warnow, as the name implies.

CONVEYANCES.—Railway to Wismar, Schwerin, and Hagenow, see page 95. Steamers to Copenhagen in 14 hours.

Schwelm.—INN.—

Märkischer Hof.

A busy place, like all the other towns in the Wupperthal, with 3,400 inhabitants. The whole country for miles round is studded with towns and villages full of life and activity, and in this respect only to be surpassed by the manufacturing towns of England. Within two leagues of Schwelm is the much-admired Schwelmer Höhle or Klutart, whose labyrinths must not, however, be visited without an experienced guide.

CONVEYANCES.—Railway to Dortmund, Elberfeld, and Dusseldorf, see pages 72 and 71.

Stargard.—On the Stettin and Posen railway with 10,000 inhabitants. Its antique fortifications and watch-towers are in good preservation. The Marienkirche, built in the 13th century by the Templars, is a fine structure well worthy of a visit; as are also the Town-hall and the Johanniskirche.

CONVEYANCES.—Railway to Stettin, Berlin, Woldenberg, and Posen see pages 100 and 101.

Stralsund.—Inns.—

Hotel de Brandenbourg, with a handsome saloon (good), Golden Lion.

16,000 inhabitants, 87 miles from Stettin, on the Strait of Gellen, which separates the Isle of Rügen from the mainland. This town is famous for the successful defence made against Wallenstein in the 30 years' war, as also for Charles XII. having been besieged in it on his return from Bender. The Rath-haus is a beautiful gothic structure. The church of St. Nicholas with its monuments and font, and the Marienkirche with its organ and paintings, are well worth seeing. There is also a cabinet of natural history and a library. The picturesque island of Rügen opposite may be visited by the ferry, which is a mile across.

Stettin.—

On the Oder, contains 39,000 inhabitants. More than 1000 ships enter her harbour yearly, and a very considerable commerce is carried on in ship-building, &c.

The Objects of Attraction are the Schloss kirche, with the tombs of the ancient dukes of Pommern; the Wall kirche, built 1124; the Jacobite tower, from the top of which you have the best sight of the town and river; the Konigs-platz, with a marble statue of Frederick the Great, by Schadow. Two Russian Empresses were born at Stettin, Catharine the Great (1729), and Maria Feodorowna, consort of Emperor Paul (1759). The principal promenade is the Plantage, before the Anclamhor.

Agent for the Sale of J. A. Farina's *Eau de Cologne*—Mr. G. A. Toepffer.

Wesel.—Inn.—

Dornbusch's.

14,000 inhabitants. This is a considerable fortress on the N.W. frontier of Prussia, at the junction of the Lippe with the Rhine. In a commercial point of view it is a rising place, especially since the improved navigation of the Lippe.

Wittenberg.—Inns.—

Stadt London, Schwarze Bär, Traube.

A fortified town, population 10,000. In the Schlosskirche, which contains the tombs of Luther, Melancthon, Frederick the Wise, and John the Steadfast, Luther's 95 theses against the doctrine of Indulgences were posted up on the 31st October, 1517, being the commencement of the Reformation. This church was much damaged in the siege of 1814. On the market place stands the great bronze statue of Luther by Schadow, with the inscription "Ist's Gottes werk so wird's bestehen, ist's menschen werk, wird's untergehen,"—(if it be God's work it will endure, if man's it will perish.) An oak tree protected by railing is shown as the place where, on the 20th December, 1520, he burned the papal bull. Numerous objects are carefully preserved in this place connected with the memory not only of Luther, but of his friends Melancthon and the painter Cranach. The ancient and renowned university of Wittenberg was in 1817 removed, and united with that of Halle.

Conveyances.—Railway to Berlin, see page 92; to Cothen, Halle, and Leipsic, see page 105.

AUSTRIA.

Short Tour through the Salzkaunner Gut from Linz, occupying two days.—Leave Linz by rail at 6 a.m.; reach Lambach at 10 a.m.; Fare, 45kr. Take a *déjeuner a la Fourchette*, at the Station; expense, about 22kr. The landlord will have a separate carriage put on for travellers visiting the Falls of the Traun. The whole expense, for it and the journey into Gmunden, will be about half a florin each person. Leave Lambach at 11, see the Falls, and arrive at Gmunden at 2; leave by steamboat at half-past 2 for Ebensee (Fare, 50kr.), reach there at half-past 3; leave by omnibus immediately (Fare, 50kr.), and reach Ischel at half-past 5 p.m. Next day—leave Ischel at 10, Ebensee at 12; reach Gmunden at 1; leave by rail at three-quarters past 2, and arrive at Linz about 9. The Lake of Gmunden is beautiful, and so are the Falls.

LONDON TO TRIESTE.—The most speedy route from London to Berlin, Leipsig, Dresden, Prague Vienna, Trieste, and the centre of Germany, is to proceed from London to Dover by the 8½ p.m. train, reaching Dover at 11¼ p.m., embark immediately, arriving in Ostend in time for the 7.15 mail a.m. train, (or by way of Calais, joining at Malines), and arriving at Cologne at 6.30 the same evening. Leave Cologne at 8 the same night, arrive at Leipsic at 3.30 p.m., Dresden at 8.30 p.m., Prague at 4 a.m., Vienna at * 7.30 p.m., and at Trieste at 4.30 a.m.—Time occupied—London to Berlin, 43¾ hours; to Trieste, 102½ hours.

* Vienna may be reached, *via* Breslau, but the journey occupies ten hours longer.

Passports—see pages 19 to 22.

Money.—See page 23 to 25

Travellers will find that some Innkeepers make out their bills in bad money, or Vienna currency (Wiener Währung), a florin of which is 10*d.* only; whereas the florin "convention money," or münz, is a zwanzigers, or 2*s.* All the respectable Hotels, and all the best shops, however, use the convention money.

NAVIGATION OF THE DANUBE.

Steamer descend the Danube from Regensburg (Ratisbon) to Passau and Linz, in one day. From Linz to Vienna, in about nine hours. From Vienna to Galaz and Constantinople, in about ten days. The ascent takes much longer time. Portions of the Danube have been considered by some superior to the Rhine.

Adelsburg.—HOTEL :—
Ungerishe Krone.
No one should pass between Trieste and Vienna, without stopping at this place, in order to see the splendid grotto in a mountain, above three quarters of a mile from the Hotel. It is, without exception, the grandest natural excavation in Eupope, if not in the whole world; and the startling effect of a river suddenly appearing in the dark bowels of a mountain, with the lights reflected from the narrow bridge in the roaring waters beneath, will never be effaced from the memory. The cost of seeing this wondrous and beautiful place, is about 10 to 14 shillings for a party of four, including lights, guides, &c. It takes about two hours to see the principal views; and Laibach may be reached the same evening comfortably, by taking a separate Eilwagen, the horses of which are paid for from post to post, and cost much the same for three or four people as the mail coach, and the comfort far greater.

Bassano.
12,000 inhabitants. Here are manufactured the fine Italian straw-hats; there is a very fine bridge over the Brenta. In the house of the great sculptor Canova, are preserved many treasures of art, and his birth-place, Posegno, about a league distant, is seldom left unvisited.

Bludenz.
A city in the Vorarlberg.
CONVEYANCES.—Eilwagens and stellwagens daily to Landeck and Innsbruck, and to Feldkirch and Bregenz on the Boden-See (Lake of Constance.)

Botzen, or Botzano.—HOTEL :—
La Corona.
A city in Tyrol, delightfully situated, 27 miles S. of Brixen, 79 S. of Innsbruck, and 40 N. of Trient.
CONVEYANCES. — Eilwagens and stellwagens to Brixen, Innsbruck, Meran, Trient, Roveredo, and Riva; also to Italy.

Bregenz.
A city in the Vorarlberg, situated on the Lake of Constance, 131 miles W. of Innsbruck, and 20 W. of Feldkirch.
CONVEYANCES.—Eilwagens and stellwagens daily to Feldkirch, Bludenz, Landeck, and Innsbruck. Steamers daily on the lake to Lindau, Rorschach, Romanshorn, Friedrichshafen, Constance, & Schaffhausen. At Friedriehshafen is the railway to Ulm, Stuttgardt, and Heilbronn.

Brixen.
A beautiful city in Tyrol, 52 miles S. of Innsbruck, and 27 N. of Bozen.
CONVEYANCES. — Eilwagens and stellwagens (a cheaper sort of conveyance) to Innsbruck and to Bozen, Meran, and Trient.

Brunn.—HOTEL :—
Three Princes.
Capital of Moravia, 40,000 inhabitants; the Leeds of Austria, a place noted for its woollen-weaving and spinning, its linen, leather, gloves, carpets, and vinegar manufactories; lively trade. Spielberg, a political prison, noted on account of the imprisonment of Baron Trenck, General Mack, and Silvio Pelico. Franzenberg: Jacob's Church (Jacob's Kirche), the residence of the Archbishop, town-house, national museum of Moravia.

CONVEYANCES. — Railway to Vienna and to Prague, see page 106.

Budweis.—HOTEL :—
Golden Sun.
Town with 7000 inhabitants, on the Moldau. Not far from Budweis lies Trocznow, where Johann Ziska was born.
CONVEYANCES.—Railway (horse) to Linz, see page 113, Eilwagen to Prague.

Chemnitz.
47 miles S.W. of Dresden; population 27,000. The most considerable manufacturing town in Saxony, producing hosiery which rivals that of England; the condition of the factory-people here is very superior to that in most other places, as they almost all possess freehold cottages, with gardens, which they cultivate themselves when the work at the looms happens to be slack; and they thus improve their means and recruit their health at the same time. Chemnitz is also famous for its manufactures of machinery for spinning. Its ancient fortifications, having been levelled, afford agreeable promenades; outside the town is the former Schloss, once the residence of the Elector, but now an inn.

Feldkirch.
A city in the Vorarlberg, 111 miles W. of Innsbruck, and 20 miles E. of Bregenz.
CONVEYANCES.—Eilwagens and stellwagens daily to Bregenz, Bludenz, Landeck, and Innsbruck. Stellwagen to Bregenz daily, at 5 a.m.; fare, 1 fl.

Gastein.—A watering-place about 80 miles south of Salzburg. The surrounding scenery is of exceeding grandeur. The Klam Strasse (near Leopoldstadt) on the road to Salzburg, may rank with the finest passes in the world.
CONVEYANCE.—Eilwagen to Salzburg.

Gmunden.—HOTEL.—
Golden Sun aud Golden Schiff.
On the Traunsee, with splendid prospect; 3,500 inhabitants; the Alps of Salzburg and Dachstein, the tops of which are covered with snow, and which surround the town, and the lake, lend to the town a majestic beauty.
CONVEYANCES.—Railway (horse) to Linz and Budweis, see page 113. Steamers, in summer, several times daily, to Ebensee, on the opposite end of the lake en route for Ischel. Fare, 50 krentzers.

Gratz.—HOTEL.—

Hotel de l'Elephant, deservedly recommended; the director speaks English, and is attentive.

Capital of Steyermark, (Styria,) with 40,000 inhabitants. It is one of the pleasantest towns of the Austrian monarchy, except Vienna and Prague, on account of its excellent situation and environs, the social feeling of its inhabitants, their cheerful calling, and cheapness of provisions.

OBJECTS OF ATTRACTION.—The cathedral, with an altar painting by Tintoretto; the arsenal, townhall, the convent of the Jesuits, castle, with a beautiful prospect; tomb of Ferdinand II., the castle in which the crown of Steyermark is kept, the theatre, the palace of Attem, the colossal statue of the Emperor Francis, the university, the Joanneum, a technical institute founded by Archduke Johann (John); the chain bridge, 318 feet long. The suburb of Jacomini is the most beautiful quarter of the town, and the most noted coffee-house is in the Jacomial haus. The town is surrounded by beautiful walks; the castle or palace of Eggenberg, with collection of paintings and park; castle and ruins of Gösling; St. John and St. Paul's churches, &c.

CONVEYANCE.—Railway to Vienna, and to Marburg, Cilly, and Laibach.

Hallstadt.—A small town on the lake of the same name, in the Salzkammergut, built on the side of a hill, almost a precipice. This lake, and the neighbouring Gosau Thal, may compare with any part of Switzerland.

Innsbruck.—HOTEL.—

Cour d'Antriche.

This is the capital city of the Tyrol, built 1754 feet above the level of the sea, and contains 13,000 inhabitants. It is the place of assemblage of the Tyrolese Estates. One of the churches contains a valuable collection of works of art, particularly the statues in bronze of the members of the house of Hapsburg. Among other objects of interest may be mentioned the Franciscan Church, containing the celebrated tomb of Maximillian the First and the the grave of Hofer; the Palace; the University, and the Museum.

CONVEYANCES.—Eilwagen (diligences) and stellwagens to Salzburg, Vienna, Munich, Verona, and Augsburg, see page 254; also to Sterzing, Brixen, Bozen, Trient, Roveredo and Riva, to Hall, Schwazt, Kufstein, to Füssen and Kempten, and to Landeck, Bludenz, Feldkirch, and Bregenz.

Ischl.

A town of 2000 inhabitants, one of the most fashionable watering-places in Austria, and the favourite summer residence of the present Emperor. It is situated in the centre of the Salzkammergut, and is good head-quarters for the tourist in that beautiful district. —Eilwagen to Vienna, Gratz, Lintz, and Salzburg.

Laibach.—HOTEL.—

HOTEL DU LION D'OR—highly recommended.

Population 15,000; 77 miles N.E. of Trieste. From the old Burg a beautiful prospect is presented to the view. The interior of the cathedral bears a strong resemblance on a small scale to that of St. Peter's at Rome; the church formerly belonging to the Jesuits is a simple but tastefully planned edifice. Besides these buildings worthy of notice are the Bishop's palace, the Lyceum, theatre, Auersperg palace and gardens, and a marble bridge over the Laibach; there is an alley on the river bank; the waterfall of Schiska within a league of the town; and, within two leagues, Kahlenberg, commanding a fine view. An excursion up the Kreuzeralpe is recommended.

CONVEYANCES.—Railway to Cilly, Gratz, and Vienna, see pages 114 to 117. Eilwagon and diligences to Trieste every day.

Lavis.

A market town in South Tyrol, a few miles N. of Trient, on the post road to Bozen. Between Lavis and St. Michell is the ferry over the water to the road, which leads to the beautiful Val di Non (Annone) and Val di Sol. There is another ferry at St. Michell for travellers coming from Bozen. In going from Lavis to the Tonal Pass, by the Val di Non, the traveller will go through the following places, viz., Mozzolombardo, Cles, Le Capelle, Caldas, Leocolas, Malé, Conviano, Preson, Ponte di Rovino, Piano, Mezzana, Pellizano, Le Fucine, and Vermiglio.

Lintz.—HOTEL.—

Stuchor Canone.

Town with 26,000 inhabitants, beautifully situated on the right shore of the Danube. Mathias Kirche (St. Matthew's Church), with the tomb of Monticuculi (1680); the hall in which the States assemble, Stephan Fadinger, the leader of the mob of rustics, was killed in one of the windows, 1626; the triangular room or hall, standing in a remarkable manner between the statues of Jupiter and Neptune; Jagermayer's garden, from whence you have the finest sight of the town: the Pödlingsberg, the highest point in the neighbourhood of the town. The fortress of Linz is remarkable on account of its peculiarity,—it is after a new plan by Prince Maximilian of Este.

CONVEYANCES.—Railway to Gmunden, see page 113. Eilwagen to Budweis, Innspruck, Munich, Passau, Regensburg, Salzburg, and Vienna, see page 255.

Steam-boats daily to Vienna, alternate days to Ratisbon.

Meran.

One of the most beautifully situated places in Tyrol, 17 miles from Bozen, and 96 from Innsbruck. From Meran, Hofer's house is only about three hours' walk.

CONVEYANCES. — Diligences and stellwagens to Prad and Mals, and also to Bozen, Brixen, and Innsbruck. To Bozen at 2 p.m., in 3 hours; fare, 48 kr. The pedestrian can walk from Meran to Hofer's house, and Sterzing by the Janfingeberge, in one day, and from thence to Innsbruck in another day. The post road is more than twice as long.

Olmutz.

In Moravia; a strong fortress, with 14,000 inhabitants. The cathedral is a noble specimen of old German architecture; in the church of St. Maurice is an organ with 2,332 pipes; the other remarkable objects are the Bishop's palace, university buildings, arsenal, and gymnasium. It is a place of considerable industry, and chief market of Moldavian and Russian horned cattle.

Prague.—HOTELS.—

ENGLISCHER-HOF, close to the railway station, a first class house, and well recommended.

HOTEL BLAUEN STERN, BLUE STAR, a good house and well conducted, close to the railway station.

(Bohemian, Praha), the capital of Bohemia, and contains 143,000 inhabitants, amongst which numbers are 12,000 Jews. Situated, and extending far on both shores of the Moldaw, and surrounded by pleasing heights, it wears, undoubtedly, the most beautiful aspect of all the German towns, being adorned with its 60 peculiar and singularly formed spires, with its lordly castle at the back of the hill (Hradschin), and the broad expanse of its streams, spanned by two noble bridges.

A Commissionaire here is indispensable, and costs 3s. a day. Here buy Bohemian glass. *Galignani's Messenger* may be seen and read at Laurentz's Casino, over a cup of delicious German coffee. The examination of baggage on the Austrian and Saxony Frontiers takes place at Bodenbach; the officers are very civil. The great demand throughout German Custom Houses, is for tobacco, which the traveller is recommended to avoid as much as possible.

Objects of Attraction.—The national Bohemian Museum, situated in the Kallowrat Stresse, near the Archbishop's Palace, with its collection of records, library, and collection of petrifactions, ; the monastery of Strahow; the edifice of Czerna; the cathedral, built in the gothic style, with the tomb of John of Nepomuk, the mausoleum, and curious mosaic; and the holy church of Loretto, in the old town. A stone bridge 1,572 feet long, erected by Charles IV, and a very chaste chain bridge lead from the Kleinseite to the old town, both affording a beautiful prospect of the town and environs; the former is known to the world through the history of John of Nepomuk; the old town house, out of the windows of which were thrown the senators of Prague. In the Jews' town—the remarkable old church yard, and the old synagogue. In the new town—the infirmary; the sick and lying-in hospitals; the monastery of Emaus, with a collection of paintings; and the Karlshof (Charles'-court.) Wallenstein's palace is also worthy of a visit, from its historical associations.

Walks.—The most beautiful prospect of the town is to be had from Laurenceberg: beautiful promenades on the bulwarks, the Sophia, or Dyers' island (with eating and bath-houses), the protection island, castle garden, and peoples' garden. Before the gates, the beautiful villa Kinsky, the orchard (2½ miles), the scharka (5 miles), Troy, Kleinbubna, Nussle, Kuchelbad.

Coffee Houses.—That in the court of the station is the best.

Agent for the Sale of J. A. Farina's *Eau de Cologne*—Mr. F. Prochaska, Perfumer.

Conveyances.—Eilwagen to Budweis, Carlsbad, and Vienna, see page 259. Steamers to and from Dresden twice daily, in connection with the Prague and Lobowitz railway.

Riva.

On the Garda-See, (Lago di Garda,) about 20 miles S.W. of Roveredo, 135 S. of Innsbruck, and 103 N. of Verona. Here they speak always Italian.

Conveyances.—Steamers on the lake daily, at half-past 6, to Garda and Peschiera, and the other places on the lake. Eilwagens and stellwagens to Roveredo, Trient, Bozen, Brixen, and Innsbruck.

Roveredo.

A city in South Tyrol, most beautifully situated, 56 miles S. of Bozen, and 40 S. of Trient.

Conveyances.—Diligences to Trient, Bozen, Brixen, and Innsbruck; and also to Riva, on the Lago di Garda. Also stellwagens (a cheaper conveyance)—also courier to Riva in 4 hours; fare, 3 Austrian lire. Here they speak always Italian.

Salzburg.—Hotel.—

Golden Ship.

A town of 11,000 inhabitants, beautifully situated on the banks of the Salza, anciently governed by an archbishop, who was a prince of the German empire, and the temporal sovereign of a district containing above 200,000 inhabitants.

The view from the Gaisberg is renowned throughout Germany.

Objects of Attraction.—The castle, the cathedral, the palace, the University church, the riding-school, the fountains, and the house in which Mozart was born. In the neighbourhood are the celebrated salt-mines of Hallein and the Lake of Königsee.

Conveyances.—Eilwagen to Bruck, Innspruck, Ischl, Landshut, Linz, Reichenhall, Villach, and Vienna, see page 260.

Treviso.

17 miles N.W. of Venice, with 16,000 inhabitants. Many elegant villas are met with on approaching the town, which is itself adorned with a number of churches and palaces, and has a handsome Town-hall and an Academy of Arts and Sciences. Among the churches the most worthy of note are that of St. Nicholas, an antique structure, and the yet unfinished cathedral of St. Peter's, in which are paintings by Titian, Domenichino, &c.; it has two theatres, and near it is the magnificent villa Manfrini.

Trient (Trento.)

52 miles N. of Verona, population 13,000. This is the wealthiest and most considerable town of the Tyrol, and lies in a plain, surrounded by wooded mountains, from whose sides flow many noble streams. In front of the cathedral is a fountain with some mediocre sculpture; the best picture is at the first altar on the left hand of the main entrance; the church of St. Maria Maggiore, wherein was held the famous council, is fast falling to decay. The environs of this town are very beautiful; the Etsch traverses the valley, while villages in a triple row rise one above another on the fruitful declivity of the mountain-range; beyond these is a marbl pillar commemorative of the French victory a Rivoli. Here they speak principally Italian.

Conveyances.—Diligences to Bozen, Brixen, and Innsbruck, also to Roveredo and Riva. Stellwagen to Riva, 5 Austrian lire (zwanzigers.)

Trieste.—Hotel.—

Hotel de la Ville also an excellent establishment.

Hotel Elysio, a first-rate new house.

The Tergest of the Romans, situated in a creek of the Adriatic sea, and at the foot of a ridge of hills called the Karst hills, has, with outskirts, 83,114 inhabitants; is a free port, and the first seaport town of the Austrian monarchy; is one of the most important commercial places of the Adriatic sea. The population is a mixed one, coming out of all the commercial nations of the Mediterranean; the Dalmatians and Italians, however, are the root of the townspeople; the country people are of the Illyrian race.

Trieste can now be reached from London in about 132 hours, including a stoppage of some time in Vienna. (For route, see page 210.) The return journey occupies longer, in consequence of a detention in Berlin and Cologne.

Travellers arriving here by sea, should at once change their money into paper currency. Gold, especially English sovereigns, bears a high premium. The prices are published daily, and the list may be seen at any money changer's. If it be intended to proceed to Vienna, the luggage should be taken in the morning to the Custom House, there to be examined and plombé, which will save a most vexatious search at Op Shina, on the top of the mountain outside the town; then procure your passport from the police office, and take it with the luggage to the post-house, to secure places in the coach for Adelsburg—a six or seven hours' drive—where the coach arives at about nine p.m. If you remain longer than one day in Trieste, a letter should be at once dispatched (in German or Italian) to the landlord of the Ungerishekrone, at Adelsburg, to secure rooms.

OBJECTS OF ATTRACTION.—The Cathedral, an old building in the Byzantine style, in which is the tomb of Winkelman, who was murdered in Trieste; the piazetta of Ricardo, a small square, with a triumphal arch of Roman origin; the Corso, the principal street between the old and new town; the Exchange, a beautiful building, standing in Exchange-place, with the Casino club, into which a stranger may easily be introduced. There are likewise to be seen the Nautical Real-Academy, the Theresian molo, with light-house; the Grande Lazaretto, or hospital; and the ship docks. Let the stranger above all visit the Tergesteum, with noble conversazioni rooms, and superb reading-rooms for the journals.

BANKERS doing English business—Falkner and Co., George Moore and Co., Grant Brothers & Co., Morpurgo and Pasente.——English Chaplain, the Rev. B. W. Wright.

CONVEYANCES.—*Public.*—To Vienna every day, at 10 a.m. and 3 p.m., by Diligence to Laibach, and railroad to Vienna. Distance 72 German miles, average passage 37 hours.—To Fiume, by Diligence, every day at 8 p.m.—To Milan, by Diligence, every day, at 6 a.m. and 8 p.m. Distance 69 German miles; average passage 48 hours.—To Istria every Wednesday and Sunday, at 6 a.m., by Diligence.—*Private Diligences.*—To Goritz every day, four times. —To Laibach every day, at 3 a.m., 4 & 8 p.m. To Udine every day, at 8 p.m. Average passage, 12 hours.—*Steamers.*—See Alphabetical List, p. 138.

Udine.

In the Tyrol, 47 miles N.W. of Trieste; a busy town with a population of 19,000. The most remarkable buildings are the cathedral, a fine structure, the palace of the Proveditori, a handsome opera-house, the Bishop's palace, and the chapel of the Toreani, in which are some excellent reliefs by Toretti. The principal square is adorned with he monuments of the Peace of Campo Formio and of Francis I. There is a noble prospect from the tower of the castle. The Campo Santo is considered to be one of the most beautiful cemeteries in Europe.

CONVEYANCES.—Diligence to Trieste daily, in 12 hours.

Vienna (Wien, German).—HOTEL:—

ARCHDUKE CHARLES HOTEL, a first-rate house, highly recommended, the proprietor, Mr. Schneider, is both attentive and obliging.

HOTEL MUNSCH, an excellent house, deserving our recommendations.

HOTEL ZUM GOLDENEN LAMM, a capital house, deservedly recommended.

WAITERS— Waiters are called "Kellner."

The city of Vienna, (the Emperor's city, as it is called in Germany,) lies on both sides of an arm of the Danube, (Donau,) of the canals, and of the rivulets. It contains 9286 houses, and without military in the boundary, a population of 410,000. The traffic in Vienna is great, and what materially adds to it, is the size of the city, taken as a manufacturing place, and as a place of residence, as likewise its shops, situated in the most noted streets, (the Stock am, Eiser, Platz, Graben, Kohlmarkt, Kärntner, Strasse, &c). Its principal trade consists in gold, silver, jewellery, and silk manufactures. The best points from which to see the town and its suburbs are, the steeple of St. Stephen's, the female spinner at the cross, the terrace on Upper Belvedere the Turk's Bulwark, the Gloriette in Schönbrun, the top of Leopold and Kahlen hills, the Krapfenwaldchen, the Hemmel, the Gallizenberg, and the Spinnerin am Kreuz.

A COMMISSIONER, or GUIDE, through the city, and to all the principal objects of attraction, costs 2 florins a day. There is no table d'hôte at Vienna, which is a very great disadvantage—as, by ordering from the Carte, the chances are that you call for unseasonable dishes, and pay much more than you wish. Itis best to dine in Vienna, at the *fixed* price of the hotel, which is generally four or five shillings. The wines called the Hungarian clarets, "Ofner," "Voslaner," and "Adelsburger," are excellent, and are to be procured throughout Austria, at reasonable prices. If about to leave the Austrian dominions, calculate how much money you will require up to last moment, and change your gold into a sufficient quantity of paper florins.

AGENT for the Sale of J. A. Farina's *Eau de Cologne*—Messrs. Jac. Manner & Co.

OBJECTS OF ATTRACTION.—The cathedral of St. Stephen's, built by Duke Henry Jasomirgott (1144); the steeple, the giant gate, the pulpit, the sarcophagus of Emperor Frederick III., the tomb of the royal family, from the 14th to the 17th century. The entrance into the steeple, leads from a small house, No. 873, Stephen's-platz. It is 428 feet high. The building of it was begun in 1359, and completed in 1433. The largest bell is cast out of 180 Turkish cannon, and weighs 357 cwt. There is to be seen, in the interior of the church, the chapel of the cross (kreuzkapelle) where lies buried the celebrated Prince Eugene. The traveller will be well repaid by a visit to the church of the Capuchins in the New-market, with the vault of the royal family, and the sarcophagus of young Napoleon, Duke of Reichstadt; the church of St. Augustin, with a noble marble monument to the memory of the Duchess Christiania, of Sax-Teschen, the most beautiful work of Canova. There is to be seen here likewise, the death-chapel of the Emperor Leopold II., of the distinguished General Daun, and of the Professor of Swieten; in the Loretto Chapel, the hearts of the members of the Emperor's family are preserved in silver urns; the St. Michael's Church, with the burial-place of Metastasius. A church well worth seeing in the suburbs is the St. Carlo Boromeo, built in fulfilment of a vow which the Emperor Charles VI. made when the plague raged in Vienna, after a drawing by Fisher of Erlach, 1737. The palace of Archduke Charles. The treasure-room in Sweizerhof, with the regalia of Charles the Great, and of the German crowns, as well as many other valuables and rarities. The royal riding-school; the royal coach-house. In the upper Belvedere, built by Prince Eugene, is the imperial picture gallery; in the lower Belvedere are the Ambras museum, Egyptian museum, and collection of antiquities. The imperial cabinets of antiquities, of minerals, of the plastic arts, are in different buildings. The several picture galleries of Prince Lichtenstein, Prince Esterhazy, Count Czernin, and Count Schönborn, are at their several palaces, as are the Schönfield museum of Baron Dietrich, and the collection of Count Harrach. The university, the polytechnic (Wieden), the Josephine, with the richest collection of anatomical properties, collected by Chevalier Fontana, of Florence (Alsergund, Wahringergasse); the normal school, founded by Maria Theresa (Anna Gasse); the geographical institution, (Alsen Vorstadt); mineralogical institution, one of the finest collections of minerals to be found in Europe; Lichtenstein palace (Landstrasse); the public infirmary, with 2,200 beds; the lunatic asylum, with 250 beds; the deaf and dumb institute, the hospital of the benevolent brotherhood, and also the new mint.

Gardens and Walks.—The Bastey, a very pleasant walk round the walls of the town; the Glacis, between the town and suburbs, with innumerable alleys of lime and chesnut trees; the Cemetery, particularly recommended in stormy weather, on account of its low situation; the Prater, in which are celebrated all the peoples' holidays (the Hyde-park of Vienna); the Park, with alleys thickly studded with trees, in the old French style; the Brigittenau, a large but irregular wood, with meadows—the royal court garden, the botanical garden of the university, in the Reunivege; the royal botanical garden for Austrian plants, the botanical garden of Joseph's academy, in the Alser burgh; the princely Liechtenstein garden, with the noted winter garden (Rossau, No. 130); the princely Schwarzenberg garden (Rennweg, 641), always open to the public; the garden of Prince Metternich, laid out in the most splendid manner (Rennweg, 545); the garden of the royal horticultural society, in which are two annual exhibitions; the garden of Rupprecht (Gumpendorf, 54), where the exhibition of potatoes takes place; the garden of M Klier (under the Weisgarbern, 92), with more than 800 kinds of pelargoniums; Adams' garden, in Matzleinsdorf, with rich tulip and auricula plants. There are also the following gardens, where concerts and balls take place, viz., the Sperl in the Leopoldstadt, the Augers garden, the Paradise garden, the Au garden, and the Volk's garden near the Bourg, the latter of which is much frequented, and contains the noted statue of Theseus, by Canova. Entrance to the concerts, about 10 kr.; to the balls, about 20 kr.

The Post Office is situated between the Alter and Heisch Mart and the Bastei, or rampart, and is a very large and splendid building. Letters are received till 6 in the evening, and even later, on payment of a small fine. Stamps are now in use, both for the kingdom and for the pre-payment of foreign letters. It is singular, that while a letter to or from Austria, if paid for in England, costs 1s. 8d.; costs, if paid for in Austria, only 29 kreuzers, less than a shilling. The rates for the kingdom are in the town, 2 kreuzers; under 10 German miles, 3 kreuzers; from 10 to 20 miles, 6 kreuzers; above 20 miles, 9 kreuzers. A letter can be insured as to delivery for a small charge. The post-office authorities have the sole privilege of carrying small parcels. Money, if sent, must be sealed up at the office in the presence of a proper officer, who delivers a receipt. The former post-office in the Wollzerle, is now only a filial office. There has been, within the last few months, receiving boxes for letters placed in different parts of the town and suburbs.

Coffee Houses.—The first coffee house in Europe is said to have been established at Vienna, 1684, by a certain Koltschitzky, a Polish spy in the quarters of the Turks, who received permission to open it, as a recompense for his services. The coffee houses in the city are not very showy; most of them have a billiard table, smoking room, and an ordinary supply of newspapers. A cup of coffee without milk, (called black coffee,) costs 8 kr. C.M., a cup with milk is called a mixture, (mélange). The most noted coffee house is Daun's, No. 278, in the Coal-market, (kohlmarkt); Neun's, in the Plankengasse, into which ladies may be taken. Fiacres, when hired by the week, are allowed to go without their number. They are, in general, very neat and clean. Hanson's Cabriolets are now being introduced.—Fare, 15 kr. per quarter, if in town. In the coffee houses of Leopold's town, (Leopoldstadt), near to Ferdinand's-bridge, (Ferdinand's-brucke,) are to be found in general many Turks and Greeks, in their national costume. Club-houses are very scarce, but there is one excellent Institution of this kind, the Judicial-political-reading Institute, in which are to be found almost all periodicals and literary news, inland and foreign, and access to it can easily be obtained. Access to the aristocratic club-house can be most easily secured by means of the Banker by whom recommended.

Beer Houses.—These are well worthy of a visit. There are 700 in the city and its suburbs. They are much frequented by foreigners. The best is Neuling's in the Ungergassen.

Passports.—Each stranger arriving at Vienna

will be asked by a police officer, as soon as the train reaches the terminus, for his travelling pass, for which a certificate will be handed him, which binds him to enquire after the pass at the Police-office, (Spenglergasse, No. 564), within the twenty-four hours. He receives here a ticket, empowering him to reside in the place six weeks, which will be renewed without delay at the expiration of that time—the traveller must be particular in observing when the time expires. If the traveller wish to make excursions during his stay in the city, he must procure a pass to that effect from the same office, either personally or by means of his servant, which will be given him upon his producing his pass entitling him to a sojourn in the city. When he wishes to leave Vienna, the pass of his residence is exchanged for his travelling passport—he must be particularly mindful to get it signed by the authorities of every country through which he wishes to pass.

LUGGAGE—The inspection of luggage takes place immediately upon arrival, and the traveller must be cautious not to carry upon his person, or to smuggle anything that pays a duty; amongst which may be particularly noticed, tobacco, playing cards, and books,--forbidden books are placed in the Central Inspection Office, and remain in oficial custody until his departure.

CABS.—These stand in all streets, but the rate of fare is not fixed, 30 kr. C.M. is the ordinary charge for a drive in the town, for a drive from the town to the suburbs, 1 fl. C.M. If the traveller have many places to call at, the best plan for him is to hire the cab for half a day, or for the whole day. On the week-days he pays from 5 to 6 fl. C.M., but on the Sundays, and in fine weather, the cab is not to be obtained for less than 10 fl. C.M. The town coaches are to be hired either by the day, the week, or the month. Cafe Francais, in the Stephen's Platz, in which is an upper room for ladies; and, in summer, the Cur Saloon, on the Wasser Slacio, with music every evening.

ENGLISH PHYSICIAN.---Maurice Jacobovics, M.D., 1150 Kohlmarkt, Fellow of the Royal Medical and Chirurgical Society of London, and late professor of external Pathology in the Royal Hungarian University.

CONVEYANCES.—Steamers on the Danube, see page 139. Railway to Presburg Pesth, and Szolnok, see page 110; to Oderberg, see page 112; to Olmutz, Brunn, Prague, Dresden, see pages 112 and 106; to Bruck and Stockerau, see page 18; to Neustadt, Glognitz, Cilly, and Laibach; and from thence by diligence to Trieste, see page 114. For Diligences, see page 262.

The Environs of Vienna. — Schönbrunn and Hitzing. You reach here either by the Vienna and Gloggnitz railway, or by the Company's coaches. Schönbrunn is the summer residence of his Majesty the Emperor; it was begun under the superintendence of Fisher, in the reign of the Emperor Mathias, and completed in the reign of Maria Theresa. The Duke of Reichstadt lived and died here (1832). The garden is well attended, particularly on the Sunday. Stapps, the German student, who made an attempt upon the life of Napoleon, was shot and buried here. The beautiful well, from whence the castle derives its name; the Gloriette, with a beautiful view of Vienna, the flower garden with the palm-house, and a menagerie are worth looking through. On the other side of the garden of Schönbrunn lies Ober-Meidling, with its Tivoli, and its Vauxhall, or the Grande Chaumière of Vienna—Hitteldorf, where the Emperor's deer park may be seen, containing 3000 wild boars, an unusual sight. —Laxenburg, to which at this present time a railway carries you: Castle, with beautiful park; Temple of Diana, the little Pretor, Temples of the Eintracht, Einsiedleref, Fisher Dorfchen, artificial waterfall — the Ringelspiel, the Holzstoss, the Meierei; above all, is the Knight's Castle (Ritterschloss) to be observed, a correct imitation of a fasthold of the middle ages. Mödling: the road to it leads by the Spinner at the Cross (Spinnerin am Kreutz), a gothic cross, erected by Crispinus Pellitzer, 1547, adorned with the statue of Crispinus and Crispianus. In Mödling is to be seen the old Knight-Templars' church of Holy Ottmar, the castle and the park of Prince Liechtenstein; the ruins of the old family castle of the Babenberger; numerous pleasant walks and eating-houses.—The Kahlenberg (Mons Citius), above 1000 feet high. The way to it is over Döbling, where there is a good picture-gallery belonging to M. Arthaber and the splendid coffee-house near the observatory; the latter affording the best sight around the neighbourhood of the city.—The Leopoldsberg, with an old castle. From this point may be taken pleasant walks on the Cobenziberg, to the Krapfenwaldchen, to Severing on the Himmel, to Grinzing and Heiligenstadt; as likewise to Nussdorf and Klosternenberg, adjoining. The ruins of Greifenstein lay one mile from the convent-castle (Klosternenberg); Richard, the Lion-hearted, lay in prison there; another road on the Vienna Wald leads through Dornbach, where Prince Schwarzenberg possesses a noble villa, with superb park. From this part you can reach the Upper Wald, and from thence you descend, and walking in the shade of a fine wood of beech-trees you reach Hainbach, Steinbach, and lastly, Mauerbach, where there is capital refreshment to be had; from thence, through a lovely valley, you get to the Huts of the Passover (Passauer Hütten), and in half an hour to the Tulbinger Kogel, a hill, from the top of which you enjoy the most beautiful prospect. A pleasant out is one to Pötzleindorf (village of Pötzlein), vulgarly called Potzelsdorf. To this place YOU MUST HAVE the Company's coaches.

REMARKS.—The Company's coaches can also be made use of as omnibuses, in order to reach a distant suburb, such as the Heitzinger, or to go to Newbaw or Shottenfeld; the coachman receives a small allowance—from 3 to 6kr. C.M. On the Sunday and on holidays the prices of the Company's coaches are raised 1 kreutzer.

Days and hours for visiting the most remarkable establishments and curiosities in Vienna:—

MONDAY. — The royal mint and cabinet of

antiquities, 10 o'clock, A.M.—The city arsenal, No. 332, from 9 to 12, A.M., and from 3 to 6 P.M.

TUESDAY.—Royal cabinet of Egyptian antiquities (Landstrass, No. 641), from the end of April to the end of September from 9 to 12, A.M., and from 3 to 6, P.M.; from the end of September to the end of April, from 9, A.M. to 2, P.M.—The royal Ambras collection (in the same building and on the same hours).—The royal gallery of paintings, in Upper Belvidere, in the summer, from 9 to 12 o'clock and from 3 to 5 o'clock; in the winter, from 9 to 2 o'clock.

WEDNESDAY.—The royal cabinet of mineralogy, from 9 to 1 o'clock.—Technical collection of his Majesty, the Emperor, in the Polytechnic Institute, at 10 A.M.

THURSDAY.—The royal cabinet of curiosities Joseph's-platz), 10 o'clock.—City arsenal (like Monday).—Blind institute (Joseph's-platz, No.188); there is a public examination of the children every Thursday, which every visitor will find very interesting.

FRIDAY.—The royal mint and cabinet of curiosities (same as Monday).—Royal cabinet of Egyptian antiquities (ditto).—Royal Ambras museum (same as Tuesdays).—Royal gallery of paintings (ditto).—Royal treasure-room, at 10, A.M., and only in the summer season.

SUNDAY.—The royal cabinet of minerals (same as Wednesday).—Royal treasure-room (same as Friday).—Josephine academy (Wahrengergassi, No. 221), in the summer months every week, in the winter every fortnight.—Royal collection of pictures of the royal academy of plastic arts (city, No. 980).—Royal Polytechnic institute, only in the summer.—Royal Deaf and dumb institution (Wieden, No. 162); public examination from 10 to 12 o'clock.

TYROL.

The following tour of from six to eight weeks in the Tyrol, &c., can be recommended:—

Munich to Innspruck, Solstein, Schonberg, Ambras, Zeil, Martinswand, Umhausen, Oetzthal, and Gletscher, Timbler Joch, Hofers haus, Meran, Finstermunz, Wormser, Joch (Monte Stelvio,) Bormio, Tonal Pass, Cles in Val di Non, Val di Non (Annone,) Trient, Riva and Garda-See (Lago di Garda), Roveredo, return to Trient, Botzen, Castrel, Groden, Enneberg, Brunecken, Pusterthal, Taufers, Antholz, Teffereckenthal, Windisch-Matray, Pass of St. Ruprecht, Heiligenblut, Rauriser Tauern, Bad Gastein, Werfeu, Pass Lueg, Abtenau, Gosau, and thence to Hallstadler-See, Ischl, Aussee, Gmunden, Fraunfall and Salzburg.

SWITZERLAND AND SAVOY.

Switzerland, or the Alpine country, has been divided by naturalists into seven regions, each successively rising above the other—the first, or lowest of which, terminates at the height of 1,700 feet above the level of the sea; the second, or region of oaks, reaches the height of 2,800 feet, and is succeeded by the region of the birch, which rises to 4,000 feet. The higher Alpine regions commence at an elevation of 6,500 feet; and above 8,000 feet is the region of glaciers and of eternal snows. Along the chain of the Alps, from Mont Blanc to the frontiers of Tyrol, there are reckoned to be above 4,000 glaciers, many of which are 18 or 21 miles long, 1½ to 2¼ miles wide, and from 100 to 600 feet thick. Altogether, the glaciers of Switzerland are presumed to form a sea of ice more than 1,000 miles in extent; and from its inexhaustible sources flow the waters of some of the principal rivers in Europe. Switzerland is also intersected by mountains, the greater part of which are ramifications of the Alps, whilst the remainder belong to the chain of Jura. From Mount St. Gothard—the central Alps—extend two ranges, which form a mass of the highest mountains in Europe. The snows accumulated on the top of the Alps are continually falling down their precipitous sides into the lower regions, where they often produce serious injury. The chain of Jura presents to the eye of the traveller a deep contrast to that of the Alps. It stretches in several parallel ridges for about 240 miles along the western and north-western frontiers of Switzerland, from the bend of the Rhone, below Geneva, at the banks of the Rhine, eastward of Basel, and is clothed from top to bottom with luxuriant pine forests.

Switzerland is also pre-eminently a land of lakes, the principal of which are the Lake of Constance, the Lake of Geneva, or Lake Leman, the Lake of Zurich, the Lake of Lucerne, and the Lake of Neuchatel, with some minor ones.

TOUR IN SWITZERLAND.

London to Ostend, Cologne, Frankfort, and Freiburg, and from thence to Schaffhausen, Constance, Roschach, St. Gall, Weisbad, Sennewald, Werdenberg, Ragatz, Pfeffers, Wallenstadt, Wesen-Wesen, Rapperschwyl, Zurich, Zug, Goldau, Righi, Lucerne, Fluelen, Andermatt, St. Gothard, Grimsel Hospice Meyringen, Grindelwald, Lauterbrunnen, Interlacken, Thun, Berne, Soluthurn, Weissenstein, Bienne, Neufchatel, Morat, Aventicum, Fribourg. Lausanne, Geneva, Vevay, Bex, Martigny, Orsieres, Liddes, St Bernard, Martigny, Trient, Chamounix, Montanvert, St. Gervais, St. Martins, Geneva, Lyons, and Paris, London. For the shorter route through France via Paris and Strasburg, see page 29, route 35.

London to Basle or Schaffhausen.—See Route 35, page 29.

London to Geneva, through France, see Route 16, page 27.

Time of Travelling.—The best time for a tour is the latter part of June, July, August, or September.

Transport of Luggage.—By applying at the Post-office, the traveller may have his luggage conveyed to any part of Switzerland. A receipt will be given, on application, at a small charge. This mode of transit, though the safest and speediest, is very expensive, and heavy articles should be sent, if time be no object, by the *roulage* or carrier's waggon.

Conveyances.—There is only one Railway in Switzerland, from Zurich to Baden (a watering-place). Diligences, generally belonging to Government, and carrying the mail, traverse all the chief roads; the fare is however high, and three or four travelling together, will find it more convenient to hire a conveyance. Return fare must also be paid, and the traveller should ascertain whether a return carriage may not be in the town before hiring one belonging to the place. Steamers navigate all the chief lakes.

Guides.—As a general rule it may be said they are absolutely necessary in mountain excursions' at any other times than the months named for a tour, since the paths are liable to be obliterated by snow. Their almost invariable honesty and good temper render them on all occasions useful.

Money.—By a decree of the Diet, 1850, the Swiss coinage has been reduced to the same standard as that of France. Francs and centimes constitute the current money, and in these accounts are now kept, the old Swiss batz being no longer a legal tender. French Napoleons and francs are the best coins the traveller can take with him. In the Cantons of St. Gall, Appenzell, and Grisons, which border on Germany, and where Bavarian florins (20 pence) and kreutzers occur, zwanzigers or 24 kreutzer pieces will be found very convenient coins, and will often be found to go as far as a franc in payment of fees, pour boires. English sovereigns are taken at the Swiss Towns at a value of 25 francs. English circular notes, or Bank of England notes, are exchanged at all the chief places of resort in the country.

Route of Three Weeks through Switzerland.—The route given supposes the traveller to enter Switzerland at Schaff hausen (by diligence from Freiburg in the Breisgau), and to leave it at Basel.

Schaffhausen.*
1 Zurich, D.
2 Righi; S. & D. to Arth
3 Lucerne ; S. from Weggis.
4 Fluellen, S ; Andermat, D.
5 Grimsel, M.
6 Meyringen, M.
7 Grindelwald, M.
8-9 Interlacken
9-10 Thun, S.; Berne, D.
11 Freiburg, D.†
12 Vevay, D.
13 Martigny, D.
14-16 Chamouni, M.
17-18 Geneva, D.
19 Lausanne, S
20 Yverdun, D.; Neufchatel, S.
21 Bienne, S.; Basle, D

Abbreviations—D. diligence; S. steamer; C. private carriage; M. mule.

Variations—* Constance, S; Bath of Pfeffers, D; Rapperschwl, D; Zurich, S; three days extra would be requiréd. Return to Thun, (either by Berne, or on foot through Schwarzenburg);
† Kandersteg, C; over the Gemmi to Leuk; Martigny, D; two days extra.

DESCRIPTIONS, &c., OF TOWNS.

Aix-les-Bains (in Savoy.)—HOTELS:—

LA POSTE—the best, and good; MAISON VENATZ; BOARDING HOUSE OF CHARPENTIER, &c.

A watering place much frequented during the season. Population about 2,500.

CONVEYANCES.—Diligences to and from Geneva and Chambery daily.

STEAMER to Lyons during the season in about 7 hours.

Arth.

A village at the foot of the Righi, beautifully situated at the head of the small Lake of Zug, and in the vicinity of Goldau, the scene of the awful desolation caused by the fall of the Rossberg mountains in 1806, when three villages and 450 persons were overwhelmed. The ascent of the Righi from either of these villages is easy, and the whole route commands rich and pastoral scenery; the descent, on the other side, to Weggis, on the Lake of Lucerne, forms a pleasing variety.

From Arth, Conveyances may be obtained to Zug and Horgen, on the Lake of Zurich.

Bale.—HOTELS:—

HOTEL OF THE THREE KINGS, Trois Rois, highly recommended; good rooms and clean; excellent cuisine and attentive servants.

HOTEL DU SAUVAGE—an excellent house, well known to English travellers, and the host gives much satisfaction by his obliging civility and attention.

Basel, or Bale, is situated at the north-western corner of Switzerland, on the north side of the Jura, and is made up of several fertile valleys bordered by mountains covered with excellent pasturage. It is the capital of one of the States, and is placed on the Rhine at the point where it verges northward. It is a well-built and large city, consisting of two towns, divided by the Rhine, and spanned by a magnificent bridge. It contains a population of 50,000 souls, and is the seat of a very fine Cathedral, built in the Gothic style of architecture, an l possessing one of the highest towers in Swiizerland next to that of Freiburg. The Mansion House, in which is the Hall where the famous Ecclesiastical Council was held between 1431 and 1438; the Masgra Fisherhof, and the Arsenal, are well worth visiting.

Basel is the seat of a University, and of a number of other Scientific Insitutions; its inhabitants are also remarkable for their intelligence and industry.

Within about six miles south-east of Bale, at Augst, near the confluence of the Ergoliz with the Rhine, are several interesting remains of the Roman town, Augusta Raurocrusan; and about three miles distant, at Arlesheim, in the Berse, are very fine baths, and a celebrated garden, laid out in the English style, by Baron de Gleresse.

The road to Bienne through the Val Moutiers or Munster Thal, is one of the finest in Switzerland, it is traversed by diligence to Berne and Neufchatel.

BANKERS.—M. Passavant & Co. cash English Bank Notes and the Circular Notes of all the Banks and Banking Houses of London, Dublin, Edinburgh, and New York. The Offices of the Bank are close to the Post-office and principal hotels.

CONVEYANCES. — Railway trains to Mulhouse, Thann, Colmar, Strasburg, and Paris (see Time Table, page 77 and 53); to Freiburg, Offenburg, Kehl, Baden, Carlsruhe, Heidelburg, Manheim, Darmstadt, and Frankfort, (pages 79, 75.) Diligences for Berne, Geneva, Neufchatel, Zurich, Lucerne, Solothurn, Schaffhausen, and every part of Switzerland, see page 246.

Baveno.—HOTEL:—

DE LA POSTE, close to the lake.

A small village on the Lake Maggiore, of no importance but as a posting station on the road to Milan, and from its proximity to the Borromean Islands. The Isola Bella is about half an hour's row from Baveno. On this island the Palace and Gardens of the Count Borromeo are situated, and liberally shown to strangers. The gardens are raised on terraces cut out of the solid rock, and, at immense cost and labour, transformed into a prolific soil, teeming with aromatic odours of oranges, citrons, and tropical plants in the open air. The Isola Madre is also well worth visiting.

After visiting the Islands, the boat should be taken to Palanza, one of the calling places of the steamer which navigates the lake daily, from Magadino, at the northern or Swiss end, to Sesto Calende, in the Austrian territory, at the south, from which there is a conveyance to Milan.

Travellers returning to Switzerland can procure tickets on board the steamer in correspondence with the diligences from Bellinzona, as far as Horgen, on the Lake of Zurich, by the St. Gothard Pass; or to Coire, by the Bernardino Pass, and through the Via Mala. By the latter route passengers are landed at Locarno, and conveyed at once to Bellinzona, to await the arrival of the diligence from Milan. From Bellinzona to Coire the journey is performed in from sixteen to eighteen hours.

Bellinzona (Bellenz, German).—HOTEL:—

HOTEL L'ANGELO.

Bellinzona is the capital of the canton of Tessin, which is situated on the south side of the great chain of Alps, possessing a mild climate and a fertile soil, but an idle and wretched population. The capital is a small trading town, with about 15,000 inhabitants, situated on the Tessin, in the lower part of the great vale Levantine, and is one of the most important points in Switzerland in a military and commercial point of view, on account of the great roads which meet there, viz.:—that of St. Gothard, between Ariolo in this canton and Andumadt in the canton of Uri, a very fine carriage road; the road Lukmanier, between Faido in Tessin and Santa Maria in the Grisons; that of Bernardin, which connects the vale Misocco with the great road of the Splugen; and that of Monte Cenera, between Bellinzona and Lugarno, terminating at Como; and, lastly, the road by Milan, along the lake Maggiore, by Sesto Calendee. Besides, Bellinzona is picturesquely situated, and a fortified city, and a place of some importance as to its traffic, on the great routes to Italy by the St. Gothard Pass to Lucerne, and the Bernardino Pass to Splugen and Coire. Diligences also to Magadino and Locarno, on Lago Maggiore, about half-past 3 a.m., in connection with the steam-boat, which plies daily, at 6 a.m. from Magadino. Bellinzona, though a Swiss town, partakes of the Italian style of architecture,

Berne.

Berne is one of the largest of the cantons of Switzerland. The mountains of this canton are very rich in metallic veins, whilst they also abound in mineral springs. Berne, the capital of the canton, is situated on the left bank of the Aar, in north latitude 46.57, seventy feet above the level of the sea, and is looked upon as one of the finest towns in Europe. The streets are broad and regular, and the prospects are very beautiful, particularly from the terrace near the Cathedral—a beautiful Gothic building with a magnificently wrought steeple. It is the seat of Government, and contains a population of 23,000 inhabitants. There is an Academy there, but it is no ways worth visiting. In the centre of the streets is a stone channel filled with a rapid stream; the streets are further embellished with a profusion of beautiful fountains surrounded with statues. The University, Veterinary School, Military Academy, and Theological College, might be visited with interest.

Until the appointment of Capt. Pictet as British Consular Agent at Geneva, Berne was the only place where an English passport could have the necessary *visa.* Berne is the general starting place for excursions into the Bernese Oberland. Travellers will do well to leave their superfluous luggage here. Carriages, servants, and guides are to be had at every hotel. Ministers for England, France, Bavaria, Austria, and Italy, reside at Berne, and passports should here be countersigned by the representatives of those States through which the traveller purposes journeying. The Town Clock should be seen by all travellers as it strikes the hour of twelve.

AGENT for the Sale of J. A. Farina's *Eau de Cologne*.—Mr. J. B. Lind, Apothecary.

CONVEYANCES. — Diligences to Aarau, Basel, Freiburg, Geneva, Lausanne, Lucerne, Neufchatel, Solothurn, Thun, Vevay, and Zurich, see page 246.

Bienne.

Bienne is an old fashioned town, situated at the foot of the Jura mountains, at a short distance from the lake of Bienne. Travellers generally make excursions to this lake and the island of St. Peter. to visit the residence of the celebrated Jean J, Rousseau. The distance from Berne to Bienne is about six leagues. The road leaves Berne by the forest of Brangastin, and passes by Maykirch to Serdorf. The lake adjoining the latter place, together with the castle of Frenisberg, formerly a convent, are worth a visit.

Chambery.—HOTELS.—None of them clean.

HOTEL DE LA POSTE—good cuisine.

HOTEL DU PETIT PARIS—good.

Chambery is distant from Geneva about 23½ leagues, and from Lyons 29 leagues. The town itself is the capital of Savoy—a dependency of the Sardinian kingdom—and contains a population of 10.000 souls. It is beautifully situated in a valley, on the two small rivers of Albano and Leisse. It contains a large market place, and some ancient ruins, which, with the fountain of the Place de l'Ans, and the Ter de l'Arquebuse, or "shooting place," are worth visiting. The other public edifices worthy notice are the Santo Chapelle, the Castle, founded in 1230 by the Count of Maurianne, the staircase of which is well worth observation; the Town-house, the Academy, the Poor-house and Hospital, erected at the expense of Count de Bigne, who amassed great wealth in the service of Tippoo Saib, which he employed in embellishing his birthplace; the Theatre, and the Barracks.

The promenades are those of Vernay, a planted Boulevard, and the Terrace.

The environs of Chambery are remarkably pleasant, and are diversified with hills covered with orchards, gardens, and vineyards, intersected by valleys. The views from the neighbouring mountains are magnificent in the extreme; and to be appreciated, should be seen.

The roads from Lyons and Geneva to Turin, over the Mont Cenis, meet here.

CONVEYANCES.—Diligences daily to and from Aix-les-Bains, Geneva, Lyons, and Turin. Courier to Geneva, Lyons, and Turin, daily between 10 and 12 night.

Chamounix.

3,150 feet above the level of the sea. A village in the valley of the same name, at the foot of Mont Blanc, distant about fifty miles from Geneva, Diligences in the season; fares, 14 francs. Several days may be well devoted to explore the wonders of this celebrated region. The Montauvert, which can be ascended on mules, and commands a view of the Mer de Glace, ought to be the first excursion. It is an elevated pasture on the summit of a mountain under the Aiguilles de Charmoz. Half way up the ascent is an agreeable resting-place, at the fountain Caillet, beside which Florian is said to have commenced his tale of Claudine. From this are seen to advantage the valleys of the Breven and of the Arguilles Rongis. At the summit of Montanvert is a small building, where refreshment, &c., may be obtained. In this house, which is dedicated to nature, is an album, called the *Livre des Amis*, wherein visitants usually inscribe their names. Among the many effusions written in it is one by Madame de Stael, and a copy of one by the Empress Josephine, the original of which was pilfered. An English gentleman named Blair erected here an hôpital, called the Chateau de Blair; but it is now used as a cow-house. The height of Montanvert above the valley of Chamounix is 2,565 feet. The Glacier de Bossons, which may be seen the same day, at the other end of the valley, is remarkable for the purity of the ice, and for the picturesque formation of the blocks of ice, resembling a ruined temple of pyramids and arches. The Brevent, on the opposite side of the valley, 8,000 feet above the sea, affords the most magnificent view of the whole range of Mont Blanc, with its numerous peaks covered with snow, and the glaciers pouring down into the valley. The Flegère, on the same side, commands the same view at a less elevation, and may be accomplished in half a day. The active tourist would be well repaid by a day's excursion to the Jardin, across the Mer de Glace, 9,100 feet above the sea—a small portion of green earth, in a region of snow and ice, commanding a view of the recesses of this wonderful range of snowy peaks. From Chamounix to Martigny, by the passes of the Tête Noire or the Col de Balme, about nine hours would be required; these roads are practicable for mules only. The Tête Noire is one of the most picturesque passes in Switzerland, abounding in glens and woody heights, the rocks frequently overhanging. Chamounix being in Savoy, travellers proceeding thither either by Geneva or Martigny, must be provided with the visé of the Sardinian government.

CHARGES.—The following are about the sums charged at the Hotels:—Dinner, 3 to 4 francs, breakfast, 1½ to 2 francs; bed, 1½ to 2 francs.

CONVEYANCES.—There is a diligence from Martigney to Villeneuve on the lake of Geneva, whence steamers may be taken to Vevay, Lausanne, and Geneva. There is also a daily diligence between Chamounix and Geneva.

Coire (Chur, German).—HOTELS: —

LA CROIX BLANCHE, LE CAPRICORN, LA POSTE—all good.

It occupies a picturesque site on the Plessour, about two miles from its confluence with the Rhine, and on the great road to Italy by the Splugen; and contains a population of 5,000 inhabitants. The public places worth visiting are the Cathedral, built in 780—in it are some very fine monuments; the Episcopal Palace, containing a very large number of paintings; the Catholic School; the Town-hall, containing the public library; and the Lyceum. The Roman Catholic Church, outside the city gates, is remarkable from its extreme antiquity, part of it dating from the seventh century. The Romansch, a dialect of the Latin, is still spoken in this vicinity. The environs of Coire are worthy the tourist's attention, and command fine views of the Galander, as well as of the mountains on the valley of the Rhine, with the glaciers of the Bodus. The Cascade, the baths of Lurli, the fountain of Aroschka, and the valley of the Albula, form delightful excursions from Coire, and will well repay a visit.

CONVEYANCES.—Diligences daily to Milan, by the Via Mala and Splugen; also to Constance and St. Gall, and to Zurich, in connexion with steamers on the lakes of Wallenstadt and Zurich.

Constance.—HOTELS:—

HECHT (LE BROCHET), KRONE (LA COURONNE)—both well spoken of.

Constance is an important town of the Grand Duchy of Baden. It contains a population of 6,000 souls, and should be Swiss, from its natural position. It is very pleasantly situated at the point where the Rhine issues from the Lake of Constance to enter the lower lake, or Lake of Zell. Constance is in a very neglected state, and contains a number of deserted convents; its mills are of a singular construction; its edifices and institutions are worthy the traveller's notice, particularly the cathedral—a Gothic building—the summit of which commands a very fine view; the carving of the doors is much admired. In the council-hall of this cathedral was pronounced the sentence against John Huss, who, as well as Jerome of Prague, was burnt alive by a decree of the famous council of Constance. The serge mantle worn by Huss, as he went to the pile, is still seen. The Church of St. Maurice, the convent where Huss was imprisoned, the dominican convent, wherein is seen the epitaph of Chrystolora, the former college of the Jesuits, the episcopal palace, the arsenal, and the chancery house, in which are some rare and valuable manuscripts. In the environs are several interesting places, particularly the spot where Huss suffered, in the suburbs of Bruel.

The navigation of Lake Constance is accomplished by seven or eight steamers, which keep up a communication two or three times a day with the principal places upon its banks. The traffic upon this Lake has received a considerable impetus from the formation of a port at Friedrichshafen and the southern terminus of the Wurtemburg railway; and it is likely to be still further augmented by the completion of the Bavarian railway to Lindau, which is anticipated in the course of next year, 1853, and by which it will be brought into communication with the system of railways in that kingdom, also with those of Northern Germany.

The northern banks of the lake are flat; but the southern side presents a series of picturesque views, having the mountains of Appengell and St. Gall, together with those of the Tyrol, in the back ground.

CONVEYANCES.—Steam-boats on the lake daily. Diligences to all parts of Switzerland.

Fluellen.—HOTEL.—

LA CROIX BLANCHE—primitive and comfortable.

A village at the south end of the Lake of Lucerne. The scenery at this end of the lake, commonly called the Bay of Uri, is the grandest in Switzerland, if not in Europe. Tell's chapel, erected on a piece of rock, where he escaped from the boat in which Gessler had him prisoner, is a conspicuous object on approaching Fluellen. Altorf, where he shot the apple from his son's head, is a few miles from Fluelien, on the St. Gothard route

Pages 222-223 not present in original guide

lenche one of the most imposing in Switzerland. The valley of the Rhone, from Martigny to Villeneuve, through St. Maurice and Bex, is replete with all that can constitute picturesque scenery—the Dent du Midi and the Dent de Morcles, crowned with snow, being conspicuous objects on each side of the valley. Along the valley of the Rhone, from Martigny to Brieg, at the foot of the Simplon Pass, is about sixty-five miles through Sion, Sierre, Leuk, and Visp. These towns have an air of decayed splendour; and the scenery around, from the width of the valley, does not partake of the usual Swiss character.

At Brieg, the ascent of the Simplon begins at once, and is a continued steep to the summit, carried round the edge of precipices, and frequently through tunnels blasted in the rock. Houses of refuge are erected at frequent intervals, to protect travellers from the avalanches in spring. At the village of Simplon, a little beyond the summit, is a rude, but clean and comfortable, inn. The descent from Simplon, through the gorge of Gondo, into Italy, is perhaps unrivalled for sublimity and wildness of scenery, and a triumph of engineering skill. At Isella, the Sardinian custom-house is situated; soon after which, at a sudden turn of the road, the Val d'Ossola bursts upon the astonished gaze of the traveller. The transition from the snows at the summit of the Simplon Pass to the sunny climate of Italy, in the course of a few hours, is truly marvellous.

From Isella, the Sardinian frontier, through the thoroughly Italian town of Domo d'Ossola, to Baveno, on the Lago Maggiore, is nearly forty miles.

The Great St. Bernard, 30 miles from Martigny, is so much visited by travellers for the romantic beauty of its scenery, that we devote a small space to a notice of it. The summit is about 11,000 feet above the sea, and 8,000 feet is the height of the highest pass. The monastery erected here has existed under thirty-four superiors for over nine centuries. The most elevated part of the passage of the Great St. Bernard is a long and narrow valley, whereof the middle is occupied by a lake, at the eastern extremity of which is the Hospice, built on the side of the ancient Roman redoubt of Steleure; and at the opposite side, towards Italy, is the Place de Jupiter—a small plain—wherein once stood a temple dedicated to that deity. The convent was founded in 962 by St. Bernard, since which it has remained unchanged in its rules, and unrivalled in its hospitalities to strangers, who, with their mules or horses, are gratuitously entertained for three days. The bodies of those who have died on the mountains are to be seen in the Morgue in a state free from decomposition. The chain of Alps in which Mount St. Bernard is situated has witnessed four military expeditions, viz., those of Hannibal, Charlemagne, Francis I., and Napoleon. The latter crossed Mount St. Bernard immediately before his descent into the plains of Lombardy, where he fought the battle of Marengo.

Meyringen.—Hotels:—

De Sauvage, or Wild Man.

A thoroughly Swiss village; a central point for many of the most interesting excursions in the Oberland. The only carriage road from it is to Brienz, along the beautiful vale of Meyringen, abounding with waterfalls. A steamer plies daily on the lake of Brienz, from Interlachen, calling at the Giesbach Fall.

From Meyringen the Lake of Lucerne may be reached in one day, over the Pass of the Brunig to Lungern, and thence along the lovely pastoral vale of Sarnen to Beckenried, on the Lake of Lucerne.

The pedestrian will find the route from Meyringen, by the Sheideck, to Grindelwald, one of the finest excursions in Switzerland, passing the Falls of the Reichenbach and the glacier of Rosenlaui.

From Meyringen to the Hospice of the Grimsel is a long and rather arduous day's journey, by the splendid Falls of the Aar, at Handek, where is a good chalêt, where comfortable refreshment may be obtained. From this point, to the summit of the Grimsel Pass, vegetation gradually ceases, and the road is carried along the precipitous rocks for many miles, the river Aar foaming beneath.

The Inn, which was burned last summer, at the Hospice of the Grimsel, 6000 feet above the sea, far removed from any human habitation, was a welcome sight to the wearied traveller in this bleak and sterile region. It was inhabited only in summer, but in the season was a constant resort for travellers, connecting the tour of the Oberland, by the Furca Pass, with the great St. Gothard route to Italy, and the Lake of Lucerne.

Neufchatel.

Neufchatel is a small canton situate among the ridges of the Jura, between the lake to which it gives its name and the borders of France; and is composed of six or seven valleys, the principal of which are the Val Trams, the Val de Sagne, and the Val de Ruz. Neufchatel, the capital, is a well-built and thriving town on the slope of a hill, at the mouth of the Seyon. It contains several remarkable buildings, particularly the Chateau, the ancient residence of the princes of Neufchatel—and the Cathedral, a Gothic building, erected in 1161, adjoining the Chateau.

The chief article of exportation is wine, produced from the neighbouring vineyards; it is much esteemed. There are also printed cottons and linens made here; but the principal article of manufacture are watches. Population about 8,000.

The environs of Neufchatel are worth visiting, especially the Abbaye de la Fontaine André, half a league distant; the Rochet de la Tablette, and the Jardin du Chanal.

Agent for the Sale of J. A. Farina's *Eau de Cologne*—Messrs. Jeanneret and Boreb.

Conveyances.—Diligences to Basle, Bern, Besancon, Chaud-de-fonds, Freiburg, Geneva, Lausanne, Locle, Paris, and Solothurn, see page 257.

Cuchy.—A small village on the Lake of Geneva. The steamers land the passengers here for Lausanne. Omnibuses to and from Lausanne, in connection with the steamers on the lake.

Pfeffers, Baths of—2 and 2½ miles from Ragatz Baths; distance about 50 miles to the Splugen. This is one of the most remarkable spots in Switzerland, the situation having features of the wildest character, and the surrounding country most picturesque. There is also a large convent, built in 1665; as a religious foundation it dates from the eighth century.

Schaffhausen.—HOTEL:—

HOTEL DU KRONE (CROWN)—very clean, moderate charges, and a most obliging host, who speaks English fluently.

Population 9,000, contains little to interest beyond the antique architecture of its houses; three miles from it, however, are the falls of the Rhine, which, from the vast body of water, more than from the height may be ranked with the chief waterfalls of Europe.

CONVEYANCES.—Diligences to Freiburg in the Bresgau, to Bale and to Zurich; steamers to Constance.

Schwytz.—HOTELS.—

HIRSCH (Stag), well spoken of; and ROESSLI'S.

Capital of the Canton. Population 5,225.

CONVEYANCES.—Diligences to Lucern, St. Gallen, Uznach, Zug, Zurich, &c.

Soleure.—HOTEL.—

LA COURONNE—good.

Capital of the Canton. Population 4,500

Splugen.

A village in the canton of the Grisons, near the source of the Rhine, and 4700 feet above the sea. Here the roads from Bellinzona, by the Bernardino Pass, and from Milan and Chiavenna, by the Splugen Pass, unite, and one diligence takes the passengers forward to Coire and Zurich.

At Splugen is one of the best country inns to be found in Switzerland.

The road from Splugen to Coire passes the celebrated defile of the Via Mala, or gorge of the Rhine, where the rocks are 1600 feet above the river.

St. Gall.—HOTELS:—

LE BROCHET—clean and comfortable; LE CHEVAL—also good.

St. Gall is a large canton extending from the Rhine and the Lake of Constance, to the Lakes of Zurich and Wallenstadt, and is divided into eight districts. It has for its capital St. Gallen, or St. Gall, a considerable town, very industrious and commercial, situate upon the Steinach, and containing a population of 11,000 souls. Its edifices and institutions are very well worth the traveller's attention, particularly the Abbey, founded at tho close of the seventh century. St. Gall, an Irishman, who journeyed into Helvetia, became its patron. The libraries and benevolent societies are well worth the tourist's attention. A number of very agreeable excursions may be made in the vicinity of St. Gall, viz.: to the Convent of Nothersack, the Bridge of St. Martin, the Spire, &c.

AGENT for the Sale of J. A. Farina's *Eau de Cologne*—Mr. L. Zolliksfer.

CONVEYANCES.—Diligences daily to most parts of Switzerland.

Thun.—HOTEL:—

HOTEL DE BELLE VUE, well conducted and agreeably situated, with very extensive grounds, and every convenience. English Divine Service is performed every Sunday during the season, in the chapel of this Hotel.

Thun, the chief town of the Oberland, is situate upon the Aao, to the north-west of the Thumner See, and is one of the most picturesque towns in Switzerland, eighteen miles from Berne, with a population of 5,000. It is one of the best points for commencing the tour of the Bernese-oberland. It contains the Military School of the Confederation, and near it are the baths of the Stanbach, which are very much frequented. Its castle and church, with its library, are the only objects of public notice.

CONVEYANCES.—Diligences to Berne three times a day. Return carriages always to be had.

Steam-boat on the Lake to Neuhaus, for Interlachen, twice daily, after arrival of the morning Diligence from Berne, and about noon.

Vevay.

Vevay is the second town of the canton of Vaud, and is situate close to the north shore of the Lake of Geneva. It contains about 5,000 inhabitants. It is beautifully and picturesquely situated at the mouth of the Gorge.

EDIFICES AND INSTITUTIONS.—The Cathedral Church, St. Martin's, built above the town, in the centre of orchards and vineyards. It is a building of the fifteenth century, and is surrounded by a planted terrace, commanding a magnificent view. In this church are buried Edmund Ludlow, the regicide, and Andrew Broughton, who read the sentence of death on Charles the First. These men sought refuge here at the Restoration, and were protected by the Bernese, who then ruled the canton of Vaud, though the English government made very many applications to have them given up. In this church are also monuments to the traveller Matte and J. Martin Couvreu, a liberal benefactor to the town. On Sundays, in summer, divine service is performed there at 1 p.m., and in the Hotel de Ville at 3.30.

The Castle of Chillon, the scene of Byron's "Prisoner of Chillon," is not far from Vevay.

CONVEYANCES.—Diligences daily to Berne, Geneva, and Milan, see page 263. STEAMER daily to Lausanne and Geneva.—Carriages are easily procured here, with two or more horses, to go to Lucerne—with two horses, 120fr.: time about 2½ days, starting early; stopping first night at Freiburg; next day at Berne; arriving at Lucerne about 4 p.m. of the third day.

Winterthur.—Winterthur is a prettily situated town in the canton of Zurich, and is met by the excursionist in his journey from the capital of the canton to Constance. It is seated in a fertile plain on the river Alach, twelve miles E.N.E. of Zurich. It is an industrious and manufacturing town, containing 4,600 inhabitants, who profess Protestantism. There is no object to be met with worth the tourist's attention save the new school, which will repay a visit.

AGENT for the Sale of J. A. Farina's *Eau de Cologne*—Madame Weerli Bidermaunn.

Yverdun.—HOTEL:—

HOTEL DE LONDRES—the best. It is both comfortable and reasonable.

This town is selected as a place of residence, to enable travellers to take excursions to the several picturesque scenes in the environs, from whence some of the finest views may be obtained.

Zug.—HOTEL.—

HIRSCH (the Stag).

The small capital of the smallest canton of the Confederation. It is situated at the east end of the Lake, and contains a population of 3,200. Its chief edifices and institutions are the Cathedral, the Church of the Capuchins, the Town Hall, and the Arsenal. The remarkable church-yard here should be visited by the traveller.

There are few objects of attraction here. The Capuchin convent and nunnery are worth a visit. Some guide-books attribute a picture in the former to Carracci; but it is not his work, but the work of an inferior artist—Fiamingo.

The bone-house attached to the Church of St. Michael, a little way outside the town, should attract a special visit from the traveller. It contains many hundred skulls, each having inscribed upon it the name of its owner, his birth, and death. The churchyard is filled with very nice ornaments. The Cemetery is also well worth a visit, on account of its display of armorial bearings, coats, and crests.

The Lake of Zug is situated partly in the canton of the same name, partly in that of Schuytz. It is four leagues in length by one in breadth, abounding in a species of fish called "rotheli," much prized. The vicinity of the Lake affords a facility for many short and pleasant excursions along its borders. For instance, to the village of Cham, the Castle of Hunenberg, the Convent of Francuthal, the Gubel, the Fenter See, and the battle-field of Morgarten, the most interesting of them all.

During the summer months the steamboat on the Lake of Zug runs three times a day in connection with the omnibuses conveying passengers from the steamboats on the Lake of Zurich, and affords a cheap, quick, and pleasant mode of conveyance for tourists to the foot of the Rigi, the Bernese, Oberland, and Luzerne.

CONVEYANCES.—Diligences daily to Arth (Rigi), at 12½ noon, and to Lucerne at 12 noon and 1.10 p.m., and Zurich at 12½ noon and 12.10 p.m.

Zurich.—HOTELS.—

HOTEL DE L'EPEE, exceedingly good in every respect, well situated, with fine view.

HOTEL BELLE VUE, facing the lake, a first-rate house, good, cheap, and comfortable.

Zurich Canton is a country of great extent, beautiful, and fertile, with a dense population. Zurich or Zurch, the capital, is situate at the northwest end of the beautiful and extensive current gushing from its broad and impetuous stream; containing a population of 16,000 inhabitants. It is built along both banks of the river in a valley hemmed in by mountains. The large town on the right bank extends to the foot of the Zoorechberg and the Sussenberg, and contains a great number of sloping streets; and the same is the case with the little town on the left bank, which is built on the hills of Sinderhoff and St. Peter's.

The Library was founded in 1620, and contains about 40,000 volumes, several rare manuscripts, many Roman antiquities, and a cabinet of 4,000 medals.

AGENT for the Sale of J. A. Farina's *Eau de Cologne*—Mr. J. Finsler, au Meyershof.

OBJECTS OF ATTRACTION.—The Cathedral; Library; Asylum for the Blind; Corn Market; Post Office; Platz Promenade, with Gessner's Monument; the Arsenal, and the Museum.

The Lake of Zurich consists of a great and lesser basin; is ten leagues in length by one and a half in breadth. The tour of the Lake is very delightful, and may be made either by land or water. Perhaps the most agreeable mode of accomplishing it would be to proceed in a carriage to Kapperschwyl, where the two basins unite along the south-western shore, (which is so elevated as to command delightful views, and leads through several very fine villages), to return also by route to Zurich along the north-eastern shore. There is a road leading from Kapperschwyl to Woznach, a little farther than the south-eastern extremity of the lake, in three hours, and another to Zurich in six hours.

CONVEYANCES.—Railway to Dietekon and Baden, see page 119. Diligences to all parts of Switzerland daily. Steamer to Wallenstadt, on the lake, every morning, see Alphabetical List of Steamers, page 139. By this steamer, the travellers for the Righi reach Horgen in an hour; and a diligence takes them to Arth, at the foot of the Righi by 2 o'clock—Total fare, 5 francs. The Righi may be ascended in the same day, the view from the summit; (where there is a very good Hotel,) is one of the sights of Switzerland. The next day, by descending to Weggis, the best views may be obtained, and thence is a steamer to Lucerne.

Roads over the Alps.—Mount Cenis, situated between France and Italy, is traversed by diligences from Lyons, and from Geneva to Turin. The pass is 6,700 feet high, and the road was constructed by Napoleon.

The pass of the Simplon (also by Napoleon) is 6,500 feet high. Diligence from Geneva and Lausanne to Milan. This is, in many respects, the most remarkable road on the Alps.

St. Gothard.—Diligence from Lucerne to Milan. Height 6,800. (See Lucerne.)

Bernardin 7,100 feet; Splugen 6,800 feet—both these passes are traversed by diligences from Coire (Zurich and Constance) to Milan, the road separating at the village of Splugen; the latter pass is the most frequented, and the road was constructed by the Austrians to oppose the Swiss route over the Bernardin. The road from Coire to Splugen passes through the Via Mala, a defile of the utmost grandeur, exceeded by none in Switzerland.

The Stelvio, connecting the Tyrol with Italy, is the highest carriage road in Europe, being 9,700 feet high. It is not, however, much traversed.

The pass of Ampezzo affords the nearest road from Innspruck to Venice. There is not, however, any public conveyance, and the traveller would find the route by Botzen, Trent, and Verona (whence there is a railway to Venice), more convenient, and superior in attractions.

In winter the journey over the chief passes is performed by sledges. Besides these carriage roads, the Pass of the Grand St. Bernard, near Martigny, in the valley of the Rhine, has much traffic over it. It is besides much visited on account of its celebrated monastery or hospital, on the summit of the pass, 8,200 feet high.

ITALY.

Italy consists of two distinct portions—the continental and the insular. The latter includes the three large Islands of Sicily, Sardinia, and Corsica, with the smaller ones of Malta, Gozo, Comino, &c. The continental portion forms a long narrow peninsula, extending from N. W. to S. E., the greatest length of which measures about 695 or 700 miles, from the sources of the River Toza to Cape Cimiti in Calabria, or Cape Lucca in Otranto. The breadth is various; its northerly measurement, from the western border of Savoy to the eastern border of Friuli, being 365 miles; about 275 miles from Mount Genevre to the mouth of the Po, through the middle of Lombardy; 105 miles from the coast of Lucca to the coast of Ravenna; 156 miles from Piombino to Ancona; 98 from the Gulf of Naples to the Gulf of Manfredonia; and only 20 miles in some parts of Calabria and straits. The superficial area, including the Islands, is 122,167 English square miles. The northern border of Italy is formed by the stupendous range of the Alps, extending in a long curve line from the shores of the Mediterranean Sea near Genoa to the head of the Adriatic. The Alps are connected with the Appenines at their extremity, a smaller but still important range, which stretches in an uninterrupted line, parallel to the shores of the Gulf of Genoa, and then through the peninsular part of Italy to the Strait of Messina, dividing the country into two narrow sections of lowland, which run along from the mountains to the adjacent seas. The great Plain of Lombardy lies between the Alps and the Appenines in Northern Italy, and is traversed by the Po, as also watered by innumerable streams which flow down from the adjacent mountains. The length of Lombardy is about 250 miles from east to west, its average breadth being 50 miles. Many narrow but fertile valleys are enclosed by the Appenines in their progress southward.

Italy is divided into nine Sovereign States, in all of which, with the exception of the petty Republic of San Marino, the government is vested in an absolute Monarch, and is everywhere exercised with the most rigorous despotism.

For the **Route** from **London to Italy,** *viâ* **Switzerland,** see London to Basle and Geneva, page 218. At Basle, the traveller may choose between the Simplon, St. Gothard, and Splugen; at Geneva, the *first* is the most convenient.

London to Italy, through France.—The following information will be useful to persons visiting Italy for the *first* time, as furnishing a programme of the most desirable *route.*

A Railway communication being now established between Paris and Chalons, travellers may proceed, by rail and steam, all the way from London to Florence, viz.,—London to Dover or Folkestone, rail; Folkestone to Boulogne, steamboat; Boulogne to Paris and Chalons, rail; steam down the Soane to Lyons, and down the Rhone to Avignon; from thence to Marseilles, by rail; from Marseilles, steamboat to Leghorn, and rail to Florence. Persons preferring a land journey to Italy, instead of taking the boat at Marseilles, should proceed thence by diligence to Toulon, Frejus, Antibes, Nice, and along the coast of the Mediterranean to Genoa and Lucca. This *route* presents a magnificent scenery of wood and water, intersected by very fine roads.

At Lyons, the traveller may proceed by diligence through Chambery, over Mount Cenis, to Turin, from which place he may take the railway to Allesandria, Novi, and Arquato. From Arquato he is taken, by diligence, to Genoa. The views by this road are magnificent. The two finest roads are the Riviere de Ponenbe, or Cornice Pass, from Nice to Genoa; and the Riviere de Levante, from Genoa to Lucca, both of which are daily traversed by good diligences.

MONEY EXCHANGE.

English currency not being understood in Italy, Napoleons and 5-franc pieces are the best coins, as as they are known all over Italy.

Sardinia and Piedmont, Duchy of Parma. Same as France.

Lombardy.—The Lire Austrian or Zwanziger is the current silver coin; 100 Lire Austrian are equal to 87 Francs, consequently a Napoleon is worth about 23 Zwanzigers; 20 Kreutzers or 100 Centesimi, are equal to 1 Austrian Lira or Zwanziger; 3 Zwanzigers equal to 1 Florin; 6 Zwanzigers equal to 1 Cour Thaler. The bills at the hotels are usually made out in French Francs.

Modena.—French, Sardinian, and Parmesan coins are current; the currency of the State, however, is the Lira of 20 Sous, subdivided into 12 Deniers; 100 Liras of Modena are equal to 38½ Francs, less a fraction.

Tuscany.—Theaccounts are kept in various ways; the legal currency is the Lire. 5 Liards are equal to 1 Crazia; 8 Crazias to 1 Paul; and 1½ Pauls to 1 Lire. An English sovereign is worth about 45 Pauls, or 30 Lire; the Napoleon is worth about 36 Pauls, or 24 Lire. The larger silver coins are the Colonata or Spanish Dollar (common throughout Italy) and the Roman Dollar, worth each 10 Pauls; the 5-Franc-piece is equal to 9 Pauls.

Lucca.—Accounts are kept in Lire, Soldi, and Denari. The Lire is equal to 75 Centimes, or 7½d.; 12 Denari equal to 1 Soldo; 20 Soldo equal to 1 Lira.

States of the Church.—The current coin of the country is in Bajocco, Pauls, and Scudo. 5 Quattrini equal to 1 Bajocco; 10 Bajocco equal to 1 Paul; 10 Pauls equal to 1 Scudo. A Napoleon is worth 37 Pauls; a Sovereign about 45 Pauls. At present paper money is universally current in Rome, and you get it at about 16 per cent. discount; by this the traveller obtains a great advantage, as it is taken for its full value at the hotels, &c. The paper money of the republic is at a further discount, the notes for 24 bajocco being current for 16 only, and the larger notes in proportion.

Naples.—The coinage here is in Grana, Carlini, and Ducats. 10 Grana are equal to 1 Carlino; and 10 Carlini equal to 1 Ducat. The Scudo is here worth 12 Carlini.

Luggage.—The Luggage is opened on the Tuscan Frontier; it is advisable to get it plombé, as it saves trouble on entering Florence.

Servants are now charged for in the Bills throughout Italy; in Lombardy, 1 Zwanziger; Tuscany, Paul; Papal States, 2 Pauls; Naples, 2 Carlini.

Waiters.—The Waiter at an Hotel is called "Cameriére," and at a Caffé, "Bottega."

Passports.—See pages 19 to 22.

Frontier, and Custom House.—In the Papal States the Custom House regulations are less severe than in the other *States* of Italy, and a small fee of a couple of Pauls will save the traveller much inconvenience. As books are the particular object of enquiry, caution should be observed in their selection.

DESCRIPTIONS, &c., OF TOWNS.

Ancona is a city and seaport town of the Roman States. It is an episcopal see, and is built in the form of an amphitheatre, on the slope of two hills rising from the shores of the Adriatic, 132 miles north-east of Rome. It is a busy commercial town, in which is erected a citadel. Ancona also possesses a very fine harbour and quay; the former is formed by a pier 2,000 feet in length, 100 in breadth, and 65 above the water, having at its extremity a lighthouse with a revolving light at the end. Its population is about 35,000, a large proportion of which are Jews, Greeks, and Moslems. It is divided into two portions—the Citta Vecchia and the Citia Nuova. The former occupies the highest grounds, and is inhabited by the poorer classes; the latter is situated in the lower slopes, and along the shores of the sea. The city contains some fine buildings, but they are badly arranged. It contains a famous port; it has two moles—one erected by Trajan, and the other by Clement XII. The triumphant arch of Trajan, which has been pronounced the finest marble arch in the world, is worth attention. Within the harbour is the lazaretto, built in the form of a pentagon by Clement XII. in 1732, and completed by Velletellin. Travellers landing at this lazaretto from the Levant or Greece, may shorten their quarantine by going through the *Spoglio*, or Bath, as it is called. The Cathedral, dedicated to St. Cireaco, the first bishop of Ancona, is an edifice of the tenth century, with the exception of the Façade, erected by Marguritone of Arezzo in the thirteenth century. Its architectural and other relics will repay the trouble of an ascent. The Church of St. Francescone, now an hospital; the Church of St. Domenico, containing a crucifixion by Titian; the grave of Rinaldo degli Albozzi, the rival of Cosmo de Medici, who died here in exile in 1425; the Loggia di Mercanta, or Exchange; and the Palazzo del Governe—are the only public buildings worth a visit.

CONVEYANCES.—A diligence leaves Ancona for Rome on Tuesdays at noon, and on Saturdays at 9 p.m.; and for Ferrara and Bologna on Tuesdays at noon, and on Saturdays at midnight.

STEAMERS belonging to the Austrian Lloyd's leave Ancona for Corfu, Patras, Syra, Athens, Smyrna, Constantinople, and Alexandria, on the 2nd and 17th; and return to Trieste on the 18th and 23rd of every month. There is also a steamer twice a month from Ancona to Trieste.

Bologna.—HOTELS.—

La Pension Suisse, St. Marc, and La Pélérin.

BOLOGNA, the capital of the most important Legation of the Holy See, is a city of two miles in length by one in breadth, and is divided into four quarters. It is entered by twelve gates, and contains a population of 71,500 inhabitants. The people of Bologna are remarkable for their intelligence and agreeable manners, as also for the independence of their opinions. The aspect of the town is gloomy and antique; the streets are irregular and narrow, whilst the thoroughfares and arcades are broad and noble. Anciently called Felsina, derived, it is said, from the Etruscan king of that name, it was, in 984 B.C., the capital of the twelve Etruscan cities. It was afterwards called Bononia, from Bono, successor to Felsina, some say from the Boii, who occupied the city in the reign of Tarquinius Priscus Owing to internecine feuds, Bologna was subject alternately to the tyranny of the Popes, of the Visconti, or to popular anarchy. It was afterwards seized on by the family of the Bentivoglio, who were dispossessed by Pope Julius the II., and the supremacy of the Holy See established by force. In 1814, during Napoleon's last struggle, it was occupied by British troops, under General Nugent. The events of 1848 will long continue to make Bologna remarkable. In 270 it was an Episcopal seat, and was afterwards raised, by Gregory XIII., to the dignity of an Archiepiscopal See. It has given six Popes to Rome, and nearly 100 cardinals. The School of Bologna has also given many illustrious names to the arts, among whom is Oderigi di Gublio, immortalised by Dante; it also produced the Caracci and their pupils. The Accademia delle Belle Arte is a noble institution, and well worth a visit.

Bologna is also the seat of a University, founded in 1119 by Wernerus, called "Luvena Juris;" it will well repay a visit, particularly the Cabinet of Natural Philosophy, and the University Library which contains many very valuable and interesting manuscripts.

CHURCHES.—This city contains 100 churches, all remarkable for their noble architecture and magnificent paintings; its piazzas are remarkably beautiful. The environs of Bologna are picturesque and elegant, and the Cemetery worth a visit. The Bolognese dialect is the most puzzling and corrupt, but in both the arts and civilization Bologna stands pre-eminently forward among the first of European cities

CONVEYANCES.—Courier to Mantua and Florence, see page 247.

A DILIGENCE plys twice a week between Rome and Milan, and the journey occupies ninety hours. The Courier is most certain. A procaccio passes twice each week, by the canal Naviglio, between Bologna and Ferrara.

Civita Vecchia.—HOTEL.—

Orlandi's.

The above city is the sea capital of the Papal states, and is the portal through which the generality of travellers enter into Southern Italy: steam navigation has raised it from insignificance to im portance as a seaport. The fine line of steamer plying between Marseilles and Naples regularly touch here, and contribute greatly to its importance and prosperity. Its commercial character possesses some interest, it being the place from whence are shipped the exports of the other "states," a large proportion of which are shipped for England. The above line of steamers, together with the French Government Packets, afford great convenience to parties proceeding to Malta and the Levant, and have brought London and Rome within a journey of ten days, making Civita Vecchia the grand point from which a rapid transit may be made to any part of the Mediterranean. Travellers are not permitted to land here uutil the passports and ship's papers are shown and examined. The traveller on landing is beset with *facchini*, or porters, and should take care to make his arrangements before leaving the vessel Civita Vecchia is remarkable for its port, which is called "Trajani Portus;" It is the capital of the smallest of the Delagation of the Ecclesiastical States, embracing a superficial extent of sixty square leagues, containing a population of 19,600 souls, 6,900 of which live in the town itself. Leo XII. erected it into an Episcopal See in 1825, and created Cardinal Pacca its first Bishop. It is now connected with the diocese of Porto and Sta Rufina. The prisons of Civita Vecchia are very large, and generally filled; they are capable of containing 1,200 persons. In one of them was confined, for eighteen years, the notorious brigand, Gasperoni, and twenty of his followers. He admitted that he committed thirty murders, and that he paid the police 100 scudi per month for information; he has now been dead for eight years. Three miles distant from Civita Vecchia are situated the Bagni di Ferrata mineral springs, called by Pliny "Aqua Tauri." At Tolfa, fifteen miles distant, are the alum works, yielding a considerable revenue to the government. The ancient Etrurian cities can be easily visited from this port. In the Town Hall is a small gallery of Etruscan antiquities, viz., sarcophagi, female heads, &c.

CONVEYANCES.—The Post Diligence conveys you to Rome, leaving Civita Vecchia at 5 a.m., arriving at Rome at 2 o'clock; the fare is 20 pauls. Steamers sail almost daily to and from Naples and Marseilles, and the intermediate ports.

Ferrara is the capital of a delegation of the same name, in the Roman States. This city was once the residence of a court celebrated throughout Europe; but grass now grows on its pavements, whilst its magnificent palaces are deserted, and crumbling into atoms The chief interest of Ferrara arises from its connexion with the House of D'Este, from which the House of Brunswick and the royal family of England trace their direct descent. Ferrara was once famous throughout Christendom for its university, within whose walls so many English students were collected as to form a distinct nation in that learned body.

The School of Ferrara, founded and patronised by the D'Este family, boasts of many illustrious names in all departments of the arts and sciences. It cherished a series of poets, from Ariosto and Bogardo down to our times. Ferrara is also remarkable for the impulse which it gave to the Reformation. It also afforded an asylum to Calvin, to Marsh, to the Duchess of Venice, the noble-minded daughter of Louis XI., and the wife of Ercole!

The public buildings worth visiting are its churches; its castle, formerly the Ducal Palace, now the residence of the Cardinal Legate: its Gallery of Pictures, lately transferred to the "Pinacothua," one of the most beautiful palaces of Ferrara. This gallery contains many excellent paintings worth the traveller's notice, particularly Garafalo, the Agony in the Garden; the Nativity, by Bastiamno; Dosso Dosse, Noah's Ark, and the Fall of Macina, by Agostine Caracco.

The Palazzo del Magistrato, in a hall of which is the Ariostean Academy, the *studio publico*, or Schools of Medicine and Jurisprudence, containing a rich cabinet of Medals, and a collection of Grecian and Roman inscriptions and antiquities; amongst which is the celebrated Sarcophagus of Aurelia. Eutychia, wife of P. Rubens. Its chief interest is the public library, containing 80,000 volumes, and 900 M.S., among which are the Greek Palempsists of Gregory, Nazeander, St. Chrysostom: together with the manuscript of Ariosto and Tasso; together with the former's arm-chair of walnut wood, the beautifully executed medal bearing his profile, which was found in his tomb, and his bronze inkstand, and the Piazza d' Aristir. The most interesting object in Ferrara is the Cell—the hospital of St. Anna, shown as the Prison of Tasso. It is below the ground floor, and lighted by a grater window from the yard. On the walls of Tasso's prison are the names of Lord Byron, Lamartine, &c. The theatre and Citadel are also worth attention.

Florence.—HOTELS.—

GRAND HOTEL DES ISLES BRITANNIQUE, in a fine situation commanding a pleasant view of the Arno, deservedly recommended.

GRAND HOTEL DE NEW YORK, an excellent first-rate house, with a delightful view of the Arno.

HOTEL DU NORD, a clean and very comfortable house, the landlord was formerly cook to Jerome Bonaparte. An excellent Table d'Hote—servie à la Français.

The journey from Florence to Rome can be made by Siena in 23½ posts, or by diligence, which performs the journey in 36 hours. The courier's carriage is still more expeditious, but the vetturini require five or six days. Post horses accomplish the journey in four days, giving plenty time to visit Siena, and making Radicofani and Viterbo the sleeping places between Rome and Siena.

Florence is the capital of Tuscany; contains a population of 106,899 souls, and is remarkable for the beauty of its site and position. The picturesque grandeur of its buildings, its wooded plains, sloping hills, and majestic mountains, can be seen to great advantage from the Boboli ground from the Church of St. Mariato, and from the Bello Sguardo, a villa once the abode of Gallileo. In general, the streets are narrow; its palaces are noble in their architectural beauty, grand design, and exquisite execution.

Modern Florence is built like a pentagon. It contains a very fine cathedral, called Santa Maria del Fiore. It was commenced in 1298 by Arnolfo di Lasso, whose design may be seen in Muro's fresco, on the east wall of the chapter house of Santa Maria Novella. The walls of the cathedral are almost entirely cased with marble. It is 454 feet long and 387 feet high; the transept is nearly 334 feet long, the height of the nave 152 feet, and that of the side aisles 96½ feet. Many architects of great talent were employed in carrying out the erection, among whom were Giotto, Taddeo, Gaddi, Andrea Orgagna, Filippo di Lorrenzo, and Brunelleschi, to whom its completion was entrusted. In 1558 it was destroyed by the Provedotore Benedetto Ungucionio, who so defaced it, that not a slab or a column was left entire; and the traveller may now see Giotto's façade, in the back ground of a lunetto in the outer cloister of St. Marco. The re-building was commenced in 1420, and entrusted to Brunelleschi, who, before his death, in 1446, saw the cupola all but finished. This cupola is octagonal in the plan, and is 138 feet 6 inches; this served as a model for Michael Angelo, for St. Peter's. The best view of it is obtained from the south-east; and the traveller should go up the dome rather than up the campanile, as a better view can be obtained by his doing so. Over the first door on the north side there are statues attributed to Jacopo della Quirini; and over the second is an "Assumption," by Nani d'Anton di Banca, called La Mandola; on the Donatello are the two small statues by Alessandro Benedetto; and in the lunetto is an "Annunciation," by Don Ghulando; on the south side, the Madonna over the door is attributable to Niccolo Arietino, and that over the other door to Gio Pisano.

The small dimensions of the windows, and the rich colours of the glass, cause the interior to look sombre and gloomy. The arches, though pointed, are not truly gothic. The pavement is tessalated with red blue and white marble. The stained glass is said to have been executed by a Florentine artist, Domenico Lisi di Gambrasin, in 1434. Above the side door in the west, to the north of the principal entrance, is the monumental fresco painting of Sir John Hawkwood. The tomb of Balthasar Cossa (John XXIII., 1419) is in this Cathedral, and deserves notice. The White Marble Tabernacle, constructed for holding the miracle-working picture by Orgagna, and surmounted by the statue of St. Michael, is worth the traveller's inspection.

The church of Santa Croce, belonging to the Black Friars, will repay a visit—it is called the "Westminster Abbey" of Florence. The principal other churches worth visiting, are Santa Maria Novella, San Lorenzo, which contains the Laurentian Library, designed by Michael Angelo; the church of San Marco, the Annunciation, and Santo Sparto. The Florentine Palaces will also be interesting to the traveller, among which is the Palazzo Bicchio. In this city are two markets, the Mercato Vecchio, and the Mercato Nuovo, these stand in the very centre of the Primo Cerchio. Among the public buildings are, Casa Bounarotti, in the Viâ Ghibellina, the house of Michael Angelo, one of the most interesting objects in Florence. It is still inhabited by his descendants; and not only is the internal arrangement preserved, but a large portion of the furniture occupies its original position, the Cas Martelli, &c. The Galleria Imperialée Reale is open to the public every day, except Sundays and holidays, between the hours of 9 a.m. and 3 p.m.: in its vestibules and galleries is the richest and most celebrated collection in the world. On the second floor, is the Magliabechian Library, of which Bosari was the architect: it is so called from its founder, Antonio Magliabec. This library, also called the Pitti Library, contains 80,000 volumes, besides 1,500 manuscripts, including one of Tasso, several of Machiavelli, and of Gallileo. The Laurentian Library contains 3,000 manuscripts, including the Panvacts, a manuscript of Virgil, two of Tautus, one of Plutarch, the Decarneson, and several by Dante. The Ricardi Library contains 23,000 volumes and 3,500 manuscripts. The Marnulli contains 45,000 volumes.

Among the places worth a visit in the environs of Florence, are Porta Alla Croce, Toggis Imperiale La Certosa, in Val d'emo, and the Sanctuaries of Valambrosa, which are 18½ English miles from Florence.

Post Office.—A letter from Florence to London takes seven days in transmission.

Divine Service is performed twice each Sunday, by the Rev. G. Robins, in the new English Church, situated in Vel Maglio, behind San Marco.

A Swiss church is opened next the Casa Schneiderf, on the Lung Arno, where a morning service in French, and an evening service in English, are gone through each Sunday, after the Presbyterian form.

British Ambassador — Right Honourable Sir Henry Lytton Bulwer, G.C.B., &c. &c.

English Physician.—Dr. Wilson, licentiate of the Royal Colleges of Physicians of Surgeons of London and Gottingen, late physician to a metropolitan hospital, and Physician to the British Legation at Florence, No. 4190, Via Tornabuoni, over the English Chemist.

English Apothecary—Mr. H. Robert, opposite the Palazzo Corsi, Via Tornabuoni, No. 4190, Pharmacy of the British Legation.

Bank and Exchange and English Warehouse. —Mr. J. H. Brown, No. 4203, Via Rondinelli, gives the best exchange; and his establishment will be found deserving our highest recommendation.

Stationer, Printseller, and Depot for Guide-Books, Maps, &c.—Edward Goodban, No. 4183, Via Legnaioli, opposite the Café Doney, has an excellent stock of the above articles. Depôt for Bradshaw's Guide, &c.

English Tailor and Hosier —T. Haskard, from London, Lungo Arno No. 1184, can be recommended as the best tailor in Florence.

Conveyances.—Railroad to Leghorn and to Siena, on the road to Rome, three or four times a day, see page 121; diligences to Rome several times a week, and to Genoa. The Couriers leave Florence with passengers, Tuesday, Thursday, and Saturday, for Bologna and Mantua, for Rome, Pisa, and Genoa. Steamers almost daily at Leghorn to Genoa and Marseilles, Civitta Vecchia, and Naples.

Genoa.—HOTELS.—

HOTEL DE LA VILLE—a good and comfortable house.

HOTEL DE LA CROIX DE MALTE—an excellent first-rate house, deservedly recommended.

HOTEL ROYAL—very good, and highly spoken of.

HOTEL FEDER—a first-rate house and highly recommended. The proprietor keeps a house of the same name at Turin.

These Hotels are facing the port, with a beautiful southern aspect, commanding a magnificent view of the sea.

GENOA, called "La Superba," is the chief port of the Sardinian states, containig a population of 144,000.

The Genoese are industrious and robust, and use a dialect unintelligible to a stranger. The women are, in general, elegant and nicely dressed. Genoa is like Bath, very up and down. It is remarkable for its palaces, and looks like a city of kings. The Palazzo Doria Tursi, in the Strada Nuova, late residence of the Queen Dowager, and afterwards the Jesuits College; the Palazzo Leïra, the Palazzo Spinola, and the Palazzo Palavacino, No. 327, Strado Carlo, attract attention. It is called Palavacino, or "Strip my neighbour," from the family name. The Cathedral of St. Lorenzo is a noble pile, and was built in the eleventh century. The columns of its portals were taken from Almeria as part of the spoils won at the capture of the city. The curious pilasters of the door on the north side of the church, are worth attention. The richest portion of the church is the chapel of St. John the Baptist, into which no female is permitted to enter except on one day of the week, an exclusion imposed by Pope Innocent the 8th. The best of the churches worth visiting are the Cathedral, St. Annunerata, and St. Maria Carignano. From the summit of the latter there is a good view of the town, port, and of the sea. The Academia Lefrestica delle Belle Arte is worth a visit. It is situated in the Piazzo Carlo Felice, close to the theatre. Genoa, and the numerous beautiful villas covering the hills about it, are seen to the greatest advantage from the entrance to the harbour. The climate is one of the worst in Italy.

FILIGREE WORK IN SILVER.—The manufactory of this celebrated article, so much admired at the Great Exhibition, at the Hotel de la Croix de Malte, can be seen without visiters being expected to purchase.

ENGLISH CONSUL, L. G. Brown, Esq.

THE BRITISH CONSULATE OFFICE is situated opposite the Theatre di Carlo Felice.

BANKERS, Messrs. Gibbs.

PHYSICIAN, Dr. A. Millingen, 664, Strada Carlo, Alberto; S. Tomaso, 3, Piano.

VETTURINI are plenty and good, and ply in the Piazza della, in Pazo.

POST OFFICE is situate in the Piazzo del Fontane. Letters arrive daily, and are distributed at 9 a.m. Boxes close for English letters, &c., at 2 p.m.

ENGLISH CHURCH.—The Rev. Mr. Strattle officiates at the English church, where service is regularly gone through on Sundays.

CONVEYANCES.—Carriages leave Genoa to meet the train at Arquata, for Turin. See table page 118.

STEAMERS ply between Genoa and Leghorn, Civita Vecchia, Naples, Messina, Palermo, Malta, and Marseilles. Days and hours of sailing announced by posting-bills.

Leghorn.—HOTEL—

HOTEL DES ISLES BRITANNIQUE, a good house, situated in the Grand Rue; the landlord is attentive and obliging.

HOTEL DES DEUX PRINCES, on the Piazzi dei Grand-Duchi, an excellent, well-conducted, good house, strongly recommended.

HOTEL DE L'AIGLE NOIR, beautifully situated, and a first-rate house.

Leghorn is the commercial capital of Tuscany, and one of the most improving towns on the Continent of Europe. It is a free port, and the great emporium of the foreign goods and manufactures required for the consumption of the Grand Duchy. The squares are spacious, the streets regular, well paved, and lighted with gas, with wide and convenient foot-paths on either side. The air is pure and salubrious, the heat of summer and the winter cold being tempered by the sea breeze. Leghorn is the favourite resort of the rank and fashion of Rome, Florence, Bologna, Sienna, &c. in the summer season, the influx of strangers frequently amounting to 20,000 persons. The Strada Ferrata Leopolda, or Leopolda Railway affords the greatest facility for visiting Pisa, Lucca, Florence, Sienna, &c., see our railway table. The Government are now at a great expense, enlarging the port to accomodate the increasing trade of the place; and to those unacquainted with the same, it would be difficult to convey an adequate idea of the enjoyment of a sail at sunset under an Italian sky among vessels gay with the flags of almost every nation of the Globe.

Travellers will do well to provide themselves here with whatever specie they are likely to require. The foreign goods for the supply of all Tuscany and the Papal States are imported and paid for by Leghorn, consequently a much better exchange will be obtained on circular notes, letters of credit, &c., than at Florence, Rome, or other inland towns which have no direct trade with England, France, or the United States, nor any occasion to make remittances to those countries.

ENGLISH CONSULS.—Alexander Macbean, Esq., Via Borra.

AMERICAN CONSULS.—Joseph A. Binda, Esq., Via Goldoni.

BANKERS.—Messrs. Maquay, Pakenham, and Smyth. Offices.—7 and 8, Via Borra; correspondents of the Uuion and Oriential Banks, and of the principal Bankers of London; also of Messrs. George Peabody & Co., and other American Bankers in London; and Messrs. Duncan, Sherman & Co., of New York, &c.

ENGLISH WAREHOUSE.—H. Dunn, No. 11, Via Grande. Travellers are recommended to purchase every thing they require here, as the articles can be had 20 per cent cheaper than at any town in the interior.

CONVEYANCES.—Railroad to Pisa Pontedera and Florence, see page 121. Steamers almost daily, during the season, to Civita Vecchia, Naples, and Sicily, Genoa, Nice, and Marseilles; the French government mail steamers arrive from Marseilles on the 1st, 11th, and 21st; they arrive from

Naples and Civita Vecchia on the 6th, 16th, and 26th of every month.

Mantua is a city of Austrian Italy, and the capital of a province of the same name. It is located on an island in the middle of a lake 20 miles in circumference, and two in breadth, and possesses one of the strongest fortresses in Europe. The streets are regular and spacious. The cathedral is a noble building, and contains some celebrated paintings, by celebrated masters. In the Church of St. Frances are some very interesting relics, which the piety or superstition of the people connected with miraculous cures, &c. A village near this city, called Mantua, was the birth-place of Virgil, and the cradle of his infancy.

Milan.—Hotel—

Grande Albergo Reale, a first-rate house, and strongly recommended.

Hotel de Grande Bretagne, a remarkably good house, gives general satisfaction.

Grand Hotel St. Marc, an old established good house.

Milan, founded by the Insubrian Gauls, is the chief city of Lombardy, and contains a population of 175,000 souls. It was sacked by Attila, A.D. 452, but its destruction was not effected until its surrender to Frederick I., 1162. The city was restored in 1167. Its restoration was effected by the combined forces of Cremona, Brescia, Bergamo, Mantua, and Verona. Milan fell again in 1535, under the power of Charles the Fifth, who fixed the succession of the Duchy in his nephew. The Utrechtian Treaty of 1713 handed Milan over to Austria. The city has ten gates, all identified with some traditionary recollection, and remarkable for their massive proportions and architectural designs. The Decomo, called by St. Ambrose in his letter to Sister Marcellina, "The great new Basilica," will repay a visit. The different churches are likewise equally worth attention; among the foremost are the churches of the Porta Orientale, Porta Kosnana, of the Porta Tiernesse, &c, The Ospedale Maggiore is a grand establishment for the sick. It was founded by Francesco Sforza in 1456. Milan is celebrated for its theatres, the principal of which is La Scala, opened at the close of 1779. It has greatly fallen off since 1840, the Milanese nobility having ceased to visit it. The climate in winter is cold and damp. The traveller will find the drive from Milan to the Lakes of Como, Maggiore, Garda, and Lacco, very pleasant and agreeable, the country along being beautifully fertile, and embellished with neat villas. There is a railway from Milan to Como.

English Bankers, Carli di Tommaso and Co., and Ulrich L'Brot.

English Chemist and Apothecary—Mr. C. Riva, Palazzi, near the Theatre, La Scala Milan. N.B.—At this address every English and foreign medicine may be obtained, and Prescriptions are most accurately prepared.

Conveyances.—Railway to Monza and Como, also to Treviglio, (18½ miles) see page 19. Diligences, see page 256.

Naples.—Hotels: —

Hotel de Russie, an excellent Hotel.

Hotel de New York, on the Quay, commanding a beautiful view of the bay and of Mount Vesuvius. It is a very comfortable hotel, and has a capital reading-room.

Naples is the chief city of the Two Sicilies, with a population of more than 360,000 souls, and has a south eastern aspect. There are five principal entrances; that by the Bridge de la Madeline, near the sea, is the most striking. Most of the houses are lofty and the streets narrow; but, with the exception of the Largo del Castello, in which are the palace and theatre of St. Carlos, and of the open space in front of the Church St. Giovanni Paluo, there are no spacious squares or places. The number of churches at Naples is small, and those best worth a visit are the St. Giovanni and Paulo, the Santa Maria Maggiore, and the San Martino, the latter of which is extremely rich in paintings and precious marbles. The interior of the royal palace may be viewed by special permission, for which one or two dollars must be paid. The Museo Borbonico will repay a good many visits, it possessing, besides a picture gallery, the fresco paintings, mosaics, gold and silver ornaments, Etruscan vases, &c., discovered in the excavations of Pompeii and Herculaneum. The Albergo dei Toveri is also a fine establishment for paupers and orphans. The Royal Library is annexed to the Borbonico Museum, and contains 250,000 volumes, besides more than 1700 papyri, found in Herculaneum. The Brancacciana Library contains 50,000 volumes. Naples also possesses an institution called the Monte de Misericordia, founded in the year 1500. It affords fixed relief to the poor, pays the debts of deserving individuals, if not exceeding 100 ducats, and sends patients to the baths of Ischia. The environs of Naples cannot be surpassed for scenic beauty and delightful reminiscences. They are painted over Virgil's tomb, in the stupendous grotto of Pausilipo, and in the ruins of Possnoli. Lake Avernus, the classic shores of Baiæ and Misenium, the islands of Ischia, Procida, and Capri, the coast to Castellamare, the orange groves of Sorrento, the fields of lava, and the streets of Pompeii, all afford to the traveller food for the most pleasing study and recollection.

The ruins of Pæstum may be visited in a day and a quarter, leaving by the railroad for Nocera at 5 p.m. (one hour), then takingacarriage to Salerno, sleeping there, and starting next morning in a carriage, reach Pæstum at 9, remain three hours, and return by same carriage to Nocera, in time for the 7½ o'clock train to Naples. A most interesting excursion, the three temples being in a very fine state of preservation; they are supposed to be 4000 years old. Another delightful excursion is by railway to Castellamare (one hour), and from thence to Sorrento by carriage along the side of the bay (1¾ hours;) one of the most beautiful rides in the world

The 8th of September (the Nativity of the Virgin) is the greatest festival in the year, and travellers should make a point of being in Naples on that day, if they can conveniently do so.

Travellers are cautioned against the depreciated copper coinage at Naples; it is only worth about half of what is marked on it.

British Ambassador, The Honourable Wm. Temple.

English Consul, Captain Gallway, R.N.

English Physicians, Drs. Strange, Roskelley, and Jackson.

English Chemist and Apothecary.—Mr. Jos. Kernot, opposite the St. Carlo Theatre.

Bankers, Rothschild and Co., J. W. Furze and Co., J. W. Turner & Co., W. Iggulden, &c.

English Ship Brokers and Shipping Agents for England, G. Caracciolo and A. Delucca, Vico 3, Piliero No. 5.

Reading Room and Library on the Chiaja, kept by Mrs Dovant.

Conveyances.— Railway to Pompeii, Nocera, Castellamare, Caserta, Capua and Nola, see page 121. Steam—see alphabetical list of Steamers, page 135.

Nice.—

In the duchy of Piedmont, situated at the foot of Mount Montalbano, with a fortified fort, and about 35,000 inhabitants, engaged in the preparation of tobacco, silk, thread, perfumery, &c. The old town has few attractions, being dark and dirty; but the new portion is finely built. The town and environs are highly celebrated for a pure healthy air, and great mildness of climate, even in the middle of winter; accounted for by the situation of the neighbouring mountains, which are connected with the Alps, and protect the country from storms. The commerce of the town is considerable, consisting in oil and spun silk.

For details see Mr Edwin Lee's book.—" Nice et son climat avec des notices sur le Littoral de la Mediterranée de Marseille à Gênes."—Just published. Nice, Visconte: Paris, Galignani: London, Bailliere, Regent Street.

British Consul and Banker, A. Lacioix, Esq.

English Physician, (established since 1841), N. A. Travis, M.D., (Edinburgh,) Fellow of the Royal College of Physicians.

English Church, — Chaplain, Rev. Charles Childers, M. A. Service at 11 a m. and 3 p.m. on Sundays, and at 11 a.m. on Wednesdays.

Surgeon Accoucheur, Dr. Gurney.

Steamers to Marseilles and Genoa twice a week, in 12 hours; fares, 31 frs. and 21 frs.

Padua.—Hotels—

Hotel de la Croix d'Or and Aquila doro.

Padua is a fine old city, containing about 51,000 inhabitants. It followed the fortunes of Venice, and is now, like Venice, part of the Lombardo-Venetian Kingdom. Its Palace of Justice and Cathedral possessing one of the most beautiful sanctuaries in existence, together with its University. Every part of the town is well worth seeing. The Café Peddrochi is the finest building of the kind in Italy.

Conveyances.—Railroad to Vicenza, Verona, and Venice. Royal diligence to Genoa daily.

Pisa (Tuscany).—Hotels—

Hotel de la Grande Bretagne.—a first-rate, capital house.

One of the most ancient and beautiful cities of Italy. situated in a fertile plain, about eight miles from the entrance of the Arno into the sea. The celebrated leaning tower, built in the twelfth century, a cathedral of the eleventh century, and numerous other ancient ecclesiastical buildings, will arrest the attention and awaken the admiration of every traveller. Van Lint, the best alabaster worker in Europe, lives here.

English Church.—During the six winter months service is performed twice each day—Chaplain, Rev. H. C. Woodward.

English Physician—Dr. Gason.

English Warehouse—J. Cordon.

Conveyances.—Railroad to Lucca and Piscia, see page 122.

Rome.—Hotels—

Hotel d'Allemagne, a first-rate house; and highly recommended, commanding a fine view over the Piazza d'Espagne.

Rome, the capital of the "Ecclesiastical States," the seat of the Popes, and once the citadel of the Cæsars, is situate on the banks of the Tiber, partly on a plain, and partly on low hills, with their intersecting valleys, about sixteen miles from the mouth of the river. The Tiber divides the city into two unequal parts. The smaller on the right bank is called the Leonine city and Trastevere. Walls of 15 miles in circuit surround the entire city. The modern city is built upon the Campus Martius of the ancient Romans, lying along the banks of the Tiber, to the north of the seven hills which formed the site of ancient Rome. Four of these hills, once the scene of so many exciting events, are now almost entirely deserted, or covered by gardens, vineyards, broken buildings, or ruins. The streets, though spacious, are winding and badly kept. Rome is entered by the Porta del Popolo, built by Vignola, from designs by Michael Angelo, in 1561. The gate opens upon the spacious Piazza del Popolo, a rather broken area at the foot of Monte Pincio. In the centre stands the fine obelisk of Rhamses I. The inns of Rome are generally situated within the triangular space lying between the Porta del Popolo, the Piazza di Spagna, the Via Conditti, and the Corso. The charges are generally for dinner, from 7 to 10 pauls; breakfast, 5 pauls; tea, 3 pauls. A bedroom generally costs from 2 to 5 pauls per diem. A suite of apartments, from 20 to 50 pauls per day. Lodgings in private houses are very easily obtained, and at reasonable prices. The best situations are the Piazza di Spagna, the Via Babunio, the Corso, and the intervening streets.

The churches in Rome form the greatest object

of attraction for the traveller, and claim his first attention. They are 364 in number, seven of which are called Basilicœ. or Cathedrals; the principal ones are as follows:—St. Peter's, St. John Lateran, Santa Maria, Maggiore, and Santa Croce, in Geraeselomme, within the city; and St. Paulo, San Lorenzo, and San Sebastian, *extra muros*. St. Peter's stands on a slight acclivity, in the Leonine city, in the north-western corner of Rome. It is built in the form of a Latin cross, the nave being 607 feet long and the transept 444 feet. The east front is 396 feet wide and 160 feet high, whilst the pillars composing it are each 88 feet high and 8¼ in diameter. The height of the dome, from the pavement to the top of the cross, is 448 feet. In front of the church there is a large piazza. The church occupies the place of Nero's Circus, and is erected on the spot where St. Peter was martyred. It occupied a period of 176 years in building, and required 350 years to perfect it. It cost £10.000,000; it covers eight English acres, and is kept in repair at a cost of £6,300 per annum.

The English traveller cannot fail to be interested by a visit to the Chapel of the Presentazione, in which is the tomb of Maria Clementina Sobieski, wife of the Pretender, James III.; she died at Rome in 1745. Opposite to this is Canova's celebrated "Monument of the Stuarts." The expense of this monument was defrayed by George IV.

San Giovani, in Laterano, St. John Lateran, is the Pope's church, he being its official minister. It is in this church, also, that the Popes are crowned. It contains the famous chapel of the Corsini, reckoned the finest in the world. and stated to have cost £400,000. The Latern Palace and Museum should be visited.

The other basilicas and churches are equally interesting to the traveller.

The palaces rank next in the order of merit, but cannot here receive any but a very short notice.

The Vatican stands prominent among the palaces of the world, as invested with the greatest interest, whether we regard its identification with all eclesiastical history. or the influence it exercised over christendom for 400 years. Its existence dates from the eighth century; being dilapidated, it was rebuilt by Innocent III. in the twelfth century. It is the winter palace of the Pope, and stands over the Vatican hill, near to St. Peters. It covers a large space, and is 1,151 English feet long, and 767 feet broad. It contains 4,422 chambers, and has eight grand staircases and two hundred smaller ones, and twenty courts In it are the Pioclimentine and Chiaramonti Museums, both filled with the masterpieces of modern art. Here are also the Cupollor Sistina, or Sistine Chapel, built in 1473, and the Vatican Library, containing the richest collection of manuscripts and pictures in the world.

The Quirinal, or the Palace of Monte Carollo. built on the Quirinal hill, is the Pope's summer residenc, and will repay a visit.

The Capitol now occupies the square of the Capitoline hill, under the name of the Piazza del Campe Doglio. It occupies the site of the ancient Capitol, and contains the palaces of the Senator and Municipal Magistrates of Rome. The Collegio della Lapunza, a university of Rome, founded by Innocent IV. in 1244, is one of the oldest in Europe. The Roman College, and the College de Propagande Fide, are likewise worth visiting.

The English Burial Ground is situated near the Porto San Paulo, adjoining the Pyramid of Caius Cestus. Among the Britsh buried here are the poets Shelley and Keats, Wyatt the sculptor, and Bell the celebrated anatomist. The climate of Rome is mild and soft, but rather relaxing and oppressive. The vilas of Rome are very elegant, and its environs worth visiting.

English Consul—Mr. Freeborn.

Physician.—Dr. Smyth, M.D.M.R.C.S., Licentiate Accoucheur, 9, Piazza di Spagna.

English Apothecary.—Balestro Borioni, 98, Via del Babaino, Piazza d'Espagne.

English Dentist.—Mr. Kemble, 17, Trinita di Monti.

English and American Bankers.—Packenham, Hooker, and Co., 20, Piazza d 'Espagne, gives the highest exchange on letters of credit, circular notes, &c., whether addressed to them or not, in correspondence with Messrs. Maquay and Pakenham, Florence.

House and Commission Agent.—J. P. Shea's House and Commission Agency Offices, 14 and 15, Piazza di Spagne, a useful and necessary establishment, where persons requiring large or small furnished apartments can, at a fixed and moderate charge, obtain correct information and efficient assistance, thus avoiding doubtful services of ambulant agents or self-interested advisers

English Reading Rooms, Monaldine, in the Piazza di Spagna, supplied with London Daily Papers, Galignani, a small English Library of Books, Maps of Rome, &c.

English Club is held at No. 11, Via Condotti.

Hackney Carriages may be hired by the hour or day. The principal stands are the Piazza di Spagna, Monte Citorio, the Corso, and the Piazza of St. Peter's. The charges are 4 pauls per hour 3 pauls for the second hour, 10 pauls for four hours, and 3 scudi for the day.

Post Office.—If possible, have letters addressed to the care of some banker, or to some respectable hotel, rather than to the *Poste Restante*. Letters for England take eleven days in transmission.

English Church.—Divine service is solemnized each Sunday, at the hours of 11 a.m. and 3 p.m., from the first Sunday of October to the end of June. The church is a large granary outside the city.

The population of Rome numbers about 180,000, the Jews excepted, who number about 8000.

Conveyances.—There are no railroads yet in the States of the Church; several are projected. Travellers proceeding southward to Naples have the choice of two diligences, one taking the route inland by Ceprano, the other by the Pontine Marshes, Terracina, and the coast. The courier has a roomy carriage, and also takes passengers; at the frontier he transfers the travellers to the Neapolitan courier, whose carriage is neither clean nor comfortable. The traveller's best plan is to proceed to Civita Vecchia, a journey of 6 hours by diligence, and there avail himself of the almost daily steam communication with Naples. *Departure of Couriers carrying Passengers:*—Monday, Tuesday, Wednesday, and Friday, at 3 p.m., Saturday, at 5 p.m. to Naples, Bologna, and Florence. To Naples, 30 hours, fare 16 scudi; Florence, 36 hours, 18.50 scudi; Bologna, 52 hours, 22 scudi; with ½ paul additional per cost for the postillion. *Diligence* to Naples by Ceprano, Monday, Wednesday, and Friday, at 8 a.m., in 36 hours; fare 10¾ scudi; by Terracina, Tuesday, Thursday, and Saturday, at 11 a.m. in 30 hours; fare 11¼ scudi. To Florence Tuesday and Saturday, at 11 a.m, by Sienna, in 36 hours; fare 14¼ scudi. To Civita Vecchia, Monday, Wednesday, and Friday, at 4 a.m., in 8 hours; fare 2 scudi. Monday, Tuesday, Thursday, Friday, and Saturday, at 8 p.m., in 8 hours; fare 2½ scudi.

Tivoli is situated in the Campagna di Roma, 18 miles from Rome, in a delightful situation. It is the seat of several remarkable antiquities, as the remains of the temple of Vesta is of the sybil, the villa of Macenas, the villa of the Emperor Adrian. The Teverone formed a picturesque cascade at Tivoli. but this has recently been destroyed, by diverting the river into a new channel.

Turin.—HOTEL.—

HOTEL DE LONDRES, good and comfortable.

HOTEL FEDER—a first-rate house, and highly recommended. The proprietor has a house of the same name in Genoa.

Turin is the capital of Piedmont, and contains a population of 125,000 inhabitants. It is situated on the left bank of the Po, near its confluence with the Dora Riparia. It contains about 110 churches and chapels, all of which are remarkable for their architecture and for the splendour of their ornaments. It is an Archiepiscopal see, and the seat of the Piedmotese Senate. The University, the Military Academy, the Royal Academy of Sciences, the Academy of Arts, the superb Museum of Egyptian Antiquities, and the Hydraulic Building, with many others, are well worth a visit. The walks around Turin are remarkably beautiful, and in its delightful neighbourhood rises the chain of heights called Collina, on which are built superb and picturesque villas. Several small but elegant towns surrounds Turin, within a radius of a few miles, all of which possess objects of interest, such as the Royal Palace at Stupianigi, one of the finest summer residences in Europe; the Veterinary School at Venerria Reale; the magnificent church at La Supergo, five miles from Turin, containing the masoleum of the Royal Family; Agri, Rivoli, and Moncaliere, with their royal palaces and chateaux, are worth visiting.

The Post Office, situated in the Palazzo Cangnano, is shut on Sundays and holydays. The latest hour for posting English letters is 3 p.m., and on Saturday all letters requiring to be franked must be posted before 6 p.m., and all others before 10 p.m.

There are no regular fiacres; but carriages ply for hire in the Piazza Castello, and answer as well as the expensive carriages of the hotels.

BRITISH AMBASSADOR—Mr. Hudson.

ENGLISH DENTIST.—Mr. Kemble, dentist to the Queen, Hotel Feder.

CONVEYANCES.—Railway from Turin to Novi and Arquata, see page 118. The Sardinian couriers have clean, well-appointed, and fast carriages, and leave Turin every afternoon for the following places:—Geneva; by the Mont Cenis, in 36 hrs., fare 80fr.; Lyons in 36 hours, fare 80fr.; Genoa, fare 40fr.; Nice, fare 39fr. 50c; Milan, fare 27fr. Diligences of Bonafous Fières, daily, for Geneva and Lyons, over Mont Cenis; Genoa, Milan, Venice, Modena, Bologna, Ancona, and Rome. Fares, to Genoa, 30fr. 25c.; to Milan 18fr. 16c.; to Venice. 47fr. 45c.; to Chambery, 50fr. 47c.; to Geneva, 65fr. 59c.

Venice.—HOTELS.—

GRAND HOTEL DE L'EUROPE, a capital house, highly recommended, good table d'hote.

Venice, one of the capitals of the Lombardo-Venetian kingdom, is built on a cluster of islands in the midst of a salt lagune, or shallow lake, and contains a population of 106,000 souls. It is divided into two unequal parts by the Canalazzo, or Grand Canal, the course of which through the city follows the form of an inverted S; is 30 feet wide, and crossed near the middle of its course by the Ponte di Rialto, a splendid marble structure of one spacious arch. In the midst of her labyrinth of canals and streets there are several large piazzas, nearly all of which are adorned with fine churches or palaces. The principal of these is the Piazza di San Marco, a large oblong area 562 feet by 232, surrounded by elegant buildings, and containing at its eastern extremity the metropolitan church of San Marco, a singular but brilliant combination of the Gothic and the Oriental style of architecture.

In the Piazza is also a lofty square tower 316 feet high, and 42 feet square, with a pyramidal top, to which top ascent is made by an inclined plane. Adjoining that church is the ancient palace of the Doge, the prisons, and other public offices of the late Venetian Republic. San Marco was erected into a cathedral in the year 1817, when the patriarchal seat was removed to it from San Pietro. It was founded in the year 828 by the Doge Guistiniano Participazio for the purpose of receiving the relics of St. Marc, which had just then been translated from Alexandria by Bono the Tribune of Malamocco, and Rustico of Torcello. The Library of St. Marc is a nobly designed building, and consists of two orders—the Doric and Ionic. The Zecca or Mint adjoins the Library on the Molo. The Doge's Palace, or the Palazza Ducale, is situated on the eastern side of the Piazzetta. The first palace built on the spot was in 820. This was destroyed in a tumult, and the Doge Pietro Ursolio built a second one in 970, which was destroyed by a great fire in 1120, and rebuilt in 1354-5 by the Doge Marino Fallerio.

The Academia delle Belle Arte is located in the ancient Convento della Carità, and is well worth attention. The house of Titian is also of great interest, and will repay a visit. The chief Theatres are those of La Fenice and San Benedetto. The islands about Venice, in the Lagoon, contain many buildings worth seeing.

The price for a Gondola, for the first hour is 1 Zwanziger, for every subsequent hour or hours, half Zwanziger. There are upwards of 4,000 Gondolas at Venice. The tide rises three feet.

English Consul.—

English Bankers, Messrs. Tatamand Mudie.

Reading Room.—There is a News Room at the north-west angle of the Piazza St. Marco in the Procuratie Vecchie, in which French, English and Italian newspapers may be found. Persons can pay for one week, or subscribe per month.

Conveyances.—Steamers to Trieste, see alphabetical list, page 139. Railroad to Padua, Vicenza and Verona, see page 120. Diligences daily to Laibach, Milan, Udine, and Vienna.

Verona.—Hotels—

Hotel des Due Torri, a first-rate capital house, highly recommended.

An ancient city, containing about 65,000 inhabitants, connected with Venice by railway. It has a pleasant and picturesque situation, the Adige flowing through it, which is crossed by four stone bridges; the interior of the city does not correspond with the beauty of its position, many of the streets being narrow and dirty.

Viterbo is a neatly built episcopal city, with 13,000 inhabitants, at the foot of a hill, surrounded with gardens, vineyards, and country houses, 42 miles north-west of Rome. The streets are broad and well paved. The public buildings are of no importance, its churches only being worth visiting. Near the city is a hot mineral spring, much frequented. It is situated at the foot of the mountain in a beautiful valley.

ISLANDS.

Capri.—Situated about 4 miles from Massa, 8 from Sorrento, and 24 from Naples; is remarkable for its picturesque scenery and salubrious air. There is no trace of volcanic formation in this island, and to this fact is attributed by many the healthiness of the climate, and the superiority of its vegetable productions; the oil, wine. and the other produce of Capri being regarded as the finest in the kingdom. Perhaps there is no spot in this neighbourhood so little known, yet so well adapted to the English taste. Here a sportsman will find abundance of quails and woodcocks twice in the year, and excellent fishing at all times—the artist, the boldest and most magnificent marine and rocky scenery—the antiquary, ruins of Roman grandeur—and the economist, cheap and excellent living. There are two very clean and decent hotels, called respectively the Vittoria, kept by Signor Pagani, and the Londra, by Signor Petagua; and were there a greater concourse of strangers, many are the small houses, now lying vacant, which could be fitted up for a trifle.

Amongst the natural curiosities of the island should be mentioned the Blue Grotto, the Green Grotto, and one recently discovered; but the lover of splendid scenery should never leave this island without spending a day on the heights. To its other attractions may be added the peculiar character of the air, which is singularly well suited to cases of bronchitis, where the soundness of the lungs can be guaranteed.

ENGLISH PHYSICIAN— Dr. Clark.

CONVEYANCES.—There is daily communication with the coast by excellent boats, which may be met with at the Porto di Massa in Naples. Other boats leave twice or three times a week for Massa, Sorrento, and Cstellamare. A steam boat goes about once a week from Naples to Capri; in the summer, leaves and returns in the evening.

Comino is a small island, two miles in length, between Malta and Gozo, and partakes more of the character of the latter. The two channels which it forms have from 12 to 20 fathoms water, and are safely passable by the largest ships in mid-channel, in which also there is good anchoring ground of fine sand.

Corfu.—HOTELS.—

Girolamo's Hotel (del Club), and Taylor's.

This beautiful island, the principal of the Ionian Republic, is under the protection of, and is garrisoned by the English. Steamers run between Trieste and the capital, Corfu, once a week at least, in connexion with Alexandria, Smyrna, Patras, Zante, Athens, Constantinople, Venice, Ancona, and Brindis. Her Majesty's mail boats once every fortnight from Malta. The Austrian Lloyd's Company from Trieste is excellent. The fare from Trieste to Corfu is £5, 10s.; eating on board, 5s. a-day, and a very good table kept. The passage, two days on an average, skirting the Dalmatian coast along the eastern shores of the Adriatic, and three days by Ancona; to Athens in two days by Patras; to Otranto in 12 hours, but sometimes several days. Fares 5 Spanish Dollars. Fares to Athens 45 fl., 30 fl., and 15 fl.; to Constantinople, 80 fl., 54 fl., and 20 fl. The Albanian mountains, forming the most splendid view on approaching Corfu. On arrival there one may land at once without any trouble. Spanish, English, and Austrian silver money taken. Excellent roads all over the country, and plenty of horses and carriages to be hired. The view from the top of the Citadel is magnificent, and there is a delightful evening walk along the shore past the village of Castrades, through olive and orange groves to the One-Gun-Battery, where fable and tradition say Ulysses' ship was wrecked, and transformed into the chapel-crowned inlet underneath the spectator's eye. An excursion to Pantaleone, a mountain pass 16 miles inland; there the view is superb. A drive to the village of Benitza, 8 miles distant; and a sea excursion to Govino, the old Venetian harbour; thence to Ipso, with its ancient olive trees; and on to Karagol, the extremity of the bay, would each and all well repay a visit. A Greek boat costs about 12s. a-day, with four rowers. To visit the harbours on the opposite coast of Albania it is necessary to take a guardiano to avoid a quarantine of twenty-four hours on return. This costs 2s. 6d. a-day besides the expenses of the man.

MONEY.—English gold and silver; also the Spanish pillar, or Mexican dollar, value 4s. 4d.; imperial Neapolitan dollar, 4s.; Roman dollar, 4s. 2d.; and copper pence, halfpence, farthings, grains; 10 grains make a penny.

Gozo, the most northerly, and is more elevated than Malta, and is entirely circumscribed with perpendicular rocks, the highest of which are to the west and south, where they are very steep. The surface of this island is not so uneven as that of Malta. The grapes of Gozo are peculiarly fine, and are highly esteemed. Cotton and grain are also cultivated here; the air very salubrious and healthy; whilst the country also possesses very beautiful prospects.

Malta.—HOTELS.—

Bentley's, Clarence, Clarendon, Dunsford's, Mediterranean, Minerva, Morell's, Princes's Royal, Royal and Victoria. The lodging-Houses are numerous and good.

Malta is distant 160 miles from Cape Paparo, the Southern point of Sicily, and 200 miles from the African coast, 220 French leagues from Marseilles, and 180 from Athens (the Piræus.)

Malta is of an irregular oval figure, about sixteen miles in length, by eight or nine in breadth, and is composed of calcareous rocks, which slope like an inclined plane, from the level of the sea towards the south and east, where they attain the height of nearly 200 yards.

Gardens are numerous in Malta, especially towards the east. They are generally ornamented with orange and lemon trees, to which the greatest attention is paid. Bees are also to be found here in great abundance; the honey is delicious, and remains always liquid. There are numerous asses of strong breed. The sheep are very prolific, and number about 12,000. There are about six or seven thousand beeves maintained here; also, five or six thousand horses of all races. Besides the food produced from the soil, there are several hundred boats employed in the fisheries for the daily supply of the markets. The climate of Malta is delightful, the four seasons are regularly defined, and the air is very salubrious and healthy. The Maltese are of a mixed race, principally Italian and Arabic; and their language, like themselves, is an Italian-Arabic dialect, intelligible to the nations of the opposite African shore. The mercantile and higher classes speak pure Italian; and English, which is the language of Government, is also spoken by the natives. The Maltese are a robust, an active, and a temperate people; but owing to a want of employment are still very poor, wasting their energies in idleness. Their condition, however, has become greatly improved since they became British subjects, new sources of industry being opened up to them, and some of them have become the best sailors in the Mediterranean.

Bookseller and Publisher, G. Muir, 247, Strada Reale, where travellers will find all necessary Guide Books and information connected with the Island or the continuance of their voyage

Steam-packets leave Malta for Marseilles, Alexandria, the Ionian Isles, Athens, Gibraltar, England, &c.

Money.—The money is that of England. The Maltese scudo, 1ls. 8d. English, is divided into 12 tari of 20 grains each; also South American dollars of the value of 4s. 2d.

The chief town of Malta is Valetta, which is built upon a tongue of land extending into a bay, and forming a splendid harbour on each side, the projecting points of which are occupied by forts and towers, the city itself and suburbs being surrounded by impregnable fortificatious, parts of which are cut out of the solid rock. The streets of Valetta are narrow and steep; but it contains some splendid buildings, which still attest the magnificence and devotion of its former masters, the Knights of St. John, to whom the island was gifted by Charles V. after they had lost Rhodes; in 1798 they were dispossessed by the French. Valetta surrendered to the British after a two years' blockade, and was ceded to Britain by the treaty of 1815.

Civitta Vecchia, or the old town, is situated in the centre of the island, and is called Medina by the natives. Its situation is so high that, on a clear day, the whole islands and the coasts of Sicily and Africa may be seen at the distance of about 60 miles. The catacombs are very extensive, and of great celebrity. Near the western part of the north coast is the Calle de Sum Paulo, or haven, where St. Paul is said to have tarried after his shipwreck, though some writers consider the island of Meleda on the Dalmatian coast to be that on which the apostle was cast.

SICILY.

This beautiful island is situate in the Mediterranean Sea, adjoining the south-western extremity of Italy, from which it is separated by the narrow strait of Messina. Its greatest length is about 190 miles, and its greatest breadth about 106, the superficial area being 8,067 square English miles, and the population about 2,000,000. The island is studded with mountains, among which, and on their tops, are plains of moderate extent, some of which are 1,000 feet above the level of the sea.

Sicily forms a portion of the kingdom of the Two Sicilies, and possesses, virtually at least, a representative constitution, established in 1812; but since 1815 this has fallen into complete abeyance, and the island is now all under the absolute power of the king. Sicily produces silk in quantities, to the extent of about 400,000 lbs., the greater part of which is manufactured into ordinary silk stuffs. At Catena cotton is also slightly cultivated. Its fishery and sulphur trades are productive. Sicily is divided into seven *valli* or intendancies, and has for its capital Palermo.

Aci Reale, north-east of Catena, a clean and well-built town, standing on streams of lava, and containing 16,000 inhabitants. *Burte* gave the title of Duke to the celebrated Lord Nelson, but his estate to which the title was attached has been entirely destroyed by eruptions of Ætna, at whose base it is situated.

Alcamo—an archiepiscopal city, with a royal college, and 20,000 inhabitants, twenty-five miles west of Palermo. In the neighbourhood is the site of the ancient Ægesta, where is a temple in good preservation.

Arragona is a small town with about 800 inhabitants, six miles north-east of Girgenti. It is remarkable for its picturesque gallery and antiquities, and also for the singular mud volcano of Macalubo in its neighbourhood. Here, on a level surface, are numbers of scarcely perceptible openings, from which, at regular intervals, and with a hissing sound, little explosions of gas burst forth; whilst, at the same time, a white and very delicate marly slime swells out and flows in a sluggish stream.

Catania, a large archiepiscopal city, with wide and straight streets, and a good harbour stands at the foot of Mount Ætna. Though having suffered much from earthquakes, it yet preserves the remains of an amphitheatre, larger than the remains of the colosseum at Rome. It contains a University, a Lyceum, a Public Library, a Museum, and other literary institutions. The silk stuffs of Catania rival the best in the kingdom. Its population is about 42,000. The drive from Catania to Messina is one of the most beautiful in the world in scenery, far surpassing that of the Rhine. An excellent road, close to the shore of the Medditeranean; and high up on the right are numerous towns, cities, villages, and castles, some on the very summits of the mountain, as travellers going to the scene of the present eruption of Ætna, near Zaffarana, should stop at the village of Giacrre, 30 miles south of Messina, where they take mules.

Girgenti, an irregularly built and episcopal city on the south-west coast, is situate on a hill 1,100 feet above the sea, not far from the shore, where it has a harbour. It has some fortifications, and about 16,000 or 17,000 inhabitants. In its neighbourhood are objects calculated to excite the traveller's warmest interest, viz.: the remains of Agrigentum, consisting of the Temple of Concord, the Temple of Juno, and the ruins of the Temples of Ceres, Proserpine, Hercules, Apollo, Diana, Castor and Pollux, Esculapius, and the Olympian Jupiter. The last was never finished, but was constructed with enormous columns 120 feet high. The pier of the harbour of Girgenti has been built from the ruins of these magnificent temples.

Marsala is a large seaport town, about twenty miles south by west of Trapani, has a large College; and 23,000 inhabitants. Its harbour is encumbered with sand; but its celebrated wines form an important article of export. There are here six wine establishments, four British, and two Sicilian. Three of the British are on a large scale, and have from 8,000 to 20,000 pipes annual deposit. The fourth, recently established, only requires time to be equally extensive. The wines only came into repute since 1802, when Admiral Lord Nelson introduced them for the use of the British fleet.

Messina, a large and fine city, and also an Episcopal See. Contains a commercial and industrious population of 90,000 souls. It posseses one of the finest harbours in the kingdom, and one of the best in Europe. The city has been rebuilt since 1783, when it was almost entirely destroyed by an earthquake. It has a citadel, and is otherwise strongly fortified; and its environs are the most densely inhabited and the best cultivated part of the island. The harbour is large, and the surrounding scenery exquisite. Mount Ætna is about 50 miles south of Messina, and 30 north of Catania.

Steamers to Naples and to Malta. The Anglo-Italian Company's vessels also touch at Messina and Palermo.

Palermo.—Hotel.—

The Trinacria—by Raguseo.

Palermo is a large and fine archiepiscopal city agreeably situated on the northern coast, commanding a beautiful sea view, and in a luxuriantly fertile and well cultivated plain called La Conca d'Oro, (the golden shell), which is enclosed on three sides by mountains, and opens on the north to a spacious bay. The houses are all flat-topped, and have balconies with glass doors instead of windows. The streets are well laid out, and nearly all terminate at the principal entrances. Several fine public buildings, seven squares, and fine walks; the best of which is the Marina, lying along the shore; a university, several literary establishments, an active commerce, with 150,000 inhabitants, entitle Palermo to rank among the principal cities of Europe.

Steamers to Messina and Naples, also to Malta, Marseilles, and Liverpool.

Saracca is a little seaport town, 32 miles west of Girgenti, built on a green hill, amidst a profusion of Cactus, off which, at a distance of 20 miles, a volcanic mount rose from the sea to a considerable height in 1833, and soon after disappeared leaving only a bank in its place.

Siragosa, a fortified episcopal city on the east coast, with 16,000 inhabitants. A splendid Natural Harbour, a Royal College, two Seminaries, a Library, and Museum stand amidst the ruins of the ancient Syracusa, which cover a space of twenty miles in circumference: and of whose five magnificent populous districts the island of Ortygia is the only one now inhabited. Its harbour, one of the finest in the Mediterranean, was long believed to be so choked with sand as only to admit chebecks and brigantines, until Lord Nelson proved otherwise in 1798, when he sailed into it with his ships of war and frigates, and fouud excellent anchorage. The celebrated fountain of Arethusa, which flows through the town in a stream four feet deep, has become turbid and muddy, and is used as a washing stream.

Taormina, 30 miles south of Messina. A small town in a beautiful situation on the coast. Contains a Roman theatre cut in the rock, a *naumachia*, a cistern, and an aqueduct worth seeing. It maintained a siege of eighty years' duration against the Saracens. Directly above Taormina is Mola, a village of 400 inhabitants, built on the very top of a lofty rock, perpendicular on three sides. Ten miles south is Mascali, a little village on the right of the road, beautifully located and surrounded by hills and mountains. Zaffarana has been partially buried up by the stream of lava; and the remaining houses are deserted by the inhabitants. The eruption is about 8 miles above Giarre, and up to this, November 10th, continues as it has been going on for months.

Trapani is a busy commercial fortified town, with a royal college, a tribunal of commerce, and 25,000 inhabitants, built on a peninsula at the western extremity of Sicily. Its inhabitants are largely engaged in fishing coral. part of which is carved into necklaces, and exported even to India, by way of Alexandria.

SPAIN.

Aranjuez is situated in a dead level, on the banks of the Tagus, 27 miles south by east of Madrid. The Palace is a large and fine building, and the grounds form one of the most delightful retreats attached to any palace.

Barcelona. The capital of Catalonia, it is situated on the Mediterranean, and is a place of great trade, containing manufactures of various sorts.

Conveyances.—Steamboats to Marseilles, Valencia, Alicante, Carthagena, Malaga, Gibraltar, and Cadiz, about four times a-month. Distance to Marseilles, 67 French leagues; to Valencia, 47 French leagues. Fares to Marseilles, 80f. and 70f. For fares to Valencia, &c., see page 127. Railway to Mataro, see page 122.

Mataro—a town of Catalonia.

Conveyance.—Railway to Barcelona, see pages 122.

ITALIAN ROUTES.

PASS OF THE SPLUGEN.—ST. GALL TO MILAN.

Diligences several times a week.—$24\frac{1}{2}$ Posts.

	Posts.
St. Gall to Horsbach	1
,, Rheinegg	$2\frac{1}{2}$
,, Alstetten	$3\frac{3}{4}$
,, Sennwald	5
,, Swelen	$6\frac{1}{4}$
,, Ragaby	$7\frac{3}{4}$
St. Gall to Coire	9
,, Tusis	$10\frac{3}{4}$
,, Splugen	$12\frac{1}{2}$
,, Campo Doleino	15
,, Chiavenna	16
,, Riva	17
St. Gall to Colico	18
,, Varenna	$19\frac{1}{4}$
,, Lecco	$20\frac{3}{4}$
,, Carsaniga	$22\frac{1}{4}$
,, Monza	$23\frac{1}{4}$
,, Milan	$24\frac{1}{2}$

PASS OF THE ST. GOTHARD.—LUCERNE TO MILAN.

23 Posts.

Lucerne to Fluellen by Steamer twice daily.—Diligences from Fluellen several times a week.

	Posts.
Fluellen to Altorf	$0\frac{1}{2}$
,, Hospital	4
,, St. Gothard	$5\frac{1}{2}$
,, Airolo	$7\frac{1}{2}$
Fluellen to Faido	$9\frac{1}{2}$
,, Pollegio	$11\frac{1}{2}$
,, Bellinzona	14
,, Lugano	$17\frac{1}{2}$
Fluellen to Como	20
,, Barlassina	$21\frac{1}{2}$
,, Milan	23

GENEVA TO TURIN, BY CHAMBERY AND THE MONT CENIS.

45 Posts, or 220 miles.

	Posts.
Geneva to St. Julien	$1\frac{1}{4}$
,, Frangy	4
,, Mionnas	$5\frac{1}{2}$
,, Rumilly	7
,, Albens	$8\frac{1}{4}$
,, Aix-les-Bains	$9\frac{3}{4}$
,, Chambery	$11\frac{3}{4}$
,, Montmeillan	$13\frac{3}{4}$
Geneva to Maltaverne	$15\frac{1}{2}$
,, Aiguebelle	17
,, La Grande Maison	$19\frac{3}{4}$
,, St. Jean	$21\frac{3}{4}$
,, St. Michel	$23\frac{3}{4}$
,, Modane	$26\frac{1}{4}$
,, Verney	28
,, Lanslebourg	30
Geneva to Mont Cenis	33
,, Molaret	36
,, Suze	38
,, Bruzolo	$39\frac{3}{4}$
,, St. Ambroise	$41\frac{1}{2}$
,, Rivoli	$43\frac{1}{4}$
,, Turin	45

TURIN TO GENOA.—$24\frac{1}{2}$ Posts, or 120 Miles.

	Posts.
Turin to Truffarello	$1\frac{3}{4}$
,, Poirino	$3\frac{1}{4}$
,, Dusino	$4\frac{3}{4}$
,, Gambetta	$6\frac{1}{4}$
,, Asti	$7\frac{3}{4}$
Turin to Annone	$9\frac{1}{4}$
,, Felizano	$10\frac{3}{4}$
,, Alexandria	13
,, Brencia	$14\frac{3}{4}$
,, Novi	$16\frac{1}{2}$
Turin to Arquata	18
,, Ronco	20
,, Pontedecimo	$22\frac{1}{2}$
,, Genoa	$24\frac{1}{2}$

GENEVA TO MILAN, BY SAVOY AND THE SIMPLON.

53 Posts, or 255 miles.

	Posts.
Geneva to Dovaine	$2\frac{1}{2}$
,, Thonon	$4\frac{1}{2}$
,, Evian	6
,, St. Gingolph	$8\frac{1}{2}$
,, Vionne	$10\frac{3}{4}$
,, St. Maurice	13
,, Martigny	$15\frac{1}{4}$
,, Riddes	$17\frac{1}{2}$
,, Sion	$19\frac{3}{4}$
Geneva to Sierre $\frac{1}{2}$	22
,, Tourtemagne	$24\frac{1}{4}$
,, Viége	$26\frac{1}{2}$
,, Brigue (ascent of the mountain)	28
,, Bérisal	$30\frac{1}{2}$
,, Simplon	34
,, Isella (frontier)	$36\frac{1}{4}$
,, Domo-d'Ossola	$38\frac{1}{2}$
Geneva to Vogogna	$40\frac{1}{2}$
,, Baveno	$43\frac{1}{2}$
,, Arona	46
,, Sesto-Calende	$47\frac{1}{4}$
,, Galarata	$48\frac{3}{4}$
,, Legnanello	$50\frac{1}{4}$
,, Rho	$51\frac{3}{4}$
,, Milan	53

MILAN TO GENOA.—$20\frac{3}{4}$ Posts, or 102 Miles.

	Posts.
Milan to Binasco	$1\frac{1}{2}$
Pavia	$2\frac{3}{4}$
Casteggio	$6\frac{1}{4}$
Vogliére	$7\frac{1}{2}$
Milan to Tortone	$9\frac{3}{4}$
,, Novi	$12\frac{1}{4}$
,, Arquata	$13\frac{3}{4}$
Milan to Ronco	$15\frac{1}{4}$
,, Ponte Decimo	$17\frac{3}{4}$
,, Genoa	$20\frac{3}{4}$

	Posts.		Posts.		Posts.
Milan to Cascina de Pecchi..	1½	Milan to Ponte S. Marco....	9¾	Milan to Vicenza	17¼
,, Canonica..........	2½	,, Deseuzano	10¾	,, Arslesega	18½
,, Bergamo..........	3¾	,, Castelnovo.........	12¼	,, Padua	19½
,, Cavernago	4¾	,, Verona*	13¾	,, Dolo.............	21
,, Palazzolo	5¾	,, Caldiero	14¾	,, Mestre	22½
,, Ospedaletto	7¼	,, Montèbello.........	16¼	,, Venice............	23½
,, Brescia	8¼				

* The Railroad from Verona to Venice is now open.

MILAN TO BOLOGNA, BY MANTUA.—21 Posts.

	Posts.		Posts.		Posts.
Milan to Meleguano	1½	Milan to Piadena	9½	Milan to Novi..............	15¾
,, Lodi.............	2¾	,, Bozzolo	10¼	,, Carpi	16¾
,, Casalpusterlengo ..	4¼	,, Castellucio	11¾	,, Modena	18
,, Pizzigbettone......	5¼	,, Mantua	12¾	,, Samoggia	19½
,, Cremona..........	7¼	,, S. Benedetto	14¼	,, Bologna	21
,, Cicognolo	8¼				

BOLOGNA TO FLORENCE.—9 Posts.

	Posts.		Posts.		Posts.
Bologna to Pianoro	1½	Tuscan Frontier.		Bologna to Cafaggiolo	7
,, Lojano..........	3	Bologna to Covigliajo	5	,, Fontebuona	8
,, Filigare	4	,, Monte Carelli ..	6	,, Florence........	9

FLORENCE TO LEGHORN, BY PONTEDERA.—4 Posts.

	Posts.		Posts.	
Florence to Lastra..........	1	Florence to Scala	3	Pontedera to Leghorn by rail.
,, Ambrogiana	2	,, Castel del Bosco .	4	

FLORENCE TO ROME, BY SIENNA.—23¼ Posts.

	Posts.		Posts.		Posts.
Florence to S. Casciano	1	Florence to La Poderma	9	,, Viserbe	17
,, Tavernelle	2	,, Ricorsi	10	,, L'imposta	18
,, Poggibonsi	3	,, Radicofain	11	,, Rosiceglione	19
,, Castiglioncello ..	4	,, Pontecentino....	12	,, Monterosi	20
,, Sienna	5	,, Acquapendente..	13	,, Baccano	21
,, Montarone......	6	,, S. Lorenzo......	13¾	,, La Storta	22
,, Buoncomento ..	7	,, Bolsena	14¾	,, Rome	23¼
,, Torreineri	8	,, Montefiascone ..	16		

FLORENCE TO ROME, BY AREZZO AND FOLIGUO.—27½ Posts.

	Posts.		Posts.		Posts.
Florence to Pontassieve	1½	Florence to Magione........	11½	Florence to Otricoli	21
,, Tucisa	3	,, Perugia	13	,, Borghetto	21¾
,, S. Giovanni	4	,, Sante Maria	14	,, Civita Castellana.	22½
,, Levane	5	,, Foliguo	15	,, Nepi	23½
,, Ponticino	6	,, Le Vene........	16	,, Monterosi	24¼
,, Arezzo	7	,, Spoleto	17	,, Baccano	25¼
,, Rigutino	8	,, La Strettura .. .	18	,, La Storta	26¼
,, Camuscia	9	,, Terni	19	,, Rome	27½
,, Case del Piano ..	10½	,, Narni	20		

CIVITA VECCHIA TO ROME.—7 Posts.

	Posts.		Posts.		Posts.
Civita Vecchia to S. Severo.	2	Civita Vecchia to Castel Guido	5	Civita Vecchia to Rome....	7
,, Palo	3½				

ROME TO NAPLES, BY TERRACINA.—20¾ Posts.

	Posts.		Posts.		Posts.
Rome to Torre di Mezzavia	1½	Rome to Mesa	8¾	Rome to Carigliano	15¼
,, Albano	2⅓	,, Ponte Maggiore....	9¾	,, S. Agata	16¼
,, Geuzano	3¼	,, Terracina	10¾	,, Sparanisi..........	17¼
,, Velletri	4¼	,, Fondi	12¼	,, Capua	18¼
,, Cisterna	5¼	,, Stri	13¼	,, Aversa	19¾
,, Torre de'tre Ponti..	6¾	,, Mola di Gaeta	14¼	,, Naples	20¾
,, Bocca di Fierne ...	7¾				

FOREIGN DILIGENCES, POST AND MAIL COACHES.

The fares may be reckoned at from 1½d. to 2d. per English mile.

ENG. MLS.	**Aalen** to
10¼	Ellwangen, 4½ a.m. & 11 p.m., in 2 hours
10¼	Heidenheim, 4.10 a.m., in 2¼ hours
20¾	Nordlingen, 4 a.m., in 4½ hours
74	Nurenberg, 4 a.m. (per Nordlingen) in 9½ hours
46	Stuttgart, 9¼ p.m., in 7¾ hrs.
32¼	Ulm, 4.10 a.m., in 6⅔ hours

	Aarau to
..	Baden, 1.50 and 5 a.m., and 1.45 p.m., and 4½ p.m. (per Brugg)
..	Basel, 12.30 noon and 9¾ p.m.
..	Bern, 12.15 noon, and 11¼ p.m., in 7¾ hours
..	Luzern, 6 a.m. (per Munster,) and 12 noon (per Sursee,) in 5¼ hours
..	Neufchatel, 11.20 p.m., in 10¾ hours
..	Schaffhausen, 2 a.m. (per Brugg), in 8 hours
..	Sins, 5 a.m. (per Muri), in 6¼ hours
..	Solothurn, 12.30 noon, and 11.20 p.m., in 4¾ hours
..	Zurich, 1.50 and 5 a.m., and 2.30 p.m., in 4½ hours

	Achim to
49½	Stade, 8 p.m.

	Aix-la-Chapelle to
11½	Eupen, 6 a.m., 7 p.m., in 2 hours
15¾	Julich, 5¾ a.m., in 3 hours
19¾	Maestricht, 6 a.m., 12½ and 3 p.m., in 3½ hours
20½	Montjoie 7 a.m., 6 (in winter 5) p.m., in 4½ hours
92	Trier, 7 a.m., in 20½ hours

ENG. MLS.	**Alsfeld** to
47¾	Friedberg, 4 a.m. (per Homberg)
26½	Fulda, 4.40 p.m., in 9 hours
31¼	Giessen, 12.30 p.m., in 4¾ hrs.
26¼	Grunberg, 4 a.m. (per Homberg,) and 12.30 p.m. (per Romrod), in 5 hours
22	Hersfield, 8¾ a.m., in 3½ hrs.
10¼	Lauterbach, 4.40 p.m., in 4½ hours
15⅔	Neustadt, 11.55 p.m., in 2 hrs.

	Altenburg to
27¾	Chemnitz, 1½ p.m., in 5 hours
93¼	Coburg, 8 a.m. and 7 p.m.
17	Gera, 8 a.m. and 3 & 7 p.m.
15½	Glauchau, 7.10 a.m., 12.55 and 6.10 p.m., in 2¼ hours
22	Hohenstein, 6¾ p.m., returning at 3 a.m., in 4¼ hours
40¼	Jena, 3 p.m., in 9¾ hours
38	Neustadt-on-the-Oder, 8 a.m. and 7 p.m., in 9 hours
19½	Rochlitz, 1½ p.m., in 3½ hours
56½	Saalfeld, 8 a.m. and 7 p.m.
12¼	Waldenburg, 6¾ p.m.
52	Weimar, 3 p.m., in 12½ hours
14½	Zeiz, 7 p.m., in 3¼ hours

	Altenkirchen to
32½	Coblentz, 4 a.m., in 6¾ hours
40¼	Cologne, 4½ a.m., in 8½ hours
32½	Limburg, 10¾ p.m., in 6 hrs.
43¾	Olpe, 4 a.m., in 11½ hours
23	Siegburg, 4½ a.m., in 5½ hrs.
34¾	Siegen, 4 a.m., in 7½ hours

	Alzey to
..	Creuznach, 7.55 p.m., in 3 hrs
35¾	Darmstadt, 5 a.m., in 5¾ hrs.
28¾	Kaiserslaut, 11 p.m., in 5 hrs.
20¾	Mayence, 5 a.m. and 3½ p.m.
18½	Worms, 6¼ a.m. (per Westhofen,) and 4 p.m. (per Pfeddersh), in 2¾ hours

ENG. MLS.	**Amberg** to
112	Augsburg, 2 a.m. (per Regensburg), in 25¾ hours
41½	Bayreuth, 12¼ a.m., in 9 hrs.
100¾	Donauworth, 12 night, in 27 hours
66	Eger, 9½ p.m., in 13½ hours
67¼	Eichstadt, 12 night, in 13¼ hours
24¼	Neumarkt, 12 night, in 4¾ hrs
39¼	Nurnberg, 5¾ a.m., in 7½ hrs.
	Regensburg, 2 a.m., in 8 hrs.

	Anclam to
32½	Demmin, 5¾ a.m., 8 p.m., in 5½ hours
22	Greifswalde, 5¼ a.m., 11.30 and 7.15 p.m., in 3½ hours
31½	N. Bradenburg, 8 a.m., in 5½ hours
28¾	Pasewalk, 7 a.m., and 3¼ and 9¾ p.m., in 5 hours
60	Passow (Berlin), 7 a.m., 3¼ and 9¾ p.m., in 10 hours
43¾	Prenzlau, 7 a.m., and 3¼ and 9¾ p.m., in 7½ hours
54½	Stettin, 7 a.m., and 3¼ and 9¾ p.m., in 10¼ hours
42½	Stralsund, 5 and 11.30 a.m., and 7.15 p.m., in 7 hours
27½	Swinemunde, 7½ a.m., returning at 10 a.m., in 9 hours

	Angermund to
26½	Boizenburg, 8 p.m., returning at 8½ a.m., in 4½ hrs.
..	Konigsberg, 8¼ a.m. and 7½ p.m., in 4¼ hours
12¼	Schwedt, 2½ and 8¾ a.m., and 7½ p.m., in 2¼ hours

	Annaberg to
35¾	Carlsbad, Mondays, Tues., Thurs., & Sat., at 4½ a.m.
22	Chemnitz, 10½ a.m., and 2½ and 10 p.m., in 5 hours
57¾	Dresden, 2 a.m., in 13 hours

ENG. MLS.	
	Annaberg to
33½	Freiberg, 2 a.m., in 8 hours
71⅓	Leipsic, 2½ p.m., in 14 hours
13½	Marienberg, 2 a.m. and 8½ p.m. on Tuesdays and Fridays., in 5 hours
22	Schneeberg, 6 a.m., in 5¾ hrs.
	Ansbach to
86	Augsburg, 5½ a.m. & 12 noon & 7½ p.m. (per Gunzenhausen.), in 9⅓ hours
26	Crailsheim, 10½ a.m., in 5½ hours
17	Gunzenhausen, 5½ a.m. and 12 noon and 7½ p.m., in 3¼ hours
43½	Hall, 10½ a.m., in 8½ hours
76½	Heilbronn, 10½ a.m. (per Hall)
..	Munich, 5½ a.m. and 12 noon and 7½ p.m., in 12 hours
42½	Nordlingen, 5½ a.m., 12 noon, and 7½ p.m., in 6 hours
25½	Nuremberg, 6 a.m. & 3½ & 4 p.m.
20¼	Rothenburg, 3¾ p.m., in 4½ hours
46	Wurzburg, 6½ a.m., in 10 hours
	Antwerp to
...	Amsterdam, 3 p.m., in 19¼ hours
...	Utrecht, 4½ a.m., 3 p.m, in 12½ hours
	Apolda to
9¼	Jena, 9.15 a.m. and 5 p.m., in 1¾ hours
40¼	Schleiz, 5 p.m., in 9½ hours
	Appenweyer to
17	Petersthal, 12½ p.m., in 3 hours
	Arnheim to
..	Emmerich, 11½ & 11½ a.m., 9½ and 10 p.m., in 2½ hours.
..	Lingen, 11 a.m., in 18½ hours
	Arnsberg to
48½	Arolsen, 12 noon, in 10¼ hours.
54¼	Battenberg, 3 p.m. on Mon. & Thurs., in 12¾ hours
77½	Cassel, 12 noon., in 17 hours
93¼	Giessen, 3 p.m. on Mondays & Thursdays, in 21¾ hours
44¾	Hallenberg, 12 noon, in 8¾ hours
28¾	Hamm (Munster), 6 a.m. and 4¾ and 11½ p.m., in 5½ hours
24¼	Iserlohn, 6 a.m., 4¾ and 11½ p.m., in 4½ hours
12½	Meschede, 12 noon, in 2½ hours
42½	Olpe, 10½ p.m., in 8¾ hours
13¼	Schmallenberg. 11 p.m., returning at 8½ p.m., in 6¾ hours
58¾	Siegen, 9.20 a.m. and 10.30 p.m., in 13½ hours
13½	Soest, 10.35 a.m. & 6.25 p.m., in 2¾ hours
18½	Werl, 6 a.m., and 4¾ and 11½ p.m., in 3½ hours
	Arnstadt to
7½	Dietendorf, 4½ and 10¾ a.m., and 1¾ p.m., in 1½ hours
11	Ilmenau, 3 p.m., in 2¾ hours
21½	Rudolstadt, 9½ a.m., in 4¾ hours
28¾	Saalfeld, 9¼ a.m., in 6 hours
30	Schleusingen, 3 p.m., in 7¼ hours
	Arnswalde to
38	Landsberg, 9 p.m., in 10 hours
9	Reetz, 1 p.m., returning at 8½ a.m., in 2 hours
	Arolsen to
49	Arnsberg, 6 p.m., in 10¼ hours
29	Cassel, 10.40 p.m., in 6½ hours
73	Iserlohn, 6 p.m., in 16½ hours
49	Marburg, 4 a.m., in 11 hours
36	Meschede, 6 p.m., in 7½ hours
31	Paderborn, 9½ a.m., in 5½ hours
53	Pyrmont, 9½ a.m., in 10½ hours
	Arona to
..	Bellinzona, 1 p.m., in 7 hours
..	Domo d'Ossola, 12 noon.
51	Milan, 7 a.m., in 7 hours
79	Turin, 1 p.m., in 15 hours
	Artern to
38	Erfurt, 2 a.m., in 8¼ hours
15	Frankenhausen, 2 a.m. (per Sachsenbach), in 3¾ hours
15	Querfurt, 11 p.m., in 2¾ hours
8	Sangerhausen. 6½ a.m., in 1½ hours
25	Sondershausen, 2 a.m. (per Sachsenbach). in 6¼ hours
16	Weissensee, 2 a.m., in 4 hours
	Aschaffenburg to
98	Bamberg, 10.10 a.m., 4.10 p.m. and 11.10 night, in 18 hours
58	Bischofsheim, 11½ night (per Wertheim), in 10 hours
24	Frankfort-on-the-Maine, 2.40 a.m. and 4½ p.m. (per Seligenstadt), and 8½ a.m. (per Hanau), in 6 hours
31	Gemunden, 10.15 a.m. (per Lohr,) in 5¼ hours
15	Hanau, 8½ a.m., in 2½ hours
58	Kissingen (in summer only), in 10¾ hours
23	Lohr, 10¼ a.m., in 4 hours
67	Mergentheim, 11½ night (per Wertheim), in 12 hours
24	Miltenberg, 11½ night, in 4 hours
19	Offenbach, 2.40 a.m., and 4½ p.m., in 3½ hours
44	Wertheim, 11½ night, in 7 hours
56	Wurzburg, 10.15 a.m. (per Lohr), 10.10 a.m., 4.10 and 11.10 p.m. (per Hessenth), in 9¼ hours
	Augsburg to
86	Ansbach, 8¼ a.m., 1.35 & 8.30 p.m. (per Gunzenhausen), in 6¾ hours
44½	Eichstadt, 10½ p.m. (per Pornbach) and 8.30 p.m., (per Donauworth), in 9 hours
..	Frankfort on the Maine, at 8.30 p.m. (per Gunzenhausen); and also at 8¼ a.m., 1.35 and 8½ p.m., (per Bamberg), in 34¼ hours
62	Fussen, 8½ a.m. (per Biessenhofen), and 7.30 p.m. (per Kempten), in 9¾ hours
32½	Gunzburg, at 7¾ a.m. and 9 p.m., in 5½ hours
112¼	Innsbruck, at 1.10 p.m. (per Munich), in 24½ hours
..	Memmingen at 8¼ a.m. (per Buchloe), in 7¼ hours
31½	Neuburg, at 8.30 p.m. (per Donauworth), and 2 p.m., in 7 hours
87½	Neuenmarkt, 10½ p.m., in 20 hours
80¾	Regensburg, at 10½ p.m. (per Neustadt); & 8 a.m. (per Munich), in 20½ hours
97	Stuttgardt, at 7¾ a.m. & 9 p.m. (per Ulm), & 8¼ a.m. & 1.35 p.m. (per Nordlingen), in 13 hours
47¼	Ulm, 7¾ a.m., and 9 p.m., in 8 hours
134½	Wurzburg, at 8¼ a.m., and 1.35 and 8.30 p.m. (per Bamberg); also at 8.30 p.m., in 18 hours
	Aurich to
16	Emden, 6 & 7 a.m., 12 noon, 2-3, and 7¾ p.m., in 4½ hours
15	Esens, 8 a.m., in 3½ hours
22	Leer, 8 and 12 p.m., in 4½ hours
16	Norden, 7 a.m., and 7¾ p.m., in 3 hours
47	Oldenburg, 8 p.m., in 8 hours
15	Wittmund, 8 a.m., in 3½ hours

Aussig to

ENG. MLS.	
..	Peterswalde, 5 a.m., returning at 5 p.m., in $3\frac{3}{4}$ hours
9	Teplitz, $1\frac{1}{2}$ and $11\frac{1}{4}$ a.m., and 2 and $5\frac{1}{2}$ p.m., in 2 hours

Avignon to

ENG. MLS.	
..	Lyons, 4.40 and $8\frac{1}{2}$ p.m., in $14\frac{3}{4}$ hours

Baden to

ENG. MLS.	
..	Aarau, 9 a.m., 5 and 8 p.m.; also 6 a.m. (per Brugg), in 3 hours
..	Basle, $6\frac{1}{2}$ and 9 a.m., 8.5 p.m., in 7 hours
..	Zurzach, 5 p.m., in 3 hours

Bamberg to

ENG. MLS.	
37	Bayreuth, 7.40 a.m., and 4.10 & 10 p.m. (per Culmbach), in 5 hours
..	Coburg, 7.40 a.m. & 4.10 p.m.
..	Eger, 7.40 a.m. and 4.10 p.m., in $11\frac{1}{2}$ hours
121	Frankfurt-on-the-Maine, 11 a.m., 4.30 and 10 p.m., in 22 hours
50	Kissingen, $7\frac{3}{4}$ and 11 a.m., and $4\frac{1}{2}$ p.m., in 5 hours
38	Kitzingen, 10 p.m., in $7\frac{1}{4}$ hrs.
49	Wurtzburg, 7.45 and 11 a.m., and 4.30 and 10 p.m., in 9 hours

Basle to

ENG. MLS.	
..	Aarau, 2 p.m. (per Fredrichsfeld); 7 a.m. and 7 p.m. (per Olten), in 6 hrs.
..	Baden, $9\frac{1}{2}$ a.m., 1 & 10 p.m.
..	Bern, 6 & 9 a.m., and $6\frac{1}{2}$ and $7\frac{1}{2}$ p.m. (per Solothurn)
..	Chaud de Fonds, 6 a.m. and $6\frac{1}{2}$ p.m., in 13 hours
..	Geneva, 6 a.m. and $6\frac{1}{2}$ p.m. (per Biel), 9 a.m. and $7\frac{1}{2}$ p.m. (per Bern), in 31 hrs.
64	Lucerne, 7 a.m. and 7 p.m.
..	Neufchatel, at 6 a.m., and $6\frac{1}{2}$ p.m. (per Biel), & $7\frac{1}{2}$ p.m. (per Solothurn), in 14 hrs.
..	Paris, 6, 7, and $11\frac{1}{2}$ a.m. (per Strasburg)
..	Schaffhausen, at 7 a.m. and $10\frac{3}{4}$ p.m. (per Waldshut) in 10 hours
..	Solothurn, 9 a.m. and $7\frac{1}{2}$ p.m.
..	Zurich, $9\frac{1}{2}$ a.m. and 10 p.m.

Bautzen to

ENG. MLS.	
17	Camenz, 4 p.m., returning at 4 a.m., in $3\frac{1}{4}$ hours
	Cottbus, $7\frac{1}{2}$ p.m., in $9\frac{1}{4}$ hours
47	Ebersbach, $6\frac{1}{2}$ p.m., return-at $3\frac{1}{2}$ a.m., in $3\frac{1}{4}$ hours
15	Schluckenau, 4 p.m., returning at 6 a.m., in $3\frac{3}{4}$ hours
15	Spremberg, $7\frac{1}{2}$ p.m., in $6\frac{3}{4}$ hrs

Bayreuth to

ENG. MLS.	
42	Amberg, 5 p.m., in $8\frac{1}{2}$ hours
37	Bamberg, 5 a.m., and 1 & 7 p.m. (per Culmbach)
14	Culmbach, 5 a.m., & 1 & 7 p.m.
..	Eger, $3\frac{1}{4}$ p.m., in $12\frac{1}{4}$ hours
..	Hof, 7 a.m. and $3\frac{1}{2}$ p.m., in 6 hours
81	Regensburg, 5 p.m., in $16\frac{1}{2}$ hours
30	Wunsiedel, $3\frac{1}{2}$ p.m., in $8\frac{1}{4}$ hours

Bebra to

ENG. MLS.	
23	Eschwege, 12 noon, in $4\frac{3}{4}$ hrs.
35	Fulda, $10\frac{1}{4}$ a.m. and $9\frac{3}{4}$ p.m.
9	Hersfeld, $10\frac{1}{4}$ a.m., $5\frac{1}{2}$ and $9\frac{3}{4}$ p.m., in $1\frac{1}{2}$ hours

Bellinzona to

ENG. MLS.	
..	Arona, $2\frac{1}{2}$ a.m. (per Magadino), in $8\frac{1}{2}$ hours
..	Chur, 1 a.m., in $17\frac{1}{2}$ hours
..	Faido, 1.25 night, in $4\frac{3}{4}$ hrs.
$75\frac{1}{2}$	Fluelen, 1.25 night, in $14\frac{3}{4}$ hrs
..	Locarno, 5 a.m., in 2 hours
..	Luzern, 1.25 night, in $17\frac{1}{4}$ hrs
..	Magadino, $2\frac{1}{2}$ a.m., in $1\frac{3}{4}$ hrs
..	Milan, 8.40 a.m.; also 11.40 night (per Camerlata), in $10\frac{1}{2}$ hours
..	St. Gotthard, 1.25 night, in 10 hours
..	Splugen, 1 a.m. (℣ Bernhardin), in $11\frac{1}{4}$ hours

Belluno to

ENG. MLS.	
119	Brixen, at $12\frac{1}{2}$ noon on Mondays & Fridays., & Briefpost daily, in $22\frac{1}{4}$ hours
33	Conegliano, 4 p.m. on Wednesdays and Saturdays, returning at 2 a.m. on Mondays and Fridays, in $4\frac{1}{4}$ hrs
74	Padua, 1 p.m. on Mondays and Fridays, in 20 hours
66	Trient, 1 p.m. on Mondays and Fridays, in $22\frac{1}{2}$ hours

Benrath to

ENG. MLS.	
11	Solingen, $9\frac{1}{4}$ a.m. & $7\frac{3}{4}$ p.m.,

Bensheim to

ENG. MLS.	
11	Worms, $8\frac{1}{2}$ and 10 a.m., $12\frac{1}{2}$ and $6\frac{1}{2}$ p.m., in 2 hours

Berchtesgadch to

ENG. MLS.	
97	Munich, 4 p.m. (per Reichenhausen), in 21 hours

Berlin to

ENG. MLS.	
82	Cottbus, $5\frac{1}{2}$ a.m. (per Lubben)
$52\frac{3}{4}$	Custrin, 10 p.m., in $8\frac{3}{4}$ hours
82	Landsberg, 10 p.m., in $14\frac{1}{2}$ hours
53	Lubben, $5\frac{1}{2}$ a.m. and 8 p.m., in $9\frac{1}{2}$ hours
$50\frac{1}{2}$	Luckau, $5\frac{1}{2}$ a.m. and 8 p.m., in 9 hours
63	Neustrelitz, $5\frac{1}{2}$ a.m. and 7 p.m., in $11\frac{1}{4}$ hours
$67\frac{1}{2}$	Prenzlaus, at $7\frac{1}{2}$ a.m. (per Templin), in 14 hours

Bern to

ENG. MLS.	
..	Aarau, $5\frac{1}{4}$ a.m. and 6 p.m., in 8 hours
..	Basel, $5\frac{1}{2}$ and 9 a.m., and 1 & $5\frac{1}{2}$ p.m. (per Solothurn), in $10\frac{1}{2}$ hours
..	Freiburg, $8\frac{1}{2}$ a.m. and 5 p.m., in $3\frac{1}{2}$ hours
..	Geneva, 9 a.m. and 9 p.m. (per Murten), in $16\frac{1}{2}$ hours
..	Lausanne, 9 a.m. and 9 p.m. (per Murten), in 11 hours
..	Lucerne, 6 p.m. (per Huttwyl), and 8 a.m. (per Langnau), in 10 hours
..	Neufchatel, 7 a.m. and 4 p.m., in 5 hours
..	Solothurn, 9 a.m. & $5\frac{1}{2}$ p.m., in 16 hours
..	Thun, 5 and $10\frac{1}{2}$ a.m. and 4 p.m.; also $12\frac{1}{2}$ p.m. (per Belp), in 5 hours
..	Vevey (Vivis), $8\frac{1}{2}$ a.m. (per Freiburg), in 11 hours
..	Zurich, $5\frac{1}{4}$ a.m. and 6 p.m., in 13 hours

Bernburg to

ENG. MLS.	
9	Alsleben, $3\frac{1}{2}$ p.m., returning at 8 a.m., in 2 hours
14	Aschersleben, $10\frac{1}{4}$ a.m., $3\frac{1}{2}$ & $9\frac{1}{2}$ p.m., in $2\frac{3}{4}$ hours
9	Calbe, 4 p.m., returning at $7\frac{1}{2}$ a.m., in 2 hours
9	Connern, 4 p.m., in 2 hours
34	Harzgerode, $10\frac{1}{4}$ a.m., in 7 hours
16	Hettstadt, $10\frac{1}{2}$ a.m. and $9\frac{1}{2}$ p.m., in $3\frac{1}{4}$ hours
33	Quedlinburg, at $9\frac{1}{2}$ p.m., in $6\frac{1}{2}$ hours

Biberach to

ENG. MLS.	
..	Kempten, 7.12 a.m. (per Waldsee), in $10\frac{1}{2}$ hours
21	Memmingen, 9 a.m., in $4\frac{1}{4}$ hrs

Bielefeld to

ENG. MLS.	
20	Detmold, 7 p.m., in $3\frac{1}{4}$ hours
10	Halle, $12\frac{1}{2}$ a.m., returning at 4 p.m., in $1\frac{1}{2}$ hours
34	Osnabruck, 7 p.m., in $6\frac{1}{4}$ hrs

ENG. MLS.

Bingen through **Bingerbruck** to

39 Coblentz, 9 a.m. & 11¼ p.m., in 6 hours
9 Creuznach, 1¼ (in winter 9¼ p.m.), 7 and 11½ p.m., in 1½ hours
16 Mayence, 9 a.m., and 7-8 p.m., in 3 hours
22 Simmern, 12½ night, in 4 hours
78 Trier, 12½ night, in 14½ hours

Birkenfeld to

42½ Creuznach, 12.20, 10.50 p.m., in 8 hours
33⅗ Saarlouis, 3 a.m., in 6½ hours
14½ St. Wendel, 2⅔ a.m., 2¼ p.m.
33⅗ Trier, 3 a.m., in 7½ hours

Bischofsheim to

58 Aschaffenberg, 3.24 p.m., in 9¾ hours
67 Heidelberg, 11 a.m., 10 p.m.
10 Mergentheim, 9.35 a.m., in 1¾ hours
34 Miltenberg, 3.24 p.m.
15 Wertheim, 3.24 p.m.,
19 Wurzburg, 4 and 8¾ a.m., in 3 hours

Bitterfeld to

8 Delitzsch, 5 a.m., in 1½ hours
20 Halle, 4 a.m., in 3¾ hours
24 Wittenberg, 3½ a.m in 5 hours

Blankenburg to

10 Halberstadt, 6¼ a.m., 2¼ p.m.
27 Nordhausen, 2.20 p.m., in 5¼ hours
43 Osterode, 5 a.m. on Sundays & Thursdays, in 11½ hours
27 Walkenried, 2.20 p.m. on Mondays and Thursdays, in 6¼ hours

Blomberg to

32½ Carlshafen, 8 p.m., in 7 hours
11¼ Detmold, 6 a.m., in 2¼ hours
7½ Horn, 10.40 a.m., in 1½ hours
23 Paderborn, 10.40 a.m., in 4¾ hours
12¼ Pyrmont, 4 p.m., in 2½ hours
18½ Rinteln, 5.10 p.m., in 4 hours

Boizenburg to

7 Lauenburg, 9 a.m., in 1¼ hours
20 Luneburg, 9 a.m., in 4 hours

Bologna to

.. Florence, at 5 p.m. on Mondays, Wednesdays, and Fridays, and Briefpost daily.
.. Mantua, 10 a.m. on Sundays, Wednesdays, and Fridays, and Briefpost daily.
.. Modena, 10 a.m. on Sundays, Wednesdays, and Fridays, and Briefpost daily.

ENG. MLS.

Bonn to

37 Coblentz, 9 a.m., 9½ p.m., & 12.42 night
16 Euskirchen, 6 p.m., in 3 hours
7 Siegburg, 8 a.m., 2½ and 7½ p.m., in 1¼ hours
86¾ Trier, 11¼ a.m. (per Wittlich), in 14 hours

Boppard to

25¼ Bingen, 8¼ a.m., 3 (in winter 4⅗) p.m., in 4 hours
13½ Coblentz, 3½ and 11½ a.m.
34¾ Creuznach, 8¼ a.m., 3 (in winter 4⅗) p.m.
20¾ Simmern, 3½ (in winter 5½) p.m., in 4¼ hours

Botzen to

27 Brixen, 12 noon, and 9 p.m.
79 Innsbruck, 12 noon & 9 p.m.
98 Landeck, 2 p.m. on Mondays and Thursdays, and Briefpost daily, in 20¼ hrs.
54 Mals, 2 p.m. on Mondays and Thursdays, in 11 hours
17 Meran, 5 a.m., and 2 p.m. on Mondays and Thursdays
56 Roveredo, 10 a.m., in 9½ hours
40 Trient, 10 a.m., in 6 hours
103 Verona, 10 a.m., and 8½ p.m., in 17¼ hours

Brandenburg to

22 Belzig, 2½ p.m., returning at 1¼ a.m.
19 Rathenow, 2½ p.m., on Mondays, Wednesdays, Fridays and Saturdays.

Bregenz to

176¼ Botzen, 4 p.m. on Tuesday and Friday, in 36½ hours
56½ Chur, 4 p.m., in 10 hours
20¼ Feldkirch, 4 p.m., in 3 hours
131¼ Innsbruck, 4 p.m., in 27¾ hours
6¾ Lindau, 5 a.m., in 1 hour

Bremen to

.. Bombay (per Marseilles), the 4th and 21st of each month in 34 days; (per Trieste) the 5th and 22nd of each month in 33 days
37 Bremerhafen, 10 p.m.
.. Calcutta (per Marseilles), 4th & 21st of month, 7 p.m., & 5th & 22nd of each month (per Trieste)—In 47 days.
67½ Harburg (Hamburg), 7½ p.m. in 10 hours
.. London, 10.10 a.m. (per Ostend), 10.10 a.m. (per Calais), in 36 hours
27 Oldenburg, 8 a.m. and 5 p.m.
76¼ Osnabruck, 5½ p.m., in 13½ hours

ENG. MLS.

Bremen to

56¼ Stade, 7 p.m., in 11 hours
12½ Sycke, 5½ p.m., returning at 6 a.m., in 2 hours

Breslau to

55 Glatz, 6 a.m. & 7 p.m., in 12 hours
69¾ Kalisch, 6½ p.m. (per Oels), in 15 hours
49 Krotoschin, 10½ a.m. and 10 p.m.
59 Lissa, 12 noon and 10 p.m., in 10½ hours
18½ Oels, 5 and 11½ a.m., and 6½ and 10 p.m.
55 Ostrowo, 6½ p.m. (per Oels.)
111 Posen, 12 noon and 10 p.m., in 18½ hours
219½ Warsaw, 1 p.m. by railway; and 6½ p.m. (per Oels), in 30½ hours

Brixen to

119 Belluno, 11 a.m. Tuesdays and Fridays, and (in summer only) 12 noon, in 21¼ hours
27 Botzen, 4¾ a.m., in 4¾ hours
144 Conegliano, 11 a.m. on Tuesdays and Fridays, returning on Mondays and Fridays at 3¼ a.m., also Briefpost daily, in 31½ hours
52 Innsbruck, 5 p.m., in 11 hrs.
163 Klagenfurt, 11 a.m. on Mondays, Thursdays, and Saturdays, in 32 hours
162 Treviso, 11 a.m. on Tuesdays and Fridays; also Briefpost daily, in 38 hours
139 Villach, 11 a.m. on Mondays, Thursdays, and Saturdays also Briefpost daily, in 27½ hours

Brody to

66 Lemberg, 6 p.m. on Sundays, Tuesdays, Thursdays, and Saturdays; also Briefpost daily, in 11½ hours

Bromberg to

51 Conitz, 7 a.m., in 13 hours
.. Culm, 8.19 a.m., 12.10, and 6.8 p.m., in 3½ hours
51 Gnesen, 11.45 a.m., in 12¼ hours
43 Graudenz, 8.19 a.m., & 12.10 and 6.8 p.m., in 5 hours
27 Inowraclaw, 11 a.m. and 7 p.m., in 4½ hours
67 Marienwerd, 8.19 a.m. and 12.10 and 6.8 p.m., in 4¼ hours
33 Thorn, 9 a.m., and 8½ p.m., in 7½ hours

Bruck to

ENG. MLS.	
106½	Ischl, 9 p.m., in 23 hours
39¼	Judenburg, Tuesday & Friday, 8 a.m., returning on Monday and Thursday at 5 a.m., in 13 hours
106½	Klagenfurt, 8.50 a.m., in 20 hours
123½	Linz, Wednesday 8.50 a.m., Monday and Thursday 9 p.m. (per Lietzen), and Briefpost daily, in 35 hours
142¼	Salzburg, 9 p.m., in 29¾ hrs.

Brunnen to

ENG. MLS.	
..	Arth, 7.50 a.m. (per Schwyz)
..	Einsiedeln, 5 p.m. (per Bingerbruck)
..	Zug, 7.50 a.m. (per Arth)

Brunswick to

ENG. MLS.	
91	Cassel, 10½ a.m. and 8½ p.m. in 18¾ hours
16	Gifhorn, 8 p.m, on Sundays and Thursdays; 7 p.m. on Tuesdays and Fridays
61	Gottingen, 10.30 a.m., 8½ p.m.
23	Helmstedt, 8 a.m., & 6 (in winter 5) p.m., in 4 hours
72	Holzminden, 8½ p.m., in 14½ hours
80	Hoxter (Hamm), 8½ p.m.
50	Neuhaldensleben, 5 a.m. on Mondays and Thursdays, in 12 hours
49	Nordheim, 10.30 a.m., 8½ p.m. in 10 hours
57	Salzwedel, 5 a.m. on Mondays and Thursdays
33	Seesen, 10.30 a.m. & 8½ p.m.
50	Uelzen, 7 p.m. on Tuesdays and Fridays, in 9 hours
20	Vorsfelde, 5 a.m. on Mondays and Thursdays; also 9 a.m. on Wednesdays and Saturdays, in 5½ hours

Budweis to

ENG. MLS.	
66	Klattau, 7 p.m., in 13 hours
62½	Linz, Mond., Tuesd., Thurs., and Saturday, at 4¾ p.m., and Briefpost daily, in 12 hours
91	Pilsen, 7 p.m., in 21¼ hours
91	Prague, 2 p.m. (per Tabor), Monday, Tuesday, Thursday, and Saturday, 8½ a.m. (per Pisek), in 19¾ hours

Bunzlau to

ENG. MLS.	
33½	Hirschberg, 7½ a.m. and 4¼ p.m., in 7¼ hours
11¼	Löwenberg, 7½ a.m., 4¼ and 10 p.m., in 2¼ hours
43¾	Neusalz, 9½ p.m., in 9½ hrs.

Burg to

ENG. MLS.	
25¼	Zerbst, Sunday, Tuesday, and Friday, 12 noon, in 5¾ hours

Burxdorf to

ENG. MLS.	
13½	Elsterwerda, 11¼ a.m., in 4 hours
38	Luckau, 11¼ a.m., in 8¼ hrs.

Butzbach to

ENG. MLS.	
30	Dillenburg, 10 p.m., in 6 hrs
48½	Siegen, 10 p.m., in 11½ hrs.
11½	Wetzlar, 10 p.m., in 2¼ hrs.

Camerlata to

ENG. MLS.	
..	Bellinzona, 8½ a.m. & 6 p.m., in 7¼ hours
..	Luzern, 6 p.m., in 24¾ hours

Carlsbad to

ENG. MLS.	
78½	Prague, (5 a.m. in summer), 12 noon, and 6 p.m., in 15½ hours

Carlshafen to

ENG. MLS.		
37	Barntrup	10¼ p.m.
31½	Blomberg	
39¼	Detmold	
12	Hoxter	
30	Pyrmont	
50½	Rinteln	

Carlsruhe to

ENG. MLS.	
21¼	Landau, 6.10 a.m., in 3½ hrs.
19	Pforzheim, 9 a.m., 12.5 and 7½ p.m., in 2¾ hours
48¼	Stuttgardt, 9 a.m., 12.5 and 7½ p.m., in 8 hours
33½	Wildbad, 12.5 p.m. in summer only, in 6¾ hours
50½	Zweibrucken, 6.10 a.m., in 11½ hours

Cassel to

ENG. MLS.	
77½	Arnsberg, 11½ a.m., in 16¾ hours
28¾	Arolsen, 11½ a.m., in 6½ hrs.
91	Brunswick, 10½ a.m. and 9 p.m., in 20 hours
115½	Coburg, 8 a.m., in 21½ hours
39¼	Eschwege, 10 a.m. and 10 p.m. (per Bischhausen)
108¾	Frankfurt-o-M., by railway, see page 76.
68	Fulda, 8 a.m. and 6½ p.m.
30	Göttingen, 6 and 10½ a.m. & 9 p.m., in 5½ hours
199	Hamm, 9¼ a.m. and 7.50 p.m. (per Hümme), in 9 hours
98¼	Harburg, 10½ a.m. & 9 p.m., (per Hanover), in 24 hours
35¾	Hanover, 6 and 10½ a.m. and 9 p.m.
42½	Heiligenstadt, 10 a.m., in 8 hours
83¼	Hersfeld, 8 a.m., 2¾ and 6½ p.m. (per Bebra), in 4 hrs.
77½	Hildesheim, 10½ a.m. and 9 p.m., in 15¾ hours
65	Meiningen, 8 a.m. (per Eisenach), in 10½ hours
51	Meschede, 11½ a.m., in 14 hrs
12¼	Mühlhausen, 10 p.m. (per Bischhausen), in 12 hours
68½	Münden, 6 and 10½ a.m. and 9 p.m., in 2½ hours
42	Nordhausen, 10 a.m., in 17 hours
..	Nordheim, 6 & 10½ a.m. & 9 p.m., in 8 hours
68	Paderborn, 9¼ a.m. and 7.50 p.m., in 7½ hours
46	Schmalkalden, 8 a.m. (per Frottstedt), and 2¾ p.m. (per Schwall), in 9½ hours
22	Wanfried, 10 a.m.; also 10 p.m. (per Bischhausen), in 8¾ hours
130½	Witzenhausen, 10 a.m., in 5 hours
25½	Wurzburg, 8 a.m., in 22¾ hrs

Celle to

ENG. MLS.	
28	Gifhorn, 3½ p.m., returning at 6½ a.m., in 5 hours
..	Harburg, 8½ p.m. (per Soltau) in 12 hours
..	Verden, 8½ p.m. (per Walsrode), in 9¾ hours

Chalon to

ENG. MLS.	
..	Lyons, 5 and 10 a.m. (per steam-boat), and 9½ p.m., in 8½ hours

Chambery to

ENG. MLS.	
..	Geneva, 8½ a.m., 2 and 10 p.m., in 9 hours
.	Turin, 9 a.m., in 20 hours

Chemnitz to

ENG. MLS.	
27¾	Altenburg, 7½ a.m., in 5 hrs.
19¾	Annaberg, 6 a.m.; 12½ and 4½ p.m., in 5 hours
47	Dresden, 12 noon and 8 p.m., in 10 hours
24	Freiberg, 12 noon and 8 p.m., in 4½ hours
19¼	Glauchau, 12 night, in 4 hrs.
14¼	Hainichen, 7½ a.m. & 7 p.m., in 3 hours
49½	Leipsic, 8 p.m., in 9 hours
19¼	Marienberg, 6 a.m. & 4½ p.m., in 4 hours
39½	Meissen, 7½ a.m. (per Nossen), in 9 hours
25	Schneeberg, 6½ a.m., and 4¾ p.m., in 5½ hours
23	Zwickau (Hof), 12½ noon & 12 night, in 5 hours

ENG. MLS.	**Chur** to
..	Bellinzona, 5 a.m., 17¼ hours
..	Bregenz, 7½ p.m., in 11½ hours
..	Chiavenna, 5 a.m., & 7.30 p.m., in 13¾ hours
..	Feldkirch, 5 a.m. (per Haag), in 7¾ hours; and 7½ p.m. (per Belzers), in 6 hours
..	Hanz, 5 a.m., Tues., Thurs., & Sat., returning at 3½ p.m., in 4¾ hours.
..	Küblis, 5 a.m., returning at 3½ p.m.; in winter, Tues., Thurs. and Saturday only; in 4¾ hours
..	Milan, 5 a.m. (per Lecco), in 29½ hours; 5 a.m. (per Bellinzona), in 28 hours; and 9.30 p.m. (per Como), in 22½ hours
..	Ragaz, 5 a.m., 1¼ and 9 p.m., in 2 hours.
..	Rorschach, 5 a.m. and 9 p.m., in 10½ hours
..	St. Gallen, 5 a.m. and 9 p.m., in 13½ hours
..	Splügen, 5 a.m., and 9.30 p.m. in 7 hours
..	Samader, 4½ a.m.; in winter, Mon., Wed., & Fri., only; returning at 5½ a.m., in 13½ hours
..	Uznach, 5 a.m., and 2½ p.m., in from 7½ to 9¼ hrs.
..	Wesen, 5 a.m., and 2½ p.m., in 5¾ hours
..	Zurich, 5 a.m., and 2½ p.m., in 17 hours

ENG. MLS.	**Cleve** to
39¼	Crefeld, 9½ a.m., 10 p.m., in 6½ hours.
33⅓	Dusseldorf, at 5 a.m. (per Xanten), 9½ a.m. and 10 p.m. (per Geldern.)
5½	Emmerich, 11 a.m., and 8¼ p.m., in 1½ hours
13½	Nymwegen, at 7½ a.m. and 6½ p.m., in 2½ hours

ENG. MLS.	**Coblentz** to
106½	Aix-la-Chapelle, 3 p.m. (per Losheim), in 22 hours.
32½	Altenkirchen, 8½ p.m., in 6¾ hours
39¼	Binger, 7 a.m. and 1 (in winter 3) p.m., in 6 hours
37	Bonn, 6¼ a.m., 7½ p.m., in 8 hours.
13½	Boppard, 7 a.m. and 1 (in winter 3) p.m., in 2 hours
53½	Cologne (Deutz), 6¼ a.m. and 7¼ p.m., in 10 hours.
48½	Creuznach, 7 a.m. and 1 (in winter 3) p.m. in 7¾ hours
17	Dierdorf, 8½ p.m., in 3 hours
11¼	Ems, 7¼ a.m. In summer, 2½ p.m., in 2 hours
76½	Frankfurt-o-M., 1 (in winter 3) p.m.; also 7¼ a.m. (per Wiesbaden), in 15 hours.
65	Giessen, 9 a.m., in 13½ hours
27¾	Limburg, 9 a.m. and 5 p.m.
25¼	Linz, 5 (in winter 4) p.m.
66	Losh, 3 p.m., in 12½ hours
55½	Mayence, 1 (in winter 3) p.m.
18½	Mayen, 7 a.m. and 3 p.m.
11¼	Neuwied, 5 (in winter 4) p.m.
76¼	Olpe, 8½ p.m., in 19½ hours
37	Schwalbach, 7¼ a.m., in 6 hours.
67	Siegen, 8½ p.m., in 14½ hours
33½	Simmern, 1 (in winter 3) p.m.
70½	Trier, 7 a.m. and 3 p.m.
55½	Wetzlar, 9 a.m., in 11½ hours
46½	Wiesbaden, 7¼ a.m., in 8½ hours

ENG. MLS.	**Coburg** to
93½	Altenburg, 6 a.m. & 1½ p.m.
..	Culmbach, 6¼ a.m. & 3 p.m.
68	Eisenach, 9 p.m., in 13½ hrs.
76½	Gera, 6 a.m. and 1½ p.m.
65	Gotha, 6 a.m. and 9 p.m.
19½	Hildburghausen, 6 a.m. and 9 p.m., in 3½ hours.
9¼	Lichtenfels, 6¼ a.m. & 3 p.m.
38	Meiningen, 9 p.m., in 7¾ hrs.
55½	Neustadt-on-the-Oder, 6 a.m. and 1½ p.m., in 14 hours
..	Nürnberg, 6¼ a.m. & 3 p.m.
43¾	Rudolstadt, 6 a.m. & 1½ p.m.
37	Saalfeld, 6 a.m. and 1½ p.m.
53½	Schmalkalden, 9 p.m., in 9¾ in hours
11¼	Sonneberg, 6 a.m. & 1½ p.m.
37	Suhl, 6 a.m. and 9 p.m.
67¼	Weimar, 6 a.m. and 1½ p.m.

ENG. MLS.	**Cologne** to
40¼	Altenkirchen, 2 (in W. 1) p.m.
9¼	Bensberg, 8 a.m., 5 & 10 p.m.
53½	Coblentz, 6½ (in winter 7.50) a.m.; & 10½ p.m., in 9 hrs.
22	Euskirchen, 5 and 10¼ a.m., 2.45 and 7 p.m. (per Brühl)
112	Frankfurt-o-M., 2 (in winter 1) p.m. (per Limburg); 8¼ p.m. (per Dpfsch), in 23½ hours
32½	Gladbach, 7¼ a.m. (per Rheydt), in 6 hours
35¾	Gumersbach, 8 a.m. & 10 p.m.
26½	Julich, 5½ p.m., in 4¾ hours
12¼	Kerpen, 6 a.m. and 5 p.m.
24¼	Lennep, 6½ a.m. and 5 p.m.
72¾	Limburg, 2 (in winter 1) p.m.
43¾	Lüdenscheid, 6½ a.m., in 11 hours
22	Neuss, 5 a.m. and 4½ p.m.
48½	Olpe, 8 a.m. and 10 p.m., in 10¾ hours
17	Siegburg, 2 (in winter 1) & 6 (in winter 5) p.m., in 3¼ hrs.
67¼	Siegen, 8 a.m. and 10 p.m., in 14 hours.
103	Trier, 5 a.m. and 7 p.m., in 23 hours
35¾	Wipperfürth, 7 a.m. (per Engelskirchen), returning at 7½ p.m., in 8½ hours

ENG. MLS.	**Constance** to
11½	Romanhorn, 6½ a.m., in 2 hrs
..	Schaffhausen, 8 a.m., in 4½ hr
..	St. Gallen, 6½ a.m., in 5 hrs.
24	Stockach, 10 p.m., in 4 hours
..	Winterthur, 8 a.m., in 6 hrs.
70½	Zurich, 8 a.m., in 8½ hours.

ENG. MLS.	**Cothen** to
7½	Aken, 8¾ a.m. & 7¾ p.m., returning at 5¼ a.m. and 3¼ p.m., in 1¾ hours

ENG. MLS.	**Cracow** to
..	Breslau, 10 a.m., and 4 p.m.
222	Lemberg, 12 a.m., 7 p.m., in 32½ hours
9½	Michalowice, 3 p.m. Tues. & Sat., returning on Sun. & Wednesday at 2½ a.m., in 1¾ hours
83½	Teschen, 7 p.m., returning at 5¼ p.m., in 15 hours
..	Warsaw, 10 a.m (per Graniey), in 29 hours
..	Vienna, 10 a.m. (per Cosel) in 22½ hours

ENG. MLS.	**Crefeld** to
39½	Cleve, 11.20 a.m., and 11½ p.m., in 7 hours
24½	Venlo, 6 a.m. (per Breyel), in 4¾ hours

ENG. MLS.	**Creuznach** to
9	Bingen, at 7½ a.m.
42½	Birkenfeld, 6 a.m., and 5½ p.m., in 7½ hours
48¼	Coblentz, 7½ a.m., 9½ p.m.
34¾	Kaiserslautern, 10 p.m., in 6¾ hours
25¼	Mayence, 4 & 7½ a.m., 5 p.m., in 5 hours
47	Mannheim, 9¾ (in Winter 11¾) p.m., in 7 hours
74	Saarlouis, 5½ p.m., in 15¾ hrs
76½	Trier, 9½ p.m. (per Bingerbruck), and 5½ p.m. (per Birkenfeld); 5½ p.m. (per Thalfang), in 17¼ hours
..	Worms, 3½ a.m. (per Alzey).

ENG. MLS.	**Culmbach** to
13½	Bayreuth, 2 and 10 a.m., and 6½ p.m., in 2¾ hours
..	Coburg, 8.34 a.m. & 4.17 p.m.
48½	Eger, 9.37 a.m., and 6.8 p.m., in 9½ hours
..	Wundsiedel, 9.37 a.m., and 6.8 p.m., in 5¾ hours

ENG. MLS.

Custrin to

53¼ Berlin, 9½ p.m., in 8¼ hours

19½ Frankfurt-on-the-Oder, 1¾ & 11¼ a.m., and 8¼ p.m., in 3 hours

33½ Konigsburg, 3 a.m., in 7¾ hours

28¾ Landsberg, 6½ a.m., and 3½ & 12½ p.m., in 5 hours

48½ Pyritz, 3½ p.m., in 11¾ hours

40¼ Schwedt, 3 a.m., in 12 hours

39¼ Schwerin, 2½ a.m., in 6½ hours

56½ Woldenberg, 3½ p.m., and 12½ night, in 9½ hours

26½ Wrietzen, 10 a.m., in 5 hours

Dantzic to

82 Stolp, 1½ p.m. and 12 night, in 11¾ hours

Darmstadt to

.. Alsey, 4 p.m. (per Worrstadt), in 5¾ hours

.. Creuznach, 4 p.m. (per Wollstein), in 6¾ hours

.. Dieburg, 6 p.m., returning at 8 a.m., in 1½ hours

.. Erbach, 7.30 a.m. and 6 p.m., in 4¾ hours

.. Mayence, 6 a.m. and 4 p.m., in 3¼ hours

.. Oppenheim, 4 p.m., in 2½ hours

.. Seligenstadt, 6 p.m., returning at 5 a.m., in 4 hours

Dessau to

.. Zerbst, 8½ a.m. and 5¼ p.m., in 2½ hours

Detmold to

.. Bielefeld, 6 a.m., in 3½ hours

.. Blomberg, 5 p.m.; also at 1.25 p.m. (per Horn), in 2¼ hours

.. Buckenburg, 8 p.m., in 7 hours

.. Carlshafen, 5 p.m., in 10 hours

.. Herford, 3 p.m., in 3 hours

.. Horn, 11½ a.m., & 1.25 p.m., in 50 minutes

.. Hoxter, 1.25 and 5 p.m., in 6 hours

.. Lemgo, 8½ a.m., and 8 p.m.

.. Paderborn, 11½ a.m., in 4 hours

.. Pyrmont, 1.25 p.m. (per Horn) and 8 p.m. (per Lemgo), in 5 hours

.. Rinteln, 8 p.m., in 5½ hours

.. Steinheim, 1.25 p.m., returning at 11 a.m., in 2½ hours

.. Vlotho, at 3 p.m., in 4½ hours

ENG. MLS.

Dijon to

.. Basel, 3½ a.m., in 17½ hours

.. Geneva, 3½ a.m., in 14½ hours

Donauesching to

39¼ Freiburg, at 9.25 p.m., in 7¼ hours

32½ Hornberg, at 9 p.m., in 5 hours

56¾ Offenburg, at 9 p.m., in 10 hours

22 Rottweil, 11 p.m., in 4 hours

24 Schaffhausen, 10 p.m., in 4¼ hours

28 Stockach, at 8½ p.m., in 6¼ hours

Donauworth to

16½ Dillingen, at 5 a.m., in 3¼ hours

30 Gunzburg, at 5 a.m., in 7 hours

34¾ Ingolstadt, at 11 p.m., in 6½ hours

21¼ Neuburg, at 11 p.m., in 3½ hours

76¼ Neuenmarkt, 11 p.m., in 20 hours

79¾ Regensburg, at 11 p.m., in 15½ hours

Dortmund to

16½ Iserlohn, at 9½ a.m. & 4½ p.m. and 12 night, in 3½ hours

Dresden to

58 Annaberg, at 8½ a.m., in 14¼ hours

48¼ Chemnitz, 12 noon, and 6½ p.m., in 8½ hours

59 Cottbus, 9½ p.m., in 12½ hours

23 Freiburg, at 8½ a.m., 12 noon, and 6½ p.m., in 4¼ hours

51 Marienberg, at 8½ a.m. on Sunday, Tuesday, and Fri.; also at 12 noon, on Sun., Tuesday, and Friday, in 12 hours

15¼ Meissen, 10 p.m., in 2¼ hours

22¼ Nossen, 12 noon, and 6 p.m.

98½ Prague, (by Railway).

49 Spremberg, 9½ p.m., in 10¼ hours

Driburg to

20¾ Hoxter, 10½ p.m., in 3 hours

12¼ Paderborn, 11¾ a.m., in 2½ hours

15¾ Steinheim, 11 p.m., returning at 7½ a.m., in 2¾ hours

Dusseldorf to

52 Cleve, 9.20 a.m. and 9½ p.m. (per Crefeld), and 6½ a.m. (per Xanten), in 8½ hours

12½ Crefeld, 9.20 a.m., & 9½ p.m., in 2 hours

23 Essen, 5 p.m., in 4½ hours

21¼ Gladbach, 9.5 p.m., in 3¾ hours

ENG. MLS.

Dusseldorf to

11¼ Mettmann, 6 p.m., in 2 hours

20 Meurs, 5½ p.m. (returning at 4½ a.m.), in 3½ hours

6¾ Ratingen, 7 p.m. (returning at 6.55 a.m.), in 1 hour

Eichstadt to

67¼ Amburg, 11—11½ a.m., in 13¼ hours

63¾ Augsburg, 2 p.m. (per Pornbach), in 13¾ hours

15¾ Ingolstadt, 2 p.m., in 3 hours

65 Munich, 2 p.m., in 14¼ hours

12¼ Neuburg, 2 p.m., in 2½ hours

42½ Neumarkt, 11—11½ a.m., in 7¾ hours

19½ Pleinfeld, 11½ a.m., in 4½ hours

13½ Weissenburg, 11½ a.m., in 3 hours

Eisenach to

47¼ Cassel, 4½ p.m., in 12 hours

68 Coburg, 2½ p.m., in 14 hours

26½ Eschwege, 4½ p.m., in 5 hours

107½ Frankfort-on-the-Maine, 7¾ a.m. (per Giessen), and 8 p.m. (per Fulda), in 12½ hours

47¼ Fulda, 8 p.m. (per Vacha), in 9½ hours

98¼ Hanau, 8 p.m. (per Fulda), in 19½ hours

48½ Hildburghausen, 2½ and 9 p.m., in 12 hours

14½ Liebenstein, summer only.

30 Meiningen, 2½ and 9 p.m., in 6¼ hours.

51¾ Mellrichstadt, 6 a.m., Tuesday and Saturday; returning on Sunday and Wednesday at 5 a.m., in 13½ hours

22 Muhlhausen, 3 p.m., in 4¼ hours

6¾ Ruhla, 3 p.m., returning at 8 a.m., in 1½ hours

19½ Salzungen, 2½ p.m., in 3¼ hours

22 Schmalkalden, 11½ a.m. (per Waltershausen), and 9 p.m., in 4¾ hours

20¾ Vacha, 1.55 a.m. (per Gerstung), and 8 p.m., in 4 hrs.

19½ Wanfried, 4½ p.m., in 4 hours

Elberfeld to

33½ Gummersbach, 2¼ p.m., in 7 hours

7½ Lennep, at 6 & 10 a.m., 2¼, 8, and 10¾ p.m., in 1¾ hours

7½ Mettmann, 6½ p.m., returning at 7 a.m., in 2 hours

ENG. MLS.	**Elberfeld** to
46	Olpe, 6 a.m. and 8 p.m., in 12 hours
$6\frac{3}{4}$	Remscheid, 6 a.m. $2\frac{1}{4}$ & 8 p.m.
65	Siegen, 6 a.m. and 8 p.m., in 15 hours
$7\frac{1}{2}$	Solingen, $9\frac{1}{2}$ p.m., in $1\frac{3}{4}$ hrs.
20	Wipperfurth, $2\frac{1}{4}$ and 8 p.m., in $4\frac{1}{2}$ hours
	Elbing to
$13\frac{1}{2}$	Pr. Holland, 1.44 and 11.12 a.m., 3.14 and 5 p.m., direct, in $2\frac{1}{4}$ hours
	Ellwangen to
$10\frac{1}{4}$	Aalen, 2.10 a.m. and 7.20 p.m., in $1\frac{3}{4}$ hours
$15\frac{1}{2}$	Crailshein, $1\frac{1}{4}$ a.m., in $2\frac{1}{2}$ hrs.
$25\frac{1}{4}$	Gmünd, 7.20 p.m., in $4\frac{1}{4}$ hrs.
$25\frac{1}{4}$	Hall, $5\frac{1}{2}$ a.m. and $8\frac{3}{4}$ p.m., in $4\frac{3}{4}$ hours
$57\frac{3}{4}$	Heilbronn, $5\frac{1}{2}$ a.m. & $8\frac{3}{4}$ p.m. in 11 hours
23	Nordlingen, $5\frac{1}{2}$ a.m., in $3\frac{3}{4}$ hrs
..	Nürnberg, $5\frac{1}{2}$ a.m. (per Nordlingen), in $8\frac{1}{4}$ hours
$58\frac{3}{4}$	Stuttgart, 7.20 p.m. (per Gmünd), in $9\frac{3}{4}$ hours
51	Ulm, 2.10 a.m., in $8\frac{1}{2}$ hours
	Emden to
$15\frac{3}{4}$	Aurich, $4\frac{1}{2}$ and $6\frac{1}{4}$ a.m., and $2\frac{1}{4}$, $3\frac{1}{4}$ (Winter $12\frac{1}{4}$ noon), and $4\frac{1}{4}$ p.m., in $4\frac{1}{4}$ hours
$18\frac{1}{2}$	Leer, $9\frac{1}{2}$ p.m., in $3\frac{1}{2}$ hours
$18\frac{1}{2}$	Norden, $4\frac{1}{2}$ a.m. and $4\frac{1}{4}$ p.m., in $3\frac{1}{4}$ hours
	Emmerich to
$18\frac{1}{2}$	Arnheim, 3 and $3\frac{1}{4}$ a.m., and 1.21 and $1\frac{1}{2}$ p.m., in 3 hrs.
$5\frac{1}{2}$	Cleve, 7 a.m.; in summer, also 3 p.m.; also Monday, Wednesday, Thursday and Saturday, 4 p.m., in 2 hours
$71\frac{3}{4}$	Münster, $3\frac{1}{2}$ p.m. (per Bocholt), in $16\frac{1}{4}$ hours
$43\frac{3}{4}$	Oberhausen, $1\frac{1}{2}$ a.m., 2 & 2.20 p.m., 12.20 & 12.45 night, in $6\frac{1}{4}$ hours
$24\frac{3}{4}$	Wesel, 2 p.m. & 12.20 night, in $3\frac{1}{4}$ hours
23	Zütphen, $2\frac{1}{2}$ p.m., in $3\frac{1}{4}$ hrs.
	Ems to
$11\frac{1}{4}$	Coblenz, $3\frac{1}{2}$ and 10 a.m., and $4\frac{3}{4}$ p.m., in 2 hours
$25\frac{1}{4}$	Schwalbach, $8\frac{3}{4}$ a.m., in $4\frac{1}{4}$ hours
$34\frac{1}{2}$	Wiesbaden, $8\frac{3}{4}$ a.m., in $6\frac{1}{4}$ hrs.
	Erfurt to
38	Artern, $2\frac{1}{2}$ p.m., in 8 hours
$72\frac{3}{4}$	Merseburg, $2\frac{1}{4}$ p.m., in $14\frac{1}{2}$ hours
$49\frac{1}{2}$	Nordhausen, 8 a.m. and 10 p.m., in $8\frac{1}{2}$ hours

ENG. MLS.	**Erfurt** to
$53\frac{1}{4}$	Querfurt, $2\frac{1}{2}$ p.m., in $11\frac{1}{4}$ hrs.
37	Sondershausen, 8 a.m. and 10 p.m., in $6\frac{1}{4}$ hours
$20\frac{3}{4}$	Weissensee, $2\frac{1}{2}$ p.m., in $3\frac{3}{4}$ hours
	Essen to
$10\frac{1}{4}$	Bochum, $7\frac{3}{4}$ a.m. & 4.20 p.m., in 2 hours
17	Dorsten, 6.30 p.m., in 3 hrs.
$12\frac{1}{4}$	Duisburg, 8 a.m. & 6.10 p.m., in $2\frac{1}{4}$ hours
23	Dusseldorf, 7.10 a.m., in 4 hrs
$4\frac{1}{2}$	Steele, 4.10 and 9.55 a.m., & 5.10 p.m., in 55 minutes
17	Witten, $7\frac{3}{4}$ a.m. & 4.20 p.m., returning at $5\frac{1}{2}$ a.m. and 2.35 p.m., in $3\frac{1}{4}$ hours
	Feldkirch to
$20\frac{3}{4}$	Bregenz, 9 p.m., in 4 hours
30	Chur, $6\frac{1}{2}$ p.m., in 7 hours
111	Innsbruck, 11 p.m., in $20\frac{1}{2}$ hours
60	Landeck, 11 p.m., in $11\frac{1}{4}$ hrs
..	Lichtensteig, 1.40 p.m. (per Wattwyl), in $7\frac{1}{4}$ hours
$27\frac{3}{4}$	Lindau, 9 p.m., in 6 hours
30	St. Gallen, 4 a.m. (per Allstetten), in $5\frac{1}{4}$ hours
74	Zurich, 4 a.m. (per St. Gallen, & 1.40 p.m. (per Wattwyl), in $17\frac{1}{2}$ hours
	Finsterwalde to
$31\frac{1}{4}$	Cottbus, 6 a.m., in $6\frac{3}{4}$ hours
	Flensburg to
$34\frac{3}{4}$	Hadersleben, $7\frac{1}{4}$ p.m., in $6\frac{1}{4}$ hours
38	Rendsburg, 8 a.m. & 11 p.m., in $6\frac{1}{4}$ hours
	Florence to
$83\frac{1}{4}$	Bologna, 5 p.m., in 14 hours. FARES--45 pauls, coupe; 40 pauls, interieur; and 30 pauls, banquette.
$159\frac{1}{2}$	Mantua, } Tues., Thurs. & Sat. at 5 p.m.; also Briefpost daily.
111	Modena, }
	Frankenhausen to
$14\frac{1}{2}$	Artern, 7 p.m., in 4 hours
$35\frac{3}{4}$	Erfurt, $2\frac{1}{4}$ a.m., in $7\frac{3}{4}$ hours
$25\frac{1}{4}$	Nordhausen, 2 a.m., in $4\frac{1}{2}$ hrs
$6\frac{3}{4}$	Sachsenburg, $2\frac{1}{4}$ a.m. and 7 p.m., in 1 hour
$12\frac{3}{4}$	Sondershausen, 2 and $6\frac{1}{4}$ a.m.
$32\frac{1}{2}$	Weimar, $2\frac{1}{4}$ a.m., in $7\frac{1}{4}$ hours
	Frankfort-on-Maine to
..	Amsterdam, 8 a.m. and 8 p.m., in 38 hours
126	Ansbach, 7 p.m., in 24 hours
23	Aschaffenburg, $12\frac{1}{2}$ noon (per Hanau), also 6 a.m. and 7 p.m. (per Seligenstadt), in 4 hours

ENG. MLS.	**Frankfurt-on-Maine** to
$211\frac{1}{2}$	Augsburg, 6 and 7 a.m.; $12\frac{1}{4}$, $12\frac{1}{2}$, and 7 p.m.
121	Bamberg, 6 a.m., $12\frac{1}{2}$ noon, & 7 p.m. (per Wurzburg), in $30\frac{1}{4}$ hours
320	Berlin, per railway, see page 99
$80\frac{3}{4}$	Bischofsheim, 7 p.m., in $15\frac{1}{2}$ hours
200	Brunswick, 12.10 & $7\frac{1}{4}$ p.m. (per Cassel), 8 a.m. (per Cologne), in 23 hours
..	Bremen, 12.10 and $7\frac{1}{4}$ p.m.; also 8 a.m. (per Cologne), in $26\frac{1}{4}$ hours
$108\frac{3}{4}$	Cassel, by railway, see page 76
$76\frac{1}{4}$	Coblentz, 8 a.m. (per Wiesbaden), 6 p.m. (per Mayence), $6\frac{1}{2}$, 8, and 11 a.m., in summer, per steamer, and 8 p.m., in $8\frac{1}{2}$ hours
156	Coburg, 6 a.m. and 7 p.m. (per Wurzburg), and $7\frac{1}{4}$ p.m (per Marburg), in 33 hours
112	Cologne, 1 p.m. (per Limburg), 6 p.m. (per Mayence), and 8 p.m.; also $6\frac{1}{2}$, 8, & 11 a.m. (by steamer in summer), in 10 hours
..	Eger, 7 p.m. (per Bamberg), in 32 hours
$107\frac{1}{2}$	Eisenach, $7\frac{1}{4}$ a.m. (per Fulda) in 20 hours
60	Fulda, $7\frac{1}{4}$ a.m. and 7 p.m., in $9\frac{3}{4}$ hours
$54\frac{1}{4}$	Gemünden, 6 a.m., in $9\frac{1}{2}$ hrs
$302\frac{3}{4}$	Harburg (Hamburg), 8 a.m., in summer, and $7\frac{1}{4}$ p.m., in $39\frac{1}{4}$ hours
$204\frac{1}{2}$	Hanover, 8 a.m. in summer; 12.10 & $7\frac{1}{4}$ p.m., in $21\frac{1}{4}$ hrs
52	Heidelberg, $8\frac{3}{4}$ p.m., in $7\frac{1}{4}$ hrs
$191\frac{1}{2}$	Hildesheim, 12.10 a.m. and $7\frac{1}{4}$ p.m., in 31 hours
$9\frac{1}{4}$	Homburg 9 and 11 a.m.; 1, 5, and 7 p.m., in $1\frac{1}{2}$ hrs.
$80\frac{3}{4}$	Kissingen, 7 p.m. (per Wurzburg), in $21\frac{3}{4}$ hours
$57\frac{3}{4}$	Lauterbach, $8\frac{1}{4}$ a.m., in $10\frac{1}{2}$ hours
215	Leipsic, $7\frac{1}{4}$ a.m. (per Fulda), in $29\frac{3}{4}$ hours
$39\frac{1}{4}$	Limburg, 1 p.m., in $7\frac{1}{2}$ hours
..	London, 8 a.m. (per Ostend), in $44\frac{1}{2}$ hours
..	Lubeck, $7\frac{1}{4}$ p.m., in 60 hours
$20\frac{3}{4}$	Mayence, at 8 p.m., in $3\frac{1}{2}$ hours
$89\frac{3}{4}$	Mergentheim, 7 p.m., in $16\frac{1}{2}$ hours
$117\frac{3}{4}$	Meiningen, 8.15 a.m., and $7\frac{1}{4}$ p.m., in 19 hours

ENG. MLS.	**Frankfort-on-Maine** to
47¼	Miltenberg, 7 p.m., in 8¼ hrs.
250¾	Munich, 6 a.m. and 12½ noon, & 7 p.m. (per Bamberg), 7 a.m. (per Heilbron), and 7 p.m. (per Wurzburg an Gunzenhausen), in 37 hrs.
32½	Nidda, 8¼ a.m., in 4¾ hours
134¼	Nurnberg, 6 a.m. & 12½ noon, and 7 p.m. (per Bamberg), and 6 a.m. (per Kitzingen), in 25 hours
3¼	Offenbach, 11¼ a.m. 5 and 10 p.m., in ⅜ of an hour
122¼	Paris, 6 a.m. (per Mannheim) in 21½ hours
..	Prague, 8.15 a.m. & 7½ p.m. (per Dresden), in 44 hours
192¾	Regensburg, 12½ noon (per Bamberg), 7 p.m. (pr Seligenstadt), in 39 hours
74	Siegen, 7¼ p.m., in 14 hours
123½	Stuttgart, 7 a.m. and 4.15 p.m. (per Heilbronn), and 12¼ noon (per Carlsruhe), in 12¾ hours
37	Weilburg, 5 p.m., returning at 3 a.m., in 7 hours
66	Wertheim, 7 p.m., in 11½ hrs.
37	Wetzlar, 7¼ p.m., in 4½ hrs.
20¾	Wiesbaden, 8 p.m., in 2½ hrs.
78½	Wurzburg, 6 a.m., and 12½ noon, and 7 p.m. (per Seligenstadt), in 12½ hours

ENG. MLS.	**Frankfurt** on the Oder to
32½	Crossen, 11 a.m. and 9 p.m.
20	Custrin, 3½ & 11½ a.m., and 9½ p.m., in 3 hours.
52	Gruneberg, at 11 a.m. and 9 p.m., in 9½ hours
48¼	Landsberg, at 3½ & 11½ a.m., and 9½ p.m., in 8½ hours.
42½	Lubben, at 4 p.m., in 10 hrs.
52¼	Luckau, at 4 p.m., in 13 hrs.
49	Meseritz, at 9 p.m., returning at 10 a.m., in 14 hours
49	Schwiebus, at 4 a.m., in 12 hours
76¾	Woldenberg, 11½ a.m. & 9½ p.m., in 13 hours

ENG. MLS.	**Freiburg** to
15¾	Altbreisach, 6 a.m., 2½ p.m.
39¼	Donaueschingen, 11½ a.m., in 8¾ hours
52	Schaffhausen, 6 p.m., in 10¾ hours
70½	Stockach, 11½ a.m., in 15 hrs.

ENG. MLS.	**Freiburg** (Switzerland) to
..	Bern, 5 a.m. and 5.5 p.m., in 3½ hours
..	Geneva, 10 a.m., 12¼ noon, & 10½ p.m., in 15¼ hours
..	Lausanne, 10 a.m., 12¼ noon, and 10½ p.m., in 8¼ hours
..	Neuenburg, 5 p.m. (per Murten), in 4½ hours
..	Vevay, 12½ noon, and 10½ night (per Moudon), in 10 hours
..	Yverdun, 10 a.m., in 8½ hrs.

ENG. MLS.	**Freiburg** (Silesian) to
29	Hirschberg, at 8¼ p.m. (per Bolkenh); also 9½ (in Winter 11) a.m., and (in Summer) 3½ p.m. (per Landeshut), in 8 hours
14½	Landeshut, 9½ (in Winter 11) a.m., 8 p.m., and (in Summer) 3½ p.m., in 3 hours
5½	Salzbrunn, 9 a.m., and 3½ & 8 p.m., in 1¼ hours
9	Waldenburg, 9 (in Winter 10½) a.m. and 8 p.m. (per Altwas), in 2½ hours

ENG. MLS.	**Friedrichsfeld** to
4½	Schwetzingen, 7.9 a.m. and 12.5 & 4¼ p.m.; returning at 5¾ & 10 a.m., & 3 p.m., in 50 minutes

ENG. MLS.	**Friedrichshafen** to
..	Chur, 5½ a.m. and 4 p.m. in 12 hours
..	Rorshach, 5½ a.m. 12 & 4 p.m.
..	St. Gallen, 5½ a.m., 12 and 4 p.m., in 3½ hours
..	Zurich, 7¾ a.m. and 4 p.m. (per Romanshorn) in 9 hours

ENG. MLS.	**Fulda** to
26½	Alsfeld, 7 a.m., in 4¾ hours.
34¾	Bebra, 4½ and 10½ a.m., in 6¼ hours
18½	Brüchenau, 6½ p.m., in 4¼ hrs.
68	Cassel, 4½ and 10½ a.m., in 9 hours
47¼	Eisenach, 10½ a.m. (per Bebra), and 5¾ p.m. (per Vacha), in 8½ hours
60	Frankfurt, 6 a.m. & 8 p.m. in 10½ hours
57¾	Giessen, 7 a.m., in 11¾ hours.
51	Hanau, 6 a.m. and 8 p.m., in 9½ hours
25¼	Hersfeld, 4½ and 10½ a.m., in 4¾ hours
33¾	Kissingen, 6½ p.m. in summer, in 9 hours

ENG. MLS.	**Furth** to
31¼	Aix-la-Chapelle, 11½ a.m., in 6 hours
11¼	Neuss, 5 a.m. and 12 noon, in 2 hours

ENG. MLS.	**Gemunden** to
30	Aschaffenberg, 11 a.m., in 5 hours
53½	Frankfurt, 11 a.m., in 10½ hours
24	Wurzburg, 3¾ p.m., in 3¾ hours

ENG. MLS.	**Geneva** to
..	Basel, 12 noon (per Bern) and 10½ p.m. (per Biel or Solothurn), in 29 hours
..	Bern, 12 noon and 10½ p.m., in 16¼ hours
..	Chambery, 7 a.m., 8½ and 9 p.m.
..	Chamouny, 7 a.m., returning at 8 a.m., in 11½ hours
..	Freiburg, 10½ p.m., in 17½ hrs
..	Lausanne, 8 a.m., 12 noon, & 10½ p.m., in 6¼ hours
..	Lyons, 6 & 10 a.m., & 3 & 5¾ p.m.
..	Milan, 11 a.m., in 51 hours
..	Martigny, 11 a.m. & 10½ p.m., in 12¼ hours
..	Neufchatel, 12 noon and 10½ p.m., in 14¼ hours
..	Paris, 7, & 10 (per Chalons), and 10 a.m. (per Dijon), in 30 hours
..	St. Maurice, 11 a.m., in 9¼ hours
..	Turin, 8½ p.m., in 20½ hours

ENG. MLS.	**Genoa** to
109½	Milan, 2 & 7 p.m., in 18 hours

ENG. MLS.	**Giessen** to
31¼	Alsfeld, 7 a.m., in 6¼ hours
93¼	Arnsberg, Sunday and Wed., at 7 a.m., in 23½ hours
30¼	Battenberg, 7 a.m., returning at 4 a.m., in 8¾ hours
28¾	Biedenkopf, 7 a.m., in 6¼ hrs.
38	Büdingen, 8½ a.m., in 7¼ hrs.
65	Coblentz, 6 a.m., in 14 hours
57¾	Fulda, 7 a.m., in 14½ hours
12¼	Grünberg, 7 a.m., in 2¾ hrs.
41½	Lauterbach, 7 a.m., in 11½ hrs
37	Limburg, 6 a.m., in 7½ hours
24¼	Nidda, 8½ a.m., in 4¼ hours.
9½	Wetzlar, 6 a.m., in 6½ hours.

ENG. MLS.	**Glogau** to
20¾	Guhrau, 2 p.m., in 4 hours.
35¾	Liegnitz, 1 and 10 a.m., in 6 hours
27¾	Lissa, 3½ and 8½ a.m., and 5¼ p.m., in 5 hours
22	Lüben, 1½ & 10 a.m., in 3¾ hrs.
70½	Meseritz, 6 p.m., in 16¾ hours
22	Neusatz, 2 p.m.. in 3¾ hours.
61¼	Nimkau, 6 p.m., in 14 hours
76¼	Posen, 3¼ a.m., and 5¼ p.m., in 13½ hours
23	Steinau, 7 p.m. Tues., Thur., and Sat., in 5½ hours

ENG. MLS.	**Gmund** to
14½	Aalen, 1½ a.m., in 2½ hours
33½	Stuttgardt, 11.30 night, in 5½ hours
12¼	Sussen, 12¾ p.m., in 2½ hours

ENG. MLS.	**Gorlitz** to
44¾	Hirschberg, 9½ p.m., in 9½ hours
14½	Lauban, 3 and 9½ p.m., in 2¾ hours
48½	Spremberg, 4½ p.m., in 8½ hrs.
22	Zittau, 12½ p.m., in 4½ hours

ENG. MLS.	**Gotha** to
65	Coburg, 8 a.m. and 3 p.m., in 14½ hours
61½	Gottingen, 1½ p.m., in 13 hrs.
43¾	Heligenstadt, 1½ p.m., in 9 hours
44¾	Hildburghausen, 8 a.m. and 3 p.m., in 10½ hours
11¼	Langensalza, 8 a.m., 1½ and 6½ p.m., in 2¼ hours
39¼	Meiningen, 1 p.m. (per Waltershausen), 5.50 p.m. (per Eisenach), & 3 p.m., in 9¼ hours
23	Muhlhausen, 8 a.m., 1½ and 6½ p.m., in 4½ hours
37	Schleusingen, 8 a.m. and 3 p.m., in 8½ hours
23	Schmalkalden, 1 p.m. (per Walterhausen), in 10 hours
27¾	Suhl, 8 a.m. and 3 p.m., in 5¾ hours
101¾	Würzburg, 3 and 5.50 p.m. (per Eisenach), in 24 hours

ENG. MLS.	**Gottingen** to
29¼	Cassel, 1.5 and 10.10 a.m., 4.25 p.m., in 5½ hours
56¾	Gotha, 11 night, in 12 hours
68	Hanover, 2.40 and 11.35 a.m., 4.10 p.m.
16½	Heiligenstadt, 11 night, in 3¼ hours
53¼	Hildesheim, 2.40 a.m. and 4.10 p.m., in 10 hours
46	Hoxter, 8½ a.m., in 9¾ hours
49	Langensalza, 11 night, in 9½ hours
38	Mulhausen, 11 night, in 7½ hours
16½	Munden, 1.5 and 10.10 a.m., 4.25 p.m., in 3½ hours
12	Nordheim, 2.40 and 11.35 a.m., 4.10 p.m.
..	Witzenhausen, 7 a.m. on Sun., Tuesday and Thursday, in 3 hours

ENG. MLS.	**Gunzburg** to
32½	Augsburg, 1 a.m. & 1½ p.m., in 5¼ hours
13½	Dillingen, 2 p.m., in 2¾ hours
31¼	Donauworth, 2 p.m., in 7 hours
14½	Ulm, 2½ a.m. and 1¼ p.m., in 2½ hours

ENG. MLS.	**Gunzenhausen** to
7	Ansbach, 2.40 a.m., 12 noon, and 5½ p.m., in 3 hours
65	Würzburg, 2.40 a.m., in 13¾ hours

ENG. MLS.	**Gustrow** to
37	Demmin, 11½ a.m., in 9 hours
12¼	Lage, 11½ a.m., in 1¾ hours
51	Ludwigslust, 6½ p.m., in 10½ hours
52	New Brandenburg, 11½ a.m.
68	Neustrelitz, 11½ a.m., in 12 hours
26½	Plaue, 11½ a.m., in 4½ hours
68	Röbel, 11½ a.m., in 10 hours
33½	Stavenhagen, 11½ a.m. and 6¾ p.m., in 5¾ hours
42½	Wahren, 11½ a.m., in 6¾ hrs.
69½	Wittstock, 11½ a.m., in 13½ hours

ENG. MLS.	**Halberstadt** to
10½	Blankenburg, 12¾ noon and 6½ p.m., in 1¾ hours
23	Hornburg, 7½ p.m., returning at 3¾ a.m., in 4½ hours
46	Nordhausen, 6½ & 12¾ a.m., and 6¾ p.m., in 7 hours
9¾	Quedlingburg, 6½ a.m.; 12¼, 4 and 6½ p.m., in 1½ hours
12¼	Wernigerode, 6¾ a.m. and 6¾ p.m., in 2½ hours

ENG. MLS.	**Hall** to
49½	Ansbach, 4¼ a.m. (per Crailsheim), in 9½ hours
19½	Crailsheim, 4¼ a.m., in 3¼ hrs.
25¼	Ellwangen, 2¼ p.m., & 12.25 night, in 4¾ hours
32½	Heilbronn, 10½ a.m., and 10½ p.m., in 6¼ hours
13½	Künzelsau, 1¾ and 10½ a.m., in 3½ hours
33½	Mergentheim, 1¾ a.m., in 7¾ hours
48½	Nördlingen, 12.25 night.
76¼	Nürmberg, 4½ a.m. (pr Crailsheim), and 12.25 night (per Nordlingen), in 13 hours
43¾	Stuttgart, 5 a.m. and 4 p.m.
34¾	Waiblingen, 5 a.m., in 7½ hrs.

ENG. MLS.	**Halle** to
20	Bitterfeld, 4 p.m., in 4 hours
15¾	Connern, 7 p.m., in 3 hours
21¼	Eisleben, 10 a.m., 3½, and 10 p.m., in 3½ hours
88½	Heiligenstadt, 10 a.m. and 10 p.m., in 19 hours
56½	Nordhausen, 10 a.m., and 10 p.m., in 10¾ hours
33½	Sangerhausen, at 10 a.m. & 10 p.m., in 6½ hours

ENG. MLS.	**Haltingen** to
..	Basle, 9.35 a.m ; 12½, 4½, 5¾, and 9½ p.m., in 1 hour
..	Lörrach, 12.35, 5¼ & 9½ p.m., in 1¼ hours
62½	Schaffhausen, 9.40 a.m., in 11 hours

ENG. MLS.	**Hamburg** to
56¾	Bremen, 8 p.m. (per Harburg), also 11 p.m., daily, except Sunday, in 9 hours
196½	Cassel, 9.20 a.m. & 4.40 p.m.
67¼	Celle, 6 p.m. (℘ Harburg).
57¾	Kiel, 10 p.m., in 8¾ hours
..	London, at 9 20 a.m. (per Ostend); 9.20 a.m. (per Calais), in 36¾ hours
39¼	Lubeck, 11 p.m., in 6 hours
27	Stade, 11½ a.m., & 10½ p.m. in 5¼ hours

ENG. MLS.	**Hamm** to
28¾	Arnsberg, 5.15 & 7.30 a.m., 1¼, 4.18, & 10¼ p.m., in 5 hrs
..	Cassel, 7½ a.m. & 9½ p.m., in 10¾ hours
..	Iserlohn, 5¼ a.m., 1¼, and 10¼ p.m., in 5¾ hours
10¼	Werl, 5¼ a.m., 1¼ and 10¼ p.m., in 1¾ hours

ENG. MLS.	**Hanau** to
13½	Aschaffenburg, 1½ p.m., in 2½ hours
29¼	Birstein, 4 p.m., in 6¼ hours
16½	Büdingen, 4 p.m., in 3 hours
97½	Eisenach, 9.50 a.m., in 19 hrs.
51	Fulda, 9.50 a.m., & 7 p.m.
57¾	Wurzburg, 1½ p.m., in 11¼ hours

ENG. MLS.	**Hanover** to
98½	Cassel, 7 a.m., 3½ & 10½ p.m., in 17¼ hours
206⅓	Frankfurt-on-the-Maine, 3½ and 10½ p.m., in 36½ hours
68	Göttingen, 7 a.m., 3½ and 10½ p.m.
27	Hameln, 11½ a.m., 4 and 10¾ p.m., in 4¾ hours
19½	Hildesheim, 9 p.m. daily, except Sunday, in 8¼ hours
55½	Holzminden, 3½ and 10½ p.m.
55½	Nordheim, 7 a.m., 3½ & 10½ p.m.
41½	Pyrmont, 11½ a.m., in 8 hours
38	Walsrode, Sunday, Tuesday, and Friday, at 7 a.m. returning Monday, Wednesday, & Saturday, at 6 a.m.

ENG. MLS.	**Harzburg** to
6¾	Goslar, 10 a.m., in 1¼ hours
37	Nordhausen, 9¾ a.m., in 9 hrs.
14½	Wernigerode, 10 a.m., in 3 hrs

ENG. MLS.	**Heidelberg** to
67¼	Bischofsheim, 4 and 9½ p.m., in 12 hours

Heidelberg to

Eng. Mls.	
43¾	Heilbronn, 9 p.m. (per Wimpfen), 10 a.m., (per Furfeld), in 7½ hours
44½	Miltenberg, 12¾ p.m, in 7¾ hours
74	Stuttgart, at 9 p.m. (per Wimpfen; 10 a.m., in 10 hours
85¼	Wurzburg, 4 and 9½ p.m., in 15¼ hours

Heilbronn to

Eng. Mls.	
76¼	Ansbach, 10½ p.m., in 14¾ hours
51	Ellwangen, 8¼ a.m. and 5¾ p.m., in 11¾ hours
23	Hall, 8¼ a.m., 5¾ & 10½ p.m.
43¾	Heidelberg, 8¼ a.m. (per Furfeld), 10½ p.m. (per Wimpfen), in 6¼ hours
41½	Mergentheim, 11¼ p.m.; 10½ p.m. (per Schonth), in 8 hours
98½	Nuremberg, 10½ p.m., in 20½ hours
55½	Rothenburg, 11¼ p.m. (per Blaufelden), in 13 hours
67½	Wurzburg, 11¼ p.m., in 15¼ hours

Herford to

Eng. Mls.	
17	Detmold, 10¼ a.m. (per Lage) in 3 hours
12¾	Lemgo, 7¼ p.m., in 2½ hours
15¾	Lübbecke, 7½ p.m., returning at 9 a.m., in 3¼ hours
32½	Pyrmont, 7¼ p.m., in 7 hours

Hildburghausen to

Eng. Mls.	
19½	Coburg, 12½ a.m. & 6½ p.m.
48½	Eisenach, 5 p.m. and 1 night
44¾	Gotha, 9¾ a.m., 5 p.m, and 1 night., in 9¾ hours
23	Meiningen, 5 p.m. & 1 night.
7½	Schleusingen, 9¾ a.m. and 1 night, in 2 hours
33½	Schmalkalden, 1 night, in 6¾ hours

Hildesheim to

Eng. Mls.	
84¼	Cassel, 2½ and 12 night
28¾	Goslar, 9 p.m., in 5½ hours
54¼	Göttingen, 2½ p.m. and 12 night, in 12 hours
32½	Hameln, 3 p.m., in 6 hours
19½	Hanover, 10½ p.m. daily, except Sunday, in 8¼ hours
49½	Holzminden, 2½ p.m. and 12 night, in 12 hours
41½	Nordheim, 2½ p.m. and 12 night, in 8 hours
37	Osterode, 10½ a.m. (per Seesen), in 6¾ hours
24¼	Seesen, 10½ a.m, in 4 hours

Hof to

Eng. Mls.	
..	Gera, at 2 p.m., in 10¼ hours
116½	Regensburg, 5.35 a.m. (per Nuremberg), in 22½ hours
21¼	Schleiz, at 2 p.m., in 4¼ hrs.
77	Weissenfels, at 2 p.m., in 16½ hours
23	Wunsiedel, 5.35 a.m. (per Schwarzeb), in 4½ hours
63½	Zeiz (Halle), at 2 p.m., in 13¼ hours

Homberg to

Eng. Mls.	
6¾	Wabern, 5½ a.m. and 4 p.m., in 1½ hours

Homburg (Höhe) to

Eng. Mls.	
9¼	Frankfurt-o-M., 9 & 11 a.m.; 1, 3½, and 7 p.m., in 1½ hrs
27¾	Weilburg, 6½ p.m., in 5½ hrs

Homburg (in Rheinbayern) to

Eng. Mls.	
6¾	Zweibrücken, 9½ a.m. and 8½ p.m., in 1 hour

Innsbruck to

Eng. Mls.	
132	Augsburg, 7 a.m. (pr Munich)
79¾	Botzen, 5 p.m., in 16½ hours
52	Brixen, 5 p.m., in 11¼ hours
111	Feldkirch, 4-5 a.m., in 20¼ hours
51	Landeck, 4-5 a.m. & 8 p.m.
186	Linz, 9 p.m., in 37¼ hours
94½	Munich, 7 a.m., in 21¾ hrs.
103	Salzburg, 9 p.m.; also 2 p.m. on Tuesdays and Fridays
181½	Verona, 5 p.m., in 34½ hours
300½	Vienna, 9 p.m., in 62¾ hours

Jena to

Eng. Mls.	
40	Altenburg, 6½ p.m., in 11½ hours
9	Apolda, 2 a.m. and 1¾ p.m.
23	Gera, 6½ p.m., in 5½ hours
18½	Neustadt, 6¾ p.m., in 4¾ hrs.
21¼	Rudolstadt, 6¾ p.m., in 4¾ hrs
30	Schleiz, 6¾ p.m., in 7½ hours
11¼	Weimar, 1¼ night in 2½ hours

Jungbunzlau to

Eng. Mls.	
47¼	Friedland, 10¾ p.m., in 8½ hours
25¼	Kolin, 11 a.m. and 11¼ p.m.
32½	Prague, 11½ p.m., in 5¾ hrs
33½	Reichenberg, 10¾ p.m., in 6 hours
46	Rumberg, 11¼ p.m., in 10¼ hrs
53¼	Trautenau. 10¾ p.m., returning at 12 noon, in 10¼ hrs.

Juterbogk to

Eng. Mls.	
30	Luckau, 12 noon, in 6 hours

Kaufbeuern to

Eng. Mls.	
25½	Fussen, 10½ a.m. (per Biessenh), in 5¼ hours
..	Schongau, 10¼ a.m. (per Biessenh), in 4½ hours

Kempten to

Eng. Mls.	
23	Füssen, 11¾ p.m., in 5½ hrs.
40	Lindau. 12¾, 6.25 & 11¾ p.m.
20½	Memmingen, 6½ & 12 p.m.
55½	Ulm, 12 night, in 10 hours

Kiel to

Eng. Mls.	
16¾	Eckernforde, at 12 noon, on Mondays, Weds., Thursdays, and Saturdays, returning at 2¼ a.m., in 2¾ hours
27	Eutin, at 11½ a.m., in 6 hrs.
54	Heiligenhafen, 11½ a.m., in 12½ hours
49	Lübeck, at 11½ a.m., in 11 hours
31¼	Schleswig, 11½ a.m. on Sunday & Tuesday, in 5¼ hrs.

Kissingen to

Eng. Mls.	
17	Bruckenau, 4¼ p.m., in 3¾ hours
81	Frankfurt-on-the-Maine, in summer only
35½	Fulda, 4¼ p.m., in 10¾ hours
33½	Meiningen, at 1½ p.m. in 8½ hours
13½	Schweinfurt, 4¾ & 9¾ a.m., and 1 p.m. in 2¾ hours
33½	Wurzburg, 4¾ & 9¾ a.m., and 1 p.m., in 8 hours

Kohlfurt to

Eng. Mls.	
24¼	Greifenberg, 6¾ a.m., returning at 3½ p.m., in 4½ hours

Koniggratz to

Eng. Mls.	
51	Glatz, 9½ p.m., in 11 hours
14½	Pardubitz, 4 a.m. & 12½ noon
65	Prague, 5 p.m., in 11½ hours
58½	Reichenberg, 1 p.m., in 11½ hours

Konigsberg to

Eng. Mls.	
71¾	Gumbinnen, 10½ a.m. and 9 p.m., in 12½ hours
71¾	Tilsit, 10¼ & 10½ a.m., and 5 and 9 p m., in 15¾ hours

ENG. MLS.	**Laibach** to
99½	Agram, 8¼ a.m., in 14½ hrs.
87¾	Carlstadt, 3 p.m. Wednesday and Saturday, and Briefpost daily, in 17 hours
54¼	Klagenfurt, 6 p.m., & Briefpost daily, in 12½ hours
..	Treviso, 6 a.m. and 6 p.m.
76¼	Triest, 6 a.m.; 6 & 6½ p.m.
111	Udine, 6 p.m., in 19¼ hours
67¼	Villach, 6 p.m., in 14¼ hours

	Landsberg to
38	Arnswalde, 7 p.m., in 10¾ hrs.
28¾	Cüstrin, 6 a.m., and 3 and 9 p.m., in 5 hours
48½	Frankfort-on-the-Oder, 6 a.m., and 3 and 9 p.m., in 8 hours
27¾	Woldenberg, 5¾ a.m. and 8½ p.m., 4¼ hours
35½	Züllichau, 10 p.m., in 14 hrs.

	Landshut to
55½	Deggendorf, at 6¼ a.m., in 9 hours
41½	Munich, 5½ a.m. & 1 & 9 p.m.
81	Passau, 5 & 6¼ a.m. (per Plattling); 6 p.m. (per Vilsbiburg)
39¼	Regensburg, 1 & 8 p.m.
82	Salzburg, 6 p.m., in 16 hours
33½	Straubing, 6½ a.m. & 1 p.m.
72½	Waldmunchen, 6½ a.m., in 15½ hours

	Lausanne to
..	Bern, 6 a.m. (per Murten); 9 a.m. (per Romont); and 6¼ p.m (per Murten), in 10 hours.
49¼	Besançon, 10.40 a.m., in 18¾ hours
..	Frieburg, 6 & 9 a.m., 6¼ p.m.
..	Geneva, at 7½ a.m., 2½, & 7½ p.m.
..	Milan, 3.40 p m., in 47 hours
..	Neufchatel, 6 a.m. and 8 p.m.
..	Paris, at 10.40 a.m.
..	St. Maurice, 6½ a.m. & 3.40 p.m
..	Vevay, 6½ a.m., & 3.40 p.m.

	Lauterbach to
10¼	Alsfeld, 9¾ a.m., in 2 hours
46	Friedberg, 5 a.m., in 8¾ hrs.
15¾	Fulda, 6¾ p.m., in 2¾ hours.
41½	Giessen, 9¾ a.m. (per Grünberg), in 8¼ hours
26½	Hersfeld, 7 p.m., in 4¾ hours
28¾	Nidda, 5 a.m. (per Schotten)
9¼	Schlitz, 7 p.m., in 1½ hours

	Leipsic to
72½	Annaberg, at 8 p.m., in 15 hours
53½	Chemnitz, 8 p.m., in 9 hours
13½	Delitzsch, 10 p.m., in 2½ hrs.
11¼	Eilenburg, 12 noon & 9½ p.m.
214	Frankfurt-on-Maine, 12 noon (per Fulda) and by railway.
17¼	Grimma, 6 a.m., 12 noon, & 6 p.m., in 3¼ hours
13	Lutzen, 7 (in Winter 6) p.m.
30½	Rochlitz, 12½ noon, 5 p.m.
40¼	Waldheim, 12 noon, in 8 hrs.
27	Zeiz, 5 p.m., in 5 hours

	Lemberg to
66	Brody, at 6 p.m. (on Sun., Tues., Th., and Sat.), and Briefpost daily, in 11½ hrs.
..	Odessa, 6 p.m. on Monday and Fri.; and 2 p.m. Sun., Wed., and Thur., in 88 hrs.

	Lichtenfels to
9¼	Coburg, 10 a.m. and 5½ p.m., in 1½ hours

	Liegnitz to
67¼	Glatz, at 6 p.m. (per Schweidnitz), in 13¾ hours
35½	Glogau, 10½ a.m. & 8 p.m., in 6½ hours
35½	Hirschberg, 10½ a.m., in 7½ hours
13½	Lüben, 10½ a.m. & 8 p.m.
30	Schweidnitz, 9 a.m., and 6 p.m., in 6 hours

	Limburg to
32½	Altenkirchen, 9 p.m., in 6½ hours
27¾	Coblentz, 5½ a.m. (in winter 6), and 1½ p.m., in 5½ hrs.
72¾	Cologne, 9 p.m., in 14¾ hrs.
3¼	Diez, 9 a.m., 3 and 9.10 p.m.
31¾	Dillenburg, 3 p.m., in 7½ hrs.
39¼	Frankfurt-o M., 6 a.m., in 7¾ hours
37	Giessen, 3 p.m., in 7½ hours
39¼	Siegen, 3 p.m. Mon., Wed., and Fri., in 9½ hours
27¾	Wetzlar, 3 p.m., in 5½ hours
27¾	Wiesbaden, 8 a.m. and 4 p.m.

	Lindau to
99½	Augsburg, 7 a.m. & 7 p.m. (per Kempten), in 13 hrs.
6¾	Bregenz, 1 p.m, in 1½ hrs.
57¼	Chur (per Rorschach)
27	Feldkirch, 5 a.m., in 5½ hrs.
40	Kempten, 7 p.m.
116½	Munich (per Augsburg)
..	St. Gallen, 5½ a.m., 1½ p.m.
..	Zurich, at 5½ & 1½ a.m., and 5½ a.m. & 1½ p.m. (per St. Gallen), in 16 hours

	Linz to
61½	Budweis, 7 p.m. on Sunday, Mon., Wed., & Friday, and Briefpost daily., in 12½ hrs.
186	Innsbruck, 2 p.m., in 35½ hrs.
150	Munich, 1 p.m., in 27½ hours
61	Passau, 1 p.m., in 10½ hours
136½	Regensburg, 1 p.m., in 23 hrs.
83	Salzburg, 2 p.m., in 14½ hrs.
49	Scharding, 1 p.m., in 7½ hrs.
115½	Vienna, at 1 & 2 p.m., in 17 hours

	Lubeck to
20½	Eutin, 2 p.m., in 2¾ hours
38	Hamburg, 11 p.m., in 6 hours
49	Kiel, 2 p.m., in 11 hours
51	Neumunster, 2 p.m., in 15 hours
39¼	Schwerin, 10½ p.m, in 6½ hrs.
35½	Wismar, 7¾ a.m., in 6 hours.
40½	Wittenburg, 10½ p.m. on Wed. and Sat., in 9¾ hours

	Lucerne to
..	Aarau, 8¼ a.m. (per Sursee); 2 p.m. (per Munster); 7 p.m. (per Kreuzstr)., in 6½ hours
64	Basel, 8¼ a.m. & 7 p.m., in 11 hours. FARES—12 frs. 80c. interieur; and 2 p.m. (per Aarau).
..	Bellinzona, at 6 a.m.
..	Bern, 8 p.m. (per Huttwyl) and 8 a.m. (per Langnau).
..	Brunnen, 11 a.m. (per Arth) 6 a.m. and 1 p.m. (per steam-boat), in 1¾ hours
..	Escholzmatt, at 8 a.m., in 4¾ hours
..	Milan, 6 a.m., in 27¼ hours
..	St. Gallen, 1 p.m. (per Brunnen and per Zurich), in 17½ hours
..	Solothurn, 8¼ a.m. & 7 p.m., in 9 hours
..	Uznach, 1 p.m., in 10¾ hours
..	Zurich, 9 a.m. (per Albis), & 10 p.m. (per Horgen)

	Ludwigsburg to
14½	Backnang, 6½ p.m., returning at 5½ a.m., in 3 hours
11¼	Gr. Bottwar, 6½ p.m., returning at 5¼ a.m., in 2½ hours

	Ludwigshafen to
6¾	Frankenthal, 9¾ p.m., in 1 hr.
12¼	Worms, 12 noon and 9¾ p.m., in 2 hours

	Luneburg to
14½	Blekede, 3 p.m., returning at 5 a.m., in 4 hours
22	Boizenburg, 12 noon, in 4 hrs.
33½	Dannenberg, 7½ a.m., returning at 6½ a.m., in 8½ hours
12¼	Lauenburg, 12 noon, in 2¾ hrs

Luxemburg to

ENG. MLS.	
30	Metz, 11 a.m., in 7 hours
19½	Thionville, 11 a.m., in 4 hrs.
25¼	Trier, 6 a.m. and 3 p.m., in 5½ hours

Lyons to

ENG. MLS.	
146¾	Avignon, 4 a.m., & 2½ p.m.
213¼	Marseilles, 4 a.m. & 2½ p.m.
230¾	Muhlhausen, 5 a.m. & 3 p.m.
300½	Paris, 5 & 9 a.m. and 7 p.m.
292½	Strasburg, 3 p.m.

Mannheim to

ENG. MLS.	
47½	Creuznach, 11.50 a.m., in 7 hours

Mantua to

ENG. MLS.	
..	Bologna, 3½ a.m. Monday, Wednesday, and Friday, and Briefpost daily, in 12 hours
..	Florence, 3½ a.m. Monday, Wednesday, and Friday, and Briefpost daily, in 26½ hours
..	Modena, 3½ a.m. Monday, Wednesday, and Friday, and 5 a.m. Tuesday, Thursday, and Saturday, and Briefpost daily, in 7¾ hours

Marburg (in Kurhessen) to

ENG. MLS.	
..	Arolsen, 6½ a.m., in 12½ hrs.
..	Biedenkopf, 5 p.m., in 3¾ hours
..	Olpe, 5 p.m. (per Creuznach)
..	Siegen, 5 p.m., in 12½ hours

Marburg (in Steiermark) to

ENG. MLS.	
..	Agram, 12 noon, returning at 4 p.m., in 18½ hours
..	Klagenfurt, 10¾ p.m. (in winter 12 noon), in 15¾ hours
..	Warasdin, 12 noon, returning at 4 a.m., in 9¾ hours

Marienbad to

ENG. MLS.	
139	Budweis, at 8½ p.m., in 32½ hours
25¼	Carlsbad, 5 and 11 a.m. in summer, in winter 5 a.m.
18½	Eger, 2 a.m.; in summer also 3¼ p.m., in 3¼ hours
22½	Franzensbad, 2 a.m., 3¼ p.m.
72½	Klattau, at 8½ p.m., in 13½ hours
47	Pilsen, 8, 8¼ a.m. and 8½ p.m.

Marseilles to

ENG. MLS.	
208¼	Lyons, 12.40 noon & 4 p.m.
522¼	Paris, 12.40 noon & 4 p.m., in 48 hrs. FARES—108 frs. coupé; 72 frs. banquette.
..	Strasburg, 12.40 noon.

Mayence to

ENG. MLS.	
20¾	Alzei, 6 a.m. and 6 p.m., in 4 hours
15¾	Bingen, 10 a.m. and 8 p.m.
55½	Coblentz, 8 p.m.
25¼	Creuznach 10 a.m. and 5 and 8 p.m.
20¾	Darmstadt, 6 a.m. & 4½ p.m.
20¾	Frankfort-o-M., 1–2 a.m.
..	Homburg, 11 a.m. (per Frankfurt), and 6 p.m. (per Alzey), in 14 hours
51	Kaiserslautern, 6 p.m., in 10 hours
..	Paris, 10.50 a.m., 2½ and 7.10 p.m. (per Frankfurt), in 33 hours
94½	Saargemünd, 6 p.m., in 25½ hours
18½	Sprendlingen, 5 p.m., in 3½ hours
106¾	Trier, 8 p.m. (per Simmern)
27¾	Worms, 5 p.m., in 4½ hours

Meiningen to

ENG. MLS.	
38	Coburg, at 8½ p.m., in 8 hrs.
29¼	Eisenach, 5 a.m., & 10 p.m.
39¼	Gotha, 2 p.m. (per Zella), & 5 a.m. and 10 p.m. (per Eisenach), in 8¾ hours
18½	Hildburghaus, 5½ a.m. (per Romhild); also at 8½ p.m.
33½	Kissingen, 4½–5 a.m., in 12 hours
20¾	Liebenstein, (in summer only), in 4½ hours
14½	Schmalkalden, 5 a.m., and 10 p.m., in 4¾ hours
42½	Schweinfurt, 4½–5 a.m., in 8¼ hours
39¼	Sonneberg, 5½ a.m., in 9¾ hours
66	Wurzburg, 4½–5 a.m., in 12¾ hours

Metz to

ENG. MLS.	
33½	Luxemburg, 7 a.m. (per Tionville), in 8 hours
28	Trier, 6 p.m., in 8½ hours

Milan to

ENG. MLS.	
78½	Bellinzona, 6 am., and 3.30 p.m. (per Camerlata), in 9¾ hours
155½	Chur, 3.30 p.m. (per Splugen)
..	Geneva, 12 night (per Sitten), in 62 hours
307	Innsbruck, at 9 p.m. (per Verona), in 55¼ hours
393½	Laibach, 9 p.m. (per Verona)
213	Lindau, (per Rorschach)
147½	Lucerne, 3.30 p.m. (per Camerlata). FARES — 40 frs. 30 cts. (French money) interieur, in 27¼ hrs.
117½	Mantua, 6 p.m., in 16 hours
..	Rome, daily Courier, also on Mon., Wed., & Friday, by Diligence.
216	Rorschach, Como), 3.30 p.m. (per Lecco), in 38 hours
207¾	St. Gallen, 3.30 p.m. (per Lecco), in 42¼ hours
..	St. Gothard, 3.30 p.m. (per Camerlata), in 20 hours
166½	Schaffhausen, 3.30 p.m. (per Camerlata), in 44 hours
40	Sesto Calende, 12 night
..	Trieste, 9 p.m. (per Venice)
99½	Turin, 3½ p.m., in 13 hours
247½	Udine, 9 p.m. (per Padua)
113¼	Verona, at 4 & 9 p.m.
147½	Vicenza, 9 p.m., in 19 hours
..	Vienna, 9 p.m. (per Trieste)
169½	Zürich, 3.30 p.m. (per Camerlata), in 36½ hours

Minden to

ENG. MLS.	
13½	Lübbecke, 1 and 9 a.m., and 4½ p.m., in 2½ hours
42½	Osnabruck, 9 a.m., and 4½ p.m., in 2½ hours
23	Rahden, 4½ p.m., returning at 8½ a.m., in 4½ hours
19½	Stolzenau, 5 p.m. Sunday, Tuesday, Thursday, and Friday, in 4½ hours
31¼	Sulingen, 3 p.m. Monday, Wednesday, and Saturday.

Modena to

ENG. MLS.	
27¾	Bologna, 11½ a.m. Monday, Wednesday, and Friday, in 4 hours
123½	Milan, 1 p.m., in 20 hours
48½	Mantua, 6 a.m. Monday, Wednesday, and Friday; also 1 p.m. Sunday, Wednesday, and Friday, in 9 hrs.

Muhlhausen (in Prussia) to

ENG. MLS.	
51	Cassel, 5 a.m. (per Bischhausen), in 12½ hours
22	Eisenach, 6.40 a.m., in 4¼ hours
23	Gotha, 6 a.m., 3 and 10 p.m., in 4½ hours
38	Göttingen, 6 p.m., in 8 hours
20¾	Heiligenstadt, 6 p.m., in 4 hours
11¼	Langensalza, 6 a.m., 3 and 10 p.m., in 2 hours
41½	Nordhausen, 7½ a.m., and 4½ p.m., in 7 hours
13½	Wanfried, 5 p.m., in 3 hours

Muhlhausen (in France) to

ENG. MLS.	
93¼	Besancon, 5 and 9 p.m.
228⅓	Lyon, 8 a.m., 12 noon, and 9 p.m., in 38 hours
305¼	Paris, 7 a.m., in 15 hours

Munich to

ENG. MLS.	
201	Amberg, 6 a.m. (per Nuremberg), 10½ p.m. (per Regensburg), in 26 hours
..	Ansbach, 6 & 11 a.m. & 6¼ p.m. (per Gunzenhausen), in 12 hours
97½	Berchtesgad, 10½ p.m. (per Traunstein), in 19¾ hours
48¼	Ingolstadt, 10½ p.m., in 9¼ hrs
97½	Innsbruck, 5 p m., in 21 hrs.
40	Kreuth, 6 a.m., in 7½ hours
41½	Landshut, 5 a.m., 12 noon, and 10½ p.m., in 7¼ hours
150	Linz, at 6 a.m., in 29¾ hours
117½	Passau, 12 noon (per Eggenfeld) and 10½ p.m. (per Landshut), in 24 hours
81	Regensburg, 5 a.m., 12 noon, and 10½ p.m., in 15½ hours
86	Reichenhall, 10½ p.m., in 17 hours
81	Salzburg, 1 p.m. (per Rosenheim) and 10½ p.m. (per Wasserberg), in 16½ hours
107½	Scharding, at 6 a.m. (per Altotting), in 18½ hours
75	Straubing, 10½ p.m., in 14½ hours
33½	Tegernsee, 6 a.m., in 6 hours
33½	Tolz, 6 a.m., in 6½ hours
271	Vienna, 6 a.m. (per Scharding), and 10½ p.m. (per Salzburg), in 60 hours
116½	Waldmunchen, 10½ p.m.
78½	Weissenburg, 10½ p.m. (per Eichstadt), in 17¾ hours
154½	Wurzburg, 6 & 11 a.m. and 6¼ p.m. (per Bamberg); and 6¼ p.m. (per Gunzenhausen), in 21¼ hours

Munster to

ENG. MLS.	
18½	Burgsteinfurt, at 1 & 7½ p.m., in 3½ hours
71¾	Emmerich, 6½ p.m. (per Cosfeld), in 18 hours
39¼	Enschede, 1 p.m., in 7¾ hrs.
46	Lingen, at 10½ a.m., in 11½ hours
33½	Osnabruck, 10½ a.m., in 7 hrs.
30	Rheda, 9½ a.m., in 7½ hours.
15¾	Warendorf, 9½ a.m. and 7 p.m., returning at 6½ a.m. and 6½ p.m., in 2¾ hours
51	Wesel, 11½ a.m.

Neisse to

ENG. MLS.	
29¼	Freiwaldau, 11.55 a.m., in 5¼ hours
32½	Glaz, 11½ a.m., in 7¼ hours
17	Neustadt, 12½ noon & 11 p.m., in 3 hours
53¾	Ratibor, 11 p m., in 10½ hours

Neuburg to

ENG. MLS.	
32½	Augsburg, 11¾ p.m. (per Donauworth), in 7 hours
20¾	Donauworth, 11¾ p.m., in 3¾ hours
12	Eichstadt, 3 a.m., in 2½ hours
13½	Ingolstadt, 2½ a.m., in 2¼ hrs
55½	Neuenmarkt, 3 a.m., in 15¾ hours
32½	Pleinfeld, 3 a.m., in 13¼ hrs.
58½	Regensburg, 2½ a.m., in 11⅝ hours
26	Weissenburg, 2½ a.m., in 12¼ hours

Neufchatel to

ENG. MLS.	
..	Basel, 6 a.m. and 1½ p.m. (per Biel), in 14½ hours
..	Bern, 1½ and 10 p.m., in 7½ hours
..	Besançon, 1 and 10 p.m.
..	Chauxde fonds, 3½ and 8 a.m.. 3 p.m.
..	Freyburg, 4 a.m. (per Murten)
..	Geneva, 10¾ a.m., and 10 p.m.
..	Lausanne, 10¾ a.m. & 10 p.m.
..	Locle, 8 a.m. and 3 p.m. & 3½ a.m. (per Ponts), in 5 hours
..	Paris, 10 and 1 p.m., in 30 hours
..	Solothurn, 1½ p.m., in 5½ hrs.
..	Yverdun, 10¾ a.m. & 10 p.m.

Neumarkt to

ENG. MLS.	
24¼	Amberg, 7½ p.m., in 5 hours
42½	Eichstadt, 5 a.m., in 8¾ hours
55½	Neuburg, 5 a.m., in 11¾ hrs.
22	Nürnberg, 6½ a.m. and 11¼ p.m., in 4¼ hours
40¼	Regensburg, 2½ a.m. and 7¾ p.m., in 7½ hours

Neustadt-on-the-Oder to

ENG. MLS.	
27¾	Apolda, 9¾ p.m., in 6 hours
9¼	Cahla, 4½ a.m. and 9¾ p.m., returning at 4 and 9 p.m.
55½	Coburg, 4 a.m. and 4½ p.m.
10¾	Gera, 3.10 a.m. and 8¼ p.m.
18½	Jena, 9¾ p.m., in 4¾ hours
18½	Saalfeld, 4 a.m. and 4½ p.m.
12¼	Schleiz, 11¾ night, in 2¾ hrs.

Neuwied to

ENG. MLS.	
11¼	Coblentz, 7¾ (in winter 8¼) a.m., in 2¼ hours
13½	Dierdorf, 6 p.m., returning at 8 a.m., in 3 hours
13½	Linz, 7½ (in winter 6½) p.m., in 2½ hours

Nordhausen to

ENG. MLS.	
26½	Blankenburg, 8 a.m., in 6¼ hours
68	Cassel, 10 p.m., 17¾ hours
35¾	Eisleben, 4¼ a.m. and 7¾ p.m.
49½	Erfurt, 7 a.m. and 7 p.m.
24¼	Frankenhausen, 7 p.m., in 5½ hours
46	Halberstadt, 3½ a.m. (per Quedlinburg), 8 a.m. (per Blankenburg), and 9½ p.m. (per Wernigerode), in 11 hours
56½	Halle, 4¼ a.m. and 7¾ p.m.
37	Harzburg, 12 night, in 9 hrs.
17	Hasselfelde, 8 a.m., in 4 hrs.
32½	Heiligenstadt, 10 a.m. and 10 p.m., in 6 hours
41½	Mühlhausen, 10 a.m. & 10 p.m., in 8½ hours
44¾	Nordheim, 11 a.m. Sunday and Thursday, in 11 hours
34¾	Osterode, 11 a.m. Sunday and Thursday, in 8 hours
35¾	Quedlinburg, 3½ a.m.
12¼	Sondershausen, 7 a.m. and 7 p.m., in 2½ hours
55½	Weimar, 7 p.m., in 14½ hrs.
32½	Weissensee, 7 p.m., in 11¼ hours
30	Werginerode, 9½ p.m., in 7½ hours
32½	Witzenhausen, 10 p.m., in 11 hours

Nordlingen to

ENG. MLS.	
22	Aalen, 5 p.m., in 4 hours
18½	Dinkelsbühl, 12¼ night, in 3½ hours
23	Ellwangen, 5 p.m.
48½	Hall 5 p.m.
24¼	Heidenheim, 2¼ and 10¾ a.m.
80¾	Heilbronn, 5 p.m.
70½	Stuttgart, 2¼ and 10¾ a.m. (per Süssen), and 5 p.m. (per Aalen), in 12 hours
44¾	Süssen, 2¼ and 10¾ a.m., in 7¼ hours
49½	Ulm, 2¼ a.m. (per Heidenheim), in 8½ hours
83¼	Würzburg, 12¼ night, in 15¾ hours

Nuremberg to

ENG. MLS.	
39¼	Amberg, 2 p.m., in 7½ hours
26	Ansbach, 5 a.m. & 5 p.m., in 5 hours
40	Baireuth, 5.35 a.m., 2.10 and 7½ p.m. (per Culmbach) in 9¼ hours
..	Coburg, 5.35 a.m., & 2.10 p.m.
54	Crailsheim, 5 a.m., in 11 hrs.
105	Eger, 2 p.m. (per Amberg) 2.10 p.m. (per Culmbach)

Nuremberg to

Eng. Mls.	
..	Eichstadt, at 7¼ a.m. (per Pleinfeld), in 6½ hours
68	Ellwangen, 1.35 p.m. (per Nordlingen), in 6½ hours
133	Frankfurt on the Maine, 5 p.m. (per Kitzingen); 7¼ a.m., 2.10 & 7½ p.m. (per Bamberg), in 25 hours
70½	Hall, 5 a.m., in 14 hours
99½	Heilbronn, at 5 a.m. (per Hall); 1.35 p.m. (per Nordlingen), in 18½ hours
22½	Neuenmarkt, 3½ and 10 p.m.
22	Prague, at 2 p.m., (per Amberg), in 44½ hours
62½	Regensburg, 3½ and 10 p.m.
107½	Stuttgart, at 7¼ a.m. (per Sussen); 1.35 p.m. (per Aalen); and 9 p.m. (per Sussen), in 16½ hours
115½	Ulm, 7¼ a.m. (per Sussen), & 9 p.m. (per Heidenheim)
250½	Vienna, 10 p.m., in 55½ hrs.
..	Weissenburg, 7¼ a.m. & 1.35 p.m. (per Pleinfeld), in 3 hours
63⅜	Würzburg, at 5 p.m. (per Kitzingen); 5.35 a.m., 2.10 and 7¼ a.m., & 7½ p.m. (per Bamberg), in 9½ hours

Nymwegen to

Eng. Mls.	
..	Amsterdam, 3½, 9½, and 11½ a.m., and 5¼ p.m., in 6 hrs
..	Arnheim, 3½, 9½, & 11½ a.m., and 2½ p.m., in 2 hours
13½	Cleve, 5¼ p.m., in 2¼ hours
..	Rotterdam, 6½ and 9½ a.m., and 5½ p.m., in 11½ hours
..	Utrecht, 3½ and 9½ a.m., and 2½ and 5½ p.m., in 5 hours

Oberhausen to

Eng. Mls.	
14½	Dorsten, 7 p.m., in 2¾ hours
43¾	Emmerich, 7, 8.5, & 11¼ a.m., and 8½ and 10 p.m., in 6 hours
4½	Mülheim, 10.20 a.m., and 2.10 & 8.35 p.m., in 40 mins.
19½	Wesel, 10¼ a.m. & 6.50 p.m., and 7 a.m. and 8½ p.m., in 2½ hours

Odessa to

Eng. Mls.	
..	Berlin, Monday and Friday, 9 p.m., in 176 hours
..	Lemberg, Monday and Friday 9 p.m., and Sunday and Thursday 4 p m; also 2 p.m on Wednesday
..	Warsaw, Monday and Friday 9 p.m., in 109 hours
..	Vienna, Sunday, Monday, Thursday and Friday, in the evening, in 205 hours

Offenbach to

Eng. Mls.	
8½	Aschaffenburg, 6½ a.m. and 8½ p.m., in 3½ hours
2¼	Frankfurt, 8 a.m., and 1 and 9 p.m., in 45 minutes
62½	Würzburg, 6½ a.m. and 7½ p.m., in 11¾ hours

Offenburg to

Eng. Mls.	
106⅛	Constance, 8¾ a.m., in 19¾ hours
61½	Donaueschingen, 8¾ a.m.
28	Hornberg, 8¾ a.m., in 4¾ hrs.
126¼	Schaffhausen, 8¾ a.m., in 17 hours
92	Stockach, 8¾ a.m., in 18 hrs.

Oldenburg to

Eng. Mls.	
47¼	Aurich, 10 p.m., in 8 hours
27¾	Bremen, 5 a.m. and 5 p.m.
38	Jever, 1 and 10½ p.m., in 7¼ hours
68	Lingen, 7 a.m., in 11¾ hours
58¾	Nienburg, 8 a.m., in 9¾ hrs.
67¼	Osnabruck, 7 a.m., in 11½ hours
40¼	Quakenbrück, 7 a.m. Tuesday and Saturday, in 7 hrs
19½	Varel, 1 and 10½ p.m., in 3½ hours

Olmutz to

Eng. Mls.	
45	Brunn, at 5½ a.m. & 3 p.m.
..	Troppau, 5¼ a.m., in 10¼ hrs

Olpe to

Eng. Mls.	
43¾	Altenkirchen, 7 p.m., in 9 hours
42½	Arnsberg, 7 p.m., per Esloke
10¼	Attendorn, 12½ p.m., in 2¼ hours
76¼	Coblentz, 7 p.m, in 15 hours
49½	Cologne, 9.10 a.m. and 6 p.m., in 10 hours

Olpe to

Eng. Mls.	
47¼	Elberfeld, 9¾ a.m. & 7½ p.m.
13½	Grevenbrück, 9½ a.m., returning at 3 p.m., in 2¾ hours
15¾	Gummersbach, 9.10 a.m. and 6 p.m., in 4¼ hours
32½	Hagen, 9¾ a.m. and 7½ p.m.
22	Kirchen, 11 a.m. and 7 p.m., returning at 5 & 11½ a.m.
39¼	Lennep, 9¾ a.m. and 7½ p.m.
30	Lüdenscheid, 7½ p.m., in 10¾ hours
63¾	Marburg, 10 a.m., in 17 hrs.
37	Meschede, 7 p.m., in 7½ hrs.
18½	Siegen, 10 a.m. and 7¾ p.m.

Oppeln to

Eng. Mls.	
27	Creutzburg, 11 a.m., returning at 6 a.m., in 5¼ hours
44½	Gleiwitz, 9½ p.m., in 9 hours
70¾	Gr. Strelitz, 9½ p.m., in 3¾ hrs
38	Lublinitz, 11 a.m. & 5 p.m.
32½	Neustadt, 12 noon, in 7½ hrs.

Oschersleben to

Eng. Mls.	
14	Bernburg, 2½ & 7½ a.m., and 12¼ p.m., in 2½ hours
19	Eisleben, 6 a.m., in 3½ hours
20	Harzgerode, 1 p.m., in 4¼ hrs
22	Magdeburg, 3 a.m., in 5¾ hrs
19	Quedlinburg, 12¼ noon and 12 night (per Ballenst.), 2 p.m (per Hoym), on Mondays, Wednesdays, and Fridays, in 4 hours

Paderborn to

Eng. Mls.	
31¼	Arolsen, 10¼ a.m. (per Seberfede), in 6¼ hours
23	Blomberg, 10 a.m., in 5 hrs.
46	Cassel, 10¼ a.m. & 12.5 p.m.
20	Detmold, 10¾ a.m., in 4 hrs.
12¼	Driburg, 8 p.m., in 2½ hours
14½	Horn, 10¾ a.m., in 2¾ hours
32½	Höxter, 8 p.m. and 10¾ a.m.
35¾	Pyrmont, 10¾ a.m., in 7¾ hrs
26½	Rheda, 10 a.m., in 6 hours
22	Steinheim, 10¾ a.m. (per Horn), in 5 hours
26½	Warburg, 6 and 10¼ a.m. and 12.5 p.m., in 5½ hours

Padua to

Eng. Mls.	
74	Belluno, 7 p.m., Monday and Friday, and Briefpost daily
55½	Ferrara, 9 p.m., in 10½ hours
86¾	Trient, 7 p.m. Monday and Friday, and Briefpost daily

Pardubitz to

ENG. MLS.	
67¼	Glatz, 7 p.m., in 20 hours
14½	Königgratz, 7¾ a.m. and 7 p.m., in 3½ hours
74	Reichenberg, 9½ a.m.., in 15 hours
89¾	Zittau, 9½ a.m., in 23 hours

Passau to

ENG. MLS.	
76¼	Landshut, 1 a.m. (per Plattling), 1 p.m. (per Vilsbiburg); also at 5 a.m., in 14 hours
60	Linz, at 11 p.m., in 12½ hrs.
117¾	Munich, at 1 a.m. (per Landshut), 1 p.m. (per Erding), and 7 a.m. (per Altotting), in 27¼ hours
74	Regensburg, 1 a.m., in 12 hrs
11¼	Scharding, 11 p.m., in 2½ hrs
176	Vienna, 11 p.m., in 30 hours

Pepinster to

ENG. MLS.	
..	Spa, 7.50 and 11¾ a.m., 2.15, 7¾, and 9½ p.m., in 1½ hour

Pesth to

ENG. MLS.	
136½	Füntkirchen, 7 p.m. Wednesday, in 29¼ hours
158¼	Kaschau, 7 p.m., Sunday, Monday, Wednesday, and Friday, in 30 hours
..	Klausenburg, 4.37 p.m. Saturday, in 59 hours
306¼	Semlin, 7 p.m. Saturday, in 60¼ hours
..	Temesvar, 4.37 p.m. Monday and Thursday; 4½ p.m. on Tuesday (per Grosswerden); returning Wednesday and Saturday 6 a.m.; also 12 noon on Saturday

Plauen to

ENG. MLS.	
13½	Adorf, 10½ a.m., and 5 p.m.
34½	Eger (Franzenbad), 12 noon in Summer only, in 6½ hours

Pleinfeld to

ENG. MLS.	
19½	Eichstadt, 9 a.m., in 4¼ hours

Posen to

ENG. MLS.	
112	Breslau, 10½ a.m., and 6 p.m., in 18¼ hours
92	Crossen, 9½ p.m., in 24 hours
..	Custrin, 6 a.m. (pr Schwerin)
76¼	Glogau, 10½ a.m., and 6 p.m.
29¼	Gnesen, 9½ a.m. and 6½ p.m.
63½	Krotoschin, 7 p.m., in 11¾ hours
48¼	Lissa, 10½ a.m., & 6 p.m.
53¼	Pleschen, 9½ a.m. returning at 7 a.m., in 12 hours
186	Warsaw, 12½ night, in 32 hours
67¼	Züllichau, 9½ p.m., in 17 hours

Potsdam to

ENG. MLS.	
41½	Wittenberg, 5½-6 p.m., in 7 hours

Prague to

ENG. MLS.	
90½	Budweis, 6 p.m. (per Tabor) also 7 p.m. Sunday, Monday, Wednesday, Friday.
78½	Carlsbad, 2 and 9 p.m.; also 5 a.m. (in summer only)
58½	Commotau, 4 p.m., returning 6 p.m.
107½	Eger, 2 (in summer only) and 9 p.m., in 21 hours
117½	Freiburg, 4 p.m., in 26¾ hrs.
137½	Hof, 9 p.m., in Summer.
82	Iglau, 6 p.m., in 16 hours
33½	Jungbunzlau, 4 p.m., in 5¾ hours
85¼	Klattau, 7 p.m., in 15¼ hours
155½	Linz, on Sun., Mon., Wed. & Fri., at 7 p.m., & Briefpost daily, in 33½ hours
60	Pilsen, 7 p.m., in 10 hours
152½	Regensburg, 7 p.m., in 36 hours
66	Reichenberg, 4 p.m., in 12 hours
187	Vienna, 6 p.m. (per Iglau); also on Sun., Tues., Thur. and Sat. at 6 p.m. (per Tabor), in 36 hours
108½	Waldmunchen, 7 p.m., in 22¾ hours

Prenzlau to

ENG. MLS.	
42½	Anclam, 4 a.m., 12 noon, and 10½ p.m., in 7 hours
68	Berlin, 3 a.m., in 14 hours
12¼	Boitzenburg, 3 p.m., in 2¼ hours
13½	Brüssow, 3 p.m. Monday, Wednesday and Saturday
66	Greifswalde, 4 a.m., 12 noon, and 10½ p.m., in 11 hours
32½	N. Brandenburg, 12½ p.m.
58¾	Neuruppin, 3 a.m. (per Templin), in 14 hours
14½	Pasewalk, 4 a.m., 12 noon, & 10½ p.m., in 2 hours
15¾	Passow, 4 and 10½ a.m., and 1¼ and 9½ p.m., in 2½ hours
86¾	Stralsund, 4 a.m., 12 noon, & 10½ p.m., in 14 hours
13½	Strasburg, 3 p.m. Sunday, Wednesday and Friday, returning at 4 a.m., in 3¾ hours

Pyrmont to

ENG. MLS.	
54¼	Arolsen, 6 a.m., in 11¼ hours
12¼	Blomberg, 8 a.m., in 2½ hours
27¾	Detmold, 10 a.m. (per Lemgo), and 8 a.m. (per Horn)
13½	Hameln, 4 a.m., in 2½ hours
41½	Hanover, 4 a.m., in 7½ hours
32½	Herford, 10 a.m., in 7 hours
46	Hildesheim, 4 a.m., in 10 hours
18½	Höxter, 8½ p.m., in 4 hours
19½	Lemgo, 10 a.m., in 4 hours
35¾	Paderborn, 8 a.m., in 7½ hours

Ratibor to

ENG. MLS.	
9	Katscher, 2¼ p.m., in 2 hours
53¼	Neisse, 2 p.m., in 10¾ hours
35½	Neustadt, 2 p.m., in 7½ hours
37	Pless, 7 p.m., returning at 12½ night
18¼	Troppau, 2 p.m., in 3½ hours

Ravensburg to

ENG. MLS.	
..	Tettnang, 9.5 a.m., 3 & 9 p.m.
..	Wolfegg, 9½ a.m., returning 4¼ a.m., in 2¼ hours

Regensburg (Ratisbon) to

ENG. MLS.	
39¼	Amberg, 4½ p.m., in 7¾ hours
82	Augsburg, at 11½ a.m. (per Neustadt), in 16¼ hours
79¾	Bayreuth, at 4½ p.m. (per Amberg), in 16¼ hours
79¾	Donauworth, 11½ a.m., in 15½ hours
89¾	Eger, 4½ p.m., in 18½ hours

ENG. MLS.	**Regensburg** (Ratisbon) to
193	Frankfort-on-the-Maine, at 3 and 10 p.m. (per Bamberg), in 39 hours
44½	Ingoldstadt, at 11½ a.m.
39¼	Landshut, 5 a.m. & 9½ p.m.
136½	Linz, 11 a.m., in 24 hours
81	Munich, 5 a.m.; 11½ a.m. (per Neustadt) and 9½ p.m. (per Landshut), in 16¼ hours
58½	Neuburg, 11½ a.m., in 11½ hours
40	Neuenmarkt, 3 and 10 p.m. in 8¼ hours
62½	Nuremberg, 3 and 10 p.m., in 12½ hours
74	Passau, 11 a.m., in 11½ hours
92	Pilsen, 4½ p.m., in 24 hours
152½	Prague, 4½ p.m., in 35¼ hours
125½	Ulm, 11½ a.m. (per Donauworth), 9½ p.m. (per Munich)
250½	Vienna, 11 a.m., in 42 hours
43¾	Waldmunchen, 4½ p.m., in 11½ hours
126½	Wurzburg, 3 p.m. (per Windsheim), 3 and 10 p.m. (per Bamberg), in 25 hours

	Rendsburg to
56	Apenrade, 12 noon, in 10¾ hours
38½	Flensburg, 12 noon & 9½ p.m.
72	Hadersleben, 12 noon, in 14 hours
17½	Schleswig, 12 noon & 9½ p.m.

	Reutlingen to
20¾	Plochingen, 9¼ a.m. and 2¾ p.m., in 3½ hours
26½	Stuttgart, 4¾ a.m., in 4¾ hrs.
9¼	Tübingen, 6½ a.m. & 7½ p.m.
46	Ulm, 7½ p.m., in hours
12¼	Urach, 7¾ p.m., in 2¼ hours

	Rochlitz to
19	Altenburg, 6 a.m., in 4 hours
31	Leipsic, 5 and 10½ a.m., in 6 hours
12½	Waldheim, 6½ a.m., in 2½ hours

	Romanshorn to
..	Constance, 6¾ p.m., in 2 hours
..	St. Gallen, 8¾ p.m., in 2¾ hours
..	Schaffhausen, 9 a.m. (per Frauenf), in 10¼ hours
..	Winterthur, 9 a.m. and 5.10 p.m., in 5 hours
..	Zurich, 9 a.m. & 5.10 p.m., in 7½ hours.

ENG. MLS.	**Rostock** to
..	Demmin, 12 noon, in 8¼ hours
..	Doberan, 11½ a.m. & 7 p.m., in 1¼ hours
..	Stralsund, 12 noon and 7 p.m., in 7½ hours
..	Wismar, 11½ a.m., in 5¼ hours

	Rudolstadt to
..	Arnstadt, 10½ p.m., in 4¾ hours
..	Coburg, 5¾ a.m. and 6½—7 p.m., in 11 hours
..	Dietendorf, 10½ p.m., in 7¼ hours
..	Gera, 2 and 6½—7 p.m., in 12 hours
..	Jena, 9 p.m., in 4¾ hours
..	Ilmenau, 2½ a.m. Tuesday, Thursday and Saturday
..	Königsee, 4½ a.m. Monday, Wednesday, Friday and Sunday; also 2½ a.m. on Tuesday, Thursday and Saturday, in 2½ hours
..	Neustadt-on-the-Order, 2 & 6½—7 p.m., in 8 hours
..	Saalfeld, 5¾ a.m. and 2 and 6½—7 p.m., in 1¼ hours
..	Weimar, 6 a.m., and 5½ p.m., in 4½ hours.

	Saarbruck to
..	Creuznach, 5.35 a.m and 4.25 p.m., in 14 hours
..	Frankfort-on-the-Maine, 5.35 a.m. (per Mannheim), in 10¼ hours
..	Saarlouis, 8½ a.m. and 4 p.m.
..	Trier, 8½ a.m. and 4 p.m.; also 4 p.m. (per Wadern)

	Saargemund to
..	Forbach, 2½ and 8½ a.m., & 2 p.m., in 2 hours
65	Strasburg, 4 a.m. and 2 p.m.

	Saarlouis to
34½	Birkenfeld, 2½ p.m., in 6¾ hours
77	Creuznach, 2½ p.m., in 15½ hours
..	Metz, 8 p.m., in 5 hours
15¾	Saarbruck, 5¾ a.m., and 4.20 p.m., in 2½ hours
40	Trier, 11¼ a.m. and 6¾ p.m. (per Wadern), in 8 hours

ENG. MLS.	**Salzburg** to
143½	Bruck, 7 p.m., in 31¼ hours.
9	Hallein, 6 a.m. and 4 p.m. on Mon. and Fri. in winter
103	Innsbruck, 5-6 a.m. and 8.20 p.m. on Mon. and Fri.
33½	Ischl, 7 a.m. and 7 p.m. in summer, in 7 hours
82	Landshut, 1 p.m., in 15¾ hrs.
83	Linz, 7½ p.m., in 14 hours
81	Munich, 6 a.m. (per Wasserburg), 1 p.m. (per Rosenheim), in 17 hours
10	Reichenhall, 5-6 a.m., in 1¼ hours
145½	Villach, Mon. & Fri. 4 p.m.; Sun., Tues., Wed., and Sat., at 6 p.m., in 30 hours
197	Vienna, 7 p.m. (per Bruck), 7½ p.m. Courier., in 39 hours

	St. Gallen to
..	Chur, 7½ a.m., 4½ p.m., & 5¼ p.m. (per Altstetten), & 6 a.m., & 8 p.m. (per Uznach.)
..	Constance, 4¾ p.m., in 4 hrs.
..	Feldkirch, 5¼ p.m., in 5½ hours
..	Glarus, 6 a.m., and 8 p.m.
..	Herisau, 6 a.m. and 8 p.m.
..	Lindau, 7½ a.m. and 4½ p.m.
..	Lucerne, 8 p.m. (per Zurich)
..	Milan, 4½ p.m. (per Lecco.)
..	Pfafers and Ragaz (Baden) 6, 7½ a.m. 4½, and 8 p.m. (per Uznach), in 12½ hours
..	Rorschach, 7½ a.m., and 12¼ and 4½ p.m., in 1 hour
..	Schaffhausen, 10 a.m., 9 p.m.
..	Uznach, 6 a.m. and 8 p.m.
..	Winterthur, 10 a.m., 9 p.m.
..	Zurich, 10 a.m. and 9 p.m.; 6 a.m. and 8 p.m. (per Uznach), in 11¾ hours

	St. Wendel to
15¾	Birkenfeld, 9¼ a.m. & 7½ p.m.
55½	Creuznach, 9¼ a.m. & 7½ p.m.
28¾	Grumbach, 5½ a.m. Monday, Wednesday, Friday and Saturday, in 6¼ hours
10¼	Neunkirchen, 4.5 a.m. and 4¾ p.m., in 2¼ hours
41½	Trier, 5¼ p.m., in 9¼ hours

	Schaffhausen to
..	Aarau, 2½ p.m., in 8 hours
61½	Basel, 5¼ a.m. in summer, (per Waldshut,) & 7½ p.m.

Schaffhausen to

ENG. MLS.	
..	Constance, at 12½ noon (per Steckborn), in 4½ hours
2	Donaueschinng, 3½ p.m., in 4½ hours
52	Freiburg, 1 p.m., (per Hollenthal), 3½ p.m. (per Donaueschinng), in 13¾ hours
..	Lucerne, 6 a.m. and 1½ p.m., in 12 hours
..	Milan, 1½ p.m., in 43½ hours
85¼	Offenburg, 3½ p.m. (per Donaueschinng) in 15½ hours
..	St. Gallen, 7 a.m. (per Frauenf.), and 12 noon (per Winterthur), in 18 hours
26	Stockach, 8½ p.m., in 6½ hours
103	Stuttgardt, at 8½ p.m. (per Stockach), in 31½ hours
84	Tubingen, at 8½ p.m. (per Stockach), in 26¼ hours
40	Tuttlingen, 8½ p.m., in 16 hours
..	Winterthur, 6 a.m., 12 noon.
..	Zurich, 6 a.m. (per Winterth.) 12 noon and 1½ p.m., in 6 hours

Schleswig to

ENG. MLS.	
39¼	Apenrade, 3¼ p.m., in 7¾ hrs.
13½	Eckenforde, at 12 night, on Tuesdays and Saturdays, in 2¾ hours
30¾	Flensburg, 3¼ p.m., in 3½ hours
55½	Hadersleben, 3¼ p.m., in 10¼ hours
30	Kiel, 12 p.m. Tu. and Sat., in 5¼ hours
17	Rendsburg, 2½ and 11¼ a.m., in 3 hours

Schwalbach to

ENG. MLS.	
37	Coblentz, 12½ noon, 1 night, in 6 hours
23¾	Ems, 12½ noon, 1 night, in 3 hours
29	Wiesbaden, 2 p.m., in 2 hrs.

Schwerin to

ENG. MLS.	
11¼	Crivitz, 2½ p.m.; also 10½ a.m. Sunday and Thursday, in 1¾ hours
39	Goldberg, Monday & Thursday 2½ p.m. (per Bruel), in 7 hours
39¼	Lübeck, 2½ p.m., in 6½ hours
23¼	Parchim, 10½ a.m. Sunday and Thursday, in 5¾ hours
27¾	Ratzeburg, 7 a.m., in 4½ hrs.

Solothurn to

ENG. MLS.	
..	Aarau, 8.15 a.m. and 7½ p.m.
..	Basel, 12.55 & 9.15 p.m. and 8.15 a.m. & 7½ p.m. (per Olten), in 8½ hours
..	Bern, 2½ a.m. and 4.15 p.m., in 3½ hours
..	Lucern, 8.15 a.m. & 7½ p.m.
..	Neufchatel, 4.40 a.m., in 5½ hours
..	Zurich, 8.15 a.m. and 7½ p.m., in 12 hours

Spa to

ENG. MLS.	
..	Pepinster, 1.20, 4.50, 7.10, & 9.25 a.m., 12.25, 3.25, 6.40, and 7.55 p.m., in 1¼ hours.

Spremberg to

ENG. MLS.	
33½	Bautzen, 10¾ p.m., in 6¾ hours
13½	Cottbus, 2¾ and 8 a.m., in 2¼ hours
49½	Dresden, 5½ p.m., in 10 hours
17	Forste, 3½ a.m., in 4 hours
47¼	Görlitz, 11 p.m., in 9½ hours
38	Sorau, 1 p.m., in 8¼ hours

Stettin to

ENG. MLS.	
54	Anclam, 2 & 10 a.m., 9 p.m., in 8¼ hours
83	Colberg, 11½ a.m. & 10 p.m.; returning at 12½ and 11¼ p.m., in 16½ hours
76¼	Greifswalde, 2 & 10 a.m., & 9 p.m., in 13 hours
25¼	Pasewalk, 2 & 10 a.m., 9 p.m.
28	Pyritz, 3¼ a.m., in 6 hours
134½	Stolp, 11½ a.m., and 10½ p.m.
97½	Stralsund, 2 & 10 a.m., 9 p.m.
42½	Uckermunde, 5½ p.m. Monday, Wednesday & Saturday, in 12 hours

Stralsund to

ENG. MLS.	
42½	Anclam, 7 a.m., 4 & 11 p.m., in 7 hours
33½	Demmin, 3½ p.m., in 6½ hours
20¾	Greifswalde, 7 a.m., 11 night, and 4 p.m., in 3¼ hours
71¾	Pasewalk, 7 a.m. 11 and 4 p.m., in 12 hours
103	Passow (Berlin) 8 a.m., 12, 3¼, and 4, p.m., in 17¼ hours
86	Prenzlau, 8 a.m., 12 and 4 p.m., in 14½ hours
46	Rostock, 8 a.m. and 9 p.m.
97½	Stettin, 8 a.m., 12 and 4 p.m., in 17½ hours

Strasburg to

ENG. MLS.	
17	Landau, 9 p.m. and 7 a.m. Briefpost, in 23¼ hours
290	Lyons, 5 p.m. (per Mulhouse) and 9 a.m. in 41 hours
37	Weissenburg, 7 a.m., 9 p.m. 1 a.m., Briefpost, returning at 9 p.m., in 9 hours

Straubing to

ENG. MLS.	
52	Altotting, 3½ p.m., in 10 hours
25¾	Cham, 1¼ p.m., in 5 hours
33½	Landshut, 2½ p.m., in 6½ hours
48½	Passau. 3 p.m., in 7½ hours
25¼	Regensburg, 9¼ a.m., in 4 hours
41½	Waldmünchen, 1¼ p.m., in 8½ hours

Stuttgardt to

ENG. MLS.	
46	Aalen, 7¾ p.m., in 8¼ hours
97½	Augsburg, 5¾ a.m., 5¾ and 7¾ p.m. (per Nordlingen), in 12 hours
23	Calw, 10¼ (in Winter, 10½) a.m. and 6 p.m., in 5¼ hours
46	Carlsruhe, 10.5 a.m. and 8½ p.m., in 8 hours
42½	Durlach, 10.5 a.m. & 8½ p.m.
60	Ellwangen, at 7¾ p.m. (per Aalen), in 10¾ hours
41½	Freudenstadt, 8¼ p.m., in 9 hours
32½	Gmund, 7¾ p.m.
37¼	Hall, 9 a.m. and 7¾ p.m. (per Schornd)
29	Hechingen, 7¾ a.m. and 8½ p.m.
74	Hornberg, Tuesday, Thursday, and Saturday, at 8½ p.m., in 16¼ hours
102	Lindau, (per Friedrichshafen)
71¾	Mergentheim, 8¼ p.m.
67¼	Nordlingen, 5¾ a.m., & 2 p.m. (per Sussen), & 7¾ p.m. (per Aalen.). in 10¼ hours
111	Nuremberg, at 5¾ a.m. and 2 p.m. (per Sussen), 7¾ p.m., (per Aalen,) in 14¾ hours
23	Reutlingen, 5 p.m., in 4¾ hours
51	Rottweil, 7¾ a.m., & 8½ p.m.
103	Schaffhausen, 8½ p.m. (per Stockach), in 23 hours
57¾	Sigmaringen, 7¾ a.m., (per Balinger) Tues., Thurs., and Sat., 6½ p.m., in 12 hours

Stuttgardt to

ENG. MLS.	
76¼	Stockach, 8½ p.m., in 17 hours
20¾	Tubingen, 7¾ a.m., 4 and 8½ p.m.
62½	Tuttlingen, 8½ p.m., in 14¼ hours
51	Ulm, 5 p.m. (per Urach).
34¾	Wildbad, 10½ a.m. (in summer), 6 p.m. (per Leonberg)
97½	Wurzburg, 8¼ p.m., in 18½ hours

Sussen to

ENG. MLS.	
18½	Heidenheim, 8.20 a.m., & 4¼ p.m., in 3¼ hours

Teplitz to

ENG. MLS.	
11¼	Altenburg, 6 a.m., returning at 5½ p.m., in 3¼ hours
9¼	Aussig, 7¾ and 10½ a.m., 2½ and 8¼ p.m., in 2 hours
65	Carlsbad, 5 a.m. (per Klosterle), and 4½ p.m. in summer, in 12¾ hours
97	Franzenbad, 4½ p.m., in 18 hours
89¾	Marienbad, 4½ p.m., in 19½ hours

Tilsit to

ENG. MLS.	
42½	Gumbinnen, 10 a.m. Sunday, Tuesday and Friday, in 9¾ hours
71¾	Konigsberg, 6 a.m., and 4½ p.m.
57¾	Memel, 9½ p.m., in 11¼ hours
20¾	Tauroggen, 4.15 a.m.; 2 p.m. Tuesday and Saturday; also 12 noon Wednesday and Sunday in 5 hours

Treviglio to

ENG. MLS.	
..	Cremona, 7½ a.m., in 6½ hours

Treviso to

ENG. MLS.	
162	Brixen, 11¼ p.m. Sunday and Thursday, and Briefpost daily, in 36¾ hours
13½	Laibach, 12 noon, and 8½ p.m., in 30½ hours
71¾	Udine, 11 a.m. and 8½ p.m., in 13 hours

Trient to

ENG. MLS.	
66	Belluno, 5¼ p.m. Monday and Friday, in 17¾ hours
40¼	Botzen, 2½ a.m., in 7¼ hours
42½	Malé, 4 a.m., returning at 4 a.m., in 10½ hours
85½	Padua, 5¼ p.m. Monday and Friday, & Briefpost daily
14½	Roveredo, 5½ p.m., in 2¾ hours
61¼	Verona, 5½ p.m., in 10½ hours

Trier to

ENG. MLS.	
92	Aix-la-Chapelle, 8 p.m., in 20 hours
76¼	Bingerbruch, 3 (in Winter 4½) a.m., in 15 hours
34¾	Birkenfeld, 2¼ p.m., in 7 hours
86¾	Bonn, 1¾ p.m. (per Wittlich)
72¾	Coblentz, 4 a.m. and 1¾ p.m.
103	Cologne, 6 a.m. and 8 p.m. (per Losheim), in 23 hours
76¼	Creuznach, 4 a.m. (per Thalfang), 2¼ p.m. (per Birkenfeld), in 15½ hours
84¼	Eupen, 8 p.m. (per Montjoie)
55½	Kirn, 4 a.m. (per Thalfang), 2¼ p.m. (per Birkenfeld)
25¼	Luxemburg, 5 a.m., 3 and 10 p.m., in 5 hours
..	Malmedy, 8 p.m. (per Butgenb), in 16¼ hours
28¾	Metz, 4½ p.m., in 10 hours
52	Neunkirchen, 4¼ p.m., in 12 hours
56½	Saarbrück, 8 a.m., and 4¼ and 10 p.m. (per Wadern)
40¼	Saarlouis, 8 a.m. and 10 p.m., in 8 hours

Trieste to

ENG. MLS.	
76¾	Laibach, 3 a.m., & 4 & 8 p.m., in 10 hours
48¼	Milan, 6 a.m. (per Venice).
..	Udine, 8 p.m., in 8¾ hours
..	Venice, 6 a.m. (Steamer), in 6 hours
..	Vienna, 3 a.m., 4 and 8 p.m., in 37 hours

Tubingen to

ENG. MLS.	
23	Cawl, 8 a.m. Tuesday, Thursday and Saturday, in 4¾ hours
38	Freudenstadt, 9 p.m., in 8¼ hours.

Tubingen to

ENG. MLS.	
13½	Hechingen, 12.30 noon, and 1.9 a.m., in 2¼ hours
55½	Hornberg, 1.10 a.m., Sunday, Wednesday, and Friday
..	Reutlingen, 7¼ a.m. & 6¼ p.m.
9¼	Rottweil, 12.30 noon, and 1.9 a.m., in 7 hours
91	Schaffhausen, 1.9 a.m. (per Stockach), in 18¾ hours
52	Schramberg, 1.10 a.m., in 9¼ hours
41½	Sigmaringen, 1.9 a.m., Sunday, Wednesday, and Friday, also 12½ noon, (per Balingen), in 13½ hours
65	Stockach, 1.9 a.m, in 12¼ hours
22	Stuttgart, 7 a.m., and 1 and 11.40 p.m., in 4¼ hours
49½	Tuttlingen, 1.9 a.m., in 9½ hours
55½	Ulm, 6¼ p.m. (per Urach)
22	Urach, 6¼ p.m., in 3¾ hours
37	Wildbad, 8 a.m. Tuesday, Thursday, and Saturday, in summer, in 10 hours

Turin to

ENG. MLS.	
..	Chambery, 5 p.m., in 10 hrs.
..	Geneva, 5 p.m., in 31 hours.

Tuttlingen to

ENG. MLS.	
35¾	Hechingen, 12.50 p.m., in 7¼ hours
41½	Schaffhausen, 11 a.m., in 8¼ hours
14½	Stockach, 11 a.m., in 2½ hrs.
71¾	Stuttgart, 12.50 p.m., in 15 hours
49½	Tübingen, 12.50 p.m., in 9¾ hours

Udine to

ENG. MLS.	
108¾	Klagenfurt, 11 a.m., Sunday, Tuesday, and Thursday, in 19 hours
111	Laibach, 8–9 a.m., in 20 hrs.
293¾	Milan, 9 p.m., in 35 hours
71¾	Treviso, 5 and 9 p.m., in 16 hours
48½	Triest, 9½ p.m., in 8¾ hours
168¾	Verona, 9 p.m., in 19 hours
84¼	Villach, 10½ a.m., Sunday, Tuesday, and Thursday, in 14¾ hours

ENG. MLS.	**Ulm** to
32½	Aalen, 3.55 p.m., in 6¾ hours
6	Augsburg, 10½ a.m. & 10½ p.m.
444½	Donauworth, 10½ a.m. (per Gunzburg), in 10½ hours
43¾	Ellwangen, 3.55 p.m., in 9 hours
76¼	Fussen, 12½ noon, in 16⅓ hrs.
13½	Gunzburg, 10½ a.m. & 10½ p.m., in 2¾ hours
20¾	Heidenheim, 3.55 p.m., in 4¼ hours
53¼	Kempten, 12½ noon, in 10 hours
32¼	Memmingen, 12½ noon., in 6 hours
53¼	Nordlingen, at 3.55 p.m., in 8¼ hours
106½	Nuremberg, at 3.55 p.m. (per Nordlingen), in 13¾ hours
125½	Regensburg, at 10½ a.m. (per Donauworth), & 10½ p.m. (per Munich), in 28 hours
39¼	Reutlingen, 10.15 p.m.
90½	Schaffhausen (per Aulendorf)
39¼	Sigmaringen (per Aulendorf)
62½	Stockach (per Aulendorf)
46	Tubingen, 10.15 p.m., in 9½ hours

ENG. MLS.	**Uznach** to
..	Brunnen, 2 a.m., in 6½ hours
..	Chur, 12.40 noon & 2¼ a.m.
..	Einsiedeln, 2 a.m., in 4½ hrs.
..	Glarus, 2¼ a.m. & 12.40 noon
..	Herisau, 1¼ and 11.40 p.m.
..	Luzern, 2 a.m., in 1¼ hours
..	Ragaz, 2¼ a.m. & 12.40 noon
..	St. Gallen, 1¼ and 11.40 p.m.
..	Wesen, 2¼ a.m. & 12.40 noon
..	Zürich, 2¼ a.m. & 12¾ noon

ENG. MLS.	**Venice** to
196¼	Milan, 7.18 and 10.38 a.m., & 3.4 p.m., in 20¼ hours
..	Trieste, 12 night, (Steamer)
..	Verona, (per Railway) see page 120

ENG. MLS.	**Verona** to
79¼	Bologna, 10 p.m. on Sundays, Tuesdays and Thursdays, in 17½ hours
102	Botzen, 5 and 9½ p.m.. in 17 hours
55½	Florence, 10 p.m., Sundays, Tuesdays and Thursdays, & also daily Mail., in 32 hrs.
183¼	Innsbruck, 5 p.m., in 35¼ hrs.
17	Milan, at 3½, 4, and 8½ p.m.
122½	Mantua, 8¾ p.m., in 4½ hours.
55½	Modena, 10 p.m. on Sundays, Tuesdays and Thursdays, also daily mail, in 13 hours
55½	Rome, at 10 p.m. on Sundays, and Thursdays, and mail on Mon., Tues. and Fri., in 87 hours
47	Roveredo, 5 p.m., in 7¼ hours
61½	Trient, 5 p.m., in 10¼ hours
194	Trieste, 4½ p.m. (per Venice).
145½	Udine, 1½-2 p.m., in 18 hours
92	Venice, (per Railway) see page 120

ENG. MLS.	**Vevay** to
..	Berne, 9 a.m. (per Bulle), and 4½ p.m. (per Moudon), in 11¼ hours
..	Freiburg, 9 a.m., (per Bulle), in 7½ hours
..	Lausanne, 7.55 a.m., and 3½ p.m., in 2 hours
..	St. Maurice, 8½ a.m., and 5.40 p.m., in 33¼ hours
..	Saanen, 9 a.m. (per Bulle), in 13¾ hours, returning 5 a.m., in 14½ hours
..	Sion, (Leuk), 8½ a.m., and 5.40 p.m.

ENG. MLS.	**Vienna** to
118¾	Budweis, 7½ p.m. (per Horn or Krems,) in 23¾ hours
411½	Feldkirch, 7 p.m., in 78 hrs.
144½	Gmunden, 7 p.m. (per Steyer)
300½	Innsbruck, 1 and 7 p.m., in 54 hours
134½	Ischl, 7¼ a.m. (per Bruck), in 40 hours
46	Krems, 6 a.m. and 7 p.m., in 7½ hours
115½	Linz, 1 and 7 p.m., in 21½ hours
..	Milan, 9 p.m., (per Trieste)
272½	Munich, at 1 & 7 p.m. (per Linz); 1 & 7 p.m. (per Salzburg), in 52 hours
..	Odessa, 7 p.m., excepting Saturdays in 203 hours
177	Passau, 1 and 7 p.m., in 35 hours
..	Prague, 7 p.m. (per Iglau); also 7½ p.m., Sunday, Tuesday, Thursday, & Saturday
250½	Regensburg, 1 and 7 p.m., in 49 hours
197	Salzburg, 7 a.m., 1 and 7 p.m., in 39 hours
106½	Steyer, 7 p.m., in 14 hours
..	Venice, 9 p.m. (per Trieste), in 39 hou s
57¾	Znaim, 7 p.m., in 9 hours

ENG. MLS.	**Waldmunchen** to
100¾	Budweis, 6 a.m., in 23 hours
34¾	Klattau, 6 a.m., in 9¼ hours
72¾	Landshut, 5 a.m. (per Straubing), in 15½ hours
116½	Munich, 5 a.m. (per Straubing), in 24 hours
48½	Pilsen, 6 a.m., in 10½ hours
108¾	Prague, 6 a.m., in 22 hours
43¾	Regensburg, 10 p.m., in 11 hours

ENG. MLS.	**Wiesbaden** to
46	Coblentz, 10 a.m. & 10½ p.m. in 8 hours
62½	Dillenburg, 8.25 a.m., in 12¼ hours
35	Ems, 10 a.m. and 10½ p.m., in 5 hours
27	Limburg, 8.25 a.m. & 3 p.m. in 5½ hours
20¾	Rudesheim, 7.45 a.m., & 3½ p.m., in 3.35 hours
9	Schwalbach, at 10 a.m. and 10½ p.m., in 1½ hours

ENG. MLS.	**Wildbad** to
13½	Calw, 5 a.m. in summer only, also at 9½ a.m., in 2¾ hours
35¾	Carlsruhe, 6½ a.m. in summer only, in 6½ hours
33½	Durlach, 6½ a.m., in summer
27¾	Freudenstadt, 6 a.m. Sunday and Wednesday, in 5½ hours
41½	Stuttgart; 5 a.m. (per Leonberg) and 9½ a.m. in summer only, in 8 hours
37	Tübingen, 9½ a.m. Tuesday, Thursday, and Saturday, in 8 hours

ENG. MLS.	**Wismar** to
23	Doberan, 9¾ a.m., in 3½ hrs.
12¼	Grevismühlen, 10½ a.m. and 8¼ p.m., in 1¾ hours
35¾	Lübeck, 10½ a.m., in 5¼ hrs.
34¾	Rostock, 9¾ a.m., in 5¼ hrs.

ENG. MLS.	**Wittenberg** to
24¼	Bitterfeld, 12 noon, in 5 hrs.
37	Eilenburg, 11½ a.m., in 8 hrs.
41½	Potsdam, 11½ night, in 7 hrs.
28¾	Torgau, 11½ noon, in 6¼ hours

ENG. MLS.	**Woldenberg** to
56½	Custrin, 4 p.m., & 12½ night, in 10 hours
76½	Frankfort-on-Oder, 4 p.m., and 12½ night, in 13 hours
27	Landsberg, 4 p.m., and 12½ night, in 4¼ hours

ENG. MLS.	**Worms** to
$13\frac{1}{2}$	Alzey, 6 a.m. (per Pfeddersh), and 5 p.m. (per Westhofen)
$11\frac{1}{4}$	Bensheim, $5\frac{1}{2}$, and $11\frac{1}{2}$ a.m., and $2\frac{1}{2}$ p.m., in 2 hrs.
$33\frac{1}{2}$	Creuznach, 5 p.m. (per Alzey)
$12\frac{1}{4}$	Ludwigshafen, 2 a.m., in 2 hours
$27\frac{3}{4}$	Mayence, $5\frac{1}{2}$ a.m., in $4\frac{3}{4}$ hrs.

ENG. MLS.	**Wurzburg** to
47	Ansbach, $8\frac{1}{2}$ a.m., in 9 hours
$43\frac{3}{4}$	Aschaffenberg, 8 a.m., $6\frac{1}{4}$ p.m. & 12 night (per Esselbach), and 6 a.m. (per Lohr), in $9\frac{3}{4}$ hours
$135\frac{1}{2}$	Augsburg, $8\frac{1}{2}$ a.m. (per Gunzenhausen); $3\frac{1}{4}$ & $11\frac{1}{2}$ a.m.,
$48\frac{1}{4}$	Bamberg, $3\frac{1}{4}$, $8\frac{1}{4}$, and $11\frac{1}{2}$ a.m. and 7 p.m., in 9 hours
$94\frac{1}{4}$	Bayreuth, $8\frac{1}{4}$ & $11\frac{1}{2}$ a.m., and 7 p.m., in $17\frac{1}{4}$ hours
$18\frac{1}{2}$	Bischofsheim, 8 a.m., & 7 p.m., in 3 hours
$43\frac{3}{4}$	Bruckenau, 2 p.m., in $8\frac{3}{4}$ hrs.
...	Eger (Prague), $8\frac{1}{4}$ a.m. (per Bamberg and Culmbach).
95	Eisenach, $8\frac{1}{4}$ a.m., in $19\frac{3}{4}$ hours
$79\frac{3}{4}$	Frankfort-on-the-Maine, at 8 a.m., and $6\frac{1}{4}$ p.m. (per Esselbach and Seligenstadt); 12 night (per Esselbach and Hanau), in $14\frac{1}{2}$ hours
$57\frac{3}{4}$	Fulda, 2 p.m., in $13\frac{1}{4}$ hours
24	Gemunden, $6\frac{1}{2}$ a.m., in $3\frac{3}{4}$ hrs.
65	Gunzenhausen, $8\frac{1}{2}$ a.m., in $13\frac{1}{4}$ hours
$58\frac{1}{2}$	Hanau, 12 night, in 11 hours
86	Heidelberg, 8 a.m., 7 p.m.
$71\frac{3}{4}$	Heilbronn, 1 p.m., in 16 hrs.
$67\frac{1}{4}$	Hof, $3\frac{1}{4}$, $8\frac{1}{4}$, & $11\frac{1}{2}$ a.m. and 7 p.m., in $17\frac{3}{4}$ hours
$33\frac{1}{2}$	Kissingen, $3\frac{1}{4}$, 6, $8\frac{1}{4}$, & $11\frac{1}{2}$ a.m. (per Schweinfurt, in $7\frac{1}{2}$ hours
12	Kitzingen, $8\frac{1}{4}$ a.m., 8 p.m., in 2 hours
66	Meiningen, $8\frac{1}{4}$ a.m., in 13 hours
$25\frac{1}{4}$	Mergentheim, 1 p.m., in $5\frac{1}{4}$ hours
38	Miltenberg, 4.50 p.m., in 7 hrs
$155\frac{1}{2}$	Munich, $8\frac{1}{2}$ a.m. (per Gunzenhausen); $3\frac{1}{4}$ & $11\frac{1}{4}$ a.m., (per Bamberg) in $20\frac{1}{2}$ hrs.
83	Nordlingen, $8\frac{1}{2}$ a.m., in $15\frac{3}{4}$ hours
$63\frac{1}{2}$	Nuremberg, 8 p.m. (per Kitzingen) $3\frac{1}{4}$, $8\frac{1}{2}$, & $11\frac{1}{2}$ a.m., and 7 p.m., (per Bamberg.)
$126\frac{1}{2}$	Regensburg, $3\frac{1}{4}$, $8\frac{1}{2}$ & $11\frac{1}{2}$ a.m. (per Bamberg) in $24\frac{3}{4}$ hrs.
23	Schweinfurt, $3\frac{1}{4}$, $8\frac{1}{4}$, and $11\frac{1}{2}$ a.m., in $4\frac{1}{2}$ hrs.
$97\frac{1}{2}$	Stuttgart, 1 p.m., in $18\frac{3}{4}$ hrs.
$22\frac{1}{2}$	Wertheim, 4.50 p.m., in $3\frac{3}{4}$ hrs

ENG. MLS.	**Yverdun** to
..	Bern, 6 and 9.20 a.m. (per Murten and Neufchâtel), in $9\frac{3}{4}$ hours.
..	Freiburg, 6 a.m. (per Payerne), in 8 hours
..	Lausanne, $1\frac{3}{4}$ and 10 a.m., and 2.20 p.m., in $3\frac{1}{4}$ hours
..	Motiers, $11\frac{1}{2}$ p.m., in 5 hours
..	Moudon, 5 a.m., returning at 4 p.m., in $3\frac{1}{2}$ hours
..	Neufchâtel, 9 20 a.m. and 11.20 p.m., in $3\frac{1}{2}$ hours

ENG. MLS.	**Zittau** to
..	Gorlitz, 5 a.m., in $4\frac{1}{2}$ hours
..	Gr. Schönau, 12 noon and 4 p.m., in 1 hour
..	Neustadt, 9 a.m., in $7\frac{1}{4}$ hours
..	Niedergrund, 12 noon, in $2\frac{1}{2}$ hours
..	Prague, 12 noon (per Niedergr), in $17\frac{1}{2}$ hours
..	Reichenberg, 5 a.m. and $3\frac{1}{2}$ p.m., in $3\frac{1}{2}$ hours

ENG. MLS.	**Zug** to
..	Arth (Rigi), 12.20 noon, in $1\frac{1}{4}$ hours
..	Brunnen, 12.20 noon, in $3\frac{1}{4}$ hours
..	Luzern, $12\frac{1}{4}$ noon, 1.35 night
..	Sins, $11\frac{1}{4}$ a.m., returning at $12\frac{1}{2}$ noon, in $1\frac{1}{4}$ hours
..	Zürich, 12.5 noon and 12.50 night, in 4 hours

ENG. MLS.	**Zurich** to
..	Aarau, 8 a.m., $1\frac{1}{2}$ & 7 p.m.
..	Basle, $5\frac{1}{2}$ & 8 a.m., & 7 p.m.
..	Bern, 8 a.m. and 7 p.m.
..	Chur, 8 a.m. and $5\frac{1}{2}$ p.m. (per Steamer)
..	Constance, $7\frac{1}{2}$ a.m., in $9\frac{1}{4}$ hours
..	Feldkirch, 7 a.m., in $15\frac{3}{4}$ hrs.
..	Frauenfeld, $7\frac{1}{2}$ a.m. & $10\frac{1}{2}$ p.m.
..	Friedrichshafen, $7\frac{1}{2}$ a.m. and $10\frac{1}{2}$ p.m. (per Romanshorn)
..	Glarus, 8 a.m. (per Lachen), and $5\frac{1}{2}$ p.m. (per Uznach).
..	Lindau, $7\frac{1}{2}$ a.m. and $10\frac{1}{2}$ p.m., also $7\frac{1}{2}$ a.m. and 9 p.m. (per St. Gallen). in 12 hrs.
..	Lucern, $8\frac{1}{2}$ a.m. and $9\frac{1}{2}$ p.m.
..	Milan, $9\frac{1}{2}$ p.m. (per St. Gotthardt), in $35\frac{1}{2}$ hours
..	Schaffhausen, at $7\frac{3}{4}$ a.m. (per Rafz); 2 and $10\frac{1}{2}$ p.m. (per Winterthur) in $7\frac{1}{2}$ hours
..	St. Gallen, $7\frac{3}{4}$ a.m. & 9 p.m. (per Winterth.); also by Steamer, at 8 a.m. and $5\frac{1}{2}$ p.m. (per Uznach), in 12 hours
..	Winterthur, $7\frac{1}{2}$ and $7\frac{3}{4}$ a.m. & 2, 5, 9, and $10\frac{1}{2}$ p.m., in $1\frac{1}{4}$ hours
..	Zug (Rigi), $8\frac{1}{2}$ a.m. & $9\frac{1}{2}$ p.m., in 4 hours

ENG. MLS.	**Zwickau** to
$53\frac{1}{4}$	Carlsbad, (in summer only).
$70\frac{1}{4}$	Dresden, (per Riesa)
$13\frac{1}{2}$	Schneeberg, 10 a.m. $3\frac{1}{2}$ & $9\frac{1}{2}$ p.m., in $3\frac{1}{4}$ hours

---

From pages 265 to 328, see SPECIAL EDITION, Price 3s. 6d., Published on the 1st of each Month, which contains an additional amount of useful Information and Maps not found in the 1s. 6d. Edition.

SPECIAL EDITION.

CONTINENTAL ROUTES.

Being desirous of making BRADSHAW'S CONTINENTAL RAILWAY GUIDE every way suitable for the instruction and amusement of Travellers, as well as with a view of pointing out to them Routes of the most approved and agreeable character, we have determined to give in our future Special Editions brief but interesting particulars in reference to the Routes most useful to be followed in travelling through the various countries. We commence with—

ROUTE 1.

A Route of Three Weeks through Switzerland.

We may first premise that the *route* given underneath, applies to travellers entering Switzerland from Freiburg-in-Breisgau, at Schaffhausen, and leaving it at Bâsle.

Freiburg-in-Breisgau to Schaffhausen, by the Hollenthal.—The distance from the former to the latter place is about 50, or perhaps 52, English miles; and the mode of conveyance is by diligence, which performs the journey direct in about ten or twelve hours. The *route* is accomplished through the charming valley of the Hollenthal, or Infernal Valley, which presents the appearance, at its opening, of a flat and fertile plain, enclosed amid sloping and sylvan hills. Nearing the ascent, its original width becomes slowly contracted; and at about 42 miles from Schaffhausen, assumes a magnificently beautiful shade of romantic grandeur. Its woods rich in foliage, cover the steep sides, from which project out sharpened fragments of rock, rugged and naked, having running at their base the Dreisam, whose banks are verdant with turf, and studded with mills. The scenery here will impress the mind of the tourist as partaking of a majestic wildness, blended with a picturesque beauty; Steig and Hirschsprung are the spots most remarkable for the exhibition of this wild and rugged grandeur. On the journey we pass Burg, remarkable by the fact of 1796, when Moreau accomplished a retreat with his army. Ninety-four years previous to this, Marshal Villars was deterred from attempting this pass, saying that he was not daredevil enough. On our onward way we meet Steig, a post station, where the traveller may enjoy good accommodation, on reasonable terms. Here a steep slope of the road leads the tourist out of the Hollensteig, or Valley of Hell; and leaving it, he parts with the finest scenery. At this juncture an extra horse is required for the ascent of the Hollensteig, for which 1fl. 12kr. must be paid. Opening in the distance is Himmelreich, *alias* the Kingdom of Heaven—called so, we presume, from the very elevated position of the country constituting it. Passing Lenzkirch, Bondorf, (nineteen miles from which is the magnificent Benedictine Abbey of St. Blaize,) we arrive at the top of the ascent, from whence may be had a magnificent view of the Lake of Constance. Close by is the Castle of Hohenlupfen; and a little further on, after passing Stuhlingen, we cross a stream, and journeying on a distance of 11½ miles, we enter

Schaffhausen.—For a description of which, see page 225.

Schaffhausen to Zurich, by Eglisau.—Distance, twenty-eight miles; the mode of conveyance is by diligence, which makes the journey in about from four to six hours. Hearing the roar of the Rhine Fall, and traversing a small portion of the Baden territory, we arrive at

Eglisau is situated on the Rhine, about 13 miles from Schaffhausen, and contains about 1700 inhabitants. The scenery of the passage of the Rhine here is very romantic. The waters flow between hills covered with trees, and is crossed by an embowered wooden bridge. We next meet, at a distance of about four miles, Bulach, a town of about 5,000 inhabitants, having some good inns. From here a magnificent view of the Alps, with their tops crowned by eternal snows, may be had. The descent to Zurich is very picturesque and romantic; passing through beautifully laid out gardens and vineyards, interspersed with beautiful villas and cottages. About two miles to the right is the hill of Weid, from which a rich view of the town and neighbourhood may be enjoyed. After this, nothing worth special notice presents itself, until our arrival at Zurich, described at page 226.

Zurich to Lucerne, across the Alb's, per Hausen.—Distance 33 English miles.—The journey is made by diligence, occupying about eight hours in the transit. A very fair new carriage-road leads to Zug, and crosses the High Albis.

Though in the ascent the road is very zigzag and circuitous, yet the ascent can be accomplished per carriage with two horses. All along the route a very beautiful view of the Alpine chain, and of the greater portion of Switzerland, can be enjoyed. After skirting the Lake for a little, it crosses the Sihl, and wends to the inn of the Albis, where the tourist can get well accommodated, and indulge in a magnificent prospect. Above the inn about one mile is a height commanding an excellent view of the entire Zürichsee. Situated at the foot is the vale of Sihl, which is beautiful in its wooded slopes and picturesque scenery, and remarkable as having been the favourite sanctum of the pastoral poet Gessner. On the south is seen the Lake of Turl; not far from which is the Church of Kappel, where Zwingli died. Remoter off is the Lake of Zug, behind which rise aloft in sublime grandeur Mounts Pilatus and Righi. At this point the horizon, reflecting the snowy chain of the Alps from Sentes to the Jungfrau, presents a remarkably brilliant aspect. Attaining the summit, 2,500 feet above the sea and 1,000 feet above the lake, we descend, touching on the right the small Lake of Turl. After traversing the new road along the western slope of the Albis, we arrive at Hausen. Near this place is Albisbrunn—a water-cure establishment—where general travellers can board and lodge for 6 or 7fr. a day. From here the Bernese Alps can be seen to advantage.

Hausen.—A village of 6,000 inhabitants, painfully remarkable as being the scene of a sanguinary conflict, in which brother met brother in hostile combat, and, in the name of religion, sacrificed each other in remorseless fury. Here Zwingli fell on the battle-field. A monument is now erected on the spot where he fell, bearing on its entablature a Latin and German inscription. We next arrive at

Rifferschwyl.—Lucern to Knonau, 10 English miles; Knonau to St. Wolfgang, 6¾ miles. A good road to Zug, the Righi, St. Wolfgang, Gisiikerbrucke, Brucke, Dierikon, and Ebikon; from which, passing the monument of the Swiss guards, we enter

Lucerne—described at page 223.—From Lucerne the tourist may proceed per steamer to Fluellen, distance about twenty-four English miles; the voyage is made in about three hours; see alphabetical list of steamers. The fare varies from 1 franc to 4 francs, and the boat generally touches at Weggis. The journey, though short, will interest. The lake, deeply interesting in its natural proportions, is yet singularly so by its historic recollections. Its shores witnessed the memorable events that guaranteed freedom to Switzerland, and built unto Liberty a home and a sanctuary.

Leaving Lucerne, we pass Hof Brücke, after which we hail Meggenhorn, and sail along through undulating hills, rich in verdure, and studded with picturesque villas and cottages—a scene beautiful in itself, but shadowed into a dark grandeur by Mount Pilatus. Further up, near the Bay of Kussnacht, to the right, is the Castle of Neu Habsburg. At the other side of the bay appears the stupendous mass of the Righi, whose sides are studded with forests, at the base of which lie fields, gardens, and cottages. Athwart the promontory of Tanzenburg the village of Weggis is seen; there tourists anxious to ascend the Righi disembark. To facilitate the tourist in his ascent, we here notice the

Ascent to the Righi from Weggis.—The ascen presents many features of inducement not generally found surrounding other pleasure trips. In its mountain majesty and stupendous structures—in its variegated splendour of beauteous scenery, representing nature in all her manifold glories, in all her eternal properties—the traveller finds a continual subject for mighty, grand, and holy thoughts, calculated to inspire the soul with feelings of the most awful reverence for nature's great parent, who, by His single fiat, had hewn out from the machinery of nature the great mount which he looks upon, to stand forth as a landmark and monument, silent but eloquent, of His power for ever. The ease of the ascent, and the facility for obtaining accommodation at every stage, combined with the sublimity of the scene from the summit, render the excursion desirable and delightful. The visit should be made in order; and for this purpose the traveller should set out early, as, if he do not, it will be impossible for him to reach Staffel or Culon in time to witness the sun set—one of the most glorious scenes ever written on the picture page of nature; as any one who has ever beheld from the Righi the gorgeous luminary, bathed in floods of light and lustre, sinking calmly and silently, yet regally and grand, into the golden ocean of his western dominions, can attest. All the interesting objects can be visited in a day, and are below particularised for the convenience of the traveller. A mule-path leads up the ascent, commanding a constant view of the lake. It first passes the Heiligen Kreutz, after which we next encounter the Cold Baths, where we find a wooden inn, a small Chapel of the Virgin, and the Spring of the Sisters' Fountain. The first crucifix on the Kussnacht side is met at Leeboden, and a walk or ride through a succession of rich pasturage, intersected by beautiful and romantic paths, brings the tourist to the Righi Staffel, an elevated plain or platform chosen for viewing the effects of sunset. There the traveller can rest and enjoy the unrivalled scenery before him, after which he finds a very good inn, where he can get comfortable accommodation. Half-an-hour's walk further on brings him to Culm, the most celebrated summit, where is also a good inn. The Kesisboden boch is famed in the ascent to the Culm. Another path branches off from Leeboden towards the right, which leads the tourist to pass the following interesting objects:—the Lieterli, the Kawseli, and the Kaltenbud or Chwesterbrunnen. From the north side very good views are obtainable of the Lake of Zug and of the town of Arth. On the west Lucerne can be distinctly seen; whilst on the south the objects seen are the Lakes of Alpnach and Saren, the Stanzer and Buochserhorn Mountains, behind which are The Alps, Berne, Unterwalden, and

Uri—an unbroken reef—with their glaciers, embracing the Engelberger, Rothstock, and the Bristentock, central between which and the Seelisberg runs the road of St. Gothard. On the east, the Alpine chain is seen to stretch along the horizon.

Resuming our journey towards Fluellen, the steamer proceeds through the Noses, immediately after passing which, we find ourselves shut out by high mountains. Running through the oval basin called the Gulf of Buochs, we touch at Beckenreid, Gersau, and Brunnen, opposite which we change our entire course and sail along the Bay of Uri, for Grutli, a short mile or two from which is Tell's Chapel. After this, we arrive at

FLUELLEN—described at page 221.—From Fluellen we proceed to visit the PASS OF ST. GOTHARD, per Altorf; Amsteg, where are good inns; and Wasen, a village of about 6000 inhabitants, on the left bank of the Ruys. Close by here is a toll, where each tourist is charged a small sum, equal to about one halfpenny English, and each carriage from 1½ to 2 frs. The first part of the way to the St. Gothard is rich in beautiful scenery; but from Wasen, up towards the Goschenen, there is an aspect of savage grandeur, not at all diminished by the narrow ravine of the Schellenen, circled for nearly four miles by stupendous rocks of granite.

THE DEVIL'S BRIDGE.—The stern and savage grandeur of this portion of the Pass far excels that of all the rest. The fearful gorge shoots out a lofty cataract, the fall of which is awfully majestic; its sheets of water rolling down in sublime grandeur, lash the opposite sides in broken fury, and laving with foam the surrounding space, until again dashed back and broken into spray. Two bridges span the torrent. The Devil's Bridge and the defile of Schellinen were the scenes of an obstinate contest during the campaign of 1799, when, on the 14th of August, the French columns, under Lecourbe and Loison, drove the Austrians up the valley of the Reuss. Just above the bridge, the road passes through a tunnel cut through the rock, called "*Hole of the Uri.*" Emerging from out this, the traveller finds himself in the beautiful valley of the Urseren, which forms a deep contrast to the savage gorge just left behind. About one mile further brings us to

ANDERMATT.—A small village with about 700 inhabitants, and the chief place of the valley, 4,450 feet above the level of the sea. Honey, cheese, and splendid trout can be had here. Behind Andermatt a bridle-path leads over the Oberalp, and by its lake to Disentis, in the Grisons.

Taking a direct road from Andermatt, we arrive at Hospital. From here a mule-path over the Furca leads to the glacier of the Rhone, (a journey of about six hours,) from whence the Hospice of the Grimsel can be made in about two.

From Hospital the journey to the Grimsel can be made in about six hours. A splendid panoramic view of the Grimsel, and of the adjacent peaks and glaciers, can be enjoyedfrom the summit of the Sidelhorn, on the right of the path to the Furca.

FROM GRIMSEL TO THE GRINDELWALD, *via* MEYRINGEN — Distance, forty-one English miles. — Leaving Grimsel, we pass through a forest of fir, and arrive at the Handek, where we can find comfortable refreshment. This spot is situated a few yards' distance from the Falls of the Aar—the noblest cataract in Switzerland. From here a short walk of about an hour brings us to

GUTTANEN.—A small and retired village. Proceeding on, we enter a ravine created by the expansion of the Im Boden; and going further, we enter the basin valley of Upper Hasli. Meeting the vale of Hasli, and crossing the Aar, we arrive at MEYRINGEN—described at page 224. From this place to the Grindelwald the distance is about 21 English miles; and the journey is accomplished in about eight hours. The journey is made at first by a path through a delightful valley, at either side of which are heard resounding the cadence of beautiful waterfalls. Passing the Baths of Rosenlaui, where we find a few rude tubs, serving as baths, the waters of which are mineral, we reach the Scheideck, the ascent of which is rather easy. From here we reach the Grindelwald in about three or four hours.

From the Grindelwald we move on through Wergeralp to Lauterbrunen--a village containing about 1400 inhabitants. The houses are all wooden, and broadly scattered over the banks of the torrent. It is 2450 feet above the level of the sea, and buried, as it were, among precipices. The Stanbbach fall of water is worth seeing. It is about one mile from the inn, and is one of the loftiest in Europe. Visiters should not leave here without exploring the upper valley of Lauterbrunnen. Very little of interest is to be met with on the route to INTERLACHEN—described at page 223.

INTERLACHEN TO THUN.—A good carriage-road exists by the southern shore of the lake. The journey by water is preferable. A diligence conveys the tourists to Neuhaus, where the steamer takes them up for Thun. On the voyage up the lake we see the village of Mertgin, at the rear of which is the Juster Thal. Sailing by the rocky promontory called the "Nose," we proceed to pass the Castle of Spietz, founded, it is said, by Attila. As we get into Thun, we find the banks on the south side studded with picturesque villas and romantically planned gardens—whilst on its northern side are uninteresting hamlets and rugged scenery.

THUN — described at page 225. — The distance from Thun to Berne is about 17 English miles, and the journey is made by diligence or per voiturier which costs 17 or 18 frs., unless it be a return one, when 11 or 12 frs. suffice. The road is an excellent one, and on a clear day commands a very fine view of the Alps. The scenery of the valley of the Aar is also beautiful, and will delight the tourist. The principal place met on the route is the little village of Munsingen, only remarkable as having been the spot where the oligarchical rule was overturned, in 1849, and a new constitution adopted. The Stockhorn is also passed, and presents an agreeable aspect.

BERNE—described at page 220.—We leave Berne

through the Gate of Mora, and proceeding through a very fertile though rather commonplace country, we arrive at Neuerieck. Here we cross the stream separating the two cantons, Berne and Freiburg. We get into the new road at this point, after crossing the bridge. The way leads along the bank of the river, through beautiful scenery. Before entering Freiburg, the view is impressive in the extreme. Its picturesque beauty is deeply reflective of solemn and romantic grandeur, as, rounding the hill leading into the valley of the Saarine, the venerable battlements, capped with innumerable towers, burst upon the vision, revealing the deep gorge of the opposite side. Close to the summit of the hill is the large old building once the Jesuits' Pensionat: near it the Jesuits' College, the Tower, and Church of St. Nicholas; beyond which is seen the Suspension Bridge, over which the traveller enters

FREIBURG—described at page 222.—We leave this place by diligence, and proceed through a fairly interesting country, until we arrive at

BULLE, about 15 miles from Vevay.—Bulle is a very industrious town, containing 1600 inhabitants. It is half way between Freiburg and Vevay. From Bulle we proceed again by diligence through the road skirting the west base of the Moleson, and passing Chatel St. Denis, remarkable for its picturesque beauty and elevated castle on the left bank of the Vevayse. A very good road carries us, by an easy descent, to

VEVAY—described at page 225.—From Vevay to Martigny, by Montreaux, Villeneuve, Aigle, and Bex, the journey is made by diligence. Leaving Vevay, the first object of interest met with is the Tour de Peibz—a small town, built in 1239 by Count Peter of Savoy. It contains the ruins of a fortified castle, and is about 1 mile from Vevay and 2½ from

CLARENS.—This spot must be ever associated with sentiment and song, as described by Rousseau in Nouvelle Heloise. From here a splendid view of the lake and valley of the Rhone, and of the opposite shore, can be had. Our own Byron has also immortalised it in a poem, in a part of which he sings—

" 'Twas not for fiction chose Rousseau this spot,
Peopleing it with affections; but he found
It was the scene which passion must allot
To the mind's purified beings."

Here jutting rocks, towering awkwardly from the banks of the lake, supplant the gorgeous scenery of hills and vine-clad undulations that characterise and adorn its banks all through from Geneva.

MONTREAUX.—Here there are one or two good inns. The climate, owing to the sheltered position of the place, is healthy and mild, rendering the village a delightful winter quarter for invalids unable to cross the Alps. From the eminence on which it is built very good views can be commanded; and under the rock, on which the parish church is erected, there is a magnificent grotto, adorned with incrustations of mosses, stalactites, and other concretions, called Confette di Tivoli. Two miles beyond Montreaux is the celebrated Castle of Chillon. It communicates with the road by a wooden bridge, and stands solitary and alone—a striking monument of feudal despotism. It is a building of the thirteenth century, and owes its origin to Amedeus IV. of Savoy. Byron has consecrated it as a part of history for ever, in his celebrated poem, "The Prisoner of Chillon," in which he thus apostrophises it:—

"Chillon! Thy prison is a holy place,
And thy sad floor an altar; for 'twas trod
Until his very steps have left a trace,
Worn as if the cold pavement were a sod,
By Bonnevard! May none those marks efface!
For they appeal from Tyranny to God."

On our way from here we meet

VILLENEUVE is built on the eastern extremity of the Lake of Geneva, and contains about 1500 in-inhabitants. Here the road leaves the borders of the lake, and enters the valley of the Rhone. A diligence takes us on, passing Lasingli, to

BEX.—A village on the road to the Simplon, containing about 4000 inhabitants, and only remarkable for its salt mines and works; situated on the valley of La Gryonne, about three miles from Bex, from which there is an excellent carriage-road through picturesque and delightful scenery, to the mines.

BRIDGE OF ST. MAURICE.—This bridge connects the cantons Vaud and Vallais. Immediately beyond it, on the left bank of the Rhone, is the old town itself, embedded among mountains.

ST. MAURICE contains about 11,000 inhabitants, and derives its name from the traditional surmise that, by order of Maximilian, the Theban Legion under St. Maurice were put to death in 302 because they would not apostatize from the Christian faith. The tourist who visits St. Maurice should make it a point to see the Abbey, a building of the fourth century. Its objects of attraction are the Museum of Ancient Art—a vase of Saracen execution, presented by Charlemagne—a golden crozier of a spire-like form, exquisitely carved—and a second one presented by Bertha, Queen of Burgundy.

Leaving ST. MAURICE, we can see the Bath House of Savoy. It is built on the right bank of the Rhone, over a sulphureous spring. We also see rising far above the road the Hermitage of our Lady of the Rock. Passing on for about seven miles, we see the celebrated waterfall of the Sallenches, the fall of which is about 120 feet. Crossing the stream of the Trient, as it descends from the Tete Noire, and meeting the Castle of La Batie, we arrive at

MARTIGNY—described at page 223.—The distance from Martigny to Chamonix is about twenty-three or twenty-four miles, and may be accomplished in from nine to eleven hours by mule or foot. The road commands a very good view of Mont Blanc. The path from Martigny leads over the Forclaz. The hamlet of Trent lies to the left far deep in the valley, beautifully situated among meadows. From here the journey begins to be accomplished through the forest of the Forclaz, emerging up the valley of the Trent, and crossing the pulverised excrescences of the winter floods, opposite the forest pointing to the Col di Balme. After climbing up a fatiguing ascent, the traveller enters on the pasturages and farm-houses of Herbageres. From here the ascent is rather slow and facile to the top, where bursts upon the astonished vision one of the most glorious scenes ever painted by the hand of Almighty intelligence on the large volume of nature. Mont Blanc, reposing in the vale of Chamounix, surrounded by the needle-peaked La Tour l'Argentiére, Verte de Dru, Charinez, and Midi, each of which is separated by its own polished glaciers, reflecting back the mighty proportions of their giant monarch, appears like a model Atlas bearing heaven on his shoulders. At his feet lies the vale, and at its extreme point the Col di Vesa. To the right are the Arguilles Rouges, whilst beyond them, enclosing the valley, stretches the Brevent, to the rear of which is seen the Mortine, supporting the snow-capped summit of the Buet. The scene, after being viewed, will remain written on the mind for ever. Its gorgeous grandeur, rugged majesty, and brilliant scenery, can never be forgotten. Descending, we pass the source of the Arve, and traverse the fine pasturage of Charmillian to the village of La Tour, a little below which the path meets the road to Chamounix by the Tete Noire.

CHAMOUNIX—described at page 220.—The distance from here to Geneva is about 52 English miles, and the journey is performed by mule or *char-à-banc* to St. Martin, thence by diligence to Geneva, and the time occupied is twelve or thirteen hours. Leaving the village, we proceed about a league and meet the Mer de Glace; and crossing the Arve above the Glacier of Bossons, we follow the road to the right bank of the stream for about a mile, when, if it so suits, we can turn off and visit the Cascades des Pelérins, remarkable for its singular beauty. Passing numerous torrents, we traverse a valley, and arrive at Les Montets through some meadows leading out of the village of Les Ouches. At Montets, Mont Blanc appears brilliant in the extreme. Crossing Pont Pelissiar, we reach

SERVOZ—We emerge from here through a forest to the road, and proceed through Chêde to the valley of the Arve, a little at this side of St. Martin. Proceeding on, we reach

SALLENCHES—A small town about 36 or 37 miles from Geneva, containing 2100 inhabitants. Entering St. Martin we cross the bridge of the Arve. From this bridge we enjoy one of the best Alpine views of Mount Blanc. On coming within a short distance of Maglan, the road nears Nant d'Arpenaz, one of the highest waterfalls in Savoy. Outside Maglan, where the precipices retire a little to the left; and at the summit of the mountain, 900 feet above the valley, is the Grotto of Balm, approached by a mule-path. Proceeding on through a narrow valley we reach

CLUSES—A small village containing about 2000 inhabitants, and famous for its watchmaking trade. It was burned down in 1843, but has since been rebuilt. Crossing the Arve by a stone bridge, we leave Cluses and pass the villages of Vaugier and Scionzier, shortly after arriving at

BONNEVILLE—A small place containing about 2000 inhabitants.

NANGY.—A small village.

CHESNE.—Before arriving here, and on reaching Annemasse, the tourist's passport is examined, and if found *en regle*, no trouble is given in reference to the baggage. Passing for some miles through a road lined with neat gardens and cottages, we arrive at

GENEVA.—See page 222.—From here we set out for Lausanne. The journey can be made by diligence or steamer daily. Leaving Geneva, we pass through a country studded with picturesque villas and neatly laid out gardens. There is scarcely one spot in Europe presents so many attractive features, in reference to situation and beauty, as the shores of the lake. Passing Versoix, now an inconsiderable village, we arrive at

COPPET.—A small village containing about 700 inhabitants, and possessing no objects of interest, save its chateau, once the residence of Madame de Stael.

NYON.—A town containing about 3000 inhabitants, built on an eminence, but possessing no objects worthy of notice.

ROLLE.—A small village surrounded by hills studded with vineyards.

MORGES.—A small town, with three thousand inhabitants. Adjoining its Port is the venerable old Castle of Wufflens, said to have been built by Queen Bertha. Before entering Lausanne, the view of the town is very beautiful indeed. At the entrance of the suburbs is the village of Ouchy, where we find a inn, in which Lord Byron wrote the "Prisoner of Chillon," finishing the poem in two days, in June 1816, being detained at the inn by severe weather. Passing through the Promenade of Montbanon, we enter

LAUSANNE.—See page 223.—LAUSANNE to BASLE, by YVERDUN, NEUFCHATEL, and BIENNE. The journey from Lausanne to Yverdun, is made by diligence. The country through which we pass is rich and picturesque, and the first place of note met with is

ECHALLENS—Situated on the river Talent, with 800 inhabitants.

YVERDUN.—See page 225.—From here we sail up the lake, passing Grandson, a small town, containing 900 inhabitants, and arrive at

NEUFCHATEL—described at page 224.—The steamer carries us on to

BIENNE.—See page 220.

Bienne to Basle.—Conveyance by diligence.

Leaving Bienne, we ascend the valley by the left bank of the Suze, meeting on our way several small cascades.

Sonceboz.—A small village of nc note.

Pass of Pierre Pertuis.

Proceeding through a valley, and up an ascent, we arrive at

Tavernus.

Mallery.

Journeying through the small plain of Taverney, we pass through a magnificent defile, and see the Birs foaming at the bottom, overshadowed by cliffs and firs; after which we arrive at

Montiers.—The village contains about 1,250 inhabitants, and derives its name from an ancient minister of St. Germanus.

Courrendelin.—Passing Délémont and St. Jacob, we enter

Basle, from whence we proceed home through France.

ROUTE 2.

Martigny to Milan, by Sion, Brieg, Domo d'Ossola, and the Passage of the Simplon.

(Distance 179 English miles.)

Passports.—Tourists intending to cross the Simplon should have their passports *visé* by the Sardinian Minister at Geneva or Lausanne.

Conveyances.—Diligences run daily to Milan, making the journey in 58 or 60 hours, and making Brieg a sleeping-place.

Quitting Martigny, we proceed for a short time through sterile rocks and mountains. Passing Reddes, the aspect of the country altogether changes—the luxuriant pasturages, rich vineyards, picturesque villages with churches, and the ruins of ancient castles, &c., now met with, presenting a deep contrast to the barren ruggedness just left behind. And, as we approach Sion through the valley of the Rhone, we behold nothing but scenes on which the eye loves to rest and memory to linger. The low grounds intersected with rivers, the adjacent mountains studded with villas and chastely-wrought buildings, and the extreme horizon bounded by the Alpine heights—all form a group scene deeply touching.

Sion.—Is the chief town of Vallais, with a population of three thousand souls. It stands on a declivity of three hills, and possesses three extensive castles, built on each declivity. The third castle, called Tourbillon, contained portraits of the bishops of Sion from the year 300; it is now in ruins. Here we find several Roman antiquities, one of which is a half-effaced inscription to the memory of Augustus, near the door of the cathedral. The landscape painter will find the castles of Sion and Montargis, seated on rocks above the town to the right, special objects of interest. The Hospital is worth a visit. Leaving Sion, we proceed through a beautiful country, rich in rural beauty, and fruitful of vineyards and pasture lands, irrigated by the Rhone.

Sierre.—A pretty little village. The people here, and indeed throughout the Vallais, speak German. Quitting Sierre, we cross the Rhone, traverse the forest of Fuiges, and pass Leuk, nine miles above which are the Baths, worth seeing—the gorge of the Dela opening behind it. Travellers in carriages usually turn off here to visit the Baths, and ascend the lofty and sterile Mount Gemmi.

Tourtemagne.—Remarkable only for the cascade behind it. The approach to this place presents us with a view of the entire Alpine chain, connecting the Simplon and St. Gothard. From here we drive to

Visp.—Is seated on the banks of the Visp—a river as large as the Rhone. It was once the residence of very many noble families, whose stately palaces are now in ruins. It is now a miserable village. From here we proceed to Brieg, passing Glys, where the ascent of the Simplon begins.

Brieg.—Is a small town, containing about eight hundred inhabitants, and is the usual resting-place for travellers crossing the Simplon. The only buildings worth notice are the Chateau of Baron Stockalper and the Jesuits' College. At this town the Simplon road leaves the valley of the Rhone. The distance from Brieg to Domo d'Ossola is about fifty English miles. It takes seven hours to reach the Simplon, and three or four to Domo d'Ossola. Before describing the ascent, it may be well to observe that the route over the Simplon was planned by the Emperor Napoleon in 1801, immediately after the sanguinary battle of Marengo. It was constructed at the united expense of France and Italy. On the side of the Haut Vallais, the work was carried on by M. Céard, representing France; and by Giovanni Fabroni on the part of Italy. Commenced on the Italian side in 1800, and on the Swiss side, in 1801, the work occupied six years in completion, giving employment to over 30,000 men. This road is the only one over the Alps, where human skill and labour have succeeded in hewing out a practicable passage for waggons and artillery. Between Brieg and Siesto, it passes over 611 bridges, besides the colossal constructions of masonry, consisting of ten galleries of solid stone, and twenty houses of refuge. It is twenty-five feet broad. It cost £5000 per mile.

Ascent of the Simplon.—The first work of the ascent of the Simplon is a bridge thrown over the Salatine, consisting of a lofty and spacious arch. On the left we pass a chapel, with several small oratories leading to it; from here we ascend to a forest of fir through beautiful windings The openings of the forest presents us with delightful views of the valley of the Rhone, shrouded by snow-capped Alps, with their queen, Mont Blanc, towering majestically above them. Traversing precipices, we reach the first gallery, and crossing the lofty

PONT DU GANTHER, fine cascades, and romantic glens present themselves, until we reach the third refuge, called

BERESAL.—It consists of two buildings connected by a roof. Passing this refuge, we see a splendid variety of Alpine flowers growing amid verdant lawns of turf; and crossing the bridges of Orsback and Saltine, (close to the bottom is a magnificent cascade,) we enter a grotto, leaving on our left the Kaltwasser glacier, from which falls four cascades, whose waters dash themselves into the chasms below. Following out our ascent, we reach an eminence over which nature seems mourning in desolate abandonment. No tree, no shrub, no green spot greets the vision ; all is melancholy and awful desolation. Close to this desolate spot is the glacier grotto, to the right of which is the Hospice, inhabited by monks belonging to Mount St. Bernard. Here there is no stabling or fodder for horses, but travellers are very comfortably accommodated.

An extensive valley of considerable width occupies the summit of the Simplon ; all about is devoid of picturesque interest. A gentle descent brings us to the seventh refuge, situated about three miles from the village of the

SIMPLON.—Travellers should take care not to be imposed on by representations to the effect of there being no horses. A wooden sabot should also be procured, to save the cross drag of the carriage, as the descent is steep and rapid. As we descend, on the right are lofty barren rocks, and roaring torrents on the left. Nine miles from Brieg and five from Domo d'Ossola, we reach the Gallerie d'Algaby, the first excavation on the Italian side. The road passes through this gallery ; and sloping gradually, enters the Gorge of Gondo—the grandest but yet most awfully savage in the Alps. Crossing the Doveria by a wooden bridge, we next pass over the Frascumnone waterfall ; and after wending through several zigzag turnings, we arrive at

GONDO, and leave the Vallais. This village consists of a few miserable huts congregated round a tower seven stories high. A short walk down the right of the torrent leads us to the gold mine of Zurichbergen. We enter Italy a short time before our arrival at the village of

ISELLA.—Here the passports and luggage of travellers are examined. This part of the road, for nearly eight miles, was destroyed by the tempests in 1834 and 1839. The road altogether, on the Sardinian side of the Pass, is in very bad repair. At this point of the journey the scenery assumes a different aspect. In place of naked ruggedness it puts on green foliage, and shrouds the road with the shade of the sombre fir, that clothes the tops of the mountains. The last gallery of the Pass is traversed previous to meeting Crevola, at which point we cross the Doveria by a bridge ninety-six feet high, with two arches. The changed aspect of the scenery and climate here proclaim our entrance into Italy.

DOMO D'OSSOLA.—A small Italian town, remarkable for its grotesque appearance and its idle lazzaroni only. From here the ascent of the Simplon occupies seven or eight hours, and twelve or thirteen from here to Milan.

VOGOGNA.—Is a small village, with the valley of Anzasca, leading up to Monte Rosa, opening up before it ; a scene worthy the tourist's special notice.

ORNAVASCA.—Near here are the white marble quarries, from which stone for the Milan Cathedral was procured. At Gravellona we cross a large bridge, and following the road leading up its left bank, we arrive, in a couple of hours, at the lake of Orta, one of the most beautiful on the Italian border. Lake Maggiore, and Isola Madre—the most northern of the Borromean Islands—burst on the vision here with great effect. Not far beyond this place will be found the rose granite quarries ; the colour is produced, it is said, by the influence of the felspar in it, which mineral abounds here in elegant flesh-coloured crystals.

BAVENO.—Close to the lake. Diligences from here to Milan in 9 hours.

BOATS.—Parties wishing to visit the Borromean Islands, will here find boats at the following rate :—For two hours, with two rowers, 5 fr , and 1 fr. per hour after ; an hour once commenced is counted as full.

ASSES may also be hired here at 4 frs. each, to ascend the Mont Monterone, towering in the rear of the village, and commanding a magnificent panoramic view of the Alps. The top is 4,350 feet above the level of the sea. The descent may be made by the opposite side to Orta, accomplishing the descent in three hours, and returning to Omegna in about two hours' walk.

CUSTOM-HOUSE OFFICERS are constantly met with along the western shore of the lake as far as Sesto. At Severn search is made on travellers landing or embarking for Austria or Switzerland. The release of baggage costs ½ fr.

THE BORROMEAN ISLANDS.—We embark at Baveno on the lake Maggiore for these islands. Travellers proceeding to Milan by carriage, should send it round to meet them at Stressa. Each morning the steamer navigating the lake, passes near the islands *en voyage* to Sesto, and touches there again on its return in the afternoon. This enables the tourist to see them ; and if he will leave Baveno early, he can reach Sesto.

PALENZA.—The steamer calls here for passengers every morning at about half past 8 o'clock, and a boat plies between here and Baveno.

LAGO MAGGIORE.—This lake, on which these islands are situated, was anciently called *Verbanus.* It is computed to be 56 Italian miles long and 6 to 9 broad, and towards its centre is about eighty fathoms deep. It presents an enchanting picture. Forest trees, olives, and vineyards, interspersed with picturesque hamlets, adorn and ornament its banks; whilst from out its placid bosom rise three small islands, two of which contain beautiful palaces and gardens—the property of the Borromean family. Passing Isola del Piscatore, Isola Bella is met with. This island is looked upon as the most beautiful of the three. It is a magnificent garden, consisting of ten terraces, the lowest of which rests on piers shooting into the lake, studded with beautiful sculpture, lined with cypresses, and rising like a pyramid, one above the other. A very great variety of fruits and flowers grows on them, such as the orange, citron, myrtle, &c. The Palace is worth seeing, and contains many very excellent paintings. We also find a very good inn on the island.

The Isola Madre rears a good many rare plants, and it will be found worth a visit.

After visiting the islands, the tourists embark for Sesto. Before reaching Arona we meet, a short mile distant, approached through a beautiful country, the magnificent statue of Charles Borromeo, wrought in bronze, by Zonelli, and measuring 112 ft. in height. The statue is erected on a hill overlooking

ARONA—A small old town, containing about 4,400 inhabitants, built on the margin of the lake, and having the Simplon road running through a part of it. At the lower end of the lake a splendid view of the snowy Monte Rosa is enjoyed; and a ferry-boat carries us over the Tecino into the Austrian-Lombardo territory met with at

SESTO CALENDE.—Here passports are *strictly* examined; and no traveller is permitted to pass the frontier, without his passport is provided with the *visa* of the Austrian minister. If he have not that, he has to return to Turin or Berne to procure it. The town is built on the left bank of the Tecino, shortly below the place it leaves the lake, and contains only one structure worthy of notice, the church of St. Donato, a building of the middle ages. From here we pursue our route to Milan through the great Lombardo plain, a splendid route made between gardens and fruit trees; the country along is fertile and rich in the extreme. Passing

GALLERATI, CASCENA DELLE CORDE, and RHO, outside which is a beautiful church, we enter Milan through the

ARCO DEL SEMPIONE—A structure begun by Napoleon, and finished in 1839 by the Austrians.

MILAN.—Described at page 233.

ROUTE 3.

A Fortnight's Tour in the Autumn, 1852.

[BY H. C.]

LONDON TO PARIS, *via* FOLKESTONE AND BOULOGNE, in 12 hours.

The attention of visiters to Paris should be directed to the Chapelle St. Ferdinand, erected on the spot where the Duke of Orleans died in 1842, and to the Chapelle Expiatoire, on the spot where the remains of Louis XVI. and Marie Antoinette were interred after being guillotined.

PARIS TO STRASBURG by Railway, in 12 hours.

The beautiful monument erected in memory of Marshal Saxe, in the Protestant Church of St. Thomas, at Strasburg, should be visited by every one.

STRASBURG TO FREIBERG, by Railway from KEHL, in $3\frac{1}{2}$ hours.

At Freiburg, travellers should ascend the Schlesberg, a little hill about a quarter of an hour's walk from the Neustell, and which commands a beautiful view of the valley of the Treisano, having the hills of the Black Forest in the distance.

FREIBERG to SCHAFFHAUSEN, through the HOLLENTHAL and BLACK FOREST (51 miles). Eilwagen in 11 hours.

Though the distance is only fifty-one miles, yet the road is so hilly eleven hours are required. The Hollenthal, a magnificent defile, through which the waters of the Treisane force their way to join the Rhine, ought to be visited by every lover of picturesque scenery. An omnibus leaves Freiberg every morning, in the season, for Steig, at the extremity of the Pass, returning in the afternoon or evening. The road to Schaffhausen, after climbing out of the Hollenthal by a very long and steep hill, passes through the Black Forest by Lenzkirch, Boudorf, and Stuhlingen; it is a picturesque route, though inferior in scenery to the Hollenthal. Shortly after leaving Stuhlingen the road crosses the Wulach, a small stream which separates Baden from Switzerland.

SCHAFFHAUSEN.

Steamers daily to Constance up the Rhine—a beautiful sail—in 6 hours. Eilwagen daily, along the south side of the river, in $4\frac{1}{2}$ hours.

SCHAFFHAUSEN to CONSTANCE. Eilwagen in $4\frac{1}{2}$ hours.

The road to Constance is carried along the Swiss, *i.e.*, south side of the Rhine, and presents many beautiful views of the river, whose banks are here and there richly wooded; also of the Unter See, or Lower Lake of Constance. Steckborn is the only considerable place on the route. At Constance Baden is re-entered.

CONSTANCE.—This is an ancient and apparently decayed city, situated at the point where the Rhine flows out of the Lake. It is chiefly noted for the Council held here 1414–1418, by which John Huss and Jerome of Prague were condemned to death as heretics, and burnt, in violation of the safe conduct given to them by the Emperor Sigismund. The Hall where the council was held is shown; Huss's bible and other relics of him; also, in the Cathedral, the flag upon which he stood to receive sentence of excommunication. The place of martyrdom is in the suburb of Bruhl, a little distance outside the city.—The Rhine is crossed at Constance by a curious, long, covered wooden bridge. The navigation of Lake Constance is accomplished by seven or eight steamers, which keep up a communication two or three times a day with the principal places upon its banks. The traffic upon Lake Constance has received a considerable impetus from the formation of a port at Friedrichshafen, the southern terminus of the Wurtemberg railway, and it is likely to be still further augmented by the completion of the Bavarian railway to Lindau, which is anticipated in the course of the present year (1853), and by which it will be brought into communication with the system of railways in that kingdom, also with those of northern Germany. The northern banks of the lake are flat, but the southern side presents a series of picturesque views, having the mountains of Appengall and St. Gall, together with those of the Tyrol, in the background.

CONSTANCE to LINDAU, by Steamer on the Lake, in 5 hours.

LINDAU.—The Bavarian frontier town is built on an island in the north-eastern corner of the lake, and connected with the mainland by a long wooden bridge. It is a place of great antiquity, having formerly been a Roman station. A fragment still exists of a wall, called the "Heidenmauer," attributed to that people. This town suffered greatly during the thirty years' war, having, in common with many other parts of the territories of the Elector of Bavaria—their most formidable opponent—been devastated by the Swedes. At present, Lindau has a population of upwards of 3000, the majority of whom are Protestants. The railway from Augsburg, which at present is only open as far as Kempten, is expected to be completed to Lindau the present summer, 1853, and will bring a considerable traffic to the town.

A pleasant excursion of 6½ miles may be made from here to Bregenz. The road lies along the shores of the lake, and at Loschau crosses the Austrian frontier. Bregenz is a good starting-point for an excursion into the Tyrol, as Innsbruck can be reached from here in about 2½ days' posting. Travellers should not omit to ascend the "Gebhardsberg" — a hill behind Bregenz — the summit of which may be reached in about twenty minutes, and commands a magnificent view, embracing the whole expanse of Lake Constance, the snow-capped mountains and glaciers of Appengell, together with the lofty peaks of the Rhchan or Tyrolese Alps.

LINDAU to AUGSBURG. EILWAGEN to KEMPTEN, in 8 hours, and railway, 4 hours.

The road to Kempten is very hilly, and requires nearly eight hours, passing through Niederstaufen, Rörhenbach, and Nellenbruck, small and dirty looking Bavarian towns, the railway, owing to the difficulties of the country, will take a more devious course. There is nothing remarkable on the route; the country is, however, pleasantly diversified, being here and there richly wooded. Occasional views are obtained of the snowy mountain ranges in Switzerland and the Tyrol. Large forests abound in these parts of Bavaria.

Kempten was formerly an imperial city; it lies on the Iller, and has upwards of 6000 inhabitants; it is believed to be an old Roman station.

The railway from Kempten to Augsburg requires 3¾ hours, the curves being very frequent, and the gradients difficult, a great speed cannot be attained. The only important place passed is Kaufbeuern, once an imperial city, and at present containing about 4000 inhabitants.

AUGSBURG.—The Hotel "Drei Mohren," was formerly the mansion of the Fuggers, the merchant princes of Augsburg; and the apartment is still preserved and shown, in which Count Anthony Fugger entertained the Emperor Charles V. on his return from the campaign against Tunis; on which occasion he destroyed in a fire of cinnamon, the emperor's bond for a large amount, which he held as security for the funds supplied by him to enable the Emperor to undertake the campaign. Augsburg has been the seat of many important diets of the empire. The Allgemeine Zeitung, the leading German newspaper, is published here by Baron Cotta.

AUGSBURG to MUNICH, Railway (39 miles) in 2 hours.

The Bavarian railways having only one line of rails, and the trains having to wait at certain stations for others to pass, considerable delays frequently occur. The country between Augsburg and Munich is flat, and the scenery only enlivened by occasional distant glimpses of the mountains in the Tyrol. Shortly before reaching Munich, the royal palace of Nympbenburg is passed.

MUNICH.—The colossal statue of Bavaria, by Schwanthaler, a female figure in bronze, 61⅓ ft. high, of most beautiful proportions, advantageously placed on a slope which rises gently from the west side of the Theresien Wirse, is the finest work of art in Europe. The many other bronze statues, in various parts of the city, are well worthy of observation.

The English garden on the northern side of the city, a plot of land four miles long, and through which the waters of the Isau are conveyed, is beautifully laid out, and forms a delightful promenade.

Returned to Augsburg.

AUGSBURG to ULM. Elwagen, in 8 hours (47 miles.)

Railway in progress of construction, to be completed in 1854. The country is undulating, and in some parts richly wooded. The road passes through Tusmarshausen, Burgau, and Gunzburg, dirty Bavarian cities of little or no interest. From the latter the road is carried nearly parallel with, though not in sight of, the Danube to Ulm, where it crosses that river which here forms the boundary between Bavaria and Wurtemberg.

ULM is now being strongly fortified by the German confederation, to defend the valley of the Danube against France. It was formerly an imperial city, and enjoyed an extensive commerce; at present contains only about 1,600 inhabitants. Large quantities of snails are fattened in this neighbourhood, and exported to Austria, where they are considered a great delicacy, and much consumed during Lent. The emperor Maximilian I., in order to refute the accusation brought against him by the citizens of Ulm, that he had drank too much wine to be able to attend to public business, climbed to the top of the tower of the cathedral, (316 English feet high,) and there balanced himself on one foot, swinging the other round in the air, which foolhardy feat is recorded by an inscription. Ulm was surrendered to the French without resistance, by the Austrian General, Maek, in 1805, when 3000 of his troops were made prisoners of war.

ULM to STUTTGART. Railway, in 4 hours.

Passing through a picturesque country, being carried along the side of the Swabian Alps, and affording many beautiful views of the valleys of the Fils and Neckar, one of the most striking of which is at Geislingen, a considerable town situated at the mouth of a deep defile, one side of which is richly clothed with foliage, while the other presents a series of gigantic rocks. The curves in the line of railway afford many different views of the gorge, at the bottom of which is seen the narrow stream of the Fils making its way to mingle its waters with those of the Neckar, to which point the railway follows its course. Before reaching Goppingen, a town of 5000 inhabitants, on the Fils, the Hohenstaufenberg, a conical hill about two miles to the right of the line, should be noticed; on it stood the castle of the noble family of Hohenstaufen, which for upwards of a century (1140 to 1250) furnished emperors to Germany. The railway then passes Plochingen, at the junction of the Fils and Neckar, and follows the valley of the latter by Esslingen (described at page 198 of Guide) to Cannstadt, an ancient Roman station, and now much frequented by the inhabitants of Stuttgart on account of its mineral waters, which are believed to be beneficial in disorders arising from indigestion, and thence to Stuttgart.

The Russian, or rather Greek, chapel, alluded to at page 198, is erected on the spot where formerly stood the feudal castle of Wurtemburg, the cradle or Stammseliloss of the powerful dukes the ancestors of the present reigning family.

STUTTGART.—A pleasant clean city. The railway station is in the Schloss Gasse, close to the palace, and quite in the centre of the town. The palace gardens, which extend upwards of two miles along the Valley of the Nesen to the elegant Grecian villa of Rosenstein, are open to the public, and form a very pleasant promenade. The orange trees are remarkably fine. There are several handsome public buildings here, among which may be specified the old and new Palaces; the interior court of the latter is curious. But here, as well as in most other German capitals, it is painful to see the numerous barracks and great display of military.

STUTTGART to HEILBRONN. Railway, in 2 hours.

Chiefly along the banks of the Neckar and Euz, many pleasing views of which are presented passing Ludwigsburg, a city with 7000 inhabitants, once intended for the capital of Wurtemburg; then winding round the base of Hohenasperg, an isolated hill with a fortress on its summit, now used as a prison, it reaches Bietigheim station, from which a railway is in progress to join the Baden line at Bruchsal; then crossing the Euz by a curious lattice bridge, reaches the valley of the Neckar, the course of which it follows very closely, being carried on an embankment rather above the level of the stream, by Besigheim and Lauffen to Heilbronn.

HEILBRONN contains upwards of 10,000 inhabitants, almost entirely protestants; it is pleasantly situated on the right bank of the Neckar. There is a covered wooden bridge across the stream, similar to those seen in Switzerland. Its chief architectural ornament is the church of St. Kilian, whose tower upwards of 220 feet high, is very beautiful. The holy spring, "der Keilige brunnen," from which the city derives its name, is near the church. About three miles east of Heilbronn are the ruins of Weinsberg, called "Weibers Treue," woman's fidelity, to commemorate an occurrence in the wars between the Guelphs and Ghibelines, when Conrad III., having taken the castle, and intending to put all the garrison to the sword, permitted the women to leave the place in safety, along with whatever they could carry; the women accordingly marched out of the castle, each bearing her husband or her lover on her shoulders.

HEILBRONN to HEIDELBERG. Steamer, in 6 hours.

The descent of the Neckar can be made in 6 hours, but the return requires nearly 12, the current being strong. Steamers ply twice a-day in summer. Refreshments can be had on board; but the cuisine is only indifferent. The route is most pleasant and interesting; the scenery is almost everywhere lovely; and though occasionally tame, many parts will bear comparison with the finest parts of the Rhine, though on a smaller scale.

The most remarkable places are (right) Juxtfield, visited on account of its brine baths, and with Ealensen salt-works in the neighbourhood; (left) Wimpfen, beautifully situated on the top of the steep and richly wooded bank of the river—a very ancient town, with a beautiful gothic church, whose three spires form very prominent objects; (left) Heinsheim, a village of Baden, prettily situated at the foot of the ruined castle of Ehrenberg, one of the most beautiful on the Neckar; (right) Gundelsheim, with the Castle of Horneck, formerly a stronghold of the Teutonic knights; (right) Ruins of Hornberg, picturesquely situated, and overgrown with ivy; (left) Obrigheim, where the river is crossed by a bridge of boats; (left) Meimeburg, an ancient castle in ruins, believed to have been destroyed during the thirty years' war; (right) Zwingenberg, formerly an extensive feudal fortress, defended by eight towers, five of which still remain: it belongs to the Margrave of Baden, who resides here a portion of every year; (right) Eberbach, a very ancient village, and in the nhighbourhood the Katzenbuchel, the highest mountain in the Odenwald; (right) Hirschhorn, with its walls and towers in ruins; (right) Neckarsteinach, the most charming of all the scenes on the banks of this picturesque stream—the four castles of Vorderburg, Mittelburg, Hinterburg, and Schadeck, rising one above another, and, in close proximity, form a *toute ensemble* not soon to be forgotten. They were formerly inhabited by the family of Landschaden. The highest of them, called by the peasantry the "Swallow's Nest," is situated on the verge of a steep and inaccessible precipice, and presents a good specimen of a fastness of the robber knight of the middle ages. (Left) Neckargemund, at the mouth of the Elseuz; (left) the Wolfsbrunnen, about two miles above Heidelberg, from which it is a pleasant walk along the banks of the river. In returning, a road, carried on the top of the high land, conducts to the castle of Heidelberg. Wolfsbrunnen is famous for its trout, which are preserved in reservoirs, and attain an enormous size. It is a favourite resort of the students from the university. (Left) Heidelberg.

HEIDELBERG to FRANKFORT, by Railway, in 3 hours.

FRANKFORT to COLOGNE, by Railway and Rhine Steamer, in 9½ hours.

COLOGNE to BRUSSELS, by Railway, in 7 hours.

BRUSSELS to LONDON, *via* CALAIS, in 13 hours.

ROUTE 4.

Zurich to Coire, by the Lakes of Zurich and Wallenstadt.

(Distance, 76 English miles.)

CONVEYANCE.—Steamers thrice daily to Rapperschwyl, and once daily to Schmerikon, from whence diligences take us on to Wesen, where we embark again for Wallenstadt; from here by coach to Coire (Chur, German). Places through should be engaged at Zurich.

FARES.—Zurich to Wallenstadt, 9 fr. 50 c.; to Schmerikon, 4 fr. 50 c.

We embark and sail along the Lake of Zurich, described at page 226.

In our voyage we meet many villages, only remarkable for their flourishing industry. We particularise a few of them, first premising that the high ridge seen rising on the west of Zurich, and stretching along the lake for a dozen or more miles, is the Albis.

KUSSNACHT.—A small village with 300 inhabitants.

WADENSCHWYL.—A sweet little village, remarkable for its many silk factories, and containing a population of about 5000 souls. A fine old castle, once the residence of the bailiff Oberamtman, but now possessed by a private individual.

RUSCHLIKON.—To the rear of this are the baths of Nydelbad. Passing Meilen and Thalwyl, we arrive at

HORGEN.—Passengers wishing to visit Righi, via Zug, must disembark here.

RICHTERSWYL.—Situated on the frontier line of the two cantons of Zurich and Schwytz. Pilgrims for the famous shrine of the Black Virgin at Einsielden disembark here. Here also is one of the largest cotton factories in Switzerland.

STAFA.—A village with four thousand inhabitants, remarkable as being the residence of Göethe. Nearing Rapperschwyl, the Isle of Aufnau forms a remarkable feature and ornament of the landscape. It is celebrated as being the scene of the refuge and death of Ulric Von Hutten.

RAPPERSCHWYL.—Situated on a neck of land advancing into the Lake of Zurich, eighteen miles south-east of Zurich. Its bridge traverses the lake for a distance of nearly five thousand feet. It is twelve feet broad, and is built of loose planks, not nailed, and without railing. The toll charged is enormous, being nearly 2s. 6d. English, for a *char-a-banc*. The original bridge was built by Leopold of Austria in 1358, and the present one is a construction of 1819.

SCHMERIKON.—Is located at the eastern extremity of the Lake of Zurich; at it the road leaves its margin

UZNACH.—A small town of nine hundred inhabitants. Here the road to St. Gall turns off; and close by at Oberkirch, are the brown coal mines. Leaving Uznach, we perceive the valley of Glarus with its snowy mountains; passing through which, we arrive at

WESEN.—A little village containing about six hundred inhabitants, situated at the extreme point of the Lake of Wallenstadt. The journey is made through a pretty country.

GLARUS to WESEN, 10 miles.

WESEN to WALLENSTADT, by steam up the Lake of Wallenstadt.—The voyage is accomplished in about two hours, and the fare is 1s. 6d. We pass through stupendous cliffs of lime stone for the northern shore. The southern side presents an aspect of verdure and cultivation. At the foot of the picturesque peak of the Sieben Churfirsten is the village of

WALLENSTADT.—A considerable village, with about eight or nine hundred inhabitants. Leaving Wallenstadt, we meet with some beautiful scenery in the valley of the Seaz, and reach

SARGANS.—A small town, situated on an eminence close to the junction of the St. Gall and Zurich roads to Coire, and containing about eight hundred inhabitants. Entering the valley of the Rhine, we pass Ragatz Zizers, and arrive at

COIRE.—Described at page 221.

ROUTE 5.

Coire to Splugen, by the Via Mala.

(Distance, 32 English miles.)

CONVEYANCE.—Diligence daily, occupying about e hours in the journey.

RICHENAU.—A small town, built where the two Rhines unite. This place is remarkable as having been the scene of Louis Phillippe's (late King of the French) professional labours as an usher. He arrived here in 1793, with a pack on his back and a staff in his hand; and, proceeding to the school-house—once the family château of the Planta—presented a letter of introduction to the principal, M. Jost, who engaged him under the assumed name of Chabot. He was then Duke de Chartres; and for six or ten months gave lessons in French, history, and mathematics. He was beloved by both scholars and master; and whilst residing here, heard of his father's death by the guillotine, and of his mother's transportation.

From here the road to the Splugen proceeds along the Henter-Rhein, on the right of which may be seen the Gallows; and on the left bank of the Rhine, further on, is seen the castle of Rhoetzuns, standing on the top of a lofty rock. A great portion of the Rheinthal, called the Valley of Domleschg, is studded with old castles, and is remarkable as being the emporium of various languages and diversified religions.

As we approach Katzis, on the other side of the Rhine, a magnificent view through the Valley of Oberhabstein may be had; and this, in its extraordinary beauty, is greatly added to by the snows of Mount Albula closing the Vista before us in the distanc.e

THUSIS.—A very small village, beautifully located at the mouth of the Via Mala gorge. It contains about 700 inhabitants. A little beyond Thusis the Nolla is crossed by a very beautiful bridge.

The VIA MALA opens short of half a mile above Thusis, and extends about 4½ miles. It is one of the most awfully savage and fearfully tremendous defiles in Switzerland. Language is barren in conveying anything like a precise idea of the colossal dimensions of this gorge—passing through precipices often times 1650 feet high, and not more than ten or twelve yards in width. The road is on the whole pretty good, and is protected by a parapet wall; and is conveyed across the Rhine by three bridges.

The middle bridge is approached by a small gallery, and is about 400 feet high. The road is here half hewn out the precipice, forming almost a subterranean passage. Close to the third bridge we pass a very fine structure, enter the valley of Schams, and passing the village of Zillis, arrive at

ANDEER.—The chief village of Schams contains about five hundred inhabitants. If the tourists wish, they can explore the Val Ferrara. It is to the left of the road, and is represented as being far more wild and terrible than the Via Mala, taking about five hours to explore it. The road having crossed the mouth of the Val Ferrara and the stream of the Aversa, it ascends into the gorge of the Rofla, where the Rhine descends in the form of a cataract. The scenery about is very fine. Soon after the new road, leaving the bridge, runs through a small gallery cut in the rock, and crossing the left bank of the Rhine, arrives at

SPLUGEN.—A small village, situated on the Rhine, at the point where the Splugen and Bernardine Passes commence. It is 4711 feet above the level of the sea.

ROUTE 6.

Splugen to Bellinzona, by the Bernardine Pass.

(Distance, 46 English miles.)

CONVEYANCE by diligence daily.

The road, leaving the Splugen bridge to the left, proceeds up the valley of Henter-Rhein. The scenery along the bank by Nufannen is wild and barren.

HENTER-RHEIN.—A small village, about 176 feet over the Splugen. From here we proceed by the Pass of the Bernardine. The road leaves the Rhine at Henter-Rhein, which it crosses by a bridge, and ascending the steep slope of the mountain, gives a very fine view, over the head of the Rhine on the left, and of the stupendous mass of the Moschel Horn on the right. The Pass hangs on the left black peak of the Mittag Horn. The summit of this Pass is about 7115 feet above the sea, and about 2400 above the village of Splugen. At its point we find a very good though plain inn. Proceeding a little down the mountain, we pass the Moesa over a handsome bridge, called after Victor Emmanuel, King of Sardinia. The carriage-road here is roofed in for some distance to protect it from the avalanches.

ST. BERNARDINE.—The first and highest village met with in the valley of Misocco. Here there is a mineral spring; and our descent to the lower valley is made through beautiful and romantic scenery.

MISOCCO.—A small village with about 1000 inhabitants. Its castle and churchyard will repay a visit. The scenery all about is very beautiful. Proceeding through the valley of Misocco, after passing Cama, Rovendo, and St. Vittore, we arrive at Bellinzona, described at page 220.

ROUTE 7.

Berne to Thun, (see Route 1, page 267.)

Thun to Vevay, by the Simmenthal, Saanen, Chateau d'Oex & Gruyeres, and Pass of the Dent de Jaman.

(Distance, 81 English miles.)

A splendid road leads through the Simmenthal, and a diligence runs in summer. The journey through the valley is rendered delightful by the beautiful and charming scenery with which it abounds, commanding brilliant landscapes of wood and water, enlivened by picturesque villages and homesteads. We enter the Simmenthal between the Stockhorn on the right and the Niesen on the left. From Thun we approach it through the road extending along the margin and by the banks of the Kander, to the spot where it meets the Simmen, a short distance from the castle of Wemmis, passed on our left.

ERLENBACH is a couple of miles further on, with the Stockhorn rising immediately behind it.

WEISSENBERG.—The Baths of Weissenberg are distant 2½ miles Conveyance by mule or chair, to be procured at the inn here. The path to the Baths wends along a romantic and picturesque defile. The Bath-house is constructed of wood; expense of baths and living, 9 or 10 fr. a day.

BOLTINGEN.—A small village built to the south of the castle of Simmeneck, 2600 feet above the level of the sea. A steep ascent presents itself, but is avoided by the wind of the road, which, as it were, radiates round it. Above us is the ruins of the castle of Lanbeck. Enjoying the scene of splendour presented by the gorge of Lanbeck, and crossing the river thrice, we reach

ZWEISIMMEN—A village of wooden houses, containing about 1300 inhabitants; and is built where the great and lesser Simmen join. Here the road to Bulle and Vevay, verging towards the S.W., leaves the Simmenthal; and crossing the Saanen Moser, leads into

SAANEN.—The principal village of the Valley of the Uppér Sarine; remarkable as being all in pasture, and possessing a population exclusively engaged in past oral occupation, and famous for the manufacture of cheese, known as "Gruyères." From here is made the ascent of the SANETSCH PASS. The road, on leaving, is rugged and steep. We leave Berne, and enter the Canton of Vauda about a mile below Saanen.

ROUGEMONT.—A small village of no note.

CHATEAU D'OEX.—A small village of 700 inhabitants. It is 3030 feet above the sea, and was rebuilt after a terrible conflagration. Crossing the Saane we traverse the narrow pass of La Tine amid mountains, rocks, and pines. The road, though rather narrow, is accessible to carriages. 10½ hours will suffice to accomplish the journey from here to Vevay, with a carriage and pair of stout horses.

MONTBOVON.—A small but pretty village situated in the Canton of Freiburg. A horse path over the Pass of Dent de Jaman, brings the traveller to Vevay in 6 hours. The views and scenery are charming. The carriage road leading from Montbovon to Vevay, descends into the valley of the same. After making a long détour, it passes round the base of the Moleson, (6181 feet), and wending under the hills, passes by

GRUYERES.—A filthy little town or village containing about 400 inhabitants. Its position is very picturesque, being built on the face of a hill, crowned with a castle, which is very remarkable, and an object worthy a visit. The district in which the town is situated is renowned for its cheeses. The old chapel of St. Theodull is also worth a visit. Within it is a monument and effigy of a Count of Gruyére, remarkable for their antiquity. Bulle to Vevay, see Route 1, page 268.

ROUTE 8.

Martigny to Aosta, Pass of the St. Bernard.

The distance from Martigny to the Hospice can be traversed in a walk of about eight or ten hours, and from thence to Aosta in about seven or eight.

Chars take the travellers from Martigny (see Route 1,) to Liddes, from whence the ascent to the Hospice is accomplished on mules. We pass through the Bourg Martigny, and cross to the left bank of the Drance. From here the road follows the course of the river as far as the villages of Valette and Bouvernier. The road again crossing and recrossing the river, and continuing its course by the right bank along the Valley of the Drance, it proceeds up the left bank to St. Branchier—a miserable village situated at the foot of Mount Catogne—where the two branches of the Drance unite. A little above this place, very beautiful views in the Val d'Entremont may be enjoyed, differing, in no way however, from the general character of Alpine views.

ORSIERES.—A path from here leads to ISSERT and the Val de Ferret. As we leave the villa e behind us, the scenery met with is rugged and wild, though not to any great extent. Nor is the landscape remarkable for anything worth notice, until we enter at the forest of St Pierre, and enter

LIDDES.—A *char* from here to Martigny costs 12 frs.; and mules from thence to the Hospice, 6 frs.

ST. PIERRE.—A small and wretched village, venerable by its antiquity. Not far from here is a magnificent cascade, in the Val Orsey. Beyond St. Pierre the path passes through a larch forest, far below which, in the distance, can be seen the course of the Drance. We enter the plain called the Sommet de Prou, as being the most elevated point of the pasturage of Prou. Above this plain is the Glacier of Menone, topped by the lofty peak of Mont Velan—the highest part of the Great St. Bernard. Shortly after, the Hôpital is reached; this appears incorporated with the skies, and is elevated 8200 feet above the level of the sea. The Hospice, or Convent, is about one mile distant from the Hôpital. At midway we cross a torrent that rises on the summit. The Convent of St. Bernard is the point of separation between the waters that flow into the Adriatic Sea and those that flow to the Mediterranean. The Hospice of the Great St. Bernard has acquired a world-wide fame for the hospitality of its inmates. It is a stone building, massive and strong, built on the loftiest point of the Pass, exposed on its north-east and south-west sides to every storm, but sheltered on the north-west by Mont Chenelletaz and Mort Mart. The chief building has seventy or eighty beds for the use of travellers, and is capable of affording shelter to over 300. Some days 600 or 700 receive aid and succour. Independent of this building, there is on the other side of the way a house of refuge, called the Hotel de St. Louis, in which ladies are chiefly accommodated. On the ground floor are the stabling, store-rooms, &c. Above these are the sleeping-rooms, the church, and refectory. A flight of steps between the two corridors leads to the drawing-room, where visiters are received by the brethren. The reception-room is chastely furnished, and ornamented with paintings, &c., presented by visitors in token of their gratitude to the brethren. The cabinet attached to this room is interesting and attractive; it contains a number of the plants, insects, and minerals indigenous to the Alps. It also contains a great many relics of the Temple of Jupiter, which, tradition states, once stood on the Pass, close to the Hospice. The figures of bronze, arms, metals, and coins, will deeply interest the antiquarian. The chapel of the Hospice is a very handsome one, and contains a monument erected by Napoleon to the memory of General Desaix, slain at Marengo. This monastery was founded in the tenth century by St. Bernard—a member of the noble family of Menthon, in Savoy—who was a canon and archdeacon of Aoste. He governed the convent for forty years, and died in 1008. All the documents, &c., likely to throw light on the circumstances of its foundation, were destroyed by two terrible conflagration of 1552. The monks of the community are regular canons of St. Augustine. Ten or twelve usually live at the convent. Their duty is to assist travellers in the dangers to which they are here continually exposed from the storm and the avalanche, in the discharge of which duty these devoted men often lose their lives. Scarcely a traveller ever passes without paying a visit to the

MORGUE—in which are deposited the bodies of the unclaimed dead who perish on the mountains. The scene it presents is awful and melancholy, yet faithful and true. The ashes of mouldering humanity, the bleached bones, the calcined particles of what was once life and vigour—all present a spectacle that awakens in the bosom of the spectator thoughts of the most serious considerations. Death, as it were, *lives* before him in all its terror: the scene opens up the portals of two states—he sees what he is, and what he will be. At one end are the remains of those who are dried up and withered. Close by are skeletons, partly preserved and partly in a state of decomposition; and all round are the broken fragments of human nature in all the plenitude of its dissolution, pointing out to the spectator his being—his end. The house in which these bodies are placed is rather a low building, situate a few yards from the east extreme point of the convent.

The visitor can scarcely leave without seeing the dogs of the Hospice. They are a noble breed, said to be a cross between the Newfoundland and the Pyrean. They are powerful, of great muscular strength, and deeply astonishing in their rational intelligence. Very many of them have perished with the guides. One of them, called "Barry," is reported to have saved fourteen individuals. His skin is stuffed, and may be seen at the Museum of Berne. Leaving the Hospice, we proceed downwards to the Val d'Aosta. Our road lies between the Lake and the Plain of Jupiter. Passing rst a sho t defile, the scene towards Italy reveals itself, showing us the large basin of the Vacherie. Turning shortly to the right, and sweeping round the basin, we descend to the plain. A very fine view may be had on looking out from the gorge on Mont Mart, towards Vacherie. After this, we arrive by a rapid descent at St. Remy. From here to St. Oyen we pass no picturesque scenery. At this place the passports are rigidly examined; and unless perfectly correct, the traveller is not permitted to pass. The baggage is closely examined at Etroubles, where also is crossed the branch of the Buttier. From here the road goes down to the village of Gignod. Beautiful indeed, and rich in all the glories of picturesque grandeur, is the scenery of the country we now pass through. The Val d'Aosta, with its trellised vine and luxuriant vegetation relieved by the back ground, filled with the beautiful forms reflected by the snowy tops of the mountains above the Val de Cogne—render interesting and delightful our entrance into

AOSTA.—A city built at the confluence of the Buttier and the Doire, in a valley rich and beautiful. It contains about seven thousand inhabitants, and is remarkable for its antiquities and historical recollections, and for the beauteous scenery surrounding it on every side. Formerly called Civitas Augusti, or the City of Augustus, it fills a large space in the page of antiquity. Known under the name of Cordéle, its history dates further back than its conquest by Terentius Varro. Its foundation is set down as being 406 years earlier than that of Rome by Romulus, and as having occurred 1158 B.C. Twenty years before Christ, its inhabitants were reduced to captivity by the Emperor Augustus. He gave his own name to it on its being rebuilt, and established there a large number of the Prætorian cohorts. Its greatness at that time cannot be doubted. The mouldering ruins and broken fragments of its stupendous buildings, now withering into clay, sufficiently attest its antique greatness. Its triumphal arches with their façades, its broken bridges, the ruins of its amphitheatre, Prætorian palaces and towers—are living attestations of its having been under the dominion of, and as having been erected by, the Emperor who swayed Rome's mighty sceptre, and wore her imperial purple when she counted the empires of the earth her pasture-lands and vineyards, and her slave-roll the broad register of the human race. It gave one archbishop to England—Anselm, the Archbishop of Canterbury, in the eleventh century, who was born there. The Cathedral likewise deserves a visit.

———

ROUTE 9.

Berne to Lausanne, by Morat and Avenches.

(Distance, 57 English Miles.)

Conveyance.—Diligence daily, making the journey in ten or eleven hours. As we go on the Alps are seen on our left, and we cross the Saarine at

Guminen—A short distance from which the road enters the Canton of Freyburg.

Morat (Murten, German).—Situated on the east side of the Lake of Morat, and contains about 1,900 inhabitants. Its streets are narrow, and it is surrounded by feudal fortresses. It is only remarkable for the sanguinary battle of 1476. The hill of Munchwyler gives the best view of the scene of the battle, and of the lake. Five miles beyond Morat is

Avenches.—Situated on the south-west angle of the area formerly occupied by the Aventicum, capital of ancient Helvetia. The town is surrounded by walls, and contains a population of 1,060 inhabitants. The antiquarian will here find much food for study and contemplation. His research will be amply compensated by exploring the mouldering fragments of the broken walls and battlements, and other records of the reigns of Vespasian and Titus, as well as of the hostile invasions of Alemanni and Atilla. A Corinthian column, 37 feet high, is seen on the left of the road as we enter the town. The castle is a building of the seventh century.

Domdee.—From here we proceed to Freyburg, described at page 222

Payerne.—A small town, no ways remarkable. The church contains a remarkable relic, said to be Queen Bertha's saddle. This church also contains her tomb. Ascending the valley of the Broye, we reach

Moudon.—A town containing about 1,600 inhabitants.

Carouge.—To the left is the road to Vevay. The road from here is very hilly, and requires extra horses to accomplish it. At our arrival on the summit of the Jorat from the southern side, a very beautiful view opens up before us, disclosing Lake Leman, &c.

Lausanne—described at page 223.

ROUTE 10.

Lyons to Pont de Beauvoisin, by Les Echelles, Chambery, and the Pass of Mont Cenis, to Turin.

(Distance, something about 180 English miles.)

Lyons to Pont De Beauvoisin.
Conveyance by diligence.

Pont Beauvoisin.—A frontier village of France, situated on the banks of the Guiers Vif, which is crossed by a bridge having French and Sardinian custom-houses at either side, where passports and baggage are severally examined. The road from this place is at first flat, but becomes an ascent after a couple of miles are passed. At the height of the ascent, we find splendid views opening up before us. Beneath us lies the sunny field of France. Soon after, we enter the magnificent gorge of La Chelle. The road is constructed of solid masonry. Extending along the edge of the precipice, rugged stupendous cliffs, many hundred feet high, line the other side; whilst in the depths below rushes the impetuous torrent.

Les Echelles.—A village situated on the Guiers, being the starting point of a road leading to the Grand Chartaeuse. We next enter the valley, and pass through a tunnel 25 feet high and 100 feet long. We follow our route through a rocky ravine.

St. Thibaud de Coux.—A waterfall not far from here has been written of by Rousseau as "La plus belle que je vis de ma vie."

Chambery—described at page 220. From here some very pleasant excursions can be made, particularly those to the baths of Aix and the Lac de Bourges.

The Dent de Nivolet and Les Charmettes.—Our road proceeds through the valleys of the Arc and Isére. On the right we see Mont Grinier, 5700 feet high. The Château Bayard stands on the left bank of the river, a few miles below.

Montmeillant.—Situated on the left bank of the Isére, where the four roads—that of the Mont Cenis, that of the Tarentaise, and those of the little St. Bernard and Grenoble—meet. Several handsome country seats, forming a handsome suburb, are around here. At this point the valley of the Isére divides itself into two large plains. Crossing the Isére, we ascend a hill, and can enjoy a magnificent view of the Arque and Isére. The hamlet of Maltaverne is the next place met with. This place commands a very good view of the lofty mountain Cerim, at the opposite side of the Isére. The rivers Arque and Isére join between Maltaverne and

Aiguebelle—Situated at the foot of Mont Cenis. The country about is very unhealthy, the rivers at their junction forming very pestilential marshes, which generate malaria, &c. Issuing from Aiguebelle, he passes under a triumphal arch; and passing a number of poor hamlets, reaches

La Grande Maison.—A short distance beyond La Chambre, on the east, a large valley, called La Magdeleine, opens a road to Mousten, the chief place in the valley of the Tarantaise, situated on the high way from the little St. Bernard to Italy. Crossing the bridge of the Hermillon, and following the base of the mountain of Rocheray, we reach

St Ivan de Marienne.—It is the chief place in the valley, and has a very good suburb. The vineyards of St. Julien produce some good wines. Beyond the town we cross the Arvan, and a little further on. the Arque, after which we arrive at

St. Michel —A very picturesque little town, surrounded by orchards and meadows.

Modane —A town famous for its cultivation of hemp, and remarkable as being the last scene of "Sterne's sentimental journey." In this part of the valley the bed of the Arque is much confined, and has to flow through a narrow gorge. The road here has been cut for about a league through the mountain. Beyond is the fort Lusseilon, having the gorge of the Arc as a *fosse*. The Point du Diable is a very striking object.

Verney.—The mountains about here are very interesting, from the singularity of their appearance. They are without a human residence, and their summits abound in dens of bears. Chamois, marmots, and pheasants are also to be found there. The path of the Col de Vanoise meets our road at Termignon.

Lans le Bourg —A large village situated at the foot of Mont Cenis, inhabited by porters and muleteers On leaving the village, a very large barrack is passed on the left. The road crossing the Are, begins its ascent to Mont Cenis. Travellers for the ascent abandon the valley of Maurienne.

Mont Cenis.—This remarkable mountain is one of the chief routes from France and Switzerland into Italy. It is situated partly in Savoy and partly in Piedmont. We are enabled to accomplish the journey from valley to valley in one day—that is, from Lauselbouрg, on the Savyard, to Suza, on the Italian side—a distance of about sixteen leagues. Many historians assert that it was by this mountain Hannibal penetrated into Italy There are houses of refuge erected all along the Pass; and we pass 23 of them between Louisburg and Suza. They are occupied by cantoniers, who keep the road in order, and render travellers any assistance they may need. The first remarkable spot met with is La Romasse When the snow has filled all the hollows in winter, travellers from Italy descend from the summit to Lauselbourg in a sledge with almost inconceivable rapidity, accomplishing the descent in about seven minutes, the sledge being guided by a peasant. The perpendicular descent is 2000 feet. The most elevated point of the road is called Point Culminant, which is commanded by very excellent views of the five peaks of Roche Melon, Roche Michel, Ronche, Corne Reusse, and Vanese. A spacious platform or plain extends from here to the Grand Croix; and the road is so guided as to avoid some dangerous avalanches. Les Tavernettes is next met with. It is a little below the Point Culminant, and not far within the entrance to the plain. At this place there is a station of *cantonniers*, under the control and direction of regular officers, to whom the tourists can complain against their drivers or post-boys for *unnecessary* delay, &c. At the seventeenth refuge a toll of 5 francs per horse is charged. From here a short distance brings us to the culminating point of the Pass, viz., 6,780 feet above the level of the sea. Continuing to traverse the plain, we reach the post-house, where we may get a plain but substantial repast. The road is magnificent; and is another monument of the enterprise and genius of Napoleon. We soon after reach the Hospice—a long range of buildings, near the extremity of the Lake, six leagues from Lans-le-Bourg. It was originally founded by Charlemagne, and re-esablished by Napoleon. It contains 1012 beds, and 1000 or 2000 more could be accommodated on the loft. There is a barrack connected with it, now occupied by a troop of carbineers, who examine the passports of tourists. The Hospice, properly so called, is inhabited by monks, who exercise hospitality towards all travellers Travellers ought to be particular in having their passports countersigned, as, unless they do so, they would be stopped at Chambery or Turin. The gorge of the little Mont Cenis is seen on the opposite side of the lake. Further on, we meet the bridge of La Rouch—a torrent following the direction of a new road.

Grand Croix.—A group of taverns. Here we cross the La Rouch, and find terminated the Mont Cenis. The road wending above the plain of St Nicholas, opens through a perpendicular granite rock of considerable elevation. Arches of masonry are to be seen along the road, constructed to protect travellers from the rocks, which very often fall. The scenery of the plain is wild and terrific. We obtain a commanding view of the hills of Charmont before we reach

Molaret—the first Piedmontese village met with. Near it is a small inn.

Susa.—A small town with about 2000 inhabitants, situated at the point where the roads over St. Genévre and Mont Cenis meet. It is a very old town, but noways remarkable. Outside the town is a triumphal arch, erected in honour of Augustus eight years before the Christian era. Passing Bruzzolo, St. Ambrogio, and Rivoli, we arrive at

Turin—described at page 236.

ROUTE 11.

Route up the Rhine.

For the skeleton routes to the Rhine, its navigation, and other synoptical details, see pages 183, 184.

The Rhine.—This river, over the entire aspect and character of which the supreme architect seems to have shed brilliant streaks of glorious scenery and picturesque grandeur, is no less remarkable for the combination of natural loveliness that characterizes its scenery, than for the historical traditions interwoven with every phase of its history, representing Roman conquests and defeats; feudal events full of chivalry and daring; and of the wars and negotiations of modern days. Its banks possess an interest, as having reposing beside them the bones and ashes of emperors and heroes. It takes its rise from three small springs flowing from three different mountains. Multitudes of torrents increase it until it falls into the Lake of Constance, which it crosses with great impetuosity for about 18 miles, passing away from it between the villages of Styger and Eschenez The picturesque grandeur of the Rhine first shadows forth its beautiful brilliancy at the magnificent cluster of mountains called the Siebengebirge, about 20 miles above Cologne. From this place, along the banks of the river as far as Mayence, are scenes of surpassing loveliness and romantic beauty; nor can the tourist, hurriedly passing up the stream in a steam-boat, have any idea of the natural beauty and grandeur of the scenery through which he passes. A mere trip up the Rhine, as English travellers generally confine themselves to, is nothing. Below Bonn or Godesberg, the river scenery is scarcely worth a glance. In a word, it is impossible for the tourist to explore or appreciate the beauties of the Rhine, unless he halt at intervals at Bonn, Coblentz, St. Goar, Bingen, or Rüdesheim.

COLOGNE TO BONN--18 English miles--journey is made by rail in about one hour, and by steam-boat in about three hours. The line passes through a beautiful country of corn fields close to the Rhine and adjacent to the Vorgebirge hills.

KALSCHEUREN STATION.

BRUHL STATION--A small town with about 2100 inhabitants, opposite the Chateau, erected in 1728 by the Episcopal Elector, Clement Augusta. In it are several portraits of the German Princes. It was here the King of Prussia entertained our gracious sovereign Queen Victoria in 1845, when she visited it during the Beethoven festival at Bonn.

WALDORF--The remains of a Roman aqueduct, stretching along the course of the Erft, is here.

RORSDORF STATION.--A brilliant view of the outline of the seven mountains beyond the Rhine may be had here.

BONN--See page 186. Here the beauties of the Rhine begin to unfold themselves. They are written on every single character that meet the eye, and painted alike on the rugged rock, the stupenduous cliff, the placid face of the waters, as on the venerable castles reflected on their smooth surface.

PITTERSDORF.--Here the steamer stops to take up passengers to or from Godesberg.

GODESBERG.--Is a small village near the Rhine, containing about 1000 inhabitants. The Draitscher Brunnen mineral spring and the baths are close by it. The castle keep, on the top of the hill, is an interesting object; it is approached by a serpentine path, and is a building of the 13th century, erected by the Archbishops of Cologne, on the site of a Roman fort. It was taken and blown up by the Bavarians in 1583. A magnificent view of the Rhine can be enjoyed from the Donjon keep, which is 100 feet high. From Godesberg excursions can be made to the volcanic hill of Rodesberg, the seven mountains. The shortest way to reach them is by crossing to Konigswinter over the Rhine by ferry-boat. A very interesting and delightful excursion, of about one day's length, may be made from the foot of the Drachenfels, by ascending the left bank of the Rhine to Rolandsbeck, and again going down the river to Konigswinter. A tour up the Arve valley can also be profitably made; and with the excursion to the seven mountains, a visit can be made to the celebrated Cistercian Abbey of Heisterbach.

KONIGSWINTER.—Is met on the left, a village of about 1600 inhabitants, situated at the foot of the Drachenfels, the ascent of which from here can be made in about half an hour.

THE SEVEN MOUNTAINS are seen on the left, and are a beautiful opening to the magnificent scenery of the Rhine. They rise in towering majesty above its banks, and are seven in number, as follows:—Stromberg, 1,053 feet; Niederstromberg, 1,066 feet; Oelberg, 1,456 feet; Wolkenberg, 1,057 feet; Drachenfels, 1,051 feet; and Lowenberg and Hemmerich. On their respective summits are the remains of an antique church, or castle. Drachenfels, or the Dragon Rock, is the most remarkable, and derives double interest from having been the subject of Byron's muse.

"The castled crag of Drachenfels
Frowns o'er the wide and winding Rhine,
Whose breast of waters broadly swells
Between the banks which bear the vine;
And hills all rich with blossom'd trees,
And fields which promise corn and wine;
And scatter'd cities crowning these,
Whose far white walls along them shine,
Have strew'd a scene, which I should see
With double joy wert thou with me."

The summit of this mountain can be arrived at in little less time than an hour from Konigswater. From its top a magnificent view may be enjoyed of the country and objects all round. In our ascent up we pass the quarry from which was taken the stone used in the erection of the Cologne Cathedral. Close to the top is a very good inn, where the traveller will find comfortable accommodation, and enjoy a magnificent view of the sun rise, should he stop over night and sleep there. From here the view extends down the river for about 20 miles, closed in by high and picturesque rocks, which impart a wild aspect to the scene, greatly relieved however by the villages and farm-houses filling up the foreground. The chief objects of attraction are the summits of the Seven Mountains, the Dungeon of Godesberg, the Volcanic Chain of the Eifel, and the Island of Nonenworth. On the summit of the Lowenberg are the ruins of the castle in which Melancthon and Bucer dwelt for a short period with the Archbishop Herman Von Weid. Close to Mehlem we find an extinct volcano, one of the most interesting on the Rhine, called the Rodesberg. Its crater is a quarter of a mile round, and 100 feet deep. A good prospect of the Rhine may be had from the arch and turrets of the Castle of Rolandseck, approached through the Eliasschluct Gorge. The road from Rolandseck to Remagen is carried through a rock. It was begun by the Bavarians, continued by the French, and perfected by the Prussians. To the right, beyond Remagen, are to be seen the Erpeler Lei basaltic precipices, 700 feet high. Here the traveller will have cause to be delighted at the successful effort, made by industry and skill, to turn a barren rock into a fruitful vineyard. The vines flourish in luxuriant grandeur, and are planted in baskets, placed in the crevices of the basalt, where they are preserved from being washed away by the rains.

LINZ.—Is on the left, situated on the bank of the river, and containing about two thousand three hundred inhabitants. The tower standing near the Rhine Gate was built by one of the Archbishops of Cologne, as a defence against the burghers of Andernach. A splendid view is enjoyed from the Pfaurkiche, in which there are some very interesting monuments, and a couple of pictures, dated 1463. The battle of Leipzig is commemorated by a cross, 40 or 50 feet high, erected on the top of the Hummelsberg, a mount to the rear of Linz, opposite which the Ahr flows into the Rhine. From its mouth we can see up the Ahr valley, discerning the black conical summit of the Landskrone.

SINZIG.—See page 187.—The village of Niedersbreisig is to the left, with Oberbreisig and its old church close by. To the left is also seen the Castle of Rheineck, built for Professor Bethman Hollweg, of Bonn. It contains some paintings by Steinle, and from its garden a very fine view may be obtained.

BROHL.—A small town on the right, near the mouth of the stream and valley of the Brohl. The Paper Mill here is worth a visit; it has a collection of Dutch pictures. This mill, and many others, are driven by the stream, and are employed in grinding tuff stone into cement. About five miles up the valley of the Ahr is the mineral spring, called Tonnisstein. From Brohl an agreeable excursion can be made to the Lake of Laach. To the right are seen the broken walls of Hammerstein Castle, erected in the 12th century, and remarkable as having been the refuge of Henry IV. of England in, 1105, who fled there to avoid the persecution of his son. It was destroyed in 1660; within it is a little old church, deeply interesting.

NAMEDY to the right, with a pretty church.

ANDERNACH.—(See page 187.)

NEUWEID is met on the left—(See page 187.)

WEISSENTHURM.—(See page 187.)—A little further on the road leaves the Rhine, and is not seen until we near Coblenz. To the left is Engers, a small village, with a remarkably built Château; and above it are the ruins of a Roman bridge, built, it is said, thirty-eight years B.C. The ruins are seen in the bed of the river.

MULHOFEN.—A small village to the left, at the mouth of the river Sayn. A road leading from Engers, three miles distant, and from Coblenz, eight miles distant, to the village and chateau of Sayn, wends up the valley. At the rear of the village of Bindorf, close by, are the Cannon Foundry and Ironworks, as large as any of the great ironworks in England. The Præmonstrant Abbey at Sayn, founded in 1202, will interest deeply. At the extreme point of the valley is the castle of the Counts of Isenburg. The valley is certainly a delightful one, containing summer-houses, &c. It forms a favourite object of summer visits to the people of Coblenz. The venerable and noble Abbey of Rommersdorf is seen on the slope of a hill north of the valley, about two miles north of Sayn, and the same distance north-east of Engers. To the right is next seen the walls of the Castle of Ehrenbreitstein.

NEUENDORF.—Here the rafts are formed. As the traveller will see these rafts, it may be interesting to observe, they are the produce of the forests covering the hills and mountains watered by the Rhine and its tributaries,—the Necker, the Murz, Main, and Moselle. After being thrown down from their lofty heights, they are felled, and cast into some stream sufficient to float them. Thus is tree after tree bound together, and conveyed from stream to stream, until floating islands are formed, which are bound into one great fabric and navigated to Dortrecht, where it is sold. As the mass floats along, it presents the appearance of a little village. On its broad surface are built 10 or 14 wooden huts. Four or five hundred rowers and assistants are required. These are directed by pilots and the proprietor, who lives on board the raft, in a house built expressly for him, superior in size, &c. to the others. The workpeople are accompanied by their wives and children, and knitting, sewing, &c. are carried on during the day. A very large quantity of provisions is consumed during the voyage; so much as 46,000 lbs. of bread, 31,000 lbs. of meat, 600 tuns of beer, and 8 or 10 butts of wine. The timber is sold at the end of the voyage, and often produces as much as £25,000, and oftentimes £30,000. The duration of the voyage is generally from eight days to six weeks.

To the left, near Kesselheim, are the remains of the Château of Schönbornlust, the residence of the Bourbon princes during their exile from France at the French revolution. Near the confluence of the Moselle and Rhine, to the left, is the monument to General Marceau, who fell on the field of Altenkirchen, in endeavouring to check the retreat of Jordan. Passing under the works of the Fort Emperor Francis, the road crosses the Moselle by a stone bridge, and enters Coblenz. Described at page 188.

At Coblenz the direct road to the Brunnen of Nassau leaves the Rhine. A great part of it is uninteresting, whilst some of the finest scenery of the Rhine lies between Coblenz and Bingen; and hence, to those wishing to explore its beauties, the post-road by the left bank as far as Bingen, where it crosses the river Rheingau and turns off to Wiesbaden, is preferable. In this case an excursion to Ems ought to be made, and to the Castle of Nassau, eight miles further. The cost of a carriage to Ems is 4½ dollars.

The tour of the MOSELLE to Treves can be made from Coblenz, returning on the river by steamer; or, if not all the way to Treves, a two days excursion might be made to Munster-Maifeld, the Castle of Elz, and the village of Alf—situated on the Moselle, at a point where the most beautiful scenery exists—and to the Baths of Bertrich.

A good day's excursion can be made by carriage, from Coblenz, by the Treves post-road, through Metternich to Lorinig, to Munster-Maifeld, to the hill above Elz, where we leave the carriage, going to Gondorf, crossing the Moselle by a ferry to Niederfell, where refreshment is taken. Elz can be seen, a walk made to Moselkern or to Hatzenport, where a boat takes us down the river to Gondorfor-Cobern, where we recross the river, meet our carriage, and return to Coblenz by the right bank of a new and bad carriage road.

COBLENZ TO MAYENCE—(Distance, 57 English miles.)—There are 5 or 6 steamers daily performing the up voyage in about eight or nine hours, and the down voyage in five or six. Above Coblenz the long ridges of the mountains begin to hem in the Rhine, which extends as far as Bingen, flowing through a contracted gorge. An unrivalled scenery here presents itself to the eye. The broken fragments of feudal castles, the mouldering ruins of their dismantled battlements, with the walled towns and venerable buildings, form the most prominent features in the scene, which is doubly heightened by the historical associations connected with each and every object that bursts upon the astonished vision. Leaving Coblenz we pass Forts Alexander and Constantine on the left and on the right banks; see the fortified fort which surmounts the heights of Pfaffendorf, situated above a village of the same name. Proceeding on, we pass Horchheim, which is the last Prussian village, and see opposite to it the island of Oberweith, on which is built the country house of Count Pfaffenhofen. Three miles or so above Coblenz we see one of the most interesting castles on the Rhine, beautiful in its picturesque outline and commanding position, it may justly be-styled the Proud Rock. It is called the castle of Stolzenfels, and was built by one of the archbishops of Treves. The wife of the Emperor Frederick II., and sister of Henry III., King of England, was received and lodged in this castle in 1235. A very good carriage road leads up to it, and about it there are very pretty plantations and shrubberies; it will well repay a visit. Its principal objects of attraction are the Rittersaal, an apartment painted with frescoes by Stilke. The subjects are numerous, representing very many scenes from history. In another room there is some armoury; and in it are to be seen the swords of Tilly, Blucher, Napoleon, Murat, &c. Queen Victoria, accompanied by the King of Prussia, visited it in 1845. From here to Mayence, both banks of the Lahn, and the right bank of the Rhine belong to Nassau. The church of St. John, a venerable ruin, is below the mouth of the Lahn. Its choir and columns are worth inspection. At a short distance from it, on the right hand bank of the Lahn, is the village of Nieder-Lahnstein, from whence we cross to Stolzenfels by ferry. A good carriage road leads up the right bank to Ems. (See page 188.)

The CASTLE of LAHNECK, OBERLAHNSTEIN, and RHENSE—(See page 189.)

BRAUBACH—A little town to the right, standing at the base of a lofty rock, on which stands the strong and feudal fortress—the Castle of Marksburg. In it is shown the cell where Henry II. was confined. It is worth a visit; and a magnificent view can be enjoyed from off the summit, of the Donjon keep. The castle is distant about seven miles from Ems, and is approached by a very passable road. Outside the town is a beautiful mineral spring of delicious water. Persons desirous of visiting Marksburg from the left bank of the Rhine, must cross the river at Nierderspay, where there is a ferry.

MARKSBURG.—(See page 189.)

We next meet the three small villages, Mittlespay, Peterspay, and Oberspay, adjoining each other. The Rhine bends terribly at this point, and does not again resume its original position until we pass Boppart. To the right, about two-and- -half miles beyond Braubach is the Dinkholder Brunnen, a famous mineral spring, whilst the white walls of the castle of Liebeneck rise to the right above Ostberspay.

BOPPART.—(See page 189.)—To the rear of this place is a medical boarding-house for the water cure. There is another similar establishment near the river called the Muhlbad.

Approaching Salzig on the left, the mountains recede a little from the banks, and give place to corn fields and meadows. We next see the mouldering battlements and ruined towers of the castles of Sternberg and Liebenstein opposite, to the right of Salzig, seated on a lofty rock, clothed with vines. The traditions connected with their history make them interesting. They are called the brothers, from the fact of two brothers having resided in them. The brothers fell in love with the one lady, and became foes, and fell by each other's sword.

EHRENTHAL.—(See page 189.)—Above this is the small village of Welmich, situated at the base of a mountain. At its top are the ruins of the Castle of Thurnberg, built by Kuno V., Falkenstein, Archbishop of Treves, in 1363. It was called the Mouse, to distinguish it from the castle called the Cat, which is above St. Goarshausen. The view obtained here is beautiful, and deserves some little lingering o'er its scenery.

ST. GOAR.—(See page 189.) To the right, some delightful excursions and views may be had from the Nassau bank of the Rhine, and boats are always at hand to bring visiters over the river to

GOARHAUSEN.—(See page 189.)

OBERWESEL.—(See page 190.)

To the left, the next object of interest we meet is Schomberg, a ruined castle built on a rock, and once the dwelling of an illustrious family of the same name, from which sprung Marshal Schomberg, the general of William the Third at the battle of the Boyne, in Ireland. Gutenfels is seen to the right, a ruined castle, situated above the town of Caul. Tradition derives its name from that of a beautiful girl called Gaudar, a favourite of Richard, Emperor of Germany, and brother of Henry III. of England. The castle was in pretty good condition until 1807, when the roof and wood-work were sold by auction, and the fine old structure became a ruin.

CAUB.—(See page 190.)—A toll is paid here to the Duke of Nassau by all vessels navigating the Rhine. The Duke is the only chieftain who exacts this feudal impost, though a couple of centuries since vessels had to pay 32 tolls on their voyage or the Rhine. Opposite Caub, in the centre of the river, we see the fine old Castle of Pfalz, built in the 13th century by the Emperor Lewis. There

Louis le Débonnaire retired to die. The castle can only be approached by a ladder.

BACHARACH.—(See page 190.)—On the right is Lorchhausen, and a little further up the river are the ruins of the Castle of Nollingen; whilst on the left, above the village of Rheindebach, are the broken walls and round tower of Furstenburg, reduced to ruins in 1689.

LORCH.—(See page 190.)—Approaching Bingen and Assmanshausen, we see what may be truly styled the castellated Rhine. These castellated ruins, the moss-covered stones, and prostrated halls, all speak forcibly of the past; and, whilst calling up in every one of their broken particles the memory of other days, cannot but remind the student, the historian, and the traveller of the happy change which has been effected from feudal barbarism to civil and constitutional principles. As we proceed along, we are attracted by the Castle of Reichaustein, or Falkenburg, which stands on our left, on a lofty jut of the rock; whilst further up, on the same bank, is the Castle of Rheinstein, built on a projecting rock that rises from the bank of the river. Not far from here, between the road and the river, rises beautiful and grand the Gothic church, dedicated to St. Clement. All, or nearly all, these strongholds of feudal robbery were destroyed at the close of the 13th century, by a decree of the Diet of the Empire. The Castle of Rheinstein is seen to the left; the ruins have been partially restored, so as to serve as a summer retreat for Prince Frederick of Prussia. The interior is well worth a minute inspection, and travellers will find no difficulty in getting access to it, there being a servant constantly there, who will shew visiters round it.

ASSMANSHAUSEN.—(See page 190.)

BINGEN.—(See page 191.)—The heights above Rudesheim and Assmanshausen, called the Niederwald, forms a favourite excursion, and can be made in three or four hours. A boat may be taken from Bingen, and descend the Rhine to the Castle of Rheinstein in about half an hour. By crossing the Nahe in the ferry, a mile will be saved. The Rhine can again be crossed to Assmanhausen, after inspecting the castle. And then we descend for about one mile through the gully; behind the village we find a path leading from the right to the Jagd Schloss, where refreshments can be had. This excursion can be made in about an hour, and a few minutes more suffices to bring us to the Bezanberte Höhle, or Magic Cave. Here three magnificent landscapes of the Rhine may be enjoyed, one different from the other, and presenting the appearance of a beautiful diorama. The Rossel, an artificial ruin, on the very outpost of the precipice, is not far from the cave; overlooking the boisterous eddies of the Bingerloch. Here the ruin of Ehrenfels is seen clinging to the outer surface of the rock. This is one of the most magnificent views of the Rhine. Here the waters present rather a curious appearance, exhibiting three different colours. In the centre, the Rhine is a clear green; the Nahe, close to the left bank, a heavy brown: and the Maine, at the right bank, a dirty red. Though the Maine joins the Rhine more than 20 miles beyond Bingen, yet the waters, it is asserted, do not mingle until their arrival at the deep pool of the Lurlei. The path now again sinks into the wood, and merges, after a mile, at the Temple, a round building seen to the right. It rests on pillars, constructed on the edge of the hill. A splendid prospect, extending up the Rhine and across the hills of the Bergstrasse and Odenwald, can be enjoyed here. The eye and mind will linger unconsciously on its beauties, until, after drinking in all the inspiration excited by the glorious developement of the wild, the romantic, and the picturesque scenery with which it abounds, it must be confessed that it is the "loveliest landscape on earth." We descend from the Temple in about half an hour to Rudesheim, by a path in the midst of vineyards.

RUDESHEIM.—Tourists can make the excursion to the Niederwald from here. Paths also lead from here to the Temple on the right, and on the left to Jagd Schloss, and to Rossel. A picturesque old tower is seen at the upper end of the town. The stupendous quadrangular castle of Brömserberg stands at the other extremity. It is a building of the 12th century, and consists of three vaulted stories, resting on walls of from ten to sixteen feet thick. Its present proprietor, Count Ingelheim, has it preserved from decay so far as possible A lofty square tower stands close to it. The castle of Brömserhof is in the centre of the town, and is interesting because of the tradition interwoven with its history. The family residence of the noble family of Brömser of Rudesheim. one of its illustrious knights, on being made prisoner by the Saracens, vowed that, if he ever returned to his native castle, he would consecrate his only daughter to the church, by devoting her to the cloister. Gisela was a beautiful girl, and loved and was beloved by a noble knight. On her father's return, he ordered her to prepare for the cell, and on her refusal threatened her with his curse. She, to avoid her fate, threw herself from off the battlements into the Rhine during a violent storm. Her body was found next day by fishermen. Up to the present the villagers and fishermen fancy they see the ghost-like form of Gisela hovering over the scene of her destruction, mingling her lamentations with the sighing of the winds. The greatness and feudal grandeur of other days has now departed from the Brömserhof, its antiquities, &c., having been transferred to Johannisberg, and its area metamorphised into common dwelling-houses. Between Kempten and Rudesheim there is a ferry that conveys parties over the Rhine. Mainz and Wiesbaden can be reached by carriages always ready for hire. Diligences start daily from Rudesheim to Wiesbaden.

The shortest road from Bingen to Mayence is by Ingelheim. Visitors to Brunnen of Nassau cross the ferry to Rudesheim. and proceed by the beautiful road by the right bank of the Rhine. Halts should be made at Rudesheim to see the Neiderwald; at Johannisberg to see the château and vineyard; at Hattenheim to dine, and see the old Convent of Eberbach, about two miles distant from the town. But before setting out, an understanding should be come to with the driver, to make these stops. Visitors to Schlangenbad face to the left, turning away from the Rhine at Walluff. Parties for Wiesbaden go on to Bieberich before leaving the Rhine, continuing by its side to Castel and Mayence. The distance to Castel from Rudesheim is about fourteen or fifteen miles. A scene of surpassing loveliness is here formed, by the mountains subsiding into gentle slopes, and the ridges of the Taunus receding to the river. The next district possesses many traits of soft picturesque beauty, delicate and sweet, mingled with richness and brilliancy.

GEISSENHEIM.—(See page 191.)—The vineyards of Johannisberg, producing the most famous of the Rhenish wine, was the property of the late Prince Metternich. The house was built in 1716, and was considerably enlarged by its late owner. The view enjoyed from its terrace and balcony is very fine. At this place the Rhine finds its greatest breadth, of 2000 feet, stretching itself out to double the width which it does near Rudesheim. Its breadth at Cologne is 1,300 feet, and at Wesel 1,500. From here up to Mayance small islands are scattered in the centre of the channel. To the right we see Winkel, called Vini Cella, from the fact of Charlemagne's wine-cellar being here. A very remarkable church, a building of the 12th century, is seen at Mittelheim, near Winkel. Proceeding on, we see to the right Reichartshausen. Count Schonborn's Chateau, a little below the village of Hattenheim, which contains about 1,200 inhabitants. In this castle there is a very fine collection of paintings. Not far from this, higher up the river, is the hill of Strahlanberg, where grows the vine which produces the famous Markobrunner wine.

ERBACH.—A small village. An excursion can be made from here, or from Hattenheim, to the Cistercian Convent of Eberbach, formerly the most important monastic establishment on the Rhine. It stands in a beautiful position at the foot of the hills, surrounded by woods that shroud it like a garment. It is a building of the 12th century, and was founded by St. Bernard de Clairvaux, but now belongs to the Duke of Nassau, and is used as a prison and asylum. Its churches, which can be easily explored, are deeply interesting. Scattered among them are some very curious monuments; those of Katzenelnbogen and Von Stein (de Lapide) are worth notice, as are also the long Dormitory and Chapter House. Up the slope of the hill, close to the Convent, is the famous Steinberg vineyard, consisting of about 100 acres. A magnificent view of the surrounding scenery can be had from the Moss-house, on the Boss, a height close by here. To the left can be seen Ingelheim, once the favourite residence of Charlemagne, but now a miserable village.

ELFELD.—A small town, with about 2,300 inhabitants, remarkable for its situation and picturesque Gothic towers. In the suburbs are very many pretty villas. The village of Kidrich, with its beautiful Gothic church, lies beyond the village, in a sweet valley. It is here the Grafenberg wine is produced. A wide path, seven miles in length, leads through the woods to Schangenbad. Nieder Walluff is to the right. Rauenthal, famous for its wine, is four miles distant.

SCHIERSTEIN, a small village, containing 1,400 inhabitants, is seen to the right, and is remarkable as being the spot where the Rheingau ends; as also for the picture gallery of M. Habel, which contains many paintings by the old masters. From here is a road to Schlangenbad, eight miles distant. The village of Fraunstein is four or five miles from Schierstein.

BIBERICH.—(See page 191.)

MAYENCE.—(See page 191.)—Mayence is connected with Cassel by a bridge of boats, 1,666 feet long, built across the Rhine; carriages passing this bridge are charged a very heavy toll. Travellers can proceed from here to Frankfort, by railway in one hour, and to Wiesbaden *viâ* Biberich in about a quarter of an hour. Excursions can be made from Mayence to Frankfort and Wiesbaden by railway, and on their way the château and garden of Biberich can be visited. Tourists so inclined can proceed by steam-boat from Mayence to Coblenz and Cologne twice each day, and during the summer to Manheim, and daily to Strasburg.

THE AHR VALLEY.—REMAGEN TO AHRWEILER AND ALTENAHAR.—Distance from Remagen to Altenahar, 19 English miles; from Bonn to Altenahar, by carriage-road, 18 English miles. The route to and from Bonn, by Remagen, will occupy a long day. A conveyance starts daily from Bonn to Altenahar, accomplishing the journey in about five hours, and to Treves in about 20, or sometimes 18 hours. At Preussischer Hof, in Remagen, a one-horse carriage may be engaged to Altenahar and back, for 3 thalers. (See foreign money, page 23.) Passengers by steamer landing at Lintz, and crossing the Rhine at Kripp, may engage a carriage there, or go on at once from Sinzig. The scenery of this valley is not less beautiful nor less interesting than that of the Rhine, and tourists visiting that river will find themselves amply repaid by an excursion by the valley of Ahr. This carriage-road ascends the valley by the left bank of the stream, passing by Badendorf and Lorsdorf, and the basalt capped hill of Landskrone. A splendid view may be enjoyed from off the hill. Near to the road side there is a mineral spring.

AHRWEILER—Is a small town with 1300 inhabitants, situated twelve miles distant from Remagen by the direct post road, and ten by the road over the hill. This place is rich in vineyards, and is the centre of the wine trade in the valley, which produces yearly about 76,000 English gallons. Though the town itself is pretty, yet its objects of attraction are not many. However, the town gates, its beautiful gothic church, and the Ursuline nunnery, situated on the opposite side of the Ahr, will attract attention and repay a visit. The gate tower also is an object of interest. Leaving Ahrweiler we meet Walporzheim, where the Burgundy grape is cultivated.

AHRBLEICHART.—Here the scenery is magnificently wild and beautiful, rocky cliffs towering upwards in their rugged majesty, hem in the valley which becomes greatly contracted here. The ruins of a convent are seen to the right at Marienthal, and the road is shadowed by lofty precipices. To the rear of Dernau a path is found to lead over the hills to Altenahr, whilst the carriage road continues its course along the left bank of the Ahr, passing the beautiful village of Recho.

LOCHMUHLE.—Here is the chief fishery depot.

Before entering Altenahr a brilliant scene indeed presents itself before us; precipices of slate tower around and above us to the height of 400 feet, having seated on their highest peak the ruins of the castle of Altenahr. Above Reimerzhofen a footpath leads to the *cross*, where the best and most distinct view in the valley may be had. Another path on the opposite side leads up to the castle or down to the town. Travellers should send on the carriage from this spot and walk up to the *cross*.

ALTENAHR.—Is a small village with about five hundred inhabitants. The place is a neat and clean little spot. A good view of the windings of the Ahr can be enjoyed from the hill on the west of the town. Travellers should return to the Rhine by the sweet valley of Brohl, having first visited the Abbey of Laach, twenty miles from the vale of Ahr. If we proceed on the road by way of Altenburg, the castle of Kreuzberg and the church of Putzfeld form prominent objects of view.

ADENAU.—A small town with about 1300 inhabitants, situated under the mountain called Hohe Acht, 2434 feet above the sea, from which a magnificent view can be obtained Not far from the town is the ruined castle of Nurberg.

THE RHINE.—MAYENCE to STRASBURG by WORMS, MANNHEIM, and SPIRES.—A little above Mayence we notice a singular change in the aspect of the scenery; indeed it may be said the Rhine loses all its beauty. The plain through which it flows is flat and unvaried, whilst the fall of the river is not more than twenty-two or twenty-three feet between Spires and Mannheim.

CONVEYANCE—By railway.

Steamers proceed up the Rhine daily from Mayence to Mannheim. Steamers go from Mannheim to Strasburg daily, accomplishing the journey in about twenty-one hours, stopping at Daxlanden or Leopoldshafen to drop passengers for Carlsruhe.

From STRASBURG to COLOGNE in two days, and from Mayence to Rotterdam in thirty-eight hours.

OPPENHEIM.—(See page 191.)

GERNSHEIM.—(See page 192.)

WORMS.—(See page 192.)

OGGERSHEIM.—To the right the Neckar joins the Rhine about a quarter of a mile below Mannheim. A bridge of boats crosses the Rhine into

MANNHEIM.—(See page 193.)—A visit ought to be made from this place to Schwetzingen, distant about nine or ten miles. Its gardens are very beautiful, and its château will repay a visit. From here there is a railroad to Heidelberg, (see page 75,) 16 miles distant; and to Frankfort and Carlsruhe; and from Ludwigshafen to Spires; to Kaiserslautern, Homberg, and Bexbach. Steamers also go several times a day to Mayence and Coblenz, and to Strasburg daily. We proceed from Ludwigshafen to Spires by rail, and leaving the station we see, on the side of the Kaiserstuhl, the castle of Heidelberg in the distance.

MUTTERSTADT and SCHIFFERSTADT are passed, and we enter

SPIRES.—An old and venerable town, situated on the left bank of the Rhine. It contains a population of about 10,500 inhabitants. At one period the number was 27,000. The history of Spires has been a varied and remarkable one. At one period the residence of Charlemagne, and other German Emperors; it was the seat of the Diet, and the Free City of the Empire. During the middle ages imperial *fetes*, court magnificence, and citizen violence were alternately the scenes to be heard of in this city. In 1697 it was burned by the French, and was not rebuilt until after the peace of Ryswick, in 1697. The revolutionary army, under Custine, besieged the city in 1794, but evacuated it next year, and again took possession of it in 1794. In 1816 it was ceded to Bavaria, since which period it has been considerably enlagerd, and much of its old splendour restored. Its Cathedral will be well worth the tourists' notice. This old and spacious building resisted all the efforts of the French miners to blow it up. The present Bavarian authorities have done much towards its partial restoration. It has been opened for public worship since 1824, though it was a complete ruin in 1816. The Hall of Antiquities, at the north-east side, is worth especial notice. A broken wall near the Protestant Church is the only relic now remaining of the Imperial Palace, in which werheld twenty-nine diets. From here a good road leads to Landau, and to the Castle of Trifels, the prison-house of Richard Cœur-de-Lion.

We continue our voyage up the Rhine, and pass Phillipsburg to the right.

GERMERSHEIM.—A bridge of boats is here. Passing Lauterberg, Leopoldshafen, Knielinegen, and Fort Louis, we arrive at Strasburg. (See page 160.)

MANNHEIM.—TO FRANKFORT BY RAIL.—Distance, 53¼ English miles. Frankfort to Basle, by Darmstadt, Heidelberg, Carlsruhe, and Frieberg. Frankfort to Heidelberg, 53¼ English miles; Heidelberg to Haltinger, 4 miles from Basle, 157 English miles.

BASLE.—(See pages 194 and 219.)

DESCRIPTION OF THE RAILWAY FROM PARIS TO STRASBURG.

The Paris and Strasburg Railway being the longest, and one of the most important lines in France, we give the following short account of the works, &c., believing it to be interesting to our readers:— The railway from Paris to Strasburg is the longest as yet completed in France, being 120 leagues, besides having several important branches. It traverses provinces differing in their genealogical constitution, their appearance, produce, manners, and the character of their inhabitants. Between the rising and the setting of the sun, a traveller may have quitted the banks of the Seine and reached the banks of the Rhine; he may have contemplated the lofty towers of Notre Dame in the morning, and admired the magnificent spire of the Cathedral of Strasburg in the afternoon; or, if he prefer, take supper on the banks of the Thames one evening, and before the next may be enjoying the magnificent scenery on the banks of the Rhine. The stupendous terminus in Paris requires no description; nearly all are aware of its grand proportions, skilful arrangements, and commodious accommodation. The railway, on quitting the terminus, takes a northern direction between the Faubourgs St. Denis and St. Martin, passes by Bondy, Villemoble, and Gagny, and joins the valley of the Marne at Chelles, touches Laguy on the right bank of the Marne, crosses that river twice at Chalifert and at Isle, proceeds between Villency and the Marne to skirt the Faubourg St. Remy at Meaux, and joins Armentières after having crossed the canal of the Ourcq and the Marne above Trilport. On quitting the tunnel, it proceeds by the side of the Marne to the south-west of the village, touches at Ussy, to the north of La Ferté-sous-Jouarre, passes the river a second time at Saussay, a third time at the south of Courcelles, traverses Nanteuil with a tunnel, crosses the Marne a fourth time, following the left bank touches at Nogent l'Artaud and Chezy l'Abbaye, and cuts through a corner with a tunnel. It crosses the Marne an eighth time between Chateau-Thierry and Vitry-le-Français; the line follows the left bank constantly, touches at Dormans, Port-a-Buison, Epernay, Jalox & Chalons. The railway leaves Vitry by the south-east, turns off to the left to penetrate into the valley of the Saulx, touches Sermaize, following the course of that river, and then skirts the valley of the Ornain to gain Bar-le-Duc. Thence it continues through the valley of the Ornain and the dale of Malval, over the hills of Loxevile and Coutance-aux-Bois, without any tunnel.

The line passes at Commercy through the valley of the Meuse. It crosses that river at Ville-Yssey, over a bridge of ninety yards; it then passes near Paguy, under a fort, by a tunnel 570 yards long, and reaches Toul by the valley of the Ingressein, which it enters by a tunnel, 1,120 yards long. From the terminus at Toul, which presents the appearance of a Swiss cottage, the railway runs along the left bank of the Moselle, while approaching the canal of the Marne to the Rhine. It follows the valley of the Moselle on the right bank, crosses that river at Fontenoy over a bridge of seven arches, of sixteen yards span each, turns the picturesque fort of Liverdun, and crosses the Moselle twice, on bridges raised sufficiently high to allow vessels to pass underneath. These bridges are formed of five arches, of twenty-four yards diameter. The road then stops at the terminus of Frouard, its point of junction with the branch to Metz. From Frouard the road runs to Nancy, by the village of Champigneuille. It crosses the canal there by a bridge placed bias; it reaches Nancy, to the south of which the terminus, situated between the Faubourgs Stanilas and Saint-Jean, had been constructed on a lake, where it is recorded that Charles the Rash was killed. After having passed Nancy, the railway joins the canal from the Marne to the Rhine, alongside of which it runs as far as Varangeville. A single bridge, that of St. Plin, nineteen yards wide, serves both for the railway and the canal to cross the Meurthe. The line follows the valley of the Meurthe as far as Luneville. There it passes the various arms of the river over bridges of a remarkable construction; thence from Luneville the railway turns to the valley of the Vezouse, near Marrainvillers. It ascends the stream of the Amiscuts, the hill which separates the waters of the Savon from the Sarre, above Richecourt, arrives at Sarrebourg, and proceeds towards Hommarting. It was at this point that it became necessary to cross the chain of the Vosges. From Hommarting to Strasburg the line is 63 kilometres and 987 metres The section between Hommarting and the limits of the department of the Bas-Rhin comprises the immense and difficult labour of the passage of the Vosges, which is accomplished by a tunnel of 2,678 yards in length. On the side of Loraine this tunnel is placed at the left of, and on the same level as the tunnel of the canal of the Marne to the Rhine; but, in place of remaining on that level, it descends into the mountain, becoming thus excavated under the canal, so that it reappears on the side of Alsace on the right of the canal, and 12 metres below it. Beyond that great tunnel 5 others of less dimensions are met —one 245, one 432, one 395, one 500, and one 308 metres in length. The latter, the entrance of which presents the appearance of a feudal fortress, is immediately followed by a great viaduct which crosses the canal and the Zorn, and terminates in a trench cut almost perpendicularly in the rock, and of which the form resembles that of a fort. Nothing can be more picturesque than the country in which these works of art are to be found. The ruins of the Castle of Lutzelburg are also to be seen above the tunnel of 432 metres, and the two Castles of Haut-Barr and Geroldseck show themselves on the mountains at this side of Saverne. The railway, on quitting Saverne, continues in the valley of the Zorn as far as Brumath. The Paris railway joins that of Basle on the glacis of Strasburg, and it proceeds into the town by four lines of rails.

RUSSIA.

RUSSIA is a vast and mighty empire, situated partly in Europe and partly in Asia, between 43° and 70° north latitude, and 18° and 65° east longitude. Its greatest extent from the southerly point of the Cremea to the north coast of Lapland, or the mouth of the White Sea, is 1,720 miles, and from the western border of Poland to the 60th meridian, along the 52° parallel, 1,791 miles. The superficial area exceeds 2,000,000 English square miles. The entire of this large territory belongs to the great plain which extends through the middle of Europe, from the German Ocean to the Caspian Sea and the Ural Mountains, with the exception of Finland, the Great Lakes, and the White Sea.

In Climate, that of Russia is of an extreme character, the winters being colder, and the summers warmer, than in the corresponding latitudes of western Europe. The Spring, however, is mild and temperate in the south, though the summer is of long duration, with oppressive heat and little rain. Autumn sets in rather late, and the winter is short, with little snow, though sometimes cold and severe. The middle region, extending from 50° to 57°, has a rough winter, and, in the more northerly region, it is long and severe, during which travelling is practicable only on sledges over the frozen snow. At St. Petersburg the duration of winter ranges from the end of September to the beginning of May, when winter all at once disappears. In the Artic region, extending from 67° to 74°, the climate is very rigorous in winter, and warm in summer.

Geology and Mineral Productions.—The predominating formations are the tertiary and alluvial, the older formations being less frequent.

Soil and Vegetation.—There is a vast tract of country, about 796,000 square miles, which possesses a peculiar and rather remarkable soil, consisting entirely of decomposed vegetable matter, which forms a stratum varying in thickness from three to five feet. A great part of Western Russia is sandy, and intersected by extensive marshes and bogs. The middle region, extending from 50° to 70°, is the wealthiest and most densely peopled portion of Russia, and consists of wide, open, undulating plains, with very slight elevations to break the monotony. The Russian forests are the most important of her vegetable productions, not only from their enormous extent, but from their supplying in profusion timber, tar, pitch, potash, and turpentine, which form a principal part of the commercial exports, and supplying fuel, in a country nearly destitute of that commodity. The population of Russia is about 60,000,000, divided into six great classes—nobles, clergy, citizens, peasants, serfs, and slaves. Education is subject to the direct control of the Government.

Government.—All power emanates from the Czar, whose authority is absolute, limitless, and without control.

Administrative Divisions.—Russia, in Europe, is divided into forty-seven Governments This does not include the sort of Military Republic of the Don Cossacks, or the Grand Duchy of Finland, which have a separate Administration, and the Kingdom of Poland.

FORMALITIES

To be observed by Foreigners on Entering Russia, and on Departing from the Empire.

Every Foreigner who arrives in Russia furnished with a Passport duly authenticated, ought to present himself, in the chief town of the first government on his road, before the civil governor, in order to deliver to him his Passport and get a ticket for his journey, that he may be able to prosecute the same into the interior of the Empire. This ticket must be renewed in every government town through which he passes on his road; and on his arrival at the place of his destination, he ought again to present himself before the respective civil governor, in order to have this ticket exchanged for a permission of residence. In both the metropolies of the Empire, viz., Moscow and St. Petersburg—his permission, or ticket of residence, is to be obtained at the Address-office for Foreigners (Bureau d'addresse pour les étrangers.)

Every Foreigner who wishes to leave Russia ought to present a petition to that effect to the Military Governor, Governor-general, or Civil Governor, accompanied with a certificate from the police that there is no legal impediment to his leaving the Empire. Besides, he must advertise his intended departure in the town in which he resides. After having observed these formalities, the Foreigner receives his Passport without delay; and, in case of necessity, he can also obtain the Passport with which he crossed the frontiers of the Empire.

The Passports for departure delivered to Foreigners on the governments of the frontiers, are valid for the term of three weeks; and those from the governments of the interior for three months. After the lapse of this term, these Passports must be revised by the Governor, in order to enable the Foreigner to pass the frontiers of the Empire.

St. Petersburgh is seated on the banks of the Neva, where it enters the Gulf of Finland. It is the metropolis of Russia, and is 400 miles N.W. of Moscow, 430 N.E. of Stockholm, and 1400 N.E. of London. The principal part of the city, named the "admiralty quarter," is situated on the mainland, along the south side, or left bank, of the Neva. Another large portion occupies the eastern half of the Vassilii Ostroff (Basil's Island.) A third portion, containing the citadel and Old St. Petersburgh. occupies a large island between the Neva, the little Neva, and the Nevka. A summer communication is maintained between these by means of three large floating bridges; and a winter one, by the solid frozen surface of the Neva. Stupendous granite quays line the bank of the river, along which are arranged very many of the principal public buildings and ornaments of the city. In general, the streets are wide and very regular, running in straight lines, but intersecting each other at different angles, except in the Vassilii Ostroff and some other places, where they come at right angles. The greater part of the streets are from 70 to 130 feet wide, the length various—some being 6000; another—the Nevski Prospekt—2¼ miles long; and the great Prospective, in the Vassilii Ostroff, 10,220 feet. The mansions of the nobility consist of vast piles of buildings furnished with great cost, and occupying the south side of the Neva, either in the admiralty quarter, or in the suburbs of Livonia and Moscow—the finest part of the city. The views on the banks of the Neva are magnificent in the extreme. On the N. of the fortress, the Academy of Sciences and Arts will attract attention; whilst on the opposite side are the Admiralty—a beautiful building, having a richly gilt spire in the centre—and a dockyard, enclosed between it and the river; the Imperial Palace—a stupendous pile; the Hermitage, the Marble Palace, and the Barracks of the Guards—all forming a unique and magnificent line of splendid edifices, unrivalled by any European city. Opposite this brilliant range stands the Citadel, its low bastions of granite encircled by the Neva, conspicuous by the delicately slender and richly gilt spire of the Church of St. Peter and Paul, in which is the mausoleum of the royal family. Towards the east from the citadel the Neva spreads itself into a wide expanse, after the fashion of a bay; on the far-stretching shore of which are several pretty buildings—especially the great Naval and Military Hospitals; whilst to the west can be seen the magnificent portico of the Exchange, built between two colossal rostral columns. At the eastern point of Vassilii Ostroff, and beyond them the Palaces and the Observatory of the Academy of Sciences, situated in the area to the west of the Admiralty, is a colossal statue of Peter the Great, the Senate, the War Office, and the Church of St. Isaak. This church, though in progress of erection for the last forty years, was not finished until within the past couple of years. It is now the finest structure in the world, whether in regard to its material or its sumptuousness. It is of a square form, with an octostyle portico on each of its four faces, and is surmounted by a dome 400 feet high. The Taurida Palace, the Palace of the Grand Duke Michael, the Hotel of the Staff, and the Cottage of Peter the Great, are also worthy of notice. But amongst the noblest of the ornaments of St. Petersburgh is an equestrian statue of Peter the Great, erected at great expense, in 1782, by Catherine II.

Twenty miles west of the city, on the Gulf of Finland, is situated the large imperial palace of Peterhof—the favourite residence of Peter the Great. Fifteen miles south is the splendid Palace Czarskocelo—the Versailles of Russia; and fifteen miles further is the Palace Gatchina, and a town of the same name, with a fine china works, and large hospitals. Several other towns of interest are to be found all round; one of which is Cronstadt—a powerful fortress and naval arsenal, about seventeen miles up the mouth of the Neva. It is impregnable, and is the station for the Russian Baltic fleet, and port of St. Petersburgh.

Commission Agent.—Mr. Sharp, English Hotel.

Moscow is the metropolis of the empire, though not the seat of government. It is a large city, regularly built, on the banks of the Moskra, 400 miles S.E. of St. Petersburgh, in 55·45 N. latitude, and in 37·33 E. longitude. In 1812 it was all but destroyed by fire. This fire has rendered the city memorable in history, as being connected with the invasion of Russia by the French, under Napoleon. On the 7th of September the battle of Borodino took place, at which the French were victorious; and the Russians retreated, leaving Moscow to its fate. The city was set on fire by the governor, Count Rostopchin, and was in ruins when the French entered it, on the 14th of the same month. In the fire 30,000 sick and wounded soldiers perished This conflagration destroyed more than three parts of the town; but it is now all rebuilt, and its improvements considerably added to. The city is divided into five divisions—the Krumlin, containing the ancient palace of the Czars, where Peter the Great was born; the Kithagorod, containing the university, the printing-house, and very many valuable buildings; the Bielgorod, or White Town; the Semliangorod; and the Sloboda, or suburbs. Its churches are worth a visit; and it is crowded with palaces, monasteries, arsenals, museums, and other public buildings, representing the various styles of architecture—Grecian, Gothic, Italian, Tartar, and Hindoo—rude, fanciful, grotesque, gorgeous, magnificent, and beautiful, overtopped by upwards of thirty gilt cupolas. The Cathedral of the Assumption, founded in 1325, and rebuilt in 1472, is decked out with gorgeous and extravagant ornaments. In this church the emperors are invested with the ancient crown of the Czars. Towering far above all other objects is the tower of Ivan Velek, or John the Great. It is 270 feet high; and contains thirty-three bells, the smallest of which is 70,000, and the largest more than 124,000 lbs. weight, English. They are decidedly worth hearing, as they toll on Sundays and festival-days. The Great Bell of Moscow, cast in the reign of the Empress Anne, and weighing 443,772 lbs., has been recently raised from a pit, in which it was sunk for a century, and placed upon a pedestal. Though now cracked and useless, it is yet a great object of veneration with the Russians. Moscow is also the seat of many scientific and literary institutions, and is the centre of a vast inland commerce. The population is about 350,000. A railway communication is established between St. Petersburgh and Moscow, (see page 118.) It is about 400 miles long, 300 of which passes through a wood. A rather remarkable—but, as one would say, an imperial—accident led to the construction of this railway on its present *site*. Very many eminent scientific men were consulted as to the course the line should take, but could not decide in reference to it. The fact being communicated to the Emperor, he at once took up a pen, and dashed it at random through the map; and forthwith ordered the railway to be constructed on the site his random shot indicated. About sixty miles west of Moscow is Borodino and Moyarsk—the scenes of two desperately contested and sanguinary battles between the French and the Russians, in 1812.

Odessa is situated on the north-western coast of the Black Sea, and is a fortified seaport in the government of Kherson, founded in 1792 by Catherine II. The harbour is an excellent one, and capable of accommodating a numerous fleet. The principal portion of the town is built upon the top of a long range of cliffs, which commands a splendid sea view. A public walk, planted with flowering trees and shrubs, extends along the top of the cliff, having the governor's house at one end, the Exchange at the other, and a statue of the Duc de Richelieu in the centre. The houses in the best localities are built of a soft, light-coloured stone, and roofed with sheets of iron, or painted wood. Its chief branch of trade consists of grain. Wool is also fast rising into importance. The carrying trade is performed chiefly in Austrian ships. The Sardinian, Russian, English, Grecian, Turkish, Swedish, and French vessels are also engaged in this trade. The inhabitants are chiefly Polish Jews, Italians, Greeks, and Germans, with a few French and English. It is a free port, and one of the cheapest towns in the world to live in. In it is a very important academic institution—the Richelieu Lyceum—having attached to its foundations professorships of Greek and the higher branches of science, together with natural and civil history. Its chief imports are sugars and other colonial products, cottons, silks, &c. The Cathedral of St. Nicholas will repay a visit, its interior being sumptuously decorated.

Riga is situated on the Dwnia, about five miles from its mouth, in the Gulf of the Baltic, designated the Gulf of Riga. It is a very strong town, and is capital of the Government of Livonia. Its commercial position is very high, being next to that of St. Petersburgh. Foreign merchants carry on its trade, and those connected with the English Factory there enjoy the greatest share of the commerce. Corn, hemp, flax, iron, timber, masts, leather, and tallow, form the principal articles of export. There is a very large floating bridge over the Dwnia, 2,600 feet long and 40 broad; this bridge is removed in winter, when the ice sets in. The population of Riga is estimated to be about 68,000.

Saratov is situated on the right bank of the Volga, proverbial for the industry of its inhabitants, which has raised it among the principal of the Russian cities, and created for it a flourishing trade. It has some very excellent buildings; and is divided into the upper and lower towns, the population of which consists of about 36,000. It has a handsome archiepiscopal palace, several elegant churches, a large bazaar, a gymnasium, and an ecclesiastical seminary.

POLAND.

POLAND.—The Polish towns are nearly all built of wood, and miserable cottages or huts constitute the villages. The country is very fertile in corn; and supplies to a great extent both Holland and Sweden with that grain. It has also extensive pastures. Peat, Ochre, Chalcedony, Chalk, Agate, Cornelian, Onyxes, Jasper, Rock Crystals, Amethysts, Sapphires, Rubies, and even Diamonds, are found in Poland; as also Talc, Spar, Lapis, Calmanaris, Coal, Iron, Lead, and Quicksilver. Leather, Fur, Hemp, Flax, Saltpetre, Alum, Manna, Honey, and Wax, are likewise produced; and it is remarkable for the beauty of its breed of Cattle.

Warsaw.—It is built partly on a plain and partly on a gentle rise from the Vistula, extending with the suburbs of Kraka and Praga, over a vast extent of ground, and containing about 150,000 inhabitants.

The streets of this city are very spacious but ill-paved, and the churches and public buildings are large and magnificent. The suburbs present rather an uncouth looking aspect, the houses being nothing more than mean, ill-constructed hovels. Its productive industry represents the manufacture of woollen-stuffs, carpeting, gold and silver wire, soap, tobacco, &c. There are also several wholesale mercantile houses employed in the import and export trades. There are two great fairs held here yearly—one in May, the other in November. They continue for three weeks, after the fashion of those at Leipsic and Frankfort.

This city was besieged, in July 1794, by the King of Prussia, but he was compelled to raise the siege the September following. The Russians attacked the city in November, and took the suburb of Praga, after which the city at once surrendered, and was made over to the King of Prussia by the Russians.

Warsaw was the Vice-Regal residence, and the place of meeting of the Polish Parliament up to 1833, when, the Polish insurrection being unsuccessful, the political existence of the Poles was annihilated; since which Poland must be looked upon as a part of the Russian Empire. It is 170 miles S. of Konigsberg and 180 E.N.E. of Breslau.

Cracow.—Situated on the left bank of the Vistula, 144 miles S.W. of Warsaw, in a fine valley, with a number of fine buildings, but narrow, irregular, and ill-paved streets. In its cathedral—regarded as the finest and most interesting church in Poland—are the tombs of kings and great men of the country, from Boleslaus the Frisean and Casimee the Just, to Joseph Poniatowski and Thaddeus Kosciusko. The university is one of the oldest in Europe, possessing a rich library and a botanic garden. It has a population of 25,000. The legislative power is vested in an Assembly of Deputies, chosen by the Communes and Executive, in a Senate consisting of twelve members, and a President, who is elected every year.

On a rock near the Vistula is the ancient Royal Palace, surrounded by brick walls and old towers, which form a kind of citadel. The University is one of the most ancient in Europe, possessing a fine library, and a botanic garden. Cracow communicates with its suburb of Padgoze, in Gallacia, by a bridge across the Vistula.

Though the city and suburbs occupy a vast tract of ground, they scarcely contain 26,000 inhabitants. The Great Square is spacious and well built, and many of the streets are broad and handsome, but on almost every building is the mark of ruined grandeur. The work of destruction was first commenced in 1702, when Charles XII. of Sweden took the city, and though his rude barbarism effected much Vandal desecration on the buildings and monuments therein, yet it had to suffer much more profanation from the Russians and the confederates. In the year 1794 the Poles, whose individual courage remained unshaken, raised their standard at Cracow, headed by the illustrious Kosciusko; and notwithstanding the almost total want of regular troops, succeeded in driving a combined force of Russians and Prussians from before Warsaw. But the Russians, under Suwarroff, poured into the country in such numbers as to make resistance hopeless; and the insurrection received a death-blow from the loss of Kosciusko, who was taken prisoner at the battle of Maczieiowicz. Warsaw was stormed by Suwarroff, and 20,000 of its brave garrison and inhabitants brutally put to the sword. Poland's last hour had struck! she was no more! Her king was sent a prisoner to Russia. The remains of Kosciusko's veteran bands disdained to live under Muscovite dominion: they sought and found a home in the armies of France, and contributed by their valour to bring Napoleon in triumph to the Kremlin. Its independence, with 487 square miles of territory, was restored by the Congress of Vienna, and a sort of a Republic created, under the joint protection of Russia, Prussia, and Austria, who exercise some partial authority in the legislation.

The monument erected to Kosciusko stands on the west, about a league from the city, and consists of a large artificial tumulus, raised by the people in 1820.

Great changes have, since 1814, been made in its constitution.

SWEDEN.

SWEDEN extends 1000 miles from N. to S., and 300 from E. to W. It is in general a very flat country; and from Gottenburg, in the W., to Stockholm, in the E., there is scarcely an acclivity to be seen.

It was formerly divided into five general parts:—Sweden proper, Gothland, Nordland, Lapland, and Finland, which were subdivided into provinces. The entire country is divided into twenty-three governments. The country is well watered by rivers (though it has scarcely a navigable one), by numerous lakes and inland pieces of water, on which the palaces and villas are usually built. In winter the cold is excessive, and in summer the heat is intense, but modified by the influence of a very serene air. In summer, all the rocks are quite covered with flowers, and the gardens plentifully abound in fruit. Horses, Cows, Hogs, Goats, Sheep, Elks, Reindeer, Bears, Wolves, Foxes, Wild Cats, and Squirrels are the animals principally found in the country. In some parts are rich silver and copper mines, and vast forests of timber-trees. Boards, Gunpowder, Leather, Iron, Copper, Tallow, Skins, Pitch, Resin, and Masts, are the principal articles of export. The inhabitants are of a strong and vigorous constitution. The Swedish houses are generally constructed of wood, and exhibit very little art in their erection. Turf generally covers the roofs in many places, and the goats may be seen browsing from off the houses.

The form of the Swedish Government has frequently varied. It was elective Monarchy before the accession of Gustavus I. In 1397, by the union of Calmar, it was stipulated that Denmark, Sweden and Norway should be ruled over by the same monarch, and hence Sweden became a mere tributory to the Danish kingdom. Gustavus Vasa rescued it from this degradation, and had the sovereignty of the country conferred upon him in 1523, and the crown made hereditary in his male issue, and afterwards extended to the female line in his family. In the regency of his daughter the nobles assumed a power offensive to the clergy and people, and Charles XI. obtained a formal cession of the absolute sovereignty, which afterwards devolved on his son Charles XII. From this monarch the crown passed in succession to his sister Ulrica, who resigned it to her consort, Frederick I. Gustavus III., in 1772, effected a revolution, whereby he secured many of the royal prerogatives forced from the throne of Sweden since the reign of Frederick I., at which period it was regarded as the most limited monarchy in the world. This monarch fell in 1792, by the hands of the assassin, leaving his son, Gustavus Adolphus, a minor, who became of age in 1796. This prince was deposed on the 1st of May, 1809, and his uncle, the Duke of Seedermania, was called to the throne. This monarch's son dying, he resigned the throne, and the Swedish Diet met to elect a successor, which they did, in the person of the brave Bernadotte, a French Marshal, a Prince of Ponte Corvo. This person, though a Frenchman, and though he owed all his eminence to Bounaparte, yet fought against him, with the allies, in 1813, and, in 1814, secured Norway to Sweden by the Treaty of Kiel.

The established religion of Sweden is the Luthercan.

Stockholm lies in a situation remarkable for its beauteous scenery. It is long, and irregularly constructed, occupying three rocky islands, besides two peninsulas. Numerous rocks of granite, rising boldly from the surface of the water, create a variety of beautiful views. The harbour of Stockholm is a very fine one, admitting ships of the largest burden. At its extremity rise several streets, one above the other, in the form of an amphitheatre; and at the summit is the palace—a magnificent building. The principal objects of attraction are the Cathedral, the Bank, and the House of the Diet. This city also contains a very large number of literary and scientific institutions. The population is about 80,000.

There is here a Royal Academy of Science, founded by the celebrated Linnœus, associated with a few other learned men, in 1741; and also a Royal Academy of Arts. The Arsenal has within it an immense number of trophies and standards taken from different nations.

Stockholm, with the small territory surrounding it, constitutes a separate government, and manufactures glass, china, silk, woollen, &c.

It is 320 miles N.E. of Copenhagen; 1000 N.E. of Paris; and 900 N.E. of London.

Upsala is 41 miles N.N.W. of Stockholm, built on a gentle height and part of an adjoining plain, in a very level and fertile country; and is one of the most beautiful and old-fashioned cities in Europe. It has about 16,000 inhabitants—a greater portion of which depend on the old and celebrated university, still enjoying a flourishing existence among them. It was founded in 1478, and is usually attended by about 1000 students, or alumni.

Gothaberg is a large commercial town, situated on the left bank of the Gothalf, near the sea, 245 miles W.S.W. of Stockholm, and has about 25,000 inhabitants, and enjoys very active commerce.

The Gotha is navigable from the sea to the Falls of Trollhalten, where the navigation is continued by a canal along the river, which here rushes impetuously down a gorge, a height of 190 feet, a d between the canal and the river there is a range of saw-mills belonging to a Glasgow company.

Fahlun, the capital of Delecarlia, is 120 miles N.W. of Stockholm, containing a population of 4000 souls. Its streets are long and wide. It is situated in the midst of a region of copper mines, extending about twenty-eight miles in length and seven in breadth. This wide space is enclosed, and partly penetrated by rocks of reddish granite, which, towards the middle, gradually merge into a uncaceous rock, the greater part of which is composed of iron and copper pyrites. During many centuries these mines were the most productive in the world, yeilding annually eight millions of pounds of pure metal. The present annual produce is thus estimated:—copper, 4,500 skip pounds; gold, 250 ducats; silver, 500 marks; lead, from 100 to 150 skip pounds; vitriol, 600 or 800 tons; ochre, 1000 tons; brimstone, 20 to 30 pounds. The ore is not rich, and the best is said to yeild 20, but the poorest only 1½ per cent

Hernosand, an Episcopal city in Norsland; has a harbour, with a considerable trade. A Gymnasium, a College, a Botanic Garden, and a Printing Press, from which mostly all the books for the use of the Laplanders have been produced.

DENMARK.

DENMARK is almost an uniformly level country. The kingdom is divided into two great divisions—the continental and the insular. The former consists of a long narrow peninsula, projected from Germany; and the latter of a number of islands, placed between that peninsula and the Kingdom of Sweden. The productive industry of Denmark is chiefly confined to agricultural produce.

The aspect of the Continental part is flat and undiversified, containing neither mountains nor rivers of any magnitude. The Keil is the only canal of importance, it admits vessels of 120 ton burthen, and extends from the Baltic to Eyder at Rendsburge, where the river becomes navigable, thus opening up a communication between the two seas, or through 105 miles of territory. This canal was commenced in 1777, and completed at an expense of £800,000. The lands are in general excellently cultivated, and rich in pasturage. The monarchy of Denmark is the oldest in Europe. Its regal puisance stands contemporaneously with the proudest epoch of the Roman Empire; and the advancement of the people in discipline and arms in the 10th century can be learned from the fact of their descent on England, and the complete subjugation of the country by them in the early part of the following century. In 1397, Norway by inheritance and Sweden by conquest, became united to Denmark, under Queen Margaret, denominated the "Semeramis of the North," on account of her heroism.

Copenhagen is situated on the east coast of Zealand, where the small isle of Armack forms a superb harbour. It is one of the finest cities of Europe, and laid out in regular though narrow streets, and adorned with very fine buildings, viz., several palaces, churches, the hospitals, Town-house, Exchange, and mansions of the nobility. The royal library contains 400,000 volumes, and the university 112,000. A large collection of northern antiquities adorn the rooms of the palace. It has a population of about 130,000, and is defended by a citadel, said to be impregnable; and also by several strongly defended forts, mounted with 1680 cannon. In the vicinity are very many beautiful and picturesque sights. The other principal towns are Roskild—the ancient capital, 20 miles W. by S. of Copenhagen—a small town with only 1300 inhabitants, containing a gothic cathedral, an excellent library, and the tombs of the royal family; Altona, on the north bank of the Elbe, near to Hamburg; Schlessing, the capital of South Jutland; and Odense, in Funen, containing a lyceum, two libraries, and about 7000 inhabitants. Besides these, Denmark claims foreign possession, represented by several islands.

The streets are well paved, but are altogether unprovided with water or gas. The Exchange is a beautiful Gothic building, built of brick, and stone quoins, after a design by Inigo Jones. It is surmounted by a singular spire, representing in its formation four dragons, with their twisted tails tapering upwards, after the fashion of a corkscrew, with their heads turned to the four points of the compass. The church of the Trinity has a very fine tower 200 feet high, and on its top there is an observatory. The Saviour's Church has a very curious winding staircase, and is surmounted with a tower 288 feet high. The church of the Holy Ghost, and Notre Dame, are very fine buildings. The interior of the latter will be found well worth a visit. In it are beautifully wrought marble statues of the twelve Apostles, Christ, and a kneeling Angel. They were executed by Thorwalden, and are supported by pedestals in full view. The view from any of these churches is magnificent in the extreme. Stretching out in chastely delineated symmetry before us is the city and harbour, surrounded by their bastions and windmills, the citadel, line-of-battle ships, frigates and corvettes, dockyards, arsenals, wharehouses, palaces, parks, gardens, plantations, squares, streets, canals, and market-places; whilst the general population is industriously engaged with horses and vehicles in the ordinary avocations of a commercial life. A long wide plain, interspersed with forests and lakes, is seen to the westward; whilst towards the east appears the blue sea, covered with craft of all description, with the coast of Sweden in the background.

A great many bathing places are to be found at Copenhagen, and the water of the Baltic is half salt and half fresh. We also find numerous theatres there, which are open on every night, not even excepting Sunday. One of its chief objects of attraction is the Tivoli Gardens, outside the Western Gate. These are the nightly resort of a numerous port on of the people. In it is a very tastefully arranged conservatory, and an excellent band is in attendance and performs several delightful pieces of music. A small Comic Theatre, a Bowling Alley, Menagerie, a Museum of Curiosities, and numerous Cafés are to be found in the gardens.

The city itself is entered by four archway gates, having drawbridges across the moat, guarded by soldiers. A toll is demanded for horses and vehicles entering the city. Another object of attractive interest is the Royal Palace of Christiansborg, built of white stone, after the Italian style of architecture, The eye will be taken by the four colossal statues ornamenting its stupendous façade. Coloured silk damask and silver ornament its empanelled walls. The ball room should be particularly noticed; its walls and arched ceiling representing a pure white marble and gold. A colonnade is formed by the Corinthian columns on either side; chandeliers, with cut glass pendants and spangles, suspended from the ceiling and adorning it; the whole being reflected by the plate glass at either side. The floors are of oak, maple, and ebony, diamonded. The stables should also be visited: they contain stalls for 200 horses.

Near the Palace is Thorwaldsen's Musem, which is well worth a special notice. It contains an immense and beautiful collection of works, all being the creation of one man, who is thus spoken of, in a work lately published, by a Liverpool Gentleman, and entitled, *A Trip to Denmark.*

"Albert Thorwaldsen, the son of a poor ship-carpenter from Iceland, was born in Copenhagen 1770. His genius, at an early age, impelled him to Rome, where he arrived almost penniless; but, having soon afterwards obtained employment in Canova's studio, his talent very quickly developed itself by the beauty and genius of his designs. Ultimately, he took a studio of his own, and modelled his famed statue of "Jason," but, as he obtained no order for it, he, in despair, determined to quit Rome, and return to Denmark. All his arrangements were made for that purpose, when Mr. Hope, of London, seeing the cast of "Jason," was so much struck with its beauty, that he immediately ordered it in marble.

"This turned the tide of Thorwaldsen's fortune; from that time his fame was established, and commissions poured in upon him. He then fixed his residence in Rome, making occasional visits to Denmark, and finally settled in Copenhagen in the year 1838.

"With an ample fortune, elected President of the Academy of Arts, a suite of apartments allotted to him in the Palace of Charlottenborg, decorated with the highest orders of merit of his own country and others, and almost adored by every person who knew him, he now devoted himself to the duties of his honourable office.

"Having intimated his intention of presenting the casts of all his works, as well as several of his statues in marble, to his native town, a magnificent museum was erected for their reception by public subscription."

OVERLAND ROUTE TO INDIA.

ROUTE via MARSEILLES.

For information respecting the journey from London to Marseilles, *via* Paris, the hours of departure, modes of conveyance, cost, &c., see pages 27, 30. 34, 35, 36, 39, 50, and 54. A conveyance leaves the office of the Administration des Services Maritimes des Messageries Nationales, Rue Notre-Dame-des-Victoires, Paris, each morning at half past 9 a.m., and arrives at Marseilles at 9 p.m. the following evening. Fares—87, 70, and 55 frs.

The railways and the steamboats on the rivers Saone and Rhone have so considerably facilitated the performance of the journey from London to Marseilles, as to render it easy of accomplishment in a few hours. Thence travellers can proceed to Malta, Alexandria, and Constantinople, or to any of the intermediate ports, either rapidly per direct packets, or more leisurely by the line of Italy, thereby visiting *en route* the most remarkable towns of that country—such as Genoa, Florence, Rome, Naples, &c.,—all of which will be found described in the GUIDE under the head of Italy.

The steam-ships of the "Administration des Services Maritimes des Messageries Nationales," Rue Notre-Dame-des-Victoires, convey the mails between Marseilles and the principal ports of the Mediterranean Sea, under arrangements detailed in pages 268 and 269. They average from 120 to 220 horse-power. For particulars in reference to tickets, accommodation, &c., see pages already mentioned (268 and 269.)

For notice of the different lines, viz., the Italian, Levant, Greek, Egypt and Syria, between Constantinople and Alexandria, and the various lines they correspond with, see pages 268 and 269, where the most ample information will be found recorded.

Passengers wishing to visit Genoa, Leghorn, Florence, Rome, Naples, and Messina, *en route* for Malta, or any destination beyond it, can embark on the packets of the line of Italy, leaving Marseilles on the 19th and 29th of each month. They are privileged to stay ten days or more at any of the intermediate stations, proceeding to their destination by subsequent packets, within a delay of four months. On re-embarking, they are only entitled to such berths as are vacant when due notice of the departure is given at the company's office. The passage-money is in all cases to be paid in advance, and in no case returned.

Passengers must follow and adhere to board regulations. They cannot pretend to the exclusive occupation of a state-room, unless engaging all the berths contained in it. The tariff of luggage is given in pages of the GUIDE already referred to; and the following refers to the charge for *extra* luggage, which is charged on board the packets at the rate of 10 frs. per 70 kilos. between Marseilles and Malta, and 25 frs. per 70 kilos. to any destination beyond Malta. Goods and merchandise are not admitted as luggage. CARRIAGES are charged as follows:—

Large size .... at 1½ fares of 1st class passages.
Small size (2 wheels) ditto. ditto.

In addition to the instructions given in reference to Passports, both under the column of "General Instructions," at page 19, and under the column of "Observations," at page 269, the following tariff of charges will be found useful for the traveller to know:—French police *visé*, gratis; British, 2 frs. 80 c.; Sardinian, 4 frs.; Tuscan, 2 frs., Roman, 3 frs 50 c.; Neapolitan, 6 frs; Greek, 1 fr. 50 c.; Russian, 6 frs.; Spanish, 5 frs. 50 c.; Dutch, 5 frs.; Belgian, 4 frs. 50 c.; Prussian, 4 frs.; Austrian, 3 frs. 90 c.; Swiss, 2 frs. 50 c.; Turkish, 2 frs. 50 c.; American, 10 frs. 50 c.; Danish, 5 frs.

For information as regards LIVING, EMBARKATION, BAGGAGE, CHILDREN, PASSPORTS, PASSAGES BY SHORT STAGES, RETURN TICKETS, FAMILY TICKETS, and the Departure from Marseilles for Syra, see the column of Observations at page 269.

NOTICE TO HOMEWARD TRAVELLERS RETURNING FROM INDIA.—The Packets of the Marine Service of the "Messageries Nationales," on their return voyage from Alexandria, are accompanied by Health Officers, and perform quarantine during the passage, so as to be admitted into *pratique* on arrival at Marseilles. In consequence of this, on their calling at Malta, no passengers are admitted but those who are not subjected to quarantine. Travellers should then bear in mind, that in order to avail themselves of the advantages offered by the French route, they must embark on board the French Packets at Alexandria, for should they proceed to Malta by any other steamer arriving there in quarantine, they would not be admitted on board the French Packets.

EXCURSIONS TO UPPER EGYPT.—The following information will prove useful to the general mass of travellers visiting Egypt.

The steamers of the Egyptian Transit Administration began since last year to perform regular trips on the Nile, from Cairo to Upper Egypt, by which means that interesting voyage—once so difficult and expensive—can be accomplished most comfortably and economically in about eighteen days.

The Transit Administration will renew the excursions this year, thus opening up an easy, interesting and agreeable route to an almost unknown land, which offers to the highest historical interest the advantage of a mild and salubrious climate during the season through which the severest cold is experienced in Europe.

Few who have not explored Upper Egypt can imagine the deep interest shrouding every feature of its historical character, or rightly analyse the features of its territorial monuments and ruins.

ROUTE via TRIESTE.

General Instructions, &c.—Baggage.—A recent regulation enables passengers for India, *viâ* Trieste, who are encumbered with heavy baggage, to ship it at Southampton by one of the steamers leaving that port for Alexandria, on the 20th of each month. The adoption of this course will save them a world of trouble, and render it unnecessary to take more baggage with them through the Continent than is requisite for their journey to Alexandria. Passengers returning from India should adopt a similar course, and leave the cumbersome portion of their baggage at Alexandria for shipment to Southampton. Much inconvenience, arising from delay, &c., will be avoided by parties forwarding keys of packages subject to duty, with the address of the owner, and the list and value of the contents, to 127, Leadenhall-street, London; or to Hecker, Bowman, and Co., Oriental-place, Southampton. Personal baggage, when declared for transit at Ostend, can be forwarded to Trieste free of Custom-House examination. The same course is adopted in reference to baggage from Trieste, which need not be examined until arrival in London. It may be well to understand that luggage declared for transit cannot be used until its arrival at its destination.

Passengers, on their arrival at Trieste from Alexandria, can have the extra quantity forwarded to England, &c., by giving the necessary instructions at Trieste. Two pounds per cwt. is charged as carriage to England, exclusive of Custom-House charges.

Passengers should not bring sealed letters into Austria, it being opposed to the postal regulations of that country. Persons purposing to reach Trieste, *viâ* Ostend and Vienna, are recommended to have their passport obtained at the Foreign Office, signed first by the Austrian Ambassador, and afterwards by the Belgian Consul, if *viâ* Ostend. If there be different members of a family travelling together, their names can all be included in the one passport. (See pages 19 to 22.)

Money.—Circular notes, sovereigns, francs, and Prussian dollars, are the best to take from England. Austrian paper money, or coin, should not be taken beyond her frontiers, as it will be refused.

Though we give, in connection with the furnished details of the various routes, the probable hours of arrival and departure of the different conveyances, yet we recommend, as a general course, that the tourist or traveller should refer himself to the Railway Time Tables and Alphabetical List of Steamers, to be found in their proper places in the Guide, where he can accurately ascertain the exact hour.

We give the following *routes*, in order that the tourist may be enabled to chose such as he deems most worthy of his adoption.

Route 1.

London to Trieste, by Cologne, Dresden, and Vienna.—See Route 5, page 26.— The distance is 1,507 miles, and the time occupied is five days sixteen hours. Fares: first class, £10 11s.; second class, £7 13s. 5d.; and third class, £5 13s. 10d. At Magdeburg the traveller can continue onward to Berlin, he can reach Vienna by rail, through Breslau, but the expense will be a little more than by the direct route.

Route 2.

By Ostend, Cologne, Frankfort, Ratisbon, the Danube, and Vienna, at the cost of £8 19s. 6d. for first class, £6 10s. 2d. 2nd class, and £5 8s. 9d. third class.

Route 3.

By Mayence, Frankfort, Ratisbon, Bruck, and Labach.—London to Mayence, Railway and Steamboat, Mayence to Frankfort by rail, Frankfort to Ratisbon by diligence, Ratisbon to Linz by steamer and diligence, Linz to Bruck by diligence, Bruck to Laibach by rail, Laibach to Trieste by diligence. Cost: 1st class, £7 16s. 8d.; 2nd class, £6 7s. 8d.; 3rd class, £6 3s.

Route 4.

By Mannheim, Carlsruhe, Stuttgard, Augsburg, Munich, Salzburg, and Bruck.—Journey performed in 134½ hours. Cost: 1st class, £7 14s. 2d; 2nd class, £6 3s. 6d.; 3rd class, £5 15s. 5d.

ROUTE 5.

By Ulm, Fussen, Innspruck, and Conegliano.-The journey is made in 142½ hours, at the cost of £6 11s. 8d. 1st class, and £5 9s. 10d. 2nd class.

ROUTE 6.

By Bale, Lucerne, Milan, Verona, and Venice. Cost: 1st class, £6 19s. 4d.; 2nd class, £5 8s. 10d. Time occupied, 127 hours.

ROUTE 7.

By Amiens, Paris, Geneva, and Milan. Cost: 1st class, £11 2s. 2d.; 2nd class, £9 4s. 8d. Time, 121 hours.

ROUTE 8.

By Hamburgh, Berlin, Breslau, and Vienna.—1st class. £10 8s. 2d.; 2nd class, £7 9s. 3d.: 3rd class, £5 14s. 10d Time occupied, 128½ hours.

Travellers anxious to enjoy the magnificent scenery between Vienna and Trieste, should proceed by the day train from Vienna to Gratz, where they should make a halt, and proceed by day train to Laibach. Conveyances from Laibach may be had at the Imperial Diligence Office; by taking four seats, a separate post carriage can be got. The traveller can delay at Adelsberg sufficient time to see the magnificent grotto close to the station, if he will start over night or early in the morning.

At Cologne, Vienna, Berlin, and Breslau, the stations of the North and South Railways are at opposite ends of the town. The conveyance thereto and from, as the case may be, will cost a small trifle. The station porter will be found useful to travellers, and his services could be secured for 6d. or 3d.; for this trifle he will attend to the luggage, see it weighed, marked, and bring a ticket, which must be produced before the baggage will be given up on arrival at the station for which it is booked.

From Trieste, parties anxious to visit the Ionian Islands, Greece, Constantinople, Asia Minor, and Egypt, can do so at a comparatively small outlay. Travellers from Greece and the Ionian Islands are admitted to free *pratique* Those from the Levant and Greece are accompanied by health officers, and the quarantine is performed on the voyage, so that passengers can now proceed on shore immediately on arrival at Trieste, provided the vessel has a clean bill of health. Tickets are good upon all the lines for two months; and travellers so disposed may land at any port on the line, provided they inform the captain of their intention. They can proceed on by the Company's next vessel.

The departure of the Austrian Lloyd's *indirect* steamers to Alexandria, *viâ* Smyrna, twice each month, in eleven days, at 4 p.m. To the Levant, every Thursday, at 4 p.m. To Greece, every Thursday, at 4 p.m. To Ancona, Brindisi, Ionian Islands, Patras, &c., across the Isthmus, to Athens and Syria, on every alternate Monday, at 4 p.m To Dalmatia, on each Monday, at 4 p.m., excepting in the months from October to April, when the boat leaves every Monday, at 6 p.m. To Istria, on every Wednesday and Saturday, at 7 p.m. To Venice daily, at 6 a.m. From Trieste to Venice a first class return ticket may be had for £1 0s. 8d., and is valid for seven days.

Passengers embarking on board, or landing from the Austrian Lloyd's steamers, each passenger requiring a boat to himself must pay 2s.; several passengers in one boat, to pay each 8d.; families, 4s.; and luggage—viz., trunks, boxes, mattresses, and portmanteaus, for each package, 2d.; hat-cases, carpet bags, &c., are free.

In Germany few travel in 1st class, and the 2nd is scarcely inferior to the English 1st class. In Belgium and Austria the 2nd class is pretty good; but travellers will exercise their own discretion in reference to this matter.

For further information see "General Instructions to Continental Travellers," pages 6 to 9.

ALEXANDRIA, the ancient capital of Lower Egypt, is situated in the Mediterranean, between the Lake Mariotis and the Isle of Pharos. Few cities present more attractive features to the traveller than this. Its ruins and desolation, its traditions and its departed glories, are alike worthy the student's consideration, who will find much to admire in its present appearance and position, as well as much to be delighted with in the inspection of its antiquities. It is enclosed by walls of Saracenic structure, supposed to have been built by one of the successors of Saladin, in the 13th century. The original city was built by Alexander the Great, soon after the fall of Tyre, about 333 B.C. Built for a mighty purpose, and with a grand design, it realised the hopes of its founder, as, not long after its erection, it became the emporium, not only for merchandise, but also for all the arts and sciences of Greece. Strabo tells us that ancient Alexandria was 30 stadia in length from east to west, and 7 or 8 stadia even where narrowest. The circumference was 9 miles, but Pliny, including no doubt the suburbs, reckons it at 15 miles. Lake Mariotis bathed its walls on the south, and the Mediterranean on the north. It was also intersected by straight parallel streets lengthways, and a free passage was left to the northern wind, which alone conveys coolness and salubrity into Egypt. At the gate of the sea, a street of 2,000 feet began and terminated at the gate of Canopos. This street was decorated with magnificent houses, temples, and buildings. Along its extensive range the eye was never tired of admiring its marble, the porphyry and obelisks which at some future day were destined to embellish Rome and Constantinople. The great street, the handsomest in the world, was intersected by another of the same breadth, which formed a square of half a league in circumference at their junction. From the middle of this great place the two gates were to be seen at once, and vessels arriving under full sail from the north and from the south. The

Palace, which advanced beyond the promontory of Lochras, occupied more than a quarter of the city. Each of the Ptolomies added to its magnificence. It contained within its enclosure the Museum, an Asylum for learned men, groves, and buildings worthy of royal majesty, and a Temple, in which was deposited the body of Alexander in a gold coffin. This beautiful monument was violated by the infamous Seleucus Cibyofactus, who carried off the gold coffin, putting a glass one in its place. Alexandria also extended along the northern bank of the lake, and in its eastern view presenting the Gymnasium, with its portico of more than 600 feet long, supported by several rows of marble pillars. Without the gate of the Canopos there was a spacious circuit for chariot races, whilst beyond that the suburb of Nicopolis ran along the sea shore, and seemed a second Alexandria. A superb amphitheatre was built there, with a race-ground for the celebration of the Quinquenalia. Such is the description left us of Alexandria by the ancients, but, above all, by Strabo.

The architect employed by Alexander for the construction of this city was the celebrated Dinocratus, who acquired such great reputation by building the Temple of Diana at Ephesus Ptolemy Soter, one of Alexander's captains, was the first to render this city populous. He was appointed Governcr of Egypt soon after the death of the Macedonian monarch, assumed the title of King, and made Alexandria the royal residence, B.C 304 years Ptolomy Philadelphus also added much to the embellishment and grandeur of Alexandria. In the first year of his reign, the celebrated watch-tower of Pharos was erected, which, when finished, was looked upon as one of the wonders of the world. The tower was a large square structure of white marble, on the top of which fires were kept constantly burning, for the direction of sailors. The building cost, if Attic, 800 talents, or £165,000; if Alexandrian, twice that sum. A curious stratagem was resorted to by the architect of this tower to perpetuate his name in connection with it, and take all the glory to himself. Being ordered to engrave upon it the following inscription—" King Ptolemy, to the Gods the Saviours, for the benefit of Sailors"—instead of the king's name he substituted his own, and then, filling up the hollow of the marble with mortar, wrote upon it the above-mentioned inscription. In process of time, the mortar being fallen off, the following inscription appeared:—" Sostratus, the Cnidian, the son of Dexiphanus, to the Gods the Saviours of Sailors."

The Temple of Serapeum had within its verge the celebrated Alexandrian Library, containing 700,000 volumes In collecting books for this library, the following plan was adopted, viz., to seize all the books which were brought into Egypt by Greeks, or other foreigners. The books were transcribed by persons appointed for that purpose. The copies were then handed back to the proprietors, and the *original* laid up in the library. The works of Sophocles, Euripides, and Æschylus, were borrowed from the Athenians by Ptolemy Eurgertus, who returned them the copies transcribed in as beautiful a manner as possible, presenting them at the same time with £30,000 for the exchange.

This city, like all others of note in the early ages, was often the scene of terrible massacres. About 141 years before Christ, it was all but destroyed by Ptolomy Physcon. At this epoch nearly all the learned men fled to Greece, Asia Minor, and to the Islands of the Archipelago, where they revived learning, and the arts. From this period the fortunes of Alexandria were dimmed by feuds and scenes of carnage, until taken by Amron, who, astonished at the richness and grandeur of the city, wrote to the Caliph:—" I have taken the City of the West. It is of immense extent; I cannot describe to you how many houses it contains. There are 4,000 palaces, 4,000 baths, 12.000 dealers in fresh oil, 40,000 Jews who pay tribute, and 400 theatres, or places of amusement." From this period until the year 924 the city remained subject to the Caliphs, and then fell into the hands of the Magrebians. The chief thing contributing to raise Alexandria to the pitch of extraordinary splendour which it enjoyed for so long a period, was its being the centre of commerce between the eastern and western world. And, though the revolutions occurring in the government of Egypt, after it fell into the hands of the Mahometans, frequently affected this city to a very great extent, yet the excellence of its port, and the innumerable conveniences resulting from the East India trade to the different Governors of Egyat, preserved it from total destruction when in the hands of the most barbarous nations. And in the thirteenth century, when the European nations began to acquire a taste for the elegancies of life, the old mart of Alexandria again revived, and its port grew famous once more as the centre of commerce. But it again declined from its ancient greatness since 1499, in which year it became subject to the Turks, when a passage was discovered around the Cape of Good Hope by the Portuguese in that year. In the ruins of ancient Alexandria we see a total wreck of ancient grandeur, in each broken fragment of which there is an inspiring reflection, and in the utter desolation of which is painted the utter fallacy of human greatness.

Alexandria Modern.—The present city is a peninsula, situated between the two ports, and presents little more than half-ruined houses and rubbish, with the ruins of a few of those magnificent dwellings erected on its site. Its population varies from between 15,000 to 20,000. Dr. Madden estimates the number at 16,000; of whom 9,000 are Arabs, 2,000 Greeks, 2,000 Europeans, and the rest Jews, Copts, &c. The commerce of Alexandria is still most extensive, as all the exports from and imports to Egypt pass through its port. The British and French Governments have Consuls at Alexandria, and there are several eminent British mercantile houses established there. There are also there Jewish merchants, who are numerous and wealthy. The late extensive importation of cotton from Egypt has added considerable importance to Alexandria; and a great stir has been created by the naval expeditions equipped there by the Pacha. It has two ports, viz.,—the old and the new one; the former of which is far the better. Turkish vessels only are allowed to land there, and the new one is reserved for European vessels, or the Christians. It is clogged with sand; and in stormy weather, vessels are subject to bilge: the bottom being also rocky, the cable soon breaks, so that, one vessel dashing against another, many are perhaps lost. A very fatal instance of this occurred many years ago, when forty-two vessels were dashed to pieces on the Mole, in a gale of wind from the north-west; and numbers have been since wrecked there. To the inquiry, why do not the Turks repair the port? we answer, that in Turkey they destroy everything, and repair nothing. The old harbour will also be destroyed, as the ballast of vessels has been thrown into it for the last 200 years. And it has been well remarked, that the spirit of the Turkish government is to destroy the labours of past ages and the hopes of future times, because *ignorant* despotism never considers to-morrow.

The country all round Alexandria is completely destitute of water, excepting that which is brought from the Nile by a canal of twelve leagues, each year, at the time of the inundation. Vaults and reservoirs are dug under the ancient city to receive the supply which must last until the next year. The canal is the only link of communication between Alexandria and Egypt, it being without the Delta; and from the nature of the soil, it truly belongs to the African deserts. Some parts of the old wall are yet standing, and are flanked with large towers about 200 paces distant one from the other; below are magnificent casements, which serve as galleries to walk in. The lower part of the towers contain a large square hall, the roof of which rests on thick columns of Thebac stone; and above this are several rooms, over which are platforms more than twenty paces square. The reservoirs are vaulted with much art; and though 2000 years have rolled by since their construction, they are still perfect. Only a few porphyry pillars and the front portico remain of Cæsar's palace; they appear very beautiful. The palace of Cleopatra was built upon the walls facing the port, having a gallery on the outside supported by several fine columns. Not far from the palace are two obelisks, commonly called Cleopatra's Needles; they are of Thebac stone, and covered with hieroglyphics; one is upturned, and is seen lying on the strand; the other stands on its pedestal. One of these has been presented to the British government by the authorities of the country. It is now being conveyed to England; and on its arrival, will be placed in the New Crystal Palace at Sydenham. These two obelisks are about sixty feet high by seven feet square, and it is supposed they decorated the palaces of the Ptolemies. Near the gates of Rosetta are five columns of marble, on the place formerly occupied by the porticos of the Gymnasium. The barbarism of the Turks has since destroyed the remainder of the colonnade. But the chief object of attention is Pompey's Pillar, situated about a quarter of a league from the southern gate: it is built of red granite: the capital, which is Corinthian with palm leaves, and not indented, is nine feet high; the shaft and upper member of the base are of one piece, of nearly ninety ft. long, and nine ft. in diameter. The base is a square of about fifteen feet on each side. This block of marble, sixty feet in circumference, rests on two layers of stones bound together with lead, which has not prevented the Arabs from forcing out several stones to seek for imaginary treasure. The entire column, ninety-five feet high, is beautifully polished, and only shivered a little at one side. Nothing can equal the majesty of this monument. Seen at a distance, it overtops the town, and serves as a signal for ships; whilst on a nearer approach it produces astonishment mixed with awe. Admiration is never lost on the beauty of the capital, the height of the shaft, or the extraordinary symplicity of the pedestal. The column was considered inaccessible until within the last half century, when, in a wild frolic, a party of English sailors, who conceived the project of emptying a bowl of punch on the top of it, scaled it by means of a rope. They dexterously availed themselves of the movements of a paper kite, by which they succeeded in fastening a rope to the summit; and by this they ascended, and performed this great achievement. It has since been rendered more accessible. Dr. Maddens mentions an English lady who breakfasted and wrote a letter on the top of it. Much research and fruitless study have been expended in attempting to discover in whose honour the pillar was erected. Dennon on this subject expresses himself thus:—"After having observed that the column is very chaste both in style and execution; that the pedestal and capital are not formed of the same granite as the shaft; that their workmanship is heavy, and appears to be merely a rough draught, and that the foundations, made up of fragments, indicate a modern construction—it may be concluded this monument is not antique, and that it may have been erected either in the time of the Greek emperors or of the caliphs, since if the capital and pedestal are of sufficiently good workmanship to belong to the former of these periods, they are not so perfect but that art may have reached so far in the latter." The catacombs are also worth a visit. They begin at the extremity of the old city and extend some distance along the coast, forming the Necropolis, or City of the Dead. The excavation is from 30 to 40 feet wide, 200 feet long, and 25 feet deep, and is terminated by gentle declivities at each end. One of these openings can be easily entered. Within there are no mummies: but the places which they occupied, the order in which they were ranged, is still to be seen. Niches 20 inches square, sunk six feet horizontally, narrowed at the bottom, and separated from each other by partitions in the rock seven or eight inches thick, divides into checkers the two walls of this subterranean vault.

Alexandria never ranked as a fortress; and in 1798, when Napoleon Buonaparte attacked it, it surrendered without a blow. The place where Sir Ralph Abercrombie fell is about four miles from the city, in the direction of Rosetta.

Passengers are carried from Alexandria to Sicily by the transit administration of his Highness the Pacha of Egypt. The transit occupies about three days. The following extracts from the Transit Guide will prove useful.

"In order to facilitate the conveyance of luggage through Egypt, travellers are recommended to limit the size of their trunks to the following dimensions:—

Length .... 3 feet.
Width................ 1 foot 3 inches.
Depth .... 1 „ 2 „

The weight of each trunk not to exceed eighty lbs.

Passengers should take as few packages or articles with them on their *route* as possible, as they are solely responsible for any such under their own personal charge. On landing from any steamer or embarking therein, First Class Passengers pay 1s., and Children and servants 6d. Parties are requested to embark only from the transit wharf.

Omnibuses are provided at the expense of the transit administration to and from the landing places and the hotel, and the hotel and canal at Alexandria, and likewise between Boulac and the hotels at Cairo, and *vice versa*. These conveyances will leave the hotels half an hour before the appointed time of starting.

No large packages of luggage can be put in the omnibuses, there being other conveyances for them at Alexandria. Payments for transit fares, overweight of luggage, &c., must be made in English gold, Egyptian piastres, Spanish or German dollars, napoleons or five-franc pieces, at the government rate of exchange. Neither will English bank notes be received. Passengers from India proceeding to Europe by the Austrian Lloyd's steamers, must separate their luggage from that of the booked-through passengers on its arrival at Alexandria, otherwise it will go on to Southampton.

The departure of the Austrian Lloyd's *direct* steamers from Alexandria for Trieste altogether depends on the arrivals of the mail packets at Suez. They generally leave for Trieste in twenty-four hours after the arrival of the mails and passengers at Alexandria.

English or Dutch subjects proceeding from India, China, or Java, *viâ* Trieste, to England or Holland, should obtain a passport from their respective Governments, and obtain the visa of the Austrian Consul, either at Bombay, Madras, Calcutta, Ceylon, China, Singapore, or Battavia, as the case may be.

All passengers by the East India Company's steamers from Bombay, without exception, obtain precedence of carriage according to priority of personal application and payment at Suez.

Two children from two to five years of age are entitled to one seat in the van, and three to four children exceeding five and under ten years of age, to the place of two first class passengers. Men servants will not be admitted to a van with first class passengers, if the consent of the other members comprising the party be not first obtained, and that the agent also sanctions the arrangement. Infants and children under two years of age are conveyed free.

In order to ensure celerity of transit, it is particularly requested that all possible expedition be used by passengers in landing at Suez, that no obstruction or delay take place in delivery of the luggage to the officers sent on board to receive it, and that every article of luggage be legibly addressed and properly secured. All luggage, except 5 lbs. weight allowed in the van for special purposes, will be conveyed direct to the transit wharf at Boulac, port of Cairo, when it will be accessible to the owner after it has been weighed; but parties who intend stopping at Cairo are requested to give notice of their intention to the agents at Suez and Cairo, and deliver to both a list of their packages, that the necessary assistance may be given for the separation of their luggage.

Passengers are conveyed to Egypt by the transit administration of His Highness the Pacha of Egypt. The mode of transit is as follows:—

Alexandria to Atfeh by the Mahmoudiah canal, in track boats towed by steam tug or by horses. From Atfeh, a distance of 120 miles by the Nile, in steam boats to

Boulac—about two miles distant from Cairo, of which it is the port. The journey is performed by omnibus, or on donkeys. The appearance is not at all striking, and possesses only one building worth notice — the palace of Ismael Pacha — a singular intermixture of Italian, Greek and Arabian architecture.

Cairo, the capital of Egypt, is situated in a plain at the foot of a mountain, in long. 32° E., lat. 30° N. It is entered by a pretty good road; and as we approach it, the city presents a very imposing appearance. Jawhar, a Moggrebin general, founded it in the middle of the tenth century, and named it "Alkahira," or the victorious. It soon became the residence of the Caliphs, and, as a consequence, the capital of that country.

It is divided into the old and new cities; the former of which, on the left bank of the Nile, is almost uninhabited. The new city is situated on a sandy plain, about 2½ miles from the old city, on the same side of the river. The citadel rising above the lofty buildings, all springing, as it were, out of a grove of the richest foliage, presents a most imposing appearance The streets are narrow and unpaved, whilst the houses are gloomy. Each street has a gate, which is closed at nightfall. The number of inhabitants is about 300,000, though some travellers estimate it at 400,000. A canal, called Khalis, runs along the city from one end to the other, with houses on either side. In its progress it forms very many small lakes, called berks, the principal of which is in the great square near the castle. On its banks are built the most beautiful houses in the city, but, being dependent for its supply of water on the inundation of the Nile, it is dry for several months in the year, and is covered with charming verdure. In the water season the barges and barks of the people of rank may be seen constantly gliding up and down on its surface, especially in the evenings, when curious fireworks and a variety of music enliven the scene. Stone walls and handsome battlements, with very fine towers at every hundred paces, surround the modern city of Cairo, which is very scarce in places of defence. The fortified palace, erected by Saladin in the 12th century, was the only place of defence in the city, and yet the Turks let it fall into ruin, until it was thoroughly repaired, not long since, by the Pacha. Guides and asses are in constant requisition to go up to it, passing on their way through the Bazaars, by the Mosque of Hassan, and through the gate memorable for the slaughter of the Mamelukes. Its principal apartment was a magnificent hall, environed with twelve columns of granite, of prodigious height ahd thickness, brought from the ruins of Alexandria. These sustained an open Dome, under which the Saladin distributed justice to his subjects. A glorious view of the city, and above 30 miles along the Nile, including the ruins of Old Cairo, the suburbs of Boulac, and Djiah, the site of Memphis, the great Pyramids, the Obelisk of Heliopolis, the ruins of Mateko, the Pyramids of Sahhara, and the "Eternal Nile," may be had from this palace. The Pacha does not now reside there, he having removed to a still more magnificent one in the vicinity. It contains a pavilion 250 feet by 200 feet, each wall of which is adorned with colonnades of white marble. A Military College, and other institutions, have been founded lately, with the view and for the purpose of introducing European arts and improvements. In the city there are about 300 mosques, some of which have six minarets, and are adorned with beautiful granite columns, brought from Heliopolis and Memphis. The largest mosque is that of Azhar, standing in the centre of the city. The next in size is that of Sultan Hassan, the finest structure in modern Egypt, and extremely light and elegant. It is built in the form of a parallelogram, and has a deep frieze running round all the wall, adorned with Gothic and Arabesque sculpture. In the neighbourhood is an extensive Necropolis, in which there are many splendid tombs, including a magnificent one built by the Pacha for his family, adorned with five spacious domes. There are several Khans and Caravanseries. These are in general several stories high, and are always full of people and merchandise, Cairo being the great centre of the trade of the interior of Africa, and having caravans departing at intervals from it for Fezzan, Darfur, and other quarters. The visitor will be particularly struck with the Slave Market, which presents natives brought from almost every portion of that great continent.

Old Cairo.—Here we find very little to interest or amuse, except the Granaries of Joseph, which, as subject of special notice in the page of Inspiration, must deeply interest the christian traveller. They consist of merely a high wall enclosing a square spot where the farmers deposit barley and other grain as a tribute to the Pacha. In it we also find a pretty church, used by the Christians and Copts, the latter being the original inhabitants of Egypt.

The apartment built over against Old Cairo and above the river is worth notice: it admits the water, and a column, with lines at a distance of every inch, marks at every two feet as far as thirty. Joseph's Well will also interest: it is situated in the fortified palace, and is said to have been made by King Mohammed 700 years ago, because the Egyptians attribute every thing to this remarkable character. The well is cut in a rock, and is 280 feet deep. The water is drawn to the top by means of oxen, placed on platforms at proper distances, which turn about the machine that raises it. Moors, Greeks, Turks, Jews and Copts constitute the population of this celebrated city, which contains 240 principal streets, 46 public squares, 11 bazaars, 140 schools, 300 public cisterns, 1,166 coffee houses, 65 public baths, 400 mosques, and *one* hospital for the mad and infirm. English hotels and lodging houses are established at Cairo. English medical men are also practising there. The Cemetery of the Mamelukes is the finest burial place in Europe: it is not far from the city, on the way of the Desert: the tombs present various forms, some of them being magnificent, having domes supported by finely carved transparent marble columns. At the distance of a mile, in another direction, are the tombs of the Caliphs: they are beautiful structures, being of the light and elegant style of the Saracenic architecture, and have some exquisitely worked domes and minarets. On the edge of the Desert, which he was attempting to explore, is Burkhardt's grave, under a small tombstone scarcely discernable.

Should the traveller prolong his stay at Cairo for some days, and visit the Pyramids, he is recommended to take a guide and a supply of provisions and candles. In returning, he can visit the Isle of Rhoda and Nilometer; Sakhara and the site of Memphis will require another day. The other objects worth seeing are the mosques, the Obelisks of Heliopolis (three hours ride), Shonha, a palace of the Pacha (two hours distance), Gardens of Rhoda, Petrified Forest, and the Toura Qurries.

Memphis, it will be remembered, was taken and sacked by Cambyses, the Persian king; it was afterwards visited by Alexander the Great, previous to the foundation of Alexandria.

The final ruin of Memphis was accomplished by the Arabs, who used up its materials in building Old Cairo in 638.

Heliopolis, or the City of the Sun—the oldest city perhaps in this land of antiquities—was a sort of sacerdotal and university town, where the illustrious Plato is said to have graduated. It consisted for the most part of temples and colleges. Nothing, however, of these now remain but a few isolated mounds, and one solitary obelisk said to have been erected by the Pharoah mentioned in the history of Joseph.

CAIRO TO SUEZ—a Distance of 70 miles across the Desert, performed in carriages or on donkeys, the latter being considerably less expensive.—Suez is a wretched looking and very uncomfortable place; mud and wooden houses abound. It is bounded by the desert and the sea. Scarcely a blade of grass or foliage of a tree is to be seen about Large salt marshes filled with stagnant waters render the air very bad, and there is not a spring any where about.

The journey from Alexandria to Suez is performed in about sixty hours, including a stoppage of one night at Cairo, and a sufficient time for refreshment and repose at the central station between Cairo and Suez.

THE RED SEA.—At the head of this sea Suez is situated. It is 1200 miles in length, in its greatest breadth not more than 200 miles broad, being comparatively a long and narrow sea. The coral reefs with which the channel abounds are very beautiful in their appearance, though extremely dangerous in navigation to sailing vessels, but not so to steamers, which keep the middle of the sea.

The shores present scenes of desolation unparalleled on the face of nature. Neither verdure, nor grass, nor one green spot on which the eye could rest with pleasure can be seen. On the east side of the head of the Red Sea a good view can be had of Mount Sinai, and the steamers on their way down touch at Cosseir, at Juddah, and Aden, taking up passengers at the two first mentioned places.

ADEN, a seaport of Arabia, now occupied by the British East India Company as a depôt for the steamers, &c. traversing the Red Sea. It was ceded to them after the unsuccessful treaty for Socrota, and has since been a scene of warfare. Here the vessel puts in for coal, during the shipping of which the voyagers have an opportunity of surveying the curious places about, and of refreshing themselves at the inn. Leaving this station, they sail through the Straits of Babelmandel into the Indian Ocean.

BOMBAY is an island city and the seat of government for the northern part of India. It came into the hands of the English by the marriage of Charles II. with Catharine of Portugal, and was made over to the East India Company in 1688, at which time it was made the seat of government of all their possessions on that side of Hindostan, which was previously at Surat. Bombay is now one of the three Presidencies by which their Oriental territories are governed. Its length from north to south is six and a half miles, and its breadth near the fort is about a mile and a half, separated from the mainland by an arm of the sea. In conjunction with the adjacent islands of Colabah, Salselte, Butcher's Island' Elephanta, and Carujah, it forms a commodious and well sheltered harbour. It contains a strong and capacious fortress, a city, dockyard, and marine arsenal. The best and finest merchant ships are built here of teak, which is brought from the neighbouring countries, and is found more durable than the best English oak. The ground here is in general barren, and very scarce of good water, but it abounds in cocoa-nuts, and its markets are supplied with every delicacy.

The town of Bombay is nearly a mile in length from the Apollo gate to that of the Bazaar, and about a quarter of a mile broad in the widest part, from the Custom-House across the Green to Church gate, which is in the centre between the Apollo and Bazaar gates. There are two gates towards the sea, which have commodious wharfs and cranes built out from each, with a landing-place for passengers. Bombay Castle—a regular quadrangle, built of hard and durable stone, and having the advantage, in one of the bastions, of a large reservoir of water—is situated between these gates. There are about the town numerous fortifications, which have been strengthened from time to time, as the importance of the place grew greater. They are particularly strong towards the sea, the harbour being completely commanded by a range of batteries. Many large and beautifully-built houses are centered in the space called the Green. The Church, which has a very neat and light appearance, is in this localty, and on the left of its gate is the Government House, presenting a very showy appearance. The Bazaar, which is crowded and populous, is on the right of the gate. The native merchants live here; and the Theatre—a handsome building—stands at the extreme end of the street. A conflagration, in 1803, nearly destroyed this portion of the town. In it three-fourths of the Bazaar, the Barracks, Custom-House, and several other public buildings were destroyed, and fears were entertained for the safety of the magazine. The trade and commerce of Bombay is very extensive. It carries on a valuable trade with the countries situated in the Arabian and Persian gulfs, with the western coast of India, its eastern parts, and the islands in the eastern ocean, and a wool trade with China. In 1808 the quantity brought to Bombay for re-exportation amounted to 85,000 bales, of 375 lbs. each, which were partly procured from the country on the Nerbuddah. It also enjoys a considerable trade with Europe, and different parts of America. It contains about 220,000 inhabitants, three-fourths of which are Hindoos, and the other fourth is composed of persons from almost every Asiatic nation.

The Company's naval force consists of twenty fighting vessels, besides armed boats, advice boats, and other craft. The annual expense for the maintenance of the Anglo-Indian army is about £10,000,000. The army, native and European, is distributed throughout the country at appointed stations, forming a chain of military posts, and keeping up a continual communication with the seats of the various Presidencies.

The Bombay Court of Judicature consists of a Chief Justice and three or more puisne judges, and its jurisdiction extends over all the territories subject to the Presidency. The climate is insalubrious.

The Government of Bombay is vested in a Governor and three Councillors, subject to the control of the Supreme Government of Bengal, whose orders they are in all cases to obey. The Court of Directors appoint the Governor and Members of the Council and likewise the Commander-in-chief of the forces, who, though not officially a Member of the Council, yet may receive such an appointment from the Directors, in which case he takes precedence of all the other members.

The travelling distance from Bombay to Calcutta is 1,300 miles; to Delhi, 965; to Hyderbad, 480; to Madras, 770; to Poonah, 90; to Seringapatam, 620; and to Surat, 177 miles.

The tariff from Suez to Bombay is, for a person occupying a berth in cabin with two or three others, £60; for a married couple occupying a cabin on main deck, with a w.c., £185; without a w.c., £165; for children with their parents, five years old and under ten, £28; two years old and under five, £14; for European servants, £25; for Native servants, £15.

CEYLON.—An island of the Indian ocean, lying off the S.W. coast of the promontory of Hindostan, from which it is separated by the Gulf of Manara and Polk's Strait. Its early history is involved in obscurity; but it is supposed to have ranked high among the cities of Asia, in population and influence, if it be the Taprobane referred to by Strabo Pomponius, Mela and Pliny. Little was known of Ceylon beyond its existence as an island, until it was visited by the Portuguese after the discovery of the passage by the Cape of Good Hope. It was in 1505 divided into many sovereignties, which afterwards were merged into one, under the title of Candy. The Dutch expelled the Portuguese, and possessed themselves of the entire circuit of the coast for ten or twenty miles from the sea, and the whole of the north part of the island, confining the dominion of the King of Candy entirely to the interior. These possessions were surrendered to the English in 1796, having first sustained a siege of three weeks. In 1815 the British marched in with an armed force, and, after deposing the king, incorporated the whole island as a part of the British dominions.

The island is mountainous and woody, and is divided into two parts by lofty mountains. Spring sets in about Oct., and the hottest season is from Jan. to April. The island abounds with very fine fruit, and produces pepper, ginger and cardamoms, with different kinds of rice, which ripen one after the other. One of the most remarkable trees in the island is the *talepot*, which grows straight and tall, and is as large as the mast of a ship; the leaves are so large as to cover fifteen men, and when dried they are round, and fold up like a fan; every soldier carries one, and it serves for his tent. But the most important of all its vegetable productions is the cinnamon tree, the bark of which is distributed over every part of the habitable globe. Topazes, garnets, rubies, and other gems, also abound in Ceylon, besides ores of copper and iron, and veins of black crystal; and in addition to the various productions of Ceylon previously enumerated, connected with it is the pearl fishery, carried on in the Gulf of Manaar, which is considered the richest source of that article in the world; however, it is a Government monopoly, and only opened periodically. There are likewise numerous other productions of considerable commercial importance.

CALCUTTA is the capital of Bengal, and the seat of the Governor-General of the British dominions in the East Indies. It is one of the largest and most beautiful cities of Asia, and is the modern capital of Hindostan. It is sit ated upon the river Hoogly, which forms the western channel of the Ganges, and is one of the principal of its numerous branches navigable for large vessels. Its name is derived from Culta—a temple dedicated by the Hindoos to Caly, the goddess of time, situate between the villages of Chultametty and Goburdpore, where the agents of the English E. India Co.'s Service, in 1680, obtained permission of Aurungzebe to establish a trading factory, which, in consequence of the disturbed state of the Province of Bengal, they were allowed to fortify in 1690. The town stands on almost a perfect level of alluvial and marshy ground, covered with jungle and stagnant pools about a century ago, and which still betrays its unsoundness everywhere, by the cracks conspicuous in its best best houses. The town is about 100 miles from the mouth of the river, the navigation of which is difficult, and very often dangerous, it being filled with numerous sand-banks, constantly shifting their position. The larger vessels load and unload at Diamond Harbour, from whence passengers are conveyed to the city (60 miles distant) by smaller vessels, or in boats. From the mouth of the Hoogly to Diamond Harbour the country is dreary in the extreme. the banks of the river are high, and the land perfectly flat at each side, forming a complete wilderness of timber and brushwood—the haunt of tigers and other beasts of prey.

As we advance up the river, however, the scene gradually improves and becomes more cultivated, the shipping and bustle on the river increase, and the beautiful country-seats on its banks announce the approach to the capital. The town and suburbs extend about six miles up along the left bank of the river. An immense square is in the middle of it, which, together with the adjacent buildings, forms the town of Calcutta properly so called. The intermediate space is the esplanade. The Citadel of Fort William is the most regular fortress in India, but would require 10,000 men with 600 pieces of cannon to defend it. It was erected by Lord Clive, in 1757, immediately after the battle of Plassey. The Government House, the largest and most beautiful in the town, built by the Marquis of Wellesley, is seen on the west of the esplanade. In it the Governor-General resides, and transacts all the Government business. The other public buildings are the Town House, the Hall of Justice, the Hospital, and the Jail (all of which are within the esplanade); the two English churches, the Portuguese, the Greek and Armenian churches, together with several small Hindoo pagodas, Mahommedan mosques, and a Sikh temple.

The traveller to India will, beside the places above described, find much to attract and interest in his wanderings through that land of sunbeams and of flowers. Several works are at present extant that will be an invaluable acquisition to him in his wanderings through the East, with whose history are identified so many interesting traditions and reminiscences of historical beauty.

Pages 305-328 not present in original guide

SARDINIAN ROYAL MAIL STEAM NAVIGATION COMPANY.

REGULAR SERVICE between MARSEILLES AND ITALY,

Performed by Splendid and Powerful Steamers, calling at

GENOA, LEGHORN, CIVITA VECCHIA, AND NAPLES.

DEPARTURES FROM MARSEILLES TO NAPLES,

and vice versa.

From Marseilles.........4th, 14th, 24th of every month, in 18 hours.
,, Genoa ....5th, 15th, 25th ,, 8 ,,
,, Leghorn ....6th, 16th, 26th ,, 10 ,,
,, Civita Vecchia, 7th, 17th, 27th ,, 13 ,,

From Naples............6th, 16th, 26th.
,, Civita Vecchia, 7th, 17th, 27th.
,, Leghorn ....8th, 18th, 28th.
,, Genoa ....9th, 19th, 29th.

TABLE OF FARES,

INCLUDING PROVISIONS FOR FIRST AND SECOND CLASS.

	Genoa.			Leghorn.			Civita Vecchia.			Naples.		
CLASSES....	1	2	3	1	2	3	1	2	3	1	2	3
Marseilles (francs)	70	40	20	80	50	30	105	65	35	150	90	40
Genoa (frs.)				40	25	10	80	50	20	125	80	30
Leghorn (frs.)							45	30	15	90	60	25
Civita Vecchia (frs.)										45	30	15

20 per cent. reduction allowed to persons taking Return Tickets and paying for them in advance. These tickets are available four months.

20 per cent. reduction allowed to families of not less than four persons.

And vice versa.

N.B.—The Freights for Goods, Carriages, &c., are established on the most favourable terms.

REGULAR SERVICE between GENOA and SARDINIA,

(CARRYING THE MAIL.)

From Genoa to Cagliari......1, 10, 20th of every month, in 40 hours.
,, Genoa to Portotorres, 5, 15, 25th ,, 24 ,,

From Cagliari to Genoa.....5, 15, 25th.
,, Portotorres to Genoa, 1, 10, 20th.

FARES, *including Provisions for first and second Class.*

From Genoa to Cagliari......and *vice versa*—1st class, 70 francs; 2nd class, 45 francs: 3rd class, 18 francs.
From Genoa to Portotorres, and *vice versa*—1st class, 55 francs; 2nd class, 35 francs; 3rd class, 12 francs.

SERVICE between GENOA and TUNIS (via Cagliari).

From Genoa, 10th and 20th of every month.
,, Tunis, 20th and 30th ,,

Fares, 1st Class, 115 francs. 2nd Class, 75 francs. 3rd Class, 30 francs.

Between NICE, GENOA and LEGHORN, regularly.

From Nice to Genoa, every Monday evening.
From Genoa to Leghorn, every Wednesday evening.

From Leghorn to Genoa, every Thursday evening.
From Genoa to Nice, every Saturday evening.

Genoa to Nice, and *vice versa*, in 12 hours; **Fares**—1st Class, 25 francs; 2nd Class, 15 francs.
Genoa to Leghorn, and *vice versa*, in 10 hours; **Fares**—1st Class, 35 francs; 2nd Class, 20 francs.

For Terms of Freight, Plans of Cabins (having superior accommodation), apply—in Marseilles, to Mr. L. A. Fontana; Nice, Messrs. A. Gilly & Co.; Leghorn, Mr. S. Palau; Civita Vecchia, Messrs. F. De Filippi & Co.; Rome, Mr. J. Freeborn, British Consul; Naples, Messrs. C. Di Lorenzo & Co.; Milan, Mr. J. Mangili; Turin, Messrs. Bonafons Brothers; and in Genoa, to the Directors of the Company—

RAPHAEL RUBATTINO & Co. [5

12

MAIL STEAM PACKETS OF THE MEDITERRANEAN.

FROM MARSEILLES.

MARINE SERVICE OF THE MESSAGERIES NATIONALES.

CHIEF OFFICES:

PARIS, Rue Notre-Dame des Victoires. MARSEILLES, Rue Mongrand, Place Royale, No. 1.
LONDON, Messrs. Lightly & Simon, 123, Fenchurch-street, & 314A, Oxford-street (Mr. J. E. Puddick, Agent.)

Lines.	THE PORTS.	Departure.				THE PORTS.	Returning.			
		Arrival.		Departure.			Arrival.		Departure.	
		Days.	Hours.	Days.	Hours.		Days.	Hours.	Days.	Hours.
The Italian Line.	Marseilles	...	...	9,19,29	10 a.m.	Malta	...	...	2,12,22	2 p.m.
	Genoa..........	10,20,30	9 a.m.	10,20,30	7 p.m.	Messina	3,13,23	8 a.m.	3,13,23	10 a.m.
	Leghorn	1,11,21	5 ,,	1,11,21	5 ,,	Naples	4,14,24	8 ,,	4,14,24	2 p.m.
	Civita Vecchia	2,12,22	8 ,,	2,12,22	2 ,,	Civita Vecchia	5,15,25	6 ,,	5,15,25	3 ,,
	Naples	3,13,23	7 ,,	3,13,23	3 ,,	Leghorn......	6,16,26	6 ,,	6,16,26	6 ,,
	Messina	4,14,24	1 p.m.	4,14,24	3 ,,	Genoa.........	7,17,27	4 ,,	7,17,27	2 ,,
	Malta (*a*)	5,15,25	9 a.m.	...	...	Marseilles ...	8,18,28	noon.	...	...
The Levant Line (b.)	Marseilles	...	...	1,11,21	2 p.m.	Constantinople	...	...	5,15,25	5 p.m.
	Malta (*c*)	5,15,25	6 a.m.	5,15,25	6 ,,	Gallipoli......	6,16,26	4 a.m.	6,16,26	5 a.m.
	Syra	8,18,28	4 p.m.	9,19,29	10 a.m.	Dardanelles	6,16,26	noon.	6,16,26	1 p.m.
	Smyrna	10,20,30	8 a.m.	10,20,30	4 p.m.	Metelin	6,16,26	10 p.m.	6,16,26	11 ,,
	Metelin	11,21, 1	1 ,,	11,21, 1	2 a.m.	Smyrna	7,17,27	7 a.m.	7,17,27	4 ,,
	Dardanelles ...	11,21, 1	11 ,,	11,21, 1	noon	Syra	8,18,28	2 p.m.	8,18,28	10 ,,
	Gallipoli	11,21, 1	8 p.m.	11,21, 1	9 p.m.	Malta (*g*).....	11,21, 1	8 ,,	12,22, 2	3 ,,
	Constantinople	12,22, 2	9 a.m.	...	...	Marseilles ...	16,26, 6	7 ,,	...	,,
The Greek Line	Marseilles.......	...	...	1,11,21	2 p.m.	Piræus........	...	...	7,17,27	6 p.m.
	Syra	8,18,28	4 p.m.	8,18,28	6 ,,	Syra	8,18,28	5 a.m.	8,18,28	10 ,,
	Piræus	9,19,29	5 a.m.	...	...	Marseilles ...	16,26, 6	7 p.m.	...	...
	Marseilles	...	...	1	2 p.m.	Salonica......	...	...	13	5 p.m.
	Piræus.	9	5 a.m.	11	6 a.m.	Piræus........	15	7 a.m,	17	6 ,,
	Salonica.........	13	3 ,,	...	...	Marseilles ...	26	7 p.m.	...	...
	Marseilles	...	...	11	2 p.m.	Calamata (*h*)	...	...	23	9 a.m.
	Piræus	19	5 a.m.	21	5 a.m.	Marathonisi..	23	6 p.m.	24	6 ,,
	Nauplia	21	4 p.m.	21	7 p.m.	Nauplia	24	10 ,,	25	10 ,,
	Marathonisi ...	22	11 a.m.	22	7 ,,	Piræus........	25	9 ,,	27	6 p.m.
	Calamata (*d*)...	23	4 ,,	...	...	Marseilles ...	6	7 ,,	...	...
	Marseilles	...	...	21	2 p.m.	Chalcies......	...	...	3	7 a.m.
	Piræus	29	5 a.m.	1	11 ,,	Piræus........	3	9 p.m.	7	6 p.m.
	Chalcies.........	2	1 p.m.	...	...	Marseilles ...	16	7 ,,	...	...
Egyptian L.	Marseilles	...	...	4,23	8 a.m.	Alexandria..	...	...	7, 18	5 p.m.
	Malta	7,26	noon	7,26	6 p.m.	Malta	12,23	6 a.m.	12, 23	noon.
	Alexandria	12, 1	6 a.m.	...	...	Marseilles ...	15,26	3 p.m.	...	...
The Syrian Line (1.)	Constantinople	...	...	8,18,28	3 p.m.	Alexandria...	...	...	23,13, 3	8 a.m.
	Smyrna (*e*)......	10,30,20	9 a.m.	10,30,20	6 ,,	Jaffa	24,14, 4	8 a.m.	24,14, 4	1 p.m.
	Rhodes	12, 2,22	5 ,,	12, 2,22	11 a.m.	Beyrout	25,15, 5	6 ,,	27,17, 7	7 a.m.
	Marsina	14, 4,24	11 ,,	14, 4,24	8 p.m.	Tripoli.........	27,17, 7	2 p.m.	27,17, 7	7 p.m.
	Alexandretta...	15, 5,25	5 ,,	15, 5,25	6 ,,	Latakia	28,18, 8	4 a.m.	28,18, 8	5 ,,
	Latakia	16, 6,26	5 ,,	16, 6,26	9 ,,	Alexandretta	29,19, 9	4 ,,	29,19, 9	6 ,,
	Tripoli	16, 6,26	6 ,,	16, 6,26	10 ,,	Marsina	30,20,10	3 ,,	30,20,10	noon.
	Beyrout	17, 7,27	5 ,,	19, 9,29	6 ,,	Rhodes	2,22,12	noon.	2,22,12	6 p.m.
	Jaffa	20,10,30	11 ,,	20,10,30	4 ,,	Smyrna (*i*)...	4,24,14	5 a.m.	8,28,18	5 ,,
	Alexandria (*f*)	22,12, 2	6 ,,	...	...	Constantinople	10,30,20	11 ,,	...	...

The above vessels carry the mail and passengers between Marseilles and the principal ports of the Mediterranean. They are commanded by officers of the French navy, by special authorization of government. Besides a full crew, every packet carries an experienced surgeon, and as many stewards and stewardesses as may be required for the best attention. The greatest care has been taken by the company of the fitting up of cabins, bedding, and state rooms, so as to afford superior accommodation and comfort.

Passengers going to Syria have no quarantine to perform on arrival. If going *via* Alexandria they are transhipped there without landing.

TARIFF OF FARES.

FROM

MARSEILLES

TO

Lines.	THE PORTS.	1st class.	2nd class.	3rd class.	4th class.
		Frs.	Frs.	Frs.	Frs.
The Italian Line.	Genoa	68	41	27	17
	Leghorn	80	48	32	20
	Civita Vecchia	105	63	42	26
	Naples	150	90	60	37
	Messina	192	116	77	48
	Malta	210	132	88	55
The Levant Line.	Syra and Piræus	330	210	140	87
	Smyrna	370	240	160	100
	Metelin	390	247	165	103
	Dardanelles	400	252	168	105
	Gallipoli	410	265	180	116
	Constantinople	420	279	186	116
The Greek Line.	Hydra	15	10	7	5
	Spezzia	16	12	8	6
	Nauplia	24	16	10	8
	Marathonisi	...	...	...	...
	Calamata	50	40	22	18
	Chalcies	25	16	10	8
	Salonica	75	48	22	18
	Syra	15	10	7	5
Egyptian Line.	Alexandria	450	280	190	120
The Syrian Line. (By Smyrna.)	Rhodes	410	260	178	112
	Marsina	460	305	203	125
	Alexandretta	467	312	207	125
	Latakia	470	315	218	127
	Tripoli	471	315	211	128
	Beyrout	463	308	207	128
	Jaffa	482	321	217	133
The Syrian Line. (By Alexandria.)	Jaffa	493	311	214	133
	Beyrout	512	323	224	138
	Tripoli	518	325	227	138
	Latakia	528	332	232	141
	Alexandretta	540	340	243	147
	Marsina	550	346	243	147
	Rhodes	556	351	243	147

(*a*) Correspondence with **the Levant** Packets, which leave Malta on the 5th, 15th, and 25th.

(*b*) The Steam Packets of the Levant Line have an arrangement with the Austrian Lloyds, for the conveyance of merchandise from Syra for Patras, Zante, Corfu, Cephalonia, Brindisi, Ancona, Trieste, Fiume, and Venice; from Constantinople for Varna, Tulcia, Galatz, Ibraila, Inaboli, Sinope, Samsoun, and Trebisonde.

(*c*) Correspondence with the Italian Packets.

(*d*) Stoppage under steam at Hydra and Spezzia.

(*e*) Correspondence with the Packet going from Marseilles to Constantinople.

(*f*) Correspondence, the 2nd and 12th, with the Packets of the Egyptian Line.

(*g*) Correspondence with the Italian Packets.

(*h*) Stoppage under steam at Hydra and Spezzia.

(*i*) Quarantine of five days.

(1) The departures from Marseilles for Syria will take place as follows:—
By way of Smyrna, 11th June.
By way of Alexandria, 4th and 23rd June.

OBSERVATIONS.

Living.—Not included in the preceding fares:—1st class, 6 frs.; 2nd class, 4 frs. per day. Passengers of 3rd and 4th class are charged according to the accommodation they require.

Embarkation.—Conveyance of passenger and luggage on board the packet, police and sanitary permit, 5 frs.

Baggage.—1st class, 100 kilos free; 2nd class, 60 kilos; 3rd class, 30 kilos, or 60 lbs. English.

Children.—From two to ten years of age, half fare, for passage and living.

Passports.—Passengers must call at the Office of the Company, in Marseilles, in the afternoon of the day preceding the departure, to deposit their passports. The Agents of the Company undertake to perform gratuitously all the formalities required at Marseilles for the embarkation, such as obtaining the necessary *visas* of passports from the respective Consuls, only requiring payment of the fees paid for the *visas*.

Passage by Short Stages.—Passengers are allowed to land at one or more intermediate places, and continue their passage by the succeeding Packets of the Company, during the term of four months.

Return Tickets.—Persons taking Out and Home Tickets, and paying the fare in advance, are allowed 20 per cent. reduction. The Return Tickets are available for four months.

Family Tickets.—Families composed of three persons, at least, enjoy the privilege of a reduction of 20 per cent. In the event of a Family taking a Return Ticket, the reduction is 30 per cent

COMPAGNIE VALERY, FRÈRES.

FRENCH STEAMERS

For carrying the Despatches between MARSEILLES & CORSICA.

REGULAR SERVICE BETWEEN MARSEILLES & LEGHORN,

Performed in 24 hours, viz. :—

18 between MARSEILLES & BASTIA, and 6 between BASTIA & LEGHORN, CALLING AT BASTIA FOR THE DESPATCHES.

Other regular Services between MARSEILLES and AJACCIO, MARSEILLES and CALVI, or L'ILE ROUSSE.

DEPARTURES, &c.

FROM	DESTINATION.	ARRIVAL.
Marseilles	Leghorn, calling at Bastia every Sunday at 9 a.m.	Bastia, Monday morning Leghorn, Mond. evening
	Ajaccio, every Friday at 9 a.m.	Ajaccio, Satur. morning
	Calvi, or L'Ile Rousse, every Tuesday, noon	Calvi, or L'Isle Rousse, Wednesday morning
Leghorn	Marseilles, calling at Bastia, Wednesday evening...	Bastia, Thurs. morning Marseilles, Fri. morning
Ajaccio	Marseilles, every Tuesday at 9 a.m.	Marseilles, Wed. morning
Calvi, or L'Ile Rousse...	Marseilles, every Saturday, noon	Marseilles, Sun morning

3d Class is only for Sailors and Labourers, who are not allowed to enter the Cabins, but must remain on deck. Children under 10 years of age are charged half-fare. Passengers of the 1st Class are allowed 50 Kilogrammes of luggage, 2nd Class, 40 Kilogrammes, and 3d Class, 20 Kilogrammes. Excess luggage will be charged 3 frs. for 100 Kilogrammes between Marseilles and Corsica, and 6 frs. for 100 Kilogrammes between Marseilles and Leghorn. The fare for Provisions must be paid in advance.

Passengers missing the boat, and who have previously paid their fares, will not have their money returned, but may proceed by the following Steam-boat.

Dogs will be kept on deck, and will be charged 6 frs. between Marseilles and Corsica, and 10 frs. between Marseilles and Leghorn.

The freight of Goods between Marseilles and Corsica is regulated by a fixed rate under the Government, and that between Marseilles and Leghorn is according to the same contract.

All goods, which are not removed six hours after the arrival of the Steam-boat, are placed in the Custom-house at the risk of the owners. The loading and unloading of carriages, luggage, and goods, are at the expense of the owners.

TABLE OF FARES, &c.

NAMES OF PLACES.		TABLE OF FARES.			FARE FOR PROVISIONS.	
FROM.	TO	1st Class.	2nd Class.	3rd Class.	1st Class.	2nd Class.
Marseilles	Bastia	30 frs.	20 frs.	15 frs.	6 frs.	4 frs.
	Leghorn	60 ,,	40 ,,	21 ,,	9 ,,	6 ,,
	Ajaccio	30 ,,	20 ,,	15 ,,	6 ,,	4 ,,
	Calvi, or L'Ile Rousse	30 ,,	20 ,,	15 ,,	6 ,,	4 ,,
Bastia	Leghorn, and *vice versa*	15 ,,	12 ,,	6 ,,	—	—

N.B.—Passengers who book for Leghorn or Marseilles may land in Corsica, Bastia, Ajaccio, Calvi, or L'Ile Rousse, and may remain one month. Passports must be sent to the Offices of the Steam-boats the evening before the departure of the boats by which they wish to proceed.

For further particulars, apply to Messrs. VALERY, BROTHERS, at Marseilles; VALERY, SONS, at Leghorn; FORCIOLI, BROTHERS, at Ajaccio; VALERY, BROTHERS, at Bastia; Mr. ROCCA RUTILI, at Calvi; JAMES SEMIDEI, at L'Ile Rousse. [7

SOUTH EASTERN RAILWAY.—The Continental Route.

LONDON TO PARIS, IN TWELVE HOURS,

By Special Tidal Trains and Steamers, *viâ* Folkestone and Boulogne.

A Special Express Train *leaves London for Paris every day.—By this Route Passengers always walk on board and on shore; small boats are never used.*

JUNE.		Leave London.	† Leave Folkestone.	Leave Boulogne.	Arrive in Paris.
1	Wednesday	1 55 p.m.	4 45 p.m.	8 0 p.m.	4 45 a.m.
2	Thursday...	2 55 ...	5 45 ...	8 45 ...	4 45 ...
3	Friday	5 30 a.m.	*8 15 a.m.	12 30 ...	6 40 p.m.
4	Saturday ...	5 55 ...	*8 45 ...	12 30 ...	6 40 ...
5	Sunday......	6 0 ...	*8 45 ...	12 30 ...	6 40 ...
6	Monday......	5 55 ..	*8 45 ...	12 30 ...	6 40 ...
7	Tuesday.....	5 55 ...	8 45 ...	12 30 ...	6 40 ...
8	Wednesday.	8 10 ...	11 0 ...	3 0 ...	8 45 ...
9	Thursday...	8 10 ...	11 0 ...	3 0 ...	8 45 ...
10	Friday.......	8 10 ...	11 0 ...	3 0 ...	8 45 ...
11	Saturday....	10 30 ...	1 15 p.m.	5 15 ...	10 45 ...
12	Sunday......	8 10 ...	1 45 ...	5 15 ...	10 45 ...
13	Monday ...	10 50 ...	1 45 ...	5 15 ...	10 45 ...
14	Tuesday ...	10 50 ...	1 45 ...	5 15 ...	10 45 ...
15	Wednesday	11 50 ...	2 45 ...	6 30 ...	12 0 midnt.
16	Thursday..	1 10 p.m.	4 0 ...	8 0 ...	4 45 a.m.
17	Friday	1 55 ...	4 45 ...	8 0 ...	4 45 ...
18	Saturday ...	2 55 ...	5 45 ...	8 45 ...	4 45 ..
19	Sunday......	5 30 a.m.	*8 15 a.m.	12 30 ...	6 40 p.m.
20	Monday	5 55 ...	*8 45 ...	12 30 ...	6 40 ...
21	Tuesday ...	5 55 ...	*8 45 ...	12 30 ...	6 40 ...
22	Wednesday	8 10 ...	11 0 ...	3 0 ...	8 45 ...
23	Thursday...	8 10 ...	11 0 ...	3 0 ...	8 45 ...
24	Friday	8 10 ...	11 0 ...	3 0 ...	8 45 ...
25	Saturday ...	10 50 ...	1 45 p.m.	5 15 ...	10 45 ..
26	Sunday......	8 10 ...	1 45 ...	5 15 ...	10 45 ...
27	Monday ...	10 50 ...	1 45 ...	5 15 ...	10 45 ...
28	Tuesday ...	10 50 ...	2 0 ...	5 15 ...	10 45 ...
29	Wednesday	12 10 p.m.	3 0 ...	6 30 ...	12 0 midnt.
30	Thursday...	1 10 ...	4 0 ...	8 0 ...	4 45 a.m.

† *Weather permitting.*

* *There is another Departure from Folkestone on these days.* *See next page.*

Fares by Through Tickets:

London to Paris.......................First Class, £2 11s. 6d.; Second Class, £1 17s.
London to Boulogne ....First Class, £1 9s. 0d.; Second Class, £1 0s.
Return Ticket, *London to Paris, First Class, £4 10s. 0d.; Second Class, £3 0s.*
The Return Tickets are available for One Month from the date of issue, via Calais or Boulogne.

PARIS TO LONDON, IN TWELVE HOURS,

By Special Tidal Trains and Steamers, *viâ* Folkestone and Boulogne.

A Special Express Train *leaves Paris for London every day.—By this Route, Passengers always walk on board and on shore; small boats are never used.*

JUNE.		Leave Paris.	† Leave Boulogne.	Leave Folkestone.	Arrive in London.
1	Wednesday	10 0 a.m.	5 0 p.m.	8 30 p.m.	11 0 p.m.
2	Thursday ..	10 0 ...	5 45 ...	9 15 ...	11 45 ...
3	Friday	10 0 ...	*6 30 ...	10 0 ...	12 30 a.m.
4	Saturday ..	10 0 ...	*7 15 ...	10 15 ...	12 45 ...
5	Sunday	10 0 ...	*7 45 ...	10 45 ...	1 15 ...
6	Monday	5 0 ...	*10 30 a.m.	2 3 ...	6 0 p.m.
7	Tuesday ..	5 0 ...	11 0 ...	3 10 ...	5 45 ...
8	Wednesday	5 30 ...	11 30 ...	3 10 ...	5 45 ...
9	Thursday ..	6 25 ...	12 0 noon	3 45 ...	6 15 ...
10	Friday	6 25 ...	12 15 p.m.	3 45 ...	6 15 ...
11	Saturday ..	7 30 ...	1 30 ...	5 18 ...	9 15 ...
12	Sunday	7 30 ...	1 45 ...	5 50 ...	9 45 ...
13	Monday	7 30 ...	1 45 ...	5 18 ...	9 15 ...
14	Tuesday ..	10 0 ...	4 0 ...	7 30 ...	10 15 ...
15	Wednesday	10 0 ...	4 0 ...	7 30 ...	10 15 ...
16	Thursday ..	10 0 ...	4 0 ...	7 30 ...	10 15 ...
17	Friday	10 0 ...	4 45 ...	8 0 ...	10 30 ...
18	Saturday ..	10 0 ...	5 45 ...	9 15 ...	11 45 ...
19	Sunday	10 0 ...	*6 45 ...	10 15 ...	12 45 a.m.
20	Monday ..	10 0 ...	*7 45 ...	10 45 ...	1 15 ...
21	Tuesday ..	5 0 ...	*10 30 a.m.	2 3 ...	6 0 p.m.
22	Wednesday	5 0 ...	11 0 ...	3 10 ...	5 45 ...
23	Thursday ..	6 25 ...	12 0 noon.	3 45 ...	6 15 ...
24	Friday	6 25 ...	12 15 p.m.	3 45 ...	6 15 ...
25	Saturday ..	7 30 ...	1 45 ...	5 18 ...	9 15 ...
26	Sunday	7 30 ..	1 45 ...	5 50 ...	9 45 ...
27	Monday	7 30 ...	1 45 ...	5 18 ...	9 15 ...
28	Tuesday ..	10 0 ...	4 0 ...	7 30 ...	10 15 ...
29	Wednesday	10 0 ...	4 0 ...	7 30 ...	10 15 ..
30	Thursday ..	10 0 ...	4 0 ...	7 30 ...	10 15 ...

† *Weather permitting.*

* *There is another Departure from Boulogne on these days.* *See next page.*

Fares by Through Tickets:

Paris to London, via Boulogne ... First Class, £2 11s. 6d.; Second Class, £1 17s.
Boulogne to London.................. First Class, £1 9s. 0d.; Second Class, £1 0s.
Return Ticket, *London to Paris, First Class, £4 10s. 0d.; Second Class, £3 0s.*
The Return Tickets are available for One Month from the date of issue, via Calais or Boulogne.

LONDON TO PARIS, BRUSSELS, COLOGNE, &c.,
Via DOVER AND CALAIS.

Daily Direct Service, Morning and Evening, between **London and the Continent,** by Steamers sailing at fixed hours, weather permitting.

FROM LONDON.

London ......depart.	8 10 a.m.	8 30 p.m.
Dover .... ,,	11 0 ...	*11 15 ...
Calais .... ,,	3 0 p.m.	2 0 a.m.
Lille ....arrive.	5 15 ...	4 0 ...
Paris............ ,,	10 45 ...	9 0 ...
Brussels .... ,,	10 10 ...	10 45 ...
Cologne ...... ,,	5 0 a.m.	6 0 p.m.

* On Sundays the Mail Packet does not sail from Dover.

TO LONDON.

Cologne. depart.	11 30 p.m.	...	8 0 a.m.
Brussels ,,	6 30 a.m.	10 30 a.m.	4 30 p.m.
Paris ... ,,	7 30 ...	11 45 ...	7 30 ...
Lille...... ,,	12 35 p.m.	6 30 p.m.	12 0 midnt.
Calais ... ,,	3 30 ...	10 0 ...	2 30 a.m.
Dover ... ,,	7 30 ..	2 0 a.m.	5 20 ...
London arrive.	10 15 ...	4 50 ...	8 6 ...

The depatrures of the Trains from Dover and Calais correspond with the arrivals of the Steamers; but the Trains do not wait when the Vessels are detained by stress of weather; in those cases, Through Passengers must proceed by the next regular Train.

Fares by Through Tickets.

	First Class.		Second Class.
London to Paris, *via* Calais.........	£3 1 0	...	£2 3 9
London to Calais	1 10 0	...	1 0 8
London to Brussels, *via* Calais.....	2 7 7	...	1 14 0
London to Cologne.......................	3 6 4	...	2 7 8
Return Tickets, London to Paris and back	4 10 0	...	3 0 0

The Return Tickets are available for One Month from the date of issue, via *Calais or Boulogne.*

FOLKESTONE AND BOULOGNE, AND DOVER AND CALAIS,

The South Eastern and Continental Steam Packet Company's unrivalled Steam Ships sail every day, each way, weather permitting.

	JUNE.	From Folkestone.	From Boulogne.
1	Wednesdy.	4 45 p.m.	5 0 p.m.
2	Thursday .	5 45 ...	5 45 ...
3	Friday ...	8 15a.m., 7 30p.m.	8 15a.m., 6 30 p.m.
4	Saturday...	8 45 ,, 7 30 ,,	8 15 ,, 7 15 ,,
5	Sunday ...	8 45 ,, 7 45 ,,	9 30 ,, 7 45 ,,
6	Monday ...	8 45 ,, 8 30 ,,	10½ ,, 8 30 ,,
7	Tuesday ...	8 45 a.m.	11 0 a.m.
8	Wednesdy.	11 0 ...	11 30 ...
9	Thursday .	11 0 ...	12 0 noon
10	Friday	11 0 ...	12 15 p.m.
11	Saturday...	1 15 p.m.	1 30 ...
12	Sunday.....	1 45 ...	1 45 ...
13	Monday ...	1 45 ...	1 45 ...
14	Tuesday ...	1 45 ...	4 0 ...
15	Wednesdy.	2 45 ...	4 0 ...
16	Thursday .	4 0 ...	4 0 ...
17	Friday ...	4 45 ...	4 45 ..
18	Saturday...	5 45 ...	5 45 ...
19	Sunday.....	8 15a.m., 6 45p.m.	8 15 a.m., 6 45 p.m.
20	Monday....	8 45 ,, 7 45 ,,	8 15 ,, 7 45 ,,
21	Tuesday ...	8 45 ,, 8 45 ,,	10½ ,, 8 45 ,,
22	Wednesdy.	11 0 a.m.	11 0 a.m.
23	Thursday .	11 0 ...	12 0 noon.
24	Friday	11 0 ...	12 15 p.m.
25	Saturday..	1 45 p.m.	1 45 ...
26	Sunday	1 45 ...	1 45 ...
27	Monday ...	1 45 ...	1 45 ...
28	Tuesday ...	2 0 ...	4 0 ...
29	Wednesdy.	3 0 ...	4 0 ...
30	Thursday..	4 0 ...	4 0 ...

From DOVER, every day at 11 a.m.
From CALAIS, every day at 3½ p.m.
For Special Trains in correspondence with the above, see page 333.

Fares.—Chief Cabin, 8s.; Fore Cabin, 6s.; Children, 4s. Carriages, 4-wheel, £2 2s.; 2-wheel, £1 1s; Horses £1 5s.; Dogs, 2s. 6d. Double Journey Tickets at a fare-and-a-half, are issued on Saturdays, and are available until the following Monday Evening. [L.O.—8.

OCEAN PARCELS' DELIVERY COMPANY,

4, AGAR STREET, STRAND (Opposite CHARING CROSS HOSPITAL.)

THIS COMPANY has been formed with the view of supplying a cheap, rapid, and certain conveyance for Small Parcels, as well as large quantities of Goods, by the best established Steamers and Sailing Vessels, to all parts of the world. Every one having correspondents or relations abroad, must have felt the want of such a medium of communication; and it shall be the constant effort of this Company to supply this great desideratum, directing their attention to the three chief points—Rapidity, Certainty, and Cheapness. Despatches are regularly made up for Australia, India, North and South America, the West Indies, the Continent of Europe, and all Parts of the World.

Insurances effected free of Commission. **G. W. FIELD, Manager.**

[L.O.—242

PARIS AND THE CONTINENT,
DIRECT SERVICE
VIA NEWHAVEN AND DIEPPE.

THE BRIGHTON STEAM PACKET COMPANY'S NEW AND POWERFUL STEAMERS

are intended to sail (wind and weather permitting),

At the times stated in the Table on the outside Cover of this Book.

If a bound Special Edition, look to the second page of the fly-leaf at the commencement of the Book; also to BRADSHAW'S (MONTHLY) GENERAL RAILWAY AND STEAM NAVIGATION GUIDE for Great Britain and Ireland.

THROUGH FARES.—LONDON TO PARIS.
First Class, 24s.; Second Class and Best Cabin, 20s.; Second Class, 17s.

These Tickets are available for four days including the date of issue, thus giving passengers who do not desire to proceed direct to Paris, the opportunity of staying a short time at Dieppe or Rouen, and they are available by any of the ordinary trains, as well as by the special and express trains running in connection with the steamers.

PASSPORTS MAY BE HAD AT THE STEAM PACKET OFFICE, NEWHAVEN, AT A COST OF 5S.

FARES.—Newhaven to Dieppe, First Class, 12s.; Second Class, 9s. Horses, 25s. Carriages, 4-wheels, 40s.; 2-wheel ditto, 25s.; Dogs, 3s. each. London to Dieppe, First Class, 18s.; Second Class, 14s.; Horses, 40s.; Carriages, 4-wheels, 60s.; 2-wheel ditto, 40s.; Dogs, 4s. Through Tickets from Newhaven to Paris, or from Dieppe to London, must be obtained at the Offices of the Company, at Newhaven or Dieppe, as they are not delivered on board the Steamer. The baggage of passengers, proceeding direct from London to Paris, will be examined at the Custom House at Dieppe.

For further particulars, apply to A. D. BOSSON, 36, Rue Basse du Rempart, Paris; and 35, Quai Henri IV., Dieppe; Rouen, H. DELAFOSSE, Grand Hotel d'Angleterre; to H. P. MAPLES, at the Company's Offices, 5, Arthur Street East, opposite the Monument, London Bridge; or to any Station on the London, Brighton, and South Coast, or Paris and Dieppe lines of Railway.

LONDON TO JERSEY, via NEWHAVEN.

FROM NEWHAVEN.

SATURDAY, June 4	at 12.30 noon.	Last Train,	10 a.m.
,, ,, 11	at 4.30 p.m.	,,	2 p.m.
,, ,, 18	at 9.30 p.m.	,,	7 p.m.
,, ,, 25	at 4.30 p.m.	,,	2 p.m.

FROM JERSEY.

MONDAY, June 6	at 3 p.m.
,, ,, 13	at 7 p.m.
,, ,, 20	at 3 p.m.
,, ,, 27	at 7 p.m.

FARES (including Steward's Fee):—

	1st Class and Best Cabin.	2nd Class and Fore Cabin.	3rd Class and Steerage.
From London to Jersey	21s. 0d.	16s. 0d.	10s. 0d.
From Newhaven to Jersey	15s. 0d.	12s. 0d.	7s. 6d.

Parcels of every description will be received at the London Bridge Terminus, or 5, Arthur Street East, London Bridge. Goods will be Carted or Lightered at very low rates. All Goods should be addressed as follows:—"*To Jersey, per London, Brighton, and South Coast Railway and Steam Boat.*"

N.B.—Bonded Goods must be sent to the Station before 6 p.m., two days, and Free Goods not later than the evening, before sailing.

For further particulars apply to A. D. BOSSON, Newhaven; JAMES WILLIAM DEAL, Jersey; H. P. MAPLES, 5, Arthur Street East, London Bridge; or at any Station on this Company's line of Railway. [L.O.—10

NETHERLANDS STEAM PACKET COMPANY.

STEAM NAVIGATION BETWEEN LONDON AND ROTTERDAM, by the powerful Steam-Ship "BATAVIER," WM. SMITH Commander, 200 Horse power, burthen 500 Tons, from St. Katharine's Steam Wharf, provided with 42 berths and 23 sofas, dining-room, two state cabins, containing seven berths and three sofas, which can be had separately. Leaving Rotterdam every Tuesday, and London every Sunday morning, regularly.

Also the fine Dutch Screw Steamer, "FYENOORD," **leaves London** (off the Tower) on **Thursday Mornings,** and **Rotterdam** on **Sundays.** For hours of departure, &c., see below; and also Bradshaw's General Railway and Steam Conveyance Guide, for Great Britain and Ireland, for June.

Steam Navigation on the Rhine, between Rotterdam and Mannheim; from Rotterdam by way of Arnhem or Nymegen, Emmerich, Wesel, Dusseldorf, Cologne, Bonn, Neuwied, Coblenz, Bingen, Biebrich, Wisbaden, Mayence, Frankfort, Worms, Ludwigshafen, and Mannheim, daily, at 6 a.m. Brom Mannheim to Rotterdam also daily, arriving at Rotterdam $1\frac{1}{2}$ days after leaving Mannheim.

The steamers of the Netherland Steam-Boat Company on the Rhine, running in communication with the "BATAVIER," as also most other steamers of this company, are provided with separate rooms, containing each two berths and one sofa. **Fares for Passengers between London and Mannheim going by the Steamers of the Netherland Steam Boat Company.**

TO OR FROM LONDON AND	SINGLE JOURNEY.												OUT AND HOME.								
	STATE CABIN.			SALOON.			FORE CABIN.			DECK.			STATE CABIN.			SALOON.			FORE CABIN.		
	£	s.	d.	£	s.	d.	£	s.	d.	£	s.	d.	£	s.	d.	£	s.	d.	£	s.	d.
Rotterdam	2	2	0	1	10	0	0	17	6	0	14	0	2	16	0	2	5	0	1	6	3
Nymegen, Arnhem	2	8	0	1	12	0	0	19	0	0	15	0	3	4	0	2	8	0	1	8	6
Dusseldorf	2	10	0	1	14	0	1	0	0	0	16	9	3	6	8	2	11	0	1	10	0
Cologne	2	12	0	1	16	0	1	1	0	0	17	6	3	9	4	2	14	0	1	11	6
Wesseling	2	13	2	1	16	9	1	1	5	0	17	10	3	10	11	2	15	2	1	12	1
Bonn	2	13	6	1	17	0	1	1	6	0	17	11	3	11	4	2	15	6	1	12	3
Plittersdorf	2	13	9	1	17	2	1	1	7	0	18	0	3	11	8	2	15	9	1	12	5
Königswinter	2	14	1	1	17	4	1	1	8	0	18	1	3	12	1	2	16	0	1	12	6
Rolandseck	2	14	4	1	17	7	1	1	9	0	18	1	3	12	5	2	16	4	1	12	8
Unkel, Remagen	2	14	11	1	17	11	1	2	0	0	18	3	3	13	3	2	16	11	1	13	0
Linz	2	15	6	1	18	4	1	2	2	0	18	5	3	14	0	2	17	6	1	13	3
Brohl	2	16	1	1	18	9	1	2	4	0	18	7	3	14	9	2	18	1	1	13	7
Andernach	2	16	8	1	19	1	1	2	7	0	18	8	3	15	7	2	18	8	1	13	10
Neuwied	2	17	3	1	19	6	1	2	9	0	18	10	3	16	4	2	19	3	1	14	2
Engers	2	18	2	2	0	1	1	3	1	0	19	1	3	17	7	3	0	2	1	14	7
Coblenz	2	18	5	2	0	3	1	3	2	0	19	2	3	17	11	3	0	5	1	14	9
Branbach	2	19	4	2	0	10	1	3	5	0	19	4	3	19	1	3	1	3	1	15	2
Boppard	2	19	11	2	1	3	1	3	8	0	19	5	3	19	10	3	1	11	1	15	6
St. Goar	3	0	9	2	1	10	1	3	11	0	19	9	4	1	0	3	2	9	1	15	11
Oberwesel, Caub	3	1	8	2	2	5	1	4	3	0	19	11	4	2	2	3	3	8	1	16	4
Bacharach, Lorch	3	2	3	2	2	10	1	4	5	1	0	2	4	3	0	3	4	3	1	16	7
Bingen, Rudesheim, Geisenheim	3	3	1	2	3	5	1	4	8	1	0	4	4	4	1	3	5	1	1	17	1
Oestrich, Eltville, Walluf	3	4	3	2	4	2	1	5	1	1	0	7	4	5	8	3	6	3	1	17	8
Biebrich, Mainz	3	4	7	2	4	4	1	5	2	1	0	7	4	6	1	3	6	6	1	17	10
Oppenheim	3	5	9	2	5	2	1	5	7	1	1	0	4	7	8	3	7	9	1	18	4
Gernsheim	3	6	7	2	5	9	1	5	10	1	1	2	4	8	9	3	8	7	1	18	10
Rheindurkheim	3	7	2	2	6	1	1	6	1	1	1	4	4	9	7	3	9	2	1	19	1
Worms	3	8	1	2	6	8	1	6	4	1	1	7	4	10	9	3	10	0	1	19	6
Ludwigshafen, Mannheim	3	9	6	2	7	8	1	6	10	1	1	11	4	12	8	3	11	6	2	0	3

SAILINGS OF THE "BATAVIER" DURING JUNE, 1853.

From London.

Sunday, June 5, ... 12.0 noon.
" " 12, ... 9.0 a.m.
" " 19, ... 12.0 noon.
" " 26, ... 9.0 a.m.

From Rotterdam.

Tuesday, June 7, ... 11.0 a.m.
" " 14, ... 8.0 a.m.
" " 21, ... 11.0 a.m.
" " 28, ... 7.0 a.m.

"FYENOORD" from London on Thursdays.
" from Rotterdam on Sundays.

N.B.—Tickets for Deck places are only issued to those who can show official certificates of their indigence. The fare for a two-wheel Carriage is equal to the fare in the State Cabin. The fare for a four-wheel Carriage is twice the fare in the Chief Cabin. The fare for a Carriage packed in a case is 50 per cent. additional. The fare for a Horse is equal to the fare in the State Cabin. The fare for a Dog to Rotterdam, 7s. 6d. Agents in London: PHILLIPS, GRAVES & PHILLIPS, 11, Rood-lane, City.

RHINE STEAM NAVIGATION.

(DUSSELDORF COMPANY.)

THE ONLY COMPANY NAVIGATING THE RHINE BETWEEN

ROTTERDAM, COLOGNE, AND MANNHEIM,

In Direct Connexion with the GENERAL STEAM NAVIGATION COMPANY from and to LONDON *viâ* Rotterdam, Antwerp, or Ostend, and the GRAND DUCAL BADEN RAILWAY between Mannheim and Basle.

This Company possess the *Fastest Steamers on the Rhine, fitted up in the most elegant manner, with every accommodation and convenience for the Traveller, and propelled by Low-pressure Engines, made by those well-known Engineers, Messrs. Miller, Ravenhill, and Co., and Messrs. Maudsley, Field, and Co.*

The Departures, as well as the arrivals at the principal Towns, and at the different places on the Rhine, visited by the Tourist for its Splendid Scenery, are several times DAILY, and so arranged as to correspond at Mannheim, Mayence, Biebrich, Bonn, Cologne, and Arnhem, with the Departures and Arrivals of the Railway Trains, affording the opportunity of a continuous travelling, and of performing the distances in an unprecedented short time.

Travellers can book direct, *viâ* Rotterdam, Antwerp, or Ostend, and obtain Bills containing Fares and the Hours of Departures, as well as every other information—

In England. LONDON, at the General Steam Navigation Company's Offices, 71, Lombard-street, and 37, Regent Circus, Piccadilly; and of all the Agents of that Establishment in the Country and on the Continent—in the Monthly Bills, and in their useful, much-sought-after Yellow Book.

In Holland and on the Rhine. ROTTERDAM, of Mr. J. P. de Cock, and at all the Agents of the Lower and Middle Rhine Dusseldorf Company.

In Belgium .. BRUSSELS, Mr. Wm. Middleton, 94, Montagne de la Cour.—AIX-LA-CHAPELLE, Mr. Wengler, Library, next door to the Hotel "The Grand Monarch."

In Frankfurt on the Main Of Mr. Fletcher, at Messrs. Gogel, Koch, and Co., and of Mr. G. Krebs, Zeil, opposite the Post Office.

Paris .... Mr. F. Spiers, 13, Rue de la Paix.

In Baden ...... MANNHEIM, Mr. Reichard, and at all the Offices at the Station of the Grand Ducal Baden Railway.

For Hours of Departure and Fares, see following pages.

FARES ON THE RHINE.

		Chief Cabin.				Fore Cabin.			
		th.	sg.	s.	d.	th.	sg.	s.	d.
ROTTERDAM to	Cologne	5	10	15	6	2	20	7	9
	Coblence	7	16	22	0	3	23	11	0
	Mainz	9	22	28	4	4	26	14	2
	Mannheim	11	10	33	0	5	20	16	6
COLOGNE to	Coblence	2	6	6	5	1	3	3	3
	Mainz	4	12	12	10	2	6	6	5
	Mannheim	6	0	17	6	3	0	8	9
BONN to	Coblence	1	22	5	0	0	26	2	6
	Mainz	3	28	11	6	1	29	5	9
	Mannheim	5	16	16	2	2	23	8	1
COBLENCE to	Mainz	2	6	6	6	1	3	3	3
	Mannheim	3	24	11	1	1	27	5	7
MAINZ to	Manheim	1	18	4	8	0	24	2	4

NOTE.—Return tickets are issued on the Rhine, for any place, at a fare and a half

[*For Continuation see next page.*

Dusseldorf Steam Navigation Company, in correspondence with the **General Steam Navigation Company and Grand Ducal Baden Railway.—From Rotterdam**—Monday, Wednesday, Friday, and Saturday, at 6 a.m., to Dusseldorf, Cologne, Coblence, Mayence, and Mannheim. N.B.—Passengers leaving Rotterdam on the days mentioned, arrive the next evening at Coblence, and the following day at Mayence and Mannheim.

From Dusseldorf.

7 a.m. daily, to Coblence, Mayence, & Mannheim.

$11\frac{3}{4}$ p.m., Monday, Wednesday, Thursday, and Saturday, to Rotterdam; Monday and Thursday, in correspondence with the London Mail Ships of the General Steam Navigation Company, leaving Rotterdam every Wednesday and Saturday morning.

From Cologne.

$5\frac{3}{4}$ a.m. daily, to Mayence (Frankfurt) in 1 day.

$12\frac{1}{2}$ noon, daily to Coblence.

$6\frac{3}{4}$ p.m. daily to Dusseldorf.

$6\frac{3}{4}$ p.m., Monday, Wednesday, Thursday, and Saturday, to Dusseldorf and Rotterdam.

$3\frac{1}{4}$ p.m. to Mayence and Mannheim.

From Bonn

3 a.m. to Mayence in one day, after arrival of first train from Cologne.

$3\frac{3}{4}$ p.m. to Coblence.

$2\frac{1}{4}$ p.m. daily, to Cologne and last train to Aix.

$3\frac{3}{4}$ p.m. to Coblence.

4 p.m. to Cologne and Dusseldorf.

4 p.m. on Monday, Wednesday, Thursday, and Saturday, to Rotterdam, as by Dusseldorf.

$6\frac{3}{4}$ p.m. to Cologne.

$10\frac{3}{4}$ p.m. to Mayence and Mannheim, arriving at Bieberich and Mayence in time to proceed with train to Frankfurt.

From Coblence.

$3\frac{1}{2}$ a.m. daily, to Mayence & to Mannheim in one day, also at Bieberich and Mayence, in time to proceed to Frankfurt.

From Coblence—Continued.

$6\frac{1}{2}$ a.m. to Mainz and Mannheim.

12 noon, daily to Mainz.

$11\frac{3}{4}$ a.m. to Cologne.

$1\frac{1}{2}$ p.m. to Cologne and Dusseldorf.

$1\frac{1}{2}$ p.m., on Monday, Wednesday, Thursday, and Saturday, to Rotterdam, as by Dusseldorf.

$4\frac{1}{4}$ p.m. to Cologne.

From Bieberich.

$7\frac{3}{4}$ a.m. daily, to Cologne.

$9\frac{1}{4}$ a.m. daily, to Cologne.

$9\frac{1}{4}$ a.m. daily, to Mannheim.

$12\frac{1}{4}$ noon daily, to Cologne and Dusseldorf.

$9\frac{1}{4}$ a.m. daily, on Monday, Wednesday, Thursday, and Saturday, to Rotterdam.

$1\frac{1}{2}$ p.m. daily to Mannheim.

From Mayence.

Daily, to Mannheim.

$7\frac{1}{2}$ a.m. daily, to Cologne.

9 a.m. daily, to Cologne and Dusseldorf.

12 noon daily, to Cologne.

9 a.m., on Monday, Wednesday, Thursday, and Saturday, to Rotterdam.

$10\frac{1}{2}$ a.m. daily, to Mannheim.

$2\frac{1}{2}$ p.m. daily, to Mannheim

From Mannheim.

5 a.m. daily, to Mayence, Cologne, and Dusseldorf.

5 a.m. on Monday, Wednesday, Thursday, and Saturday, to Dusseldorf, and Rotterdam, as by Dusseldorf.

$4\frac{3}{4}$ p.m. daily, to Mainz.

DIRECT FARES FROM LONDON	Via Rotterdam.								Via Antwrp and from Cologne, exclusive of Belgian Railway fare.				Via Ostend and from Cologne, exclusive of Belgian Railway fare.			
	Out, or Single Journey.				Out & Home, or Double Journey.											
TO	Chief Cabin.		Fore Cabin.		Chief Cabin.		Fore Cabin.		Chief Cabin.		Fore Cabin.		Chief Cabin.		Fore Cabin.	
	s.	d.	s.	d.	s.	d.	s.	d.	s.	d.	s.	d.	s.	d.	s.	d.
Dusseldorf	34	0	20	0	51	0	30	0	..		..		..		..	
Cologne	36	0	21	0	54	0	31	6	..		..		..		..	
Bonn	37	0	21	6	55	6	32	3	31	4	20	8	21	4	15	8
Neuwied	39	6	22	9	59	3	34	2	35	3	22	10	25	8	17	10
Coblence	40	3	23	2	60	5	34	9	36	6	23	3	26	6	18	3
Bingen	43	5	24	8	65	1	37	1	41	1	25	7	31	1	20	8
Bieberich	44	4	25	2	66	6	37	10	42	10	26	5	32	10	21	6
Wiesbaden	45	0	25	10	67	9	39	2	43	6	27	0	33	3	22	0
Mayence	44	4	25	2	66	6	37	10	42	10	26	5	32	10	21	6
Mannheim	47	8	26	10	71	6	40	3	47	6	28	9	34	6	23	9
Baden-Baden	55	8	32	4	..		..		56	0	34	7	46	0	29	7
Kehl (Strasbourg)	58	0	34	1	92	2	54	9	58	6	36	4	48	6	31	4
Freiburg	62	4	36	10	100	10	60	3	62	6	39	1	52	6	34	1
Basle	67	2	40	10	..		..		67	6	42	2	57	6	39	1

ENGLISH & BELGIAN GOVERNMENT NEW FAST STEAMERS BETWEEN

DOVER AND OSTEND.

PERFORMING THE VOYAGE IN ABOUT FOUR HOURS,

Carrying the Prussian, Hamburgh, and Rotterdam Mails, and Commanded by Officers of the Royal Navy. The shortest and most agreeable route, as regards Customs, Passports, non-changing of Carriages, &c.

A Steamer leaves OSTEND every evening (except Saturday), at 6.30
,, ,, DOVER every night (except Sunday), at 11.15

Routes to and from England to Belgium, the Rhine, and Germany.

NOTE.—The distance to Cologne, the Rhine, and all Germany, is 110 Kilometres, or nearly 70 Miles less from Ostend than from Calais.

From LONDON.

LONDON	Dep.	8.30 p.m.
DOVER	Arr.	11. 0 ,,
,,	Dep.	11.15 ,,
OSTEND	Dep.	7.15 a.m.
MALINES	Arr.	10 10 ,,
BRUSSELS	Arr.	10.45 ,,
*COLOGNE	Arr.	6. 0 p.m.
COLOGNE, for Hamburgh, Leipsic, Berlin, Vienna, Trieste, &c.	Dep.	8. 0 ,,

By no route can Cologne be reached from England earlier than 6.0 p.m.

From GERMANY, the RHINE, and BELGIUM.

COLOGNE (Night Train)	Dep.	11.30 p.m.
BRUSSELS	Arr.	7.25 a.m.
OSTEND	Arr.	11.30 a.m.
COLOGNE, Mail Day Train.*	Dep.	8. 0 a.m.
OSTEND	Arr.	6.20 p.m.
BRUSSELS	Dep.	2.45 ,,
MALINES	Arr.	2.55 ,,
MALINES	Dep.	3.10 ,,
OSTEND	Arr.	6.20 ,,
,, (Steamer)	Dep.	6.30 ,,
DOVER	arrive about	11.0 ,,
,,	Dep.	2. 0 a.m.
LONDON	Arr.	4.50 ,,

There are also Trains at 5.20, 7.15, 8, 9.15, 11.45, and 2, from Dover to London.

*Travellers must leave Cologne by 7 a m. Train. No other reaches Ostend or Calais the same night.

Travellers may obtain Through Tickets and Pay their Fares to and from

		£	s.	d.		Fr.	c.		£	s.	d.		Fr.	c.
LONDON and OSTEND	1st Class.	1	17	3	or	47	20	2nd Class.	1	5	3	or	31	45
,, ,, BRUSSELS		2	6	6	or	57	70		1	11	6	or	39	35
,, ,, AIX-LA-CHAPELLE		2	17	6	or	71	50		1	19	9	or	49	30
,, ,, COLOGNE		3	5	0	or	81	00		2	6	3	or	57	50

By Express Trains on South Eastern, 1st Class Tickets admitted **without extra charge**; 2nd Class pay 7s. 4d. extra. These Tickets, or any portions of them, are available AT ANY TIME, THEY need not be used on the day they are purchased.

They also entitle the holder, during One Month from date of Continental Railway portion of Ticket, TO STOP at all the principal towns between Ostend and Cologne, or vice versa, and to continue his route at pleasure; the names of the towns are attached to the tickets.

BY STEAMERS ONLY.

FARES—First Class, 15s.; 2nd Class, 10s.; Children, 7s. 6d. and 5s.

OFFICES, AGENTS, AND CORRESPONDENTS OF THE BELGIAN AND ENGLISH GOVERNMENT STEAMERS.

Those marked * issue Direct Through Tickets.

LONDON, Mail and Continental Parcels' Daily Express Office, 52, Gracechurch-street; Admiralty and Universal Office, 34, Regent Circus; 9, Weymouth-st., Portland-place (Belgian Legation); 52, Gracechurch-st. (Belgian Consulate); *London Bridge Station South-Eastern Railway, and 40, Regent Circus; all the principal Hotels, Clubs, &c.—LIVERPOOL, 13, Water-street, H. Smith & Co.—EDINBURGH, 23, Waterloo-place, Harthill & Co.—MANCHESTER, T. C. Cartwright, 32, Cooper-st.—OSTEND, 15, Georges-st., Louis Carbon, Exchange Office.—*BRUSSELS, 74, Montagne de la Cour, John Piddington, General Agent; and *North Railway Station.—*MALINES Railway Station.—ANTWERP, C. Froment, bookseller, 665, Marché aux Souliers.—BRUGES, 2, Rue des Pierres, J. Molhant.—GHENT, 1, Rue de Brabant, A. Daele—LIEGE, 8, Place-Verte.—*AIX-LA-CHAPELLE, E. Ter Meer, Book and Musicseller, Holegraben, No. 478, *Railway Station,—*COLOGNE, 6 and 8, Frederic-Willem-street, Ristelhueber, Expéditeur; *2, Frederic-Willem-street, Assenheimer, bookseller; and the *Rhenish Railway Station. PARIS, Jonas's British and Foreign Advertiser Office, 72, Rue Basse du Rempart.

See also Bradshaw's British Railway and Steam Navigation Guide, and South Eastern Time Book.

Travellers must be provided with Passports, see page 6.—Commodious **Waiting Room** on the Quay at OSTEND, with Refreshments. Luggage and Passports (which are indispensable) examined in the same Building. Luggage belonging to Passengers proceeding to or from Germany is not examined by the Belgian Customs, if declared for transit, at Ostend, Cologne, or Aix-la-Chapelle.—At DOVER and OSTEND, Luggage of Passengers arriving by Mails IS NOW examined at any hour of the day or night.—**The opening of the Admiralty Pier at Dover, will in future render Boating unnecessary.**—NOTE—At the Brussels Office the highest rate of Exchange is given for all monies.

N.B.—These Packets convey Parcels and Samples, daily, to and from all parts of the Continent, at a fixed and moderate charge WHICH TRAVEL WITH THE MAIL THROUGHOUT. Office, 52, Gracechurch Street. [15

STEAM COMMUNICATION

MONTHLY FROM

LIVERPOOL TO NEW YORK, BALTIMORE, PITTSBURG, CINCINNATI, CHARLESTON, HAVANA, &c. BY WAY OF PHILADELPHIA.

THE LIVERPOOL & PHILADELPHIA STEAM-SHIP COMPANY

Intend sailing their new Iron Screw Steam-ships, as follow:—

CITY OF PHILADELPHIA ......(new)......2,189 Tons...........Capt. R. Leitch.
CITY OF MANCHESTER ....2,125 ,, ...Capt. W. Wylie.
CITY OF GLASGOW ....1,610 ,, ...Capt. K. Morrison.

From LIVERPOOL.

CITY OF GLASGOW.........Wed., 8th June, 1853.	CITY OF MANCHESTER...Wed., 24th Aug., 1853.
CITY OF MANCHESTER...Wed., 6th July, ,,	CITY OF GLASGOW ......Wed., 14th Sept., ,,
CITY OF GLASGOW ......Wed., 27th July, ,,	CITY OF MANCHESTER..Wed, 12th Oct., ,,

From PHILADELPHIA.

CITY OF MANCHESTER....Sat., 11th June, 1853.	CITY OF GLASGOW.........Sat., 2nd July, 1853.

RATES OF CABIN PASSAGE FROM LIVERPOOL.

After Saloon State-rooms (2 berths in each) ....Twenty Guineas.
Ditto, and Midship (3 berths in each) ....Fifteen ,,
Ditto, ditto, Forward State-rooms...........................Thirteen ,,

Including Provisions and Steward's Fee,
All having the same privilege, and messing together.

A limited number of Passengers to Philadelphia will be taken at Seven Guineas; to New York at Seven Pounds Fifteen Shillings, and supplied with Provisions of a superior quality, properly cooked, and as much as is required; and these Passengers are hereby informed, that, in order to satisfy the requirements of the Government Officers, the Date filled into their Contract Tickets will be, in every case, the date of the day preceding the fixed day of sailing; and those Passengers booked for New York, will, on their arrival in Philadelphia, be provided by the Agents of the Steamers with a Ticket entitling them to a Free Passage by Steam-boat or Railway to New York.

These Steamers carry "Phillips's Patent Fire-Annihilators."

An experienced Surgeon is attached to each Steamer.

Passengers will find PHILADELPHIA the most central Port, BEING ON THE DIRECT MAIL ROUTE from New York to the Western and Southern States.

RATES OF FREIGHT.

Freight on Goods, 60s. per Ton, with the exception of Unmanufactured Produce, &c., which will be taken subject to agreement, payable here or in Philadelphia, at 4 dollars 80 cents per pound sterling. Private arrangements have been made by the Agents to transport fine goods to New York, by Steam-boat (including insurance) and Canal, at four cents per foot, or about 6s. 8d. per ton measurement, and by steamer to Charleston eight cents, and to Norfolk and Richmond Va., at six cents per foot.

Goods intended for the interior of the United States, if consigned to the Agents at Philadelphia will be forwarded without charge for commission.

DOGS AT THREE POUNDS EACH.

Apply in Philadelphia and New York, to THOMAS RICHARDSON; in Belfast, to RICHARDSON BROTHERS and Co.; in Glasgow, to PATRICK HENDERSON and Co.; in Dublin, to CORNELIUS CARLETON; in London, to EDWARDS, SANDFORD, & Co., for Passengers, and PICKFORD & Co., for Goods; in Paris, to FRED. REDFERN, 8, Rue de la Paix; in Havre, to W. DAVIDSON; in Manchester, to GEORGE STONIER; and to

RICHARDSON BROTHERS & Co., 12 and 13, Tower Buildings, LIVERPOOL.

[T.F.—16

The Imperial and Royal

DANUBE STEAM NAVIGATION COMPANY

HAS just Established an Accelerated and distinct LINE OF PACKETS from VIENNA TO GALATZ, without changing Steamer at ORSOVA, which, during the present year, will have **ONE DEPARTURE WEEKLY,** from FRIDAY, 29th APRIL, and will correspond with the Boats of the Austrian Lloyd's, going to Constantinople, and with the Russian Steamers for Odessa; which Service will be kept up with punctuality and despatch.

These Vessels will not take Passengers on board from the Intermediate Stations above Orsova, being exclusively destined for the communication with the Ports of the Lower Danube, the Levant, and Russia.

The Service will be regulated as follows:-

There will be a Departure from VIENNA every FRIDAY at 9 A.M. At PESTH, (where the Boat arrives at 8 P.M.,) at MOHACS, and at SEMLIN, the stoppages will be only for the time requisite for taking in coal; and it will arrive at ORSOVA on the SUNDAY, between 1 and 3 P.M.

In order to avoid all unnecessary delay, arrangements have been made for simplifying and expediting the examination of Luggage and Passports, so that the Steamer will be able to pass the Irongate Cataracts, and arrive in the afternoon at Turnu-Severin—the first station in Wallachia. The departure from that place will be in the Evening, so as to arrive at Giurgevo the next day at 5 o'clock in the afternoon, and at Galatz on the Tuesday, between noon and 2 P.M.; the passage from Vienna being thus accomplished in about 100 hours.

Passengers for Constantinople are sent on for Galatz the same evening by the Lloyd's Steamer, which reaches the Bosphorus in the afternoon of the following Thursday, where the Passengers will be landed on the seventh day after the departure from Vienna; so that Travellers from Paris or London can thus reach Constantinople on the tenth day.

The Accelerated Boats are also in correspondence with the Steamers of the Russian Government, proceeding to Odessa where it will be possible to arrive on the eighth day after departure from Vienna, and on the eleventh from London or Paris.

The Departure from Galatz for Vienna takes place early every Friday morning, after the Passengers from Odessa have embarked, as well as those arrived the previous evening from Constantinople, having left that city on the preceding Tuesday at noon. In the passage to Orsova, which is reached on the Sunday afternoon, the Boat touches at Rustzuk and Widdin, on the Turkish bank—and at Braila, Giurgevo, Calafat, and Turnu-Severin, on the Wallachian bank; at the two last places, however, under quarantine, and for the sole purpose of landing the Passengers brought by sea, and embarking those destined for the Stations above Orsova.

The Boat arrives at Pest on the Wednesday, and at Vienna on the Thursday following—being the tenth day after the departure from Constantinople and Odessa, and the seventh from Galatz.

DEPARTURES.

From Linz to Vienna, and Return.—From 1st May, every day.

At Linz there is a correspondence with the Bavarian Steamers from Ratisbon and Donawert.

From Vienna to Presburg and Pesth, and Return.—Daily.

From Vienna to Semlin and Belgrade.—In May—every Sunday, Tuesday, Thursday, and Friday. In June—every day.

From Semlin and Belgrade to Vienna.—Daily, during May.

From Vienna to Orsova, Galatz, and Constantinople.—1st. BY ORDINARY CONVEYANCE.—In April, every Tuesday, along the Wallachian—and every Friday, along the Turkish bank. Departure from Galatz for Constantinople on the following Tuesday. From 10th May, every Tuesday, along both banks (Turkish and Wallachian.) Departure for Constantinople the following Tuesday. In addition, from Friday, 6th May, every fortnight, along the Turkish bank: departure for Constantinople on the following Friday.

The duration of the voyage from Vienna to Constantinople by the ordinary conveyance, is 10 days. N.B.—The Boat passing along the Turkish bank, performs quarantine at Galatz.

2nd. BY THE ACCELERATED CONVEYANCE.—From 29th April, every Friday, along the Wallachian bank, and without changing Steamer at Orsova, in direct correspondence with the Lloyd's Boats for Constantinople.

The duration of the passage from Vienna to Galatz, by the accelerated conveyance, is 100 hours. From Vienna to Constantinople, 160 hours.

From Galatz to Odessa.—The Boats of the Wallachian bank are in correspondence with the Russian Steamers from Odessa, arriving at Galatz every fortnight.

From Galatz to Orsova and Vienna.—1st. BY ORDINARY CONVEYANCE.—In May, every Tuesday, along both banks of the river; and, in addition, from 13th May, every Friday, along the Turkish bank.

2nd. BY ACCELERATED CONVEYANCE.—From 6th May, every Friday, the Boat touching at Braila, Giurgevo, Rustzuk, Calafat, Widdin, and Turnu-Severin.

From Constantinople to Galatz and Vienna.—Every Tuesday, the Boat arriving on the following Thursday at Galatz, where it is in correspondence with the ordinary Danube Steamer; going the next day to Orsova and Vienna, along the Turkish bank.

From Odessa to Galatz and Vienna.—Every fortnight.

Table of Fares (in Convention Money) for Passengers and Goods.

	1st Class.				2nd Class.				Berths.				Carriages.		Horses.		Goods	
	Up Passage.		Down Passage		Up Passage.		Down Passage.		Up Passage.		Down Passage.		Up and Down Passage.		Up and Down Passage.		Up and Down Passage.	
	fl.	kr.	fl.	kr.	fl.	kr.	fl.	kr.	fl.	kr.	fl.	kr.	fl.	kr.	fl.	kr.	fl.	kr.
Linz to Vienna	8	...	6	...	5	20	4	...	6	...	15	...	25	...	15	...	...	50
Vienna. **Pesth**	7	30	5	30	5	...	4	...	12	...	25	...	25	...	25	...	...	54
Semlin	18	30	15	30	12	20	10	40	30	...	49	...	57	...	40	...	1	40
Orsova	27	30	22	30	18	20	15	20	36	...	59	...	70	...	50	...	2	10
Widdin and Calafat	32	30	27	30	21	50	18	40	50	...	79	...	77	...	65	...	2	20
Giurgevo	42	30	37	30	28	50	25	50	60	...	89	...	87	...	70	...	2	36
Rustzuk	42	30	37	30	28	50	25	50	6	...	89	...	87	...	70	...	2	30
Silistria	46	10	41	10	31	25	28	25	80	..	100	...	94	...	80	...	2	40
Ibraila	51	50	46	50	35	25	32	25	80	...	100	...	97	...	80	...	2	40
Galatz	52	30	47	30	35	50	32	50	80	...	100	...	100	...	80	...	2	40
Cons'nople	92	30	87	30	65	50	62	50	...	...	...	...	150	...	100	...	3	...
Odessa	The Fare from Vienna to Galatz, with the additional Russian Fare to Odessa.																	

Rates for the Accelerated Conveyance, Up or Down, Board included.

	Orsova and Turnu-Severin.								Widdin and Calafat.								Rustzuk, Giurgevo.							
	Passage.		Berths.			Cars.&Hrses	Goods per Cwt.		Passage.		Berths.			Cars.&Hrses	Goods per Cwt.		Passage.		Berths.			Cars.&Hrses	Goods per Cwt.	
	1st Cls	2d Cls	1st Cls	2d Cls	3d Cls				1st Cls	2d Cls	1st Cls	2d Cls	3d Cls				1st Cls	2d Cls	1st Cls	2d Cls	3d Cls			
FROM	f.	f.	f.	f.	f.	f.	f.	kr.	f.	f.	f.	f.	f.	f.	f.	kr.	f.	f.	f.	f.	f.	f.	f.	kr.
Vienna	55	35	75	60	40	80	4	20	65	45	100	80	50	85	4	40	90	60	110	99	55	100	5	...
Pesth	40	25	45	35	25	52	3	...	50	35	65	55	35	60	3	50	70	45	80	65	45	70	4	20

	Braila and Galatz.								Constantinople.							
	Passage		Berths.			Carriages and Horses.	Goods per Cwt.		Passage.		Berths.			Carriages and Horses.	Goods per Cwt.	
	1st Cls.	2nd Cls.	1st Cls.	2nd Cls.	3rd Cls.				1st Cls.	2nd Cls.	1st Cls.	2nd Cls.	3rd Cls.			
FROM	f.	f.	f.	f.	f.	f.	f.	kr.	f.	f.	f.	f.	f.	f.	f.	kr.
Vienna	100	70	120	100	60	110	5	30	140	100	...	...	...	160	6	30
Pesth	90	60	105	85	55	85	4	40	130	90	...	...	...	135	5	40

Children under Ten Years pay half fare.

For more ample particulars, apply to

Messrs. DRAPER, PIETRONI & CO.,
81, London Wall, London.

[L.O.—17

STEAM FROM LIVERPOOL TO ITALY.

ANGLO-ITALIAN STEAM NAVIGATION COMPANY'S

Splendid, Powerful, and Unrivalled Steam Ships,

Genova, Capt. Walter Paton; **Livorno,** Capt. W. O. Campbell; **Trinacria** (New), Capt. ——,

The **LIVORNO,** for GENOA and LEGHORN, sails on TUESDAY, JUNE 7th, (receiving Goods up till midnight of the 6th).

CABIN PASSAGE, including Provisions and Steward's Fee.

Liverpool to Gibraltar,	10 Guineas.	Liverpool to Leghorn, 14 guineas.
„ Genoa,	13 „	For the Round, *via* Marseilles, 25 „

For terms of Freight or Passage, and Plans of Cabins, (having very superior accommodation for Passengers, and carries a Stewardess,) apply to P. HENDERSON & Co., Bothwell Street, Glasgow; J. F. CAMPBELL & Co., 53, Cornhill; or to

M'KEAN, M'LARTY, & Co., 31, Water Street, Liverpool.

[T.F.—22

STEAM BETWEEN LIVERPOOL AND CANADA.

The Swift and Powerful First-class Steam Ships,

Cleopatra .. .. H. R. CUMMING, Commander
Lady Eglinton .. .. ——— Do.
Genova .. .. WALTER PATON. Do.

Are intended to be dispatched as under:—

FROM BIRKENHEAD DOCK FOR QUEBEC AND MONTREAL

DIRECT,

Lady Eglinton.....on Thursday, 16th June. | **Cleopatra**....on Thursday, 14th July.

The **Lady Eglinton** is quite new, and one of the fastest Screw Steamers afloat. She is expected to make a very rapid passage to Canada, and has excellent accommodation for Passengers.

Stewardesses attend both First and Second Cabins.

CABIN PASSAGE, exclusive of Wines and Liquors, ... 21 Guineas.
SECOND CABIN, Do. Do. .. .. 12 Do.

FREIGHT, 60s. per ton, and 5 per cent. primage.

For Freight or Passage, and Plans of Cabins, &c., apply to Patrick Henderson and Co., 4 Bothwell Street, Glasgow; or to

M'KEAN, M'LARTY & CO.,
31, Water Street, Liverpool.

Liverpool, 24th May, 1853. [T.F.—23

JOHN HILL,

TRAVELLING EQUIPAGE MANUFACTURER TO THE ARMY & NAVY.

THIS ARTICLE HAS FIVE COMPARTMENTS.

A to contain Linen.
B „ „ Bonnets.
C „ „ Mantles and Shawls.
D „ „ Dresses.
E „ „ Light Articles.

97, REGENT ST., QUADRANT,
AND
122, PICCADILLY,
Six Doors West of Regent Circus,
LONDON.

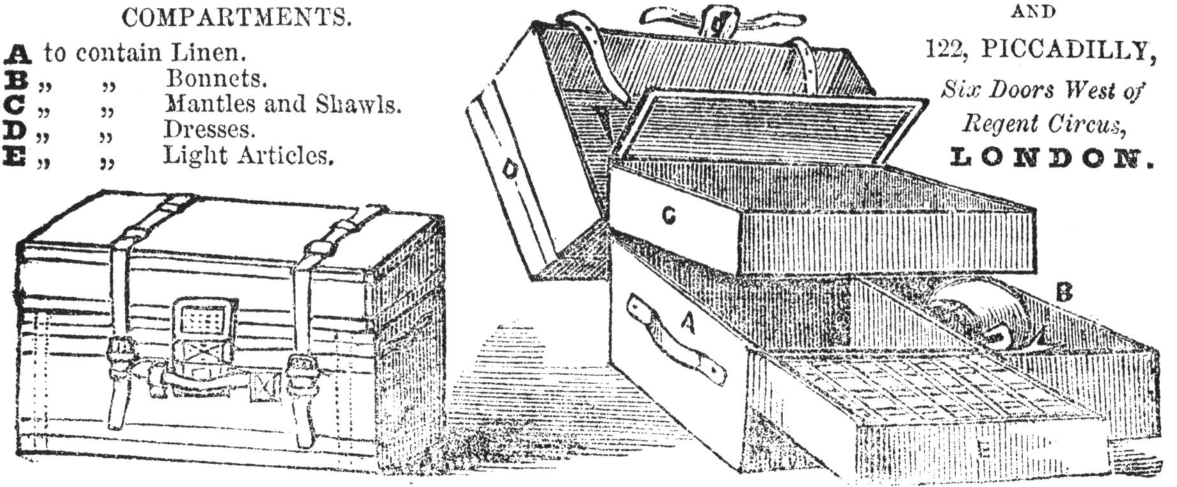

MANUFACTURER OF REGISTERED PORTMANTEAUS.

JOHN HILL respectfully solicits the attention of the Nobility, Gentry, and all persons travelling to any part of the globe, to his newly-invented LADY'S EXPANDING PORTMANTEAU, which for strength, portability, and capacity for containing, excels all others ever invented; is strongly recommended for continental, railway, and general travelling. To be had only of the inventor, where every other article connected with the business are of first-rate quality. Leather and carpet bags, various descriptions of hat-cases, boxes, and trunks; writing, dressing, and brush cases of every description; air-tight tin boxes for India; wood cases made and lined with tin, zinc, or copper; paper boxes.

PATENTEE OF THE CHORETIKOPAS. L.O.—240.

TO TRAVELLERS VISITING LONDON.

MECHI'S SHOW-ROOMS,

4, LEADENHALL STREET,

Near the India House.

ALL persons of taste should hasten to inspect the unique and *récherché* STOCK of ELEGANCIES now exhibited by Mechi, in his new SHOW-ROOMS, 4, Leadenhall Street, near the India House. Determined to take the lead in taste, he has brought out some most superb and novel specimens in Papier Mache. Finding it impossible to display them advantageously in his former space, he has fitted up splendid Show-Rooms, to which he invites those who are desirous of seeing the most brilliant specimens this country can produce. MECHI has the best stock in London of Ladies' and Gentlemen's Dressing-cases, Work-boxes, Writing-desks, Tea-trays, and every thing for the Toilet and Work-table.

M ost people complain that shaving's a bore,
E ach day's painful scrape only chafes an old sore;
C hoose the cutler who stands at the head of the trade,
H alf the battle depends on a well-temper'd blade—
I n the front of these lines his name is displayed.

MECHI'S RAZOR STROPS and MAGIC PASTE are renowned throughout the civilized world. His Needles also command the approbation of the Ladies. Mechi's famous Bagatelle Tables, affording a charming amusement on a wet day. Illustrated Catalogues gratis.

4, Leadenhall Street, a few doors from Gracechurch Street. [L.O.—28

THE NEW REGISTERED PORTMANTEAU,

Registered and Manufactured by

JOHN SOUTHGATE,

76, WATLING STREET, LONDON.

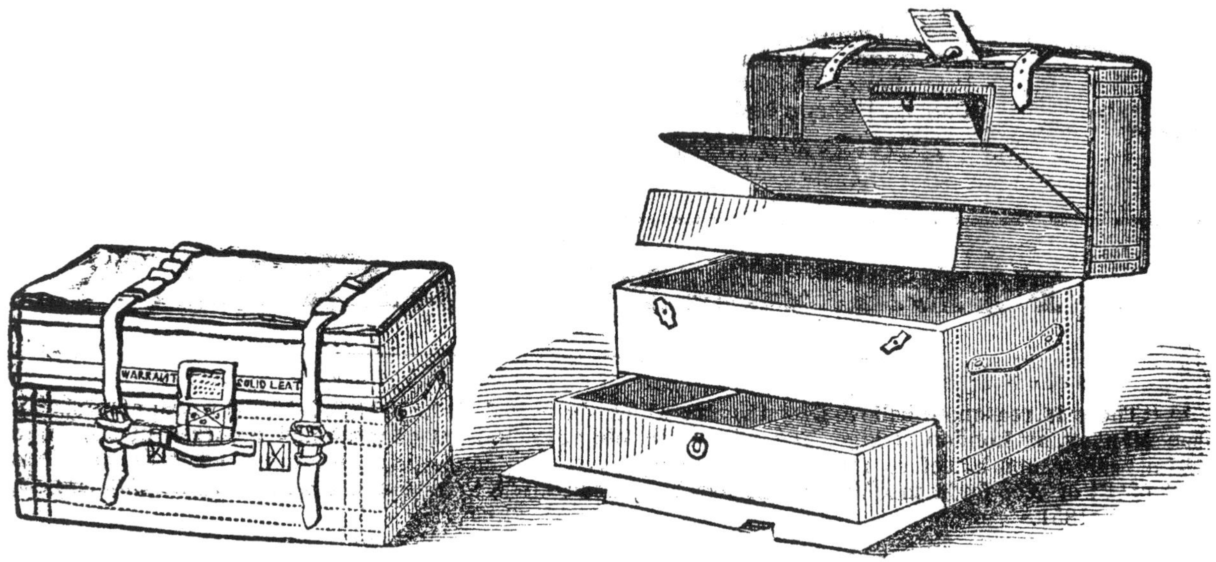

THIS PORTMANTEAU is admitted by all who have used it, to be the most PERFECT and USEFUL of any yet invented, and to combine all the advantages so long desired by all who travel.

The peculiar conveniences of this Portmanteau are, that it contains *separate compartments* for each description of Clothes, Boots, &c.: each division is kept entirely distinct, and is immediately accessible on opening the Portmanteau, without lifting or disturbing any thing else. Every article is packed perfectly flat, and remains so during the whole of the journey.

It may be obtained of Mr. Wilkinson, 30, *Cockspur Street; of* Messrs. Moore and Co., 14, *St. James's Street, London; of* Mr. Hunt, *Above-Bar, Southampton; of* Mr. Bays, *Hatter, Cambridge; of* Mr. Ellenger, *Grainger Street, Newcastle-on-Tyne; of most Outfitters and Saddlers throughout the Kingdom; and of*

JOHN SOUTHGATE,

Manufacturer of every description of Portmanteaus and Travelling Equipage,

76, WATLING STREET, CITY;

AGENT FOR

GALT'S REGISTERED CLARENCE WRAPPER AND CAPE,

Suitable for the use of both Ladies and Gentlemen travelling either by Rail or Carriage.

Its peculiar construction prevents its sliding down when used as a Wrapper, and forms an elegant Cape when walking or riding.

Travellers en Route to and from the Continent.

THE QUEEN'S HOTEL,
St. Martin's-le-Grand,
LONDON.

OPPOSITE
THE
GENERAL POST OFFICE.

THIS MAGNIFICENT HOTEL, having recently undergone extensive Alterations, and a great portion of it newly furnished, WILL BE FOUND, ON TRIAL, TO HAVE NO RIVAL IN THE METROPOLIS EITHER IN POINT OF ACCOMMODATION OR MODERATE CHARGES. The Coffee-room is one of the largest and most comfortable in England. A Night Porter, and a fixed moderate Charge for Servants.

[L.O.—35

Travellers en Route to and from the Continent.

HENRY HOLT, Successor to the late Mr. RADLEY.

FAMILIES and GENTLEMEN visiting the Continent, by way of the Metropolis, will find that this Hotel is most admirably situated, being within a few minutes' drive of the Dover and Brighton Railway Stations, and all the Places of Embarkation, *per Steamer*, to all parts of the Continent.

The arrangements for Families consist of lofty and well-ventilated Sitting-rooms, and quiet Back Bed-rooms, with a private entrance, distinct from the public Coffee-room, &c. Families of three or more may arrange to board by the week, at a reduction of the daily charges. Bed, Breakfast, and Attendance in the Coffee-room, Six Shillings per Night. Small Private Rooms for Parties, for Luncheons, Dinners, &c.

Hot and Cold Baths.

[L.O.—36

Hotel Advertisements.

The following **ADVERTISEMENTS** are arranged in the Alphabetical Order of the Towns, irrespective of Geographical Position.

AIX-LA-CHAPELLE.

HOTEL DU GRAND MONARQUE.—DREMEL'S HOTEL at AIX LA CHAPELLE. —This magnificent and large Hotel, for Families and single Travellers, continues to maintain its European reputation for being the favoured residence of travellers of all nations. The proprietor, Mr. FRITZ DREMEL, obtained this unusual patronage by the cleanliness and comfort of his apartments, (all the beds being of new construction,) the richness and excellence of its viands and wines, added to the attention and civility of the attendants. The first Mineral Bath Establishment is attached to the Hotel. [38

HOTEL DES QUATRE SAISONS.—Situated in the best part of the city, opposite the Opera-House, and in the vicinity of the Baths, and all public amusements.—The Proprietor, G. Y. HUBER, having entirely refitted it, with a view to the comfort of those who may honour him with their patronage, pledges to devote his best energies to merit the continued favours of the Nobility and Gentry. Apartments, large and small, handsomely furnished, and waited upon by attentive servants. Two superior Table D'Hôtes a day. Mr. HUBER also begs to recommend the HOTEL DES BAINS DE LA ROSE, BOURCETTE, of which he is likewise Proprietor. It is within two minutes' walk of the city, and has Hot Mineral Springs, and Baths, and very superior accommodations. [39

HOTEL NUELLENS, opposite the Fontaine Eliza, and situated in the most fashionable part of the city, has great attractions to tourists and travellers. This house possesses excellent accommodation for single persons or large families, and the Cuisine department will afford satisfaction to the most fastidious taste. Extract from the 18th Edition of Murray's Hand Book:—This Hotel in the best situation, &c. &c., is recommended as capital. Table d'hôte at 1½, and 5 o'clock. [37

AMIENS.

HOTEL DE FRANCE ET D'ANGLETERRE, 23, Rue Royale—by M. FONTAINE.— Persons visiting or passing through Amiens will find this Hotel combines superior accommodation, with the most moderate scale of charges. It is one of the oldest establishments on the Continent; and, having been honoured with the patronage of the nobility and gentry of England during a great many years, Mr. Fontaine is desirous that every attention be paid to the comfort of English Travellers. Families and Gentlemen accommodated with convenient suites of apartments, or single rooms, well furnished. Attendance good. Refreshments of the first quality, and Wines of the best vintage, at moderate prices. [41

HOTEL DU RHIN, PLACE ST. DENIS, close to the Railway Stations, AMIENS. This Hotel is situated in the handsomest part of the town, and is extensively patronised by the English Nobility, Clergy, and Gentry The present proprietor begs to assure Travellers and others, that no exertion on his part shall be wanting to render this Hotel the most comfortable in Amiens.

Table d'Hôte at Five o'Clock. Breakfasts and Dinners at any hour

BEAUTIFUL APARTMENTS FOR FAMILIES.—TOWN AND TRAVELLING CARRIAGES [42

HOTEL DE LONDRES AND DU NORD—Kept by Mr. LAUGE—conveniently situated opposite the Railway Station, with a southern aspect. The accommodation consists of a handsome Saloon, elegantly Furnished Apartments for Families, and large Bedrooms for Single Travellers--all of which will afford satisfaction to English visiters. The Cuisine department is carefully superintended by Mr. LAUGE; and the prices are reasonable. [40

AMSTERDAM.

BRACK'S DOELEN HOTEL—Situated in the centre of the Town, and most convenient for Visiters on pleasure or business. It commands a splendid view of the Quays, &c.; and, being conducted on a liberal scale, it is patronised by the highest classes of society in Holland. It is also much frequented by English Travellers for the comfort and first-rate accommodation it affords, as well as for the invariable civility shown to visiters. Cold and warm baths may be had at any hour—Carriages for hire—Table d'Hôte at half-past 4, or dinner à la carte. [43

ANTWERP.

HOTEL St. ANTOINE, PLACE VERTE.—This Hotel, already favourably known to all Travellers, increases daily in reputation, and the Proprietor, Mr. SCHMIDT SPANHOVEN, pledges himself to spare no exertions to merit the patronage of the Nobility and Gentry by civility and attention. A superior Cuisine, and a very extensive stock of the finest wines. Large and small apartments elegantly furnished, attentive servants, and good table d'Hote. Carriages of every description. English and French Newspapers taken in. [44

PARK HOTEL, Place Verte (Park Square). This Hotel, situate in the pleasantest part of the City, opposite the celebrated Cathedral, and next door to the General Post-Office, increases daily in repute as a first-rate Family Hotel. Considered one of the most respectable establishments on the Continent, it combines not only the greatest comfort, with superior cookery, and excellent wines, but also affords the luxury and advantages of Baths in the House.

Table d'Hôte at One and Six o'clock. The Proprietor, Mr. L. DELAPRE, speaks English and several languages fluently, and respectfully solicits the patronage of the English Nobility and Gentry. [45

BADEN BADEN.

THE RHINE HOTEL—by F. SCHLUND—is admirably situated near the Post-Office, the Promenade, and facing the Palace of the Grand Duchess Stephanie. Table d'Hôte at 1 and 5 o'clock. Restaurant à la Carte at all hours. The Cuisine Department is conducted by first-rate French Cooks. Rhine and other Wine of excellent quality. Large and small apartments, comfortable, and well-furnished. The prices are exceedingly reasonable. The Poste Restante being in this Hotel, is a great advantage to residents. [47

HOTEL DE HOLLANDE, F. A. Zachmann and A. Roessler, proprietors. This favourite and first-class Hotel, situate near the Kursaal, commands one of the most charming views in Baden. It consists of an hundred sleeping apartments, elegant sitting-rooms, a well supplied reading-room, and a garden for the use of visiters, from whence you hear playing the music band of the Kursaal. Is conducted under the immediate superintendence of the proprietors, who endeavour by the most strict attention, and exceedingly moderate prices, to merit the continued patronage of English visiters. The wines of this Hotel are reputed of the best quality in Baden. Breakfast, 36 kr.; Tea, 42 kr.; Dinner at table d'hôte at one, including wine, 1 fl. 12 kr.; Dinner at five, exclusive of wine, 1 fl. 36 kr. [46

HOTEL DE RUSSIE.—G. Lungl, Proprietor—most delightfully situate near the Kersaal and Railway Station, is patronised by the élite and fashionable visiters to Baden-Baden. English Families will find this a very desirable residence, at which there is a choice of large or small Apartments, well furnished and comfortable; and no expense is spared to render the Hotel deserving their patronage. The Hotel is celebrated for its cuisine, cleanliness, and good attendance. [251

BALE, OR BASLE.

HOTEL OF THE THREE KINGS.—This Hotel is in the best situation in Bale, overlooking the Bridge and the Rhine. It has lately been re-built and newly furnished, and contains 150 chambers. There is a Table d'Hôte at 1 and 5 o'clock. The Prices are moderate, and the Servants attentive. A List of Prices is in each chamber. [244

HOTEL DU SAUVAGE—Proprietor, T. T. PFANDER—Enjoying an extensive and high reputation among English Travellers for cleanliness, civility, good fare, and very moderate charges. Situated in the centre of the town, nearest to the Cathedral, the Museum, the Post and Diligence Offices. The German and Strasburg Railway Offices being in this hotel, is a great advantage for residents. [48

BATHS OF ISCHL, NEAR SALZBURG, AUSTRIA.

THE GRAND AND NEW HOTEL TALLACHIUI.—This magnificent Establishment having a new Proprietor, now affords accommodation equal to any Hotel on the Continent. In addition to large and small Apartments, there are Drawing-Rooms for distinguished Visitors; Reading Rooms; a Billiard Room; Smoking Room, &c. Two Table d'Hôtes. Private Dinners at any hour. Prices moderate. Foreign monies taken at the rate of Exchange. A. BAUER, the Proprietor, formerly of the Arch-Duke Charles Hotel at Linz, being in correspondence with the principal Hotel-Keepers at Munich, Salzburg, Linz, Innspruck, &c., is enabled to assist Travellers in their journies with respect to Lounkutscher or Veturino's, by recommending only the most completent and trustworthy. Carriages and Horses to Let, or Travelling Carriages for hire, always ready for Travellers. [257

BERLIN.

HOTEL DU NORD, No. 35, UNTER DEN LINDEN, near the Opera House, the Museum, the King's Palace, the Palace of the Prince of Prussia, and the Monument of Professor Rauch.—Proprietor, J. BRANDT. This Hotel, the largest and most superbly furnished in Berlin, has a great number of spacious saloons and airy bedrooms, furnished with every comfort the traveller can desire.

A first-rate Cuisine for French or English cookery. Dinner at all hours.

Good society may always be met with at this Hotel.

The English Episcopal Chapel is in this Hotel—the Rev. —— Bellson performs the service. [50

HOTEL DE RUSSIE, near the Chlossbrücke—Proprietor, MR. EHRENREICK—First-rate Hotel in the centre of the town, within five minutes' walk of the principal Public Buildings, the Palace, Museum, Arsenal, Post-Office, Grand Opera, and the Monument of Frederick the Great, the Royal Library, Theatres, &c. The Proprietor begs leave to say, that no Hotel in Berlin is really more conveniently situated for travellers either on business or pleasure. Mr. E. and the attendants speak English, and they will be found attentive to the wants and wishes of visiters. Baths in the Hotel, and Carriages may be hired for town use or excursions. [49

BIEBERICH (on the Rhine, near Wiesbaden.)

AN ENGLISH LADY has established a highly respectable BOARDING-HOUSE, where Families and Tourists will find superior accommodation and English comforts for long or short periods. The house faces the Rhine, and is close to the landing-place. Address, ALBERT HOUSE, BIEBERICH, Duchy of Nassau. [51

BONN.

GRAND HOTEL BELLE VUE, by Mme. N. STAMM. This well-known establishment is situated on the banks of the Rhine, close to the landing-place of the Rhine steamers, and near the railway station. It commands a splendid view of the seven mountains, and it combines every comfort with moderate charges. The English Club established in this hotel admits the visiters to its saloons. Table d'hôte at 1 and 5 o'clock. [53

BONN—Continued.

THE GRAND HOTEL ROYAL, facing the landing-place of the Rhine Steamers, and near the Railway Station. This Hotel combines every comfort with moderate charges, and its situation is so convenient and agreeable, that travellers will find it a highly desirable place of residence, or of temporary sojourn. Table d'Hôte at half-past 1 and 5 o'clock. [54

THE GOLDEN STAR HOTEL, patronised by the English Royal Family, the English Nobility, and Gentry, is the nearest Hotel to the Railway Terminus, and to the landing places of the Rhine Steam-boats. The Proprietor, MR. J. SCHMIDT, begs leave to recommend his Hotel to English Tourists. The apartments are furnished and carpeted throughont in the best English style, and the charges are moderate. Advantageous arrangements can be made, by single persons or families, for Board and Lodging during the Winter months. [52

BOULOGNE-SUR-MER.

HOTEL DE L'EUROPE.—Parties about to visit Boulogne for the benefit of its pure air and invigorating sea breezes, or *en route* to the Metropolis of France, are respectfully informed that this first-rate Establishment is the oldest in the place, and is situated on the Quay, opposite the Steam-packet Station, and near the Paris Railway Terminus. The apartments combine French elegance with English comfort; the bed-rooms are scrupulously clean, lofty, and airy; it has an excellent Table d'Hôte; and the Wines are of the choicest vintages. Board for Families on the most reasonable terms. Attached to the Hotel are Warm Baths, a fine Garden, Smoking-room, Sitting-room for Boarders, with English Papers daily on the tables. It is also replete with Stabling, Lock-up Coach-houses, &c. The Carriage of the Establishment is always in attendance for Travellers on the arrival of the Trains and Steamers, and conveys them without charge to the Hotel. [56

BRIGHTON HOTEL.—This comfortable Hotel, entirely restored, considerably enlarged, and situated in the middle of large and beautiful gardens, in the neighbourhood of the Valley of the VERTE-VOIE, of the railroad, and port, for the departure of Trains and Steamers—is the only one that can offer the united advantages of the town and country. A Play-ground is established in one of the three large gardens attached to the house. Bathing-rooms are annexed to the establishment. The carriages of the Hotel are charged to conduct gratuitously, in town or to the port, the Travellers who wish to go out; and they find on the port the carriages of the Hotel, to bring them back when they desire it. Price per day, 10 francs—Breakfast, Lunch, Dinner, Tea, Lodging, Attendance, and Candles. Per Week, 60 or 70 francs—according to the Apartments (Private Room included), Private Dinner, or at the Table d'Hôte, without any extra charge. Three children, from 3 to 4 years of age, will pay the same as an adult. Two children, from 10 to 12 years of age, will pay the same as an adult. [58

THE BEDFORD HOTEL.—This splendid first-rate Establishment, opposite the Steam-packet Station, and next door to the Custom-house, with a good Sea View, Garden, Lock-up Coach-houses and Stabling.——Prices:—Bedrooms, 2 francs; Table d'Hôte Dinners, 3 francs; Breakfast, 1 franc 50 cents. Good Private Sitting-rooms.

N.B.—A Carriage is always in attendance at the Railway Station, to convey passengers and their baggage to the Hotel *without charge*. An English waiter and chambermaid in the Hotel. English and French newspapers daily. [55

BOULOGNE-SUR-MER.—36, RUE DE BOSTON.

ROYAL GEORGE HOTEL (30 Beds), Back of Custom-House, on the Port. Breakfast, Eggs, &c., 1s.; Ditto, Steaks and Chops, 1s. 6d.; Dinner, 1s. 6d.; Tea and Supper, 1s.; excellent Beds, 1s. Private Rooms. Bordeaux Wine, 1s. 3d. per bottle; Champagne ditto, 3s., 4s., and 5s. per bottle; see priced Wine List. Money exchanged. London Porter, Ales, &c.—Travellers are particularly requested to ask (upon passing through the Custom-House) for the "ROYAL GEORGE HOTEL." Bed and Breakfast, 2s. [59

MRS. LEA begs to intimate that she receives Boarders by the day, week, or month. Her Boarding House, No. 12, Rue de l'Ecu, being recently furnished direct from Paris, is now peculiarly suited, by its elegance and comfort, for the superior classes who favour her with their patronage. The accommodation and provisions are unexceptionable, although the charges are moderate. A man-servant is kept. The "Times" received daily. Letters, prepaid, to be addressed, "MRS. LEA, 12, Rue de l'Ecu, Boulogne-sur-Mer. [60

BREMEN.

HOTEL DE L'EUROPE — ALBERTI and C. A. SCHULGE, Proprietors.— This splendid Hotel has been newly opened, and offers the greatest advantages for Families and Travellers visiting Bremen. It is situated on the Boulevards, within a few minutes' walk of the Railway Station, Post-Office, and Theatres. A first-rate Table d'Hôte every day at 2 o'clock. English and French spoken by both Proprietors and servants of the Hotel. Advantageous arrangements made with Families remaining for a period. This Hotel has 80 first-class Beds, independent of several suites of Apartments for Families. The English and French journals are taken in. [62

BRUGES.

HOTEL DE LA FLEUR DE BLÉ.—A large Hotel, with a fine Garden, situated in the centre of the town, adjoining the Theatre—recently taken by Mr. MEES GARNOT, who has newly furnished and re-embellished it throughout. Large and small Apartments, elegantly and comfortably furnished, to be hired at moderate prices. Superior Table d'Hôte, and Wines of the best quality. Two handsome Carriages start daily, during the summer months, from this Hotel for Blankenberghe; and an Omnibus from the Hotel waits the arrival of every train at the railway station. English, French, and German spoken. [65

HOTEL DE FLANDRE.—This old-established Hotel will be found equally desirable for Families, single Travellers, or parties visiting Bruges on business or pleasure, in consequence of its central sitnation and comfortable accommodation. Murray's Hand-Book recommends this House for "its moderate charges," adding that the Table d'Hôte is at 1, and that the Fish Dinners on Fridays are renowned. [64

HOTEL DE COMMERCE, near the Grande Place and the Railway Station, has long been favourably known to English families for its splendid and well-furnished apartments, its excellent accommodation, good cuisine and wines. An elegant omnibus conveys travellers to and from the railway station, the baggage being transported gratis. Mr. VANDENBERGH, in recommending his old established Hotel to the notice of visitors, begs they will not permit themselves to be misled by touters. [63

BRUNSWICK.

HOTEL D'ANGLETERRE.—This long-established and first-rate Hotel keeps up its superiority for real comfort and cleanliness under the present Proprietor, Mr. BECKER, who has lately fitted up the rooms in elegant style, and continues to ensure the preference given so long to this house, particularly by the English Nobility and Gentry. [66

BRUSSELS.

HOTEL DE BELLE VUE, PLACE ROYALE.—This unrivalled Establishment, under the superintendence of MADAME DE PROFT, maintains its European reputation, and recommends itself to the patronage of the Nobility, Gentry, and Travellers, indiscriminately of all Countries. Carriages belonging to the Hotel may be had for visiting the town or the environs of Brussels. [68

HOTEL DE FRANCE, RUE ROYALE, facing the Park.—MISS PORTER, the Proprietress, respectfully tenders her grateful thanks for the patronage she continues to be honoured with; and begs to assure Travellers visiting Brussels, it is her constant study to render the Hotel de France worthy of its reputation. It has been considerably enlarged this year, by the addition of the adjoining house, which has been fitted up in a superior manner for the accommodation of Families or single persons, and which can be hired separately during the winter months. The Proprietress exercises the strictest surveillance over every part of her establishment. She is likewise particularly anxious to protect visiters during their stay at the Hotel, from being imposed upon by Commissioners, &c. Table d'Hôte at 5. [70

BRUSSELS—Continued.

BOARDING and LODGING HOUSE.—MRS. HAYDON'S highly-respectable Establishment, No. 27, QUARTIER LOUISE, is situated in the most pleasant and salubrious Boulevard of Brussels. It combines the quiet comfort of a desirable home with the advantages of good society. Terms Moderate. [79

FIRST CLASS ENGLISH BOARDING-HOUSE.—Families and Parties visiting this beautiful city will find very superior accommodation by the week or month in the Establishment of an English Protestant Family long resident on the Continent, and occupyIng a spacious House, delightfully situate close to the Park, the Boulevards, and the Palace. No. 10, RUE THERESIENNE—RUE DE NAMUR. [80

ENGLISH BOARDING-HOUSE, 2, Impasse du Parc, Rue Royale.—This Establishment, overlooking the Park, affords accommodation for Families, Single Ladies, and Gentlemen. A liberal Table is kept; and the House combines the domestic comforts of a private family, with a first-class residence. Terms moderate. [69

BOOKSELLERS.—KIESLING & CO., GERMAN BOOKSELLERS, 26, Montagne de la Cour, BRUSSELS, (also in OSTEND, 7, Rue des Capucins.)—A large choice of Books in English and all the Continental Languages, Guides, Maps, &c. Murray's Handbooks. Bradshaw's Guides. German and French Circulating Library. [81

GLOVER.—J. AUVRAY, Breveté, No. 9, Passage des Princes, Galeries St. Hubert, manufacturer of Kid Gloves, warranted of the best quality. Wholesale and retail warehouse for all descriptions of Gloves. Manufactured by J. AUVRAY after the newest and most approved Parisian fashions and colours. [82

LACE MANUFACTORY.—Ladies desirous of purchasing the genuine Brussels and Valenciennes Lace, or Mechlin Point, are invited to visit the Celebrated Establishment of Mr. VANDERKELEN BRESSON, No. 248, and No. 1, Rue du Marquis, near the Cathedral of St. Gudule, where they may witness the process of manufacturing lace of the finest texture, and inspecting an Unrivalled Stock of Royal Black Lace, and various articles of the Richest and Newest Patterns, at fixed prices. Mr. V. B. is the recipient of the Prize Medal of the Great Exhibition, and the Gold Medal of the Belgian Government. Visiters should be particular in not mistaking the House, or confounding this Establishment with others, which may be easily avoided, AS THE NAME IS ON THE DOOR. [83

LIBRARY, 84, MONTAGNE DE LA COUR. FROMENT'S LIBRARY—READING ROOMS and CIRCULATING LIBRARY. English residents and visitors to Brussels are respectfully informed that the Reading Rooms are supplied with a great variety of English, French, German, American, and Belgian Newspapers, viz.:—The Times, Morning Chronicle, Herald, Post, Globe, Standard, Sun, Express, Galignani's Messenger, Bell's Life in London, Sunday Times, Examiner, Naval and Military Gazette, &c. &c.

Bradshaw's British and Continental Railway Guides are on sale at this Establishmen [84

MILLINERY.—MLLE. MARIE SERRARIS, 73, RUE DE LA MONTAGNE, near the General Post Office. The assortment of articles for the Toilette is constantly supplied with the latest Parisian Fashions, and whether for Trousseaux, Coiffures, Layettes, Flowers, &c., every article will be found of a superior quality and of exquisite work. [85

NOUVEAUTES.—À la Fabrique Européenne et des Indes, Cluzeau, Ainé, 86 Rue de la Montagne, opposite the General Post-Office. *Wholesale and Retail House. Fixed Prices.* French Shawls of all descriptions, plain or brocaded. Lyons Silks of all descriptions, plain or brocaded. Woollen Tissues, and other articles for dresses, of the choicest patterns, and remarkable for elegance and variety. Cloaks and Mantles made for Ladies (articles for Mourning). The strictly honourable principles of this House, established for the last quarter of a century, are a guarantee to purchasers. The extensive rooms are always open to the public, and visitors are invited to view them without being bound to purchase. [86

PIANOFORTE REPOSITORY, 23, RUE DE RUYSBROCK.— MR. FELIX JASTRZEBSKI has always for Sale or Hire a number of excellent Pianofortes of improved action, great power and richness of tone, consisting of Boudoir, Cottage, Grand or Semi-Grand, in elegant varieties, and at moderate prices. Mr. F. J. was awarded the Prize Medal by the Commissioners of the Great Exhibition. [87

TAILOR.—J. B. COLLARD, 42, RUE DE LA MADELEINE.—Mr COLLARD employs the most able workmen in the trade, and is thus enabled to keep the greates variety of Garments of the latest fashions and novelties, at the most moderate prices. English Traveller are respectfully invited to visit this Establishment, where English is spoken. [88

THE OLD ENGLISH BANK AND EXCHANGE OFFICE, 8, Rue Royale, Brussels. Messrs. SALTER & BIGWOOD respectfully inform travellers that their Bank, Insurance and House Agencies are removed to the above address. Persons intending to reside in this city may always procure good furnished houses, for large or small families, by applying at this establishment between 10 and 4 Sundays excepted [89

WATCHMAKER.—H. PLET, 52, RUE DE LA MADELEINE, Watch and Chronometer Manufacturer.—The best description of highly-finished flat horizontal Stop Watches. A selection of fine Repeaters, with second-hand distinct, by the most eminent makers, at Geneva prices, and warranted. Exquisitely small Watches, elegantly ornamented and set with stones. Beautiful Time-Pieces. Plain good Watches of all descriptions. Repairs carefully and promptly executed.

ENGLISH SPOKEN. [90

EDUCATION.—FRENCH BOARDING-SCHOOL FOR YOUNG LADIES.

CONDUCTED BY MADAME FLASSCHEON-MICHAUX,

RUE THERESIENNE, VILVORDE, NEAR BRUSSELS.

THIS Establishment has been carried on for the last 15 years, to the greatest satisfaction of numerous English parents, on account of the progress their children have made in their Education, and the parental care bestowed on them. The young ladies are instructed in every branch of Polite Literature, including the English, French, and German languages. An English Governess accompanies the young ladies to the services of the English Protestant Church at Brussels. Terms, including washing, table linen, bed furniture complete, and every necessary for the school, £22 per annum. [91

CALAIS.

A QUILLACQ begs to inform the Nobility, Gentry, and Travellers, that they will find in his great Establishment (Quillacq's Hotel), every accommodation and comfort, combined ith very reduced charges. [93

HOTEL DESSIN.—Ever since Calais has been the principal Sea-port of communication between France and England, the Hotel Dessin has enjoyed the patronage of the English Nobility and Gentry; and the Proprietor, L. DESSIN, endeavours, by personal superintendence, and the introduction of every modern improvement, to render his Hotel deserving of their continued favours, and of being classed with the best in Europe.

Bradshaw's British and Continental Railway Guides are Sold at this Hotel. [92

CARLSRUHE.

THE GOLDEN CROSS HOTEL, close to the Railway Station, affords exceedingly good accommodation, and excellent Refreshments at moderate prices; these, combined with cleanliness, good attendance, and superior wines, render this Hotel an agreeable residence for Travellers.

TABLE D'HÔTE AT 1 AND 5. [94

CHALONS-SUR-SAONE.

HOTEL DU PARC—Kept by E. PRATA, and situated in front of the Steam Packet Station, is one of the oldest Hotels in France, conducted with a view to offer the best of accommodation at reasonable prices. Suitable and elegant Apartments for large families or single persons. Refreshments and Wines of the best description; these, combined with prompt attendance and civility, render this Hotel deserving the general patronage of Travellers. Post Carriages can be had for Geneva, also for Lyons, when the navigation is stopped. [95

HOTEL DES DILIGENCES—M. SOUDAN, Proprietor—opposite the Lyons and Marseilles Steam-Packet Wharf.—Travellers will find the situation of this Hotel exceedingly convenient; and the Landlord, who speaks English, will be happy to give them every information they may require. Large and small Apartments. An excellent Cuisine, with good attendance, and prices very liberal. Coach-house and Stabling. Omnibuses in attendance at the Railway Stations, to convey Passengers who honour this Hotel with their patronage. [96

CHAUFONTAINE.

HOTEL DES BAINS.—This Hotel, so favourably known to travellers, is still conducted by Monsieur A. HENRARD, proprietor of the equally well-known Hotel de l'Europe at Liege. The Baths at this Establishment are supplied from the warm mineral springs for which the village is so deservedly celebrated. Monsieur HENRARD respectfully informs travellers to and from Germany, that, independent of the accommodation afforded at this Hotel, he has several well-furnished Houses always to Let—by the Month, the Quarter, or the Year—at reasonable prices. [97

COLOGNE.

HOTEL DISCH, situated in Bridge Street. A first-rate house, very highly recommended, as combining good accommodation with moderate charges. The proprietors, Messieurs DISCH & CAPELLAN, keep a large assortment of the best stock of Moselle Wines for wholesale. [99

THE HOTEL DE HOLLANDE is delightfully situated near the landing-place of the Rhine Steamers. The apartments at this Hotel are well furnished, and suited to large families. The windows overlook the Rhine. The accommodation will be found to combine comfort and cleanliness, with moderate prices. Travellers are respectfully recommended to remember the above name, to avoid being conducted to another house instead. [101

THE HOTEL ROYAL, facing or overlooking the Rhine, commands an extensive view of this noble river. This well-known hotel contains numerous suites of apartments for the accommodation of families visiting Cologne. And in consequence of the Hotel having been recently enlarged, there are several apartments on the ground floor. Travellers will find this House extremely convenient for landing from, or embarking on board of the Rhine Steamers. Table d'Hôte at 1 and 5 o'clock. Omnibuses and private carriages belonging to the Hotel. [98

FREDERICK'S HOTEL—by Mr. Toos.—Lodging and Breakfast (Tea or Coffee), 2 francs; Dinner (Table d'Hôte), including half a Bottle of Wine, 2 francs. Attendance, half a franc per day. This Hotel is situated in the most beautiful part of the city, close to the Cathedral and the Casino—only five minutes' distance from the Rhine, and where the Steamers start from for Coblentz, Mayence, and Frankfort. It is also the nearest Hotel to the railway for Bonn. The landlord speaks French and English. [103

HOTEL DE GERMAINE (Germanischer Hof), situated close to the Cathedral, commanding a fine view of the Rhine, and within a short distance of the Paris and Berlin Railway Stations. This new and splendid Hotel possesses excellent accommodation for Families and Visitors to the Continent. The Rooms are furnished in first-rate style, and exceedingly pleasant, comfortable, and airy.

The Proprietor has much pleasure to add, that those who have once visited this Hotel, invariably honour it again with their presence. Terms exceedingly moderate. [100

HOTEL DE BRUSSELS—situated close to the Belgian and Paris Railway Station, is recommended to the notice of Travellers for its comfortable accommodation and moderate charges; viz:—Bed-room and Breakfast, 2 frs. 25 cts.; Table d'Hôte Dinner and Wine, 2 frs. 50 cts.; Tea, 1 fr. Omnibuses convey travellers from the Hotel to and from the Railway Stations and Steam-boats' Wharf. [102

DUSSELDORF.

HOTEL DE L'EUROPE—Facing the Railway Station, and close to the Landing-place of the Rhine Steamers.—The Belvidere at this Hotel commands the finest view of the Town and Environs. Well-furnished apartments for Families or single Travellers may be hired by the month at very moderate prices. The Proprietor, Mr. Ed. Goetzen, is particularly desirous to give satisfaction. Good attendance. Table d'Hôte at half-past 4. English and French spoken. [113

FLORENCE.

GRAND HOTEL DES ISLES BRITANNIQUES, opposite the river Arno, and near the Trinity Bridge, kept by JOSEPH DEL-BELLO, and directed by F. LASCIALFARE.—The above old-established house will be found, on trial, to be replete with every comfort. Families will find it most agreeably situated, commanding a splendid view, and combining all that can be desired in accommodation and convenience. [115

GRAND HOTEL DE NEW YORK (formerly the RICASOLI PALACE), is situate on the Quay, and commands a delightful and extensive view of the river Arno. The Proprietor makes it his constant study to render the Hotel every thing that can be desired by Families and Single Gentlemen. An excellent Table d'Hôte. Baths in the house. Good Stabling.

The Proprietor begs travellers not to confound this Hotel with the Hotel de York. [116

HOTEL DU NORD, F. PONSSON, Proprietor.—Situate in the centre of the town, in the PLACE DE LA SAINTE TRINITE.—This Hotel is considered very convenient for Travellers. Large and small apartments, elegantly furnished. The *cuisine* department reputed excellent, and charges moderate. Stabling and Coach-house. An excellent Table d'Hôte, servie à la Française [114

ENGLISH BANK AND EXCHANGE.—J. H. BROWN, VIA RONDINELLI, Nos. 4203 and 4204—Gives the highest Exchange for Bills, Circular Notes, and Letters of Credit (whether addressed to him or not), *without any Commission or Charges whatever*, by which a saving is effected of 4 or 5 dollars on every £100 exchanged. *The Rate of Exchange is posted up daily, outside the Bank door*, for the information of the public. Mr. Brown's London bankers are the Royal British Bank, 429, Strand.

Attached to the Bank, is the WINE and TEA WAREHOUSE, for sale of WINES, TEA, ALE, PORTER, SPIRITS, GROCERIES, and a great variety of ENGLISH and FOREIGN ARTICLES, at moderate prices.

Also a GENERAL AGENCY OFFICE, for Shipping GOODS and WORKS OF ART to all parts of the world; or Procuring Apartments, Letting Houses, and for giving to the traveller much useful information, to nable him to avoid imposition. [117

FRANKFORT-ON-THE-MAINE.

HOTEL OF THE ROMAN EMPEROR.—Proprietors, MESSRS. LOHR AND ALTEN.—This favourite and first class Hotel, situate in the centre of this fine City, is conducted under the immediate superintendence of the Proprietors, who endeavour, by the most strict attention and moderate rates, to merit the continued patronage of English visiters. Breakfast, 36 kr.; Tea, 42 kr.; Dinner at Table d'Hôte, including Wine, 1 fl. 30 kr. Dinner at 5, exclusive of Wine, 1 fl. 45 kr. [119

THE WEIDENBUSCH HOTEL.—GUSTAV MEVI.—Among the Hotels for which Frankfort is celebrated, the Weidenbusch has always been considered one of the best and least expensive. The magnificent saloon of this Establishment can accommodate one thousand persons at dinner. Travellers wishing to stay some time in this town, can make most advantageous arrangements for board and lodging. This Hotel combines all the comforts of a first-rate Hotel with moderate charges, and its situation is convenient for business or pleasure. [120

HOTEL DE RUSSIE.—P. RIED, late of the Mainlust Hotel, and successor to Mr. Sarg, begs to call the attention of English Families and Gentlemen visiting Frankfort, to the above Establishment, feeling assured, from his long experience in the business, that visiters may rely on every comfort and attention. Reading-Room attached to the Hotel. [118

FRANKFORT-ON-THE-MAINE—Continued.

LANDSBERG HOTEL.—Noblemen and Gentlemen who may be pleased to honour me with their patronage, will find every convenience and comfort in my Hotel. With other advantages, are combined those of the promptest and most civil attendance (for which, indeed, the Landsberg has long been famed throughout Germany); an extensive stock of the choicest wines ranging back to the year 1811; an *excellent cuisine;* a spacious coffee-room; a hundred and fifty bed-chambers, (many with double beds,) with a number of elegantly furnished private sitting-rooms; and the *strictest integrity* and *moderation* with regard to charges. Licensed Commissioners are constantly at hand. There are Private Carriages on the premises. FRED. ORTENBACH, Landlord. [245

FREIBURG IN BRESGAU, DUCHY OF BADEN.

HOTEL D'ALLEMAGNE—M. GUSTAV. RETFUS, Proprietor, (formerly proprietor of the Zacringerhof Hotel). - This Hotel having been conducted the last three years by Mr. R., it has already acquired an excellent reputation; and, from the circumstance of Mr. R. having resided in England, he is acquainted with the customs and habits of English Travellers, and is always ready to assist them in their travelling arrangements. The house itself has the finest situation, near the Promenade, and is reputed a comfortable clean Hotel. [122

HOTEL ZAHRINGHER HOF—By B. G. H. SOMMER.—This comfortable Family Hotel, newly furnished and embellished, is the best situated in the town. Carriages and Horses for excursion to the Hollenthall and Switzerland, are procured by the landlord of this Hotel at a moment's notice; and, to avoid any misunderstanding with the coachman, Mr. S. writes the agreements. [121

GENEVA.

HOTEL DE L'ECU.—This unrivalled and admirably conducted Hotel has long enjoyed an extensive and high reputation among English Travellers. Situated in the finest part of the town, and facing the lake, it commands a beautiful view of the environs. Its accommodation is of so superior a character, that Tourists will find it a highly desirable place of residence, or of temporary sojourn. [123

MILLINERY, DRESSMAKERS, &c.—MME. BAUD, who speaks English fluently, respectfully invites the attention of the English Ladies to her Warehouse, 176, RUE DU RHONE, for every article of Millinery, Parisian Toilettes, Coiffures, Lace, Silks, &c. &c. [248

GENOA.

HOTEL DE LA VILLE.—This Hotel is at present one of the most comfortable in Italy. The refreshments of the first quality, superior accommodation, and attendance equal to that of the first Hotels in the North of Europe. The Proprietor, MR. J. SMITH, has also a depôt of JEWELLERY, and manufactures the SILVER FILIGREE WORK. [125

HOTEL DE LA CROIX DE MALTE.—VITTORIA PERNETTI BIANCHI, Director and Proprietor.—This Hotel is situated in the centre of the town, commands a view of the sea, and is the nearest to the Steam-packet Wharf. It has lately been much enlarged and embellished, and all the modern improvements conducive to comfort have been introduced, to render this Establishment worthy the patronage of the English Nobility and Gentry. There is also a manufactory of the celebrated Filigree Work in Silver attached to the Hotel, which is highly interesting to visiters. [126

HOTEL ROYAL, kept by MESSRS. S. STEPHANINI & BIANCHI.—This Hotel commands a delightful Marine View, and is respectfully recommended as deserving the notice of English travellers. The Proprietors beg to assure English visiters that every attention is paid to those who honour them with their patronage. Table d'Hôte. Breakfast and Dinner at any hour. [127

HOTEL FEDER, formerly the Admiralty Palace, is situate at the corner of the Palace Bianche, opposite the Port, and commands a magnificent view of the sea. This Hotel will be found to merit, in every respect, the patronage with which it is honoured by the English nobility and gentry, from its perfect cleanliness, high respectability, and the increasing attention to the comforts of Travellers. Table d'Hôte, and private dinners à la Carte. Coach-House and stabling. [124

GHENT.

HOTEL DE VIENNE.—This Hotel is old-established, situate in an open and airy situation, in the centre of the town, near to the Hotel de Ville, the Cathedral, and other Churches, so much the admiration of visiters.

A. ROZZMAN has been the Proprietor of this Hotel for two years, is well-known, and in soliciting the patronage of the Public, pledges himself to spare no exertion to promote the greatest comfort to his visiters. His BEDS are noted for their cleanliness, his WINES are of the first quality, and his Viands and Cookery very superior. His charges are considered, by his visiters, extremely moderate.

A ROZZMAN and his waiters speak English, French, German, Flemish, and Dutch. Table d'Hôte at 1 and 5 o'clock. The public are requested to pay no attention to *interested* Omnibus-drivers and Cabmen. [129

HOTEL ROYAL, PLACE d'ARMES. This Hotel is situated in the centre of the Town, contiguous to all the public establishments, and Railway Station. Travellers will find every comfort at this Hotel, and experience prompt attention from the attendants. Arrangements made with Families at very moderate prices during the Winter Season. [130

HOTEL DE LA POSTE.—A first-rate house, situated in the Place d'Armes.—The accommodation it affords is both elegant and comfortable. The apartments are spacious and airy, well-furnished and convenient, adapted for large Families or single Travellers. Mr. PAUW begs to inform the English nobility and gentry visiting Ghent, they will find his Establishment a cheerful and respectable residence, where every attention will be paid to their comfort. An excellent Table d'Hôte and good Wines, with prompt attendance. [131

HOTEL DE FLANDRE.—Mr. C. Dubus, the proprietor of this old established and favourite Hotel, has the honour to acquaint visiters to this city that his house is fitted up with every regard to comfort travellers can desire. Breakfast, 1 fr.; Dinner, 2fr.; half a bottle of Wine, 1 fr. 50 cents; Tea, 1 fr. Civil and attentive servants.

The Hotel is situated in the centre of the town, close to all the principal buildings, churches, &c. Families will find it a desirable residence. Large and small apartments at moderate prices. Advantageous arrangements made with Families during the winter season. [128

GRATZ.

HOTEL DE L'ELEPHANT. — The ELEPHANT HOTEL, kept by M. LISTE, MURVORSTADT PLATZ, No. 890.—This Hotel is situated in the centre of the town, and is the nearest to the Railway Station. It offers good accommodation. Refreshments of the best quality, and genial comfort. The Director of the Establishment speaks English. [132

THE HAGUE.

HOTEL BELLE VUE—R. Maitland, proprietor. This favourite and first-class Hotel, pleasantly situate opposite the Royal Park, in the most delightful part of the Hague, commanding a most beautiful prospect near the promenade and public buildings, is fitted up in a very superior style, and conducted by the proprietor, who is of English extraction, in a manner to render it deserving the extensive patronage it enjoys among the nobility and gentry of the Continent. English travellers will find it a most desirable residence for comfort and accommodation which nothing can surpass, and for civility and attention. In addition to the beautiful rural scenery in front of the House, there is a fine extensive garden, with shaded lawns and a pavillion. Arrangements made by the month on favourable terms. ☞ Table d'Hôte at half-past four o'clock. [133

HOTEL PAULEZ.—MR. T. PAULEZ, Proprietor.—This Hotel has been entirely refitted and refurnished throughout, in the best taste possible, and it is now re-opened to the public. It is situated in the finest quarter of the city, facing the Theatre. The Table d'Hôte at half past four, served with the greatest care, and *trés recherché* is frequented by good society. Every comfort and convenience of modern invention that the most fastidious traveller can wish, will be found in this Establishment. [252

HAMBURG.

HOTEL DE L'EUROPE.—Messrs. HARTMAUN & BRETTSCHNEIDER, Proprietors.—This first-rate Hotel, which has no rival in Hamburg, either as regards situation or accommodation, is particularly suitable to English Travellers. [134

ENGLISH HOTEL, 2, ADMIRALITASTRASSE—Mr. A. H. BARGSTEDT, Proprietor. —This Hotel offers superior accommodation for Families, Commercial Travellers, and Tourists. Its central situation renders it equally convenient for Travellers on business or pleasure, to the Merchant or Tourist. The Apartments are well furnished, and will be found exceedingly comfortable. The charges are moderate, and the attendance exact. [135

HANOVER.

THE UNION HOTEL.—C. M. REISS, is the nearest Hotel to the Railway Station. It is conveniently situated for travellers, and commands a fine and salubrious aspect. Furnished in the best modern style, it affords accommodation for a large number of travellers, who will find the best of refreshments are supplied at reasonable prices. [137

HOTEL ROYAL, close to the Railway Station, in the best part of the city. The *Cuisine* and Wines are of first-rate quality, and the accommodation excellent for families or single travellers. The Reading Room is well supplied with Newspapers and Periodicals. [136

HAVRE.

WHEELER'S HOTEL, 19, PETIT-QUAI, NOTRE-DAME.—This Family and Commercial Hotel, near the Custom House and Steam Packets, has been newly fitted up in the English style, with those domestic comforts so essentially necessary to travellers. It will be found to combine comfort with moderate charges. Omnibuses to and from every Train. [138

LEONARD HYMAN, Wine and Commission Merchant, 38, Rue d'Orleans.—Goods received and forwarded to all parts of the world. L. H. being Agent for the Royal Western Yacht Club of England, will be most happy to supply persons with Wines of superior quality, at low prices; and respectfully offers his services to English and American Travellers desirous of forwarding Goods, &c., from Havre. [139

HEIDELBERG.

THE EAGLE (or ADLER) HOTEL, in the GRANDE PLACE, commands a beautiful view of the celebrated Castle of Heidelberg and surrounding country. Families as well as single gentlemen visiting this highly interesting town will find this house every thing desirable,—comfortable, clean, well conducted, and reasonable. Table d'Hôte at 1 and 5 o'clock. [141

THE GOLDEN FALCON HOTEL is admirably situated in the Market Place, and nearest the castle. J. GAUZEMULLER begs to recommend his Hotel to English Travellers. There are also well furnished apartments for families, as well as single gentlemen and ladies, who wish to make a longer residence during the winter months at a very moderate rate. [142

HOTEL DU PRINCE CHARLES, on the Corn Market, nearest to the Castle. We, the proprietors, respectfully recommend this establishment to families and single gentlemen, as being the largest and best situated in the town. It commands beautiful views of the Castle, and the valley of the Neckar; is light, airy, cheerful, and truly comfortable. It has been lately embellished and re-furnished, and is conducted on a most liberal scale, under the personal superintendence of the proprietor, Mr. Sebastian Frank. Good attendance and moderate prices.

[143

HEIDELBERG—Continued.

THE COURT OF BADEN HOTEL.—Ranks amongst the best in Germany. Situate in the centre of the town, nearest to the Railway Station, commanding a beautiful view of the environs. The rooms are comfortably furnished for families or single gentlemen. Attendance good, and prices moderate. [140

HOTEL DE HOLLANDE.—Conveniently situated in the centre of the town, the nearest to the landing-place of the Steam-Boats, in the immediate neighbourhood of the Neckar, the celebrated Castle, and all the most attractive points of view. Quiet, and reasonable charges; strongly recommended for its cleanliness, civility, and good attendance. [247

PIANOFORTES.

GEORGE TRAU has always on hand a Large Assortment of very Superior PIANOFORTES, of the best quality, and German manufacture, for SALE or HIRE, at very moderate prices. Orders received by letter (pre-paid), will be punctually attended to by

GEORGE TRAU, No. 7, HAUPTSTRASSE, OPPOSITE HOTEL DE BADEN, HEIDELBERG. [144

INTERLACHEN.

HOTEL D'INTERLACHEN.—This first-rate Establishment, which has been very considerably enlarged, is very highly recommended by English Travellers in general. It has a Table d'Hôte daily, at 1 and 4. Travellers sojourning eight days, can be accommodated at 5 or 8 francs per day. During the season, the Hotel is supplied with French, English, and German newspapers. The landlord also furnishes Guides, or Carriages and Horses, for excursions among the mountains. [145

KEHL.

HOTEL DU PIED DE CHEVREUIL—Mr. JERD. RETFUS, Proprietor.—This Hotel is beautifully situated between the Station and the Bridge, in the middle of the two. The landlord is very active, and exceedingly obliging. Travellers who intend visiting Strasbourg, generally leave their Luggage at this Hotel, which may be termed a clean and comfortable house. [146

LEGHORN.

GRAND HOTEL DES ISLES BRITANNIQUES, 33, Grand Rue, opposite the PORT.—MR. ANGIOLO BIANCHI, Proprietor, assures travellers that they will be perfectly satisfied with the comfortable accommodation afforded at this Establishment. It has the advantage of being situated in the centre of the town, and close to the sea. The apartments are well furnished; the attendants speak English. Table d'Hôte, or private Dinners. [148

HOTEL DES DEUX PRINCES, PRAZZI DEI GRAN-DUCHI, opposite to the NEW POST-OFFICE.—MR. THOMSON, Proprietor, in returning thanks for the kind patronage of English travellers, respectfully informs strangers that his Hotel is the most centrally and pleasantly situated in Leghorn. Large and small apartments, elegantly furnished. Table d'Hôte, and private Dinners. [149

HOTEL DE L'AIGLE NOIR.—This Hotel, having been newly furnished and decorated, will be found to afford every thing required by travellers. It is situated on the PORT, opposite the landing-place of the Steam-packets, and is likewise close to the Railway station. Table d'Hôte at 2½ and 5 o'clock. [147

ENGLISH WAREHOUSE.

HENRY DUNN, No. 11, VIA GRANDE, LEGHORN (Established 36 Years), Dealer in WINES, SPIRITS, ALE, PORTER, &c., of the best quality; TEA, of all sorts; LINEN, HOSIERY, ENGLISH FLANNEL, IRISH LINEN and MANUFACTURED GOODS, SILKS, &c. H. D. has for sale a small Gallery of Paintings, by the old Italian, Flemish, and Dutch Masters. Goods received and forwarded to England, or any part of the Continent. [150

LEIPSIC.

HOTEL DE RUSSIE, PETERSTRASSE, G. M. CRAMER, Proprietor.—Travellers visiting this town will find the above Hotel exceedingly comfortable. English Visiters in particular will be gratified with the manner it is conducted, and the information and assistance Mr. Cramer is always ready to afford. [152

HOTEL DE POLOGNE.—Messrs. GROSSBERGER and KUHL beg to call the attention of Visitors to Leipsic to their well-known commodious Establishment, situate in the centre of the town, near the Railway Station and Theatre, replete with every comfort, and containing 136 Bed-rooms, Two large and elegant Saloons, Reading Room, Refreshment Room, and Bathing Rooms. Terms moderate. Suitable accommodation for Nobility, Families, or Single Travellers, on business or pleasure. [L.O.—153

HOTEL DE BAVIERE—GUILLAUME REDSLOB, Proprietor.—The situation of this Hotel, the manner in which it is conducted, and the reputation it enjoys throughout Germany, induce the Proprietor to take the liberty of recommending it to the attention of English and other Travellers, and to assure them no pains will be spared to merit their patronage. The accommodation for Families or Single Persons is of the best description—the apartments being exceedingly airy, well furnished, and carpeted. [151

LIEGE.

HOTEL DE L'EUROPE, Place de la Comedie.—This first-rate House affords excellent accommodation, combining elegance and comfort. The apartments, well furnished, are large and airy, adapted to families or single travellers. Table d'Hôte at One o'Clock and Four o'Clock afternoon. Prices moderate. French, German, and English spoken. Monsieur A. HENRARD begs to inform travellers that he is also Proprietor of the Hotel des Bains at Chaufontaine, at which Hotel arrangements are made for boarding and lodging families or single persons on most advantageous terms. [155

HOTEL D'ANGLETERRE, near the Theatre—Mr. CLUCK, Proprietor.—This large and fine Hotel—the nearest to the Railway-Station and Steam Packets—is situated in the most salubrious part of the town, contiguous to the Promenades and Public Establishments. It is celebrated for its cleanliness, good attendance, and reasonable prices. Large and small Apartments, suitable for Families or Single Travellers. Fixed Prices. Bed, 1 fr. 50 c. to 2 frs. Table d'Hôte at 1 and 6 o'clock afternoon. ENGLISH, FRENCH, AND GERMAN SPOKEN. [156

To Travellers between England and Germany.

HOTEL DE BELLE VUE, AT LIEGE.—GME. RIEGELS DELAFOSSE.—This Hotel, recently built on the left bank of the Meuse, at its junction with the Ourthe, within 400 yards of the New Railway Station, is recommended for the *convenience*, the *quietness*, and the *beauty* of its situation. It will be found to possess the comforts of the best English, with the advantages of the best Continental Hotels. Charges moderate. Servants included in the bill. Table d'Hôte daily, at 2½ francs. N.B.—The opening of the railway from Namur to Liege, through the picturesque valley of the Meuse, and the junction, at Liege, of all the lines of railway from Calais, Ostend, and Cologne, make the Hotel de Belle Vue at Liege a no less desirable than pleasant resting-place. [157

HOTEL DE SUEDE (proprietor, Mr. DALIMIER), one of the finest and best in Belgium, is admirably situated, facing the Royal Theatre, the Boulevards, and nearest the Railway Station. Patronised by travellers of all nations, it possesses an excellent cuisine, and is favourably known for its scrupulous cleanliness. Large Apartments, combining every domestic comfort. The Coffee-Room is splendid and elegant, and well supplied with English and Foreign Newspapers. English spoken. Fixed prices, Table d'Hôte 2½ francs, Bed-rooms 1½ to 2 francs, Sitting-room 3 to 6 francs, per day. [154

LILLE.

HOTEL DE L'EUROPE, Nos. 30 and 32, RUE BASSE.—This well-known Establishment is situated in the centre of the public buildings, close to the Theatre and Railway Terminus. A Pavilion has been recently added, which contains numerous large apartments and saloons looking into the beautiful garden of the Hotel. Hot Baths to be had at all hours. MR. JM. FERRU, having been honoured during many years with the patronage of English Travellers, hopes, by unceasing attention to the comforts of his visiters, to merit a continuance of their favours. [158

LOUVAIN.

HOTEL DE SUEDE—the principal Hotel at Louvain—a favourite resting-place of Travellers to and from the Rhine, will be found for situation, comfort, cleanliness, and moderation of charges, to merit the extensive patronage of English Travellers; as also the recommendation in "Murray's Hand-Book." Table d'Hôte, 2 francs. [159

LYONS.

GRAND HOTEL DE L'UNIVERS, 4, Rue de la République, or late Rue de Bourbon, 4, Place Bellecour, situated near the Post-Office. The Rhone and Soane Steam Boats. —Messrs. GLOVER & VUFFRAY have the honour to inform the Nobility and Travellers, that their new, excellent, and splendid Hotel, was opened in May 1846—the furniture quite new, and fitted up in the English style, one of the partners being an Englishman. The Hotel is patronized by families of the first distinction of every nation, and acknowledged to be one of the best and cleanest in France. *Travellers are particularly requested not to attend to Postmasters, Postillions, Touters, Porters, &c., either on or at the arrival of Steamboats or Diligences; for, as they receive no bribe, they will be sure to say that the Hotel is shut up, quite full, or too far off, so that those who listen to the suggestions of those interested individuals will certainly be deceived.* Charges moderate. Large and small apartments. Excellent Table d'Hôte. Private Dinners. Stabling and Lock-up Coach-houses. Several Languages spoken. [161

HOTEL DE L'EUROPE.—MR. JOLY, Proprietor.—The excellent accommodation and comfort of this long-established house commend themselves to all Visiters; its situation on the quay of the Saône is one of the most central and delightful, commanding a view of the charming scenery of Lyons. The Apartments are excellent and well-furnished, the Cuisine recherché, the Table d'Hôte proverbially good, and prices moderate. English spoken. [160

MAGDEBURG.

STADT LONDON, HOTEL DE LONDON, RUDOLF GAERTNER, Proprietor.—This Establishment is situated close to the Railway Station, and English Travellers will find it a comfortable Residence, offering superior accommodation aud good living, at moderate prices. Baths attached to the establishment. Fixed price for attendance. [162

MALINES.

HOTEL DE LA GRUE, GRANDE PLACE, MALINES, BELGIUM.—Kept by D. BREUGELMANS.—This is decidedly the largest and best Hôtel at Malines. Good Beds, excellent Wines, Baths, with every comfort of a private House. Families may be accommodated with Private Apartments for any length of time, and as cheap as at home. The Landlord and Waiters speak English. General Changarnier has apartments at this Hotel. [163

MANNHEIM.

HOTEL DE L'EUROPE.—Messrs. SCHOTT & FOHR.—This first-class establishment, opposite the landing-place of the Rhine Steamers, and enjoying an excellent reputation, has been recently embellished and fitted up in a most superior manner, enabling it to vie with the best houses on the Continent. Possessing 120 bed-rooms, and numerous large and moderate-sized suites of apartments, it offers the advantages of the best of accommodation, with excellent Refreshment and good Wines. Table d'Hôte at 1 and 5. [164

MARSEILLES.

HOTEL DES COLONIES, 13, Rue Vacon.—Messrs. BERGEYVET & RENCUREL, Proprietors.—This Hotel has been built on the newest principles, and has 100 large and small apartments. From its proximity to places of business or pleasure, it is a most desirable residence for Visiters. There are forty elegant pavilions for dinner-parties in the beautiful garden; and no expense has been spared to render this establishment worthy the patronage of English Travellers. Bath attached to the Hotel. English spoken. [166

MARSEILLES—Continued.

HOTEL BRISTOL, 8, Rue Saffron.—Mr. AUGUSTUS BOULBENE, Proprietor. This Hotel is situated in the best part of the city, close to the Post-Office, Foreign Consul's Office, Steam-Boats, Diligences, and Railway Offices. The Proprietor having travelled for several years with English Families, many comforts will be found at this House not to be obtained at any other Hotel. Charges strictly moderate. An excellent Table d'Hôte. Several languages spoken. [167

HOTEL DES AMBASSADEURS.—Travellers visiting Marseilles for business or pleasure, are recommended to patronise this Hotel, as being both highly respectabl- and comfortable, conveniently and pleasantly situated near the Steam-Packets, Diligence, and Post-Offices, with a fine view of the Port. It is furnished in a superior style, and the living will be found firste rate, at as moderate prices as in inferior hotels. The attendance is good; and English, German, Italian, and Spanish is spoken. [165

MAYENCE.

COURT OF HOLLAND HOTEL—Opposite the landing-place of the Rhine Steamers. J. B. MAIER-KERN respectfully invites attention to his old-established Hotel, as having well-furnished and comfortable Apartments for Families and single Gentlemen. Refreshments of the best quality; and the house is celebrated for its fine Wines, produced from Mr. MAIER's own vineyards. The Poste Restante is also in this Hotel—a great advantage to travellers. [169

HOTEL D'ANGLETERRE.—H. SPECHT.—This Hotel, situated in front of the Bridge leading to the Frankfort Railway, and opposite the landing-place of the Rhine Steam-Boats, commands an extensive view of the Rhine and the picturesque environs of Mayence. Travellers honouring this Hotel with their patronage, will find good accommodation, choice wines, and refreshments of the best quality, at exceedingly reasonable prices. Table d'Hôte at 1 and 5 o'clock. [168

MILAN.

GRAND ROYAL HOTEL, only two stories high, kept by G. BRUSCHETTI, who, having been frequently in England, is well acquainted with the comforts required by Travellers. He can also afford them every information regarding the different roads.

Excellent Table d'Hôte; Baths, Carriages, &c. A large collection of Antique and Modern Pictures, by the best and most admired painters, are to be seen in the Hotel.

N.B.—Please to observe BRUSCHETTI'S Grand Royal Hotel. [170

HOTEL DE LA GRANDE BRETAGNE, CORSIA DELLA PALLA, M. VITAL° BIGANZOLI, Proprietor.—The central position and comforts of this long-established house commend it to the patronage of all visiters—Families or Single Gentlemen. It consists of good apartments, Sitting-rooms, &c., all elegantly furnished. Table d'Hôte at 5. Baths in the Hotel. [172

GRAND HOTEL ST. MARC, MR. P. CASNEDI, Proprietor.—This Hotel has recently undergone extensive alterations, and a great portion of it newly furnished, and fitted up with every modern convenience. Its situation is most central, being close to the Post and Diligence offices, to the Cathedral, and public Places of Amusement. It offers first-rate accommodation and good attendance. TABLE D'HÔTE. [171

MUNICH.

HOTEL DU CERF D'OR—THE GOLDEN STAG.—The Proprietor, Mr. PHILIPPE HAVARD, respectfully informs English Travellers, that this Hotel is situated in the most beautiful part of this fine city, close to the Theatres, the Post-Office, and the Jardin Anglais. The Hotel has been completely refurnished throughout, and affords the best of accommodation. Refreshments à l'Anglaise ou à la Francaise, of the choicest quality, and at moderate prices, [174

NAMUR.

HOTEL D'HARSCAMP.—Travellers visiting Namur will find this Hotel a central and commodious Hotel, newly and elegantly furnished, and adapted in all respects to the improved taste of the Age. Reputed for many years as one of the best in Belgium for its respectability, its wine, of the first quality, and its viands of the best description. Mr. F. Hoogen, the present Proprietor, will endeavour to render this Hotel deserving this high standing, and the support of its distinguished and numerous visiters. [175

NANCY.

HOTEL DE L'EUROPE.—This old-established first-rate Hotel will be found equally desirable for Families or single Travellers visiting Nancy on business or pleasure, in consequence of its comfortable accommodation, moderate terms, central situation, and proximity to the Railway Station. Mr. Malthis, the Proprietor, speaks English. Superior Table d'Hôte. English Newspapers. [176

OSTEND.

HOTEL DES BAINS.—This Hotel, which has enjoyed the patronage of English travellers for a great many years, is particularly recommended for the attention shown to strangers. The apartments, elegantly furnished, are light, quiet, and airy. This establishment is situated in the centre of the town, close to the landing-place of the steam-packets, and not far from the Railway Station. Prices:—Table d'Hôte Dinner, 3 fr.; Breakfast, 1 fr. 25 cents; Breakfast with Eggs, 1 fr. 50 cents; Tea. 1 fr. 25 cents; Wine, 3 fr. per bottle. Apartments—Bed-room, 1 fr. 50 cents 2 fr. [178

PARIS.

LAWSON'S HOTEL BEDFORD, No. 17 and 19, Rue de l'Arcade, near the Madeleine Church (formerly Rue St. Honore.)—This Hotel has long been known to English Travellers for its comfort and many advantages. The Proprietor, in acknowledging with grateful thanks past favours, begs to assure his numerous patrons, that he has spared no expense to provide his guests with every convenience and comfort in this establishment. The Hotel is situated in the quiet and beautiful quarter of the Madeleine, free from noise and bustle; and it is within a minute's walk of the Champs Elyseés, the Railway Station, and the Boulevards. Table d'Hôte at 5 o'clock daily, in time for the Theatres. Omnibuses to and from every train. Moderate charges, and good attendance. [180

GRAND HOTEL D'ANGLETERRE, Rue des Filles St. Thomas, No. 10.—Mr. COURTOIS, Proprietor.—English Visiters to the French Metropolis will find the above Establishment very central and quietly situated, affording every comfort, combined with economy. Refreshments, Wines, &c., of the best quality. Good Table d'Hôte at 5 30 p.m. Mr. Courtois, having been educated in England, knows what an English visiter requires. Fixed prices for attendance. Travellers are requested not to mistake Mr. Courtois' Establishment for one of a similar name. [181

HOTEL WAGRAM.—MR. JULES BOULLE, Proprietor, 28, Rue de Rivoli, facing the Tuileries Gardens, in the immediate vicinity of the Champs Elysées, and principal places of amusement in Paris. English Visiters will find this Hotel worthy of their patronage, both as regards comfort and economy. Large and small Apartments. Dinners à la Carte, at a fixed price. This Hotel enjoys the reputation of being a well-conducted, highly respectable house; and the Landlord endeavours to render it more attractive by paying every attention to his visiters. [182

HOTEL VICTORIA, Rue Chaveau la Garde, No. 3, near the Church of the Madeline, the best quarter of Paris.—Established in 1837, and patronised by the ex-Royal Family.—The accommodation is of the best description, and the charges are exceedingly moderate; for the daily expense of apartment, breakfast, dinner with wine, tea or supper in the evening, and servants, do not exceed seven shillings per day. [183

HOTEL DE NORMANDIE, 240, RUE ST. HONORE.—The above Hotel possesses advantages for travellers rarely to be met with. It is in the vicinity of the principal Public Establishments, in the most favourable situation for pleasure as well as business, and it is the constant aim of the Proprietor to merit patroage by affording every comfort at the most moderate charges. Each Visiter may be furnished with a Bed-room, Breakfast, Dinner at Table d'Hôte, with a bottle of good Burgundy Wine, at 5s. and 5s. 6d. per day, including light and servants; 30s. per Week during the winter. N.B.—English spoken by the landlord and servants. [184

HOTEL DE LILLE AND D'ALBION,

323, RUE ST. HONORE,

PARIS.

There is a communication with the Rue de Rivoli from the Garden of the Hotel opposite the principal entrance to the

TUILLERIES GARDENS.

TABLE D'HÔTE—BATHS—STABLE AND COACH HOUSE.

English Attendants. [185

HOTEL DE FOLKSTONE, 9, Rue Castellane, Paris, L. OLIVIER, Proprietor.—This Establishment, situated in the fine quarter of the Madeleine, near the Boulevards, the Tuieries, and the Champs Elysées, It is particularly noted for itselegant furnitnre, good arrangement, and cleanliness, and nothing is spared by the Proprietors to render this Hotel one of the most comfortable in Paris. Bed-rooms at 2, 3, and 4 francs per day. Apartments for families. Arrangements made by week or month. English Breakfasts at 1 fr. 50 c. and 2 francs. Table de Hôte at 3 francs. English, German, Spanish and Italian Interpreters. [186

HOTEL DES ETRANGERS, 3, RUE VIVIENNE, M. GIRARD, Proprietor, near the Palais Royal, the Bourse, the Boulevards, and the Theatres. Restaurant—Table d'Hôte, 4 fr. Large and small well furnished apartments. Bedrooms at 2, 3, or 4 francs. French, English, and German newspapers. Mr. GIRARD requests gentlemen and families who are recommended to his Hotel, not to allow themselves to be misled by touters or other interested persons, who frequently deceive passengers by conducting them to other establishments of the same name as the above respectable Hotel. [187

GRAND HOTEL DE LYON, No 12, RUE DES FILLES ST. THOMAS, with a large frontage in the Rue Richelieu, and near the Bourse. No hotel is better situated for travellers who visit Paris for pleasure or business. Board and lodging at 5fr., 6fr., or 6½fr.; admission to dinner "de famille," at 2frs., wine included; single room, at 1½, 2, or 3 francs. Also, small and large apartments for families. Restaurant à la Carte, or board and lodging by the week, month, or year. Newspapers and periodicals are provided for the use of travellers.

Mr. MERIMEE, the landlord, being in communication with the principal Hotels throughout France and Europe, recommends those best suited to travellers. Omnibuses for all parts of Paris; also to and from every Train. English, German, and Spanish spoken. [179

BROWN'S ALBION HOTEL AND COMMERCIAL TAVERN (late J. DRAKE'S,) 30, FAUBOURG ST. HONORE, COUR DES COCHES, and 17, RUE DE LA MADELINE, in the immediate vicinity of the British Embassy, Tuileries, &c., is peculiarly convenient for those visiting the capital on either business or pleasure. An excellent Table d'Hôte, at 6 daily. Good Beds and comfortable accommodation. [188

BRITISH TAVERN—104, RUE RICHELIEU—NEAR THE BOULEVART.—English Restaurant, suited to the accommodation of the superior orders. This Establishment, situate in the centre of Paris, is distinguished by the noble elegance of its *locale*, combining the advantage of free respiration, both in its lofty salons, and its GARDEN, in which latter can be taken one's repast in the fine weather of summer; and is remarkable for the true character and quality of its Wines, which are served without the absurdly exorbitant prices exacted in almost all the public establishments, and that for wines neither true nor in good order. [189

PARIS—Continued.

TO PERSONS VISITING PARIS.—FURNISHED APARTMENTS, combining English comforts with economy, situated in the centre of Paris, and on one of the best Boulevards, near the Grand Opera, Exchange, and all the principal Promenades, between the Rue Richelieu and the Rue Vivienne. Excellent attendance, and English spoken.

No. 19, BOULEVARD, MONTMARTRE, PARIS. [190

APARTMENT and COMMISSION AGENT.—A. WEBB, 36, RUE DE RIVOLI.—Houses and Apartments to Let, Furnished or Unfurnished; Merchandise packed and forwarded to all parts of the world, with economy and despatch; Goods Warehoused by the month or year. Letters, Parcels, or Goods may be consigned to M. A. Webb, until wanted. Information concerning apartments, acking, conveyances, duties, &c., given gratis.—*Importer & Dealer in Foreign and French Wines.* [191

DANCING ACADEMY, No. 320, RUE SAINT HONORE, exactly opposite the Hotel de Lille and d'Albion. —At this admirably conducted establishment, now under the direction of MADEMOISELLE VICTORINE and MONSIEUR COULON, of the Grand Opera, the elite of Parisian society dance the Valse à 2 et à 3 Temps, Polka, Redowa, Schottische, Sicilienne, &c. For terms and hours of public repetitions, private lessons, &c., see the Prospectus, in English and French, to be had gratis at the above address. N.B.—Pupils attended at their own residences. Lessons of grace and deportment. [192

DENTIST.—WILLIAM ROGERS, 270, Rue St. Honoré, author of the "Buccomancie, or the Art of Knowing the Past, Present, and Future of a Person, after examining the Mouth," and several other medical and scientific works. Mr. ROGERS is sole inventor of the HOCHET DE DENTITION—a substitute for the coral mouthpiece—which obviates convulsions and accidents during infant dentition. The HOCHET DE DENTITION is 2 francs, or 20 francs per dozen. Sold by WM. ROGER Dentist, 270, Rue St. Honoré; or of the principal Chemists. [193

ENGLISH ALE AND PORTER STORES.—B. HARRIS & Co, 17 Boulevard de la Madeleine (Cité Vindé), Paris. Importers of every description of English Ale, Porter, and Stout, direct from the Breweries, and at lower prices than have ever been delivered in the trade. Bass & Co.'s, Allsopp's & Co.'s, East India Pale, and Burton Ales, 12 francs per dozen. Campbell & Co.'s Scotch Ales, 12 francs per dozen. Guiness & Co.'s Dublin Stout, 10 francs per dozen. Barclay & Co.'s, Reid & Co.'s, Truman & Co.'s, London Porter, 8 francs per dozen. Sherry Wines, pure, from the first houses in Cadiz, 42 francs per dozen. Old Crusted Port, of the finest vintages, 48 francs per dozen; superior Ports, 42 francs per doz. Choice old Cognac, from 2 to 3 francs per bottle. English Gin, 1 franc 25 cts. per bottle. Fine Burgundy, Clarets, and Champagne, at equally low prices. Prime Cheshire Cheese. Yorkshire Hams and Tongues. For the convenience of private families, the above Ales, Porter and Stout may be had in pint bottles. The Trade supplied in barrels of 18, 36, and 54 gallon casks at a great reduction. [194

THE ESTABLISHMENT OF

Mr. HOGG,

ENGLISH CHEMIST TO THE EMBASSY,

2, RUE CASTIGLIONE, (THREE DOORS FROM RUE DE RIVOLI,) PARIS,

Enjoys a reputation equal to the first London Houses for the excellent quality of its Medicines, and the exactitude with which Prescriptions are prepared.

BRANCH ESTABLISHMENT IN LONDON—9, ALBION PLACE, HYDE PARK SQUARE. [195

NOUVEAUTES—AUX TROIS QUARTIERS.—GALLOIS, GIGNAUX, & CO., MAGAZIN DE NOUVEAUTES, 21 AND 23, BOULEVARD DE LA MADELINE.—This well-known Establishment, by its immense sale, and the constant supply of the newest articles from the first manufactories of France, is enabled to offer an unrivalled choice of Silks and Velvets of special patterns; Mantles, Merinos, French Cashmeres, Woollen Stuffs, Lace, &c., &c., at comparatively low prices. The business is conducted on the strictest principles of honour English assistants in attendance. [197

POTSDAM.

PRAGUE.

ROME.

ROME—Continued.

J. P. SHEA, HOUSE AND COMMISSION AGENT, 14 and 15, PIAZZA DI SPAGNA, in soliciting the patronage of Visiters who may require large or small Apartments, begs leave to assure them that his registers will always afford the best means of obtaining what they really require. Twenty years' experience in Italy, and the attention which he pays to the drawing up of agreements, the proper filling up of inventories, the fair estimation of damages, &c., &c., ensuring increase of comfort, and in many instances preventing unnecessary trouble, annoyance, and expense. From his friends, and the numerous distinguished families by whom he has the honour to be known, J. P. S. hopes to be favoured with that confidence and support which he always has, and ever will earnestly endeavour to deserve. FURNITURE, LINEN, &c., &c., LET ON HIRE. BAGGAGE, WORKS OF ART, &c., PACKED, FORWARDED, OR WAREHOUSED. London Correspondent, J. A. GODDARD, Custom-House Chambers, 67, Lower Thames-street. [205

ROTTERDAM.

GRAND HOTEL DES PAYS-BAS This is one of the best Hotels in Holland. It is clean and comfortable, and conveniently situated on the Broompjes, the landing and embarking place of all the Steam-Boats. Large and small apartments; Prices moderate. In this Hotel there are Baths, likewise, excellent stabling and coach-houses. Table d'Hôte at half-past four. A person from the Hotel is always in attendance on the arrival of every Packet, to afford assistance and information. [206

NEW BATH HOTEL.—Passengers and Families visiting or returning from the Rhine, will find the best of accommodation at this Hotel. It is near the landing and embarking-place of the Steam-boats, and offers great advantages from its proximity to the Quay. A person from the Hotel is always in attendance on the arrival of every Packet, to afford information and assistance. [249

ROUEN.

HOTEL D'ALBION, VVE. SMITH, QUAI DE LA BOURSE, 16.—Mrs. Smith, in returning her grateful thanks for the patronage she has so long been favoured with, begs to inform travellers who visit the fine old city of Rouen, that it is her constant study to render her Hotel worthy of the reputation it has enjoyed of combining comfortable accommodation with reasonable prices. It has been recently enlarged and splendidly fitted up, and now contains large and small apartments. Restaurants and Table d'Hôte. Omnibuses attached to the Chemin de Fer convey passengers to and from the Hotel. [207

SPA.

HOTEL DE FLANDRE—Mr. PIERRE SURY, Proprietor.—This old-established House has been entirely re-furnished and embellished. Several additional Sleeping and Private Apartments have been added to it, for the convenience of large Families visiting Spa; and Mr. SURY respectfully solicits the attention of Travellers to his Hotel, as one combining comfort with cleanliness and economy. Table d'Hôte at 4 o'clock. There is a charming Garden for the use of Visitors. [208

GRAND HOTEL BRITTANIQUE.—Situated in the finest part of the town, and having a spacious English garden, offers every attraction Travellers can desire. The Proprietor has engaged the most competent persons, to ensure the strictest attention being paid to the rules of the Establishment, which are made with a view of rendering it a cheap and agreeable residence. It will be open all the year; and Families passing the winter may engage Apartments on advantageous terms. Table d'Hôte at 4 o'clock. Private Dinners. [246

STRASBOURG.

HOTEL DE PARIS.—The Proprietor of this unrivalled Establishment respectfully offers his grateful acknowledgments to the English Nobility and Gentry for their continued patronage, and avails himself of this occasion to assure Travellers visiting Strasbourg that no efforts will be spared on his part to render their sojourn at the above Hotel both comfortable and satisfactory. [250

STRASBOURG—Continued.

HOTEL DE LA MAISON ROUGE.—GRANDE PLACE.—This old-established Hotel will be found equally desirable for Families or single Travellers, in consequence of its central situation, comfortable accommodation, and moderate charges. And the Proprietor, in returning thanks to the Public for their liberal patronage, ventures to hope for their continued support. Table d'Hôte at $12\frac{1}{2}$ and at 5. Dinners and Breakfasts à la Carte. Wines of excellent vintage. Omnibuses convey Passengers to and from the Railway Station and Steam-boats. [209

THUN.

HOTEL DE BELLE VUE.—Families and Single Travellers will find first-class accommodation at this Hotel, on a most moderate scale of charges. The landlord is Proprietor of the Steam-Boat running between Thun and Interlachen; and his civility and *prevenance* to English Travellers is proverbial. Murray's Hand-book does him the honour to describe his establishment as a first-rate Hotel, well situated, and admirably conducted. The Proprietor has recently built a Saloon in the Garden for the use of the residents; and he has also opened walks leading to the celebrated Pavili n, St. Jaques, and other picturesque sites in the environs. [210

TURIN.

HOTEL DE LONDRES.—This Hotel will be found a convenient, comfortable, and economical residence for strangers. Parties remaining several weeks, will be accommodated upon liberal terms. An excellent Table d'Hôte. Mr. VIRANGE, the Proprietor, will endeavour to render English travellers as comfortable as possible. [212

HOTEL FEDER—formerly the Palais de Sonnar—Rue St. Francois de Paul, corner of the Rue de Po.—The position of this Hotel is particularly open and healthy; and from its consisting of Suites of Apartments for Families and Gentlemen, it is peculiarly suited to English Travellers, by whom it has long been patronised. It offers extreme cleanliness and comfort, combined with elegance and economy. English spoken. [211

VENICE.

GRAND HOTEL DE L'EUROPE.—This first-rate Establishment is situate in the finest part of Venice. Visiters to this beautiful city will find this Hotel worthy of patronage, both as regards comfort and economy. MR. MARSEILLE, the Proprietor, respectfully recommends his house to the notice of English travellers. [214

GRAND HOTEL DE LA VILLE, CANAL GRANDE—This Establishment, from its moderate charges, its excellent *cuisine*, and first-rate accommodation, is one of the best Hotels, not only in Venice, but in Italy. The new Director, Mr. D. LODOMEZ, will endeavour to give the utmost satisfaction in his power, to deserve the patronage of those who honour this Hotel with their confidence.

*** English and French spoken. [213

VERONA.

HOTEL DES DUE TORRI—A. and P. BARBERI, Proprietors—Situate in the Place de S. Anastasie.—This Hotel is the most central in Verona. Excellent Sitting-rooms and Sleeping apartments, with every comfort to afford satisfaction. Table d'Hôte at 3 and 5 o'clock. Large and small apartments for Families. Rooms for single Gentlemen, price 2 francs. [215

VIENNA.

THE ARCHDUKE CHARLES HOTEL.—A. SCHNEIDER'S is a large and excellent first-rate establishment, much frequented by English travellers for its moderate charges, comfort, and cleanliness. It is centrally situated, and near the theatres. There is no Table d'Hôte at this or any other hotel in Vienna, but dinners à la Carte are supplied at all hours. English spoken by all the servants. The only Hotel in Vienna where English Travellers can see the "Times" and "Galignani's Messenger." [216

VIENNA—Continued.

HOTEL MUNSCH, Vienna, Neumarkt, No. 1045, formerly the Casino. The undersigned begs to inform travellers, that he has transformed the building formerly known as the Casino into a first-rate hotel. The *Hotel Munsch* more particularly deserves the attention of strangers, as facing the Neumarkt on the one side, and the Kännther Street on the other; it is close to the Imperial Palace, the Volksgarthen, and Theatres. The hotel, which contains several sitting-rooms, large and small apartments, and bath-rooms, is furnished in a most elegant and comfortable style. Besides the principal dining-room, which is one of the most spacious and handsome in *Vienna*, there are others on the first and ground floors. The best German, English, and French papers are taken in. Excellent cuisine à la carte, and first-rate private dinners at any hour of the day. English spoken by all the servants. F. MUNSCH. [218

HOTEL ZUM GOLD LAMM.—THE GOLDEN LAMB HOTEL, J. F. HAUPTMAUN, Proprietor.—This Establishment, one of the largest in Europe, is beautifully situate on the side of the Danube. It has 150 large and small apartments, suitable for Families or single Travellers. The strictest attention is paid to the comforts of each visiter. English newspapers taken in, and the landlord speaks English. [217

WATERLOO.

"A VOICE FROM WATERLOO," by the late Sergeant-Major COTTON, many years Waterloo Guide, is admitted to be the best compendium of the great historical events which preceded and resulted in this memorable battle, the description of which is deemed most graphic and correct. The fourth edition is just published, copies of which may be procured at "Cotton's Waterloo Museum," Mount St. Jean, village of Waterloo; at Todd's, and other Libraries in Brussels. [219

WIESBADEN.

ROSE HOTEL AND BATH HOUSE, which obtains its supply of Mineral Water from the principal Spring (Kochbrunnen), kept by M. Schmidt, many years Maitre d'Hotel at Meurice's Hotel, Paris. Large and spacious apartments, airy sleeping-rooms, commanding a fine view of the Taunus Mountains. Families can be accommodated during the winter with elegantly furnished suites of Apartments, comprising kitchen and every convenience, on moderate terms. Table d'Hôte at 1 and 4. [221

HOTEL AND BATHS—DE L'AIGLE ET DE LA POSTE—situated in the vicinity of the Mineral Springs, possesses a splendid Garden containing a warm spring, which supplies eighty Baths in the establishment. This Hotel is recommended to the attention of the English visiters, for the superiority of its Accommodation, the qualities of its Refreshments and Wines, and lowness of its Charges. Attendance good. [222

ENGLISCHER HOF—HOTEL D'ANGLETERRE; Proprietor, LUDWICZ GOETZ, near the Promenade and Kochbrunnen. Mineral Water Baths supplied by the Kochbrunnen: large and small Apartments for Families, and excellent Bedrooms for single Gentlemen. This House has been known for many years among the elite of English Visiters to Wiesbaden, and it is still conducted in its ancient style of comfort and elegance. Prices very mode te After the season, Apartments, including kitchen, &c are let at this Hotel on the same terms as private apartments in the town [220

YVERDUN.

HOTEL DE LONDRES.—Mr. EMERY SUISSE has the honour to return his grateful acknowledgments for the patronage bestowed upon him so many years; and, respectfully soliciting its continuance, he begs to inform Travellers that his Hotel, having been recently improved, will still be found the best at Yverdun, offering every advantage, with economical charges. [223

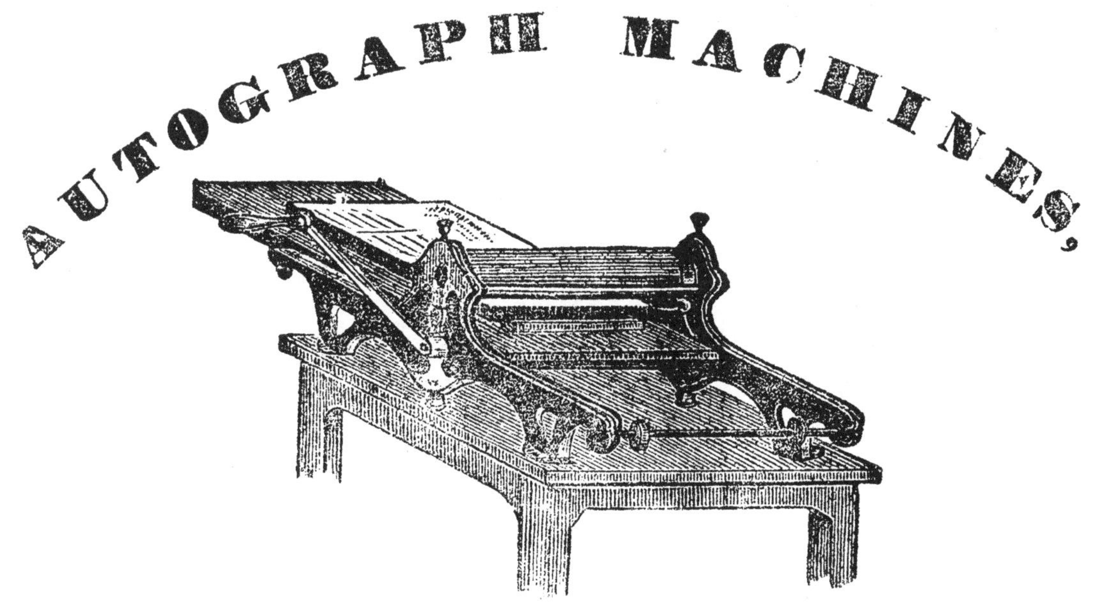

FOR COUNTING HOUSE USE,

By means of which any person can Print, with ease and rapidity, any number of Circulars, Letters, &c., &c., on their own premises.

		Including the Requisites	With Mahogany Stand.
To Print a subject	11 × 9	£6 6s.	
Extra strong ditto	11 × 9	£7 7s.	£10 10s.
Ditto ditto	16½ × 10½	£8 8s.	£11 11s.
Ditto ditto	18 × 13½	£9 9s.	£12 12s.

Instructions for using the Machines are Printed, and supplied to Purchasers.

ALSO

LETTER COPYING MACHINES.

	Ritchie's Lever.	Screw. Good Quality.	Screw. Best Make.
Large Quarto	30s.	35s., 40s., & 45s.	70s.
Foolscap	40s.	45s.	100s.
Folio Post	50s.	55s.	
Extra Ditto	60s.	65s.	120s.

GEORGE M'CORQUODALE & CO. LIVERPOOL.

HEAL & SON'S

ILLUSTRATED CATALOGUE OF BEDSTEADS,

AND PRICE LIST OF BEDDING

SENT FREE BY POST.

IT CONTAINS DESIGNS AND PRICES OF

UPWARDS OF ONE HUNDRED BEDSTEADS.

196, Tottenham Court Road, London.

[L.O.—]

NO ONE SHOULD GO TO SEA WITHOUT A LIFE-BELT.

The best and most portable at CORDING'S —Post free for 10s.

AIR BEDS, for Sea or Land travelling; CUSHIONS, for railways and invalids
COMPRESSIBLE SPONGING BATHS;
PORTABLE INDIA-RUBBER BOATS for one, two, or six persons.

CORDING'S WATERPROOFS

Have been tested for several years; their general use by the NOBILITY and GENTRY of the United Kingdom, and the OFFICERS of the ARMY and NAVY in all parts of the world, is a guarantee of their service and durability. They are made of various fabrics, suitable for LADIES' and GENTLEMEN'S WEAR, and are acknowledged by those who have used them, to be the best and only ones TO BE RELIED ON IN ALL CLIMATES.

CORDING'S GOSSAMER WATERPROOF COAT FOR THE POCKET, WEIGHT ONLY 9 OZ.

CORDING'S FISHING BOOTS

Are superior to any thing hitherto made for the comfort of ANGLERS and SNIPE SHOOTERS; they are light, pliable, and never crack; impervious to water for any length of time, and require no dressing to keep them in condition.

A LARGE STOCK OF WATERPROOFS ON HAND, AND ANY ARTICLE MADE TO ORDER.

CAUTION—All Genuine Goods are Stamped with the Name,

J. C. CORDING, 231, STRAND,

FIVE DOORS WEST OF TEMPLE BAR, LONDON. [L.O.—234

COMFORT IN A STORM!!!

EDMISTON'S POCKET SIPHONIA, OR WATERPROOF OVERCOAT.

Weight 10 Ounces.

SOLE Manufacturers of the celebrated Pocket Siphonia, remarkable for its lightness and softness of texture, easily folded to carry in the Pocket or on saddle. The most important feature in this Waterproofing is being mineralized, which effectually resists the powerful heat of the sun, and most violent rains—also obviating the stickiness and unpleasant smell peculiar to all other Waterproofs.

Price according to size............ **40s. to 55s.**
All Silk throughout........ **50s. to 65s.**

MEASUREMENT.—Length, and Size round the Chest, over the Coat

Stock Siphonias, from 25s. to 35s.
Yacht Jackets, from 18s. 6d.; Overalls, 10s. 6d
Knapsacks, &c.

NOTICE.—" EDMISTON, 416, STRAND," stamped inside. None other are genuine.

Ladies' Capes and Hoods, Petticoats, Gloves, Goloshes, Driving-Aprons, Sou'-westers, Fishing Boots, soft and pliable, require no dressing. WATER BEDS on Sale or Hire. Water Pillows, &c., &c.

TO SHIPPERS A LIBERAL DISCOUNT ALLOWED.

VICTORIA STEAMER.—LIFE BELTS.—The "Times" of the 17th February records another instance of the utility of a Life Belt at sea for emigrants, boating, and bathing purposes. EDMISTON'S Improved Belts, renowned in all parts of the world, 9s. to 12s. 6d., post-free. Portable Air Beds for ship's use, folding up in a small compass, for carrying up the country as a knapsack. Shippers and Emigrant Parties supplied by contract.—**EDMISTON'S POCKET SIPHONIA DEPOT, 416, Strand, four doors west of the Adelphi.** [L.O.—243

SHORTEST AND CHEAPEST ROUTE

TO

PARIS AND THE CONTINENT,

Via NEWHAVEN AND DIEPPE.

DAILY DIRECT SERVICE

IN CONNECTION WITH

The Brighton Steam Packet Company's New and Powerful Steamers.

	FROM LONDON.				FROM PARIS.			
JUNE.	TRAIN LEAVES LONDON.	STEAMER LEAVES NEWHAVEN	TRAIN LEAVES DIEPPE.	ARRIVES AT PARIS.	TRAIN LEAVES PARIS.	STEAMER LEAVES DIEPPE.	TRAIN LEAVES NEWHAVEN	ARRIVES AT LONDON.
Wednesday 1	8 0 a.m.	10 45 a.m.	6 45 p.m.	11 0 p.m.	9 25 a.m.	4 0 p.m.	9 30 p.m.	11 30 p.m.
Thursday.. 2	8 0 ..	11 0 ..	6 45 ..	11 0 ..	12 30 noon	10 30 ..	7 35 a.m.	9 50 a.m.
Friday...... 3	10 0 ..	12 30 noon	6 45 ..	11 0 ..	12 0 ..	11 30 ..	7 35 ..	9 50 ..
Saturday.... 4	10 0 ..	12 30 ..	9 45 ..	5 0 a.m.	12 0 ..	12 0 night	7 50 ..	10 30 ..
Monday.... 6	10 0 ..	2 0 p.m.	9 45 ..	5 0 ..	12 0 ..	1 0 a.m	10 20 ..	1 0 p.m.
Tuesday.... 7	6 0 ..	8 30 a.m.	6 45 ..	11 0 p.m.	12 0 ..	1 30 ..	10 20 ..	1 0 ..
Wednesday 8	12 0 noon	2 45 p.m.	9 45 ..	5 0 a.m.	9 25 a.m.	2 40 p.m.	9 30 p.m.	11 30 ..
Thursday.. 9	8 0 a.m.	9 45 a.m.	6 45 ..	11 0 p.m.	12 0 noon	2 0 a.m.	1 10 ..	3 45 ..
Friday......10	2 0 p.m.	4 30 p.m.	7 0 a.m.	3 0 ..	12 0 ..	9 0 p.m.	7 35 a.m.	9 50 a.m.
Saturday...11	8 0 a.m.	10 30 a.m.	6 45 p.m.	11 0 ..	9 25 a.m.	4 0 p.m.	7 50 ..	10 30 ..
Monday....13	2 0 p.m.	6 0 p.m.	7 0 a.m.	3 0 ..	12 0 noon	11 30 ..	7 35 ..	9 50 ..
Tuesday....14	10 0 a.m.	1 30 ..	9 45 p.m.	5 0 a.m.	9 25 a.m.	6 0 ..	7 35 ..	9 50 ..
Wednesdy.15	5 10 p.m.	8 30 ..	7 0 a.m.	3 0 p.m.	9 25 ..	2 30 ..	8 30 p.m.	10 30 ..
Thursday..16	8 0 a.m.	9 45 a.m.	6 45 p.m.	11 0 ..	12 0 noon	8 30 ..	7 35 a.m.	9 50 ..
Friday......17	8 0 ..	10 45 ..	6 45 ..	11 0 ..	9 25 a.m.	4 0 ..	9 30 p.m.	11 30 p.m.
Saturday...18	8 0 ..	11 0 ..	6 45 ..	11 0 ..	12 0 noon	10 30 ..	7 50 a.m.	10 30 a.m.
Monday ...20	10 0 ..	12 30 noon	9 45 ..	5 0 a.m.	12 0 ..	12 0 night	7 35 ..	9 50 ..
Tuesday ...21	10 0 ..	2 0 p.m	9 45 ..	5 0 ..	12 0 ..	2 0 a.m.	10 20 ..	1 0 p.m.
Wednesdy.22	12 0 noon	2 45 ..	9 45 ..	5 0 ..	9 25 a.m.	2 40 p.m.	9 30 p.m.	11 30 ..
Thursday..23	8 0 a.m.	9 45 ..	6 45 ..	11 0 p.m.	12 0 noon	2 0 a.m.	1 10 ..	3 45 ..
Friday......24	2 0 p.m	4 30 ..	7 0 a.m.	3 0 ..	12 0 ..	9 0 p.m.	7 35 a.m,	9 50 a.m.
Saturday..25	8 0 a.m.	10 30 a.m.	6 45 p.m.	11 0 ..	9 25 a m.	4 0 ..	7 50 ..	10 30 ..
Monday....27	2 0 p.m.	6 30 p.m.	7 0 a.m.	3 0 ..	12 0 noon	11 30 ..	7 35 ..	9 50 ..
Tuesday....28	10 0 a.m.	2 0 ..	9 45 p.m.	5 0 a.m.	9 25 a.m.	6 0 ..	7 35 ..	9 50 ..
Wednesdy.29	5 10 p.m.	8 30 ..	7 0 a.m.	3 0 p.m.	9 25 ..	2 30 ..	8 30 p.m.	10 30 p.m.
Thursday..30	8 0 a.m.	9 45 a.m.	6 45 p.m.	11 0 ..	12 0 noon	8 30 ..	7 35 a.m.	9 50 a.m

Weather permitting.

The Steamers sail from the Railway Wharf at Newhaven, adjoining the Terminus, the Hotel, and the Custom House.

THROUGH FARES.—LONDON TO PARIS.

First Class .... **24s.**
Second Class and Best Cabin.............. **20s.**
Second Class .... **17s.**

These Tickets are available for four days, including the date of issue.

For further particulars see page 335; and also "Bradshaw's General Guide for Great Britain and Ireland.

MESSRS FUTVOYE AND COMPANY

Desire to call the attention of the Nobility and Gentry to the elegant and extensive SHOW-ROOMS they have recently opened in REGENT STREET, and the adjoining premises in BEAK STREET. These SHOW-ROOMS are of that commodious character as to readily admit of articles of every variety being properly displayed, consequently, a most extensive stock, comprising ENGLISH and FRENCH JEWELLERY, WATCHES, CLOCKS, BRONZES, PAPIER MACHE, LEATHER and CABINET GOODS, GLASS and CHINA ORNAMENTS, MUSICAL INSTRUMENTS, BUSTS and STATUETTES of the DUKE OF WELLINGTON, in Ivory and Parian, and all the most recent NOVELTIES in FANCY GOODS, as well as articles of UTILITY, of English and Foreign Manufacture, will be found arranged for inspection. Those articles MANUFACTURED by the firm are in every case after the most approved designs, and will invariably be found to display an elegance of taste, combined with the most superior workmanship. With regard to IMPORTED GOODS, Messrs. FUTVOYE AND COMPANY believe that their many years' experience in the WHOLESALE TRADE, together with their extensive Continental connections, have secured for them unusual facilities for obtaining all the best productions of FOREIGN MANUFACTURE on the most advantageous terms.

Messrs. FUTVOYE AND COMPANY can refer to the continued patronage they have been favoured with from members of the ROYAL FAMILY, and some of the most distinguished of the ARISTOCRACY as a guarantee for the SUPERIOR CHARACTER of the articles of which their stock consists, while, as regards price, the extensive nature of their transactions enables them to enter into successful competition with any other house in the trade.

Messrs. FUTVOYE AND COMPANY, in soliciting an inspection of their EXTENSIVE STOCK and MAGNIFICENT PREMISES, beg to assure all who may honour them with a visit, that they will meet with a polite reception, whether purchasers or otherwise, and to intimate, that it will be with them an invariable rule to exchange any article purchased at their ESTABLISHMENT, which may not be approved of.

FUTVOYE'S RACING GAME,

The most interesting amusement yet produced can now be had from three to six guineas, in oak, walnut, or mahogany; also smaller sizes for children, from 2s. to 15s.

THE PARIS CHOCOLATE COMPANY,

Distinguished by the Patronage of Her Majesty the Queen,

And the unanimous awards of both

"COUNCIL" AND "PRIZE MEDALS" AT THE GREAT EXHIBITION OF 1851.

Such is the perfection attained in the manufacture of the Company's preparations, that they may be used either as Food or Beverage.

And Chocolate or *properly prepared Cocoa* is now universally recommended by the medical profession as more conducive to health than any other vegetable production which enters into the human dietary.

BREAKFAST CHOCOLATE, in ½ and ¼lb. tablets, plain, from 1s. 4d. to 3s. per lb.; with vanille, from 3s. to 6s. per lb.

HONEY CHOCOLATE, a combination of the purest heather Honey with the mildest French Cocoa, in Pots 1s. 3d. each.

THE CHOCOLATE BONBONS, as supplied to the most distinguished families in the Kingdom, and pronounced an unrivalled dessert, 3s. 3d., 4s. 4d., and 6s. per lb., and in fancy boxes, 6d., 1s., 1s. 3d., 2s., and 2s. 6d. each.

FANCY CHOCOLATES, in Medallions, Railway Pastilles, Penny Sticks, Statuettes, Cigars, &c.

CHOCOLATE POWDER.—Exhibition Quality, with vanille, in canisters and packets, 2s. per lb., plain quality loose, and in canisters and packets at 1s. per lb. and upwards.

FRENCH SYRUPS, ARE UNRIVALLED SUMMER BEVERAGES, in bottles, from 1s. 2d. to 2s. 6d. each, prepared from the choicest fruits, and when mixed with cold water, form an anti-alcoholic drink not to be surpassed; peculiarly adapted for evening and juvenile parties, extensively used for flavouring Jellies, Creams, Puddings, &c.

SUPERIOR TO COFFEE, BUT LOWER IN PRICE.—Breakfast Chocolate, prepared from the choicest Cocoas of the English markets, and manufactured by the most approved French method. ¼lbs., 6d. each. ⅛lbs., 3d. each. 1 oz., 1d. each. ½ oz., 6d. per doz.

Travellers will find the above articles invaluable, as they are portable, require no preparation, and are warranted to keep good in any climate.

Consumers are particularly requested to observe the Company's name and address on each packet, and to purchase only of their regularly appointed agents.

AGENTS WANTED FOR VACANT TOWNS.

Sold Wholesale and Retail by the principal Grocers, Confectioners, and Druggists in the Kingdom.

CHOCOLATE MILLS, ISLEWORTH—Wholesale Depôt, 35, Pudding-lane, City.

Post-office orders, and applications for Agencies, to be addressed to

SAMUEL SANDERS, Wholesale Depôt.

WHOLESALE AGENTS,

By whom Price Lists are sent (post free), and Retailers supplied upon the best terms.

LONDON.

Akhurst, J., family grocer, 10, Grove-terrace, Notting-hill

Austen & Co., tea-dealers, 101, High-st., Camden Town

Hatfield, John, 221, Regent st

Pearse, Mr., confectioner, High-st., Hampstead

Russell, T., family grocer, 72, Borough, and 22, New-st, Covent-garden

Wortley and Hanbury, tea-dealers, grocers, and Italian Warehousemen, 54, Upper Baker-st., Regent's-park

COUNTRY.

Bedford—Brashier & Son, Foreign Warehousemen

Blackburn—Dickson and Wells, tea-dealers, 11, Ainsworth-street

Boston—Noble, J. & Co., Market-place

Brighton—Maynard, J. G., confec., 40, West-st

Cambridge—Moore J. V., tea-dealer, 24, Trinity-st

Cheltenham—Jul & Co., grocers, opposite Queen's hotel

Edinburgh—Maclean & Son, Foreign Warehousemen, 27, Princes st, and 61, Queen-street

Gravesend—Jewesson, R. W., 25½, Harmer-st

Greenwich—Barber, C. W., family grcr, Church-st

Guildford—Copeman & Lacy, tea-dealers, High-st

Harrow—Hutton, S., tea-dealer, &c

Ludlow—Foster, E., dispensing chemist

Lymington—Hayward, J., grocer

Oxford—Cooper, F. T., tea dealer, High-st

Portsea—Bizwood, J., chemist, 44, St. James-st

Salisbury—Whitlock, E., dispensing chemist

Sunderland—Young, John, wholesale druggist, 130, High-street

Swansea—Day, William, 1, Mount-street

Wellingborough—Hensman, C., wholesale druggist

SOLE CONSIGNEES—Bombay—Stevens Brothers, Merchants.

LONDON RETAIL AGENTS APPOINTED.

Abbis & Co., tea-dealers and grocers, 60, Gracechurch-st
Akhurst, Mr., grocer, Notting-hill
Armstrong, G., tea-dealer, 42, Old Bond-st, Piccadilly
Ashton, W., Post-office, City-rd
Austin and Co., 86, Gray's-inn-ln
Barber, C. W., grocer, Greenwich
Budgen, Mr., grocer, 23, High-st., Kensington
Carter, Mr., confectioner, 36, Portman-pl., Edgeware-rd
Clifford, E., French and Italian warehouseman, Lr.Grosvenor-st
Cooper, Mr., 27, Brompton-row
Cooper, Mr., 209, Tot.-court-rd.
Dennis & Son, Church-st. Hackney
Elwin, T., Manor-rise, Brixton
Eve, John O., tea-dealer, 435, West Strand
Foster, W., tea-dealer, 5 and 6, Philpot-lane
Grignon and Co., Italian warehousemen, 2 and 3 Suffolk-st., Pall-mall, East
Grinham, G. J., 13, Mortimer-st., and St. John-st-rd
Hall R., 63, South Audley-street
Handscombe, grocer, Mile-end
Hill and Dibdin, Brompton-rd
Holland, W., tea, coffee, and spice dealer, 127, Oxford-st
Johnson, 4, Pont-st., Belgrave-sq
Johnston, Mr., grocer, Lower Clapton
Jones, Mr., grocer, Up. Clapton
Knowles, H., Lower Belgrave-st
Lawrence, W. C., 158, Oxford-st
Lawrence, C. B., 98, Strand
Lund S., family tea warehouse, Newgate-st
Masters and Co., Bishop's-road, Paddington
Millard, Camden-broadway
Miller, A., grocer, Tottenham
Payne & Son, foreign warehousemen, tea, coffee, and spice merchants, 328, Regent-st
Pearse, confectioner, Hampstead
Phillips, R. M., wine merchant, grocer, &c., 4, Grove-terrace, Brompton
Russel, T., family grocer, 72, Boro' & 22, New-st., Covent-garden
Searcy, W., Upper Berkley-st., west
Shepard, S., 37, Frederick-place, Hampstead-rd
Snowden, R., coffee merchant, City-rd
Stevens, Mr., grocer, 6, Derville's row, Hammersmith
Warton, A., French and Italian warehousemen, 13, N. Audley-st
Wortley & Hanbury, grocers, &c., Upper Baker-st, Regent's-park

COUNTRY RETAIL AGENTS APPOINTED.

Aberdeen—Farquharson and Co, 131, Union-st.; Lockhart and Co., 92, Union-st.; Lumsden and Co., 95, Union-st.; M'Leod, Mr., 3, Market-st.; Milne & Son, 185, Union-st.; Walker, W., 52, Union-st
Accrington — Marshall, G., chemist, Blackburn-st
Alford—Hildred, J. S., confec
Aspley Beds—Turney, A. P
Banbury—Austin, J. B., wholesale and retail druggist
Bangor—Birket, T., grocer
Barnstaple—Gregory, Mr., family grocer; Arnoll, R., confectioner
Barnsley—Guest, T., tea-dealer Market-pl
Bath—Amery, J., confectioner, 8, N. Bond-st.; Fisher, Mr., confectioner, Northgate; Fortt and Son, confec., Milsom-st.; Slade & Co., grocers, Milsom-st
Bawtry—Nettleship, T., chemist
Beaumaris—Barker, chemist
Bedford—Brashier and Son
Berwick—Elliott, J., grocer, Hide-hill
Bideford—Dingle, E., chemist
Biggleswade—Spong, T. W
Birmingham—Birch, A., grocer, 8, High-st.; Lisseter, E., confectioner, 53, New-st.; Parker, T., grocer, Bull-st.; Partridge, J., grocer, Worcester-st.; Simpson, E., grocer, Broad-st.; Taylor, James, grocer, Broad st.; Webb, E. T., grocer, Grea Brook-st
Blackburn—Dickson & Wells grocers, 11, Ainsworth-st
Blackpool—Booth and Co., grocers, Market-st
Boston—Noble, J. & Co., Market-place
Bradford — Alderson & Sons, grocers, Bridge-st.; Bartle, confectioner; Britton, R., grocer; Denison, P., grocer, Manchester-road; Hall, Mr., confectioner, Bank-st.; Outhwaite, chemist, Kirkgate; Shackleton, Miss, Hustler-gate
Brecon—Bright, chemist, Medical hall
Brentford—Wood, H., chemist
Bridlington-Quay--Stephenson, Mr., chemist
Bridgewater--Heard and Son, chemists and druggists
Brighton—Fortt, W., confec., 70, East-st.; Maynard, J. G., confec., West-st.; Mutton, confec., 82, King's-row
Bristol—Coleman and Co., 64, Redcliff-st.; Duck and Co., grocers, Wine-st; Ferris and Score, chemists to Her Majesty, 4, & 5, Union-st.; Langridge, T., 60, Wine-st.; Mackrel & Co., Wine-st.; Nattriss, John, confectioner, Wine-st.; Wedmore, J. & S., family grocers
Bungay—Howard, F., grocer, Earsham-st.; Owles J., chemist
Burnley—Thomas, R., druggist, Market-st
Bury — Holt, S., chemist, 14, Bolton-st
Bury St. Edmunds—Oliver, J. G., family grocer
Cambridge—Moore, J. V., 24, Trinity-st
Canterbury — Pond, Misses, confectioners
Cardiff—Bird, W. & Son, grocers, Duke-st
Carnarvon—Griffith, R., chemist; Owen, G., chemist
Carlisle—Mackereth, English-st.; Taylor, C., 76, Market-place
Castletown — Stowell, J. J., chemist, Malew-st
Coleford—Herbert, J., grocer
Coleshill—Dale, J., grocer, &c
Chatham—Perry, (late Dunn), confectioner, High-st
Chelmsford—Copland, Henry, chemist; Fry, J. S., confec
Cheltenham — Jull and Co., grocers, opposite the Queen's Hotel
Chertsey—Robinson and Co., confec
Chester—Platt, Mr., chemist
Christchurch — Tucker, W
Chichester—Finch, H., confectioner, East-st; Stokes, W., family grocer; Wright, Mrs., confectioner
Chippenham—Nicholls, W.
Clifton—Pomeroy, J., confec.; Warren, T. A., confectioner
Clitheroe—Bailey, W., jun., grocer, Castle-st
Cockermouth—Taylor, T F., chemist, Main-st
Colchester—Carr, J.O., family grocer, High-st
Coventry—Slingsby, W., and F., Broadgate
Cowbridge — Williams, W., grocer, High st
Crediton—Searle, J

Crewkerne—Strawson, H., ch

Darlington—Heron, W., Prospect-pl.; Spence, H., 5, Bond-gt.; Thompson, 5, Blackwall-gt

Dartford—Langlands, grocer

Dawlish—Ferris, W., grocer

Deal — Fitch, E. J., grocer, Beech-st

Derby—Bakewell, J. and C., grocers, Market Head; Brentnall, T., 50, St. Peter-st.; Clark, J., Italian warehousemen; Hollingshead, confec., Irongate

Devizes—Giddings, E., Brittox

Diss—Musket, C., Crown-st

Doncaster—Berrill, G. Baxtergate; Parkinson, S., and Son

Dorchester — Biggs, confectioner; Bishop, J., grocer

Dorkin—Butler, W. T., grocer

Douglas—Higgins, Robert, ch; Quine, Mr., chemist

Dover—Lilley, J., grocer, Market-pl.; Pierce, J. S., grocer, Snargate-st

Driffield—Rawlinson, J., grocr.

Dumfries— Sloane Brothers, Queensbury-sq

Dundee—Fyffe, Jas., grocer, 63, High-st.; Keiller, C., confec., 1, Castle-st.; Marshall and Co., 99, Nethergate; Stuart, P., grocer, 38, Nethergate

Durham—Shields, J., 12 and 13, Market-pl

Edinburgh—Calderwood, confectioner; Kirkhope, J., grocer, Melville-pl.; Maclean and Son, purveyors of wines and provisions to Her Majesty, 27, Prince's-st.; Mackie, J. W., 108, Prince's-st.; Melrose & Co., 93, George-st.; Redpath, D., confectioner, Nicholson-st

Ely—Pate & Hogg, Wholesale druggists

Evesham—Beckingsale & Co

Exeter—Gould, W., family grocer; March, J., confec.; Ridgway, Hall, and Co., tea-dealers; Salter, T., confec; Tucker, C., grocer

Exmouth — Farncombe, H., confec.; Foster, R., grocer; Nicks J. T., grocer

Eye (Suffolk)—Bishop, grocer

Fakenham—Burrell, J. G., confectioner; Hubbard, grocer

Falmouth—Downing, grocer

Farnham—Williams, chemist

Folkestone—Pledge, G., grocer, Rendezvous-st

Fordingbridge—Fulford, Mrs

Glasgow—Aylward, & Co., 102, Argyle-st.; Baxter & Sons, 157, Buchanan-street; Burton and Thompson, grocers, 93, St. Vincent-st.; Duncan, A., 106, Buchanan-st.; M'Lerie, & Co., 36, Buchanan-st.; Smith, R., grocer Sauchiehall-st

Gloucester—Bellamy, J., grocer, Westgate-st

Gosport—Biddle, J., grocer, Forton-road; Wright, A., grocer

Greenock—Alexander, J., 9, Westblackhall-st.; Macfarlane, J. A., 8, Westblackhall-st

Guildford—Copeman & Lacy, grocers, and foreign warehousemen

Haddington — Wilson, W., grocer, High-st

Halifax—Parker, T., chemist, 14, Crown-st

Harrogate—Harper, J., grocer; Robinson, James, confec

Hastings—Amoore, confect.

Hertford—Gilbertson and Son

Hexham—Newbegin, T., grocer, Market-pl

Hitchen—Clisby, E., chemist, Sun-st

Horsham—Chatfield, T. confec

Huddersfield — Hoskin, W., grocer, 94, King-st

Hull—Field, W., grocer, Market-pl.; Fullerton, Mrs., 47, Saville-st.; Gill, R. J., 19, Trinity House-lane; Hammond, J., 5, Witham; Pickering, A., 45., Lowgate; Rimmington, J., wholesale and family tea-dealer, coffee and spice merchant, 28, Market-pl

Huntington—Ridgely, grocer

Inverness—Macbean, Angus, 15, High-st

Ipswich—Miller, R., Old Butter-market

Kendal—Greaves, E., Strickland-gate; Severs, J., ditto

Kidderminster—Rickett, Brothers, High-st

Lancaster—Jackson, E., chemist, Market-place

Landport—Wells, T. & Co., Railway tea establishment

Launceston—Powell, J., grocer

Leamington—Jacks, P., grocer Upper Parade; Oldham, S., 24, Lower Parade; Surcomb and Heard, 21, Bath-st

Leeds—Buck & Jackson, tea-dealers; Ellison, Upperhead-row; Robinson, A., 26, Upper-head-row; Wood, G., confec., Commercial-st

Leek—Haynes, S. N., grocer Derby-st

Leicester—Sarson & Simpkin, Hotel-st

Lewes—Hammond, 42, High-st

Lichfield — Harris, W. R., chem; Tanner, W. H., grocr, &c

Lincoln — Tomlinson, chemist, 292, High-st.; Turner, & Co., Above-hill

Liskeard—Elliot, S., chemist

Liverpool—Beynon, J., grocer, Ranelagh-st.; Choffin, C. E., 43, South Castle-st.; Chapman, T., grocer, James'-st; Fisk, A., confec., St. Luke's-pl.; Fisk & Son, confec., Castle-st.; Gaskell & Fair, Clayton-sq.; Goodacre, S. and T., Old Haymarket; Herring and Co., 80, Renshaw-st.; Miller & Co, 8, Dale-st; Nixon, T. and Co., 1, Castle-st; Sowden, J. T., 20, Great George-st; Syers, T. H., 16, Ranelagh-st; Thompson, J. & Co., 48, Berry-st.; Woodville, I., grocer, & Italian warehouseman, 78, Bold-st

Louth—Hurst, John, chemist, Market-pl

Lowestoft—Devereux, Jas & Thos., grocers

Ludlow—Foster, E., chemist

Lymington—Hayward, J., grcr

Lynn—Bayes, J., chemist

Maidstone—Bayfield, J., chemist, Gabriel's-hill; Jackson, Mr., confectioner, High-st.; Wraith, J., grocer, Week-st

Malton—Sewell & Son, grocers

Manchester—Binyons, Robinson, and Co., tea and coffee dealers, 18, St. Ann's-sq., 51, Oldham-st, and 216, Deansgate; Brown, L. F., chem., Gt. Ducie-st.; Croxton and Bedford, grocers, 98, Oxford-st.; Dadd, S., grocer, 123, Oxford-rd; Darbyshire and Co., 49, Market-st; Entwistle and Co., Bank-parade Salford; Gill, G., Post-office, Strangeways; Gould Brothers, 3, Market-pl.; Hodgson, T., 109, Oxford-st.; Holt, G., chemist, 11, Lloyd-st., Greenheys; Holyoake, W., 37, Downing-st.; Howarth, J., grocer, Princess-st.; Hutchinson, Mrs., Palatine-bdgs; Lett, W., chemist, 183, Oxford-st; Mace, C., Grocer, 240, Deansgate; Nield, S., 223, Stretford new-rd.; Phythian, Post-office, Rusholme; Richardson and Roebuck, grocers to Her Majesty, Market-pl.; Roach, E., Market-st.; Satterthwaite, W., grocer, 63, Piccadilly, and 147, Oldham st; Sayce and Co., grocers, 35, Deansgate; Seelig, J., Cross-st., King-st.; Stewart, confectioner, Old Exchange, King-st Storey, chemist, 75, Oxford-st;

Tamplin, E.C., chem., 75, Oxford-st.; Whitley John, confec., 113, Piccadilly; Yates, R. S., confec., 3, St. Ann's-sq

March—Davies, P H, chemist

Margate—Brashier, S. and J., confectioners

Market Harborough—Higgs, J. S., chemist; Shepard, chemist

Newcastle—Bell, J. and M., confec., Pilgrim-st.; Brightwen, C., grocer, Grey-st.; Watson and Son, head of Grey-st

Newbury—Fidier, T., chemist, Market-pl

Newmarket—Rogers, J., chemist

Newport (Isle of Wight)—Way, W., family grocer

Newton Abbott—Gaskell, W. J., chemist

Northampton—Adkins W., chemist, Sheep-st.; Mayger W. D., chem, Regent-sq.; Greville H. M. and E., chem., Wood-hl.

Norwich—Norgate and Co., grocers, &c

Nottingham—Barber, John, tea-dealer; Bowers and Co., 22, Chapel-rd.; Clarke and Emms, Long-row; Eggleston, Bridlesmith-gate; Fox, T., confec., 16, Long-row; Goodacre, R., grocer, Pelham-st

Nuneaton—Iliffe, T., chemist.

Oldham—Heywood, T., family grocer

Oundle—Hilliam, J. L., grocer

Oxford—Cooper, 46, High-st

Peel (Isle of Man)—Carran, chem

Penzance—George, R., confec

Perth—Fenwick and Son, confectioners, 27, John-st.; Keiller, Mr., 45, George-st

Peterborough—Bedells, T., grocer

Plymouth—Ford, confec.; Wills, J, grocer, 18, George-St.; Wearing, W. H., chemist, George-st

Pontefract—Phillips, J. & Co

Poole—Green, George, confec

Portsea—Bigwood, J., dispensing chemist, 44, St. James'-st

Portsmouth—Chambers, grocer, 83, High-st.; Fraser, W., confectioner, High-st

Preston—Dawson, T., chemist, Fishergate; Edmondson, J., 100, Fishergate; Myers, F., Wholesale grocer and tea dealer, 118, and 119, Fishergate; Thornley, J, Market-pl

Ramsbury—Seymour, S., conf

Ramsey (Isle of Man)—Carran, chem.; Stowell, Thos., chem., &c

Ramsgate—Austen and Son., Harbour-st

Reading—Gregory, T., 32, Market-pl

Reigate—Deane, J., grocer, High-st

Rhyl—Hilditch, W., chemist

Richmond—Hall and Son, grocers, George-st.; Keay, G., grocer, Up Hill-st.; Pentelow, grocer, Lower George-st

Ringwood (Hants)—Lowe, George, grocer

Rochdale—Baker, P. P., chemist; Booth, J., chemist

Royston—Bull, W., chemist.

Rugby—Freen, G., chemist: Jacomb, S., confec., School-st

Rugely—James T., stationer

Ryde—Riddet and Sons, grocers, &c

Salisbury—Whitlock, chemist.

Sandgate—Jenner, R. B., dispensing chemist

Sandwich—Baker, J., grocer

Scarborough—Sleightholm, A., confectioner

Selby—Fish, G., Market-pl

Sheffield—Allshorn, A., Fargate; Appleyard & Co., 21, Old Haymrkt.; Ballans & Co., Angel-st.; Davey, J. H., 19, Fargate; Fox, W., 6, Barkerpool; Hall, H., 118, West-st.; Millns, F., Castle-st.; Porter T. and Son 7, King-st.; Sharman, J., Spring-house; Thompson, S., 1, High-st.; Waterfall, John G., grocer; Watson, T., grocer, 6 Fargate.

Shepton Mallett—Wason, J., perfumer, High-st

Sherborne—Gosney, G, grocer; Sharpe, W.G., confectioner

Shrewsbury—Crump, V., confectioner, Wyle Cop; Davies and Son, confec., Market-pl.; Wilding, Eliz., Corn-market

Sidmouth—Trump, J., grocer; Webber, J., confectioner

Slough—Griffith, R., chemist

Southampton—Cooksey Brothers, grocers; Randal and Son, chemists to Her Majesty

Southsea—Wearn, W, grocer

Stamford—Patterson G., chem. Freeman, E., chemist

Stockport—Patten, W. H., chemist, 50 and 52, Heaton-lane

Stowmarket—Jackson, W., chemist and druggist

St. Austell—Geldard, chemist

St. Bees—Reay, J., chemist

St. Helens—Thompson R., chemist

St. Ives—Johnson, J., grocer.

St. Leonard's—Beck, J., confectioner, 44, Marina

St. Neots—Topham F., statnr

Tavistock—Perry, chemist, &c

Teignmouth—Musgrave, J., grocer

Thrapston—Sanderson grocer

Tiverton—Ward, R., tea-dealer, Angel-hill

Torquay—Lodge, T., chemist; Narracott Brothers, grocers; Webber and Alderton, chemists

Truro—Job, R. O, chemist

Tunbridge-Wells—Delves & Jull, grocers, Parade; Field, F., confectioner; Gates, A. D., grocer, High-st.; Lovegrove, T., confectioner, Parade

Ventnor (Isle of Wight)—Joliffe, J, confec., Church-st

Walsall—Abbey, T., grocer

Wareham—Barfoot, grocer

Warwick—Hopkins, Thomas, druggist

Watlington—Spyer, W. G., chemist

Wellingbro'—Bland and Son, grocers

Weston-Super-Mare—Griffiths, C., chemist, High-st

Weymouth—Ayling, Joshua, grocer; Drew and Son, confectioners; Lundie, J., grocer; Slyfield and Co., Thomas st

Whitehaven—Davies E. and Co., grocers; Fletcher, J grocer, 47, King-st

Wimbourne—Huntley, grocer

Winchester—Benny & Hayles High-st

Windsor—Layton, C., confec.

Wisbeach—Oldham T, chem.

Woburn—Heighington, family grocer, &c

Woolwich—Davisson, J., confectioner, Hare-st.; Harrison, confec., Green's-end; Parkes, H. chemist, Green's end; Parkes, Thomas, Hare-st

Worcester—West, R., grocer, High-st.; Hambler, J., confectioner, High-st

Worthing—Potter, W., grocer, 3, High-st

Yarmouth—Fenn, J., grocer; Owles, J., chemist

York—Barker and Co., 1 High Westgate; Pinder, G. E., 8, High Westgate; Tindell, Mrs., 14, High Ousegate; Winn, J., grocer, 39, Coney-st

---

Post-office orders, and applications for agencies, to be addressed to Samuel Sanders, wholesale depôt.

SECTION 2

MAPS

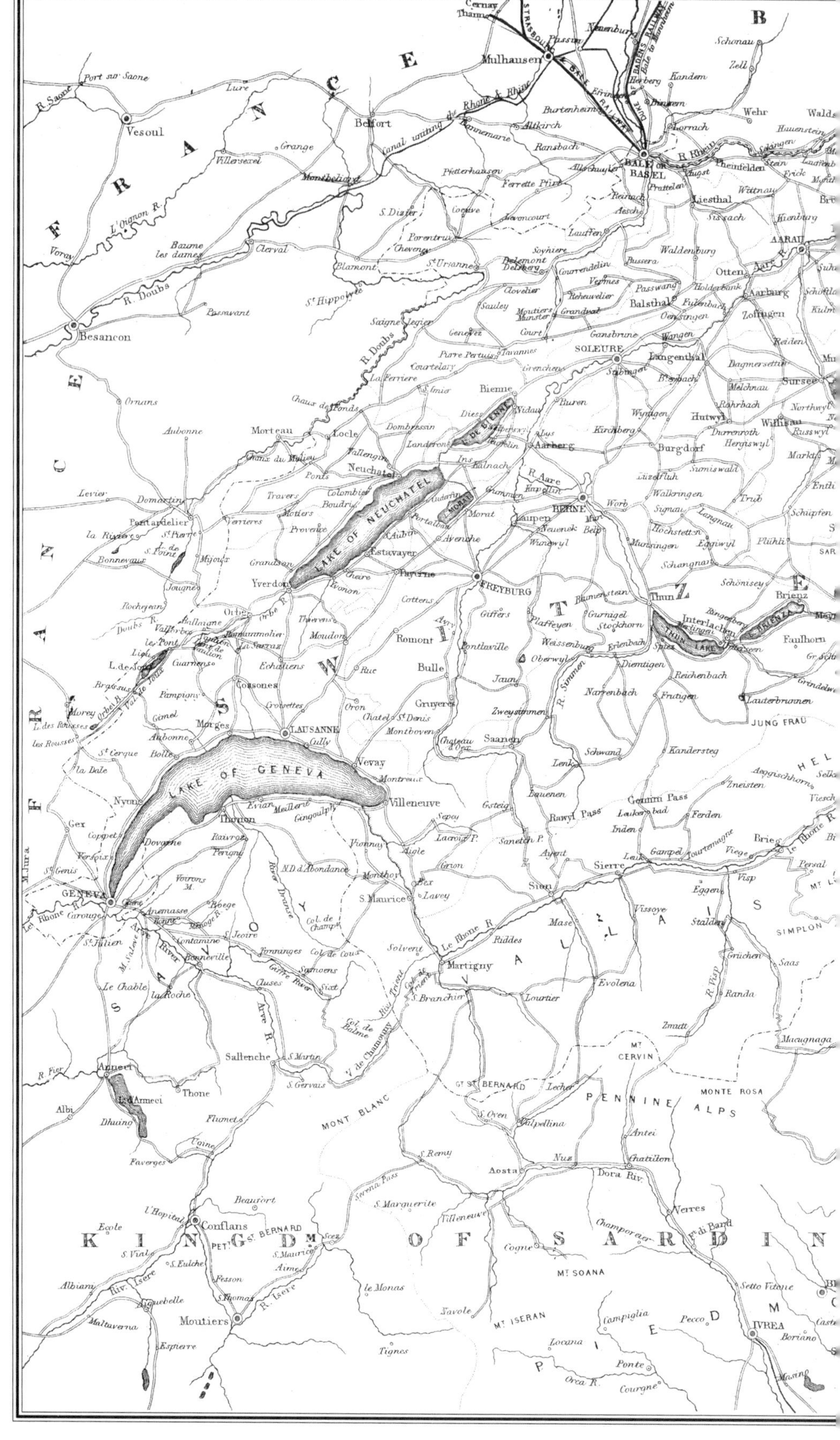

FRANCE
Mulhausen
Belfort
Vesoul
Besancon
BALE OR BASEL
AARAU
SOLEURE
Bienne
Neuchatel
LAKE OF NEUCHATEL
BERNE
FREYBURG
Yverdon
LAUSANNE
LAKE OF GENEVA
GENEVA
Thonon
Villeneuve
Martigny
Sion
Sierre
Thun
Interlachen
Lauterbrunnen
JUNG FRAU
MONT BLANC
GT ST BERNARD
MT CERVIN
MONTE ROSA
PENNINE ALPS
Aosta
Annecy
Conflans
Moutiers
IVREA
KINGDM OF SARDIN
SIMPLON

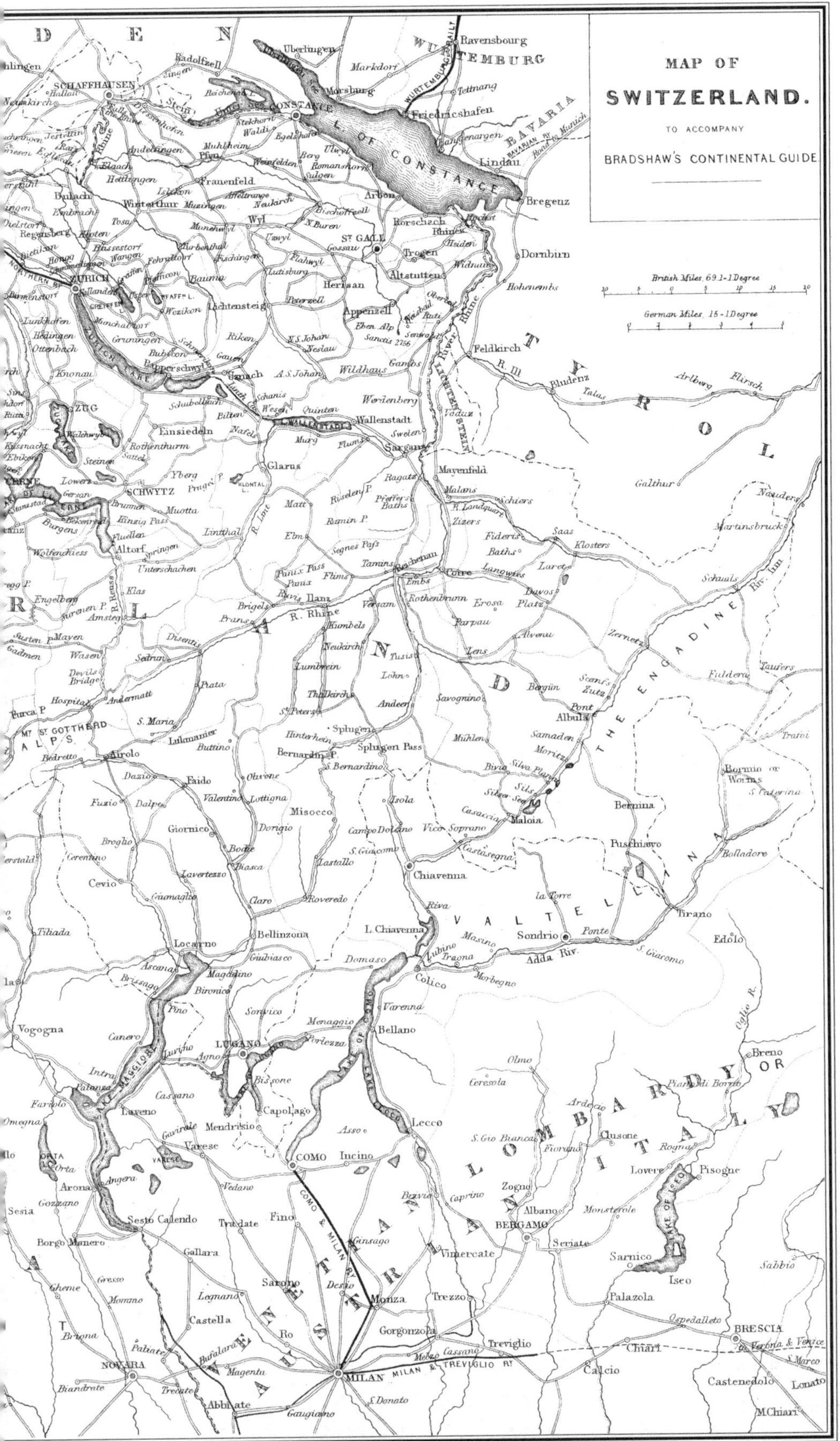
MAP OF
SWITZERLAND.
TO ACCOMPANY
BRADSHAW'S CONTINENTAL GUIDE
British Miles, 69.1 = 1 Degree
German Miles, 15 = 1 Degree
B.R.Davies fc. George Str. Euston Squ.
BADEN
WURTEMBURG
BAVARIA
TYROL
GRISONS
LOMBARDY OR ITALY
VALTELLINA
THE ENGADINE
L. OF CONSTANCE
ZURICH LAKE
L. MAGGIORE
LAKE OF COMO
LAKE OF ISEO
MT. ST. GOTTHERD ALPS
R. Rhine
Adda Riv.
Riv. Inn
Schaffhausen
Constance
Ravensbourg
Friedrichshafen
Lindau
Bregenz
Dornbirn
Feldkirch
Bludenz
Zurich
St. Gall
Appenzell
Herisan
Winterthur
Frauenfeld
Rorschach
Zug
Schwytz
Altorf
Glarus
Wallenstadt
Sargans
Ragatz
Mayenfeld
Coire
Reichenau
Ilanz
Disentis
Andermatt
Airolo
Faido
Splugen
Bernardin P.
Thusis
Bergün
Samaden
Maloja
Chiavenna
Sondrio
Tirano
Bormio or Worms
Bellinzona
Locarno
Lugano
Como
Lecco
Bergamo
Milan
Monza
Novara
Brescia
Varese
Arona
Sesto Calendo
Colico
Clusone
Lovere
Pisogne
Iseo
Treviglio
Chiari
Lonato
Como & Milan Ry.
Milan & Treviglio Ry.

Namur and Liége and Mons and Manage Railwa
Lines shewing direct Communication.

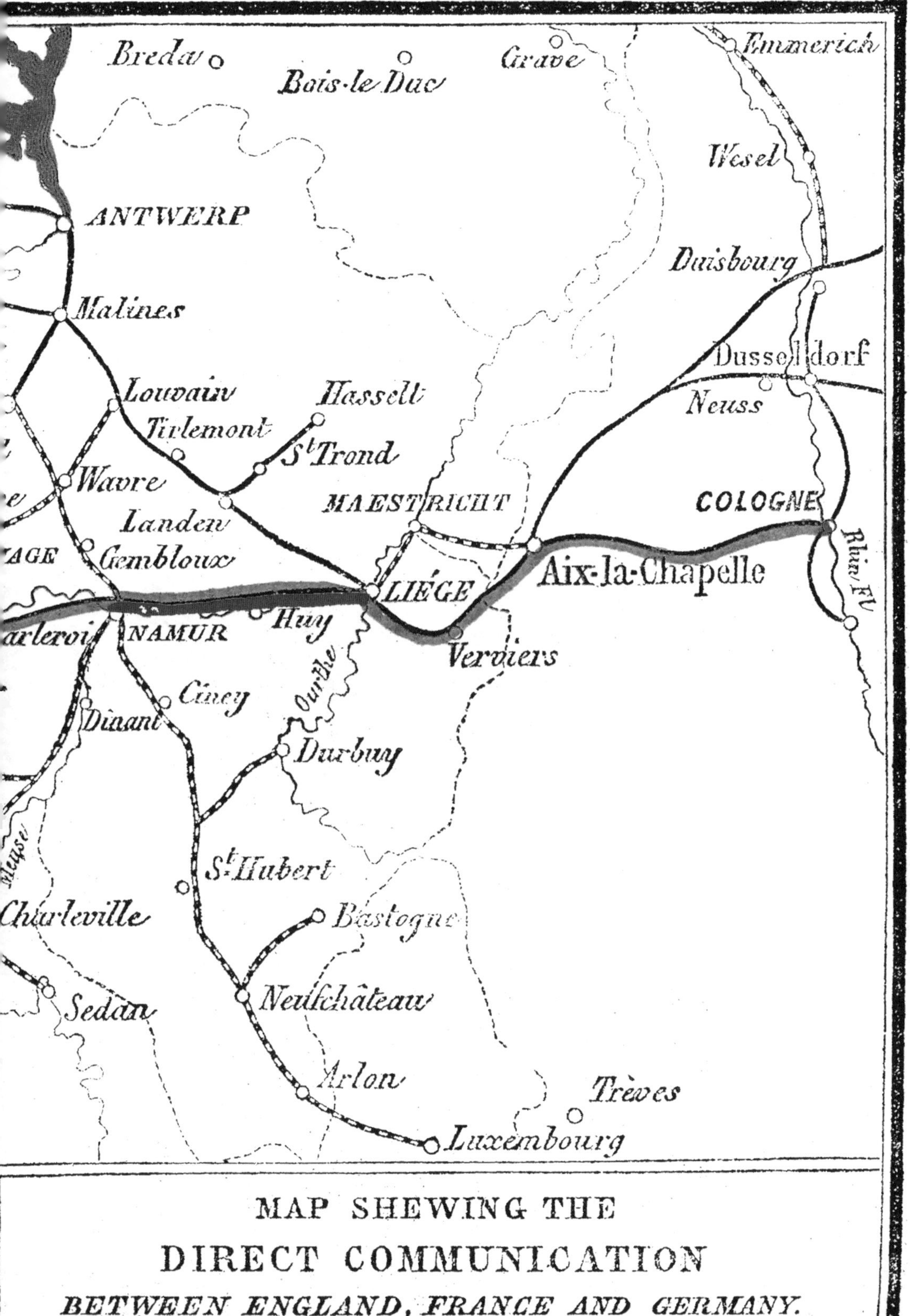

MAP SHEWING THE
DIRECT COMMUNICATION
BETWEEN ENGLAND, FRANCE AND GERMANY.

Lines open.
Lines Constructing or projected.

HAGUE'S

Explanation of the numbers:

1. Royal Palace .... Paleis v. z. M. d. Koning
2. King's Mews .... 's Konings Stallen
3. Prince of Orange's Palace
   Paleis v. z. K. H. de Prins van Orange
4. Minister of Finance's office . Ministerie van Finantien
5. .... Salon d'Exposition
6. Cloister Church .... Klooster Kerk
7. Royal Riding school ... 's Konings Manège
8. Barracks .... Oranje Kazerne
9. Library .... Bibliotheek
10. Portuguse Synagogue. Portugeesche Synagoge
11. Estabt. for boring Canon. Boorhuis
12. Canon foundery .... Konongietery
13. Post horses office .... Paardenpostery
14. Prince Frederic's Palace. Paleis v. z. K. H. Prins Frederik
15. Government offices for South Holland
    Gouvernement van Zuid Holland
16. French Roman cath: Chh. Fransche Roomsche Kerk
17. Theatre .... Schouwburg, Theâtre
18. King's Palace .... Paleis v. z. M. den Koning (Plein)
19. Poor house .... Arme inrigting
20. Museum .... Museum
21. Government offices .... Ministerium
22. States General 1. Chamb. ...... Staaten Generaal 1. Kammer
23. " 2. " " " 2. "
24. Roman Cathc. Chapel .... Roomsche Kapel
25. Lottery office and Criminal Court of Justice
    Binnenhof, Loteryzaal en Hoog Geregtshof
26. Principal Guard house Hoofdwacht
27. Government offices of National and Colonies,
    and Minister of Justice's offices
    Ministerie v. d. nationale Nyverheid en Kolonien
    & Ministerie v. Justice
28. French Church .... Fransche Waalsche Kerk
29. .... Pastors Kerk
30. Old Men's Hospital ...... Oude Mannenhuis
31. English Chapel .... Engelsche Kerk
32. Jansenist Chapel .... Jansenist Kerk
33. Exhibition of Works of Art
    Tentoonstelling van Kunstwerken
34. Town Hall .... Stadhuis
35. Post office .... Postkantoor
36. Principal Church .... Groote Kerk
37. .... Fundatiehuis
38. Rom. Cathoc. Church ... Roomsche Kerken
39. Lutheran Church .... Luthersche Kerk
40. New Church .... Nieuwe Kerk
41. Old Women and Children's Hospital
    Oude Vrouwen en Kinderhuis

I. Ledig Erf II. Breed Straat
III. Snoek Straat
IV. Korte Molen Straat
V. Molen Straat
VI. Het Korte Bosch
VII. Slik Einde VIII. De Geest
IX. Nobel Str. X. Groen Markt
XI. Loosduiner Brug
XII. Slop de drie Boeren
XIII. Groote Lou
XIV. Lorren of A
XV. Jan Hend
XVI. School St
XVII. Nieuwe
XVIII. Veene St
XIX. Goort St
XX. De Laan

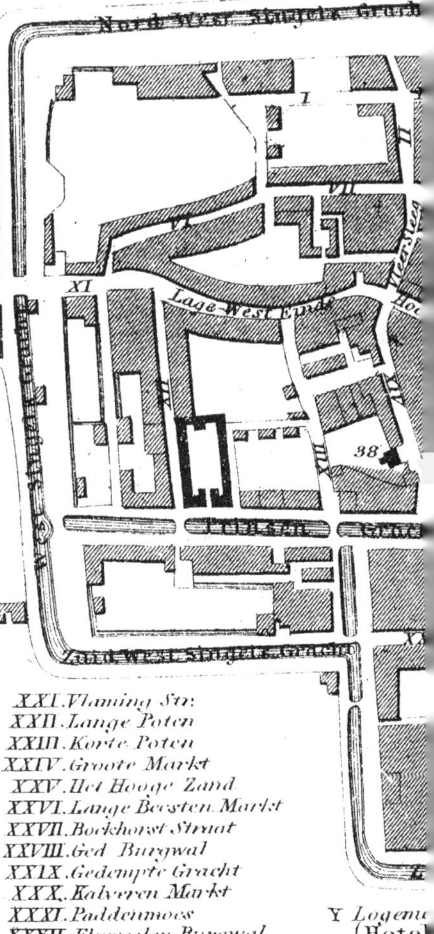

GRAVENHAGE.- LA HAYE.

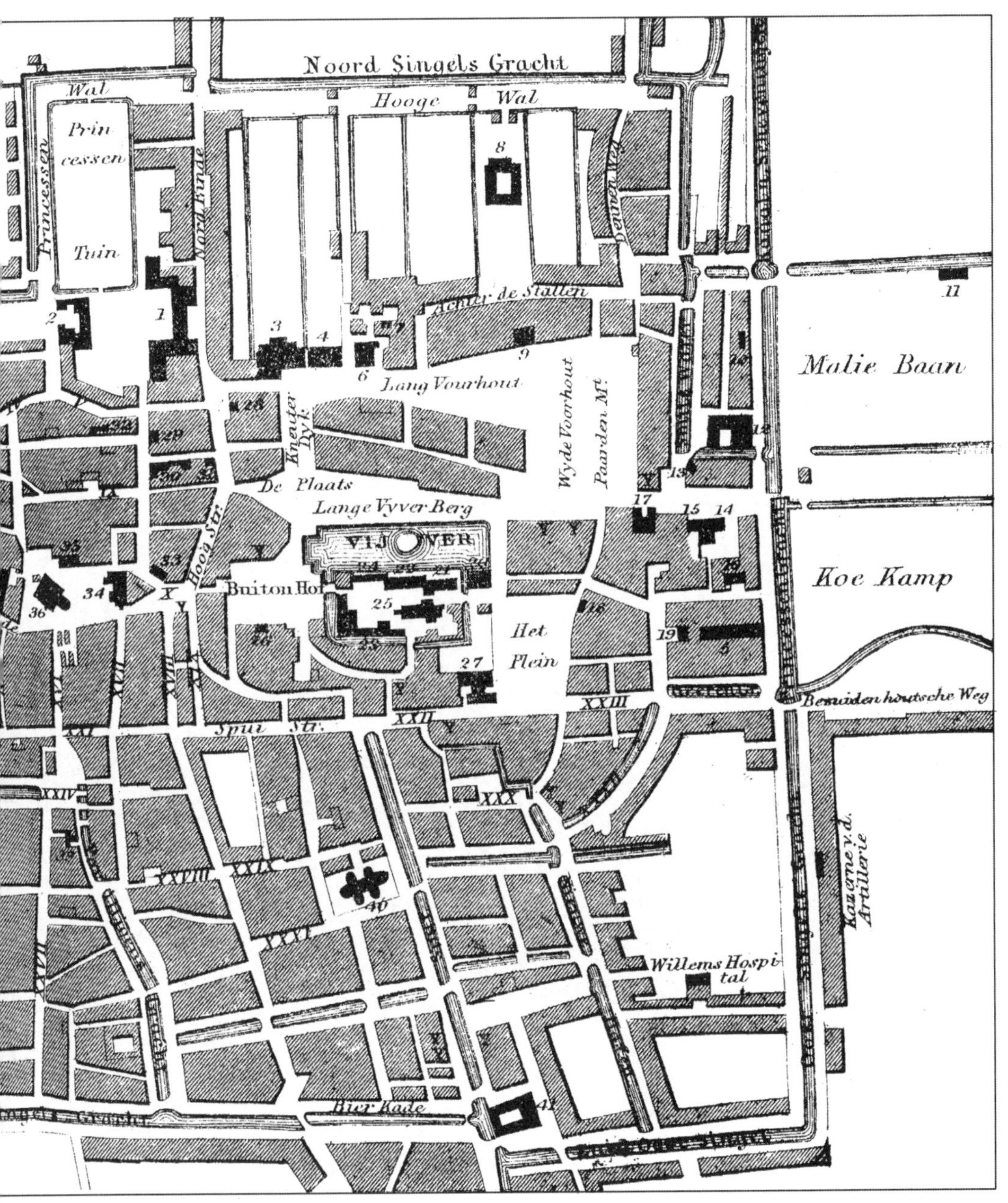

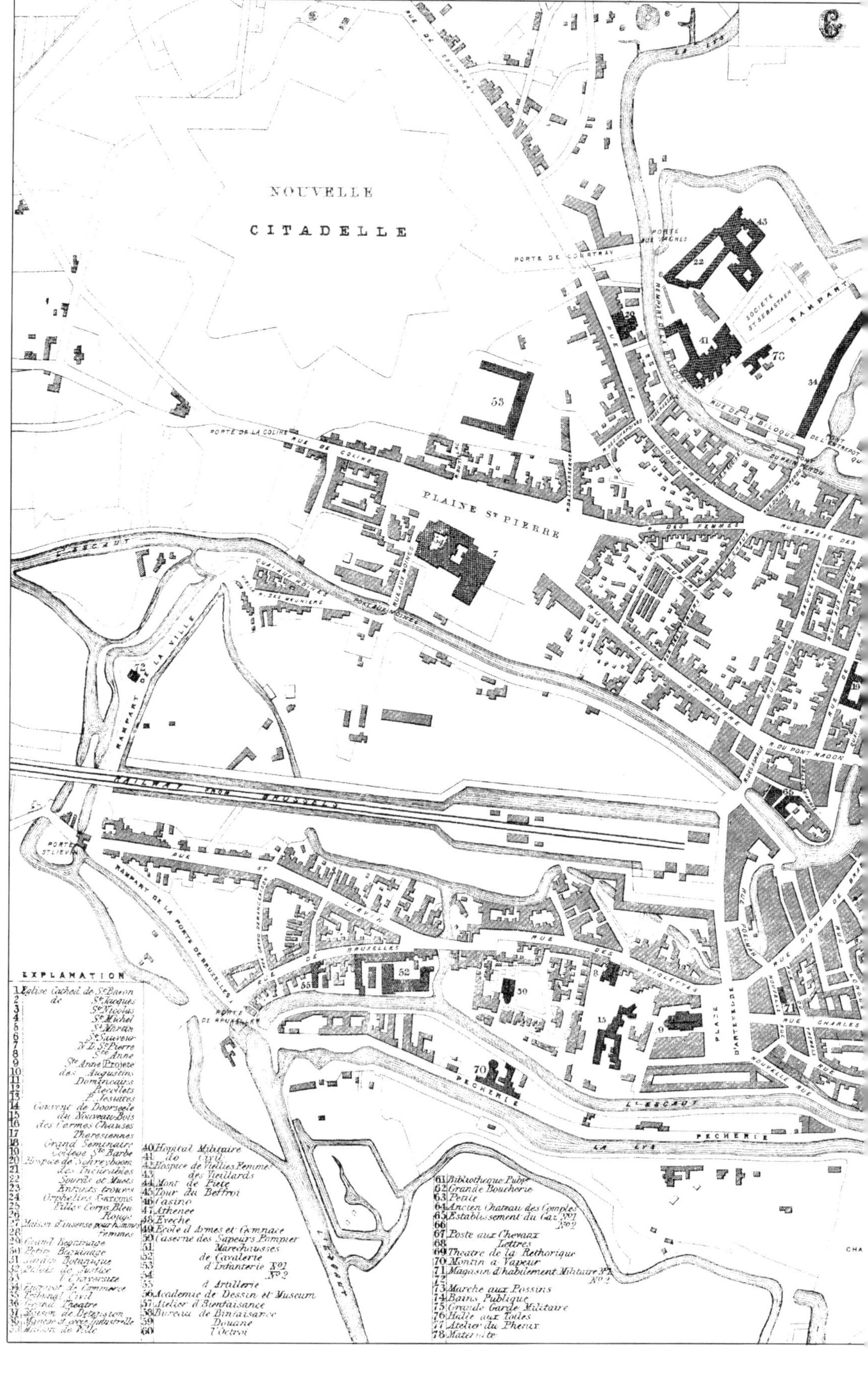
6
NOUVELLE
CITADELLE
PLAINE St PIERRE
RUE DE COURTRAY
PORTE DE COURTRAY
PORTE AUX VACHES
SOCIETE St SEBASTIEN
RAMPART
RUE DE LA BILOQUE
PORTE DE LA COLINE
RUE DE COLINE
QUAI AUX MOINES
PONT AUX MOINES
RUE AUX MOINES
R. DES FEMMES
RUE BASSE DES
RUE NEUVE St PIERRE
R. DU PONT MADOU
RAMPART DE LA VILLE
RAILWAY POUR BRUXELLES
PORTE St LIEVIN
RUE St LIEVIN
RAMPART DE LA PORTE DE BRUXELLES
RUE DE BRUXELLES
PORTE DE BRUXELLES
RUE DES VIOLETTES
PLACE D'ARTEVELDE
RUE DIGNE DE BRABANT
RUE CHARLES
NOUVELLE RUE
PECHERIE
L'ESCAUT
LA LYS
EXPLANATION
1 Eglise Cathed. de St Baron
2 de St Jacques
3 St Nicolas
4 St Michel
5 St Martin
6 St Sauveur
7 N. D. St Pierre
8 Ste Anne
9 Ste Anne Projete
10 des Augustins
11 Dominicains
12 Recollets
13 P. Jesuites
14 Couvent de Doorseele
15 du Nouveau Bois
16 des Carmes Chausses
17 Theresiennes
18 Grand Seminaire
19 College Ste Barbe
20 Hospice de Schreyboom
21 Les Incurables
22 Sourds et Muets
23 Enfants trouves
24 Orphelins Garcons
25 Filles Corps Bleu
26 Rouge
27 Maison d'insense pour hommes
28 femmes
29 Grand Beguinage
30 Petit Beguinage
31 Jardin Botanique
32 Palais de Justice
33 l'Universite
35 Tribunal Civil
36 Grand Theatre
37 Maison de Detention
39 Maison de Ville
40 Hopital Militaire
41 do Civil
42 Hospice de Viellies Femmes
43 des Vieillards
44 Mont de Piete
45 Tour du Beffroi
46 Casino
47 Athenee
48 Eveche
49 Ecole d'Armes et Gymnace
50 Caserne des Sapeurs Pompier
51 Marechausses
52 de Cavalerie
53 d'Infanterie No1
54 No2
55 d'Artillerie
56 Academie de Dessin et Museum
57 Atelier d'Bienfaisance
58 Bureau de Bienfaisance
59 Douane
60 l'Octroi
61 Bibliotheque Publ.
62 Grande Boucherie
63 Petite
64 Ancien Chateau des Comptes
65 Establissement du Gaz No1
66 No2
67 Poste aux Chevaux
68 Lettres
69 Theatre de la Rethorique
70 Moulin a Vapeur
71 Magasin d'habilement Militaire No1
72 No2
73 Marche aux Poissons
74 Bains Publique
75 Grande Garde Militaire
76 Halle aux Toiles
77 Atelier du Phenix
78 Maternite

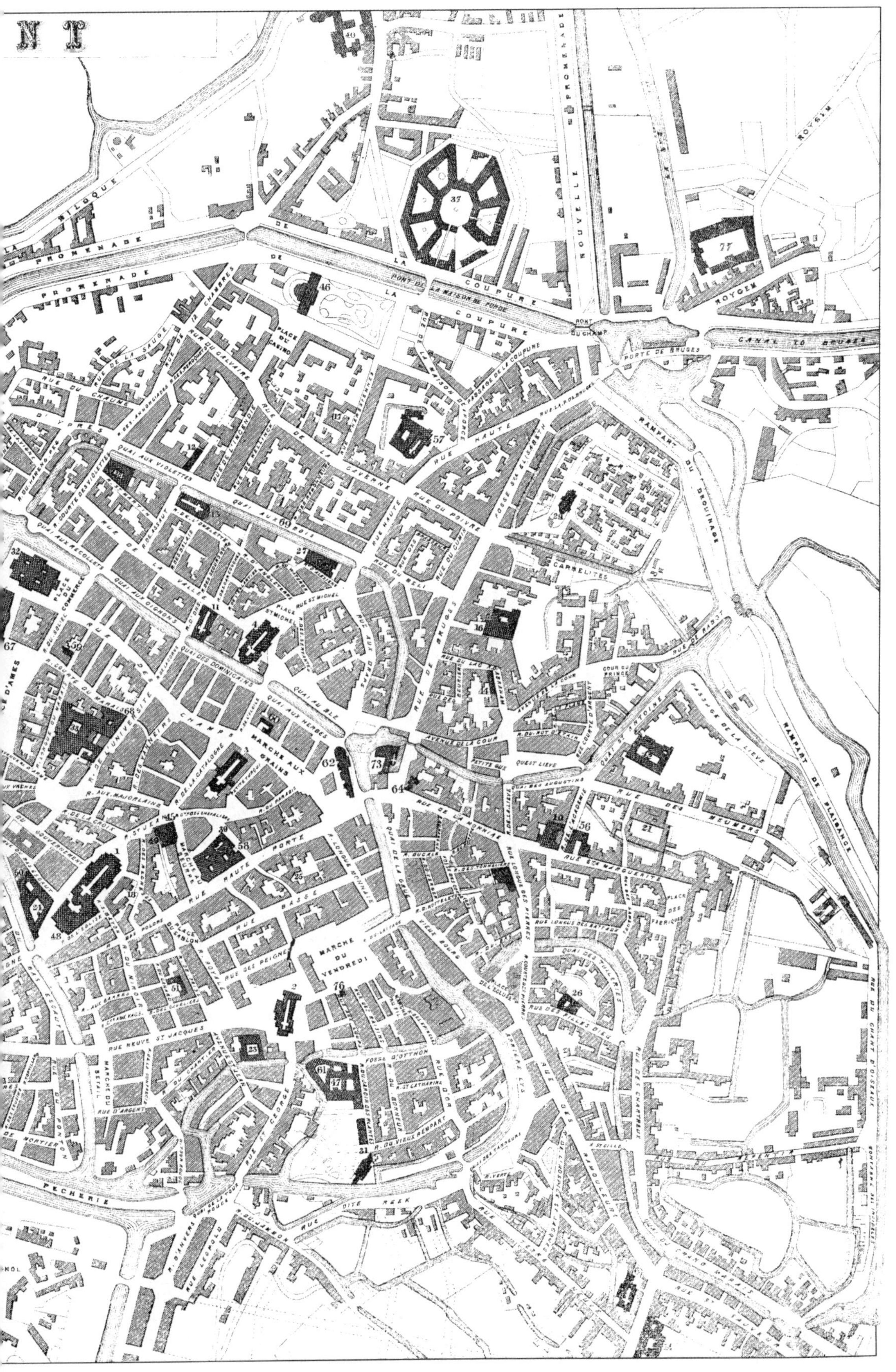
N T
PROMENADE DE LA COUPURE
PONT DE LA MAISON DE FORCE
NOUVELLE PROMENADE
ROYGEM
PONT DU CHAMP
CANAL TO BRUGES
PORTE DE BRUGES
RAMPART DU BEGUINAGE
RUE HAUTE
RUE DU POIVRE
CARMELITES
QUAI AUX VIOLETTES
QUAI AUX BOIS
QUAI AUX RECOLLETS
QUAI AUX OIGNONS
QUAI DES DOMINICAINS
QUAI AU BLE
QUAI AUX HERBES
MARCHE AUX GRAINS
RUE DE BRUGES
RUE DES MEUNIERS
RUE STE MARGUERITE
RAMPART DE PLAISANCE
PASSAGE DE LA LIEVE
RUE HAUTE PORTE
RUE BASSE
MARCHE DU VENDREDI
RUE NEUVE ST JACQUES
RUE D'ARGENT
RUE ST GEORGE
PECHERIE
RUE DITE REEK
RUE DU CHANT D'OISEAUX

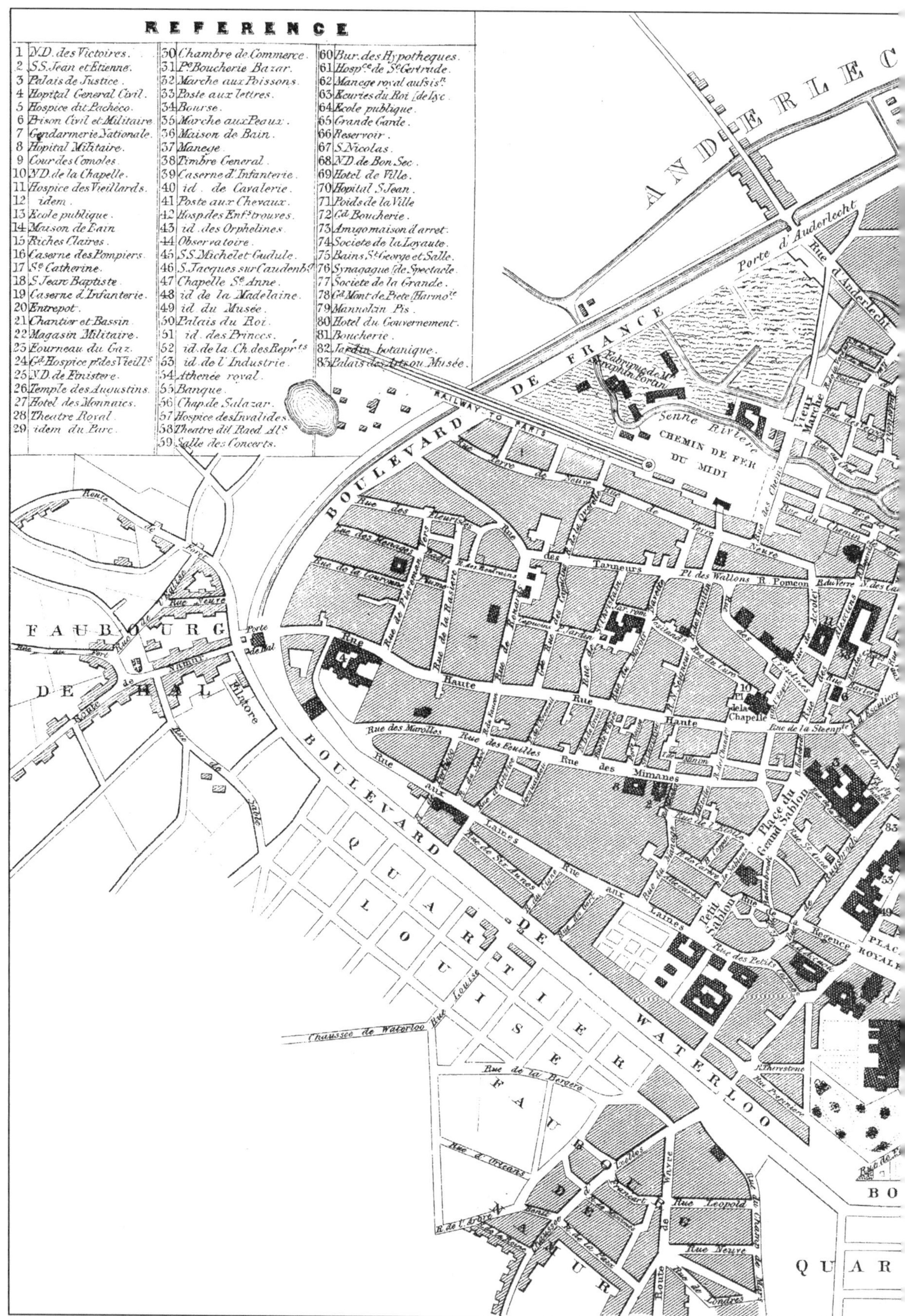
REFERENCE
1 N.D. des Victoires.
2 SS. Jean et Etienne.
3 Palais de Justice.
4 Hopital General Civil.
5 Hospice dit Pachéco.
6 Prison Civil et Militaire.
7 Gendarmerie Nationale.
8 Hopital Militaire.
9 Cour des Comoles.
10 N.D. de la Chapelle.
11 Hospice des Vieillards.
12 idem.
13 Ecole publique.
14 Maison de Bain.
15 Riches Claires.
16 Caserne des Pompiers.
17 Ste Catherine.
18 S. Jean Baptiste.
19 Caserne d'Infanterie.
20 Entrepot.
21 Chantier et Bassin.
22 Magasin Militaire.
23 Fourneau du Gaz.
24 Gd Hospice pr des Vieills.
25 N.D. de Finistere.
26 Temple des Augustins.
27 Hotel des Monnaies.
28 Theatre Royal.
29 idem du Parc.
30 Chambre de Commerce.
31 Pe Boucherie Bazar.
32 Marche aux Poissons.
33 Poste aux lettres.
34 Bourse.
35 Marche aux Peaux.
36 Maison de Bain.
37 Manege.
38 Timbre General.
39 Caserne d'Infanterie.
40 id. de Cavalerie.
41 Poste aux Chevaux.
42 Hosp. des Enfs trouves.
43 id. des Orphelines.
44 Observatoire.
45 SS. Michel et Gudule.
46 S. Jacques sur Caudenbg.
47 Chapelle Ste Anne.
48 id de la Madelaine.
49 id du Musée.
50 Palais du Roi.
51 id. des Princes.
52 id. de la Ch. des Reprts
53 id. de l'Industrie.
54 Athenée royal.
55 Banque.
56 Chap. de Salazar.
57 Hospice des Invalides.
58 Theatre dit Raed Als
59 Salle des Concerts.
60 Bur. des Hypotheques.
61 Hospce de Ste Gertrude.
62 Manege royal aufsisn.
63 Ecuries du Roi [de Lyc.
64 Ecole publique.
65 Grande Garde.
66 Reservoir.
67 S. Nicolas.
68 N.D. de Bon Sec.
69 Hotel de Ville.
70 Hopital S. Jean.
71 Poids de la Ville
72 Gd Boucherie.
73 Amigo maison d'arret.
74 Societe de la Loyaute.
75 Bains St George et Salle.
76 Synagague [de Spectacle.
77 Societe de la Grande.
78 Gd Mont de Piete [Harmoie
79 Mannekin Pis.
80 Hotel du Gouvernement.
81 Boucherie.
82 Jardin botanique.
83 Palais des Arts ou Musée.
ANDERLECHT
Porte d'Anderlecht
Rue d'Anderlecht
BOULEVARD DE FRANCE
RAILWAY TO PARIS
CHEMIN DE FER DU MIDI
Senne Riviere
Vieux Marche
Rue des Tanneurs
Pl. des Wallons
R. Pomeon
FAUBOURG DE HAL
Porte de Hal
Rue Haute
Rue des Marolles
Rue des Mimanes
Rue aux Laines
Place du Grand Sablon
Petit Sablon
Rue de la Regence
PLACE ROYALE
Rue des Petits Carmes
BOULEVARD DE WATERLOO
QUARTIER LOUISE
Chaussée de Waterloo
Rue Louise
Rue de la Bergere
Rue d'Orleans
FAUBOURG DE NAMUR
Rue Leopold
Rue Neuve
Rue de Londres
R. Thérésienne
QUAR

BRUSSELS.
ENGRAVED FOR BRADSHAW'S CONTINENTAL GUIDE
FAUBOURG DE FLANDRE
Molenbeek St J
MOLENBEEK
Etablt Geographique
B.BARTHELEMY
Pte de Flandre
Rue du Rempart des Moines
Nour. M Grains
Marché aux Grains
Bassin
Gd Bassin
Quai aux Houils
Quai à la Chaux
Quai aux Briques et Tuilles
Quai aux Bois
Canal de Willebroek
Allee Verte
Chemin de Fer
Rue du Frontispice
FAUBOURG DE LAEKEN
Route de Malines et d'Auvers
rue de Laeken
Place d'Anvers
BOULEVARD D' ANVERS
Rue de la Fiancée
Rue du St Pierre
SENNE REVIERE
Longue Rue
Neuve Longue
Place des Martyrs
Rue d'Argent
Rue du Damier
Rue des Cendres
Rue Poulie
Rue du Marais
Chemin de Fer
RAIL TO OSTEND ANTWERP & COLOGNE
Port de Cologne
Rue des Pierres
Rue Verte
Grande Place
Place de la Monn
Rue des Fripiers
Montagne a Herb Pot
Rue des Comediens
Rue de Schaerbeek
Rue Lachero
Chemin de Terre
BOULEVd. DU JARDIN BOTANIQUE
FAUBOURG DE SCHAERBEEK
Rue de la Poste
Porte de Schaerbeek
Rue Royale
RUE ROYALE
PARC
Rue de la Loi
Pl. des Barri
Rue du Nord
Rue Neuve
BOULEVARD DE L' OBSERVATOIRE
Chaussée de Schaerbeek
Rue de la Limite
RUE DUCALE
ARD DU REGENT
R. de l'Astronomie
FAUBOURG DE LOUVAIN
QUARTIER LEOPOLD
St JOSSE-TEN-NOODEN

ESCAUT
Chantier
Porte de Fer
Fort du Kiel
Quai Plantin
Arsenal Militaire
Rue du Convent
Entrée de la Citadelle
CITADELLE
Bains
Gazométre
Ruelle du Livre
Fort St. Laurent
ESPLANADE
OU
PLACE D' ARMES
Magasin a Poudre
Porte des Beguines
R. des Beguines
R. Large
Petit Marché
Longue R. de l'Hôpital
Jardin de l'Harmonie
Fort Montebello
Jardin Botanique
Leopold
Magasin a Poudre
Road to Mechlin
Lunette Herenthals
ANTWERP.
SCALES
Yards
English
Mile
Metres
RAILWAY FROM BRUSSELS

S C H E L D E
Werf
Quai Vandyck
Quai Jordaens
Place Ste Walburge
R. des Nattes
R. Harengs
Quai Tavernicrs
Fort St Laurent
Cuisine
PETIT BASSIN
GRAND BASSIN
Quai de l'Entrepôt
Entrepôt
Maison Anseatique
Place Nassau
Chantier du Kattendyck
Bonnet de Prêtre
Batterie des
GRANDE PLACE
Hotel de Ville
Canal des Recolets
Rue Neuve
Place de Meir
Rue du Chene
R. Rouge
Marché aux Chevaux
Canal d'Amidon
Le Cage
Magasin à Poudre
Route de Hollande
Porte de Borgerhout
Station du Chemin de Fer
Borgerhout
1
2 „ St Jacques.
3 „ St Pauls (Dominicains).
4 „ St Andre.
5 „ St Augustin.
6 „ St Charles (Jesuites).
7 „ St Antoine (Capucins).
8 „ St Joseph (Theresiennes).
9 Chapelle Gallicane.
10 Librairie Anglaise et Francaise.
11 Poste aux Lettres.
12 Grand Theatre.
13 Theatre des Varieties.
14 Hotel de Ville.
15 Banque.
16 Bourse.
17 Hotel du Gouvernement.
18 Musee et Academie de Peinture
19 Salle d'Exposition.
20 Moulin à Vapeur.
21 La Prison.
HOTELS
22 Hotel St Antoine
23 „ du Parc (Bains)
24 „ du Laboureur.
25 „ d Angleterre (Bains)
26 „ des Pays Bas.
27 Binges Hotel.
28 Hotel des Etrangers.

MAYENCE.

Str. von Paris
B.
Martin
Bonifaci
B.
Ale
xander B.
Georg
Kästrich
Phillippe B.
Johannis B.
Eichelstein
Pulverthurm
Citadelle
Thiermarkt Strasse
Ludwigs St.
Holz
magazin
am Holzthor
Fischthor
am eisernen Thor
Ankerplatz der
Dampfschiffe
RHEIN STRO

MAINZ.

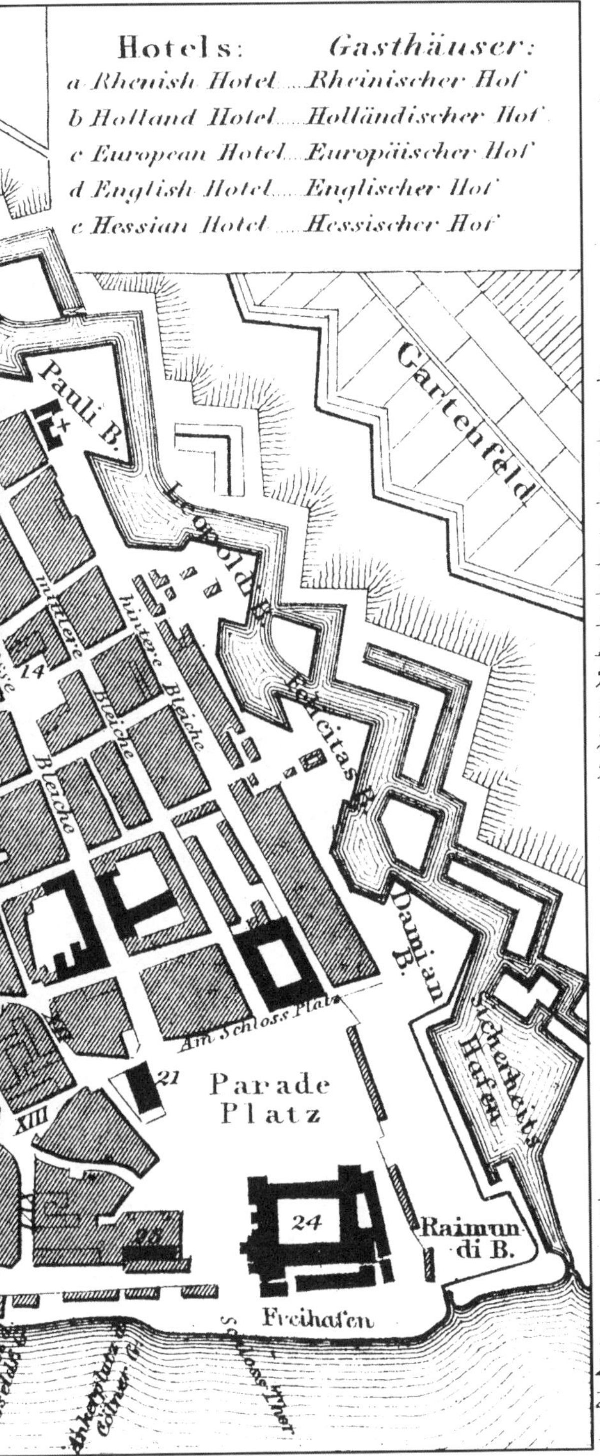

Explanation of the numbers:

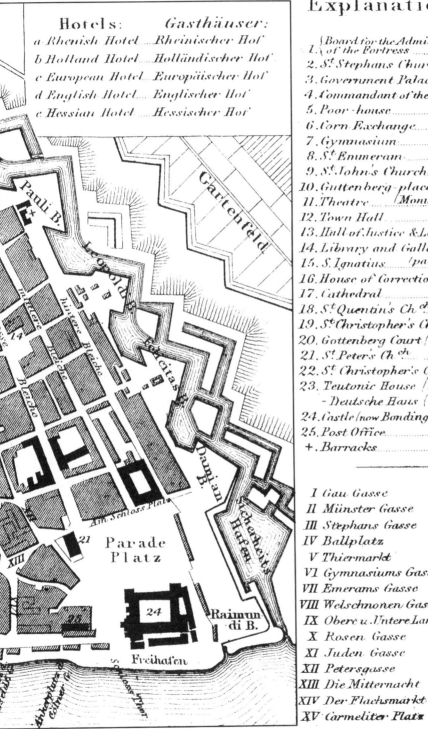

1. Board for the Administrat.n of the Fortress	Festungs Gouvernement
2. St. Stephans Church	Stephans Kirche
3. Government Palace	Regierungs Pallast
4. Commandant of the Fortress	Festungs Commandant
5. Poor-house	Armenhaus
6. Corn Exchange	Fruchthalle
7. Gymnasium	Gymnasium
8. St. Emmeran	S. Emmeran
9. St. John's Church	Johannes Kirche
10. Guttenberg-place & Monument	Gutenbergs Platz u. Monum.t
11. Theatre	Theater
12. Town Hall	Stadthaus
13. Hall of Justice & Lockup	Justiz u. Arresthaus
14. Library and Gallery of paintings	Bibliotheck u. Gallerie
15. S. Ignatius	St. Ignatz
16. House of Correction	Correctionshaus
17. Cathedral	Dom
18. St. Quentin's Ch.ch	St. Quintin
19. St. Christopher's Ch.ch	St. Christoph
20. Gottenberg Court (Casino)	Hof zum Gottenberg (Casino)
21. St. Peter's Ch.ch	Peters Kirche
22. St. Christopher's Ch.ch	Kirche St. Christoph
23. Teutonic House (Residence of the Governor) - Deutsche Haus (Wohnung des Gouverneurs)	
24. Castle (now Bonding Wareh.e	Schloss jetzt Lagerhaus
25. Post Office	Postamt (drey Kronen)
+. Barracks	Casernen

I Gau Gasse	XVI Mitternachts Gasse
II Münster Gasse	XVII Bauern Gasse
III Stephans Gasse	XVIII Schuster Gasse
IV Ballplatz	XIX Das Höfchen
V Thiermarkt	XX Der Speisemarkt
VI Gymnasiums Gasse	XXI Liebfrau Platz und Heumarkt
VII Emerams Gasse	XXII Auf dem Brand
VIII Welschnonen Gasse	XXIII Rheinstrasse
IX Obere u. Untere Langgasse	XXIV Obere u. Unt. Leer Gass.
X Rosen Gasse	XXV Hundsgasse
XI Juden Gasse	XXVI Augustiner Gasse
XII Petersgasse	XXVII Gräber Gasse
XIII Die Mitternacht	XXVIII Kapuziner Gasse
XIV Der Flachsmarkt	XXIX Quintins Gasse
XV Carmeliter Platz	

CHURCHES | KIRCHEN.

I. Aus dem Mittel Alter

1. *Der* **Dom** *oder die* **St. Bartholomäus-Kirche** *mit dem* **Pfarrthurm** *(dem grössten. 222 Fuss hohen Thurm der Stadt), dem Grabmal Günther's von Schwarzburg und der Wahlkapelle. am Domplatz.*
2. *Die restaurirte* **Nicolaikirche.** *am Römerberg.*
3. *Die* **Leonhardskirche.** *vielleicht an der Stelle des Palastes von Karl dem Grossen). am Main.*
4. *Die* **Liebfrauenkirche.** *am Liebfrauenberg.*
5. *Die* **Weissfrauenkirche.** *in der Nähe des Gallus-Thors*

II AUS NEUERER ZEIT

6. *Die* **Katharinenkirche** *(luth. Hauptkirche). an d. Hauptwache.*
7. *Die* **St. Paulskirche.** *am Paulsplatz.*
8. *Die* **deutsch-reformirte Kirche.** *auf dem Kornmarkt.*
9. *Die* **französisch-reformirte Kirche.** *an der Stadt-Allee.*

CHARITIES & THEIR ESTABTS. | WOHLTHATICKEITS ANSTALTEN

10. *Das* **Senckenbergische Stift.** *Hospital für Burger und Beisassen. am Eschenheimer Thor.*

Das **Hospital zum heil. Geist** *(für Fremde u. Dienstboten). auf der Langen-Strasse.*

12. *Das* **israelitische Hospital.** *am Judenmarkt.*
13. *Das* **Irrenhaus** *und* **Hospital für Epileptische.** *in der Nähe des Theaters.*

Das **Rochus-Hospital** *(für Unreine) ist vor dem Affenthor (Sachsenhausen). das* **Militär-Hospital** *und das* **Christ'sche Kinder-Krankenhaus** *sind vor dem Allerheiligen-Thor*

14. *Das* **Waisenhaus.** *am Friedberger Thor.*
15. *Das* **Versorgunghaus.** *auf dem Klapperfeld.*

Das **Taubstummen-Institut** *ist am Wege zum Friedhof. vor dem Eschenheimer und Friedberger Thor.*

MUSEUMS &c. | WISSENSCHAFTLICHE ANSTALTEN UND SAMMLUNGEN

16. *Die* **Stadt-Bibliothek** *am Obermainthor (mit der Statue Gothe's von Marchesi).*

Die **wissenschaftlichen Sammlungen** *im Senckenbergischen Stift (No. 10). namlich. a) die* **Senckenberg. medicinisch-naturwissensch. Bibliothek** *bestehend aus der Bibliothek des medicin. Instituts. der naturforsch. Gesellschaft und des physik. Vereins (b) die* **Bibl. des geogr. Vereins.** *c) die* **Anatomie.** *d) der* **botanische Garten.** *e) das* **Senckenberg. Museum** *oder das* **Naturalienkabinet** *der Senckenb. naturforsch. Gesellschaft. f) die* **chemische und physik. Sammlung** *des physik. Vereins.*

17. *Der* **polytechnische Verein** *an der Katharinenkirche mit Bibliothek und Modellen-Sammlung.*
18. *Die* **Bibliothek** *des* **Städel'schen Instituts** *in der neuen Mainzerstrasse.*
19. *Die* **Lese-Gesellschaft.** *am Rossmarkt.*

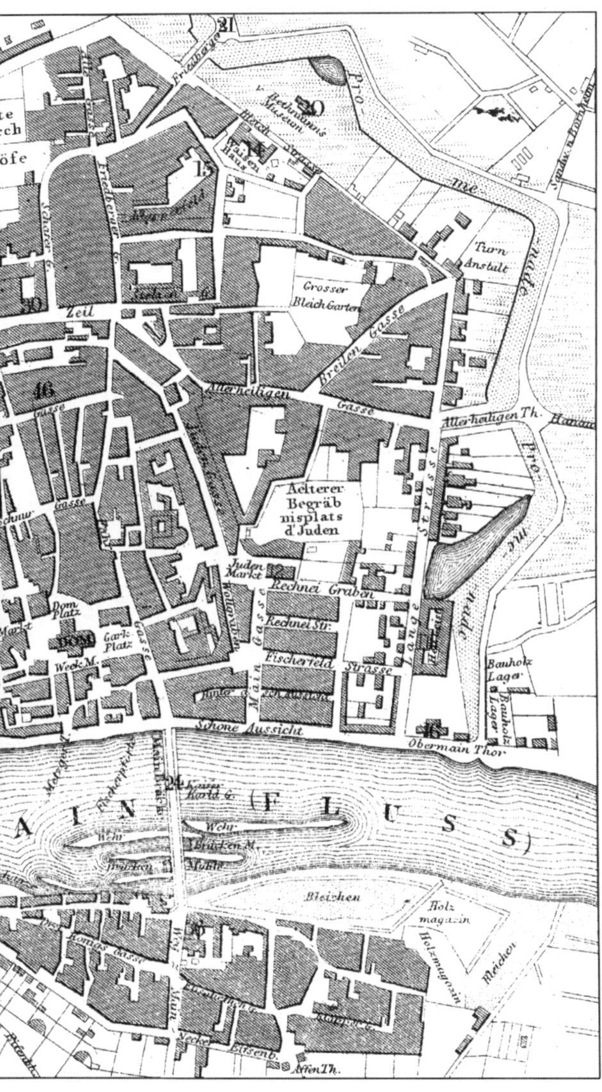

COLLECTIONS OF PAINTINGS – KUNST SAMMLUNGEN

Das **Städel'sche Institut** *(N.º 18). in der neuen Mainzerstrasse (besonders Gemäldesammlung).*

20 . *Das* **von Bethmann' sche Museum** . *am Friedberger Thor. mit der Ariadne von Dannecker.*

Die **Prehn' sche Gemälde-Sammlung** . *in der Stadt-bibliothek (N.º 16).*

MONUMENTS – MONUMENTE.

21 . *Das* **Monument** *der 1792 bei der Erstürmung der Stadt durch die Franzosen gefallenen* **Hessen** . *vor dem Friedberger Thor.*

22 . **Göthe's Statue** *von* **Schwanthaler** . *in der Stadt-Allee.*

Göthe's Statue *von* **Marchesi** . *in der Stadt-Bibliothek (N.º 16).*

23 . *Das von* **Launitz** *gefertigte Denkmal* **Guiollett's** *welcher die Promenade am die Stadt angelegt . vor dem Bockenheimer Thor.*

24 . *Die Statue* **Karls d. Grossen** . *von* **Wendelstadt** . *auf d. Brücke.*

THE MOST FREQUENTED HOTELS – DIE BESUCHTESTEN GASTHOFE.

25 . *Der* **Schwanen** . *am Komödienplatz.*

26 . *Der* **Weidenbusch** . *dem Schwanen gegenuber.*

27 . *Der* **englische Hof** . *am Rossmarkt.*

28 . *Der* **Pariser Hof** . *am Paradeplatz.*

29 . *Der* **russische Hof** . *auf der Zeil.*

30 . *Der* **römische Kaiser** . *ebendaselbst.*

31 . *Der* **Landsberg** . *am Liebfrauenberg.*

SONSTIGE BEMERKENSWERTHE GEBAUDE UND ORTE.

32 . *Der* **Römer** *(regierungsgebäude). am Römerberg. mit dem Kaiser Saal und dem kurfürstl. Wahlzimmer Im dortigen Stadtarchiv die goldene Bulle.*

33 . *Der* **Saalhof** *mit einer alten Kapelle . am Main (Platz. wo Ludwig des Frommen Palast gestanden).*

34 . *Das* **Thurn- u. Taxis'** *sche* **Palais** . *auf der Eschenheimer Strasse . Sitz der Bundesversammlung.*

35 . *Die* **Börse** *an der neuen Kräme.*

36 . *Das* **Deutschordenshaus** . *in Sachsenhausen . an der Brücke*

37 . **Göthe's Geburtshaus** . *auf dem Grossen Hirschgraben.*

38 . *Das* **Postgebäude** . *auf der Zeil.*

39 . *Das* **Münzgebaude** . *in der Münzgasse.*

40 . *Die* **Kaserne** . *ehemaliges Kloster ebendaselbst.*

41 . *Das* **Theater** . *am Komödienplatz.*

. *Das* **Casino** . *auf dem Rossmarkt in demselben Hause. wo die Lese-Gesellschaft (N.º 19).*

42 . *Die* **Mainlust** . *vor dem Untermainthor.*

43 . *Der* **Taunus-Eisenbahnhof** . *vor dem Gallusthor Rechts und links davon die noch unvollendeten Bahnhöfe der Main-Neckar- und der Frankfurt-Casseler Bahn (Der provis. Haupt-Bahnhof der Main-Neckarbahn ist vor dem Affenthor in Sachsenhausen).*

44 . *Die* **Hauptwache** . *an der Katharinenpforte und Zeil.*

45 . *Das* **Zollgebäude** . *am Main.*

Der **Friedhof** . *vor dem Friedberger und Eschenheimer Thor. mit Denkmalen von* **Thorwaldsen. Launitz . Zwerger** *u. A.*

A
B
C
D
1
2
3
4
5
6
7
MÜNCHEN.
Thore, Brücken und Strassen:
1 Isarthor G5
2 Siegesthor G1
3 Isarbrucke H6
4 Ludwigstrasse G2
5 Carol Platz Obelisk E2
6 Maximilians Platz E3
7 Maxim Joseph Platz F4
8 Promenade Platz E4
9 Schrannen Platz F5
10 Universitats Platz G1
11 Wittelsbacher Platz F3
Kirchen u Paläste:
12 Allerheil Hof Capelle G4
13 Bonifaciuskirche D2
14 Frauenkirche E4
15 S Johanniskirche E5
16 Kreuzkirche D5
17 Ludwigskirche G1
18 Maria Hilfkirche in der Vorstadt Au H7
19 Michaelis Hofkirche E4
20 S Peterskirche F5
21 Protestantische Kirche D4
22 Theatinerkirche F3
23 Synagoge
24 Der allgem Friedhof D7
25 Die alte Residenz F3
26 Der neue Konigsbau F4
27 Der neue Saalbau G3
28 Palast des Herzogs von Leuchtenberg F3
29 Palast des Herzogs Max in Bayern F2
Andere öffentliche Gebäude:
30 Acad d bild Kunste E4
31 Allgem Krankenhaus C6
32 Arcad d Hofgartens F3
33 Bergwerks und Salinen Administrat Gebaude G1
34 Bibliothek G1
35 Blinden Institut G1
36 Botanischer Garten D3
37 Die konigl Erzgiesserei Nymphenburgerstrasse verlangerte Briennerstrasse
Schleissheimer Str
Casernen Str
Augusten Str
Brienner Str
Karls Strasse
Luisen Str
Carolinen Platz
Sophien Strasse
Botanischer Garten
Elisen Str
Bahnhof
Bayer Strasse
Karls Platz
Karls Thor
Neuhauser
Karls Str
Lerchen Strasse
Sonnen Strasse
Sendlinger Thor Platz
Sendlinger Landstrasse
Thalkirchner Str
Friedhof
40
41
43
13
16
30
31

F
G
H
I
38 Frohnveste E 6
39 Gewehrkammer G 3
40 Glasmalerei Anstalt D 2
41 Glyptothek D 2
42 Kriegsministerium G 2
43 Kunstausstellungs Gebaude D 2
44 Kunstverein F 3
45 Odeon F 3
46 Pinakothek E 1
47 Postgebaude F 4
48 Rathhaus F 5
49 Reitbahn G 4
50 Theater G 4
51 Universitat G 1
52 Vereinigte Samml. G 3
53 Zeughaus G 4
54 Hofgarten G 3
55 Englischer Garten H 2
56 Eisenbahnhof C 4
Lowen Strasse
Ludwigs Strasse
Ob. Garten-Strasse
Konigin Strasse
Englischer Garten
Feld Strasse
Fruhlings Str
Hofgarten Str.
Residenz
Max Joseph Platz
Residenz Strasse
Theatiner Str
Promenade Str
Wittelsb. Platz
Kaufinger Str
Wein Str
Haupt Platz
Rosenthal
Thal
Herrn Str
Isar Thor
Rumforder Str
Zweibrucken Str
FLUSS
Haidhausen
Gasteig
Wiener Strasse
JSAR
Vorstadt Au
Frauenhofer Str

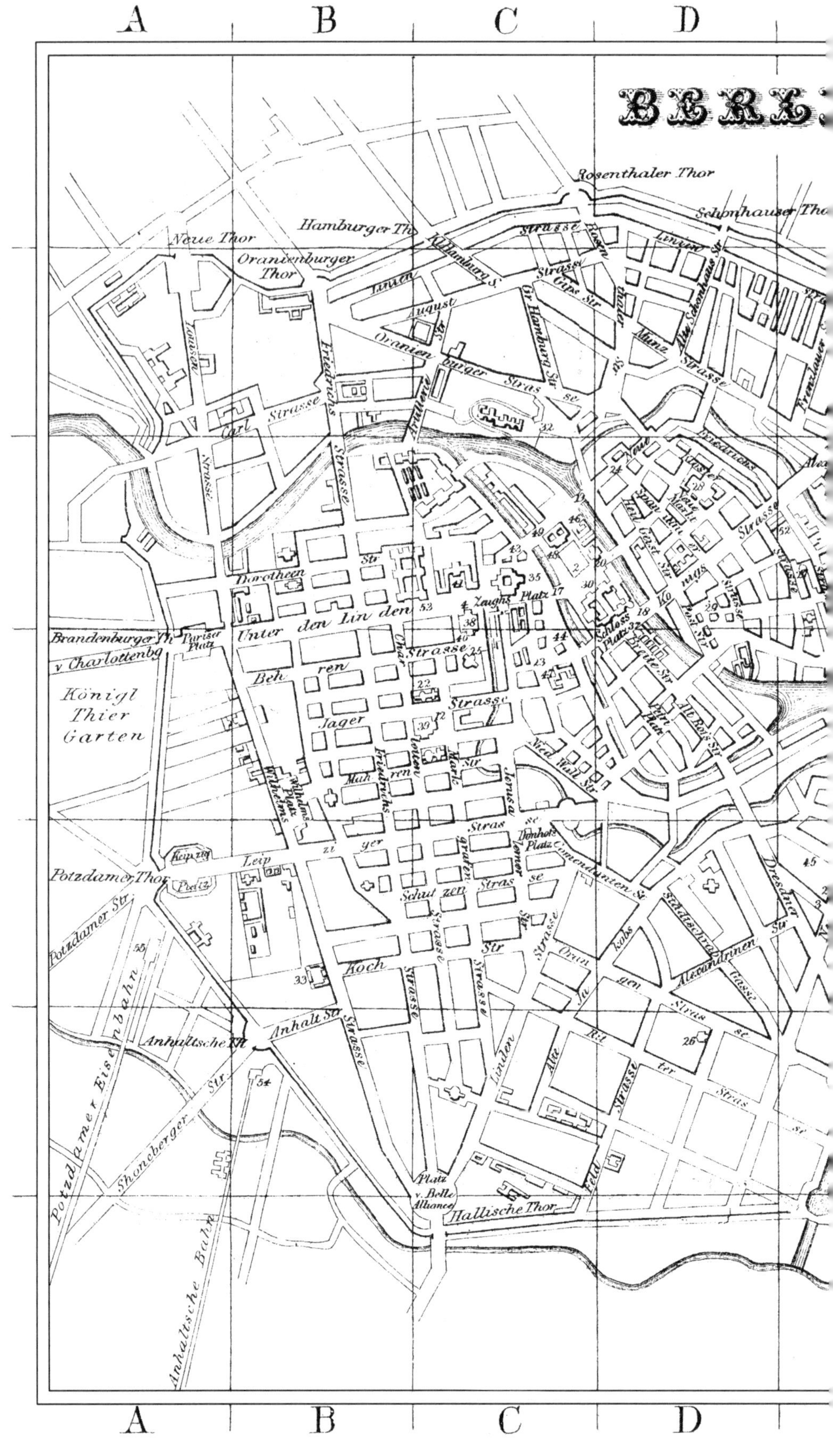

A
B
C
D
BERL
Rosenthaler Thor
Schonhauser Thor
Hamburger Th
Neue Thor
Oranienburger Thor
Linien
August
Oranien burger Stras se
Friedrichs Strasse
Carl Strasse
Dorotheen Str
Unter den Linden
Zeughs Platz
Brandenburger Th
v Charlottenbg
Pariser Platz
Königl Thier Garten
Beh ren Strasse
Char
Jager Strasse
Wilhelms Platz
Wilhelms
Mah ren
Friedrichs
Jerusa lemer
Donhofs Platz
Leipziger Platz
Potzdamer Thor
Potzdamer Str
Leip zi ger Stras se
Schut zen Stras se
Koch Str
Anhalt Str
Anhaltsche Th
Potzdamer Eisenbahn
Shoneberger Str
Anhaltsche Bahn
Platz v. Belle Alliance
Hallische Thor
Alte Rit ter Stras se
Dresdner
Alexandrinen Strasse
Schloss Platz
A
B
C
D

F G H I

Oeffentliche Plätze:

1 Der Schlossplatz D3
2 Der Lustgarten C3
3 Der Zeughausplatz C3
4 D Platz am Opernhaus C3
5 Der Platz an der Königswache, sche 42.
6 Der Platz vor den Linden, siche 13.
7 Der Pariser Platz A4
8 Der Wilhelms Platz B4
9 Der Leipziger Pl A5
10 D Belle Alliance Pl C6
11 Der Dönhofs Platz C5
12 …ensdarm Markt C4
13 Unter den Linden B3
14 Friedrichsstrasse B4
15 Leipzigerstrasse B5
16 Königsstrasse D3

Brücken:

17 Schlossbrücke C2
18 Die lange Brücke D3
19 D neue Friedrichsbr C3

Kirchen und andere öffentliche Gebäude:

20 Die Domkirche D3
21 Dorotheenkirche B3
22 Französische Kirche C4
23 Friedrichswerdersche K C4
24 Garnisonkirche D3
25 Hedwigskirche C4
26 Die neue Jacobskirche D6
27 Klosterkirche E3
28 Marienkirche D3
29 Nicolaikirche D3
30 Das königl Schloss C3
31 Königliches Palais C3
32 Monbijon C2
33 Palais d Prinzen Albert B5
34 Pal. d. Prinz v. Preussen C3
35 Zeughaus C3
36 Palais des Prinzen Carl B4
37 Marstall D3
38 Opernhaus C3
39 D neue Schauspielhaus C4
40 Die Bibliothek C4
41 D Universitätsgebäude C3
42 Neue Königswache C3
43 Singakademie C3
44 Die Bauakademie C4
45 D Festungsmodellhaus E5
46 Börse C3
47 Die neue Münze C4
48 Das Museum C3
49 Das neue Museum C3
50 Hospit d. Schwanenord F6
51 Das Zellengefängniss A1
52 Das Lagerhaus E3
53 Die Akadem d Künste B3

Eisenbahnhöfe:

54 Bahnhof d. Anhalt schen Bahn B6
55 d Potsdamer Bahn A5
56 d Frankfurter Bahn G5
57 d Berl Stettin Bahn B1

F G H I

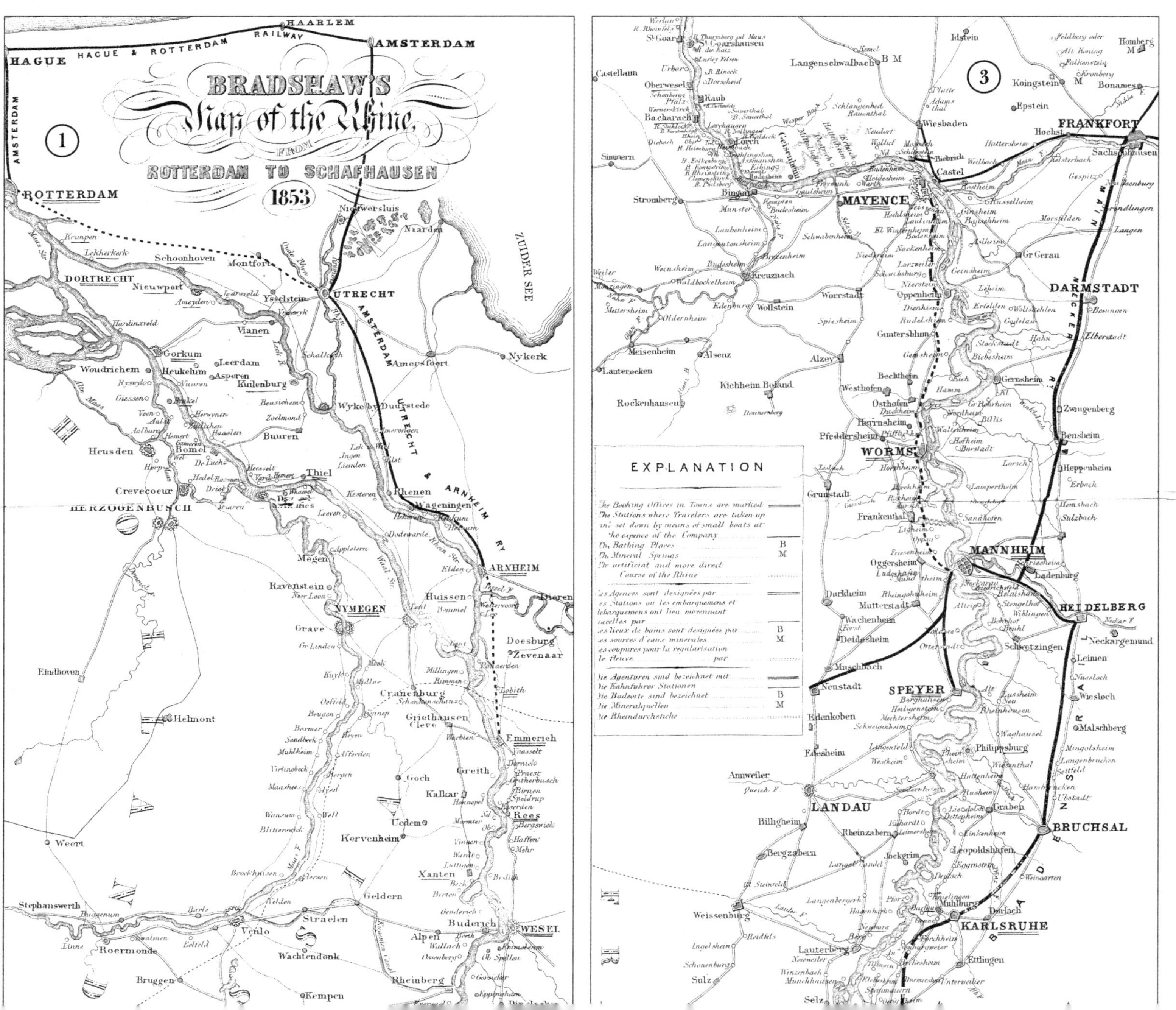

BRADSHAW'S
Map of the Rhine,
FROM
ROTTERDAM TO SCHAFHAUSEN
1853
1
3
HAGUE
HAGUE & ROTTERDAM RAILWAY
HAARLEM
AMSTERDAM
ROTTERDAM
ZUIDER SEE
DORTRECHT
UTRECHT
AMSTERDAM UTRECHT & ARNHEIM RY
ARNHEIM
NYMEGEN
HERZOGENBUSCH
Emmerich
WESEL
Venlo
Roermonde
Stephanswerth
Eindhoven
Helmont
Weert
Gorkum
Woudrichem
Heusden
Crevecoeur
Thiel
Rhenen
Wageningen
Amersfoort
Nykerk
Naarden
Schoonhoven
Nieuwport
Vianen
Kulenburg
Grave
Cranenburg
Cleve
Kalkar
Xanten
Geldern
Kervenheim
Straelen
Wachtendonk
Kempen
Rheinberg
Buderich
Rees
Doesburg
Zevenaar
FRANKFORT
MAYENCE
DARMSTADT
WORMS
MANNHEIM
HEIDELBERG
SPEYER
LANDAU
BRUCHSAL
KARLSRUHE
Wiesbaden
Biebrich
Castel
Bingen
Kreuznach
St Goar
Bacharach
Oberwesel
Kaub
Lorch
Oppenheim
Alzey
Frankenthal
Dürkheim
Neustadt
Philippsburg
Schwetzingen
Bensheim
Weissenburg
MAIN
NECKER RY
BADEN
EXPLANATION
The Booking Offices in Towns are marked
The Stations where Travelers are taken up and set down by means of small boats at the expence of the Company
Do Bathing Places B
Do Mineral Springs M
Do artificial and more direct Course of the Rhine
Les Agences sont designées par
Les Stations ou les embarquemens et debarquemens ont lieu moyennant
Les lieux de bains sont designées par B
Les sources d'eaux minerales M
Les coupures pour la regularisation le fleuve par
Die Agenturen sind bezeichnet mit
Die Bahnfuhrer Stationen
Die Badeorte sind bezeichnet B
Die Mineralquellen M
Die Rheindurchstiche

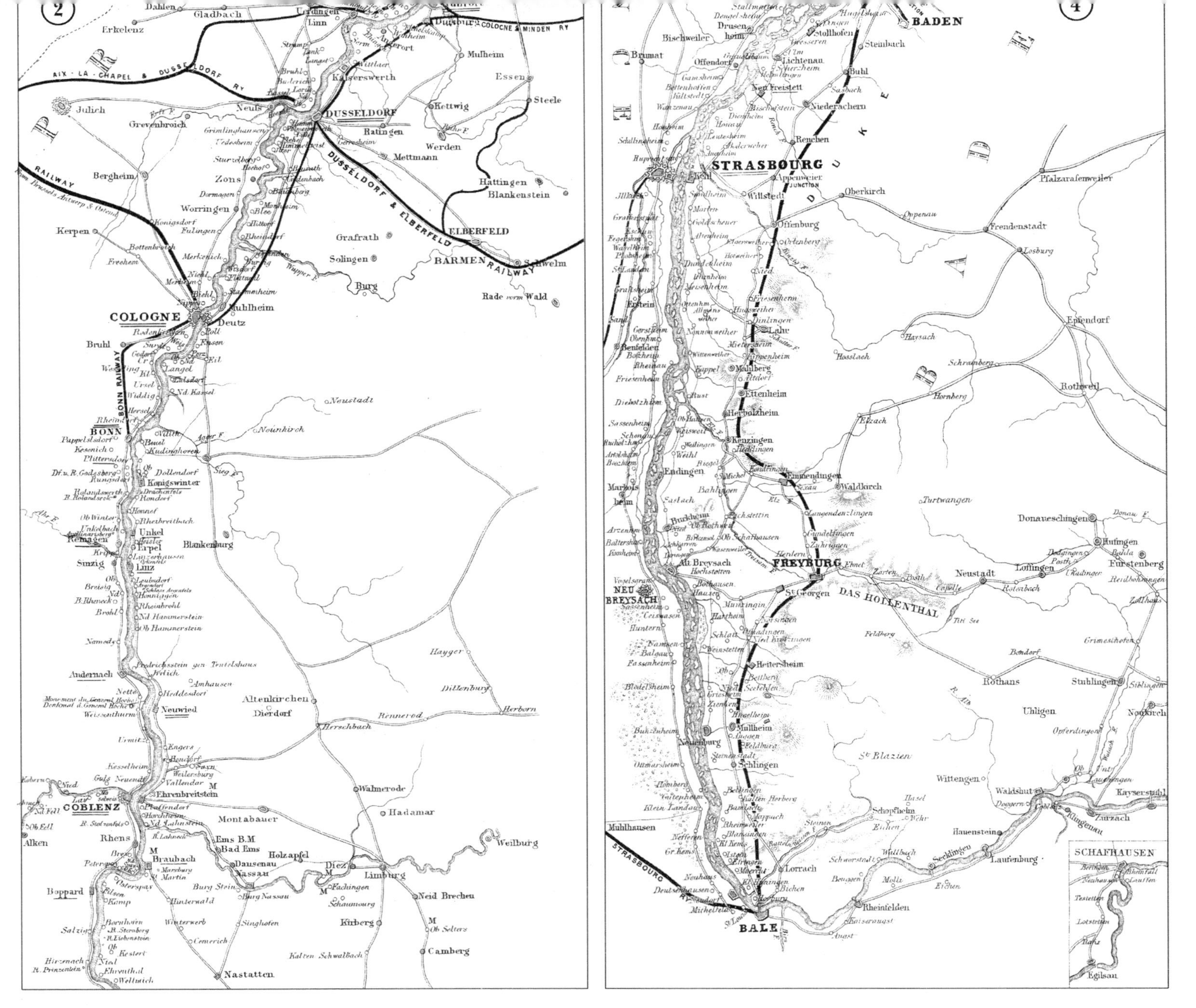

2
COLOGNE
DUSSELDORF
BONN
COBLENZ
AIX-LA-CHAPEL & DUSSELDORF RY
DUSSELDORF & ELBERFELD
BARMEN RAILWAY
COLOGNE & MINDEN RY
BONN RAILWAY
ELBERFELD
Erkelenz
Gladbach
Dahlen
Uerdingen
Linn
Duisburg
Mulheim
Essen
Steele
Kettwig
Werden
Julich
Grevenbroich
Neuss
Kaiserswerth
Ratingen
Mettmann
Hattingen
Blankenstein
Schwelm
Bergheim
Kerpen
Zons
Worringen
Grafrath
Solingen
Burg
Rade vorm Wald
Muhlheim
Deutz
Bruhl
Neustadt
Konigswinter
Unkel
Remagen
Erpel
Linz
Sinzig
Blankenburg
Andernach
Neuwied
Altenkirchen
Dierdorf
Hayger
Dillenburg
Herborn
Ehrenbreitstein
Montabauer
Walmerode
Hadamar
Weilburg
Alken
Rhens
Braubach
Ems B.M
Bad Ems
Dausenau
Nassau
Holzapfel
Diez
Limburg
Neid Brechen
Boppard
Kirberg
Camberg
Nastatten
4
STRASBOURG
BADEN
FREYBURG
BALE
NEU BREYSACH
DAS HOLLENTHAL
SCHAFHAUSEN
STRASBOURG
Bischweiler
Drusen heim
Brumat
Offendorf
Stollhofen
Lichtenau
Steinbach
Buhl
Neu Freistett
Niederachern
Renchen
Kehl
Appenweier JUNCTION
Willstedt
Oberkirch
Offenburg
Pfalzarafenweiler
Frendenstadt
Losburg
Lahr
Epfendorf
Rothweil
Mahlberg
Ettenheim
Herbolzheim
Kenzingen
Endingen
Emmendingen
Waldkirch
Elzach
Hornberg
Turtwangen
Donaueschingen
Hufingen
Furstenberg
Alt Breysach
St Georgen
Neustadt
Loffingen
Heitersheim
Mullheim
Neuenburg
Schlingen
St Blazien
Rothans
Stuhlingen
Uhligen
Nordkirch
Wittengen
Waldshut
Kayserstuhl
Zurzach
Schopfheim
Lorrach
Rheinfelden
Seckingen
Laufenburg
Hauenstein
Mulhhausen
Egilsau

SECTION 3

ADVERTISEMENTS

PRIZE MEDAL OF THE

GREAT EXHIBITION

AWARDED TO

PIERCE,

5, JERMYN STREET, REGENT STREET,

For IMPROVEMENTS in the construction of **Fire-Lump Grates,** and his **Economical Radiating Grates** upon the same principle of using Fire-Lumps in all Grates manufactured by him, and where may be seen a splendid assortment of these very superior Grates, suitable for the *Drawing Room, Library, Dining Room, Saloon, &c.*, finished in the most splendid and simplest designs at *moderate prices*, adapted to the *Louis Quatorze, Elizabethan, Renaissance, or Gothic Styles* of Architecture.

The best and cheapest Grate for all useful purposes is

PIERCE'S UNIVERSAL FIRE-LUMP GRATE,

Which requires no fixing, being made in one piece, having strong octagon bars and bottom, with a loose trivet, capacious and safe hobs, complete.

Prices, **11s. 6d., 13s. 6d., 22s. 6d., 25s.**

PIERCE'S IMPROVED COTTAGER'S GRATE,

For warming Two Rooms with only One Fire. Prices, **27s.** and **30s.**

PIERCE'S PYRO-PNEUMATIC STOVE-GRATE,

For the economical enjoyment of health, warmth, ventilation and comfort, being the only *pure warm-air Stove-Grate* yet invented that is constructed *entirely of fire-lumps,* without any *heating surface of iron;* is peculiarly adapted for the efficient WARMING and VENTILATING CHURCHES, CHAPELS, SCHOOLS, PUBLIC ROOMS, HOTELS, INVALIDS' APARTMENTS, &c.

This Stove-Grate possesses the *cheerful open fire*, and from the *novelty of its principle, economy in use*, and *elegance of design*, renders it more suitable than any other, where, these advantages, combined with purity of atmosphere, are important.

Price **£7., £9 10s., £13 10s.,** and **£16** in plain design.

These *Fire-lump bodies* may be seen cased in elegant designs of *Ormolu, Bronze China, Glass, Ground Steel, &c.* ONE is always in use warming Pierce's Show Rooms, No. 5, Jermyn Street.

These newly-invented Stove-Grates have received the most favourable notices of the public press, for which see the prospectuses with numerous testimonials, which will be forwarded on application, and every information afforded. Also his

IMPROVED METHOD OF WARMING

Churches, mansions, galleries, staircases, and entrance-halls, by **Hot Water,** whereby *warmth* is combined with *ventilation*, and the salubrity of the air produced from its use, with perfect safety from accident, having fully established its reputation.

Warm Baths fitted up from the boiler of the range, or a servants' room, which are always ready at a minute's notice.

Kitchens, Laundries, and Drying Rooms fitted with every improvement, and on the most economical arrangement.

Manufactory and Show Rooms, 5, Jermyn St., Regent St.

[29.

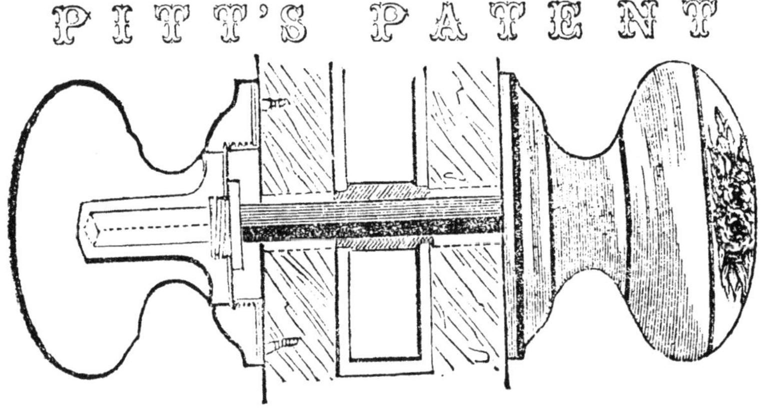

F. & C. OSLER,

44, OXFORD STREET, LONDON

(MANUFACTORY, BROAD STREET, BIRMINGHAM),

ESTABLISHED 1807.

MANUFACURERS OF

GLASS CHANDELIERS, GLASS LUSTRES,

TABLE GLASSES, &c. &c.

A Select and Extensive Stock, in every variety of pattern, of

RICHLY CUT CRYSTAL GLASS CHANDELIERS,

WITH GLASS BRANCHES, FOR DRAWING ROOMS, &C.

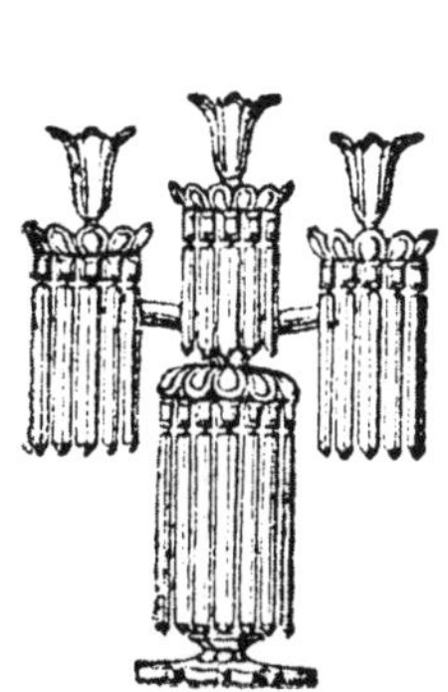

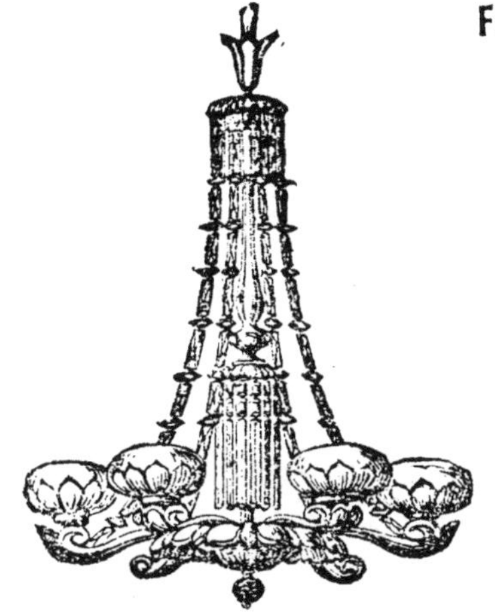

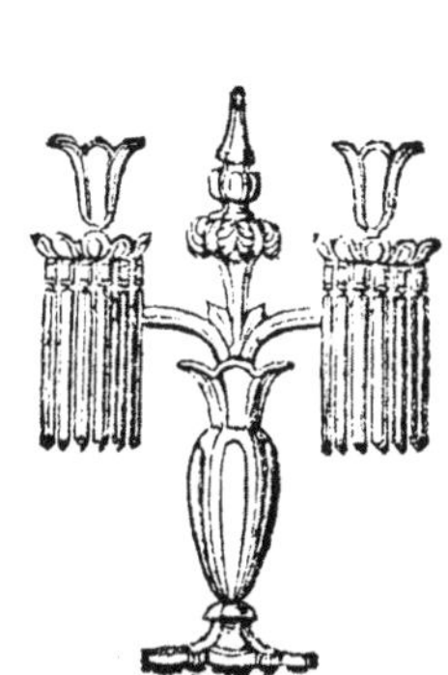

Elegant Crystal Glass Chandeliers, for Gas

(Made from "Registered" designs), with Glass Branches, &c., suitable for Drawing Rooms and Ball Rooms.

Theatres, Concerts, Assembly, and Ball Rooms, Lighted by Estimate, on the Lowest Terms.

A Large and Choice Assortment, in new and beautiful designs, of

HANDSOMELY-CUT GLASS LUSTRES AND GIRONDOLES.

Cut-Glass Ice Dishes and Pails, also Ice Plates, and all Articles in Glass required for Ice,

BEST CUT TABLE GLASS, IN EVERY VARIETY.

FAMILY CRESTS AND REGIMENTAL BADGES ENGRAVED.

ORNAMENTAL GLASS, ENGLISH AND FOREIGN,

(The Latter selected and imported by Messrs. Osler), in the greatest variety

Wholesale, Export, and General Furnishing Orders for Glass promptly executed.

NO MORE GRAY HAIR.

THE COLUMBIAN

INSTANTANEOUS HAIR DYE

IMPARTS immediately to Gray Hair or Whiskers a Natural and Permanent Brown or Black, without staining the skin. rivate Hair Dyeing Rooms. The Head of Hair Dyed in an Hour; Whiskers and Moustachioes in a few Mii utes.—Mr. and Mrs. UNWIN may be consulted daily.—Prepared and sold Wholesale and Retail by UNWIN & ALBERT, Court Hair Dressers, &c., 24, PICCADILLY, London, and 112, RUE RICHELIEU, Paris, in Cases at 5s. 6d., 7s. 6d., and 10s. 6d. Forwarded on receipt of a Post Office Order. [3

SOYER'S NECTAR,

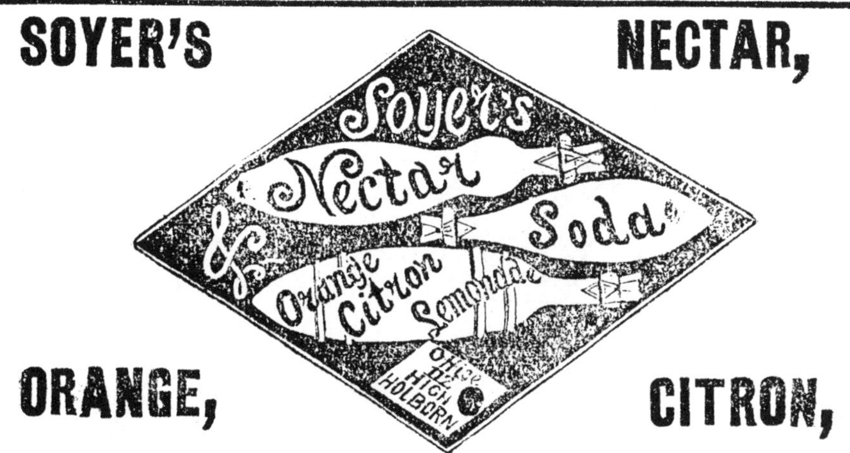

ORANGE, CITRON,

LEMONADE, & CARBONATED SODA WATER.

MANUFACTORY,

112, HIGH HOLBORN LONDON.

Delivered, free of Charge, to any part of London within the Post Office town delivery. [13

IMPROVED MODERATOR LAMPS.

THOMAS PEARCE & SON recommend their LAMPS with great confidence to the public. They are made expressly for their house by the first manufacturer in Paris, and bear T. P. & Son's name. Besides being cheaper, they possess the advantage over those usually offered for sale, of being on an improved principle—are finished with more care, and the patterns are in much better taste; while their cleanliness, simplicity of management, and the extreme economy of a brilliant and unfading light, are generally acknowledged.

THOMAS PEARCE & SON, 23, Ludgate Hill. [24.

B. BARRETT BROTHERS,

184, Oxford Street,

PATENTEES AND MANUFACTURERS OF THE BEST QUALITY OF

SOLID LEATHER

PORTMANTEAUS AND TRUNKS,

ON THE NEWEST CONSTRUCTION.

SOLE INVENTORS OF THE
IMPROVED RAILWAY DRESS IMPERIAL,
WITH REGISTERED PORTION FOR BONNETS.

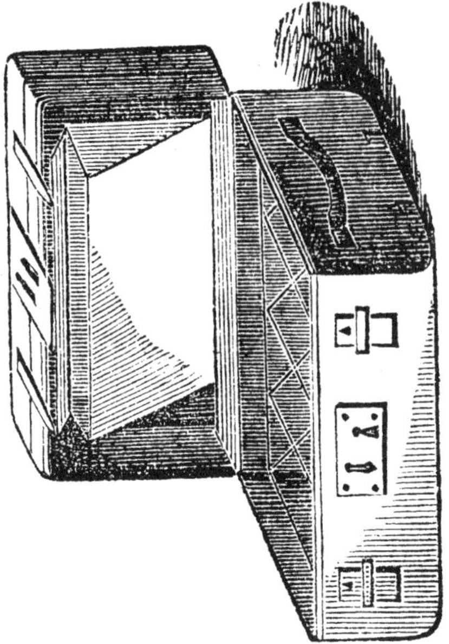

This is the most useful Trunk for Ladies' Appare' that has yet been invented, which we can with confidence recommend for its lightness and durability.

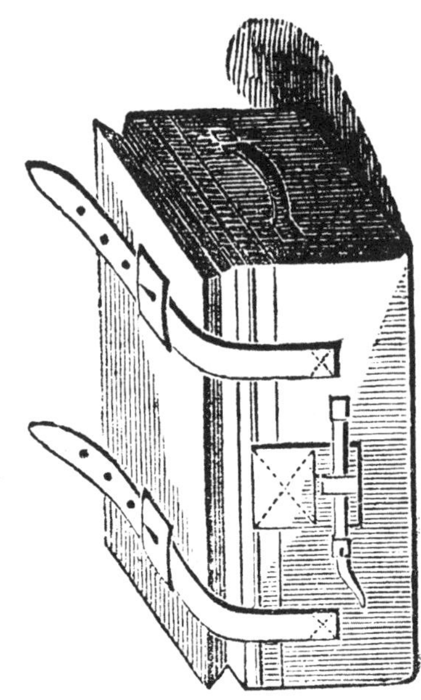

EXPANDING TOP DRESS IMPERIAL.

THE REGISTERED UNITED SERVICE.

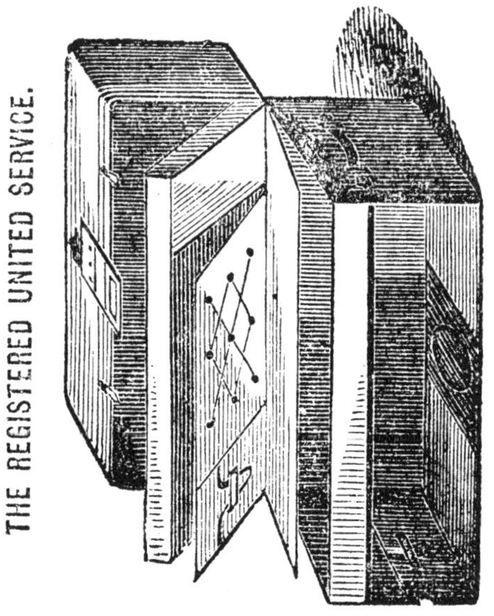

This Portmanteau has four compartments, forming excellent Wardrobes, with convenience for packing Hat, if required.

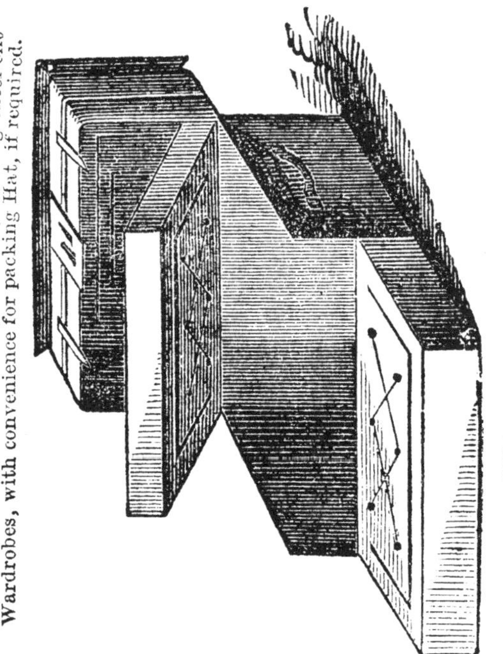

FOLDING PORTMANTEAU.

184, OXFORD STREET.

BARRETT'S IMPROVED LIGHT TRUNKS FOR THE OVERLAND ROUTE.

TIN CASES & BULLOCK TRUNKS FOR INDIA.

A LARGE ASSORTMENT OF BAGS OF EVERY DESCRIPTION.—WHOLESALE PRICES.

☞ 184, *OXFORD STREET (Between Duke Street & Orchard Street).* [6.

PRESENTS.

FOREIGN
FANCY ESTABLISHMENT,

58,
OXFORD STREET.

THE LARGEST AND MOST ELEGANT
COLLECTION OF

FANCY GOODS

IN LONDON;

Selected with due regard to English taste.

MODERATOR LAMPS

WITH THE LATEST IMPROVEMENTS,

FROM 16s. TO £20.

BRONZES, CLOCKS

OPERA GLASSES,

Dresden and Sevres Ghina, Bohemian and French Glass, both useful and ornamental.

SAME PRICES AS ABROAD,

AT

58, Oxford Street,

WHOHACK AND SCHLOEZER,

MANUFACTORY, 72, BERNERS STREET,

Where Lamps, Bronzes, and all kinds of Fancy Goods are cleaned and repaired at Moderate Charges.

FRENCH LAMP OIL, AT 3s. 9d. PER GALLON. [7.

COLLINS'

FOUR FOLDING & QUINTIPARTITE PORTMANTEAU.

Registered No. 2,845, *pursuant to the Act* 6 *and* 7 *Victoria, cap.* 65.

THIS original article, Manufactured of SOLID LEATHER is adapted to contain every kind of wearing apparel, in five separate and easily accessible compartments, dividing the woollen goods from the linen, also a convenient space for boots, all the divisions affording a great width and length, to avoid folding the clothes, and obviates the necessity of disturbing one portion to gain access to another

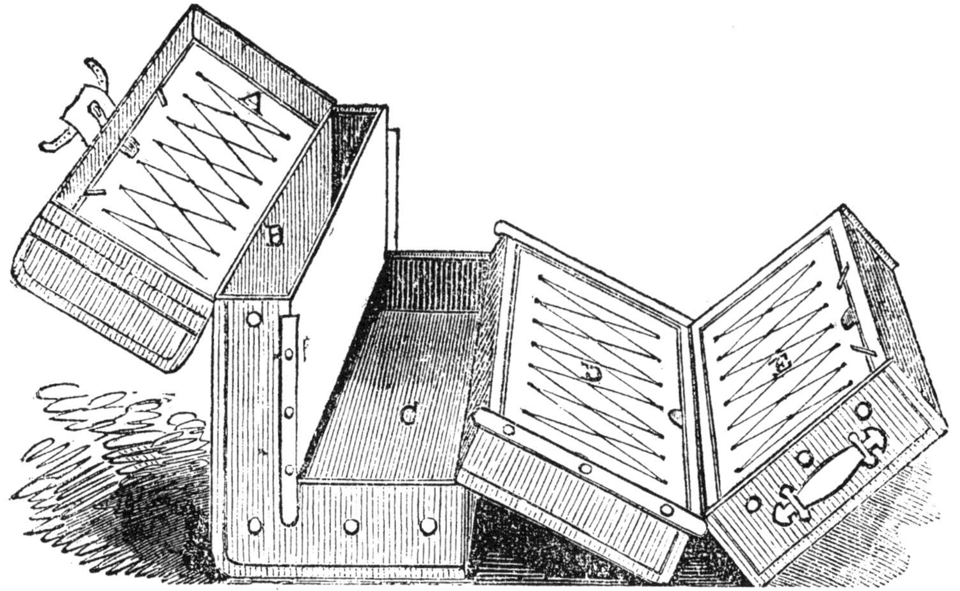

Fig. 1 represents the Portmanteau open.

Compartment	**A**	adapted for	containing	Coats.
Ditto	**B**	,,	,,	Boots.
Ditto	**C**	,,	,,	Trousers.
Ditto	**D**	,,	,,	Waistcoats and Under Clothing.
Ditto	**E**	,,	,,	Shirts, Cravats, and Collars.

The great facility for packing without moving the Portmanteau, its simplicity of construction, rendering the opening and folding together the operation of a moment, and its compactness and portability when closed, have not been equalled by any modern invention; these qualities render it invaluable for railway and Continental travelling.

IMPERIALS & TRUNKS
Fitted to Carriages.
CARPET AND LEATHER BAGS
Of every description.
LADIES' RAILWAY PORTMANTEAUS
With Bonnet Slides and Trays.
OIL CLOTH & CANVAS COVERS,
Made to open with the Trunk.
REGULATION OVERLAND
PORTMANTEAUS AND TRUNKS,
PACKING AND TIN CASES,
PAPER BOXES,
UNITED PORTMANTEAU & BAG,
In Leather and Carpet.
CASH BELTS & BAGS,
TIN, BRASS, AND IRON TRUNKS.

Fig. 2 represents the Portmanteau when closed, ready for travelling.

DANIEL COLLINS,

WHOLESALE AND RETAIL PORTMANTEAU & TRUNK MANUFACTURER,

(ESTABLISHED 1779), [2.

310, OXFORD STREET, LONDON, NEAR BOND STREET.

ELLWOOD'S

PATENT AIR-CHAMBER HAT

FOR INDIA.

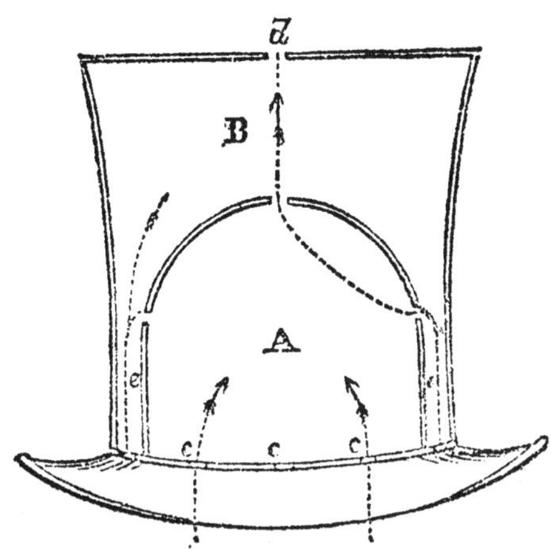

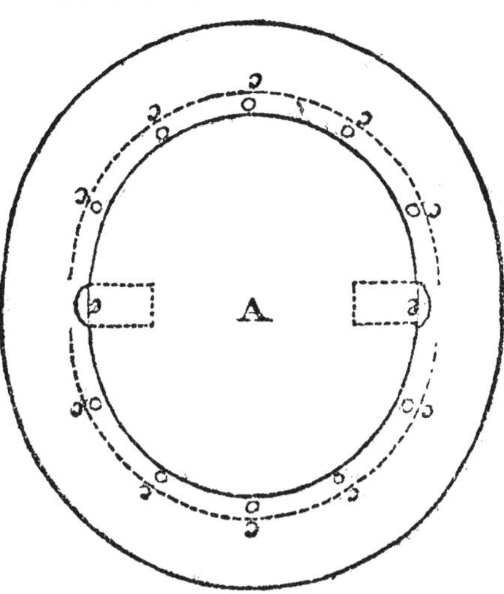

A.—The inner crown which fits the head.

B.—The air chamber into which the air is admitted by means of C C C, small aperture on the under side of brim.

d.—Small aperture at upper part of outer crown, to allow the air to pass out.

ee.—Are small tubes for ventilating the inner crown.

By consulting the above diagrams it will be seen that this hat consists of two parts—the outer part forming an air-chamber round the inner one. On the underside of the brim is a series of perforations, and as the heat of the sun warms, or rarifies the air in the inner chamber between the two parts, a rapid circulation of air takes place through the perforations in the brim, escaping at the top of the outer crown: this circulation of air has the effect of keeping the head perfectly cool, and renders the hat comfortable to the wearer.

This principle is applicable to all kinds of Hats, Military Helmets, Chakos, Hunting Caps, &c., and would be a great acquisition to our Army in India; it would enable the men to do their duty with greater comfort, and prevent many deaths and much illness from "*Coup de Soleil.*"

To be had wholesale of the Patentees and Manufacturers, J. Ellwood and Sons, Great Charlotte Street, Blackfriars Road, London; or wholesale and retail of Ashmead and Tyler, 7, Mount Street, Grosvenor Square; Barber and Son, 13, Royal Exchange; Bailey, 46, Fleet Street; Beardmore, 60, New Bond Street; Briggs, 98, Gracechurch Street; Chatting, 5, Newgate Street; Cole and Son, 23, Bridge Street; Westminster; Donaldson, 33, Warwick Street, Regent Street; Jupp and Son, 222, Regent Street: Lea, 1, Pall Mall; Lock, 6, St. James' Street; Melton, 194, Regent Street; Preedy, 2, Fleet Street; Reynolds, 125, Strand; Thredder, 74, Fleet Street; Mander and Allenders, Liverpool. [36

THE SIX DAYS CAB COMPANY.

Offices—15, Duke Street Chambers, Adelphi (provisionally registered pursuant to act of parliament), for supplying the public with *Cabs at 4d. per mile*, and Brougham, Clarence, and all other carriages at a much reduced rate. Principal stables, Adelphi. In 10,000 shares of £1 each, with power to increase the capital to £50,000. Deposit, 5s. per share.

Directors.

Frederick Bull, Esq., Drayton Grove, Brompton.
Frederick J. Sewell, Esq., Ecclestone Street South, Eaton Square.
Charles Henry Price, Esq., Crescent, Avenue Road, Old Kent Road.
(With power to add to their number.)

Standing Counsel.—Trevethan Spicer, Esq., LL.D., M.A., 4, Gray's Inn Square.
Solicitor.—Grantham Robt. Dodd, jun., Esq., F.L.S., 26, New Broad-st., City.
Mr. Henry Spicer, *Manager*. Mr. S. Watkins Evans, *Secretary*.

Notwithstanding the existence of several cab companies, it is admitted, on all hands, that there is ample room for another. The directors on that account have determined upon starting the Six-Days Cab Company, to run at reduced fares and to abolish all Sunday traffic.

The degree of success that has attended similar associations proves that there is very little speculation in the objects of this company.

The following are among the advantages which this company presents:—

1st, To supply the public with first-rate horses and carriages, the latter to be provided with improved indicators, by which it will be at once seen the distance travelled.

2nd, To abolish the insult and extortion now too prevalent, by employing men of known respectability of character, who will be provided with livery coats and hats, and paid a regular weekly salary.

3rd, To afford their servants the opportunity of moral and religious instruction, by entirely abolishing all Sunday work, thereby constituting this, what the title imports, viz., a Six-Day Conveyance Company.

4th, To bring the luxury of cabriolet riding within the reach of all classes, by reducing the fares to (one-half of the present legal charge) 4d. per mile, which, by the calculations subjoined, are clearly shown to be both possible and profitable.

The following statement is submitted to the public for consideration. It is calculated that each £1,000 will purchase 10 cabs, 20 horses and harness complete.

Receipts from each £1,000 Capital.			
Weekly income derived from 20 horses, each horse travelling 25 miles per diem, for 6 days, at 4d. per mile	£50	0	0
Deduct expenditure as on other side	33	10	0
Gross weekly profit	£16	10	0
or £858 per annum.			

Payments.			
Keep for 20 horses	£13	0	0
Ten drivers	10	10	0
Duty on 10 Cabs	5	0	0
Wear and tear	5	0	0
	£33	10	0

After allowing a deduction of 25 per cent. from the above for expenses of management, there will be left a profit of 60 per cent. per annum.

Applications for shares to be made in the form annexed, to Mr. Evans, Secretary, at the offices of the company, 15, Duke Street, Adelphi, London.

FORM OF APPLICATION FOR SHARES.

To the Directors of the Six-Days Cab Company.

Gentlemen,—I hereby apply for shares of £1 each in the above company, and I hereby agree to accept the same, or any less number allotted to me, and to pay the deposit thereon, and the further calls when required; also to execute the deed of settlement when called upon to do so.—Dated this day of 185

Name ....
Address ....
Occupation ....
Reference and Address..............................

F. & C. OSLER,

44, OXFORD STREET, LONDON

(MANUFACTORY, BROAD STREET, BIRMINGHAM),

ESTABLISHED 1807.

MANUFACURERS OF

GLASS CHANDELIERS, GLASS LUSTRES,

TABLE GLASSES, &c. &c.

A Select and Extensive Stock, in every variety of pattern, of

RICHLY CUT CRYSTAL GLASS CHANDELIERS,

WITH GLASS BRANCHES,

FOR DRAWING ROOMS, &C.

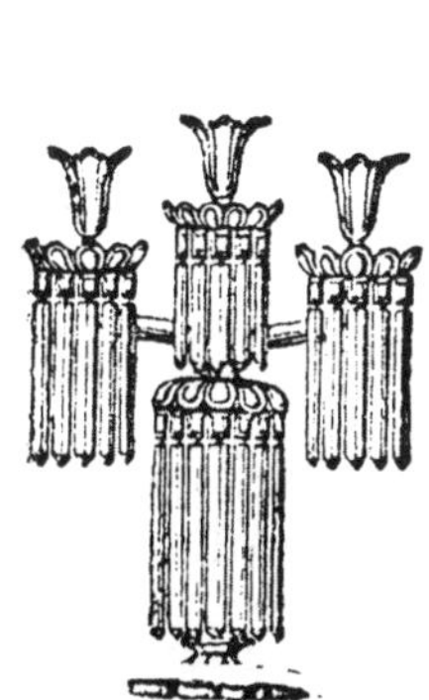

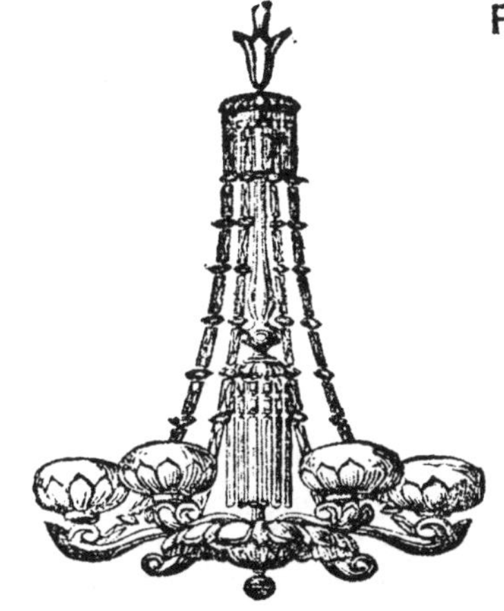

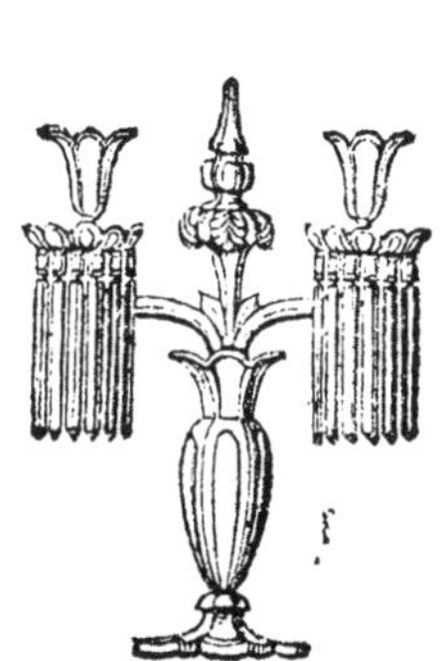

Elegant Crystal Glass Chandeliers, for Gas

(Made from "Registered" designs), with Glass Branches, &c., suitable for Drawing Rooms and Ball Rooms.

Theatres, Concerts, Assembly, and Ball Rooms, Lighted by Estimate, on the Lowest Terms.

A Large and Choice Assortment, in new and beautiful designs, of

HANDSOMELY-CUT GLASS LUSTRES AND GIRONDOLES.

Cut-Glass Ice Dishes and Pails, also Ice Plates, and all Articles in Glass required for Ice,

BEST CUT TABLE GLASS, IN EVERY VARIETY.

FAMILY CRESTS AND REGIMENTAL BADGES ENGRAVED.

ORNAMENTAL GLASS, ENGLISH AND FOREIGN,

(The Latter selected and imported by Messrs. Osler), in the greatest variety

Wholesale, Export, and General Furnishing Orders for Glass promptly executed.

[4

THE SIX DAYS CAB COMPANY.

Offices—15, Duke Street Chambers, Adelphi (provisionally registered pursuant to act of parliament), for supplying the public with *Cabs at 4d. per mile*, and Brougham, Clarence, and all other carriages at a much reduced rate. Principal stables, Adelphi. In 10,000 shares of £1 each, with power to increase the capital to £50,000. Deposit, 5s. per share.

Directors.

Frederick Bull, Esq., Drayton Grove, Brompton.
Frederick J. Sewell, Esq., Ecclestone Street South, Eaton Square.
Charles Henry Price, Esq., Crescent, Avenue Road, Old Kent Road.
(With power to add to their number.)

Standing Counsel.—Trevethan Spicer, Esq., LL.D., M.A., 4, Gray's Inn Square.
Solicitor.—Grantham Robt. Dodd, jun., Esq., F.L.S., 26, New Broad-st., City.
Mr. Henry Spicer, *Manager*. Mr. S. Watkins Evans, *Secretary*.

Notwithstanding the existence of several cab companies, it is admitted, on all hands, that there is ample room for another. The directors on that account have determined upon starting the Six-Days Cab Company, to run at reduced fares and to abolish all Sunday traffic.

The degree of success that has attended similar associations proves that there is very little speculation in the objects of this company.

The following are among the advantages which this company presents:—

1st, To supply the public with first-rate horses and carriages, the latter to be provided with improved indicators, by which it will be at once seen the distance travelled.

2nd, To abolish the insult and extortion now too prevalent, by employing men of known respectability of character, who will be provided with livery coats and hats, and paid a regular weekly salary.

3rd, To afford their servants the opportunity of moral and religious instruction, by entirely abolishing all Sunday work, thereby constituting this, what the title imports, viz., a Six-Day Conveyance Company.

4th, To bring the luxury of cabriolet riding within the reach of all classes, by reducing the fares to (one-half of the present legal charge) 4d. per mile, which, by the calculations subjoined, are clearly shown to be both possible and profitable.

The following statement is submitted to the public for consideration. It is calculated that each £1,000 will purchase 10 cabs, 20 horses and harness complete.

Receipts from each £1,000 Capital.

	£	s.	d.
Weekly income derived from 20 horses, each horse travelling 25 miles per diem, for 6 days, at 4d. per mile	£50	0	0
Deduct expenditure as on other side	33	10	0
Gross weekly profit	£16	10	0

or £858 per annum.

Payments.

	£	s.	d.
Keep for 20 horses	£13	0	0
Ten drivers	10	10	0
Duty on 10 Cabs	5	0	0
Wear and tear	5	0	0
	£33	10	0

After allowing a deduction of 25 per cent. from the above for expenses of management, there will be left a profit of 60 per cent. per annum.

Applications for shares to be made in the form annexed, to Mr. Evans, Secretary, at the offices of the company, 15, Duke Street, Adelphi, London.

FORM OF APPLICATION FOR SHARES.

To the Directors of the Six-Days Cab Company.

Gentlemen,—I hereby apply for shares of £1 each in the above company, and I hereby agree to accept the same, or any less number allotted to me, and to pay the deposit thereon, and the further calls when required; also to execute the deed of settlement when called upon to do so.—Dated this day of 185

Name ....
Address ....
Occupation ....
Reference and Address..........................

THE ELECTRIC TELEGRAPH COMPANY,

INCORPORATED 1846.

THE following are now the Charges for the transmission of messages not exceeding Twenty Words,

WITHIN A CIRCUIT OF 100 MILES....2s. 6d.

BEYOND A CIRCUIT OF 100 MILES....5s. 0d.

(DISTANCE CALCULATED AS THE CROW FLIES).

An addition of one half the above rates for each Ten Words or fraction of Ten Words additional—or a charge of Threepence per word, at the option of the party sending the message.

TELEGRAPH STATIONS.

Ambergate
Audley End
Banbury
Bangor
Basingstoke
BATH
Belper
BERWICK-ON-TWEED
Beverley
Biggleswade
Birkenhead
BIRMINGHAM
Bishop Stortford
Bletchley
Boston
BRADFORD
Brandon
Brentwood
BRIDGEWATER
Bridlington
BRIGHTON
***BRISTOL**
Bromsgrove
Broxbourne
Buckingham
BURTON-ON-TRENT
Carnarvon
CAMBRIDGE
CARLISLE
Chelmsford
CHELTENHAM
CHESTER
Chesterfield
Chesterford
Chippenham
Church Fenton
COLCHESTER
Colwich
Congleton
Conway
COVENTRY
Crewe
Darlington
DERBY
Didcot
DONCASTER
DORCHESTER
Dunbar
DURHAM
***EDINBURGH**
ELY
EXETER
Ferry Hill
Firsby
Gainsborough
***GLASGOW**
Glossop
GLOUCESTER
Gobowen
Gosport
Grantham
GREAT GRIMSBY
HALIFAX
Harecastle
Harrogate
Hadfield
Hayward's Heath
HEREFORD
Hertford
Hitchin
HOLYHEAD
HUDDERSFIELD
***HULL**
Huntingdon
Kendal
Knottingley
LANCASTER
***LEEDS**
Leek
Leicester
Leighton
Leith
Lewes
LINCOLN
***LIVERPOOL**
Do. Lime Street
LONDON
Longport, or Burslem
Longton
Loughborough
Louth
LOWESTOFT
Ludlow
Lymington
MACCLESFIELD
Malton
***MANCHESTER**
Do. Victoria
Do. London Road
March
Market Harbro'
MARYPORT
Masbro'
Melton Mowbray
Milford Junction
Mirfield
Morpeth
Mottram
Newark-on-Trent
NEWCASTLE-ON-TYNE
*Do. Central Station
Newcastle-uuder-Lyne
Newhaven
NEWMARKET
Normanton
Northallerton
NORTHAMPTON
North Dean
North Shields
Norton Bridge
NORWICH
NOTTINGHAM
Oxenholme
OXFORD
Penistone
Penrith
PETERBOROUGH
PLYMOUTH
Poole
PORTSMOUTH
PRESTON
READING
Retford
Rhyl
Richmond (Yorkshire)
Rocester
Rochdale
Romford
Ruabon
Rugby
St. Ives
St. Neots
SCARBOROUGH
Selby
SHEFFIELD
Shiffnal
SHREWSBURY
Skipton
Slough
Somer Leyton
SOUTHAMPTON
South Shields
Spalding
Spetchley (Worcester)
STAFFORD
Staleybridge
Stamford
STOCKPORT
STOKE-ON-TRENT
Stone
Stratford (Essex)
Stroud
SUNDERLAND
SWINDON
TAMWORTH
TAUNTON
Thetford
Thirsk
Thrapston
Todmorden
TOTNESS
Tring
Wakefield
Warrington
Water Lane
Weedon
Wellington (Shropshire)
WHITEHAVEN
WIGAN
WINCHESTER
Winchfield
Windsor
Winslow
Wisbeach
Witham
WOLVERHAMPTON
Wolverton
Worksop
Wrexham
Wymondham
YARMOUTH
***YORK**

Remittances to London from the Stations marked thus * can be made through this Company.

OFFICES IN LONDON AT WHICH MESSAGES ARE RECEIVED AND FORWARDED:

CENTRAL STATION, Lothbury. BRANCH STATIONS :—General Post Office, St. Martin's-le-Grand; West Strand, No. 448, Corner of Adelaide Street (open day and night): No. 17A, Great George Street, Westminster; No. 53, Waterloo Road; No. 7, Knightsbridge Terrace, opposite Albert Gate; at the Great Northern Railway Station, King's Cross; at the London and North Western Railway Stations, Euston Square and Camden Town; at the Eastern Counties Railway Station, Shoreditch; at the London and South Western Railway Station, Waterloo Road; at the London and Brighton Railway Station, London Bridge; at the Great Western Railway Station, Paddington.

By order, J. S. FOURDRINIER, Secretary. [5

SUBMARINE TELEGRAPH COMPANY

BETWEEN GREAT BRITAIN AND THE CONTINENT OF EUROPE,

VIA FRANCE AND BELGIUM.

OFFICES:

30, CORNHILL, LONDON; CLARENCE PLACE, DOVER; AND 83, RUE RICHELIEU, PARIS.

The following Cities and Towns are in Electric Communication with Great Britain:

- Adelsberg
- Agram
- Aix-la-Chapelle
- Altenburg
- Amiens
- **Amsterdam**
- Angers
- Angouleme
- Ansbach
- **Antwerp**
- Arras
- Aschaffenburg
- **Augsburg**
- Avignon
- **Baden**
- Bamburg
- Bautzen
- Bergamo
- **Berlin**
- Bielitz
- Bietigheim
- Blois
- Bodenbach
- Bonn
- **Bordeaux**
- Burgoforto
- Botzen (in Tyrol)
- **Boulogne Sur Mer**
- Bourges
- Brain le Compte
- Breda
- Bregenz
- **Bremen**
- Brescia
- **Breslau**
- Brixen
- Bromberg
- Bruchsal
- Bruges
- Brunn
- **Brunswick**
- **Brussels**
- Buchen
- **Calais**
- Carlsruhe
- Cassel
- Chalons Sur Marne
- Chalons Sur Saone
- Chartres (Eure et Loir)
- Chateauroux
- Chemnitz
- Cilly
- Cittanuova
- Coblentz
- Colmar (Alsace)
- **Cologne**
- Courtrai
- **Cracow**
- Czegled
- Czernowitz
- **Dantzic**
- Dessau
- Deutz
- **Dieppe**
- Dijon
- Dirschaw
- Dordrecht
- **Dresden**
- Duisburg
- Dunkirk
- Dusseldorf
- Eisenach
- Elberfeld
- Elbing
- Erfurt
- Essek
- Feldkirk
- **Florence**
- **Frankfort-on-Main**
- Frankfort-on-Oder
- Friburg
- Friedrichshafen
- **Ghent**
- Giessen
- Glognitz
- Gorlitz
- Gotha
- Govitz
- Gratz
- Guastalla
- Haarlem
- Hagenau
- Halle
- Haltingen-Bale
- **Hamburg**
- Ham
- Hanau
- **Hanover**
- Harburg
- Hasselt
- **Havre**
- Hazebrook
- Heidleberg
- Heilbrun
- Hermannstadt
- Hof
- Hohenschwangau
- Ingolstadt
- Inspruck
- Ischl
- Juterburg
- Karlsburgh
- **Kehl-Strasbourg**
- Kempten
- Kikinda
- Klagenfurt
- Klausenburg
- Kohlfurt
- **Konigsburg**
- Kothen
- Kreutz
- Kufstein
- Kosel
- La Haye
- Laibach
- Landen
- Landshut
- **Leghorn**
- **Leipzic**
- Lemburg
- Liegnitz
- Lindau
- Linz
- **Lisle**
- Louvain
- Lucca
- **Lyons**
- Metz
- Macon
- Magdeburg
- Malines
- Mannheim
- **Mantua**
- Marburg
- **Marseilles**
- Massa
- **Mayence**
- **Milan**
- Minden
- Mons
- Mulhouse
- **Munich**
- Munster
- Murzzuschlag
- **Modena**
- **Nantes**
- Neuhausel
- Nevers
- Nuremburg
- Nancy
- Oderberg
- Offenburg
- Olmutz
- Oppeln
- Orleans
- Oschersleben
- **Ostend**
- Paderborn
- Padua
- **Paris**
- Passau
- Peschiera
- **Pesth-Bude**
- Peterwardin
- Pirano
- Pisa
- Plauen
- Poictiers
- Pola
- Posen
- Potsdam
- **Prague**
- **Presburg**
- Przmysl
- Parma
- Quievrain
- Rastadt
- Ratibor
- Ratisbon
- Rieza
- Rosenheim
- **Rotterdam**
- **Rouen**
- Roveredo
- Rovigno
- Rzeszow
- Reggio
- Salzburg
- Semlin
- Sienna
- St. Etienne
- St. Omer
- **Stettin**
- **Stuttgard**
- Swinnemunde
- Szolneck
- Szegedin
- **Strasbourg**
- Tarnow
- Temeswar
- Termonde
- Tirlemont
- Tonnerre
- Tournay
- Tours
- Trento
- Treves
- Treviglio
- Trevisa
- **Trieste**
- Troppau
- Trubau
- Turbise
- Udine
- Ulm
- Valenciennes
- **Venice**
- **Verona**
- Verviers
- Vicenza
- **Vienna**
- Weimar
- Werden
- Wesel
- Wittenburg
- Wurzburg

J. W. and T. ALLEN,

MANUFACTURERS,

18 & 22, WEST STRAND, LONDON.

Registered November 25th, 1851, No. 3,027.

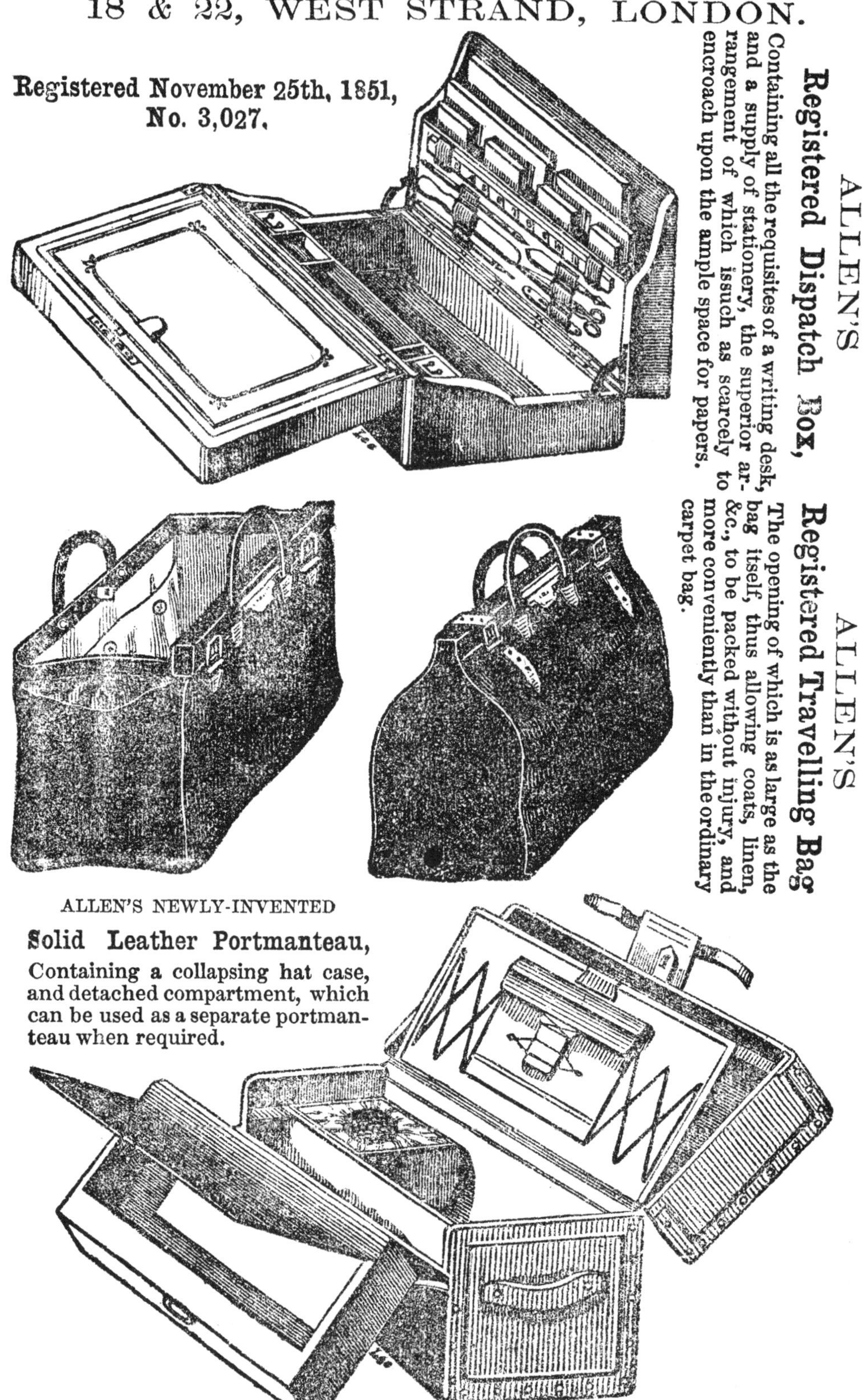

ALLEN'S
Registered Dispatch Box,
Containing all the requisites of a writing desk, and a supply of stationery, the superior arrangement of which issuch as scarcely to encroach upon the ample space for papers.

ALLEN'S
Registered Travelling Bag
The opening of which is as large as the bag itself, thus allowing coats, linen, &c., to be packed without injury, and more conveniently than in the ordinary carpet bag.

ALLEN'S NEWLY-INVENTED

Solid Leather Portmanteau,

Containing a collapsing hat case, and detached compartment, which can be used as a separate portmanteau when required.

Gentlemen are invited to inspect these articles before purchasing any of the old kinds. Illustrated Catalogues, with prices, gratis.

ALLEN, 18 and 22, WEST STRAND, LONDON.

IMPORTANT FAMILY MEDICINE.

NORTON'S CAMOMILE PILLS,

THE

MOST CERTAIN PRESERVER OF HEALTH;

A MILD, YET SPEEDY, SAFE, AND

EFFECTUAL AID IN CASES OF INDIGESTION,

AND ALL STOMACH COMPLAINTS,

AND, AS A NATURAL CONSEQUENCE,

A PURIFIER OF THE BLOOD, AND A SWEETENER OF THE WHOLE SYSTEM.

INDIGESTION is a weakness or want of power of the digestive juices in the stomach to convert what we eat and drink into healthy matter, for the proper nourishment of the whole system. It is caused by every thing which weakens the system in general, or the stomach in particular. From it proceed nearly all the diseases to which we are liable; for it is very certain that if we could always keep the stomach right, we should only die by old age or accident. Indigestion produces a great variety of unpleasant sensations: amongst the most prominent of its miserable effects are a want of, or an inordinate appetite, sometimes attended with a constant craving for drink, a distension or feeling of enlargement of the stomach, flatulency, heartburn, pains in the stomach, acidity, unpleasant taste in the mouth, perhaps sickness, rumbling noise in the bowels: in some cases of depraved digestion there is nearly a complete disrelish for food, but still the appetite is not greatly impaired, as at the stated period of meals persons so afflicted can eat heartily, although without much gratification; a long train of nervous symptoms are also frequent attendants, general debility, great languidness, and incapacity for exertion. The minds of persons so afflicted frequently become irritable and desponding, and great anxiety is observable in the countenance; they appear thoughtful, melancholy, and dejected, under great apprehensions of some imaginary danger, will start at any unexpected noise or occurrence, and become so agitated that they require some time to calm and collect themselves; yet for all this the mind is exhilarated without much difficulty; pleasing events, society, will for a time dissipate all appearance of disease; but the excitement produced by an agreeable change vanishes soon after the cause has gone by. Other symptoms are, violent palpitations, restlessness, the sleep disturbed by frightful dreams and startings, and affording little or no refreshment; occasionally there is much moaning, with a sense of weight and oppression upon the chest, nightmare, &c.

It is almost impossible to enumerate all the symptoms of this first invader upon the constitution, as in a hundred cases of *Indigestion* there will probably be something peculiar to each; but be they what they may, they are all occasioned by the food becoming a burden rather than a support to the stomach; and in all its stages the medicine most wanted is that which will afford speedy and effectual assistance to the digestive organs, and give energy to the nervous and muscular systems — nothing can more speedily or with more certainty effect so desirable an object than *Norton's Extract of Camomile Flowers.* The herb has, from time immemorial, been highly esteemed in England as a grateful anodyne, imparting an aromatic bitter to the taste, and a pleasing degree of warmth and strength to the stomach; and in all cases of indigestion, gout in the stomach, windy colic, and general weakness, it has for ages been strongly recommended by the most eminent practitioners as very useful and beneficial. The great, indeed, only objection to their use, has been the large quantity of water which it takes to dissolve a small part of the flowers, and which must be taken with it into the stomach. It requires a quarter of a pint of boiling water to dissolve the soluble portion of one drachm of camomile flowers; and, when one or even two ounces may be taken with advantage, it must at once be seen how impossible it is to take a proper dose of this wholesome herb in the form of tea; and the only reason why it has not long since been placed the very first in rank of all restorative medicines is, that in taking it, the stomach has always been loaded with water, which tends in a great measure to counteract, and very frequently wholly to destroy, the effect. It must be evident that loading a weak stomach with a large quantity of water, merely for the purpose of conveying into it a small quantity of medicine, must be injurious; and that the medicines must possess powerful renovating properties only to counteract the bad effects likely to be produced by the water. Generally speaking, this has been the case with camomile flowers, a herb possessing the highest restorative qualities, and, when properly taken, decidedly the most speedy restorer, and the most certain preserver of health.

These PILLS are wholly CAMOMILE, prepared by a peculiar process, accidentally discovered, and known only to the proprietor, and which he firmly believes to be one of the most valuable modern discoveries in medicine, by which all the essential and extractive matter of more than an ounce of the flowers is concentrated in four moderate-sized pills. Experience has afforded the most ample proof that they possess all the fine aromatic and stomachic properties for which the herb has been esteemed; and, as they are taken into the stomach unencumbered by any diluting or indigestible substance, in the same degree has their benefit been more immediate and decided. Mild in their operation and pleasant in their effect, they may be taken at any age, and under any circumstance, without danger or inconvenience; a person exposed to cold and wet a whole day or night could not possibly receive any injury from taking them, but, on the contrary, they would effectually prevent a cold being taken. After a long acquaintance with and strict observance of the medicinal properties of *Norton's Camomile Pills*, it is only doing them justice to say, that they are really the most valuable of all TONIC MEDICINES. By the word tonic is meant a medicine which gives strength to the stomach sufficient to digest in proper quantities all wholesome food, which increases the power of every nerve and muscle of the human body, or, in other words, invigorates the nervous and muscular systems. The solidity or firmness of the whole tissue of the body which so quickly follows the use of *Norton's Camomile Pills*, their certain and speedy effects in repairing the partial dilapidations from time or intemperance, and their lasting salutary influence on the whole frame, is most convincing, that in the smallest compass is contained the largest quantity of the tonic principle, of so peculiar a nature as to pervade the whole system, through which it diffuses health and strength sufficient to resist the formation of disease, and also to fortify the constitution against contagion; as such, their general use is strongly recommended as a preventive during the prevalence of malignant fever or other infectious diseases, and to persons attending sick rooms they are invaluable, as in no one instance have they ever failed in preventing the taking of illness, even under the most trying circumstances.

As *Norton's Camomile Pills* are particularly recommended for all stomach complaints or indigestion, it will probably be expected that some advice should be given respecting diet, though, after all that has been written upon the subject, after the publication of volume upon volume—after the country has, as it were, been inundated with practical essays on diet, as a means of prolonging life, it would be unnecessary to say more, did we not feel it our duty to make the humble endeavour of inducing the public to regard them not, but to adopt that course which is dictated by nature, by reason, and by common sense. Those persons who study the wholesomes, and are governed by the opinions of writers on diet, are uniformly both unhealthy in body and weak in mind. There can be no doubt that the palate is designed to inform us what is proper for the stomach, and of course that must best instruct us what food to take, and what to avoid: we want no other adviser. Nothing can be more clear than that those articles which are agreeable to the taste were by nature intended for our food and sustenance, whether liquid or solid, foreign or of native production; if they are pure and unadulterated, no harm need be dreaded by their use; they will only injure by abuse. Consequently, whatever the palate approves, eat and drink, always in moderation, but never in excess; keeping in mind that the first process of digestion is performed in the mouth, the second in the stomach; and that, in order that the stomach may be able to do its work properly, it is requisite the first process should be well performed; this consists in masticating or chewing the solid food, so as to break down and separate the fibres and small substances of meat and vegetables, mixing them well, and blending the whole together before they are swallowed; and it is particularly urged upon all to take plenty of time to their meals, and never eat in haste. If you conform to this short and simple, but comprehensive advice, and find that there are various things which others eat and drink with pleasure and without inconvenience, and which would be pleasant to yourself only that they disagree, you may at once conclude that the fault is in the stomach; that it does not possess the power which it ought to do, that it wants assistance, and the sooner that assistance is afforded the better. A very short trial of this medicine will best prove how soon it will put the stomach in a condition to perform with ease all the work which nature intended for it. By its use you will soon be able to enjoy, in moderation, whatever is agreeable to the taste, and unable to name one individual article of food which disagrees with or sits unpleasantly on the stomach. Never forget that a small meal well digested affords more nourishment to the system than a large one, even of the same food, when digested imperfectly. Let the dish be ever so delicious, ever so enticing a variety offered, the bottle ever so enchanting, never forget that temperance tends to preserve health, and that health is the soul of enjoyment. But should an impropriety be at any time, or ever so often, committed, by which the stomach becomes overloaded or disordered, render it immediate aid by taking a dose of *Norton's Camomile Pills*, which will so promptly assist in carrying off the burden thus imposed upon it, that all will soon be right again.

It is most certainly true that every person in his lifetime consumes a quantity of noxious matter, which if taken at one meal would be fatal: it is these small quantities of noxious matter, which are introduced into our food, either by accident or wilful adulteration, which we find so often upset the stomach, and not unfrequently lay the foundation of illness, and perhaps final ruination to health. To preserve the constitution, it should be our constant care, if possible, to counteract the effect of these small quantities of unwholesome matter; and whenever, in that way, an enemy to the constitution finds its way into the stomach, a friend should be immediately sent after it, which would prevent its mischievous effects, and expel it altogether; no better friend can be found, nor one which will perform the task with greater certainty, than NORTON'S CAMOMILE PILLS. And let it be observed that the longer this medicine is taken the less it will be wanted; it can in no case become habitual, as its entire action is to give energy and force to the stomach, which is the spring of life, the source from which the whole frame draws its succour and support. After an excess of eating or drinking, and upon every occasion of the general health being at all disturbed, these PILLS should be immediately taken, as they will stop and eradicate disease at its commencement. Indeed, it is most confidently asserted, that by the timely use of this medicine only, and a common degree of caution, any person may enjoy all the comforts within his reach, may pass through life without an illness, and with the certainty of attaining a healthy OLD AGE.

On account of their volatile properties they must be kept in bottles; and if closely corked, their qualities are neither impaired by time nor injured by any change of climate whatever. Price 13½d. and 2s. 9d. each, with full directions. The large bottle contains the quantity of three small ones, or PILLS equal to fourteen ounces of CAMOMILE FLOWERS.

Sold by nearly all respectable Medicine Vendors.

Be particular to ask for "NORTON'S PILLS," and do not be persuaded to purchase an imitation.

and Birmingham Railway).—Cameron and Martin, agents.

West Cornwall.—J. Dorington and Co., agents.

West End of London and Crystal Palace.—Wm. Bryden. agent.

Wexford Junction.—George Lewis Smyth, agent.

Whitehaven and Furness Junction.—Roy and Co., agents.

Wimbledon and Croydon (Incorporation of Company for making a Railway from Wimbledon to Croydon; Power to use the line of the London and South Western Railway Company, and make Arrangements for the purpose; Amendment of Acts of that Company).—H. & W. Toogood, agents.

Woodford (to incorporate a Company for making a Railway from the East and West India Docks and Birmingham Junction Railway at Hackney Wick to Woodford).—Tyrrell, Paine and Layton, agents.

Worcester and Hereford.—Pritt & Co., agents.

Worcester and Hereford Junction.—Dyson and Co.; J. Dorington and Co., agents.

York, Newcastle and Berwick, York and North Midland and Leeds Northern Companies (Amalgamation, &c.)—Pritt and Co., agents.

Advertisements.

THE NEW REGISTERED PORTMANTEAU,

Registered and Manufactured by

JOHN SOUTHGATE,

76, WATLING STREET, LONDON.

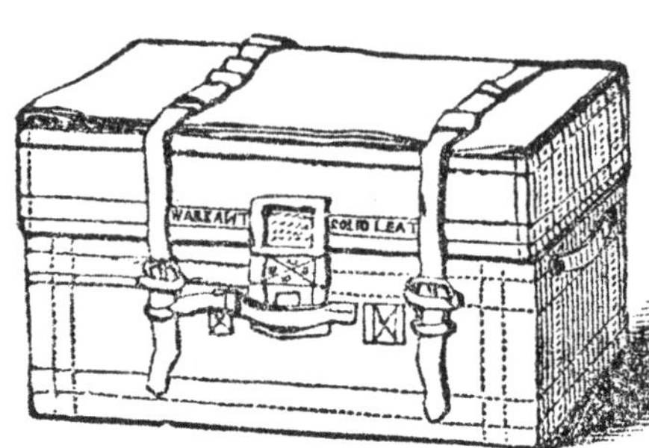

THIS PORTMANTEAU is admitted by all who have used it to be the most PERFECT and USEFUL of any yet invented, and to combine all the advantages so long desired by all who travel.

The peculiar conveniences of this Portmanteau are, that it contains separate compartments for each description of Clothes, Boots, &c.; each division is kept entirely distinct, and is immediately accessible on opening the Portmanteau, without lifting or disturbing anything else Every article is packed perfectly flat, and remains so during the whole of the journey.

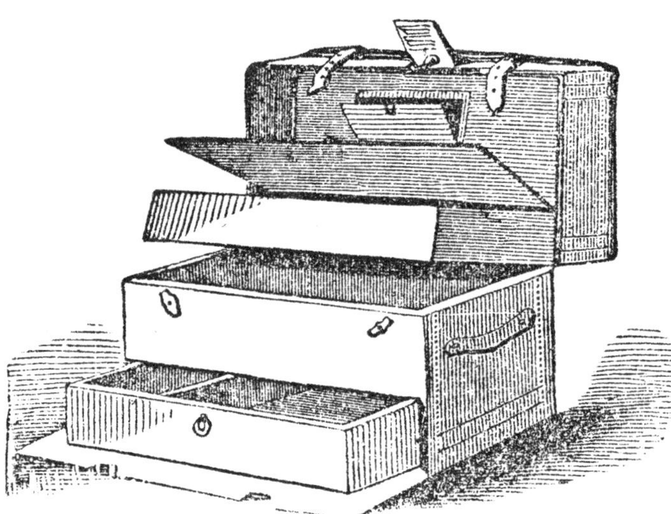

It may be obtained of Mr. WILKINSON, 30, Cockspur Street; of Messrs. MOORE & Co., 14, St. James's Street, London. Of Mr. HUNT, Above-Bar, Southampton; of Mr. BAYS, Hatter, Cambridge; of Mr. ELLENGER, Granger Street, Newcastle-on-Tyne; of most Outfitters and Saddlers throughout the Kingdom; and of

JOHN SOUTHGATE,

Manufacturer of every Description of Portmanteaus and Travelling Equipage.

76, WATLING STREET, CITY;

AGENT FOR

GALT'S REGISTERED CLARENCE WRAPPER & CAPE,

Suitable for the use of both Ladies and Gentlemen travelling either by rail or carriage.

Its peculiar construction prevents it sliding down when used as a Wrapper, nad forms an elegant Cape when walking or riding.

CLERICAL, MEDICAL, AND GENERAL
LIFE ASSURANCE SOCIETY.

ADVANTAGES OFFERED. EXTENSION OF LIMITS OF RESIDENCE.—The Assured may reside in most parts of the world without extra charge, and in all parts, by payment of a small extra premium.

MUTUAL SYSTEM WITHOUT THE RISK OF PARTNERSHIP.

The small share of profit devisible in future among the Shareholders being now provided for, without intrenching on the amount made by the regular business, the Assured will hereafter derive all the benefits obtainable from a Mutual Office, with, at the same time, complete freedom from liability, secured by means of an ample Proprietary Capital—thus combining in the same office all the advantages of both systems.

The Assurance Fund already invested amounts to **£850,000**, and the Income exceeds **£136,000** per Annum.

CREDIT SYSTEM.—On policies for the whole of Life, one-half of the Annual Premiums for the first five years may remain on credit, and may either continue as a debt on the Policy, or may be paid off at any time.

LOANS.—Loans are advanced on Policies which have been in existence five years and upwards, to the extent of nine-tenths of their value.

BONUSES.—Five Bonuses have been declared; at the last in January, 1852, the sum of £131,125 was added to the Policies, producing a Bonus varying with the different ages, from 24½ to 55 per cent. on the Premiums paid during the five years, or from **£5 to £12 10s. per cent.** on the Sum Assured.

The Bonuses applied in reduction of Premium on many of the Policies which have participated in three or more divisions, have been sufficient not only to extinguish the whole of the premiums, but also to add a Bonus to the sum assured, which will be further augmented at every succeeding division.

The following are examples:—

Sums Assured.	No. of Bonuses.	Original Premium.		Bonus already added to Sums Assured since the extinguishment of all the Premiums.
£		£ s. d.		£ s. d.
1000	5	82 11 10	Extinguished.	337 11 0
1000	4	82 0 10	Ditto.	114 0 0
1000	3	125 0 0	Ditto.	193 5 0
1000	3	100 5 0	Ditto.	106 10 0

PARTICIPATION IN PROFITS.—Policies participate in the Profits in proportion to the number and amount of the premiums paid between every division, so that if only one year's Premium be received prior to the Books being closed for any division, the Policy on which it was paid will obtain its due share. The books close for the next Division on 30th June, 1856, therefore those who effect Policies before the 30th June next will be entitled to one year's additional share of Profits over later assurers.

APPLICATION OF BONUSES.—The next and future Bonuses may be either received in Cash, or applied at the option of the assured in any other way.

NON-PARTICIPATING.—Assurances may be effected for a Fixed Sum at considerably reduced rates, and the Premiums for term Policies are lower than at most other Safe Offices.

PROMPT SETTLEMENT OF CLAIMS.—Claims paid *thirty* days after proof of death, and all Policies are *Indisputable* except in cases of fraud.

INVALID LIVES may be assured at rates proportioned to the increased risk.

POLICIES are granted on the lives of persons in any station, and of every age, and for any sum on one life from £50 to £10,000.

PREMIUMS may be paid yearly, half-yearly, or quarterly, but if a payment be omitted from any cause, the Policy can be revived within *fourteen* Months.

The accounts and Balance Sheets are at all times open to the inspection of the Assured, or of *Persons desirous to assure.*

A copy of the last Report, with a Prospectus and forms of Proposal, can be obtained f any of the Society's Agents, or will be forwarded free by addressing a line to

GEORGE H. PINCKARD, Resident Secretary

99, Great Russell Street, Bloomsbury, London. [40

NORWICH UNION FIRE INSURANCE SOCIETY.

ESTABLISHED 1797. CAPITAL, £550,000.

DIRECTORS.

President—ANTHONY HUDSON, Esq., Banker.

Vice-President—GEORGE MORSE, Esq.

Lieut-Gen. Sir R. J. Harvey, C.B.
C. Evans, Esq., Chancellor of Norwich.
Edward Steward, Esq.
Lewis Evans, Esq., M.D.
Thomas Blakiston, Esq., R.N.

Timothy Steward, Esq.
George Durrant, Esq.
R. J. H. Harvey, Esq.
Sir William Foster, Bart.
Henry S. Patteson, Esq.

Secretary—Samuel Bignold, Esq. | London Agent—C. J. Bunyon, Esq.

Insurances are granted by this Society on buildings, goods, merchandise, and effects, ships in port, harbour or dock, from loss or damage by fire in any part of the united kingdom of great Britain and Ireland.

It is provided by the constitution of the society, that the insured shall be free from all responsibility; and to guarantee the engagements of the office, a fund of £550,000 has been subscribed by a numerous and opulent proprietary, which fund has been further increased by the accumulation of an additional reserve, now amounting to £96,800. Returns of three-fifths of the profits of the company are periodically made to parties insuring, who have thus, from time to time, received from the Society sums amounting in the aggregate to nearly £380,000. The rates of premium are in no case higher than those charged by other principal offices making no returns to their Insurers.

The business of the company exceeds £62,000,000, and, owing to the liberality with which its engagements have been performed, is rapidly increasing. The Duty paid to government for the year 1851 was £74,101 15s. 3d.; and the amount insured on farming stock was upwards of £9,156,898.

Norwich Union Life Insurance Society (Established 1808)

DIRECTORS.

Committee.
President—Lieut-Gen. Sir ROBERT J. HARVEY, C.B.
Vice-Presidents—JOHN WRIGHT, Esq. LEWIS EVANS, Esq., M.D.
Timothy Steward, Esq. George Durrant, Esq. James Winter, Esq.

Charles Turner, Esq.
Peter Finch, Esq.
James Neave, Esq.

I. O. Taylor, Esq.
Frank Noverre, Esq.
J. H. Barnard, Esq.

W. Rackham, Esq.
R. Griffin, Esq.

Auditors—Mressrs. E. Willet, James Hardy, Anthony Bailey,

Secretary—Samuel Bignold, Esq. | London Agent—Chas. John Bunyon, Esq.

This society has now been established upwards of 44 years, upon the principles of MUTUAL ASSURANCE; during which period it has paid to claimants on terminated policies upwards of £3,000,000 sterling; in addition to which nearly *One Million and a Quarter* sterling has been assigned by way of bonuses; while the accumulated capital for meeting existing engagements (and which is almost wholly invested on real and government securities) exceeds £2,100,000. There is no *Proprietary* to divide with the *Assured* the profits of this institution, which is one of the very few purely Mutual Insurance Offices. In addition, however, to the entire profits of the Society, persons now effecting insurances will be entitled to participate in the benefits to be derived from the Reserved Fund, now amounting to £215,197 12s. 7d., and which, affording all the protection of a Proprietary Capital, will at the same time increase instead of diminishing their future bonuses. The Rates of Premium are below those of most Insurances Offices, and under the age of 45 not less so than 10 per cent., a benefit in itself equivalent to an annual bonus.

One half of the first five Annual Premiums may remain as a permanent charge upon Policies granted for the whole duration of Life.

Division of Profits.

No. of Pol.	Sum Insurd.	Bonus prior to June, 1852			Bonus declared in June, 1852			Totl amnt Payable.			No. of Pol.	Sum Insrd	Bonus prior to June, 1852			Bonus declared in June, 1852.			Totl. amnt Payable.		
	£	£	s.	d.	£	s.	d.	£	s.	d.		£	£	s.	d	£	s.	d.	£	s.	d.
206	499	270	15	9	68	3	1	837	18	10	1062	200	115	8	11	30	19	1	346	8	0
233	1,000	504	12	11	126	17	0	1631	9	11	1088	200	102	10	2	27	9	4	329	19	6
864	499	290	8	11	77	15	3	867	4	2	1094	1000	597	17	4	159	18	0	1757	15	4
870	100	58	18	5	15	15	8	174	14	1	1372	300	141	0	1	39	2	0	480	2	1
933	250	158	15	0	42	10	9	451	5	9	1444	1000	685	15	7	190	0	0	1875	15	7
944	2,000	904	9	4	241	18	0	3146	7	4	1946	2500	1031	1	0	309	10	10	3840	11	10

For Prospectuses and Copies of the Directors' and Actuary's Reports, apply to the Societies' Offices, 6, Crescent, New Bridge Street, Blackfriars; and Surrey Street, Norwich.

[15

IMPERIAL LIFE INSURANCE COMPANY,
1, OLD BROAD STREET,
LONDON.

THOMAS NEWMAN HUNT, Esq., *Chairman.*
JOHN HORSLEY PALMER, Esq., *Deputy-Chairman.*

A SCALE OF PREMIUMS on Insurances for the whole term of life has recently been adopted, by which a material reduction has been made at all ages below 50 years.

FOUR-FIFTHS, or 80 per cent. of the Profits, are assigned to Policies *every fifth year*, and may be applied to increase the sum insured to an immediate payment in cash, or to the reduction and ultimate extinction of future Premiums.

The following will shew the effect of the Bonus on Policies of 30 years' duration, on the 31st January, 1851:—

Age when Insured.	Sum Insured.	Annual Premium.	Addition to Sum payable at death.	Value of Addition in Cash.	Or Premium Extinguished and Cash Paid.
	£	£ s. d.	£	£	£
21	1000	22 5 0	560	276	5
26	2000	49 1 8	1120	617	93
31	3000	81 17 6	1680	1027	282
36	4000	122 13 4	2240	1505	582
41	5000	174 7 6	2800	2043	992

ONE-THIRD of the Premium on Insurances of £500 and upwards for the whole term of life may remain as a debt upon the Policy to be paid off at convenience; by which means £1,500 may be insured for the present outlay otherwise required for £1,000.

LOANS.—The Directors will lend sums of £50 aud upwards on the security of Policies effected with this Company for the whole term of life, when they have acquired an adequate value

SECURITY.—Those who effect Insurances with this Company are protected by its large Subscribed Capital from the risk incurred by members of Mutual Societies.

INSURANCES without participation in profits, may be effected at reduced rates.

16] SAMUEL INGALL, Actuary.

CHAPMAN,
22, EDWARD ST., PORTMAN SQUARE.

BATH, BRIGHTON, AND WHEEL CHAIRS,
Of every description;

SPINAL CARRIAGES, INCLINED PLANES, INVALID SOFAS AND TABLES, EASY ARM CHAIRS, &c., &c.

Or on Hire on very moderate terms.

N.B. An Assortment of Dressing Cases, Writing Desks, Tea Chests, Ink Stands, and various articles, selling off at a great loss. [22

BATTAM'S
ONE GUINEA TROUSER
COMBINES ALL THE REQUISITES, VIZ.:—

Really excellent Material (in great variety for choice), first-rate Style, Elegance and Comfort in Fit, and the Very Best Workmanship.

160, TOTTENHAM COURT ROAD,
NEAR SHOOLBRED'S.

Gentlemen who may prefer seeing patterns at their own residences, will be waited upon without delay. [56.

THE GREAT EXHIBITION OF ALL NATIONS,

1851.

Prize Medal.
TO
COACH MAKERS,
UPHOLSTERERS,
BOOKBINDERS,
BOOT & SHOE MAKERS
requiring first quality,
MOROCCO, ROAN,
SKIVER, KID,
AND
CALF LEATHER,
SHEEP & LAMB SKIN
WOOL RUGS
IN FAST AND
BRILLIANT COLOURS.
J. S. DEED, MANUFACTURER,
NOS. 8. 9. 10,
Little Newport Street,
LEICESTER SQUARE,
LONDON.
IMPORTER OF FRENCH AND
GERMAN LEATHER.

A LIST OF GOODS SENT FREE TO ALL PARTS OF GREAT BRITAIN, IRELAND, AND THE CONTINENTS.

THE STOCK

IS COMPLETE IN EVERY DEPARTMENT,

AND WORTHY THE ATTENTION OF BUYERS AND MANUFACTURERS

REQUIRING AN EXTENSIVE SELECTION

AND SUPERIOR QUALITY

[53.

TO RAILWAY  COMPANIES.

IMPROVED PACKING FOR STEAM ENGINES,

GLANDS, PUMPS, &c.

This Packing is more durable and economical than any other at present in use, as it saves time, and consumes less Oil and Tallow than the ordinary Packing, and can be applied with greater facility. It answers equally well for Steam and Hot or Cold Water Pumps.

GUTTA PERCHA FEED PIPES FOR LOCOMOTIVE ENGINES

Offer similar advantages, as far as cheapness, durability, and resistance to the effects of steam, hot or cold water are concerned.—Every variety of Gutta Percha articles suitable for Manufacturers may be had, viz.:—

Mill Bands,	Tubing,	Shuttle Beds,	Syphons,	Bowls,
Pump Buckets,	Lining for Tanks,	Washers,	Carboys for Acids,	Ladles,
Felt Edging,	Flax Holders,	Covers for Rollers,	Funnels, &c., &c.	&c., &c.

MANUFACTURED BY THE

GUTTA PERCHA COMPANY, PATENTEES,

18, Wharf Road, City Road, London; and sold by their Wholesale Dealers in town and country.

SUB-MARINE & SUBTERRANEAN ELECTRIC TELEGRAPH WIRES,

INSULATED WITH GUTTA PERCHA.

Perfect Insulation.—The Gutta Percha Company having completed the Covering of the Insulated Wires for the Submarine Telegraph Communication between France and England, are prepared to undertake contracts on favourable terms. By means of their improved machinery, they are enabled to insure perfect insulation.

DESCRIPTION OF THE SUB-MARINE TELEGRAPH LAID BETWEEN ENGLAND & FRANCE.

A The four conducting Copper Wires. *B* Covering of Gutta Percha. The DOUBLE COVERING of Gutta Percha is more clearly explained by the section *E*. *C* Spun Yarn, saturated with tar, wound round the covered wires, and filling up the interstices, so as to form a core upon which the Galvanized Wires are laid. *D* Outer protection, consisting of ten Galvanized Iron Wires. *E* Section of the cable complete. [43.

THE GUTTA PERCHA COMPANY, PATENTEES, 18, WHARF ROAD, CITY ROAD, LONDON.

GLASS SHADES

FOR the protection of Wax Flowers and all other ornaments which may be injured by exposure.

The Prices having been greatly reduced, are now very moderate.

PLATE GLASS, PATENT PLATE GLASS,

SHEET AND CROWN WINDOW GLASS,

HARTLEY'S ROUGH PLATE GLASS AND HORTICULTURAL SHEET GLASS

FOR CONSERVATORIES, &C.

Lists of the prices sent free, on application.

PAINTED AND STAINED GLASS,

And every variety of coloured and ornamental Window Glass, at

CLAUDET AND HOUGHTON'S,

89, HIGH HOLBORN, LONDON.

UNDER THE PATRONAGE OF HER MAJESTY.

MR. CLAUDET'S

DAGUERREOTYPE PORTRAIT ROOMS,

ARE OPEN DAILY, AT

107, REGENT STREET, QUADRANT.

Mr. Claudet's Portraits are taken non-inverted (viz. the right and left side as in nature), for which, and his other improvements in photography, the *Great Exhibition Council Medal* was awarded to him.

Mr. Claudet also produces, in the highest perfection, Stereoscopic Daguerreotype Portraits, Groups, and Views, which, when seen through the Stereoscope, present the really marvellous appearance of perfect relief as though they were real tangible objects.

Specimens on view. **Admission Free.** [49.

THE ROUND OF THE HEAD	INCHES	EIGHTHS
FROM EAR TO EAR........		
FROM FOREHEAD TO POLL		

KERR & STRANG most respectfully inform the Nobility, Gentry, and the Public, that they have invented or brought to the greatest state of perfection, the following leading articles, besides numerous others. Their VENTILATING NATURAL CURL Ladies' and Gentlemen's PERUKES, either Crops or Full Dress, with Partings and Crowns, so natural as to defy detection, and with or without their improved Metallic Springs. VENTILATING FRONTS, BANDEAUX BORDERS, NATTES, BANDS A LA REINE, &c. &c. Their INSTANTANEOUS LIQUID HAIR DYE, the only Dye that really answers for all colours, and never fades nor acquires that unnatural red or purple tint, common to all other Dyes. Ladies or Gentlemen requiring it are requested to have it done at their Establishment the first time, and to bring a friend or servant with them to see how it is used, which will enable them to do it afterwards, without the chance of failure.

Forwarded to all parts, on receipt of Post Office Order or Stamps.

MEXICAN BALM, or Restorative for the Hair.—The constant use of this Balm will encourage the growth and strengthen the weakest Hair, and causes it to assume, if ever so harsh or thin, a luxuriant, soft, and flexible appearance.

KERR & STRANG,

HAIR DRESSERS, PERFUMERS,

AND

WIG MANUFACTURERS,

124, LEADENHALL STREET,

LONDON.

WEDGWOOD'S

PATENT IMPROVED MANIFOLD WRITER.

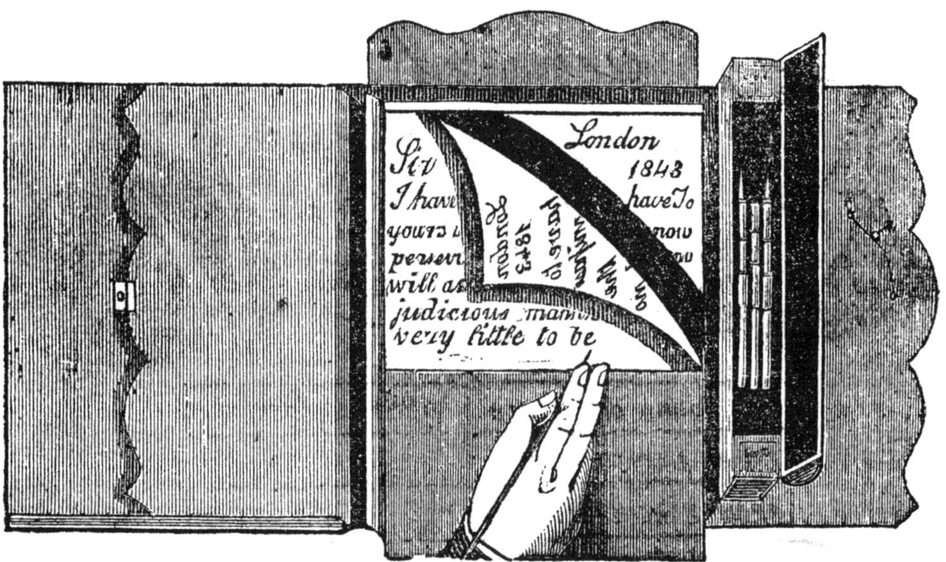

THIS INVENTION will produce a LETTER and its COPY at ONE OPERATION; or, if required, a **Letter, Duplicate,** and a **Copy,** all in Durable Ink, and with a Pen that requires no repairs; it is simple in its operation, is cheap and portable in its construction, and is capable of effecting an immense saving of time and expense. To Merchants, Bankers, Members of Parliament, and Solicitors, and indeed to all persons who have occasion to write much, and who desire to retain Copies of their Letters, or to send Duplicates abroad, this invention will prove invaluable.

Wedgwood's Clip Desk, for holding down the leaves of the Copying Book while writing.

MANUFACTORY, **84, Lombard Street, London.**

*** Fresh supplies of **Copy Books** and **Carbonic Paper** may be had, to recruit Old Cases.

Also, **Wedgwood's Patent Noctograph,** to assist the Blind.

Gentlemen's Writing Desks, first quality, with Patent Ink and Light, warranted to stand tropical climates; also Despatch Boxes, with copying apparatus complete.

Agents at Liverpool:—J. Mawdsley, F. L. Hausburg, G. M'Corquodale.—Manchester: Love and Barton, J. Parkes, Collins and Hall.—Birmingham: J. Bell (late Wrightson and Webb), J. H. Beilby, B. Hall.—Bristol: H. Oldland, Evans and Abbott.—Bradford: Mawson.—Leeds: J. Knight.—Newcastle-upon-Tyne: Thomas Horn.—Hull: Goddard and Lancaster.—York: Bellerby and Sampson—Southampton: Stebbing.—Glasgow: Geo. Gallie, Lumsden and Son.—Aberdeen: D. Wyllie and Son.—Dublin: J. Chambers, Jun. and Co.; O'Neil and Duggan. [31.

DOUCET & CO.

FRENCH SHIRT MAKERS, &c., &c.,

133, REGENT STREET.

(Established in 1817, 21, *Rue de la Paix, Paris.)*

Collars, Cravats, Flannel Waistcoats, Hunting and Boating Shirts, Dressing Gowns, and Gentlemen's Morning Costumes, of an entirely new style. The only French Shirt Maker, to whom was awarded the Great Medal at the Exhibition.

133, Regent Street, London; 31, Rue de la Paix, Paris.

[42.

PULVERMACHER'S PATENT PORTABLE

HYDRO-ELECTRIC CHAIN

EXHIBITED with the greatest success before the Royal Coll. of Physicians, Royal Coll. of Surgeons, Royal Brit. Association, Prov. Med. Chirurgical Association, Academie de Médicine, at Paris, a (vote of thanks to the Inventor). Highly favourable Testimonials in Writing from the most distinguished Members of the Profession, and now extensively used and prescribed in the Hospitals of London, Edinburgh, Manchester, Nottingham, Birmingham, Paris, &c. Constructed to be worn on the body under the garments, SUPPLYING MILD STREAMING ELECTRICITY, or Vital Functional Energy to the System. Immediate Relief from Acute Pains. Radical Cure of Rheumatic, Catarrhal, Neuralgic, Spasmodic, Nervous and Functional Disorders, Female Complaints, &c., within an incredibly short space of time, by this simple and painless remedy, which can be freely tested beforehand, at C. MEINIG'S Head Depots, 103, Leadenhall Street, and 71, Regent Street. 600 Cases of Cures within the last Eight Months, signed by Physicians, Noblemen, Clergymen, Magistrates, &c.—Price 4s. 6d., 6s., 12s., 18s., 22s., and 26s. 6d., according to Power.—Full description gratis (or per post for two stamps).

......"I can scarcely recommend Dr. P.'s ingenious invention too strongly to the notice of my Medical Brethren."—*From that eminent Physician of Guy's Hospital, Dr. Golding Bird, M.D., F.R.S., &c., &c.* [57

MEDICAL ELECTRICITY.

123, NEWGATE STREET.

HORNE, THORNTHWAITE, & WOOD'S ELECTRO-GALVANIC MACHINES, for the administration of Medical Electricity, as manufactured by them for the principal London and Provincial Hospitals, the Medical Profession, and public generally, so simple in their application that they may be used at a minute's notice, and without trouble. Price £3 3s., £5 5s., and £8 8s., complete in case, with directions.—See Guide to the Correct Administration of Medical Galvanism, by J. H. HORNE, price 2s.

INSTANTANEOUS PHOTOGRAPHIC PICTURES.

HORNE, THORNTHWAITE, & WOOD, OPTICIANS, 123 and 121, Newgate-street, London, beg to call the attention of Photographers, and all persons desirous of obtaining fac-simile representations of their friends, or the places they visit, to the use of the PREPARED COLLODION, which instantaneously produces both positive and negative pictures on the same medium. Persons having Photographic Cameras may be supplied with the materials for practising this beautiful department of Photography in large or small quantities. The articles required are: Prepared Collodion, 9d. per oz.; Pyro-Gallic Acid, 3s. per drachm; Acetic Acid Glacial, 1s. per oz.; Nitrate of Silver, 5s. per oz.; Hypo-Sulphate of Soda, 3s. per lb.; Ammonia Nitrate of Silver, 1s. per oz. Cameras complete, with all the apparatus and material required for taking pictures by the Collodion or Talbotype processes, £5 5s.; larger sizes, £10 10s.; £15 15s.; and £21.—See THORNTHWAITE's Guide to Photography, fifth edition, in boards, 2s. 6d. [35

ORNAMENTAL STOVES.

JEREMIAH EVANS & Co. respectfully invite the attention of Noblemen and Gentlemen furnishing or refitting their mansions to the most extensive and varied Stock of DRAWING-ROOM and other STOVES in the kingdom, which combine many recent improvements, producing great heat with small consumption of fuel, and are manufactured of every description of pattern, including the Gothic, Grecian, French, and Elizabethan; also Fenders and Fire Irons ensuite IMPROVED KITCHEN RANGES, with or without steam apparatus. Hot and Cold Baths of all descriptions, and every requisite in Furnishing Ironmongery at wholesale prices. Improved Hot Water Apparatus for warming buildings, conservatories, &c.—Manufactory and Show Rooms, 33, KING WILLIAM STREET, LONDON BRIDGE.—Established in 1815. [47

HUBBUCK'S

PATENT WHITE ZINC PAINT,

(*The "Permanent White" of the Ancient Artist.*)

ELEGANT, HEALTHFUL, DURABLE, ECONOMICAL.

NOW OFFERED UNDER THE ORDINARY PRICE OF WHITE LEAD.

THE WHITE PAINT MADE FROM PURE ZINC was pronounced by scientific men of the last century, to be the most beautiful of all White Paints, and unchangeable for hundreds of years. Experience has justified these high commendations, and conclusively established its superiority over white lead, and every other White Paint hitherto known. Notwithstanding this, the cost being several shillings per pound, restricted its use to Artists.

HUBBUCK AND SON, the original manufacturers of White Zinc Paint on a large scale in this country, have been enabled, by an extended and peculiar process of manufacture (which is patented), to remove this obstacle to its general use, and to supply their Pure White Zinc Paint at a less price than the ordinary White Lead.

For FRESCOE and ARTISTIC works in general, this material possesses avdantages unattainable by any other paint. Ceilings coloured by it are not effected by Gas.

CHEAPNESS.—The price per hundred weight is now less than the price of the best White Lead, whilst two hundred weight of this paint, with seven gallons of oil and urpentine, covers as much surface as three hundred weight of white lead, and twelve gallons of oil and turpentine.

To a CONTRACTOR for extensive works, taken at competition prices, this is important—cheapness with him depending not alone on the price per hundred weight. The saving on the cost of the paint and oil is 25 per cent. This applies to buff, lead colour, and every purpose for which white lead was formerly used as an ingredient.

HUBBUCK'S paint is entirely free from any injurious properties whatever; it is healthful in the manufacture, healthful in use, and healthful to occupants of rooms newly painted with it.

As a necessary guard against the substitution of inferior Zinc Paints, each cask is stamped "HUBBUCK, LONDON, PATENT;" and if the cask is not so marked the reason is obvious.

For all uses, for painting, light-houses, sluice-gates, iron roofing, and bridges, the interior and exterior of buildings, and for all ormanental, decorative, and sanitary purposes, HUBBUCK'S Patent White Zinc Paint has proved to be superior to every other Paint known, and equally adapted for all climates.

THOMAS HUBBUCK & SON,

COLOUR AND VARNISH MANUFACTURERS,

OPPOSITE THE LONDON DOCKS.

HUBBUCK'S PATENT WHITE ZINC PAINT.—"We have received a specimen of white zinc paint, manufactured by Messrs. Hubbuck and Son, near the entrance to the London Docks, who have succeeded in producing this pigment at a less cost, and in retaining its numerous advantages over lead. The white oxide of zinc has, for a century past, been known to make the most perfect white, and to be more durable than any known substance; but its costliness confined its use to artists. It retains its whiteness for years; gases have no injurious effect on it; the hold of a ship retains its pristine hue, even after a voyage, whatever the character of the bilge-water may have been. For the preservation of iron, it is superior to every other coating, for on its application a galvanic action ensues, by which it forms an amalgam, thoroughly protecting it from rust or decay. Apartments may be immediately occupied, without injury to the most delicate constitution. For public schools, and all rooms occupied by children, there will now be no excuse for using posionous paints. Parents have remarked that their children, on returning from the country to newly-painted houses. have suffered in health. The reason is evident; the breath extracts the position from paint, even after several months' drying, and the lungs draw in the deadly vapour."—*Wesleyan Times, August 5th*

DUNN'S

TAILORS' LABOUR AGENCY

IS THE PRACTICAL DEVELOPMENT OF A THEORY

BASED ON THE ASSOCIATION PRINCIPLE,

By which it is sought to stem the downward tendency of wages in the TAILORING TRADE, consequent upon the large Establishments having engrossed the supply, and obtained such a command over the labour market as to enable them to fix the wages at a standard that is regulated only by the *unscrupulousness of the middle men*, who bid against one another for the Making-up Garments (providing they can be supplied with a certain quantity), at prices that entail misery and privation, together with *moral and social degradation upon the unfortunate operatives driven, by stern necessity, to toil under those unfeeling task masters.*

This undertaking owes its origin to Mr. MAYHEW's able exposition of the sufferings and misery entailed on thousands. The new system now introduced is conducted by the promoter, at a *charge equal only to 10 per cent.* on the amount paid as Journey-men's Wages; the *remaining profits*, after being divided to reduce the price to the customer on one hand, and to paying the men the standard wages on the other, are appropriated to the advancement of the social position of the operatives and employees ENGAGED IN CARRYING OUT THIS GREAT PRINCIPLE. Yet in its infancy, and, comparatively, unknown, it nevertheless lifts a proud trophy of the success of its practical working in the works now in progress, namely, the establishment, at an estimated COST OF SEVEN HUNDRED POUNDS, of an

EXTENSIVE SCHOOL AND LECTURE ROOM,

WITH WARM BATHS ATTACHED,

To be opened in March, 1853, for the use of the men and their families, all of which advantages are secured to them, and rendered self-supporting, by a payment of *sixpence in the pound* from their improved weekly wages.

Mainly depending for success upon the advantages it offers to the public in the way of purchase, it will be found the FIRST HOUSE IN LONDON for those who, either from motives of economy or philanthrophy, lend it their support. Omnibuses reach it from all parts of the metropolis and suburbs, in one or two stages of 3d. each—the premises being in the NEIGHBOURHOOD of the ELEPHANT AND CASTLE, and numbered

13 and 14, NEWINGTON CAUSEWAY,

AND 39 & 40, BRIDGE HOUSE PLACE,

Opposite the Borough End, and near the Queen's Bench Prison.

AS A GUIDE TO PRICES,

The Working Man May here obtain a useful Black Dress Coat for.....................	1	5	0	Wages paid,	0	10	0
The Gentleman a First-class Dress Coat (a pattern of workmanship) for	2	15	0	„	0	15	0
A variety of Strong and useful Trowsers, from 10s. to	0	13	0	„ 3s. to	0	3	6
Ditto Best quality, in Patterns, from 17s. to	1	4	0	„	0	4	0
An Excellent Black Vest for	0	7	6	„	0	2	6

Boys' Clothing, Ladies' Habits, Liveries, and everything in the Trade at the same Moderate Price.

[2

CORNER OF HANOVER SQUARE.
ESTABLISHED, 1769.
HONI·SOIT·QUI·MAL·Y·PENSE
DIEU·ET·MON·DROIT
K. DINSDALE.
314, OXFORD STREET,
LONDON.
SADDLER & HARNESS MANUFACTURER
TO THE QUEEN & ROYAL FAMILY.
OPPOSITE CAVENDISH SQUARE.

NOVELTY IN HARNESS.

"GREAT NOVELTY IN HARNESS.—We were yesterday admitted to a private view of a magnificent set of harness, for two carriage horses and two out-riders, made by the express command of Her Most Gracious Majesty the Queen, at Mr. KAY DINSDALE'S, Saddler and Harness Manufacturer, 314, Oxford Street. Of the artistic merit of the work it is impossible to speak too highly, and to Mr. Dinsdale great credit is due. This gentlemen has the merit of having given an impetus to this peculiar mode of decorative art, which was scarcely known until within the last few years. We have witnessed with admiration and delight the work of South American Indians in small basket work, and in other forms, and we had imagined that the working in 'quills' was almost exclusively confined to such latitudes. But it appears that in reference to the beautiful example of quill work, as exemplified in the marvellous specimens placed before us, that the art is not confined to southern latitudes. The artists engaged to work out the elaborate designs which beautify the various parts of the harness are Tyrolese, and assuredly their artistic taste and their singular knowledge of the art of working the peacock's quills is marvellous. The set of harness which we viewed is the private harness for Her Majesty, and is intended to be used only when His Royal Highness Prince Albert drives through Windsor Park, attended by two out-riders. To Mr. Kay Dinsdale the greatest credit is due, for having matured a very beautiful artistic work. But the peculiar and singular charm of this splendid work of art, for such it may well be termed, is, that the materials used to decorate the harness for Her Majesty are the tail feathers of the most beautiful peacocks, wrought in most elegant devices. The winkers are surrounded by the rose, shamrock, and thistle, and in the centre the royal motto in garter, surmounted by the crown, with "V. R." in centre, the pads and most prominent parts to correspond, and the traces and breechings are a beautiful scroll of England's rose, with rose leaves—in fact, every part is diversified with elegant patterns, and the general effect is so truly elegant as to have all the appearance of frosted silver, possessing all the charms of novelty and decorative effect, combined with the additional advantage of cleanliness and durability. A more beautiful work of the kind we cannot imagine. To the artistic taste of Mr. Dinsdale we gladly pay our tribute of respect."—*From Morning Herald, of Sept.*, 1852. [65

PAPETERIE MARION,

152, REGENT STREET, LONDON;

14, CITE BERGERE, PARIS.

MARION & CO.,

MANUFACTURING STATIONERS,

AND IMPORTERS OF

FRENCH FANCY GOODS,

FANCY PAPERS AND ENVELOPES,

OF EVERY DESCRIPTION.

FOREIGN POST PAPER,

MOURNING AND WEDDING STATIONERY,

ORNAMENTS

And Accessories for the Bureau and Ladies' Writing Table.

BRONZES. [64

RIDLER'S HOTEL, HOLBORN LONDON.

V. RIDLER begs to inform the public that, by his alterations and improvement, he is enabled to offer to Ladies and Gentlemen convenient suites of rooms. A Ladies' Coffee Room and other arrangements, which will be found peculiarly acceptable to families. In returning his best thanks to the public for the great increase of his business, he hopes for a continuance of their patronage.

N.B.—A fixed charge for servants. [69

EXTRAORDINARY RELIEF

And BENEFIT has been experienced by a vast number of Persons afflicted with **RHEUMATISM, GOUT, PARALYSIS, SPINAL AFFECTIONS, WEAKNESS, and GENERAL DEBILITY,** from perusing a Pamphlet, which may be obtained, Post Free, by addressing a letter paid, to Mr. CABBURN'S Dispensary, King's Cross, London, with three Postage Stamps inclosed.

The testimonials of Noblemen, Clergy, Physicians, Medical Gentlemen, and many others, may be seen, particularly of the Rev. G. W. Cockburn, of Pembroke Rectory, who, from experience in his own family and neighbourhood, strongly recommends it to his brother Clergy, as a cheap, yet safe and efficacious remedy, for general suffering, [70

SECTION 4

TRAVEL JOURNAL PAGES